IF FOUND, please notify and arrange return to owner. This written test b the owner's/pilot's preparation for the Federal Aviation Administration pilot l airline transport pilot or aircraft dispatcher certificate. Thank you.

Pilot's Name P. M. GARDNER

Address 8, THE MEWS, STOKE.

PLYMOUTH. DEVON

City State Zip Code

Telephone (_____) 0752 561392.

Additional copies of *Airline Transport Pilot FAA Written Exam* are available from

FAR/.

Gleim Publications, Inc.
P.O. Box 12848
University Station
Gainesville, Florida 32604
(352) 375-0772
(800) 87-GLEIM
FAX: (352) 375-6940
Internet: www.gleim.com
E-mail: admin@gleim.com

The price is $26.95 (subject to change without notice). Orders must be prepaid. Use the order form on page 818. Shipping and handling charges apply to all orders. Add applicable sales tax to shipments within Florida.

Gleim Publications, Inc. guarantees the immediate refund of all resalable materials returned in 30 days. Shipping and handling charges are nonrefundable.

REVIEWERS AND CONTRIBUTORS

Karen A. Hom, B.A., University of Florida, is our book production coordinator. Ms. Hom coordinated the production staff, reviewed the manuscript, and provided production assistance throughout the project.

Barry A. Jones, ATP, CFII, MEI, B.S. in Air Commerce/Flight Technology, Florida Institute of Technology, is our aviation project manager and also a flight instructor and charter pilot with Gulf Atlantic Airways in Gainesville, FL. Mr. Jones assembled the text, added new material, incorporated numerous revisions, and provided technical assistance throughout the project.

Travis A. Moore, M.B.A., University of Florida, provided editorial assistance, composed the page layout, and reviewed the final drafts of the text.

Nancy Raughley, B.A., Tift College, is our editor. Ms. Raughley reviewed the manuscript, revised it for readability, and assisted in all phases of production.

The CFIs who have worked with me throughout the years to develop and improve my pilot training materials.

The many FAA employees who helped, in person or by telephone, primarily in Gainesville, Orlando, Oklahoma City, and Washington, DC.

The many pilots who have provided comments and suggestions about *Airline Transport Pilot FAA Written Exam* during the past 5 years.

A PERSONAL THANKS

This manual would not have been possible without the extraordinary efforts and dedication of Jim Collis, Terry Hall, and Gail Luparello, who typed the entire manuscript and all revisions, as well as prepared the camera-ready pages.

The author also appreciates the proofreading and production assistance of Chad Houghton, Katandra Littles, Jennifer Menge, Mark Moore, Shana Robbins, and Chad Young.

Finally, I appreciate the encouragement, support, and tolerance of my family throughout this project.

Groundwood Paper and Highlighters -- This book is printed on high quality groundwood paper. It is lightweight and easy-to-recycle. We recommend that you purchase a highlighter specifically designed to be non-bleed-through (e.g., Avery *Glidestick*™) at your local office supply store.

THIRD EDITION

ATP

AIRLINE TRANSPORT PILOT

FAA WRITTEN EXAM

for the FAA Computer-Based Pilot Knowledge Test

Airline Transport Pilot - FAR Part 121
Airline Transport Pilot - FAR Part 135
Aircraft Dispatcher
Airline Transport Pilot - Added Rating - Airplane

by Irvin N. Gleim, Ph.D., CFII

with the assistance of
Barry A. Jones, ATP, CFII, MEI

ABOUT THE AUTHOR

Irvin N. Gleim earned his private pilot certificate in 1965 from the Institute of Aviation at the University of Illinois, where he subsequently received his Ph.D. He is a commercial pilot and flight instructor (instrument) with multiengine and seaplane ratings, and is a member of the Aircraft Owners and Pilots Association, American Bonanza Society, Civil Air Patrol, Experimental Aircraft Association, and Seaplane Pilots Association. He is also author of flight maneuvers and practical test prep books for the private, instrument, commercial, and flight instructor certificates/ratings, and study guides for the private/recreational, instrument, commercial, flight/ground instructor, fundamentals of instructing, airline transport pilot, and flight engineer FAA knowledge tests. Two additional pilot training books are *Pilot Handbook* and *Aviation Weather and Weather Services*.

Dr. Gleim has also written articles for professional accounting and business law journals, and is the author of widely used review manuals for the CIA exam (Certified Internal Auditor), the CMA exam (Certified Management Accountant), the CFM exam (Certified in Financial Management), and the CPA exam (Certified Public Accountant). He is Professor Emeritus, Fisher School of Accounting, University of Florida, and is a CFM, CIA, CMA, and CPA.

Gleim Publications, Inc.
P.O. Box 12848 • University Station
Gainesville, Florida 32604

(352) 375-0772
(800) 87-GLEIM

FAX: (352) 375-6940
Internet: www.gleim.com
E-mail: admin@gleim. com

ISSN 1088 615X

ISBN 0-917539-49-4

Seventh Printing: December 1998

This is the seventh printing of the third edition of
Airline Transport Pilot FAA Written Exam.
Please e-mail update@gleim.com with ATP 3-7 as the subject or text. You will receive our current update as a reply.

EXAMPLE:

To: update@gleim.com
From: your e-mail address
Subject: ATP 3-7

SOURCES USED IN AIRLINE TRANSPORT PILOT FAA PILOT KNOWLEDGE TEST

The first lines of the answer explanations contain citations to authoritative sources of the answers. These publications can be obtained from the FAA, the Government Printing Office, and aviation bookstores. These citations are abbreviated as provided below:

AC	Advisory Circular
ACL	Aeronautical Chart Legend
A/FD	Airport/Facility Directory
AFNA	Aerodynamics for Naval Aviators
AIM	Aeronautical Information Manual
AMR	Aircraft Maintenance and Repair - McGraw-Hill
A&PM AH	Airframe and Powerplant Mechanics Airframe Handbook
AvW	Aviation Weather
AWS	Aviation Weather Services
	En Route High Altitude Chart
FAA-P-8740-48	On Landings, Part I
FAA-P-8740-50	On Landings, Part III
FAR	Federal Aviation Regulations
FTH	Flight Training Handbook
FTP	Flight Theory for Pilots - Jeppesen Sanderson, Inc.
FTW	Fly the Wing - Iowa State University Press/Ames
HMT	Hazardous Material Table
IAP	Instrument Approach Procedures
IFH	Instrument Flying Handbook
MHP	Medical Handbook for Pilots
NTSB	National Transportation Safety Board Regulations
PHAK	Pilot's Handbook of Aeronautical Knowledge
PWBH	Pilot's Weight and Balance Handbook
SID	Standard Instrument Departure Chart
STAR	Standard Terminal Arrival Chart
TCAS	Transport Category Aircraft Systems - Jeppesen Sanderson, Inc.

HELP !!

This is the Third Edition, designed specifically for professional pilots who aspire to obtain the airline transport pilot certificate. Please send any corrections and suggestions for subsequent editions to the author, c/o Gleim Publications, Inc. The last page in this book has been reserved for you to make comments and suggestions. It can be torn out and mailed to us.

Save time, money, and frustration -- see the order form on page 818. Please bring Gleim books to the attention of flight instructors, fixed-base operators, and others with a potential interest in flying. Wide distribution of Gleim books and increased interest in flying depend on your assistance, good word, etc. Thank you.

NOTE: ANSWER DISCREPANCIES and UPDATES

Our answers have been carefully researched and reviewed. Inevitably, there will be differences with competitors' books and even the FAA. If necessary, we will develop an UPDATE for *Airline Transport Pilot FAA Written Exam*. Send e-mail to update@gleim.com as described at the top right of this page, and visit our Internet site for the latest updates and information on all of our products. To continue providing our customers with first-rate service, we request that questions about our books and software be sent to us via mail, e-mail, or fax. The appropriate staff member will give each question thorough consideration and a prompt response. Questions concerning orders, prices, shipments, or payments will be handled via telephone by our competent and courteous customer service staff.

TABLE OF CONTENTS

If you are preparing for the aircraft dispatcher knowledge test, prepare for the ATP-121 knowledge test as discussed on page 5 of this book.

PREFACE

The primary purpose of this book is to provide you with the easiest, fastest, and least expensive means of passing the ATP (airplane) or aircraft dispatcher knowledge test. We have

1. Reproduced each of the 1,509 actual FAA test questions that can possibly be used on your FAA pilot knowledge test.
2. Reordered the questions into 171 logical topics.
3. Organized the 171 topics into 17 chapters.
4. Explained the answer immediately to the right of or below each question.
5. Provided an easy-to-study outline of exactly what you need to know (and no more) at the beginning of each chapter.

Accordingly, you can thoroughly prepare for the FAA pilot knowledge test by

1. Studying the brief outlines at the beginning of each chapter.
2. Answering the question on the left side of each page while covering up the answer explanations on the right side of each page.
3. Reading the answer explanation for each question that you answer incorrectly or have difficulty with.
4. Using Gleim's *FAA Test Prep* software which facilitates this process. See pages 13 through 19.

Most books create additional work for the user. In contrast, my books facilitate your effort. They are easy to use. The outline format, type styles, and spacing are designed to improve readability. Concepts are often presented as phrases rather than as complete sentences.

Read Chapter 1, The FAA Pilot Knowledge Test, carefully. Also, recognize that this study manual is concerned with **airplane** flight training, not helicopter or flight navigator training. I am confident this manual will facilitate speedy completion of your pilot knowledge test. I also wish you the very best as you complete your ATP training and pursue your aviation career. Thank you very much for your interest in my pilot training books; hopefully, you will recommend them to others.

Enjoy Flying -- Safely!

Irvin N. Gleim

December 1998

SEVENTH PRINTING (12/98) CHANGES

1. Chapter 9, IFR Navigation Equipment, Holding, and Approaches
   a. Module 9.2, Navigation Systems/Miscellaneous Questions, includes four new questions, which were previously OMEGA-related questions (Q: 1, 2, 3, and 4).
   b. Module 9.7, Holding, includes two revised questions (Q: 42 and 44).
2. Chapter 11, BE-1900 Operating/Performance Data, includes the correct Figure 18 -- Time, Fuel, and Distance to Cruise Climb (p. 542).
3. Chapter 16, Terminal Aerodrome Forecast (TAF), includes one revised question (Q: 64).

CHAPTER ONE
THE FAA PILOT KNOWLEDGE TEST

The beginning of this chapter provides an overview of the process to obtain an airline transport pilot (ATP) or aircraft dispatcher certificate and explains the content and procedure of the Federal Aviation Administration (FAA) pilot knowledge test, including how to take the test at a computer testing center. The remainder of this chapter discusses and illustrates Gleim's ***FAA Test Prep*** software.

NOTE: This book is to be used for ATP-FAR Part 121-airplane, ATP-FAR Part 135-airplane, ATP-FAR Part 135 -- added rating-airplane, and aircraft dispatcher, but **not** for helicopter or flight navigator certificates. A complete discussion is provided on page 5.

Airline Transport Pilot FAA Written Exam is one of two related books, each in outline/illustration format, for obtaining an ATP certificate. The other book is *Aviation Weather and Weather Services*.

Aviation Weather and Weather Services combines all of the information from the FAA's *Aviation Weather* (AC 00-6A), *Aviation Weather Services* (AC 00-45E), and numerous FAA publications into one easy-to-understand book. It will help you study all aspects of aviation weather and provide you a single weather reference book.

1.1 WHAT IS AN ATP CERTIFICATE?

An ATP certificate is identical to your commercial pilot certificate except it allows you to

1. Act as pilot in command (PIC) of an aircraft under Part 121 for a domestic, flag, or supplemental air carrier, with an appropriate type rating for that aircraft
   a. Or as second in command (SIC) of an aircraft in a flag or supplemental operation that requires three or more pilots

2. Act as PIC under Part 135 passenger-carrying operations of a turbojet airplane, of an airplane having a passenger seating configuration of 10 seats or more, or of a multiengine airplane in a commuter operation, with an appropriate type rating for the aircraft, if required
3. Serve as director of operations or chief pilot under Part 121 or 135, with the appropriate experience
4. Instruct other pilots in air transportation service in aircraft of the category, class, and type for which you are rated

Part 121 operators are precluded from having pilots 60 years and older on flight status. ATPs 60 years and older may exercise their certificate privileges under Parts 91, 125, and 135.

Your ATP certificate will be sent to you by the FAA upon satisfactory completion of your training program, a pilot knowledge test, and a practical test. A sample ATP certificate is reproduced below.

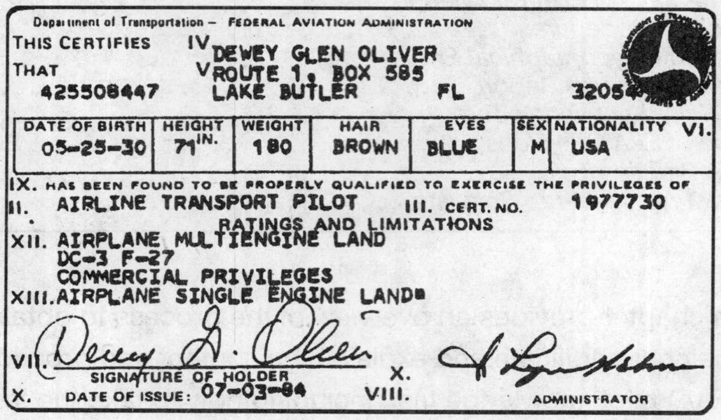

Department of Transportation – FEDERAL AVIATION ADMINISTRATION

THIS CERTIFIES IV DEWEY GLEN OLIVER
THAT V ROUTE 1, BOX 585
425508447 LAKE BUTLER FL 3205

DATE OF BIRTH	HEIGHT	WEIGHT	HAIR	EYES	SEX	NATIONALITY VI.
05-25-30	71 IN.	180	BROWN	BLUE	M	USA

IX. HAS BEEN FOUND TO BE PROPERLY QUALIFIED TO EXERCISE THE PRIVILEGES OF
II. AIRLINE TRANSPORT PILOT III. CERT. NO. 1977730
RATINGS AND LIMITATIONS
XII. AIRPLANE MULTIENGINE LAND
DC-3 F-27
COMMERCIAL PRIVILEGES
XIII. AIRPLANE SINGLE ENGINE LAND

VII. SIGNATURE OF HOLDER X. VIII. ADMINISTRATOR
X. DATE OF ISSUE: 07-03-84

1.2 REQUIREMENTS TO OBTAIN AN ATP CERTIFICATE

1. Be at least 23 years of age.
2. Be able to read, speak, write, and understand the English language. (Certificates with operating limitations may be available for medically related deficiencies.)
3. Be of good moral character.
4. Meet at least one of the following:
   a. Hold at least a commercial pilot certificate and an instrument rating.
   b. Meet the military experience requirements (listed in FAR 61.73) to qualify for a commercial pilot certificate and an instrument rating.
   c. Hold either a foreign ATP or a foreign commercial pilot license and an instrument rating, without limitations, issued by a member nation of the International Civil Aviation Organization (ICAO).
5. Hold at least a current FAA third-class medical certificate. Later, if your flying requires an ATP certificate, you must hold a first-class medical certificate.
   a. You must undergo a routine medical examination which may be administered only by FAA-designated doctors called aviation medical examiners (AME).
      1) A first-class medical certificate is valid for 6 months and expires on the last day of the 6th month after the month of issuance (when another medical examination is required) for those operations requiring an ATP certificate.
   b. If you have a physical handicap, medical certificates can usually be issued. Operating limitations may be imposed depending upon the nature of the disability.

c. The FAA publishes a directory that lists all authorized AMEs by name and address. Copies of this directory are kept at all FAA offices, Air Traffic Control (ATC) facilities, and Flight Service Stations (FSS).

6. Use this book and *Aviation Weather and Weather Services* to prepare yourself for the ATP knowledge test, which covers the following areas (61.155):

   a. *Applicable Federal Aviation Regulations . . . that relate to airline transport pilot privileges, limitations, and flight operations.*

   b. *Meteorology, including knowledge of and effects of fronts, frontal characteristics, cloud formations, icing, and upper-air data.*

   c. *General systems of weather and NOTAM collection, dissemination, interpretation, and use.*

   d. *Interpretation and use of weather charts, maps, forecasts, sequence reports, abbreviations, and symbols.*

   e. *National Weather Service functions as they pertain to operations in the National Airspace System.*

   f. *Windshear and microburst awareness, identification, and avoidance.*

   g. *Principles of air navigation under instrument meteorological conditions in the National Airspace System.*

   h. *Air traffic control procedures and pilot responsibilities as they relate to en route operations, terminal area and radar operations, and instrument departure and approach procedures.*

   i. *Aircraft loading, weight and balance, use of charts, graphs, tables, formulas, and computations, and their effect on aircraft performance.*

   j. *Aerodynamics relating to an aircraft's flight characteristics and performance in normal and abnormal flight regimes.*

   k. *Human factors.*

   l. *Aeronautical decision making and judgment.*

   m. *Crew resource management to include crew communication and coordination.*

7. Pass a pilot knowledge test with a score of 70% or better. All FAA tests are administered at FAA-designated computer testing centers. The ATP and aircraft dispatcher tests consist of 80 multiple-choice questions (except that the ATP airplane-added rating consists of 50 questions) selected from the 1,509 airplane-related questions among the 1,730 questions in the FAA's ATP, aircraft dispatcher and flight navigator knowledge test bank; the balance of 221 questions are for helicopters and flight navigators. Each of the FAA's 1,509 airplane-related questions is reproduced in this book with complete explanations to the right of (or below) each question.

   a. A knowledge test is not required for you to add another aircraft type rating to your ATP certificate if your ATP certificate lists the aircraft category and class rating that is appropriate to the type rating sought.

8. Accumulate flight experience (FAR 61.159).

   a. Except as provided in b. and c. on the next page, you must log at least 1,500 hr. of total time as a pilot that includes at least

      1) 500 hr. of cross-country flight time
      2) 100 hr. of night flight time

a) A person who has performed at least 20 night takeoffs and landings to a full stop may substitute each additional night takeoff and landing to a full stop for 1 hr. of night flight time, limited to not more than 25 hr. of night flight time.

3) 75 hr. of actual or simulated instrument flight time

a) The maximum time that may be accumulated in a flight simulator or flight training device, representing an airplane, is either

i) 25 hr., if the training is not conducted under FAR Part 142, or
ii) 50 hr., if the training is conducted under FAR Part 142.

4) 250 hr. of flight time as PIC of an airplane, or as SIC performing the duties and functions of a PIC under the supervision of a PIC, or by any combination of the two. This requirement must include

a) 100 hr. of cross-country time
b) 25 hr. of night flight time

NOTE: Not more than 100 hr. of the total aeronautical experience requirements may be obtained in a flight simulator or a flight training device that represents an airplane, provided the experience was obtained in a course conducted under FAR Part 142.

b. A commercial pilot may credit the following flight time toward the 1,500 hr. of total pilot time.

1) SIC time, provided the time is acquired in an airplane, under one of the following conditions:

a) Required to have more than one pilot flight crewmember by the airplane's flight manual, a type certificate, or the regulations under which the flight is being conducted

b) Engaged in operations under Part 121 or 135 for which a SIC is required

c) Required under the FARs to have more than one pilot flight crewmember

2) Flight-engineer time, provided the time

a) Is acquired in an airplane required to have a flight engineer by the airplane's flight manual or type certificate

b) Is acquired while in operations conducted under Part 121 for which a flight engineer is required

c) Is acquired while the person is participating in a pilot training program under Part 121

d) Does not exceed more than 1 hr. for each 3 hr. of flight-engineer flight time for a total credited time of not more than 500 hr.

c. You may be issued an ATP certificate with the endorsement *"Holder does not meet the pilot in command aeronautical experience requirements of ICAO,"* if you

1) Credit SIC or flight-engineer time toward the 1,500 hr. total flight time requirement

2) Do not have at least 1,200 hr. of flight time as a pilot, including no more than 50% of your SIC time and none of your flight-engineer time

3) Otherwise meet the aeronautical experience requirements

NOTE: The endorsement described in item c. above will be removed when you present satisfactory evidence of the accumulation of 1,200 hr. flight time as a pilot including no more than 50% of your SIC time and none of your flight-engineer time.

9. Successfully complete a practical flight test given as a final exam by an FAA inspector or designated pilot examiner and conducted as specified in the FAA's Airline Transport Pilot and Type Rating Practical Test Standards [FAA-S-8081-5C dated August 1998, with Change 1 (October 1998)].
   a. FAA inspectors are FAA employees and do not charge for their services.
   b. FAA-designated examiners are proficient, experienced flight instructors and pilots who are authorized by the FAA to conduct flight tests. They do charge a fee.
   c. The ATP practical test covers the following areas of operations:
      1) Preflight preparation
      2) Preflight procedures
      3) Takeoff and departure phase
      4) In-flight maneuvers
      5) Instrument procedures
      6) Landings and approaches to landings
      7) Normal and abnormal procedures
      8) Emergency procedures
      9) Postflight procedures

1.3 PART 121 vs. PART 135 PILOT KNOWLEDGE TEST

1. The FAA gives you an option between either a Part 121 or a Part 135 ATP knowledge test.
   a. Study suggestions
      1) ATP-121 knowledge test: Study all chapters **except** Chapters 5 and 11. In Chapter 10, study only Modules 7 through 11.
      2) ATP-135 knowledge test: Study all chapters **except** Chapters 4, 12, 13, and 14. In Chapter 10, study only Modules 1 through 6.
   b. If you are studying for the ATP airplane add-on rating (i.e., you are already a helicopter ATP), you have the ATP-135 option only.

1.4 FAA PILOT KNOWLEDGE TEST

1. This book is designed to help you prepare for the following FAA pilot knowledge tests:
   a. Airline Transport Pilot (FAR Part 121)-Airplane (ATP), which consists of 80 questions and has a time limit of 3 hr.
   b. Airline Transport Pilot (FAR Part 135)-Airplane (ATA), which consists of 80 questions and has a time limit of 3 hr.
   c. Airline Transport Pilot (FAR Part 135)-Added Rating-Airplane (ARA), which consists of 50 questions and has a time limit of 2 hr. 30 min.
      1) This test is for a person who currently holds an ATP certificate with a helicopter class rating and wants to add an airplane category rating to his/her ATP certificate.
   d. Aircraft Dispatcher (ADX), which consists of 80 questions and has a time limit of 3 hr.
      1) The ADX knowledge test covers basically the same material as the ATP-121 knowledge test because only Part 121 certificate holders are required to have aircraft dispatchers and the test does not include helicopter questions.
2. This book contains only airplane-related questions; we cover neither helicopter nor navigator questions.

3. All of the 1,509 questions in the FAA's ATP test bank that are applicable to airplanes have been grouped into the following 17 categories, which are the titles of Chapters 2 through 18:

Note that the FAA questions are **not** grouped together by topic. We have unscrambled them for you in this book.

4. Within each of the chapters listed, questions relating to the same subtopic (e.g., thunderstorms, load factor, approach and landing, etc.) are grouped to facilitate your study program. Each subtopic is called a module.

5. To the right of (or below) each question are
   a. The correct answer
   b. The FAA question number
   c. A reference for the answer explanation
      1) See page iv for a listing of abbreviations used for authoritative sources.
      2) EXAMPLE: *FTH Chap 1* means *Flight Training Handbook*, Chapter 1.

6. Each chapter begins with an outline of the material tested on the FAA pilot knowledge test. The outlines in this part of the book are very brief and have only one purpose: to help you pass the FAA ATP or aircraft dispatcher knowledge test.
   a. **CAUTION:** The **sole purpose** of this book is to expedite your passing the FAA pilot knowledge test for the ATP or aircraft dispatcher certificate. Material not directly tested on the FAA pilot knowledge test is omitted. Much more information and knowledge are necessary to fly safely. Some of this additional material is presented in Gleim's *Aviation Weather and Weather Services*.

Follow the suggestions given throughout this chapter and you will have no trouble passing the ATP or aircraft dispatcher knowledge test the first time you take it.

1.5 HOW TO PREPARE FOR THE FAA PILOT KNOWLEDGE TEST

1. Begin by carefully reading the rest of this chapter. You need to have a complete understanding of the examination process prior to beginning to study for it. This knowledge will make your studying more efficient.
2. After you have spent an hour studying this chapter, set up a study schedule, including a target date for taking your pilot knowledge test.
   a. Do not let the study process drag on, i.e., the quicker the better.
   b. Determine where and when you are going to take your pilot knowledge test.
3. Work through each of Chapters 2 through 18.
   a. Each chapter begins with a list of module titles. The number in parentheses after each title is the number of FAA questions that cover the information in that module. The two numbers following the parentheses are the page numbers on which the outline and the questions for that particular module begin, respectively.

b. Begin by studying the outlines slowly and carefully.

c. Next, answer the multiple-choice questions under exam conditions. Cover the answer explanations on the right side (or the bottom) of each page with your hand or a piece of paper while you answer the multiple-choice questions.

1) Remember, it is very important to the learning (and understanding) process that you honestly commit yourself to an answer. If you are wrong, your memory will be reinforced by having discovered your error. Therefore, it is crucial to cover up the answer and make an honest attempt to answer the question before reading the answer.

2) Study the answer explanation for each question that you answer incorrectly, do not understand, or have difficulty with.

3) Use our *FAA Test Prep* software to assure that you do not refer to answer explanations before committing to an answer AND to simulate actual computer testing center exam conditions.

4. Note that this test book (in contrast to most other question and answer books) contains the FAA questions grouped by topic. Thus, some questions may appear repetitive, while others may be duplicates or near-duplicates. Accordingly, do not work question after question (i.e., waste time and effort) if you are already conversant with a topic and the type of questions asked.

5. As you move from module to module and chapter to chapter, you may need further explanation or clarification of certain topics. You may wish to obtain and use Gleim's *Aviation Weather and Weather Services* described on page 1.

6. Keep track of your work!!! As you complete a module in Chapters 2 through 18, grade yourself with an A, B, C, or ? (use a ? if you need help on the subject) next to the module title at the front of the respective chapter.

a. The A, B, C, or ? is your self-evaluation of your comprehension of the material in that module and your ability to answer the questions.

A means a good understanding
B means a fair understanding
C means a shaky understanding
? means to ask your instructor or others about the material and/or questions and read the pertinent sections in *Aviation Weather and Weather Services*

b. This procedure will provide you with the ability to see quickly (by looking at the first page of Chapters 2 through 18) how much studying you have done (and how much remains) and how well you have done.

c. This procedure will also facilitate review. You can spend more time on the modules you had difficulty with.

d. *FAA Test Prep* software provides you with your historical performance data.

1.6 WHEN TO TAKE THE PILOT KNOWLEDGE TEST

1. You must be at least 21 years of age to take the ATP or aircraft dispatcher knowledge test.

2. Take the pilot knowledge test within the next 30 days.

a. Get your pilot knowledge test behind you.

3. Your practical test must follow within 24 months.

a. Otherwise, you will have to retake your pilot knowledge test.

4. You may take the ATP practical test with an expired pilot knowledge test report, provided you are employed as a flight crewmember
   a. By a certificate holder under Part 121 or 135 (except an on-demand operation) at the time of the practical test and have satisfactorily accomplished that operator's approved
      1) Pilot in command aircraft qualification training program that is appropriate to the certificate and rating sought or
      2) Qualification training requirements appropriate to the certificate and rating sought
   b. In scheduled U.S. military air transport operations at the time of the practical test, and have accomplished the pilot in command aircraft qualification training program that is appropriate to the certificate and rating sought

1.7 COMPUTER TESTING CENTERS

The FAA has contracted with several computer testing services to administer FAA pilot knowledge tests. Each of these computer testing services has testing centers throughout the country. You register by calling an 800 number. Call the following testing services for information regarding the location of testing centers most convenient to you and the cost to take the ATP (airplane) and/or aircraft dispatcher knowledge test.

CATS	(800) 947-4228
LaserGrade	(800) 211-2754
Sylvan	(800) 274-1900

Also, about twenty Part 141 schools use the AvTEST computer testing system, which is very similar to the computer testing services described previously.

1.8 GLEIM'S *FAA TEST PREP* SOFTWARE

Computer testing is consistent with modern aviation's use of computers (e.g., DUATS, flight simulators, computerized cockpits, etc.). All FAA pilot knowledge tests are administered by computer.

Computer testing is natural after computer study. Computer-assisted instruction is a very efficient and effective method of study. Gleim's *FAA Test Prep* software is designed to prepare you for computer testing. *FAA Test Prep* contains all of the questions in this book (but not the outlines and figures). You choose either STUDY MODE or TEST MODE.

In STUDY MODE, the software provides you with an explanation of each answer you choose (correct or incorrect). You design each study session:

Topic(s) you wish to cover
Number of questions
Order of questions -- FAA, Gleim, or random
Order of answers to each question -- FAA or random
Questions missed from last session -- test, study, or both
Questions missed from all sessions -- test, study, or both
Questions never answered correctly

In TEST MODE, you decide the format -- CATS, LaserGrade, Sylvan, AvTEST, or Gleim. When you finish your test, you can study the questions missed and access answer explanations. The software imitates the operation of the FAA-approved computer testing companies above. Thus, you have a complete understanding of exactly how to take an FAA computer test before you go to a computer testing center.

To use *FAA Test Prep*, you need an IBM-compatible computer with a hard disk and 2.0 MB of disk space, 2.0 MB of RAM, and a high-density 3.5 in. diskette drive. Learn more details about how Gleim's *FAA Test Prep* software functions beginning on page 13. Call (800) 87-GLEIM or use the order form at the back of this book to obtain your copy of this useful interactive software.

1.9 PART 141 SCHOOLS WITH PILOT KNOWLEDGE TEST EXAMINING AUTHORITY

The FAA permits some FAR Part 141 schools to develop, administer, and grade their own pilot knowledge tests as long as they use the FAA pilot knowledge test questions, i.e., the questions in this book. The FAA does not provide the correct answers to the Part 141 schools, and only reviews the Part 141 school test question selection sheets. Thus, some of the answers used by Part 141 test examiners may not agree with the FAA or this book. The latter is not a problem but may explain why you may miss a question on a Part 141 knowledge test using an answer presented in this book.

1.10 AUTHORIZATION TO TAKE THE PILOT KNOWLEDGE TEST

Neither an authorization nor an instructor endorsement is required for a pilot to take the ATP or aircraft dispatcher knowledge tests; however, (s)he must be at least 21 years of age.

1.11 FORMAT OF THE PILOT KNOWLEDGE TEST

The FAA's ATP knowledge test for airplanes and aircraft dispatcher knowledge test consist of 80 multiple-choice questions selected from the 1,509 questions that appear in the next 17 chapters. The ATP -- airplane-added rating test consists of 50 questions.

Note that the FAA test will be taken from exactly the same questions that are reproduced in this book. If you study the next 17 chapters, including all the questions and answers, **you should be assured of passing your FAA pilot knowledge test.**

Additionally, all of the FAA legends and figures are contained in a book titled *Computer Testing Supplement for Airline Transport Pilot and Aircraft Dispatcher*, which you will be given for your use at the time of your test. All of the airplane-related figures and most of the legends are reproduced in this book. We did not reproduce Legend 8, Radar Minima; Legends 12 through 14 and 16 through 21, *Airport/Facility Directory* Legend; Legends 23 through 33, Excerpt from 49 CFR Part 175 (hazardous materials regulations); and Legends 39 through 41, General Information on SIDs, STARs, and Profile Descents.

1.12 WHAT TO TAKE TO THE FAA PILOT KNOWLEDGE TEST

1. The same flight computer that you use to solve the test questions in this book, i.e., one you are familiar with and have used before
2. A pocket calculator you are familiar with and have used before (no instructional material for the calculator allowed)
3. U.S. commercial pilot certificate, foreign ATP certificate, or evidence of U.S. military experience
4. Proper identification that contains your
   a. Photograph
   b. Signature
   c. Date of birth
   d. Actual residential address, if different from your mailing address

NOTE: Paper and pencils are supplied at the examination site.

1.13 COMPUTER TESTING PROCEDURES

To register for the pilot knowledge test by computer, you should call one of the computer testing services listed in Module 1.7, Computer Testing Centers, on page 8, or you may call one of their testing centers. These testing centers and telephone numbers are listed in Gleim's *FAA Test Prep* software under Vendors in the main menu. When you register, you will normally pay the fee with a credit card.

When you arrive at the computer testing center, you will be required to provide positive proof of identification and documentary evidence of your age. Some centers require two forms of ID; check when you schedule your test. Next, you sign in on the testing center's daily log. On the logsheet there must be a statement that your signature certifies that, if this is a retest, you meet the applicable requirements (see Module, 1.16, Failure on the Pilot Knowledge Test, on page 12) and that you have not taken and passed this test in the past 2 years.

Next, you will be taken into the testing room and seated at a computer terminal. A person from the testing center will assist you in logging on the system, and you will be asked to confirm your personal data (e.g., name, Social Security number, etc.). Then you will be prompted and given an online introduction to the computer testing system and you will take a sample test. If you have used our *FAA Test Prep* software, you will be conversant with the computer testing methodology and environment, and you will probably want to skip the sample test and begin the actual test immediately. You will be allowed 3.0 hr. (2.5 hr. for the ATP -- added rating-airplane) to complete the actual test. This is approximately 2.25 minutes per question. Confirm the time permitted when you call the testing center to register to take the test by computer. When you have completed your test, an Airman Computer Test Report will be printed out, validated (usually with an embossed seal), and given to you by a person from the testing center. Before you leave, you will be required to sign out on the testing center's daily log.

Each testing center has certain idiosyncrasies in its paperwork, scheduling, and telephone procedures, as well as in its software. It is for this reason that our *FAA Test Prep* software emulates each of these FAA-approved computer testing companies.

1.14 FAA QUESTIONS WITH TYPOGRAPHICAL ERRORS

Occasionally, FAA test questions contain typographical errors such that there is no correct answer. The FAA test development process involves many steps and people, and as you would expect, glitches occur in the system that are beyond the control of any one person. We indicate "best" or "may be correct" rather than correct answers for some questions. Use these best answers for the indicated questions.

Note that the FAA corrects (rewrites) defective questions on the computer tests, which it cannot currently do with respect to faulty figures printed in FAA Computer Testing Supplements. Thus, it is important to study questions carefully that are noted to have a best answer in this book.

1.15 YOUR PILOT KNOWLEDGE TEST REPORT

1. You will receive your Airman Computer Test Report upon completion of the test. An example computer test report is reproduced below.
   a. Note that you will receive only one grade as illustrated.
   b. The expiration date is the date by which you must take your FAA practical test, unless you are employed by a Part 121 or 135 air carrier (see Module 1.6, When to Take the Pilot Knowledge Test, on page 6).
   c. The report lists the FAA subject matter knowledge codes of the questions you missed, so you can review the topics you missed prior to your practical test.

Federal Aviation Administration
Airman Computer Test Report

EXAM TITLE: Airline Transport Pilot -- Airplane (FAR Part 121)

NAME: Jones David John

ID NUMBER: 123-45-6789 TAKE: 1

DATE: 08/14/97 SCORE: 92 GRADE: Pass

Knowledge area codes in which questions were answered incorrectly. A code may represent more than one incorrect response.

A20 D10 G02, I13, J18, X07

EXPIRATION DATE: 08/31/99

<u>DO NOT LOSE THIS REPORT</u>

Authorized instructor's statement. (If Applicable)

I have given Mr./Ms. ____________________ additional instruction in each subject area shown to be deficient and consider the applicant competent to pass the test.

Last ____________________ Initial ______ Cert. No. ________ Type ______
(Print Clearly)

Signature ______________________________

CTD's Embossed Seal

2. Use the FAA's list of subject matter knowledge codes on pages 795 to 799 to determine which topics you had difficulty with.
   a. Look them over and review them with your instructor so (s)he can certify that (s)he reviewed the deficient areas and found you competent in them when you take your practical test.
3. Keep your Airman Computer Test Report in a safe place, as you must submit it to the FAA examiner when you take your practical test.

1.16 FAILURE ON THE PILOT KNOWLEDGE TEST

1. If you fail (less than 70%) the pilot knowledge test (almost impossible if you follow our instructions on how to prepare), you may retake it after your instructor endorses the bottom of your Airman Computer Test Report certifying that you have received the necessary ground training to retake the test.
2. Upon retaking the test, everything is the same except you must also submit your Airman Computer Test Report indicating the previous failure to the computer testing center.
3. Note that the pass rate on the ATP pilot knowledge test is about 80%; i.e., 2 out of 10 fail the test initially. Reasons for failure include
   a. Failure to study the material tested (contained in the outlines at the beginning of Chapters 2 through 18 of this book);
   b. Failure to practice working the FAA exam questions under test conditions (all of the FAA questions on airplanes appear in Chapters 2 through 18 of this book); and
   c. Poor examination technique, such as misreading questions and not understanding the requirements.

1.17 REORGANIZATION OF FAA QUESTIONS

1. The questions in the FAA ATP test bank are numbered 8001 to 9730. The FAA questions appear to be presented randomly.
   a. We have reorganized the FAA questions into chapters and modules.
   b. The FAA question number is presented in the middle of the first line of the explanation of each answer.
2. Pages 800 through 813 contain a list of the FAA questions numbers 8001 to 9720 with cross-references to the FAA's subject matter knowledge codes and the chapters and question numbers in this book.
   a. For example, we have coded FAA question number 8001 as E-01 and 5-6, which means it is covered under the FAA subject code, "FAR Part 135, General," and is found in Chapter 5 as question 6 in this book.
   b. Note that, although 8001 to 9730 implies 1,730 questions, only 1,509 apply to airplanes.
      1) There are 130 questions that relate to helicopters and have been omitted from this book (indicated as H in our cross-reference table).
      2) There are 91 questions that relate to the flight navigator knowledge test and have been omitted from this book (indicated as N in our cross-reference table).

With this overview of exam requirements, you are ready to begin the easy-to-study outlines and rearranged questions with answers to build your knowledge and confidence and PASS THE FAA's ATP KNOWLEDGE TEST.

The feedback we receive from users of our books and software indicates that they reduce anxiety, improve FAA test scores, and build knowledge. Studying for each test becomes a useful step toward advanced certificates and ratings.

1.18 SIMULATED FAA PRACTICE TEST

Appendix A, Airline Transport Pilot (Part 121) Practice Test, beginning on page 795, and Appendix B, Airline Transport Pilot (Part 135) Practice Test, beginning on page 779, allow you to practice taking either the ATP-121 or ATP-135 FAA pilot knowledge test without the answers next to the questions. Each test has 80 questions that have been randomly selected from the 1,509 airplane-related questions in the FAA's ATP test bank. Topical coverage in each practice test is similar to that of either the FAA's Airline Transport Pilot (Part 121) Airplane or the Airline Transport Pilot (Part 135) Airplane knowledge test.

It is very important that you answer all 80 questions at one sitting. You should not consult the answers, especially when being referred to figures (charts, tables, etc.) throughout this book where the questions are answered and explained. Analyze your performance based on the answer key which follows each practice test in Appendix A and Appendix B.

Also rely on Gleim's *FAA Test Prep* software to simulate actual computer testing conditions including the screen layouts, instructions, etc., for CATS, LaserGrade, Sylvan, and AvTEST.

1.19 INSTRUCTIONS FOR THE CD-ROM VERSION OF THE *FAA TEST PREP* SOFTWARE

To install *FAA Test Prep*, put your CD-ROM in your CD-ROM drive. If an autoplay window (shown below) appears after you insert the CD, click on "Setup" to begin the installation procedure. If no screen appears after you have inserted the CD, click on the Windows Start button, and select "Run" from a list of options. Type x:\setup.exe (if x is the drive letter of your CD-ROM), and click "OK." Follow the on-screen instructions to finalize the installation.

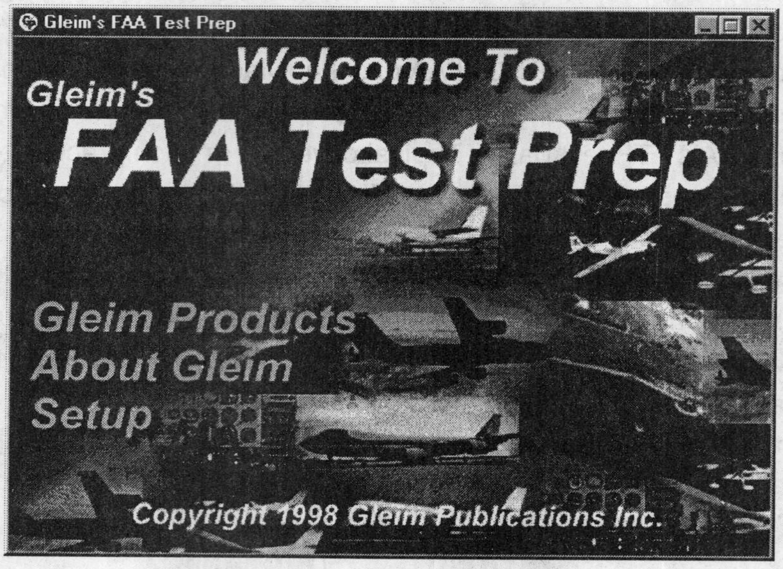

Gleim Publications requires all *FAA Test Prep* users to register their software for unlimited use, free updates, and technical support. To register, simply use the Personal Registration Number and Library Passkey(s) that were shipped with your CD-ROM, call (800) 87-GLEIM, or register online at (http://www.gleim.com/license.html). NOTE: For Windows 3.1 and DOS users, Gleim offers an updated DOS version of *FAA Test Prep* to be used in conjunction with each of the written exam books.

Once you have installed *FAA Test Prep* onto your system, you can begin studying at any time by clicking on the icon placed on your desktop. Use the Tutorial in HELP to go step by step through the study process, or start studying right away by clicking on Create Session in the Session menu. *FAA Test Prep* allows you to customize your study process using several different options.

Study Mode

Using Study Mode gives you immediate feedback on why your answer selection for a particular FAA question is correct or incorrect and allows you to access the context-sensitive outline material that helps to explain concepts related to the question. Choose from several different question sources: all questions available for that library, questions from a certain topic (chapters and modules from Gleim books), questions that you missed or marked in the last session you created, questions that you have never answered correctly, questions from certain FAA subject codes, etc. You can mix up the questions by selecting to randomize the question and/or answer order so that you do not memorize answer letters.

You may then grade your study sessions and track your study progress using the performance analysis charts and graphs. The Performance Analysis information helps you to focus on areas where you need the most improvement, saving you time in the overall study process. You may then want to go back and study questions that you missed in a previous session, or you may want to create a study session of questions that you marked in the previous session, and all of these options are made easy with *FAA Test Prep*'s Study Mode.

After studying the outlines and questions in Study Mode, you can switch to Test Mode, which gives you the option of taking your pilot knowledge test under actual testing conditions using one of the emulations of the major testing centers.

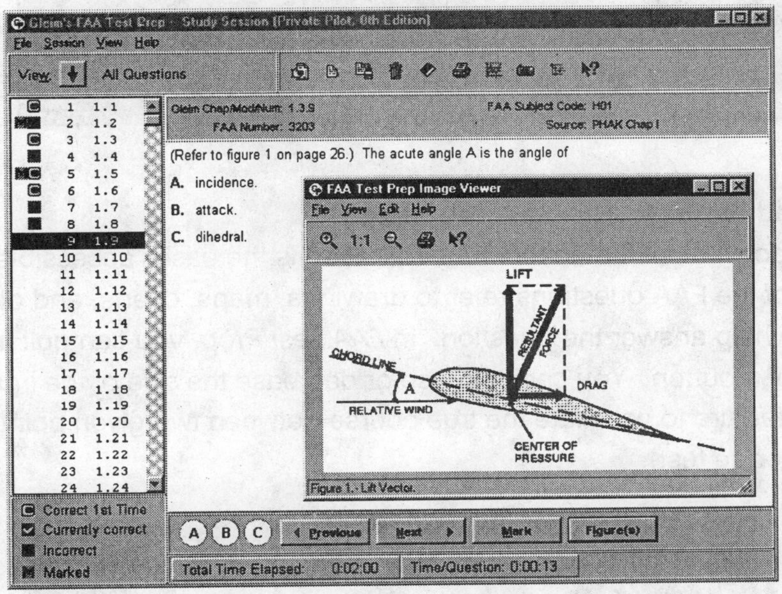

Test Mode

Take an exam in the actual testing environment of any of the major testing centers: CATS, Sylvan, AvTest, or Lasergrade. *FAA Test Prep* emulates the testing formats of these testing centers making it easy for you to study FAA questions under actual exam conditions. After studying with *FAA Test Prep*, you will know exactly what to expect when you go in to take your pilot knowledge test.

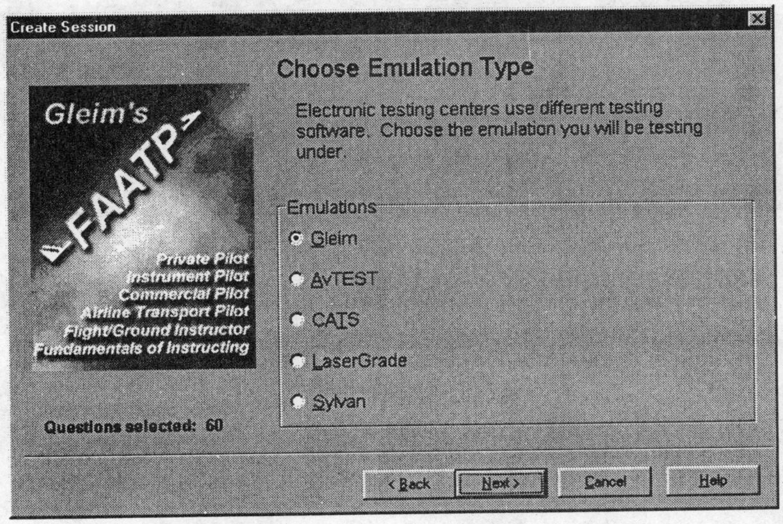

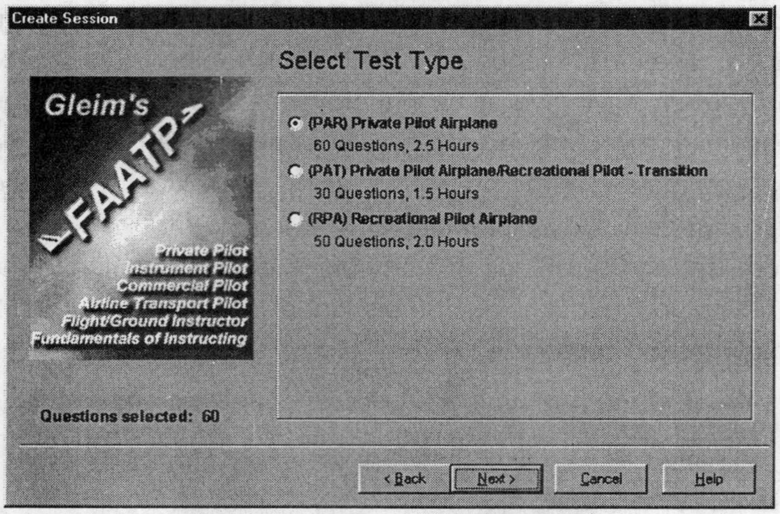

On-Screen Charts and Figures

One of the most convenient features of *FAA Test Prep* is the easily accessible on-screen charts and figures. Several of the FAA questions refer to drawings, maps, charts, and other pictures that provide information to help answer the question. In *FAA Test Prep*, you can pull up any of these figures with the click of a button. You can increase or decrease the size of the images, and you may also use our drawing feature to calculate the true course between two given points (required only on the private pilot knowledge test).

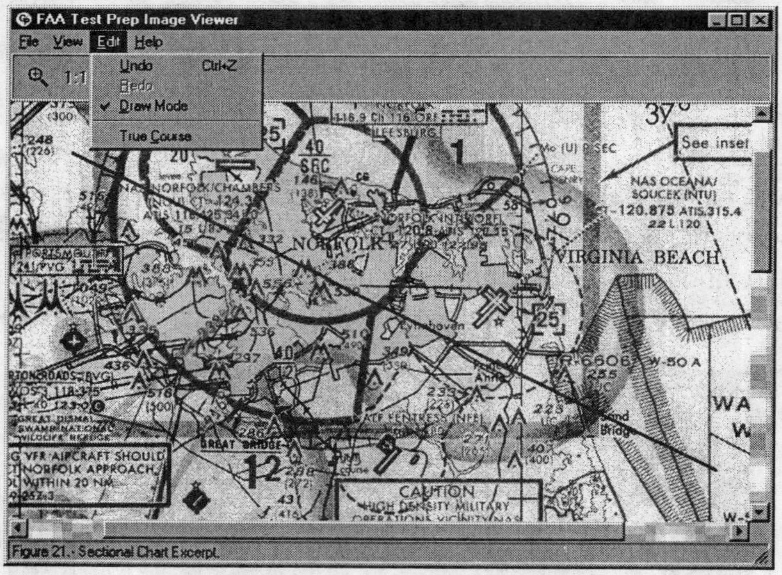

Instructor Print Options

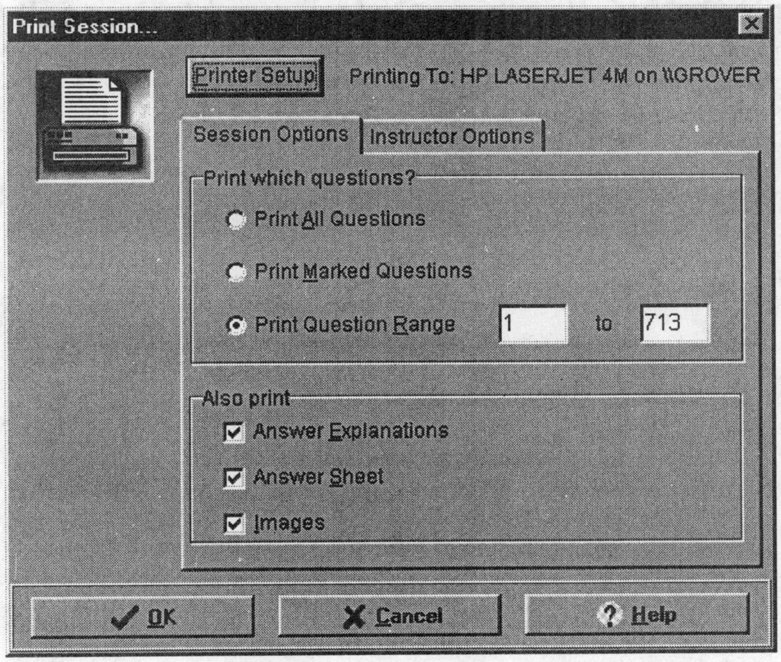

FAA Test Prep is also a useful tool for instructors who want to create quizzes and assignments for their students. An instructor may mark questions in a session and then choose to print marked questions to create a quiz or test. (S)he may select to print an answer sheet, a blank answer sheet, and a renumbered printout of questions marked and any instructions that go along with the quiz or test.

FAA Test Prep also contains a listing by state of all major testing center locations for CATS, AvTest, LaserGrade, and Sylvan as well as instructor sign-off forms needed to take the pilot knowledge tests. Gleim's *FAA Test Prep* is an all-in-one program designed to help anyone with a computer and an interest in flying to pass the pilot knowledge tests.

FREE Updates and Technical Support

Gleim offers FREE technical support to all registered users. Call (800) 87-GLEIM, send e-mail to support@gleim.com, or fill out the technical support request form online (www.gleim.com/techform.html). Downloadable library updates will also be available free to registered users of our CD-ROM software. For more information on update service by e-mail, turn to page 817.

Diskette Version Available for Windows 3.1 or DOS Users

The diskette version of FAA Test Prep uses the same database of questions as the CD-ROM version and includes emulations of all the major testing centers (CATS, AvTest, LaserGrade, and Sylvan). The diskette version does not contain outlines and requires the appropriate Gleim book to reference charts and figures. Customers may upgrade from the diskette to the CD-ROM version by mailing in the diskette with a check for $25 (Private Pilot) or $35 (all other libraries).

END OF CHAPTER

CHAPTER TWO
NTSB PART 830, FAR PART 1, FAR PART 61, FAR PART 119

This chapter contains outlines of major concepts tested; all FAA test questions and answers regarding NTSB Part 830 and FAR Parts 1, 61, and 119; and an explanation of each answer. Each module is listed above with the number of questions from the FAA pilot knowledge test pertaining to that particular module. For each module, the first number following the parentheses is the page number on which the outline begins, and the next number is the page number on which the questions begin.

There are 46 questions in this chapter. We separate and organize the FAA questions into meaningful study units, i.e., chapters and modules. As an analogy, it is easier to deal with the "trees" if you understand the "forest." In this context, "trees" are individual FAA questions, and the "forest" is the ATP knowledge test. The organizational units between the overall ATP knowledge test and individual ATP test questions are chapters and modules in this book.

CAUTION: The **sole purpose** of this book is to expedite passing the FAA knowledge test. Topics or regulations not directly tested on the FAA knowledge test are omitted. Much more information and knowledge are necessary to fly safely. This additional material is presented in Gleim's other pilot training books and in many FAA books and circulars, as well as in airplane *POH*s and other commercial textbooks.

2.1 NTSB PART 830

830.2 Definitions (Questions 1-3)

1. A **serious injury**, as defined by the NTSB, includes
   a. An injury which caused severe tendon damage
   b. An injury requiring hospitalization of at least 48 hr. commencing within 7 days after the date of the injury
2. **Substantial damage**, as defined by the NTSB, includes failure of a component that adversely affects the airplane's performance and requires replacement of the affected component.

830.5 Immediate Notification (Questions 4-5)

1. Several types of incidents require immediate notification to the NTSB, including flight control system malfunction.
2. The NTSB must be notified immediately when an aircraft accident results in substantial damage.

830.15 Reports and Statement to Be Filed (Questions 6-7)

1. The operator of an aircraft involved in an accident must file a report with the NTSB within 10 days.
2. The operator of an aircraft involved in an incident must submit a report to the NTSB only if requested to do so by the NTSB.

2.2 FAR PART 1

1.1 General Definitions (Questions 8-11)

1. **Clearway** -- for turbine-engine-powered airplanes certificated after August 29, 1959, an area beyond the runway, not less than 500 ft. wide, centrally located about the extended centerline of the runway and under the control of the airport authorities. The clearway is expressed in terms of a clearway plane, extending from the end of the runway with an upward slope not exceeding 1.25%, above which no object or terrain protrudes. However, threshold lights may protrude above the plane if their height above the end of the runway is 26 in. or less and if they are located on each side of the runway.
2. **Crewmember** -- a person assigned to perform duty in an aircraft during flight time
3. **Operational control** -- with respect to a flight, the exercise of authority over initiating, conducting, or terminating a flight
4. **Stopway** -- an area beyond the takeoff runway, no less wide than the runway and centered upon the extended centerline of the runway, able to support the airplane during an aborted takeoff without causing structural damage to the airplane, and designated by the airport authorities for use in decelerating the airplane during an aborted takeoff

1.2 Abbreviations and Symbols (Questions 12-20)

1. V_C is design cruising speed.
2. V_2 is takeoff safety speed.
3. V_{MO}/M_{MO} is the maximum operating limit speed for an airplane.
4. V_{MU} is minimum unstick speed.
5. V_S is the stalling speed or the minimum steady flight speed at which the airplane is controllable.
6. V_{S0} is the minimum steady flight speed or stalling speed in a landing configuration.
7. V_{EF} is the speed at which the critical engine is assumed to fail during takeoff.
8. V_1 is the maximum speed in the takeoff at which the pilot must take the first action (e.g., apply brakes, reduce thrust, deploy speed brakes) to stop the airplane within the accelerate-stop distance.
    a. V_1 also is the minimum speed in the takeoff, following a failure of the critical engine at V_{EF}, at which the pilot may continue the takeoff and achieve the required height above the takeoff surface.

2.3 FAR PART 61

61.13 Issuance of Airman Certificates, Ratings, and Authorizations (Questions 21-23)

1. Upon the original issuance of a Category II (ILS) pilot authorization, the authorization contains a limitation of 1,600 ft. RVR (runway visual range).

2. A Category II limitation is removed when the holder shows that, within the past 6 months, (s)he has made three Category II ILS approaches with a 150-ft. decision height to a landing under actual or simulated instrument conditions.

61.15 Offenses Involving Alcohol or Drugs (Question 24)

1. No later than 60 days after conviction for driving while intoxicated by alcohol or drugs, a pilot must report the action to the FAA, Civil Aviation Security Division.

61.23 Medical Certificates: Requirement and Duration (Questions 25-27)

1. A person is not required to hold a medical certificate when taking a practical test for a certificate or type rating that is conducted entirely in a flight simulator or flight training device.

61.29 Replacement of Lost or Destroyed Airman or Medical Certificate or Knowledge Test Report (Question 28)

1. The maximum time a temporary replacement certificate is valid is 60 days.
2. If you need a replacement certificate, call (405) 954-3261.

61.31 Type Rating Requirements, Additional Training, and Authorization Requirements (Question 29)

1. The pilot in command is required to hold a type rating when operating an aircraft with a gross weight of more than 12,500 lb. or any turbojet-powered airplane.

61.39 Prerequisites for Practical Tests (Questions 30-31)

1. To take an entire practical test or only a portion of the test, the person is required to hold at least a current third-class medical certificate.

61.51 Pilot Logbooks (Question 32)

1. In an airplane requiring two pilots, all of the time during which the second in command is controlling the airplane solely by reference to flight instruments may be logged by him/her as instrument flight time.

61.57 Recent Flight Experience: Pilot in Command (Questions 33-35)

1. To maintain instrument experience, you must have logged, within the past 6 months, at least six instrument approaches, holding procedures, and tracking courses through the use of navigation systems.
    a. This experience must be logged in the appropriate category of aircraft or in a flight simulator or flight training device that is representative of the category of aircraft for the instrument privileges sought.
    b. Thus, to be current for IFR operations in an airplane, all of the requirements must be met in an airplane, an airplane flight simulator, or an airplane flight training device.
2. Alternatively, an instrument proficiency check may be completed every 6 months.

61.67 Category II Pilot Authorization Requirements (Questions 36-37)

1. To be eligible for the practical test for the original issue or renewal of a Category II authorization, the pilot must fly six ILS approaches, three of which may be flown to the Category I decision height by use of an approach coupler (autopilot).

61.157 Flight Proficiency (Questions 38-39)

1. Any type rating(s) on the pilot certificate of an applicant who successfully completes an ATP practical test shall be included on the ATP certificate, provided the applicant passes the practical test in the same category and class of aircraft as the type rating(s).
    a. If a type rating is limited to VFR, that limitation shall be carried forward to the person's ATP certificate level.

61.167 Privileges (Questions 40-41)

1. An airline transport pilot may instruct other pilots in air transportation service, excluding briefings and debriefings, for a maximum of
   a. 8 hr. in any 24-consecutive-hour period
   b. 36 hr. in any 7-consecutive-day period

2.4 FAR PART 119

119.3 Definitions (Questions 42-43)

1. **Provisional airport** means an airport approved by the Administrator for use by a certificate holder for the purpose of providing service to a community when the regular airport used by the certificate holder is not available.

119.5 Certifications, Authorizations, and Prohibitions (Questions 44-45)

1. A person who is not authorized to conduct direct air carrier operations, but who is authorized by the Administrator to conduct operations as a U.S. commercial operator, will be issued an Operating Certificate.
2. The operations specifications specifically authorize a Part 121 or 135 certificate holder to operate an aircraft in a particular geographical area.

119.49 Contents of Operations Specifications (Question 46)

1. The kinds of operations that a certificate holder is authorized to conduct are specified in the certificate holder's operations specifications.

2.1 NTSB PART 830

830.2 Definitions

1.
8320. Which of the following meets the requirements of a "serious injury" as defined by the NTSB?

A—A simple fracture of the nose or other extremity.
B—An injury which caused severe tendon damage.
C—First-degree burns over 5 percent of the body.

Answer (B) is correct (8320). *(NTSB 830.2)*

Serious injury means any injury which (1) requires hospitalization for more than 48 hr., commencing within 7 days from the date the injury was received; (2) results in a fracture in any bone (except simple fractures of the fingers, toes, or nose); (3) causes severe hemorrhages, nerve, muscle, or tendon damage; (4) involves any internal organ; or (5) involves second- or third-degree burns, or any burns covering more than 5% of the body surface.

Answer (A) is incorrect because simple fractures, such as of the finger, toe, or nose, are not considered a serious injury. Answer (C) is incorrect because only second- and third-degree burns or first-degree burns over more than 5%, not just 5%, of the body are defined as a serious injury. First-degree burns are less serious than second- and third-degree burns.

2.
8317. What period of time must a person be hospitalized before an injury may be defined by the NTSB as a "serious injury"?

A—72 hours; commencing within 10 days after date of injury.
B—48 hours; commencing within 7 days after date of the injury.
C—10 days, with no other extenuating circumstances.

Answer (B) is correct (8317). *(NTSB 830.2)*

Serious injury means any injury which requires hospitalization for more than 48 hr., commencing within 7 days from the date the injury was received.

Answer (A) is incorrect because 72 hr. is not a time frame requirement defined in NTSB Part 830. Answer (C) is incorrect because 10 days is the amount of time required to file a report to the NTSB after an accident.

3.
8319. Which of the following constitutes "substantial damage" according to NTSB Part 830?

A—Ground damage to landing gear, wheels, or tires.
B—Damage to wingtips (or rotor blades, in the case of a helicopter).
C—Failure of a component which would adversely affect the performance, and which would require replacement.

Answer (C) is correct (8319). *(NTSB 830.2)*

Substantial damage means damage or failure that adversely affects the structural strength, performance, or flight characteristics of the aircraft and requires major repair or replacement of the affected component.

Answer (A) is incorrect because ground damage to landing gear, wheels, or tires is not considered "substantial damage" for the purpose of NTSB Part 830. Answer (B) is incorrect because damage to wingtips (or rotor blades, in the case of a helicopter) is not considered "substantial damage" for the purpose of NTSB Part 830.

830.5 Immediate Notification

4.
8321. Which incident requires an immediate notification to NTSB?

A—Aircraft colliding on the ground.
B—Flight control system malfunction.
C—Damage to property, other than the aircraft, estimated to exceed $10,000.

Answer (B) is correct (8321). *(NTSB 830.5)*

The NTSB must be notified immediately and by the most expeditious means possible when an aircraft accident or any of various listed incidents occurs or when an aircraft is overdue and believed to have been in an accident. The following are considered incidents:

1. Flight control system malfunction or failure
2. Inability of any required flight crewmember to perform normal flight duties as a result of injury or illness
3. Failure of structural components of a turbine engine, excluding compressor and turbine blades and vanes
4. In-flight fire
5. Aircraft collision in flight

Answer (A) is incorrect because a ground collision does not require immediate notification. Answer (C) is incorrect because immediate notification is required for damage to property of more than $25,000, not $10,000.

5.
8318. Within what time period should the nearest NTSB field office be notified when an aircraft is involved in an accident which results in substantial damage?

A—Immediately.
B—7 calendar days.
C—10 days.

Answer (A) is correct (8318). *(NTSB 830.5)*

The NTSB must be notified immediately and by the most expeditious means possible when an aircraft accident, which results in substantial damage, or any of various listed incidents occurs or when an aircraft is overdue and believed to have been in an accident.

Answer (B) is incorrect because a written report, not notification, is required after 7 days if an overdue aircraft is still missing, not after an aircraft is involved in an accident which results in substantial damage. Answer (C) is incorrect because a written accident report, not notification, is required within 10 days.

830.15 Reports and Statement to Be Filed

6.
8322. Within how many days must the operator of an aircraft involved in an accident file a report to the NTSB?

A—3 days.
B—7 days.
C—10 days.

Answer (C) is correct (8322). *(NTSB 830.15)*

The operator of an aircraft shall file a report on NTSB Form 6120.1 or Form 7120.2 within 10 days after an accident.

Answer (A) is incorrect because a written report to the NTSB is required within 10 days, not 3 days, after an accident. Answer (B) is incorrect because a written report to the NTSB is required within 7 days for an overdue aircraft that is still missing, not for an aircraft involved in an accident.

7.
8323. When is an operator of an aircraft, which has been involved in an incident, required to submit a report to the nearest field office of the NTSB?

A—Within 7 days.
B—Within 10 days.
C—Only if requested to do so by the NTSB.

Answer (C) is correct (8323). *(NTSB 830.15)*

The operator of an aircraft shall file a report on NTSB Form 6120.1 or Form 7120.2 on an incident for which notification is required only if requested to do so by the NTSB.

Answer (A) is incorrect because a written report to the NTSB is required within 7 days for an overdue aircraft that is still missing, not for an incident. Answer (B) is incorrect because a written report to the NTSB is required within 10 days of an accident, not an incident, involving an aircraft.

2.2 FAR PART 1

1.1 General Definitions

8.
9324. What is the name of a plane beyond the end of a runway which does not contain obstructions and can be considered when calculating takeoff performance of turbine-powered aircraft?

A—Clearway.
B—Stopway.
C—Obstruction clearance plane.

Answer (A) is correct (9324). *(FAR 1.1)*
A clearway is an area beyond the runway, not less than 500 ft. wide, centrally located about the extended centerline of the runway and under the control of the airport authorities. The clearway is expressed in terms of a clearway plane, extending from the end of the runway with an upward slope not exceeding 1.25%, above which no object or terrain protrudes. However, threshold lights may protrude above the plane if their height above the end of the runway is 26 in. or less and if they are located on each side of the runway.
Answer (B) is incorrect because a stopway is an area beyond the takeoff runway, no less wide than the runway and centered upon the extended centerline of the runway, able to support the airplane during an aborted takeoff. Answer (C) is incorrect because an obstruction clearance plane is used in calculating the effective length of a runway for landing limitations, not for calculating takeoff performance in a turbine-powered aircraft.

9.
9325. Which is a definition of the term "crewmember"?

A—Only a pilot, flight engineer, or flight navigator assigned to duty in an aircraft during flight time.
B—A person assigned to perform duty in an aircraft during flight time.
C—Any person assigned to duty in an aircraft during flight except a pilot or flight engineer.

Answer (B) is correct (9325). *(FAR 1.1)*
A crewmember is a person assigned to perform duty in an aircraft during flight time.
Answer (A) is incorrect because crewmember includes cabin crew as well as cockpit crew. Answer (C) is incorrect because crewmember includes cockpit crew as well as cabin crew.

10.
9326. Regulations concerning the operational control of a flight refer to

A—the specific duties of any required crewmember.
B—exercising authority over initiating, conducting, or terminating a flight.
C—exercising the privileges of pilot in command of an aircraft.

Answer (B) is correct (9326). *(FAR 1.1)*
Operational control of a flight refers to the exercise of authority over initiating, conducting, or terminating a flight.
Answer (A) is incorrect because crewmember refers to any person assigned to perform duty in an aircraft during flight time, which includes cabin crew as well as cockpit crew. Answer (C) is incorrect because pilot in command refers to the pilot responsible for the operation and safety of an aircraft during flight time.

11.
9327. What is an area identified by the term "stopway"?

A—An area, at least the same width as the runway, capable of supporting an airplane during a normal takeoff.
B—An area designated for use in decelerating an aborted takeoff.
C—An area, not as wide as the runway, capable of supporting an airplane during a normal takeoff.

Answer (B) is correct (9327). *(FAR 1.1)*
A stopway is an area beyond the takeoff runway, no less wide than the runway and centered upon the extended centerline of the runway, able to support the airplane during an aborted takeoff without causing structural damage to the airplane.
Answer (A) is incorrect because an area, at least the same width as the runway, capable of supporting an airplane during a normal takeoff describes the nonlanding portion of a runway, which is before a displaced threshold and may be suitable for taxiing, landing rollout, and takeoff of aircraft. Answer (C) is incorrect because an area, not as wide as the runway, capable of supporting an airplane during a normal takeoff describes an area that exists before a displaced threshold.

1.2 Abbreviations and Symbols

12.
9321. Which is the correct symbol for design cruising speed?

A—V_C.
B—V_S.
C—V_{MA}.

Answer (A) is correct (9321). *(FAR 1.2)*
V_C is design cruising speed. Design cruising speed is established by the manufacturer and is used to define the flight envelope parameters in the aircraft certification.
Answer (B) is incorrect because V_S is the stalling speed or minimum steady flight speed at which the airplane is controllable. Answer (C) is incorrect because V_{MA} is a nonsense concept in that it is not defined in FAR 1.2.

13.
9317. Which is a definition of V_2 speed?

A—Takeoff decision speed.
B—Takeoff safety speed.
C—Minimum takeoff speed.

Answer (B) is correct (9317). *(FAR 1.2)*
V_2 is takeoff safety speed. Takeoff safety speed means a referenced airspeed obtained after liftoff at which the required one-engine-inoperative climb performance can be achieved.
Answer (A) is incorrect because V_2 is takeoff safety speed, not takeoff decision speed. There is no symbol for takeoff decision speed. Answer (C) is incorrect because V_{2MIN}, not V_2, is minimum takeoff safety speed.

14.
9320. Which speed symbol indicates the maximum operating limit speed for an airplane?

A—V_{LE}.
B—V_{MO}/M_{MO}.
C—V_{LO}/M_{LO}.

Answer (B) is correct (9320). *(FAR 1.2)*
V_{MO}/M_{MO} is maximum operating limit speed. Maximum operating limit speed is also known as maximum Mach number, which is analogous to V_{NE} of a small airplane.
Answer (A) is incorrect because V_{LE} is maximum landing gear extended speed. Answer (C) is incorrect because V_{LO} is the maximum speed for operating the landing gear.

15.
9319. What is the correct symbol for minimum unstick speed?

A—V_{MU}.
B—V_{MD}.
C—V_{FC}.

Answer (A) is correct (9319). *(FAR 1.2)*
V_{MU} is minimum unstick speed. Minimum unstick speed is the minimum airspeed at which the airplane can be made to take off without demonstrating hazardous characteristics while continuing the takeoff.
Answer (B) is incorrect because V_{MD} is a nonsense concept in that it is not defined in FAR 1.2. Answer (C) is incorrect because V_{FC}/M_{FC} is maximum speed for stability characteristics.

16.
9323. Which is the correct symbol for the stalling speed or the minimum steady flight speed at which the airplane is controllable?

A—V_{S0}.
B—V_S.
C—V_{S1}.

Answer (B) is correct (9323). *(FAR 1.2)*
V_S is the stalling speed or the minimum steady flight speed at which the airplane is controllable.
Answer (A) is incorrect because V_{S0} is the stalling speed or the minimum steady flight speed in the landing configuration. Answer (C) is incorrect because V_{S1} is the stalling speed or the minimum steady flight speed obtained in a specific configuration.

17.
9322. Which is the correct symbol for the minimum steady-flight speed or stalling speed in the landing configuration?

A—V_S.
B—V_{S1}.
C—V_{S0}.

Answer (C) is correct (9322). *(FAR 1.2)*
V_{S0} is the stalling speed or the minimum steady flight speed in the landing configuration.
Answer (A) is incorrect because V_S is the stalling speed or the minimum steady flight speed at which the airplane is controllable. Answer (B) is incorrect because V_{S1} is the stalling speed or the minimum steady flight speed obtained in a specific configuration.

18.
8780. The symbol for the speed at which the critical engine is assumed to fail during takeoff is

A—V_2.
B—V_1.
C—V_{EF}.

Answer (C) is correct (8780). *(FAR 1.2)*
V_{EF} means the speed at which the critical engine is assumed to fail during takeoff.
Answer (A) is incorrect because V_2 is the takeoff safety speed, not the speed at which the critical engine is assumed to fail during takeoff. Answer (B) is incorrect because V_1 is the maximum speed in the takeoff at which the pilot must take the first action to stop the airplane within the accelerate-stop distance, not the speed at which the critical engine is assumed to fail during takeoff.

19.
8774. The maximum speed during takeoff that the pilot may abort the takeoff and stop the airplane within the accelerate-stop distance is

A—V_2.
B—V_{EF}.
C—V_1.

Answer (C) is correct (8774). *(FAR 1.2)*

V_1 means the maximum speed in the takeoff at which the pilot must take the first action (e.g., apply brakes, reduce thrust, deploy speed brakes) to stop the airplane within the accelerate-stop distance.

Answer (A) is incorrect because V_2 is the takeoff safety speed, not the maximum speed during takeoff that the pilot may abort the takeoff and stop the airplane within the accelerate-stop distance. Answer (B) is incorrect because V_{EF} means the speed at which the critical engine is assumed to fail during takeoff, not the maximum speed during takeoff that the pilot may abort the takeoff and stop the airplane within the accelerate-stop distance.

20.
8775. The minimum speed during takeoff, following a failure of the critical engine at V_{EF}, at which the pilot may continue the takeoff and achieve the required height above the takeoff surface within the takeoff distance is indicated by symbol

A—V_{2MIN}.
B—V_1.
C—V_{LOF}.

Answer (B) is correct (8775). *(FAR 1.2)*

V_1 is the minimum speed in the takeoff, following a failure of the critical engine at V_{EF}, at which the pilot can continue the takeoff and achieve the required height above the takeoff surface within the takeoff distance.

Answer (A) is incorrect because V_{2MIN} is the minimum takeoff safety speed, not the minimum speed during takeoff, following a failure of the critical engine at V_{EF}, at which the pilot may continue the takeoff and achieve the required height above the takeoff surface within the takeoff distance. Answer (C) is incorrect because V_{LOF} is the liftoff speed, not the minimum speed during takeoff, following a failure of the critical engine at V_{EF}, at which the pilot may continue the takeoff and achieve the required height above the takeoff surface within the takeoff distance.

2.3 FAR PART 61

<u>61.13 Issuance of Airman Certificates, Ratings, and Authorizations</u>

21.
9348. What is the lowest HAT for which a Category II applicant can be certified during the original issuance of the authorization?

A—100 feet AGL.
B—150 feet AGL.
C—200 feet AGL.

Answer (B) is correct (9348). *(FAR 61.13)*

Upon original issuance of a Category II pilot authorization, the authorization contains a limitation for Category II operations of 1,600 ft. RVR (runway visual range) and a 150-ft. decision height.

Answer (A) is incorrect because a 100-ft. decision height is allowed after completion of three Category II ILS approaches with a 150-ft. DH within the previous 6 months. Answer (C) is incorrect because 200 ft. is the standard Category I ILS decision height.

22.
9347. A Category II ILS pilot authorization, when originally issued, is normally limited to

A—Category II operations not less than 1600 RVR and a 150-foot DH.
B—pilots who have completed an FAA-approved Category II training program.
C—Category II operations not less than 1200 RVR and a 100-foot DH.

Answer (A) is correct (9347). *(FAR 61.13)*

Upon original issuance of a Category II authorization, the authorization contains a limitation for Category II operations of 1,600 ft. RVR and a 150-ft. DH. This initial limitation is removed when three Category II ILS approaches within a 150-ft. DH have been flown.

Answer (B) is incorrect because a Category II pilot authorization is issued as a part of a pilot's instrument rating or ATP certificate, not a Category II training program. Answer (C) is incorrect because a 1,200 RVR and a 100-ft. DH are the Category II minimums after the initial limitation is removed by the pilot's completing three ILS approaches to a 150-ft. DH in the preceding 6 months.

23.
9346. When may a Category II ILS limitation be removed?

A — When three Category II ILS approaches have been completed to a 150-foot decision height and landing.
B — When six ILS approaches to Category II minimums and landings have been completed in the past 6 months.
C — 120 days after issue or renewal.

Answer (A) is correct (9346). *(FAR 61.13)*

The Category II limitation is removed when the holder shows that, since the beginning of the sixth preceding month, (s)he has made three Category II ILS approaches with a 150-ft. decision height to a landing under actual or simulated instrument conditions.

Answer (B) is incorrect because the removal of the Category II limitation requires only three, not six, Category II ILS approaches to a 150-ft. decision height. Answer (C) is incorrect because 120 days is the expiration of a temporary airman certificate and is not related to Category II limitations.

61.15 Offenses Involving Alcohol or Drugs

24.
9332. How soon after the conviction for driving while intoxicated by alcohol or drugs shall it be reported to the FAA, Civil Aviation Security Division?

A — No later than 30 working days after the motor vehicle action.
B — No later than 60 days after the motor vehicle action.
C — Required to be reported upon renewal of medical certificate.

Answer (B) is correct (9332). *(FAR 61.15)*

Each individual convicted of driving while intoxicated by alcohol or drugs shall provide a written report of each motor vehicle action to the FAA, Civil Aviation Security Division, not later than 60 days after the motor vehicle action.

Answer (A) is incorrect because the report will be sent no later than 60 days, not 30 days, after the motor vehicle action. Answer (C) is incorrect because, although conviction of driving while intoxicated by alcohol or drugs is reported on medical certificates, notification of a motor vehicle action for these offenses is required to be reported to the FAA in Oklahoma City no later than 60 days from that date.

61.23 Medical Certificates: Requirement and Duration

25.
9333. An applicant who is scheduled for a practical test for an airline transport pilot certificate, in an approved flight simulator, is

A — required to have at least a current third-class medical certificate.
B — not required to have a medical certificate.
C — required to have a first-class medical certificate.

Answer (B) is correct (9333). *(FAR 61.23)*

When taking the practical test for an airline transport pilot certificate in a flight simulator, an applicant is not required to have a medical certificate.

Answer (A) is incorrect because an applicant is required to have at least a third-class medical certificate if the ATP practical test is conducted in an airplane, not a flight simulator. Answer (C) is incorrect because an applicant is required to have a first-class medical certificate to exercise the privileges of an ATP certificate, not to take the ATP practical test.

26.
9335. An applicant who is taking a practical test for a type rating to be added to a commercial pilot certificate, in an approved simulator, is

A — required to have a first-class medical certificate.
B — required to have a second-class medical certificate.
C — not required to have a medical certificate.

Answer (C) is correct (9335). *(FAR 61.23)*

A person who is taking a practical test for a type rating to be added to a commercial pilot certificate, in a flight simulator, is not required to have a medical certificate.

Answer (A) is incorrect because a person is required to have a first-class medical certificate to exercise the privileges of an ATP certificate, not to take a practical test for a type rating in a flight simulator. Answer (B) is incorrect because a person is required to have a second-class medical certificate to exercise the privileges of a commercial pilot certificate, not to take a practical test for a type rating in a flight simulator.

27.
9343. When a type rating is to be added to an airline transport pilot certificate, and the practical test is scheduled in an approved flight training device and/or approved flight simulator, the applicant is

A — required to have at least a third-class medical certificate.
B — is not required to have a medical certificate.
C — required to have a first-class medical certificate.

Answer (B) is correct (9343). *(FAR 61.23)*

A person who is taking a practical test in a flight simulator or flight training device for a type rating to be added to an ATP certificate is not required to have a medical certificate.

Answer (A) is incorrect because a third-class medical certificate is required if any part of the practical test is conducted in an airplane, not if the practical test is conducted entirely in a flight simulator or flight training device. Answer (C) is incorrect because a person is required to have a first-class medical certificate to exercise the privileges of an ATP certificate, not to take a practical test to add a type rating to an ATP certificate.

61.29 Replacement of Lost or Destroyed Airman or Medical Certificate or Knowledge Test Report

28.
9351. When a temporary replacement is received for an airman's medical certificate, for what maximum time is this document valid?

A—30 days.
B—60 days.
C—90 days.

Answer (B) is correct (9351). *(FAR 61.29)*
A person who has lost an airman certificate or medical certificate may obtain a fax from the FAA confirming that it was issued. The fax may be carried as a certificate for a period not to exceed 60 days pending his/her receipt of a duplicate certificate.
Answer (A) is incorrect because the fax that may be carried as a certificate is valid for 60 days, not 30 days. Answer (C) is incorrect because the fax that may be issued as a certificate is valid for 60 days, not 90 days.

61.31 Type Rating Requirements, Additional Training, and Authorization Requirements

29.
9350. Unless otherwise authorized, when is the pilot in command required to hold a type rating?

A—When operating an aircraft that is certificated for more than one pilot.
B—When operating an aircraft having a gross weight of more than 12,500 pounds.
C—When operating a multiengine aircraft having a gross weight of more than 6,000 pounds.

Answer (B) is correct (9350). *(FAR 61.31)*
A person may not act as pilot in command of any turbojet or other large aircraft (an aircraft of more than 12,500 lb. maximum certificated takeoff weight) unless (s)he holds a type rating for that aircraft.
Answer (A) is incorrect because, although an aircraft may require two pilots for its operation, only turbojet aircraft and other aircraft in excess of 12,500 lb. require a type rating. Answer (C) is incorrect because large aircraft are those aircraft in excess of 12,500 lb., not 6,000 lb. They can be either single-engine or multiengine aircraft.

61.39 Prerequisites for Practical Tests

30.
9340. An applicant who is scheduled for a practical test for an airline transport pilot certificate, in an aircraft, needs

A—a first-class medical certificate.
B—at least a current third-class medical certificate.
C—a second-class medical certificate.

Answer (B) is correct (9340). *(FAR 61.39)*
A person who is scheduled for an ATP practical test in an airplane must hold at least a current third-class medical certificate.
Answer (A) is incorrect because a person is required to have a first-class medical certificate to exercise the privileges of an ATP certificate, not to take the ATP practical test in an airplane. Answer (C) is incorrect because a person is required to have a second-class medical certificate to exercise the privileges of a commercial pilot certificate, not to take the ATP practical test in an airplane.

31.
9349. When a type rating is to be added to an airline transport pilot certificate, and the practical test is scheduled in an approved flight simulator and an aircraft, the applicant is

A—required to have at least a current third-class medical certificate.
B—required to have a current first-class medical certificate.
C—not required to hold a medical certificate.

Answer (A) is correct (9349). *(FAR 61.39)*
When a type rating is to be added to an ATP certificate, and the practical test is scheduled in a flight simulator and an airplane, the person is required to have at least a current third-class medical certificate.
Answer (B) is incorrect because a person is required to have a first-class medical certificate to exercise the privileges of an ATP certificate, not to take a practical test for a type rating to be added to an ATP certificate. Answer (C) is incorrect because the person is required to hold at least a current third-class medical certificate since a portion of the practical test will be conducted in an airplane. If the entire test will be completed in a flight simulator, a person does not need a medical certificate.

61.51 Pilot Logbooks

32.
9342. What instrument flight time may be logged by a second in command of an aircraft requiring two pilots?

A—All of the time the second in command is controlling the airplane solely by reference to flight instruments.
B—One-half the time the flight is on an IFR flight plan.
C—One-half the time the airplane is in actual IFR conditions.

Answer (A) is correct (9342). *(FAR 61.51)*
A pilot may log as instrument flight time only that time during which (s)he operates the aircraft solely by reference to the flight instruments under actual or simulated instrument flying conditions.
Answer (B) is incorrect because only when the pilot is flying in actual or simulated instrument flying conditions as sole manipulator of the controls may (s)he log instrument flight time. Answer (C) is incorrect because a pilot may log all flight time in which (s)he is sole manipulator of the controls in IFR conditions as instrument flight time.

61.57 Recent Flight Experience: Pilot in Command

33.
9344. To satisfy the minimum required instrument experience for IFR operations, a pilot must accomplish during the past 6 months at least

A—six instrument approaches, holding, intercepting, and tracking courses through the use of navigation systems in an approved flight training device/simulator or in the category of aircraft to be flown.
B—six instrument approaches, three of which must be in the same category and class of aircraft to be flown, plus holding, intercepting, and tracking courses in any aircraft.
C—six instrument approaches and 6 hours of instrument time, three of which may be in a glider.

Answer (A) is correct (9344). *(FAR 61.57)*
To satisfy the minimum required instrument experience for IFR operations, a pilot must accomplish six instrument approaches, holding, and intercepting and tracking courses through the use of navigation systems in a flight simulator or flight training device (representative of the category of aircraft to be flown) or in the appropriate category of aircraft to be flown.

Answer (B) is incorrect because, to meet the instrument currency, all of the instrument approaches, holding, and intercepting and tracking courses must be completed in the category of aircraft to be used or in a flight simulator or training device that is representative of the aircraft to be used, not any aircraft. Answer (C) is incorrect because no minimum instrument time is required and all of the requirements must be accomplished in the category of aircraft to be used. In addition to six approaches, the pilot must also accomplish holding and intercepting and tracking courses.

34.
9339. A pilot, acting as second in command, successfully completes the instrument competency check specified in FAR Part 61. How long does this pilot remain current if no further IFR flights are made?

A—12 months.
B—90 days.
C—6 months.

Answer (C) is correct (9339). *(FAR 61.57)*
A pilot acting as either pilot in command or second in command will remain current for 6 months after an instrument competency check if no further IFR flights are made.

Answer (A) is incorrect because, upon completion of an instrument competency check, a pilot will remain current for 6 months, not 12 months. Answer (B) is incorrect because 90 days defines the three takeoffs-and-landings experience required to carry passengers.

35.
9338. Within the past 6 months, a pilot has accomplished:

Two approaches in a helicopter.
Two approaches in an airplane.
Two approaches in a glider.

What additional instrument experience must the pilot obtain prior to acting as second in command (under 14 CFR Part 135) on an IFR flight?

A—Four approaches in an aircraft, approved training device, flight simulator (that is representative of the aircraft category), holding, intercepting and tracking courses using the navigation systems.
B—Passes an instrument proficiency check in any cate-gory aircraft, approved simulator or training device.
C—Holding, intercepting and tracking courses (using the navigation systems) in an aircraft, approved simulator or approved flight training device.

Answer (A) is correct (9338). *(FAR 61.57, 135.245)*
FAR 135.247 requires that the second in command on an IFR flight meet the instrument experience requirements of Part 61. FAR 61.57 requires that in the past 6 months a pilot must have accomplished at least six instrument approaches, holding procedures, and intercepting and tracking courses through the use of navigation systems in an aircraft, flight simulator, or flight training device that is representative of the aircraft category for the instrument privileges sought.

Answer (B) is incorrect because an instrument proficiency check must be in an aircraft, flight simulator, or flight training device that is appropriate to the aircraft category, not any category of aircraft. Answer (C) is incorrect because six instrument approaches, holding, and intercepting and tracking courses must be done in the same category (airplane) of aircraft for which instrument privileges are sought; thus the pilot must accomplish four approaches in an airplane or an airplane flight simulator or training device for his/her instrument experience to be current.

61.67 Category II Pilot Authorization Requirements

36.
9334. What recent experience is required to be eligible for the practical test for the original issue of a Category II authorization?

A—Within the previous 6 months, six ILS approaches flown manually to the Category I DH.
B—Within the previous 12 calendar months, six ILS approaches flown by use of an approach coupler to the Category I or Category II DH.
C—Within the previous 6 months, six ILS approaches, three of which may be flown to the Category I DH by use of an approach coupler.

Answer (C) is correct (9334). *(FAR 61.67)*
An applicant for the original issuance of a Category II authorization must have made at least six ILS approaches since the beginning of the sixth month before the practical test. These approaches must be under actual or simulated instrument flight conditions down to the minimum landing altitude for the ILS approach in the type of airplane in which the flight is to be conducted. At least three of these approaches must be conducted manually, without the use of an autopilot (approach coupler).
Answer (A) is incorrect because only three of the six approaches must be flown manually to Category I DH.
Answer (B) is incorrect because the six ILS approaches must be flown within the preceding 6, not 12, calendar months, and three of the approaches must be flown manually, not with an approach coupler.

37.
9345. To be eligible for the practical test for the renewal of a Category II authorization, what recent instrument approach experience is required?

A—Within the previous 6 months, six ILS approaches, three of which may be flown to the Category I DH by use of an approach coupler.
B—Within the previous 6 months, six ILS approaches flown by use of an approach coupler to the Category I DH.
C—Within the previous 12 calendar months, three ILS approaches flown by use of an approach coupler to the Category II DH.

Answer (A) is correct (9345). *(FAR 61.67)*
For a pilot to renew his/her Category II authorization, (s)he must meet the same requirements as those established for the original issuance; i.e., at least six ILS approaches must have been made under actual or simulated instrument flight conditions down to the minimum landing altitude for the ILS approach in the type of airplane in which the flight is to be conducted, and they must have been completed since the beginning of the sixth month before the test. At least three of these approaches must have been flown manually without the use of an approach coupler.
Answer (B) is incorrect because only three of the six approaches may be flown using an approach coupler.
Answer (C) is incorrect because the requirement is for a total of six, not three, approaches, only three of which may be flown by use of an approach coupler. The approaches are not required to be flown down to Category II DH. Also, they must have been flown within the preceding 6, not 12, calendar months.

61.157 Flight Proficiency

38.
9328. A commercial pilot has a type rating in a B-727 and B-737. A flight test is completed in a B-747 for the Airline Transport Pilot Certificate. What pilot privileges may be exercised regarding these airplanes?

A—Commercial - B-737; ATP - B-727 and B-747.
B—ATP - B-747; Commercial - B-727 and B-737.
C—ATP - B-747, B-727, and B-737.

Answer (C) is correct (9328). *(FAR 61.157)*
When a person successfully passes the ATP practical test, all type ratings will be included at the ATP certificate level, provided that the aircraft used on the practical test is the same category and class of aircraft as the type ratings. Since the B-727, 737, and 747 are all airplanes (category) and multiengine land (class), the ATP certificate privileges may be exercised for the B-727, 737, and 747.
Answer (A) is incorrect because all three airplanes, not only the B-727 and 747, will be included at the ATP certificate level, since they are all the same category and class of aircraft.
Answer (B) is incorrect because all three airplanes, not only the airplane in which the practical test was taken, will be at the ATP certificate level, since they are all the same category and class of aircraft.

39.
9329. A commercial pilot has DC-3 and DC-9 type ratings. A flight test is completed for an Airline Transport Pilot Certificate in a B-727. What pilot privileges may be exercised?

A—ATP - B-727 and DC-3; Commercial - DC-9.
B—ATP - B-727, DC-9, and DC-3.
C—ATP - B-727 and DC-9; Commercial - DC-3.

Answer (B) is correct (9329). *(FAR 61.157)*
When a person successfully passes the ATP practical test, all type ratings will be included at the ATP certificate level, provided that the aircraft used on the practical test is the same category and class of aircraft of the type ratings. Since the B-727, DC-3, and DC-9 are all airplanes (category) and multiengine land (class), the ATP certificate privileges may be exercised for the B-727, DC-9, and DC-3.
Answer (A) is incorrect because all three aircraft, not only the B-727 and DC-3, will be included at the ATP certificate level, since they are all the same category and class of aircraft.
Answer (C) is incorrect because all three aircraft, not only the B-727 and DC-9, will be included at the ATP certificate level, since they are all the same category and class of aircraft.

61.167 Privileges

40.
9330. In a 24-hour consecutive period, what is the maximum time, excluding briefing and debriefing, that an airline transport pilot may instruct other pilots in air transportation service?

A—8 hours.
B—6 hours.
C—10 hours.

Answer (A) is correct (9330). *(FAR 61.167)*
An airline transport pilot may instruct other pilots in air transportation service, excluding briefings and debriefings, for a maximum of 8 hr. in any 24-hr. consecutive period.
Answer (B) is incorrect because an airline transport pilot may instruct for a maximum of 8 hr., not 6 hr., in any 24-hr. consecutive period. Answer (C) is incorrect because an airline transport pilot may instruct for a maximum of 8 hr., not 10 hr., in any 24-hr. consecutive period.

41.
9331. The flight instruction of other pilots in air transportation service by an airline transport pilot is restricted to

A—36 hours in any 7-consecutive-day period.
B—7 hours in any 24-consecutive-hour period.
C—30 hours in any 7-consecutive-day period.

Answer (A) is correct (9331). *(FAR 61.167)*
The period of time that an airline transport pilot may instruct other pilots in air transportation service, excluding briefings and debriefings, is restricted to 36 hr. in any 7-consecutive-day period.
Answer (B) is incorrect because an airline transport pilot may instruct other pilots in air transportation for a maximum of 8 hr., not 7 hr., in any 24-consecutive-hour period. Answer (C) is incorrect because an airline transport pilot may instruct other pilots in air transportation for a maximum of 36 hr., not 30 hr., in any 7-consecutive-day period.

2.4 FAR PART 119

119.3 Definitions

42.
8429. An airport approved by the Administrator for use by an air carrier certificate holder for the purpose of providing service to a community when the regular airport is not available is a/an:

A—destination airport.
B—provisional airport.
C—alternate airport.

Answer (B) is correct (8429). *(FAR 119.3)*
Provisional airport is defined as an airport approved by the Administrator (FAA) for use by a certificate holder for the purpose of providing service to a community when the regular airport used by the certificate holder is not available.
Answer (A) is incorrect because a destination airport is the airport of intended landing when departing on a flight, not necessarily an airport approved by the FAA for use by an air carrier certificate holder for the purpose of providing service to a community when the regular airport is not available. Answer (C) is incorrect because an alternate airport means an airport at which an aircraft may land if a landing at the intended airport becomes inadvisable, not necessarily an airport approved by the FAA for use by an air carrier certificate holder for the purpose of providing service to a community when the regular airport is not available.

43.
8430. A provisional airport is an airport approved by the Administrator for use by an air carrier certificate holder for the purpose of

A—obtaining provisions and fuel when unable, due to winds, to proceed direct to the regular airport.
B—having the aircraft catered (foods, beverages, or supplies).
C—providing service to a community when the regular airport is unavailable.

Answer (C) is correct (8430). *(FAR 119.3)*
A provisional airport is an airport approved by the Administrator (FAA) for use by an air carrier certificate holder for the purpose of providing service to a community when the regular airport used by the certificate holder is unavailable.
Answer (A) is incorrect because an alternate airport, not a provisional airport, is an airport used to obtain provisions and fuel when an aircraft is unable, due to winds, to proceed direct to the regular airport. Answer (B) is incorrect because a provisional airport is an airport approved by the FAA for use by an air carrier certificate holder for the purpose of providing service to a community when the regular airport is unavailable, not for the purpose of having the airplane catered.

119.5 Certifications, Authorizations, and Prohibitions

44.
8767. A person who is not authorized to conduct direct air carrier operations, but who is authorized by the Administrator to conduct operations as a U.S. commercial operator, will be issued

A — an Air Carrier Certificate.
B — a Supplemental Air Carrier Certificate.
C — an Operating Certificate.

Answer (C) is correct (8767). *(FAR 119.5)*
A person who is not authorized to conduct direct air carrier operations, but who is authorized by the Administrator (FAA) to conduct operations as a U.S. commercial operator, will be issued an Operating Certificate.
Answer (A) is incorrect because an Air Carrier Certificate is issued to a person who is authorized, rather than to a person who is not authorized, to conduct direct air carrier operations. Answer (B) is incorrect because a person who is not authorized to conduct direct air carrier operations, but who is authorized by the FAA to conduct operations as a U.S. commercial operator, will be issued an Operating Certificate, not a Supplemental Air Carrier Certificate. Additionally, there is no certificate called a Supplemental Air Carrier Certificate.

45.
8003. Which document specifically authorizes a person to operate an aircraft in a particular geographic area?

A — Operations Specifications.
B — Operating Certificate.
C — Dispatch Release.

Answer (A) is correct (8003). *(FAR 119.5)*
Under Part 121 or 135, no person may operate an aircraft in a geographical area unless its operations specifications specifically authorize the certificate holder to operate in that area.
Answer (B) is incorrect because an operating certificate is issued to a business to conduct Part 121 or 135 operations; it does not state where the aircraft can operate. Answer (C) is incorrect because a dispatch release authorizes a flight to begin, not the geographic area in which a person can operate an aircraft.
FAR Part 119 contains certification rules for Parts 121, 125, and 135.

119.49 Contents of Operations Specifications

46.
8768. The kinds of operation that a certificate holder is authorized to conduct are specified in the

A — certificate holder's operations specifications.
B — application submitted for an Air Carrier or Operating Certificate, by the applicant.
C — Air Carrier Certificate or Operating Certificate.

Answer (A) is correct (8768). *(FAR 119.49)*
The kinds of operation that a certificate holder is authorized to conduct are specified in the certificate holder's operations specifications, i.e., domestic, flag, supplemental, commuter, or on-demand operations.
Answer (B) is incorrect because, while an applicant must inform the FAA as to what kinds of operation (s)he wants to operate when applying for an Air Carrier or Operating Certificate, the kinds of operation that a certificate holder is authorized to conduct are specified in the operations specifications. Answer (C) is incorrect because the kinds of operation that a certificate holder is authorized to conduct are specified in the operations specifications, not on the Air Carrier or Operating Certificate.

END OF CHAPTER

CHAPTER THREE
FAR PART 91, FAR PART 108, HAZARDOUS MATERIALS

This section contains outlines of major concepts tested, all FAA test questions and answers regarding FAR Parts 91 and 108 and hazardous materials, and an explanation of each answer. Each module, or subtopic, within this chapter is listed above with the number of questions from the FAA pilot knowledge test pertaining to that particular module. For each module, the first number following the parentheses is the page number on which the outline begins, and the next number is the page number on which the questions begin.

There are 84 questions in this chapter. We separate and organize the FAA questions into meaningful study units, i.e., chapters and modules. As an analogy, it is easier to deal with the "trees" if you understand the "forest." In this context, "trees" are individual FAA questions and the "forest" is the ATP knowledge test. The organizational units between the overall ATP knowledge test and individual ATP test questions are chapters and modules in this book.

CAUTION: The **sole purpose** of this book is to expedite your passing the FAA pilot knowledge test for the ATP certificate. Topics or regulations not directly tested on the FAA pilot knowledge test are omitted. Much more information and knowledge are necessary to fly safely. This additional material is presented in Gleim's other pilot training books (see the order form on page 818) and in many FAA books and circulars, as well as in airplane *POH*s and other commercial textbooks.

3.1 FAR PART 91

91.17 Alcohol or Drugs (Question 1)

1. No person may act or attempt to act as a crewmember of a civil aircraft within 8 hr. after the consumption of any alcoholic beverage, while under the influence of drugs or alcohol, or while having .04 percent by weight or more alcohol in the blood.

91.117 Aircraft Speed (Questions 2-6)

1. The maximum indicated airspeed below 10,000 ft. MSL (including Class B airspace) is 250 kt.
2. The maximum indicated airspeed at or below 2,500 ft. AGL within 4 NM of the primary airport of a Class C or Class D airspace area is 200 kt.
3. The maximum indicated airspeed in the airspace underlying Class B airspace, or in a VFR corridor designated through Class B airspace, is 200 kt.

91.123 Compliance with ATC Clearances and Instructions (Questions 7-8)

1. Each pilot in command who (though not deviating from an FAR) is given priority by ATC in an emergency shall submit a detailed report of that emergency within 48 hr. to the manager of that ATC facility, if requested by ATC.

91.129 Operations in Class D Airspace (Questions 9-11)

1. An airplane approaching to land on a runway served by a visual approach slope indicator shall maintain an altitude at or above the glide slope until a lower altitude is necessary for a safe landing.
2. A turbine-powered airplane or a large airplane (more than 12,500 lb.) shall enter Class D airspace at an altitude of at least 1,500 ft. AGL and maintain at least 1,500 ft. AGL until further descent is required for a safe landing.
   a. Each pilot of a turbine-powered or large airplane shall climb to an altitude of 1,500 ft. AGL as rapidly as practicable after takeoff.

91.155 Basic VFR Weather Minimums (Questions 12-18)

Airspace	Flight Visibility	Distance from Clouds
Class A	Not applicable	Not applicable
Class B	3 SM	Clear of clouds
Class C	3 SM	500 ft. below 1,000 ft. above 2,000 ft. horiz.
Class D	3 SM	500 ft. below 1,000 ft. above 2,000 ft. horiz.
Class E: Less than 10,000 ft. MSL	3 SM	500 ft. below 1,000 ft. above 2,000 ft. horiz.
At or above 10,000 ft. MSL	5 SM	1,000 ft. below 1,000 ft. above 1 SM horiz.

Airspace	Flight Visibility	Distance from Clouds
Class G: 1,200 ft. or less above the surface (regardless of MSL altitude)		
Day Night, except as provided in 1. below	1 SM 3 SM	Clear of clouds 500 ft. below 1,000 ft. above 2,000 ft. horiz.
More than 1,200 ft. above the surface but less than 10,000 ft. MSL		
Day	1 SM	500 ft. below 1,000 ft. above 2,000 ft. horiz.
Night	3 SM	500 ft. below 1,000 ft. above 2,000 ft. horiz.
More than 1,200 ft. above the surface and at or above 10,000 ft. MSL	5 SM	1,000 ft. below 1,000 ft. above 1 SM horiz.

1. An airplane may be operated clear of clouds in Class G airspace at night below 1,200 ft. AGL when the visibility is less than 3 SM but more than 1 SM in an airport traffic pattern and within ½ NM of the runway.

91.157 Special VFR Weather Minimums (Question 19)

1. Special VFR may be conducted in controlled airspace clear of clouds with a minimum of 1 SM visibility.

91.171 VOR Equipment Check for IFR Operations (Questions 20-25)

1. In addition to the VOR check that must be made at least every 30 days, the altimeter system and the transponder must have been inspected within 24 calendar months.
2. When conducting a VOR operation check, the following must be entered in an aircraft log or other record:
   a. Date
   b. Place
   c. Bearing error
   d. Pilot's signature
3. The maximum allowable tolerance when performing an operational check of a dual VOR system is 4° variation between the two indicated bearings (whether on the ground or in the air).
4. For VOT checks, the maximum error is ±4°.
   a. The CDI must center on 360° ± 4° (i.e., 356°-004°) with the TO/FROM reading FROM.
5. For airborne checkouts, the maximum permissible error is ±6°.

91.173 ATC Clearance and Flight Plan Required (Question 26)

1. No person may operate an aircraft in controlled airspace under IFR unless that person has
   a. Filed an IFR flight plan, and
   b. Received an appropriate ATC clearance.

91.175 Takeoff and Landing under IFR (Questions 27-38)

1. The standard takeoff minimum for a Part 121 or 135 airplane with more than two engines is ½ SM visibility.
2. Each pilot shall immediately execute an appropriate missed approach procedure
   a. Upon arrival at a specified DH if the required visual references are not acquired, or
   b. At any time thereafter if the visual references are lost below the DH.
3. When "cleared for the approach" while being radar vectored on an unpublished route, a pilot shall maintain the last altitude assigned to him/her until the aircraft is established on a segment of a published route.
4. The approach light system can be used as a visual reference, except that descent below 100 ft. above TDZE requires that the red light bars be visible and identifiable.
5. In the case of a radar vector to a final approach course or fix, for which the approach procedure specifies "NO PT," no pilot may make a procedure turn unless cleared to do so by ATC.
6. When proceeding to the alternate airport, the actual minimums shown on the IAP chart for the airport apply.
7. If RVR (runway visual range) minimums for takeoff or landing are prescribed in an instrument approach procedure, but RVR is not reported for the runway of intended operation, the RVR minimum shall be converted to ground visibility.
   a. RVR 40 = 3/4 SM
   b. RVR 32 = 5/8 SM
   c. RVR 16 = 1/4 SM
8. On an ILS, a compass locator or precision radar may be substituted for the middle marker.

91.185 IFR Operations: Two-Way Radio Communications Failure (Questions 39-44)

1. If the failure occurs while IMC, one of the following routes should be flown:
   a. The last route assigned by ATC
   b. If under radar vectors, a direct route to the fix, route, or airway to which you were being vectored
   c. If no route was assigned, the route ATC advised you to expect
   d. The filed flight plan route
2. The altitudes to be flown should be the highest of the following:
   a. The last altitude ATC assigned
   b. The MEA for that route
   c. The altitude ATC advised you to expect

3. Once you arrive at your destination, you may execute an instrument approach. If more than one approach is available, you may choose any one. The altitudes to be flown should correspond to those given by the IAP chart. You should attempt to execute the approach as close as possible to the ETA in your flight plan (add your estimated time en route per your flight plan to your departure time). Or if an EFC time was given, you should begin the descent and approach as close to the EFC as possible.
4. If you are holding when the failure occurs or if you are ahead of the filed times, you should continue holding or slow the aircraft to meet the EFC or filed ETA.

91.187 Operation under IFR in Controlled Airspace: Malfunction Reports (Questions 45-48)

1. The pilot in command of each aircraft operated in controlled airspace under IFR shall report as soon as practicable to ATC any malfunction of navigational, approach, or communication equipment occurring in flight.
   a. The report is required no matter how slightly the malfunction may affect the conduct of the flight.

91.189 Category II and III Operations: General Operating Rules (Question 49)

1. Unless otherwise authorized, no pilot operating an aircraft in a Category II approach may descend below 100 ft. above the touchdown zone elevation using the approach lights as a reference **unless** the red terminating bars or the red side row bars are distinctly visible and identifiable.

91.205 Powered Civil Aircraft with Standard Category U.S. Airworthiness Certificates: Instrument and Equipment Requirements (Question 50)

1. For flights at or above FL 240, DME is required if navigating by VORs.

91.213 Inoperative Instruments and Equipment (Question 51)

1. A function of the minimum equipment list (MEL) is to indicate required items (instruments and/or equipment) which may be inoperative prior to beginning a flight in an aircraft.

91.215 ATC Transponder and Altitude Reporting Equipment and Use (Question 52)

1. No person may operate an aircraft at and above 10,000 ft. MSL, excluding the airspace at and below 2,500 ft. AGL, unless that aircraft is equipped with an operable Mode C transponder.

91.609 Flight Recorders and Cockpit Voice Recorders (Questions 53-55)

1. Information obtained from flight data and cockpit voice recorders shall be used only for determining possible causes of accidents or incidents.
   a. The FAA does not use the cockpit voice recorder for any civil penalty or certificate action.
2. In the event of an accident or occurrence that results in the termination of the flight, an operator shall keep the recorded information from flight recorders and cockpit voice recorders for at least 60 days.

91.611 Authorization for Ferry Flight with One Engine Inoperative (Questions 56-60)

1. A ferry flight of a three-turbine-engine aircraft with one engine inoperative to a repair base may be made only if the weather conditions at the takeoff and destination airports are VFR.
   a. The same requirement applies when one engine of a four-engine reciprocating airplane is inoperative.
2. Only required flight crewmembers may be aboard; i.e., no passengers may be aboard.

91.705 Operations within the North Atlantic Minimum Navigation Performance Specifications Airspace (Questions 61-62)

1. No person may operate a civil aircraft of U.S. Registry in North Atlantic (NAT) airspace designated as Minimum Navigation Performance Specifications (MNPS) airspace unless the FAA Administrator authorizes deviations from the requirements of this section in accordance with Section 3 of Appendix C to Part 91.

3.2 FAR PART 108

108.11 Carriage of Weapons (Questions 63-64)

1. When a passenger notifies an air carrier that an unloaded weapon is in his/her baggage, the baggage must remain locked and be carried in an area inaccessible to the passenger, but only the passenger may retain the key.
2. Persons specifically authorized to carry a deadly weapon aboard an aircraft must notify the air carrier at least 1 hr. before departure (except in an emergency).

108.21 Carriage of Passengers under the Control of Armed Law Enforcement Escorts (Questions 65-66)

1. No more than one person in the custody of law enforcement personnel may be carried on a flight if the person is considered to be in a maximum risk category, and that person must have at least two armed law enforcement escorts.
2. A person in custody of law enforcement personnel must board before all other passengers board and must deplane after all other passengers have left the aircraft.

3.3 HAZARDOUS MATERIALS (49 CFR) (Questions 67-84)

This section includes 18 questions on hazardous materials, which come from title 49 of the Code of Federal Regulations (49 CFR). Remember, the FARs are in 14 CFR.

1. FAR 121.433(a) and FAR 135.333 require a certificate holder to provide appropriate training to persons assigned duties relating to the transport of hazardous materials as defined in 49 CFR, Part 171.8.
2. Pages 59 through 61 (Legends 34, 35, and 36) contain excerpts from 49 CFR, Part 172.101 Hazardous Materials Table (use for questions 67 through 71) which specifies
   a. Description and proper shipping ware
   b. Hazard class
   c. Label required (if any)
   d. Packaging exceptions and specific requirements
   e. Maximum quantity in one package
      1) Passenger-carrying aircraft
      2) Cargo only
   f. Water shipment, i.e., nonaviation

3. Questions 72 through 84 test rules in 49 CFR Part 175.
   a. These regulations will be available to you during your knowledge test in Appendix 2, Legends 23 through 33, of the FAA *Computerized Testing Supplement for Airline Transport Pilot and Aircraft Dispatcher*.
4. The originating aircraft operator must retain for 90 days one copy of each shipping paper describing and certifying hazardous materials.
5. If the hazardous material is not permitted aboard passenger-carrying aircraft, it must be labeled with a **Cargo Aircraft Only** label.
6. Lost or detached labels for packages of hazardous materials must be replaced in accordance with the information provided in the shipping papers.
7. Written reports must be filed within 15 days of fires involving hazardous materials.
8. If magnetized material affects the accuracy of the magnetic compass, a special aircraft swing and compass calibration may be made.
9. Corrosive materials cannot be next to, or in a position that will allow contact with, a package of flammable solids, oxidizing materials, or organic peroxides.
10. Not more than 50 lb. of hazardous materials may be carried in an accessible cargo compartment of a passenger-carrying aircraft.
11. No limitation applies to the number of packages of ORM (other regulated material) aboard a passenger-carrying aircraft.
12. Packages containing radioactive materials, when their combined transport indices exceed 50, may not be carried in a passenger-carrying aircraft.
13. If dry ice is carried aboard an aircraft, proper ventilation of the aircraft should be assured.
14. If radiological advice or assistance is needed, the U.S. Energy and Research Development Administration should be notified.
15. **Radioactive Yellow II** labeled packages having a transport index of 15 may be no closer to passengers than 4 ft. from a space continuously occupied by people.
16. A small aircraft operating into a remote area in the United States, and in other than scheduled passenger operations, may carry not more than 20 gal. of flammable liquid fuel.

QUESTIONS AND ANSWER EXPLANATIONS

All the FAA questions from the pilot knowledge test for the ATP certificate relating to FAR Part 91, FAR Part 108, and hazardous materials and the material outlined previously are reproduced on the following pages in the same modules as the outlines. To the immediate right of each question are the correct answer and answer explanation. You should cover these answers and answer explanations while responding to the questions. Refer to the general discussion in Chapter 1 on how to take the FAA pilot knowledge test.

Remember that the questions from the FAA pilot knowledge test bank have been reordered by topic, and the topics are organized into a meaningful sequence. Accordingly, the first line of the answer explanation gives the FAA question number and the citation of the authoritative source for the answer.

3.1 FAR PART 91

91.17 Alcohol or Drugs

1.
9354. A person may not act as a crewmember of a civil aircraft if alcoholic beverages have been consumed by that person within the preceding

A—8 hours.
B—12 hours.
C—24 hours.

Answer (A) is correct (9354). *(FAR 91.17)*
No person may act or attempt to act as a crewmember of a civil aircraft within 8 hr. after the consumption of any alcoholic beverage, while under the influence of drugs or alcohol, or while having .04 percent by weight or more alcohol in the blood.
Answer (B) is incorrect because a person is required to wait only 8 hr., not 12 hr., after the consumption of alcohol to act as a crewmember provided that (s)he is not still under the influence. Answer (C) is incorrect because a person is required to wait only 8 hr., not 24 hr., after the consumption of alcohol to act as a crewmember provided that (s)he is not still under the influence.

91.117 Aircraft Speed

2.
9398. At what maximum indicated airspeed may a reciprocating-engine-powered airplane be operated within Class D airspace?

A—156 knots.
B—180 knots.
C—200 knots.

Answer (C) is correct (9398). *(FAR 91.117)*
Unless otherwise authorized or required by ATC, no person may operate an aircraft at or below 2,500 ft. AGL within 4 NM of the primary airport of a Class C or Class D airspace area at an indicated airspeed of more than 200 kt.
Answer (A) is incorrect because the maximum indicated airspeed within Class D airspace is 200 kt., not 156 kt. Answer (B) is incorrect because the maximum indicated airspeed within Class D airspace is 200 kt., not 180 kt.

3.
9399. What is the maximum indicated airspeed a turbine-powered aircraft may be operated below 10,000 feet MSL?

A—288 knots.
B—250 knots.
C—230 knots.

Answer (B) is correct (9399). *(FAR 91.117)*
Unless otherwise authorized by ATC, no person may operate an aircraft below 10,000 ft. MSL at an indicated airspeed of more than 250 kt. (288 MPH).
Answer (A) is incorrect because 288 MPH, not 288 kt., is the maximum authorized airspeed below 10,000 ft. MSL. Answer (C) is incorrect because 230 kt. is the maximum authorized holding speed for civil turbojets from above 6,000 ft. through 14,000 ft., not the maximum airspeed below 10,000 ft. MSL.

4.
9400. At what maximum indicated airspeed can a reciprocating-engine airplane operate in the airspace underlying Class B airspace?

A—180 knots.
B—200 knots.
C—230 knots.

Answer (B) is correct (9400). *(FAR 91.117)*
No person may operate an aircraft in the airspace underlying a Class B airspace area, or in a VFR corridor designated through a Class B airspace area, at an indicated airspeed of more than 200 kt. (230 MPH).
Answer (A) is incorrect because the maximum indicated airspeed in the airspace underlying Class B airspace is 200 kt., not 180 kt. Answer (C) is incorrect because 230 MPH, not 230 kt., is the maximum authorized airspeed in the airspace underlying a Class B airspace area.

5.
9397. At what maximum indicated airspeed can a B-727 operate within Class B airspace without special ATC authorization?

A—230 knots.
B—250 knots.
C—275 knots.

Answer (B) is correct (9397). *(FAR 91.117)*
Unless otherwise authorized or required by ATC, no person may operate an aircraft in Class B airspace at an indicated airspeed of more than 250 kt.
Answer (A) is incorrect because 230 kt. is the maximum authorized holding speed for civil turbojet aircraft operating from above 6,000 ft. through 14,000 ft., not for aircraft operating within Class B airspace. Answer (C) is incorrect because the maximum indicated airspeed within Class B airspace is 250 kt., not 275 kt.

6.
9396. What is the maximum indicated airspeed a reciprocating-engine-powered airplane may be operated within Class B airspace?

A—180 knots.
B—230 knots.
C—250 knots.

Answer (C) is correct (9396). *(FAR 91.117)*
Unless otherwise authorized or required by ATC, no person may operate an aircraft in Class B airspace at an indicated airspeed of more than 250 kt.
Answer (A) is incorrect because the maximum indicated airspeed within Class B airspace is 250 kt., not 180 kt. Answer (B) is incorrect because 230 kt. is the maximum authorized holding speed for civil turbojet aircraft from 6,000 ft. through 14,000 ft., not for aircraft operating within Class B airspace.

91.123 Compliance with ATC Clearances and Instructions

7.
9388. When may ATC request a detailed report on an emergency even though a rule has not been violated?

A—When priority has been given.
B—Anytime an emergency occurs.
C—When the emergency occurs in controlled airspace.

Answer (A) is correct (9388). *(FAR 91.123)*
Each pilot in command who (though not deviating from an FAR) is given priority by ATC in an emergency shall submit a detailed report of that emergency within 48 hr. to the manager of that ATC facility, if requested by ATC.
Answer (B) is incorrect because, during an emergency when no rule has been violated, ATC may request a detailed report only if priority is given, not anytime an emergency occurs. Answer (C) is incorrect because, during an emergency when no rule has been violated, ATC may request a detailed report only if priority is given, not anytime an emergency occurs.

8.
9379. During an emergency, a pilot in command does not deviate from an FAR rule but is given priority by ATC. To whom or under what condition is the pilot required to submit a written report?

A—To the manager of the General Aviation District Office.
B—To the manager of the facility in control at the time of the deviation.
C—Upon request by ATC, submit a written report to the ATC manager.

Answer (C) is correct (9379). *(FAR 91.123)*
Each pilot in command who (though not deviating from any FAR) is given priority by ATC in an emergency shall submit a detailed report of that emergency within 48 hr. to the manager of that ATC facility, if requested by ATC.
Answer (A) is incorrect because, if requested by ATC, the detailed report is to be given to the manager of the ATC facility in control at the time that the emergency occurred, not to the general aviation district office. Answer (B) is incorrect because a detailed written report is to be submitted only if it was requested by ATC (it is not mandatory).

91.129 Operations in Class D Airspace

9.
9378. A pilot approaching to land a turbine-powered aircraft on a runway served by a VASI shall

A—not use the VASI unless a clearance for a VASI approach is received.
B—use the VASI only when weather conditions are below basic VFR.
C—maintain an altitude at or above the glide slope until a lower altitude is necessary for a safe landing.

Answer (C) is correct (9378). *(FAR 91.129)*
An airplane approaching to land on a runway served by a visual approach slope indicator shall maintain an altitude at or above the glide slope until a lower altitude is necessary for a safe landing.
Answer (A) is incorrect because a VASI should be used at all times when available and is not considered an instrument approach. Answer (B) is incorrect because a VASI should be used at all times both in VFR and during the transition out of IFR weather.

10.
9395. At what minimum altitude is a turbine-engine-powered, or large airplane, required to enter Class D airspace?

A—1,500 feet AGL.
B—2,000 feet AGL.
C—2,500 feet AGL.

Answer (A) is correct (9395). *(FAR 91.129)*
A turbine-powered airplane or a large airplane (more than 12,500 lb.) shall, unless otherwise required by the applicable distance-from-clouds criteria, enter the traffic pattern of an airport in Class D airspace at an altitude of at least 1,500 ft. above the elevation of the airport and maintain at least 1,500 ft. until further descent is required for a safe landing.
Answer (B) is incorrect because the minimum traffic pattern altitude for turbine-powered aircraft is 1,500 ft. AGL, not 2,000 ft. Answer (C) is incorrect because the minimum traffic pattern altitude for turbine-powered aircraft is 1,500 ft. AGL, not 2,500 ft.

11.
9401. A pilot of a turbine-powered airplane should climb as rapidly as practicable after taking off to what altitude?

A—1,000 feet AGL.
B—1,500 feet AGL.
C—5,000 feet AGL.

Answer (B) is correct (9401). *(FAR 91.129)*
Unless otherwise required by departure procedure or the applicable distance-from-clouds criteria, each pilot of a turbine-powered airplane and each pilot of a large airplane shall climb to an altitude of 1,500 ft. above the surface as rapidly as practicable after takeoff.
Answer (A) is incorrect because turbine-powered or large aircraft (in excess of 12,500 lb.) should climb as rapidly as possible to 1,500 ft., not 1,000 ft., above the surface. Answer (C) is incorrect because all turbine-powered or large aircraft should climb as rapidly as possible to 1,500 ft., not 5,000 ft., above the surface.

91.155 Basic VFR Weather Minimums

12.
8893. What is the required flight visibility and distance from clouds if you are operating in Class E airspace at 9,500 feet with a VFR-on-Top clearance during daylight hours?

A—3 statute miles, 1,000 feet above, 500 feet below, and 2,000 feet horizontal.
B—5 statute miles, 500 feet above, 1,000 feet below, and 2,000 feet horizontal.
C—3 statute miles, 500 feet above, 1,000 feet below, and 2,000 feet horizontal.

Answer (A) is correct (8893). *(FAR 91.155)*

In Class E airspace less than 10,000 ft. MSL, the basic VFR weather minimums are in-flight visibility of 3 SM and a distance from clouds of 500 ft. below, 1,000 ft. above, and 2,000 ft. horizontal.

Answer (B) is incorrect because the visibility requirement is 3 SM, not 5 SM, and the distances from clouds should be 1,000 ft. above and 500 ft. below. Answer (C) is incorrect because the distances from clouds should be 1,000 ft. above, not below, and 500 ft. below, not above.

13.
8900. What is the minimum flight visibility and distance from clouds for flight at 10,500 feet, in Class E airspace, with a VFR-on-Top clearance during daylight hours?

A—3 statute miles, 1,000 feet above, 500 feet below, and 2,000 feet horizontal.
B—5 statute miles, 1,000 feet above, 1,000 feet below, and 1 mile horizontal.
C—5 statute miles, 1,000 feet above, 500 feet below, and 1 mile horizontal.

Answer (B) is correct (8900). *(FAR 91.155)*

In Class E airspace at or above 10,000 ft. MSL, the basic VFR weather minimums are in-flight visibility of 5 SM and a distance from clouds of 1,000 ft. above or below and 1 SM horizontal.

Answer (A) is incorrect because 3 SM, 1,000 ft. above, 500 ft. below, and 2,000 ft. horizontal are the VFR weather minimums for below, not at or above, 10,000 ft. MSL. Answer (C) is incorrect because the vertical separation from clouds is 1,000 ft. both above and below.

14.
8898. (Refer to figure 128 on page 45.) What is the minimum in-flight visibility and distance from clouds required for an airplane operating less than 1,200 feet AGL during daylight hours in the circle 6 area?

A—3 miles; (I) 1,000 feet; (K) 2,000 feet; (L) 500 feet.
B—1 mile; (I) clear of clouds; (K) clear of clouds; (L) clear of clouds.
C—1 mile; (I) 500 feet; (K) 1,000 feet; (L) 500 feet.

Answer (B) is correct (8898). *(FAR 91.155)*
In uncontrolled airspace below 1,200 ft. AGL (area 6 in Fig. 128), the basic VFR weather minimums during daylight hours are in-flight visibility of 1 SM and clear of clouds.
Answer (A) is incorrect because 3 SM visibility, 1,000 ft. above, 500 ft. below, and 2,000 ft. horizontal are the VFR weather minimums for a flight in controlled, not uncontrolled airspace. Answer (C) is incorrect because the distance from clouds is clear of clouds, not 500 ft. above and below and 1,000 ft. horizontal.

15.
8897. (Refer to figure 128 on page 45.) What in-flight visibility and distance from clouds is required for a flight at 8,500 feet MSL (above 1,200 feet AGL) in VFR conditions during daylight hours for the circle 4 area?

A—1 mile; (E) 1,000 feet; (G) 2,000 feet; (H) 500 feet.
B—3 miles; (E) 1,000 feet; (G) 2,000 feet; (H) 500 feet.
C—5 miles; (E) 1,000 feet; (G) 1 mile; (H) 1,000 feet.

Answer (A) is correct (8897). *(FAR 91.155)*
In uncontrolled airspace at more than 1,200 ft. AGL but less than 10,000 ft. MSL (area 4 in Fig. 128), the basic VFR weather minimums are in-flight visibility of 1 SM and a distance from clouds of 500 ft. below, 1,000 ft. above, and 2,000 ft. horizontal.
Answer (B) is incorrect because 3 SM, 1,000 ft. above, 2,000 ft. horizontal, and 500 ft. below are the VFR weather minimums for controlled, not uncontrolled, airspace below 10,000 ft. MSL. Answer (C) is incorrect because 5 SM, 1,000 ft. above, 1 SM horizontal, and 1,000 ft. below are the VFR weather minimums for controlled and uncontrolled airspace at or above, not below, 10,000 ft. MSL.

16.
8894. (Refer to figure 128 on page 45.) What is the minimum in-flight visibility and distance from clouds required for a VFR-on-Top flight at 9,500 feet MSL (above 1,200 feet AGL) during daylight hours for the circle 3 area?

A—2,000 feet; (E) 1,000 feet; (F) 2,000 feet; (H) 500 feet.
B—5 miles; (E) 1,000 feet; (F) 2,000 feet; (H) 500 feet.
C—3 miles; (E) 1,000 feet; (F) 2,000 feet; (H) 500 feet.

Answer (C) is correct (8894). *(FAR 91.155)*
In Class E airspace below 10,000 ft. MSL (area 3 in Fig. 128), the basic VFR weather minimums are in-flight visibility of 3 SM and a distance from clouds of 500 ft. below, 1,000 ft. above, and 2,000 ft. horizontal.
Answer (A) is incorrect because the minimum visibility required is 3 SM, not 2,000 ft. Answer (B) is incorrect because, in Class E airspace at or above 10,000 ft., not below 10,000 ft., the minimum visibility is 5 SM.

17.
8896. (Refer to figure 128 on page 45.) What is the minimum in-flight visibility and distance from clouds required in VFR conditions above clouds at 13,500 feet MSL (above 1,200 feet AGL) during daylight hours for the circle 2 area?

A—5 miles; (A) 1,000 feet; (C) 2,000 feet; (D) 500 feet.
B—3 miles; (A) 1,000 feet; (C) 1 mile; (D) 1,000 feet.
C—5 miles; (A) 1,000 feet; (C) 1 mile; (D) 1,000 feet.

Answer (C) is correct (8896). *(FAR 91.155)*
In uncontrolled airspace at more than 1,200 ft. AGL and at or above 10,000 ft. MSL (area 2 in Fig. 128), the basic VFR weather minimums are in-flight visibility of 5 SM and a distance from clouds of 1,000 ft. above or below and 1 SM horizontal.
Answer (A) is incorrect because 1,000 ft. above, 2,000 ft. horizontal, and 500 ft. below are the minimum cloud distances for VFR in uncontrolled airspace above 1,200 ft. AGL and below, not above, 10,000 ft. MSL. Answer (B) is incorrect because visibility minimum is 5 SM, not 3 SM.

18.
8895. (Refer to figure 128 on page 45.) A flight is to be conducted in VFR-on-Top conditions at 12,500 feet MSL (above 1,200 feet AGL). What is the in-flight visibility and distance from clouds required for operation during daylight hours for the circle 1 area?

A—5 miles; (A) 1,000 feet; (B) 2,000 feet; (D) 500 feet.
B—5 miles; (A) 1,000 feet; (B) 1 mile; (D) 1,000 feet.
C—3 miles; (A) 1,000 feet; (B) 2,000 feet; (D) 1,000 feet.

Answer (B) is correct (8895). *(FAR 91.155)*
In Class E airspace at or above 10,000 ft. MSL (area 1 in Fig. 128), the basic VFR weather minimums are in-flight visibility of 5 SM and a distance from clouds of 1,000 ft. above or below and 1 SM horizontal.
Answer (A) is incorrect because the distance from cloud requirements listed are for below, not above, 10,000 ft. MSL. Answer (C) is incorrect because the visibility requirement is 5 SM, not 3 SM, and the horizontal separation requirement from clouds is 1 SM, not 2,000 ft.

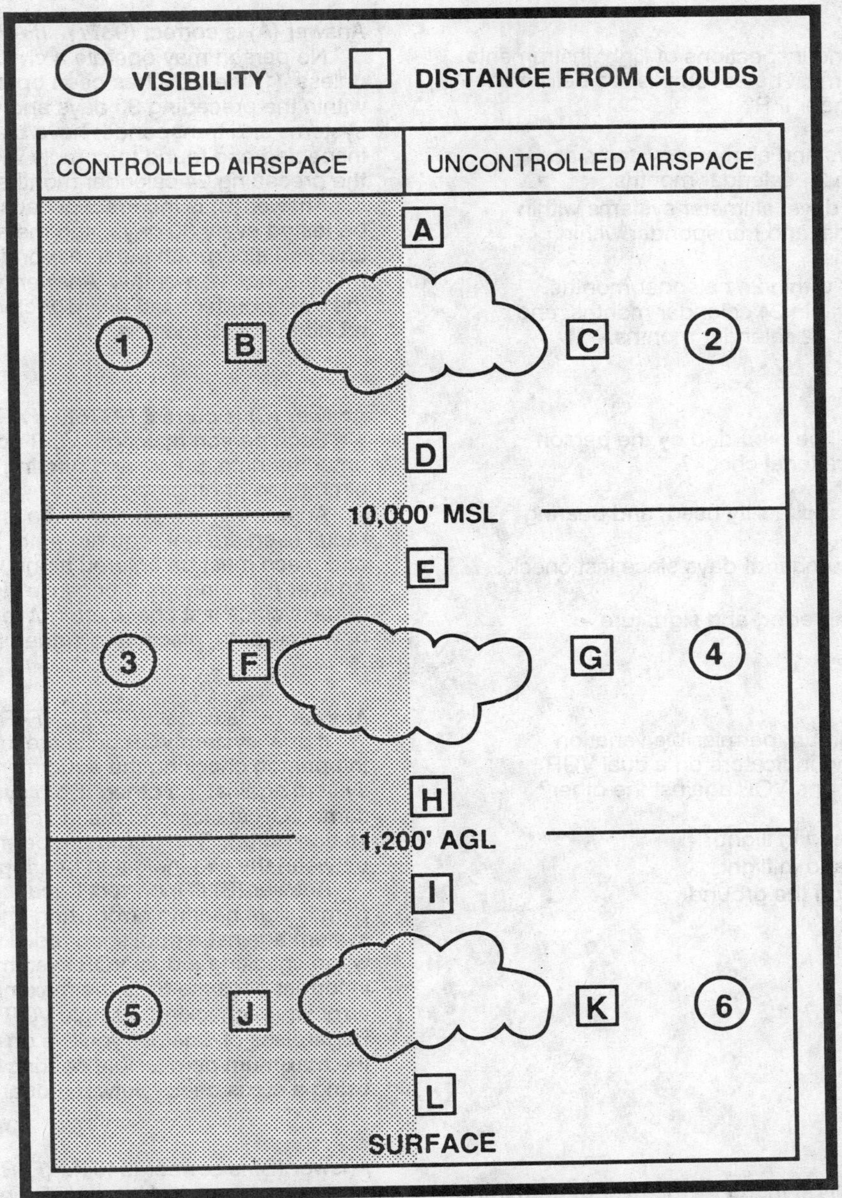

FIGURE 128.—Minimum In-Flight Visibility and Distance From Clouds.

91.157 Special VFR Weather Minimums

19.
8899. (Refer to figure 128 above.) What is the minimum in-flight visibility and distance from clouds required for an airplane operating less than 1,200 feet AGL under special VFR during daylight hours in the circle 5 area?

A—1 mile; (I) 2,000 feet; (J) 2,000 feet; (L) 500 feet.
B—3 miles; (I) clear of clouds; (J) clear of clouds; (L) 500 feet.
C—1 mile; (I) clear of clouds; (J) clear of clouds; (L) clear of clouds.

Answer (C) is correct (8899). *(FAR 91.157)*
In controlled airspace below 1,200 ft. AGL (area 5 in Fig. 128) when operating an airplane under special VFR, the distance-from-clouds requirement is clear of clouds. No one may take off or land an airplane under special VFR unless ground visibility is at least 1 SM. If ground visibility is not reported, the in-flight visibility during takeoff or landing must be at least 1 SM.

Answer (A) is incorrect because special VFR permits operating clear of clouds. Answer (B) is incorrect because special VFR permits clear of clouds and a minimum visibility of 1 SM, not 3 SM.

91.171 VOR Equipment Check for IFR Operations

20.
9377. Which checks and inspections of flight instruments or instrument systems must be accomplished before an aircraft can be flown under IFR?

A—VOR within 30 days and altimeter systems and transponder within 24 calendar months.
B—ELT test within 30 days, altimeter systems within 12 calendar months, and transponder within 24 calendar months.
C—Airspeed indicator within 24 calendar months, altimeter system within 24 calendar months, and transponder within 12 calendar months.

Answer (A) is correct (9377). *(FAR 91.171, 91.411)*
No person may operate a civil aircraft under IFR unless (1) the VOR has been operationally checked within the preceding 30 days and (2) the altimeter systems and transponder have been tested and inspected and found to comply with FAA standards within the preceding 24 calendar months.
Answer (B) is incorrect because ELTs do not have to be tested every 30 days, and the altimeter must be checked along with the transponder every 24 calendar months, not 12 months. Answer (C) is incorrect because the transponder must be inspected every 24 calendar months, not 12 months.

21.
9376. Which entry shall be recorded by the person performing a VOR operational check?

A—Frequency, radial and facility used, and bearing error.
B—Flight hours and number of days since last check, and bearing error.
C—Date, place, bearing error, and signature.

Answer (C) is correct (9376). *(FAR 91.171)*
Each person making a VOR operational check shall enter the date, place, and bearing error, and sign the aircraft log or other record.
Answer (A) is incorrect because the frequency and radial used are not required entry items; however, date and place must be entered along with signature. Answer (B) is incorrect because flight hours and number of days since last check are not required entry items; however, date, place, and signature must be included.

22.
9375. What is the maximum permissible variation between the two bearing indicators on a dual VOR system when checking one VOR against the other?

A—4° on the ground and in flight.
B—6° on the ground and in flight.
C—6° in flight and 4° on the ground.

Answer (A) is correct (9375). *(FAR 91.171)*
If dual-system VOR units are installed in the aircraft, the person checking the equipment may check one system against the other. Both systems are tuned to the same VOR station and the indicated bearings to that station noted. The maximum permissible variation between the two indicated bearings is 4°.
Answer (B) is incorrect because 6° is the maximum permissible bearing error when checking a single VOR system against a published radial while in the air, not when checking a dual VOR system. Answer (C) is incorrect because 6° is the maximum permissible bearing error when checking a single VOR system while in the air. Regardless of whether you are on the ground or airborne, the maximum permissible bearing error is only 4° when using a cross-check between dual VORs.

23.
9404. What record shall be made by the pilot performing a VOR operational check?

A—The date, frequency of VOR or VOT, number of hours flown since last check, and signature in the aircraft log.
B—The date, place, bearing error, and signature in the aircraft log or other record.
C—The date, approval or disapproval, tach reading, and signature in the aircraft log or other permanent record.

Answer (B) is correct (9404). *(FAR 91.171)*
Each person making a VOR operational check shall enter the date, place, and bearing error, and sign the aircraft log or other record.
Answer (A) is incorrect because neither the frequency nor the number of hours flown since the last check need be entered in the log or record. However, bearing error and place must be entered in the log. Answer (C) is incorrect because neither the tach reading nor approval or disapproval need be entered in the record of a VOR operational check. Also, if the VOR systems are not within the permissible bearing error, the aircraft cannot be flown in IFR operations, but it may still be flown under VFR.

24.
9405. During a VOT check of the VOR equipment, the course deviation indicator centers on 356° with the TO/FROM reading FROM. This VOR equipment may

A—be used if 4° is entered on a correction card and subtracted from all VOR courses.
B—be used during IFR flights, since the error is within limits.
C—not be used during IFR flights, since the TO/FROM should read TO.

Answer (B) is correct (9405). *(FAR 91.171, AIM 1-4)*
When using an FAA-approved VOT station or a test signal radiated by a certificated and appropriately rated radio repair station, the maximum permissible bearing error is plus or minus 4°. To use the VOT service, tune in the VOT frequency on your VOR receiver. With the course deviation indicator (CDI) centered, the omni-bearing selector should read 0° with the TO/FROM indication showing "FROM." Since the CDI for this aircraft reads 356°, it is within the 4° permissible bearing error, so the VOR equipment may be used during IFR flights.
Answer (A) is incorrect because 4° is the maximum permissible bearing error for a VOT check, and no correction card exists for VORs. VORs are either within or not within acceptable limits. Answer (C) is incorrect because a "TO" reading would be indicated if the omni-bearing selector were selected to 180°, not 0°.

25.
9406. If an airborne checkpoint is used to check the VOR system for IFR operations, the maximum bearing error permissible is

A—plus or minus 6°.
B—plus 6° or minus 4°.
C—plus or minus 4°.

Answer (A) is correct (9406). *(FAR 91.171)*
If neither a test signal nor a designated checkpoint on the surface is available, use an airborne checkpoint designated by the FAA Administrator or, outside the United States, by an appropriate authority. The maximum permissible bearing error is plus or minus 6° for airborne checks.
Answer (B) is incorrect because the maximum bearing error is plus or minus 6°, not plus 6° or minus 4°. Answer (C) is incorrect because plus or minus 4° is the maximum permissible bearing error when using a VOT check or a radio repair facility, not when checking a single VOR while in the air.

91.173 ATC Clearance and Flight Plan Required

26.
9374. A pilot is operating in Class G airspace. If existing weather conditions are below those for VFR flight, an IFR flight plan must be filed and an ATC clearance received prior to

A—takeoff if weather conditions are below IFR minimums.
B—entering controlled airspace.
C—entering IFR weather conditions.

Answer (B) is correct (9374). *(FAR 91.173)*
No person may operate an aircraft in controlled airspace under IFR unless that person has (1) filed an IFR flight plan and (2) received an appropriate ATC clearance.
Answer (A) is incorrect because, if IFR weather conditions exist and you wish to depart, an ATC clearance and IFR flight plan are not required in Class G airspace. Answer (C) is incorrect because an IFR flight plan and an ATC clearance are not required to fly in IMC (instrument meteorological conditions) in Class G airspace.

91.175 Takeoff and Landing under IFR

27.
9370. When takeoff minimums are not prescribed for a civil airport, what are the takeoff minimums under IFR for a three-engine airplane?

A—1 SM.
B—1/2 SM.
C—300 feet and 1/2 SM.

Answer (B) is correct (9370). *(FAR 91.175)*
Unless otherwise authorized by the FAA, no pilot operating an aircraft under FAR Part 121, 125, 127, 129, or 135 may take off from a civil airport under IFR unless weather conditions are at or above weather minimums for IFR takeoff prescribed for that airport under FAR Part 97. If takeoff minimums are not prescribed under FAR Part 97 for a particular airport, the minimum visibility for aircraft having more than two engines is ½ SM visibility.
Answer (A) is incorrect because 1 SM visibility is for aircraft, other than helicopters, having two engines or less, not three engines. Answer (C) is incorrect because minimum ceilings are not specified in FAR Part 91 for takeoff minimums.

28.
9382. Assuming that all ILS components are operating and the required visual references are not acquired, the missed approach should be initiated upon

A—arrival at the DH on the glide slope.
B—arrival at the visual descent point.
C—expiration of the time listed on the approach chart for missed approach.

Answer (A) is correct (9382). *(FAR 91.175)*

When conducting an ILS approach, each pilot operating a civil aircraft shall immediately execute an appropriate missed approach procedure upon arrival at the DH (decision height) on the glide slope when the required visual references are not acquired.

Answer (B) is incorrect because a visual descent point is used for nonprecision approaches (e.g., VOR/DME), not on an ILS approach. Answer (C) is incorrect because the expiration of the time listed on the approach chart is used for nonprecision approaches (e.g., VOR, ADF), not for an ILS approach.

29.
9383. What action should be taken when a pilot is "cleared for approach" while being radar vectored on an unpublished route?

A—Descend to minimum vector altitude.
B—Remain at last assigned altitude until established on a published route segment.
C—Descend to initial approach fix altitude.

Answer (B) is correct (9383). *(FAR 91.175)*

When operating on an unpublished route or while being radar vectored, the pilot, when (s)he receives an approach clearance, shall maintain the last altitude assigned to him/her until the aircraft is established on a segment of a published route or instrument approach procedure unless a different altitude is assigned by ATC.

Answer (A) is incorrect because a pilot should maintain the last altitude assigned by ATC, not descend to minimum vector altitude. Answer (C) is incorrect because a pilot should maintain the last altitude assigned by ATC, not descend to initial approach fix altitude.

30.
9384. Under which condition, if any, may a pilot descend below DH or MDA when using the ALSF-1 approach light system as the primary visual reference for the intended runway?

A—Under no condition can the approach light system serve as a necessary visual reference for descent below DH or MDA.
B—Descent to the intended runway is authorized as long as any portion of the approach light system can be seen.
C—The approach light system can be used as a visual reference, except that descent below 100 feet above TDZE requires that the red light bars be visible and identifiable.

Answer (C) is correct (9384). *(FAR 91.175)*

When a DH or an MDA is applicable to an instrument approach, no pilot may operate a civil aircraft at any airport below the authorized MDA or continue an approach below the authorized DH unless a visual reference, e.g., the approach light system, for the intended runway is clearly visible, except that the pilot may not descend below 100 ft. above the touchdown zone elevation using the approach lights as a reference unless the red terminating bars or the red side row bars are distinctly visible and identifiable.

Answer (A) is incorrect because approach lighting systems can be used as a reference below the DH or MDA up to 100 ft. above the TDZE, at which point the runway environment must be in sight. Answer (B) is incorrect because the approach lighting system can be used only to within 100 ft. of the TDZE, at which point the runway environment must be in sight.

31.
9369. If being radar vectored to the final approach course of a published instrument approach that specifies "NO PT," the pilot should

A—advise ATC that a procedure turn will not be executed.
B—not execute the procedure turn unless specifically cleared to do so by ATC.
C—execute a holding-pattern type procedure turn.

Answer (B) is correct (9369). *(FAR 91.175)*

In the case of a radar vector to a final approach course or fix, a timed approach from a holding fix, or an approach for which the procedure specifies "NO PT," a pilot may not make a procedure turn unless cleared to do so by ATC.

Answer (A) is incorrect because a procedure turn is not authorized or expected to be executed for this instrument approach; therefore, advising ATC of your intention to omit a procedure turn is not necessary. Answer (C) is incorrect because, if the published instrument approach specifies "NO PT," you should follow the published approach procedure and not execute a holding-pattern-type procedure turn.

32.
9385. What altitude is a pilot authorized to fly when cleared for an ILS approach? The pilot

A—may begin a descent to the procedure turn altitude.
B—must maintain the last assigned altitude until established on a published route or segment of the approach with published altitudes.
C—may descend from the assigned altitude only when established on the final approach course.

Answer (B) is correct (9385). *(FAR 91.175)*

When operating on an unpublished route or while being vectored to an ILS approach, the pilot, upon receiving an approach clearance, shall maintain the last altitude assigned to him/her until the aircraft is established on a segment of a published route or instrument approach procedure unless a different altitude is assigned by ATC.

Answer (A) is incorrect because descent to the procedure turn altitude can be commenced only when you are established on that segment of the instrument approach. Answer (C) is incorrect because the pilot does not have to be established on the final approach course to descend from the last assigned altitude, if (s)he is established on a published route segment with a specified lower minimum altitude than the last assigned altitude.

33.
9368. When must the pilot initiate a missed approach procedure from an ILS approach?

A—At the DH when the runway is not clearly visible.
B—When the time has expired after reaching the DH and the runway environment is not clearly visible.
C—At the DH, if the visual references for the intended runway are not distinctly visible or anytime thereafter that visual reference is lost.

Answer (C) is correct (9368). *(FAR 91.175)*

Each pilot operating a civil aircraft shall immediately execute an appropriate missed approach procedure upon arrival at the missed approach point (DH on an ILS approach) if the visual runway references are not distinctly visible or at any time thereafter if those visual references are lost below the DH.

Answer (A) is incorrect because the runway itself does not have to be visible at the DH to continue with the approach. A pilot may use the approach lighting system to within 100 ft. of the TDZE or any of the following: (1) threshold lights, (2) REIL lights, (3) VASI lights, (4) TDZ lights, or (5) runway lights. Answer (B) is incorrect because, as soon as the DH is reached on an ILS approach, regardless of the elapsed time, a missed approach procedure should be executed if visual references are not obtained or if, at any time after the DH is reached, visual reference is lost.

34.
9394. When proceeding to the alternate airport, which minimums apply?

A—The IFR alternate minimums section in front of the NOAA IAP book.
B—2000-3 for at least 1 hour before until 1 hour after the ETA.
C—The actual minimums shown on the IAP chart for the airport.

Answer (C) is correct (9394). *(FAR 91.175)*

No pilot operating a civil aircraft may land that aircraft when the flight visibility is less than the visibility prescribed in the standard instrument approach procedure being used.

Answer (A) is incorrect because the alternate minimums listed in the NOAA IAP (National Oceanic and Atmospheric Administration Instrument Approach Procedure) book refer to the ceiling and visibility requirements for that airport in order to file it as an alternate, not the ceiling and visibility required to execute an instrument approach. Answer (B) is incorrect because 2000-3 minimums apply to the destination airport. If your destination airport has a forecast ceiling of at least 2,000 ft. and a visibility of at least 3 SM 1 hr. before to 1 hr. after your ETA, an alternate airport need not be filed in the flight plan.

35.
9393. The visibility criteria for a particular instrument approach procedure is RVR 40. What minimum ground visibility may be substituted for the RVR value?

A—5/8 SM.
B—3/4 SM.
C—7/8 SM.

Answer (B) is correct (9393). *(FAR 91.175)*
If RVR (runway visual range) minimums for takeoff or landing are prescribed in an instrument approach procedure, but RVR is not reported for the runway of intended operation, the RVR minimum shall be converted to ground visibility. An RVR of 40 is equivalent to 3/4 SM visibility.

Answer (A) is incorrect because a 5/8 SM visibility is equivalent to an RVR of 32, not 40. Answer (C) is incorrect because a 7/8 SM visibility is equivalent to an RVR of 45, not 40.

36.
9392. The prescribed visibility criteria of RVR 32 for the runway of intended operation is not reported. What minimum ground visibility may be used instead of the RVR value?

A—3/8 SM.
B—5/8 SM.
C—3/4 SM.

Answer (B) is correct (9392). *(FAR 91.175)*
If RVR (runway visual range) minimums for takeoff or landing are prescribed in an instrument approach procedure, but RVR is not reported for the runway of intended operation, the RVR minimum shall be converted to ground visibility. An RVR of 32 is equivalent to 5/8 SM visibility.

Answer (A) is incorrect because a 3/8 SM visibility is not a published RVR value used on instrument approach procedure charts. Answer (C) is incorrect because a 3/4 SM visibility is equivalent to an RVR of 40, not 32.

37.
9391. What minimum ground visibility may be used instead of a prescribed visibility criteria of RVR 16 when that RVR value is not reported?

A—1/4 SM.
B—3/4 SM.
C—3/8 SM.

Answer (A) is correct (9391). *(FAR 91.175)*
If RVR (runway visual range) minimums for takeoff or landing are prescribed in an instrument approach procedure, but RVR is not reported for the runway of intended operation, the RVR minimum shall be converted to ground visibility. An RVR of 16 is equivalent to 1/4 SM visibility.

Answer (B) is incorrect because a 3/4 SM visibility is equivalent to an RVR of 40, not 16. Answer (C) is incorrect because a 3/8 SM visibility is not a published RVR value used on instrument approach procedure charts.

38.
9403. Which facility may be substituted for the middle marker during a Category I ILS approach?

A—VOR/DME FIX.
B—Surveillance radar.
C—Compass locator.

Answer (C) is correct (9403). *(FAR 91.175)*
The basic ground components of an ILS are the localizer, glide slope, outer marker, and middle marker. A compass locator or precision radar may be substituted for the outer or middle marker.

Answer (A) is incorrect because VOR/DME can be substituted for the outer marker only, not the middle marker. Answer (B) is incorrect because surveillance radar may be substituted for the outer marker only, not the middle marker.

91.185 IFR Operations: Two-Way Radio Communications Failure

39.
9363. If a pilot is being radar vectored in IFR conditions and loses radio communications with ATC, what action should be taken?

A—Fly directly to the next point shown on the IFR flight plan and continue the flight.
B—Squawk 7700 and climb to VFR on Top.
C—Fly direct to a fix, route, or airway specified in the vector clearance.

Answer (C) is correct (9363). *(FAR 91.185)*
If two-way radio communications failure occurs in IFR weather conditions and the pilot is being vectored by ATC, the pilot should proceed by the direct route from the point of radio failure to the fix, route, or airway specified in the vector clearance.
Answer (A) is incorrect because the route shown on the flight plan should be used only if an assigned route, vector, or expected route has not been received. Answer (B) is incorrect because a climb should be initiated only in order to establish the highest of either the assigned, MEA, or expected altitude, and the transponder should be set to 7600, not 7700, to indicate communications failure.

40.
9390. While in IFR conditions, a pilot experiences two-way radio communications failure. Which route should be flown in the absence of an ATC assigned route or a route ATC has advised to expect in a further clearance?

A—The most direct route to the filed alternate airport.
B—An off-airway route to the point of departure.
C—The route filed in the flight plan.

Answer (C) is correct (9390). *(FAR 91.185)*
If two-way radio communications failure occurs in IFR conditions, each pilot shall continue with the flight according to the following: (1) by the route assigned in the last ATC clearance; (2) if being radar vectored, by the direct route from the point of radio failure to the fix, route, or airway specified in the vector clearance; (3) in the absence of an assigned route, by the route that ATC has advised may be expected in a further clearance; or (4) by the route filed in the flight plan.
Answer (A) is incorrect because, upon two-way radio communications failure, an approach and landing should be made or attempted at the destination airport first before going to the filed alternate airport. Answer (B) is incorrect because, in the absence of an assigned route or expected route, only the filed route in the flight plan may be used. An off-airway route should not be used unless it was filed as part of the flight plan.

41.
9389. What altitude and route should be used if the pilot is flying in IFR weather conditions and has two-way radio communications failure?

A—Continue on the route specified in the clearance and fly the highest of the following: the last assigned altitude, altitude ATC has informed the pilot to expect, or to the MEA.
B—Descend to MEA and, if clear of clouds, proceed to the nearest appropriate airport. If not clear of clouds, maintain the highest of the MEA's along the clearance route.
C—Fly the most direct route to the destination, maintaining the last assigned altitude or MEA, whichever is higher.

Answer (A) is correct (9389). *(FAR 91.185)*
If radio communication failure occurs in IFR conditions and a clearance has been received, the pilot should fly the route assigned in the last ATC clearance and the highest of either the assigned altitude, MEA, or altitude to be expected when informed by ATC.
Answer (B) is incorrect because the highest of either the MEA, expected altitude, or assigned altitude should be used. Answer (C) is incorrect because, if ATC advises the pilot that (s)he may expect an altitude after reaching a clearance limit, and it is higher than the published MEA or assigned altitude, the expected altitude should be used. The route to be used should be the one assigned by ATC, as specified in a vector clearance, the route ATC has advised may be expected, or in the absence of all of these, the route as filed in the flight plan, not the most direct route.

42.
9364. A pilot is flying in IFR weather conditions and has two-way radio communications failure. What altitude should be used?

A—Last assigned altitude, altitude ATC has advised to expect, or the MEA, whichever is highest.
B—An altitude that is at least 1,000 feet above the highest obstacle along the route.
C—A VFR altitude that is above the MEA for each leg.

Answer (A) is correct (9364). *(FAR 91.185)*
If a pilot experiences two-way radio communications failure, (s)he should maintain the highest of the following altitudes or flight levels for the route segment being flown: (1) the altitude or flight level assigned in the last ATC clearance received, (2) the minimum altitude/flight level, or (3) the altitude or flight level ATC has advised may be expected in a further clearance.
Answer (B) is incorrect because 1,000 ft. above the highest obstacle along the route is what a MOCA, or minimum obstruction clearance altitude, provides. Answer (C) is incorrect because VFR altitudes or regulations should never be used while flying in IFR weather conditions. A VFR altitude should be used only in VFR weather conditions if VFR-on-top clearance has been approved by ATC.

43.
9362. After experiencing two-way radio communications failure en route, when should a pilot begin the descent for the instrument approach?

A—Upon arrival at any initial approach fix for the instrument approach procedure but not before the flight plan ETA as amended by ATC.
B—Upon arrival at the holding fix depicted on the instrument approach procedure at the corrected ETA, plus or minus 3 minutes.
C—At the primary initial approach fix for the instrument approach procedure at the ETA shown on the flight plan or the EFC time, whichever is later.

Answer (A) is correct (9362). *(FAR 91.185)*
If two-way radio communication failure occurs en route and your clearance limit is not a fix from which an approach begins, leave the clearance limit at the expect-further-clearance time if one has been received, or if no EFC has been received, proceed to clearance limit, and proceed to the appropriate initial approach fix. Commence descent and approach to coincide as closely as possible with the ETA.
Answer (B) is incorrect because an approach should begin at the initial approach fix, not at a holding fix, as close as possible to the ETA. Answer (C) is incorrect because an EFC time supersedes a flight plan ETA and should be used if one has been received (no matter if the EFC is sooner or later than the flight plan ETA).

44.
9365. A pilot is holding at an initial approach fix after having experienced two-way radio communications failure. When should that pilot begin descent for the instrument approach?

A—At the EFC time, if this is within plus or minus 3 minutes of the flight plan ETA as amended by ATC.
B—At flight plan ETA as amended by ATC.
C—At the EFC time as amended by ATC.

Answer (C) is correct (9365). *(FAR 91.185)*
Unless otherwise authorized by ATC, each pilot who has two-way radio communications failure when operating under IFR should leave the clearance limit (when the clearance limit is a fix from which an approach begins), commence descent or descent and approach as close as possible to the expect-further-clearance (EFC) time if an EFC has been received, or if one has not been received, as close as possible to the estimated time of arrival (ETA) as calculated from the filed or amended estimated time en route.
Answer (A) is incorrect because the approach should begin at the EFC time, regardless of whether it is close to the planned ETA or not; i.e., ETA is used only if an EFC has not been received. Answer (B) is incorrect because a pilot who is holding at an initial approach fix after having experienced a two-way radio communication failure without an EFC time should begin descent for the instrument approach as closely as possible to the filed or amended (with ATC) ETA.

91.187 Operation under IFR in Controlled Airspace: Malfunction Reports

45.
9387. While flying in controlled airspace under IFR, the ADF fails. What action is required?

A—Descend below Class A airspace.
B—Advise dispatch via company frequency.
C—Notify ATC immediately.

Answer (C) is correct (9387). *(FAR 91.187)*
The pilot in command of each aircraft operated in controlled airspace under IFR shall report as soon as practicable to ATC any malfunction of navigational, approach, or communication equipment occurring in flight.
Answer (A) is incorrect because controlled airspace exists far below Class A airspace (base of 18,000 ft. MSL), and any loss of a navigational aid should be reported to ATC. Answer (B) is incorrect because, although the operations manual may require that the dispatcher be notified, the pilot in command must report the failure to ATC immediately.

46.
9386. While flying IFR in controlled airspace, if one of the two VOR receivers fails, which course of action should the pilot in command follow?

A—No call is required if one of the two VOR receivers is operating properly.
B—Advise ATC immediately.
C—Notify the dispatcher via company frequency.

Answer (B) is correct (9386). *(FAR 91.187)*
The pilot in command of each aircraft operated in controlled airspace under IFR shall report as soon as practicable to ATC any malfunction of navigational, approach, or communication equipment occurring in flight.
Answer (A) is incorrect because any malfunction of a navigational radio should be reported, no matter how slightly it may affect the conduct of the flight. Answer (C) is incorrect because, although the operations manual may require that the dispatcher be notified, the pilot in command must report the failure to ATC immediately.

47.
9380. What action is necessary when a partial loss of ILS receiver capability occurs while operating in controlled airspace under IFR?

A—Continue as cleared and file a written report to the Administrator if requested.
B—If the aircraft is equipped with other radios suitable for executing an instrument approach, no further action is necessary.
C—Report the malfunction immediately to ATC.

Answer (C) is correct (9380). *(FAR 91.187)*
The pilot in command of each aircraft operated in controlled airspace under IFR shall report as soon as practicable to ATC any malfunction of navigational, approach, or communication equipment occurring in flight.
Answer (A) is incorrect because any malfunction of approach equipment must be reported in flight, not by a written report. Answer (B) is incorrect because, although another type of instrument approach may be executed if permission is granted by ATC, any malfunction of approach equipment should be reported.

48.
9381. What action should be taken if one of the two VHF radios fail while IFR in controlled airspace?

A—Notify ATC immediately.
B—Squawk 7600.
C—Monitor the VOR receiver.

Answer (A) is correct (9381). *(FAR 91.187)*
The pilot in command of each aircraft operated in controlled airspace under IFR shall report as soon as practicable to ATC any malfunction of navigational, approach, or communication equipment occurring in flight.
Answer (B) is incorrect because, although a communications failure has been experienced, it is only a partial one. One operational VHF radio is still available, and all other radios are working normally. Thus, a squawk of 7600 is not needed. Answer (C) is incorrect because an operable VHF radio is still available for communication. Monitoring a NAVAID is not needed. The only pilot action required is notification to ATC of the problem.

91.189 Category II and III Operations: General Operating Rules

49.
9412. When may a pilot descend below 100 feet above the touchdown zone elevation during a Category II ILS instrument approach when only the approach lights are visible?

A—After passing the visual descent point (VDP).
B—When the RVR is 1,600 feet or more.
C—When the red terminal bar of the approach light systems are in sight.

Answer (C) is correct (9412). *(FAR 91.189)*
Unless otherwise authorized, a pilot operating an aircraft in a Category II approach may not descend below 100 ft. above the touchdown zone elevation using the approach lights as a reference unless the red terminating bars or the red side row bars are distinctly visible and identifiable.
Answer (A) is incorrect because a VDP is not used in conjunction with Category II ILS instrument approaches. Answer (B) is incorrect because, although 1,600 ft. may be the required in-flight visibility, descending below 100 ft. above the touchdown zone elevation based on the approach lights also requires sight of the red terminating bars.

91.205 Powered Civil Aircraft with Standard Category U.S. Airworthiness Certificates: Instrument and Equipment Requirements

50.
9408. When is DME required for an instrument flight?

A—At or above 24,000 feet MSL if VOR navigational equipment is required.
B—In terminal radar service areas.
C—Above 12,500 feet MSL.

Answer (A) is correct (9408). *(FAR 91.205)*
For flights at or above FL 240, DME is required if navigating by VORs.
Answer (B) is incorrect because the only requirement for operation in a terminal radar service area is two-way radio communication, not DME. Answer (C) is incorrect because 12,500 ft. MSL is not an altitude significant to airspace definition or other operating rules.

91.213 Inoperative Instruments and Equipment

51.
9407. A function of the minimum equipment list is to indicate required items which

A—are required to be operative for overwater passenger air carrier flights.
B—may be inoperative for a one-time ferry flight of a large airplane to a maintenance base.
C—may be inoperative prior to beginning a flight in an aircraft.

Answer (C) is correct (9407). *(FAR 91.213)*
A function of an approved minimum equipment list (MEL) is to indicate the required items (instruments and/or equipment) which may be inoperative prior to beginning a flight in an aircraft and to state under what conditions the flight can be operated with that inoperative equipment.
Answer (A) is incorrect because an MEL prescribes which instruments and equipment may be inoperative prior to beginning a flight, not which items are required to be operative for overwater air carrier flights. Answer (B) is incorrect because a special flight permit, not an MEL, authorizes a one-time ferry flight of a large airplane to a maintenance base with inoperative instruments and/or equipment.

91.215 ATC Transponder and Altitude Reporting Equipment and Use

52.
9409. In what altitude structure is a transponder required when operating in controlled airspace?

A—Above 12,500 feet MSL, excluding the airspace at and below 2,500 feet AGL.
B—Above 10,000 feet MSL, excluding the airspace at and below 2,500 feet AGL.
C—Above 14,500 feet MSL, excluding the airspace at and below 2,500 feet AGL.

Answer (B) is correct (9409). *(FAR 91.215)*
No person may operate an aircraft at and above 10,000 ft. MSL, excluding the airspace at and below 2,500 ft. AGL, unless that aircraft is equipped with an operable Mode C transponder.
Answer (A) is incorrect because 12,500 ft. MSL is not an altitude significant to airspace definition or other operating rules. Answer (C) is incorrect because 14,500 ft. MSL is the floor of Class E airspace (unless designated at a lower altitude), not the floor at which an operable Mode C transponder is required.

91.609 Flight Recorders and Cockpit Voice Recorders

53.
9410. Information obtained from flight data and cockpit voice recorders shall be used only for determining

A—who was responsible for any accident or incident.
B—evidence for use in civil penalty or certificate action.
C—possible causes of accidents or incidents.

Answer (C) is correct (9410). *(FAR 91.609)*
Information obtained from flight data and cockpit voice recorders is used to assist in determining the cause of accidents or occurrences in connection with investigations under NTSB Part 830. The FAA does not use the cockpit voice recorder for any civil penalty or certificate action.
Answer (A) is incorrect because flight data or cockpit voice recorders are used only to determine causes of accidents or incidents, not to determine who was responsible or at fault. Answer (B) is incorrect because flight data or cockpit voice recorders may not be used for any civil penalty or certificate action.

54.
9356. For what purpose may cockpit voice recorders and flight data recorders **NOT** be used?

A—Determining causes of accidents and occurrences under investigation by the NTSB.
B—Determining any certificate action, or civil penalty, arising out of an accident or occurrence.
C—Identifying procedures that may have been conducive to any accident, or occurrence resulting in investigation under NTSB Part 830.

Answer (B) is correct (9356). *(FAR 91.609)*
Information obtained from flight data and cockpit voice recorders is used to assist in determining the cause of accidents or occurrences in connection with investigations under NTSB Part 830. The FAA does not use the cockpit voice recorder for any civil penalty or certificate action.
Answer (A) is incorrect because cockpit voice recorders and flight data recorders are used to determine causes of accidents or occurrences. Answer (C) is incorrect because flight data recorders and cockpit voice recorders are used to identify any procedure, malfunction, or failure that may have contributed to an accident or occurrence.

55.
9357. How long is cockpit voice recorder and flight recorder data kept, in the event of an accident or occurrence resulting in terminating the flight?

A—60 days.
B—90 days.
C—30 days.

Answer (A) is correct (9357). *(FAR 91.609)*
In the event of an accident or occurrence that results in the termination of the flight, any operator who has installed approved flight recorders and cockpit voice recorders shall keep the recorded information for at least 60 days or, if requested by the FAA or the NTSB, for a longer period.
Answer (B) is incorrect because the information need be kept for only 60 days, not 90 days. Answer (C) is incorrect because the information must be kept for a minimum of 60 days, not 30 days.

91.611 Authorization for Ferry Flight with One Engine Inoperative

56.
9359. Which operational requirement must be observed when ferrying an air carrier airplane when one of its three turbine engines is inoperative?

A—The weather conditions at takeoff and destination must be VFR.
B—The flight cannot be conducted between official sunset and official sunrise.
C—Weather conditions must exceed the basic VFR minimums for the entire route, including takeoff and landing.

Answer (A) is correct (9359). *(FAR 91.611)*
The holder of an air carrier operating certificate or a certificate issued under Part 125 may conduct a ferry flight of an aircraft equipped with three turbine engines, one of which is inoperative, to a base for the purpose of repairing that engine only if the weather conditions at the takeoff and destination airports are VFR.
Answer (B) is incorrect because a ferry flight may be conducted after sunset and before sunrise as long as the takeoff and destination airports are VFR. Answer (C) is incorrect because the weather conditions must be VFR only for takeoff and landing, not over the entire route.

57.
9360. Which operational requirement must be observed when ferrying a large, turbine-engine-powered airplane when one of its engines is inoperative?

A—The weather conditions at takeoff and destination must be VFR.

B—Weather conditions must exceed the basic VFR minimums for the entire route, including takeoff and landing.

C—The flight cannot be conducted between official sunset and sunrise.

Answer (A) is correct (9360). *(FAR 91.611)*

The holder of an air carrier operating certificate or a certificate issued under Part 125 may conduct a ferry flight of an aircraft with one of its engines inoperative to a base for the purpose of repairing that engine only if the weather conditions at the takeoff and destination airports are VFR.

Answer (B) is incorrect because the weather conditions must be VFR only for takeoff and landing, not over the entire route. Answer (C) is incorrect because a ferry flight may be conducted after sunset and before sunrise as long as the takeoff and destination airports are VFR.

58.
9361. When a turbine-engine-powered airplane is to be ferried to another base for repair of an inoperative engine, which operational requirement must be observed?

A—Only the required flight crewmembers may be on board the airplane.

B—The existing and forecast weather for departure, en route, and approach must be VFR.

C—No passengers except authorized maintenance personnel may be carried.

Answer (A) is correct (9361). *(FAR 91.611)*

The holder of an air carrier operating certificate or a certificate issued under Part 125 may conduct a ferry flight of an aircraft with one of its turbine engines inoperative to a base for the purpose of repairing that engine with only the required flight crewmembers on board the airplane.

Answer (B) is incorrect because the weather conditions must be VFR only for takeoff and landing, not over the entire route. Answer (C) is incorrect because only the required flight crewmembers may be aboard. Maintenance personnel, mechanics, and others may not be carried.

59.
9355. Which operational requirement must be observed by a commercial operator when ferrying a large, three-engine, turbojet-powered airplane from one facility to another to repair an inoperative engine?

A—The computed takeoff distance to reach V_1 must not exceed 70 percent of the effective runway length.

B—The existing and forecast weather for departure, en route, and approach must be VFR.

C—No passengers may be carried.

Answer (C) is correct (9355). *(FAR 91.611)*

The holder of an air carrier operating certificate or a certificate issued under Part 125 may conduct a ferry flight of an aircraft with one of its turbine engines inoperative to a base for the purpose of repairing that engine with only the required flight crewmembers on board the airplane. No passengers may be carried.

Answer (A) is incorrect because runway length allowing V_1 in less than 70% of the runway is not required for ferry flights with one engine inoperative. Answer (B) is incorrect because the weather conditions must be VFR only for takeoff and landing, not over the entire route.

60.
9358. A commercial operator plans to ferry a large, four-engine, reciprocating-engine-powered airplane from one facility to another to repair an inoperative engine. Which is an operational requirement for the three-engine flight?

A—The gross weight at takeoff may not exceed 75 percent of the maximum certificated gross weight.

B—Weather conditions at the takeoff and destination airports must be VFR.

C—The computed takeoff distance to reach V_1 must not exceed 70 percent of the effective runway length.

Answer (B) is correct (9358). *(FAR 91.611)*

The holder of an air carrier operating certificate or a certificate issued under Part 125 may conduct a ferry flight of an aircraft with one of its reciprocating engines inoperative to a base for the purpose of repairing that engine only if the weather conditions at the takeoff and destination airports are VFR.

Answer (A) is incorrect because gross weight restrictions do not exist for ferry flights with one engine inoperative. Answer (C) is incorrect because runway length allowing V_1 in less than 70% of the runway is not required for ferry flights with one engine inoperative.

91.705 Operations within the North Atlantic Minimum Navigation Performance Specifications Airspace

61.
9352. Which publication includes information on operations in the North Atlantic (NAT) Minimum Navigation Performance Specifications Airspace?

A—FAR Part 121.
B—ICAO Annex 1, Chapter 2.
C—FAR Part 91.

Answer (C) is correct (9352). *(FAR 91.705)*
Operations within the North Atlantic (NAT) Minimum Navigation Performance Specifications (MNPS) Airspace is the title of both FAR 91.705 and Appendix C of Part 91.
Answer (A) is incorrect because FAR Part 121 provides rules in the United States regarding operating requirements of domestic, flag, and supplemental air carriers. Answer (B) is incorrect because ICAO Annex 1, Chapter 2, concerns pilot certificates and ratings.

62.
9353. How may an aircraft operate in North Atlantic (NAT) Minimum Navigation Performance Specifications Airspace with less than the minimum navigation capability required by FAR Part 91, appendix C?

A—By operating under VFR conditions only.
B—By requesting a deviation from the Administrator.
C—By operating only between 2400Z and 0600Z.

Answer (B) is correct (9353). *(FAR 91.705)*
No person may operate a civil aircraft of U.S. Registry in North Atlantic (NAT) airspace designated as Minimum Navigation Performance Specifications (MNPS) airspace unless the FAA authorizes deviations from the requirements of this section in accordance with Section 3 of Appendix C of FAR Part 91.
Answer (A) is incorrect because NAT flights, with or without MNPS, may be conducted in IFR weather conditions as well as VFR. Answer (C) is incorrect because NAT flights, with or without MNPS, do not have time restrictions.

3.2 FAR PART 108

108.11 Carriage of Weapons

63.
8137. When a passenger notifies the certificate holder prior to checking baggage that an unloaded weapon is in the baggage, what action is required by regulation regarding this baggage?

A—The baggage may be carried in the flightcrew compartment, provided the baggage remains locked, and the key is given to the pilot in command.
B—The baggage must remain locked and carried in an area that is inaccessible to the passenger, and only the passenger retains the key.
C—The baggage must remain locked and stored where it would be inaccessible, and custody of the key shall remain with a designated crewmember.

Answer (B) is correct (8137). *(FAR 108.11)*
When a passenger notifies the certificate holder prior to checking baggage that an unloaded weapon is in his/her baggage, that baggage must remain locked, and only the passenger who checked the baggage may retain the key or combination. The baggage containing the weapon is carried in an area, other than the flight crew compartment, that is inaccessible to passengers.
Answer (A) is incorrect because the baggage containing the unloaded weapon must be carried in an area other than, not in, the flight crew compartment, and the person who checked the baggage, not the PIC, should retain the key. Answer (C) is incorrect because the person who checked the baggage, not a designated crewmember, retains custody of the key.

64.
8131. A certificate holder is notified that a person specifically authorized to carry a deadly weapon is to be aboard an aircraft. Except in an emergency, how long before loading that flight should the air carrier be notified?

A—Notification is not required, if the certificate holder has a security coordinator.
B—A minimum of 1 hour.
C—A minimum of 2 hours.

Answer (B) is correct (8131). *(FAR 108.11)*
Except in an emergency, a certificate holder should be notified at a minimum of 1 hr. before the flight on which a person who is specifically authorized to carry a deadly weapon is to be aboard that aircraft.
Answer (A) is incorrect because, except in an emergency, a certificate holder must be notified at a minimum of 1 hr. before a flight, regardless of whether the certificate holder is required to have a security coordinator. Answer (C) is incorrect because, except in an emergency, a certificate holder must be notified at a minimum of 1 hr., not 2 hr., before a flight.

108.21 Carriage of Passengers under the Control of Armed Law Enforcement Escorts

65.
8136. Which applies to the carriage of a person in the custody of law enforcement personnel?

A—The air carrier is not allowed to serve beverages to the person in custody or the law enforcement escort.
B—No more than one person considered to be in the maximum risk category may be carried on a flight, and that person must have at least two armed law enforcement escorts.
C—The person in custody must be seated between the escort and the aisle.

Answer (B) is correct (8136). *(FAR 108.21)*
No more than one person who the certificate holder has been notified is in a maximum risk category may be carried on the airplane, and that person must have at least two armed law enforcement escorts.
Answer (A) is incorrect because the air carrier can serve nonalcoholic beverages to the law enforcement escort. Additionally, food or beverage may be served to the person in custody with the authorization of the law enforcement escort. Answer (C) is incorrect because the law enforcement escort must be seated between the person in custody and the aisle; the person in custody is not to be seated between the escort and the aisle.

66.
8132. When a person in the custody of law enforcement personnel is scheduled on a flight, what procedures are required regarding boarding of this person and the escort?

A—They shall be boarded before all other passengers board, and deplaned after all the other passengers have left the aircraft.
B—They shall be boarded after all other passengers board, and deplaned before all the other passengers leave the aircraft.
C—They shall board and depart before the other passengers.

Answer (A) is correct (8132). *(FAR 108.21)*
Each person in the custody of law enforcement personnel will be boarded before all other passengers board and deplaned after all other passengers have left the aircraft.
Answer (B) is incorrect because the person in custody will be boarded before, not after, all other passengers board and deplaned after, not before, all other passengers leave the aircraft. Answer (C) is incorrect because the person in custody will be deplaned after, not before, all other passengers leave the aircraft.

3.3 HAZARDOUS MATERIALS (49 CFR)

67.
8299. (Refer to legend 34 on page 59, excerpt from CFR 49, Part 172.) If not excepted, what label, if any, must be placed on a package containing acetone?

A—No label is required.
B—POISON.
C—FLAMMABLE LIQUID.

Answer (C) is correct (8299). *(HMT)*
The hazardous materials classification of acetone is flammable liquid, and it is required to be labeled (if not excepted) as a "flammable liquid."
Answer (A) is incorrect because most hazardous materials require labeling. Answer (B) is incorrect because acetone is to be labeled "flammable liquid," not "poison."

68.
8300. (Refer to legend 34 on page 59, excerpt from CFR 49, Part 172.) What is the maximum, if any, net quantity of acetyl bromide in one package that may be carried in a cargo-only aircraft?

A—1 quart.
B—1 gallon.
C—No limit is specified.

Answer (B) is correct (8300). *(HMT)*
One gallon of acetyl bromide is the maximum quantity per container that may be carried aboard a cargo-only aircraft.
Answer (A) is incorrect because 1 quart is the maximum per container that may be carried aboard any passenger-carrying, not cargo-only, aircraft. Answer (C) is incorrect because a maximum of 1 gal. per container may be carried aboard any cargo-only aircraft.

EXCERPT FROM CFR 49 PART 172

Chapter 1—Research and Special Programs Administration §172.101

§172.101 Hazardous Materials Table (cont'd)

(1)	(2)	(3)	(4)	(5)		(6)		(7)		
				Packaging		Maximum net quantity in one package		Water shipments		
/W/A	Hazardous materials descriptions and proper shipping names	Hazard class	Label(s) required (if not excepted)	(a) Exceptions	(b) Specific requirements	(a) Passenger carrying aircraft or railcar	(b) Cargo only aircraft	(a) Cargo vessel	(b) Passenger vessel	(c) Other requirements
	Accumulator, pressurized (pneumatic or hydraulic), containing nonflammable gas	Nonflammable gas	Nonflammable gas	173.306		No limit	No limit	1,2	1,2	
	Acetal	Flammable liquid	Flammable liquid	173.118	173.119	1 quart	10 gallons	1,3	4	
	Acetaldehyde (ethyl aldehyde)	Flammable liquid	Flammable liquid	None	173.119	Forbidden	10 gallons	1,3	5	
A	Acetaldehyde ammonia	ORM-A	None	173.505	173.510	No limit	No limit			
D	Acetic acid (aqueous solution)	Corrosive material	Corrosive	173.244	173.245	1 quart	10 gallons	1,2	1,2	Stow separate from nitric acid or oxidizing materials.
	Acetic acid, glacial	Corrosive material	Corrosive	173.244	173.245	1 quart	10 gallons	1,2	1,2	Stow separate from nitric acid or oxidizing materials. Segregation same as for flammable liquids
	Acetic anhydride	Corrosive material	Corrosive	173.244	173.245	1 quart	1 gallon	1,2	1,2	
	Acetone	Flammable liquid	Flammable liquid	173.118	173.119	1 quart	10 gallons	1,3	4	
	Acetone cyanohydrin	Poison B	Poison	None	173.346	Forbidden	55 gallons	1	5	Shade from radiant heat. Stow away from corrosive materials.
	Acetone oil	Flammable liquid	Flammable liquid	173.118	173.119	1 quart	10 gallons	1,2	1	
	Acetonitrile	Flammable liquid	Flammable liquid	173.118	173.119	1 quart	10 gallons	1	4	Shade from radiant heat.
	Acetyl benzoyl peroxide, solid	Forbidden								
	Acetyl benzoyl peroxide solution, not over 40% peroxide	Organic peroxide	Organic peroxide	None	173.222	Forbidden	1 quart	1,2	1	
	Acetyl bromide	Corrosive material	Corrosive	173.244	173.247	1 quart	1 gallon	1	1	Keep dry. Glass carboys not permitted on passenger vessels.

LEGEND 34.—Hazardous Materials Table (CFR 49 Part 172).

EXCERPT FROM CFR 49 PART 172

§172.101 Title 49—Transportation

§172.101 Hazardous Materials Table (cont'd)

(1)	(2)	(3)	(4)	(5)		(6)		(7)		
				Packaging		Maximum net quantity in one package		Water shipments		
□/W/A	Hazardous materials descriptions and proper shipping names	Hazard class	Label(s) required (if not excepted)	(a) Exceptions	(b) Specific requirements	(a) Passenger carrying aircraft or railcar	(b) Cargo only aircraft	(a) Cargo vessel	(b) Passenger vessel	(c) Other requirements
	Acetyl chloride	Flammable liquid	Flammable liquid	173.244	173.247	1 quart	1 gallon	1	1	Stow away from alcohols. Keep cool and dry. Separate longitudinally by an intervening complete compartment or hold from explosives.
	Acetylene	Flammable gas	Flammable gas	None	173.303	Forbidden	300 pounds	1	1	Shade from radiant heat.
A	Acetylene tetrabromide	ORM-A	None	173.505	173.510	10 gallons	55 gallons			
	Acetyl iodide	Corrosive material	Corrosive	173.244	173.247	1 quart	1 gallon	1	1	Keep dry. Glass carboys not permitted on passenger vessels.
	Acetyl peroxide solution, not over 25% peroxide	Organic peroxide	Organic peroxide	173.153	173.222	Forbidden	1 quart	1,2	1	
	Acid butyl phosphate	Corrosive material	Corrosive	173.244	173.245	1 quart	5 gallons	1,2	1,2	Glass carboys in hampers not permitted under deck.
	Acid carboy empty. See Carboy, empty									
□	Acid, liquid, n.o.s.	Corrosive material	Corrosive	173.244	173.245	1 quart	5 pints	1	4	Keep cool.
□	Acid, sludge	Corrosive material	Corrosive	None	173.248	Forbidden	1 quart	1,2	1	
	Acrolein, inhibited	Flammable liquid	Flammable liquid and Poison	None	173.122	Forbidden	1 quart	1,2	5	Keep cool. Stow away from living quarters.
	Acrylic acid	Corrosive material	Corrosive	173.244	173.245	1 quart	5 pints	1	1	
	Acrylonitrile	Flammable liquid	Flammable liquid and Poison	None	173.119	Forbidden	1 quart	1,2	5	Keep cool.

LEGEND 35.—Hazardous Materials Table (CFR 49 Part 172) (Cont'd).

EXCERPT FROM CFR 49 PART 172

§172.101 Hazardous Materials Table (cont'd)

(1)	(2)	(3)	(4)	(5) Packaging		(6) Maximum net quantity in one package		(7) Water shipments		
□/ W/ A	Hazardous materials descriptions and proper shipping names	Hazard class	Label(s) required (if not excepted)	(a) Exceptions	(b) Specific requirements	(a) Passenger carrying aircraft or railcar	(b) Cargo only aircraft	(a) Cargo vessel	(b) Passenger vessel	(c) Other requirements
	Alkyl aluminum halides. See Pyrophoric liquid, n.o.s.									
A	Allethrin	ORM-A	None	173.505	173.510	No limit	No limit			
	Allyl alcohol	Flammable liquid	Flammable liquid and Poison	173.118	173.119	1 quart	10 gallons	1,2	1	
	Allyl bromide	Flammable liquid	Flammable liquid	173.118	173.119	Forbidden	10 gallons	1,2	1	
	Allyl chloride	Flammable liquid	Flammable liquid	None	173.119	Forbidden	10 gallons	1,3	5	
	Allyl chlorocarbonate	Flammable liquid	Flammable liquid	None	173.288	Forbidden	5 pints	1	5	Keep dry. Separate longitudinally by an intervening complete hold or compartment from explosives. Segregation same as for corrosive materials.
	Allyl chloroformate. See Allyl chlorocarbonate									
	Allyl trichlorosilane	Corrosive material	Corrosive	None	173.280	Forbidden	10 gallons	1	1	Keep dry.
	Aluminum alkyls. See Pyrophoric liquid n.o.s.									
	Aluminum bromide, anhydrous	Corrosive material	Corrosive	173.244	173.245b	25 pounds	100 pounds	1,2	1,2	Keep dry.
	Aluminum dross, wet or hot. See Sec. 173.173									
	Aluminum hydride	Flammable solid	Flammable solid and Dangerous when wet	None	173.206	Forbidden	25 pounds	1,2	5	Segregation same as for flammable solid labeled Dangerous When Wet.

LEGEND 36.—Hazardous Materials Table (CFR 49 Part 172) (Cont'd).

69.
8301. (Refer to legend 35 on page 60, excerpt from CFR 49, Part 172.) What is the maximum, if any, net quantity of acetylene in one package that may be carried in a passenger-carrying aircraft?

A—Any amount is forbidden.
B—300 pounds.
C—No limit is specified.

Answer (A) is correct (8301). *(HMT)*
Any amount of acetylene is forbidden aboard passenger-carrying aircraft.
Answer (B) is incorrect because 300 lb. of acetylene may be carried aboard a cargo-only, not passenger-carrying, aircraft. Answer (C) is incorrect because any amount of acetylene is forbidden aboard passenger-carrying aircraft.

70.
8302. (Refer to legend 36 on page 61, excerpt from CFR 49, Part 172.) If not excepted, what label, if any, must be placed on a package containing allethrin?

A—ORM-A.
B—None.
C—CORROSIVE.

Answer (B) is correct (8302). *(HMT)*
No label is required on allethrin, which is an ORM-A (other regulated material) classification.
Answer (A) is incorrect because ORM-A is the hazardous materials classification by which the proper label is placed on the container. In this case, no label is required. Answer (C) is incorrect because no label is required on allethrin.

71.
8303. (Refer to legend 36 on page 61, excerpt from CFR 49, Part 172.) What is the maximum, if any, net quantity of aluminum hydride in one package that may be carried in a passenger-carrying aircraft?

A—No limit is specified.
B—25 pounds.
C—Any amount is forbidden.

Answer (C) is correct (8303). *(HMT)*
The Hazardous Materials Table indicates that any amount of aluminum hydride is forbidden on passenger-carrying aircraft.
Answer (A) is incorrect because any amount of aluminum hydride is forbidden aboard a passenger-carrying aircraft. Answer (B) is incorrect because 25 lb. of aluminum hydride is allowable only on cargo-only, not passenger-carrying, aircraft.

72.
8304. Hazardous material shipped on an aircraft must be described and certified on a shipping paper. For what period of time must the originating aircraft operator retain one copy of this document?

A—30 days.
B—60 days.
C—90 days.

Answer (C) is correct (8304). *(49 CFR Part 175.30)*
The originating aircraft operator must retain for 90 days one copy of each shipping paper describing and certifying hazardous materials.
Answer (A) is incorrect because the shipping paper describing and certifying hazardous materials must be retained for 90 days, not 30, by the originating aircraft operator. Answer (B) is incorrect because the shipping paper describing and certifying hazardous materials must be retained for 90 days, not 60, by the originating aircraft operator.

73.
8305. Certain classes of hazardous material may be shipped by air but are not permitted aboard passenger-carrying aircraft. How must such material be labeled?

A—DANGEROUS.
B—HAZARDOUS/CLASS X.
C—CARGO AIRCRAFT ONLY.

Answer (C) is correct (8305). *(49 CFR Part 175.30)*
If hazardous material as presented is not permitted aboard passenger-carrying aircraft, it must be labeled with a "Cargo Aircraft Only" label.
Answer (A) is incorrect because hazardous material not permitted aboard passenger-carrying aircraft must be labeled "Cargo Aircraft Only," not "Dangerous." Answer (B) is incorrect because hazardous material not permitted aboard passenger-carrying aircraft must be labeled "Cargo Aircraft Only," not "Hazardous/Class X."

74.
8306. The aircraft operator discovers that the label on a container of hazardous material is missing. How should the appropriate replacement label be determined?

A—Shipping papers.
B—Hazardous material index.
C—Hazardous Materials Tables of CFR 49.

Answer (A) is correct (8306). *(49 CFR Part 175.40)*
Lost or detached labels for packages of hazardous materials must be replaced in accordance with the information provided on the shipping papers.
Answer (B) is incorrect because the shipping papers, not the hazardous material index, are used to determine the contents of a package with a missing label. Answer (C) is incorrect because the Hazardous Materials Tables of 49 CFR Part 172 are used to determine the labeling requirements, but the shipping papers will identify the hazardous material in the container.

75.
8307. An operator makes a telephone report of an incident involving fire during the loading of hazardous materials. Within what period of time must a written report be submitted?

A—48 hours.
B—10 days.
C—15 days.

Answer (C) is correct (8307). *(49 CFR Part 175.45)*

Each operator who transports hazardous materials shall report in writing within 15 days of the date of discovery each incident that occurs during the course of transportation (including loading, unloading, or temporary storage) in which, as a direct result of hazardous materials, fire, breakage, spillage, or suspected contamination occurs.

Answer (A) is incorrect because 48 hr. is not a time limit specified in 49 CFR Part 175. Answer (B) is incorrect because 10 days is the time within which a report concerning an aircraft accident or fire, not a hazardous materials fire, must be reported.

76.
8308. Which procedure must be followed if an operator, when loading magnetized material, cannot avoid placing it in a position where it affects the accuracy of the magnetic compass?

A—Placard the compass "unreliable."
B—Rely solely on electronic navigation.
C—Make a special compass swing and calibration.

Answer (C) is correct (8308). *(49 CFR Part 175.85)*

No person may load magnetized material (which might cause an erroneous magnetic compass reading) on an aircraft, in the vicinity of a magnetic compass, in a manner that affects its operation. If this requirement cannot be met, a special aircraft swing and compass calibration may be made.

Answer (A) is incorrect because a reliable magnetic compass is required. Thus, the airplane cannot be operated until the compass is made reliable by a special compass swing and calibration. Answer (B) is incorrect because a reliable magnetic compass is required. Thus, the airplane cannot be operated until the compass is made reliable by a special compass swing and calibration.

77.
8309. Which class of hazardous material must be loaded aboard an aircraft in a position that allows no contact with containers of corrosive materials?

A—Organic chemicals.
B—Oxidizing materials.
C—Catalytic agents.

Answer (B) is correct (8309). *(49 CFR Part 175.78)*

No person may stow a package of a corrosive material on an aircraft next to, or in a position that will allow contact with, a package of flammable solids, oxidizing materials, or organic peroxides.

Answer (A) is incorrect because not all organic chemicals are classified as organic peroxides. Answer (C) is incorrect because catalytic agents cause a chemical reaction, and they are not necessarily only oxidizing materials.

78.
8310. What is the maximum weight of hazardous material (other than nonflammable compressed gas) that may be carried in an accessible cargo compartment of a passenger-carrying aircraft?

A—50 pounds, unless otherwise specifically permitted.
B—10 pounds, if classified as corrosive.
C—25 pounds, if classified as ORM-D.

Answer (A) is correct (8310). *(49 CFR Part 175.75)*

Not more than 50 lb. net weight of hazardous material (other than nonflammable compressed gas) may be carried in any freight container within an accessible cargo compartment of a passenger-carrying aircraft.

Answer (B) is incorrect because up to 50 lb., not 10 lb., of hazardous material, even if corrosive, can be carried in an accessible cargo compartment of a passenger-carrying aircraft. Answer (C) is incorrect because there is no limitation to the amount of ORM material aboard a passenger-carrying aircraft.

79.
8311. What is the maximum, if any, number of packages of ORM material that may be transported in a passenger-carrying aircraft?

A—No limit applies.
B—A number whose combined transportation indices total 50.
C—A number whose combined transportation indices total 100.

Answer (A) is correct (8311). *(49 CFR Part 175.75)*

No limitation applies to the number of packages of ORM material aboard a passenger-carrying aircraft.

Answer (B) is incorrect because combined transportation indices of 50 refer to the maximum number of packages of radioactive materials, not ORM. Answer (C) is incorrect because combined transportation indices of 100 do not apply to any hazardous material that can be carried on a passenger-carrying aircraft.

80.
8312. If transported in a passenger-carrying aircraft, what is the maximum combined transportation indices of packages containing radioactive materials?

A—100.
B—50.
C—25.

Answer (B) is correct (8312). *(49 CFR Part 175.75)*

Packages containing radioactive materials when their combined transport indices exceed 50 may not be carried in a passenger-carrying aircraft.

Answer (A) is incorrect because, on a passenger-carrying aircraft, the maximum combined transportation indices of packages containing radioactive materials are 50, not 100. Answer (C) is incorrect because, on a passenger-carrying aircraft, the maximum combined transportation indices of packages containing radioactive materials are 50, not 25.

81.
8313. What precaution, if any, should be taken if dry ice is carried aboard an aircraft?

A—This material does not require special precautions.
B—A waiver to carry this material should be requested from the certificating FAA district office.
C—Proper ventilation of the aircraft should be assured.

Answer (C) is correct (8313). *(AC 103-4)*

Dry ice is not a corrosive and therefore does not require special packaging or containment. It does require proper ventilation because its vapors displace oxygen, and there is a limit on the amount that may be carried on each type of transport aircraft.

Answer (A) is incorrect because there are ventilation and maximum load limitations on dry ice. Answer (B) is incorrect because a waiver is not required; dry ice may be carried if certain precautions are taken.

82.
8314. Who should be notified if there is a suspected radioactive contamination involving a radioactive materials shipment and it is determined that radiological advice is needed?

A—Office of Hazardous Materials Regulation.
B—U.S. Energy Research and Development Administration.
C—Nuclear Regulatory Commission.

Answer (B) is correct (8314). *(49 CFR Part 175.700)*

If radiological advice or assistance is needed, the U.S. Energy Research and Development Administration should be notified.

Answer (A) is incorrect because the Office of Hazardous Materials Regulation would be notified along with the FAA in the event of a fire, injury, or fatality. However, the U.S. Energy Research and Development Administration handles radioactive contamination. Answer (C) is incorrect because the U.S. Energy Research and Development Administration, not the Nuclear Regulatory Commission, provides radiological advice and assistance.

83.
8315. What is the minimum distance that a package of radioactive materials bearing the label "RADIOACTIVE YELLOW II," and having a transport index of 15, may be placed from a space continuously occupied by people?

A—3 feet.
B—4 feet.
C—5 feet.

Answer (B) is correct (8315). *(49 CFR Part 175.700)*

Radioactive Yellow II labeled packages having a transport index of 15 may be no closer than 4 ft. to a space continuously occupied by people.

Answer (A) is incorrect because 3 ft. is the minimum required distance of a radioactive package having a transport index of 5.1 to 10.0, not 15. Answer (C) is incorrect because 5 ft. is the minimum required distance of a radioactive package having a transport index of 20.1 to 30.0, not 15.

84.
8316. What is the maximum quantity of flammable liquid fuel that may be carried in the cabin of a small, nonscheduled, passenger-carrying aircraft being operated in a remote area of the United States?

A—10 gallons.
B—15 gallons.
C—20 gallons.

Answer (C) is correct (8316). *(49 CFR Part 175.310)*

A small aircraft operating into a remote area in the United States may carry, in other than scheduled passenger operations, not more than 20 gal. of flammable liquid fuel.

Answer (A) is incorrect because 20, not 10, gal. is the maximum amount of flammable liquid fuel that may be carried in the cabin of a small aircraft. Answer (B) is incorrect because 20, not 15, gal. is the maximum amount of flammable liquid fuel that may be carried in the cabin of a small aircraft.

END OF CHAPTER

CHAPTER FOUR
FEDERAL AVIATION REGULATIONS: PART 121

(Continued next page)

NOTE: This chapter applies to only the ATP-Part 121 and aircraft dispatcher knowledge test.

(Continued next page)

This chapter contains outlines of major concepts tested, all FAA test questions and answers regarding FAR Part 121, and an explanation of each answer. Each module, or subtopic, within this chapter is listed on the previous two pages with the number of questions from the FAA pilot knowledge test pertaining to that particular module. For each module, the first number following the parentheses is the page number on which the outline begins, and the next number is the page number on which the questions begin.

There are 165 questions in this chapter. We separate and organize the FAA questions into meaningful study units, i.e., chapters and modules. As an analogy, it is easier to deal with the "trees" if you understand the "forest." In this context, "trees" are individual FAA questions and the "forest" is the ATP knowledge test. The organizational units between the overall ATP knowledge test and individual ATP test questions are chapters and modules in this book.

CAUTION: The **sole purpose** of this book is to expedite your passing the FAA pilot knowledge test for the ATP certificate. Topics or regulations not directly tested on the FAA pilot knowledge test are omitted. Much more information and knowledge are necessary to fly safely. This additional material is presented in Gleim's other pilot training books (see the order form on page 818) and in many FAA books and circulars, as well as in airplane *POH*s and other commercial textbooks.

4.1 APPROVAL OF ROUTES: DOMESTIC AND FLAG OPERATIONS

121.99 Communications Facilities (Question 1)

1. The cockpit crews of domestic and flag air carriers must be able to communicate with their company dispatch offices along their entire route of flight.

4.2 AIRPLANE PERFORMANCE OPERATING LIMITATIONS

121.189 Transport Category Airplanes: Turbine Engine Powered; Takeoff Limitations (Question 2)

1. A runway "clearway" is considered in computing takeoff weight limitations for turbine-engine-powered transport airplanes certificated after September 30, 1958.

121.195 Transport Category Airplanes: Turbine Engine Powered: Landing Limitations: Destination Airports (Question 3)

1. 115% of the dry runway length is required for a turbojet-powered airplane at the destination airport if the runways are forecast to be wet or slippery at ETA.

4.3 SPECIAL AIRWORTHINESS REQUIREMENTS

121.285 Carriage of Cargo in Passenger Compartments (Questions 4-6)

1. Cargo may be carried aft of a divider in a passenger compartment if properly secured by a safety belt or other tiedown devices to withstand certain load stresses.
2. A cargo bin in a passenger compartment may not be in a position that restricts access to, or use of, any aisle in the passenger compartment.
   a. The bin must withstand the load factor required of passenger seats, multiplied by 1.15, using the combined weight of the bin and the maximum weight of the cargo that may be carried in the bin.

4.4 INSTRUMENT AND EQUIPMENT REQUIREMENTS

121.309 Emergency Equipment (Questions 7-11)

1. If a passenger cabin has a seating capacity of more than 99 passengers, regardless of how many passengers are actually being carried, two megaphones must be carried: one at the forward end and the other in the most rearward location in the passenger cabin.
   a. If only one portable battery-powered megaphone is required, it should be placed in the most rearward location in the passenger cabin.
2. The number of passenger seats in the airplane determines the minimum number of hand fire extinguishers that are required.
3. Emergency equipment installed in an air carrier airplane must be clearly identified and clearly marked to indicate its method of operation.

121.310 Additional Emergency Equipment (Questions 12-15)

1. The emergency lights on a passenger airplane must be armed or turned on during taxi, takeoff, and landing.
   a. Interior emergency lights must be operable manually from the flight crew station and from a point in the passenger compartment.
2. An automatic deploying escape slide system on a passenger-carrying land plane must be armed during taxi, takeoff, and landing.

3. If there is a required emergency exit located in the flight crew compartment, the door separating the flight crew compartment from the passenger cabin must be latched open during takeoff and landing.

121.311 Seats, Safety Belts, and Shoulder Harnesses (Question 16)

1. Two persons may share one safety belt in a lounge seat only during the en route portion of the flight.

121.315 Cockpit Check Procedure (Question 17)

1. In the event of an engine emergency, the use of a cockpit check procedure by the flight crew is required to prevent reliance on memorized procedures.

121.318 Public Address System (Question 18)

1. An air carrier airplane must have an operating public address system if it has a seating capacity of more than 19 passengers.

121.319 Crewmember Interphone System (Question 19)

1. A crewmember interphone system is required on airplanes with more than 19 passenger seats.

121.327 Supplemental Oxygen: Reciprocating Engine Powered Airplanes (Question 20)

1. For flights in a reciprocating-engine-powered airplane of more than 30 min. duration at cabin pressure altitudes above 8,000 ft. up to and including 14,000 ft., there must be enough oxygen for 30 min. for 10% of the passengers.
   a. EXAMPLE: For a 2-hr. flight at a cabin pressure altitude of 12,000 ft., there must be enough oxygen for 30 min. for 10% of the passengers.

121.329 Supplemental Oxygen for Sustenance: Turbine Engine Powered Airplanes (Questions 21-22)

1. For flights with cabin pressure altitude above 15,000 ft., there must be enough oxygen available for each passenger for the entire flight above 15,000 ft. cabin pressure altitude.

121.333 Supplemental Oxygen for Emergency Descent and for First Aid; Turbine Engine Powered Airplanes with Pressurized Cabins (Questions 23-31)

1. For flights in a pressurized turbine-powered airplane above 10,000 ft. MSL, there must be a minimum of a 2-hr. supply of supplemental oxygen for each flight crewmember on flight deck duty in the event of an emergency descent.
2. The highest flight level at which operations may be conducted without the pilot at the controls wearing and using an oxygen mask, while the other pilot is away from the duty station, is FL 250.
   a. Thus, if either pilot of an air carrier airplane leaves the duty station while flying at FL 410, the other pilot shall put on the oxygen mask and breathe oxygen.
3. Each air carrier flight deck crewmember on flight deck duty must be provided with an oxygen mask that can be rapidly placed on his/her face (i.e., a quick-donning oxygen mask) when operating at flight altitudes above FL 250.
   a. A flight crewmember must be able to don and use a quick-donning oxygen mask within 5 sec.

4. If a pressurized turbine-powered airplane is not equipped with quick-donning oxygen masks, the maximum altitude authorized without one pilot wearing and using an oxygen mask is FL 250.
5. Each airplane must carry at least two oxygen-dispensing units for first aid treatment of occupants who might require undiluted oxygen for physiological reasons.
6. Prior to flights conducted above FL 250, a passenger briefing by a crewmember shall be given instructing passengers on the necessity of using oxygen in the event of cabin depressurization.
7. Oxygen requirements for passengers on flights operated at or below FL 250 are dependent upon the airplane's ability to make an emergency descent to a flight altitude of 14,000 ft. within 4 min.

121.339 Emergency Equipment for Extended Over-Water Operations (Questions 32-33)

1. For extended over-water operations, an appropriately equipped survival kit must be attached to each required life raft.
2. Also, a life preserver equipped with a survivor locator light must be provided for each person on the airplane.

121.340 Emergency Flotation Means (Questions 34-35)

1. Each large aircraft operating over water must have a life preserver for each aircraft occupant.
   a. A life preserver must be stored within easy reach of each seated occupant.

121.343 Flight Recorders (Question 36)

1. For the purpose of testing a flight recorder system, a total of 1 hr. of the oldest recorded data accumulated at the time of testing may be erased.

121.349 Radio Equipment for Operations under VFR over Routes Not Navigated by Pilotage or for Operations under IFR or Over-the-Top (Questions 37-42)

1. Air carrier flights (including turbojet operations) operated IFR or VFR over-the-top must have VOR equipment installed in duplicate.
2. Air carrier airplanes must be DME equipped whenever VOR navigational receivers are required.
   a. When a pilot is operating under IFR in controlled airspace, (s)he must report a failure of DME to ATC immediately.
3. When a flight in an air carrier airplane using NDB NAVAIDS is planned, the airplane must have sufficient fuel to proceed safely by means of VOR NAVAIDS to a suitable airport and complete an instrument approach by use of the remaining airplane radio system.

121.353 Emergency Equipment for Operations over Uninhabited Terrain Areas: Flag, Supplemental, and Certain Domestic Operations (Questions 43-47)

1. Flag and supplemental air carriers and commercial operators flying over uninhabited terrain must have
   a. Suitable pyrotechnic signaling devices
   b. A survival kit for each occupant of the airplane
   c. An approved survival-type emergency locator transmitter

121.357 Airborne Weather Radar Equipment Requirements (Questions 48-50)

1. **An air carrier may dispatch an aircraft with inoperative airborne radar only in day VFR conditions if thunderstorms are forecast along the proposed route of flight.**
2. **An air carrier airplane's airborne radar must be in satisfactory operating condition prior to dispatch if the flight will be conducted in night VFR conditions with scattered thunderstorms reported en route.**
3. **If airborne weather radar becomes inoperative en route and thunderstorms are possible, the flight should proceed in accordance with approved instructions and procedures specified in the operations manual.**

121.359 Cockpit Voice Recorders (Questions 51-53)

1. **Information recorded during normal operations by required cockpit voice recorders in passenger-carrying airplanes may be erased except the last 30 min.**
2. **Required cockpit voice recorders must be operated from the start of the before-starting-engine checklist to the completion of the final checklist upon termination of the flight.**

121.360 Ground Proximity Warning-Glide Slope Deviation Alerting System (Question 54)

1. **All turbine-powered airplanes are required to be equipped with a ground proximity warning-glide slope deviation alerting system.**

4.5 AIRMAN AND CREWMEMBER REQUIREMENTS

121.383 Airman: Limitations on Use of Services (Question 55)

1. **The "age 60" rule applies to all required pilot crewmembers.**

121.385 Composition of Flight Crew (Questions 56-58)

1. **If a flight engineer becomes incapacitated during a flight, his/her duties may be performed by any flight crewmember if the crewmember is qualified to perform flight engineer functions.**
   a. **Thus, when a flight engineer is a required crewmember, at least one other flight crewmember must be qualified to perform flight engineer duties, but that flight crewmember is not required to hold a flight engineer certificate.**

121.387 Flight Engineer (Questions 59-60)

1. **For all airplanes for which a type certificate was issued before January 2, 1964, with a maximum certified takeoff weight of more than 80,000 lb., a flight engineer is required.**
   a. **After January 1, 1964, the requirement for a flight engineer is determined by the airplane's type certificate.**

121.389 Flight Navigator and Specialized Navigation Equipment (Questions 61-63)

1. **A flight navigator or special navigation equipment is required on routes listed in the certificate holder's operations specifications.**
2. **A flight navigator or a specialized means of navigation is required on all flights outside the 48 contiguous United States when the airplane's position cannot be reliably fixed for a period of more than 1 hr.**

121.391 Flight Attendants (Questions 64-67)

1. The number of flight attendants required is based upon seating capacity.
2. Two flight attendants are required for the first 51 to 100 seats.
   a. One additional flight attendant is required for each 50 seats over 100.
   b. EXAMPLE: An air carrier airplane with a seating capacity of 187 requires four flight attendants, regardless of the number of passengers actually carried.

121.397 Emergency and Emergency Evacuation Duties (Questions 68-69)

1. The certificate holder's manual shall include descriptions of required crewmember functions to be performed in the event of an emergency.
2. The certificate holder assigns required crewmember functions to be performed in the event of an emergency.

4.6 TRAINING PROGRAM

121.400 Applicability and Terms Used (Questions 70-72)

1. **Initial training** describes training required for a flight crewmember who has not qualified and served in the same capacity on another airplane of the same group, e.g., turbojet powered.
2. **Upgrade training** is required for a crewmember who has qualified and served as second in command or flight engineer on a particular airplane type before (s)he serves as pilot in command or second in command.
3. **Transition training** is required for a crewmember or dispatcher who has qualified and served in the same capacity on another airplane of the same group.
   a. EXAMPLE: A captain on a DC-9 becomes captain on a B-737; i.e., both airplanes are turbojets (same group).

121.401 Training Program: General (Question 73)

1. Whenever a flight crewmember who is required to take recurrent training, a flight check, or a competence check takes the check or completes the training in the calendar month before or after the month in which the training or check was required, (s)he is considered to have completed it in the calendar month in which it was required.

121.417 Crewmember Emergency Training (Questions 74-75)

1. Air carriers must give instruction on respiration, hypoxia, and decompression to each crewmember serving on pressurized airplanes operated above FL 250.
2. Crewmembers must actually operate the airplane emergency equipment once every 24 calendar months.

4.7 CREWMEMBER QUALIFICATIONS

121.433a Training Requirements: Handling and Carriage of Dangerous Articles and Magnetized Materials (Question 76)

1. Any person whose duties include handling or carriage of dangerous articles and/or magnetized materials must have satisfactorily completed an established and approved training program within the preceding 12 calendar months.

121.439 Pilot Qualification: Recent Experience (Questions 77-78)

1. A required pilot flight crewmember who has not made three takeoffs and landings within the preceding 90 days must reestablish recency of experience by performing
   a. At least one full stop landing
   b. At least one ILS approach to the lowest ILS minimums authorized for the certificate holder and a landing from that approach
   c. At least one takeoff with a simulated failure of the most critical powerplant

121.440 Line Checks (Question 79)

1. A line check for the pilot in command is required each 12 calendar months in one of the types of airplanes (s)he is to fly.

121.441 Proficiency Checks (Questions 80-81)

1. A pilot in command must have completed either a proficiency check or simulator training within the preceding 6 months.
2. A pilot flight crewmember, other than pilot in command, must have received either a proficiency check or line-oriented simulator training within the previous 24 months.

4.8 AIRCRAFT DISPATCHER QUALIFICATIONS AND DUTY TIME LIMITATIONS: DOMESTIC AND FLAG OPERATIONS; FLIGHT ATTENDANT DUTY PERIOD LIMITATIONS AND REST REQUIREMENTS: DOMESTIC, FLAG, AND SUPPLEMENTAL OPERATIONS

121.463 Aircraft Dispatcher Qualifications (Question 82)

1. To remain current as an aircraft dispatcher, a person (in addition to fulfilling other requirements) must have spent, within the preceding 12 calendar months, at least 5 hr. observing flight deck operations in one of the types of airplanes in each group that (s)he is to dispatch.

121.465 Duty Time Limitations: Domestic and Flag Operations (Questions 83-86)

1. Normally, dispatchers can be scheduled for no more than 10 consecutive hours of duty.
2. If a dispatcher is scheduled for more than 10 hr. of duty in 24 consecutive hours, the carrier shall provide him/her with a rest period of at least 8 hr. at or before the completion of 10 hr. of duty.
3. Aircraft dispatchers must have 24 consecutive hours of rest during any 7 consecutive days or the equivalent thereof within any calendar month.

4.9 FLIGHT TIME LIMITATIONS AND REST REQUIREMENTS: DOMESTIC OPERATIONS

121.471 Flight Time Limitations and Rest Requirements: All Flight Crewmembers (Question 87)

1. Duty and rest period rules for domestic air carrier operations require that a flight crewmember not be assigned any duty with the air carrier during any required rest period.

4.10 FLIGHT TIME LIMITATIONS: FLAG OPERATIONS

121.481 Flight Time Limitations: One or Two Pilot Crews (Questions 88-89)

1. The maximum flight time in 24 consecutive hours that a flag air carrier may schedule a pilot in a two-pilot crew without a rest period is 8 hr.
2. The maximum number of hours a pilot may fly in 7 consecutive days in a two-pilot crew for a flag air carrier is 32 hr.

121.483 Flight Time Limitations: Two Pilots and One Additional Flight Crewmember (Question 90)

1. A flag air carrier may schedule a pilot to fly in an airplane, having two pilots and one additional flight crewmember, for no more than 12 hr. during any 24 consecutive hours.

121.491 Flight Time Limitations: Deadhead Transportation (Question 91)

1. For the computation of flight time limits for flag air carrier flight crewmembers, time spent in deadhead transportation to or from a duty assignment is not considered to be part of a rest period.

4.11 FLIGHT TIME LIMITATIONS: SUPPLEMENTAL OPERATIONS

121.503 Flight Time Limitations: Pilots: Airplanes (Question 92)

1. A supplemental air carrier pilot may fly a maximum of 100 hr. in any 30 consecutive days.

121.507 Flight Time Limitations: Three Pilot Crews: Airplanes (Question 93)

1. A supplemental air carrier pilot on a three-pilot crew may be scheduled for flight deck duty for a maximum of 8 hr. in any 24-hr. period.

121.517 Flight Time Limitations: Other Commercial Flying: Airplanes (Question 94)

1. The flight time limitations established for flight crewmembers include all commercial flying in any flight crewmember position.

121.521 Flight Time Limitations: Crew of Two Pilots and One Additional Airman as Required (Question 95)

1. The maximum number of hours that a supplemental air carrier airman may be aloft in any 30 consecutive days, as a member of a flight crew that consists of two pilots and at least one additional flight crewmember, is 120 hr.

4.12 FLIGHT OPERATIONS

121.537 Responsibility for Operational Control: Supplemental Operations (Question 96)

1. The pilot in command and the director of operations have joint responsibility for the initiation, continuation, diversion, and termination of a supplemental air carrier or commercial operator flight.

121.542 Flight Crewmember Duties (Questions 97-98)

1. The **critical phases of flight** include taxi, takeoff, landing, and all other operations conducted below 10,000 ft. MSL, excluding cruise flight.
2. Nonsafety-related cockpit activities by flight crewmembers are prohibited in the critical phases of flight, i.e., below 10,000 ft. MSL, except when in cruise flight.

121.547 Admission to Flight Deck (Question 99)

1. The pilot in command has the emergency authority to exclude any and all persons from admittance to the flight deck in the interest of safety.

121.549 Flying Equipment (Questions 100-101)

1. Each flight crewmember shall have available for individual use on each flight a flashlight in good working order.
2. Assuring that appropriate aeronautical charts are aboard an aircraft is the responsibility of the pilot in command.

121.557 Emergencies: Domestic and Flag Operations (Questions 102-105)

1. Whenever a pilot in command or a dispatcher exercises emergency authority, (s)he shall keep the appropriate ATC facility and dispatch centers fully informed of the progress of the flight.
   a. The person who declares the emergency is required to submit a written report on any deviation that occurs during an emergency.
   b. When the pilot in command is responsible for a deviation during an emergency, the pilot should submit a written report within 10 days after returning to home base.
   c. When an aircraft dispatcher declares an emergency for a flight and a deviation results, a written report shall be sent through the air carrier's operations manager to the FAA Administrator within 10 days.
2. If an aircraft dispatcher cannot communicate with an air carrier flight during an emergency, the aircraft dispatcher should take any action considered necessary under the circumstances.

121.565 Engine Inoperative: Landing; Reporting (Questions 106-108)

1. When an engine's rotation is stopped in flight, the pilot in command must, as soon as practicable, first report the occurrence to the appropriate ground radio station.
2. If one of two available engines is shut down on an air carrier airplane, the pilot should land at the nearest suitable airport in point of time at which a safe landing can be made.
3. When one engine on a domestic air carrier three-engine turbojet airplane is shut down, the pilot in command may continue to the planned destination if this is considered as safe as landing at the nearest suitable airport.

121.571 Briefing Passengers before Takeoff (Question 109)

1. "Keep seat belts fastened while seated" should be stated as a passenger announcement after each takeoff.

121.575 Alcoholic Beverages (Question 110)

1. When an intoxicated person creates a disturbance aboard an air carrier aircraft, the certificate holder must submit a written report concerning the incident to the FAA Administrator within 5 days.

121.583 Carriage of Persons without Compliance with the Passenger-Carrying Requirements of This Part (Question 111)

1. The pilot in command may authorize a passenger to be admitted to the crew compartment aboard an all-cargo aircraft.

4.13 DISPATCHING AND FLIGHT RELEASE RULES

121.593 Dispatching Authority: Domestic Operations (Questions 112-113)

1. A domestic air carrier flight may remain on the ground at an intermediate airport for not more than 1 hr. before a redispatch release is required.

121.595 Dispatching Authority: Flag Operations (Questions 114-116)

1. A flag air carrier may continue from an intermediate airport without redispatch if the airplane has been on the ground for not more than 6 hr.

121.601 Aircraft Dispatcher Information to Pilot in Command: Domestic and Flag Operations (Questions 117-119)

1. The pilot of a domestic or flag air carrier airplane can find the latest FDC NOTAMs at any company dispatch facility.
2. The aircraft dispatcher must provide the pilot in command of a domestic or flag air carrier airplane with information concerning irregularities of facilities and services.
   a. The aircraft dispatcher is also responsible for briefing the pilot in command on all available weather information.

121.603 Facilities and Services: Supplemental Operations (Questions 120-121)

1. The pilot in command is responsible for obtaining information on all current airport conditions, weather, and irregularities of navigation facilities for a supplemental air carrier flight.
   a. During a supplemental air carrier flight, the pilot in command is responsible for obtaining information on meteorological conditions.

121.617 Alternate Airport for Departure (Questions 122-125)

1. If weather conditions at the airport of takeoff are below the landing minimums of the certificate holder's operations specifications for that airport, no person may dispatch or release an aircraft from that airport unless the dispatch or flight release specifies an alternate airport for takeoff.
   a. For aircraft having two engines, if a departure alternate airport is required, it cannot be more than 1 hr. from the departure airport at normal cruising speed in still air with one engine inoperative.
   b. For aircraft having three or more engines, if a departure alternate airport is required, it cannot be more than 2 hr. from the departure airport at normal cruising speed in still air with one engine inoperative.

121.619 Alternate Airport for Destination: IFR or Over-the-Top: Domestic Operations (Question 126)

1. For domestic air carriers, when the weather conditions forecast for the destination and the first alternate airport are marginal, at least one additional alternate must be designated.

121.621 Alternate Airport for Destination: Flag Operations (Questions 127-128)

1. A flag air carrier airplane operating under IFR must list at least one alternate airport for each destination airport in the dispatch release if the flight is scheduled for more than 6 hr.
   a. An alternate is not required if the flight is less than 6 hr. and the visibility at the destination is at least 3 SM, or 2 SM more than the lowest applicable minimum from 1 hr. before to 1 hr. after the ETA.

121.623 Alternate Airport for Destination: IFR or Over-the-Top: Supplemental Operations (Question 129)

1. A supplemental air carrier in the contiguous United States must list at least one alternate airport for each destination in the flight release, regardless of existing or forecast weather conditions.

121.625 Alternate Airport Weather Minimums (Questions 130-131)

1. The minimum weather conditions that must exist for an airport to be listed as an alternate in the dispatch release of a domestic air carrier are specified in the certificate holder's operations specifications for that airport when the flight arrives.

121.627 Continuing Flight in Unsafe Conditions (Question 132)

1. If a required instrument on a multiengine airplane becomes inoperative while en route, the pilot in command must comply with the approved procedures as specified in the certificate holder's manual.

121.629 Operation in Icing Conditions (Questions 133-134)

1. One cannot dispatch or release an aircraft or continue to operate an aircraft en route when the pilot in command or aircraft dispatcher expects icing conditions that might adversely affect the safety of the flight.
2. Before takeoff, frost, snow, or ice adhering to the wings, control surfaces, or propellers of the aircraft must be removed.

121.637 Takeoffs from Unlisted and Alternate Airports: Domestic and Flag Operations (Questions 135-138)

1. Airports not listed in operations specifications and not having prescribed takeoff weather minimums require weather minimums of 800-2, 900-1½, or 1,000-1 for a takeoff, whether a foreign or domestic airport.

121.639 Fuel Supply: All Operations: Domestic Operations (Question 139)

1. The reserve fuel supply for domestic air carriers is required to be 45 min. at normal fuel consumption in addition to the fuel required to fly to and land at the most distant alternate airport.

121.641 Fuel Supply: Nonturbine and Turbo-Propeller-Powered Airplanes: Flag Operations (Question 140)

1. Upon arrival at the most distant airport, the fuel reserve requirement for a turbopropeller flag air carrier airplane is 30 min. plus 15% of the total time required or 90 min. at normal cruise, whichever is less.

121.643 Fuel Supply: Nonturbine and Turbo-Propeller-Powered Airplanes: Supplemental Operations (Questions 141-143)

1. The fuel reserve requirement for a commercially operated or supplemental air carrier reciprocating-engine-powered airplane within the 48 contiguous United States is 45 min. at normal cruising fuel consumption after arrival at the most distant alternate airport.
2. The fuel reserve required for a turbopropeller supplemental air carrier upon arrival at a destination airport for which an alternate is not specified is 3 hr. at normal cruising fuel consumption.

121.645 Fuel Supply: Turbine-Engine-Powered Airplanes, Other Than Turbo Propeller: Flag and Supplemental Operations (Questions 144-148)

1. The fuel reserve required by a flag air carrier turbojet airplane on a domestic flight after reaching the most distant alternate airport is 45 min. at normal cruising fuel consumption.
2. The reserve fuel requirement for a flag air carrier turbojet airplane released to an island airport for which an alternate airport is not available is the fuel needed to fly to that airport and then fly for 2 hr. at normal cruising fuel consumption.
3. If a supplemental or commercial air carrier is operating a turbojet-powered airplane on an IFR flight **outside** the U.S. and an alternate is not required, 2 hr. at normal cruising fuel consumption is required as a reserve.
   a. If an alternate is required, the reserve fuel requirement is 30 min. at holding speed, at 1,500 ft. over the airport.
4. The fuel requirement to release a turbine-engine-powered flag air carrier which has no available alternate is 2 hr. at normal cruise fuel consumption.

121.651 Takeoff and Landing Weather Minimums: IFR: All Certificate Holders (Question 149)

1. An air carrier pilot may continue an instrument approach to the DH or MDA after receiving a weather report indicating that less than minimum published landing conditions exist **only** when the pilot has begun the final approach segment of the instrument approach.

121.652 Landing Weather Minimums: IFR: All Certificate Holders (Questions 150-151)

1. Category II ILS operations below 1,600 RVR and 150-ft. DH may be approved after the pilot has logged 100 hr. flight time in the make and model airplane under FAR Part 121 and made three Category II ILS approaches in actual or simulated IFR conditions with 150-ft. decision heights since the beginning of the preceding sixth month.
2. If a pilot in command of an airplane has not served 100 hr. as pilot in command of operations in the type of airplane being operated, the MDA or decision height and visibility minimums in the certificate holder's operations specifications are increased by 100 ft. and ½ SM.

121.657 Flight Altitude Rules (Question 152)

1. In order for a supplemental air carrier to conduct day, over-the-top flight below the specified IFR minimum en route altitude, the flight must be conducted at least 1,000 ft. above an overcast or broken cloud layer and have at least 5 SM flight visibility with any higher broken or overcast layer being a minimum of 1,000 ft. above the IFR MEA.

4.14 RECORDS AND REPORTS

121.687 Dispatch Release: Flag and Domestic Operations (Questions 153-156)

1. The dispatch release must contain the following information for each flight:
   a. Identification number of the aircraft
   b. Trip number
   c. Departure airport, intermediate stops, destination airports, and alternate airports
   d. A statement of the type of operation (e.g., IFR, VFR)
   e. Minimum fuel supply
   f. Current weather information for the complete flight

121.689 Flight Release Form: Supplemental Operations (Questions 157-158)

1. Supplemental and commercial air carriers must include the name of each flight crewmember, flight attendant, and designated pilot in command in the flight release.

121.695 Disposition of Load Manifest, Dispatch Release, and Flight Plans: Domestic and Flag Operations (Questions 159-161)

1. The pilot in command of a domestic or flag air carrier flight shall carry in the airplane the
   a. Load manifest
   b. Dispatch release
   c. Flight plan
2. Domestic and flag air carriers shall keep copies of flight plans, dispatch releases, and load manifests for at least 3 months.

121.697 Disposition of Load Manifest, Flight Release, and Flight Plans: Supplemental Operations (Questions 162-163)

1. The pilot in command of a supplemental air carrier flight or commercial operator shall carry in the airplane to the destination airport the
   a. Load manifest
   b. Flight release
   c. Airworthiness release
   d. Pilot route certification
   e. Flight plan
2. Supplemental air carriers and commercial operators shall retain a copy of the load manifest, flight release, airworthiness release, pilot route certification, and flight plan for 3 months.

4.15 APPENDIX G

Doppler Radar and Inertial Navigation System (INS): Request for Evaluation; Equipment and Equipment Installation; Training Program; Equipment Accuracy and Reliability; Evaluation Program (Questions 164-165)

1. Operators using inertial navigation systems (INS) must have at least a dual system, and both must be operational at takeoff.
   a. The dual system may consist of two INS units or one INS unit and one Doppler radar unit.

QUESTIONS AND ANSWER EXPLANATIONS

All the FAA questions from the pilot knowledge test for the ATP certificate relating to FAR Part 121 and the material outlined previously are reproduced on the following pages in the same modules as the outlines. To the immediate right of each question are the correct answer and answer explanation. You should cover these answers and answer explanations while responding to the questions. Refer to the general discussion in Chapter 1 on how to take the FAA pilot knowledge test.

4.1 APPROVAL OF ROUTES: DOMESTIC AND FLAG OPERATIONS

121.99 Communications Facilities

1.
8135. Who must the crew of a domestic or flag air carrier airplane be able to communicate with, under normal conditions, along the entire route (in either direction) of flight?

A—ARINC.
B—Any FSS.
C—Appropriate dispatch office.

Answer (C) is correct (8135). *(FAR 121.99)*
Each domestic and flag air carrier must show that a two-way air/ground radio communication system is available at points that will ensure reliable and rapid communications under normal operating conditions over the entire route (either direct or via approved point-to-point circuits) between each airplane and the appropriate dispatch office, and between each airplane and the appropriate air traffic control unit. For all domestic air carrier operations and for flag air carrier operations in the 48 contiguous states and the District of Columbia, the communications systems between each airplane and the dispatch office must be independent of any system operated by the United States.

Answer (A) is incorrect because the crew of a domestic or flag air carrier airplane must be able to communicate directly with the appropriate dispatch office, not just ARINC. ARINC is largely owned by a group of airlines and is contracted by the FAA to provide communications support for ATC and meteorological services in portions of international airspace. Answer (B) is incorrect because the crew of a domestic or flag air carrier airplane must be able to communicate with the appropriate dispatch office, not any FSS, along the entire route.

4.2 AIRPLANE PERFORMANCE OPERATING LIMITATIONS

121.189 Transport Category Airplanes: Turbine Engine Powered; Takeoff Limitations

2.
8134. For which of these aircraft is the "clearway" for a particular runway considered in computing takeoff weight limitations?

A—Those passenger-carrying transport aircraft certificated between August 26, 1957 and August 30, 1959.
B—Turbine-engined-powered transport airplanes certificated after September 30, 1958.
C—U.S. certified air carrier airplanes certificated after August 29, 1959.

Answer (B) is correct (8134). *(FAR 121.189)*
The takeoff distance may include a clearway distance, but the clearway distance included may not be greater than one-half of the takeoff run for turbine-engine-powered transport airplanes certificated after September 30, 1958.

Answer (A) is incorrect because the clearway for a particular runway may be considered in computing takeoff distance for turbine-engine-powered, not just passenger-carrying, transport aircraft certificated after, not before, September 30, 1958. Answer (C) is incorrect because a turbine-engine-powered transport, not an air carrier airplane, certificated after August 29, 1959 may include the clearway in determining takeoff distance.

121.195 Transport Category Airplanes: Turbine Engine Powered: Landing Limitations: Destination Airports

3.
8133. What effective runway length is required for a turbojet-powered airplane at the destination airport if the runways are forecast to be wet or slippery at the ETA?

A—70 percent of the actual runway available, from a height of 50 feet over the threshold.
B—115 percent of the runway length required for a dry runway.
C—115 percent of the runway length required for a wet runway.

Answer (B) is correct (8133). *(FAR 121.195)*
No person may take off a turbojet-powered airplane when the appropriate weather reports and forecasts, or a combination thereof, indicate that the runways at the destination airport may be wet or slippery at the estimated time of arrival unless the effective runway length at the destination airport is at least 115% of the runway length required for a dry runway.

Answer (A) is incorrect because 70% of the actual runway available is a landing limitation for a turbopropeller airplane, not a turbojet-powered airplane landing at an airport that forecasts the runways to be wet or slippery at the ETA. Answer (C) is incorrect because, if the runways are forecast to be wet or slippery at the ETA, the effective runway length for a turbojet-powered airplane is 115% of the runway length required for a dry, not wet, runway.

4.3 SPECIAL AIRWORTHINESS REQUIREMENTS

121.285 Carriage of Cargo in Passenger Compartments

4.
8138. What restrictions must be observed regarding the carrying of cargo in the passenger compartment of an airplane operated under FAR Part 121?

A—All cargo must be separated from the passengers by a partition capable of withstanding certain load stresses.
B—All cargo must be carried in a suitable flame resistant bin and the bin must be secured to the floor structure of the airplane.
C—Cargo may be carried aft of a divider if properly secured by a safety belt or other tiedown devices to withstand certain load stresses.

Answer (C) is correct (8138). *(FAR 121.285)*
Cargo may be carried aft of a bulkhead or divider in any passenger compartment provided the cargo is restrained and is properly secured by a safety belt or other tiedown devices having enough strength to eliminate the possibility of shifting under all normally anticipated flight and ground conditions.
Answer (A) is incorrect because cargo may be carried in the passenger compartment if it is carried in an approved cargo bin that meets certain requirements. A partition separating the cargo from the passengers is not required. Answer (B) is incorrect because the cargo bin may be attached to either seat tracks or the floor structure, not only the floor structure, of the airplane.

5.
8139. What requirement must be met regarding cargo that is carried anywhere in the passenger compartment of an air carrier airplane?

A—The bin in which the cargo is carried may not be installed in a position that restricts access to, or use of, any exit.
B—The bin in which the cargo is carried may not be installed in a position that restricts access to, or use of, any aisle in the passenger compartment.
C—The container or bin in which the cargo is carried must be made of material which is at least flash resistant.

Answer (B) is correct (8139). *(FAR 121.285)*
A cargo bin installed in the passenger compartment may not be installed in a position that restricts access to, or use of, any emergency exit or aisle in the passenger compartment.
Answer (A) is incorrect because the cargo bin may not be installed in a position that restricts access to, or use of, any emergency exit, not any exit, in the airplane. Answer (C) is incorrect because the container or bin in which the cargo is carried must be made of material which is at least flame, not flash, resistant.

6.
8175. Which restriction applies to a cargo bin in a passenger compartment? The bin

A—may have an open top if it is placed in front of the passengers and the cargo is secured by a cargo net.
B—must withstand the load factor required of passenger seats, multiplied by 1.15, using the combined weight of the bin and the maximum weight of the cargo that may be carried in the bin.
C—must be constructed of flame retardant material and fully enclosed.

Answer (B) is correct (8175). *(FAR 121.285)*
A cargo bin installed in a passenger compartment must withstand the load factors and emergency landing conditions applicable to the passenger seats of the airplane in which the bin is installed, multiplied by a factor of 1.15, using the combined weight of the bin and the maximum weight of cargo that may be carried in the bin.
Answer (A) is incorrect because the cargo bin must be fully enclosed, not have an open top if it is placed in front of the passengers. Answer (C) is incorrect because the bin must be constructed of flame resistant, not retardant, material.

4.4 INSTRUMENT AND EQUIPMENT REQUIREMENTS

121.309 Emergency Equipment

7.
8160. Where should the portable battery-powered megaphone be located if only one is required on a passenger-carrying airplane?

A—The most forward location in the passenger cabin.
B—In the cabin near the over-the-wing emergency exit.
C—The most rearward location in the passenger cabin.

Answer (C) is correct (8160). *(FAR 121.309)*
One megaphone is required on each airplane with a seating capacity of more than 60 and less than 100 passengers at the most rearward location in the passenger cabin, where it would be readily accessible to a normal flight attendant seat.
Answer (A) is incorrect because the portable battery-powered megaphone must be in the most rearward, not forward, location in the passenger cabin. Answer (B) is incorrect because the portable battery-powered megaphone must be in the most rearward location in the cabin, not near the over-the-wing emergency exit.

8.
8161. How many portable battery-powered megaphones are required on an air carrier airplane with a seating capacity of 100 passengers on a trip segment when 45 passengers are carried?

A—Two; one at the forward end, and the other at the most rearward location in the passenger cabin.
B—Two; one at the most rearward and one in the center of the passenger cabin.
C—Two; one located near or accessible to the flight crew, and one located near the center of the passenger cabin.

Answer (A) is correct (8161). *(FAR 121.309)*
Two megaphones are required in the passenger cabin on each airplane with a seating capacity of more than 99 passengers, one installed at the forward end and the other at the most rearward location, where it would be readily accessible to a normal flight attendant seat.
Answer (B) is incorrect because one megaphone must be at the forward end, not in the center, and the other in the most rearward location in the passenger cabin. Answer (C) is incorrect because the megaphones are located in the passenger cabin, one at the forward end, not necessarily accessible to the flight crew, and the other at the most rearward location, not the center, of the passenger cabin.

9.
8162. How many portable battery-powered megaphones are required on an air carrier airplane with a seating capacity of 150 passengers on a trip segment when 75 passengers are carried?

A—Two; one located near or accessible to the flight crew, and one located near the center of the passenger cabin.
B—Two; one at the most rearward and one in the center of the passenger cabin.
C—Two; one at the forward end, and the other at the most rearward location of the passenger cabin.

Answer (C) is correct (8162). *(FAR 121.309)*
Two megaphones are required in the passenger cabin on each airplane with a seating capacity of more than 99 passengers, one installed at the forward end and the other at the most rearward location, where it would be readily accessible to a normal flight attendant seat.
Answer (A) is incorrect because one megaphone must be located at the forward end, not necessarily near or accessible to the flight crew, and the other at the most rearward location, not near the center, of the passenger cabin. Answer (B) is incorrect because one megaphone must be at the forward end, not center, and the other at the most rearward location in the passenger cabin.

10.
8176. Which factor determines the minimum number of hand fire extinguishers required for flight under FAR Part 121?

A—Number of passengers and crewmembers aboard.
B—Number of passenger cabin occupants.
C—Airplane passenger seating accommodations.

Answer (C) is correct (8176). *(FAR 121.309)*
An airplane's passenger seating accommodations determine the minimum number of hand fire extinguishers required for flight under FAR Part 121.
Answer (A) is incorrect because the minimum number of hand fire extinguishers required is determined by the airplane passenger seating accommodations, not the actual number of passengers and crew aboard a given flight. Answer (B) is incorrect because the minimum number of hand fire extinguishers required is determined by the airplane passenger seating accommodations, not the actual number of passenger cabin occupants.

11.
8177. Which requirement applies to emergency equipment (fire extinguishers, megaphones, first-aid kits, and crash ax) installed in an air carrier airplane?

A—All emergency equipment must be readily accessible to the passengers.
B—Emergency equipment cannot be located in a compartment or area where it is not immediately visible to a flight attendant in the passenger compartment.
C—Emergency equipment must be clearly identified and clearly marked to indicate its method of operation.

Answer (C) is correct (8177). *(FAR 121.309)*
All emergency equipment installed in an air carrier airplane must be clearly identified and clearly marked to indicate its method of operation.
Answer (A) is incorrect because only that emergency equipment located in the passenger compartment, not all emergency equipment, must be readily accessible to passengers. Answer (B) is incorrect because there is no requirement that the emergency equipment be visible to a flight attendant in the passenger compartment. Emergency equipment can be carried in a compartment or container as long as it is marked as to the contents.

121.310 Additional Emergency Equipment

12.
8144. The emergency lights on a passenger-carrying airplane must be armed or turned on during

A—taxiing, takeoff, cruise, and landing.
B—taxiing, takeoff, and landing.
C—takeoff, cruise, and landing.

Answer (B) is correct (8144). *(FAR 121.310)*
The emergency lights on a passenger-carrying airplane must be armed or turned on during taxiing, takeoff, and landing.
Answer (A) is incorrect because the emergency lights must be armed or turned on during taxiing, takeoff, and landing, not cruise. Answer (C) is incorrect because the emergency lights must be armed or turned on during taxiing, takeoff, and landing, not cruise.

13.
8157. If a passenger-carrying landplane is required to have an automatic deploying escape slide system, when must this system be armed?

A—For taxi, takeoff, and landing.
B—Only for takeoff and landing.
C—During taxi, takeoff, landing, and after ditching.

Answer (A) is correct (8157). *(FAR 121.310)*
Automatic deploying escape slide systems must be armed during taxi, takeoff, and landing.
Answer (B) is incorrect because an automatic deploying escape slide system must be armed for taxi as well as takeoff and landing. Answer (C) is incorrect because an automatic deploying escape slide system may be deployed, not armed, after ditching.

14.
8158. If there is a required emergency exit located in the flight crew compartment, the door which separates the compartment from the passenger cabin must be

A—unlocked during takeoff and landing.
B—locked at all times, except during any emergency declared by the pilot in command.
C—latched open during takeoff and landing.

Answer (C) is correct (8158). *(FAR 121.310)*
If it is necessary to pass through a doorway separating the passenger cabin from other areas to reach any required emergency exit from any passenger seat, the door must have a means to latch it in open position, and the door must be latched open during each takeoff and landing.
Answer (A) is incorrect because the door must always be latched open, not unlocked, during takeoff and landing. Answer (B) is incorrect because the door must always be latched open, not locked, during takeoff and landing.

15.
8159. Federal Aviation Regulations require that interior emergency lights must

A—operate automatically when subjected to a negative G load.
B—be operable manually from the flight crew station and a point in the passenger compartment.
C—be armed or turned on during taxiing and all flight operations.

Answer (B) is correct (8159). *(FAR 121.310)*
Interior emergency lights must be operable manually both from the flight crew compartment and from a point in the passenger compartment that is readily accessible to a normal flight attendant seat.
Answer (A) is incorrect because interior emergency lights must operate automatically in a crash landing, which would cause a positive, not negative, G force. Answer (C) is incorrect because the interior emergency lights must be armed or turned on during taxiing, takeoff, and landing, not all flight operations (e.g., cruise).

121.311 Seats, Safety Belts, and Shoulder Harnesses

16.
8153. When may two persons share one approved safety belt in a lounge seat?

A—When one is an adult and one is a child under 3 years of age.
B—Only during the en route flight.
C—During all operations except the takeoff and landing portion of a flight.

Answer (B) is correct (8153). *(FAR 121.311)*
Two persons occupying a berth may share one approved safety belt and two persons occupying a multiple lounge or divan seat may share one approved safety belt during en route flight only.
Answer (A) is incorrect because the regulations do not specify an age of persons sharing a seat belt on a lounge seat. Sharing a seat belt in a lounge seat can be done only during en route flight. Answer (C) is incorrect because two persons may share one seat belt in a lounge seat only during the en route portion of the flight, which excludes taxi, takeoff, and landing.

121.315 Cockpit Check Procedure

17.
8163. In the event of an engine emergency, the use of a cockpit check procedure by the flight crew is

A—encouraged; it helps to ensure that all items on the procedure are accomplished.
B—required by regulations to prevent reliance upon memorized procedures.
C—required by the FAA as a doublecheck after the memorized procedure has been accomplished.

Answer (B) is correct (8163). *(FAR 121.315)*

Each certificate holder shall provide an approved cockpit check procedure for each type of aircraft. The approved procedures must include each item necessary for flight crewmembers to check for safety before starting engines, taking off, or landing, and in engine and systems emergencies. The procedures must be designed so that a flight crewmember will not need to rely upon his/her memory for items to be checked.

Answer (A) is incorrect because the use of a cockpit check procedure is required, not encouraged, by regulations. Answer (C) is incorrect because the purpose of the checklist is to avoid having the flight crew rely upon memory.

121.318 Public Address System

18.
8179. An air carrier airplane must have an operating public address system if it

A—has a seating capacity of 19 passengers.
B—has a seating capacity for more than 19 passengers.
C—weighs more than 12,500 pounds.

Answer (B) is correct (8179). *(FAR 121.318)*

No person may operate an air carrier airplane with a seating capacity of more than 19 passengers unless it is equipped with an operating public address system.

Answer (A) is incorrect because an air carrier airplane must have an operating public address system if it has a seating capacity of more than, not equal to, 19 passengers. Answer (C) is incorrect because an air carrier airplane is required to have an operating public address system if it has a seating capacity of more than 19 passengers, not if it weighs more than 12,500 lb.

121.319 Crewmember Interphone System

19.
8178. A crewmember interphone system is required on which airplane?

A—A large airplane.
B—A turbojet airplane.
C—An airplane with more than 19 passenger seats.

Answer (C) is correct (8178). *(FAR 121.319)*

No person may operate an airplane with a seating capacity of more than 19 passengers unless the airplane is equipped with a crewmember interphone system.

Answer (A) is incorrect because the crewmember interphone system requirement is based upon the number of seats, not the size of the airplane. A crewmember interphone system is required if the airplane has more than 19 passenger seats. Answer (B) is incorrect because the number of passenger seats, not the type of propulsion, determines whether a crewmember interphone system is required.

121.327 Supplemental Oxygen: Reciprocating Engine Powered Airplanes

20.
8185. For a 2-hour flight in a reciprocating-engine-powered airplane at a cabin pressure altitude of 12,000 feet, how much supplemental oxygen for sustenance must be provided? Enough oxygen for

A—30 minutes for 10 percent of the passengers.
B—10 percent of the passengers for 1.5 hours.
C—each passenger for 30 minutes.

Answer (A) is correct (8185). *(FAR 121.327)*

For flights in a reciprocating-engine-powered airplane of more than 30 min. duration at cabin pressure altitudes above 8,000 ft. up to and including 14,000 ft., enough oxygen must be provided for 30 min. for 10% of the passengers.

Answer (B) is incorrect because enough oxygen for 10% of the passengers for 1.5 hr. is the oxygen required for a 2-hr. flight at a cabin pressure altitude of 12,000 ft. for a turbine-engine-powered airplane, not a reciprocating-engine-powered airplane. Answer (C) is incorrect because there must be enough oxygen for 10% of the passengers, not each passenger, for 30 min.

121.329 Supplemental Oxygen for Sustenance: Turbine Engine Powered Airplanes

21.
8174. What is the passenger oxygen supply requirement for a flight, in a turbine-powered aircraft, with a cabin pressure altitude in excess of 15,000 feet? Enough oxygen for

A—each passenger for the entire flight above 15,000 feet cabin altitude.
B—30 percent of the passengers.
C—10 percent of the passengers for 30 minutes.

Answer (A) is correct (8174). *(FAR 121.329)*
For flights at cabin pressure altitudes above 15,000 ft. in a turbine-powered airplane, there must be enough oxygen available for each passenger carried during the entire flight at those altitudes.
Answer (B) is incorrect because enough oxygen for 30% of the passengers is the oxygen supply requirement for the time at cabin pressure altitudes above 14,000 ft., up to and including 15,000 ft., not above 15,000 ft. Answer (C) is incorrect because enough oxygen for 10% of the passengers is the oxygen supply requirement for flights of more than 30 min. at cabin pressure altitudes above 10,000 ft., up to and including 14,000 ft., not for cabin pressure altitudes above 15,000 ft.

22.
8186. At which cabin altitude must oxygen be provided for all passengers during the entire flight at those altitudes?

A—15,000 feet.
B—16,000 feet.
C—14,000 feet.

Answer (B) is correct (8186). *(FAR 121.327, 121.329)*
For flights at cabin pressure altitudes above 15,000 ft., there must be enough oxygen available for all passengers during the entire flight at those altitudes. Thus, at a cabin pressure altitude of 16,000 ft., there must be enough oxygen available for all passengers during the entire flight at that altitude.
Answer (A) is incorrect because, at a cabin pressure altitude of 15,000 ft., there must be enough oxygen available for 30% of the passengers, not all passengers, during the entire flight at that altitude. Answer (C) is incorrect because, at a cabin pressure altitude of 14,000 ft., there must be enough oxygen available for 10% of the passengers, not all the passengers, for flight at that altitude that is more than 30 min. in duration, not for the entire flight at that altitude.

121.333 Supplemental Oxygen for Emergency Descent and for First Aid; Turbine Engine Powered Airplanes with Pressurized Cabins

23.
8173. How much supplemental oxygen for emergency descent must a pressurized turbine-powered air transport airplane carry for each flight crewmember on flight deck duty when operating at flight altitudes above 10,000 feet?

A—A minimum of 2-hours' supply.
B—Sufficient for the duration of the flight above 8,000 feet cabin pressure altitude.
C—Sufficient for the duration of the flight at 10,000 feet flight altitude, not to exceed 1 hour and 50 minutes.

Answer (A) is correct (8173). *(FAR 121.333)*
When operating a turbine-engine-powered airplane with a pressurized cabin at flight altitudes above 10,000 ft., there must be a minimum of a 2-hr. supply of supplemental oxygen for each flight crewmember on flight deck duty in the event of an emergency descent. The 2-hr. oxygen supply is that required for a constant rate of descent from the airplane's maximum certificated operating altitude to 10,000 ft. in 10 min., followed by 1 hr. 50 min. at 10,000 ft.
Answer (B) is incorrect because oxygen requirements at a cabin pressure altitude above 8,000 ft. is for passengers in reciprocating-engine-powered airplanes, not for flight crewmembers on a turbine-engine-powered airplane in the event of an emergency descent. Answer (C) is incorrect because a minimum of 2 hr. of supplemental oxygen is required for each flight crewmember on flight deck duty. The minimum 2-hr. supply includes 10 min. for the descent to 10,000 ft., followed by 1 hr. 50 min. at 10,000 ft.

24.
8187. What is the highest flight level that operations may be conducted without the pilot at the controls wearing and using an oxygen mask, while the other pilot is away from the duty station?

A—FL 240.
B—FL 250.
C—Above FL 250.

Answer (B) is correct (8187). *(FAR 121.333)*
If for any reason at any time it is necessary for one pilot to leave his/her station at the controls of the airplane when operating at flight altitudes above FL 250, the remaining pilot at the controls shall put on and use his/her oxygen mask until the other pilot has returned to his/her duty station. Thus, FL 250 is the highest flight level at which operations may be conducted without the pilot at the controls wearing and using an oxygen mask while the other pilot is away from the duty station.
Answer (A) is incorrect because the highest flight level at which operations may be conducted without the pilot at the controls wearing and using an oxygen mask while the other pilot is away from the duty station is FL 250, not FL 240. Answer (C) is incorrect because at flight levels above FL 250, the pilot at the controls must wear and use an oxygen mask anytime the other pilot is away from the duty station.

25.
8155. If either pilot of an air carrier airplane leaves the duty station while flying at FL 410, the other pilot

A—and the flight engineer shall put on their oxygen masks and breathe oxygen.
B—shall put on the oxygen mask and breathe oxygen.
C—must have a quick-donning type oxygen mask available.

Answer (B) is correct (8155). *(FAR 121.333)*
If for any reason at any time it is necessary for one pilot to leave his/her duty station at the controls of the airplane when operating at flight altitudes above FL 250, the remaining pilot at the controls must put on and use his/her oxygen mask until the other pilot has returned to his/her duty station.
Answer (A) is incorrect because only the remaining pilot at the flight controls, not the flight engineer, is required to put on the oxygen mask and breathe oxygen. Answer (C) is incorrect because, if one pilot leaves the duty station when above FL 250, the remaining pilot must put on the oxygen mask and breathe oxygen, not just have a quick-donning-type oxygen mask available.

26.
8156. If a turbine-engine-powered, pressurized airplane is not equipped with quick-donning oxygen masks, what is the maximum flight altitude authorized without one pilot wearing and using an oxygen mask?

A—FL 200.
B—FL 300.
C—FL 250.

Answer (C) is correct (8156). *(FAR 121.333)*
If a turbine-engine-powered, pressurized airplane is not equipped with quick-donning-type oxygen masks, the maximum altitude authorized without one pilot at the controls wearing and using an oxygen mask is FL 250.
Answer (A) is incorrect because the maximum altitude authorized without one pilot wearing and using an oxygen mask in a turbine-engine-powered, pressurized airplane that is not equipped with quick-donning-type oxygen masks is FL 250, not FL 200. Answer (B) is incorrect because the maximum altitude authorized without one pilot wearing and using an oxygen mask in a turbine-engine-powered, pressurized airplane that is not equipped with quick-donning-type oxygen masks is FL 250, not FL 300.

27.
8183. Each air carrier flight deck crewmember on flight deck duty must be provided with an oxygen mask that can be rapidly placed on his face when operating at flight altitudes

A—of FL 260.
B—of FL 250.
C—above FL 250.

Answer (C) is correct (8183). *(FAR 121.333)*
Each flight crewmember on flight deck duty must be provided with an oxygen mask that can be rapidly placed on his/her face from its ready position, properly secured, sealed, and supplying oxygen on demand, when operating at flight altitudes above FL 250.
Answer (A) is incorrect because each flight crewmember on flight deck duty must be provided with an oxygen mask that can be rapidly placed on his/her face when operating at flight altitudes above FL 250, not FL 260. Answer (B) is incorrect because each flight crewmember on flight deck duty must be provided with an oxygen mask that can be rapidly placed on his/her face when operating at flight altitudes above, not at, FL 250.

28.
8184. A flight crewmember must be able to don and use a quick-donning oxygen mask within

A—5 seconds.
B—10 seconds.
C—15 seconds.

Answer (A) is correct (8184). *(FAR 121.333)*

It must be possible to place a quick-donning oxygen mask on the face from its ready position, properly sealed, secured, and supplying oxygen on demand, with one hand within 5 seconds.

Answer (B) is incorrect because it must be possible to put on a quick-donning oxygen mask with one hand and use it within 5 seconds, not 10 seconds. Answer (C) is incorrect because it must be possible to put on a quick-donning oxygen mask with one hand and use it within 5 seconds, not 15 seconds.

29.
8180. What is the minimum number of acceptable oxygen-dispensing units for first-aid treatment of occupants who might require undiluted oxygen for physiological reasons?

A—Two.
B—Four.
C—Three.

Answer (A) is correct (8180). *(FAR 121.333)*

There must be a minimum of two acceptable oxygen-dispensing units for first-aid treatment of occupants who might require undiluted oxygen for physiological reasons.

Answer (B) is incorrect because the minimum number of oxygen-dispensing units for first-aid treatment is two, not four. Answer (C) is incorrect because the minimum number of oxygen-dispensing units for first-aid treatment is two, not three.

30.
8181. A passenger briefing by a crewmember shall be given, instructing passengers on the necessity of using oxygen in the event of cabin depressurization, prior to flights conducted above

A—FL 200.
B—FL 240.
C—FL 250.

Answer (C) is correct (8181). *(FAR 121.333)*

Before flight is conducted above FL 250, a crewmember shall instruct the passengers on the necessity of using oxygen in the event of cabin depressurization and shall point out to them the location and demonstrate the use of the oxygen-dispensing equipment.

Answer (A) is incorrect because only if the flight is conducted above FL 250, not FL 200, is an oxygen briefing required. Answer (B) is incorrect because only if the flight is conducted above FL 250, not FL 240, is an oxygen briefing required.

31.
8182. The supplemental oxygen requirements for passengers when a flight is operated at FL 250 is dependent upon the airplane's ability to make an emergency descent to a flight altitude of

A—10,000 feet within 4 minutes.
B—14,000 feet within 4 minutes.
C—12,000 feet within 4 minutes or at a minimum rate of 2,500 ft/min, whichever is quicker.

Answer (B) is correct (8182). *(FAR 121.333)*

The supplemental oxygen requirements for passengers when a flight is operated at FL 250 is dependent upon the airplane's ability to make an emergency descent to a flight altitude of 14,000 ft. or less within 4 min.

Answer (A) is incorrect because the airplane must be able to descend to 14,000 ft., not 10,000 ft., in 4 min. Answer (C) is incorrect because the regulations do not specify a rate of descent in feet per minute. The determining factor is the ability to descend to 14,000 ft., not 12,000 ft., in 4 min.

121.339 Emergency Equipment for Extended Over-Water Operations

32.
8164. Which emergency equipment is required for a flag air carrier flight between John F. Kennedy International Airport and London, England?

A—A life preserver equipped with an approved survivor locator light or other flotation device for the full seating capacity of the airplane.
B—An appropriately equipped survival kit attached to each required liferaft.
C—A self-buoyant, water resistant, portable survival-type emergency locator transmitter for each required liferaft.

Answer (B) is correct (8164). *(FAR 121.339)*
No person may operate an airplane in extended overwater operations without having an appropriately equipped survival kit attached to each required life raft.
Answer (A) is incorrect because there must be a life preserver, equipped with an approved survivor locator light, for each occupant of the airplane, not for the full seating capacity of the airplane. Answer (C) is incorrect because only one self-buoyant, water-resistant, portable survival-type emergency locator transmitter is required to be carried in the airplane, not one for each required life raft.

33.
8165. What emergency equipment is required for extended overwater operations?

A—A portable survival emergency locator transmitter for each liferaft.
B—A pyrotechnic signaling device for each life preserver.
C—A life preserver equipped with a survivor locator light, for each person on the airplane.

Answer (C) is correct (8165). *(FAR 121.339)*
No person may operate an airplane in extended overwater operations unless there is a life preserver, equipped with an approved survivor locator light, for each person on the airplane.
Answer (A) is incorrect because only one portable survival type emergency locator transmitter is required to be carried on the airplane, not one for each life raft. Answer (B) is incorrect because there should be at least one pyrotechnic signaling device for each life raft, not for each life preserver.

121.340 Emergency Flotation Means

34.
8166. Each large aircraft operating over water must have a life preserver for each

A—aircraft occupant.
B—seat on the aircraft.
C—passenger seat, plus 10 percent.

Answer (A) is correct (8166). *(FAR 121.340)*
No person may operate a large airplane in any overwater operation unless it is equipped with life preservers or with an approved flotation means for each airplane occupant.
Answer (B) is incorrect because each large airplane operating over water must have a life preserver for each occupant, not each seat, on the airplane. Answer (C) is incorrect because each large airplane operating over water must have a life preserver for each occupant, not each passenger seat plus 10%.

35.
8169. Life preservers required for overwater operations are stored

A—within easy reach of each passenger.
B—under each occupant seat.
C—within easy reach of each seated occupant.

Answer (C) is correct (8169). *(FAR 121.340)*
Life preservers required for overwater operations must be stored within easy reach of each seated occupant.
Answer (A) is incorrect because life preservers must be stored within easy reach of each seated occupant (flight crewmembers and passengers), not within easy reach of each passenger. Answer (B) is incorrect because life preservers must be stored within easy reach of each seated occupant, not under each occupant seat.

121.343 Flight Recorders

36.
8142. For the purpose of testing the flight recorder system,

A—a minimum of 1 hour of the oldest recorded data must be erased to get a valid test.
B—a total of 1 hour of the oldest recorded data accumulated at the time of testing may be erased.
C—a total of no more than 1 hour of recorded data may be erased.

Answer (B) is correct (8142). *(FAR 121.343)*
For the purpose of testing the flight recorder or flight recorder system, a total of 1 hr. of the oldest recorded data accumulated at the time of testing may be erased.
Answer (A) is incorrect because, for the purpose of testing the flight recorder system, a maximum, not minimum, of 1 hr. of the oldest recorded data may be erased. Answer (C) is incorrect because the recorded data that is erased must be the oldest at the time of testing, not just any data.

121.349 Radio Equipment for Operations under VFR over Routes Not Navigated by Pilotage or for Operations under IFR or Over-the-Top

37.
8145. When an air carrier flight is operated under IFR or over-the-top on "victor airways," which navigation equipment is required to be installed in duplicate?

A—VOR.
B—ADF.
C—VOR and DME.

Answer (A) is correct (8145). *(FAR 121.349)*

No person may operate an airplane under IFR or over-the-top on VHF (victor) airways unless the airplane is equipped with that radio equipment necessary to receive satisfactorily, by either of two independent systems, radio navigational signals from all primary en route and approach navigational facilities intended to be used, which are VOR/VORTAC stations. Equipment provided to receive signals en route may be used to receive signals on approach, if it is capable of receiving both signals.

Answer (B) is incorrect because ADF equipment is not required for a flight operated IFR or over-the-top on VHF (victor) airways. Answer (C) is incorrect because only one, not two, DME is required to be installed whenever VOR navigation equipment is required.

38.
8195. An air carrier operates a flight in VFR over-the-top conditions. What radio navigation equipment is required to be a dual installation?

A—VOR.
B—VOR and ILS.
C—VOR and DME.

Answer (A) is correct (8195). *(FAR 121.349)*

No person may operate an airplane in VFR over-the-top conditions unless the airplane is equipped with the radio navigation equipment necessary to receive satisfactorily, by either of two independent systems, radio navigation signals from all primary en route and approach facilities intended to be used. Of the choices provided, only the VOR is required to be a dual installation.

Answer (B) is incorrect because only one ILS receiver, not two, is required. Answer (C) is incorrect because only one DME, not two, is required.

39.
8146. When must an air carrier airplane be DME equipped?

A—In Class E airspace for all IFR or VFR on Top operations.
B—Whenever VOR navigational receivers are required.
C—For flights at or above FL 180.

Answer (B) is correct (8146). *(FAR 121.349)*

Whenever VOR navigational receivers are required, at least one approved distance measuring equipment unit (DME) capable of receiving and indicating distance information from VORTAC facilities must be installed on each airplane when operated in the 50 states and the District of Columbia. If the DME becomes inoperative en route, the pilot shall notify ATC of that failure as soon as it occurs.

Answer (A) is incorrect because DME is required only if VOR equipment is required, not in Class E airspace for all IFR or VFR-on-top operations. Answer (C) is incorrect because an air carrier airplane must be DME equipped whenever VOR navigational receivers are required, not for flights at or above FL 180.

40.
8147. When a pilot plans a flight using NDB NAVAIDS, which rule applies?

A—The airplane must have sufficient fuel to proceed, by means of VOR NAVAIDS, to a suitable airport and land.
B—The pilot must be able to return to the departure airport using other navigation radios.
C—The airplane must have sufficient fuel to proceed, by means of VOR NAVAIDS, to a suitable airport and complete an instrument approach by use of the remaining airplane radio system.

Answer (C) is correct (8147). *(FAR 121.349)*

When operating over routes on which navigation is based on NDB NAVAIDs, only one ADF receiver need be installed if the airplane is equipped with two VOR receivers and if VOR navigational aids are so located and the airplane is so fueled that, in the case of failure of the ADF receiver, the flight may proceed safely to a suitable airport, by means of VOR aids, and complete an instrument approach by use of the remaining airplane radio system.

Answer (A) is incorrect because the airplane must have sufficient fuel to proceed, by means of VOR NAVAIDs, to a suitable airport and complete an instrument approach, not only land. Answer (B) is incorrect because the airplane must be able to fly to a suitable airport, not necessarily the departure airport, and complete an instrument approach.

41.
8149. If an air carrier airplane is flying IFR using a single ADF navigation receiver and the ADF equipment fails, the flight must be able to

A—proceed safely to a suitable airport using VOR aids and complete an instrument approach by use of the remaining airplane radio system.
B—continue to the destination airport by means of dead reckoning navigation.
C—proceed to a suitable airport using VOR aids, complete an instrument approach, and land.

Answer (A) is correct (8149). *(FAR 121.349)*
In the case of operation over routes on which navigation is based on ADF, only one ADF receiver need be installed if the airplane is equipped with two VOR receivers and if VOR navigational aids are so located and the airplane is so fueled that, in the case of failure of the ADF receiver, the flight may proceed safely to a suitable airport, by means of VOR aids, and complete an instrument approach by use of the remaining airplane radio system.
Answer (B) is incorrect because the flight must be able to proceed to a suitable airport, not necessarily the destination airport, by means of VOR equipment, not dead reckoning navigation, and complete an instrument approach utilizing the remaining airplane radio system. Answer (C) is incorrect because the flight to the suitable airport must be done safely, and the instrument approach at the suitable airport may be completed by the use of the remaining airplane radio systems.

42.
8152. While on an IFR flight in controlled airspace, the failure of which unit will precipitate an immediate report to ATC?

A—One engine, on a multiengine aircraft.
B—Airborne radar.
C—DME.

Answer (C) is correct (8152). *(FAR 121.349)*
If the DME becomes inoperative en route while in controlled airspace, the pilot shall notify ATC of that failure as soon as it occurs.
Answer (A) is incorrect because the failure of one engine on a multiengine airplane must be reported to an appropriate ground radio station (FAR 121.565), not necessarily ATC. Answer (B) is incorrect because there is no requirement to report the failure of airborne radar to ATC. If the airborne weather radar becomes inoperative, the airplane must be operated in accordance with the certificate holder's operations manual.

121.353 Emergency Equipment for Operations over Uninhabited Terrain Areas: Flag, Supplemental, and Certain Domestic Operations

43.
8167. For a flight over uninhabited terrain, an airplane operated by a flag or supplemental air carrier must carry enough appropriately equipped survival kits for

A—all of the passengers, plus 10 percent.
B—all aircraft occupants.
C—all passenger seats.

Answer (B) is correct (8167). *(FAR 121.353)*
No flag or supplemental air carrier may conduct an operation over an uninhabited area or any other area that (the FAA specifies in its operations specifications) requires equipment for search and rescue in case of an emergency unless it has enough survival kits, appropriately equipped for the route to be flown, for the number of occupants of the airplane.
Answer (A) is incorrect because there must be enough appropriately equipped survival kits for all occupants on the airplane (including the crew), not enough for all the passengers plus 10%. Answer (C) is incorrect because there must be enough appropriately equipped survival kits for all aircraft occupants, not all passenger seats.

44.
8168. When a supplemental air carrier is operating over an uninhabited area, how many appropriately equipped survival kits are required aboard the aircraft?

A—One for each passenger seat.
B—One for each passenger, plus 10 percent.
C—One for each occupant of the aircraft.

Answer (C) is correct (8168). *(FAR 121.353)*
No supplemental air carrier may conduct an operation over an uninhabited area or any other area that (the FAA specifies in its operations specifications) requires equipment for search and rescue in case of an emergency unless it has enough survival kits, appropriately equipped for the route to be flown, for the number of occupants of the airplane.
Answer (A) is incorrect because an appropriately equipped survival kit is required for each occupant, not for each passenger seat. Answer (B) is incorrect because an appropriately equipped survival kit is required for each occupant of the airplane (including crew), not for each passenger plus 10%.

45.
8172. An airplane operated by a flag air carrier operator flying over uninhabited terrain must carry which emergency equipment?

A—Suitable pyrotechnic signaling devices.
B—Colored smoke flares and a signal mirror.
C—Survival kit for each passenger.

Answer (A) is correct (8172). *(FAR 121.353)*
No flag air carrier may conduct an operation over an uninhabited area or any other area that (the FAA specifies in its operations specifications) requires equipment for search and rescue in case of an emergency unless the airplane has suitable pyrotechnic signaling devices.
Answer (B) is incorrect because, although some colored smoke flares may be of a pyrotechnic nature, they are not specified in the FARs. Answer (C) is incorrect because a survival kit is required for each occupant of the airplane, not each passenger.

46.
8170. An airplane operated by a supplemental air carrier flying over uninhabited terrain must carry which emergency equipment?

A—Survival kit for each passenger.
B—Suitable pyrotechnic signaling devices.
C—Colored smoke flares and a signal mirror.

Answer (B) is correct (8170). *(FAR 121.353)*
No supplemental air carrier may conduct an operation over an uninhabited area or any other area that (the FAA specifies in its operations specifications) requires equipment for search and rescue in case of an emergency unless the airplane has suitable pyrotechnic signaling devices.
Answer (A) is incorrect because a survival kit is required for each occupant of the airplane, not each passenger. Answer (C) is incorrect because, although some colored smoke flares may be of a pyrotechnic nature, they are not specified in the FARs.

47.
8171. An airplane operated by a commercial operator flying over uninhabited terrain must carry which emergency equipment?

A—A signal mirror and colored smoke flares.
B—Survival kit for each passenger.
C—An approved survival-type emergency locator transmitter.

Answer (C) is correct (8171). *(FAR 121.353)*
No airplane operated by a commercial operator may conduct operations over an uninhabited area or any other area that (the FAA specifies in its operations specifications) requires equipment for search and rescue in case of an emergency unless the airplane has an approved survival-type emergency locator transmitter.
NOTE: The FAA may change "commercial operator" to flag, supplemental, or domestic air carrier in the future.
Answer (A) is incorrect because a signal mirror is not required for a flight over uninhabited terrain, but a suitable pyrotechnic signaling device, not colored smoke flares, is required. Answer (B) is incorrect because the airplane must carry a survival kit for each occupant (including the crew), not each passenger.

121.357 Airborne Weather Radar Equipment Requirements

48.
8150. If an air carrier airplane's airborne radar is inoperative and thunderstorms are forecast along the proposed route of flight, an airplane may be dispatched only

A—when able to climb and descend VFR and maintain VFR/OT en route.
B—in VFR conditions.
C—in day VFR conditions.

Answer (C) is correct (8150). *(FAR 121.357)*
If an air carrier airplane's airborne weather radar is inoperative and thunderstorms are forecast along the proposed route of flight, that airplane may be dispatched only in day VFR conditions.
Answer (A) is incorrect because, with an inoperative airborne weather radar, the airplane may be dispatched to fly only during the day, not night, in VFR weather conditions. Answer (B) is incorrect because, with an inoperative airborne weather radar, the airplane may be dispatched to fly only during day, not night, VFR weather conditions.

49.
8151. An air carrier airplane's airborne radar must be in satisfactory operating condition prior to dispatch, if the flight will be

A—conducted under VFR conditions at night with scattered thunderstorms reported en route.
B—carrying passengers, but not if it is "all cargo."
C—conducted IFR, and ATC is able to radar vector the flight around areas of weather.

Answer (A) is correct (8151). *(FAR 121.357)*
No person may dispatch an airplane (or begin the flight of an airplane in the case of an air carrier or commercial operator that does not use a dispatch system) under IFR or night VFR conditions when current weather reports indicate that thunderstorms, or other potentially hazardous weather conditions that can be detected with airborne weather radar, may reasonably be expected along the route to be flown, unless the airborne weather radar equipment is in satisfactory operating condition.
Answer (B) is incorrect because the requirement that the airplane be equipped with an operating airborne weather radar applies to a transport-category aircraft, regardless of whether the airplane is used to carry passengers or cargo. Answer (C) is incorrect because an airplane's airborne weather radar must be satisfactorily operating before conducting an IFR flight if thunderstorms can be expected along the route to be flown, not if ATC is able to provide vectors for weather.

50.
8148. What action should be taken by the pilot in command of a transport category airplane if the airborne weather radar becomes inoperative en route on an IFR flight for which weather reports indicate possible thunderstorms?

A—Request radar vectors from ATC to the nearest suitable airport and land.
B—Proceed in accordance with the approved instructions and procedures specified in the operations manual for such an event.
C—Return to the departure airport if the thunderstorms have not been encountered, and there is enough fuel remaining.

Answer (B) is correct (8148). *(FAR 121.357)*
If the airborne weather radar becomes inoperative en route, the pilot in command must proceed in accordance with the approved instructions and procedures specified in the operations manual for such an event.
Answer (A) is incorrect because, if the airborne weather radar becomes inoperative en route, the pilot in command must follow the instructions and procedures specified in the operations manual, not request radar vectors from ATC to the nearest suitable airport and land. Answer (C) is incorrect because, if the airborne weather radar becomes inoperative en route, the pilot in command must follow the instructions and procedures specified in the operations manual, not return to the departure airport if the thunderstorms have not been encountered and if there is enough fuel remaining.

121.359 Cockpit Voice Recorders

51.
8140. Information recorded during normal operation of a cockpit voice recorder in a large pressurized airplane with four reciprocating engines

A—may all be erased or otherwise obliterated except for the last 30 minutes.
B—may be erased or otherwise obliterated except for the last 30 minutes prior to landing.
C—may all be erased, as the voice recorder is not required on an aircraft with reciprocating engines.

Answer (A) is correct (8140). *(FAR 121.359)*
All of the information recorded during normal operation of a cockpit voice recorder, in a large pressurized airplane with four reciprocating engines, may be erased or otherwise obliterated except for the last 30 min.
Answer (B) is incorrect because the information recorded on a cockpit voice recorder may be erased or otherwise obliterated except for the last 30 min., not the last 30 min. prior to landing. Answer (C) is incorrect because an approved cockpit voice recorder is required on large turbine-powered airplanes and on large pressurized airplanes with four reciprocating engines.

52.
8141. Which rule applies to the use of the cockpit voice recorder erasure feature?

A—All recorded information may be erased, except for the last 30 minutes prior to landing.
B—Any information more than 30 minutes old may be erased.
C—All recorded information may be erased, unless the NTSB needs to be notified of an occurrence.

Answer (B) is correct (8141). *(FAR 121.359)*
An approved cockpit voice recorder having an erasure feature may be used so that, at any time during the operation of the recorder, information recorded more than 30 min. earlier may be erased or otherwise obliterated.
Answer (A) is incorrect because only information more than 30 min. old may be erased, not all information except the last 30 min. prior to landing. Answer (C) is incorrect because only information older than 30 min., not all information, may be erased. If an occurrence requiring immediate notification of the NTSB results in the termination of a flight, the certificate holder must keep the recorded information for at least 60 days.

53.
8143. A cockpit voice recorder must be operated

A—from the start of the before starting engine checklist to completion of final checklist upon termination of flight.
B—from the start of the before starting engine checklist to completion of checklist prior to engine shutdown.
C—when starting to taxi for takeoff to the engine shutdown checklist after termination of the flight.

Answer (A) is correct (8143). *(FAR 121.359)*
No certificate holder may operate a large turbine-engine-powered airplane or a large pressurized airplane with four reciprocating engines unless an approved cockpit voice recorder is installed in that airplane and is operated continuously from the start of the use of the checklist (before starting engines for the purpose of flight) to completion of the final checklist at the termination of the flight.

Answer (B) is incorrect because the cockpit voice recorder must be operated to completion of the final checklist upon termination of the flight, not the checklist prior to engine shutdown. Answer (C) is incorrect because the cockpit voice recorder must be operated from the beginning of the start-engine checklist, not from the start of the taxi for takeoff, to the final checklist after engine shutdown, not just engine shutdown.

121.360 Ground Proximity Warning-Glide Slope Deviation Alerting System

54.
8154. Which airplanes are required to be equipped with a ground proximity warning glide slope deviation alerting system?

A—All turbine-powered airplanes.
B—Passenger-carrying turbine-powered airplanes only.
C—Large turbine-powered airplanes only.

Answer (A) is correct (8154). *(FAR 121.360)*
No person may operate a turbine-powered airplane unless it is equipped with a ground proximity warning-glide slope deviation alerting system.

Answer (B) is incorrect because all turbine-powered airplanes are required to be equipped with a ground proximity warning-glide slope deviation alerting system, regardless of whether that airplane is used for passenger or cargo operations. Answer (C) is incorrect because all, not only large, turbine-powered airplanes are required to be equipped with a ground proximity warning-glide slope deviation alerting system.

4.5 AIRMAN AND CREWMEMBER REQUIREMENTS

121.383 Airman: Limitations on Use of Services

55.
8191. The "age 60 rule" of FAR Part 121 applies to

A—any required pilot crewmember.
B—any flight crewmember.
C—the pilot in command only.

Answer (A) is correct (8191). *(FAR 121.383)*
No certificate holder may use the services of any person as a pilot on an airplane engaged in operations under Part 121 if that person has reached his/her 60th birthday. No person may serve as a pilot on an airplane engaged in operations under Part 121 if that person has reached his/her 60th birthday.

Answer (B) is incorrect because the "age 60" rule applies to pilot crewmembers, not to flight crewmembers such as flight engineers and flight attendants. Answer (C) is incorrect because the rule applies to every pilot crewmember, not just to the pilot in command.

121.385 Composition of Flight Crew

56.
8188. If a flight engineer becomes incapacitated during flight, who may perform the flight engineer's duties?

A—The second in command only.
B—Any flight crewmember, if qualified.
C—Either pilot, if they have a flight engineer certificate.

Answer (B) is correct (8188). *(FAR 121.385)*
On each flight requiring a flight engineer, at least one flight crewmember, other than the flight engineer, must be qualified to provide emergency performance of the flight engineer's functions for the safe completion of the flight if the flight engineer becomes ill or is otherwise incapacitated. A pilot need not hold a flight engineer's certificate to perform the flight engineer's functions in such a situation.

Answer (A) is incorrect because any qualified flight crewmember, not only the second in command, may provide emergency performance of the flight engineer's duties. Answer (C) is incorrect because, if the flight engineer becomes incapacitated during flight, a pilot is not required to hold a flight engineer certificate to provide emergency performance of the flight engineer's duties.

57.
8212. An air carrier uses an airplane that is certified for operation with a flightcrew of two pilots and one flight engineer. In case the flight engineer becomes incapacitated,

A—at least one other flight crewmember must be qualified to perform flight engineer duties.
B—one crewmember must be qualified to perform the duties of the flight engineer.
C—one pilot must be qualified and have a flight engineer certificate to perform the flight engineer duties.

Answer (A) is correct (8212). *(FAR 121.385)*
On each flight requiring a flight engineer, at least one flight crewmember, other than the flight engineer, must be qualified to provide emergency performance of the flight engineer's functions for the safe completion of the flight if the flight engineer becomes ill or is otherwise incapacitated. A pilot need not hold a flight engineer's certificate to perform the flight engineer's functions in such a situation.
Answer (B) is incorrect because the requirement is for at least one flight crewmember, not just one crewmember, to be qualified to perform the flight engineer's duties. Answer (C) is incorrect because, if the flight engineer becomes incapacitated, a pilot may perform the duties of the flight engineer if that pilot is qualified to perform the duties, but (s)he is not required to have a flight engineer certificate.

58.
8213. When a flight engineer is a required crewmember on a flight, it is necessary for

A—one pilot to hold a flight engineer certificate and be qualified to perform the flight engineer duties in an emergency.
B—the flight engineer to be properly certificated and qualified, but also at least one other flight crewmember must be qualified and certified to perform flight engineer duties.
C—at least one other flight crewmember to be qualified to perform flight engineer duties, but a certificate is not required.

Answer (C) is correct (8213). *(FAR 121.385)*
On each flight requiring a flight engineer, at least one flight crewmember, other than the flight engineer, must be qualified to provide emergency performance of the flight engineer's functions for the safe completion of the flight if the flight engineer becomes ill or is otherwise incapacitated. A pilot need not hold a flight engineer's certificate to perform the flight engineer's functions in such a situation.
Answer (A) is incorrect because it is not necessary for either of the pilots to hold a flight engineer certificate, but at least one flight crewmember must be qualified to perform the flight engineer's duties during the remainder of a flight in an emergency. Answer (B) is incorrect because at least one other flight crewmember must be qualified, but not certified, to perform the flight engineer's duties during the remainder of a flight in an emergency.

<u>121.387 Flight Engineer</u>

59.
8189. Under which condition is a flight engineer required as a flight crewmember in FAR Part 121 operations?

A—If the airplane is being flown on proving flights, with revenue cargo aboard.
B—If the airplane is powered by more than two turbine engines.
C—If required by the airplane's type certificate.

Answer (C) is correct (8189). *(FAR 121.387)*
No certificate holder may operate an airplane for which a type certificate was issued before January 2, 1964, having a maximum certificated takeoff weight of more than 80,000 lb., without a flight crewmember holding a current flight engineer certificate. For each airplane type certificated after January 1, 1964, the requirement for a flight engineer is determined under the type certification requirements.
Answer (A) is incorrect because the requirement to have a flight engineer as a member of the flight crew is based on the airplane's type certificate, not on the type of flight the airplane is conducting. Answer (B) is incorrect because the number of engines is not a factor in determining the need for a flight engineer. The airplane's type certificate determines the need for a flight engineer.

60.
8190. When the need for a flight engineer is determined by aircraft weight, what is the takeoff weight that requires a flight engineer?

A—80,000 pounds.
B—more than 80,000 pounds.
C—300,000 pounds.

Answer (B) is correct (8190). *(FAR 121.387)*
No certificate holder may operate an airplane for which a type certificate was issued before January 2, 1964, having a maximum certificate takeoff weight of more than 80,000 lb., without a flight crewmember holding a current flight engineer certificate. For each airplane type certificated after January 1, 1964, the requirement for a flight engineer is determined under the type certification requirements.
Answer (A) is incorrect because a flight engineer is required if the maximum certificated takeoff weight is more than, not equal to, 80,000 lb. Answer (C) is incorrect because 300,000 lb. is the weight above which airplanes are classified as "heavy."

121.389 Flight Navigator and Specialized Navigation Equipment

61.
8196. Routes that require a flight navigator are listed in the

A—International Notices to Airmen.
B—International Aeronautical Information Manual.
C—Certificate holder's Operations Specifications.

Answer (C) is correct (8196). *(FAR 121.389)*

Routes that require a flight navigator are listed in the certificate holder's operations specifications.

Answer (A) is incorrect because international NOTAMs contain information concerning the establishment or condition of, or change in, any facility, service, or procedure or hazards for flights outside the U.S., not a listing of particular routes that require a flight navigator. Answer (B) is incorrect because the *International Aeronautical Information Manual* is a publication designed primarily as a preflight planning guide for international flights, not as a source for determining if a particular route requires a flight navigator.

62.
8197. Where are the routes listed that require special navigation equipment?

A—Certificate holder's Operations Specifications.
B—International Aeronautical Information Manual.
C—International Notices to Airmen.

Answer (A) is correct (8197). *(FAR 121.389)*

Routes that require special navigation equipment are listed in the certificate holder's operations specifications.

Answer (B) is incorrect because the *International Aeronautical Information Manual* is a publication designed primarily as a preflight planning guide for international flights. It does not list routes which require special navigation equipment. Answer (C) is incorrect because international NOTAMs contain information concerning the establishment or condition of, or change in, any facility, service, or procedure or hazards for flights outside the U.S. They do not list routes which require special navigation equipment.

63.
8199. A flight navigator or a specialized means of navigation is required aboard an air carrier airplane operated outside the 48 contiguous United States and District of Columbia when

A—operations are conducted IFR or VFR on Top.
B—operations are conducted over water more than 50 miles from shore.
C—the airplane's position cannot be reliably fixed for a period of more than 1 hour.

Answer (C) is correct (8199). *(FAR 121.389)*

No certificate holder may operate an airplane outside the 48 contiguous states and the District of Columbia, when its position cannot be reliably fixed for a period of more than 1 hr., without a flight crewmember who holds a current flight navigator certificate or approved specialized means of navigation which enables a reliable determination to be made of the position of the airplane by each pilot seated at his duty station.

Answer (A) is incorrect because, whether IFR or VFR on top, the requirement applies if the airplane's position cannot be reliably fixed for more than 1 hr. Answer (B) is incorrect because the requirement applies over water or land if the airplane's position cannot be reliably fixed for more than 1 hr.

121.391 Flight Attendants

64.
8192. An airplane has seats for 149 passengers and eight crewmembers. What is the minimum number of flight attendants required with 97 passengers aboard?

A—Four.
B—Three.
C—Two.

Answer (B) is correct (8192). *(FAR 121.391)*

The number of required flight attendants is based upon passenger seating capacity, not the number of passengers on a given flight. A seating capacity of 51 to 100 requires two flight attendants, after which one flight attendant is required for each unit of 50 seats. A seating capacity of 149 requires three flight attendants.

Answer (A) is incorrect because four flight attendants are required on an airplane with a seating capacity between 151 and 200, not 149. Answer (C) is incorrect because two flight attendants are required on an airplane with a seating capacity of 97, not 149. The number of required flight attendants is based on passenger seating capacity, not the number of passengers on a given flight.

65.
8193. When an air carrier airplane with a seating capacity of 187 has 137 passengers on board, what is the minimum number of flight attendants required?

A—Five.
B—Four.
C—Three.

Answer (B) is correct (8193). *(FAR 121.391)*

The number of required flight attendants is based upon passenger seating capacity, not the number of passengers on a given flight. A seating capacity of 51 to 100 requires two flight attendants, after which one flight attendant is required for each unit of 50 seats. A seating capacity of 187 requires four flight attendants.

Answer (A) is incorrect because five flight attendants are required on an airplane with a passenger seating capacity between 201 and 250, not 187. Answer (C) is incorrect because three flight attendants are required on an airplane with a seating capacity of 137, not 187. The number of flight attendants required is based on passenger seating capacity, not the number of passengers on a given flight.

66.
8201. What is the minimum number of flight attendants required on an airplane having a passenger seating capacity of 188 with only 117 passengers aboard?

A—Five.
B—Four.
C—Three.

Answer (B) is correct (8201). *(FAR 121.391)*

The number of required flight attendants is based upon passenger seating capacity, not the number of passengers on a given flight. A seating capacity of 51 to 100 requires two flight attendants, after which one flight attendant is required for each unit of 50 seats. A seating capacity of 188 requires four flight attendants.

Answer (A) is incorrect because five flight attendants are required on an airplane with a seating capacity between 201 and 250, not 188. Answer (C) is incorrect because three flight attendants are required on an airplane with a seating capacity of 117, not 188. The number of flight attendants required is based on passenger seating capacity, not the number of passengers on a given flight.

67.
8202. What is the minimum number of flight attendants required on an airplane with a passenger seating capacity of 333 when 296 passengers are aboard?

A—Seven.
B—Six.
C—Five.

Answer (A) is correct (8202). *(FAR 121.391)*

The number of required flight attendants is based upon passenger seating capacity, not the number of passengers on a given flight. A seating capacity of 51 to 100 requires two flight attendants, after which one flight attendant is required for each unit of 50 seats. A seating capacity of 333 requires seven flight attendants.

Answer (B) is incorrect because six flight attendants are required on an airplane with a seating capacity of 296, not 333. The number of flight attendants required is based on passenger seating capacity, not the number of passengers on a given flight. Answer (C) is incorrect because five flight attendants are required on an airplane with a seating capacity between 201 and 250, not 333.

121.397 Emergency and Emergency Evacuation Duties

68.
8198. Which document includes descriptions of the required crewmember functions to be performed in the event of an emergency?

A—Airplane Flight Manual.
B—Certificate holder's manual.
C—Pilot's Emergency Procedures Handbook.

Answer (B) is correct (8198). *(FAR 121.397)*

The certificate holder's manual must include descriptions of the required crewmember functions to be performed in the event of an emergency.

Answer (A) is incorrect because the airplane flight manual contains emergency procedures appropriate to the airplane, not the required crewmember functions during an emergency. Answer (C) is incorrect because the description of the required crewmember functions in an emergency is found in the certificate holder's manual, not a pilot's emergency procedures handbook.

69.
8200. The required crewmember functions that are to be performed in the event of an emergency shall be assigned by the

A—pilot in command.
B—air carrier's chief pilot.
C—certificate holder.

Answer (C) is correct (8200). *(FAR 121.397)*
The certificate holder must assign the required crewmember functions that are to be performed in the event of an emergency.
Answer (A) is incorrect because the required crewmember functions that are to be performed in the event of an emergency must be assigned by the certificate holder, not the pilot in command. Answer (B) is incorrect because certificate holder, not the chief pilot, must assign the required crewmember functions that are to be performed in the event of an emergency.

4.6 TRAINING PROGRAM

121.400 Applicability and Terms Used

70.
8215. The training required by flight crewmembers who have not qualified and served in the same capacity on another airplane of the same group (e.g., turbojet powered) is

A—upgrade training.
B—transition training.
C—initial training.

Answer (C) is correct (8215). *(FAR 121.400)*
Initial training is required for flight crewmembers who have not qualified and served in the same capacity on another airplane of the same group (e.g., turbojet powered).
Answer (A) is incorrect because upgrade training is required for a flight crewmember who has qualified and served as second in command or flight engineer on a particular airplane type, before (s)he serves as pilot in command or second in command, respectively, on that airplane. Answer (B) is incorrect because transition training is required for flight crewmembers who have qualified and served in the same capacity on another airplane in the same group.

71.
8216. A crewmember who has served as second in command on a particular type airplane (e.g., B-727-100), may serve as pilot in command upon completing which training program?

A—Upgrade training.
B—Recurrent training.
C—Initial training.

Answer (A) is correct (8216). *(FAR 121.400)*
Upgrade training is required for a crewmember who has served as second in command on a particular type airplane (e.g., B-727-100) before (s)he may serve as pilot in command on that airplane.
Answer (B) is incorrect because recurrent training is a scheduled periodic training requirement to ensure that a crewmember is adequately trained and currently proficient with respect to the type of airplane and crewmember position involved. Answer (C) is incorrect because initial training is required for a crewmember who has not qualified and served in the same capacity on another airplane of the same group.

72.
8217. The training required for crewmembers or dispatchers who have been qualified and served in the same capacity on other airplanes of the same group is

A—difference training.
B—transition training.
C—upgrade training.

Answer (B) is correct (8217). *(FAR 121.400)*
Transition training is required for crewmembers and dispatchers who have qualified and served in the same capacity on another airplane of the same group.
Answer (A) is incorrect because difference training is required for crewmembers and dispatchers who have qualified and served on a particular type airplane, when the FAA finds difference training is necessary. Answer (C) is incorrect because upgrade training is required for a crewmember who has qualified and served as second in command or flight engineer on a particular airplane type, before (s)he serves as pilot in command or second in command, respectively, on that airplane.

121.401 Training Program: General

73.
8214. If a flight crewmember completes a required annual flight check in December 1987 and the required annual recurrent flight check in January 1989, the latter check is considered to have been taken in

A—November 1988.
B—December 1988.
C—January 1989.

Answer (B) is correct (8214). *(FAR 121.401)*

Whenever a flight crewmember is required to take recurrent training, a flight check, or a competence check, and takes the check or completes the training in the calendar month before or after the calendar month in which that training or check is required, (s)he is considered to have taken or completed it in the calendar month in which it was required.

Answer (A) is incorrect because the check taken in January is considered to have been taken in December, not November. The annual flight check can be taken 1 month before the month due. Answer (C) is incorrect because the check taken in January is considered to have been taken in December, the month the flight check was due. The annual flight check can be taken 1 month after the month due.

121.417 Crewmember Emergency Training

74.
8204. The air carrier must give instruction on such subjects as respiration, hypoxia, and decompression to crewmembers serving on pressurized airplanes operated above

A—FL 180.
B—FL 200.
C—FL 250.

Answer (C) is correct (8204). *(FAR 121.417)*

Crewmembers who serve in operations above FL 250 must receive instruction on such subjects as respiration, hypoxia, and decompression.

Answer (A) is incorrect because crewmembers who serve in operations above FL 250, not FL 180, must receive instruction on such subjects as respiration, hypoxia, and decompression. Answer (B) is incorrect because crewmembers who serve in operations above FL 250, not FL 200, must receive instruction on such subjects as respiration, hypoxia, and decompression.

75.
8218. How often must a crewmember actually operate the airplane emergency equipment, after initial training? Once every

A—6 calendar months.
B—12 calendar months.
C—24 calendar months.

Answer (C) is correct (8218). *(FAR 121.417)*

During initial training and once each 24 calendar months during recurrent training, each crewmember must perform certain emergency drills and operate specified emergency equipment.

Answer (A) is incorrect because a crewmember must actually operate emergency equipment once every 24 calendar months, not 6 calendar months. Answer (B) is incorrect because a crewmember must actually operate emergency equipment once every 24 calendar months, not 12 calendar months.

4.7 CREWMEMBER QUALIFICATIONS

121.433a Training Requirements: Handling and Carriage of Dangerous Articles and Magnetized Materials

76.
8206. A person whose duties include the handling or carriage of dangerous articles and/or magnetized materials must have satisfactorily completed an established and approved training program within the preceding

A—24 calendar months.
B—12 calendar months.
C—6 calendar months.

Answer (B) is correct (8206). *(FAR 121.433a)*

No certificate holder may use any person to perform, and no person may perform, any assigned duties and responsibilities for the handling or carriage of dangerous articles and/or magnetized materials unless within the preceding 12 calendar months that person has satisfactorily completed training in an established and approved program.

Answer (A) is incorrect because any person involved with dangerous articles and/or magnetized materials must have completed an approved training program within the preceding 12 calendar months, not 24 calendar months. Answer (C) is incorrect because any person involved with dangerous articles and/or magnetized materials must have completed an approved training program within the preceding 12 calendar months, not 6 calendar months.

121.439 Pilot Qualification: Recent Experience

77.
8209. What is one of the requirements that must be met by an airline pilot to re-establish recency of experience?

A—At least one landing must be made from a circling approach.
B—At least one full stop landing must be made.
C—At least one precision approach must be made to the lowest minimums authorized for the certificate holder.

Answer (B) is correct (8209). *(FAR 121.439)*
A required pilot flight crewmember who has not made three takeoffs and landings within the preceding 90 days must reestablish recency of experience as follows: Under the supervision of a check airman, make at least three takeoffs and landings in the type airplane in which that person is to serve or in an advanced simulator or visual simulator,

1. At least one takeoff with a simulated failure of the most critical powerplant
2. At least one landing from an ILS approach to the lowest ILS minimum authorized for the certificate holder
3. At least one landing to a full stop

Answer (A) is incorrect because one landing must be made from an ILS approach to the lowest ILS minimums, which implies a straight-in approach, not a circling approach. Answer (C) is incorrect because a landing must be made, not just an approach, from an ILS approach, not any precision approach, to the lowest ILS minimum authorized for the certificate holder.

78.
8208. Which is one of the requirements that must be met by a required pilot flight crewmember in re-establishing recency of experience?

A—At least one landing must be made with a simulated failure of the most critical engine.
B—At least one ILS approach to the lowest ILS minimums authorized for the certificate holder and a landing from that approach.
C—At least three landings must be made to a complete stop.

Answer (B) is correct (8208). *(FAR 121.439)*
A required pilot flight crewmember who has not made three takeoffs and landings within the preceding 90 days must reestablish recency of experience as follows: Under the supervision of a check airman, make at least three takeoffs and landings in the type airplane in which that person is to serve or in an advanced simulator or visual simulator,

1. At least one takeoff with a simulated failure of the most critical powerplant
2. At least one landing from an ILS approach to the lowest ILS minimum authorized for the certificate holder
3. At least one landing to a full stop

Answer (A) is incorrect because at least one takeoff, not landing, is required with a simulated failure of the most critical engine. Answer (C) is incorrect because only one landing, not three landings, to a complete stop is required.

121.440 Line Checks

79.
8210. What are the line check requirements for the pilot in command for a domestic air carrier?

A—The line check is required every 12 calendar months in one of the types of airplanes to be flown.
B—The line check is required only when the pilot is scheduled to fly into special areas and airports.
C—The line check is required every 12 months in each type aircraft in which the pilot may fly.

Answer (A) is correct (8210). *(FAR 121.440)*
No certificate holder may use any person, nor may any person serve, as pilot in command of an airplane unless, within the preceding 12 calendar months, that person has passed a line check in which (s)he satisfactorily performed the duties and responsibilities of a pilot in command in one of the types of airplanes (s)he is to fly.
Answer (B) is incorrect because a pilot must complete special types of navigation qualifications and airport qualifications, not a line check, within the preceding 12 calendar months before the pilot is scheduled to fly into special areas and airports. Answer (C) is incorrect because a line check is required in only one of the types of aircraft flown by the pilot in command, not in each type in which the pilot may fly.

121.441 Proficiency Checks

80.
8205. A pilot in command must complete a proficiency check or simulator training within the preceding

A—6 calendar months.
B—12 calendar months.
C—24 calendar months.

Answer (A) is correct (8205). *(FAR 121.441)*
A pilot in command must have completed a proficiency check within the preceding 12 calendar months and, in addition, within the preceding 6 calendar months, either a proficiency check or simulator training.
Answer (B) is incorrect because, within the preceding 12 calendar months, a pilot in command must have completed a proficiency check, not a proficiency check or simulator training. Answer (C) is incorrect because, within the preceding 24 calendar months, all pilots other than the pilot in command must have completed a proficiency check or line-oriented simulator training.

81.
8207. A pilot flight crewmember, other than pilot in command, must have received a proficiency check or line-oriented simulator training within the preceding

A—6 calendar months.
B—12 calendar months.
C—24 calendar months.

Answer (C) is correct (8207). *(FAR 121.441)*
No certificate holder may use any person, nor may any person serve, as a required pilot flight crewmember other than a pilot in command unless that person has satisfactorily completed within the preceding 24 calendar months either a proficiency check or the line-oriented simulator training course.
Answer (A) is incorrect because, within the preceding 6 calendar months, a pilot in command, not any other pilot, must have completed a proficiency check or simulator training. Answer (B) is incorrect because, within the preceding 12 calendar months, all pilots other than the pilot in command must have completed a proficiency check or any approved simulator training course, not necessarily line-oriented simulator training.

4.8 AIRCRAFT DISPATCHER QUALIFICATIONS AND DUTY TIME LIMITATIONS: DOMESTIC AND FLAG OPERATIONS; FLIGHT ATTENDANT DUTY PERIOD LIMITATIONS AND REST REQUIREMENTS: DOMESTIC, FLAG, AND SUPPLEMENTAL OPERATIONS

121.463 Aircraft Dispatcher Qualifications

82.
8230. To remain current as an aircraft dispatcher, a person must, in addition to other requirements,

A—within the preceding 12 calendar months, spend 2.5 hours observing flight deck operations, plus two additional takeoffs and landings, in one of the types of airplanes in each group he/she is to dispatch.
B—within the preceding 12 calendar months, spend at least 5 hours observing flight deck operations in one of the types of airplanes in each group he/she is to dispatch.
C—within the preceding 12 calendar months, spend at least 5 hours observing flight deck operations in each type of airplane, in each group that he/she is to dispatch.

Answer (B) is correct (8230). *(FAR 121.463)*
No domestic or flag air carrier may use any person, nor may any person serve, as an aircraft dispatcher unless within the preceding 12 calendar months (s)he has satisfactorily completed operating familiarization consisting of at least 5 hr. observing flight deck operations in one of the types of airplanes in each airplane group (s)he is to dispatch.
Answer (A) is incorrect because a dispatcher may reduce the 5 hr. of observing flight deck operations requirement to a minimum of 2.5 hr. by the substitution of one additional takeoff and landing for an hour of flight. In this case, the aircraft dispatcher must spend 2.5 hr. observing flight deck operations plus three, not two, additional takeoffs and landings in one of the types of airplanes in each airplane group (s)he is to dispatch. Answer (C) is incorrect because the aircraft dispatcher is required to spend at least 5 hr. observing flight deck operations in one of the types of airplanes, not each type of airplane, in each airplane group (s)he is to dispatch.

121.465 Duty Time Limitations: Domestic and Flag Operations

83.
8211. Normally, a dispatcher should be scheduled for no more than

A—8 hours of service in any 24 consecutive hours.
B—10 hours of duty in any 24 consecutive hours.
C—10 consecutive hours of duty.

Answer (C) is correct (8211). *(FAR 121.465)*
Except in cases in which circumstances or emergency conditions beyond the control of the air carrier require otherwise, no domestic or flag air carrier may schedule a dispatcher for more than 10 consecutive hr. of duty.
Answer (A) is incorrect because a dispatcher should normally be scheduled for no more than 10 consecutive hr. of duty, not 8 hr. of service in any 24 consecutive hr. Answer (B) is incorrect because a dispatcher may be scheduled for more than 10 hr. of duty in any 24 consecutive hr. if the air carrier provides the dispatcher a rest period of at least 8 hr. at or before the end of 10 hr. of duty.

84.
8238. The maximum number of consecutive hours of duty that an aircraft dispatcher may be scheduled is

A—12 hours.
B—10 hours.
C—8 hours.

Answer (B) is correct (8238). *(FAR 121.465)*
No domestic or flag air carrier may schedule a dispatcher for more than 10 consecutive hr. of duty.
Answer (A) is incorrect because an aircraft dispatcher may be scheduled for a maximum of 10 consecutive hr. of duty, not 12 consecutive hr. Answer (C) is incorrect because an aircraft dispatcher may be scheduled for a maximum of 10 consecutive hr. of duty, not 8 consecutive hr.

85.
8229. If a domestic or flag air carrier schedules a dispatcher for 13 hours of duty in a 24-consecutive-hour period, what action is required?

A—The dispatcher should be given a rest period of 24 hours at the end of the 13 hours.
B—The dispatcher should refuse to be on duty 13 hours as 121.465(1) limits the duty period to 10 consecutive hours.
C—The dispatcher should be given a rest period of at least 8 hours at or before the completion of 10 hours of duty.

Answer (C) is correct (8229). *(FAR 121.465)*
If a domestic or flag air carrier schedules a dispatcher for more than 10 hr. of duty in 24 consecutive hr., the carrier must provide the dispatcher a rest period of at least 8 hr. at or before the end of 10 hr. of duty.
Answer (A) is incorrect because the air carrier must provide the dispatcher a rest period of at least 8 hr., not 24 hr., at or before the end of 10 hr. of duty, not at the end of 13 hr. of duty. Answer (B) is incorrect because there will be no violation of FAR 121.465 if the air carrier provides the dispatcher a rest period of at least 8 hr. at or before the end of 10 hr. of duty.

86.
8231. An aircraft dispatcher shall receive at least 24 consecutive hours of rest during

A—every 7 consecutive days.
B—any 7 consecutive days or the equivalent thereof within any calendar month.
C—each calendar week.

Answer (B) is correct (8231). *(FAR 121.465)*
An aircraft dispatcher must be relieved of all duty with the air carrier for at least 24 consecutive hr. during any 7 consecutive days or the equivalent thereof within any calendar month.
Answer (A) is incorrect because an aircraft dispatcher must receive at least 24 consecutive hr. of rest during any 7 consecutive days within any calendar month, not every 7 consecutive days. Answer (C) is incorrect because an aircraft dispatcher must receive at least 24 consecutive hr. of rest during any 7 consecutive days within any calendar month, not during each calendar week.

4.9 FLIGHT TIME LIMITATIONS AND REST REQUIREMENTS: DOMESTIC OPERATIONS

121.471 Flight Time Limitations and Rest Requirements: All Flight Crewmembers

87.
8228. Duty and rest period rules for domestic air carrier operations require that a flight crewmember

A—not be assigned to any duty with the air carrier during any required rest period.
B—not be on duty aloft for more than 100 hours in any 30-day period.
C—be relieved of all duty for at least 24 hours during any 7 consecutive days.

Answer (A) is correct (8228). *(FAR 121.471)*
No domestic air carrier may assign any flight crewmember and no flight crewmember may accept assignment to any duty with the air carrier during any required rest period.
Answer (B) is incorrect because the total flight time limitation is 100 hr. in any calendar month, not in any 30-day period. Answer (C) is incorrect because a domestic air carrier must relieve a flight crewmember from all duty for at least 24 consecutive hr., not just 24 hr., during any 7 consecutive days.

4.10 FLIGHT TIME LIMITATIONS: FLAG OPERATIONS

121.481 Flight Time Limitations: One or Two Pilot Crews

88.
8220. The maximum flight time in 24 consecutive hours that a flag air carrier may schedule a pilot in a two-pilot crew without a rest period is

A—8 hours.
B—10 hours.
C—12 hours.

Answer (A) is correct (8220). *(FAR 121.481)*
A flag air carrier may schedule a pilot to fly in an airplane that has a crew of one or two pilots for 8 hr. or less during any 24 consecutive hr. without a rest period during these 8 hr.
Answer (B) is incorrect because a pilot of a domestic air carrier, not a flag air carrier, may be scheduled for 10 hr. of scheduled flight time without a rest period. Answer (C) is incorrect because 12 hr. is the limit for a crew consisting of two pilots and one additional flight crewmember, not a two-pilot crew.

89.
8221. The maximum number of hours a pilot may fly in 7 consecutive days as the pilot in command in a two-pilot crew for a flag air carrier is

A—35 hours.
B—32 hours.
C—30 hours.

Answer (B) is correct (8221). *(FAR 121.481)*
No pilot of a two-pilot crew for a flag air carrier may fly more than 32 hr. during any 7 consecutive days, and each pilot must be relieved from all duty for at least 24 consecutive hr. at least once during any 7 consecutive days.
Answer (A) is incorrect because the maximum number of hours that either pilot in a two-pilot crew for a flag air carrier may fly in 7 consecutive days is 32 hr., not 35 hr. Answer (C) is incorrect because the maximum number of hours that any pilot for a domestic air carrier, not a flag air carrier, may fly in any 7 consecutive days is 30 hr.

121.483 Flight Time Limitations: Two Pilots and One Additional Flight Crewmember

90.
8219. A flag air carrier may schedule a pilot to fly in an airplane, having two pilots and one additional flight crewmember, for no more than

A—8 hours during any 12 consecutive hours.
B—10 hours during any 12 consecutive hours.
C—12 hours during any 24 consecutive hours.

Answer (C) is correct (8219). *(FAR 121.483)*
A flag air carrier may not schedule a pilot to fly, in an airplane that has a crew of two pilots and at least one additional flight crewmember, for more than 12 hr. during any 24 consecutive hr.
Answer (A) is incorrect because a flag air carrier may not schedule a pilot to fly, in an airplane that has a crew of two pilots and one additional flight crewmember, for more than 12 hr. during any 24 consecutive hr., not 8 hr. during any 12 consecutive hr. Answer (B) is incorrect because a flag air carrier may not schedule a pilot to fly, in an airplane that has a crew of two pilots and one additional flight crewmember, for more than 12 hr. during any 24 consecutive hr., not 10 hr. during any 12 consecutive hr.

121.491 Flight Time Limitations: Deadhead Transportation

91.
8227. How does deadhead transportation, going to or from a duty assignment, affect the computation of flight time limits for air carrier flight crewmembers? It is

A—considered part of the rest period if the flightcrew includes more than two pilots.
B—considered part of the rest period for flight engineers and navigators.
C—not considered part of a rest period.

Answer (C) is correct (8227). *(FAR 121.491)*
For the computation of flight time limits for a flag air carrier flight crewmember, time spent in deadhead transportation to or from a duty assignment is not considered to be a part of a rest period.
Answer (A) is incorrect because time spent in deadhead transportation to or from a duty assignment is not considered to be a part of a rest period, regardless of the number of pilots in the flight crew. Answer (B) is incorrect because time spent in deadhead transportation to or from a duty assignment is not considered to be a part of a rest period. This requirement includes pilots, flight engineers, and flight navigators.

4.11 FLIGHT TIME LIMITATIONS: SUPPLEMENTAL OPERATIONS

121.503 Flight Time Limitations: Pilots: Airplanes

92.
8222. The maximum number of hours that a supplemental air carrier pilot may fly, as a crewmember, in a commercial operation, in any 30 consecutive days is

A—100 hours.
B—120 hours.
C—300 hours.

Answer (A) is correct (8222). *(FAR 121.503)*
No pilot may fly as a crewmember of a supplemental air carrier more than 100 hr. during any 30 consecutive days.
Answer (B) is incorrect because the maximum number of hours that a supplemental air carrier airman, not pilot, may be aloft as a member of a flight crew that consists of two pilots and at least one additional flight crewmember, is 120 hr. during any 30 consecutive days. Answer (C) is incorrect because the maximum number of hours that a supplemental air carrier pilot may fly, in an airplane that has a crew of two pilots and at least one additional flight crewmember, is 300 hr. during any 90 consecutive days, not any 30 consecutive days.

121.507 Flight Time Limitations: Three Pilot Crews: Airplanes

93.
8223. A supplemental air carrier may schedule a pilot, on a three-pilot crew, for flight deck duty during any 24 consecutive-hour period for not more than

A—6 hours.
B—8 hours.
C—10 hours.

Answer (B) is correct (8223). *(FAR 121.507)*
No supplemental air carrier may schedule a pilot for flight deck duty in an airplane that has a crew of three pilots for more than 8 hr. in any 24 consecutive hr.
Answer (A) is incorrect because the maximum flight time that a supplemental air carrier may schedule a pilot for flight deck duty on an airplane that has a crew of three pilots is 8 hr., not 6 hr., during any 24 consecutive hr. Answer (C) is incorrect because the maximum flight time that a supplemental air carrier may schedule a pilot for flight deck duty on an airplane that has a crew of three pilots is 8 hr., not 10 hr., during any 24 consecutive hr.

121.517 Flight Time Limitations: Other Commercial Flying: Airplanes

94.
8224. The flight time limitations established for flight crewmembers include

A—only commercial flying in any flight crewmember position in which FAR Part 121 operations are conducted.
B—all flight time, except military, in any flight crewmember position.
C—all commercial flying in any flight crewmember position.

Answer (C) is correct (8224). *(FAR 121.517)*
The flight time limitations established for flight crewmembers employed by a supplemental air carrier or commercial operator include all commercial flying in any flight crewmember position.
Answer (A) is incorrect because the flight time limitations established for flight crewmembers include all commercial flying, not only FAR Part 121 operations, in any flight crewmember position. Answer (B) is incorrect because the flight time limitations established for flight crewmembers include all commercial flying, not all flight time, in any flight crewmember position.

121.521 Flight Time Limitations: Crew of Two Pilots and One Additional Airman as Required

95.
9714. Which is the maximum number of hours that a supplemental air carrier airman may be aloft in any 30 consecutive days, as a member of a flight crew that consists of two pilots and at least one additional flight crewmember?

A—100 hours.
B—120 hours.
C—300 hours.

Answer (B) is correct (9714). *(FAR 121.521)*
The maximum number of hours that a supplemental air carrier airman may be aloft in any 30 consecutive days as a member of a flight crew that consists of two pilots and at least one additional flight crewmember is 120 hr.
Answer (A) is incorrect because 100 hr. is the maximum number of hours that a supplemental air carrier pilot may fly in any 30 consecutive days, not an airman that is a member of a flight crew that consists of two pilots and at least one additional flight crewmember.
Answer (C) is incorrect because 300 hr. is the maximum number of hours that a supplemental air carrier airman may be aloft in any 90, not 30, consecutive days as a member of a flight crew that consists of two pilots and at least one additional flight crewmember.

4.12 FLIGHT OPERATIONS

121.537 Responsibility for Operational Control: Supplemental Operations

96.
8243. The persons jointly responsible for the initiation, continuation, diversion, and termination of a supplemental air carrier or commercial operator flight are the

A—pilot in command and chief pilot.
B—pilot in command and director of operations.
C—pilot in command and the flight follower.

Answer (B) is correct (8243). *(FAR 121.537)*

The pilot in command and the director of operations are jointly responsible for the initiation, continuation, diversion, and termination of a supplemental air carrier flight. The director of operations may delegate the functions for the initiation, continuation, diversion, and termination of a flight, but (s)he may not delegate the responsibility for those functions.

NOTE: The FAA may delete the term "commercial operator" in the future.

Answer (A) is incorrect because the pilot in command and the director of operations, not the chief pilot, of a supplemental air carrier are jointly responsible for the initiation, continuation, diversion, and termination of a flight. Answer (C) is incorrect because the pilot in command and the director of operations, not a flight follower, of a supplemental air carrier are jointly responsible for the initiation, continuation, diversion, and termination of a flight.

121.542 Flight Crewmember Duties

97.
8298. With regard to flight crewmember duties, which of the following operations are considered to be in the "critical phase of flight"?

A—Taxi, takeoff, landing, and all other operations conducted below 10,000 feet MSL, including cruise flight.
B—Descent, approach, landing, and taxi operations, irrespective of altitudes MSL.
C—Taxi, takeoff, landing, and all other operations conducted below 10,000 feet, excluding cruise flight.

Answer (C) is correct (8298). *(FAR 121.542)*

No flight crewmember may perform any duties during a critical phase of flight except those duties required for the safe operation of the aircraft. The critical phases of flight include all ground operations involving taxi, takeoff, and landing, and all other flight operations conducted below 10,000 ft., except cruise flight.

Answer (A) is incorrect because the critical phases of flight include all ground operations involving taxi, takeoff, and landing, and all other operations conducted below 10,000 ft., except cruise flight. The critical phase of flight does not include cruise flight when it is conducted below 10,000 ft. Answer (B) is incorrect because the critical phases of flight include all ground operations involving taxi, takeoff, and landing, and all other operations conducted below 10,000 ft., except cruise flight.

98.
8297. Below which altitude, except when in cruise flight, are non-safety related cockpit activities by flight crewmembers prohibited?

A—10,000 feet.
B—14,500 feet.
C—FL 180.

Answer (A) is correct (8297). *(FAR 121.542)*

No flight crewmember may perform any nonsafety-related cockpit duties during the critical phase of flight. The critical phases of flight include all ground operations involving taxi, takeoff and landing, and all other flight operations conducted below 10,000 ft., except in cruise flight.

Answer (B) is incorrect because flight crewmembers are prohibited from any nonsafety-related cockpit duties below 10,000 ft., not 14,500 ft., except in cruise flight. Answer (C) is incorrect because flight crewmembers are prohibited from any nonsafety-related cockpit duties below 10,000 ft., not FL 180, except in cruise flight.

121.547 Admission to Flight Deck

99.
8244. The pilot in command has emergency authority to exclude any and all persons from admittance to the flight deck

A—except a FAA inspector doing enroute checks.
B—in the interest of safety.
C—except persons who have authorization from the certificate holder and the FAA or NTSB.

Answer (B) is correct (8244). *(FAR 121.547)*
In the interest of safety, the pilot in command has emergency authority to exclude any and all persons, without exception, from admittance to the flight deck.
Answer (A) is incorrect because, while an FAA inspector may be admitted to the flight deck during normal operations, the pilot in command has emergency authority to exclude any person from the flight deck in the interest of safety. Answer (C) is incorrect because, while persons who have authorization from the certificate holder and the FAA or NTSB may be admitted to the flight deck during normal operations, the pilot in command has emergency authority to exclude any and all persons from admittance to the flight deck in the interest of safety.

121.549 Flying Equipment

100.
8235. Each crewmember shall have readily available for individual use on each flight a

A—key to the flight deck door.
B—certificate holder's manual.
C—flashlight in good working order.

Answer (C) is correct (8235). *(FAR 121.549)*
Each crewmember shall, on each flight, have readily available for his/her use a flashlight in good working order.
Answer (A) is incorrect because a key to the flight deck door is not required equipment for each crewmember. Answer (B) is incorrect because only appropriate parts of, not the entire, certificate holder's manual must be accessible to each crewmember.

101.
8242. Assuring that appropriate aeronautical charts are aboard an aircraft is the responsibility of the

A—aircraft dispatcher.
B—flight navigator.
C—pilot in command.

Answer (C) is correct (8242). *(FAR 121.549)*
The pilot in command shall ensure that appropriate aeronautical charts containing adequate information concerning navigation aids and instrument approach procedures are aboard the aircraft for each flight.
Answer (A) is incorrect because the dispatcher may be hundreds of miles from the origination of the flight, e.g., in a central dispatch office. Answer (B) is incorrect because, although a flight navigator may be assigned the task of carrying aeronautical charts, the pilot in command is responsible for ensuring that adequate charts are aboard the aircraft.

121.557 Emergencies: Domestic and Flag Operations

102.
8246. Who is required to submit a written report on a deviation that occurs during an emergency?

A—Pilot in command.
B—Dispatcher.
C—Person who declares the emergency.

Answer (C) is correct (8246). *(FAR 121.557)*
Whenever a pilot in command or a dispatcher exercises emergency authority, (s)he shall keep the appropriate ATC facility and dispatch centers fully informed of the progress of the flight. The person declaring the emergency shall send a written report of any deviation through the air carrier's operations manager to the administrator. A dispatcher shall send his/her report within 10 days after the date of the emergency, and a pilot in command shall send his/her report within 10 days after returning to his/her home base.
Answer (A) is incorrect because either the pilot in command or the dispatcher must submit a written report, depending upon who declared an emergency. Answer (B) is incorrect because either the pilot in command or the dispatcher must submit a written report, depending upon who declared an emergency.

103.
8240. When the pilot in command is responsible for a deviation during an emergency, the pilot should submit a written report within

A—10 days after the deviation.
B—10 days after returning home.
C—10 days after returning to home base.

Answer (C) is correct (8240). *(FAR 121.557)*
When the pilot in command declares an emergency and is responsible for a deviation during that emergency, the pilot should submit a report, through the air carrier's operations manager, to the FAA within 10 days after returning to his/her home base.

Answer (A) is incorrect because, when the dispatcher, not the pilot in command, declares an emergency and is responsible for a deviation, (s)he must submit a report, through the air carrier's operations manager, to the FAA within 10 days after the deviation. Answer (B) is incorrect because, when the pilot in command declares an emergency and is responsible for a deviation during that emergency, (s)he must submit a report, through the air carrier's operations manager, to the FAA within 10 days after returning to his/her home base, not his/her home.

104.
8239. An aircraft dispatcher declares an emergency for a flight and a deviation results. A written report shall be sent by the

A—dispatcher to the FAA Administrator within 10 days.
B—air carrier's operations manager to the FAA Administrator within 10 days.
C—pilot in command to the FAA Administrator within 10 days.

Answer (B) is correct (8239). *(FAR 121.557)*
When an aircraft dispatcher declares an emergency for a flight and a deviation results, the dispatcher must submit a written report, through the air carrier's operations manager to the FAA Administrator within 10 days.

Answer (A) is incorrect because an aircraft dispatcher must submit a written report through the air carrier's operations manager before it is routed to the FAA Administrator. Answer (C) is incorrect because an aircraft dispatcher must submit a written report through the air carrier's operations manager, not the pilot in command, to the FAA Administrator within 10 days.

105.
8245. If an aircraft dispatcher cannot communicate with the pilot of an air carrier flight during an emergency, the aircraft dispatcher should

A—take any action considered necessary under the circumstances.
B—comply with the company's lost aircraft plan.
C—phone the ARTCC where the flight is located and ask for a phone patch with the flight.

Answer (A) is correct (8245). *(FAR 121.557)*
If the aircraft dispatcher cannot communicate with the pilot in command of a flight in an emergency situation that requires immediate decision and action by the aircraft dispatcher, (s)he shall declare an emergency and take any action that (s)he considers necessary under the circumstances.

Answer (B) is incorrect because, if an aircraft dispatcher cannot communicate with the pilot of an air carrier flight during an emergency, the aircraft dispatcher should take any action considered necessary under the circumstances, which may or may not include following the company's lost aircraft plan. Answer (C) is incorrect because, if an aircraft dispatcher cannot communicate with the pilot of an air carrier flight during an emergency, (s)he should take any action that (s)he considers necessary under the circumstances. One action may be to contact the ARTCC where the flight is located to ask the pilot to contact the company.

121.565 Engine Inoperative: Landing; Reporting

106.
8236. If an engine's rotation is stopped in flight, the pilot in command must report it, as soon as practicable, to the

A—appropriate ground radio station.
B—nearest FAA district office.
C—operations manager (or director of operations).

Answer (A) is correct (8236). *(FAR 121.565)*
The pilot in command shall report each stoppage of engine rotation in flight to the appropriate ground radio station as soon as practicable and shall keep that station fully informed of the progress of the flight.

Answer (B) is incorrect because, if an engine's rotation is stopped in flight, the pilot in command must report it, as soon as practicable, to the appropriate ground radio station, not the nearest FAA district office. Answer (C) is incorrect because, if an engine's rotation is stopped in flight, the pilot in command must report it, as soon as practicable, to the nearest ground radio station, not the operations manager (or director of operations).

107.
8241. What action shall the pilot in command take if it becomes necessary to shut down one of the two engines on an air carrier airplane?

A—Land at the airport which the pilot considers to be as safe as the nearest suitable airport in point of time.
B—Land at the nearest suitable airport in point of time at which a safe landing can be made.
C—Land at the nearest airport, including military, that has a crash and rescue unit.

Answer (B) is correct (8241). *(FAR 121.565)*

Whenever one engine of a two-engine air carrier airplane fails or whenever the rotation of an engine is stopped to prevent possible damage, the pilot in command shall land the airplane at the nearest suitable airport, in point of time, at which a safe landing can be made.

Answer (A) is incorrect because, whenever one engine of an air carrier airplane that has three or more engines, not a two-engine airplane, fails or its rotation is stopped, the pilot in command may land at the airport which the pilot considers to be as safe as the nearest suitable airport in point of time. Answer (C) is incorrect because, if one engine of a two-engine air carrier is shut down, the pilot in command shall land the airplane at the nearest suitable airport, in point of time, at which a safe landing can be made. While there is no requirement that the airport have a crash and rescue unit, it would be a consideration. However, military airports are not normally included as suitable airports.

108.
8237. If it become necessary to shut down one engine on a domestic air carrier three-engine turbojet airplane, the pilot in command

A—must land at the nearest suitable airport, in point of time, at which a safe landing can be made.
B—may continue to the planned destination if approved by the company aircraft dispatcher.
C—may continue to the planned destination if this is considered as safe as landing at the nearest suitable airport.

Answer (C) is correct (8237). *(FAR 121.565)*

If not more than one engine of an airplane that has three or more engines fails or has its rotation stopped, the pilot in command may proceed to an airport that (s)he selects (e.g., the destination airport) if, after considering various factors, (s)he decides that proceeding to that airport is as safe as landing at the nearest suitable airport.

Answer (A) is incorrect because, if it becomes necessary to shut down one engine of a two-engine airplane, not a three-engine airplane, the pilot in command must land at the nearest suitable airport, in point of time, at which a safe landing can be made. Answer (B) is incorrect because, if it becomes necessary to shut down one engine on a three-engine air carrier airplane, the pilot in command may continue to the planned destination if the destination is considered as safe as landing at the nearest suitable airport. The decision of the pilot in command need not be approved by the aircraft dispatcher.

121.571 Briefing Passengers before Takeoff

109.
8225. Which passenger announcement(s) must be made after each takeoff?

A—Keep safety belts fastened while seated and no smoking in the aircraft lavatories.
B—Passengers should keep seat belts fastened while seated.
C—How to use the passenger oxygen system and that there is a $1,000 fine for tampering with a smoke detector.

Answer (B) is correct (8225). *(FAR 121.571)*

After each takeoff, immediately before or immediately after turning the seat belt sign off, an announcement shall be made that passengers should keep their seat belts fastened, while seated, even when the seat belt sign is off.

Answer (A) is incorrect because the announcement that smoking is prohibited in the aircraft lavatories must be made before, not after, takeoff. Answer (C) is incorrect because the announcement that Federal law prohibits tampering with any smoke detector in an airplane lavatory must be made before, not after, takeoff. An announcement on how to use the passenger oxygen system must be made before flight is conducted above FL 250.

121.575 Alcoholic Beverages

110.
8233. If an intoxicated person creates a disturbance aboard an air carrier aircraft, the certificate holder must submit a report, concerning the incident, to the Administrator within

A—7 days.
B—5 days.
C—48 hours.

Answer (B) is correct (8233). *(FAR 121.575)*

Each certificate holder shall, within 5 days after the incident, report to the FAA Administrator any disturbance caused by a person who appears to be intoxicated aboard any of its aircraft.

Answer (A) is incorrect because, if an intoxicated person creates a disturbance aboard an air carrier aircraft, the certificate holder must submit a report concerning the incident to the FAA Administrator within 5 days, not 7 days. Answer (C) is incorrect because, if an intoxicated person creates a disturbance aboard an air carrier aircraft, the certificate holder must submit a report concerning the incident to the FAA Administrator within 5 days, not 48 hr.

121.583 Carriage of Persons without Compliance with the Passenger-Carrying Requirements of This Part

111.
8234. When carrying a passenger aboard an all-cargo aircraft, which of the following applies?

A—The passenger must have access to a seat in the pilot compartment.
B—The pilot in command may authorize the passenger to be admitted to the crew compartment.
C—Crew-type oxygen must be provided for the passenger.

Answer (B) is correct (8234). *(FAR 121.583)*

The pilot in command may authorize a passenger to be admitted to the crew compartment of an all-cargo airplane.

Answer (A) is incorrect because the passenger on an all-cargo airplane must have an unobstructed access from his/her seat to the pilot compartment or to a regular emergency exit. The passenger is not required to have access to a seat in the pilot compartment. Answer (C) is incorrect because crew-type oxygen is not required for passengers. It is only required that the passenger be briefed on the use of oxygen and emergency oxygen equipment.

4.13 DISPATCHING AND FLIGHT RELEASE RULES

121.593 Dispatching Authority: Domestic Operations

112.
8232. A domestic air carrier flight has a delay while on the ground, at an intermediate airport. How long before a redispatch release is required?

A—Not more than 1 hour.
B—Not more than 2 hours.
C—More than 6 hours.

Answer (A) is correct (8232). *(FAR 121.593)*

Except when a domestic air carrier airplane lands at an intermediate airport specified in the original dispatch release and remains there for not more than 1 hr., no person may start a flight unless an aircraft dispatcher specifically authorizes that flight.

Answer (B) is incorrect because a domestic air carrier airplane may remain at an intermediate airport for not more than 1 hr., not 2 hr., before a redispatch release is required. Answer (C) is incorrect because a flag air carrier airplane, not a domestic air carrier airplane, may be delayed on the ground at an intermediate airport for not more than 6 hr. before a redispatch release is required.

113.
8260. A domestic air carrier airplane lands at an intermediate airport at 1815Z. The latest time it may depart without a specific authorization from an aircraft dispatcher is

A—1945Z.
B—1915Z.
C—1845Z.

Answer (B) is correct (8260). *(FAR 121.593)*

A domestic air carrier airplane may remain on the ground at an intermediate airport specified in the original dispatch release for not more than 1 hr. before a redispatch release is required. Thus, if the airplane lands at 1815Z, the latest time it may depart without a specific authorization from an aircraft dispatcher is 1915Z.

Answer (A) is incorrect because a domestic air carrier airplane may remain on the ground at an intermediate airport for not more than 1 hr., not 1 hr. and 30 min., before a redispatch release is required. Answer (C) is incorrect because a domestic air carrier airplane may remain on the ground at an intermediate airport for not more than 1 hr., not 30 min., before a redispatch release is required.

121.595 Dispatching Authority: Flag Operations

114.
8259. A flag air carrier flight lands at an intermediate airport at 1805Z. The latest time that it may depart without being redispatched is

A—2005Z.
B—1905Z.
C—0005Z.

Answer (C) is correct (8259). *(FAR 121.595)*
A flag air carrier airplane may continue a flight from an intermediate airport without redispatch if the airplane has been on the ground not more than 6 hr. Thus, if the flight lands at 1805Z, the latest time it may depart without being redispatched is 0005Z.
Answer (A) is incorrect because a flag carrier airplane may remain on the ground at an intermediate airport for not more than 6 hr., not 2 hr., before a redispatch is required. Answer (B) is incorrect because 1905Z is the latest time a domestic air carrier airplane, not a flag air carrier airplane, may depart an intermediate airport without being redispatched.

115.
8266. When a flag air carrier airplane lands at an intermediate airport at 1822Z, what is the latest time it may continue a flight without receiving a redispatch authorization?

A—1922Z.
B—1952Z.
C—0022Z.

Answer (C) is correct (8266). *(FAR 121.595)*
A flag air carrier airplane may continue a flight from an intermediate airport without redispatch if the airplane has been on the ground not more than 6 hr. Thus, if the flight lands at 1822Z, the latest time it may depart without being redispatched is 0022Z.
Answer (A) is incorrect because 1922Z is the latest time a domestic air carrier airplane, not a flag air carrier airplane, may depart an intermediate airport without being redispatched. Answer (B) is incorrect because a flag air carrier airplane may remain on the ground at an intermediate airport for not more than 6 hr., not 1 hr. and 30 min., without being redispatched.

116.
8267. If a flag air carrier flight lands at an intermediate airport at 1845Z, and experiences a delay, what is the latest time it may depart for the next airport without a redispatch release?

A—1945Z.
B—2015Z.
C—0045Z.

Answer (C) is correct (8267). *(FAR 121.595)*
A flag air carrier airplane may continue a flight from an intermediate airport without redispatch if the airplane has been on the ground not more than 6 hr. Thus, if the flight lands at 1845Z, the latest time it may depart without being redispatched is 0045Z.
Answer (A) is incorrect because 1945Z is the latest time a domestic air carrier airplane, not a flag air carrier airplane, may depart an intermediate airport without being redispatched. Answer (B) is incorrect because a flag air carrier airplane may remain on the ground at an intermediate airport for not more than 6 hr., not 1 hr. and 30 min., without being redispatched.

121.601 Aircraft Dispatcher Information to Pilot in Command: Domestic and Flag Operations

117.
8283. Where can the pilot of a flag air carrier airplane find the latest FDC NOTAM's?

A—Any company dispatch facility.
B—Notices To Airmen publication.
C—Airport/Facility Directory.

Answer (A) is correct (8283). *(FAR 121.601)*
Any company dispatch facility of a flag air carrier shall provide the pilot information that may affect the safety of the flight, including FDC NOTAMs.
Answer (B) is incorrect because the *Notices to Airmen Publication* will contain only those FDC NOTAMs that are generally at least 2 weeks old, while the company dispatch facility will have the latest FDC NOTAMs. Answer (C) is incorrect because the *Airport/Facility Directory* does not contain any FDC NOTAM information.

118.
8280. By regulation, who shall provide the pilot in command of a domestic or flag air carrier airplane information concerning weather, and irregularities of facilities and services?

A—The aircraft dispatcher.
B—Air route traffic control center.
C—Director of operations.

Answer (A) is correct (8280). *(FAR 121.601)*
The aircraft dispatcher shall provide the pilot in command of a domestic or flag air carrier airplane all available current reports or information on airport conditions and irregularities of navigation facilities that may affect the safety of the flight.
Answer (B) is incorrect because, while an air route traffic control center may have information concerning irregularities of facilities and service, it is not the proper source of that information. That information must be provided by the aircraft dispatcher. Answer (C) is incorrect because the director of operations is an administrative person responsible for the day-to-day operations and is not involved in providing weather and other information to the pilot in command. Providing that information is the responsibility of the aircraft dispatcher.

119.
8284. Who is responsible, by regulation, for briefing a domestic or flag air carrier pilot in command on all available weather information?

A—Company meteorologist.
B—Aircraft dispatcher.
C—Director of operations.

Answer (B) is correct (8284). *(FAR 121.601)*
The aircraft dispatcher shall provide the pilot in command of a domestic or flag air carrier airplane with all available weather reports and forecasts of weather phenomena that may affect the safety of flight, including adverse weather phenomena, such as clear air turbulence, thunderstorms, and low-altitude wind shear, for each route to be flown and each airport to be used.
Answer (A) is incorrect because the weather briefing for a domestic or flag carrier is the responsibility of the aircraft dispatcher, not a company meteorologist. Answer (C) is incorrect because the director of operations is an administrative person responsible for the day-to-day operations. The aircraft dispatcher, not the director of operations, is responsible for providing the pilot in command with all available weather information.

121.603 Facilities and Services: Supplemental Operations

120.
8281. Who is responsible for obtaining information on all current airport conditions, weather, and irregularities of navigation facilities for a supplemental air carrier flight?

A—Aircraft dispatcher.
B—Director of operations or flight follower.
C—Pilot in command.

Answer (C) is correct (8281). *(FAR 121.603)*
Before beginning a flight, each pilot in command of a supplemental air carrier airplane shall obtain all available current weather reports or information on airport conditions and irregularities of navigation facilities that may affect the safety of the flight.
Answer (A) is incorrect because an aircraft dispatcher shall provide the pilot in command of a flag or domestic air carrier, not a supplemental air carrier, information on all current airport conditions, weather, and irregularities of navigation facilities that may affect the safety of the flight. Answer (B) is incorrect because the pilot in command, not the director of operations or flight follower, of a supplemental air carrier is responsible for obtaining information on all current airport conditions, weather, and irregularities of navigation facilities that may affect the safety of the flight.

121.
8282. During a supplemental air carrier flight, who is responsible for obtaining information on meteorological conditions?

A—Aircraft dispatcher.
B—Pilot in command.
C—Director of operations or flight follower.

Answer (B) is correct (8282). *(FAR 121.603)*
During a flight, the pilot in command of a supplemental air carrier flight shall obtain any additional information on meteorological conditions and irregularities of facilities and services that may affect the safety of the flight.
Answer (A) is incorrect because, during a flight, the aircraft dispatcher shall provide the pilot in command of a flag or domestic air carrier, not a supplemental air carrier, any additional information on meteorological conditions. Answer (C) is incorrect because the pilot in command, not the director of operations or flight follower, of a supplemental air carrier is responsible for obtaining information on meteorological conditions.

121.617 Alternate Airport for Departure

122.
8248. An alternate airport for departure is required

A—if weather conditions are below authorized landing minimums at the departure airport.
B—when the weather forecast at the ETD is for landing minimums only at the departure airport.
C—when destination weather is marginal VFR (ceiling less than 3,000 feet and visibility less than 5 SM).

Answer (A) is correct (8248). *(FAR 121.617)*
If the weather conditions at the departure airport are below the landing minimums in the certificate holder's operations specifications for that airport, no person may dispatch or release an aircraft from that airport unless the dispatch or flight release specifies an alternate airport.
Answer (B) is incorrect because an alternate airport for departure is required when the weather conditions, not forecast, are below, not equal to, the authorized landing minimums at the departure airport. Answer (C) is incorrect because an alternate airport for departure is required if weather conditions at the departure airport are below authorized landing minimums at the departure airport. Weather conditions at the destination have no effect on whether a departure alternate airport is required.

123.
8249. What is the maximum distance that a departure alternate airport may be from the departure airport for a two-engine airplane?

A—1 hour at normal cruise speed in still air with both engines operating.
B—1 hour at normal cruise speed in still air with one engine operating.
C—2 hours at normal cruise speed in still air with one engine operating.

Answer (B) is correct (8249). *(FAR 121.617)*
The maximum distance that a departure alternate airport may be from the departure airport for a two-engine airplane is 1 hr. at normal cruising speed in still air with one engine operating.
Answer (A) is incorrect because the maximum distance that a departure alternate airport may be from the departure airport for a two-engine airplane is 1 hr. at normal cruising speed with one engine, not both engines, operating. Answer (C) is incorrect because the maximum distance that a departure alternate airport may be from the departure airport for an airplane having three or more engines, not a two-engine airplane, is 2 hr. at normal cruising speed in still air with one engine inoperative.

124.
8252. When a departure alternate is required for a three-engine air carrier flight, it must be located at a distance not greater than

A—2 hours from the departure airport at normal cruising speed in still air with one engine not functioning.
B—1 hour from the departure airport at normal cruising speed in still air with one engine inoperative.
C—2 hours from the departure airport at normal cruising speed in still air.

Answer (A) is correct (8252). *(FAR 121.617)*
When a departure alternate airport is required for a three-engine air carrier flight, it must be located at a distance not greater than 2 hr. from the departure airport at normal cruising speed in still air with one engine inoperative.
Answer (B) is incorrect because, when a departure alternate airport is required for a two-engine, not a three-engine, air carrier flight, it must be located at a distance no greater than 1 hr. from the departure airport at normal cruising speed in still air with one engine inoperative. Answer (C) is incorrect because, when a departure alternate airport is required for a three-engine air carrier flight, it must be located at a distance not greater than 2 hr. from the departure airport at normal cruising speed in still air with one engine inoperative, not all engines operating.

125.
8250. If a four-engine air carrier airplane is dispatched from an airport that is below landing minimums, what is the maximum distance that a departure alternate airport may be located from the departure airport?

A—Not more than 2 hours at cruise speed with one engine inoperative.
B—Not more than 2 hours at normal cruise speed in still air with one engine inoperative.
C—Not more than 1 hour at normal cruise speed in still air with one engine inoperative.

Answer (B) is correct (8250). *(FAR 121.617)*
If a four-engine air carrier airplane is dispatched from an airport that is below authorized landing minimums, the maximum distance that a departure alternate airport may be located from the departure airport is not more than 2 hr. at normal cruising speed in still air with one engine inoperative.
Answer (A) is incorrect because the maximum distance that a departure alternate airport may be located from the departure airport for a four-engine air carrier airplane is not more than 2 hr. at normal cruising speed, not any cruise speed, in still air with one engine inoperative. Answer (C) is incorrect because the maximum distance that a departure alternate airport may be located from the departure airport for a two-engine, not a four-engine, air carrier airplane is not more than 1 hr. at normal cruising speed in still air with one engine inoperative.

121.619 Alternate Airport for Destination: IFR or Over-the-Top: Domestic Operations

126.
8247. When the forecast weather conditions for a destination and alternate airport are considered marginal for a domestic air carrier's operation, what specific action should the dispatcher or pilot in command take?

A—List an airport where the forecast weather is not marginal as the alternate.
B—Add 1 additional hour of fuel based on cruise power settings for the airplane in use.
C—List at least one additional alternate airport.

Answer (C) is correct (8247). *(FAR 121.619)*
No person may dispatch a domestic air carrier airplane under IFR or over-the-top unless (s)he lists at least one alternate airport for each destination airport in the dispatch release. When the weather conditions forecast for the destination and first alternate are marginal, at least one additional alternate airport must be designated.

Answer (A) is incorrect because the destination and first alternate can remain on the dispatch release when the weather forecast is marginal for a domestic air carrier's operation. If the weather is marginal, then at least one additional alternate airport should be designated on the dispatch release. Answer (B) is incorrect because, when the weather conditions forecast for a destination and alternate airport are considered marginal for a domestic air carrier's operation, at least one additional alternate airport should be listed on the dispatch release. Additional fuel is not required by the forecast marginal weather conditions.

121.621 Alternate Airport for Destination: Flag Operations

127.
8256. Which dispatch requirement applies to a flag air carrier that is scheduled for a 7-hour IFR flight?

A—No alternate airport is required if the forecast weather at the ETA at the destination airport is at least 1,500 feet and 3 miles.
B—An alternate airport is not required if the ceiling will be at least 1,500 feet above the lowest circling MDA.
C—An alternate airport is required.

Answer (C) is correct (8256). *(FAR 121.621)*
No person may dispatch a flag air carrier airplane under IFR or over-the-top without listing at least one alternate airport for each destination airport in the dispatch release, unless the flight is scheduled for not more than 6 hr. and certain conditions are met.

Answer (A) is incorrect because, whenever a flag air carrier flight is scheduled for an IFR flight of more than 6 hr., an alternate airport is required, regardless of the forecast weather conditions at the destination airport. Answer (B) is incorrect because, whenever a flag air carrier flight is scheduled for an IFR flight of more than 6 hr., an alternate airport is required, regardless of the forecast weather conditions at the destination airport.

128.
8262. An alternate airport is not required to dispatch a flag air carrier airplane for a flight of less than 6 hours when the visibility for at least 1 hour before and 1 hour after the ETA at the destination airport is forecast to be

A—2 miles or greater.
B—at least 3 miles, or 2 miles more than the lowest applicable minimum.
C—3 miles.

Answer (B) is correct (8262). *(FAR 121.621)*
An alternate airport is not required to dispatch a flag air carrier airplane for a flight of less than 6 hr. when the visibility for at least 1 hr. before and 1 hr. after the ETA at the destination airport, the appropriate weather reports or forecasts, or any combination of them, indicate the visibility at that airport will be at least 3 SM, or 2 SM more than the lowest applicable visibility minimums, whichever is greater, for the instrument approach procedures to be used at the destination airport.

Answer (A) is incorrect because, for an alternate not to be listed for a flag air carrier flight of less than 6 hr., the visibility for at least 1 hr. before and 1 hr. after the ETA at the destination airport must be forecast to be at least 3 SM, or 2 SM more than the lowest applicable visibility minimums, whichever is greater, not just 2 SM or greater. Answer (C) is incorrect because, for an alternate not to be listed for a flag air carrier flight of less than 6 hr., the visibility for at least 1 hr. before and 1 hr. after the ETA at the destination airport must be forecast to be at least 3 SM, or 2 SM more than the lowest applicable visibility minimums, whichever is greater, not just 3 SM.

121.623 Alternate Airport for Destination: IFR or Over-the-Top: Supplemental Operations

129.
8251. When is a supplemental air carrier, operating under IFR, required to list an alternate airport for each destination airport within the 48 contiguous United States?

A—When the forecast weather indicates the ceiling will be less than 1,000 feet and visibility less than 2 miles at the estimated time of arrival.
B—On all flights, an alternate is required regardless of existing or forecast weather conditions at the destination.
C—When the flight is scheduled for more than 6 hours en route.

Answer (B) is correct (8251). *(FAR 121.623)*

Each person releasing an aircraft of a supplemental air carrier in the 48 contiguous United States for operation under IFR or over-the-top shall list at least one alternate airport for each destination airport in the flight release.

Answer (A) is incorrect because, for a supplemental air carrier, an alternate is required regardless of weather when operating under IFR in the 48 contiguous United States. Answer (C) is incorrect because an alternate is required for each destination for a flag air carrier, not a supplemental air carrier, for a scheduled flight of more than 6 hr.

121.625 Alternate Airport Weather Minimums

130.
8254. Prior to listing an airport as an alternate airport in the dispatch or flight release, weather reports and forecasts must indicate that weather conditions will be at or above authorized minimums at that airport

A—for a period 1 hour before or after the ETA.
B—during the entire flight.
C—when the flight arrives.

Answer (C) is correct (8254). *(FAR 121.625)*

No person may list an airport as an alternate in the dispatch or flight release unless the appropriate weather reports or forecasts, or any combination thereof, indicate that the conditions will be at or above the alternate weather minimums specified in the certificate holder's operations specifications for that airport when the flight arrives.

Answer (A) is incorrect because, prior to listing an airport as an alternate in the dispatch or flight release, weather reports and forecasts must indicate that weather conditions will be at or above authorized minimums when the flight arrives, not for a period of 1 hr. before or after the ETA. Answer (B) is incorrect because, prior to listing an airport as an alternate in the dispatch or flight release, weather reports and forecasts must indicate that weather conditions will be at or above authorized minimums when the flight arrives, not for the entire flight.

131.
8255. The minimum weather conditions that must exist for an airport to be listed as an alternate in the dispatch release for a domestic air carrier flight are

A—those listed in the NOAA IAP charts for the alternate airport, at the time the flight is expected to arrive.
B—those specified in the certificate holder's Operations Specifications for that airport, when the flight arrives.
C—those listed on the NOAA IAP charts for the alternate airport, from 1 hour before or after the ETA for that flight.

Answer (B) is correct (8255). *(FAR 121.625)*

No person may list an airport as an alternate airport in the dispatch or flight release for domestic air carriers unless the appropriate weather reports or forecasts, or any combination thereof, indicate that the weather conditions will be at or above the alternate weather minimums specified in the certificate holder's operations specifications for that airport when the flight arrives.

Answer (A) is incorrect because, although the alternate minimums in the NOAA IAP chart may coincide with the air carrier's operations specifications, the operations specifications determine alternate weather minimums. Answer (C) is incorrect because, although the alternate minimums in the NOAA IAP chart may coincide with the air carrier's operations specifications, the operations specifications determine alternate weather minimums at the time the flight arrives, not 1 hr. before or after the ETA.

121.627 Continuing Flight in Unsafe Conditions

132.
8278. If a required instrument on a multiengine airplane becomes inoperative, which document dictates whether the flight may continue en route?

A—An approved Minimum Equipment List for the airplane.
B—Original dispatch release.
C—Certificate holder's manual.

Answer (C) is correct (8278). *(FAR 121.627)*

If any instrument or item of equipment required by FAR Part 121 (for the particular operation) becomes inoperative en route, the pilot in command must comply with the approved procedures as specified in the certificate holder's manual.

Answer (A) is incorrect because an approved MEL may authorize a takeoff with inoperative instruments or equipment. It does not authorize a flight to continue after the failure of a required instrument en route. Answer (B) is incorrect because a dispatch release contains flight-related information, not the procedures to follow if a required instrument becomes inoperative while en route.

121.629 Operation in Icing Conditions

133.
8258. The pilot in command of an airplane en route determines that icing conditions can be expected that might adversely affect safety of the flight. Which action is appropriate?

A—The pilot in command may continue to the original destination airport, after climbing to a higher altitude.
B—The pilot in command shall not continue flight into the icing conditions.
C—The flight may continue to the original destination airport, provided all anti-icing and deicing equipment is operational and is used.

Answer (B) is correct (8258). *(FAR 121.629)*
No person may dispatch or release an aircraft, continue to operate an aircraft en route, or land an aircraft when, in the opinion of the pilot in command or aircraft dispatcher (domestic and flag air carriers only), icing conditions are expected or met that might adversely affect the safety of the flight.
Answer (A) is incorrect because, if the pilot in command determines that icing conditions can be expected that may compromise the safety of the flight, the pilot in command shall not continue flight into the expected icing conditions regardless of altitude. Answer (C) is incorrect because, if it is determined that icing can be expected that may compromise the safety of the flight, the pilot in command may not continue regardless of the availability or use of anti-icing or deicing equipment.

134.
8265. What action is required prior to takeoff if snow is adhering to the wings of an air carrier airplane?

A—Sweep off as much snow as possible and the residue must be polished smooth.
B—Assure that the snow is removed from the airplane.
C—Add 15 knots to the normal V_R speed as the snow will blow off.

Answer (B) is correct (8265). *(FAR 121.629)*
No person may take off an air carrier airplane unless it has been checked to ensure that the snow has been removed from the wings.
Answer (A) is incorrect because the snow must be removed from the wings of the airplane and any residue cannot be polished smooth. Answer (C) is incorrect because there is no authorized adjustment to V_R to compensate for snow on the wings. The snow must be removed prior to takeoff.

121.637 Takeoffs from Unlisted and Alternate Airports: Domestic and Flag Operations

135.
8261. The weather conditions that meet the minimum requirements for a flag air carrier to take off from an alternate airport that is not listed in the Operations Specifications are

A—800–2, 900–1-1/2, 1000–1.
B—800–1/2, 900–1, 1000–2.
C—800–1, 900–2, 1000–3.

Answer (A) is correct (8261). *(FAR 121.637)*
No pilot may take off a flag air carrier airplane from a non-U.S. airport that is not listed in the operations specifications unless the weather minimums for takeoff prescribed or approved by the government of the country in which the airport is located exist, or if minimums are not prescribed or approved for the airport, the weather minimums of 800–2, 900–1½, or 1,000–1 are met.
Answer (B) is incorrect because the visibility requirements for 800-, 900-, and 1,000-ft. ceilings are visibilities of 2, 1.5, and 1 mile(s), respectively. Answer (C) is incorrect because the visibility requirements for 800-, 900-, and 1,000-ft. ceilings are visibilities of 2, 1.5, and 1 mile(s), respectively.

136.
8257. An airport is not listed in a domestic Air Carrier's Operations Specifications and does not have the prescribed takeoff weather minimums. What are the minimum weather conditions required for takeoff?

A—800–2.
B—900–1.
C—1000–1/2.

Answer (A) is correct (8257). *(FAR 121.637)*
No pilot may take off a domestic air carrier airplane from any U.S. airport that is not listed in the operations specifications unless the prescribed weather minimums for takeoff exist, or if minimums are not prescribed for the airport, the weather minimums of 800–2, 900–1½, or 1,000–1 are met.
Answer (B) is incorrect because a 900-ft. ceiling requires a minimum visibility of 1½ SM, not 1 SM. Answer (C) is incorrect because a 1,000-ft. ceiling requires a minimum visibility of 1 SM, not ½ SM.

137.
8263. The minimum weather conditions that must exist for a domestic air carrier flight to take off from an airport that is not listed in the Air Carrier's Operations Specifications (takeoff minimums are not prescribed for that airport) is

A—800-2, 1,100-1, or 900-1-1/2.
B—1,000-1, 900-1-1/4, or 800-2.
C—1,000-1, 900-1-1/2, or 800-2.

Answer (C) is correct (8263). *(FAR 121.637)*
No pilot may take off a domestic air carrier airplane from a U.S. airport that is not listed in the operations specifications unless the prescribed weather minimums for takeoff exist, or if minimums are not prescribed for the airport, the weather minimums of 800–2, 900–1½, or 1,000–1 are met.
Answer (A) is incorrect because a visibility of 1 SM requires a ceiling of 1,000 ft., not 1,100 ft. Answer (B) is incorrect because a 900-ft. ceiling requires a minimum visibility of 1½ SM, not 1¼ SM.

138.
8264. When an alternate airport outside the United States has no prescribed takeoff minimums and is not listed in a Flag Air Carrier's Operations Specifications, the minimum weather conditions that will meet the requirements for takeoff is

A—800-1-1/2.
B—600-2.
C—900-1-1/2.

Answer (C) is correct (8264). *(FAR 121.637)*
No pilot may take off a flag air carrier airplane from a non-U.S. airport that is not listed in the operations specifications unless the weather minimums for takeoff prescribed or approved by the government of the country in which the airport is located exist, or if minimums are not prescribed or approved for the airport, the weather minimums of 800–2, 900–1½, or 1,000–1 are met.
Answer (A) is incorrect because an 800-ft. ceiling requires a minimum visibility of 2 SM, not 1½ SM. Answer (B) is incorrect because a visibility of 2 SM requires a ceiling of 800 ft., not 600 ft.

121.639 Fuel Supply: All Operations: Domestic Operations

139.
8268. The reserve fuel supply for a domestic air carrier flight is

A—30 minutes plus 15 percent at normal fuel consumption in addition to the fuel required to the alternate airport.
B—45 minutes at normal fuel consumption in addition to the fuel required to fly to and land at the most distant alternate airport.
C—45 minutes at normal fuel consumption in addition to the fuel required to the alternate airport.

Answer (B) is correct (8268). *(FAR 121.639)*
No person may dispatch or take off an airplane unless it has enough fuel to fly to the airport to which it is dispatched, then fly to and land at the most distant alternate airport, and then fly for 45 min. at normal cruising fuel consumption.
Answer (A) is incorrect because the reserve fuel supply for a domestic air carrier flight is 45 min., not 30 min. plus 15%, at normal fuel consumption in addition to the fuel required to fly to and land at, not just fly to, the most distant alternate airport. Answer (C) is incorrect because the reserve fuel supply must include the fuel required to land at the most distant alternate airport, not any alternate airport, in addition to the fuel to fly to that airport.

121.641 Fuel Supply: Nonturbine and Turbo-Propeller-Powered Airplanes: Flag Operations

140.
8274. Upon arriving at the most distant airport, what is the fuel reserve requirement for a turbopropeller flag air carrier airplane?

A—90 minutes at holding altitude and speed fuel consumption or 30 minutes plus 15 percent of cruise fuel consumption, whichever is less.
B—45 minutes at holding altitude.
C—30 minutes plus 15 percent of the total time required, or 90 minutes at normal cruise, whichever is less.

Answer (C) is correct (8274). *(FAR 121.641)*
No person may dispatch or take off a turbopropeller-powered airplane unless, considering the wind and other weather conditions expected, it has enough fuel to (1) fly to and land at the airport to which it is dispatched; (2) fly to and land at the most distant alternate airport specified in the dispatch release; and (3) thereafter fly for 30 min. plus 15% of the total time required to fly at normal cruising fuel consumption to the airports specified above or for 90 min. at normal cruising fuel consumption, whichever is less.
Answer (A) is incorrect because the 90 min. is at normal fuel consumption, not at holding altitude and speed fuel consumption. Additionally, the 15% is of the total time to fly to the alternate and then to the destination, not 15% of the cruise fuel consumption. Answer (B) is incorrect because 45 min. at normal cruise, not holding altitude, is the fuel reserve requirement for a domestic air carrier, not a flag air carrier.

121.643 Fuel Supply: Nonturbine and Turbo-Propeller-Powered Airplanes: Supplemental Operations

141.
8270. What is the fuel reserve requirement for a commercially operated reciprocating-engine-powered airplane flying within the 48 contiguous United States upon arrival at the most distant alternate airport specified in the flight release? Enough fuel to fly

A—30 minutes plus 15 percent of total time required to fly at normal cruising consumption to the alternate.
B—to fly for 90 minutes at normal cruising fuel consumption.
C—45 minutes at normal cruising fuel consumption.

Answer (C) is correct (8270). *(FAR 121.643)*

Upon arrival at the most distant alternate airport specified in the flight release, a supplemental air carrier operating a reciprocating-engine-powered airplane flying within the 48 contiguous U.S. must have enough fuel to fly for 45 min. at normal cruising fuel consumption.

NOTE: The FAA may change "commercially operated" to "supplemental air carrier" in the future.

Answer (A) is incorrect because 30 min. plus 15% of the total time required to fly to the alternate, or 90 min. at normal cruising fuel consumption, whichever is less, is the fuel reserve requirement upon arrival at the most distant alternate airport if one airport of the flight is outside of, not within, the 48 contiguous U.S. Answer (B) is incorrect because 30 min. plus 15% of the total time required to fly to the alternate, or 90 min. at normal cruising fuel consumption, whichever is less, is the fuel reserve requirement upon arrival at the most distant alternate airport if one airport of the flight is outside of, not within, the 48 contiguous U.S.

142.
8277. The fuel reserve required for a reciprocating-engine-powered supplemental air carrier airplane upon arrival at the most distant alternate airport during a flight in the 48 contiguous United States is

A—45 minutes at normal cruising fuel consumption.
B—the fuel required to fly to the alternate, plus 10 percent.
C—3 hours at normal cruising fuel consumption.

Answer (A) is correct (8277). *(FAR 121.643)*

Upon arrival at the most distant alternate airport during a flight within the 48 contiguous U.S., a reciprocating-engine-powered supplemental air carrier airplane must have enough fuel to fly for 45 min. at normal cruising fuel consumption.

Answer (B) is incorrect because, upon arrival at the most distant alternate, the airplane must have enough fuel to fly for 45 min. at normal cruising fuel consumption, not the fuel required to fly to the alternate plus 10%. Answer (C) is incorrect because a fuel supply of 3 hr. at normal cruising fuel consumption is required after the airplane arrives at a destination airport outside of, not within, the 48 contiguous U.S. where an alternate airport is not required.

143.
8275. The fuel reserve required, for a turbopropeller supplemental air carrier airplane upon the arrival at a destination airport for which an alternate airport is not specified, is

A—3 hours at normal consumption, no wind condition.
B—3 hours at normal cruising fuel consumption.
C—2 hours at normal cruising fuel consumption.

Answer (B) is correct (8275). *(FAR 121.643)*

No person may release a turbopropeller-powered airplane of a supplemental air carrier to an airport for which an alternate is not specified unless it has enough fuel, considering wind and other weather conditions expected, to fly to that airport and thereafter to fly for 3 hr. at normal cruising fuel consumption.

Answer (A) is incorrect because the fuel reserve must consider wind and other weather conditions. The fuel consumption cannot be based on still air. Answer (C) is incorrect because 2 hr. of fuel at normal cruise beyond the destination is the fuel requirement for turbojet, not turbopropeller, airplanes flying to an airport where an alternate is not required.

121.645 Fuel Supply: Turbine-Engine-Powered Airplanes, Other than Turbo Propeller: Flag and Supplemental Operations

144.
8269. The minimum amount (planned) of fuel to be aboard a flag air carrier turbojet airplane on a flight within the 48 contiguous United States, after reaching the most distant alternate airport, should be

A—45 minutes at normal cruising fuel consumption.
B—2 hours at normal cruising fuel consumption.
C—enough fuel to return to the destination airport or to fly for 90 minutes at normal cruising fuel consumption, whichever is less.

Answer (A) is correct (8269). *(FAR 121.645)*
A flag air carrier turbojet airplane operating within the 48 contiguous U.S. may use the fuel requirements for domestic air carriers, which states that no person may dispatch or take off an airplane unless it has enough fuel to fly to the airport to which it is dispatched, fly to and land at the most distant alternate airport (where required) for the airport to which dispatched, and thereafter fly for 45 min. at normal cruising fuel consumption.
Answer (B) is incorrect because 2 hr. normal cruising fuel is required at the destination airport when an alternate is not specified and the flight is conducted outside of, not within, the 48 contiguous United States. Answer (C) is incorrect because there is no provision for return to the destination airport in calculating fuel requirements.

145.
8271. For a flag air carrier flight to be released to an island airport for which an alternate airport is not available, a turbojet-powered airplane must have enough fuel to fly to that airport and thereafter to fly

A—at least 2 hours at normal cruising fuel consumption.
B—for 3 hours at normal cruising fuel consumption.
C—back to the departure airport.

Answer (A) is correct (8271). *(FAR 121.645)*
No person may release a flag air carrier turbojet-powered airplane to an airport for which an alternate is not available unless it has enough fuel, considering wind and other weather conditions expected, to fly to that airport and thereafter to fly for at least 2 hr. at normal cruising fuel consumption.
Answer (B) is incorrect because flag air carrier nonturbine and turbopropeller-powered airplanes, not turbojet airplanes, must have enough fuel to fly to an airport for which an alternate is not available and thereafter to fly for 3 hr. at normal cruising fuel consumption. Answer (C) is incorrect because there is no requirement for returning to the departure airport in computing fuel supply requirements.

146.
8272. An alternate airport is not required for a supplemental or commercial air carrier, turbojet-powered airplane on an IFR flight outside the 48 contiguous United States, if enough fuel

A—is aboard to fly to the destination at normal cruise speed and thereafter at least 2 hours at normal holding speed.
B—is aboard the airplane to fly to the destination and then to fly for at least 2 more hours at normal cruising fuel consumption.
C—to fly over the destination for 30 minutes at holding airspeed at 1,500 feet AGL is carried aboard the airplane.

Answer (B) is correct (8272). *(FAR 121.645)*
No person may release a supplemental or commercial air carrier turbojet-powered airplane to an airport for which an alternate is not specified unless it has enough fuel, considering wind and other weather conditions expected, to fly to that airport and thereafter to fly for at least 2 hr. at normal cruising fuel consumption.
Answer (A) is incorrect because, once the airplane arrives at the destination, it needs enough fuel for at least 2 hr. at normal cruising, not holding, fuel consumption. Answer (C) is incorrect because 30 min. at holding airspeed at 1,500 ft. AGL is a part of the fuel requirements for turbine-powered airplanes outside the U.S. if an alternate is required.

147.
8273. The fuel reserve required for a turbine-engine-powered (other than turbopropeller) supplemental air carrier airplane upon arrival over the most distant alternate airport outside the 48 contiguous United States is

A—30 minutes at holding speed, at 1,500 feet over the airport.
B—30 minutes, over the airport, at 1,500 feet, at cruising speed.
C—2 hours at the normal cruise fuel consumption rate.

Answer (A) is correct (8273). *(FAR 121.645)*
The fuel reserve required for a supplemental air carrier turbojet airplane upon arrival over the most distant alternate airport outside the 48 contiguous United States is enough fuel to fly for 30 min. at holding speed at 1,500 ft. above the alternate airport under standard temperature conditions.
Answer (B) is incorrect because, upon arrival at the most distant alternate airport, the fuel requirement is based on holding, not cruising, speed. Answer (C) is incorrect because fuel for 2 hr. at normal cruise is the requirement after arriving at an international destination airport where no alternate was specified.

148.
8276. A turbine-engine-powered flag air carrier airplane is released to an airport which has no available alternate. What is the required fuel reserve?

A—2 hours at normal cruise speed in a no wind condition fuel consumption.

B—2 hours at normal cruise fuel consumption.

C—30 minutes, plus 10 percent of the total flight time.

Answer (B) is correct (8276). *(FAR 121.645)*

No person may release a turbine-engine-powered airplane (other than a turbopropeller airplane) to an airport for which an alternate is not specified unless it has enough fuel, considering wind and other weather conditions expected, to fly to that airport and thereafter to fly for at least 2 hr. at normal cruising fuel consumption.

Answer (A) is incorrect because the required fuel reserve upon arrival at an airport which has no available alternate is 2 hr. at normal cruising fuel consumption, not normal cruising speed. Additionally, in computing the fuel requirements, wind must be considered. Answer (C) is incorrect because, when referring to flag air carrier operations outside the 48 contiguous states where an alternate is specified, the flight must have sufficient fuel to fly to the destination airport plus 10% of the total time from departure to destination airport, then to the most distant alternate with an additional 30 min. fuel at holding speed at 1,500 ft. AGL at the alternate.

121.651 Takeoff and Landing Weather Minimums: IFR: All Certificate Holders

149.
8279. Under what conditions may an air carrier pilot continue an instrument approach to the DH, after receiving a weather report indicating that less than minimum published landing conditions exist at the airport?

A—If the instrument approach is conducted in a radar environment.

B—When the weather report is received as the pilot passes the FAF.

C—When the weather report is received after the pilot has begun the final approach segment of the instrument approach.

Answer (C) is correct (8279). *(FAR 121.651)*

If a pilot has begun the final approach segment of a precision instrument approach procedure and after that receives a later weather report indicating below-minimum conditions, the pilot may continue the approach to the DH.

Answer (A) is incorrect because, in order to continue the approach, the pilot must have begun the final approach segment. Whether or not the approach is in a radar environment is not a factor. Answer (B) is incorrect because the question refers to an IAP with a DH, which implies a precision approach. While a precision approach does not have a FAF, the final approach segment begins with the intercept of the electronic glide slope.

121.652 Landing Weather Minimums: IFR: All Certificate Holders

150.
8285. Category II ILS operations below 1600 RVR and a 150-foot DH may be approved after the pilot in command has

A—logged 90 hours' flight time, 10 takeoffs and landings in make and model airplane and three Category II ILS approaches in actual or simulated IFR conditions with 150-foot DH since the beginning of the sixth preceding month, in operations under 14 CFR Parts 91 and 121.

B—made at least six Category II approaches in actual IFR conditions with 100-foot DH within the preceding 12 calendar months.

C—logged 100 hours' flight time in make and model airplane under 14 CFR Part 121 and three Category II ILS approaches in actual or simulated IFR conditions with 150-foot DH since the beginning of the sixth preceding month.

Answer (C) is correct (8285). *(FAR 121.652)*

A Category II pilot authorization is issued as a part of the applicant's instrument rating or airline transport pilot certificate. Upon original issue, the authorization contains a limitation for Category II operations of 1,600 ft. RVR and a 150-ft. decision height. This limitation is removed when the holder shows that since the beginning of the sixth preceding month (s)he has made three Category II ILS approaches to a landing under actual or simulated instrument conditions with a 150-ft. decision height. However, Category II minimums do not apply to air carrier operations until the pilot in command has served 100 hr. as pilot in command under FAR Part 121 in the type of airplane he is operating.

Answer (A) is incorrect because the pilot-in-command experience in the make and model of airplane and the Category II currency must have all been conducted in operations under FAR Part 121 only. Answer (B) is incorrect because the requirement is at least three, not six, Category II approaches in actual (or simulated) conditions to a 150-ft., not a 100-ft., DH within the preceding 6 months.

151.
8289. When a pilot's flight time consists of 80 hours' pilot in command in a particular type airplane, how does this affect the minimums for the destination airport?

A—Has no effect on destination but alternate minimums are no less than 300 and 1.
B—Minimums are decreased by 100 feet and 1/2 mile.
C—Minimums are increased by 100 feet and 1/2 mile.

Answer (C) is correct (8289). *(FAR 121.652)*
If the pilot in command of an airplane has not served 100 hr. as pilot in command in operations under FAR Part 121 in the type of airplane, the minimums for the destination airport are increased by 100 ft. and ½ SM (or an RVR of 2,400).
Answer (A) is incorrect because, when the pilot has 80 hr. of pilot-in-command experience in a particular type airplane, the destination airport minimums are increased by 100 ft. and ½ SM; they do not remain the same. Answer (B) is incorrect because, when the pilot has 80 hr. of pilot-in-command experience in a particular type airplane, the destination airport minimums are increased, not decreased, by 100 ft. and ½ SM.

121.657 Flight Altitude Rules

152.
8253. Which in-flight conditions are required by a supplemental air carrier to conduct a day, over-the-top flight below the specified IFR minimum en route altitude?

A—The flight must remain clear of clouds by at least 1,000 feet vertically and 1,000 feet horizontally and have at least 3 miles flight visibility.
B—The flight must be conducted at least 1,000 feet above an overcast or broken cloud layer, any higher broken/overcast cloud cover is a minimum of 1,000 feet above the IFR MEA, and have at least 5 miles flight visibility.
C—The height of any higher overcast or broken layer must be at least 500 feet above the IFR MEA.

Answer (B) is correct (8253). *(FAR 121.657)*
A supplemental air carrier may conduct day over-the-top operations in an airplane at flight altitudes lower than the minimum en route IFR altitudes if the operation is conducted at least 1,000 ft. above the top of lower broken or overcast cloud cover, the top of the lower cloud cover is generally uniform and level, flight visibility is at least 5 SM, and the base of any higher broken or overcast cloud cover is generally uniform and level and is at least 1,000 ft. above the minimum en route IFR altitude for that route segment.
Answer (A) is incorrect because the flight must remain at least 1,000 ft. above the cloud layer with a flight visibility of at least 5 SM, not 3 SM. Answer (C) is incorrect because the height of any higher ceiling must be at least 1,000 ft., not 500 ft., above the IFR MEA.

4.14 RECORDS AND REPORTS

121.687 Dispatch Release: Flag and Domestic Operations

153.
8292. What information must be contained in, or attached to, the dispatch release for a domestic air carrier flight?

A—Departure airport, intermediate stops, destinations, alternate airports, and trip number.
B—Names of all passengers on board and minimum fuel supply.
C—Cargo load, weight and balance data, and identification number of the aircraft.

Answer (A) is correct (8292). *(FAR 121.687)*
The dispatch release for a domestic air carrier flight may be in any form but must contain at least the following information concerning each flight: (1) identification number of the aircraft; (2) trip number; (3) departure airport, intermediate stops, destination airports, and alternate airports; (4) a statement of the type of operation (e.g., IFR, VFR); (5) minimum fuel supply; and (6) current weather information.
Answer (B) is incorrect because the passenger names are part of the required load manifest, not the dispatch release. Answer (C) is incorrect because the cargo load and weight and balance data are part of the required load manifest, not the dispatch release.

154.
8290. Which information must be contained in, or attached to, the dispatch release for a flag air carrier flight?

A—Type of operation (e.g., IFR, VFR), trip number.
B—Total fuel supply and minimum fuel required on board the airplane.
C—Passenger manifest, company or organization name, and cargo weight.

Answer (A) is correct (8290). *(FAR 121.687)*
The dispatch release for a flag air carrier flight may be in any form but must contain at least the following information concerning each flight: (1) identification number of the aircraft; (2) trip number; (3) departure airport, intermediate stops, destination airports, and alternate airports; (4) a statement of the type of operation (e.g., IFR, VFR); (5) minimum fuel supply; and (6) current weather information.
Answer (B) is incorrect because the total fuel weight (supply) on board is found in the load manifest, not the dispatch release. Answer (C) is incorrect because a passenger list and cargo weight are found in the load manifest, not the dispatch release.

155.
8293. What information must be included on a domestic air carrier dispatch release?

A—Evidence that the airplane is loaded according to schedule, and a statement of the type of operation.
B—Minimum fuel supply and trip number.
C—Company or organization name and identification number of the aircraft.

Answer (B) is correct (8293). *(FAR 121.687)*
The dispatch release for a domestic air carrier flight may be in any form but must contain at least the following information concerning each flight: (1) identification number of the aircraft; (2) trip number; (3) departure airport, intermediate stops, destination airports, and alternate airports; (4) a statement of the type of operation (e.g., IFR, VFR); (5) minimum fuel supply; and (6) current weather information.
Answer (A) is incorrect because the proper loading of the airplane is documented in the load manifest, not the dispatch release. Answer (C) is incorrect because the company or organization name is not required on the dispatch release for a domestic air carrier.

156.
8294. A dispatch release for a flag or domestic air carrier must contain or have attached to it

A—minimum fuel supply and weather information for the complete flight.
B—trip number and weight and balance data.
C—weather information for the complete flight and a crew list.

Answer (A) is correct (8294). *(FAR 121.687)*
The dispatch release for a flag or domestic air carrier must contain, or have attached to it, weather reports, available weather forecasts, or a combination thereof, for the destination airport, intermediate stops, and alternate airports, that are the latest available at the time the release is signed by the pilot in command and the dispatcher. It may include any additional available weather reports or forecasts that the pilot in command or the aircraft dispatcher considers necessary or desirable. Additionally, the dispatch release will contain the minimum fuel supply.
Answer (B) is incorrect because weight and balance data are part of the load manifest, not the dispatch release. Answer (C) is incorrect because the crew list is part of a supplemental air carrier's flight release, not a flag or domestic air carrier's dispatch release.

<u>121.689 Flight Release Form: Supplemental Operations</u>

157.
8291. The certificated air carrier operators who must attach to, or include on, the flight release form the name of each flight crewmember, flight attendant, and designated pilot in command are

A—supplemental and commercial.
B—supplemental and domestic.
C—flag and commercial.

Answer (A) is correct (8291). *(FAR 121.689)*
Supplemental air carriers must include the name of each flight crewmember, flight attendant, and pilot designated as pilot in command in the flight release.
NOTE: The FAA may delete "and commercial" from the answer in the future.
Answer (B) is incorrect because domestic air carriers, unlike supplemental air carriers, utilize a dispatch release. Supplemental air carriers utilize a flight release. A flight release contains the crew names, but a dispatch release does not. Answer (C) is incorrect because flag air carriers, unlike supplemental air carriers, utilize a dispatch release. Supplemental air carriers utilize a flight release. A flight release contains the crew names, but a dispatch release does not.

158.
8295. The information required in the flight release for supplemental air carriers and commercial operators that is not required in the dispatch release for flag and domestic air carriers is the

A—weather reports and forecasts.
B—names of all crewmembers.
C—minimum fuel supply.

Answer (B) is correct (8295). *(FAR 121.689)*
Supplemental air carriers must include the name of each flight crewmember, flight attendant, and pilot designated as pilot in command in the flight release.
NOTE: The FAA may delete "commercial operators" in the future.
Answer (A) is incorrect because weather reports and forecasts are found in the flight release for supplemental air carriers just as they are found in the dispatch release for flag and domestic air carriers. Answer (C) is incorrect because minimum fuel supply information is found in the flight release for supplemental air carriers just as they are found in the dispatch release for flag and domestic air carriers.

121.695 Disposition of Load Manifest, Dispatch Release, and Flight Plans: Domestic and Flag Operations

159.
8286. Which documents are required to be carried aboard each domestic air carrier flight?

A—Load manifest (or information from it) and flight release.
B—Dispatch release and weight and balance release.
C—Dispatch release, load manifest (or information from it), and flight plan.

Answer (C) is correct (8286). *(FAR 121.695)*
The pilot in command of a domestic air carrier airplane shall carry in the airplane to its destination a copy of the completed load manifest (or information from it, except information concerning cargo and passenger distribution), a copy of the dispatch release, and a copy of the flight plan.
Answer (A) is incorrect because a flight release is used by supplemental air carriers, not domestic air carriers. Answer (B) is incorrect because there is no such thing as a weight and balance release. The weight and balance data are contained in the load manifest.

160.
8296. Which documents are required to be carried aboard each flag air carrier flight?

A—Dispatch release, flight plan, and weight and balance release.
B—Load manifest, flight plan, and flight release.
C—Dispatch release, load manifest, and flight plan.

Answer (C) is correct (8296). *(FAR 121.695)*
The pilot in command of a flag air carrier airplane shall carry in the airplane to its destination a copy of the completed load manifest (or information from it, except information concerning cargo and passenger distribution), a copy of the dispatch release, and a copy of the flight plan.
Answer (A) is incorrect because there is no such thing as a weight and balance release. The weight and balance data are contained in the load manifest. Answer (B) is incorrect because a flight release is used by supplemental air carriers, not flag air carriers.

161.
8288. A domestic or flag air carrier shall keep copies of the flight plans, dispatch releases, and load manifests for at least

A—3 months.
B—6 months.
C—30 days.

Answer (A) is correct (8288). *(FAR 121.695)*
A domestic or flag air carrier shall keep copies of the flight plans, dispatch releases, and load manifests for at least 3 months.
Answer (B) is incorrect because a domestic or flag air carrier shall keep copies of the flight plans, dispatch releases, and load manifests for at least 3 months, not 6 months. Answer (C) is incorrect because a domestic or flag air carrier shall keep copies of the flight plans, dispatch releases, and load manifests for at least 3 months, not 30 days.

121.697 Disposition of Load Manifest, Flight Release, and Flight Plans: Supplemental Operations

162.
8226. What information must the pilot in command of a supplemental air carrier flight or commercial operator carry to the destination airport?

A—Cargo and passenger distribution information.
B—Copy of the flight plan.
C—Names of all crewmembers and designated pilot in command.

Answer (B) is correct (8226). *(FAR 121.697)*
The pilot in command of a supplemental air carrier flight shall carry in the airplane to its destination the original or signed copy of the load manifest, flight release, airworthiness release, pilot route certification, and flight plan.
NOTE: The FAA may change "commercial operator" to "supplemental air carrier" in the future.
Answer (A) is incorrect because cargo and passenger distribution information is part of the weight and balance information contained in the load manifest. Answer (C) is incorrect because a list of the names of all crewmembers and the designated pilot in command is one element contained in the flight release.

163.
8287. How long shall a supplemental air carrier or commercial operator retain a record of the load manifest, airworthiness release, pilot route certification, flight release, and flight plan?

A—1 month.
B—3 months.
C—12 months.

Answer (B) is correct (8287). *(FAR 121.697)*

A supplemental air carrier shall retain a record of the load manifest, airworthiness release, pilot route certification, flight release, and flight plan for at least 3 months.

NOTE: The FAA may delete "commercial operator" in the future.

Answer (A) is incorrect because a supplemental air carrier shall retain a record of the load manifest, airworthiness release, pilot route certification, flight release, and flight plan for at least 3 months, not 1 month. Answer (C) is incorrect because a supplemental air carrier shall retain a record of the load manifest, airworthiness release, pilot route certification, flight release, and flight plan for at least 3 months, not 12 months.

4.15 APPENDIX G

Doppler Radar and Inertial Navigation System (INS): Request for Evaluation; Equipment and Equipment Installation; Training Program; Equipment Accuracy and Reliability; Evaluation Program

164.
8194. Which equipment requirement must be met by an air carrier that elects to use a dual Inertial Navigation System (INS) on a proposed flight?

A—The dual system must consist of two operative INS units.
B—A dual VORTAC/ILS system may be substituted for an inoperative INS.
C—Only one INS is required to be operative, if a Doppler Radar is substituted for the other INS.

Answer (C) is correct (8194). *(FAR 121 Appendix G)*

If an applicant elects to use an Inertial Navigation System, it must be at least a dual system (including navigational computers and reference units). At least two systems must be operational at takeoff. The dual system may consist of either two INS units or one INS unit and one Doppler radar unit.

Answer (A) is incorrect because the dual INS system may consist of two INS units or one INS unit and one Doppler radar unit. It does not have to be two INS units. Answer (B) is incorrect because VORTAC/ILS systems are not authorized as substitutes for an inoperative INS.

165.
8203. An air carrier that elects to use an Inertial Navigational System (INS) must meet which equipment requirement prior to takeoff on a proposed flight?

A—The INS system must consist of two operative INS units.
B—Only one INS is required to be operative, if a Doppler Radar is substituted for the other INS.
C—A dual VORTAC/ILS system may be substituted for an inoperative INS.

Answer (B) is correct (8203). *(FAR 121 Appendix G)*

If an applicant elects to use an Inertial Navigation System, it must be at least a dual system (including navigational computers and reference units). At least two systems must be operational at takeoff. The dual system may consist of either two INS units or one INS unit and one Doppler radar unit.

Answer (A) is incorrect because the dual INS system may consist of two INS units or one INS unit and one Doppler radar unit. Answer (C) is incorrect because VORTAC/ILS systems are not authorized as substitutes for an inoperative INS.

END OF CHAPTER

CHAPTER FIVE
FEDERAL AVIATION REGULATIONS: PART 135

(Continued next page)

NOTE: This chapter applies to only the ATP Part 135 knowledge test.

135.185	Empty Weight and Center of Gravity: Currency Requirement	(2 questions)	131, 158
5.4 VFR/IFR OPERATING LIMITATIONS AND WEATHER REQUIREMENTS			
135.205	VFR: Visibility Requirements	(1 question)	131, 158
135.213	Weather Reports and Forecasts	(1 question)	131, 158
135.215	IFR: Operating Limitations	(1 question)	131, 159
135.217	IFR: Takeoff Limitations	(2 questions)	131, 159
135.219	IFR: Destination Airport Weather Minimums	(1 question)	131, 159
135.221	IFR: Alternate Airport Weather Minimums	(1 question)	131, 160
135.223	IFR: Alternate Airport Requirements	(4 questions)	132, 160
135.225	IFR: Takeoff, Approach and Landing Minimums	(5 questions)	132, 161
135.227	Icing Conditions: Operating Limitations	(2 questions)	132, 162
5.5 FLIGHT CREWMEMBER REQUIREMENTS			
135.243	Pilot in Command Qualifications	(3 questions)	132, 163
135.244	Operating Experience	(5 questions)	133, 163
135.245	Second in Command Qualifications	(1 question)	133, 165
135.247	Pilot Qualifications: Recent Experience	(2 questions)	133, 165
135.253	Misuse of Alcohol	(1 question)	133, 166
5.6 CREWMEMBER FLIGHT TIME AND DUTY PERIOD LIMITATIONS AND REST REQUIREMENTS			
135.265	Flight Time Limitations and Rest Requirements: Scheduled Operations	(3 questions)	133, 166
5.7 CREWMEMBER TESTING REQUIREMENTS			
135.297	Pilot in Command: Instrument Proficiency Check Requirements	(5 questions)	134, 167
135.299	Pilot in Command: Line Checks: Routes and Airports	(3 questions)	134, 168
5.8 TRAINING			
135.321	Applicability and Terms Used	(4 questions)	134, 169
135.331	Crewmember Emergency Training	(2 questions)	134, 170
135.333	Training Requirements: Handling and Carriage of Hazardous Materials	(1 question)	134, 170
5.9 AIRPLANE PERFORMANCE OPERATING LIMITATIONS			
135.367	Large Transport Category Airplanes: Reciprocating Engine Powered: Takeoff Limitations	(2 questions)	135, 171
135.375	Large Transport Category Airplanes: Reciprocating Engine Powered: Landing Limitations: Destination Airports	(3 questions)	135, 171
135.379	Large Transport Category Airplanes: Turbine Engine Powered: Takeoff Limitations	(2 questions)	135, 172
135.385	Large Transport Category Airplanes: Turbine Engine Powered: Landing Limitations: Destination Airports	(8 questions)	135, 173
135.387	Large Transport Category Airplanes: Turbine Engine Powered: Landing Limitations: Alternate Airports	(3 questions)	135, 175
135.397	Small Transport Category Airplane Performance Operating Limitations		136
5.10 MAINTENANCE, PREVENTIVE MAINTENANCE, AND ALTERATIONS			
135.413	Responsibility for Airworthiness	(1 question)	136, 176
135.415	Mechanical Reliability Reports	(1 question)	136, 176

NOTE: This chapter applies to only the ATP Part 135 knowledge test.

This chapter contains outlines of major concepts tested, all FAA test questions and answers regarding FAR Part 135, and an explanation of each answer. Each module, or subtopic, within this chapter is listed on the previous pages with the number of questions from the FAA pilot knowledge test pertaining to that particular module. For each module, the first number following the parentheses is the page number on which the outline begins, and the next number is the page number on which the questions begin.

There are 154 questions in this chapter. We separate and organize the FAA ATP questions into meaningful study units and subunits, i.e., chapters and modules. As an analogy, it is easier to deal with the "trees" if you understand the "forest." In this context, "trees" are individual FAA questions, and the "forest" is the ATP knowledge test. The organizational units between the overall ATP knowledge test and individual ATP test questions are chapters and modules in this book.

CAUTION: The **sole purpose** of this book is to expedite your passing the FAA pilot knowledge test for the ATP certificate. Topics or regulations not directly tested on the FAA pilot knowledge test are omitted. Much more information and knowledge are necessary to fly safely. This additional material is presented in Gleim's other pilot training books (see the order form on page 818) and in many FAA books and circulars, as well as in airplane *POH*s and other commercial textbooks.

5.1 GENERAL

135.3 Rules Applicable to Operations Subject to This Part (Question 1)

1. An aircraft operated outside of the U.S., over a foreign country, by an FAR Part 135 operator must comply with the regulations of the foreign country.

135.19 Emergency Operations (Question 2)

1. The pilot in command may deviate from any rule of FAR Part 135 during an emergency involving the safety of persons or property only to the extent required to meet that emergency.

135.21 Manual Requirements (Question 3)

1. All employees of a certificate holder who are furnished copies of the certificate holder's manual are responsible for keeping their copies up-to-date with approved changes and additions.

135.23 Manual Contents (Questions 4-5)

1. The certificate holder's manual will contain the procedures for servicing the aircraft at a location where previous arrangements have not been made by the operator.
2. The manual will also contain the procedures that explain how the required return-to-service conditions have been met after the aircraft has undergone required airworthiness inspections.

135.25 Aircraft Requirements (Question 6)

1. A certificate holder must have "exclusive use" of at least one aircraft that meets the requirements of at least one kind of operation authorized in the certificate holder's operations specifications.

5.2 FLIGHT OPERATIONS

135.63 Recordkeeping Requirements (Questions 8-11)

1. For multiengine aircraft, each certificate holder is responsible for the preparation and accuracy of a load manifest containing information concerning the loading of the aircraft, which must be prepared in duplicate before each takeoff.
2. Completed load manifests must be kept for 30 days at the certificate holder's principal operations base or at another location used by it and approved by the FAA Administrator.
3. A list of passenger names and their weights is not required on the load manifest; only the number of passengers is required.

135.65 Reporting Mechanical Irregularities (Questions 12-13)

1. Before each flight, the pilot in command is directly responsible for determining the airworthiness status of a mechanical irregularity previously entered in the aircraft maintenance log.
2. Procedures for keeping copies of the aircraft maintenance log in the aircraft and available to appropriate personnel are set forth in the certificate holder's manual.

135.77 Responsibility for Operational Control (Question 14)

1. The certificate holder is required to list in the certificate holder's manual the name and title of each person authorized to exercise operational control for a particular flight.

135.85 Carriage of Persons without Compliance with the Passenger-Carrying Provisions of This Part (Question 15)

1. An individual who is necessary for the safe handling of hazardous material on the aircraft may be carried aboard a Part 135 aircraft without complying with passenger-carrying requirements.

135.87 Carriage of Cargo Including Carry-on Baggage (Questions 16-21)

1. Cargo carried in the passenger compartment must be packaged or covered to avoid possible injury to occupants.
2. Cargo not stored in an approved bin must be secured by a safety belt or an approved tie-down device.
3. All carry-on baggage must be restrained so that its movement is prevented during turbulence.
4. Cargo, including carry-on baggage, that is carried anywhere in the passenger compartment may not be located in a position that restricts access to, or use of, any required emergency or regular exit, or the use of the aisle between the crew and the passenger compartment.
5. In a cargo-only operation, cargo must be loaded in such a manner that at least one emergency or regular exit is available to all occupants.

135.89 Pilot Requirements: Use of Oxygen (Questions 22-27)

1. Each pilot of an unpressurized aircraft shall use oxygen continuously when flying
   a. At altitudes above 10,000 ft. MSL through 12,000 ft. MSL for any time in excess of 30 min. duration
   b. Above 12,000 ft. MSL
2. In a pressurized aircraft, each pilot shall use oxygen continuously anytime the cabin pressure altitude is more than 12,000 ft. MSL.
3. The maximum altitude without one pilot wearing and using an oxygen mask in a pressurized aircraft equipped with quick-donning oxygen masks is 35,000 ft. MSL.
   a. Above 35,000 ft. MSL, one pilot at the controls must wear a secured and sealed oxygen mask.
4. The remaining pilot must use an oxygen mask in a pressurized cabin airplane at altitudes above 25,000 ft. MSL if the other pilot leaves the duty station.

135.91 Oxygen for Medical Use by Passengers (Questions 28-31)

1. The equipment used to store liquid oxygen must be covered in the certificate holder's approved maintenance program.
2. A person using oxygen equipment must be seated to avoid restricting access to, or use of, any required exit.
3. No person may smoke within 10 ft. of oxygen storage and dispensing equipment.
4. If a certificate holder deviates from the provisions of the regulations regarding medical use of oxygen by passengers, a complete report of the incident shall be sent to the FAA within 10 working days.

135.93 Autopilot: Minimum Altitudes for Use (Questions 32-37)

1. Autopilots may not be used at less than 500 ft. AGL or twice the maximum altitude loss specified in the approved *Airplane Flight Manual* or equivalent for a malfunction of the autopilot, whichever is higher.
2. On other than an ILS, one cannot use an autopilot at an altitude above the ground that is less than 50 ft. below the approved minimum descent altitude for that procedure or, if higher, twice the maximum loss specified in the approved flight manual for a malfunction of the autopilot under approach conditions.
   a. EXAMPLE: The maximum altitude loss for a particular malfunctioning autopilot under approach conditions is 55 ft. If the TDZE is 571 ft. and the MDA is 1,100 ft., to which minimum altitude may you use this autopilot?
      1) You are limited to 50 ft. below the MDA (here 1,100 ft.), which is 1,050 ft. You are also limited to twice the maximum altitude loss of 55 ft., which is 110 ft. AGL or 681 ft. MSL.
      2) Since 1,050 ft. MSL is greater than 681 ft. MSL, the minimum altitude for autopilot use is 1,050 ft. MSL.
3. For ILS approaches, you may not use an autopilot with an approach coupler at an altitude that is less than 50 ft. AGL or malfunction maximum altitude loss, whichever is higher.

135.99 Composition of Flight Crew (Questions 38-39)

1. An aircraft with 10 or more passenger seats requires a second in command, i.e., a copilot.
   a. Thus, an autopilot may not be used in place of a second in command in such an aircraft.

135.100 Flight Crewmember Duties (Questions 40-41)

1. The **critical phases of flight** include all ground operations involving taxi, takeoff, landing, and all other operations conducted below 10,000 ft., excluding cruise flight.
2. Other than in cruise flight, nonsafety cockpit activities by flight crewmembers are prohibited below 10,000 ft.

135.105 Exception to Second in Command Requirement: Approval for Use of Autopilot System (Questions 42-43)

1. A commuter air carrier certificate holder may have an aircraft approved with an autopilot system and no second in command if the autopilot system is capable of operating the controls to maintain flight and to maneuver the aircraft about three axes.
2. Commuter air carriers may not use a pilot in command with less than 100 hr. of PIC flight time in the make and model to be flown if an autopilot is to take the place of a second in command.

135.107 Flight Attendant Crewmember Requirement (Question 44)

1. A flight attendant crewmember is required on aircraft having a passenger seating capacity of 20 or more.

135.115 Manipulation of Controls (Question 45)

1. Only an authorized FAA safety representative who is qualified in the aircraft and is checking flight operations may be allowed by the pilot in command to manipulate the flight controls in addition to the second in command.

135.117 Briefing of Passengers before Flight (Questions 46-48)

1. Prior to takeoff, the pilot in command of an aircraft carrying passengers shall ensure that all passengers have been orally briefed on
   a. The use of safety belts, smoking rules, and the location and operation of fire extinguishers
   b. Normal and emergency use of oxygen if the flight involves operations above 12,000 ft. MSL
2. The oral preflight briefing may be conducted by the pilot in command or a crewmember and supplemented by printed cards for the use of each passenger.

135.119 Prohibition against Carriage of Weapons (Question 49)

1. Crewmembers and/or others authorized by the certificate holder may be allowed to carry a deadly weapon on board an aircraft operated under FAR Part 135.

5.3 AIRCRAFT AND EQUIPMENT

135.149 Equipment Requirements: General (Questions 50-51)

1. All turbojet airplanes require a third gyroscopic bank-and-pitch indicator.
   a. That instrument must be capable of continuing reliable operation for a minimum of 30 min. after total failure of the aircraft's electrical generating system.

135.150 Public Address and Crewmember Interphone Systems (Questions 52-53)

1. An approved public address and crewmember interphone system is required in aircraft having a passenger seating configuration, excluding any pilot seat, of more than 19 seats.
2. The crewmember interphone system on a large turbojet-powered airplane provides a means of two-way communication between ground personnel and at least one of two flight crewmembers in the pilot compartment when the airplane is on the ground.
   a. The interphone station for use by ground personnel must be located so that those using the system from that station may avoid visible detection from within the airplane.

135.151 Cockpit Voice Recorders (Questions 54-57)

1. An approved cockpit voice recorder is required equipment in multiengine, turbine-powered airplanes having a passenger seating configuration of 20 or more seats.
2. Cockpit voice recorders must be operated continuously from the use of the checklist before the flight to completion of the final checklist at the end of the flight.
3. Information recorded during normal operations by a required cockpit voice recorder may be erased or otherwise obliterated, except for the last 30 min.

135.153 Ground Proximity Warning System (Questions 58-60)

1. Ground proximity warning systems are required for turbine-powered airplanes with a passenger seating configuration, excluding any pilot seat, of 10 seats or more.
2. Ground proximity warning systems required under FAR Part 135 must convey warnings of any deviation below glide slope and of excessive closure rate with terrain.
3. Ground proximity warning systems, if required, must incorporate a means of alerting the pilot when a malfunction occurs.

135.157 Oxygen Equipment Requirements (Questions 61-65)

1. Pressurized aircraft above 15,000 ft. MSL require oxygen availability for each occupant in the aircraft (other than pilots) for 1 hr. unless at all times during the flight above that altitude the aircraft can safely descend to 15,000 ft. MSL within 4 min.
   a. Then only a 30-min. supply is required for each passenger.
2. At altitudes above 10,000 ft. MSL through 15,000 ft. MSL, oxygen dispensers and oxygen must be available for at least 10% of the occupants of an unpressurized aircraft (other than the pilots) for that part of the flight at those altitudes of more than 30 min. duration.
   a. All passengers in an unpressurized airplane must be supplied oxygen above 15,000 ft. MSL.

135.159 Equipment Requirements: Carrying Passengers under VFR at Night or under VFR Over-the-Top Conditions (Question 66)

1. No person may operate an aircraft under FAR Part 135, carrying passengers under VFR at night, unless it is equipped with a flashlight having at least two size "D" cells or the equivalent.

135.167 Emergency Equipment: Extended Overwater Operations (Questions 67-72)

1. Each airplane being operated in extended overwater operations is required to have a life preserver, equipped with a survivor locator light, for each person on the airplane.
   a. The life preserver must be stored within easy access of each seated occupant.
2. Each airplane being operated in extended overwater operations must carry enough approved life rafts of a rated capacity and buoyancy to accommodate the occupants of the airplane.
   a. Each life raft must be equipped with one pyrotechnic signaling device.
   b. At least one life raft must be equipped with a survival-type emergency locator transmitter.

135.171 Shoulder Harness Installation at Flight Crewmember Stations (Questions 73-75)

1. Shoulder harnesses must be installed at each flight crewmember station in all turbojet airplanes.
   a. This requirement also applies to all aircraft having a seating configuration, excluding any pilot seat, of 10 seats or more.
2. Only when a pilot cannot perform the required duties with a shoulder harness fastened, may it be unfastened during takeoff and landing.

135.173 Airborne Thunderstorm Detection Equipment Requirements (Question 76)

1. Small aircraft having a passenger seating configuration of 10 seats or more, excluding any pilot seat, engaged in passenger-carrying operations must have airborne thunderstorm detection equipment.

135.175 Airborne Weather Radar Equipment Requirements (Question 77)

1. Large transport category aircraft in the United States engaged in passenger-carrying operations must have airborne weather radar equipment.

135.177 Emergency Equipment Requirements for Aircraft Having a Passenger Seating Configuration of More Than 19 Passengers (Questions 78-80)

1. Aircraft having a seating configuration, excluding any pilot seat, of more than 19 seats must have one approved first-aid kit for treatment of injuries likely to occur in flight or in a minor accident.
2. A crash ax must be located in an accessible position to the crew, but it must be inaccessible to passengers during normal operations.

135.178 Additional Emergency Equipment (Question 81)

1. Aircraft having a passenger seating configuration of more than 19 seats must have interior emergency lights that must be operable manually from the flight crew station and a point in the passenger compartment.

135.179 Inoperable Instruments and Equipment (Questions 82-83)

1. In order for an aircraft to be operated with certain equipment inoperative under the provisions of a minimum equipment list (MEL), the FAA district office having certification responsibility must have issued the certificate holder operations specifications authorizing the use of an MEL.
2. An approved MEL, as authorized by the operations specifications, constitutes an approved change to the type design without requiring recertification.

135.181 Performance Requirements: Aircraft Operated Over-the-Top or in IFR Conditions (Question 84)

1. Multiengine airplanes carrying passengers for hire in IFR weather conditions must be able to climb, with the critical engine inoperative, at least 50 fpm at the MEAs of the route to be flown, or 5,000 ft. MSL, whichever is higher.

135.183 Performance Requirements: Land Aircraft Operated over Water (Question 85)

1. Single-engine land airplanes carrying passengers must be operated at an altitude that will allow them to reach land in case of engine failure when being operated over water.

135.185 Empty Weight and Center of Gravity: Currency Requirement (Questions 86-87)

1. The empty weight and CG of a multiengine aircraft used in air taxi service must be established by actual weighing of the aircraft within the preceding 36 calendar months.

5.4 VFR/IFR OPERATING LIMITATIONS AND WEATHER REQUIREMENTS

135.205 VFR: Visibility Requirements (Question 88)

1. In Class G airspace, the Part 135 visibility requirements are 1,000-ft. ceiling and 2 SM visibility.

135.213 Weather Reports and Forecasts (Question 89)

1. The FAA must issue operations specifications to permit IFR operations from an airport that is not at the location where weather observations are made.

135.215 IFR: Operating Limitations (Question 90)

1. The FAA must issue operations specifications approving IFR departures from an airport that does not have an approved standard instrument approach procedure.

135.217 IFR: Takeoff Limitations (Questions 91-92)

1. A takeoff may not be made from an airport that is below the authorized IFR landing minimums unless there is an alternate airport with the required IFR landing minimums within 1 hr. flying time, at normal cruise speed in still air.

135.219 IFR: Destination Airport Weather Minimums (Question 93)

1. A pilot may not begin an IFR operation unless the next airport of intended landing is forecast to be at or above authorized IFR landing minimums at the estimated time of arrival.

135.221 IFR: Alternate Airport Weather Minimums (Question 94)

1. A pilot may not designate an airport as an alternative unless it is forecast to be at or above alternate minimums at the estimated time of arrival.

135.223 IFR: Alternate Airport Requirements (Questions 95-98)

1. An aircraft operating in IFR conditions must carry enough fuel to
   a. Complete the flight to the first airport of intended landing
   b. Fly from that airport to the alternate airport, if required
   c. Fly thereafter for 45 min. at normal cruising speed
2. If the required ceiling exists, an alternate airport is not required if, for at least 1 hr. before and after the ETA, the forecast visibility is at least 3 SM, or 2 SM more than the lowest applicable visibility minimums for the instrument approach procedure to be used, whichever is greater.
3. If the required visibility exists and circling is not authorized, an alternate for the destination airport is not required if, for at least 1 hr. before and after the ETA, the forecast ceiling is at least 1,500 ft. above the lowest published minimum, or 2,000 ft. above the airport elevation, whichever is higher.

135.225 IFR: Takeoff, Approach and Landing Minimums (Questions 99-103)

1. Pilots may not begin instrument approaches to an airport unless the latest weather report indicates that weather conditions are at or above the authorized IFR landing minimums.
   a. If a pilot has passed the final approach fix and learns that the weather has gone below the minimums, (s)he can continue the approach to the DH or MDA and land only if the actual weather conditions are at least equal to the minimums prescribed for the procedure.
2. Pilots may not take off under IFR at a military or a foreign airport unless the visibility is at least 1 SM.
3. One condition required for a pilot to take off under IFR with less-than-standard takeoff minimums at an airport where a straight-in instrument approach procedure is authorized and there is an approved weather reporting source is that the wind direction and velocity must be such that a straight-in approach can be made to the runway served by the procedure.

135.227 Icing Conditions: Operating Limitations (Questions 104-105)

1. No pilot may take off an aircraft that has frost, snow, or ice adhering to any propeller, windshield, wings, or stabilizing or control surface.
2. No pilot may take off an airplane anytime conditions are such that frost, ice, or snow may reasonably be expected to adhere to the airplane unless a pretakeoff contamination check has been completed within 5 min. prior to beginning takeoff.
   a. A pretakeoff contamination check is a check to make sure the wings and control surfaces are free of frost, ice, or snow.

5.5 FLIGHT CREWMEMBER REQUIREMENTS

135.243 Pilot in Command Qualifications (Questions 106-108)

1. The minimum certificate and rating requirements for the pilot in command of a multiengine airplane, including a turbojet airplane, being operated by a commuter air carrier are an ATP certificate; airplane category; multiengine class rating; and an airplane type rating, if required.

135.244 Operating Experience (Questions 109-113)

1. Prior to being designated as pilot in command of an airplane operated in passenger-carrying service by a commuter air carrier, the pilot must have the following operating experience in each make and basic model of airplane to be flown:
   a. 25 hr. in a turbojet-powered airplane
   b. 20 hr. in a multiengine, turboprop airplane
   c. 15 hr. in a multiengine, reciprocating engine-powered airplane
   d. 10 hr. in a single-engine airplane
2. A reduction of up to 50% of these times may be made by substituting one takeoff and landing for each required hour of operating experience.

135.245 Second in Command Qualifications (Question 114)

1. To satisfy the instrument approach recency experience requirement, a second in command must have made at least six approaches within the past 6 months in any airplane, helicopter, approved instrument ground trainer, or simulator.

135.247 Pilot Qualifications: Recent Experience (Questions 115-116)

1. One requirement that must be met by a pilot in command to reestablish recency of experience is to make three takeoffs and three landings as the sole manipulator of the flight controls in an aircraft of the same category and class and, if a type rating is required, of the same type in which that person is to serve.
2. For operations during the period beginning 1 hr. after sunset and ending 1 hr. before sunrise, a pilot in command of an airplane carrying passengers must have made three takeoffs and three landings during that period as sole manipulator of the flight controls in an aircraft of the same category and class and, if a type rating is required, of the same type in which that person is to serve.

135.253 Misuse of Alcohol (Question 117)

1. An employee who performs safety-sensitive functions for a certificate holder and who has actual knowledge of an accident for which (s)he performed a safety-sensitive function at or near the time of the accident shall not use alcohol for 8 hr. following the accident.

5.6 CREWMEMBER FLIGHT TIME AND DUTY PERIOD LIMITATIONS AND REST REQUIREMENTS

135.265 Flight Time Limitations and Rest Requirements: Scheduled Operations (Questions 118-120)

1. Flight time limitations are based on flight time accumulated under FAR Part 135 and in any other commercial flying.
2. The maximum number of hours that a pilot may fly as a pilot for a commuter air carrier and in other commercial flying is
   a. 34 hr. in any 7 consecutive days
   b. 120 hr. in any calendar month

5.7 CREWMEMBER TESTING REQUIREMENTS

135.297 Pilot in Command: Instrument Proficiency Check Requirements (Questions 121-125)

1. A person may not serve as pilot in command in an IFR operation unless that person has passed an instrument proficiency check under actual or simulated IFR conditions since the beginning of the 6th calendar month prior to the date to serve.
   a. A pilot must take the instrument proficiency check required in each type of aircraft to which that pilot is assigned in rotation, but not more than one flight check during each 6 calendar months.
   b. If the pilot is assigned to both single-engine and multiengine airplanes, the initial flight check is done in the multiengine airplane; then flight checks are taken alternately in single-engine and multiengine airplanes.
2. If a pilot is authorized to use an autopilot system in place of a second in command, that pilot must properly conduct instrument operations competently both with and without the autopilot during the instrument proficiency check.
   a. An autopilot check may be taken concurrently with the instrument proficiency check at 12-month intervals.

135.299 Pilot in Command: Line Checks: Routes and Airports (Questions 126-128)

1. A pilot in command must have passed a line check in one of the types of aircraft which that pilot is to fly since the beginning of the 12th calendar month before serving as pilot in command.
2. In order to serve as pilot in command in an IFR operation, a person must have passed a line check since the beginning of the 12th month before that service, which includes
   a. At least one flight over a civil airway or an approved off-airway route, or a portion of either
   b. Takeoffs and landings at one or more representative airports

5.8 TRAINING

135.321 Applicability and Terms Used (Questions 129-132)

1. **Initial training** is required for flight crewmembers who have not qualified and served in the same capacity on an aircraft.
2. **Upgrade training** is required for a flight crewmember who has served as second in command of a particular aircraft type (e.g., BE-1900) before (s)he may serve as pilot in command on that aircraft.
3. **Transition training** is required for flight crewmembers who have been qualified and have served in the same capacity on another aircraft.

135.331 Crewmember Emergency Training (Questions 133-134)

1. The certificate holder must give instruction on such topics as respiration, hypoxia, gas bubble formation, gas expansion, decompression, and length of consciousness without supplemental oxygen at altitude to crewmembers serving on aircraft operated above FL 250.

135.333 Training Requirements: Handling and Carriage of Hazardous Materials (Question 135)

1. A person whose duties include the handling or carriage of dangerous articles and/or magnetized materials must have satisfactorily completed an approved training program established by the certificate holder within the previous 12 calendar months.

5.9 AIRPLANE PERFORMANCE OPERATING LIMITATIONS

135.367 Large Transport Category Airplanes: Reciprocating Engine Powered: Takeoff Limitations (See 135.397.) (Questions 136-137)

1. When computing takeoff limitations, takeoff data based on still air may be corrected taking into account
   a. Not more than 50% of any reported headwind component
   b. Not less than 150% of any reported tailwind component

135.375 Large Transport Category Airplanes: Reciprocating Engine Powered: Landing Limitations: Destination Airports (See 135.397.) (Questions 138-140)

1. A reciprocating airplane must be able to land in 60% of the effective length of the runway (wet or dry) at the airport of intended landing.
   a. The effective runway length begins at the point where the obstruction clearance plane intersects the runway.

135.379 Large Transport Category Airplanes: Turbine Engine Powered: Takeoff Limitations (See 135.397.) (Questions 141-142)

1. For turbine-engine-powered large transport category airplanes certificated after September 30, 1958, the takeoff distance may include a "clearway" distance, but the clearway distance included may not be greater than one-half of the takeoff run.
2. The accelerate-stop distance must not exceed the length of the runway plus the length of any stopway for a turbine-powered small transport airplane.

135.385 Large Transport Category Airplanes: Turbine Engine Powered: Landing Limitations: Destination Airports (See 135.397.) (Questions 143-150)

1. A turbine-engine airplane must be able to land in 60% of the effective length of the runway (wet or dry) at the airport of intended landing.
   a. The effective runway length begins at the point where the obstruction clearance plane intersects the runway.

135.387 Large Transport Category Airplanes: Turbine Engine Powered: Landing Limitations: Alternate Airports (See 135.397.) (Questions 151-153)

1. Turboprop airplanes must be able to land in 70% of the effective length of the runway (wet or dry) at an alternate airport.
   a. The effective runway length begins at the point where the obstruction clearance plane intersects the runway.

135.397 Small Transport Category Airplane Performance Operating Limitations

1. Small reciprocating transport airplanes must comply
   a. With the landing limitations in 135.375 and 135.377
   b. With the takeoff limitations in 135.367
2. Small turbine transport airplanes must comply
   a. With the landing limitations in 135.385 and 135.387
   b. With the takeoff limitations in 135.379
3. Summary
   a. Landing limitations for both reciprocating and turbine airplanes at destination airports are 60% of effective runway length.
      1) The effective runway length begins at the point where the obstruction clearance plane intersects the runway.
   b. Landing limitations at alternate airports are 70% of effective runway length.

5.10 MAINTENANCE, PREVENTIVE MAINTENANCE, AND ALTERATIONS

135.413 Responsibility for Airworthiness (Question 154)

1. Persons other than the certificate holder who perform aircraft maintenance must perform the maintenance in accordance with the certificate holder's manual and FAR Parts 43, 91, and 135.

135.415 Mechanical Reliability Reports (Question 155)

1. Each certificate holder is responsible for submitting a mechanical reliability report.

QUESTIONS AND ANSWER EXPLANATIONS

All the FAA questions from the pilot knowledge test for the ATP certificate relating to FAR Part 135 and the material outlined previously are reproduced on the following pages in the same modules as the outlines. To the immediate right of each question are the correct answer and answer explanation. You should cover these answers and answer explanations while responding to the questions. Refer to the general discussion in Chapter 1 on how to take the FAA pilot knowledge test.

Remember that the questions from the FAA pilot knowledge test bank have been reordered by topic, and the topics are organized into a meaningful sequence. Accordingly, the first line of the answer explanation gives the FAA question number and the citation of the authoritative source for the answer.

5.1 GENERAL

135.3 Rules Applicable to Operations Subject to This Part

1.
8010. An aircraft being operated outside of the United States, over a foreign country, by a 14 CFR Part 135 operator must comply with

A—the International Civil Aviation Organization (ICAO), Annex 3, Rules of the Air.
B—regulations of the foreign country.
C—rules of the U.S. State Department and the foreign country.

Answer (B) is correct (8010). *(FAR 135.3 and 91.703)*
While operating an aircraft outside of the U.S., over a foreign country, an FAR Part 135 operator must comply with the regulations of the foreign country.
Answer (A) is incorrect because ICAO Rules of the Air is Annex 2, not Annex 3. Answer (C) is incorrect because the U.S. State Department has no authority over aviation activities over a foreign country.

135.19 Emergency Operations

2.
8819. The pilot in command may deviate from 14 CFR Part 135 during an emergency involving the safety of persons or property only

A—after ATC is notified of the emergency and the extent of deviation required.
B—to the extent required to meet that emergency.
C—if required to, by the emergency cockpit checklist.

Answer (B) is correct (8819). *(FAR 135.19)*
In an emergency involving the safety of persons or property, the pilot in command may deviate from the rules of FAR Part 135 to the extent required to meet that emergency.
Answer (A) is incorrect because ATC should be notified after, not before, the pilot in command deviates from the rules of FAR Part 135 during an emergency. Answer (C) is incorrect because the pilot in command may deviate from the rules of FAR Part 135 during an emergency to the extent required to meet that emergency, not if an emergency checklist requires the deviation.

135.21 Manual Requirements

3.
8011. Who is responsible for keeping copies of the certificate holder's manual up to date with approved changes or additions?

A—Each of the certificate holder's employees who are furnished a manual.
B—An employee designated by the certificate holder.
C—A representative of the certificate holder approved by the Administrator.

Answer (A) is correct (8011). *(FAR 135.21)*
Each employee of the certificate holder to whom a manual (or portions of it) is furnished is responsible for keeping his/her copy up-to-date with the changes and additions furnished to him/her.
Answer (B) is incorrect because all employees of the certificate holder to whom copies of the manual have been furnished are responsible for keeping them up-to-date, not an employee designated by the certificate holder. Answer (C) is incorrect because a certificate holder must furnish a copy of the manual to a representative of the FAA (the Principal Operations Inspector), and the certificate holder, not the inspector, is responsible for keeping the inspector's copy up-to-date.

135.23 Manual Contents

4.
8004. If previous arrangements have not been made by the operator, where can the procedures for servicing the aircraft be found?

A—Certificate holder's maintenance manual.
B—Certificate holder's manual.
C—Pilot's Handbook.

Answer (B) is correct (8004). *(FAR 135.23)*
The certificate holder's manual contains the procedures to be followed by the pilot in command to obtain maintenance, preventive maintenance, and servicing of the aircraft at a place where previous arrangements have not been made.
Answer (A) is incorrect because the maintenance manual describes how maintenance personnel would service the airplane, not the procedures the pilot in command would follow to have the aircraft serviced at a place where previous arrangements have not been made. Answer (C) is incorrect because the Pilot's Handbook provides information on the airplane, not the procedures to follow to have the airplane serviced at a place where previous arrangements have not been made.

5.
8012. What document contains procedures that explain how the required return-to-service conditions have been met?

A—Maintenance manual.
B—Pilot's Handbook.
C—Certificate holder's manual.

Answer (C) is correct (8012). *(FAR 135.23)*
The certificate holder's manual must include procedures for ensuring that the pilot in command knows that the aircraft has undergone the required airworthiness inspections and has been approved for return to service in compliance with applicable maintenance requirements.
Answer (A) is incorrect because the certificate holder's manual, not the maintenance manual, must contain the procedures that explain how the return-to-service conditions have been met. Answer (B) is incorrect because the certificate holder's manual, not the pilot's handbook, must contain the procedures that explain how the return-to-service conditions have been met.

135.25 Aircraft Requirements

6.
8001. A certificate holder must have "exclusive use" of

A—at least one aircraft that meets the requirements of the specific operations authorized in the certificate holder's Operations Specifications.
B—at least one aircraft that meets the requirements of at least one kind of operation authorized in the certificate holder's Operations Specifications.
C—at least one aircraft that meets the requirements of each kind of operation authorized in the Operations Specifications.

Answer (B) is correct (8001). *(FAR 135.25)*
Each certificate holder must have the exclusive use of at least one aircraft that meets the requirements for at least one kind of operation authorized in the certificate holder's operations specifications. In addition, for each kind of operation for which the certificate holder does not have the exclusive use of an aircraft, the certificate holder must have available for use under a written agreement (including arrangements for performing required maintenance) at least one aircraft that meets the requirements for that kind of operation. However, this does not prohibit the operator from using or authorizing the use of the aircraft for other than air taxi or commercial operations and does not require the certificate holder to have exclusive use of all aircraft that the certificate holder uses.
Answer (A) is incorrect because the certificate holder must have exclusive use for at least one, not all, operation(s) authorized to the certificate holder. Answer (C) is incorrect because the certificate holder must have exclusive use for at least one, not all, operation(s) authorized to the certificate holder.

Question 7 was moved to Chapter 2, FAR 119. Therefore, question numbering in this chapter is off by one.

5.2 FLIGHT OPERATIONS

136.63 Recordkeeping Requirements

8.
8009. Who is responsible for the preparation of a required load manifest?

A—PIC or the Dispatcher.
B—Company official designated by the Administrator.
C—The certificate holder.

Answer (C) is correct (8009). *(FAR 135.63)*
For multiengine aircraft, each certificate holder is responsible for the preparation and accuracy of a load manifest in duplicate containing information concerning the loading of the aircraft. The load manifest must be prepared before each takeoff.
Answer (A) is incorrect because, while the PIC must carry a copy of the load manifest in the aircraft to its destination, the PIC is not responsible for the preparation of the load manifest. Additionally, dispatchers are required for some FAR Part 121 operations, not FAR Part 135. Answer (B) is incorrect because the certificate holder, not any official designated by the FAA, is responsible for the preparation of a required load manifest.

9.
8007. Where must a certificate holder keep copies of completed load manifests and for what period of time?

A—1 month at its principal operations base, or at a location approved by the Administrator.
B—30 days at its principal operations base, or another location used by it and approved by the Administrator.
C—30 days, at the flight's destination.

Answer (B) is correct (8007). *(FAR 135.63)*
The certificate holder must keep copies of completed load manifests for at least 30 days at its principal operations base or at another location used by it and approved by the FAA Administrator.
Answer (A) is incorrect because a certificate holder must keep copies of completed load manifests for 30 days, not 1 month, at its principal operations base or at another location used by it and approved by the FAA, not at any location. Answer (C) is incorrect because, while the PIC must carry a copy of the completed load manifest to the flight's destination, the certificate holder must keep copies of completed load manifests at its principal operations base or at another location used by it and approved by the FAA.

10.
8008. Which is NOT a required item on the load manifest?

A—List of passenger names and the weight of each.
B—Aircraft registration number or flight number.
C—Identification of crewmembers and their crew position.

Answer (A) is correct (8008). *(FAR 135.63)*
A list of passenger names and their weights is not required on the load manifest; only the number of passengers is required.
Answer (B) is incorrect because the aircraft registration number or flight number must be included on the load manifest. Answer (C) is incorrect because the identification of crewmembers and their crew position assignments must be included on the load manifest.

11.
8043. The load manifest must be prepared prior to each takeoff for

A—any aircraft with a passenger seating capacity of 10 seats or more.
B—any aircraft with more than one engine.
C—all helicopters and large aircraft operated by a commuter air carrier.

Answer (B) is correct (8043). *(FAR 135.63)*
For multiengine aircraft, each certificate holder is responsible for the preparation in duplicate and the accuracy of a load manifest containing information concerning the loading of the aircraft. The manifest must be prepared before each takeoff.
Answer (A) is incorrect because a manifest is required for multiengine aircraft only, regardless of the number of passengers carried. Answer (C) is incorrect because the FAA's load manifest requirement is based on single-engine/multiengine, not class or size.

135.65 Reporting Mechanical Irregularities

12.
8006. Who is directly responsible for determining the status of each mechanical irregularity previously entered in the aircraft maintenance log?

A—Aircraft dispatcher.
B—Line maintenance supervisor.
C—The next pilot in command.

Answer (C) is correct (8006). *(FAR 135.65)*
The pilot in command shall enter or have entered in the aircraft maintenance log each mechanical irregularity that comes to the pilot's attention during flight time. Before each flight, the pilot in command shall, if the pilot does not already know, determine the status of each irregularity entered in the maintenance log at the end of the preceding flight.
Answer (A) is incorrect because the aircraft dispatcher is responsible for briefing the pilot in command on all available weather information and on irregularities of facilities and services. Answer (B) is incorrect because the pilot in command, not the line maintenance supervisor, is directly responsible for determining the status of each mechanical irregularity previously entered in the aircraft maintenance log.

13.
8019. Procedures for keeping copies of the aircraft maintenance log in the aircraft and available to appropriate personnel shall be set forth in

A—the certificate holder's manual.
B—the maintenance procedures handbook.
C—the Operations Specifications.

Answer (A) is correct (8019). *(FAR 135.65)*

Each certificate holder shall establish a procedure for keeping copies of the aircraft maintenance log in the aircraft for access by appropriate personnel and shall include that procedure in the certificate holder's manual.

Answer (B) is incorrect because a maintenance procedures handbook establishes procedures for handling different maintenance items, not procedures for keeping copies of the maintenance log in the aircraft. Answer (C) is incorrect because the operations specifications lists the time limitations for overhauls, inspections, and other items that are subject to an airworthiness maintenance program, not procedures for keeping copies of the maintenance log in the aircraft.

135.77 Responsibility for Operational Control

14.
8005. Where is the certificate holder required to list the name and title of each person authorized to exercise operational control for a particular flight?

A—Operations Specifications.
B—Attached to the load manifest.
C—Certificate holder's manual.

Answer (C) is correct (8005). *(FAR 135.77)*

Each certificate holder is responsible for operational control and shall list, in the operations manual required, the name and title of each person authorized by it to exercise operational control.

Answer (A) is incorrect because the operations specifications prescribes the area in which the certificate holder can operate, types of instrument approaches that can be flown, aircraft that can be used, etc., not who can exercise operational control. Answer (B) is incorrect because the load manifest contains specific flight data such as fuel on board, passengers, cargo, etc., not the name of each person who can exercise operational control.

135.85 Carriage of Persons without Compliance with the Passenger-Carrying Provisions of This Part

15.
8038. Which person may be carried aboard an aircraft without complying with the passenger-carrying requirements of FAR Part 135?

A—An individual who is necessary for the safe handling of hazardous material on the aircraft.
B—A representative of the Administrator, traveling to attend a meeting.
C—A member of the United States diplomatic corps on an official courier mission.

Answer (A) is correct (8038). *(FAR 135.85)*

Certain types of persons may be carried aboard an aircraft without having to comply with the passenger-carrying requirements of FAR Part 135. They include

1. A crewmember or other employee of the certificate holder
2. A person necessary for the safe handling of animals on the aircraft
3. A person necessary for the safe handling of hazardous materials (as defined in Subchapter C of Title 49 CFR)
4. A person performing duty as a security or honor guard accompanying a shipment made by or under the authority of the U.S. Government
5. A military courier or a military route supervisor carried by a military cargo contract air carrier or commercial operator in operations under a military cargo contract, if that carriage is specifically authorized by the appropriate military service
6. An authorized representative of the FAA Administrator conducting an en route inspection
7. A person, authorized by the FAA Administrator, who is performing a duty connected with a cargo operation of the certificate holder

Answer (B) is incorrect because a representative of the FAA Administrator conducting an en route inspection, not traveling to attend a meeting, may be carried aboard an aircraft without complying with the passenger-carrying requirements of FAR Part 135. Answer (C) is incorrect because a member of the U.S. diplomatic corps on an official courier mission carried aboard an aircraft must comply with the passenger-carrying requirements of FAR Part 135.

135.87 Carriage of Cargo Including Carry-on Baggage

16.
8032. Which restriction must be observed regarding the carrying of cargo in the passenger compartment?

A—It is packaged or covered to avoid possible injury to occupants.
B—All cargo must be carried in a suitable bin and secured to a passenger seat or the floor structure of the aircraft.
C—Cargo carried in passenger seats must be forward of all passengers.

Answer (A) is correct (8032). *(FAR 135.87)*
No person may carry cargo, including carry-on baggage, in or on any aircraft unless it is packaged or covered to avoid possible injury to occupants.
Answer (B) is incorrect because carry-on baggage can be stowed under a passenger seat as long as the seat is fitted with a means to prevent the baggage from sliding under the impact of a crash, which does not mean that the baggage must be secured to the passenger seat or the floor structure of the aircraft. Answer (C) is incorrect because carry-on baggage can be stowed under a passenger seat, not forward of all passenger seats, as long as the seat is fitted with a means to prevent the baggage from sliding under the impact of a crash.

17.
8040. Which is a requirement governing the carriage of cargo, on a scheduled passenger flight?

A—Cargo must be carried in an approved rack, bin, or compartment.
B—Cargo not stowed in an approved bin must be secured by a safety belt or approved tiedown device.
C—All cargo carried in the passenger compartment must be packaged and stowed ahead of the foremost seated passenger.

Answer (B) is correct (8040). *(FAR 135.87)*
Cargo not stowed in an approved bin on a scheduled passenger flight must be properly secured by a safety belt or other approved tie-down device having enough strength to eliminate the possibility of shifting under all normally anticipated flight and ground conditions.
Answer (A) is incorrect because cargo does not have to be carried in an approved bin if it is secured by a safety belt or an approved tie-down device. Answer (C) is incorrect because cargo may be carried in the passenger compartment under specified conditions; it is not required to be stowed ahead of the foremost seated passenger.

18.
8832. What requirement must be met regarding cargo that is carried anywhere in the passenger compartment of a commuter air carrier airplane?

A—Cargo may not be carried anywhere in the rear of the passenger compartment.
B—The bin in which the cargo is carried may not be installed in a position that restricts access to, or use of the aisle between the crew and the passenger compartment.
C—The container or bin in which the cargo is carried must be made of material which is at least flash resistant.

Answer (B) is correct (8832). *(FAR 135.87)*
Cargo, including carry-on baggage, that is carried anywhere in the passenger compartment may not be located in a position that restricts access to, or use of, any required emergency or regular exit, or the use of the aisle between the crew and the passenger compartment.
Answer (A) is incorrect because there is no regulation stating that cargo cannot be carried anywhere in the rear of the passenger compartment. Answer (C) is incorrect because FAR 135.87 does not specify what material the container or bin must be made of. FAR 121.285 requires the bin to be of material that is at least flame, not flash, resistant.

19.
8041. Which is a requirement governing the carriage of carry-on baggage?

A—All carry-on baggage must be restrained so that its movement is prevented during air turbulence.
B—Carry-on baggage must be stowed under the seat in front of the owner.
C—Pieces of carry-on baggage weighing more than 10 pounds must be carried in an approved rack or bin.

Answer (A) is correct (8041). *(FAR 135.87)*
All carry-on baggage must be restrained so that its movement is prevented during air turbulence.
Answer (B) is incorrect because there is no FAR requirement that carry-on baggage be stowed under the seat in front of the owner. Answer (C) is incorrect because there is no FAR requirement that carry-on baggage weighing more than 10 lb. be carried in an approved rack or bin.

20.
8042. If carry-on baggage or cargo is carried in the passenger compartment, it must be

A—stowed ahead of the foremost seated passengers and secured by approved means.
B—placed in an approved rack, bin, or compartment installed in the aircraft.
C—so located that it does not obstruct the access to, or the use of, any required emergency or regular exit.

Answer (C) is correct (8042). *(FAR 135.87)*
If carry-on baggage is not carried in an approved rack, bin, or compartment installed in the aircraft, it must be located so that is does not obstruct the access to, or the use of, any required emergency or regular exit.
Answer (A) is incorrect because there is no FAR requirement that carry-on baggage be stowed ahead of the foremost seated passengers. Answer (B) is incorrect because carry-on baggage does not have to be placed in an approved rack, bin, or compartment in the aircraft if it is carried in accordance with other specified conditions.

21.
8039. In a cargo-only operation, cargo must be loaded

A—so that it does not obstruct the aisle between the crew and cargo compartments.
B—in such a manner that at least one emergency or regular exit is available to all occupants.
C—in such a manner that at least one emergency or regular exit is available to all crewmembers, if an emergency occurs.

Answer (B) is correct (8039). *(FAR 135.87)*
In a cargo-only operation, cargo must be loaded so that at least one emergency or regular exit is available to provide all occupants of the aircraft a means of unobstructed exit from the aircraft if an emergency occurs.
Answer (A) is incorrect because cargo must be loaded so that it does not obstruct the aisle between the crew and passenger, not cargo, compartments in a passenger-carrying flight, not in a cargo-only operation. Answer (C) is incorrect because access to at least one emergency or regular exit must be available to all occupants, not just crewmembers, if an emergency occurs.

135.89 Pilot Requirements: Use of Oxygen

22.
8056. At altitudes above 10,000 feet through 12,000 feet MSL, each pilot of an unpressurized airplane must use supplemental oxygen for that part of the flight that is of a duration of more than

A—20 minutes.
B—30 minutes.
C—45 minutes.

Answer (B) is correct (8056). *(FAR 135.89)*
Each pilot of an unpressurized aircraft shall use oxygen continuously when flying at altitudes above 10,000 ft. MSL through 12,000 ft. MSL for that part of the flight at those altitudes that is of more than 30 min. duration.
Answer (A) is incorrect because, for that part of the flight that exceeds 30, not 20, min. in duration from 10,000 ft. to 12,000 ft. MSL, oxygen is required. Answer (C) is incorrect because, for that part of the flight that exceeds 30, not 45, min. in duration from 10,000 ft. to 12,000 ft. MSL, oxygen is required.

23.
8023. Which is a pilot requirement for oxygen?

A—Each pilot of a pressurized aircraft operating at FL 180 and above shall have an approved quick-donning type oxygen mask.
B—On pressurized aircraft requiring a flight crew of two pilots, both shall continuously wear oxygen masks whenever the cabin pressure altitude exceeds 12,000 feet MSL.
C—On unpressurized aircraft, flying above 12,000 feet MSL, pilots shall use oxygen continuously.

Answer (C) is correct (8023). *(FAR 135.89)*
On unpressurized aircraft, each pilot must use oxygen continuously when flying above 12,000 ft. MSL.
Answer (A) is incorrect because there is no FAR requirement that a pressurized aircraft operating at FL 180 and above have an approved quick-donning-type oxygen mask for each pilot. Answer (B) is incorrect because, on pressurized aircraft requiring a flight crew of two pilots, both must use oxygen continuously, not just wear oxygen masks, whenever the cabin pressure altitude exceeds 12,000 ft. MSL.

24.
8022. Which is a requirement for pilot use of oxygen in a pressurized airplane?

A—The pilot at the controls shall use oxygen continuously any time the cabin pressure altitude is more than 12,000 feet MSL.
B—At FL 250 and above, each pilot shall have an approved quick-donning oxygen mask.
C—At FL 250 and above the pilot at the controls must have an approved oxygen mask any time the other pilot is away from the duty station.

Answer (A) is correct (8022). *(FAR 135.89)*
Each pilot of a pressurized airplane must use oxygen continuously anytime the airplane is operated at a cabin pressure altitude above 12,000 ft. MSL. At cabin pressure altitudes above 10,000 ft. MSL through 12,000 ft. MSL, oxygen must be used continuously for flights in excess of 30 min. duration at those cabin pressure altitudes.
Answer (B) is incorrect because there is no FAR requirement that each pilot have an approved quick-donning oxygen mask when operating a pressurized airplane at FL 250 and above. Answer (C) is incorrect because, if one pilot leaves a pilot duty station of an aircraft at altitudes above, not at, FL 250, the remaining pilot must put on and use, not just have, an approved oxygen mask until the other pilot returns to the pilot duty station.

25.
8055. The two pilot stations of a pressurized aircraft are equipped with approved quick-donning oxygen masks. What is the maximum altitude authorized if one pilot is not wearing an oxygen mask and breathing oxygen?

A—41,000 feet MSL.
B—35,000 feet MSL.
C—25,000 feet MSL.

Answer (B) is correct (8055). *(FAR 135.89)*
The maximum altitude authorized if one pilot at the controls is not wearing an oxygen mask and breathing oxygen in a pressurized aircraft equipped with quick-donning oxygen masks for both pilot stations is 35,000 ft. MSL.
Answer (A) is incorrect because at 41,000 ft. at least one pilot at the controls must wear, secured and sealed, an oxygen mask that either supplies oxygen at all times or automatically supplies oxygen whenever the cabin pressure altitude exceeds 12,000 ft. MSL. Answer (C) is incorrect because 25,000 ft. MSL is the maximum altitude authorized if one pilot at the controls is not wearing an oxygen mask in an aircraft that does not have quick-donning oxygen masks for both pilot stations.

26.
8021. Above which altitude/flight level must at least one of the two pilots, at the controls of a pressurized aircraft (with quick-donning masks) wear a secured and sealed oxygen mask?

A—FL 300.
B—FL 350.
C—FL 250.

Answer (B) is correct (8021). *(FAR 135.89)*
Whenever a pressurized aircraft equipped with quick-donning masks is operated above FL 350, at least one of the two pilots at the controls must wear a secured and sealed oxygen mask that either supplies oxygen at all times or automatically supplies oxygen whenever the cabin pressure altitude exceeds 12,000 ft. MSL.
Answer (A) is incorrect because at least one of the two pilots at the controls of a pressurized aircraft, equipped with quick-donning masks, must wear a secured and sealed oxygen mask above FL 350, not FL 300. Answer (C) is incorrect because FL 250 is the maximum altitude/flight level above which at least one of the two pilots of a pressurized aircraft must wear a secured and sealed oxygen mask, if the aircraft is not equipped with quick-donning masks.

27.
8020. Which is a requirement for flight crew use of oxygen masks in a pressurized cabin airplane?

A—Both pilots at the controls shall use oxygen masks above FL 350.
B—At altitudes above 25,000 feet MSL, if one pilot leaves the pilot duty station, the remaining pilot at the controls shall use an oxygen mask.
C—At altitudes above FL 250, one of the two pilots at the controls shall use an oxygen mask continuously.

Answer (B) is correct (8020). *(FAR 135.89)*
If one pilot leaves the duty station of a pressurized airplane when operating at altitudes above 25,000 ft. MSL, the remaining pilot at the controls must put on and use an approved oxygen mask until the other pilot returns to the pilot duty station of the airplane.
Answer (A) is incorrect because at least one pilot, not both pilots, must use an oxygen mask above FL 350. Answer (C) is incorrect because one pilot is required to use an oxygen mask continuously above FL 250 only if the other pilot leaves the duty station.

135.91 Oxygen for Medical Use by Passengers

28.
8024. Which requirement applies when oxygen is stored in liquid form?

A—Smoking is not permitted within 50 feet of stored liquid oxygen.
B—Liquified oxygen is a hazardous material and must be kept in an isolated storage facility.
C—The equipment used to store liquid oxygen must be covered in the certificate holder's approved maintenance program.

Answer (C) is correct (8024). *(FAR 135.91)*
When medical oxygen is stored in the form of a liquid, the equipment must have been under the certificate holder's approved maintenance program since it was purchased new or since the storage container was last purged.
Answer (A) is incorrect because smoking is not permitted within 10 ft., not 50 ft., of oxygen storage and use. Answer (B) is incorrect because liquified oxygen can be carried aboard airplanes and used for medical reasons if in compliance with FAR 135.91.

29.
8025. Which is a condition that must be met when a person is administered medical oxygen in flight?

A—The distance between a person using medical oxygen and any electrical unit must not be less than 5 feet.
B—A person using oxygen equipment must be seated to avoid restricting access to, or use of, any required exit.
C—A person being administered oxygen must be monitored by equipment that displays and records pulse and respiration.

Answer (B) is correct (8025). *(FAR 135.91)*
When a person is administered medical oxygen in flight, the equipment must be stowed and each person using the equipment must be seated so as not to restrict access to, or use of, any required emergency or regular exit or the aisle in the passenger compartment.
Answer (A) is incorrect because there is no provision for distance from electrical units during medical oxygen use. Answer (C) is incorrect because displaying and recording pulse and respiration data during administration of medical oxygen is not required.

30.
8030. Which is a requirement regarding the carriage and operation of oxygen equipment for medical use by passengers?

A—No person may smoke within 10 feet of oxygen storage and dispensing equipment.
B—When oxygen equipment is used for the medical treatment of a patient, the rules pertaining to emergency exit access are waived.
C—No person may connect oxygen bottles or any other ancillary equipment until all passengers are aboard the aircraft and seated.

Answer (A) is correct (8030). *(FAR 135.91)*
No person may smoke and no certificate holder may allow any person to smoke within 10 ft. of oxygen storage and dispensing equipment.
Answer (B) is incorrect because medical oxygen equipment must be used so as not to restrict access to, or use of, any required emergency or regular exit or the aisle in the passenger compartment. Answer (C) is incorrect because no certificate holder may allow any person other than a person trained in the use of medical oxygen equipment to connect or disconnect oxygen bottles or any other ancillary component while any passenger(s) is (are) aboard the aircraft.

31.
8031. If a certificate holder deviates from the provisions of regulations which pertain to medical use of oxygen by passengers, a complete report of the incident shall be sent to the FAA within

A—7 working days.
B—10 working days.
C—10 days of the deviation.

Answer (B) is correct (8031). *(FAR 135.91)*
If a certificate holder deviates from the provisions of regulations which pertain to medical use of oxygen by passengers, a report shall be sent to the appropriate FAA Flight Standards District Office within 10 working days.
Answer (A) is incorrect because the report is required in 10 working days, not 7 working days. Answer (C) is incorrect because the report is required in 10 working, not calendar, days.

135.93 Autopilot: Minimum Altitudes for Use

32.
8013. What is the lowest altitude above the terrain that an autopilot may be used during en route operations, if the Airplane Flight Manual specifies a malfunction under cruise conditions?

A—1,000 feet.
B—500 feet.
C—100 feet.

Answer (B) is correct (8013). *(FAR 135.93)*
No person may use an autopilot during en route operations at an altitude above the terrain which is less than 500 ft. or less than twice the maximum altitude loss specified in the approved *Airplane Flight Manual* or equivalent for a malfunction of the autopilot, whichever is higher.
Answer (A) is incorrect because 1,000 ft. would be correct only if the maximum altitude loss specified in the *Airplane Flight Manual* for a malfunction of the autopilot was 500 ft. Answer (C) is incorrect because the lowest altitude above the terrain at which an autopilot may be used during en route operations is 500 ft., not 100 ft.

33.
8014. The maximum altitude loss specified for malfunction of a certain autopilot under cruise conditions is 50 feet. What is the lowest altitude this autopilot may be used en route?

A—500 feet AGL.
B—550 feet AGL.
C—600 feet AGL.

Answer (A) is correct (8014). *(FAR 135.93)*
No person may use an autopilot at an altitude above the terrain which is less than 500 ft. or less than twice the maximum altitude loss specified in the approved *Airplane Flight Manual* or equivalent for a malfunction of the autopilot, whichever is higher.
Answer (B) is incorrect because the lowest the aircraft may cruise is 500 ft. AGL, not 550 ft. AGL, or twice the maximum autopilot loss, whichever is higher. Answer (C) is incorrect because the altitude loss of the autopilot doubled is not added to the minimum of 500 ft. AGL.

34.
8015. The maximum altitude loss for a particular malfunctioning autopilot under approach conditions is 55 feet. If the TDZE is 571 feet and the MDA is 1,100 feet, to which minimum altitude may you use this autopilot?

A—626 feet MSL.
B—990 feet MSL.
C—1,050 feet MSL.

Answer (C) is correct (8015). *(FAR 135.93)*

When using an instrument approach facility other than ILS, no person may use an autopilot at an altitude above the terrain that is less than 50 ft. below the approved minimum descent altitude for that procedure, or less than twice the maximum loss specified in the approved *Airplane Flight Manual* or equivalent for a malfunction of the autopilot under approach conditions, whichever is higher. Note that the MDA in the question refers to a nonprecision approach.

The aircraft is allowed to descend to the higher of two altitudes. The first minimum altitude is 50 ft. below the MDA (here 1,100 ft.), which is 1,050 ft. The second is twice the maximum altitude loss of 55 ft., which is 110 ft. AGL or 681 ft. MSL. Since 1,050 ft. MSL is greater than 681 ft. MSL, the minimum altitude for autopilot use is 1,050 ft. MSL.

Answer (A) is incorrect because 626 ft. MSL is the 571 TDZE plus 55 ft. altitude loss, which implies that the autopilot can be used until an altitude is reached from which a malfunction will result in a ground strike. Answer (B) is incorrect because 990 ft. MSL is the MDA of 1,100 less twice the maximum autopilot loss of 55 ft., which is not provided for in the FARs.

35.
8017. The maximum altitude loss for a malfunctioning autopilot without an approach coupler is 45 feet. If the MDA is 1,620 feet MSL and the TDZE is 1,294 feet, to which minimum altitude may you use the autopilot?

A—1,510 feet MSL.
B—1,339 feet MSL.
C—1,570 feet MSL.

Answer (C) is correct (8017). *(FAR 135.93)*

The aircraft is allowed to descend to the higher of two altitudes. The first minimum altitude is 50 ft. below the MDA of 1,620 ft. MSL, or 1,570 ft. MSL (1,620 – 50). The second is twice the maximum altitude loss possible in an autopilot malfunction as specified in the autopilot manual. The maximum altitude loss is 90 ft. (45 x 2). Add the 90 ft. to the touchdown zone elevation of 1,294 to get a minimum altitude number of 1,384 ft. MSL. Therefore the higher or more restrictive altitude would apply, or 1,570 ft. MSL (1,570 ft. MSL is higher than 1,384 ft. MSL).

Answer (A) is incorrect because only 50 ft. below the MDA is allowed, not 90 ft. below the MDA. Answer (B) is incorrect because 1,339 ft. MSL is only 45 ft. above the TDZE.

36.
8016. The maximum altitude loss for a malfunctioning autopilot with an approach coupler is 40 feet. To which minimum altitude may the autopilot be used during an ILS approach in less than basic VFR conditions?

A—40 feet AGL.
B—50 feet AGL.
C—80 feet AGL.

Answer (B) is correct (8016). *(FAR 135.93)*

For ILS approaches, when reported weather conditions are less than basic VFR weather conditions, no person may use an autopilot with an approach coupler at an altitude that is less than 50 ft. above the terrain or the maximum altitude loss specified in the approved *Airplane Flight Manual* or equivalent for the malfunction of the autopilot with approach coupler, whichever is higher.

Answer (A) is incorrect because the aircraft is allowed to descend to only 50 ft. AGL, not down to 40 ft. AGL (40 ft. is the maximum autopilot loss). Answer (C) is incorrect because twice the autopilot loss, 80 ft. (2 x 40 ft.) in this case, is for non-ILS approaches.

37.
8037. The altitude loss for a particular malfunctioning autopilot with an approach coupler is 60 feet. If the reported weather is below basic VFR minimums and an ILS approach using the approach coupler is to be used, what minimum altitude may be used?

A—50 feet AGL.
B—55 feet AGL.
C—60 feet AGL.

Answer (C) is correct (8037). *(FAR 135.93)*
For ILS approaches, when reported weather conditions are less than basic VFR weather conditions, no person may use an autopilot with an approach coupler at an altitude above the terrain that is less than 50 ft. above the terrain or the maximum altitude loss specified in the approved *Airplane Flight Manual* or equivalent for the malfunction of the autopilot with approach coupler, whichever is higher. In this case, the maximum altitude loss is 60 ft.
Answer (A) is incorrect because the lowest altitude is the greater of 50 ft. AGL or the maximum autopilot loss. In this case, the maximum altitude loss is 60 ft. Answer (B) is incorrect because the lowest altitude is the greater of 50 ft. AGL or the maximum autopilot loss. In this case, the maximum altitude loss is 60 ft., not 55 ft.

135.99 Composition of Flight Crew

38.
8044. What is the minimum passenger seating configuration that requires a second in command?

A—15 seats.
B—12 seats.
C—10 seats.

Answer (C) is correct (8044). *(FAR 135.99)*
No certificate holder may operate an aircraft without a second in command if that aircraft has a passenger seating configuration, excluding any pilot seat, of 10 seats or more.
Answer (A) is incorrect because, excluding any pilot seat, a second in command is required with a minimum passenger seating of 10, not 15. Answer (B) is incorrect because a second in command is required with a minimum passenger seating of 10, not 12.

39.
8036. An autopilot may not be used in place of a second in command in any aircraft

A—being operated in commuter air carrier service.
B—having a passenger seating configuration, excluding any pilot's seat, of 10 seats or more.
C—having a total seating capacity of 10 or more seats and being operated in commuter air service.

Answer (B) is correct (8036). *(FAR 135.99)*
No certificate holder may operate an aircraft without a second in command if that aircraft has a passenger seating configuration, excluding any pilot seat, of 10 seats or more. Thus, an autopilot may not be used in place of a second in command in such an aircraft.
Answer (A) is incorrect because an autopilot can be used in place of a second in command if the airplane has a passenger seating configuration, excluding any pilot seat, of less than 10 seats. This includes aircraft being operated in commuter air carrier service. Answer (C) is incorrect because an autopilot may not be used in place of a second in command of any aircraft having passenger seating, not total seating, capacity of 10 or more seats. Pilot seats are excluded from the seating configuration.

135.100 Flight Crewmember Duties

40.
8106. With regard to flight crewmember duties, which operations are considered to be in the "critical phase of flight"?

A—All ground operations involving taxi, takeoff, landing, and all other operations conducted below 10,000 feet MSL, including cruise flight.
B—Descent, approach, landing, and taxi operations, irrespective of altitudes MSL.
C—All ground operations involving taxi, takeoff, landing, and all other operations conducted below 10,000 feet, excluding cruise flight.

Answer (C) is correct (8106). *(FAR 135.100)*
No flight crewmember may perform any duties during a critical phase of flight except those duties required for the safe operation of the aircraft. The critical phases of flight include all ground operations involving taxi, takeoff, and landing, and all other flight operations conducted below 10,000 ft., except cruise flight.
Answer (A) is incorrect because the critical phases of flight include all ground operations involving taxi, takeoff, and landing, and all other operations conducted below 10,000 ft., except cruise flight. The critical phase of flight does not include cruise flight when it is conducted below 10,000 ft. Answer (B) is incorrect because the critical phases of flight include all ground operations involving taxi, takeoff, and landing, and all other operations conducted below 10,000 ft., except cruise flight.

41.
8113. Other than in cruise flight, below what altitude are non-safety related cockpit activities by flight crewmembers prohibited?

A—12,000 feet.
B—10,000 feet.
C—8,000 feet.

Answer (B) is correct (8113). *(FAR 135.100)*

No flight crewmember may perform any nonsafety-related cockpit duties during the critical phases of flight. The critical phases of flight include all ground operations involving taxi, takeoff, landing, and all other flight operations conducted below 10,000 ft., except cruise flight.

Answer (A) is incorrect because flight crewmembers are prohibited from any nonsafety-related cockpit activities below 10,000 ft., not 12,000 ft., except in cruise flight. Answer (C) is incorrect because flight crewmembers are prohibited from any nonsafety-related cockpit activities below 10,000 ft., not 8,000 ft., except in cruise flight.

135.105 Exception to Second in Command Requirement: Approval for Use of Autopilot System

42.
8035. Which is a condition that must be met by a commuter air carrier certificate holder to have an aircraft approved for operation with an autopilot system and no second in command?

A—The passenger seating configuration is 10 or more, including any pilot seat.
B—The autopilot system is capable of operating the controls to maintain flight and to maneuver the aircraft about the three axes.
C—The operation is restricted to VFR or VFR over-the-top.

Answer (B) is correct (8035). *(FAR 135.105)*

Unless two pilots are required for operations under VFR, a person may operate an aircraft without a second in command if it is equipped with an operative approved autopilot system that is capable of operating the aircraft controls to maintain flight and maneuver it about the three axes.

Answer (A) is incorrect because an autopilot system, without a second in command, may be used if the passenger seating configuration is 10 or more, excluding, not including, any pilot seat. Answer (C) is incorrect because IFR operations may take place under certain conditions, including that the pilot in command must have 100 hr. in make and model of aircraft and that the certificate holder's operations specifications authorize use of an autopilot.

43.
8034. A commuter air carrier certificate holder plans to assign a pilot as pilot in command of an aircraft having eight passenger seats to be used in passenger-carrying operations. Which experience requirement must that pilot meet if the aircraft is to be flown with an operative approved autopilot and no second in command?

A—100 hours as pilot in command in the category, class, and type.
B—50 hours and 10 landings as pilot in command in the make and model.
C—100 hours as pilot in command in the make and model.

Answer (C) is correct (8034). *(FAR 135.105)*

No certificate holder may use any person, nor may any person serve, as a pilot in command of an aircraft with an autopilot and no second in command operated by a commuter air carrier in passenger-carrying operations unless that person has at least 100 hr. pilot-in-command flight time in the make and model of aircraft to be flown and has met all other applicable requirements of FAR Part 135.

Answer (A) is incorrect because the 100 hr. must be in the make and model of aircraft to be flown, not in the category, class, and type. Answer (B) is incorrect because 100 hr., not 50 hr., of flight time must be in the make and model of aircraft. The number of landings, or combination of flight hours and landings, is not specified.

135.107 Flight Attendant Crewmember Requirement

44.
8026. A flight attendant crewmember is required on aircraft having a passenger seating configuration, excluding any pilot seat, of

A—15 or more.
B—19 or more.
C—20 or more.

Answer (C) is correct (8026). *(FAR 135.107)*

No certificate holder may operate an aircraft that has a passenger seating configuration, excluding any pilot seat, of more than 19 (i.e., 20 or more) unless there is a flight attendant crewmember on board the aircraft.

Answer (A) is incorrect because aircraft with more than 19 seats, not 15, excluding any pilot seat, is the requirement for a flight attendant. Answer (B) is incorrect because the flight attendant requirement specifies "more than 19" not "19 or more."

135.115 Manipulation of Controls

45.
8018. Which person, other than the second in command, may the pilot in command permit to manipulate the flight controls?

A—A member of the National Transportation Safety Board who holds a pilot certificate appropriate for the aircraft.
B—An authorized FAA safety representative who is qualified in the aircraft, and is checking flight operations.
C—A pilot employed by an engineering firm who is authorized by the certificate holder to conduct flight tests.

Answer (B) is correct (8018). *(FAR 135.115)*
No pilot in command may allow any person to manipulate the flight controls of an aircraft during flight conducted under FAR Part 135, nor may any person manipulate the controls during such flight, unless that person is

1. A pilot employed by the certificate holder and qualified in the aircraft; or
2. An authorized FAA safety representative who has the permission of the pilot in command, is qualified in the aircraft, and is checking flight operations.

Answer (A) is incorrect because only a pilot qualified in the aircraft and employed by the certificate holder, not a member of the NTSB, may manipulate the controls. Answer (C) is incorrect because flight checks by an engineering firm may be done under FAR Part 91, not under FAR Part 135 operations.

135.117 Briefing of Passengers before Flight

46.
8028. Before takeoff, the pilot in command of an aircraft carrying passengers shall ensure that all passengers have been orally briefed on the normal and emergency use of oxygen

A—if the flight involves operations above 12,000 feet MSL.
B—regardless of the altitude at which the flight will operate.
C—if the flight involves operations at or above 12,000 feet MSL for more than 30 minutes.

Answer (A) is correct (8028). *(FAR 135.117)*
Before each takeoff, each pilot in command of an aircraft carrying passengers must ensure that all passengers have been orally briefed on the normal and emergency use of oxygen if the flight involves operations above 12,000 ft. MSL.
Answer (B) is incorrect because the pilot in command must ensure that all passengers have been orally briefed on the normal and emergency use of oxygen before a flight involving operations above 12,000 ft. MSL, not before any flight. Answer (C) is incorrect because the pilot in command must ensure that all passengers have been orally briefed on the normal and emergency use of oxygen if the flight involves operations above 12,000 ft. MSL, regardless of the amount of time above 12,000 ft. MSL.

47.
8027. Before each takeoff, the pilot in command of an aircraft carrying passengers shall ensure that all passengers have been orally briefed on the

A—location of normal and emergency exits, oxygen masks, and life preservers.
B—use of safety belts, location and operation of fire extinguishers, and smoking.
C—use of seatbelts, smoking, and location and use of survival equipment.

Answer (B) is correct (8027). *(FAR 135.117)*
Before each takeoff, each pilot in command of an aircraft carrying passengers shall ensure that all passengers have been orally briefed on

1. Smoking, which is generally not permitted
2. Use of safety belts
3. The placement of seat backs in an upright position before takeoff and landing
4. The location and means for opening the passenger entry door and emergency exits
5. The location of survival equipment
6. Ditching procedures and the use of required flotation equipment if the flight involves extended overwater operation
7. The normal and emergency use of oxygen if the flight involves operations above 12,000 ft. MSL
8. The location and operation of fire extinguishers

Answer (A) is incorrect because oxygen mask and life preserver information is required only in flight above 12,000 ft. MSL and during extended overwater operations. Answer (C) is incorrect because there is no requirement for orally briefing the passengers on the use of survival equipment.

48.
8029. The oral before flight briefing required on passenger-carrying aircraft shall be

A—supplemented by an actual demonstration of emergency exit door operation by a crewmember.
B—presented by the pilot in command or another flight crewmember, as a crewmember demonstrates the operation of the emergency equipment.
C—conducted by a crewmember or the pilot in command and supplemented by printed cards for the use of each passenger.

Answer (C) is correct (8029). *(FAR 135.117)*

The oral briefing shall be given by the pilot in command or a crewmember. The briefing shall be supplemented by printed cards, which must be carried in the aircraft in locations convenient for the use of each passenger.

Answer (A) is incorrect because there is no requirement to demonstrate the emergency door operation. Only a verbal description of the location and operation of the passenger entry door and emergency exits is required. Answer (B) is incorrect because there is no requirement to demonstrate the operation of the emergency equipment.

135.119 Prohibition against Carriage of Weapons

49.
8033. Who may be allowed to carry a deadly weapon on board an aircraft operated under FAR Part 135?

A—Official bodyguards attached to foreign legations.
B—Crewmembers and/or others authorized by the certificate holder.
C—Employees of a municipality or a state, or of the United States.

Answer (B) is correct (8033). *(FAR 135.119)*

No person may, while on board an aircraft operated under FAR Part 135, carry on or about that person a deadly or dangerous weapon, either concealed or unconcealed, except crewmembers and other persons authorized by the certificate holder to carry arms.

Answer (A) is incorrect because official bodyguards attached to foreign legations are not exempted from the prohibition against the carriage of a deadly weapon on board an aircraft operating under FAR Part 135. Answer (C) is incorrect because only those employees of a municipality, a state, or the U.S. authorized to carry arms may be allowed to carry a deadly weapon, not any employee.

5.3 AIRCRAFT AND EQUIPMENT

135.149 Equipment Requirements: General

50.
8053. What aircraft operating under FAR Part 135 are required to have a third gyroscopic bank-and-pitch indicator installed?

A—All airplanes that are turbojet powered.
B—All multiengine airplanes that require a two pilot flight crew.
C—All turbine powered aircraft having a passenger seating capacity of 30 seats or more.

Answer (A) is correct (8053). *(FAR 135.149)*

No person may operate a turbojet aircraft unless a third gyroscopic bank-and-pitch indicator is installed.

Answer (B) is incorrect because all turbojet aircraft, not only those that require a two-pilot flight crew, are required to have a third gyroscopic bank-and-pitch indicator. Answer (C) is incorrect because only turbojet aircraft, not all airplanes having a passenger seating capacity of 30 or more, are required to have a third gyroscopic bank-and-pitch indicator.

51.
8054. In airplanes where a third gyroscopic bank-and-pitch indicator is required, that instrument must

A—continue reliable operation for at least 30 minutes after the output of the airplane's electrical generating system falls below an optimum level.
B—be operable by a selector switch which may be actuated from either pilot station.
C—continue reliable operation for a minimum of 30 minutes after total failure of the electrical generating system.

Answer (C) is correct (8054). *(FAR 135.149)*

When a third gyroscopic bank-and-pitch indicator is required, that instrument must continue reliable operation for a minimum of 30 min. after total failure of the electrical generating system.

Answer (A) is incorrect because 30 min. of reliable operation is required of the third gyroscopic attitude indicator in turbojets after a total failure of the aircraft's electrical generating system, not when the system drops below an optimal level. Answer (B) is incorrect because the third (backup) gyroscopic attitude indicator in a turbojet must be automatically switched to the emergency power source after total electrical system failure. Manual switching is not allowed.

135.150 Public Address and Crewmember Interphone Systems

52.
8048. Which aircraft must be equipped with an approved public address and crewmember interphone system?

A—All turbine-engine-powered aircraft having a seating configuration of more than 19 seats.
B—Aircraft having a passenger seating configuration, excluding any pilot seat, of more than 19 seats.
C—Multiengine aircraft having a passenger seating configuration of 10 seats or more.

Answer (B) is correct (8048). *(FAR 135.150)*
All aircraft having a passenger seating configuration of more than 19 seats (excluding any pilot seat) are required to be equipped with an approved public address and crewmember interphone system.
Answer (A) is incorrect because the requirement for a public address and crewmember interphone system is based on passenger seating, excluding any pilot seat, not the total airplane seating configuration. Answer (C) is incorrect because passenger seating of 10 seats or more requires a second in command, not a public address system.

53.
8792. The crewmember interphone system on a large turbojet-powered airplane, provides a means of two-way communications between ground personnel and at least one of two flight crewmembers in the pilot compartment, when the aircraft is on the ground. The interphone station for use by ground personnel must be located so that those using the system from that station

A—are always visible from within the airplane.
B—are able to avoid the intake areas of the engines.
C—may avoid visible detection from within the airplane.

Answer (C) is correct (8792). *(FAR 135.150)*
When a large turbojet-powered airplane is on the ground, the crewmember interphone system provides a means of two-way communication between ground personnel and at least one of two flight crewmembers in the pilot compartment. The interphone station for use by ground personnel must be located so that those using the system from that station may avoid visible detection from within the airplane.
Answer (A) is incorrect because the interphone system for ground personnel use must be located to avoid visible detection, not be visible, from within the airplane. Answer (B) is incorrect because the interphone station for ground personnel use must be located to avoid visible detection from within the airplane, not to avoid the intake areas of the engines.

135.151 Cockpit Voice Recorders

54.
8046. An approved cockpit voice recorder is required equipment in

A—large turbine-powered airplanes having a maximum passenger capacity of 20 or more seats.
B—multiengine, turbine-powered airplanes having a passenger seating configuration of 20 or more seats.
C—all aircraft operated in commuter air carrier service having a passenger seating configuration of 20 seats or more.

Answer (B) is correct (8046). *(FAR 135.151)*
No person may operate a multiengine, turbine-powered airplane having a passenger seating configuration of 20 or more seats unless it is equipped with an approved cockpit voice recorder.
Answer (A) is incorrect because a cockpit voice recorder is required in multiengine, turbine-powered airplanes, not only large turbine-powered airplanes, having a maximum passenger seating capacity of 20 or more seats. Answer (C) is incorrect because a cockpit voice recorder is required in multiengine, turbine-powered airplanes, not in all aircraft operated in commuter air carrier service, having a passenger seating configuration of 20 or more seats.

55.
8833. Information recorded during normal operation of a cockpit voice recorder in a multiengine turbine-powered airplane

A—may all be erased or otherwise obliterated except for the last 30 minutes.
B—may all be erased or otherwise obliterated except for the last 30 minutes prior to landing.
C—may all be erased, prior to each flight, unless the NTSB has requested that it be kept for 60 days.

Answer (A) is correct (8833). *(FAR 135.151)*
Information recorded during normal operation of a cockpit voice recorder in a multiengine turbine-powered airplane (having a seating configuration of 20 or more seats) may all be erased or otherwise obliterated except for the last 30 min.
Answer (B) is incorrect because information recorded may be erased or otherwise obliterated except for the last 30 min., not the last 30 min. prior to landing. Answer (C) is incorrect because information recorded may be erased or otherwise obliterated except for the last 30 min., not prior to each flight.

56.
8045. During which time period must a required voice recorder of a passenger-carrying airplane be continuously operated?

A—From the beginning of taxi to the end of the landing roll.
B—From engine start at departure airport to engine shutdown at landing airport.
C—From the use of the checklist before the flight to completion of the final check at the end of the flight.

Answer (C) is correct (8045). *(FAR 135.151)*
Cockpit voice recorders must be operated continuously from the use of the checklist before the flight to completion of the final checklist at the end of the flight.
Answer (A) is incorrect because the requirement is from the use of the checklist before the flight, not the beginning of taxi, to the completion of the final checklist, not the end of the landing roll. Answer (B) is incorrect because, prior to the engine start, a pre-start checklist is usually required, and after engine shutdown, a final check is usually required.

57.
8047. Information recorded during normal operations by a required cockpit voice recorder

A—must be erased or obliterated, except for the last 30 minutes.
B—may be erased or obliterated, only once each flight.
C—may be erased or obliterated, except the last 30 minutes.

Answer (C) is correct (8047). *(FAR 135.151)*
Information recorded during normal operations by a required cockpit voice recorder may be erased or obliterated, except for the last 30 min.
Answer (A) is incorrect because the information recorded may, not must, be erased or obliterated, except for the last 30 min. Answer (B) is incorrect because the information recorded may be erased or obliterated, except for the last 30 min., not only once each flight.

<u>135.153 Ground Proximity Warning System</u>

58.
8069. In which airplanes is a ground proximity warning system required?

A—All airplanes having a passenger seating configuration, excluding any pilot seat, of 10 seats or more.
B—Turbine-powered airplanes having a passenger seating configuration, excluding any pilot seat, of 10 seats or more.
C—Turbine-powered aircraft having a passenger seating configuration, including any pilot seat, of 10 seats or more.

Answer (B) is correct (8069). *(FAR 135.153)*
No person may operate a turbine-powered airplane having a passenger seating configuration, excluding any pilot seat, of 10 seats or more, unless it is equipped with a ground proximity warning system or a system that conveys warnings of excessive closure rates with the terrain and any deviations below glide slope by visual and audible means.
Answer (A) is incorrect because only a turbine-powered airplane, not a reciprocating airplane, is required to have a ground proximity warning system if it has 10 passenger seats or more. Answer (C) is incorrect because pilot seats are excluded, not included, in the number of seats.

59.
8070. When a ground proximity warning system is required under FAR Part 135, it must

A—convey warnings of any deviation below glide slope and of excessive closure rate with the terrain.
B—convey warnings for excessive closure rates with the terrain but not for deviation from an ILS glide slope.
C—alert the pilot by an audible and visual warning signal when deviation above or below glide slope occurs.

Answer (A) is correct (8070). *(FAR 135.153)*
No person may operate a turbine-powered airplane having a passenger seating configuration, excluding any pilot seat, of 10 seats or more, unless it is equipped with a ground proximity warning system or a system that conveys warnings of excessive closure rates with the terrain and any deviations below glide slope by visual and audible means.
Answer (B) is incorrect because the ground proximity warning system must warn the pilot of both excessive closure rates with the terrain and any deviations below glide slope. Answer (C) is incorrect because the ground proximity warning system must alert the pilot by an audible and visual warning signal of excessive closure rates with the terrain and any deviations below, not above, the glide slope.

60.
8071. When a ground proximity warning system is required, it must

A—apply corrective control pressure when deviation below glide slope occurs.
B—incorporate a means of alerting the pilot when a system malfunction occurs.
C—incorporate a backup feature that activates automatically upon total failure of the aircraft's electrical generating system.

Answer (B) is correct (8071). *(FAR 135.153)*
A ground proximity warning system must have a means of alerting the pilot when a malfunction occurs in the system.
Answer (A) is incorrect because there is no requirement for auto-flight or autopilot connection to the ground proximity warning system. However, a means for alerting the pilot when a malfunction occurs is mandated by the regulation. Answer (C) is incorrect because no backup feature is required. Electrical failure does not mean that the airplane is too close to the ground or below the glide slope.

135.157 Oxygen Equipment Requirements

61.
8072. A pressurized airplane being operated at FL 330 can descend safely to 15,000 feet MSL in 3.5 minutes. What oxygen supply must be carried for all occupants other than the pilots?

A—60 minutes.
B—45 minutes.
C—30 minutes.

Answer (C) is correct (8072). *(FAR 135.157)*
Pressurized aircraft above 15,000 ft. MSL require oxygen availability to each occupant of the aircraft, other than the pilots, for 1 hr. unless, at all times during flight above that altitude, the aircraft can safely descend to 15,000 ft. MSL within 4 min., in which case only a 30-min. supply is required.
Answer (A) is incorrect because 1 hr. of oxygen for each passenger is required if a descent to 15,000 ft. MSL cannot be made within 4 min. Answer (B) is incorrect because there is no 45-min. time period specified with respect to oxygen supply under FAR Part 135.

62.
8080. The oxygen requirements for occupants of a pressurized airplane operated at altitudes above FL 250 is dependent upon the airplane's ability to descend safely to an altitude of

A—10,000 feet MSL in 4 minutes.
B—12,000 feet MSL at a minimum rate of 2,500 ft/min.
C—15,000 feet MSL in 4 minutes.

Answer (C) is correct (8080). *(FAR 135.157)*
Pressurized aircraft above 15,000 ft. MSL require oxygen availability to each occupant of the aircraft, other than the pilots, for 1 hour unless, at all times during flight above that altitude, the aircraft can safely descend to 15,000 ft. MSL within 4 min., in which case only a 30-min. supply is required.
Answer (A) is incorrect because the descent requirement is to 15,000 ft. MSL, not 10,000 ft. MSL, in 4 min. Answer (B) is incorrect because the requirement calls for a descent to be made to 15,000 ft. MSL, not 12,000 ft. MSL, in 4 min. A minimum descent rate is not specified.

63.
8074. Between what altitudes must oxygen be available to at least 10 percent of the occupants, in an unpressurized airplane, other than the pilots?

A—Above 12,000 feet through 16,000 feet MSL, for any time period.
B—Above 10,000 feet through 15,000 feet MSL, if flight at those altitudes is of more than a 30-minute duration.
C—10,000 feet to 15,000 feet MSL, if flight at those altitudes is of more than a 30-minute duration.

Answer (B) is correct (8074). *(FAR 135.157)*
At altitudes above 10,000 ft. through 15,000 ft. MSL, oxygen dispensers and oxygen must be available for at least 10% of the occupants of an unpressurized aircraft, other than the pilots, for that part of the flight at those altitudes that is of more than 30 min. duration.
Answer (A) is incorrect because oxygen must be available to at least 10% of the occupants in an unpressurized airplane, other than the pilots, from above 10,000 ft. MSL through 15,000 ft. MSL, not from above 12,000 ft. MSL through 16,000 ft. MSL, if flight at those altitudes is of more than a 30-min. duration, not of any duration. Answer (C) is incorrect because oxygen must be available to at least 10% of the occupants in an unpressurized airplane, other than the pilots, from above, not at, 10,000 ft. MSL through 15,000 ft. MSL, if flight at those altitudes is of more than a 30-min. duration.

64.
8081. An unpressurized aircraft with 20 occupants other than the pilots will be cruising at 14,000 feet MSL for 25 minutes. For how many, if any, of these occupants must there be an oxygen supply?

A—Five.
B—Two.
C—None.

Answer (C) is correct (8081). *(FAR 135.157)*
At altitudes above 10,000 ft. through 15,000 ft. MSL, oxygen dispensers and oxygen must be available for at least 10% of the occupants of an unpressurized aircraft, other than the pilots, for that part of the flight at those altitudes that is of more than 30 min. duration. This flight is only 25 min. in length.
Answer (A) is incorrect because no oxygen supply is required for flight between 10,000 ft. MSL and 15,000 ft. MSL for 30 min. or less. Answer (B) is incorrect because an oxygen supply for two occupants is the minimum requirement for more than 30, not 25, min. at 14,000 ft. MSL.

65.
8073. At what altitude, in an unpressurized airplane, must all passengers be supplied oxygen?

A—Above 12,000 feet MSL.
B—Above 14,000 feet MSL.
C—Above 15,000 feet MSL.

Answer (C) is correct (8073). *(FAR 135.157)*
Above 15,000 ft. MSL, oxygen must be supplied to all passengers in an unpressurized aircraft.
Answer (A) is incorrect because, from 10,000 ft. MSL through 15,000 ft. MSL, oxygen is required for at least 10%, not all, of the passengers if the flight is more than 30 min. in duration. Answer (B) is incorrect because only in flight at 14,000 ft. MSL for more than 30 min. is oxygen required for at least 10%, not all, of the passengers.

135.159 Equipment Requirements: Carrying Passengers under VFR at Night or under VFR Over-the-Top Conditions

66.
8808. No person may operate an aircraft under 14 CFR Part 135, carrying passengers under VFR at night, unless

A—each flight crewmember has a flashlight having at least two size "D" batteries or the equivalent.
B—it is equipped with a flashlight having at least two size "D" cells or the equivalent.
C—each crewmember has a flashlight having at least two size "D" cells and a spare bulb.

Answer (B) is correct (8808). *(FAR 135.159)*
No person may operate an aircraft carrying passengers under VFR at night, unless it is equipped with a flashlight having at least two size "D" batteries or the equivalent.
Answer (A) is incorrect because only one flashlight having at least two size "D" batteries or the equivalent is required in the airplane, not one flashlight for each flight crewmember. Answer (C) is incorrect because only one flashlight is required in the airplane, not one flashlight for each crewmember, and there is no requirement for a spare bulb.

135.167 Emergency Equipment: Extended Overwater Operations

67.
8079. In addition to fully-equipped liferafts and life preservers, what emergency equipment must be provided during extended overwater operations?

A—One water resistant, self-buoyant, portable survival-type emergency radio transmitter for each liferaft.
B—Each aircraft must have at least one liferaft, equipped with a survival-type emergency locator transmitter.
C—One pyrotechnic signaling device for each aircraft.

Answer (B) is correct (8079). *(FAR 135.167)*
No person may operate an aircraft in extended overwater operations unless there is attached to one of the required life rafts a survival-type emergency locator transmitter.
Answer (A) is incorrect because only one, not each, life raft must be equipped with a survival-type emergency locator transmitter. Answer (C) is incorrect because a pyrotechnic signaling device is required for each life raft, not one for each aircraft.

68.
8838. What emergency equipment is required for extended overwater operations?

A—A portable survival emergency locator transmitter for each liferaft.
B—A pyrotechnic signaling device for each life preserver.
C—A life preserver equipped with a survivor locator light, for each person on the airplane.

Answer (C) is correct (8838). *(FAR 135.167)*
Each airplane being operated in extended overwater operations must have a life preserver equipped with an approved survivor locator light for each person on the airplane.
Answer (A) is incorrect because an approved survival-type emergency locator transmitter is required to be attached to only one life raft, not each life raft. Answer (B) is incorrect because a pyrotechnic signaling device is required for each life raft, not each life preserver.

69.
8840. Each aircraft being operated in extended overwater operations, must have a life preserver for each

A—aircraft occupant.
B—seat on the aircraft.
C—passenger seat, plus 10 percent.

Answer (A) is correct (8840). *(FAR 135.167)*
Each aircraft being operated in extended overwater operations must have a life preserver equipped with an approved survivor locator light for each occupant of the aircraft.
Answer (B) is incorrect because a life preserver is required for each aircraft occupant, not for each seat on the aircraft. Answer (C) is incorrect because a life preserver is required for each aircraft occupant, not for each passenger seat, plus 10%.

70.
8841. Life preservers required for extended overwater operations are stored

A—within easy reach of each passenger.
B—under each occupant seat.
C—within easy access of each seated occupant.

Answer (C) is correct (8841). *(FAR 135.167)*
Life preservers required for extended overwater operations are stored within easy access of each seated occupant.
Answer (A) is incorrect because life preservers must be within easy access, not reach, of each seated occupant, not only passengers. Answer (B) is incorrect because life preservers must be within easy access of each seated occupant, not necessarily under each occupant seat.

71.
8842. An airplane, operated by a commuter air carrier, flying in extended overwater operations must carry enough approved liferafts of a rated capacity and buoyancy to accommodate the occupants of the aircraft. Each liferaft must be equipped with

A—one approved pyrotechnic signaling device.
B—colored smoke flares and a signal mirror.
C—one fishing kit for each person the raft is rated to carry.

Answer (A) is correct (8842). *(FAR 135.167)*
An airplane, operated by a commuter air carrier, flying in extended overwater operations must carry enough approved life rafts of rated capacity and buoyancy to accommodate the occupants of the aircraft. Each life raft must be equipped with one approved pyrotechnic signaling device.
Answer (B) is incorrect because colored smoke flares are not required emergency equipment for extended overwater operations. Answer (C) is incorrect because one fishing kit for each life raft, not each person the raft is rated to carry, is required emergency equipment for extended overwater operations.

72.
8078. Which is a requirement for life preservers during extended overwater operations? Each life preserver must be equipped with

A—a dye marker.
B—an approved survivor locator light.
C—one flashlight having at least two size "D" cells or equivalent.

Answer (B) is correct (8078). *(FAR 135.167)*
No person may operate an aircraft in extended overwater operations unless it carries, installed in conspicuously marked locations easily accessible to the occupants, an approved life preserver equipped with an approved survivor locator light for each occupant of the aircraft. The life preserver must be easily accessible to each seated occupant.
Answer (A) is incorrect because the dye marker is for each life raft, not each life preserver. Answer (C) is incorrect because the flashlight and associated batteries are required for each life raft, not each life preserver.

135.171 Shoulder Harness Installation at Flight Crewmember Stations

73.
8075. Which airplanes must have a shoulder harness installed at each flight crewmember station?

A—All airplanes used in commuter air service, having a passenger seating configuration of 9, excluding any pilot seat.
B—All airplanes operating under FAR Part 135, having a seating configuration for 10 persons.
C—All turbojet-powered airplanes.

Answer (C) is correct (8075). *(FAR 135.171)*
No person may operate a turbojet aircraft or an aircraft having a passenger seating configuration, excluding any pilot seat, of 10 seats or more unless it is equipped with an approved shoulder harness installed for each flight crewmember station.
Answer (A) is incorrect because the requirement is for all turbojet aircraft or aircraft having a passenger seating configuration, excluding any pilot seat, of 10 seats or more, regardless of scheduled or on-demand operations. Answer (B) is incorrect because nonturbojet-powered airplanes must have a passenger seating configuration of 10 seats or more, excluding any pilot seat, not just a total of 10 seats in the airplane.

74.
8077. Which group of aircraft must have a shoulder harness installed at each flight crewmember station?

A—Aircraft having a passenger seating configuration, excluding any pilot seat, of 10 seats or more.
B—All passenger-carrying aircraft operating under FAR Part 135, having a seating configuration for 10 persons.
C—Large aircraft being operated in commuter air service, having a passenger seating configuration of 9, excluding any pilot seat.

Answer (A) is correct (8077). *(FAR 135.171)*
No person may operate a turbojet aircraft or an aircraft having a passenger seating configuration, excluding any pilot seat, of 10 seats or more unless it is equipped with an approved shoulder harness installed for each flight crewmember station.
Answer (B) is incorrect because the requirement is for all turbojet aircraft or aircraft having 10 passenger seats or more, not all passenger-carrying aircraft operating under FAR Part 135. Answer (C) is incorrect because the requirement is for all turbojet aircraft or aircraft having 10 passenger seats or more, even if under 12,500 lb. gross takeoff weight, regardless of whether the aircraft is conducting scheduled or on-demand operations.

75.
8076. When is a pilot not required to keep the shoulder harness fastened during takeoff and landing while at a pilot station?

A—When operating an aircraft having a passenger seating configuration, excluding any pilot seat, of 10 seats or less.
B—When the pilot cannot perform the required duties with the shoulder harness fastened.
C—When serving as pilot in command or second in command of an aircraft having a total seating capacity of eight seats or less.

Answer (B) is correct (8076). *(FAR 135.171)*
Each flight crewmember occupying a station equipped with a shoulder harness must fasten the shoulder harness during takeoff and landing, except that the shoulder harness may be unfastened if the crewmember cannot perform the required duties with the shoulder harness fastened.
Answer (A) is incorrect because a flight crewmember may unfasten his/her shoulder harness to perform required duties which cannot be performed when in a shoulder harness. The number of passenger seats has no effect on this requirement. Answer (C) is incorrect because a flight crewmember may unfasten his/her shoulder harness to perform required duties which cannot be performed when in a shoulder harness. The number of passenger seats has no effect on this requirement.

135.173 Airborne Thunderstorm Detection Equipment Requirements

76.
8062. In which aircraft, or under what conditions, is airborne thunderstorm detection equipment required?

A—Large multiengine turbine-powered aircraft having a passenger seating configuration of 19 seats or more being operated by a commuter air carrier.
B—Any aircraft having a passenger seating configuration of 19 seats or more that is engaged in passenger-carrying operations under IFR or at night.
C—Small aircraft having a passenger seating configuration of 10 seats or more, excluding any pilot seat, that are engaged in passenger-carrying operations.

Answer (C) is correct (8062). *(FAR 135.173)*
No person may operate an aircraft that has a passenger seating configuration, excluding any pilot seat, of 10 seats or more in passenger-carrying operations, unless the aircraft is equipped with either approved thunderstorm detection equipment or approved airborne weather radar equipment.
Answer (A) is incorrect because the requirement is for any airplane, whether single or multiengine, piston or turbine-powered, that has a passenger seating configuration of 10, not 19, or more. Answer (B) is incorrect because the requirement is for aircraft passenger seating of 10, not 19, or more under any conditions, not just under IFR or at night.

135.175 Airborne Weather Radar Equipment Requirements

77.
8061. Airborne weather radar equipment must be installed in large transport category aircraft, in the conterminous 48 United States,

A—that are engaged in passenger-carrying operations.
B—that are engaged in either cargo or passenger-carrying operations.
C—and be fully operational, although weather forecasts indicate no hazardous conditions.

Answer (A) is correct (8061). *(FAR 135.175)*
In the conterminous 48 states, no person may operate a large transport-category aircraft in passenger-carrying operations unless approved airborne weather radar equipment is installed in the aircraft.
Answer (B) is incorrect because airborne weather radar equipment is not required for cargo operations. Answer (C) is incorrect because day-VFR flights may be conducted with the airborne weather radar inoperative, provided it is done in accordance with the operation specifications and the minimum equipment list.

135.177 Emergency Equipment Requirements for Aircraft Having a Passenger Seating Configuration of More Than 19 Passengers

78.
8059. How many, if any, approved first aid kits are required on an aircraft having a passenger seating configuration of 20 seats and a passenger load of 14?

A—None.
B—One.
C—Two.

Answer (B) is correct (8059). *(FAR 135.177)*
No person may operate an aircraft having a passenger seating configuration, excluding any pilot seat, of more than 19 seats unless it is equipped with one approved first-aid kit for treatment of injuries likely to occur in flight or in a minor accident.

Answer (A) is incorrect because one approved first-aid kit is required on each aircraft with a seating capacity of 20 passengers or more. The number of passengers aboard is irrelevant. Answer (C) is incorrect because one approved first-aid kit is required on each aircraft with a seating capacity of 20 passengers or more. The number of passengers aboard is irrelevant.

79.
8060. An aircraft has a passenger seating configuration of 19 seats, excluding any pilot seats. How many, if any, approved first aid kits are required?

A—One.
B—Two.
C—None.

Answer (C) is correct (8060). *(FAR 135.177)*
Approved first-aid kits are required only on aircraft with a seating configuration, excluding any pilot seat, of more than 19 seats.

Answer (A) is incorrect because, if the passenger seating were more than 19, one first-aid kit would be required. In this case, the configuration is 19 passenger seats, so no first-aid kit is required. Answer (B) is incorrect because, if the passenger seating were more than 19, one first-aid kit, not two, would be required. In this case, the configuration is 19 passenger seats, so no first-aid kit is required.

80.
8058. When a crash ax is required equipment on an aircraft, where should it be located?

A—In the flight crew compartment.
B—At a location inaccessible to the passengers during normal operations.
C—At a location accessible to both the crew and passengers during normal operations.

Answer (B) is correct (8058). *(FAR 135.177)*
A crash ax must be located so that it is accessible to the crew but inaccessible to passengers during normal operations.

Answer (A) is incorrect because a crash ax must be located so that it is inaccessible to passengers during normal operations but need not be in the flight crew compartment. Answer (C) is incorrect because a crash ax must be located so that it is inaccessible, not accessible, to passengers during normal operations.

135.178 Additional Emergency Equipment

81.
8834. Federal Aviation Regulations require that interior emergency lights, on aircraft having a passenger seating configuration of 20

A—operate automatically when subjected to a negative G load.
B—be operable manually from the flight crew station and a point in the passenger compartment.
C—be armed or turned on during taxiing and all flight operations.

Answer (B) is correct (8834). *(FAR 135.178)*
Aircraft having a passenger seating configuration of more than 19 seats must have interior emergency lights that must be operable manually both from the flight crew station and from a point in the passenger compartment that is readily accessible to a normal flight attendant seat.

Note: The FAA may change "seating configuration of 19 or more" to "seating configuration of more than 19" in the question in Jan./Feb. 1997.

Answer (A) is incorrect because interior emergency lights operate automatically (when properly set) in the event of failure of the primary lighting power, not when subjected to a negative G load. Answer (C) is incorrect because interior emergency lights must be armed or turned on only during taxiing, takeoff, and landing, not all flight operations (e.g., cruise flight).

135.179 Inoperable Instruments and Equipment

82.
8052. To operate an aircraft with certain equipment inoperative under the provisions of a minimum equipment list, what document authorizing it must be issued to the certificate holder?

A—Letter of Authorization from the Regional Airworthiness Office authorizing such an operation.
B—Operations specifications issued by the FAA district office having certification responsibility.
C—Letter of Authorization issued by the FAA district office having certification responsibility.

Answer (B) is correct (8052). *(FAR 135.179)*

No person may take off an aircraft with inoperable instruments or equipment installed unless the FSDO having certification responsibility has issued the certificate holder operations specifications authorizing operations in accordance with an approved minimum equipment list.

Answer (A) is incorrect because operations specifications, not a letter of authorization, must be issued by the FSDO having certification responsibility, not the Regional Airworthiness Office, to operate under the provisions of an MEL. Answer (C) is incorrect because a letter of authorization is issued for an FAR Part 91 MEL, while operations specifications are issued for an FAR Part 135 MEL.

83.
8807. Which document would constitute an approved change to the type design without requiring a recertification?

A—An approved Minimum Equipment List.
B—The Operations Specifications as approved by the Administrator.
C—A special flight permit.

Answer (A) is correct (8807). *(FAR 135.179)*

An approved minimum equipment list (MEL), as authorized by the operations specifications, constitutes an approved change to the type design without requiring recertification.

Answer (B) is incorrect because an approved MEL, not the operations specifications, constitutes an approved change to the type design without requiring a recertification. The operations specifications authorize the use of an MEL. Answer (C) is incorrect because a special flight permit is issued to allow an aircraft to make a flight, under specified conditions with inoperable instruments or equipment, to a place where maintenance can be performed.

135.181 Performance Requirements: Aircraft Operated Over-the-Top or in IFR Conditions

84.
8051. What performance is required of a multiengine airplane with the critical engine inoperative, while carrying passengers for hire in IFR weather conditions?

A—Climb at least 100 ft/min at the highest MEA of the route to be flown or 5,000 feet MSL, whichever is higher.
B—Climb at least 50 ft/min at the MEA's of the route to be flown or 5,000 feet AGL, whichever is higher.
C—Climb at least 50 ft/min at the MEA's of the route to be flown or 5,000 feet MSL, whichever is higher.

Answer (C) is correct (8051). *(FAR 135.181)*

No person may operate a multiengine aircraft carrying passengers over-the-top or in IFR conditions at a weight that will not allow it to climb, with the critical engine inoperative, at least 50 fpm when operating at the MEAs of the route to be flown or 5,000 ft., MSL, whichever is higher.

Answer (A) is incorrect because the minimum climb is 50 fpm, not 100 fpm, while operating at the MEAs of the route, not the highest MEA, or 5,000 ft. MSL, whichever is higher. Answer (B) is incorrect because the airplane must be able to climb at 50 fpm at the MEAs of the route to be flown or 5,000 ft. MSL, not 5,000 ft. AGL, whichever is higher.

135.183 Performance Requirements: Land Aircraft Operated over Water

85.
8050. Which performance requirement applies to passenger-carrying land airplanes being operated over water?

A—Multiengine airplanes must be able to climb, with the critical engine inoperative, at least 50 ft/min at 1,500 feet above the surface.
B—Single-engine airplanes must be operated at an altitude that will allow them to reach land in case of engine failure.
C—Multiengine airplanes must be able to climb, with the critical engine inoperative, at least 100 ft/min at 1,000 feet above the surface.

Answer (B) is correct (8050). *(FAR 135.183)*

No person may operate a land aircraft carrying passengers over water unless it is operated at an altitude that allows it to reach land in the case of engine failure.

Answer (A) is incorrect because a multiengine airplane must be able to climb, with the critical engine inoperative, at least 50 fpm, at 1,000 ft. above the surface, not 1,500 ft. above the surface. Answer (C) is incorrect because a multiengine airplane must be able to climb, with the critical engine inoperative, at least 50 fpm, not 100 fpm, at 1,000 ft. above the surface.

135.185 Empty Weight and Center of Gravity: Currency Requirement

86.
8049. The weight and CG of an aircraft used in air taxi service must have been calculated from those values established by actual weighing of the aircraft within what period of time?

A—Multiengine aircraft, preceding 36 calendar months.
B—Multiengine and single-engine aircraft, preceding 36 calendar months.
C—Multiengine aircraft, last 36 calendar months; single-engine, last 24 calendar months.

Answer (A) is correct (8049). *(FAR 135.185)*
No person may operate a multiengine aircraft unless the current empty weight and center of gravity are calculated from values established by actual weighing of the aircraft within the preceding 36 calendar months.
Answer (B) is incorrect because single-engine aircraft are not required to be actually weighed on a specific time schedule. Answer (C) is incorrect because single-engine aircraft are not required to be actually weighed on a specific time schedule.

87.
8067. What are the empty weight and balance currency requirements for aircraft used in air taxi service?

A—The empty weight and CG of multiengine and single-engine aircraft must have been calculated from an actual weighing within the previous 36 calendar months.
B—The empty weight and CG must have been calculated from an actual weighing within the previous 24 calendar months unless the original Airworthiness Certificate was issued within the previous 36 calendar months.
C—The empty weight and CG of multiengine aircraft must have been calculated from an actual weighing within the previous 36 calendar months.

Answer (C) is correct (8067). *(FAR 135.185)*
No person may operate a multiengine aircraft unless the current empty weight and center of gravity are calculated from values established by actual weighing of the aircraft within the preceding 36 calendar months.
Answer (A) is incorrect because single-engine aircraft are not required to be actually weighed on a specific time schedule. Answer (B) is incorrect because the empty weight and CG must have been calculated from an actual weighing within the previous 36 months, not 24 months, unless the original airworthiness certificate was issued within the preceding 36 calendar months.

5.4 VFR/IFR OPERATING LIMITATIONS AND WEATHER REQUIREMENTS

135.205 VFR: Visibility Requirements

88.
8114. What is the minimum ceiling and visibility for an airplane to operate under VFR in Class G airspace?

A—2,000-foot ceiling; 1-mile visibility.
B—2,000-foot ceiling; 1-mile flight visibility.
C—1,000-foot ceiling; 2-miles flight visibility.

Answer (C) is correct (8114). *(FAR 135.205)*
No person may operate an airplane under VFR in Class G airspace when the ceiling is less than 1,000 ft. unless flight visibility is at least 2 SM.
Answer (A) is incorrect because basic VFR weather minimums in Class G airspace are a ceiling of 1,000 ft., not 2,000 ft., and flight visibility of 2 SM, not 1 SM. Answer (B) is incorrect because basic VFR weather minimums in Class G airspace are a ceiling of 1,000 ft., not 2,000 ft., and flight visibility of 2 SM, not 1 SM.

135.213 Weather Reports and Forecasts

89.
8068. Which condition must be met to conduct IFR operations from an airport that is not at the location where weather observations are made?

A—An "Authorization Letter" permitting the procedure must be issued by the FAA district office charged with the overall inspection of the certificate holder.
B—A "Letter of Waiver" authorizing the procedure must be issued by the Administrator, after an investigation by the U.S. National Weather Service and the FSDO which find the standard of safety to be satisfactory.
C—The Administrator must issue Operations Specifications that permit the procedure.

Answer (C) is correct (8068). *(FAR 135.213)*
Weather observations made and furnished to pilots to conduct IFR operations at an airport must be taken at the airport where those IFR operations are conducted, unless the FAA issues operations specifications allowing the use of weather observations taken at a location not at the airport where the IFR operations are conducted.
Answer (A) is incorrect because the FSDO will issue operations specifications, not an authorization letter, to permit IFR operations from an airport that is not at the location where weather observations are made. Answer (B) is incorrect because the FSDO will issue operations specifications, not a letter of waiver, after an investigation by the NWS and the FSDO which find the standard of safety to be satisfactory.

135.215 IFR: Operating Limitations

90.
8057. A pilot may make an IFR departure from an airport that does not have an approved standard instrument approach procedure if

A—there is a departure alternate within 60 minutes and the weather there is above landing minimums.
B—the Administrator has issued Operations Specifications to the certificate holder approving the procedure.
C—the departure airport is within 30 minutes flying time of another airport that has an approved standard instrument approach procedure.

Answer (B) is correct (8057). *(FAR 135.215)*

The FAA may issue operations specifications to the certificate holder to allow it to depart from an airport that does not have an approved standard instrument approach procedure.

Answer (A) is incorrect because a pilot may make an IFR departure from an airport that does not have an approved standard instrument approach procedure only if it is authorized in the operations specifications, not if there is a departure alternate airport. Answer (C) is incorrect because a pilot may make an IFR departure from an airport that does not have an approved standard instrument approach procedure only if it is authorized in the operations specifications, not if there is a departure alternate airport.

135.217 IFR: Takeoff Limitations

91.
8843. No person may takeoff an aircraft under IFR from an airport that has takeoff weather minimums but that is below landing minimums unless there is an alternate airport within

A—1 hour at normal indicated airspeed of the departure airport.
B—1 hour at normal cruise speed in still air of the departure airport.
C—1 hour at normal cruise speed in still air with one engine operating.

Answer (B) is correct (8843). *(FAR 135.217)*

No person may take off an aircraft under IFR from an airport where weather conditions are at or above takeoff minimums but are below authorized IFR landing minimums unless there is an alternate airport within 1 hr. flying time, at normal cruising speed in still air.

Answer (A) is incorrect because the alternate must be within 1 hr. at normal cruise speed in still air, not at normal indicated airspeed. Answer (C) is incorrect because an alternate airport within 1 hr. at normal cruise speed in still air with one engine operating is a requirement for a two-engined airplane operating under FAR Part 121, not FAR Part 135.

92.
8065. A takeoff may not be made from an airport that is below the authorized IFR landing minimums unless

A—there is an alternate airport with the required IFR landing minimums within 60 minutes' flying time, at normal cruising speed in still air.
B—the departure airport is forecast to have the required IFR landing minimums within 1 hour.
C—there is an alternate airport with the required IFR landing minimums within 60 minutes' flying time, at normal cruising speed in still air with one engine inoperative.

Answer (A) is correct (8065). *(FAR 135.217)*

No person may take off an aircraft under IFR from an airport where weather conditions are at or above takeoff minimums but are below authorized IFR landing minimums unless there is an alternate airport within 1 hr. flying time, at normal cruising speed in still air.

Answer (B) is incorrect because the regulations state that an alternate airport is required within 1 hr. flying time. The FARs do not refer to the forecast weather at the departure airport. Answer (C) is incorrect because there is no requirement that flying time be calculated with one engine inoperative since some operations are conducted with single-engine aircraft.

135.219 IFR: Destination Airport Weather Minimums

93.
8066. A pilot may not begin an IFR operation unless the next airport of intended landing is forecast to be at or above authorized IFR landing minimums at

A—the estimated time of arrival, plus or minus 1 hour.
B—the estimated time of arrival.
C—the estimated time of arrival, plus or minus 30 minutes.

Answer (B) is correct (8066). *(FAR 135.219)*

No person may take off an aircraft under IFR or begin an IFR or over-the-top operation unless the latest weather reports or forecasts, or any combination of them, indicate that weather conditions at the estimated time of arrival at the next airport of intended landing will be at or above authorized IFR landing minimums.

Answer (A) is incorrect because the forecast or weather conditions are for estimated time of arrival, not plus or minus 1 hr. Answer (C) is incorrect because the forecast or weather conditions are for estimated time of arrival, not plus or minus 30 min.

135.221 IFR: Alternate Airport Weather Minimums

94.
8064. A pilot may not designate an airport as an alternate unless the weather reports, or forecasts, or any combination of them indicate that it will be at or above alternate airport landing minimum at the

A—time of departure.
B—estimated time of arrival, plus or minus 1 hour.
C—estimated time of arrival.

Answer (C) is correct (8064). *(FAR 135.221)*

No person may designate an alternate airport unless the weather reports or forecasts, or any combination of them, indicate that the weather conditions will be at or above authorized alternate airport landing minimums for that airport at the estimated time of arrival.

Answer (A) is incorrect because the alternate airport designation is based on the estimated arrival time, not time of departure. Answer (B) is incorrect because the alternate airport designation is based on the weather at the estimated arrival time, not plus or minus 1 hr.

135.223 IFR: Alternate Airport Requirements

95.
8088. If the weather forecasts do not require the listing of an alternate airport on an IFR flight, the airplane must carry sufficient fuel to fly to the destination airport and

A—make one missed approach and thereafter have a 45-minute reserve at normal cruising speed.
B—fly thereafter for 45 minutes at normal cruising speed.
C—fly for 45 minutes thereafter at normal cruise climb speed.

Answer (B) is correct (8088). *(FAR 135.223)*

No person may operate an aircraft in IFR conditions unless it carries enough fuel (considering weather reports or forecasts, or any combination of them) to complete the flight to the first airport of intended landing and fly after that for 45 min. at normal cruising speed, if no alternate airport is required.

Answer (A) is incorrect because there is no regulatory requirement to plan for fuel used for a missed approach. Answer (C) is incorrect because the airplane must carry enough fuel to fly to the destination airport and fly after that for 45 min. at normal cruising, not climb, speed.

96.
8089. If the weather forecasts require the listing of an alternate airport on an IFR flight, the airplane must carry enough fuel to fly to the first airport of intended landing, then to the alternate, and fly thereafter for a minimum of

A—45 minutes at normal holding speed.
B—45 minutes at normal cruise speed and then complete an approach and landing.
C—45 minutes at normal cruise speed.

Answer (C) is correct (8089). *(FAR 135.223)*

No person may operate an aircraft in IFR conditions unless it carries enough fuel (considering weather reports or forecasts, or any combination of them) to complete the flight to the first airport of intended landing, then fly to the alternate airport, and fly after that for 45 min. at normal cruising speed.

Answer (A) is incorrect because the airplane must have enough fuel to fly to the alternate airport and to fly after that for 45 min. at normal cruising, not holding, speed. Answer (B) is incorrect because there is no regulatory requirement that there should be enough fuel to complete an approach and landing after 45 min.

97.
8087. An alternate for a destination airport (circling not authorized) is not required if, for at least 1 hour before and after the ETA, the required visibility exists, and the forecast ceiling is at least

A—1,500 feet above the lowest published minimum, or 2,000 feet above the airport elevation, whichever is higher.
B—1,500 feet above the lowest MDA or 2,000 feet above the runway touchdown zone elevation, whichever is higher.
C—1,000 feet above the lowest published minimum, or 1,500 feet above the airport elevation, whichever is higher.

Answer (A) is correct (8087). *(FAR 135.223)*

If a standard instrument approach procedure for the first airport of intended landing is prescribed and, for at least 1 hr. before and after the estimated time of arrival, the appropriate weather reports or forecasts, or any combination of them, indicate that visibility for that airport is forecast to be at least 3 SM, or 2 SM more than the lowest applicable visibility minimums, whichever is the greater, for the instrument approach procedure to be used at the destination airport, no alternate landing airport is required.

If a circling instrument approach is not authorized for the destination airport and the ceiling will be at least 1,500 ft. above the lowest published minimum or 2,000 ft. above the airport elevation, whichever is higher, no alternate landing airport is required.

Answer (B) is incorrect because, if a circling approach is not authorized, the ceiling must be at least 1,500 ft. above the lowest published minimum, not necessarily the lowest MDA, or 2,000 ft. above the airport elevation, not the touchdown zone elevation. Answer (C) is incorrect because the requirement is 1,500 ft., not 1,000 ft., above the lowest published minimum altitude or 2,000 ft., not 1,500 ft., above the airport elevation.

98.
8063. Assuming the required ceiling exists, an alternate for the destination airport is not required if, for at least 1 hour before and after the ETA, the forecast visibility is at least

A—5 miles, or 3 miles more than the lowest applicable visibility minimums for the instrument approach procedure to be used, whichever is greater.
B—3 miles, or 2 miles more than the lowest applicable visibility minimums for the instrument approach procedure to be used, whichever is greater.
C—3 nautical miles, or 2 nautical miles more than the lowest applicable visibility minimums for the approach procedure to be used, whichever is greater.

Answer (B) is correct (8063). *(FAR 135.223)*
No alternate is required if the destination airport has at least one standard approach procedure and, for at least 1 hr. before and after the estimated time of arrival, the appropriate weather reports or forecasts, or any combination of them, indicate that visibility for that airport is forecast to be at least 3 SM, or 2 SM more than the lowest applicable visibility minimums, whichever is the greater, for the instrument approach procedure to be used at the destination airport.
Answer (A) is incorrect because the visibility requirement is for only 3 SM, not 5 SM, or 2 SM, not 3 SM, more than the lowest landing visibility minimums. Answer (C) is incorrect because the visibility is measured in statute miles (SM), not nautical miles (NM).

135.225 IFR: Takeoff, Approach and Landing Minimums

99.
8092. An instrument approach procedure to an airport may not be initiated unless the latest weather report issued by an authorized weather reporting facility indicates that weather conditions

A—are at or above the circling minimums for the runway the pilot intends to use.
B—are at or above the authorized IFR landing minimums for that procedure.
C—exceed the straight-in minimums for all nonprecision approaches.

Answer (B) is correct (8092). *(FAR 135.225)*
No pilot may begin an instrument approach procedure to an airport unless the latest weather report issued by the weather reporting facility at that airport indicates that weather conditions are at or above the authorized IFR landing minimums for that airport.
Answer (A) is incorrect because the approach may be initiated only if weather conditions are above the reported minimums for the intended approach. Answer (C) is incorrect because the approach may be initiated only if weather conditions are above the reported minimums for the intended approach.

100.
8086. After passing the final approach fix on a VOR approach, a weather report is received indicating the visibility is below prescribed minimums. In this situation, the pilot

A—may continue the approach and land, if at the MDA, the actual weather conditions are at least equal to the minimums prescribed for the procedure.
B—may continue the approach and land regardless of the visibility observed at the MDA, if prior to beginning the approach, the visibility was reported at or above minimums.
C—should level off and continue to fly the approach to the MAP, and execute the missed approach.

Answer (A) is correct (8086). *(FAR 135.225)*
If a pilot has begun the final approach segment (e.g., passing the final approach fix on a VOR approach) and a weather report indicates the visibility is below the prescribed minimums, the pilot may continue the approach and land if, at the MDA, the pilot finds that the actual weather conditions are at least equal to the minimums prescribed for the procedure.
Answer (B) is incorrect because, if at the MDA the weather is below published minimums, the pilot must execute a missed approach. Answer (C) is incorrect because, if at the MDA the weather conditions are at least equal to the published minimums, the pilot should continue the approach and land, not level off and continue to fly to the MAP and then execute the missed approach.

101.
8091. A pilot may not take off under IFR at a foreign airport unless the visibility is

A—1/2 mile or more above landing minimums.
B—1 mile or more and the ceiling is 500 feet or more.
C—at least 1 mile.

Answer (C) is correct (8091). *(FAR 135.225)*
Each pilot making an IFR takeoff or approach and landing at a foreign or military airport shall comply with applicable instrument approach procedures and weather minimums. In addition, no pilot may take off under IFR at that airport when the visibility is less than 1 SM.
Answer (A) is incorrect because the ½-SM visibility limit is for aircraft landing at a foreign airport, not the required takeoff visibility minimum, which is 1 SM. Answer (B) is incorrect because the requirement for taking off at a foreign airport is 1 SM visibility only. No ceiling limitations are stated.

102.
8090. At a military airport, a pilot may not take off under IFR unless the reported weather conditions indicate that the

A—visibility is at least 1 mile.
B—ceiling is at least 500 feet and the visibility is 1 mile or more.
C—airport has landing minimums.

Answer (A) is correct (8090). *(FAR 135.225)*

Each pilot making an IFR takeoff or approach and landing at a military or foreign airport shall comply with applicable instrument approach procedures and weather minimums. In addition, no pilot may take off under IFR at that airport when the visibility is less than 1 SM.

Answer (B) is incorrect because the requirement for taking off at a military airport is 1 SM visibility only. No ceiling limitations are stated. Answer (C) is incorrect because there is no requirement that the military airport have landing minimums for an IFR takeoff, unless they are required at a specific airport.

103.
8085. Which is one required condition for a pilot to take off under IFR with less-than-standard takeoff minimums at an airport where a straight-in instrument approach procedure is authorized and there is an approved weather reporting source?

A—The pilot must have at least 100 hours as pilot in command in the type airplane to be flown.
B—The certificate holder has been approved for such operation and the visibility at the time of takeoff must be at least RVR 16.
C—Wind direction and velocity must be such that a straight-in approach can be made to the runway served by the procedure.

Answer (C) is correct (8085). *(FAR 135.225)*

One required condition for a pilot to take off under IFR with less-than-standard takeoff minimums at an airport where a straight-in instrument approach procedure is authorized and there is an approved weather reporting source is that the wind direction and velocity at the time of takeoff be such that a straight-in instrument approach can be made to the runway served by the instrument approach. Other conditions are that the ground and aircraft equipment for that approach be working and that the certificate holder be approved for such operations.

Answer (A) is incorrect because the pilot must have 100 hr. as PIC in the make and model, not type, of airplane to be flown to act as PIC of a commuter air carrier that uses an autopilot in place of a second in command, not to take off under IFR with less-than-standard minimums. Answer (B) is incorrect because the only requirement for visibility is that it be equal to or better than the lowest straight-in minimum, not that it be at least RVR 16.

135.227 Icing Conditions: Operating Limitations

104.
8084. Which is an operational requirement concerning ice, snow, or frost on structural surfaces?

A—A takeoff may be with ice, snow, or frost adhering to the wings or stabilizing or control surfaces, but polished smooth, if the anti-icing and deicing equipment is operating.
B—If snow, ice, or frost is adhering to the airplane's lift or control surfaces, but polished smooth, a takeoff may be made.
C—A takeoff may not be made if ice or snow is adhering to the wings or stabilizing or control surfaces.

Answer (C) is correct (8084). *(FAR 135.227)*

No pilot may take off an aircraft that has frost, ice, or snow adhering to any propeller, windshield, wing, or stabilizing or control surface; to a power plant installation; or to an airspeed, altimeter, rate-of-climb, or flight attitude instrument system.

Answer (A) is incorrect because a takeoff may be made with frost, not ice or snow, adhering to the wings or stabilizing or control surfaces, if the frost has been polished to make it smooth. There is no requirement that the anti-icing and deicing equipment be operational. Answer (B) is incorrect because a takeoff may be made with frost, not snow or ice, adhering to the wings or stabilizing or control surfaces, if the frost has been polished smooth.

105.
9696. A pretakeoff contamination check for snow, ice or frost is required by FAR Part 135. This check is required to

A—be made within 2 minutes of starting the takeoff roll.
B—be completed within 5 minutes prior to beginning the takeoff.
C—see that the aircraft is clean, therefore, a safe takeoff can be made during the next 5 minutes.

Answer (B) is correct (9696). *(FAR 135.227)*.

A pretakeoff contamination check, which has been established by the certificate holder and approved by the FAA for the specific airplane type, is required to be completed within 5 min. prior to beginning the takeoff roll. A pretakeoff contamination check is a check to make sure the wings and control surfaces are free of frost, ice, or snow.

Answer (A) is incorrect because the pretakeoff contamination check must be completed within 5 min., not made within 2 min., prior to beginning the takeoff roll. Answer (C) is incorrect because the pretakeoff contamination check is a check of the wings and control surfaces, not of the entire aircraft, to see if they are clean of frost, ice, or snow.

5.5 FLIGHT CREWMEMBER REQUIREMENTS

135.243 Pilot in Command Qualifications

106.
8082. What are the minimum certificate and rating requirements for the pilot in command of a multiengine airplane being operated by a commuter air carrier?

A—Airline transport pilot; airplane category; multiengine class.
B—Commercial pilot; airplane category; multiengine class; instrument rating; airplane type rating, if required.
C—Airline transport pilot; airplane category; multiengine class; airplane type rating, if required.

Answer (C) is correct (8082). *(FAR 135.243)*
No certificate holder may use a person as pilot in command in passenger-carrying operations of a multiengine airplane being operated by a commuter air carrier unless that person holds an airline transport pilot certificate with appropriate category and class ratings and, if required, an appropriate type rating for that airplane.
Answer (A) is incorrect because, in addition to the category and class ratings, an aircraft type rating may be required for that airplane. Answer (B) is incorrect because, for the pilot in command of any multiengined aircraft used as a commuter air carrier, an appropriate airline transport, not a commercial, pilot certificate is required.

107.
8083. What are the minimum certificate and rating requirements for the pilot in command of a multiengine airplane in commuter air carrier service under IFR?

A—Airline transport pilot of any category; multiengine class rating.
B—Airline transport pilot; airplane category; multiengine class rating; airplane type rating, if required.
C—Commercial pilot; airplane category; multiengine class and instrument rating.

Answer (B) is correct (8083). *(FAR 135.243)*
No certificate holder may use a person as pilot in command in passenger-carrying operations of a multiengine airplane being operated by a commuter air carrier unless that person holds an airline transport pilot certificate with appropriate category and class ratings and, if required, an appropriate type rating for that airplane.
Answer (A) is incorrect because a type rating may be required for the appropriate category of aircraft being used, and the ATP must be airplane category. Answer (C) is incorrect because an appropriate airline transport, not a commercial, pilot certificate is required for the pilot in command of a commuter air carrier.

108.
8107. What are the minimum certificate and rating requirements for the pilot in command of a turbojet airplane with two engines being operated by a commuter air carrier (as defined in Part 298)?

A—Airline transport pilot; airplane category; multiengine class rating; airplane type rating, if required.
B—Airline transport pilot of any category; multiengine class rating; airplane type rating.
C—Commercial pilot; airplane category; multiengine class rating; instrument rating; airplane type rating.

Answer (A) is correct (8107). *(FAR 135.243)*
To act as pilot in command of a turbojet airplane with two engines being operated by a commuter air carrier, the PIC must have an ATP certificate with an airplane category, a multiengine class rating, and an airplane type rating, if required.
NOTE: A commuter operation is defined in FAR 119.3 as well as Part 298.
Answer (B) is incorrect because the airline transport pilot's certificate must be appropriate for the specific category (i.e., airplane vs. rotorcraft) of aircraft. Answer (C) is incorrect because, to act as pilot in command of a cargo, not passenger-carrying, turbojet, the pilot must hold a commercial pilot certificate.

135.244 Operating Experience

109.
8109. A person is acting as a pilot in command of a turbojet-powered airplane operated in passenger-carrying service by a commuter air carrier. If 10 takeoffs and landings have been accomplished in that make and basic model, which additional pilot-in-command experience meets the requirement for designation as pilot in command?

A—10 hours.
B—15 hours.
C—10 hours, and five takeoffs and landings.

Answer (B) is correct (8109). *(FAR 135.244)*
25 hr. of operating experience is required for a person to serve as pilot in command of a turbojet-powered aircraft used in passenger-carrying commuter air service. A reduction of up to 50% of the required time may be made by the substitution of one takeoff and landing for each required hour of operating experience. Since 10 takeoffs and landings have been accomplished, only 15 hr. is required (25 – 10 = 15).
Answer (A) is incorrect because 10 hr. of operating experience is required in a single-engine, not turbojet-powered, aircraft in order to serve as PIC for a commuter air carrier. Answer (C) is incorrect because only 50% of the required 25 hr. of operating experience may be substituted with takeoffs and landings. Thus 13 hr., not 10 hr., and two takeoffs and landings, not five takeoffs and landings, would meet the requirement.

110.
8103. A person is acting as pilot in command of a multiengine, turboprop-powered airplane operated in passenger-carrying service by a commuter air carrier. If eight takeoffs and landings are accomplished in that make and basic model, which additional pilot-in-command experience meets the requirement for designation as pilot in command?

A—7 hours, and two takeoffs and landings.
B—10 hours, and three takeoffs and landings.
C—10 hours, and two takeoffs and one landing.

Answer (B) is correct (8103). *(FAR 135.244)*

A minimum of 20 hr. operating experience is required for a person to act as pilot in command of a turboprop-powered airplane used in passenger-carrying service by a commuter air carrier. A maximum of 10 takeoffs and landings may be used to reduce the required experience to 10 flight hr. Therefore a minimum of 10 hr. operating experience and at least two takeoffs and landings (in addition to eight previous takeoffs and landings) are needed.

Answer (A) is incorrect because a minimum of 10 hr., not 7 hr., and two takeoffs and landings are needed to meet the requirements for designation as PIC. Answer (C) is incorrect because a minimum of 10 hr. and at least two takeoffs and two landings, not one, are needed to meet the requirements for designation as PIC.

111.
8110. A pilot's experience includes 8 hours in a particular make and basic model multiengine, turboprop airplane while acting as pilot-in-command. Which additional pilot-in-command experience meets the requirements for designation as pilot in command of that airplane when operated by a commuter air carrier in passenger-carrying service?

A—Twelve takeoffs and landings.
B—Five takeoffs and landings, and 2 hours.
C—Ten takeoffs and landings, and 2 hours.

Answer (C) is correct (8110). *(FAR 135.244)*

The pilot of a turboprop airplane must have 20 hr. of operating experience in that particular make and model of aircraft in order to serve as PIC for a commuter air carrier. A maximum reduction of 50% of this time may be made by substituting one takeoff and landing for each flight hour. In this case, a minimum of 2 additional hr. operating experience to reach 10 hr. (50% of the 20 required hr.) and 10 takeoffs and landings are required.

Answer (A) is incorrect because only 50% of the required 20 hr. may be substituted by takeoffs and landings. Thus, 10 takeoffs and landings, not 12, and 2 hr. are needed to meet the requirements for designation as PIC. Answer (B) is incorrect because 15 hr. is the experience required in a multiengine, reciprocating airplane, not a multiengine, turboprop airplane, which requires 20 hr.

112.
8108. A person is acting as pilot in command of a multiengine, reciprocating engine-powered airplane operated in passenger-carrying service by a commuter air carrier. If five takeoffs and landings have been accomplished in that make and basic model, which additional pilot-in-command experience meets the requirement for designation as the pilot in command?

A—Two takeoffs and landings, and 8 hours.
B—Five takeoffs and landings, and 5 hours.
C—Three takeoffs and landings, and 7 hours.

Answer (A) is correct (8108). *(FAR 135.244)*

15 hr. of operating experience is required for a person to serve as pilot in command of a reciprocating multiengine-powered airplane used in passenger-carrying service by a commuter air carrier. Up to 50% of these required hours may be reduced by one takeoff and landing for each required hour of operating experience. A maximum of seven takeoffs and landings may be used to reduce the required experience to 8 flight hr. Thus, two takeoffs and landings (in addition to five previous takeoffs and landings) and 8 flight hr. are needed.

Answer (B) is incorrect because an additional five takeoffs and landings would exceed the 50% of 15 hr. reduction allowed. A maximum of 7 hr. of operating experience may be substituted. Answer (C) is incorrect because an additional three takeoffs and landings would exceed the 50% of 15 hr. reduction allowed. A maximum of 7 hr. of operating experience may be substituted.

113.
8111. A person is acting as pilot in command of a single-engine airplane operated in passenger-carrying service by a commuter air carrier. If six takeoffs and landings have been accomplished in that make and basic model, which additional pilot-in-command experience meets the requirement for designation as pilot in command?

A—4 hours.
B—5 hours.
C—6 hours.

Answer (B) is correct (8111). *(FAR 135.244)*

Since 10 hr. of experience is required for a person to act as pilot in command of a single-engine airplane used in passenger-carrying service by a commuter air carrier, a maximum of five takeoffs and landings may be substituted for 5 hr. operating experience. Thus, 5 hr. (10 – 5) is required to meet the PIC requirement.

Answer (A) is incorrect because only five of the six takeoffs and landings can be substituted; thus 5 hr., not 4 hr., is needed to meet the PIC requirement. Answer (C) is incorrect because five of the six takeoffs and landings can be substituted; thus 5 hr., not 6 hr., is needed to meet the PIC requirement.

135.245 Second in Command Qualifications

114.
8105. To satisfy the instrument approach recency experience requirement, a second in command must have made at least

A—six approaches within the past 6 months; three must have been in the category aircraft to be flown.
B—six approaches within the past 6 months in any airplane, helicopter, approved instrument ground trainer, or simulator.
C—six approaches and 6 hours of instrument time within the past 6 months, in an airplane, helicopter, approved instrument ground trainer, or simulator.

Answer (B) is correct (8105). *(FAR 135.245)*

To satisfy the instrument approach recency experience requirement, a second in command must have made six approaches within the past 6 months in any airplane, helicopter, approved instrument ground trainer, or simulator.

Answer (A) is incorrect because at least 3 hr. of the required 6 hr. of instrument time, not three approaches, must be in the category of aircraft to be flown. Answer (C) is incorrect because at least 3 hr. of the required 6 hr. of instrument time must be in the category of aircraft to be flown.

135.247 Pilot Qualifications: Recent Experience

115.
8830. What is one of the requirements that must be met by a pilot in command to reestablish recency of experience?

A—At least one full stop landing must be made from a circling approach.
B—Three takeoffs and landings must be made as the sole manipulator of the controls, in the type, if a type rating is required, if not in the same category and class aircraft that the person is to serve.
C—At least one nonprecision approach must be made to the lowest minimums authorized for the certificate holder.

Answer (B) is correct (8830). *(FAR 135.247)*

No person may serve as pilot in command of an aircraft carrying passengers unless, within the preceding 90 days, that person has made three takeoffs and landings as the sole manipulator of the flight controls in an aircraft of the same category and class and, if a type rating is required, of the same type in which that person is to serve.

Answer (A) is incorrect because one of the requirements that must be met to reestablish recency of experience is three takeoffs and landings as sole manipulator of the controls, not a full stop landing from a circling approach. Answer (C) is incorrect because one of the requirements that must be met to reestablish recency of experience is three takeoffs and landings as sole manipulator of the controls, not a nonprecision approach to the lowest minimums authorized for the certificate holder.

116.
8809. For operations during the period beginning 1 hour after sunset and ending 1 hour before sunrise (as published in the Air Almanac), no certificate holder may use any person, nor may any person serve, as pilot in command of an aircraft carrying passengers unless that person has made three takeoffs and three landings, within the preceding 90 days,

A—as the sole manipulator of the flight controls in an aircraft of the same category and class and, if a type rating is required, of the same type in which that person is to serve.
B—as pilot in command of an aircraft of the same category and class and, if a type rating is required, of the same type in which that person is to serve.
C—as the sole manipulator of the flight controls in an aircraft of the same type in which that person is to serve.

Answer (A) is correct (8809). *(FAR 135.247)*

For operations during the period beginning 1 hr. after sunset and ending 1 hr. before sunrise (as published in the Air Almanac), no certificate holder may use any person, nor may any person serve, as pilot in command of an aircraft carrying passengers unless that person has made three takeoffs and three landings during that period as the sole manipulator of the flight controls in an aircraft of the same category and class and, if a type rating is required, of the same type in which that person is to serve, within the preceding 90 days.

Answer (B) is incorrect because the pilot must make the three takeoffs and three landings within the preceding 90 days as sole manipulator of the controls, not just as PIC. Answer (C) is incorrect because the three takeoffs and three landings must be in the same category and class of aircraft in which that person is to serve. The same type of aircraft means that, if a type rating is required, then the requirement must also be in the same type of aircraft.

135.253 Misuse of Alcohol

117.
8813. An employee who performs safety-sensitive functions, for a certificate holder, who has actual knowledge of an accident involving an aircraft for which he or she performed a safety-sensitive function at or near the time of the accident shall not use alcohol

A—until 4 hours after the accident.
B—within 8 hours of the accident.
C—until given a release by the NTSB or FAA.

Answer (B) is correct (8813). *(FAR 135.253)*

An employee who performs safety-sensitive functions for a certificate holder and who has actual knowledge of an accident involving an aircraft for which (s)he performed a safety-sensitive function at or near the time of the accident shall not use alcohol for 8 hr. following the accident, unless he or she has been given a post-accident test under Appendix J of FAR Part 121 or the employer has determined that the employee's performance could not have contributed to the accident.

Answer (A) is incorrect because an employee who has actual knowledge of an accident for which he or she performed a safety-sensitive function at or near the time of the accident must not use alcohol within 8 hr., not 4 hr., of the accident. Answer (C) is incorrect because an employee can use alcohol before 8 hr. if he or she has been given a post-accident test under Appendix J of FAR Part 121 or the employer, not the NTSB or FAA, has determined that the employee's performance could not have contributed to the accident.

5.6 CREWMEMBER FLIGHT TIME AND DUTY PERIOD LIMITATIONS AND REST REQUIREMENTS

135.265 Flight Time Limitations and Rest Requirements: Scheduled Operations

118.
8104. Pilot flight time limitations under FAR Part 135 are based

A—on the flight time accumulated in any commercial flying.
B—solely on flight time accumulated in air taxi operations.
C—solely on flight time accumulated during commercial flying, in the last 30 day and/or 12 month period.

Answer (A) is correct (8104). *(FAR 135.265)*

Flight time limitations under FAR Part 135 are based on the flight time accumulated during any commercial flying time.

Answer (B) is incorrect because any and all commercial flying time, such as flight instruction, is included and counted under FAR Part 135 flight time limitations. Answer (C) is incorrect because only commercial flight time, not all, is accumulated based on a 24-hr., 7-day, 30-day, and calendar-year period, not only a 30-day and 12-month period.

119.
8814. What is the maximum number of hours that a pilot may fly in 7 consecutive days as a pilot in commercial flying and as a pilot for a commuter air carrier?

A—32 hours.
B—34 hours.
C—35 hours.

Answer (B) is correct (8814). *(FAR 135.265)*

No certificate holder may schedule any flight crewmember, and no flight crewmember may accept an assignment, for flight time in scheduled operations or in other commercial flying if that crewmember's total flight time in all commercial flying will exceed 34 hr. in any 7 consecutive days.

Answer (A) is incorrect because the maximum number of hours that a pilot may fly in 7 consecutive days as a pilot in commercial flying and as a pilot for a commuter air carrier is 34 hr., not 32 hr. Answer (C) is incorrect because the maximum number of hours that a pilot may fly in 7 consecutive days as a pilot in commercial flying and as a pilot for a commuter air carrier is 34 hr., not 35 hr.

120.
8815. What is the maximum number of hours that a commuter air carrier may schedule a flight crewmember to fly in scheduled operations and other commercial flying in any calendar month?

A—100.
B—110.
C—120.

Answer (C) is correct (8815). *(FAR 135.265)*
No certificate holder may schedule any flight crewmember, and no flight crewmember may accept an assignment, for flight time in scheduled operations or in other commercial flying if that crewmember's total flight time in all commercial flying will exceed 120 hr. in any calendar month.
Answer (A) is incorrect because the maximum number of hours that a commuter air carrier may schedule a flight crewmember to fly in scheduled operations and other commercial flying is 120 hr., not 100 hr., in any calendar month. Answer (B) is incorrect because the maximum number of hours that a commuter air carrier may schedule a flight crewmember to fly in scheduled operations and other commercial flying is 120 hr., not 110 hr., in any calendar month.

5.7 CREWMEMBER TESTING REQUIREMENTS

135.297 Pilot in Command: Instrument Proficiency Check Requirements

121.
8098. A person may act as pilot in command of both type A and type B aircraft under IFR if an instrument proficiency check has been passed in

A—either type A or B since the beginning of the 12th month before time to serve.
B—type A since the beginning of the 12th month, and in type B since the beginning of the 6th month before time to serve.
C—type A since the beginning of the 12th month, and in type B since the beginning of the 24th month before time to serve.

Answer (B) is correct (8098). *(FAR 135.297)*
For instrument currency purposes, a pilot must take the instrument proficiency check required in each type of aircraft to which that pilot is assigned, in rotation, but not more than one flight check during each 6 months.
Answer (A) is incorrect because an instrument proficiency check is done every 6 months, not 12 months, and the pilot would rotate the type aircraft for each 6-month check. Answer (C) is incorrect because the required instrument proficiency check ride is valid only since the beginning of the 6th calendar month. A rotation is done every 6, not 12, months.

122.
8101. A person may not serve as pilot in command in an IFR operation unless that person has passed an

A—aircraft competency, an instrument proficiency, and auto-pilot check within the previous 6 calendar months prior to the date to serve.
B—instrument proficiency check in the airplane in which to serve, or in an approved aircraft simulator, within the previous 12 calendar months.
C—instrument proficiency check under actual or simulated IFR conditions, since the beginning of the 6th calendar month prior to the date to serve.

Answer (C) is correct (8101). *(FAR 135.297)*
No certificate holder may use a pilot, nor may any person serve, as a pilot in command of an aircraft under IFR unless, since the beginning of the 6th calendar month before that service, that pilot has passed an instrument proficiency check.
Answer (A) is incorrect because the aircraft competency and autopilot checks must have been performed within the previous 12, not 6, calendar months. Answer (B) is incorrect because the instrument proficiency check is required within the previous 6, not 12, calendar months.

123.
8100. A person is assigned as pilot in command to fly both single-engine and multiengine airplanes and has passed the initial instrument proficiency check in a multiengine airplane. Which requirement applies regarding each succeeding instrument check?

A—The instrument check must be taken every 6 calendar months in both a single-engine and a multiengine airplane.
B—The instrument check must be taken alternately in single-engine and multiengine airplanes every 6 calendar months.
C—The instrument check may be taken in either a single-engine or multiengine airplane if taken at intervals of 6 calendar months.

Answer (B) is correct (8100). *(FAR 135.297)*
If the pilot in command is assigned to pilot both single-engine and multiengine aircraft, that pilot must initially take the instrument proficiency check in a multiengine aircraft, and each succeeding check alternately in single-engine and multiengine aircraft, but not more than one flight check during each 6-month period.
Answer (A) is incorrect because, after a pilot initially takes the required instrument proficiency check in a multiengine airplane, subsequent instrument checks at 6-month intervals must be alternated between the single-engine airplane and the multiengine airplane. Answer (C) is incorrect because each succeeding instrument check must alternate between the single-engine and multiengine airplane, not be in either one.

124.
8099. A pilot in command is authorized to use an autopilot system in place of a second in command. During the instrument proficiency check, that person is required to demonstrate (without a second in command) the ability to

A—comply with complex ATC instructions with, but not without, the autopilot.
B—properly conduct air-ground communications with, but not without, the autopilot.
C—properly conduct instrument operations competently both with, and without, the autopilot.

Answer (C) is correct (8099). *(FAR 135.297)*
If the pilot in command is authorized to use an autopilot system in place of a second in command, that pilot must show, during the required instrument proficiency check, that the pilot is able (without a second in command) both with and without using the autopilot to conduct instrument operations competently.
Answer (A) is incorrect because the pilot must be able both to conduct air-ground communications and to comply with complex air traffic control instructions without, as well as with, the use of the autopilot. Answer (B) is incorrect because the pilot must be able both to conduct air-ground communications and to comply with complex air traffic control instructions without, as well as with, the use of the autopilot.

125.
8102. A pilot in command who is authorized to use an autopilot system, in place of a second in command, may take the autopilot check

A—concurrently with the instrument proficiency check, but at 12-month intervals.
B—in any aircraft appropriately equipped, providing the check is taken at 6-month intervals.
C—concurrently with the competency check, providing the check is taken at 12-month intervals.

Answer (A) is correct (8102). *(FAR 135.297)*
Each pilot taking the autopilot check must show that, while using the autopilot, the airplane can be operated as proficiently as it would be if a second in command were present to handle air-ground communications and air traffic control instructions. The autopilot check need be demonstrated only once every 12 calendar months during the required instrument proficiency check.
Answer (B) is incorrect because the instrument proficiency (and related autopilot) check must be taken in the type aircraft flown in FAR Part 135 operations, and it must be taken every 12, not 6, months. Answer (C) is incorrect because the autopilot check must be taken in conjunction with the instrument proficiency, not the competency, check every 12 months.

135.299 Pilot in Command: Line Checks: Routes and Airports

126.
8097. No certificate holder may use a person as pilot in command unless that person has passed a line check

A—since the beginning of the 12th month before serving as pilot in command.
B—since the beginning of the 6th month before serving as pilot in command.
C—within the past 6 months.

Answer (A) is correct (8097). *(FAR 135.299)*
No certificate holder may use a pilot, nor may any person serve, as a pilot in command of a flight unless, since the beginning of the 12th calendar month before that service, that pilot has passed a line check in one of the types of aircraft which that pilot is to fly.
Answer (B) is incorrect because an instrument proficiency check, not a line check, is required since the beginning of the 6th month before serving as PIC. Answer (C) is incorrect because a line check must have been passed since the beginning of the 12th month before serving as PIC, not within the past 6 months.

127.
8095. To serve as pilot in command in an IFR operation, a person must have passed a line check

A—consisting of a flight over the route to be flown, with at least three instrument approaches at representative airports, within the past 12 calendar months, in one type of aircraft which that pilot is to fly.
B—within the past 12 months, which included a portion of a civil airway and one instrument approach at one representative airport, in one of the types of aircraft which that pilot is to fly.
C—since the beginning of the 12th month before that service, which included at least one flight over a civil airway, or approved off-airway route, or any portion of either, in one type of aircraft which that pilot is to fly.

Answer (C) is correct (8095). *(FAR 135.299)*
No certificate holder may use a pilot, nor may any person serve, as a pilot in command of a flight unless, since the beginning of the 12th calendar month before that service, that pilot has passed a line check in one of the types of aircraft which that pilot is to fly. The flight check shall consist of at least one flight over one route segment and include takeoffs and landings at one or more representative airports; if authorized for IFR flight, at least one flight shall be flown over a civil airway, an approved off-airway route, or a portion of either of them.
Answer (A) is incorrect because there is no requirement for instrument approaches to be performed for the line check of routes and airports. Answer (B) is incorrect because there is no requirement for instrument approaches to be performed for the line check of routes and airports.

128.
8096. What are the minimum requirements for the line check required of each pilot in command authorized for IFR air taxi operations? The line check shall be given over

A—one route segment in each type of airplane the pilot is to fly and includes takeoffs and landings at one or more representative airports.
B—a civil airway or an approved off-airway route, or a portion of either of them, in one type of airplane the pilot is to fly and includes takeoffs and landings at one or more representative airports.
C—a civil airway or an approved off-airway route in each make and model airplane the pilot is to fly and includes takeoffs and landings at one or more representative airports.

Answer (B) is correct (8096). *(FAR 135.299)*
No certificate holder may use a pilot, nor may any person serve, as a pilot in command of a flight unless, since the beginning of the 12th calendar month before that service, that pilot has passed a line check in one of the types of aircraft which that pilot is to fly. The flight check shall consist of at least one flight over one route segment and include takeoffs and landings at one or more representative airports; if authorized for IFR flight, at least one flight shall be flown over a civil airway, an approved off-airway route, or a portion of either of them.
Answer (A) is incorrect because the line check is conducted in one, not each, type of aircraft which the pilot will fly, and for IFR operations the flight must be flown over a civil airway, an approved off-airway route, or a portion of either of them, not necessarily a route segment. Answer (C) is incorrect because the line check is conducted in one type of aircraft, not each make and model airplane, which the pilot is to fly.

5.8 TRAINING

135.321 Applicability and Terms Used

129.
8820. The training required for flight crewmembers who have not qualified and served in the same capacity on an aircraft is

A—upgrade training.
B—transition training.
C—initial training.

Answer (C) is correct (8820). *(FAR 135.321)*
Initial training is required for flight crewmembers who have not qualified and served in the same capacity on an aircraft.
Answer (A) is incorrect because upgrade training is required for a crewmember who has qualified and served as second in command on a particular aircraft type before (s)he serves as pilot in command on that aircraft. Answer (B) is incorrect because transition training is required for a crewmember who has qualified and served in the same capacity on another aircraft.

130.
8821. A crewmember who has served as second in command on a particular aircraft type (e.g., BE-1900), may serve as pilot in command upon completing which training program?

A—Upgrade training.
B—Transition training.
C—Initial training.

Answer (A) is correct (8821). *(FAR 135.321)*
A crewmember who has served as second in command on a particular aircraft type (e.g., BE-1900) may serve as pilot in command upon completing upgrade training.
Answer (B) is incorrect because transition training is required for crewmembers who have qualified and served in the same capacity on another aircraft. Answer (C) is incorrect because initial training is required for crew-members who have not qualified and served in the same capacity on an aircraft.

131.
9719. A crewmember who has served as second in command on a particular aircraft type (e.g., BE-1900), may serve as pilot in command upon completing which training program?

A—Upgrade training.
B—Transition training.
C—Initial training.

Answer (A) is correct (9719). *(FAR 135.321)*
A crewmember who has served as second in command on a particular aircraft type (e.g., BE-1900) may serve as pilot in command upon completion of upgrade training.
Answer (B) is incorrect because transition training is required for a crewmember who has qualified and served in the same capacity on another aircraft. Answer (C) is incorrect because initial training is required for a crewmember who has not qualified and served in the same capacity on an aircraft.

132.
8827. The training required for crewmembers who have been qualified and served in the same capacity on another aircraft is

A—difference training.
B—transition training.
C—upgrade training.

Answer (B) is correct (8827). *(FAR 135.321)*
The training required for crewmembers who have been qualified and have served in the same capacity on another aircraft is transition training.
Answer (A) is incorrect because difference training is required for crewmembers who have qualified and served on a particular type aircraft prior to becoming qualified in the same capacity on a particular variation of that aircraft. Answer (C) is incorrect because upgrade training is required for a crewmember who has qualified and served as second in command on a particular aircraft type, before (s)he serves as pilot in command on that aircraft.

135.331 Crewmember Emergency Training

133.
8828. The certificate holder must give instruction on such subjects as respiration, hypoxia, gas expansion, and decompression to crewmembers who serve in operations above

A—FL 180.
B—FL 200.
C—FL 250.

Answer (C) is correct (8828). *(135.331)*
The certificate holder must give instruction on such subjects as respiration, hypoxia, gas expansion, and decompression to crewmembers who serve in operations above FL 250.
Answer (A) is incorrect because the certificate holder must give instruction on such subjects as respiration, hypoxia, gas expansion, and decompression to crewmembers who serve in operations above FL 250, not FL 180. Answer (B) is incorrect because the certificate holder must give instruction on such subjects as respiration, hypoxia, gas expansion, and decompression to crewmembers who serve in operations above FL 250, not FL 200.

134.
8829. The air carrier must give instruction on such subjects as gas bubble formation, hypoxia, decompression, and length of consciousness without supplemental oxygen at altitude to crewmembers serving on aircraft operated above

A—FL 250.
B—FL 200.
C—FL 180.

Answer (A) is correct (8829). *(FAR 135.331)*
Crewmembers who serve in operations above FL 250 must receive instruction on subjects such as gas bubble formation, hypoxia, decompression, and length of consciousness without supplemental oxygen at altitude.
Answer (B) is incorrect because instruction on subjects such as gas bubble formation, hypoxia, and decompression must be given to crewmembers serving on aircraft operating above FL 250, not FL 200. Answer (C) is incorrect because instruction on subjects such as gas bubble formation, hypoxia, and decompression must be given to crewmembers serving on aircraft operating above FL 250, not FL 180.

135.333 Training Requirements: Handling and Carriage of Hazardous Materials

135.
9720. A person whose duties include the handling or carriage of dangerous articles and/or magnetized materials must have satisfactorily completed an approved training program established by the certificate holder within the previous

A—6 calendar months.
B—12 calendar months.
C—24 calendar months.

Answer (B) is correct (9720). *(FAR 135.333)*
No certificate holder may use any person to perform, and no person may perform, any assigned duties and responsibilities for the handling or carriage of hazardous materials (e.g., dangerous articles and/or magnetized materials), unless within the preceding 12 calendar months that person has satisfactorily completed initial or recurrent training in an appropriate training program established by the certificate holder.
Answer (A) is incorrect because any person involved in the handling or carriage of dangerous articles or magnetized materials must have completed an approved training program within the previous 12 calendar months, not 6 calendar months. Answer (C) is incorrect because any person involved in the handling or carriage of dangerous articles or magnetized materials must have completed an approved training program within the previous 12 calendar months, not 24 calendar months.

5.9 AIRPLANE PERFORMANCE OPERATING LIMITATIONS

135.367 Large Transport Category Airplanes: Reciprocating Engine Powered: Takeoff Limitations

136.
8115. When computing the takeoff data, what is the percentage of the reported headwind component that may be applied to the "still air" data?

A—Not more than 150 percent.
B—Not more than 100 percent.
C—Not more than 50 percent.

Answer (C) is correct (8115). *(FAR 135.367)*

When computing takeoff limitations, takeoff data based on still air may be corrected by taking into account not more than 50% of any reported headwind component.

Answer (A) is incorrect because takeoff data based on still air may be corrected by taking into account not less than, instead of not more than, 150% of any reported tailwind, not headwind, component. Answer (B) is incorrect because 100% is not a limit on headwinds or tailwinds for takeoff limitation computations.

137.
8116. When computing takeoff data, what is the percentage of the effective tailwind component which may be applied to the "still air" data?

A—Not less than 150 percent.
B—Not less than 100 percent.
C—Not more than 50 percent.

Answer (A) is correct (8116). *(FAR 135.367)*

To allow for wind effect, takeoff data based on still air may be corrected by taking into account not more than 50% of any reported headwind component and not less than 150% of any reported tailwind component.

Answer (B) is incorrect because 100% is not a limit on headwinds or tailwinds for takeoff limitation computations. Answer (C) is incorrect because 50% is the limit on the headwind, not the tailwind, component.

135.375 Large Transport Category Airplanes: Reciprocating Engine Powered: Landing Limitations: Destination Airports

138.
8124. (Refer to figure 2 below.) What is the maximum landing distance that may be used by a reciprocating-engine-powered, small transport category airplane to land on Rwy 1 (dry) at the destination airport?

A—5,010 feet.
B—5,820 feet.
C—5,845 feet.

Answer (A) is correct (8124). *(FAR 135.375)*

FAR 135.397 prescribes that FARs 135.375 and 135.377 are applicable to reciprocating-powered small airplanes. FAR 135.375 requires a reciprocating airplane to be able to land in 60% of the effective length of the runway at the destination airport.

The effective length of Rwy 1 on Fig. 2 is 8,350 ft. (9,700 – 1,350). The effective runway length begins at the point where the obstruction clearance plane intersects the centerline of the runway. Thus, the maximum landing distance is 5,010 ft. (8,350 x 60%).

Answer (B) is incorrect because 5,820 ft. is 60% of the actual, not the effective, runway length. Answer (C) is incorrect because 5,845 ft. is 70%, not 60%, of the effective runway length.

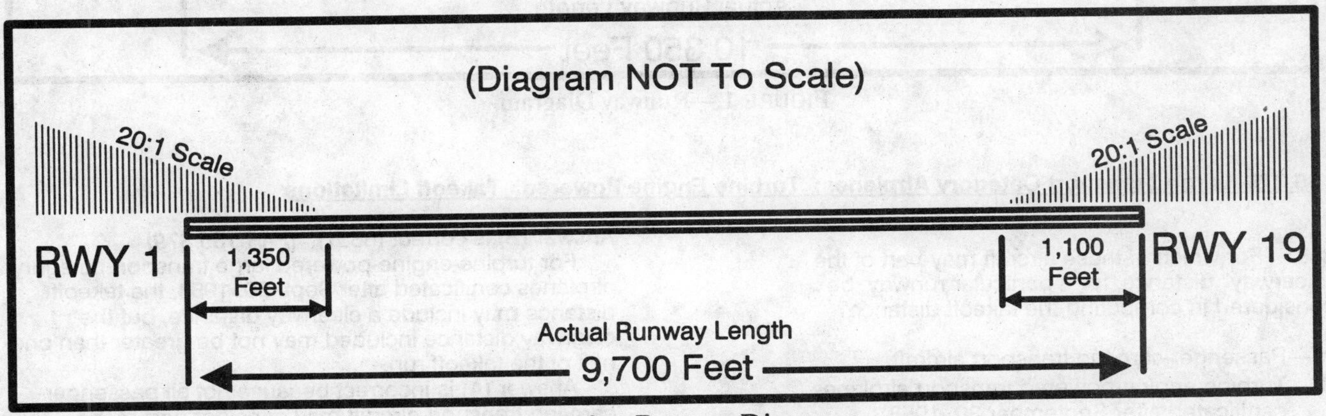

FIGURE 2.—Runway Diagram.

139.
8118. (Refer to figure 1 below.) What is the maximum landing distance that may be used by a reciprocating-engine-powered, small transport category airplane to land on Rwy 24 (dry) at the destination airport?

A—5,490 feet.
B—6,210 feet.
C—6,405 feet.

Answer (A) is correct (8118). *(FAR 135.375)*
FAR 135.397 prescribes that FARs 135.375 and 135.377 are applicable to reciprocating-powered small airplanes. FAR 135.375 requires a reciprocating airplane to be able to land in 60% of the effective length of the runway at the airport of intended landing.
The effective length of Rwy 24 on Fig. 1 is 9,150 ft. (10,350 – 1,200). The effective runway length begins at the point where the obstruction clearance plane intersects the centerline of the runway. Thus, the maximum landing distance is 5,490 ft. (9,150 x 60%).
Answer (B) is incorrect because 6,210 ft. is 60% of the actual, not the effective, runway length. Answer (C) is incorrect because 6,405 ft. is 70%, not 60%, of the effective runway length.

140.
8120. (Refer to figure 1 below.) What is the maximum landing distance that may be used by a reciprocating-engine-powered, small transport category airplane to land on Rwy 6 (dry) at the destination airport?

A—5,460 feet.
B—6,210 feet.
C—6,370 feet.

Answer (A) is correct (8120). *(FAR 135.375)*
FAR 135.397 prescribes that FARs 135.375 and 135.377 are applicable to reciprocating-powered small airplanes. FAR 135.375 requires a reciprocating airplane to be able to land in 60% of the effective length of the runway at the destination airport.
The effective length of Rwy 6 on Fig. 1 is 9,100 ft. (10,350 – 1,250). The effective runway length begins at the point where the obstruction clearance plane intersects the centerline of the runway. Thus, the maximum landing distance is 5,460 ft. (9,100 x 60%).
Answer (B) is incorrect because 6,210 ft. is 60% of the actual, not the effective, runway length. Answer (C) is incorrect because 6,370 ft. is 70%, not 60%, of the effective runway length.

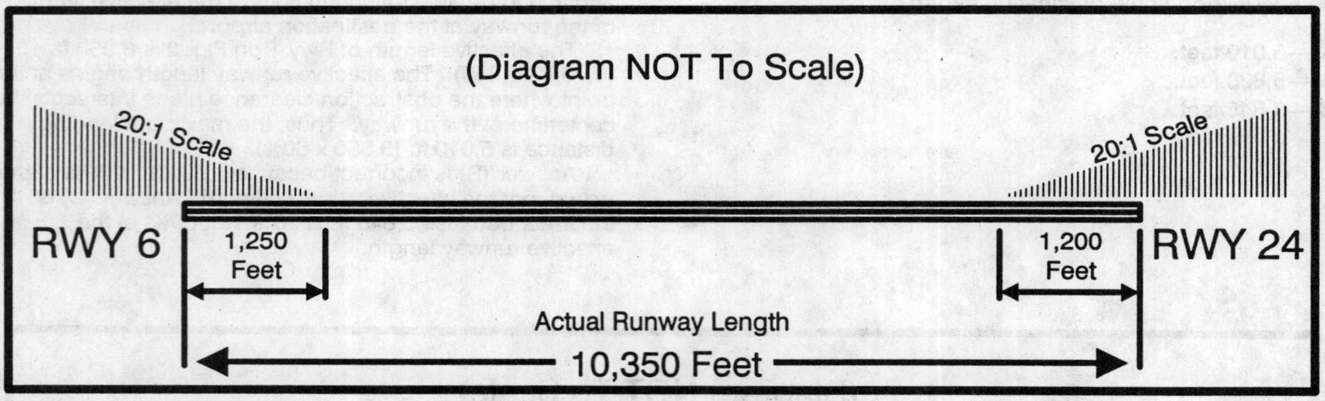

FIGURE 1.—Runway Diagram.

135.379 Large Transport Category Airplanes: Turbine Engine Powered: Takeoff Limitations

141.
8831. For which of these aircraft may part of the "clearway" distance, for a particular runway, be considered in computing the takeoff distance?

A—Passenger-carrying transport aircraft.
B—Turbine-engine-powered transport airplanes, certificated after September 30, 1958.
C—U.S. certified transport airplane, certificated before August 26, 1957.

Answer (B) is correct (8831). *(FAR 135.379)*
For turbine-engine-powered large transport category airplanes certificated after Sept. 30, 1958, the takeoff distance may include a clearway distance, but the clearway distance included may not be greater than one-half of the takeoff run.
Answer (A) is incorrect because not all passenger-carrying transport aircraft may consider part of the clearway distance in computing the takeoff distance. Answer (C) is incorrect because turbine-engine-powered large transport category airplanes certificated after Sept. 30, 1958, not any U.S.-certified transport airplane certificated before Aug. 26, 1957, can include part of the clearway distance when computing the takeoff distance.

142.
8094. Which takeoff computation must not exceed the length of the runway plus the length of the stopway for a turbine-engine-powered small transport category airplane?

A—Takeoff distance.
B—Acceleration-stop distance.
C—Acceleration-climb distance.

Answer (B) is correct (8094). *(FAR 135.379, 135.397)*
The acceleration-stop distance must not exceed the length of the runway plus the length of any stopway for a turbine-powered, small-transport-category airplane.
Answer (A) is incorrect because the takeoff distance usually is shorter than the computed acceleration-stop distance. The latter must be no greater than the length of the runway plus the length of any stopway. Answer (C) is incorrect because the acceleration-stop, not acceleration-climb, distance must not exceed the length of the runway plus the length of any stopway.

135.385 Large Transport Category Airplanes: Turbine Engine Powered: Landing Limitations: Destination Airports

143.
8121. (Refer to figure 1 on page 172.) What is the maximum landing distance that may be used by a turbine-engine-powered, small transport category airplane to land on Rwy 24 (dry) at the destination airport?

A—5,460 feet.
B—5,490 feet.
C—6,210 feet.

Answer (B) is correct (8121). *(FAR 135.385)*
FAR 135.397 prescribes that FARs 135.385 and 135.387 are applicable to turbine-engine-powered small airplanes. FAR 135.385 requires a turbine-engine-powered airplane to be able to land in 60% of the effective length of the runway at the destination airport.
The effective length of Rwy 24 on Fig. 1 is 9,150 ft. (10,350 – 1,200). The effective runway length begins at the point where the obstruction clearance plane intersects the centerline of the runway. Thus, the maximum landing distance is 5,490 ft. (9,150 x 60%).
Answer (A) is incorrect because 5,460 ft. is 60% of the effective runway length of Rwy 6, not Rwy 24. Answer (C) is incorrect because 6,210 ft. is 60% of the actual, not the effective, runway length.

144.
8122. (Refer to figure 1 on page 172.) What is the maximum landing distance that may be used by a turbine-engine-powered, small transport category airplane to land on Rwy 6 (wet) at the destination airport?

A—5,460 feet.
B—5,880 feet.
C—6,088 feet.

Answer (A) is correct (8122). *(FAR 135.385)*
FAR 135.397 prescribes that FARs 135.385 and 135.387 are applicable to turbine-engine-powered small airplanes. FAR 135.385 requires a turbine-engine-powered airplane to be able to land in 60% of the effective length of a dry (or a wet) runway at the destination airport.
The effective length of Rwy 6 on Fig. 1 is 9,100 ft. (10,350 – 1,250). The effective runway length begins at the point where the obstruction clearance plane intersects the centerline of the runway. Thus, the maximum landing distance is 5,460 ft. (9,100 x 60%).
Answer (B) is incorrect because 5,880 ft. is 60% of 9,800 ft. Answer (C) is incorrect because 6,088 ft. is 60% of 10,150 ft.

145.
8123. (Refer to figure 2 on page 171.) What is the maximum landing distance that may be used by a turbopropeller-powered, small transport category airplane to land on Rwy 19 (dry) at the destination airport?

A—6,020 feet.
B—5,820 feet.
C—5,160 feet.

Answer (C) is correct (8123). *(FAR 135.385)*
FAR 135.397 prescribes that FARs 135.385 and 135.387 are applicable to turbopropeller-powered small airplanes. FAR 135.385 requires a turbine-engine-powered airplane to be able to land in 60% of the effective length of the runway at the destination airport.
The effective length of Rwy 19 on Fig. 2 is 8,600 ft. (9,700 – 1,100). The effective runway length begins at the point where the obstruction clearance plane intersects the centerline of the runway. Thus, the maximum landing distance is 5,160 ft. (8,600 x 60%).
Answer (A) is incorrect because 6,020 ft. is 70%, not 60%, of the effective runway length. Answer (B) is incorrect because 5,820 ft. is 60% of the actual, not the effective, runway length.

146.
8125. (Refer to figure 2 on page 171.) What is the maximum landing distance that may be used by a turbine-engine-powered, small transport category airplane to land on Rwy 1 (dry) at the destination airport?

A—5,010 feet.
B—5,820 feet.
C—5,845 feet.

Answer (A) is correct (8125). *(FAR 135.385)*
FAR 135.397 prescribes that FARs 135.385 and 135.387 are applicable to turbine-engine-powered small airplanes. FAR 135.385 requires a turbine-engine-powered airplane to be able to land in 60% of the effective length of the runway at the destination airport.
The effective length of Rwy 1 on Fig. 2 is 8,350 ft. (9,700 – 1,350). The effective runway length begins at the point where the obstruction clearance plane intersects the centerline of the runway. Thus, the maximum landing distance is 5,010 ft. (8,350 x 60%).
Answer (B) is incorrect because 5,820 ft. is 60% of the actual, not the effective, runway length. Answer (C) is incorrect because 5,845 ft. is 70%, not 60%, of the effective runway length.

147.
8126. (Refer to figure 2 on page 171.) What is the maximum landing distance that may be used by a turbine-engine-powered, small transport category airplane to land on Rwy 19 (dry) at the destination airport?

A—5,160 feet.
B—5,820 feet.
C—6,020 feet.

Answer (A) is correct (8126). *(FAR 135.385)*
FAR 135.397 prescribes that FARs 135.385 and 135.387 are applicable to turbine-engine-powered small airplanes. FAR 135.385 requires a turbine-engine-powered airplane to be able to land in 60% of the effective length of the runway at the destination airport.
The effective length of Rwy 19 on Fig. 2 is 8,600 ft. (9,700 – 1,100). The effective runway length begins at the point where the obstruction clearance plane intersects the centerline of the runway. Thus, the maximum landing distance is 5,160 ft. (8,600 x 60%).
Answer (B) is incorrect because 5,820 ft. is 60% of the actual, not the effective, runway length. Answer (C) is incorrect because 6,020 ft. is 70%, not 60%, of the effective runway length.

148.
8127. (Refer to figure 2 on page 171.) May a small transport category, turbine-engine-powered airplane that has a computed landing distance of 5,500 feet use one or both of the runways depicted in the illustration at the destination airport?

A—Neither Rwy 1 nor Rwy 19 may be used if dry conditions exist.
B—Only Rwy 19 may be used provided dry conditions exist.
C—Rwy 1 or Rwy 19 may be used whether conditions are wet or dry.

Answer (A) is correct (8127). *(FAR 135.385)*
FAR 135.397 prescribes that FARs 135.385 and 135.387 are applicable to turbine-engine-powered small airplanes. FAR 135.385 requires a turbine-engine-powered airplane to be able to land in 60% of the effective length of the runway at the destination airport.
The effective length of Rwy 1 on Fig. 2 is 8,350 ft. (9,700 – 1,350). For Rwy 19, the effective length is 8,600 ft. (9,700 – 1,100). The effective runway length begins at the point where the obstruction clearance plane intersects the centerline of the runway. Thus, the maximum landing distance is 5,010 ft. (8,350 x 60%) for Rwy 1 and 5,160 ft. (8,600 x 60%) for Rwy 19.
Thus, neither Rwy 1 nor 19 may be used; i.e., the maximum landing distance for each is less than 5,500 ft.
Answer (B) is incorrect because Rwy 19's maximum landing distance is 5,160 ft. Answer (C) is incorrect because neither Rwy 1 nor 19 may be used.

149.
8128. (Refer to figure 2 on page 171.) May a small transport category, turboprop airplane that has a computed landing distance of 6,000 feet use either or both runways depicted in the illustration at the destination airport?

A—Only Rwy 19 may be used if dry conditions exist.
B—Neither Rwy 1 nor Rwy 19 may be used under any conditions.
C—Either Rwy 1 or Rwy 19 may be used whether conditions are wet or dry.

Answer (B) is correct (8128). *(FAR 135.385)*
FAR 135.397 prescribes that FARs 135.385 and 135.387 are applicable to turbine-engine-powered small airplanes. FAR 135.385 requires a turbine-engine-powered airplane to be able to land in 60% of the effective length of the runway at the destination airport.
The effective length of Rwy 1 on Fig. 2 is 8,350 ft. (9,700 – 1,350). For Rwy 19, the effective length is 8,600 ft. (9,700 – 1,100). The effective runway length begins at the point where the obstruction clearance plane intersects the centerline of the runway. Thus, the maximum landing distance is 5,010 ft. (8,350 x 60%) for Rwy 1 and 5,160 ft. (8,600 x 60%) for Rwy 19.
Thus, neither Rwy 1 nor 19 may be used; i.e., the maximum landing distance for each is less than 6,000 ft.
Answer (A) is incorrect because Rwy 19's maximum landing distance is 5,160 ft. Answer (C) is incorrect because neither Rwy 1 nor 19 may be used.

150.
8130. (Refer to figure 2 on page 171.) Which condition meets FAR Part 135 operational requirements for a small, transport category, turboprop airplane to land at the destination airport that has the runway environment given in the illustration?

A—The airport may be listed as the destination airport if the landing distance does not exceed 5,160 feet for Rwy 19.
B—The airport may NOT be listed as the destination airport if the landing distance exceeds 5,100 feet for Rwy 19.
C—The airport may be listed as the destination airport if the landing distance does not exceed 5,350 feet for either runway, wet or dry conditions.

Answer (A) is correct (8130). *(FAR 135.385)*
FAR 135.397 prescribes that FARs 135.385 and 135.387 are applicable to turbine-engine-powered small airplanes. FAR 135.385 requires a turboprop airplane to be able to land in 60% of the effective length of the runway at the destination airport.
The effective length of Rwy 1 on Fig. 2 is 8,350 ft. (9,700 – 1,350). For Rwy 19, the effective length is 8,600 ft. (9,700 – 1,100). The effective runway length begins at the point where the obstruction clearance plane intersects the centerline of the runway. Thus, the maximum landing distance is 5,010 ft. (8,350 x 60%) for Rwy 1 and 5,160 ft. (8,600 x 60%) for Rwy 19.
Thus, Rwy 19 may be used within 5,160 ft. landing distance.
Answer (B) is incorrect because the landing distance may be up to 5,160 ft. on Rwy 19. Answer (C) is incorrect because Rwy 1 landing distance cannot exceed 5,010 ft., and Rwy 19 landing distance cannot exceed 5,160 ft.

135.387 Large Transport Category Airplanes: Turbine Engine Powered: Landing Limitations: Alternate Airports

151.
8117. (Refer to figure 1 on page 172.) What is the maximum landing distance that may be used by a turbopropeller-powered, small transport category airplane to land on Rwy 24 (dry) at the alternate airport?

A—5,490 feet.
B—6,210 feet.
C—6,405 feet.

Answer (C) is correct (8117). *(FAR 135.387)*
FAR 135.397 prescribes that FARs 135.385 and 135.387 are applicable to turbine-engine-powered small airplanes. FAR 135.387 requires a turbopropeller-powered airplane to be able to land in 70% of the effective length of the runway at an alternate airport.
The effective length of Rwy 24 on Fig. 1 is 9,150 ft. (10,350 – 1,200). The effective runway length begins at the point where the obstruction clearance plane intersects the centerline of the runway. Thus, the maximum landing distance is 6,405 ft. (9,150 x 70%).
Answer (A) is incorrect because 5,490 ft. is 60%, not 70%, of the effective runway length. Answer (B) is incorrect because 6,210 ft. is 60% of the actual, not the effective, runway length.

152.
8119. (Refer to figure 1 on page 172.) What is the maximum landing distance that may be used by a turbopropeller-powered, small transport category airplane to land on Rwy 6 (dry) at the alternate airport?

A—5,460 feet.
B—6,210 feet.
C—6,370 feet.

Answer (C) is correct (8119). *(FAR 135.387)*
FAR 135.397 prescribes that FARs 135.385 and 135.387 are applicable to turbine-engine-powered small airplanes. FAR 135.387 requires a turbopropeller-powered airplane to be able to land in 70% of the effective length of the runway at an alternate airport.
The effective length of Rwy 6 on Fig. 1 is 9,100 ft. (10,350 – 1,250). The effective runway length begins at the point where the obstruction clearance plane intersects the centerline of the runway. Thus, the maximum landing distance is 6,370 ft. (9,100 x 70%).
Answer (A) is incorrect because 5,460 ft. is 60%, not 70%, of the effective runway length. Answer (B) is incorrect because 6,210 ft. is 60%, not 70%, of the actual, not the effective, runway length.

153.
8129. (Refer to figure 2 on page 171.) What is the maximum landing distance that may be used for a non-transport category, turbopropeller-driven airplane to land on Rwy 1 (dry) at the alternate airport?

A—5,010 feet.
B—5,845 feet.
C—6,020 feet.

Answer (B) is correct (8129). *(FAR 135.387)*
FAR 135.397 prescribes that FARs 135.385 and 135.387 are applicable to turbine-engine-powered small airplanes. FAR 135.387 requires a turboprop airplane to be able to land in 70% of the effective length of the runway at alternate airports.
The effective length of Rwy 1 on Fig. 2 is 8,350 ft. (9,700 – 1,350). The effective runway length begins at the point where the obstruction clearance plane intersects the centerline of the runway. Thus, the maximum landing distance is 5,845 ft. (8,350 x 70%).
Answer (A) is incorrect because 5,010 ft. is 60%, not 70%, of the effective runway length. Answer (C) is incorrect because 6,020 ft. is 70% of the effective runway length of Rwy 19, not Rwy 1.

5.10 MAINTENANCE, PREVENTIVE MAINTENANCE, AND ALTERATIONS

135.413 Responsibility for Airworthiness

154.
8093. If a certificate holder makes arrangements for another person to perform aircraft maintenance, that maintenance shall be performed in accordance with the

A—certificate holder's manual and FAR Parts 43, 91, and 135.
B—provisions of a contract prepared by a certificate holder and approved by the supervising FAA district office.
C—provisions and standards outlined in the certificate holder's manual.

Answer (A) is correct (8093). *(FAR 135.413)*

The certificate holder shall ensure that any maintenance, preventive maintenance, or alteration that is performed by another person is performed under the certificate holder's manual and under FARs 43, 91, and 135.

Answer (B) is incorrect because the FAA allows other persons to perform maintenance, preventive maintenance, or alterations only in accordance with the certificate holder's manual requirements. Answer (C) is incorrect because, while the maintenance must be performed in accordance with the certificate holder's manual, it must also be performed in accordance with FAR Parts 43, 91, and 135.

135.415 Mechanical Reliability Reports

155.
8112. Who is responsible for submitting a Mechanical Reliability Report?

A—Each certificate holder.
B—Director of maintenance at the facility that discovers the reportable condition.
C—Chief inspector at the facility where the condition is found.

Answer (A) is correct (8112). *(FAR 135.415)*

Each certificate holder shall report the occurrence or detection of each failure, malfunction, or defect in an aircraft.

Answer (B) is incorrect because someone other than a maintenance facility may discover the discrepancy. An example would be an engine shutdown during flight due to foreign object ingestion or icing. Upon landing, the certificate holder shall submit a mechanical reliability report. Answer (C) is incorrect because someone other than a maintenance facility may discover the discrepancy. An example would be an engine shutdown during flight due to foreign object ingestion or icing. Upon landing, the certificate holder shall submit a mechanical reliability report.

END OF CHAPTER

CHAPTER SIX
AERODYNAMICS AND AIRPLANES

This chapter contains outlines of major concepts tested, all FAA test questions and answers regarding aerodynamics and airplanes, and an explanation of each answer. Each module, or subtopic, within this chapter is listed above with the number of questions from the FAA pilot knowledge test pertaining to that particular module. For each module, the first number following the parentheses is the page number on which the outline begins, and the next number is the page number on which the questions begin.

There are 157 questions in this chapter. We separate and organize the FAA questions into meaningful study units, i.e., chapters and modules. As an analogy, it is easier to deal with the "trees" if you understand the "forest." In this context, "trees" are individual FAA questions and the "forest" is the ATP knowledge test. The organizational units between the overall ATP knowledge test and individual ATP test questions are chapters and modules in this book.

CAUTION: The **sole purpose** of this book is to expedite your passing the FAA pilot knowledge test for the ATP certificate. Topics or regulations not directly tested on the FAA pilot knowledge test are omitted. Much more information and knowledge are necessary to fly safely. This additional material is presented in Gleim's other pilot training books (see the order form on page 818) and in many FAA books and circulars, as well as in airplane *POH*s and other commercial textbooks.

6.1 FLIGHT CONTROLS (Questions 1-3)

1. The primary flight control surfaces allow the pilot to control an airplane's movement around its lateral, longitudinal, and vertical axes. The primary flight controls are
   a. Elevator
   b. Ailerons (inboard and/or outboard)
   c. Rudder
2. Leading-edge flaps are an example of an auxiliary flight control.

6.2 AILERONS (Questions 4-6)

1. Some large jet transports use both inboard and outboard ailerons.
   a. At low airspeeds, the outboard ailerons provide effective roll control.
   b. At high speeds, aerodynamic loads from use of outboard ailerons can twist the wing.
   c. Accordingly, the outboard ailerons are locked at high airspeeds.
2. Inboard ailerons are used for both low-speed and high-speed flight.
3. Outboard ailerons are used for low-speed flight only.

6.3 TRIM TABS (Questions 7-13)

1. A **control tab** is used on some transport aircraft as a manual backup to flight controls which are normally operated hydraulically.
   a. This manual backup, called **manual reversion**, unlocks the control tabs allowing the pilot to operate the control tabs by moving the control wheel, which will cause the flight controls to move.
2. An **elevator trim tab** modifies the downward tail load for various airspeeds in flight, reducing or eliminating flight control pressures.
   a. The trim tab maintains balance in flight by remaining fixed for all positions when the flight control is moved.
3. The **servo tab** aids the pilot in moving the primary control surface and holding it in the desired position.
   a. The servo tab moves in the opposite direction from the primary control surface.
   b. The purpose of a servo tab is to reduce the control forces by deflecting in the proper direction to move a primary flight control.
4. The **anti-servo tab** moves in the same direction as the primary flight control surface.
   a. It is a stabilizing force which increases control force pressures and prevents the control surface from moving to a full-deflection position.

6.4 WING LIFT ALTERING DEVICES (Questions 14-22)

1. High-lift devices increase lift at low airspeeds, allowing lower landing and takeoff speeds.
2. Leading-edge flaps increase the camber of the wing, which delays a stall to a higher angle of attack. The increased camber prevents airflow separation at low speeds.
3. Leading-edge slots and slats direct air from the high-pressure area under the leading edge along the top of the wing and delay airflow separation to some higher angle of attack.
   a. These devices change the stalling angle of attack to a higher angle and increase lift at relatively slow speeds.

4. Flight spoilers reduce lift without increasing airspeed.
   a. They disrupt the smooth flow of air over the wing to reduce the lifting force of the wing and are used to reduce the wings' lift upon landing.
   b. Ground spoilers are used only to reduce lift upon landing and are the same components as flight spoilers but deflect to a greater degree on the ground.

6.5 ANGLE OF ATTACK/LIFT (Questions 23-26)

1. Lift is proportional to the square of the airplane's velocity; e.g., an airplane at 200 kt. has four times the lift of the same airplane at 100 kt.
2. At high altitudes, a higher true airspeed is required for any given angle of attack because the air density decreases with altitude.
3. A lower angle of attack will produce the same lift in ground effect as out of ground effect.
4. Angle of attack controls the airplane's lift, airspeed, and drag.

6.6 DRAG (Questions 27-30)

1. When airspeed decreases below the maximum L/D airspeed, total drag increases due to increased induced drag.
   a. At maximum L/D, a propeller-driven airplane enjoys maximum range and maximum engine-out glide distance.
2. When an airplane leaves ground effect, it will require an increase in angle of attack to maintain the same lift coefficient due to an increase in induced drag.
3. As gross weight increases, induced drag increases more than parasite drag increases.

6.7 STALL SPEEDS (Questions 31-34)

1. Wing-mounted vortex generators reduce the drag caused by supersonic airflow over portions of the wing.
2. Indicated stall speed is affected by weight, load factor, and power, but not by angle of attack or air density.
3. An airfoil can stall at a higher airspeed when turbulent air results in an abrupt change in relative wind.
4. Airflow separation over the wing can be delayed by using vortex generators, making the wing surface rough, and/or directing high pressure air over the top of the wing or flaps through slots.

6.8 LOAD FACTOR (Questions 35-39)

1. Load factor is the lift divided by total weight.
   a. EXAMPLE: An aircraft subjected to a total load of 6,000 lb. in flight with a gross weight of 2,000 lb. would have a load factor of 3 Gs.
2. For any given angle of bank, the load factor of an airplane in a coordinated, constant altitude turn is constant and independent of gross weight or the rate of turn.
   a. Only the angle of bank determines the load factor for a given airplane during a level coordinated turn.
3. During a level turn, both total lift and load factor increase.

6.9 PALLET WEIGHT (Questions 40-62)

1. There are 17 questions that require you to determine the maximum allowable weight of cargo that may be carried on a given pallet.
   a. EXAMPLE: Determine the maximum allowable weight that may be carried on a pallet, given the following information:

      Pallet dimensions -- 76 x 74 in.
      Floor load limit -- 176 lb./sq. ft.
      Pallet weight -- 77 lb.
      Tie-down devices -- 29 lb.

      1) Compute the area of the pallet (multiply the dimensions); then divide by 144 sq. in./sq. ft. to determine the area of the pallet in square feet.

         $76 \times 74 = 5{,}624$ *sq. in.*
         $5{,}624 \div 144 = 39.056$ *sq. ft.*

      2) Multiply the area of the pallet (sq. ft.) by the floor load limit (lb./sq. ft.) to determine allowable gross weight of the pallet.

         $39.056 \times 176 = 6{,}873.8$ *lb.*

      3) Subtract the pallet weight and tie-down device weight to determine the maximum allowable weight that can be carried on the pallet.

         $6{,}873.8 - 77 - 29 = 6{,}767.8$ *lb.*

2. Six questions require you to determine the minimum floor load limit an aircraft must have to carry a given pallet of cargo.
   a. EXAMPLE: What is the minimum floor load limit that an aircraft must have to carry the following pallet of cargo?

      Pallet dimensions -- 39 x 37 in.
      Pallet weight -- 37 lb.
      Tie-down devices -- 21 lb.
      Cargo weight -- 1,094.3 lb.

      1) Compute the area of the pallet (multiply the dimensions); then divide by 144 sq. in./sq. ft. to determine the area of the pallet in square feet.

         $39 \times 37 = 1{,}443$ *sq. in.*
         $1{,}443 \div 144 = 10.02$ *sq. ft.*

      2) Determine the gross weight of the pallet of cargo by adding the weight of the pallet, tie-down devices, and cargo.

         $37 + 21 + 1{,}094.3 = 1{,}152.3$ *lb.*

      3) The minimum floor load limit is determined by dividing the gross weight of the pallet by the pallet area.

         $1{,}152.3 \div 10.02 = 115$ *lb./sq. ft.*

6.10 CLIMBS (Questions 63-64)

1. An airplane will climb by increasing the pitch attitude at any speed higher than maximum L/D (L/D_{max}).
2. The maximum rate of climb for a jet airplane will occur at a speed greater than that for L/D_{max}.

6.11 TURNS (Questions 65-69)

1. Increasing airspeed while maintaining a coordinated turn with a constant angle of bank and altitude will decrease the rate of turn and increase the radius of turn but will not increase the load factor.
   a. Slower airspeed and steeper bank increase the rate of turn and decrease the turn radius.
2. If no corrective action is taken by the pilot, as angle of bank increases, the vertical component of lift decreases, and the sink rate increases.
   a. The angle of attack must be increased during a turn to compensate for the loss of vertical lift if altitude is to be maintained.

6.12 STABILITY (Questions 70-74)

1. **Stability** is the inherent ability of an object (e.g., airplane), after its equilibrium is disturbed, to return to its original position. In other words, a stable airplane will tend to return to the original condition of flight if disturbed by a force such as turbulent air.
2. **Static stability** is the initial tendency that the airplane displays after its equilibrium is disturbed.
   a. **Positive static stability** can be illustrated by a ball inside a round bowl. If the ball is displaced from its normal resting place, it will eventually return to its original position at the bottom of the bowl.
   b. **Neutral static stability** can be illustrated by a ball on a flat plane. If the ball is displaced, it will come to rest at some new, neutral position and show no tendency to return to its original position.
   c. **Negative static stability** is actually instability. It can be illustrated by a ball on the top of an inverted round bowl. Even the slightest displacement of the ball will activate greater forces, which will cause the ball to continue to move in the direction of the applied force (e.g., gravity).
3. **Dynamic stability** is the overall tendency that the airplane displays after its equilibrium is disturbed.
   a. **Positive dynamic stability** is a property which dampens the oscillations set up by a statically stable airplane, enabling the oscillations to become smaller and smaller in magnitude until the airplane eventually settles down to its original condition of flight.
   b. **Neutral dynamic stability** means the oscillations remain unchanged.
   c. **Negative dynamic stability** is actually dynamic instability. It means the oscillations tend to increase.
4. An airplane is said to have
   a. Longitudinal stability about the lateral axis
   b. Lateral stability about the longitudinal axis
   c. Directional stability about the vertical axis
   d. Lateral stability or instability in turns

6.13 EFFECT OF REARWARD CG (Questions 75-76)

1. At the aft CG limit, the airplane will have its
   a. Lowest stall speed,
   b. Highest cruise speed, and
   c. Least stability about the lateral axis.

6.14 TAKEOFF AND LANDING PERFORMANCE (Questions 77-81)

1. An upsloped runway impedes acceleration, resulting in a longer ground roll on takeoff.
2. A headwind allows the airplane to reach liftoff speed at a lower groundspeed, requiring less runway length.
3. Critical engine failure speed (V_1) must be reduced as airplane gross weight increases due to the increased mass that must be decelerated and stopped in the event of a rejected takeoff.
   a. V_1 actually means takeoff decision speed (formerly denoted as critical engine failure speed)..
4. High elevation airports require a higher true airspeed to obtain the desired indicated airspeed due to the decreased density of the air.
   a. This requirement results in an increase in groundspeed.
5. Main wheel brakes are at maximum effectiveness when wing lift is reduced.

6.15 MAXIMUM RANGE (Questions 82-86)

1. Maximum range is maintained in a tailwind by decreasing speed to maximize the benefit of the tailwind.
   a. To reduce fuel consumption, you should fly at a higher airspeed in a headwind to reduce the effect of the headwind.
2. As weight decreases, so does the maximum range airspeed.
3. Maximum range for a jet airplane occurs when the proportion between velocity and thrust required is greatest. This point is at a speed greater than that for L/D_{max}.
4. As turbojet aircraft weight is reduced, the maximum range performance is obtained by increasing altitude or decreasing speed.

6.16 PROPELLER PITCH AND ENGINE PERFORMANCE (Questions 87-89)

1. Geometric pitch along the propeller varies to permit a constant angle of attack along its length when in cruising flight.
2. On large reciprocating engines, high RPM and low manifold pressure produce the most severe wear, fatigue, and damage.
3. High relative humidity causes a significant reduction of power output of reciprocating engines but negligible loss of thrust for a turbojet engine.

6.17 TURBOCHARGERS (Questions 90-91)

1. The critical altitude of a supercharged reciprocating engine is the highest altitude at which a desired manifold pressure can be obtained.
2. The waste gate of a turbocharged reciprocating engine controls the exhaust gas discharge.

6.18 MULTIENGINE AIRPLANE OPERATION (Questions 92-103)

1. Stalls should **never** be practiced with one engine inoperative or at idle power: loss of control may result.
2. The blue line on the airspeed indicator on a light twin-engine airplane represents the maximum single-engine rate of climb at gross weight.

3. Pilots of light twin-engine airplanes should be able to maintain heading at V_{MC}.
   a. V_{MC} decreases with altitude on airplanes with unsupercharged engines.
   b. V_{MC} is the highest when CG is in the most rearward allowable position.
4. When an engine on a twin-engine airplane fails, the rate of climb will be reduced by 50% or more.
5. The critical engine of a twin-engine airplane is the one with the center of thrust closest to the center line in the fuselage.
6. The ball of the slip-skid indicator may be deflected outside of its reference lines when operating on a single engine in a light twin at any airspeed above V_{MC}.
7. Slush on the runway has the effect of reducing the critical engine failure speed (V_1).
8. The safest and most efficient takeoff and initial climb procedure in a light twin is to accelerate to an airspeed slightly above V_{MC} and then lift off and climb at the best-rate-of-climb airspeed.
9. Use V_{YSE} if engine failure occurs at an altitude above the single-engine ceiling.
10. For an engine-out approach and landing, the flight path and procedures should be almost identical to the normal approach and landing.

6.19 TURBINE-ENGINE OPERATION (Questions 104-111)

1. The highest temperature in a turbojet engine is found at the turbine inlet.
   a. As temperature increases, thrust decreases on gas turbine engines.
   b. High temperatures reduce the thrust of turbine engines due to the decrease in air density.
2. As outside air pressure decreases, thrust output decreases due to higher density altitude.
3. The most important restriction to the operation of turbojet or turboprop engines is limiting the exhaust gas temperature.
4. The equivalent shaft horsepower (ESHP) of a turboprop engine is a measure of shaft horsepower and jet thrust.
5. Increases in altitude result in lower air density and engine mass flow, causing a decrease in turboprop engine power.
6. Minimum specific fuel consumption of turboprop engines is usually available above 25,000 ft.

6.20 COMPRESSOR STALL (Questions 112-115)

1. A transient compressor stall is characterized by intermittent bang as backfires and flow reversals take place.
2. Strong vibrations and a loud roar indicate that a compressor stall has developed and become steady.
3. Steady, continuous flow-reversal compressor stall has the greatest potential for severe engine damage.
4. In the event of compressor stall, one should reduce fuel flow, reduce angle of attack, and increase airspeed.

6.21 MACH SPEED FLIGHT (Questions 116-124)

1. Below .75 Mach is the subsonic flight range.
2. Transonic flight regimes usually occur from .75 to 1.20 Mach.
3. The critical Mach number produces the first evidence of local sonic flow.
   a. It is the highest speed possible without supersonic flow over the wing.
4. A severe moment, or "tuck under," is the result of shock-induced separation of air flow occurring symmetrically near the wing root of a sweptwing aircraft.
5. The center of pressure moves inward and forward when the wingtips of a sweptwing airplane are shock-stalled first.
6. Sweepback wing design increases the critical Mach number significantly over a straight wing design.
   a. One disadvantage of the sweptwing design is that the wingtip section stalls prior to the wing root.
7. Dutch roll describes gusts causing a sweptwing-type airplane to roll in one direction while yawing in another.

6.22 THRUST REVERSERS (Questions 125-126)

1. Thrust reversers or reverse thrust propellers should be applied immediately after ground contact, i.e., as soon as possible after touchdown, to reduce landing distance of turbojet or turboprop aircraft.

6.23 HYDROPLANING (Questions 127-133)

1. **Viscous hydroplaning** occurs when a film of moisture covers the painted or rubber-coated portion of the runway.
   a. It occurs at a lower speed than dynamic hydroplaning.
2. **Dynamic hydroplaning** occurs when the groundspeed is at least 8.73 times the square root of the tire pressure of the main tires.
   a. EXAMPLE: The minimum speed for dynamic hydroplaning with a tire having an air pressure of 121 PSI is 96 kt.

$$8.73 \times \sqrt{121} = 8.73 \times 11 = 96\ kt.$$

3. **Reverted rubber hydroplaning** occurs when an airplane's tires are effectively held off the smooth runway surface by steam generated by friction.
4. When hydroplaning is experienced, aerodynamic braking should be used to its fullest advantage.
5. Landing at higher-than-recommended touchdown speeds increases hydroplaning potential regardless of how you brake.

6.24 GROUND DEICING/ANTI-ICING (Questions 134-153)

1. Test data indicate that ice, snow, or frost having a thickness and roughness similar to medium or coarse sandpaper on the leading edge and upper surface of a wing can reduce lift by as much as 30% and increase drag by 40%.
   a. Increased surface roughness can cause a decreased angle of attack for stalls and/or an increased stall speed.
2. Freezing point depressant (FPD) fluids used for deicing are intended to provide ice protection on the ground only.
   a. They are highly soluble in water; however, ice is slow to absorb the fluid and to melt when in contact with it.
   b. FPD fluid residue on engine fan or compressor blades can reduce engine performance and cause surging and/or compressor stalls.
3. The practice developed and accepted by the North American air carrier industry using traditional North American fluids is to ensure that the remaining film has a freeze point of at least 20°F below ambient temperature.
4. Snow on top of deicing or anti-icing fluids must be considered as adhering to the aircraft.
5. The purpose of diluting ethylene glycol deicing fluid with water in nonprecipitation conditions is to lower the freezing point.
   a. The minimum glycol content of Type 1 deicing/anti-icing fluid is 80%.
   b. The minimum glycol content of Type 2 deicing/anti-icing fluid is 50%.
6. The one-step process for deicing/anti-icing an airplane consists of applying heated fluid onto the airplane surfaces to remove accumulated ice, snow, or frost and prevent their subsequent buildup.
   a. A disadvantage of the one-step process compared to the two-step process is that more fluid is used with the one-step method when large deposits of ice and snow must be flushed off airplane surfaces.
7. The two-step process consists of separate deicing and anti-icing steps.
   a. First, a heated, diluted Type 1 fluid is applied to remove accumulated ice, snow, or frost.
   b. Then a cold, more concentrated Type 2 fluid is applied.
   c. Using a heated Type 1 fluid followed by a cold Type 2 fluid increases holding time.
      1) Conversely, applying heated Type 2 fluid during the anti-icing (second) step will decrease the holding time.
8. Deicing procedures and equipment developed for large transport airplanes may not be appropriate for some of the smaller aircraft used under FAR Part 135.

6.25 PITOT SYSTEM (Questions 154-157)

1. If both the ram air input and the drain hole of the pitot system become completely blocked during an en route descent in a fixed-thrust and fixed-pitch attitude configuration, a decrease in indicated airspeed should be expected.
   a. If level flight is conducted, large power changes may not produce any variation in indicated airspeed.
   b. In other words, the airspeed indicator may act as an altimeter.
2. If the ram air input to the pitot tube is blocked by ice but the drain hole and static port are not, the indicated airspeed will drop to zero.

QUESTIONS AND ANSWER EXPLANATIONS

All the FAA questions from the pilot knowledge test for the ATP certificate relating to aerodynamics and airplanes and the material outlined previously are reproduced on the following pages in the same modules as the outlines. To the immediate right of each question are the correct answer and answer explanation. You should cover these answers and answer explanations while responding to the questions. Refer to the general discussion in Chapter 1 on how to take the FAA pilot knowledge test.

Remember that the questions from the FAA pilot knowledge test bank have been reordered by topic, and the topics are organized into a meaningful sequence. Accordingly, the first line of the answer explanation gives the FAA question number and the citation of the authoritative source for the answer.

6.1 Flight Controls

1.
8326. Which of the following is considered a primary flight control?

A—Slats.
B—Elevator.
C—Dorsal fin.

Answer (B) is correct (8326). *(FTH Chap 4)*
The primary flight control surfaces allow the pilot to control an airplane's movement around its lateral, longitudinal, and vertical axes. The primary flight controls are the elevator, ailerons, and rudder.
Answer (A) is incorrect because slats are high-lift devices, not a flight control device. Answer (C) is incorrect because a dorsal fin is not a flight control but is used to provide directional stability.

2.
8343. Which of the following are considered primary flight controls?

A—Tabs.
B—Flaps.
C—Outboard ailerons.

Answer (C) is correct (8343). *(FTH Chap 4)*
The primary flight control surfaces allow the pilot to control an airplane's movement around its lateral, longitudinal, and vertical axes. The primary flight controls are elevators, ailerons, and rudders.
Answer (A) is incorrect because tabs are secondary, not primary, flight controls. Answer (B) is incorrect because flaps are secondary, not primary, flight controls.

3.
8327. Which of the following is considered an auxiliary flight control?

A—Ruddervator.
B—Upper rudder.
C—Leading-edge flaps.

Answer (C) is correct (8327). *(A&PM AH Chap 1)*
Leading-edge flaps, speed brakes, spoilers, trailing-edge flaps, and leading-edge slats are auxiliary (secondary) wing flight control surfaces.
Answer (A) is incorrect because a ruddervator is a primary, not auxiliary, flight control surface that incorporates both a rudder and an elevator into one surface. This is done on "V"-tail-type airplanes. Answer (B) is incorrect because upper rudders (found on the B-727) are standby rudders, which are used in the event of a hydraulic system failure. These are primary, not auxiliary, flight controls.

6.2 Ailerons

4.
8324. When are inboard ailerons normally used?

A—Low-speed flight only.
B—High-speed flight only.
C—Low-speed and high-speed flight.

Answer (C) is correct (8324). *(TCAS Chap 5)*
Some large aircraft use two sets of ailerons (inboard and outboard). At high airspeeds, the aerodynamic loads from use of the outboard ailerons twist the wingtips. The outboard ailerons are locked in the neutral position during high-speed flight.
Answer (A) is incorrect because the inboard ailerons are used during both high- and low-speed flight. Answer (B) is incorrect because the inboard ailerons are used during both high- and low-speed flight.

5.
8325. When are outboard ailerons normally used?

A—Low-speed flight only.
B—High-speed flight only.
C—Low-speed and high-speed flight.

Answer (A) is correct (8325). *(TCAS Chap 5)*
Some large aircraft use two sets of ailerons (inboard and outboard). At high airspeeds, the aerodynamic loads from use of the outboard ailerons twist the wingtips. The outboard ailerons are locked in the neutral position during high-speed flight.
Answer (B) is incorrect because the outboard ailerons are locked during high-speed flight. Answer (C) is incorrect because the outboard ailerons are locked during high-speed flight.

6.
8342. Why do some airplanes equipped with inboard/outboard ailerons use the outboards for slow flight only?

A—Increased surface area provides greater controllability with flap extension.
B—Aerodynamic loads on the outboard ailerons tend to twist the wingtips at high speeds.
C—Locking out the outboard ailerons in high-speed flight provides variable flight control feel.

Answer (B) is correct (8342). *(TCAS Chap 5)*
Some large aircraft use two sets of ailerons (inboard and outboard). At high airspeeds, the aerodynamic loads from use of the outboard ailerons twist the wingtips. The outboard ailerons are locked in the neutral position during high-speed flight.
Answer (A) is incorrect because, while using the outboard ailerons during slow flight does increase roll stability, if they are used in high-speed flight, the aerodynamic loads would twist the wingtips. Answer (C) is incorrect because locking out the outboard ailerons reduces the aerodynamic loads on the wings, preventing overstressing at high airspeeds.

6.3 Trim Tabs

7.
8328. What is the purpose of a control tab?

A—Move the flight controls in the event of manual reversion.
B—Reduce control forces by deflecting in the proper direction to move a primary flight control.
C—Prevent a control surface from moving to a full-deflection position due to aerodynamic forces.

Answer (A) is correct (8328). *(TCAS Chap 5)*
When hydraulic pressure is lost to the primary controls, the control tabs unlock from their actuating cylinders and allow control wheel inputs. This method of secondary control is known as manual reversion.
Answer (B) is incorrect because servo, not control, tabs reduce control forces by deflecting primary flight controls in the proper direction. Answer (C) is incorrect because anti-servo, not control, tabs prevent a control surface from moving to a full-deflection position due to aerodynamic forces.

8.
8340. What is the purpose of an elevator trim tab?

A—Provide horizontal balance as airspeed is increased to allow hands-off flight.
B—Adjust the speed tail load for different airspeeds in flight allowing neutral control forces.
C—Modify the downward tail load for various airspeeds in flight eliminating flight-control pressures.

Answer (C) is correct (8340). *(PHAK Chap l)*
The elevator trim tab acts on the elevators, which in turn act upon the entire airplane. This allows the pilot to adjust the angle of attack of the elevators, thus modifying the downward tail load for any airspeed in flight and eliminating the need to exert continuous flight-control pressures.
Answer (A) is incorrect because the elevator trim tab permits hands-off flight at any airspeed, not only when the airspeed is increasing, and provides longitudinal, not horizontal, balance. Answer (B) is incorrect because the elevator trim tab adjusts the downward, not speed, tail load for various airspeeds in flight allowing neutral control forces.

9.
8339. Which direction from the primary control surface does an elevator adjustable trim tab move when the control surface is moved?

A—Same direction.
B—Opposite direction.
C—Remains fixed for all positions.

Answer (C) is correct (8339). *(FTH Chap 4)*
Once adjusted, an elevator adjustable trim tab remains fixed for all positions relative to the primary control surface as the primary control surface is moved.
Answer (A) is incorrect because adjustable trim tabs are adjusted in the opposite direction of the primary control surface as a means of trimming the control surface. Once adjusted, their relationship remains constant with respect to the primary control surface. Answer (B) is incorrect because once adjusted, trim tabs remain fixed to the primary control surface as the primary control surface is moved.

10.
8330. What is the purpose of a servo tab?

A—Move the flight controls in the event of manual reversion.
B—Reduce control forces by deflecting in the proper direction to move a primary flight control.
C—Prevent a control surface from moving to a full-deflection position due to aerodynamic forces.

Answer (B) is correct (8330). *(FTH Chap 4)*
The servo tab aids the pilot in moving a primary control surface and in holding it in the desired position.
Answer (A) is incorrect because, in the event of manual reversion on some transport category aircraft, the control, not servo, tabs would move the flight controls. Answer (C) is incorrect because to preclude full deflection of control surfaces is the purpose of the anti-servo, not servo, tab.

11.
8338. Which direction from the primary control surface does a servo tab move?

A—Same direction.
B—Opposite direction.
C—Remains fixed for all positions.

Answer (B) is correct (8338). *(FTH Chap 4)*
Movement of the servo tab in one direction causes the primary control surface to move in the opposite direction. If a servo tab on an aileron is deflected upward, the aileron is deflected downward, increasing the angle of attack on that wing, resulting in greater lift on that wing.
Answer (A) is incorrect because an anti-servo tab, as found on the trailing edge of stabilators, moves in the same direction as the stabilator to provide a feel to the pilot control pressures. Answer (C) is incorrect because servo tabs move in response to the pilot's control movements.

12.
8329. What is the purpose of an anti-servo tab?

A—Move the flight controls in the event of manual reversion.
B—Reduce control forces by deflecting in the proper direction to move a primary flight control.
C—Prevent a control surface from moving to a full-deflection position due to aerodynamic forces.

Answer (C) is correct (8329). *(AMR Chap 1)*
Since the anti-servo tab moves in the same direction as the control surface, it produces a stabilizing force that increases control force pressures.
Answer (A) is incorrect because, in the event of manual reversion, the control, not anti-servo, tabs would move the flight controls. Answer (B) is incorrect because a servo, not an anti-servo, tab reduces control forces by deflecting in the proper direction to move a primary flight control.

13.
8337. Which direction from the primary control surface does an anti-servo tab move?

A—Same direction.
B—Opposite direction.
C—Remains fixed for all positions.

Answer (A) is correct (8337). *(AMR Chap 1)*
An anti-servo tab, as found on the trailing edge of a stabilator, moves in the same direction as the primary flight control surface.
Answer (B) is incorrect because a servo, not an anti-servo, tab moves in the opposite direction from the primary control surface. Answer (C) is incorrect because trim, not anti-servo, tabs remain fixed during control inputs.

6.4 Wing Lift Altering Devices

14.
8384. The primary purpose of high-lift devices is to increase the

A—L/D_{max}.
B—lift at low speeds.
C—drag and reduce airspeed.

Answer (B) is correct (8384). *(FTP Chap 4)*
High-lift devices increase lift at low airspeeds, allowing lowered landing and takeoff speeds.
Answer (A) is incorrect because increasing the lift component is an objective of high-lift devices which increase the ratio of L/D. The primary purpose of high-lift devices is to increase lift at low speeds. Answer (C) is incorrect because increasing the drag to reduce airspeed is the function of spoilers, not high-lift devices.

15.
8331. Which is a purpose of leading-edge flaps?

A—Increase the camber of the wing.
B—Reduce lift without increasing airspeed.
C—Direct airflow over the top of the wing at high angles of attack.

Answer (A) is correct (8331). *(AMR Chap 1)*
The leading-edge flap is similar in operation to the plain flap. When actuated, the leading edge of the wing extends in a downward direction to increase the camber of the wing, providing greater lift at low flight speeds.
Answer (B) is incorrect because leading-edge flaps increase, not decrease, the lift at slow airspeeds. Answer (C) is incorrect because a slot, not a leading-edge flap, directs airflow over the top of the wing at high angles of attack.

16.
8385. What is the primary function of the leading edge flaps in landing configuration during the flare before touchdown?

A—Prevent flow separation.
B—Decrease rate of sink.
C—Increase profile drag.

Answer (A) is correct (8385). *(FTP Chap 4)*
The primary function of the leading edge flaps in the landing configuration during the flare before touchdown is to prevent flow separation at low airspeeds, therefore allowing lower landing and takeoff speeds.
Answer (B) is incorrect because, to decrease the rate of sink, the coefficient of lift (C_L) must increase. C_L is increased by the use of leading edge lift devices, slats, flaps, and other devices with the correct power setting. Answer (C) is incorrect because spoilers, not leading edge flaps, increase profile drag and are usually deployed after touchdown to reduce lift.

17.
8386. What effect does the leading edge slot in the wing have on performance?

A—Decreases profile drag.
B—Changes the stalling angle of attack to a higher angle.
C—Decelerates the upper surface boundary layer air.

Answer (B) is correct (8386). *(AMR Chap 1)*
The leading edge slot in a wing conducts the flow of high energy air into the boundary layer on the upper surface and delays airflow separation to some higher angle of attack. Thus, the slot simply delays stall to a higher angle of attack.
Answer (A) is incorrect because, at low angles of attack, there is little or no profile drag increase. At high angles of attack, the slot delays the stall characteristics of the wing. Answer (C) is incorrect because the leading edge slot actually increases airflow on the upper wing surface to allow higher angles of attack.

18.
8334. Which is a purpose of leading-edge slats on high-performance wings?

A—Increase lift at relative slow speeds.
B—Improve aileron control during low angles of attack.
C—Direct air from the low-pressure area under the leading edge along the top of the wing.

Answer (A) is correct (8334). *(AMR Chap 1)*
Leading-edge slats direct air from the high-pressure area under the wing to the upper surface, resulting in improved stall characteristics at lower speeds. They also increase lift at relatively slow airspeeds.
Answer (B) is incorrect because the leading edge slats are used during high, not low, angle of attack situations, such as takeoffs and landings. Answer (C) is incorrect because the area under the leading edge is high pressure, not low pressure.

19.
8335. Which is a purpose of leading-edge slats on high-performance wings?

A—Decrease lift at relative slow speeds.
B—Improve aileron control during low angles of attack.
C—Direct air from the high-pressure area under the leading edge along the top of the wing.

Answer (C) is correct (8335). *(AMR Chap 1)*
Leading-edge slats direct air from the high-pressure area under the wing to the upper surface, resulting in improved stall characteristics at lower speeds. They also increase lift at relatively slow airspeeds.
Answer (A) is incorrect because the purpose of leading-edge-lift slats is to increase, not decrease, the lift at low speeds. Sometimes these are referred to as high-lift devices. Answer (B) is incorrect because the leading-edge slats are used during high, not low, angle of attack situations, such as takeoffs and landings.

20.
8332. What is a purpose of flight spoilers?

A—Increase the camber of the wing.
B—Reduce lift without increasing airspeed.
C—Direct airflow over the top of the wing at high angles of attack.

Answer (B) is correct (8332). *(AMR Chap 1)*
Spoilers are mounted on the upper surface of each wing, and they reduce lift without increasing airspeed. Their purpose is to spoil or disrupt the smooth flow of air over the wing to reduce the lifting force of the wing, thus increasing the rate of descent without increasing airspeed.
Answer (A) is incorrect because flaps, not spoilers, increase the camber of the wing. Answer (C) is incorrect because slots and slats, not spoilers, direct airflow over the top of the wing at high angles of attack.

21.
8333. For which purpose may flight spoilers be used?

A—Reduce the wings' lift upon landing.
B—Increase the rate of descent without increasing aerodynamic drag.
C—Aid in longitudinal balance when rolling an airplane into a turn.

Answer (A) is correct (8333). *(AMR Chap 1)*
The purpose of spoilers is to spoil or disrupt the smooth flow of air over the wing to reduce the lifting force of the wing. Thus, flight spoilers may be used to reduce the wings' lift upon landing.
Answer (B) is incorrect because spoilers will increase the aerodynamic drag. Answer (C) is incorrect because longitudinal balance or stability is primarily achieved by the horizontal stabilizer, not a spoiler.

22.
8336. Which is a purpose of ground spoilers?

A—Reduce the wings' lift upon landing.
B—Aid in rolling an airplane into a turn.
C—Increase the rate of descent without gaining airspeed.

Answer (A) is correct (8336). *(AMR Chap 1)*
Spoilers are designed to spoil or disrupt the smooth flow of air over the wing to reduce the lifting force of the wing. Thus, ground spoilers are used to reduce the wings' lift upon landing.
Answer (B) is incorrect because a flight spoiler, not a ground spoiler, can be used to roll an airplane into a turn. Answer (C) is incorrect because flight spoilers, not ground spoilers, are used to increase the rate of descent without gaining airspeed.

6.5 Angle of Attack/Lift

23.
8377. What will be the ratio between airspeed and lift if the angle of attack and other factors remain constant and airspeed is doubled? Lift will be

A—the same.
B—two times greater.
C—four times greater.

Answer (C) is correct (8377). *(FTH Chap 17)*
Lift is proportional to the square of the airplane's velocity, if the angle of attack and other factors remain constant. For example, an airplane traveling at 200 kt. has four times the lift of the same airplane traveling at 100 kt.
Answer (A) is incorrect because lift is proportional to the square of the airplane's velocity; it is not constant. Answer (B) is incorrect because, as airspeed is doubled, the lift will be four times greater, not doubled.

24.
8378. What true airspeed and angle of attack should be used to generate the same amount of lift as altitude is increased?

A—The same true airspeed and angle of attack.
B—A higher true airspeed for any given angle of attack.
C—A lower true airspeed and higher angle of attack.

Answer (B) is correct (8378). *(FTH Chap 17)*
At an altitude of 18,000 ft., the air has one-half the density of air at sea level. Thus, in order to maintain the same amount of lift as altitude increases, an airplane must fly at a greater true airspeed for any given angle of attack.
Answer (A) is incorrect because true airspeed must be increased, not constant, as altitude increases.
Answer (C) is incorrect because true airspeed must increase, not decrease, for any given angle of attack.

25.
8379. How can an airplane produce the same lift in ground effect as when out of ground effect?

A—The same angle of attack.
B—A lower angle of attack.
C—A higher angle of attack.

Answer (B) is correct (8379). *(FTH Chap 17)*
The reduction of the wingtip vortices due to ground effect alters the spanwise lift distribution and reduces the induced angle of attack and induced drag. The wing will require a lower angle of attack in ground effect to produce the same lift coefficient as when out of ground effect.
Answer (A) is incorrect because, if the same angle of attack is maintained, an increase in lift coefficient will result. Answer (C) is incorrect because a lower, not higher, angle of attack is required to produce the same lift in ground effect as out of ground effect.

26.
8382. By changing the angle of attack of a wing, the pilot can control the airplane's

A—lift, gross weight, and drag.
B—lift, airspeed, and drag.
C—lift and airspeed, but not drag.

Answer (B) is correct (8382). *(FTH Chap 17)*
The pilot can control the airplane's lift, airspeed, and drag. As the angle of attack is increased, the lift increases to the stalling angle of attack, airspeed decreases, and induced drag increases with the increase in lift.
Answer (A) is incorrect because angle of attack cannot control the airplane's gross weight. Answer (C) is incorrect because the pilot can control the amount of induced drag by changing the angle of attack.

6.6 Drag

27.
8346. What is the effect on total drag of an aircraft if the airspeed decreases in level flight below that speed for maximum L/D?

A—Drag increases because of increased induced drag.
B—Drag increases because of increased parasite drag.
C—Drag decreases because of lower induced drag.

Answer (A) is correct (8346). *(FTH Chap 17)*
Total drag is at a minimum for the maximum lift-drag ratio (L/D_{max}) at one specific angle of attack and lift coefficient. As airspeed decreases, the induced drag will increase because a greater angle of attack is required to maintain the lift coefficient. The amount of induced drag varies inversely as the square of the airspeed.
Answer (B) is incorrect because parasite drag varies directly, not inversely, with airspeed. Answer (C) is incorrect because drag increases, not decreases, from any speed other than that for maximum L/D.

28.
8383. What performance is characteristic of flight at maximum L/D in a propeller-driven airplane?

A—Maximum range and distance glide.
B—Best angle of climb.
C—Maximum endurance.

Answer (A) is correct (8383). *(FTH Chap 17)*
At maximum L/D, total drag is at a minimum. This occurs at a particular angle of attack and lift coefficient at which the proportion between speed and power required is the greatest. Thus, the maximum range and engine-out glide distance for a propeller-driven airplane is at maximum L/D.
Answer (B) is incorrect because best angle of climb (e.g., to clear an obstacle) is at a high angle of attack with both high lift and high drag coefficients, which would not result in a maximum L/D ratio. Answer (C) is incorrect because maximum endurance would be obtained at the point of minimum power required, since this would require the lowest fuel flow to keep the airplane in steady, level flight. This point is not at maximum L/D.

29.
8375. What flight condition should be expected when an aircraft leaves ground effect?

A—An increase in induced drag requiring a higher angle of attack.
B—A decrease in parasite drag permitting a lower angle of attack.
C—An increase in dynamic stability.

Answer (A) is correct (8375). *(FTH Chap 17)*
The reduction of the wingtip vortices due to ground effect alters the spanwise lift distribution and reduces the induced angle of attack and induced drag. When leaving ground effect, the airplane will require an increase in angle of attack to maintain the same lift coefficient, which will increase induced drag.
Answer (B) is incorrect because, at slow airspeeds when taking off, induced, not parasite, drag predominates. Answer (C) is incorrect because, when leaving ground effect, expect a decrease, not increase, in stability and a nose-up change in moment.

30.
8397. What is the relationship between induced and parasite drag when the gross weight is increased?

A—Parasite drag increases more than induced drag.
B—Induced drag increases more than parasite drag.
C—Both parasite and induced drag are equally increased.

Answer (B) is correct (8397). *(FTP Chap 7)*
Increasing airplane weight increases the induced drag (more lift is required) more than the parasite drag because a higher angle of attack is required to support the increased weight.
Answer (A) is incorrect because parasite drag increases less, not more, than induced drag as airplane weight increases. Answer (C) is incorrect because induced drag increases more than parasite drag with increases in airplane gross weight.

6.7 Stall Speeds

31.
8341. Which is a purpose of wing-mounted vortex generators?

A—Reduce the drag caused by supersonic flow over portions of the wing.
B—Increase the onset of drag divergence and aid in aileron effectiveness at high speed.
C—Break the airflow over the wing so the stall will progress from the root out to the tip of the wing.

Answer (A) is correct (8341). *(ABS Chap 4)*
Even when jet aircraft do not fly at Mach 1 or greater, airflow over some portions of the upper surface of the wing may exceed Mach 1 and create a shockwave of turbulent air. This turbulent air causes a portion of the wing to partially stall, which causes a substantial increase in drag. Wing-mounted vortex generators are installed to reduce this drag caused by supersonic airflow over portions of the wing.
Answer (B) is incorrect because, although the vortex generators are most effective at high speeds, the increased drag that they produce is not their purpose. Answer (C) is incorrect because a stall strip breaks the airflow over the wing so the stall will progress from the root out to the tip of the wing.

32.
8348. What affects indicated stall speed?

A—Weight, load factor, and power.
B—Load factor, angle of attack, and power.
C—Angle of attack, weight, and air density.

Answer (A) is correct (8348). *(FTH Chap 17)*
An airplane's indicated stall speed is affected by total airplane weight, weight distribution within the airplane, angle of bank, pitch attitude, control coordination, drag, and power settings, but NOT by angle of attack or air density.
Answer (B) is incorrect because indicated stall speed is not affected by the angle of attack. Answer (C) is incorrect because indicated stall speed is not affected by angle of attack or air density.

33.
8344. How can turbulent air cause an increase in stalling speed of an airfoil?

A—An abrupt change in relative wind.
B—A decrease in angle of attack.
C—Sudden decrease in load factor.

Answer (A) is correct (8344). *(AC 61-67B)*
Turbulence can cause an aircraft to stall at a significantly higher airspeed than in stable conditions. A vertical gust or wind shear can cause a sudden change in the relative wind and result in an abrupt increase in the angle of attack and, thus, result in a stall. Although a gust may not be maintained long enough for a stall to develop, the aircraft may stall while the pilot is attempting to control the flight path, particularly during an approach in gusty conditions.
Answer (B) is incorrect because decreased angle of attack decreases, not increases, the possibility of a stall. Answer (C) is incorrect because a sudden decrease in load factor decreases, not increases, the stalling speed.

34.
8356. Airflow separation over the wing can be delayed by using vortex generators,

A—directing high pressure air over the top of the wing or flap through slots and making the wing surface smooth.
B—directing a suction over the top of the wing or flap through slots and making the wing surface smooth.
C—making the wing surface rough and/or directing high pressure air over the top of the wing or flap through slots.

Answer (C) is correct (8356). *(FTP Chap 4)*
Airflow separation over the wing can be delayed by various methods of replacing the slow-moving laminar airflow next to the wing's surface with faster-moving air. One method is the use of vortex generators, which are attached to the upper surface of the wing. Vortex generators make the wing surface rough, creating a turbulent flow that increases the speed of the air. Another method is to direct high-pressure air over the top of the wing, or flap, through slots.
Answer (A) is incorrect because a smooth wing surface does not delay airflow separation. Vortex generators create a turbulent flow of air, which increases the speed of the airflow next to the wing's surface. Answer (B) is incorrect because vortex generators create a turbulent flow of air making the wing surface rough, not smooth. Additionally, slots direct high-pressure air, not a suction, over the top of the wing or flap.

6.8 Load Factor

35.
8347. What is load factor?

A—Lift multiplied by the total weight.
B—Lift subtracted from the total weight.
C—Lift divided by the total weight.

Answer (C) is correct (8347). *(FTH Chap 17)*
A load factor is the ratio of the total airload acting on the airplane to the gross weight of the airplane. For example, if an airplane has a gross weight of 2,000 lb. and during flight is subjected to aerodynamic forces which increase the total load the wing must support to 4,000 lb., the load factor is 2 (4,000 ÷ 2,000). In this example, the airplane wing is producing lift that is equal to twice the gross weight of the airplane.
Answer (A) is incorrect because lift is divided, not multiplied, by the total weight. Answer (B) is incorrect because lift is divided by, not subtracted from, the total weight.

36.
8354. If an aircraft with a gross weight of 2,000 pounds were subjected to a total load of 6,000 pounds in flight, the load factor would be

A—2 G's.
B—3 G's.
C—9 G's.

Answer (B) is correct (8354). *(FTH Chap 17)*
Load factor is the ratio of the total airload acting on the airplane to the gross weight of the airplane. In this problem, the total airload is 6,000 lb., and the gross weight is 2,000 lb. The load factor is 3 (6,000 ÷ 2,000). Load factors are usually expressed in terms of "G," or pull of gravity, in this case three times the actual weight.
Answer (A) is incorrect because 6,000 lb. ÷ 2,000 lb. = 3, not 2. Answer (C) is incorrect because 6,000 lb. ÷ 2,000 lb. = 3, not 9.

37.
8396. For a given angle of bank, the load factor imposed on both the aircraft and pilot in a coordinated constant-altitude turn

A—is directly related to the airplane's gross weight.
B—varies with the rate of turn.
C—is constant.

Answer (C) is correct (8396). *(FTH Chap 17)*
In any airplane at any airspeed, if a coordinated constant altitude turn is maintained, the load factor for a given degree of bank is constant, which is the resultant load of gravity and centrifugal force.
Answer (A) is incorrect because load factor is not affected by changes in gross weight. Answer (B) is incorrect because, for any given angle of bank, the rate of turn varies with the airspeed; thus there is no change in centrifugal force for any given bank. The load factor remains constant.

38.
8353. Upon which factor does wing loading during a level coordinated turn in smooth air depend?

A—Rate of turn.
B—Angle of bank.
C—True airspeed.

Answer (B) is correct (8353). *(FTH Chap 17)*
The load factor for a given airplane during a level coordinated turn is determined solely by the angle of bank.
Answer (A) is incorrect because, in a coordinated turn, the rate of turn does not have any impact on the load factor, which is determined solely by the angle of bank. Answer (C) is incorrect because true airspeed has no impact on the load factor.

39.
8422. What result does a level turn have on the total lift force and load factor?

A—Lift force remains constant and the load factor increases.
B—Lift force increases and the load factor decreases.
C—Both total lift force and load factor increase.

Answer (C) is correct (8422). *(PHAK Chap 1)*
During a level turn, both total lift and load factor increase.
Answer (A) is incorrect because lift increases, not remains constant, in level turns. Answer (B) is incorrect because load factor increases, not decreases, in level turns.

6.9 Pallet Weight

40.
8431. What is the maximum allowable weight that may be carried on a pallet which has the dimensions of 36 x 48 inches?

Floor load limit – 169 lb/sq ft
Pallet weight – 47 lb
Tie-down devices – 33 lb

A—1,948.0 pounds.
B—1,995.0 pounds.
C—1,981.0 pounds.

Answer (A) is correct (8431). *(PWBH Chap 7)*
Pallet area: 36 x 48 = 1,728 sq. in.
Pallet sq. ft.: 1,728 ÷ 144 = 12 sq. ft.
Max. weight: 12 x 169 = 2,028 lb.
Max. cargo weight: 2,028 – 47 – 33 = 1,948 lb.

Answer (B) is incorrect because 1,995 lb. does not include the weight of the pallet as part of the total loaded pallet weight. Answer (C) is incorrect because 1,981 lb. does not include the weight of the tie-down devices as part of the total loaded pallet weight.

41.
8432. What is the maximum allowable weight that may be carried on a pallet which has the dimensions of 76 x 74 inches?

Floor load limit – 176 lb/sq ft
Pallet weight – 77 lb
Tie-down devices – 29 lb

A—6,767.8 pounds.
B—6,873.7 pounds.
C—6,796.8 pounds.

Answer (A) is correct (8432). *(PWBH Chap 7)*
Pallet area: 76 x 74 = 5,624 sq. in.
Pallet sq. ft.: 5,624 ÷ 144 = 39.056 sq. ft.
Max. weight: 39.056 x 176 = 6,873.8 lb.
Max. cargo weight: 6,873.8 – 77 – 29 = 6,767.8 lb.

Answer (B) is incorrect because 6,873.7 lb. is the maximum allowable weight of the pallet, which is a total of the weight of the pallet and tie-down devices, plus the amount carried on the pallet. Answer (C) is incorrect because 6,796.8 lb. does not include the weight of the tie-down devices as part of the total loaded pallet weight.

42.
8433. What is the maximum allowable weight that may be carried on a pallet which has the dimensions of 81 x 83 inches?

Floor load limit – 180 lb/sq ft
Pallet weight – 82 lb
Tie-down devices – 31 lb

A—8,403.7 pounds.
B—8,321.8 pounds.
C—8,290.8 pounds.

Answer (C) is correct (8433). *(PWBH Chap 7)*
Pallet area: 81 x 83 = 6,723 sq. in.
Pallet sq. ft.: 6,723 ÷ 144 = 46.688 sq. ft.
Max. weight: 46.688 x 180 = 8,403.8 lb.
Max. cargo weight: 8,403.8 – 82 – 31 = 8,290.8 lb.

Answer (A) is incorrect because 8,403.7 lb. is the maximum allowable weight of the pallet, which is a total of the weight of the pallet and tie-down devices, plus the amount carried on the pallet. Answer (B) is incorrect because 8,321.8 lb. does not include the weight of the tie-down devices as part of the total loaded pallet weight.

43.
8769. What is the maximum allowable weight that may be carried on a pallet which has the dimensions of 33.5 x 48.5 inches?

Floor load limit – 76 lb/sq ft
Pallet weight – 44 lb
Tie-down devices – 27 lb

A—857.4 pounds.
B—830.4 pounds.
C—786.5 pounds.

Answer (C) is correct (8769). *(PWBH Chap 7)*
Pallet area: 33.5 x 48.5 = 1,624.75 sq. in.
Pallet sq. ft.: 1,624.75 ÷ 144 = 11.283 sq. ft.
Max. weight: 11.283 x 76 = 857.5 lb.
Max. cargo weight: 857.5 – 44 – 27 = 786.5 lb.

Answer (A) is incorrect because 857.4 lb. is the maximum weight of the pallet, which includes the weight of the pallet, tie-down devices, and cargo. Answer (B) is incorrect because 830.4 lb. does not include the weight of the tie-down devices (27 lb.) as part of the total loaded pallet weight.

44.
8770. What is the maximum allowable weight that may be carried on a pallet which has the dimensions of 36.5 x 48.5 inches?

Floor load limit – 112 lb/sq ft
Pallet weight – 45 lb
Tie-down devices – 29 lb

A—1331.8 pounds.
B—1302.8 pounds.
C—1347.8 pounds.

Answer (B) is correct (8770). *(PWBH Chap 7)*
Pallet area: 36.5 x 48.5 = 1,770.25 sq. in.
Pallet sq. ft.: 1,770.25 ÷ 144 = 12.293 sq. ft.
Max. weight: 12.293 x 112 = 1,376.8 lb.
Max. cargo weight: 1,376.8 – 45 – 29 = 1,302.8 lb.

Answer (A) is incorrect because 1,331.8 lb. does not include the weight of the pallet (45 lb.) as part of the total loaded pallet weight. Answer (C) is incorrect because 1,347.8 lb. does not include the weight of the tie-down devices (29 lb.) as part of the total loaded pallet weight.

45.
8771. What is the maximum allowable weight that may be carried on a pallet which has the dimensions of 42.6 x 48.7 inches?

Floor load limit – 121 lb/sq ft
Pallet weight – 47 lb
Tie-down devices – 33 lb

A—1,710.2 pounds.
B—1,663.2 pounds.
C—1,696.2 pounds.

Answer (B) is correct (8771). *(PWBH Chap 7)*
Pallet area: 42.6 x 48.7 = 2,074.62 sq. in.
Pallet sq. ft.: 2,074.62 ÷ 144 = 14.407 sq. ft.
Max. weight: 14.407 x 121 = 1,743.2 lb.
Max. cargo weight: 1,743.2 – 47 – 33 = 1,663.2 lb.

Answer (A) is incorrect because 1,710.2 lb. does not include the weight of the tie-down devices (33 lb.) as part of the total loaded pallet weight. Answer (C) is incorrect because 1,696.2 lb. does not include the weight of the pallet (47 lb.) as part of the total loaded pallet weight.

46.
8772. What is the maximum allowable weight that may be carried on a pallet which has the dimensions of 24.6 x 68.7 inches?

Floor load limit – 85 lb/sq ft
Pallet weight – 44 lb
Tie-down devices – 29 lb

A—924.5 pounds.
B—968.6 pounds.
C—953.6 pounds.

Answer (A) is correct (8772). *(PWBH Chap 7)*
Pallet area: 24.6 x 68.7 = 1,690.02 sq. in.
Pallet sq. ft.: 1,690.02 ÷ 144 = 11.736 sq. ft.
Max. weight: 11.74 x 85 = 997.6 lb.
Max. cargo weight: 997.6 – 44 – 29 = 924.6 lb.

Answer (B) is incorrect because 968.6 lb. does not include the weight of the tie-down devices (29 lb.) as part of the total loaded pallet weight. Answer (C) is incorrect because 953.6 lb. does not include the weight of the pallet (44 lb.) as part of the total loaded pallet weight.

47.
8773. What is the maximum allowable weight that may be carried on a pallet which has the dimensions of 34.6 x 46.4 inches?

Floor load limit – 88 lb/sq ft
Pallet weight – 41 lb
Tie-down devices – 26 lb

A—914.1 pounds.
B—940.1 pounds.
C—981.1 pounds.

Answer (A) is correct (8773). *(PWBH Chap 7)*
Pallet area: 34.6 x 46.4 = 1,605.44 sq. in.
Pallet sq. ft.: 1,605.44 ÷ 144 = 11.149 sq. ft.
Max. weight: 11.149 x 88 = 981.1 lb.
Max. cargo weight: 981.1 – 41 – 26 = 914.1 lb.

Answer (B) is incorrect because 940.1 lb. does not include the weight of the pallet (41 lb.) as part of the total loaded pallet weight. Answer (C) is incorrect because 981.1 lb. is the maximum weight of the pallet, which includes the weight of the pallet, tie-down devices, and cargo.

48.
8776. What is the maximum allowable weight that may be carried on a pallet which has the dimensions of 33.5 x 48.5 inches?

Floor load limit – 66 lb/sq ft
Pallet weight – 34 lb
Tie-down devices – 29 lb

A—744.6 pounds.
B—681.6 pounds.
C—663.0 pounds.

Answer (B) is correct (8776). *(PWBH Chap 7)*
Pallet area: 33.5 x 48.5 = 1,624.75 sq. in.
Pallet sq. ft.: 1,624.75 ÷ 144 = 11.282 sq. ft.
Max. weight: 11.282 x 66 = 744.6 lb.
Max. cargo weight: 744.6 – 34 – 29 = 681.6 lb.

Answer (A) is incorrect because 744.6 lb. is the maximum weight of the pallet, which includes the weight of the pallet, tie-down devices, and cargo. Answer (C) is incorrect because 663.0 lb. is the maximum cargo weight if the floor load limit is 64 lb./sq. ft., not 66 lb./sq. ft.

49.
8777. What is the maximum allowable weight that may be carried on a pallet which has the dimensions of 36.5 x 48.5 inches?

Floor load limit – 107 lb/sq ft
Pallet weight – 37 lb
Tie-down devices – 33 lb

A—1,295.3 pounds.
B—1,212.3 pounds.
C—1,245.3 pounds.

Answer (C) is correct (8777). *(PWBH Chap 7)*
Pallet area: 36.5 x 48.5 = 1,770.25 sq. in.
Pallet sq. ft.: 1,770.25 ÷ 144 = 12.293 sq. ft.
Max. weight: 12.293 x 107 = 1,315.3 lb.
Max. cargo weight: 1,315.3 – 37 – 33 = 1,245.3 lb.

Answer (A) is incorrect because 1,295.3 lb. is the maximum cargo weight if the floor load limit is 111 lb./sq. ft., not 107 lb./sq. ft. Answer (B) is incorrect because 1,212.3 lb. is the maximum cargo weight if the floor load limit is 104 lb./sq. ft., not 107 lb./sq. ft.

50.
8778. What is the maximum allowable weight that may be carried on a pallet which has the dimensions of 42.6 x 48.7 inches?

Floor load limit – 117 lb/sq ft
Pallet weight – 43 lb
Tie-down devices – 31 lb

A—1,611.6 pounds.
B—1,654.6 pounds.
C—1,601.6 pounds.

Answer (A) is correct (8778). *(PWBH Chap 7)*
Pallet area: 42.6 x 48.7 = 2,074.6 sq. in.
Pallet sq. ft.: 2,074.6 ÷ 144 = 14.41 sq. ft.
Max. weight: 14.41 x 117 = 1,686.0 lb.
Max. cargo weight: 1,686 – 43 – 31 = 1,612 lb.

Answer (B) is incorrect because 1,654.6 lb. does not include the weight of the tie-down devices (31 lb.) as part of the total pallet weight. Answer (C) is incorrect because 1,601.6 lb. is the maximum cargo weight if the floor load limit is 116 lb./sq. ft., not 117 lb./sq. ft.

51.
8779. What is the maximum allowable weight that may be carried on a pallet which has the dimensions of 24.6 x 68.7 inches?

Floor load limit – 79 lb/sq ft
Pallet weight – 43 lb
Tie-down devices – 27 lb

A—884.1 pounds.
B—857.1 pounds.
C—841.1 pounds.

Answer (B) is correct (8779). *(PWBH Chap 7)*
Pallet area: 24.6 x 68.7 = 1,690.02 sq. in.
Pallet sq. ft.: 1,690.02 ÷ 144 = 11.736 sq. ft.
Max. weight: 11.736 x 79 = 927.1 lb.
Max. cargo weight: 927.1 – 43 – 27 = 857.1 lb.

Answer (A) is incorrect because 884.1 lb. does not include the weight of the pallet (43 lb.) as part of the total pallet weight. Answer (C) is incorrect because 841.1 lb. is the maximum cargo weight if the floor load limit is 78 lb./sq. ft., not 79 lb./sq. ft.

52.
8781. What is the maximum allowable weight that may be carried on a pallet which has the dimensions of 143 x 125.2 inches?

Floor load limit – 209 lb/sq ft
Pallet weight – 197 lb
Tie-down devices – 66 lb

A—25,984.9 pounds.
B—25,787.9 pounds.
C—25,721.9 pounds.

Answer (C) is correct (8781). *(PWBH Chap 7)*
Pallet area: 143 x 125.2 = 17,903.6 sq. in.
Pallet sq. ft.: 17,903.6 ÷ 144 = 124.33 sq. ft.
Max. weight: 124.33 x 209 = 25,984.9 lb.
Max. cargo weight:
25,984.9 – 197 – 66 = 25,721.9 lb.

Answer (A) is incorrect because 25,984.9 lb. is the maximum weight of the pallet, which includes the weight of the pallet, tie-down devices, and cargo. Answer (B) is incorrect because 25,787.9 lb. does not include the weight of the pallet (197 lb.) as part of the total loaded pallet weight.

53.
8787. What is the maximum allowable weight that may be carried on a pallet which has the dimensions of 138.5 x 97.6 inches?

Floor load limit – 235 lb/sq ft
Pallet weight – 219 lb
Tie-down devices – 71 lb

A—21,840.9 pounds.
B—21,769.9 pounds.
C—22,059.9 pounds.

Answer (B) is correct (8787). *(PWBH Chap 7)*
Pallet area: 138.5 x 97.6 = 13,517.6 sq. in.
Pallet sq. ft.: 13,517.6 ÷ 144 = 93.87 sq. ft.
Max. weight: 93.87 x 235 = 22,059.9 lb.
Max. cargo weight:
22,059.9 – 219 – 71 = 21,769.9 lb.

Answer (A) is incorrect because 21,840.9 lb. does not include the weight of the pallet (219 lb.) as part of the total loaded pallet weight. Answer (C) is incorrect because 22,059.9 lb. is the maximum weight of the pallet, which includes the weight of the pallet, tie-down devices, and cargo.

54.
8788. What is the maximum allowable weight that may be carried on a pallet which has the dimensions of 96.1 x 133.3 inches?

Floor load limit – 249 lb/sq ft
Pallet weight – 347 lb
Tie-down devices – 134 lb

A—21,669.8 pounds.
B—21,803.8 pounds.
C—22,120.8 pounds.

Answer (A) is correct (8788). *(PWBH Chap 7)*
Pallet area: 96.1 x 133.3 = 12,810.1 sq. in.
Pallet sq. ft.: 12,810.1 ÷ 144 = 88.96 sq. ft.
Max. weight: 88.96 x 249 = 22,150.8 lb.
Max. cargo weight:
22,150.8 – 347 – 134 = 21,669.8 lb.

Answer (B) is incorrect because 21,803.8 lb. does not include the weight of the pallet (347 lb.) as part of the total loaded pallet weight. Answer (C) is incorrect because 22,120.8 lb. is the approximate maximum weight of the pallet, which includes the weight of the pallet, tie-down devices, and cargo.

55.
8789. What is the maximum allowable weight that may be carried on a pallet which has the dimensions of 87.7 x 116.8 inches?

Floor load limit – 175 lb/sq ft
Pallet weight – 137 lb
Tie-down devices – 49 lb

A—12,262.4 pounds.
B—12,448.4 pounds.
C—12,311.4 pounds.

Answer (A) is correct (8789). *(PWBH Chap 7)*
Pallet area: 87.7 x 116.8 = 10,243.36 sq. in.
Pallet sq. ft.: 10,243.36 ÷ 144 = 71.134 sq. ft.
Max. weight: 71.134 x 175 = 12,448.4 lb.
Max. cargo weight:
12,448.4 – 137 – 49 = 12,262.4 lb.

Answer (B) is incorrect because 12,448.4 lb. is the maximum allowable weight of the pallet, which includes the weight of the pallet, tie-down devices, and the cargo. Answer (C) is incorrect because 12,311.4 lb. does not include the weight of the pallet (137 lb.) as part of the total loaded pallet weight.

56.
8790. What is the maximum allowable weight that may be carried on a pallet which has the dimensions of 98.7 x 78.9 inches?

Floor load limit – 183 lb/sq ft
Pallet weight – 161 lb
Tie-down devices – 54 lb

A—9,896.5 pounds.
B—9,735.5 pounds.
C—9,681.5 pounds.

Answer (C) is correct (8790). *(PWBH Chap 7)*
Pallet area: 98.7 x 78.9 = 7,787.4 sq. in.
Pallet sq. ft.: 7,787.4 ÷ 144 = 54.08 sq. ft.
Max. weight: 54.08 x 183 = 9,896.5 lb.
Max. cargo weight:
9,896.5 – 161 – 54 = 9,681.5 lb.

Answer (A) is incorrect because 9,896.5 lb. is the maximum weight of the pallet, which includes the weight of the pallet, tie-down devices, and cargo. Answer (B) is incorrect because 9,735.5 lb. does not include the weight of the pallet as part of the total loaded pallet weight.

57.
8791. What minimum floor load limit must an aircraft have to carry the following pallet of cargo?

Pallet size is 78.9 inches wide and 98.7 inches long
Pallet weight – 161 lb
Tie-down devices – 54 lb
Cargo weight – 9,681.5 lb

A—182 lb/sq ft.
B—180 lb/sq ft.
C—183 lb/sq ft.

Answer (C) is correct (8791). *(PWBH Chap 7)*
Pallet area: 78.9 x 98.7 = 7,787.4 sq. in.
Pallet sq. ft.: 7,787.4 ÷ 144 = 54.08 sq. ft.
Pallet net weight: 161 + 54 + 9,681.5 = 9,896.5 lb.
Min. floor load limit:
9,896.5 ÷ 54.08 = 183 lb./sq. ft.

Answer (A) is incorrect because a minimum floor load limit of 182 lb./sq. ft. does not include the weight of the tie-down devices (54 lb.) as part of the pallet net weight. Answer (B) is incorrect because a minimum floor load limit of 180 lb./sq. ft. does not include the weight of the pallet (161 lb.) as part of the pallet net weight.

58.
8844. What is the minimum floor load limit that an aircraft must have to carry the following pallet of cargo?

Pallet dimensions are 39 x 37 inches
Pallet weight – 37 lb
Tie-down devices – 21 lb
Cargo weight – 1,094.3 lb

A—115 lb/sq ft.
B—112 lb/sq ft.
C—109 lb/sq ft.

Answer (A) is correct (8844). *(PWBH Chap 7)*
Pallet area: 39 x 37 = 1,443 sq. in.
Pallet sq. ft.: 1,443 ÷ 144 = 10.02 sq. ft.
Pallet net weight: 37 + 21 + 1,094.3 = 1,152.3 lb.
Min. floor load limit:
1,152.3 ÷ 10.02 = 115 lb./sq. ft.

Answer (B) is incorrect because a minimum floor load limit of 112 lb./sq. ft. does not include the weight of the tie-down devices (21 lb.) as part of the pallet net weight. Answer (C) is incorrect because a minimum floor load limit of 109 lb./sq. ft. does not include the weight of the pallet (37 lb.) and the tie-down devices (21 lb.) as part of the pallet net weight.

59.
8845. What is the minimum floor load limit that an aircraft must have to carry the following pallet of cargo?

Pallet dimensions are 37.5 x 35 inches
Pallet weight – 34 lb
Tie-down devices – 23 lb
Cargo weight – 1,255.4 lb

A—152 lb/sq ft.
B—148 lb/sq ft.
C—144 lb/sq ft.

Answer (C) is correct (8845). *(PWBH Chap 7)*
Pallet area: 37.5 x 35 = 1,312.5 sq. in.
Pallet sq. ft.: 1,312.5 ÷ 144 = 9.11 sq. ft.
Pallet net weight: 34 + 23 + 1,255.4 = 1,312.4 lb.
Min. floor load limit:
1,312.4 ÷ 9.11 = 144 lb./sq. ft.

Answer (A) is incorrect because a minimum floor load limit of 152 lb./sq. ft. is required for a pallet net weight of 1,384.7 lb., not 1,312.4 lb. Answer (B) is incorrect because a minimum floor load limit of 148 lb./sq. ft. is required for a pallet net weight of 1,348.3 lb., not 1,312.4 lb.

60.
8846. What is the minimum floor load limit that an aircraft must have to carry the following pallet of cargo?

Pallet dimensions are 48.5 x 33.5 inches
Pallet weight – 44 lb
Tie-down devices – 27 lb
Cargo weight – 786.5 lb

A—79 lb/sq ft.
B—76 lb/sq ft.
C—73 lb/sq ft.

Answer (B) is correct (8846). *(PWBH Chap 7)*
Pallet area: 48.5 x 33.5 = 1,624.75 sq. in.
Pallet sq. ft.: 1,624.75 ÷ 144 = 11.28 sq. ft.
Pallet net weight: 44 + 27 + 786.5 = 857.5 lb.
Min. floor load limit: 857.5 ÷ 11.28 = 76 lb./sq. ft.

Answer (A) is incorrect because a minimum floor load limit of 79 lb./sq. ft. is required for a pallet net weight of 891.1 lb., not 857.5 lb. Answer (C) is incorrect because a minimum floor load limit of 73 lb./sq. ft. does not include the weight of the tie-down devices (27 lb.) as part of the pallet net weight.

61.
8847. What is the minimum floor load limit that an aircraft must have to carry the following pallet of cargo?

Pallet dimensions are 116.8 x 87.7 inches
Pallet weight – 137 lb
Tie-down devices – 49 lb
Cargo weight – 12,262.4 lb

A—172 lb/sq ft.
B—176 lb/sq ft.
C—179 lb/sq ft.

Answer (B) is correct (8847). *(PWBH Chap 7)*
Pallet area: 116.8 x 87.7 = 10,243.36 sq. in.
Pallet sq. ft.: 10,243.36 ÷ 144 = 71.13 sq. ft.
Pallet net weight: 137 + 49 + 12,262.4 = 12,448.4 lb.
Min. floor load limit:
12,448.4 ÷ 71.13 = 175 lb./sq. ft.

Answer (A) is incorrect because a minimum floor load limit of 172 lb./sq. ft. is required for a pallet net weight of 12,234.4 lb., which is less than the cargo weight of 12,262.4 lb. The pallet net weight includes the cargo weight, the pallet weight, and the weight of the tie-down devices. Answer (C) is incorrect because a minimum floor load limit of 179 lb./sq. ft. is required for a pallet net weight of 12,732.3 lb., not 12,448.4 lb.

62.
8848. What is the minimum floor load limit that an aircraft must have to carry the following pallet of cargo?

Pallet dimensions are 78.9 x 98.7 inches
Pallet weight – 161 lb
Tie-down devices – 54 lb
Cargo weight – 9,681.5 lb

A—180 lb/sq ft.
B—186 lb/sq ft.
C—183 lb/sq ft.

Answer (C) is correct (8848). *(PWBH Chap 7)*
Pallet area: 78.9 x 98.7 = 7,787.43 sq. in.
Pallet sq. ft.: 7,787.43 ÷ 144 = 54.08 sq. ft.
Pallet net weight: 161 + 54 + 9,681.5 = 9,896.5 lb.
Min. floor load limit:
9,896.5 ÷ 54.08 = 183 lb./sq. ft.

Answer (A) is incorrect because a minimum floor load limit of 180 lb./sq. ft. does not include the weight of the pallet (161 lb.) as part of the pallet net weight. Answer (B) is incorrect because a minimum floor load limit of 186 lb./sq. ft. is required for a pallet net weight of 10,059 lb., not 9,896.5 lb.

6.10 Climbs

63.
8399. At which speed will increasing the pitch attitude cause an airplane to climb?

A—Low speed.
B—High speed.
C—Any speed.

Answer (B) is correct (8399). *(FTP Chap 6)*
At speeds below L/D_{max}, an increase in pitch will slow the airplane down (i.e., the region of reverse command). At L/D_{max} and above, an increase in pitch will increase climb or decrease descent.
Answer (A) is incorrect because, below L/D_{max}, performance decreases, not increases, with increases in pitch. Answer (C) is incorrect because, below L/D_{max}, performance decreases, not increases, with increases in pitch.

64.
8400. At what speed, with reference to L/D_{max}, does maximum rate-of-climb for a jet airplane occur?

A—A speed greater than that for L/D_{max}.
B—A speed equal to that for L/D_{max}.
C—A speed less than that for L/D_{max}.

Answer (A) is correct (8400). *(FTP Chap 6)*
The maximum rate-of-climb for a jet airplane will occur at a speed greater than that for L/D_{max}. This occurrence is accounted for, in part, by the increase in power available with speed.
Answer (B) is incorrect because a speed equal to that of L/D_{max} is the maximum climb angle, not rate-of-climb. Answer (C) is incorrect because the maximum rate-of-climb is at a speed greater, not less, than L/D_{max}.

6.11 Turns

65.
8345. What effect does an increase in airspeed have on a coordinated turn while maintaining a constant angle of bank and altitude?

A—The rate of turn will decrease resulting in a decreased load factor.
B—The rate of turn will increase resulting in an increased load factor.
C—The rate of turn will decrease resulting in no changes in load factor.

Answer (C) is correct (8345). *(FTH Chap 17)*
Increasing airspeed while maintaining a coordinated turn with a constant angle of bank and altitude will decrease the rate of turn. For any given bank angle, the rate of turn varies with the airspeed; the higher the speed, the slower the rate of turn. This variation compensates for added centrifugal force, allowing the load factor to remain the same.
Answer (A) is incorrect because, at a constant bank angle, the higher airspeed will decrease the rate of turn to compensate for added centrifugal force, allowing the load factor to remain the same, not decrease. Answer (B) is incorrect because, for any bank angle, the rate of turn varies with the airspeed; the higher the speed, the slower, not faster, the rate of turn.

66.
8349. If no corrective action is taken by the pilot as angle of bank is increased, how is the vertical component of lift and sink rate affected?

A—Lift increases and the sink rate increases.
B—Lift decreases and the sink rate decreases.
C—Lift decreases and the sink rate increases.

Answer (C) is correct (8349). *(FTH Chap 17)*
As the angle of bank is increased, the horizontal component of lift increases, which decreases the vertical component. As this happens, weight is greater than the vertical component of lift, and lift decreases as the sink rate increases.
Answer (A) is incorrect because lift will decrease, not increase. Answer (B) is incorrect because the sink rate increases, not decreases, as the lift decreases.

67.
8352. What is the relationship of the rate of turn with the radius of turn with a constant angle of bank but increasing airspeed?

A—Rate will decrease and radius will increase.
B—Rate will increase and radius will decrease.
C—Rate and radius will increase.

Answer (A) is correct (8352). *(FTH Chap 17)*
As airspeed is increased, the angle of attack needs to be decreased, which will cause the rate of turn to decrease. At the same time, the increase in airspeed results in an increase of the turn radius.
Answer (B) is incorrect because, to maintain a constant angle of bank while increasing airspeed, the radius of turn will increase, not decrease. Answer (C) is incorrect because, to maintain a constant angle of bank while increasing airspeed, the rate of turn will decrease, not increase.

68.
8351. How can the pilot increase the rate of turn and decrease the radius at the same time?

A—Steepen the bank and increase airspeed.
B—Steepen the bank and decrease airspeed.
C—Shallow the bank and increase airspeed.

Answer (B) is correct (8351). *(FTH Chap 17)*
At slower airspeeds, an airplane can make a turn in less distance (smaller radius) and at a faster rate. Thus, to decrease the radius and increase the rate, one steepens the bank and decreases airspeed.
Answer (A) is incorrect because a decrease, not increase, in airspeed decreases the turn radius. Answer (C) is incorrect because a steeper, not shallower, bank and a decrease, not increase, in airspeed increase the rate of turn.

69.
8350. Why must the angle of attack be increased during a turn to maintain altitude?

A—Compensate for loss of vertical component of lift.
B—Increase the horizontal component of lift equal to the vertical component.
C—Compensate for increase in drag.

Answer (A) is correct (8350). *(FTH Chap 17)*
The lift during a turn is divided into two components, one vertical and the other horizontal. This division reduces the amount of lift which is opposing gravity. The angle of attack must be increased until the vertical component of lift is equal to the weight in order to maintain altitude.
Answer (B) is incorrect because angle of attack is increased in order to increase the vertical component of lift to equal weight. Answer (C) is incorrect because additional thrust (power), not angle of attack, is used to compensate for increase in drag.

6.12 Stability

70.
8367. Describe dynamic longitudinal stability.

A—Motion about the longitudinal axis.
B—Motion about the lateral axis.
C—Motion about the vertical axis.

Answer (B) is correct (8367). *(FTH Chap 17)*
Longitudinal stability is the quality which makes an airplane stable about its lateral axis. It involves the pitching motion as the airplane's nose moves up and down in flight. Dynamic stability is the overall tendency that the airplane displays after its equilibrium is disturbed.
Answer (A) is incorrect because motion about the airplane's longitudinal axis is lateral, not longitudinal, stability. Answer (C) is incorrect because motion about the vertical axis is directional, not longitudinal, stability.

71.
8366. What is a characteristic of longitudinal instability?

A—Pitch oscillations becoming progressively greater.
B—Bank oscillations becoming progressively greater.
C—Aircraft constantly tries to pitch down.

Answer (A) is correct (8366). *(FTH Chap 17)*
Longitudinal stability is the quality which makes an airplane stable about its lateral axis (pitching). A longitudinally unstable airplane has a tendency to dive or climb (oscillations) progressively into a very steep dive or climb.
Answer (B) is incorrect because longitudinal stability refers to pitch, not bank, oscillations. Answer (C) is incorrect because the aircraft constantly trying to pitch down is a characteristic of improper elevator trim, not longitudinal instability.

72.
8365. Identify the type stability if the aircraft attitude remains in the new position after the controls have been neutralized.

A—Negative longitudinal static stability.
B—Neutral longitudinal dynamic stability.
C—Neutral longitudinal static stability.

Answer (C) is correct (8365). *(FTH Chap 17)*
If the airplane's nose remains in the new position after the elevator control is pressed forward and released, the aircraft displays neutral longitudinal static stability.
Answer (A) is incorrect because a negative longitudinal static stability means the airplane tends to move even farther from the original position. Answer (B) is incorrect because, with neutral longitudinal dynamic stability, the airplane continues to oscillate without a tendency to increase or decrease.

73.
8372. Identify the type stability if the aircraft attitude tends to move farther from its original position after the controls have been neutralized.

A—Negative static stability.
B—Positive static stability.
C—Negative dynamic stability.

Answer (A) is correct (8372). *(FTH Chap 17)*
When the airplane's nose moves farther from its original position, it has the undesirable characteristic of negative static stability.
Answer (B) is incorrect because, if the aircraft had positive static stability, it would return to its original position. Answer (C) is incorrect because negative dynamic stability refers to oscillations that become progressively larger.

74.
8373. Identify the type stability if the aircraft attitude tends to return to its original position after the controls have been neutralized.

A—Positive dynamic stability.
B—Positive static stability.
C—Neutral dynamic stability.

Answer (B) is correct (8373). *(FTH Chap 17)*
Imagine that you trim the airplane for hands-off control in level flight and then momentarily give the controls a slight push to nose the airplane down. If within a brief period the nose rises to the original position and then stops, the airplane is statically stable. It is positively statically stable because it has returned to its original position after being displaced.
Answer (A) is incorrect because positive dynamic stability refers to oscillations being dampened or decreasing. Answer (C) is incorrect because neutral dynamic stability refers to oscillations continuing without a tendency to increase or decrease.

6.13 Effect of Rearward CG

75.
8380. What are some characteristics of an airplane loaded with the CG at the aft limit?

A—Lowest stall speed, highest cruise speed, and least stability.
B—Highest stall speed, highest cruise speed, and least stability.
C—Lowest stall speed, lowest cruise speed, and highest stability.

Answer (A) is correct (8380). *(FTH Chap 17)*
The airplane will stall at a higher speed with a forward CG location. The critical angle of attack is reached at a higher speed due to increased wing loading. Conversely, the airplane will stall at a lower speed with an aft CG loading. The airplane will cruise faster with an aft CG location because of reduced drag. The airplane will become less stable as the CG is moved rearward.
Answer (B) is incorrect because an aft CG causes the airplane to have the lowest, not highest, stall speed. Answer (C) is incorrect because an aft CG causes an airplane to have the highest, not lowest, cruise speed and the least, not highest, stability.

76.
8376. What characteristic should exist if an airplane is loaded to the rear of its CG range?

A—Sluggish in aileron control.
B—Sluggish in rudder control.
C—Unstable about the lateral axis.

Answer (C) is correct (8376). *(FTH Chap 17)*
The rearward CG limit is largely determined by considerations of stability. When loaded to the rear of its CG limit, an airplane will become unstable about the lateral axis, i.e., longitudinally unstable. At this point when the nose is momentarily pulled up, it may alternately climb and dive, becoming steeper with each oscillation.
Answer (A) is incorrect because an aft location of the CG has a greater effect on the longitudinal stability, not the lateral (aileron) controllability. Answer (B) is incorrect because an aft CG has a greater effect on the longitudinal stability, not vertical (rudder) controllability.

6.14 Takeoff and Landing Performance

77.
9083. What effect does an uphill runway slope have upon takeoff performance?

A—Increases takeoff distance.
B—Decreases takeoff speed.
C—Decreases takeoff distance.

Answer (A) is correct (9083). *(PHAK Chap IV)*
The upslope of a runway impedes acceleration, resulting in a longer ground run on takeoff.
Answer (B) is incorrect because indicated airspeed for takeoff remains the same. Answer (C) is incorrect because the takeoff distance is increased, not decreased.

78.
9075. Which condition reduces the required runway for takeoff?

A—Higher-than-recommended airspeed before rotation.
B—Lower-than-standard air density.
C—Increased headwind component.

Answer (C) is correct (9075). *(FTH Chap 17)*
The effect of a headwind is to allow the airplane to reach lift-off speed at a lower groundspeed. A headwind which is 10% of the takeoff airspeed will reduce the takeoff distance approximately 19%.
Answer (A) is incorrect because higher-than-recommended airspeed before rotation increases, not reduces, the required runway for takeoff. Answer (B) is incorrect because lower-than-standard air density increases, not decreases, the required runway for takeoff.

79.
9076. Which performance factor decreases as airplane gross weight increases, for a given runway?

A—Critical engine failure speed.
B—Rotation speed.
C—Accelerate-stop distance.

Answer (A) is correct (9076). *(FTP Chap 12)*
Critical engine failure speed (i.e., takeoff decision speed or V_1) is the speed to which the airplane can be accelerated, lose an engine, and then either continue the takeoff with the remaining engine(s) or stop, in the same total runway distance. Critical engine failure speed decreases as the airplane gross weight increases due to the increased mass that must decelerate and stop in the event of a rejected takeoff.
Answer (B) is incorrect because an increase in aircraft gross weight usually results in an increase in the rotation speed (V_R). Answer (C) is incorrect because the accelerate-stop distance will increase as the aircraft gross weight increases.

80.
8374. What effect does landing at high elevation airports have on groundspeed with comparable conditions relative to temperature, wind, and airplane weight?

A—Higher than at low elevation.
B—Lower than at low elevation.
C—The same as at low elevation.

Answer (A) is correct (8374). *(FTH Chap 17)*
An airplane at altitude will land at the same indicated airspeed as at sea level but, because of the reduced density (comparable conditions), the true airspeed (TAS) will be greater. Thus, with a higher TAS, the groundspeed will be higher at high elevation airports than at low elevation.
Answer (B) is incorrect because, at high elevation, there is reduced air density, and thus TAS will increase. As TAS increases, groundspeed will increase, not decrease. Answer (C) is incorrect because, under comparable conditions, TAS will increase and cause the groundspeed to be higher, not the same, at higher elevation.

81.
9084. Under which condition during the landing roll are the main wheel brakes at maximum effectiveness?

A—When wing lift has been reduced.
B—At high groundspeeds.
C—When the wheels are locked and skidding.

Answer (A) is correct (9084). *(FTW Chap 15)*

During the landing roll, the main wheel brakes are at maximum effectiveness when wing lift has been reduced and the normal force on the wheels approaches the weight of the airplane. At this point, the braking friction force is at maximum.

Answer (B) is incorrect because, at high groundspeeds, the lift is greater and the normal force on the wheels is small; thus the braking friction force is small. Answer (C) is incorrect because, when the wheels are locked and skidding, the braking friction force is small.

6.15 Maximum Range

82.
8398. What should a pilot do to maintain "best range" airplane performance when a tailwind is encountered?

A—Increase speed.
B—Maintain speed.
C—Decrease speed.

Answer (C) is correct (8398). *(FTP Chap 6)*

A pilot flying an airplane in a tailwind should decrease speed to take advantage of the wind. In a headwind, the pilot should increase speed to reduce the effect of the wind.

Answer (A) is incorrect because a pilot would increase speed with a headwind, not a tailwind. Answer (B) is incorrect because a pilot would maintain speed in a calm wind, not tailwind, condition.

83.
8381. Which maximum range factor decreases as weight decreases?

A—Angle of attack.
B—Altitude.
C—Airspeed.

Answer (C) is correct (8381). *(FTH Chap 17)*

For propeller-driven airplanes, maximum range is obtained at maximum lift-drag (L/D) ratio, the point at which the proportion between speed and power required is greatest. As weight decreases, so does this optimum airspeed due to a reduction in the maximum L/D. Additionally, for jet aircraft airspeed must be reduced as weight decreases to obtain maximum range.

Answer (A) is incorrect because the factors of maximum range are weight, altitude, and aerodynamic configuration of the airplane, not angle of attack. Answer (B) is incorrect because maximum range altitude may increase, not decrease, with a decrease in weight.

84.
9078. Which procedure produces the minimum fuel consumption for a given leg of the cruise flight?

A—Increase speed for a headwind.
B—Increase speed for a tailwind.
C—Increase altitude for a headwind, decrease altitude for a tailwind.

Answer (A) is correct (9078). *(FTP Chap 6)*

Airplanes flying in a headwind should fly at higher airspeeds to reduce the effect of the headwind. Conversely, airplanes flying in a tailwind should slow to take advantage of the wind with lower power settings.

Answer (B) is incorrect because tailwind increases performance, and slower TAS decreases fuel consumption. Answer (C) is incorrect because airspeed, not altitude, should be adjusted according to the wind.

85.
8401. At what speed, with reference to L/D_{max}, does maximum range for a jet airplane occur?

A—A speed less than that for L/D_{max}.
B—A speed equal to that for L/D_{max}.
C—A speed greater than that for L/D_{max}.

Answer (C) is correct (8401). *(FTP Chap 6)*

Maximum range for a jet airplane occurs when the proportion between velocity and thrust required is greatest, and this point is at a speed greater than that for L/D_{max}.

Answer (A) is incorrect because a speed greater, not less, than L/D_{max} will obtain maximum range for a jet airplane. Answer (B) is incorrect because a speed equal to that of L/D_{max} is a jet airplane's maximum endurance, not maximum range.

86.
9077. Maximum range performance of a turbojet aircraft is obtained by which procedure as aircraft weight reduces?

A—Increasing speed or altitude.
B—Increasing altitude or decreasing speed.
C—Increasing speed or decreasing altitude.

Answer (B) is correct (9077). *(FTP Chap 7)*
Maximum range is the consideration of maximum flying distance. "Cruise control" of an airplane implies that the airplane is operated to maintain the recommended long-range cruise condition throughout the flight. As fuel is consumed, the gross weight will vary and optimum airspeed, altitude, and power setting can vary. As the gross weight decreases, the optimum airspeed and power may decrease, or the optimum altitude may increase.
Answer (A) is incorrect because, as weight decreases, the optimum speed decreases, not increases, or altitude increases. Answer (C) is incorrect because, as weight decreases, speed decreases, not increases, or altitude increases, not decreases.

6.16 Propeller Pitch and Engine Performance

87.
8368. What is the reason for variations in geometric pitch along a propeller or rotor blade?

A—It permits a relatively constant angle of attack along its length when in cruising flight.
B—It prevents the portion of the blade near the hub or root from stalling during cruising flight.
C—It permits a relatively constant angle of incidence along its length when in cruising flight.

Answer (A) is correct (8368). *(FTH Chap 17)*
Variations in the geometric pitch of the blades permit the propeller to operate with a relatively constant angle of attack along its length when in cruising flight. Propeller blades have variations to change the blade in proportion to the differences in speed of rotation along the length of the propeller and thereby keep thrust more nearly equalized along this length.
Answer (B) is incorrect because, if there were no variation in geometric pitch, the propeller tips, not the root, would be stalled during cruising flight. Answer (C) is incorrect because variations in geometric pitch permit a constant angle of attack, not incidence, along its length.

88.
9068. Under normal operating conditions, which combination of MAP and RPM produce the most severe wear, fatigue, and damage to high performance reciprocating engines?

A—High RPM and low MAP.
B—Low RPM and high MAP.
C—High RPM and high MAP.

Answer (A) is correct (9068). *(AFNA Chap 2)*
The most severe rate of wear and fatigue damage occurs at high RPM and low MAP, on engines found on transport category airplanes, such as a DC-6. High RPM produces high centrifugal loads and reciprocating inertia loads. Thus, operating time at maximum RPM and MAP must be held to a minimum, and operation at maximum RPM and low MAP must be avoided. See page 145 of *Aerodynamics for Naval Aviators*. Note that this is the opposite from what we learn as commercial pilots regarding current high-performance engines.
Answer (B) is incorrect because high, not low, RPM and low, not high, MAP produce the most severe wear to high-performance reciprocating engines. Answer (C) is incorrect because a high RPM and a low, not high, MAP produce the most severe wear to high-performance reciprocating engines.

89.
9069. What effect does high relative humidity have upon the maximum power output of modern aircraft engines?

A—Neither turbojet nor reciprocating engines are affected.
B—Reciprocating engines will experience a significant loss of BHP.
C—Turbojet engines will experience a significant loss of thrust.

Answer (B) is correct (9069). *(PHAK Chap IV)*
Water vapor, i.e., high relative humidity, will cause a significant reduction of power output of reciprocating engines but a negligible loss of thrust for a turbojet engine.
Answer (A) is incorrect because both reciprocating and turbojet engines are affected by high relative humidity. Answer (C) is incorrect because turbojet engines will have a negligible, not significant, loss of thrust.

6.17 Turbochargers

90.
9072. Where is the critical altitude of a supercharged-reciprocating engine?

A—The highest altitude at which a desired manifold pressure can be obtained.
B—Highest altitude where the mixture can be leaned to best power ratio.
C—The altitude at which maximum allowable BMEP can be obtained.

Answer (A) is correct (9072). *(FTH Chap 2)*
Because the density of air decreases as altitude increases, the supercharger compresses the thin air to maintain the preset power (manifold pressure) as the airplane climbs. When the critical altitude is reached, the turbine is rotating at its highest speed and can no longer compensate for decreasing manifold pressure after that altitude is exceeded.
Answer (B) is incorrect because critical altitude is the highest altitude at which a manifold pressure, not fuel mixture, can be obtained. Answer (C) is incorrect because BMEP is pressure representing the mean gas load on the piston during the power stroke, not the air pressure in the manifold.

91.
9073. What is controlled by the waste gate of a turbocharged-reciprocating engine?

A—Supercharger gear ratio.
B—Exhaust gas discharge.
C—Throttle opening.

Answer (B) is correct (9073). *(FTH Chap 2)*
The waste gate allows exhaust gas to be directed to drive the turbine of the turbocharger. The waste gate is normally controlled automatically to maintain the required amount of exhaust gas flow so the turbocharger can maintain the desired manifold pressure. At the critical altitude, the exhaust gas waste gate is fully closed, and the turbine is operating at maximum speed.
Answer (A) is incorrect because the waste gate controls exhaust gas discharge, not a supercharger gear ratio. Answer (C) is incorrect because the throttle opening sets the desired manifold pressure; it does not operate a waste gate that is part of the turbocharger system.

6.18 Multiengine Airplane Operation

92.
8363. Under what condition should stalls never be practiced in a twin-engine airplane?

A—With one engine inoperative.
B—With climb power on.
C—With full flaps and gear extended.

Answer (A) is correct (8363). *(FTH Chap 16)*
The pilot of a twin-engine airplane should become familiar with imminent stalls entered with various flap settings, power settings, and landing gear positions. Because of possible loss of control, stalls with one engine inoperative or at idle power and the other developing effective power are not to be practiced.
Answer (B) is incorrect because you may be required to practice stalls with climb power on. Answer (C) is incorrect because stalls should be practiced with full flaps and gear extended, as in a stall on approach to landing.

93.
8364. What does the blue radial line on the airspeed indicator of a light, twin-engine airplane represent?

A—Maximum single-engine rate of climb.
B—Maximum single-engine angle of climb.
C—Minimum controllable airspeed for single-engine operation.

Answer (A) is correct (8364). *(FTH Chap 16)*
The airspeed indicator of a light, twin-engine airplane is marked (in addition to other normally marked airspeeds) with a red radial line at the minimum controllable airspeed with the critical engine inoperative, and a blue radial line at the best rate-of-climb airspeed with one engine inoperative.
Answer (B) is incorrect because the blue radial line is the maximum single-engine rate, not angle, of climb. Answer (C) is incorrect because minimum controllable airspeed for single-engine operation is marked by a red, not blue, radial line.

94.
8360. What performance should a pilot of a light, twin-engine airplane be able to maintain at V_{MC}?

A—Heading.
B—Heading and altitude.
C—Heading, altitude, and ability to climb 50 ft/min.

Answer (A) is correct (8360). *(FTH Chap 16)*

V_{MC} represents the minimum controllable airspeed with a critical engine inoperative. FAA regulations require that, in an airplane at V_{MC}, the pilot must at least be able to stop the turn which results when the critical engine is suddenly made inoperative within 20° of the original heading using max rudder deflection and a max bank of 5° into the operative engine. Also, after recovery, the pilot must maintain the airplane in straight flight with not more than 5° bank wing lowered toward the operating engine. This does not mean that the airplane must be able to climb or even to hold altitude. It means only that a heading can be maintained.

Answer (B) is incorrect because the ability to maintain altitude is not a requirement of V_{MC}. Answer (C) is incorrect because the ability to hold altitude and climb is not a requirement of V_{MC}.

95.
8362. What effect, if any, does altitude have on V_{MC} for an airplane with unsupercharged engines?

A—None.
B—Increases with altitude.
C—Decreases with altitude.

Answer (C) is correct (8362). *(FTH Chap 16)*

For an airplane with unsupercharged engines, V_{MC} decreases as altitude is increased; i.e., directional control can be maintained at a lower airspeed than at sea level. V_{MC} is a function of power, which decreases with altitude. It is possible for the airplane to reach a stall speed prior to the loss of directional control.

Answer (A) is incorrect because V_{MC} is always affected by altitude. Answer (B) is incorrect because V_{MC} decreases, not increases, with altitude.

96.
8371. Under what condition is V_{MC} the highest?

A—Gross weight is at the maximum allowable value.
B—CG is at the most rearward allowable position.
C—CG is at the most forward allowable position.

Answer (B) is correct (8371). *(FTH Chap 16)*

V_{MC} is greater when the center of gravity is at the most rearward allowable position. Since the airplane rotates around its center of gravity, the moments are measured using that point as a reference. A rearward CG would not affect the thrust moment but would shorten the arm to the center of the rudder's horizontal lift, which would mean that a higher force or airspeed would be required to provide the necessary rudder effectiveness.

Answer (A) is incorrect because maximum gross weight decreases, not increases, V_{MC}. Answer (C) is incorrect because a forward CG increases rudder effectiveness and reduces V_{MC}.

97.
8370. What is the resulting performance loss when one engine on a twin-engine fails?

A—Reduction of cruise airspeed by 50 percent.
B—Reduction of climb by 50 percent or more.
C—Reduction of all performance by 50 percent.

Answer (B) is correct (8370). *(FTH Chap 16)*

When one engine fails on a light twin, the climb performance loss is greater than 50% because climb performance is a function of thrust horsepower in excess of that required for level flight. When power is increased in both engines in level flight and airspeed is held constant, the airplane will climb at a rate depending on the power added. When one engine fails, however, not only does it lose power, but the drag increases considerably because of asymmetric thrust. The operating engine must carry the full burden alone, and climb performance may be reduced by 80% or more.

Answer (A) is incorrect because the power loss affects climb capability much more than it does cruise speed. Answer (C) is incorrect because climb, not all, performance is reduced by more than 50%, not by 50%.

98.
8361. What criteria determines which engine is the "critical" engine of a twin-engine airplane?

A—The one with the center of thrust closest to the centerline of the fuselage.
B—The one designated by the manufacturer which develops most usable thrust.
C—The one with the center of thrust farthest from the centerline of the fuselage.

Answer (A) is correct (8361). *(FTH Chap 16)*

On twin-engine airplanes if the propellers rotate in the same direction (most U.S.-designed engines rotate clockwise when viewed from the rear) and both engines develop an equal amount of thrust, the asymmetric propeller thrust, or "P-factor," results in a center of thrust at the right side of each engine. The turning (or yawing) force of the right engine is greater than the left engine because the center of thrust is much farther away from the centerline of the fuselage; it has a longer arm. Thus, when the right engine is operative and the left engine is inoperative, the turning (or yawing) force is greater than with a good left engine and an inoperative right engine. Directional control may be difficult when the left (or critical) engine is suddenly inoperative.

Answer (B) is incorrect because the critical engine of a twin-engine airplane is the one with the center of thrust closer to the centerline of the fuselage (propellers rotate in same direction), not one designated by the manufacturer. Answer (C) is incorrect because the critical engine is the one with the center of thrust closer, not farther, from the centerline of the fuselage.

99.
8357. In a light, twin-engine airplane with one engine inoperative, when is it acceptable to allow the ball of a slip-skid indicator to be deflected outside the reference lines?

A—While maneuvering at minimum controllable airspeed to avoid overbanking.
B—When operating at any airspeed greater than V_{MC}.
C—When practicing imminent stalls in a banked attitude.

Answer (B) is correct (8357). *(FTH Chap 16)*

Flight tests have shown that holding the ball of the turn coordinator in the center while maintaining heading with wings level increases V_{MC} as much as 20 kt. due to increased drag. Banking into the operative engine sufficiently to achieve zero sideslip (usually 5° or less) reduces V_{MC} and ensures that the airplane will be in a minimum drag configuration for best climb performance. Engine-out flight with the ball centered is never correct.

Answer (A) is incorrect because, with a 5° bank toward the good engine and the ball deflected toward the good engine, the airplane will be in a zero sideslip. There is no tendency for overbanking. Answer (C) is incorrect because stalls should never be practiced with one engine inoperative.

100.
9085. Which condition has the effect of reducing critical engine failure speed?

A—Slush on the runway or inoperative antiskid.
B—Low gross weight.
C—High density altitude.

Answer (A) is correct (9085). *(FTP Chap 12)*

Slush on the runway may dictate adjustments, such as a reduction in critical engine failure speed (V_1), an increase in required runway length, or a penalty in runway limited weight. An inoperative antiskid system may have the same requirements according to the airplane flight manual or company operations manual.

Answer (B) is incorrect because low gross weight may allow an increase in critical engine failure speed. Answer (C) is incorrect because an increase in density altitude requires a higher takeoff velocity (TAS) and critical engine failure speed.

101.
8358. What is the safest and most efficient takeoff and initial climb procedure in a light, twin-engine airplane? Accelerate to

A—best engine-out, rate-of-climb airspeed while on the ground, then lift off and climb at that speed.
B—V_{MC}, then lift off at that speed and climb at maximum angle-of-climb airspeed.
C—an airspeed slightly above V_{MC}, then lift off and climb at the best rate-of-climb airspeed.

Answer (C) is correct (8358). *(FTH Chap 16)*

On normal takeoffs, liftoff should never take place until the airspeed reaches and exceeds V_{MC}. The FAA recommends V_{MC} +5 kt. before liftoff. The safest and most efficient climb procedure is one in which the airplane leaves the ground slightly above V_{MC}, accelerates to V_Y (best rate of climb), and climbs at V_Y for both engines, not single-engine.

Answer (A) is incorrect because liftoff should occur slightly above V_{MC}, and the climb should be at the best rate-of-climb airspeed for both engines, not for an engine out. Answer (B) is incorrect because liftoff should occur slightly above V_{MC}, and the climb should be at the best rate, not angle, of climb.

102.
8369. If an engine failure occurs at an altitude above single-engine ceiling, what airspeed should be maintained?

A—V_{MC}.
B—V_{YSE}.
C—V_{XSE}.

Answer (B) is correct (8369). *(FTH Chap 16)*
When an engine failure occurs at an altitude above the single-engine ceiling, altitude will be lost. In an airplane not capable of maintaining altitude with an engine inoperative under existing circumstances, the airspeed should be maintained at V_{YSE} so as to conserve altitude as long as possible.
Answer (A) is incorrect because V_{YSE} should be maintained, not the minimum controllable airspeed. Answer (C) is incorrect because the best rate-, not angle-, of-climb airspeed should be maintained.

103.
8359. What procedure is recommended for an engine-out approach and landing?

A—The flightpath and procedures should be almost identical to a normal approach and landing.
B—The altitude and airspeed should be considerably higher than normal throughout the approach.
C—A normal approach, except do not extend the landing gear or flaps until over the runway threshold.

Answer (A) is correct (8359). *(FTH Chap 16)*
In most light twins, a single-engine approach can be accomplished with the flight path and procedures almost identical to a normal approach and landing. However, neither full flaps nor the landing gear should be extended until the landing is assured.
Answer (B) is incorrect because higher altitude and airspeed result in floating, and unnecessary runway use should be avoided. Answer (C) is incorrect because landing gear and full flaps should be extended when the landing is assured, not over the runway threshold.

6.19 Turbine-Engine Operation

104.
9058. Which place in the turbojet engine is subjected to the highest temperature?

A—Compressor discharge.
B—Fuel spray nozzles.
C—Turbine inlet.

Answer (C) is correct (9058). *(AFNA Chap 2)*
There is a relatively slow rise in temperature as the air passes through the compressor inlet to the compressor discharge. The air is discharged into the combustion chamber. At the front of the combustion chamber are the fuel spray nozzles. The temperature increases rapidly in the combustion chamber and is cooled by a secondary airflow. The turbine inlet is subjected to the highest temperature in the turbojet engine. High-temperature, high-energy combustion gas is delivered through the turbine inlet from the combustion chamber. The temperature decreases through the turbine and exhaust nozzle.
Answer (A) is incorrect because the compressor discharge has a relatively low, not high, temperature in the turbojet engine. Answer (B) is incorrect because the fuel spray nozzles are located in front of the combustion chamber and are not subjected to the highest temperature.

105.
9059. What effect would a change in ambient temperature or air density have on gas-turbine-engine performance?

A—As air density decreases, thrust increases.
B—As temperature increases, thrust increases.
C—As temperature increases, thrust decreases.

Answer (C) is correct (9059). *(AFNA Chap 2)*
A high ambient air temperature at a given pressure altitude relates to a high density altitude or a decrease in air density. Thrust is reduced because of low air density and low mass flow. Also, thrust and fuel flow are reduced further because of high compressor inlet temperature.
Answer (A) is incorrect because, as air density decreases, thrust decreases, not increases. Answer (B) is incorrect because thrust decreases, not increases, with an increase in temperature.

106.
9063. What effect, if any, does high ambient temperature have upon the thrust output of a turbine engine?

A—Thrust will be reduced due to the decrease in air density.
B—Thrust will remain the same, but turbine temperature will be higher.
C—Thrust will be higher because more heat energy is extracted from the hotter air.

Answer (A) is correct (9063). *(AFNA Chap 2)*

A high ambient temperature at a given pressure altitude relates to a high density altitude or a decrease in air density. Thrust is reduced because of the low air density and low mass flow. Also, thrust and fuel flow are reduced further because of high compressor inlet temperature.

Answer (B) is incorrect because the compressor inlet, not turbine, temperature will increase at high ambient temperature. Answer (C) is incorrect because thrust is reduced, not increased, because the hotter air is less dense, with a low mass flow.

107.
9061. As outside air pressure decreases, thrust output will

A—increase due to greater efficiency of jet aircraft in thin air.
B—remain the same since compression of inlet air will compensate for any decrease in air pressure.
C—decrease due to higher density altitude.

Answer (C) is correct (9061). *(AFNA Chap 2)*

Altitude is one factor which strongly affects the performance of the turbojet engine. An increase in altitude produces a decrease in density and pressure. This high density altitude causes a decrease in the engine air mass flow and, thus, a decrease in thrust output.

Answer (A) is incorrect because thrust output decreases, not increases, with a decrease in air pressure. Answer (B) is incorrect because the compression of inlet air does not compensate for the low air mass flow caused by higher density altitudes.

108.
9060. The most important restriction to the operation of turbojet or turboprop engines is

A—limiting compressor speed.
B—limiting exhaust gas temperature.
C—limiting torque.

Answer (B) is correct (9060). *(AFNA Chap 2)*

The operating characteristics of the turbojet or turboprop engine provide various operating limitations. Limiting exhaust gas temperature is the most important restriction to the operation of the turbojet or turboprop engine.

Answer (A) is incorrect because the turbine section is the most critical element of the turbojet engine. Temperature control is more restrictive than turbine speed, which may operate above 10,000 RPM continuously. Answer (C) is incorrect because torque is a performance measure used on turbopropeller airplanes but is not generally applicable to turbojet engines. The most important restriction is temperature, even though in cooler weather a torque limitation may be reached before the temperature limitation in a turbopropeller airplane.

109.
9070. Equivalent shaft horsepower (ESHP) of a turboprop engine is a measure of

A—turbine inlet temperature.
B—shaft horsepower and jet thrust.
C—propeller thrust only.

Answer (B) is correct (9070). *(AFNA Chap 2)*

In addition to providing jet thrust, the turboprop engine requires additional turbine stages to continue the expansion of gases in the turbine section and to extract a very large percent of the exhaust gas energy as shaft power. The turboprop is primarily a power-producing machine, and the jet thrust is a small amount of the output propulsive power. The turboprop engine is rated by equivalent shaft horsepower (ESHP), which is a measure of shaft horsepower and jet thrust.

Answer (A) is incorrect because ESHP is a measure of power, not temperature. Answer (C) is incorrect because propeller thrust is not a measurement of ESHP.

110.
9062. What effect will an increase in altitude have upon the available equivalent shaft horsepower (ESHP) of a turboprop engine?

A—Lower air density and engine mass flow will cause a decrease in power.
B—Higher propeller efficiency will cause an increase in usable power (ESHP) and thrust.
C—Power will remain the same but propeller efficiency will decrease.

Answer (A) is correct (9062). *(AFNA Chap 2)*
The ESHP will vary with altitude in a manner similar to the thrust output of the turbojet because the higher altitude produces much lower density and engine mass flow.
Answer (B) is incorrect because propeller efficiency decreases, not increases, with an increase in altitude. Answer (C) is incorrect because power will decrease, not remain the same, with an increase in altitude.

111.
9071. Minimum specific fuel consumption of the turboprop engine is normally available in which altitude range?

A—10,000 feet to 25,000 feet.
B—25,000 feet to the tropopause.
C—The tropopause to 45,000 feet.

Answer (B) is correct (9071). *(FTP Chap 6)*
The minimum specific fuel consumption is obtained at relatively high power setting and high altitudes. The low inlet air temperature reduces the specific fuel consumption, and the lowest is obtained near altitudes of 25,000 to 35,000 ft. (or to the tropopause).
Answer (A) is incorrect because the altitude range is from 25,000 to 35,000 ft., not 10,000 to 25,000 ft. Answer (C) is incorrect because the tropopause is the highest, not lowest, altitude range for minimum specific fuel consumption.

6.20 Compressor Stall

112.
9064. What characterizes a transient compressor stall?

A—Loud, steady roar accompanied by heavy shuddering.
B—Sudden loss of thrust accompanied by a loud whine.
C—Intermittent "bang," as backfires and flow reversals take place.

Answer (C) is correct (9064). *(AFNA Chap 2)*
As a compressor stall occurs, the pressure rises and the compressor does not furnish discharge at a pressure equal to the combustion chamber pressure. As a result, a flow reversal or backfire takes place. If the stall is transient and intermittent, the indication will be the intermittent "bang" as backfire and flow reversal take place.
Answer (A) is incorrect because this describes a developed and steady stall, not a transient stall. Answer (B) is incorrect because a transient stall is characterized by an intermittent "bang," not a loud whine.

113.
9065. What indicates that a compressor stall has developed and become steady?

A—Strong vibrations and loud roar.
B—Occasional loud "bang" and flow reversal.
C—Complete loss of power with severe reduction in airspeed.

Answer (A) is correct (9065). *(AFNA Chap 2)*
As a compressor stall occurs, the pressure rises and the compressor does not furnish discharge at a pressure equal to the combustion chamber pressure. As a result, a flow reversal or backfire takes place. If the stall develops and becomes steady, strong vibrations and a loud roar develop from the continuous flow reversal.
Answer (B) is incorrect because an occasional loud "bang" and flow reversal describe an indication of a transient stall, not a stall that has developed and become steady. Answer (C) is incorrect because a compressor stall will not cause a complete loss of power.

114.
9066. Which type of compressor stall has the greatest potential for severe engine damage?

A—Intermittent "backfire" stall.
B—Transient "backfire" stall.
C—Steady, continuous flow reversal stall.

Answer (C) is correct (9066). *(AFNA Chap 2)*
In a steady compressor stall, strong vibrations and a loud roar develop from the continuous flow reversal. The increase in compressor power required tends to reduce RPM, and the reduced airflow and increased fuel flow cause a rapid, immediate rise in exhaust gas temperature. The possibility of engine damage is immediate with the steady stall.
Answer (A) is incorrect because an intermittent "backfire" stall does not have as great a potential for severe engine damage as a steady stall. Answer (B) is incorrect because a transient "backfire" stall does not have as great a potential for severe engine damage as a steady stall.

115.
9067. What recovery would be appropriate in the event of compressor stall?

A—Reduce fuel flow, reduce angle of attack, and increase airspeed.
B—Advance throttle, lower angle of attack, and reduce airspeed.
C—Reduce throttle, reduce airspeed, and increase angle of attack.

Answer (A) is correct (9067). *(AFNA Chap 2)*
Since the possibility of engine damage is immediate if a compressor stall becomes steady, recovery must be accomplished immediately. The recovery from a compressor stall must entail reducing the throttle setting to reduce fuel flow, lowering angle of attack, and increasing airspeed to improve inlet conditions.
Answer (B) is incorrect because throttle is reduced, not increased, and airspeed must be increased, not decreased. Answer (C) is incorrect because airspeed is increased, not decreased, and angle of attack is decreased, not increased.

6.21 Mach Speed Flight

116.
8390. At what Mach range does the subsonic flight range normally occur?

A—Below .75 Mach.
B—From .75 to 1.20 Mach.
C—From 1.20 to 2.50 Mach.

Answer (A) is correct (8390). *(FTP Chap 17)*
Since there is a possibility of having both subsonic and supersonic flows existing on the aircraft, it is convenient to define certain regimes of flight. Subsonic flight range occurs in Mach numbers below 0.75.
Answer (B) is incorrect because from 0.75 to 1.20 Mach is the transonic, not subsonic, flight regime. Answer (C) is incorrect because from 1.20 to 2.50 Mach is part of the supersonic, not subsonic, flight regime.

117.
8387. Within what Mach range does transonic flight regimes usually occur?

A—.50 to .75 Mach.
B—.75 to 1.20 Mach.
C—1.20 to 2.50 Mach.

Answer (B) is correct (8387). *(FTP Chap 17)*
Since there is a possibility of having both subsonic and supersonic flows existing on the aircraft, it is convenient to define certain regimes of flight. Transonic flight regimes occur in Mach numbers from 0.75 to 1.20.
Answer (A) is incorrect because 0.50 to .75 Mach is part of the subsonic, not transonic, flight regime. Answer (C) is incorrect because 1.20 to 2.50 Mach is part of the supersonic, not transonic, flight regime.

118.
8389. What is the free stream Mach number which produces first evidence of local sonic flow?

A—Supersonic Mach number.
B—Transonic Mach number.
C—Critical Mach number.

Answer (C) is correct (8389). *(FTP Chap 17)*
By definition, critical Mach number is the "free stream Mach number which produces first evidence of local sonic flow." Therefore, shock waves, buffet, airflow separation, etc., take place above critical Mach number.
Answer (A) is incorrect because the free stream Mach number which produces first evidence of local sonic flow is the critical, not supersonic, Mach number. Answer (B) is incorrect because the free stream Mach number which produces first evidence of local sonic flow is the critical, not transonic, Mach number.

119.
8388. What is the highest speed possible without supersonic flow over the wing?

A—Initial buffet speed.
B—Critical Mach number.
C—Transonic index.

Answer (B) is correct (8388). *(FTP Chap 17)*
The highest speed possible without supersonic flow over the wing is termed the critical Mach number.
Answer (A) is incorrect because the initial buffet speed occurs above the critical Mach number, when an area of supersonic flow is created over the wing. Answer (C) is incorrect because the critical Mach number, not the transonic index, is the highest speed possible without supersonic flow over the wing.

120.
8392. What is the result of a shock-induced separation of airflow occurring symmetrically near the wing root of a sweptwing aircraft?

A—A high-speed stall and sudden pitchup.
B—A severe moment or "tuck under."
C—Severe porpoising.

Answer (B) is correct (8392). *(FTP Chap 17)*
When airflow separation occurs on the wing due to shock wave formation, there will be a loss of lift and a subsequent loss of downwash aft of the affected area. If the shock-induced separation occurs symmetrically near the wing root, a decrease in downwash behind this area is caused by a loss of lift. A decrease in downwash on the horizontal tail will create a diving moment and the aircraft will "tuck under."

Answer (A) is incorrect because there is a sudden pitch down, not up, when a shock-induced separation of airflow occurs symmetrically near the wing root of a sweptwing aircraft. Answer (C) is incorrect because there is a diving moment, not severe porpoising, when a shock-induced separation of airflow occurs symmetrically near the wing root of a sweptwing aircraft.

121.
8395. What is the movement of the center of pressure when the wingtips of a sweptwing airplane are shock-stalled first?

A—Inward and aft.
B—Inward and forward.
C—Outward and forward.

Answer (B) is correct (8395). *(FTP Chap 3)*
On a sweptwing airplane, the wing center of pressure shifts when the airplane is shock-stalled. On a sweptwing airplane when the wingtips are shock-stalled first, the center of pressure will move forward and inward.

Answer (A) is incorrect because, when the wingtips are shock-stalled first, the center of pressure moves forward, not aft. Answer (C) is incorrect because, when the wingtips are shock-stalled first, the center of pressure moves inward, not outward.

122.
8391. What is the principal advantage of a sweepback design wing over a straightwing design?

A—The critical Mach number will increase significantly.
B—Sweepback will increase changes in the magnitude of force coefficients due to compressibility.
C—Sweepback will accelerate the onset of compressibility effect.

Answer (A) is correct (8391). *(FTP Chap 17)*
The sweep of a surface produces a beneficial effect in high speed flight since higher flight speeds may be obtained before components of speed perpendicular to the leading edge produce critical conditions on the wing. One of the most important advantages of a sweepback wing design is an increase in the critical Mach number.

Answer (B) is incorrect because sweepback will reduce, not increase, changes in the magnitude of force coefficients due to compressibility. Answer (C) is incorrect because sweepback will delay, not accelerate, the onset of compressibility effect.

123.
8393. What is one disadvantage of a sweptwing design?

A—The wing root stalls prior to the wingtip section.
B—The wingtip section stalls prior to the wing root.
C—Severe pitchdown moment when the center of pressure shifts forward.

Answer (B) is correct (8393). *(FTP Chap 17)*
The use of sweptwing design produces certain disadvantages which are important from the standpoint of both airplane design and flight operations. One disadvantage is that, when sweepback is combined with taper, there is an extremely powerful tendency for the wingtip section to stall prior to the wing root.

Answer (A) is incorrect because a sweptwing design has a tendency for the wingtip, not wing root, to stall first. Answer (C) is incorrect because, when the center of pressure shifts forward, there is a pitch up, not down, moment.

124.
8394. What is the condition known as when gusts cause a sweptwing-type airplane to roll in one direction while yawing in the other?

A—Porpoise.
B—Wingover.
C—Dutch roll.

Answer (C) is correct (8394). *(AFNA Chap 3)*
Sweptwing design contributes to lateral stability by producing stable rolling moments with sideslip. Dutch roll is a coupled lateral-directional oscillation developed when gusts cause a sweptwing-type airplane to roll in one direction while yawing in the other.
Answer (A) is incorrect because dutch roll, not porpoise, is developed when gusts cause a sweptwing-type airplane to roll in one direction while yawing in the other. Answer (B) is incorrect because dutch roll, not wingover, is developed when gusts cause a sweptwing-type airplane to roll in one direction while yawing in the other.

6.22 Thrust Reversers

125.
9074. How should thrust reversers be applied to reduce landing distance for turbojet aircraft?

A—Immediately after ground contact.
B—Immediately prior to touchdown.
C—After applying maximum wheel braking.

Answer (A) is correct (9074). *(AFNA Chap 2)*
Reverse thrust of turbojet engines will usually employ some form of vanes, buckets, or clamshells in the exhaust to turn or direct the exhaust gases forward. Reverse thrust must be applied immediately after ground contact for maximum effectiveness in reducing landing distance.
Answer (B) is incorrect because thrust reversers should be applied immediately after, not prior to, ground contact to reduce landing distance. Answer (C) is incorrect because thrust reversers should be applied immediately after ground contact, not after applying maximum wheel braking, to reduce landing distance.

126.
9079. How should reverse thrust propellers be used during landing for maximum effectiveness in stopping?

A—Gradually increase reverse power to maximum as rollout speed decreases.
B—Use maximum reverse power as soon as possible after touchdown.
C—Select reverse-pitch after landing and use idle power setting of the engines.

Answer (B) is correct (9079). *(AFNA Chap 2)*
Reverse thrust of propellers is obtained by rotating the blade angle well below the low pitch stop and applying engine power. The action is to extract a large amount of momentum from the airstream and create negative thrust. Maximum effectiveness is achieved by use of maximum reverse power immediately after the airplane is in contact with the runway.
Answer (A) is incorrect because maximum effectiveness is achieved by use of maximum reverse power as soon as possible after touchdown, not as the rollout speed decreases. Answer (C) is incorrect because power should be at maximum, not idle, to add to drag and braking friction to increase the net retarding force.

6.23 Hydroplaning

127.
8933. A definition of the term "viscous hydroplaning" is where

A—the airplane rides on standing water.
B—a film of moisture covers the painted or rubber-coated portion of the runway.
C—the tires of the airplane are actually riding on a mixture of steam and melted rubber.

Answer (B) is correct (8933). *(FAA-P-8740-50)*
Viscous hydroplaning can occur on a thin film of water if it covers the painted or rubber-coated portion of the runway.
Answer (A) is incorrect because dynamic hydroplaning occurs when the airplane tires ride on standing water. Answer (C) is incorrect because reverted rubber hydroplaning occurs when the tires of the airplane are actually riding on a mixture of steam and melted rubber.

128.
8938. Compared to dynamic hydroplaning, at what speed does viscous hydroplaning occur when landing on a smooth, wet runway?

A—At approximately 2.0 times the speed that dynamic hydroplaning occurs.
B—At a lower speed than dynamic hydroplaning.
C—At the same speed as dynamic hydroplaning.

Answer (B) is correct (8938). *(AC 91-6)*
Viscous hydroplaning may occur at lower speeds and at lower water depths than dynamic hydroplaning.
Answer (A) is incorrect because dynamic hydroplaning usually occurs at a higher speed than viscous hydroplaning. Answer (C) is incorrect because viscous hydroplaning often occurs on smooth runway pavements or where rubber deposits are present, usually in the touchdown area where a thin film of water can significantly reduce the coefficient of friction. This usually occurs at a speed lower than dynamic hydroplaning.

129.
8935. At what minimum speed (rounded off) could dynamic hydroplaning occur on main tires having a pressure of 121 PSI?

A—90 knots.
B—96 knots.
C—110 knots.

Answer (B) is correct (8935). *(FAA-P-8740-50)*
The minimum speed in knots for dynamic hydroplaning can be calculated by the following formula:

$$8.73 \times \sqrt{\textit{Tire pressure (in PSI)}}$$

Therefore, for a tire pressure of 121 PSI, the minimum speed is 96 kt.

$$8.73 \times \sqrt{121} = 8.73 \times 11 = 96\ \textit{kt}.$$

Answer (A) is incorrect because 90-kt. hydroplaning will occur at a tire pressure of 106 PSI. Answer (C) is incorrect because 110-kt. hydroplaning will occur at a tire pressure of 159 PSI.

130.
8936. At what minimum speed will dynamic hydroplaning begin if a tire has an air pressure of 70 PSI?

A—85 knots.
B—80 knots.
C—75 knots.

Answer (C) is correct (8936). *(FAA-P-8740-50)*
The minimum speed in knots for dynamic hydroplaning can be calculated by the following formula:

$$8.73 \times \sqrt{\textit{Tire pressure (in PSI)}}$$

$$8.73 \times \sqrt{70} = 8.73 \times 8.36 = 73\ \textit{kt}.$$

Answer (A) is incorrect because hydroplaning will occur at 85 kt. with a tire pressure of 95 PSI. Answer (B) is incorrect because hydroplaning will occur at 80 kt. with a tire pressure of 84 PSI.

131.
8934. Which term describes the hydroplaning which occurs when an airplane's tire is effectively held off a smooth runway surface by steam generated by friction?

A—Reverted rubber hydroplaning.
B—Dynamic hydroplaning.
C—Viscous hydroplaning.

Answer (A) is correct (8934). *(FAA-P-8740-50)*
Reverted rubber hydroplaning is the result of a locked wheel skid in which reverted rubber becomes a barrier between the tire and the runway. Steam generated by the heat of friction will hold the wheel off a smooth runway surface.
Answer (B) is incorrect because dynamic hydroplaning occurs when there is standing water or slush on the runway which forms a wedge that lifts the tire away from contact with the runway surface. Answer (C) is incorrect because viscous hydroplaning occurs on a thin film of water on a smooth (e.g., painted or rubber coated) runway surface.

132.
8937. What is the best method of speed reduction if hydroplaning is experienced on landing?

A—Apply full main wheel braking only.
B—Apply nosewheel and main wheel braking alternately and abruptly.
C—Apply aerodynamic braking to the fullest advantage.

Answer (C) is correct (8937). *(AC 91-6)*
During hydroplaning, the tire(s) is (are) not in contact with the runway surface, so there is no friction, and application of the brakes would do nothing. Aerodynamic braking must be used to its fullest advantage.

Answer (A) is incorrect because applying full main wheel braking may increase or compound the problems associated with hydroplaning. If any brakes are used, a pumping or modulating motion like an antiskid system can be used. Aerodynamic braking is recommended. Answer (B) is incorrect because abrupt use of either the nosewheel or the mainwheel brakes will lock the wheels and compound the problem.

133.
8939. What effect, if any, will landing at a higher-than-recommended touchdown speed have on hydroplaning?

A—No effect on hydroplaning, but increases landing roll.
B—Reduces hydroplaning potential if heavy braking is applied.
C—Increases hydroplaning potential regardless of braking.

Answer (C) is correct (8939). *(AC 91-6)*
Landing at a higher-than-recommended touchdown speed increases the hydroplaning potential because the wings provide lift and reduce the contact between the tires and the runway, allowing a layer of water to form between the tire and the runway.

Answer (A) is incorrect because landing at a higher airspeed increases the hydroplaning potential. Answer (B) is incorrect because landing at a higher airspeed increases, not reduces, the hydroplaning potential, regardless of braking.

6.24 Ground Deicing/Anti-Icing

134.
9440. Which is an effect of ice, snow, or frost formation on an airplane?

A—Decreased stall speed.
B—Decreased pitchup tendencies.
C—Decreased angle of attack for stalls.

Answer (C) is correct (9440). *(AC 20-117)*
When ice, snow, or particularly frost forms on the upper surface of a wing, it provides a surface texture of considerable roughness. The increase in surface roughness increases skin friction drag and reduces the kinetic energy of the boundary layer, causing incipient stalling of the wing; i.e., separation will occur at angles of attack lower than for the clean, smooth wing. In some aircraft, stall will occur prior to activation of stall warning devices.

Answer (A) is incorrect because the formation of ice, snow, or frost on the wings of an aircraft increases, not decreases, stall speed. Answer (B) is incorrect because the formation of ice, snow, or frost on the wings of some aircraft may increase, not decrease, pitchup tendencies.

135.
9449. Which is an effect of ice, snow, or frost formation on an airplane?

A—Increased stall speed.
B—Increased pitchdown tendencies.
C—Increased angle of attack for stalls.

Answer (A) is correct (9449). *(AC 20-117)*
When ice, snow, or particularly frost forms on the upper surface of a wing, it provides a surface texture of considerable roughness. The increase in surface roughness increases skin friction drag and reduces the kinetic energy of the boundary layer, causing an increase in power required and stall speed.

Answer (B) is incorrect because the formation of ice, snow, or frost on the wings of some aircraft may increase pitchup, not pitchdown, tendencies. Answer (C) is incorrect because the formation of ice, snow, or frost on the wings of an aircraft decreases, not increases, the angle of attack for stalls. In some aircraft, stall will occur prior to activation of stall warning devices.

136.
9695. The adverse effects of ice, snow, or frost on aircraft performance and flight characteristics include decreased lift and

A—increased thrust.
B—a decreased stall speed.
C—an increased stall speed.

Answer (C) is correct (9695). *(AC 120-58)*
The adverse effects of ice, snow, or frost on aircraft performance and flight characteristics are generally reflected in the form of decreased lift, increased stall speed, decreased thrust, trim changes, and altered stall characteristics and handling qualities.
Answer (A) is incorrect because the adverse effects of ice, snow, or frost on aircraft performance and flight characteristics include a decrease, not an increase, in thrust. Answer (B) is incorrect because the adverse effects of ice, snow, or frost on aircraft performance and flight characteristics include an increase, not a decrease, in stall speed.

137.
9699. Test data indicate that ice, snow, or frost having a thickness and roughness similar to medium or coarse sandpaper on the leading edge and upper surface of a wing can

A—reduce lift by as much as 40 percent and increase drag by 30 percent.
B—reduce lift by as much as 30 percent and increase drag by 40 percent.
C—increase drag and reduce lift by as much as 40 percent.

Answer (B) is correct (9699). *(AC 120-58)*
Test data indicate that ice, snow, or frost formations having a thickness and surface roughness similar to medium or coarse sandpaper on the leading edge and upper surface of a wing can reduce wing lift by as much as 30% and increase drag by 40%. These changes in lift and drag significantly increase stall speed, reduce controllability, and alter aircraft flight characteristics.
Answer (A) is incorrect because ice, snow, or frost on the leading edge and upper surface of a wing can reduce lift by 30%, not 40%, and increase drag by 40%, not 30%. Answer (C) is incorrect because ice, snow, or frost on the leading edge and upper surface of a wing can reduce lift by 30%, not 40%.

138.
9451. Test data indicate that ice, snow, or frost having a thickness and roughness similar to medium or coarse sandpaper on the leading edge and upper surface of a wing can

A—reduce lift by as much as 40 percent and increase drag by 30 percent.
B—increase drag and reduce lift by as much as 40 percent.
C—reduce lift by as much as 30 percent and increase drag by 40 percent.

Answer (C) is correct (9451). *(AC 120-58)*
Test data indicate that ice, frost, or snow formations on the leading edge and upper surface of a wing, having a thickness and surface roughness similar to medium or coarse sandpaper, can reduce wing lift by as much as 30% and increase drag by 40%. These changes in lift and drag will significantly increase stall speed, reduce controllability, and alter aircraft flight characteristics.
Answer (A) is incorrect because ice, snow, or frost on the leading edge and upper surface of a wing can reduce lift by 30%, not 40%, and increase drag by 40%, not 30%. Answer (B) is incorrect because ice, snow, or frost on the leading edge and upper surface of a wing can reduce lift by 30%, not 40%.

139.
9450. Freezing Point Depressant (FPD) fluids used for deicing

A—provide ice protection during flight.
B—are intended to provide ice protection on the ground only.
C—on the ground, cause no performance degradation during takeoff.

Answer (B) is correct (9450). *(AC 120-58)*
FPD fluids are used to aid the ground deicing process and to provide a protective film of FPD (anti-icing) to delay formations of frost, snow, or other ice, until after takeoff. During flight, an aircraft's deice/anti-ice equipment (if installed) provides ice protection.
Answer (A) is incorrect because FPD fluids used during ground deicing are not intended for, and do not provide, ice protection during flight. Answer (C) is incorrect because some large aircraft do experience performance degradation during takeoff, and on small airplanes degradation is significant.

140.
9453. Freezing Point Depressant (FPD) fluids are highly soluble in water; however,

A—ice is slow to absorb it but fast to melt when in contact with FPD.
B—ice absorbs it very fast but is slow to melt when in contact with it.
C—ice is slow to absorb it, and to melt when in contact with it.

Answer (C) is correct (9453). *(AC 120-58)*
FPD fluids are very soluble in water. However, the rate at which ice will absorb FPD or melt is very slow. Thus, ice formations adhering to a wing surface must be melted by repeated application of FPD fluids or by application of heated fluid.
Answer (A) is incorrect because the rate at which ice will melt when in contact with FPD is very slow, not fast. Answer (B) is incorrect because the rate at which ice will absorb FPD is very slow, not fast.

141.
9454. Freezing Point Depressant (FPD) fluid residue on engine fan or compressor blades

A—can increase performance and cause stalls or surges.
B—could cause FPD vapors to enter the aircraft but would have no effect on engine thrust or power.
C—can reduce engine performance and cause surging and/or compressor stalls.

Answer (C) is correct (9454). *(AC 120-58)*
FPD fluid residue on engine fan or compressor blades can reduce engine performance or cause a stall or a surge. In addition, this residue could increase the possibility of, or the quantity of, glycol vapors entering the aircraft through the engine bleed air system.
Answer (A) is incorrect because FPD fluid residue on engine fan or compressor blades can reduce, not increase, performance. Answer (B) is incorrect because FPD fluid residue on engine fan or compressor blades can reduce, rather than have no effect on, performance.

142.
9700. What is the effect of Freezing Point Depressant (FPD) fluid residue on engine fan or compressor blades?

A—It could cause FPD vapors to enter the aircraft but would have no effect on engine thrust or power.
B—It can increase performance and cause stalls or surges.
C—It can reduce engine performance and cause surging and/or compressor stalls.

Answer (C) is correct (9700). *(AC 120-58)*
FPD fluid residue on engine fan or compressor blades can reduce engine performance and cause surging and/or compressor stalls. In addition, this residue could increase the possibility of, or the quantity of, glycol vapors entering the aircraft through the engine bleed air system.
Answer (A) is incorrect because FPD fluid residue on engine fan or compressor blades can reduce engine thrust or power in addition to allowing FPD vapors to enter the aircraft. Answer (B) is incorrect because FPD fluid residue on engine fan or compressor blades can reduce, not increase, engine performance and cause stalls or surges.

143.
9698. The practice developed and accepted by the North American air carrier industry using traditional North American fluids is to ensure that the freeze point of the remaining film is below ambient temperature by at least

A—10°F.
B—20°F.
C—20°C.

Answer (B) is correct (9698). *(AC 120-58)*
The practice developed and accepted by the North American air carrier industry using traditional North American fluids is to ensure that the remaining film has a freeze point of at least 20°F below ambient temperature.
Answer (A) is incorrect because the remaining film should have a freeze point of at least 20°F, not 10°F, below ambient temperature. Answer (C) is incorrect because the remaining film should have a freeze point of at least 20°F, not 20°C, below ambient temperature.

144.
9448. Anti-icing fluid should provide freezing point protection to

A—-20° F ambient temperature.
B—+32 °F outside temperature or below.
C—a freezing point no greater than 20° F below the ambient or airplane surface temperature.

Answer (C) is correct (9448). *(AC 20-117)*
Practice developed and accepted by the air carrier industry is to assure that the residual surface film of anti-icing fluid should provide freezing point protection to at least 20°F (11°C) below the colder of ambient or aircraft surface (skin) temperature.
Answer (A) is incorrect because anti-icing fluid should have a freezing point no greater than 20°F below ambient or surface temperature, whichever is lower, regardless of ambient temperature. Answer (B) is incorrect because anti-icing fluid should have a freezing point no greater than 20°F below ambient or surface temperature, whichever is lower, regardless of outside temperature.

145.
9452. Snow on top of deicing or anti-icing fluids

A—need not be considered as adhering to the aircraft.
B—must be considered as adhering to the aircraft.
C—must be considered as adhering to the aircraft, but a safe takeoff can be made as it will blow off.

Answer (B) is correct (9452). *(AC 120-58)*
Ice, frost, or snow on top of deicing or anti-icing fluids must be considered as adhering to the aircraft. Takeoff should not be attempted.
Answer (A) is incorrect because ice, frost, or snow on top of deicing or anti-icing fluids must be considered as adhering to the aircraft. Answer (C) is incorrect because takeoff should not be attempted.

146.
9442. The purpose of diluting ethylene glycol deicing fluid with water in non-precipitation conditions is to

A—raise the eutectic point.
B—decrease the freeze point.
C—increase the minimum freezing point (onset of crystallization).

Answer (B) is correct (9442). *(AC 20-117)*
Pure ethylene glycol will freeze at warmer temperatures than that diluted with water. For this reason, all currently available commercial and military deicing fluids contain small quantities of water.
Answer (A) is incorrect because the eutectic point, or minimum freezing point (onset of crystallization), is a fixed value that occurs with a specific mixture of glycol and water for which the freezing temperature is at its lowest. Answer (C) is incorrect because the minimum freezing point (onset of crystallization), or eutectic point, is a fixed value that occurs with a specific mixture of glycol and water for which the freezing temperature is at its lowest.

147.
9446. What is the minimum glycol content of Type 1 deicing/anti-icing fluid?

A—30 percent.
B—50 percent.
C—80 percent.

Answer (C) is correct (9446). *(AC 120-58)*
Type 1 deicing/anti-icing fluids in the concentrated form contain a minimum of 80% glycols and are considered "unthickened" because of their relatively low viscosity. These fluids are used for deicing or anti-icing but provide very limited anti-icing protection.
Answer (A) is incorrect because the minimum glycol content of Type 1 fluid is 80%, not 30%. Answer (B) is incorrect because 50% is the minimum glycol content of Type 2, not Type 1, fluid.

148.
9447. What is the minimum glycol content of Type 2 deicing/anti-icing fluid?

A—30 percent.
B—50 percent.
C—80 percent.

Answer (B) is correct (9447). *(AC 120-58)*
Type 2 deicing/anti-icing fluids contain a minimum of 50% glycols and are considered "thickened" because of added thickening agents that enable the fluid to be deposited in a thicker film and to remain on the aircraft surfaces until the time of takeoff. These fluids are used for deicing and anti-icing, and provide greater protection than do Type 1 fluids against ice, frost, or snow formation in conditions conducive to aircraft icing on the ground.
Answer (A) is incorrect because the minimum glycol content of Type 2 fluid is 50%, not 30%. Answer (C) is incorrect because 80% is the minimum glycol content of Type 1, not Type 2, fluid.

149.
9441. Which is a disadvantage of the one-step over the two-step process when deicing/anti-icing an airplane?

A—It is more complicated.
B—The holding time is increased.
C—More fluid is used with the one-step method when large deposits of ice and snow must be flushed off airplane surfaces.

Answer (C) is correct (9441). *(TCAS Chap 3)*
The one-step process for deicing/anti-icing an airplane consists of applying heated fluid onto the airplane surfaces to remove accumulated ice, snow, or frost and prevent their subsequent buildup. Its primary disadvantage is that, when large deposits of ice and snow must be flushed off of airplane surfaces, the total fluid usage will be greater than for a two-step process.
Answer (A) is incorrect because the primary advantage of the one-step process is that it is quick and uncomplicated. Answer (B) is incorrect because, since the one-step process uses heated fluid, the holding time is decreased, not increased.

150.
9443. Which procedure increases holding time when deicing/anti-icing an airplane using a two-step process?

A—Heated Type 1 fluid followed by cold Type 2 fluid.
B—Cold Type 2 fluid followed by hot Type 2 fluid.
C—Heated Type 1 or 2 fluid followed by cold Type 1 fluid.

Answer (A) is correct (9443). *(TCAS Chap 3)*
The two-step process consists of separate deicing and anti-icing steps. First, a heated, diluted Type 1 fluid is applied to remove accumulated ice, snow, or frost. Then a cold, more concentrated fluid is applied. Using a Type 2 fluid for the second step increases the holding time (i.e., the time the fluid will protect the aircraft from ice, snow, and frost) significantly due to its higher viscosity.

Answer (B) is incorrect because using a heated, not cold, fluid in the first step helps melt any accumulated ice, snow, or frost, and using a cold, not hot, fluid in the second step leaves greater amounts of residual film, increasing holding time. Answer (C) is incorrect because using a Type 2 fluid for the second step increases the holding time (i.e., the time the fluid will protect the aircraft from ice, snow, and frost) significantly due to its higher viscosity.

151.
9444. Which of the following will decrease the holding time during anti-icing using a two-step process?

A—Apply heated Type 2 fluid.
B—Decrease the water content.
C—Increase the viscosity of Type 1 fluid.

Answer (A) is correct (9444). *(AC 20-117)*
The two-step process consists of separate deicing and anti-icing steps. First, a heated, diluted Type 1 fluid is applied to remove accumulated ice, snow, or frost. Then a cold, more concentrated fluid is applied. Using a heated Type 2 fluid in the second step will leave less amounts of residual film, decreasing holding time.

Answer (B) is incorrect because decreasing the water content of the anti-icing fluid increases its viscosity, which will increase, not decrease, holding time. Answer (C) is incorrect because increasing the viscosity of Type 1 fluid requires lowering its temperature. This will increase, not decrease, holding time because it will leave greater amounts of residual film.

152.
9445. What should the deice/anti-ice fluid temperature be during the last step of a two-phase process?

A—Hot.
B—Warm.
C—Cold.

Answer (C) is correct (9445). *(AC 20-117)*
The two-step process consists of separate deicing and anti-icing steps. First, a heated, diluted Type 1 fluid is applied to remove accumulated ice, snow, or frost. Then a cold, more concentrated fluid is applied. Using a cold fluid in the second step will leave greater amounts of residual film, increasing the effectiveness of the deice/ anti-ice fluid.

Answer (A) is incorrect because using a cold, not hot, fluid in the second step will leave greater amounts of residual film, increasing the effectiveness of the deice/ anti-ice fluid. Answer (B) is incorrect because using a cold, not warm, fluid in the second step will leave greater amounts of residual film, increasing the effectiveness of the deice/anti-ice fluid.

153.
9697. Deicing procedures and equipment developed for large transport airplanes

A—will not be appropriate for the smaller aircraft, used under FAR Part 135.
B—will be appropriate for all of the smaller aircraft, used under FAR Part 135.
C—may not be appropriate for some of the smaller aircraft, used under FAR Part 135.

Answer (C) is correct (9697). *(AC 135-17)*
Deicing procedures and equipment developed for large transport airplanes may not be appropriate for some of the smaller aircraft used under FAR Part 135.

Answer (A) is incorrect because deicing procedures and equipment developed for large transport airplanes may not be appropriate for some, not all, of the smaller aircraft used under FAR Part 135. Answer (B) is incorrect because deicing procedures and equipment developed for large transport airplanes may be appropriate for some, not all, of the smaller aircraft used under FAR Part 135.

6.25 Pitot System

154.
9080. During an en route descent in a fixed-thrust and fixed-pitch attitude configuration, both the ram air input and drain hole of the pitot system become completely blocked by ice. What airspeed indication can be expected?

A—Increase in indicated airspeed.
B—Decrease in indicated airspeed.
C—Indicated airspeed remains at the value prior to icing.

Answer (B) is correct (9080). *(AC 91-43)*
If the ram air input and the drain hole are blocked, the pressure is trapped in the system, and the airspeed indicator will react as an altimeter. During a descent, the airspeed indication will decrease.
Answer (A) is incorrect because indicated airspeed will decrease, not increase, in a descent. Answer (C) is incorrect because indicated airspeed will remain at the same value during level, not descending, flight.

155.
9081. What can a pilot expect if the pitot system ram air input and drain hole are blocked by ice?

A—The airspeed indicator may act as an altimeter.
B—The airspeed indicator will show a decrease with an increase in altitude.
C—No airspeed indicator change will occur during climbs or descents.

Answer (A) is correct (9081). *(AC 91-43)*
If the ram air and the drain hole are blocked, the pressure is trapped in the system, and the airspeed indicator will react as an altimeter: higher indicated airspeed at higher altitudes and lower indicated airspeed at lower altitudes.
Answer (B) is incorrect because the airspeed indicator will show an increase, not decrease, with an increase in altitude. Answer (C) is incorrect because differential pressure between the pitot tube and static air source changes and so does indicated airspeed.

156.
9082. If both the ram air input and drain hole of the pitot system are blocked by ice, what airspeed indication can be expected?

A—No variation of indicated airspeed in level flight if large power changes are made.
B—Decrease of indicated airspeed during a climb.
C—Constant indicated airspeed during a descent.

Answer (A) is correct (9082). *(AC 91-43)*
If both the pitot tube input and the drain hole on the pitot system are blocked, the airspeed indication will be constant at any given altitude.
Answer (B) is incorrect because, during a climb, it will indicate an increase, not decrease, due to the stronger differential pressure in the blocked pitot tube relative to the static vents. Answer (C) is incorrect because indicated airspeed will change with changes in altitude.

157.
9222. How will the airspeed indicator react if the ram air input to the pitot head is blocked by ice, but the drain hole and static port are not?

A—Indication will drop to zero.
B—Indication will rise to the top of the scale.
C—Indication will remain constant but will increase in a climb.

Answer (A) is correct (9222). *(AC 91-43)*
If the ram air input to the pitot head is blocked by ice but the drain hole and static port remain open, the pressure in the line to the airspeed indicator will vent out through the drain hole. Thus, the airspeed indication will drop to zero.
Answer (B) is incorrect because the airspeed indication will drop to zero, not rise to the top of the scale, if only the ram air input is blocked. Answer (C) is incorrect because the pressure in the airspeed line will vent out through the vent hole, and the indication will drop to zero. It will not act as an altimeter.

END OF CHAPTER

CHAPTER SEVEN
AIRSPACE AND AIRPORTS

This chapter contains outlines of major concepts tested, all FAA test questions and answers regarding airspace and airports, and an explanation of each answer. Each module, or subtopic, within this chapter is listed above with the number of questions from the FAA pilot knowledge test pertaining to that particular module. For each module, the first number following the parentheses is the page number on which the outline begins, and the next number is the page number on which the questions begin.

There are 65 questions in this chapter. We separate and organize the FAA ATP questions into meaningful study units, i.e., chapters and modules. As an analogy, it is easier to deal with the "trees" if you understand the "forest." In this context, "trees" are individual FAA questions and the "forest" is the ATP knowledge test. The organizational units between the overall ATP knowledge test and individual ATP test questions are chapters and modules in this book.

CAUTION: The **sole purpose** of this book is to expedite your passing the FAA pilot knowledge test for the ATP certificate. Topics or regulations not directly tested on the FAA pilot knowledge test are omitted. Much more information and knowledge are necessary to fly safely. This additional material is presented in Gleim's other pilot training books (see the order form on page 818) and in many FAA books and circulars, as well as in airplane *POH*s and other commercial textbooks.

7.1 AIRSPACE (Questions 1-13)

1. IFR Low-Altitude En Route Charts depict **military training routes (MTR)** above 1,500 ft. AGL.
2. **Military operations areas (MOA)** have the purpose of separating military training activities from IFR traffic.
   a. Each pilot is responsible for collision avoidance in an MOA.
3. A **warning area** extends from 3 NM outward from the coast of the U.S., and the area may be located in domestic or international airspace, or both.
   a. The purpose of a warning area is to warn pilots of the potential danger from invisible hazards.

4. Large turbine-powered airplanes operating to or from a primary airport in Class B airspace must operate above the floor of the Class B airspace when within the lateral limits of the Class B airspace.
5. Class A airspace extends from 18,000 ft. MSL to and including FL 600.
6. The ceiling of Class C airspace is normally 4,000 ft. above the airport elevation.
7. The Class E airspace used for transition to/from a terminal or an en route environment begins at either 700 ft. or 1,200 ft. AGL.
   a. Below Class E airspace is Class G airspace.
8. The maximum indicated airspeed that an aircraft can be flown in Class B airspace is 250 kt.

7.2 CLASS C AIRSPACE (Questions 14-22)

1. Class C airspace consists of a surface area (formerly called the inner circle) and a shelf area (formerly called the outer circle).
   a. The surface area has a 5-NM radius from the primary airport.
      1) Extending from the surface to 4,000 ft. above the airport elevation.
   b. The shelf area is an area from 5 to 10 NM from the primary airport.
      1) Extending from 1,200 ft. to 4,000 ft. above the airport elevation.
2. Surrounding the Class C airspace is the outer area. The outer area is not classified as Class C airspace.
   a. The normal radius of the outer area is 20 NM from the primary airport.
3. Pilot and equipment requirements to operate in Class C airspace
   a. No specific pilot certification required
   b. Two-way radio
   c. Mode C transponder, unless otherwise authorized by ATC
4. ATC provides sequencing of arriving aircraft, separation of aircraft (except between VFR aircraft), and traffic advisories within Class C airspace.
   a. In the outer area, the same services are provided when communications and radar contact are established.

7.3 AIRPORT MARKINGS AND SIGNS (Questions 23-37)

1. **Hold line markings** at the intersection of taxiways and runways consist of four lines (two solid and two dashed) that extend across the width of the taxiway.
   a. These lines are yellow in color, and the dashed lines are nearest the runway.
   b. When instructed by ATC to hold short of a runway (ILS critical area, etc.), the pilot should stop so that no part of the aircraft extends beyond the hold line.
   c. An aircraft exiting a runway is considered clear of the runway when all parts of the aircraft have crossed the hold line.
2. **Holding position signs** have white inscriptions on a red background.
3. **Destination signs** have black inscriptions on yellow backgrounds indicating destinations on the airport.
4. A **runway boundary sign** (Fig. 156 on page 233), which faces the runway and is visible to the pilot, indicates a point at which the aircraft will be clear of the runway.
5. An **ILS critical area boundary sign** (Fig. 157 on page 234) has a graphic depiction of the ILS pavement holding position marking.

6. **Runway distance remaining markers** are signs that indicate distance remaining in increments of 1,000 ft.
7. On FAA nonprecision approach runways, there is a runway aiming point marking (two broad stripes parallel to the runway, one on each side of the centerline) 1,000 ft. from the threshold.
8. On ICAO nonprecision approach runways, fixed distance markers are set forth every 500 ft. and may have a runway aiming point marking approximately 1,000 ft. from the threshold.
   a. They are also used on FAA ICAO precision approach runways.

7.4 AIRPORT LIGHTING (Questions 38-49)

1. Runway remaining lighting on centerline lighting systems are alternate red and white lights from 3,000 ft. to 1,000 ft. and then red lights to the end.
2. Runway edge lights on FAA ICAO precision approach runways and ICAO nonprecision approach runways are white, except for the last 2,000 ft., which has amber (yellow) lights.
3. **Touchdown zone lighting (TDZL)** is two rows of transverse light bars disposed symmetrically about the runway centerline.
4. **Taxiway turnoff lights** associated with the centerline lighting system are flush lights spaced at 50-ft. intervals defining the curved path of aircraft travel from the runway centerline to the point of taxiway.
   a. These lights are green.
5. High-intensity runway lights (HIRL) or medium-intensity runway lights (MIRL) have amber lights replacing the white lights in the last 2,000 ft. of runway for a caution zone.
   a. VFR runway lights do not use amber lights to indicate a caution zone.
6. **Runway end identifier lights (REIL)** are for the identification of a runway surrounded by a preponderance of other lighting.
   a. They are synchronized flashing lights placed laterally at each side of the runway threshold.
7. A military airport is identified by a green and white beacon light with dual flashes of the white.
8. A lighted heliport is identified by a green, yellow, and white beacon light.

7.5 VASI (Questions 50-59)

1. A three-bar VASI provides a normal glide angle for both high- and low-cockpit aircraft.
   a. The higher glide slope is intended for use by high-cockpit aircraft.
   b. A steeper-than-normal VASI glide slope angle may result in an increased landing rollout for a high-performance airplane.
2. The tri-color VASI consists of one light projector with three colors: red, green, and amber.
   a. Amber is a high indication.
   b. Green is an on-course indication.
   c. Red is a low indication.
3. The normal range of a tri-color VASI at night is 5 mi.
4. A pulsating VASI consists of one light projector with two colors: red and white.
   a. High -- pulsating white
   b. On glide path -- steady white
   c. Slightly below glide path -- steady red
   d. Low -- pulsating red

7.6 PAPI (Questions 60-61)

1. The precision approach path indicator (PAPI) consists of a row of four lights perpendicular to the runway: red and white.
   a. High -- white
   b. On glide path -- red and white
   c. Low -- red

7.7 NOTAMs (Questions 62-65)

1. FDC NOTAMs are regulatory amendments to published instrument approach procedures (IAPs) and charts not yet available in normally published charts.
2. NOTAMs are broadcast to pilots on an hourly basis, appended to the weather broadcast.
3. NOTAMs (L) disseminate information on taxi closures, personnel and equipment near or crossing runways, airport lighting aids that do not affect instrument approach criteria, and airport rotating beacon outages.
4. NOTAMs (D) disseminate the status of navigation aids, ILSs, radar service available, and other information essential to planning.

QUESTIONS AND ANSWER EXPLANATIONS

All the FAA questions from the pilot knowledge test for the ATP certificate relating to airspace and airports and the material outlined previously are reproduced on the following pages in the same modules as the outlines. To the immediate right of each question are the correct answer and answer explanation. You should cover these answers and answer explanations while responding to the questions. Refer to the general discussion in Chapter 1 on how to take the FAA pilot knowledge test.

Remember that the questions from the FAA pilot knowledge test bank have been reordered by topic, and the topics are organized into a meaningful sequence. Accordingly, the first line of the answer explanation gives the FAA question number and the citation of the authoritative source for the answer.

7.1 Airspace

1.
9049. Which aeronautical chart depicts Military Training Routes (MTR) above 1,500 feet?

A—IFR Low Altitude En Route Chart.
B—IFR High Altitude En Route Chart.
C—IFR Planning Chart.

Answer (A) is correct (9049). *(AIM Para 3-5-2)*

IFR Low-Altitude En Route Charts depict all military training routes (IR/VR) that accommodate operations above 1,500 ft. AGL. These routes are identified by three digit numbers, e.g., IR 008, VR 009, etc. IR means IFR; VR means VFR. Note that segments of these routes may be below 1,500 ft.

Answer (B) is incorrect because IFR High-Altitude En Route Charts do not depict MTRs. Answer (C) is incorrect because VFR, not IFR, Planning Charts depict MTRs.

2.
8891. What is the purpose of MOA's?

A—To protect military aircraft operations from civil aircraft.
B—To separate military training activities from IFR traffic.
C—To separate military training activities from both IFR and VFR traffic.

Answer (B) is correct (8891). *(AIM Para 3-4-5)*
Military operations areas (MOAs) consist of airspace of defined vertical and lateral limits established for the purpose of separating certain military training activities from IFR traffic. Whenever an MOA is being used, nonparticipating IFR traffic may be cleared through the MOA if IFR separation can be provided by ATC. Otherwise, ATC will reroute or restrict nonparticipating IFR traffic. Pilots operating under VFR should exercise extreme caution while flying within an MOA when military activity is being conducted. Information regarding activities in an MOA may be obtained from any FSS within 100 mi. of the area.
Answer (A) is incorrect because MOAs are to separate, not protect, military training activities from IFR traffic. Answer (C) is incorrect because MOAs are established for the purpose of separating IFR, not VFR, traffic from military training activities.

3.
8892. Who is responsible for collision avoidance in an MOA?

A—Military controllers.
B—ATC controllers.
C—Each pilot.

Answer (C) is correct (8892). *(FAR 91.113)*
When weather conditions permit, regardless of whether a flight is conducted under VFR or IFR, each pilot is responsible to see and avoid other traffic. This includes operations in an MOA.
Answer (A) is incorrect because each pilot, not military controllers, is responsible for collision avoidance in an MOA, when weather conditions permit. Answer (B) is incorrect because each pilot, not ATC controllers, is responsible for collision avoidance in an MOA, when weather conditions permit.

4.
8890. Why are certain areas that start 3 nautical miles from the coastline of the U.S. and extend outward, classified as Warning Areas?

A—To inform pilots of participating aircraft to maintain extreme vigilance while conducting flight within the area.
B—To warn all aircraft pilots that flying within the area may be extremely hazardous to aircraft and occupants.
C—To warn pilots of nonparticipating aircraft of a potential danger within the area.

Answer (C) is correct (8890). *(AIM Para 3-4-4)*
A warning area is airspace of defined dimensions, extending from 3 NM outward from the coast of the U.S., that contains activity that may be hazardous to nonparticipating aircraft. The purpose of such warning areas is to warn nonparticipating pilots of the potential danger. A warning area may be located over domestic or international waters or both.
Answer (A) is incorrect because the purpose of a warning area is to warn nonparticipating, not participating, pilots to maintain extreme vigilance while conducting flight within the area. Answer (B) is incorrect because the purpose of a warning area is to warn nonparticipating pilots, not all pilots, that flying within the area may be hazardous.

5.
8889. What restriction applies to a large, turbine-powered airplane operating to or from a primary airport in Class B airspace?

A—Must not exceed 200 knots within Class B airspace.
B—Must operate above the floor when within lateral limits of Class B airspace.
C—Must operate in accordance with IFR procedures regardless of weather conditions.

Answer (B) is correct (8889). *(AIM Para 3-2-3)*
A large, turbine-powered airplane operating to or from a primary airport in Class B airspace must operate at or above the designated Class B airspace floors while within the lateral limits of Class B airspace, unless otherwise authorized by ATC.
Answer (A) is incorrect because the speed limit within Class B airspace is 250, not 200, kt. for all aircraft. Answer (C) is incorrect because VFR is permitted in Class B airspace; i.e., an IFR clearance is not required as it is in Class A airspace.

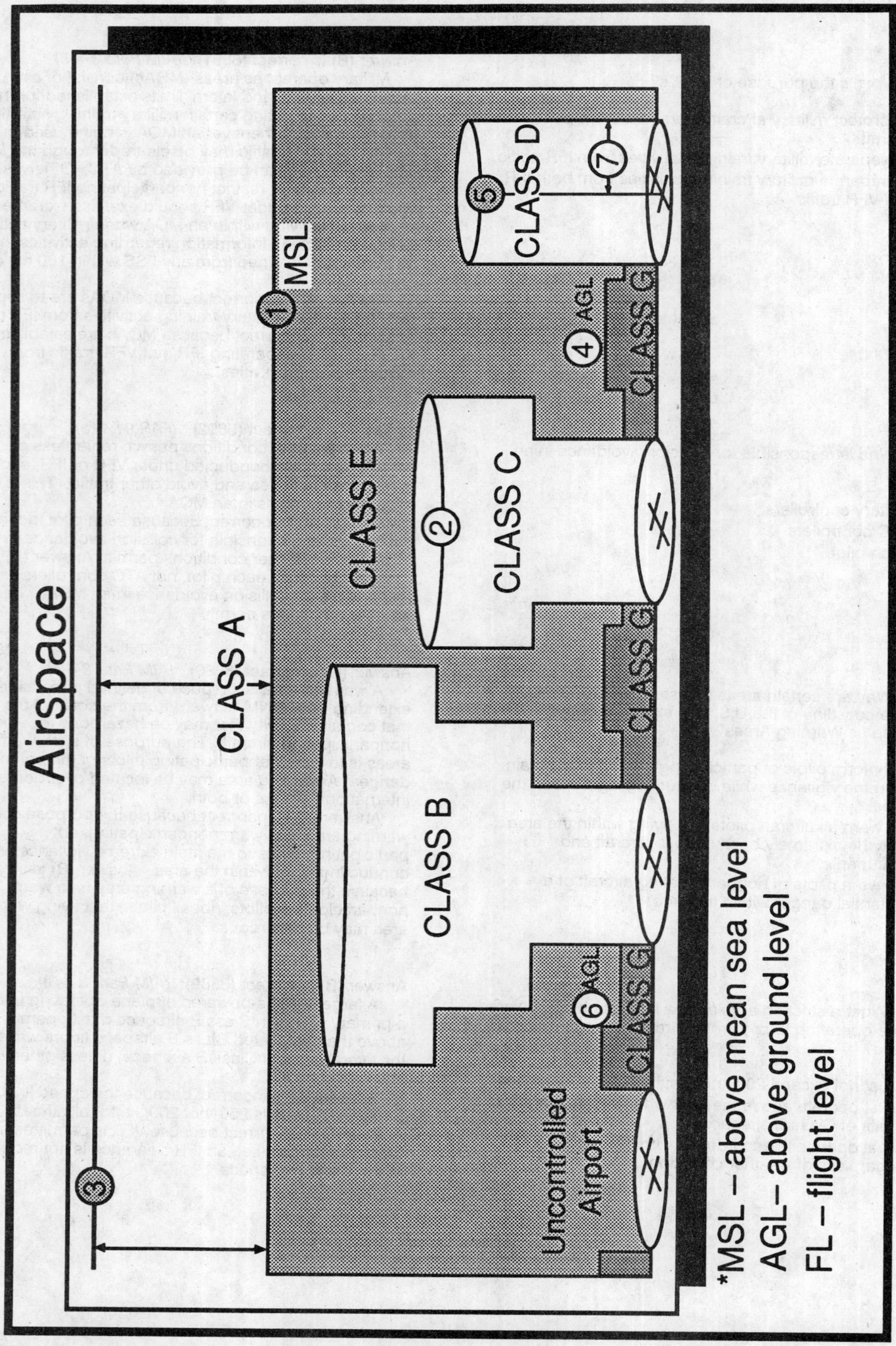

FIGURE 127.—Airspace.

6.
8888. (Refer to figure 127 on page 228.) What is the base of the Class A airspace?

A—12,000 feet AGL.
B—14,500 feet MSL.
C—FL 180.

Answer (C) is correct (8888). *(AIM Para 3-2-2)*
The base of Class A airspace is 18,000 ft. MSL (FL 180).
Answer (A) is incorrect because 12,000 ft. AGL is not an altitude which defines airspace. Answer (B) is incorrect because 14,500 ft. MSL is a base of Class E airspace, not Class A airspace.

7.
8884. (Refer to figure 127 on page 228.) Which altitude is appropriate for circle 1 (top of Class E airspace)?

A—14,000 feet MSL.
B—14,500 feet MSL.
C—18,000 feet MSL.

Answer (C) is correct (8884). *(AIM Para 3-2-6)*
Circle 1 on Fig. 127 indicates the base of Class A or top of Class E airspace, which is 18,000 ft. MSL.
Answer (A) is incorrect because 14,000 ft. MSL is not an altitude which defines airspace. Answer (B) is incorrect because 14,500 ft. MSL is the top of Class G, not Class E, airspace.

8.
8885. (Refer to figure 127 on page 228.) Which altitude is appropriate for circle 2 (top of Class C airspace)?

A—3,000 feet AGL.
B—4,000 feet AGL.
C—3,500 feet MSL.

Answer (B) is correct (8885). *(AIM Para 3-2-4)*
Circle 2 on Fig. 127 indicates the ceiling of Class C airspace, which is normally 4,000 ft. above the airport elevation.
Answer (A) is incorrect because 3,000 ft. AGL is not an altitude which defines airspace. Answer (C) is incorrect because 3,500 ft. MSL is not an altitude which defines airspace.

9.
8886. (Refer to figure 127 on page 228.) Which altitude is appropriate for circle 3 (top of Class A airspace)?

A—FL 600.
B—FL 450.
C—FL 500.

Answer (A) is correct (8886). *(AIM Para 3-2-2)*
Circle 3 on Fig. 127 indicates the ceiling of Class A airspace, which is at FL 600.
Answer (B) is incorrect because FL 450 is the ceiling of jet routes, not Class A airspace. Answer (C) is incorrect because FL 500 is not an altitude which defines airspace.

10.
8881. (Refer to figure 127 on page 228.) Which altitude is appropriate for circle 4 (top of Class G airspace)?

A—700 feet AGL.
B—1,200 feet AGL.
C—1,500 feet AGL.

Answer (B) is correct (8881). *(AIM Para 3-2-6)*
Circle 4 on Fig. 127 indicates the top of Class G airspace at 1,200 ft. AGL.
Answer (A) is incorrect because 700 ft. AGL is the floor of Class E airspace when designated in conjunction with an airport for which an approved IAP is prescribed, as shown in circle 6, not circle 4. Answer (C) is incorrect because the top of Class G airspace at circle 4 is 1,200 ft. AGL, not 1,500 ft. AGL.

11.
8883. (Refer to figure 127 on page 228.) Which altitude is appropriate for circle 6 (top of Class G airspace)?

A—500 feet AGL.
B—700 feet AGL.
C—1,200 feet AGL.

Answer (B) is correct (8883). *(AIM Para 3-2-6)*
Circle 6 on Fig. 127 indicates the floor of Class E airspace when designated in conjunction with an airport for which an approved IAP has been prescribed. The floor of Class E (or top of Class G) airspace at circle 6 is 700 ft. AGL.
Answer (A) is incorrect because 500 ft. AGL is not an altitude which defines airspace. Answer (C) is incorrect because 1,200 ft. AGL is normally the floor of Class E airspace, as shown in circle 4, not circle 6.

12.
8882. (Refer to figure 127 on page 228.) Which altitude is normally appropriate for circle 5 (top of Class D airspace)?

A—1,000 feet AGL.
B—2,500 feet AGL.
C—3,000 feet AGL.

Answer (B) is correct (8882). *(AIM Para 3-2-5)*
Circle 5 on Fig. 127 indicates the ceiling of Class D airspace. Class D airspace normally extends upward from the surface to 2,500 ft. AGL.
Answer (A) is incorrect because 1,000 ft. AGL is the normal traffic pattern altitude for piston aircraft, not the ceiling of Class D airspace. Answer (C) is incorrect because 3,000 ft. AGL was the ceiling of the old airport traffic area, not Class D airspace.

13.
8887. The maximum indicated airspeed that an aircraft may be flown in Class B airspace, after departing the primary airport, while at 1,700 feet AGL and 3.5 nautical miles from the airport is

A—200 knots.
B—230 knots.
C—250 knots.

Answer (C) is correct (8887). *(FAR 91.117)*
Unless otherwise authorized or required by ATC, no person may operate an aircraft in Class B airspace at an indicated airspeed of more than 250 kt.
Answer (A) is incorrect because 200 kt. is the maximum indicated airspeed for aircraft at or below 2,500 ft. AGL within 4 NM of the primary airport of Class C or D airspace, not in Class B airspace. Answer (B) is incorrect because 230 kt. is the maximum holding airspeed for civil turbojet aircraft operating above 6,000 ft. through 14,000 ft. MSL, not the maximum indicated airspeed while operating in Class B airspace.

7.2 Class C Airspace

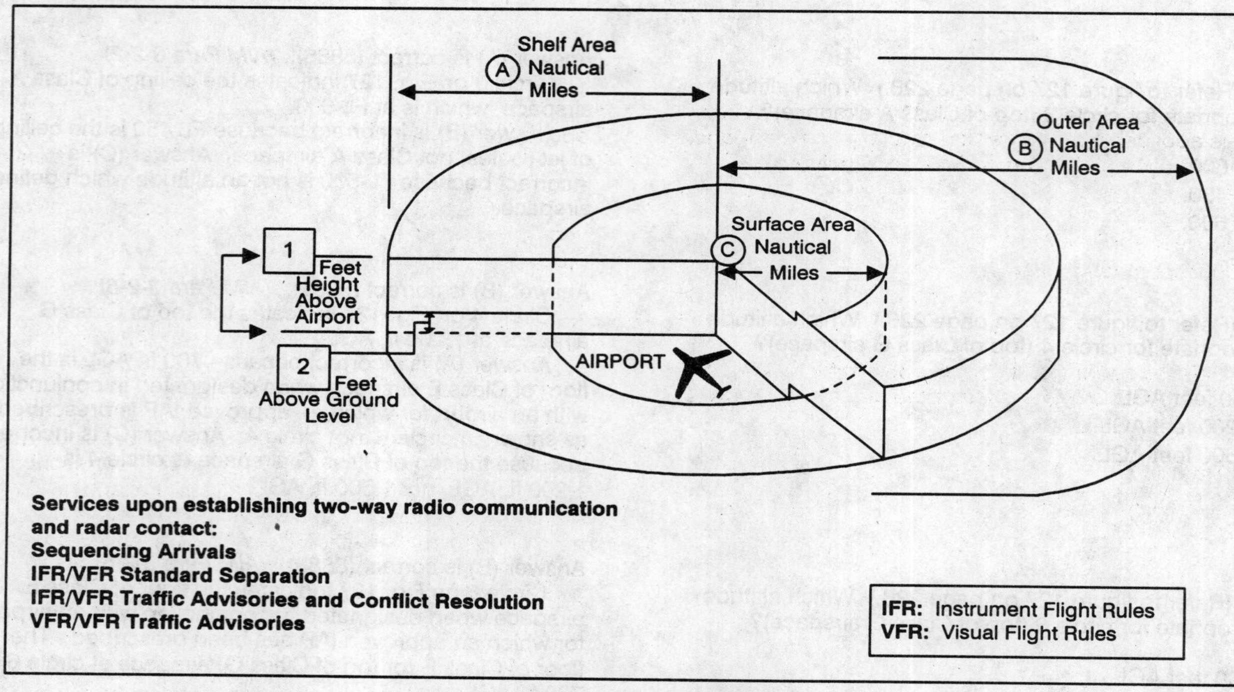

Figure 126.—Class C Airspace.

14.
8874. (Refer to figure 126 on page 230.) What is the radius from the airport of the outer circle (now called the shelf area) A?

A—5 miles.
B—10 miles.
C—15 miles.

Answer (B) is correct (8874). *(AIM Para 3-2-4)*
The radius of the shelf area of Class C airspace is 10 NM from the airport.
Answer (A) is incorrect because 5 NM is the radius of the surface, not shelf, area of Class C airspace. Answer (C) is incorrect because 15 NM is not established as the radius for any area of Class C airspace.

15.
8872. (Refer to figure 126 on page 230.) What is the normal radius from the airport of the outer area, B?

A—10 miles.
B—20 miles.
C—25 miles.

Answer (B) is correct (8872). *(AIM Para 3-2-4)*
The normal radius of the outer area is 20 NM from the airport.
Answer (A) is incorrect because 10 NM is the radius of the shelf area, not the outer area, of Class C airspace. Answer (C) is incorrect because 25 NM does not pertain to any set radius of Class C airspace.

16.
8873. (Refer to figure 126 on page 230.) What is the radius from the airport of the inner circle (now called the surface area) C?

A—5 miles.
B—7 miles.
C—10 miles.

Answer (A) is correct (8873). *(AIM Para 3-2-4)*
The radius of the surface area of Class C airspace is 5 NM from the airport.
Answer (B) is incorrect because 7 NM is not established as the radius for any portion of Class C airspace. Answer (C) is incorrect because 10 NM is the radius of the shelf, not surface, area of Class C airspace.

17.
8876. (Refer to figure 126 on page 230.) Which altitude (box 1) is applicable to the vertical extent of the inner and outer circles (now called the surface and shelf areas)?

A—3,000 feet AGL.
B—3,000 feet above airport.
C—4,000 feet above airport.

Answer (C) is correct (8876). *(AIM Para 3-2-4)*
The vertical extent of Class C airspace is 4,000 ft. above the airport elevation.
Answer (A) is incorrect because the vertical extent of Class C airspace is 4,000 ft. above the airport elevation, not 3,000 ft. AGL. Answer (B) is incorrect because the vertical extent of Class C airspace is 4,000 ft., not 3,000 ft., above the airport.

18.
8875. (Refer to figure 126 on page 230.) Which altitude (box 2) is applicable to the base of the outer circle (now called the shelf area)?

A—700 feet AGL.
B—1,000 feet AGL.
C—1,200 feet AGL.

Answer (C) is correct (8875). *(AIM Para 3-2-4)*
The base of the shelf area of Class C airspace is 1,200 ft. above the airport elevation.
Answer (A) is incorrect because 700 ft. AGL is the base of Class E airspace when designated in conjunction with an airport for which an approved IAP is prescribed, not the base of the shelf area of Class C airspace. Answer (B) is incorrect because 1,000 ft. AGL is the normal traffic pattern altitude for most propeller-driven airplanes, not the base of the shelf area of Class C airspace.

19.
8880. What pilot certification and aircraft equipment are required for operating in Class C airspace?

A—No specific certification but a two-way radio.
B—At least a Private Pilot Certificate and two-way radio.
C—At least a Private Pilot Certificate, two-way radio, and a TSO-C74b transponder.

Answer (A) is the best answer (8880). *(AIM Para 3-2-4)*
No specific certification is required to operate in Class C airspace; i.e., a student pilot may operate in Class C airspace (however, a recreational pilot may not unless with a special CFI endorsement). The aircraft must be equipped with a two-way radio and a transponder with Mode C capability, unless otherwise authorized by ATC.
Answer (B) is incorrect because a specific pilot certificate is not required, and a Mode C 4096 transponder is required. Answer (C) is incorrect because a specific pilot certificate is not required, and Mode C capability on the transponder is required.

20.
8877. What minimum aircraft equipment is required for operation within Class C airspace?

A—Two-way communications.
B—Two-way communications and transponder.
C—Transponder and DME.

Answer (B) is correct (8877). *(AIM Para 3-2-4)*
In Class C airspace, the equipment requirement is an operating two-way communications radio and a Mode C transponder.
Answer (A) is incorrect because a Mode C transponder is also required. Answer (C) is incorrect because two-way communications are also required, and DME is not required.

21.
8879. What services are provided for aircraft operating within Class C airspace?

A—Sequencing of arriving aircraft, separation of aircraft (except between VFR aircraft), and traffic advisories.
B—Sequencing of arriving aircraft (except VFR aircraft), separation between all aircraft, and traffic advisories.
C—Sequencing of all arriving aircraft, separation between all aircraft, and traffic advisories.

Answer (A) is correct (8879). *(AIM Para 3-2-4)*
ATC provides these services for aircraft operating within Class C airspace: sequencing of all arriving aircraft to the primary airport; maintaining standard IFR separation between IFR aircraft; providing traffic advisories and conflict resolution between IFR and VFR aircraft; and providing traffic advisories and safety alerts, as needed, between VFR aircraft.
Answer (B) is incorrect because the services in Class C airspace provide sequencing of all, not only IFR, aircraft to the primary airport. Answer (C) is incorrect because the services in Class C airspace do not provide separation between VFR aircraft, only traffic advisories and safety alerts.

22.
8878. What service is provided for aircraft operating within the outer area of Class C airspace?

A—The same as within Class C airspace when communications and radar contact is established.
B—Radar vectors to and from secondary airports within the outer area.
C—Basic radar service only when communications and radar contact is established.

Answer (A) is correct (8878). *(AIM Para 3-2-4)*
Within the outer area of Class C airspace, the same services are provided for aircraft as within Class C airspace. Providing these services, of course, requires establishment of two-way communications and radar contact.
Answer (B) is incorrect because providing radar vectors to and from secondary airports within the outer circle is not a mandated service of ATC. Answer (C) is incorrect because the same, not basic radar, services are provided in the outer area as within Class C airspace, once two-way communications and radar contact are established.

7.3 Airport Markings and Signs

23.
9423. Hold line markings at the intersection of taxiways and runways consist of four lines (two solid and two dashed) that extend across the width of the taxiway. These lines are

A—white in color and the dashed lines are nearest the runway.
B—yellow in color and the dashed lines are nearest the runway.
C—yellow in color and the solid lines are nearest the runway.

Answer (B) is correct (9423). *(AIM Para 2-3-5)*
Holding position markings for taxiway/runway intersections consist of four yellow lines -- two solid and two dashed, spaced 6 in. apart and extending across the width of the taxiway or runway. The solid lines are always on the side where the aircraft is to hold (i.e., away from the runway). Thus, the dashed lines are nearest the runway.
Answer (A) is incorrect because hold line markings are always yellow, not white, in color. Answer (C) is incorrect because the solid lines are farthest from, not nearest to, the runway (i.e., on the side where the aircraft is to hold).

24.
9416. When instructed by ATC to "Hold short of a runway (ILS critical area, etc.)," the pilot should stop

A—with the nose gear on the hold line.
B—so that no part of the aircraft extends beyond the hold line.
C—so the flight deck area of the aircraft is even with the hold line.

Answer (B) is correct (9416). *(AIM Para 2-3-5)*
When instructed by ATC to hold short of a runway (ILS critical area, etc.), you should stop so no part of your aircraft extends beyond the holding position marking.
Answer (A) is incorrect because you should stop before, not with the nose gear on, the hold line.
Answer (C) is incorrect because you should stop before, not so the flight deck is even with, the hold line.

25.
9417. You have just landed at JFK and the tower tells you to call ground control when clear of the runway. You are considered clear of the runway when

A—the aft end of the aircraft is even with the taxiway location sign.
B—the flight deck area of the aircraft is even with the hold line.
C—all parts of the aircraft have crossed the hold line.

Answer (C) is correct (9417). *(AIM Para 2-3-5)*
An aircraft exiting a runway is not considered clear of the runway until all parts of the aircraft have crossed the applicable holding position marking.
Answer (A) is incorrect because you are clear when the entire aircraft has crossed the hold line, not when the aft end is even with the taxiway location sign. Answer (B) is incorrect because you are clear when the entire aircraft has crossed the hold line, not when the flight deck is even with the hold line.

26.
9421. Holding position signs have

A—white inscriptions on a red background.
B—red inscriptions on a white background.
C—yellow inscriptions on a red background.

Answer (A) is correct (9421). *(AIM Para 2-3-8)*
A holding position sign has a red background with a white inscription and is used to denote an entrance to a runway or critical area.
Answer (B) is incorrect because a holding position sign has a white, not red, inscription on a red, not white, background. Answer (C) is incorrect because a holding position sign has a white, not yellow, inscription on a red background.

27.
9422. Airport information signs, used to provide destination or information, have

A—yellow inscriptions on a black background.
B—white inscriptions on a black background.
C—black inscriptions on a yellow background.

Answer (C) is the best answer (9422). *(AIM Para 2-3-11)*
Destination signs have black inscriptions on yellow backgrounds indicating destinations on the airport.
Answer (A) is incorrect because taxiway location signs, not destination signs, have yellow inscriptions on black backgrounds. Answer (B) is incorrect because runway distance remaining signs, not destination signs, have white inscriptions on black backgrounds.

28.
9436. (Refer to figure 156 below.) This sign, which faces the runway and is visible to the pilot, indicates

A—a point at which the pilot should contact ground control without being instructed by the tower.
B—a point at which the aircraft will be clear of the runway.
C—the point at which the emergency arresting gear is stretched across the runway.

Answer (B) is correct (9436). *(AIM Para 2-3-9)*
Fig. 156 is a runway boundary sign. This sign, which faces the runway and is visible to the pilot exiting the runway, is located adjacent to the holding position marking on the pavement. It is intended to provide pilots with another visual cue which they can use as a guide in deciding when they are clear of the runway.
Answer (A) is incorrect because the pilot should contact ground control when advised by the tower, not after passing the runway boundary sign. Answer (C) is incorrect because arresting gear that crosses over a runway is identified by solid yellow circles painted on the runway, not by a runway boundary sign.

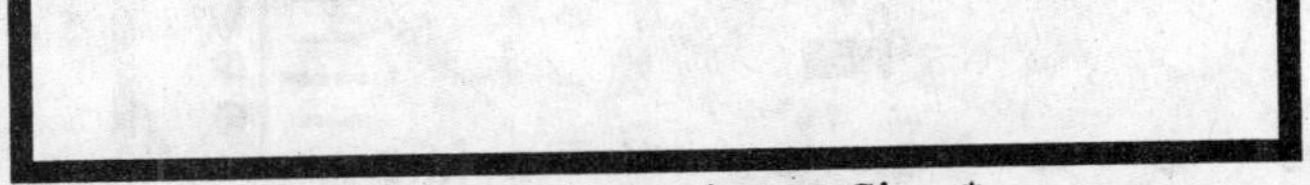

FIGURE 156.—Airport Sign.*

☐ Yellow

*NOTE: Figure 156 is in color in the FAA *Computerized Testing Supplement for Airline Transport Pilot and Aircraft Dispatcher*, which you will use during your test.

29.
9437. (Refer to figure 157 below.) This is an example of

A—an ILS Critical Area Holding Position Sign.
B—a Runway Boundary Sign.
C—an ILS Critical Area Boundary Sign.

FIGURE 157.—Airport Sign.*

*NOTE: Figure 157 is in color in the FAA *Computerized Testing Supplement for Airline Transport Pilot and Aircraft Dispatcher*, which you will use during your test.

Answer (C) is correct (9437). *(AIM Para 2-3-9)*
Fig. 157 is an ILS critical area boundary sign. This sign is located adjacent to the ILS holding position marking on the pavement and can be seen by pilots leaving the critical area. The sign is intended to provide pilots with another visual cue which they can use as a guide in deciding when they are clear of the ILS critical area.
Answer (A) is incorrect because an ILS critical area holding position sign has a red, not yellow, background with the inscription "ILS" in white, not a graphic depiction of the ILS pavement holding position marking. Answer (B) is incorrect because a runway boundary sign depicts the pavement holding position marking, i.e., four lines -- two solid and two dashed.

30.
8907. Identify the runway distance remaining markers.

A—Signs with increments of 1,000 feet distance remaining.
B—Red markers laterally placed across the runway at 3,000 feet from the end.
C—Yellow marker laterally placed across the runway with signs on the side denoting distance to end.

Answer (A) is correct (8907). *(AIM Para 2-3-13)*
Runway distance remaining signs are located along the sides of the runway to indicate the remaining runway distance in increments of 1,000 ft. The signs have white numbers on a black background and are lighted for nighttime and low-visibility operations.
Answer (B) is incorrect because distance remaining markers are along the side of, not across, the runway and are black and white, not red. Answer (C) is incorrect because distance remaining markers are signs along the side of, not across, the runway and are black and white, not yellow.

31.
8922. (Refer to figure 129 below.) What is the runway distance remaining at "A" for a daytime takeoff on runway 9?

A—1,000 feet.
B—1,500 feet.
C—2,000 feet.

Answer (A) is correct (8922). *(AC 00-54)*
"A" on Fig. 129 refers to the runway aiming point marking that is 1,000 ft. from the threshold of runway 27. Since runway 9 is being used for a takeoff, "A" would indicate 1,000 ft. of runway remaining.
Answer (B) is incorrect because the 1,500-ft. distance of runway remaining is not marked on an FAA nonprecision runway. Answer (C) is incorrect because 2,000 ft. is the distance remaining on an ICAO, not an FAA, nonprecision instrument runway where the runway edge lights are amber.

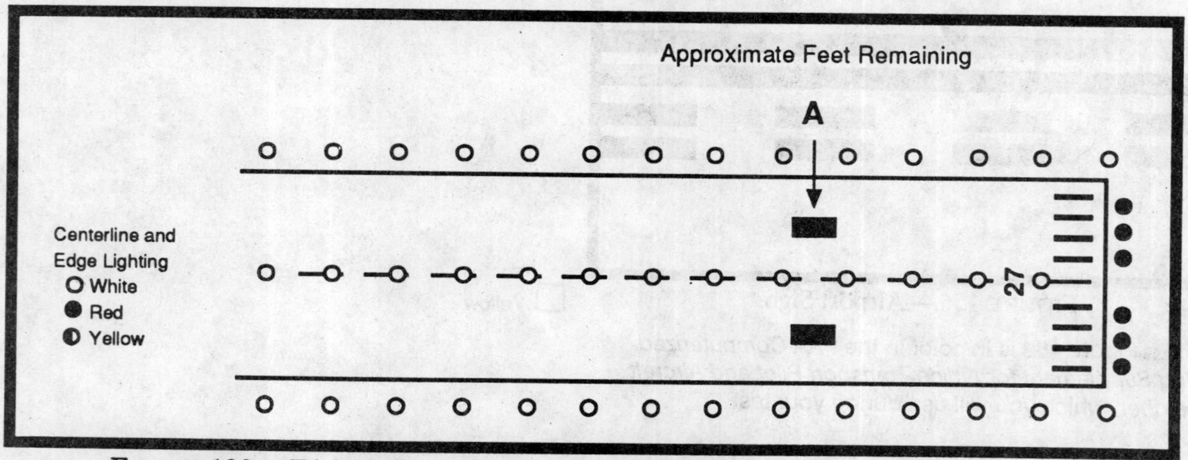

FIGURE 129.—FAA Nonprecision Approach Runway Markings and Lighting.

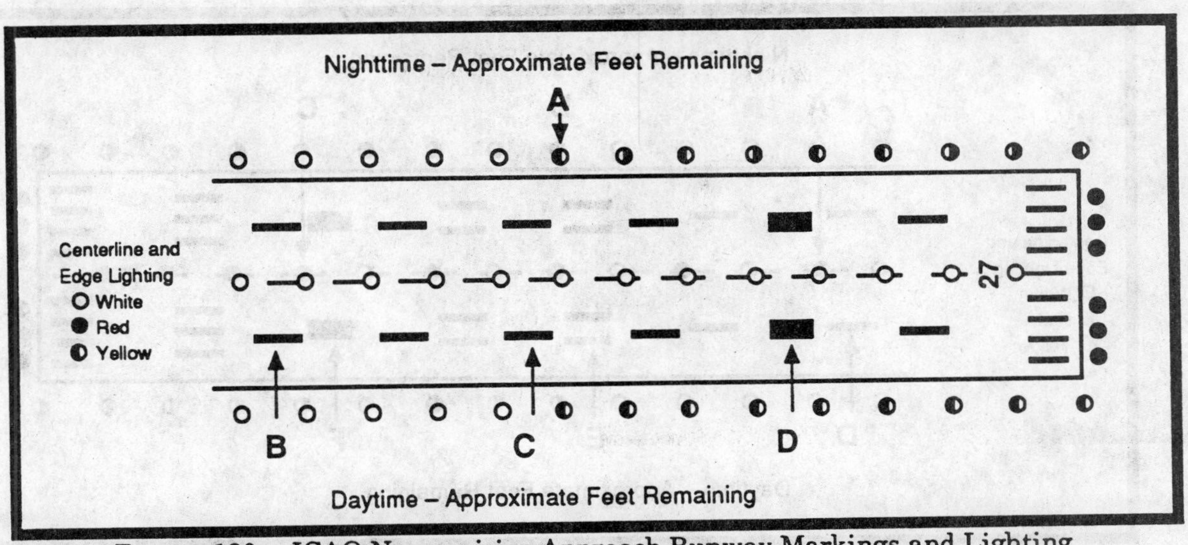

FIGURE 130.—ICAO Nonprecision Approach Runway Markings and Lighting.

32.
8924. (Refer to figure 130 above.) What is the runway distance remaining at "B" for a daytime takeoff on runway 9?

A—2,000 feet.
B—2,500 feet.
C—3,000 feet.

Answer (C) is correct (8924). *(AC 00-54)*

"B" on Fig. 130 refers to fixed distance marking which provides distance indication from the threshold of a landing position runway. The markers are spaced approximately every 500 ft. (150 meters) to a distance of approximately 3,000 ft. For a takeoff on runway 9 during the day, "B" indicates 3,000 ft. to the end of the runway because it is the first distance marker encountered.

Answer (A) is incorrect because the marker at 2,000 ft. is the third, not first, distance marker encountered. Answer (B) is incorrect because the marker at 2,500 ft. is the second, not first, distance marker encountered.

33.
8925. (Refer to figure 130 above.) What is the runway distance remaining at "C" for a daytime takeoff on runway 9?

A—2,500 feet.
B—2,000 feet.
C—1,500 feet.

Answer (B) is correct (8925). *(AC 00-54)*

"C" on Fig. 130 refers to fixed distance markings which are spaced at approximately 500-ft. (150 meters) intervals from the threshold of a landing position runway to approximately 3,000 ft. During a daytime takeoff on runway 9, "C" is the third set of distance markings encountered. The first begins at 3,000 ft., the second is at 2,500 ft., and "C" is at 2,000 ft. from the end of the runway.

Answer (A) is incorrect because the marker at 2,500 ft. is the second, not third, distance marker encountered. Answer (C) is incorrect because the marker at 1,500 ft. is the fourth, not third, distance marker encountered.

34.
8926. (Refer to figure 130 above.) What is the runway distance remaining at "D" for a daytime takeoff on runway 9?

A—500 feet.
B—1,000 feet.
C—1,500 feet.

Answer (B) is correct (8926). *(AC 00-54)*

"D" on Fig. 130 refers to the runway aiming point marking which is located approximately 1,000 ft. from the threshold. During a takeoff on runway 9, the marker at "D" on Fig. 130 indicates 1,000 ft. of remaining runway because it is the fifth distance marker encountered.

Answer (A) is incorrect because the marker at 500 ft. is the sixth, not fifth, distance marker encountered. Answer (C) is incorrect because the marker at 1,500 ft. is the fourth, not fifth, distance marker encountered.

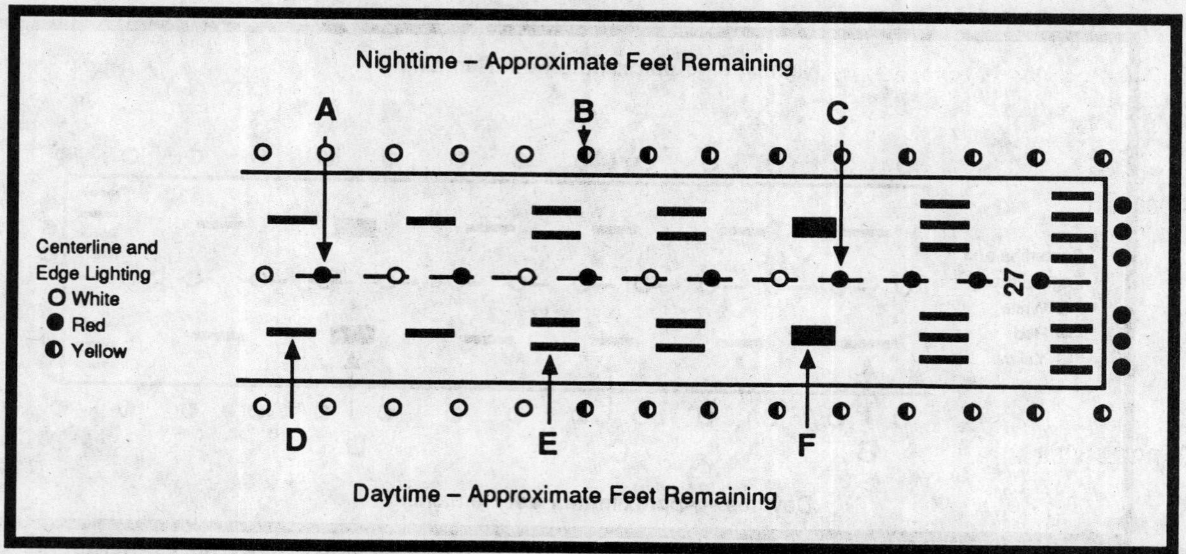

FIGURE 131.—FAA ICAO Precision Approach Runway Markings and Lighting.

35.
8929. (Refer to figure 131 above.) What is the runway distance remaining at "D" for a daytime takeoff on runway 9?

A—3,000 feet.
B—2,500 feet.
C—1,500 feet.

Answer (A) is correct (8929). *(AC 00-54)*
"D" on Fig. 131 refers to fixed distance markings which begin at the 500-ft. mark from the end of the runway and continue at 500-ft. intervals to the 3,000-ft. mark, depending on the runway length. During a daytime takeoff on runway 9, the marking at "D" on Fig. 131 indicates 3,000 ft. of remaining runway because it is the first pair of single markers on either side of the centerline.
Answer (B) is incorrect because the markers at 2,500 ft. are the second, not first, pair of single markers encountered on either side of the centerline. Answer (C) is incorrect because the markers at 1,500 ft. are the second pair of double, not single, markers encountered on either side of the centerline.

36.
8927. (Refer to figure 131 above.) What is the runway distance remaining at "E" for a daytime takeoff on runway 9?

A—1,500 feet.
B—2,000 feet.
C—2,500 feet.

Answer (B) is correct (8927). *(AC 00-54)*
"E" on Fig. 131 refers to fixed distance markings which begin at the 500-ft. mark from the end of the runway, and continue at 500-ft. intervals to the 3,000-ft. mark, depending on the runway length. During a daytime takeoff on runway 9, the marking at "E" on Fig. 131 indicates 2,000 ft. of remaining runway because it is the first pair of double markers on either side of the centerline.
Answer (A) is incorrect because the markers at 1,500 ft. are the second, not first, pair of double markers encountered on either side of the centerline. Answer (C) is incorrect because the markers at 2,500 ft. are the second pair of single, not the first pair of double, markers encountered on either side of the centerline.

37.
8931. (Refer to figure 131 on page 236.) What is the runway distance remaining at "F" for a daytime takeoff on runway 9?

A—2,000 feet.
B—1,500 feet.
C—1,000 feet.

Answer (C) is correct (8931). *(AC 00-54)*
"F" on Fig. 131 refers to the runway aiming point marking which is located 1,000 ft. from the landing threshold end of the runway. During a daytime takeoff on runway 9, the marking at "F" on Fig. 131 indicates 1,000 ft. of remaining runway.
Answer (A) is incorrect because the markers at 2,000 ft. are the first pair of double markers, not a single bold marker, encountered on either side of the centerline. At night it is marked by the beginning of amber runway edge lights. Answer (B) is incorrect because the markers at 1,500 ft. are the second pair of double markers, not a single bold marker, encountered on either side of the centerline.

7.4 Airport Lighting

38.
8928. (Refer to figure 131 on page 236.) What is the runway distance remaining at "A" for a nighttime takeoff on runway 9?

A—2,000 feet.
B—3,000 feet.
C—3,500 feet.

Answer (B) is correct (8928). *(AIM Para 2-1-5)*
"A" on Fig. 131 refers to runway centerline lights which are installed on FAA ICAO precision approach runways. They are white up to 3,000 ft. of remaining runway. Runway remaining lighting is centerline lighting in the final 3,000 ft. viewed from the takeoff position. Alternate red and white lights are seen from the 3,000-ft. point to the 1,000-ft. point, and red lights are seen for the final 1,000 ft. At point A on Fig. 131, 3,000 ft. remain, and the alternating red and white lights begin.
Answer (A) is incorrect because 2,000 ft. is marked by the beginning of amber runway edge lights. Answer (C) is incorrect because the runway remaining lights begin alternating between red and white at 3,000 ft., not 3,500 ft., of remaining runway.

39.
8932. (Refer to figure 131 on page 236.) What is the runway distance remaining at "C" for a nighttime takeoff on runway 9?

A—1,000 feet.
B—1,500 feet.
C—1,800 feet.

Answer (A) is correct (8932). *(AIM Para 2-1-5)*
"C" on Fig. 131 refers to runway centerline lights which are installed on FAA ICAO precision approach runways. Runway remaining lighting is centerline lighting in the final 3,000 ft. viewed from the takeoff position. Alternate red and white lights are seen from 3,000 ft. to 1,000 ft., and red lights are seen for the last 1,000 ft. of the runway. Point C on Fig. 131 is 1,000 ft. from the end of the runway and is the beginning of red runway centerline lights.
Answer (B) is incorrect because the start of red runway centerline lights indicates 1,000 ft., not 1,500 ft., of remaining runway. Answer (C) is incorrect because the start of red runway centerline lights indicates 1,000 ft., not 1,800 ft., of remaining runway.

40.
8930. (Refer to figure 131 on page 236.) What is the runway distance remaining at "B" for a nighttime takeoff on runway 9?

A—1,000 feet.
B—2,000 feet.
C—2,500 feet.

Answer (B) is correct (8930). *(AIM Para 2-1-4)*
"B" on Fig. 131 refers to the runway edge lights, which are white. However, on FAA ICAO precision instrument runways, amber (yellow) replaces white on the last 2,000 ft. or half of the runway length, whichever is less. During a takeoff on runway 9 at night, "B" on Fig. 131 marking the beginning of amber runway edge lights indicates 2,000 ft. of remaining runway.
Answer (A) is incorrect because 1,000 ft. is indicated by the start of red centerline lighting. Answer (C) is incorrect because the beginning of yellow runway edge lights on an instrument runway indicates 2,000 ft., not 2,500 ft., of remaining runway.

41.
8923. (Refer to figure 130 below.) What is the runway distance remaining at "A" for a nighttime takeoff on runway 9?

A—1,000 feet.
B—2,000 feet.
C—2,500 feet.

Answer (B) is correct (8923). *(AIM Para 2-1-4)*
"A" on Fig. 130 refers to the runway edge lights which are white. However, on ICAO nonprecision instrument runways, amber (yellow) replaces white on the last 2,000 ft. or half the runway length, whichever is less. At point A on Fig. 130, during a takeoff on runway 9 at night, the start of amber runway edge lights indicates that 2,000 ft. of runway remains.

Answer (A) is incorrect because the beginning of yellow runway edge lights on an ICAO nonprecision instrument runway indicates 2,000 ft., not 1,000 ft. of runway remaining. Answer (C) is incorrect because the beginning of yellow runway edge lights on an ICAO nonprecision instrument runway indicates that 2,000 ft., not 2,500 ft., of runway remaining.

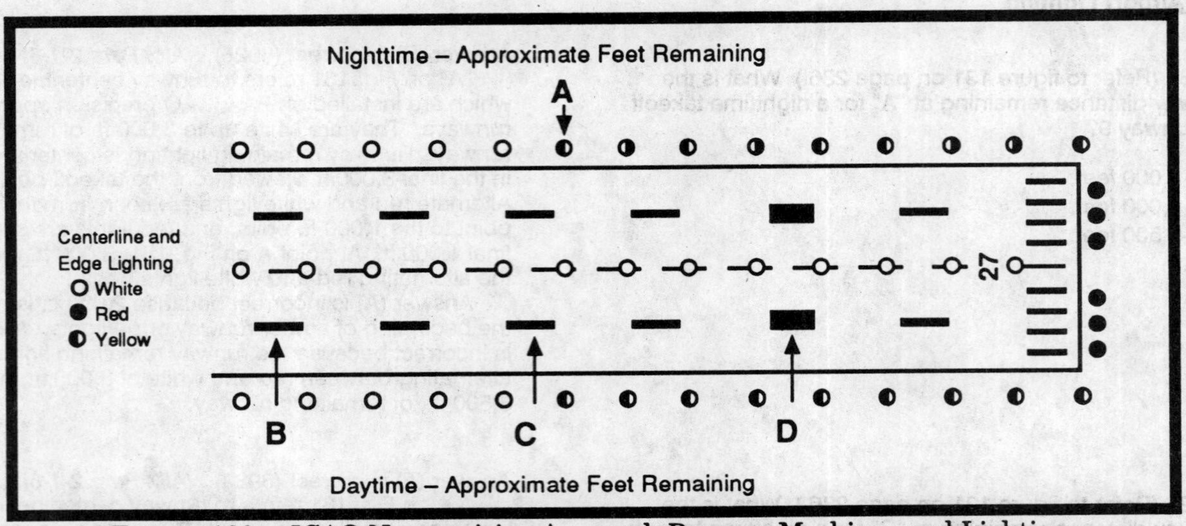

FIGURE 130.—ICAO Nonprecision Approach Runway Markings and Lighting.

42.
8903. Identify runway remaining lighting on centerline lighting systems.

A—Amber lights from 3,000 feet to 1,000 feet, then alternate red and white lights to the end.
B—Alternate red and white lights from 3,000 feet to 1,000 feet, then red lights to the end.
C—Alternate red and white lights from 3,000 feet to the end of the runway.

Answer (B) is correct (8903). *(AIM Para 2-1-5)*
Runway remaining lighting on centerline lighting systems alternates red and white lights as seen from 3,000 ft. to 1,000 ft. and has all red lights from 1,000 ft. to the runway end. From the opposite direction, these lights are seen as white lights.

Answer (A) is incorrect because alternate red and white, not amber, lights are from 3,000 ft. to 1,000 ft.; then red lights, not alternate red and white, are to the end. Answer (C) is incorrect because runway remaining lighting alternates red and white lights from 3,000 ft. to 1,000 ft. and has red lights, not alternate red and white, from 1,000 ft. to the end of the runway.

43.
8902. Identify touchdown zone lighting (TDZL).

A—Two rows of transverse light bars disposed symmetrically about the runway centerline.
B—Flush centerline lights spaced at 50-foot intervals extending through the touchdown zone.
C—Alternate white and green centerline lights extending from 75 feet from the threshold through the touchdown zone.

Answer (A) is correct (8902). *(AIM Para 2-1-5)*
Touchdown zone lighting (TDZL) consists of two rows of transverse light bars disposed symmetrically about the runway centerline in the runway touchdown zone. The system starts 100 ft. from the landing threshold and extends to 3,000 ft. from the threshold or the midpoint of the runway, whichever is less.
Answer (B) is incorrect because flush centerline lights spaced at 50-ft. intervals extending the length of the runway, including the touchdown zone, are runway centerline lighting, not TDZL. Answer (C) is incorrect because runway centerline lights, not TDZL, extend from 75 ft. from the threshold through the touchdown zone and are white, not alternating white and green.

44.
8904. Identify taxi turnoff lights associated with the centerline lighting system.

A—Alternate blue and white lights curving from the centerline of the runway to the centerline of the taxiway.
B—Green lights curving from the centerline of the runway to the centerline of the taxiway.
C—Blue lights curving from the centerline of the runway to the centerline of the taxiway.

Answer (B) is correct (8904). *(AIM Para 2-1-5)*
Taxiway turnoff lights associated with the centerline lighting system are flush lights spaced at 50-ft. intervals defining the curved path of aircraft travel from the runway centerline to a point on the taxiway. These lights are green.
Answer (A) is incorrect because taxiway turnoff lights are green, not alternate blue and white. Answer (C) is incorrect because taxiway turnoff lights are green, not blue.

45.
8901. What is the advantage of HIRL or MIRL on an IFR runway as compared to a VFR runway?

A—Lights are closer together and easily distinguished from surrounding lights.
B—Amber lights replace white on the last 2,000 feet of runway for a caution zone.
C—Alternate red and white lights replace the white on the last 3,000 feet of runway for a caution zone.

Answer (B) is correct (8901). *(AIM Para 2-1-4)*
HIRL (high-intensity runway lights) and MIRL (medium-intensity runway lights) are runway edge light systems that have variable intensity controls. The runway edge lights are white, except that on instrument runways amber replaces white on the last 2,000 ft. or half the runway length, whichever is less, to form a caution zone for landings.
Answer (A) is incorrect because MIRL and HIRL are runway edge light systems and are not spaced closer together on instrument runways. Answer (C) is incorrect because alternate red and white runway centerline, not runway edge, lights are on the last 3,000 ft. of a runway to the last 1,000 ft. of runway (the last 1,000 ft. of runway centerline lights are marked by red lights).

46.
8914. What is the purpose of REIL?

A—Identification of a runway surrounded by a preponderance of other lighting.
B—Identification of the touchdown zone to prevent landing short.
C—Establish visual descent guidance information during an approach.

Answer (A) is correct (8914). *(AIM Para 2-1-3)*
Runway end identifier lights (REIL) are installed to provide rapid and positive identification of the approach end of a particular runway. REIL is effective for the identification of a runway surrounded by a preponderance of other lighting.
Answer (B) is incorrect because the touchdown zone is identified by in-runway lighting of two rows of transverse light bars on either side of the runway centerline from 100 ft. to 3,000 ft. from the landing threshold. Answer (C) is incorrect because a VASI, not REIL, assists in providing visual descent guidance information during an approach.

47.
8915. Identify REIL.

A—Amber lights for the first 2,000 feet of runway.
B—Green lights at the threshold and red lights at far end of runway.
C—Synchronized flashing lights laterally at each side of the runway threshold.

Answer (C) is correct (8915). *(AIM Para 2-1-3)*
Runway end identifier lights (REIL) are installed to provide rapid and positive identification of the approach end of a particular runway. The system consists of a pair of synchronized flashing lights located laterally on each side of the runway threshold.

Answer (A) is incorrect because amber lights are used on the last, not first, 2,000 ft. of runway edge lights to form a caution zone on instrument runways. Answer (B) is incorrect because green lights at the threshold mark the runway edge for landing aircraft, and red lights at the far end mark the runway edge to a departing or landing aircraft.

48.
8905. How can a pilot identify a military airport at night?

A—Green, yellow, and white beacon light.
B—White and red beacon light with dual flash of the white.
C—Green and white beacon light with dual flash of the white.

Answer (C) is correct (8905). *(AIM Para 2-1-8)*
Military airports can be identified at night by an airport beacon. The beacon flashes green and white light with a dual flash of the white between the green flashes.

Answer (A) is incorrect because a sequential green, yellow, and white beacon light identifies a lighted civilian, not military, heliport. Answer (B) is incorrect because no type of airfield is marked by a beacon with a red and white light with a dual flash of the white.

49.
8906. How can a pilot identify a lighted heliport at night?

A—Green, yellow, and white beacon light.
B—White and red beacon light with dual flash of the white.
C—Green and white beacon light with dual flash of the white.

Answer (A) is correct (8906). *(AIM Para 2-1-8)*
Lighted heliports can be identified at night by an airport beacon. The beacon flashes green, yellow, and white light.

Answer (B) is incorrect because no type of airfield is marked by a beacon with a white and red light with a dual flash of the white. Answer (C) is incorrect because a green and white beacon light with a dual flash of the white identifies a military airport, not a lighted heliport.

7.5 VASI

50.
8911. What is the advantage of a three-bar VASI?

A—Pilots have a choice of glide angles.
B—A normal glide angle is afforded both high and low cockpit aircraft.
C—The three-bar VASI is much more visible and can be used at a greater height.

Answer (B) is correct (8911). *(AIM Para 2-1-2)*
The three-bar VASI provides two visual glide paths. The lower glide path is provided by the near and middle bars and is normally set at 3° while the upper glide path, provided by the middle and far bars, is normally 1/4° higher. This higher glide path is intended for use only by high cockpit aircraft to provide a sufficient threshold crossing height.

Answer (A) is incorrect because the three-bar VASI provides a glide slope for high cockpit aircraft, not a choice of glide angles for pilots. Answer (C) is incorrect because both the two- and three-bar VASI are visible from 3 to 5 mi. during the day and up to 20 mi. or more at night, and the three-bar VASI does not provide use at a greater height.

51.
8913. The higher glide slope of the three-bar VASI is intended for use by

A—high performance aircraft.
B—helicopters.
C—high cockpit aircraft.

Answer (C) is correct (8913). *(AIM Para 2-1-2)*
The three-bar VASI provides two visual glide paths. The higher glide path is intended for use only by high-cockpit aircraft to provide a sufficient threshold crossing height.

Answer (A) is incorrect because the higher glide slope of a three-bar VASI is for use only by high-cockpit aircraft, which may or may not be high-performance aircraft. Answer (B) is incorrect because the higher glide slope of a three-bar VASI is for use only by high-cockpit aircraft, not specifically for use by helicopters.

52.
8912. A pilot of a high-performance airplane should be aware that flying a steeper-than-normal VASI glide slope angle may result in

A—a hard landing.
B—increased landing rollout.
C—landing short of the runway threshold.

Answer (B) is correct (8912). *(AIM Para 2-1-2)*
Although VASI normally provides glide path angles of 3°, some locations may be as high as 4.5° to give proper clearance. Pilots of high-performance aircraft are cautioned that use of VASI angles in excess of 3.5° may cause an increase in runway length required for landing and rollout.
Answer (A) is incorrect because flying a steeper-than-normal VASI may result in an increased landing rollout, not a hard landing, in a high-performance airplane. Answer (C) is incorrect because a landing short of the runway threshold results from flying a lower-than-normal, not higher, VASI glide slope angle.

53.
8916. What does the tri-color VASI consist of?

A—Three light bars; red, green, and amber.
B—One light projector with three colors; red, green, and amber.
C—Three glide slopes, each a different color; red, green, and amber.

Answer (B) is correct (8916). *(AIM Para 2-1-2)*
Tri-color VASIs normally consist of a single light unit projecting a three-color visual approach path. The three colors are red, green, and amber. Below the glide path is red, above the glide path is amber, and on the glide path is green.
Answer (A) is incorrect because a tri-color VASI consists of a single light projector, not three light bars. Answer (C) is incorrect because a tri-color VASI projects only one glide slope, not three. Below the glide slope is red, above the glide slope is amber, and on the glide slope is green.

54.
8917. Which color on a tri-color VASI is a “high” indication?

A—Red.
B—Amber.
C—Green.

Answer (B) is correct (8917). *(AIM Para 2-1-2)*
The tri-color VASI projects a three-color visual approach path into the final approach area of the runway. A “high” indication is seen as the color amber.
Answer (A) is incorrect because a red color on a tri-color VASI indicates below, not above, the glide path. Answer (C) is incorrect because a green color on a tri-color VASI indicates on, not above, the glide path.

55.
8918. Which color on a tri-color VASI is an “on course” indication?

A—Red.
B—Amber.
C—Green.

Answer (C) is correct (8918). *(AIM Para 2-1-2)*
The tri-color VASI projects a three-color visual approach path into the final approach area of the runway. An “on course,” or on glide path, indication is seen as the color green.
Answer (A) is incorrect because a red color on a tri-color VASI indicates below, not on, the glide path. Answer (B) is incorrect because an amber color on a tri-color VASI indicates above, not on, the glide path.

56.
8919. Which color on a tri-color VASI is a “low” indication?

A—Red.
B—Amber.
C—Green.

Answer (A) is correct (8919). *(AIM Para 2-1-2)*
The tri-color VASI projects a three-color visual approach path into the final approach area of the runway. A “low” indication is seen as the color red.
Answer (B) is incorrect because an amber color on a tri-color VASI is an indication of above, not below, the glide path. Answer (C) is incorrect because a green color on a tri-color VASI is an indication of on, not below, the glide path.

57.
8920. What is the normal range of the tri-color VASI at night?

A—5 miles.
B—10 miles.
C—15 miles.

Answer (A) is correct (8920). *(AIM Para 2-1-2)*
Tri-color VASI has a useful range of approximately ½ to 1 mi. during the day and up to 5 mi. at night depending on the visibility conditions.

Answer (B) is incorrect because a tri-color VASI has a normal range of 5 mi., not 10 mi., at night. Answer (C) is incorrect because a tri-color VASI has a normal range of 5 mi., not 15 mi., at night.

58.
8909. What does the pulsating VASI consist of?

A—Three-light system, two pulsing and one steady.
B—Two-light projectors, one pulsing and one steady.
C—One-light projector, pulsing white when above glide slope or red when more than slightly below glide slope, steady white when on glide slope, steady red for slightly below glide path.

Answer (C) is correct (8909). *(AIM Para 2-1-2)*
Pulsating VASIs normally consist of a single light unit projecting a two-color visual glide path indication in the final approach area of the runway. The below glide path indication is normally pulsating red, and the above glide path is pulsating white. The on glide path indication is a steady white light. The slightly below glide path is a steady red. The answer should refer to "pulsating," not "pulsing."

Answer (A) is incorrect because the pulsating VASI is a two-, not three-, light system, with two pulsating and two, not one, steady. Answer (B) is incorrect because the pulsating VASI is a single, not double, light projecting unit.

59.
8910. What are the indications of the pulsating VASI?

A—High - pulsing white, on glidepath - green, low - pulsing red.
B—High - pulsing white, on glidepath - steady white, slightly below glide slope - steady red, low - pulsing red.
C—High - pulsing white, on course and on glidepath - steady white, off course but on glidepath - pulsing white and red; low - pulsing red.

Answer (B) is correct (8910). *(AIM Para 2-1-2)*
The pulsating VASI provides a two-color visual glide path indication in the final approach area. It provides only a glide path indication while lateral course guidance is provided by the runway or runway lights. Above glide path is pulsating white. On glide path is steady white. Slightly below glide path is steady red. Below glide path is pulsating red. Also, the answer should refer to "pulsating," not "pulsing."

Answer (A) is incorrect because the on glide path indication of a pulsating VASI is either a pulsating red and white or steady white, not green, light. Answer (C) is incorrect because the pulsating VASI provides only glide path indications, not lateral, or course, indications.

7.6 PAPI

60.
8921. What does the Precision Approach Path Indicator (PAPI) consist of?

A—Row of four lights parallel to the runway; red, white, and green.
B—Row of four lights perpendicular to the runway; red and white.
C—One light projector with two colors; red and white.

Answer (B) is correct (8921). *(AIM Para 2-1-2)*
The PAPI uses lights similar to the two- and three-bar VASI but installed in a single row of either two or four light units perpendicular to the runway. The row of lights is normally installed on the left side of the runway. Each light unit appears as either red or white. When two are red and two are white, you are on the glide path.
Answer (A) is incorrect because PAPI has a row of four lights perpendicular, not parallel, to the runway and projects red and white, not green, light. Answer (C) is incorrect because PAPI consists of a row of four, not one, light projectors emitting red or white light.

61.
8908. What are the indications of Precision Approach Path Indicator (PAPI)?

A—High - white, on glidepath - red and white; low - red.
B—High - white, on glidepath - green; low - red.
C—High - white and green, on glidepath - green; low - red.

Answer (A) is correct (8908). *(AIM Para 2-1-2)*
PAPI can indicate five possible glide path indications. All white light indicates “high” or more than 3.5° glide path. One red and three white indicate a slightly high (3.2°) glide path. Two red and two white indicate on the glide path (3°). Three red and one white indicate a slightly low (2.8°) glide path. Four red lights indicate below (less than 2.5°) the glide path.
Answer (B) is incorrect because the on glide path indication of PAPI is both red and white, not green, lights. Answer (C) is incorrect because above the glide path indication of PAPI is all white (green is not a color indication of PAPI), on glide path is two red and two white, not green, and below glide path is all red.

7.7 NOTAMs

62.
9086. What are FDC NOTAMs?

A—Conditions of facilities en route that may cause delays.
B—Time critical aeronautical information of a temporary nature from distant centers.
C—Regulatory amendments to published IAP's and charts not yet available in normally published charts.

Answer (C) is correct (9086). *(AIM Para 5-1-3)*
FDC (Flight Data Center) NOTAMs are regulatory in nature and issued to establish restrictions to flight or amend charts or published instrument approach procedures. FDC NOTAMs are published as needed and indexed in the *Notice to Airmen Publication*.
Answer (A) is incorrect because NOTAM (D) contains information on navigational facilities en route that may cause delays. NOTAMs (D) are appended to the hourly weather reports and are available from any FSS for the duration of their validity or until published. Answer (B) is incorrect because time critical aeronautical information of a temporary nature from distant centers will be included in a NOTAM (D), or distant. NOTAMs (D) are appended to the hourly weather reports and are available from any FSS for the duration of their validity or until published.

63.
9089. How often are NOTAM's broadcast to pilots on a scheduled basis?

A—15 minutes before and 15 minutes after the hour.
B—Between weather broadcasts on the hour.
C—Hourly, appended to the weather broadcast.

Answer (C) is correct (9089). *(AIM Para 5-1-3)*
NOTAMs (D) are broadcast to pilots automatically, appended to the hourly weather broadcast. NOTAM (L) information is not attached to the hourly weather reports but is distributed locally and maintained at each FSS for facilities in its area only. FDC NOTAMs are transmitted only once and are kept on file at the FSS until published or canceled.
Answer (A) is incorrect because NOTAMs (D) are appended to the hourly weather report, not broadcasted 15 min. before and after the hour. Answer (B) is incorrect because NOTAMs (D) are appended to the hourly weather broadcast, not a separate broadcast between weather reports.

64.
9088. NOTAM (L)'s are used to disseminate what type of information?

A—Conditions of facilities en route that may cause delays.
B—Taxi closures, personnel and equipment near or crossing runways, airport lighting aids that do not affect instrument approach criteria, and airport rotating beacon outages.
C—Time critical information of a permanent nature that is not yet available in normally published charts.

Answer (B) is correct (9088). *(AIM Para 5-1-3)*
NOTAMs (L), or local, disseminate information of a local nature, including taxiway closures, personnel and equipment near or crossing runways, airport lighting aids that do not affect instrument approach criteria, and airport rotating beacon outages.
Answer (A) is incorrect because conditions of facilities en route that may cause delays are disseminated by NOTAMs (D). Answer (C) is incorrect because time critical information of a permanent nature that is not yet available in normally published charts is disseminated by an FDC NOTAM.

65.
9087. What type information is disseminated by NOTAM (D)'s?

A—Status of navigation aids, ILS's, radar service available, and other information essential to planning.
B—Airport or primary runway closings, runway and taxiway conditions, and airport lighting aids outages.
C—Temporary flight restrictions, changes in status in navigational aids, and updates on equipment such as VASI.

Answer (A) is correct (9087). *(AIM Para 5-1-3)*
NOTAMs (D), or distant, are NOTAMs which are disseminated for all navigational facilities that are part of the National Airspace System (NAS) and for all public-use airports, seaplane bases, and heliports listed in the *A/FD*. They include the status of navigation aids, ILSs, radar service available, and other information essential to planning.
Answer (B) is incorrect because NOTAMs (L), or local, contain information on taxiway conditions and airport lighting aids outages that do not affect instrument approach criteria. Answer (C) is incorrect because temporary flight restrictions are normally disseminated in FDC NOTAMs.

END OF CHAPTER

CHAPTER EIGHT
AIR TRAFFIC CONTROL

This chapter contains outlines of major concepts tested, all FAA test questions and answers regarding air traffic control, and an explanation of each answer. Each module, or subtopic, within this chapter is listed above with the number of questions from the FAA pilot knowledge test pertaining to that particular module. For each module, the first number following the parentheses is the page number on which the outline begins, and the next number is the page number on which the questions begin.

There are 61 questions in this chapter. We separate and organize the FAA questions into meaningful study units and subunits, i.e., chapters and modules. As an analogy, it is easier to deal with the "trees" if you understand the "forest." In this context, "trees" are individual FAA questions and the "forest" is the ATP knowledge test. The organizational units between the overall ATP knowledge test and individual ATP test questions are chapters and modules in this book.

CAUTION: The **sole purpose** of this book is to expedite your passing the FAA pilot knowledge test for the ATP certificate. Topics or regulations not directly tested on the FAA pilot knowledge test are omitted. Much more information and knowledge are necessary to fly safely. This additional material is presented in Gleim's other pilot training books (see the order form on page 818) and in many FAA books and circulars, as well as in airplane *POH*s and other commercial textbooks.

8.1 FLIGHT PLANS (Questions 1-11)

1. When transitioning from VFR to IFR on a composite flight plan, the pilot closes the VFR flight plan with the nearest FSS and requests an IFR clearance 5 min. prior to the point at which change from VFR to IFR is proposed.
   a. Conversely, when transitioning from IFR to VFR, the pilot should cancel IFR with ATC and contact the nearest FSS to activate the VFR portion.
2. On a composite flight plan, the fix where the IFR portion is to be terminated must be included.
3. IFR flight plans should be filed at least 30 min. prior to departure, and clearance should be requested not more than 10 min. prior to taxi.
4. The route of flight on an IFR flight plan should be a simplified route via airways or jet routes with transitions.
5. Off-airway direct flights should be defined by all radio fixes over which the flight will pass.
6. RNAV routes below FL 390 must be planned to begin and end over appropriate arrival and departure transition fixes or navigational aids for the altitude being flown, and each random route waypoint must be defined using degree-distance fixes based on navigational aids appropriate to the altitude being flown.
   a. A random RNAV route must be entirely within the radar environment.
7. In order to use special or privately owned IAP, the pilot must have approval of the owner of the privately owned IAP.
8. IFR flight plans may be canceled only if the flight is in VFR conditions outside Class A airspace.
9. Civilian air ambulance flights should be so indicated with the word "LIFEGUARD" entered in the remarks block of the flight plan.

8.2 SIDs AND STARs (Questions 12-14)

1. SIDs are depicted in plan views as "Vectors" provided for navigational guidance or "Pilot NAV" with courses the pilot is responsible to follow.
2. A STAR simplifies clearance delivery procedures.
   a. STARs are issued only when ATC deems them appropriate.

8.3 ATC -- PRETAKEOFF (Questions 15-21)

1. Pretaxi clearance programs require pilots to request IFR clearance 10 min. or less prior to taxi and then to request taxi clearance from ground control.
2. In a **cleared as filed** clearance, the minimum information is
   a. Destination airport
   b. En route altitude
   c. SID, if appropriate
3. A **void time** specification in a clearance is used when a pilot is operating from an uncontrolled airport.
   a. If (s)he does not take off before the void time, the clearance is void.
4. The term **hold for release** is a procedure for delaying departure for traffic volume, weather, or a need to issue further instructions.
5. A **gate hold** requires the pilot to contact ground control prior to starting engines for sequencing.
   a. When gate hold procedures are in effect, turbine-powered aircraft are expected to be ready for takeoff when they reach the runway or warmup block.
6. A pilot should state his/her position on the airport when calling the tower for takeoff from a runway intersection, at all times.

8.4 CLEARANCES AND CLEARANCE LIMITS (Questions 22-26)

1. An **ATC instruction** is a directive issued by ATC for the purpose of requiring a pilot to take a specific action, providing the safety of the aircraft is not jeopardized.
2. Pilots should read back altitudes, altitude restrictions, and vectors in the same sequence as given in a clearance or instruction by ATC.
3. If an ATC clearance appears to violate an FAR, the pilot should request clarification from ATC.
4. If a pilot is within 3 min. of a clearance limit and a further clearance has not been received, the pilot should start a speed reduction to holding speed in preparation for holding.
5. Pilots should report time and altitude upon arriving at or leaving clearance limits.

8.5 ATC -- WHILE EN ROUTE (Questions 27-31)

1. If ATC requests "VERIFY 9,000" and the pilot is maintaining 8,000, the pilot should report "maintaining 8,000."
2. Position reports are required at all compulsory reporting points on an IFR flight on airways or routes.
3. When operating IFR in a radar environment, you should report the following information:
   a. Vacating an altitude
   b. Inability to climb at a rate of at least 500 fpm
   c. Time and altitude upon reaching a holding fix or point to which to be cleared
   d. Change in average true airspeed exceeding 5% or 10 kt.
   e. Leaving any assigned holding fix or point
4. The maximum acceptable tolerance for penetrating a domestic ADIZ is ±10 NM and ±5 min.
5. Pilots should disregard effects of nonstandard atmospheric temperatures and pressures when setting an altimeter.

8.6 ATC -- SPEED ADJUSTMENTS (Questions 32-34)

1. ATC may request a turbine-powered aircraft operating below 10,000 ft. to reduce speed to as low as 210 kt.
2. When a turbine-powered aircraft is departing an airport, ATC may request a minimum speed as low as 230 kt. in order to maintain separation.
3. If ATC requests a speed adjustment that is not within the operating limits of the aircraft, the pilot should advise ATC of the airspeed that will be used.

8.7 VFR-ON-TOP (Questions 35-38)

1. A pilot may maintain "VFR-on-top" by maintaining VFR altitudes and cloud clearances and also comply with applicable IFR rules.
2. When "VFR-on-top," a pilot must maintain VFR clearance requirements from clouds, but the clearance can be above, below, or between layers.
3. ATC will not authorize "VFR-on-top" in Class A airspace.
4. When a pilot is operating "VFR-on-top," ATC provides the pilot with traffic advisories only.

8.8 ATC -- MINIMUM FUEL AND EMERGENCIES (Questions 39-46)

1. IFR pilots should advise ATC of minimum fuel status if the remaining fuel precludes any undue delay.
   a. The term **minimum fuel** is an advisory to ATC indicating an emergency situation is possible should an undue delay occur.
2. If the remaining usable fuel supply suggests the need for traffic priority to ensure a safe landing, the pilot should declare an emergency due to low fuel and report fuel remaining in minutes.
3. Pilots should avoid switching through transponder codes of 7500, 7600, and 7700.
   a. The hijack code is 7500.
   b. The communication lost code is 7600.
   c. The emergency code is 7700.
4. A pilot should declare an emergency anytime (s)he is doubtful of a condition that could adversely affect flight safety.
5. Pilots should report a near midair collision if the proximity of another aircraft was less than 500 ft.
6. ATC issues safety alerts if the aircraft altitude is noted to be in close proximity to the surface or an obstacle.

8.9 TRAFFIC ALERT AND COLLISION AVOIDANCE SYSTEM (TCAS) (Questions 47-50)

1. TCAS I provides proximity warning only.
2. TCAS II provides traffic and resolution advisories.
3. Each pilot who deviates from an ATC clearance in response to a TCAS advisory is expected to comply with both of the following:
   a. Notify ATC of the deviation as soon as practicable.
   b. Expeditiously return to the ATC clearance in effect prior to the advisory, after the conflict is resolved.

8.10 ATC -- APPROACH AND LANDING (Questions 51-61)

1. When not in radar contact on an IFR approach, a pilot must report leaving the final approach fix (FAF) inbound or outer marker inbound and a missed approach.
2. If on radar vectors the final approach course is imminent and the pilot has not been informed of crossing the final approach, the pilot should advise ATC that (s)he is crossing the final approach course.
3. Radar service is terminated while the airplane is vectored for an IFR approach at an uncontrolled airport when the landing is completed or when the pilot is advised to change to advisory frequency, whichever occurs first.
4. After a pilot is cleared for an IFR approach to an uncontrolled airport, the pilot should broadcast intentions and continually update position on the CTAF.
5. While being vectored to the final approach course, a pilot may descend to published altitudes only when approach control clears the flight for the approach.
6. A pilot may execute a missed approach during an ASR anytime at the pilot's discretion.
7. If visual reference is lost while circling to land from an instrument approach, the pilot must follow the missed approach specified for that particular procedure.
   a. To become established on the prescribed missed approach course, the pilot should make an initial climbing turn toward the runway and continue the turn until established on the missed approach course.
8. A **visual approach** may be initiated by ATC while a **contact approach** may be initiated only by the pilot.
9. Pilots receive landing priority in turn, on a first-come, first-served basis, except in an emergency.
10. When landing at a controlled airport, a pilot should exit the runway at the nearest suitable taxiway and remain on tower frequency until instructed otherwise.
11. Braking action reports should be given as one of the following:
    a. Nil
    b. Poor
    c. Fair
    d. Good

QUESTIONS AND ANSWER EXPLANATIONS

All the FAA questions from the pilot knowledge test for the ATP certificate relating to air traffic control and the material outlined previously are reproduced on the following pages in the same modules as the outlines. To the immediate right of each question are the correct answer and answer explanation. You should cover these answers and answer explanations while responding to the questions. Refer to the general discussion in Chapter 1 on how to take the FAA pilot knowledge test.

Remember that the questions from the FAA pilot knowledge test bank have been reordered by topic, and the topics are organized into a meaningful sequence. Accordingly, the first line of the answer explanation gives the FAA question number and the citation of the authoritative source for the answer.

8.1 Flight Plans

1.
9030. When a composite flight plan indicates VFR for the first portion of the flight, what is the procedure for the transition?

A—The VFR portion is automatically canceled and the IFR portion is automatically activated when the pilot reports IFR conditions.
B—The pilot should advise ATC to cancel VFR and activate the IFR portion of the flight.
C—The pilot should close the VFR portion with the nearest FSS and request the IFR clearance at least 5 minutes prior to IFR.

Answer (C) is correct (9030). *(AIM Para 5-1-6)*
When a composite flight plan indicates VFR for the first portion of the flight, the pilot should report the departure time to the FSS where the composite flight plan was filed. To transition, the pilot should close the VFR portion with the nearest FSS and request the IFR clearance at least 5 min. prior to the point at which change from VFR to IFR is proposed.
Answer (A) is incorrect because VFR flight plans are never automatically closed; it is the pilot's responsibility to close a VFR flight plan. An IFR clearance must be requested and received before entering IFR conditions in controlled airspace. It is not automatically activated when the pilot reports IFR conditions. Answer (B) is incorrect because the pilot should cancel a VFR flight plan with the nearest FSS, not ATC.

2.
9028. When a composite flight plan indicates IFR for the first portion of the flight, what is the procedure for the transition?

A—The IFR portion is automatically canceled and the VFR portion is automatically activated when the pilot reports VFR conditions.
B—The pilot should advise ATC to cancel the IFR portion and contact the nearest FSS to activate the VFR portion.
C—The pilot should advise ATC to cancel the IFR portion and activate the VFR portion.

Answer (B) is correct (9028). *(AIM Para 5-1-6)*
When a composite flight plan indicates IFR for the first portion of flight and VFR for the latter portion, the pilot will normally be cleared to the point at which the change is proposed. Once the pilot has reported over the clearance limit and does not desire further IFR clearance, the pilot should advise ATC to cancel the IFR portion and contact the nearest FSS to activate the VFR portion.
Answer (A) is incorrect because a pilot can operate on an IFR flight plan in VFR conditions without the IFR portion being automatically canceled. When a composite flight plan indicates IFR for the first portion, the pilot will normally be cleared to the point at which transition is proposed. Here the pilot should advise ATC to cancel the IFR portion and contact the nearest FSS to activate the VFR portion. Answer (C) is incorrect because the pilot should contact the nearest FSS, not ATC, to activate the VFR portion.

3.
9029. Which IFR fix(es) should be entered on a composite flight plan?

A—All compulsory reporting points en route.
B—The VOR's that define the IFR portion of the flight.
C—The fix where the IFR portion is to be terminated.

Answer (C) is correct (9029). *(AIM Para 5-1-6)*
On composite flight plans, the IFR portion should include the items of a standard IFR flight plan. These items include points of transition from one airway to another, fixes defining direct route segments, and the clearance limit fix where the IFR portion is to be terminated.
Answer (A) is incorrect because compulsory reporting points are not listed on an IFR flight plan unless they define a point of transition, direct route segments, or the clearance limit fix. Also, there are no compulsory reporting points for a VFR flight. Answer (B) is incorrect because IFR fixes can be defined as intersections, waypoints, and DME distance, along with VORs.

4.
9031. What is the suggested time interval for filing and requesting an IFR flight plan?

A—File at least 30 minutes prior to departure and request the clearance not more than 10 minutes prior to taxi.
B—File at least 30 minutes prior to departure and request the clearance at least 10 minutes prior to taxi.
C—File at least 1 hour prior to departure and request the clearance at least 10 minutes prior to taxi.

Answer (A) is correct (9031). *(AIM Paras 5-1-7 and 5-2-1)*
Pilots should file IFR flight plans at least 30 min. prior to estimated time of departure to prevent possible delays in receiving a departure clearance from ATC. Certain airports have established pretaxi clearance programs through which pilots of IFR airplanes may contact clearance delivery or ground control not more than 10 min. prior to taxi time.
Answer (B) is incorrect because a pilot can request the clearance not more than 10 min., not at least 10 min., prior to taxi. Answer (C) is incorrect because pilots should file at least 30 min., not 1 hr., prior to departure and request the clearance not more than 10 min., not at least 10 min., prior to taxi.

5.
9032. How should the route of flight be defined on an IFR flight plan?

A—A simplified route via airways or jet routes with transitions.
B—A route via airways or jet routes with VOR's and fixes used.
C—A route via airways or jet routes with only the compulsory reporting points.

Answer (A) is correct (9032). *(AIM Para 5-1-7)*
It is vitally important that the route of flight be defined accurately and completely on an IFR flight plan. To simplify definition of the route and to facilitate ATC, pilots are requested to file via airways or jet routes with transitions.
Answer (B) is incorrect because, to simplify the route, all VORs and fixes are not used to define a route on an IFR flight plan. Answer (C) is incorrect because compulsory reporting points may not define the transitions between airways or jet routes.

6.
9033. How should an off-airway direct flight be defined on an IFR flight plan?

A—The initial fix, the true course, and the final fix.
B—All radio fixes over which the flight will pass.
C—The initial fix, all radio fixes which the pilot wishes to be compulsory reporting points, and the final fix.

Answer (B) is correct (9033). *(AIM Para 5-1-7)*
All or any portion of an off-airway direct flight must be defined on an IFR flight plan by indicating the radio fixes over which the flight will pass. These fixes automatically become compulsory reporting points for the flight, unless advised otherwise by ATC.
Answer (A) is incorrect because true course is not an item that is reported on an IFR flight plan. The initial fix and the final fix are listed as radio fixes that define the start and finish points of a flight. Answer (C) is incorrect because initial and final fixes are required to define random RNAV, not direct flight, routes. All radio fixes that define the route of a direct flight automatically become compulsory reporting points, not only those the pilot desires.

7.
9026. How are RNAV routes below FL 390 defined on the IFR flight plan?

A—Define each waypoint using degree-distance fixes based on appropriate navigational aids or by latitude/longitude.
B—List the initial and final fix with at least one waypoint each 200 NM.
C—Begin and end over appropriate arrival and departure transition fixes or navigation aids for the altitude being flown, define the random route waypoints by using degree-distance fixes based on navigation aids appropriate for the altitude being flown.

Answer (C) is correct (9026). *(AIM Para 5-1-7)*
RNAV routes below FL 390 must be planned to begin and end over appropriate arrival and departure transition fixes or navigational aids for the altitude being flown; then each waypoint is defined by using degree-distance fixes based on appropriate navigational aids. A minimum of one waypoint must be filed for each ARTCC through which the route is planned; these must be located within 200 NM of the preceding center's boundary. Also, a waypoint description is required for each turnpoint in the route.
Answer (A) is incorrect because RNAV routes defined on an IFR flight plan must also begin and end over an established radio fix. Answer (B) is incorrect because RNAV waypoints have no established distance requirement. A minimum of one waypoint must be filed for each ARTCC through which the route is planned, and this must be located within 200 NM of the preceding center's boundary.

8.
9027. What is one limitation when filing a random RNAV route on an IFR flight plan?

A—The waypoints must be located within 200 NM of each other.
B—The entire route must be within radar environment.
C—The waypoints may only be defined by degree-distance fixes based on appropriate navigational aids.

Answer (B) is correct (9027). *(AIM Para 5-1-7)*
Random RNAV routes can be approved only when the entire route is in a radar environment. ATC will monitor each random RNAV flight, but navigation on the route is the responsibility of the pilot.
Answer (A) is incorrect because VOR/VORTAC (H) facilities, not waypoints, must be within 200 NM of each other when operating above FL 450 to define a direct, not random RNAV, route. Answer (C) is incorrect because random RNAV waypoints may be defined by degree-distance fixes based on appropriate navigational aids or by latitude-longitude coordinate navigation, independent of VOR/TACAN references, operating at and above FL 390 in the conterminous U.S.

9.
9040. Under what condition may a pilot file an IFR flight plan containing a special or privately owned IAP?

A—Upon approval of ATC.
B—Upon approval of the owner.
C—Upon signing a waiver of responsibility.

Answer (B) is correct (9040). *(AIM Para 5-4-7)*
Pilots planning flights to locations served by a special or privately owned IAP should obtain advance approval from the owner of the procedure. These IAPs may require special crew training qualifications or other special considerations to execute the approach. Approval by the owner is necessary because special procedures are for the exclusive use of the owner, and these approaches may be based on privately owned navigational aids.
Answer (A) is incorrect because ATC is not required to question pilots to determine whether they have the owner's permission to use the procedure. Answer (C) is incorrect because a pilot is responsible for the safe operation of the airplane. To sign a waiver of responsibility is contrary to the pilot's responsibilities.

10.
9005. Under what condition may a pilot cancel an IFR flight plan prior to completing the flight?

A—Anytime it appears the clearance will cause a deviation from FAR's.
B—Anytime within controlled airspace by contacting ARTCC.
C—Only if in VFR conditions in other than Class A airspace.

Answer (C) is correct (9005). *(AIM Para 5-1-13)*
An IFR flight plan may be canceled at any time the flight is operating in VFR conditions outside Class A airspace by the pilot's stating, "Cancel my IFR flight plan." Once accepted by ATC, a pilot should change to the appropriate communications frequency, VFR transponder code, and VFR altitude.
Answer (A) is incorrect because, anytime a clearance appears to deviate from an FAR, the pilot should request clarification from ATC and an amended clearance. Answer (B) is incorrect because all aircraft in Class A airspace (above FL 180) or when operating in IMC must be operating under an IFR flight plan.

11.
9053. To assure expeditious handling of a civilian air ambulance flight, the word "LIFEGUARD" should be entered in which section of the flight plan?

A—Aircraft type/special equipment block.
B—Pilot's name and address block.
C—Remarks block.

Answer (C) is correct (9053). *(AIM Para 4-2-4)*
Civilian air ambulance flights responding to medical emergencies (first call to an accident scene; carrying patients, organ donors, organs, or other urgently needed lifesaving medical material) will be expedited by ATC. When expeditious handling is necessary, add the word "LIFEGUARD" in the remarks section of the flight plan. The remarks section contains information important to ATC or serves to clarify other flight plan information.
Answer (A) is incorrect because only the airplane's designator or manufacturer's name and the transponder, DME and/or RNAV equipment code are entered in the aircraft type/special equipment block. Answer (B) is incorrect because the complete name, address, and telephone number of the pilot in command are entered in the pilot's name and address block. Sufficient information is listed here to identify home base, airport, or operator. This information would be essential in the event of a search and rescue operation.

8.2 SIDs and STARs

12.
9012. In what way are SID's depicted in plan view?

A—"Vectors" provided for navigational guidance or "Pilot NAV" with courses the pilot is responsible to follow.
B—"Vectors" and "Pilot NAV" for pilots to use at their discretion.
C—Combined textual and graphic form which are mandatory routes and instructions.

Answer (A) is correct (9012). *(AIM Para 5-2-6)*
SID procedures will be depicted in one of two basic forms. "Vectors" are established where ATC will provide radar navigational guidance to a filed/assigned route or to a fix depicted on the SID. "Pilot NAV" indicates where the pilot is primarily responsible for navigation on the SID route. These may contain vector instructions which pilots are expected to comply with until notified to resume normal navigation on the filed/assigned route or SID procedure.

Answer (B) is incorrect because SIDs are departure procedures and must be followed as depicted, not at the pilot's discretion. If a pilot does not wish to use a SID, then (s)he must notify ATC. Answer (C) is incorrect because, while SIDs are published in textual and graphic form, they are mandatory only if the SID was given as part of a clearance.

13.
9034. What is the primary purpose of a STAR?

A—Provide separation between IFR and VFR traffic.
B—Simplify clearance delivery procedures.
C—Decrease traffic congestion at certain airports.

Answer (B) is correct (9034). *(AIM Para 5-4-1)*
A STAR is an ATC coded IFR arrival route established for use by arriving IFR traffic at certain airports. Its purpose is to simplify clearance delivery procedures.
Answer (A) is incorrect because separation between IFR and VFR traffic is provided by Class B or TRSA radar service, not a STAR. Answer (C) is incorrect because a STAR is used to simplify clearance delivery procedures, thus decreasing radio frequency, not traffic, congestion at certain airports.

14.
9035. When does ATC issue a STAR?

A—Only when ATC deems it appropriate.
B—Only to high priority flights.
C—Only upon request of the pilot.

Answer (A) is correct (9035). *(AIM Para 5-4-1)*
Pilots of IFR airplanes destined to locations for which STARs have been published may be issued a clearance containing a STAR whenever ATC deems it appropriate. A pilot must have at least a textual description in his/her possession. It is the responsibility of each pilot to accept or refuse an issued STAR.
Answer (B) is incorrect because any type of IFR flight can be issued a STAR. High priority flights will normally be handled in an expeditious manner by ATC.
Answer (C) is incorrect because a STAR is a clearance delivery procedure that is issued by ATC. A pilot has the responsibility to accept or refuse that clearance. A pilot can list a STAR in the flight plan, but ATC will issue one only if appropriate.

8.3 ATC -- Pretakeoff

15.
9008. What is the normal procedure for IFR departures at locations with pretaxi clearance programs?

A—Pilots request IFR clearance when ready to taxi. The pilot will receive taxi instruction with clearance.
B—Pilots request IFR clearance when ready to taxi. Pilots will receive taxi clearance, then receive IFR clearance while taxiing or on runup.
C—Pilots request IFR clearance 10 minutes or less prior to taxi, then request taxi clearance from ground control.

Answer (C) is correct (9008). *(AIM Para 5-2-1)*
Pretaxi clearance programs allow pilots of departing IFR airplanes to receive their IFR clearances before they start taxiing for takeoff. Pilot participation is not mandatory. Participating pilots should request IFR clearance 10 min. or less prior to taxi, then request taxi clearance from ground control.
Answer (A) is incorrect because, at a location with a pretaxi clearance program, the pilot will first receive the IFR clearance, then taxi instructions. The pilot should request the IFR clearance 10 min. or less prior to taxi time. Answer (B) is incorrect because, at a location with a pretaxi clearance program, the pilot will first be given the IFR clearance, then the taxi clearance. The pilot should request the IFR clearance 10 min. or less prior to taxi time.

16.
9006. What minimum information does an abbreviated departure clearance "cleared as filed" include?

A—Clearance limit and en route altitude.
B—Clearance limit, en route altitude, and SID, if appropriate.
C—Destination airport, en route altitude, and SID, if appropriate.

Answer (C) is correct (9006). *(AIM Para 5-2-3)*
The minimum information in an abbreviated IFR departure clearance will include the destination airport. "Cleared to (destination) airport as filed" does not include the en route altitude filed in the flight plan. En route altitude will be stated in the clearance, or the pilot will be advised to expect an assigned or filed altitude within a given time frame or at a certain point after departure. The SID name, the current number, and the SID transition name will be given for all departure clearances, when appropriate.
Answer (A) is incorrect because a clearance limit may be a fix, point, or location. An abbreviated clearance will be a clearance to the destination airport. In some cases, a clearance is issued to a fix (limit) from which another clearance limit will be issued. SIDs are stated in all IFR departure clearances when appropriate. Answer (B) is incorrect because, even though a clearance limit can be the destination, a "cleared as filed" clearance will state the destination airport's name.

17.
9007. Under what condition does a pilot receive a "void time" specified in the clearance?

A—On an uncontrolled airport.
B—When "gate hold" procedures are in effect.
C—If the clearance is received prior to starting engines.

Answer (A) is correct (9007). *(AIM Para 5-2-4)*
A pilot will receive a "void time" in an IFR clearance when operating from an uncontrolled airport. If the flight has not departed prior to the void time, the clearance is void. The pilot who is still on the ground at the void time must advise ATC of his/her intentions as soon as possible, normally within a maximum of 30 min.
Answer (B) is incorrect because gate hold procedures are in effect whenever departure delays exceed or are anticipated to exceed 15 min. Pilots should contact ground control or clearance delivery prior to starting engines to receive departure clearance and engine startup advisories. Answer (C) is incorrect because clearances can be issued before starting the airplane's engine(s). Only when operating from an uncontrolled airport will the clearance contain a "void time."

18.
9009. What is the purpose of the term "hold for release" when included in an IFR clearance?

A—A procedure for delaying departure for traffic volume, weather, or need to issue further instructions.
B—When an IFR clearance is received by telephone, the pilot will have time to prepare for takeoff prior to being released.
C—Gate hold procedures are in effect and the pilot receives an estimate of the time the flight will be released.

Answer (A) is correct (9009). *(AIM Para 5-2-4)*
ATC may issue "hold for release" instructions in a clearance to delay an airplane's departure for traffic management reasons (i.e., weather, traffic volume, etc.). The pilot may not depart until (s)he receives a release time or is given additional instructions by ATC.
Answer (B) is incorrect because, when a pilot receives an IFR clearance via telephone, it is normally because (s)he is departing from an uncontrolled airport. In this case, ATC issues a clearance void time, not a hold for release. Answer (C) is incorrect because gate hold procedures are in effect whenever departure delays exceed (or are expected to exceed) 15 min. This procedure is not a way for ATC to delay an airplane's departure.

19.
9056. What action should the pilot take when "gate hold" procedures are in effect?

A—Contact ground control prior to starting engines for sequencing.
B—Taxi into position and hold prior to requesting clearance.
C—Start engines, perform pretakeoff check, and request clearance prior to leaving the parking area.

Answer (A) is correct (9056). *(AIM Para 4-3-15)*
Pilots should contact ground control or clearance delivery prior to starting engines as gate hold procedures will be in effect whenever departure delays exceed or are anticipated to exceed 15 min. Pilots should monitor the ground control or clearance delivery frequency for engine startup advisories or new proposed start time if the delay changes. The sequence for departure will normally be maintained in accordance with the initial call-up.
Answer (B) is incorrect because "taxi into position" means that the pilot is on the active runway and ready for takeoff. This is not a position where ATC would issue an IFR clearance. Answer (C) is incorrect because pilots should contact ground control for sequencing before, not after, starting engines.

20.
9057. What special consideration is given for turbine-powered aircraft when "gate hold" procedures are in effect?

A—They are given preference for departure over other aircraft.
B—They are expected to be ready for takeoff when they reach the runway or warmup block.
C—They are expected to be ready for takeoff prior to taxi and will receive takeoff clearance prior to taxi.

Answer (B) is correct (9057). *(AIM Para 4-3-15)*
When gate hold procedures are in effect, ATC will consider that pilots of turbine-powered aircraft are ready for takeoff when they reach the runway or warmup block.
Answer (A) is incorrect because, when gate hold procedures are in effect, sequencing of all airplanes is based on the initial call-up to ground control or clearance delivery. Answer (C) is incorrect because a pilot of any airplane should be ready to taxi, not take off, prior to taxi, and takeoff clearance is received prior to takeoff, not taxi.

21.
9424. Pilots should state their position on the airport when calling the tower for takeoff

A—from a runway intersection.
B—from a runway intersection, only at night.
C—from a runway intersection, only during instrument conditions.

Answer (A) is correct (9424). *(AIM Para 4-3-10)*
In order to enhance airport capacities, reduce taxiing distances, minimize departure delays, and provide for more efficient movement of air traffic, controllers may initiate intersection takeoffs as well as approve them when the pilot requests. A pilot should state his/her position on the airport when calling the tower for takeoff from a runway intersection.
Answer (B) is incorrect because a pilot should state his/her position on the airport when calling the tower for takeoff from a runway intersection at all times. Answer (C) is incorrect because a pilot should state his/her position on the airport when calling the tower for takeoff from a runway intersection under all, not just instrument, conditions.

8.4 Clearances and Clearance Limits

22.
9439. An ATC "instruction"

A—is the same as an ATC "clearance."
B—is a directive issued by ATC for the purpose of requiring a pilot to take a specific action providing the safety of the aircraft is not jeopardized.
C—must be "read back" in full to the controller and confirmed before becoming effective.

Answer (B) is correct (9439). *(AIM P/C Glossary)*
An ATC instruction is a directive issued by ATC for the purpose of requiring a pilot to take a specific action, e.g., "Turn left, heading 250," "Go around," "Clear the runway," etc.
Answer (A) is incorrect because an ATC clearance is an authorization by ATC for an aircraft to proceed under specified traffic conditions within controlled airspace. An instruction is more specific, e.g., "Turn left heading 250." Answer (C) is incorrect because, although instructions should be (and some are required to be) read back to the controller, they are effective immediately.

23.
9045. What is the pilot's responsibility for clearance or instruction readback?

A—Except for SID's, read back altitude assignments, altitude restrictions, and vectors.
B—If the clearance or instruction is understood, an acknowledgement is sufficient.
C—Read back the entire clearance or instruction to confirm the message is understood.

Answer (A) is correct (9045). *(AIM Para 4-4-6)*

Pilots should read back the parts of ATC clearances and instructions containing altitude assignments or vectors as a means of mutual verification. Altitudes, altitude restrictions, and vectors should be read back in the same sequence as they are given in the clearance or instruction. Altitudes contained in charted procedures, such as SIDs, should not be read back unless they are specifically stated by the controller.

Answer (B) is incorrect because the best way to know that the clearance or instruction is understood is to read back the "numbers" as a double-check between the pilot and ATC. This practice reduces the kinds of communication errors that occur when a number is either misheard or incorrect. Answer (C) is incorrect because the pilot's responsibility is to read back the clearances and instructions containing altitude assignments, altitude restrictions, and vectors, not the entire clearance or instruction.

24.
9402. What action should a pilot take when a clearance is received from ATC that appears to be contrary to a regulation?

A—Read the clearance back in its entirety.
B—Request a clarification from ATC.
C—Do not accept the clearance.

Answer (B) is correct (9402). *(AIM Para 4-4-1)*

FAR 91.3(a) states: "The pilot-in-command of an aircraft is directly responsible for, and is the final authority as to, the operation of that aircraft." If ATC issues a clearance that would cause a pilot to deviate from a rule or regulation or, in the pilot's opinion, would place the airplane in jeopardy, it is the pilot's responsibility to request a clarification from ATC.

Answer (A) is incorrect because reading the clearance back in its entirety does not inform ATC of the possible conflict to a regulation. A pilot should actively seek clarification if there is any doubt. Answer (C) is incorrect because not accepting a clearance is not the proper procedure to use when, in a pilot's opinion, it would conflict with a regulation. First, a pilot should receive a clarification from ATC, then ask for an amended clearance, if necessary.

25.
8853. What action should a pilot take if within 3 minutes of a clearance limit and further clearance has not been received?

A—Assume lost communications and continue as planned.
B—Plan to hold at cruising speed until further clearance is received.
C—Start a speed reduction to holding speed in preparation for holding.

Answer (C) is correct (8853). *(AIM Para 4-4-3)*

When an airplane is within 3 min. from a clearance limit and a clearance beyond the fix has not been received, the pilot is expected to start a speed reduction so the airplane will initially cross the fix at or below the maximum holding speed in preparation for holding.

Answer (A) is incorrect because, if two-way communications are lost, the pilot is required to hold at the clearance limit in a standard pattern on the course that was used to approach the fix. If an expected further clearance time was received, (s)he should plan on leaving the fix at that time. If none was given and the fix is an IAP, (s)he should plan his/her arrival as close as possible to the estimated time of arrival. Answer (B) is incorrect because cruising speed may be greater than maximum holding speed. For all propeller-driven airplanes (including turboprop), the maximum holding speed is 175 KIAS. For turbojet airplanes, the maximum holding airspeed is 200 KIAS from minimum holding altitude through 6,000 ft.; 230 KIAS from above 6,000 ft. through 14,000 ft.; and 265 KIAS above 14,000 ft.

26.
8854. What report should the pilot make at a clearance limit?

A—Time and altitude/flight level arriving or leaving.
B—Time, altitude/flight level, and expected holding speed.
C—Time, altitude/flight level, expected holding speed, and inbound leg length.

Answer (A) is correct (8854). *(AIM Para 4-4-3)*

The pilot should report to ATC the time and altitude/flight level at which the airplane reaches the clearance limit, and (s)he should report leaving the clearance limit.

Answer (B) is incorrect because ATC does not need the expected holding speed reported since it will be at or below the maximum holding airspeed. Answer (C) is incorrect because inbound leg lengths are set by time or DME distance. At or below 14,000 ft. MSL, there is a 1-min. inbound leg. Above 14,000 ft. MSL, the inbound leg is 1½ min.

8.5 ATC – While En Route

27.
9013. What action should a pilot take if asked by ARTCC to "VERIFY 9,000" and the flight is actually maintaining 8,000?

A—Immediately climb to 9,000.
B—Report climbing to 9,000.
C—Report maintaining 8,000.

Answer (C) is correct (9013). *(AIM Para 5-3-1)*

At times a controller will ask a pilot to verify that (s)he is at a particular altitude. The pilot should confirm that (s)he is at the altitude stated by the controller, or (s)he should inform the controller of the actual altitude being maintained, if different. If asked by ARTCC to "Verify 9,000" and the flight is actually maintaining 8,000, the pilot should report maintaining 8,000.

Answer (A) is incorrect because a pilot should not take action to change his/her actual altitude to the altitude stated in the controller's verification request unless the controller specifically authorizes a change. Answer (B) is incorrect because a pilot should not take action to change his/her actual altitude to the altitude stated in the controller's verification request unless the controller specifically authorizes a change.

28.
9014. Where are position reports required on an IFR flight on airways or routes?

A—Over all designated compulsory reporting points.
B—Only where specifically requested by ARTCC.
C—When requested to change altitude or advise of weather conditions.

Answer (A) is correct (9014). *(AIM Para 5-3-2)*

The safety and effectiveness of traffic control depends to a large extent on accurate position reporting. A position report for an IFR flight along airways or routes is required over all designated compulsory reporting points along the route being flown. Position reports should include the following: identification, position, time, altitude/flight level, type of flight plan, ETA and name of next reporting point, the name only of the next succeeding reporting point along the route, and pertinent remarks. Compulsory reporting points are indicated on en route charts by a solid triangle.

Answer (B) is incorrect because the "on request" reporting point is indicated on en route charts by an open, not solid, triangle. Reports passing an "on request" reporting point are necessary only when requested by ARTCC. Answer (C) is incorrect because pilots on IFR flight plans must always report when changing altitude and are expected to report weather conditions which have not been forecast or any hazardous conditions.

29.
9015. Which reports are required when operating IFR in radar environment?

A—Position reports, vacating an altitude, unable to climb 500 ft/min, and time and altitude reaching a holding fix or point to which cleared.
B—Position reports, vacating an altitude, unable to climb 500 ft/min, time and altitude reaching a holding fix or point to which cleared, and a change in average true airspeed exceeding 5 percent or 10 knots.
C—Vacating an altitude, unable to climb 500 ft/min, time and altitude reaching a holding fix or point to which cleared, a change in average true airspeed exceeding 5 percent or 10 knots, and leaving any assigned holding fix or point.

Answer (C) is correct (9015). *(AIM Para 5-3-2)*
When informed by ATC that his/her airplane is in "RADAR CONTACT," the pilot should discontinue position reports over designated reporting points. A pilot will report at all times vacating an altitude, inability to climb/descend at a rate of at least 500 fpm, time and altitude upon reaching a holding fix or point to which cleared, a change in average true airspeed exceeding 5% or 10 kt., leaving any assigned holding fix or point, and a missed approach.
Answer (A) is incorrect because position reports are not required in a radar environment. A pilot must also report a change in average TAS (exceeding 5% or 10 kt.), leaving any assigned holding fix or point, and a missed approach. Answer (B) is incorrect because position reports are not required in a radar environment. A pilot must also report when leaving any assigned holding fix or point and when the approach has been missed.

30.
9100. What is the maximum acceptable tolerance for penetrating a domestic ADIZ?

A—Plus or minus 10 miles; plus or minus 10 minutes.
B—Plus or minus 20 miles; plus or minus 5 minutes.
C—Plus or minus 10 miles; plus or minus 5 minutes.

Answer (C) is correct (9100). *(AIM Para 5-6-1)*
A domestic Air Defense Identification Zone (ADIZ) is within the United States along an international boundary and is implied to be over land. The maximum acceptable tolerance for penetrating a domestic ADIZ is within 10 NM from the centerline of an intended track over an estimated penetration point and within 5 min. of the estimated time.
Answer (A) is incorrect because penetration of an ADIZ within 10 min. is not acceptable for over either water or land. Answer (B) is incorrect because the maximum acceptable tolerance for penetrating a coastal, not domestic, ADIZ is within 20 NM of the intended track and within 5 min. of the estimated penetration time.

31.
9099. When setting the altimeter, pilots should disregard

A—effects of nonstandard atmospheric temperatures and pressures.
B—corrections for static pressure systems.
C—corrections for instrument error.

Answer (A) is correct (9099). *(IFH Chap IV)*
When setting the altimeter, pilots should disregard the effects of nonstandard atmospheric temperatures and pressures. The altimeter setting system provides a means that corrects for pressure variations. Since instrument flight in controlled airspace is accomplished at assigned indicated altitudes, airplane separation is maintained because all aircraft using the same altimeter setting are equally affected by nonstandard temperatures and pressures equally at various levels.
Answer (B) is incorrect because altimeters are subject to errors in the static pressure system. A pilot should set the current reported altimeter setting on the altimeter setting scale. The altimeter should read within 75 ft. of field elevation. If not, it is questionable and should be evaluated by a repair station. Answer (C) is incorrect because altimeters are subject to instrument errors. A pilot should set the current reported altimeter setting on the altimeter setting scale. The altimeter should read within 75 ft. of field elevation. If not, it is questionable and should be evaluated by a repair station.

8.6 ATC -- Speed Adjustments

32.
9094. When a speed adjustment is necessary to maintain separation, what minimum speed may ATC request of a turbine-powered aircraft operating below 10,000 feet?

A—200 knots.
B—210 knots.
C—250 knots.

Answer (B) is correct (9094). *(AIM Para 4-4-11)*
ATC will issue speed adjustments to pilots of radar-controlled aircraft to achieve or maintain required or desired spacing. ATC will express all speed adjustments in knots based on indicated airspeed in 10-kt. increments. ATC may request a minimum speed of 210 kt. of a turbine-powered airplane operating below 10,000 ft. MSL.
Answer (A) is incorrect because 200 kt. is the maximum airspeed of any airplane operating below 2,500 ft. AGL within 4 NM of the primary airport in Class C or Class D airspace, in a VFR-designated corridor through Class B airspace, or in airspace underlying Class B airspace. Answer (C) is incorrect because 250 kt. is the maximum airspeed of any airplane operating below 10,000 ft. MSL and within Class B airspace.

33.
9095. When a speed adjustment is necessary to maintain separation, what minimum speed may ATC request of a turbine-powered aircraft departing an airport?

A—188 knots.
B—210 knots.
C—230 knots.

Answer (C) is correct (9095). *(AIM Para 4-4-11)*
ATC will issue speed adjustments to pilots of radar-controlled airplanes to achieve or maintain required or desired spacing. ATC will express all speed adjustments in knots based on indicated airspeed in 10-kt. increments. For departing turbine-powered aircraft, the minimum speed that ATC may request is 230 kt.
Answer (A) is incorrect because 188 kt. is not an applicable airspeed for any ATC operation. All airspeeds used by ATC/FARs are expressed in 10-kt. increments. Answer (B) is incorrect because 210 kt. is the minimum airspeed that ATC can request of a turbine-powered airplane operating below 10,000 ft. MSL, excluding departing airplanes.

34.
9096. If ATC requests a speed adjustment that is not within the operating limits of the aircraft, what action must the pilot take?

A—Maintain an airspeed within the operating limitations as close to the requested speed as possible.
B—Attempt to use the requested speed as long as possible, then request a reasonable airspeed from ATC.
C—Advise ATC of the airspeed that will be used.

Answer (C) is correct (9096). *(AIM Para 4-4-11)*
The pilot retains the authority to reject the application of speed adjustment by ATC. If the speed adjustment is not within the operating limits of the airplane, the pilot is expected to advise ATC of the airspeed that will be used.
Answer (A) is incorrect because, while a pilot should maintain at least the minimum safe airspeed for any particular operation, a pilot is expected to advise ATC of the airspeed being used when it differs from ATC's requested speed adjustment. Answer (B) is incorrect because a pilot who uses an airspeed that is not within the operating limits of the airplane not only is in violation of FARs but also is risking the safety of all on board the airplane. A pilot must operate the airplane in a safe manner and advise ATC of the airspeed that will be used.

8.7 VFR-on-Top

35.
9046. Under what conditions may a pilot on an IFR flight plan comply with authorization to maintain "VFR-on-Top"?

A—Maintain IFR flight plan but comply with visual flight rules while in VFR conditions.
B—Maintain VFR altitudes, cloud clearances, and comply with applicable instrument flight rules.
C—Maintain IFR altitudes, VFR cloud clearances, and comply with applicable instrument flight rules.

Answer (B) is correct (9046). *(AIM Para 4-4-7)*
A pilot on an IFR flight plan operating in VFR weather conditions may request VFR-on-top instead of an assigned altitude. When ATC authorizes maintenance of VFR-on-top, pilots on IFR flight plans must maintain VFR altitudes, maintain VFR cloud clearances and visibilities, and comply with applicable instrument flight rules. These rules include minimum IFR altitudes, position reporting, radio communications, courses to be flown, and adherence to ATC clearances.

Answer (A) is incorrect because not only will a pilot remain on the IFR flight plan and comply with VFR altitudes, visibility, and cloud clearances, (s)he must also comply with applicable IFR rules, e.g., position reporting, minimum IFR altitudes. Answer (C) is incorrect because, while operating on a VFR-on-top clearance, a pilot must maintain VFR, not IFR, altitudes.

36.
9047. What cloud clearance must be complied with when authorized to maintain "VFR-on-Top"?

A—May maintain VFR clearance above, below, or between layers.
B—Must maintain VFR clearance above or below.
C—May maintain VFR clearance above or below, but not between layers.

Answer (A) is correct (9047). *(AIM Para 4-4-7)*
ATC authorization to maintain VFR-on-top is not intended to restrict pilots so that they must operate only above a layer. Instead, it permits operation above, below, or between layers, or in areas where there is no meteorological obscuration.

Answer (B) is incorrect because an authorization to maintain VFR-on-top allows a pilot to maintain VFR clearance not only above or below, but also between layers. Answer (C) is incorrect because an authorization to maintain VFR-on-top allows a pilot to maintain VFR clearance above, below, and between layers.

37.
9048. In what airspace will ATC not authorize "VFR-on-Top"?

A—Class C airspace.
B—Class B airspace.
C—Class A airspace.

Answer (C) is correct (9048). *(AIM Para 4-4-7)*
ATC will not authorize VFR or VFR-on-top operations in Class A airspace. Class A airspace extends from FL 180 up to, and including, FL 600.

Answer (A) is incorrect because, while there may be some restrictions due to separation, a pilot can operate VFR-on-top in Class C airspace. Answer (B) is incorrect because, while there may be some restrictions due to separation, a pilot can operate VFR-on-top in Class B airspace.

38.
9093. What separation or service by ATC is afforded pilots authorized "VFR-on-Top"?

A—The same afforded all IFR flights.
B—3 miles horizontally instead of 5.
C—Traffic advisories only.

Answer (C) is correct (9093). *(AIM Para 4-4-7)*
Separation will be provided between all aircraft operating on IFR flight plans except during VFR-on-top operations outside Class B or Class C airspace. Under these conditions, ATC may issue traffic advisories, but it is the responsibility of the pilot to be vigilant in order to see and avoid other aircraft.

Answer (A) is incorrect because separation will be provided for all IFR flights except those operating with a VFR-on-top clearance. In that case, only traffic advisories may be provided. Answer (B) is incorrect because, when radar is employed for separation of aircraft at the same altitude, a minimum of 3 mi. separation is provided between airplanes operating within 40 mi. of the radar antenna site, and 5 mi. between aircraft operating beyond 40 mi. from the antenna site.

8.8 ATC -- Minimum Fuel and Emergencies

39.
9010. Under what condition should a pilot on IFR advise ATC of minimum fuel status?

A—When the fuel supply becomes less than that required for IFR.
B—If the remaining fuel suggests a need for traffic or landing priority.
C—If the remaining fuel precludes any undue delay.

Answer (C) is correct (9010). *(AIM Para 5-5-15)*
A pilot should advise ATC of minimum fuel status when the remaining fuel supply has reached a state which precludes any undue delay upon reaching destination. A pilot must be aware that this is not an emergency situation but an advisory that indicates an emergency situation is possible should any undue delay occur.

Answer (A) is incorrect because a pilot must ensure the minimum amount of fuel is on board the airplane for the planned IFR flight and alternatives, if needed, during the flight planning phase. Answer (B) is incorrect because, if the remaining fuel suggests a need for traffic or landing priority, the pilot should declare an emergency, not minimum fuel status, due to low fuel and report fuel remaining in minutes.

40.
9011. What does the term "minimum fuel" imply to ATC?

A—Traffic priority is needed to the destination airport.
B—Emergency handling is required to the nearest suitable airport.
C—Advisory that indicates an emergency situation is possible should an undue delay occur.

Answer (C) is correct (9011). *(AIM Para 5-5-15)*
When a pilot advises ATC of a minimum fuel status, ATC will handle this report as an advisory that indicates an emergency situation is possible should an undue delay occur. A minimum fuel advisory does not imply a need for traffic priority.

Answer (A) is incorrect because a pilot should declare an emergency due to low fuel and report fuel remaining in minutes if traffic priority is needed to the destination airport. Answer (B) is incorrect because emergency handling to the nearest suitable airport is required in a distress or urgent type of emergency.

41.
9420. You should advise ATC of minimum fuel status when your fuel supply has reached a state where, upon reaching your destination, you cannot accept any undue delay.

A—This will ensure your priority handling by ATC.
B—ATC will consider this action as if you had declared an emergency.
C—If your remaining usable fuel supply suggests the need for traffic priority to ensure a safe landing, declare an emergency due to low fuel and report fuel remaining in minutes.

Answer (C) is correct (9420). *(AIM Para 5-5-15)*
Advising ATC of minimum fuel status is not considered an emergency, nor does it imply a need for traffic priority. However, if the remaining usable fuel supply suggests the need for traffic priority to ensure a safe landing, you should declare an emergency due to low fuel and report fuel remaining in minutes.

Answer (A) is incorrect because a minimum fuel advisory does not imply a need for traffic priority, only that you cannot accept any undue delay. Answer (B) is incorrect because declaring minimum fuel is not an emergency situation but merely an advisory that indicates an emergency situation is possible should any undue delay occur.

42.
9052. Which range of codes should a pilot avoid switching through when changing transponder codes?

A—0000 through 1000.
B—7200 and 7500 series.
C—7500, 7600, and 7700 series.

Answer (C) is correct (9052). *(AIM Para 4-1-19)*
When making routine code changes, pilots should avoid inadvertent selection of codes 7500, 7600, or 7700, which can cause momentary false alarms at automated ground facilities. This applies to nondiscrete code 7500 and all discrete codes in the 7600 and 7700 series. Remember that 7500 is for hijack, 7600 for lost radio communications, 7700 for general emergency, and 7777 for military interceptor operations.

Answer (A) is incorrect because codes 0000 through 1000 are acceptable codes that may be used during normal operations. Answer (B) is incorrect because the 7200 series can be used during normal operations, while 7500 should be avoided except in the case of a hijack.

43.
9051. What is the hijack code?

A—7200.
B—7500.
C—7777.

Answer (B) is correct (9051). *(AIM Para 6-3-4)*

Transponder code 7500 means: "I am being hijacked/forced to a new destination." Code 7500 will never be assigned by ATC without prior notification from the pilot that his/her airplane is being subjected to unlawful interference. Code 7500 will trigger special emergency indicators in all radar ATC facilities.

Answer (A) is incorrect because 7200 is a code that is used for normal operating procedures. Answer (C) is incorrect because under no circumstances should a pilot of a civil airplane operate the transponder on Code 7777. This code is reserved for military interceptor operations.

44.
9097. What minimum condition is suggested for declaring an emergency?

A—Anytime the pilot is doubtful of a condition that could adversely affect flight safety.
B—When fuel endurance or weather will require an en route or landing priority.
C—When distress conditions such as fire, mechanical failure, or structural damage occurs.

Answer (A) is correct (9097). *(AIM Para 6-1-2)*

An emergency is defined as either a distress or an urgency condition. A distress condition can be a fire, mechanical failure, or structural damage. An airplane is in at least an urgency condition when the pilot becomes doubtful about position, fuel endurance, weather, or any other condition that could adversely affect flight safety. A pilot should declare an emergency under any of these circumstances, not after the situation has developed into a distress condition.

Answer (B) is incorrect because, if fuel endurance or weather will require an en route or landing priority, the situation has progressed beyond an urgency condition and is now a distress condition. Answer (C) is incorrect because distress condition implies a serious and/or imminent danger requiring immediate assistance. This situation is the step after an urgency condition, which is one that has the potential to become a distress condition.

45.
9098. It is the responsibility of the pilot and crew to report a near midair collision as a result of proximity of at least

A—50 feet or less to another aircraft.
B—500 feet or less to another aircraft.
C—1,000 feet or less to another aircraft.

Answer (B) is correct (9098). *(AIM Para 7-6-3)*

A near midair collision is defined as an incident associated with the operation of an airplane in which a possibility of collision occurs as a result of proximity of less than 500 ft. to another airplane. It is the responsibility of the pilot and/or flight crew to determine whether a near midair collision did actually occur and to initiate a near midair collision report.

Answer (A) is incorrect because a near midair collision is reported if the possibility of a collision occurs as a result of proximity of less than 500, not 50, ft. to another airplane. Answer (C) is incorrect because proximity of greater than 500 ft. is not considered a near midair collision and would not be reported as such.

46.
9050. Under what condition does ATC issue safety alerts?

A—When collision with another aircraft is imminent.
B—If the aircraft altitude is noted to be in close proximity to the surface or an obstacle.
C—When weather conditions are extreme and wind shear or large hail is in the vicinity.

Answer (B) is correct (9050). *(AIM Para 4-1-15)*

ATC will issue a safety alert when an airplane under its control is at an altitude which, in ATC's judgment, places the aircraft in unsafe proximity to terrain, obstructions, or another aircraft. A terrain or obstruction alert is issued to an airplane that is at an altitude believed to place the aircraft in unsafe proximity to terrain or obstructions. An aircraft conflict alert is issued when an airplane under a controller's direction is at an altitude believed to place the aircraft in unsafe proximity to another airplane not under that controller's direction.

Answer (A) is incorrect because a safety alert is issued to a pilot if ATC believes that his/her airplane is at an altitude which will place it in unsafe proximity to another airplane, not that a collision is imminent. Answer (C) is incorrect because, when weather conditions are extreme and wind shear or large hail is in the vicinity, a convective SIGMET, not a safety alert, is broadcast.

8.9 Traffic Alert and Collision Avoidance System (TCAS)

47.
9425. TCAS I provides

A—traffic and resolution advisories.
B—proximity warning.
C—recommended maneuvers to avoid conflicting traffic.

Answer (B) is correct (9425). *(AIM Para 4-4-15)*
TCAS I provides only a proximity warning to assist the pilot in the visual acquisition of intruder aircraft. No recommended avoidance maneuvers are provided or authorized as a direct result of a TCAS I warning.
Answer (A) is incorrect because TCAS II, not TCAS I, provides traffic and resolution advisories. TCAS I provides only a proximity warning. Answer (C) is incorrect because TCAS II, not TCAS I, provides recommended maneuvers to avoid conflicting traffic and resolution advisories. TCAS I provides only a proximity warning.

48.
9426. TCAS II provides

A—traffic and resolution advisories.
B—proximity warning.
C—maneuvers in all directions to avoid the conflicting traffic.

Answer (A) is correct (9426). *(AIM Para 4-4-15)*
TCAS II provides traffic and resolution advisories. Resolution advisories provide recommended maneuvers in a vertical direction (climb or descend only) to avoid conflicting traffic.
Answer (B) is incorrect because TCAS I, not TCAS II, provides only a proximity warning. TCAS II provides traffic and resolution advisories. Answer (C) is incorrect because TCAS II provides recommended maneuvers only in a vertical direction, not in all directions, to avoid conflicting traffic.

49.
9427. Each pilot, who deviates from an ATC clearance in response to a TCAS advisory, is expected to notify ATC and

A—maintain the course and altitude resulting from the deviation, as ATC has radar contact.
B—request a new ATC clearance.
C—expeditiously return to the ATC clearance in effect prior to the advisory, after the conflict is resolved.

Answer (C) is correct (9427). *(AIM Para 4-4-15)*
Each pilot who deviates from an ATC clearance in response to a TCAS II resolution advisory shall notify ATC of that deviation as soon as practicable and expeditiously return to the current ATC clearance when the traffic conflict is resolved.
Answer (A) is incorrect because, since ATC is not responsible for IFR aircraft separation during a deviation, the pilot should notify ATC of the deviation and expeditiously return to the clearance in effect after the conflict is resolved. Answer (B) is incorrect because, since deviations from clearances should be kept to the minimum necessary to satisfy a TCAS advisory, the pilot should notify ATC of the deviation and expeditiously return to the clearance in effect after the conflict is resolved.

50.
9428. Each pilot who deviates from an ATC clearance in response to a TCAS advisory is expected to

A—maintain the course and altitude resulting from the deviation, as ATC has radar contact.
B—request ATC clearance for the deviation.
C—notify ATC of the deviation as soon as practicable.

Answer (C) is correct (9428). *(AIM Para 4-4-15)*
Each pilot who deviates from an ATC clearance in response to a TCAS II resolution advisory shall notify ATC of that deviation as soon as practicable and expeditiously return to the current ATC clearance when the traffic conflict is resolved.
Answer (A) is incorrect because, since ATC is not responsible for IFR aircraft separation during a deviation, the pilot should notify ATC of the deviation and expeditiously return to the clearance in effect after the conflict is resolved. Answer (B) is incorrect because ATC clearance for a deviation in response to a TCAS advisory is not required, although the pilot is expected to notify ATC of the deviation as soon as practicable.

8.10 ATC -- Approach and Landing

51.
9016. Which reports are always required when on an IFR approach not in radar contact?

A—Leaving FAF inbound or outer marker inbound and missed approach.
B—Leaving FAF inbound, leaving outer marker inbound or outbound, and missed approach.
C—Leaving FAF inbound, leaving outer marker inbound or outbound, procedure turn outbound and inbound, and visual contact with the runway.

Answer (A) is correct (9016). *(AIM Para 5-3-3)*
When not in radar contact, a pilot is required to report when leaving final approach fix (FAF) inbound on final approach (nonprecision approach) or when leaving the outer marker inbound on final approach (precision approach). At all times, a pilot will report a missed approach.

Answer (B) is incorrect because a pilot is required to report leaving the outer marker inbound, not outbound, on final approach. Answer (C) is incorrect because a pilot is not required to report leaving the outer marker outbound, the execution of a procedure turn, and/or visual contact with the runway.

52.
9036. What action(s) should a pilot take if vectored across the final approach course during an IFR approach?

A—Continue on the last heading issued until otherwise instructed.
B—Contact approach control, and advise that the flight is crossing the final approach course.
C—Turn onto final, and broadcast in the blind that the flight has proceeded on final.

Answer (B) is correct (9036). *(AIM Para 5-4-3)*
If a pilot is being vectored to the final approach course, these vectors are used for spacing and separating aircraft. Pilots must not deviate from the headings issued by approach control. Pilots will normally be informed when it is necessary to vector across the final approach course for spacing or other reasons. If approach course is imminent and the pilot has not been informed of crossing the final approach course, the pilot should contact approach control and advise that the flight is crossing the final approach course.

Answer (A) is incorrect because the pilot should maintain last heading issued but should also advise approach control that the flight is crossing the final approach course. Answer (C) is incorrect because a pilot should broadcast in the blind that the flight has turned onto final when operating VFR at an uncontrolled airport.

53.
9038. When is radar service terminated while vectored for an IFR approach at an uncontrolled airport?

A—Only upon landing or advised to change to advisory frequency.
B—When aligned on the final approach course.
C—When cleared for the approach.

Answer (A) is correct (9038). *(AIM Para 5-4-3)*
Radar service is terminated while the airplane is being vectored for an IFR approach at an uncontrolled airport when the landing is completed or when the pilot is advised to change to advisory frequency, whichever occurs first.

Answer (B) is incorrect because, when an airplane is established on the final approach course, radar separation will be maintained and the pilot will be expected to complete the approach utilizing the approach aid designated in the clearance (ILS, VOR, etc.). Answer (C) is incorrect because, when an airplane is cleared for the approach, approach control will continue to maintain radar separation, and the pilot is expected to complete the approach utilizing the approach aid designated in the clearance (ILS, VOR, etc.).

54.
9039. When cleared for an IFR approach to an uncontrolled airport with no FSS, what precaution should the pilot take after being advised to change to advisory frequency?

A—Monitor ATC for traffic advisories as well as UNICOM.
B—Broadcast position and intentions on the Common Traffic Advisory Frequency and monitor the frequency.
C—Wait until visual contact is made with the airport and then broadcast position and intentions to land on UNICOM.

Answer (B) is correct (9039). *(AIM Para 5-4-4)*
When making an IFR approach to an uncontrolled airport with no FSS, after ATC advises, "Change to advisory frequency approved," the pilot should broadcast his/her intentions, including the type of approach and the time at which (s)he arrives over the FAF or outer marker inbound. The pilot should monitor the CTAF for reports from other pilots and for continual updates to position reports.

Answer (A) is incorrect because, after ATC advises the pilot to change to advisory frequency, ATC will no longer be able to provide traffic advisories. Answer (C) is incorrect because a pilot should always broadcast intentions and continually update position reports on the CTAF, not wait until visual contact is made with the airport. Waiting is unsafe and can contribute to an accident.

55.
9037. While being vectored to the final approach course of an IFR approach, when may the pilot descend to published altitudes?

A—Anytime the flight is on a published leg of an approach chart.
B—When the flight is within the 10-mile ring of a published approach.
C—Only when approach control clears the flight for the approach.

Answer (C) is correct (9037). *(AIM Para 5-4-7)*
While being vectored to the final approach course and being cleared for the approach, a pilot may descend to published altitudes anytime the flight is established on a segment of a published route or IAP. After the airplane is so established, published altitudes apply to descent within each succeeding route or approach segment unless a different altitude is assigned by ATC.
Answer (A) is incorrect because one must be cleared for the approach to be able to descend to published altitudes. Answer (B) is incorrect because, when the flight is within the 10-mile ring of a published approach, a pilot will maintain the minimum altitude for IFR and maintain altitude issued by approach control until established on a published segment of the approach.

56.
9041. When may a pilot execute a missed approach during an ASR approach?

A—Anytime at the pilot's discretion.
B—Only at the MAP.
C—Only when advised by the controller.

Answer (A) is correct (9041). *(AIM Para 5-4-10)*
An ASR approach is one in which a controller provides azimuth guidance only. The pilot is furnished headings to fly to align the airplane with the extended line of the runway. A pilot may execute a missed approach during an ASR anytime at the pilot's discretion.
Answer (B) is incorrect because the controller will instruct the pilot to execute a missed approach at the MAP or anytime during the approach that the controller considers that safe guidance cannot be provided. Answer (C) is incorrect because a pilot can execute a missed approach anytime at the pilot's discretion, not only when advised by the controller.

57.
9090. If visual reference is lost while circling to land from an instrument approach, what action(s) should the pilot take?

A—Make a climbing turn toward the landing runway until established on the missed approach course.
B—Turn toward the landing runway maintaining MDA, and if visual reference is not regained, perform missed approach.
C—Make a climbing turn toward the VOR/NDB, and request further instructions.

Answer (A) is correct (9090). *(AIM Para 5-4-19)*
If visual reference is lost while circling to land from an instrument approach, the missed approach specified for that particular procedure must be followed. To become established on the prescribed missed approach course, the pilot should make an initial climbing turn toward the runway and continue the turn until established on the missed approach course.
Answer (B) is incorrect because, once visual reference is lost while circling, a missed approach must be executed. While turning toward the runway, a climbing turn should be established (MDA should not be maintained). Answer (C) is incorrect because a pilot should make a climbing turn toward the runway, not VOR/NDB, to ensure obstacle clearance while becoming established on the missed approach course.

58.
9091. What is the difference between a visual and a contact approach?

A—A visual approach is an IFR authorization while a contact approach is a VFR authorization.
B—A visual approach is initiated by ATC while a contact approach is initiated by the pilot.
C—Both are the same but classified according to the party initiating the approach.

Answer (B) is correct (9091). *(AIM Para 5-4-20, 5-4-22)*
Visual approaches are initiated by ATC to reduce pilot/controller workload and expedite traffic by shortening flight paths to the airport. A contact approach must be initiated by the pilot. A pilot operating clear of clouds who has at least 1 SM flight visibility and can reasonably expect to continue to the destination airport in those conditions may request ATC authorization for a contact approach.
Answer (A) is incorrect because both a visual and a contact approach are initiated from an IFR flight plan. Answer (C) is incorrect because a visual approach is one in which the pilot has a preceding aircraft or the airport in sight and can maintain basic VFR weather minimums. A contact approach is used by a pilot in lieu of conducting a standard or special instrument approach to an airport.

59.
9092. Except during an emergency, when can a pilot expect landing priority?

A—When cleared for an IFR approach.
B—When piloting a large, heavy aircraft.
C—In turn, on a first-come, first-serve basis.

Answer (C) is correct (9092). *(AIM Para 5-4-23)*
A clearance for a specific type of approach to an airplane operating on an IFR flight plan does not mean that landing priority will be given over other traffic. Air traffic control towers handle all airplanes, regardless of the type of flight plan, on a first-come, first-served basis. A landing sequence will be issued to each airplane as soon as possible to enable the pilot to adjust his/her flight path properly.
Answer (A) is incorrect because a clearance for an IFR approach does not mean landing priority will be given over other traffic. Answer (B) is incorrect because a large, heavy aircraft will be sequenced for landing on a first-come, first-served basis, with no special priority over other traffic.

60.
9044. What action is expected of an aircraft upon landing at a controlled airport?

A—Continue taxiing in the landing direction until advised by the tower to switch to ground control frequency.
B—Exit the runway at the nearest suitable taxiway and remain on tower frequency until instructed otherwise.
C—Exit the runway at the nearest suitable taxiway and switch to ground control upon crossing the taxiway holding lines.

Answer (B) is correct (9044). *(AIM Para 4-3-20)*
After landing, unless otherwise instructed by the control tower, continue to taxi in the landing direction, proceed to the nearest suitable taxiway, and exit the runway without delay. A pilot who has just landed should not change from the tower frequency to the ground control frequency until directed to do so by the controller.
Answer (A) is incorrect because, upon landing, the pilot should exit the runway at the nearest suitable taxiway to clear the runway for other traffic and then switch to ground control when directed. Answer (C) is incorrect because, while the crossing of the taxiway hold lines indicates clearing of the active runway, a pilot should not switch to ground control until directed to do so by the controller. Switching without permission may be confusing to ATC.

61.
9055. How should a pilot describe braking action?

A—00 percent, 50 percent, 75 percent, or 100 percent.
B—Zero-zero, fifty-fifty, or normal.
C—Nil, poor, fair, or good.

Answer (C) is correct (9055). *(AIM Para 4-57)*
Pilots should describe the quality of braking action by using the terms of "nil," "poor," "fair," and "good" or a combination of these terms. In describing braking action for a portion of a runway, pilots should use descriptive terms that are easily understood.
Answer (A) is incorrect because, to describe braking action, a pilot should use nil (not 00%), poor (not 50%), fair (not 75%), or good (not 100%). Answer (B) is incorrect because, to describe braking action, a pilot should use the terms nil (not zero-zero), poor, fair (not fifty-fifty), or good (not normal).

END OF CHAPTER

CHAPTER NINE
IFR NAVIGATION EQUIPMENT, HOLDING, AND APPROACHES

This chapter contains outlines of major concepts tested, all FAA test questions and answers regarding IFR navigation equipment, holding, and approaches, and an explanation of each answer. Each module, or subtopic, within this chapter is listed above with the number of questions from the FAA pilot knowledge test pertaining to that particular module. For each module, the first number following the parentheses is the page number on which the outline begins, and the next number is the page number on which the questions begin. Note that eight pages of IAP legends are reproduced as general references.

There are 138 questions in this chapter. We separate and organize the FAA ATP questions into meaningful study units, i.e., chapters and modules. As an analogy, it is easier to deal with the "trees" if you understand the "forest." In this context, "trees" are individual FAA questions, and the "forest" is the ATP knowledge test. The organizational units between the overall ATP knowledge test and individual ATP test questions are chapters and modules in this book.

CAUTION: The **sole purpose** of this book is to expedite your passing the FAA pilot knowledge test for the ATP certificate. Topics or regulations not directly tested on the FAA pilot knowledge test are omitted. Much more information and knowledge are necessary to fly safely. This additional material is presented in Gleim's other pilot training books (see the order form on page 818) and in many FAA books and circulars, as well as in airplane *POH*s and other commercial textbooks.

9.1 NAVIGATION SYSTEMS/MISCELLANEOUS QUESTIONS (Questions 1-5)

1. When the approach procedure involves a procedure turn, the pilot should observe a maximum airspeed of 200 kt. IAS, from first overheading the course reversal initial approach fix (IAF) through completing the procedure turn maneuver, to ensure containment within the obstruction clearance area.
2. You should notify ATC on the initial contact that you have received the ATIS broadcast by repeating the alphabetical code word appended to the broadcast.
3. During a LORAN approach, the receiver must detect a loss of signal or a signal blink within 10 seconds of the occurrence and warn the pilot of the event.
4. **Off-route obstruction clearance altitude (OROCA)** is an off-route altitude that provides obstruction clearance with a 1,000-ft. buffer in nonmountainous terrain areas and a 2,000-ft. buffer in designated mountainous terrain areas within the U.S.
5. **Inertial Navigation System (INS)** is a navigation computer which provides position by signals from self-contained gyros and accelerometers.

9.2 DISTANCE MEASURING EQUIPMENT (DME) (Questions 6-7)

1. DME (distance measuring equipment) displays slant range distance in nautical miles.
2. Ignore slant range error if the airplane is 1 NM or more from the ground facility for each 1,000 ft. AGL.
   a. The greatest slant range error comes at high altitudes very close to the VORTAC.
   b. EXAMPLE: If you are 12,000 ft. AGL directly above a VORTAC, your DME will read 2.0 NM.

9.3 VOR/VORTAC IDENTIFIER (Questions 8-9)

1. When VORs are undergoing maintenance, the coded and/or voice identification is not broadcast from the VOR.
   a. The facility may transmit a coded identification T-E-S-T during maintenance.

9.4 RMI INTERPRETATION (Questions 10-13)

1. The **radio magnetic indicator (RMI)** consists of a rotating compass card and one or more navigation indicators which point to stations.
2. The knobs at the bottom of the RMI allow you to select ADFs or VORs as stations.
3. The magnetic heading of the airplane is always directly under the index at the top of the instrument.

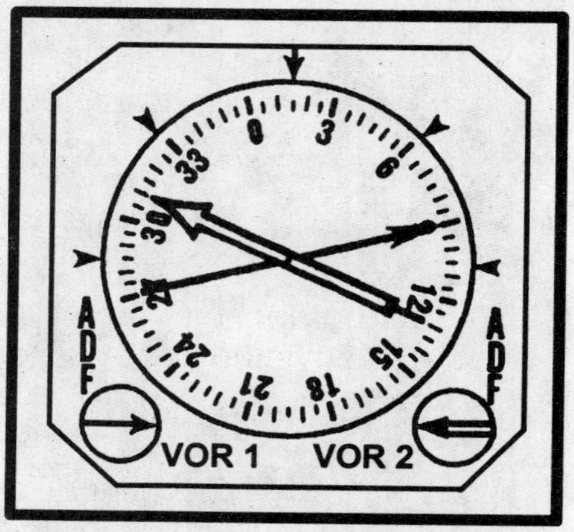

4. The bearing pointer displays magnetic bearings to selected navigation stations.
   a. The tail of the indicator tells you which radial you are on, or the magnetic bearing FROM the station.

9.5 HSI INTERPRETATION (Questions 14-25)

1. The **horizontal situation indicator (HSI)** is a combination of the heading indicator and the VOR/ILS indicator, as illustrated and explained below.

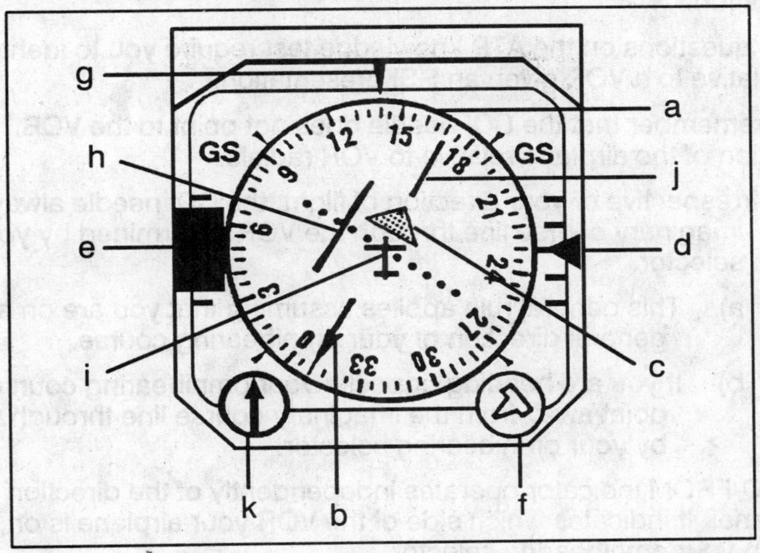

   a. The azimuth card -- rotates so that the heading is shown under the index at the top of the instrument
      1) The azimuth card may be part of a remote indicating compass (RIC), or
      2) The azimuth card must be checked against the magnetic compass and reset with a heading set knob.
   b. The course indicating arrow -- the VOR (OBS) indicator
   c. The TO/FROM indicator for the VOR
   d. Glide slope deviation pointer -- indicates above or below the glide slope, which is the longer center line
   e. Glide slope warning flag -- comes out when reliable signals are not received by the glide slope receiver
   f. Heading set knob -- used to coordinate the heading indicator (directional gyro, etc.) with the actual compass
      1) If the azimuth card is part of an RIC, this knob is normally a heading bug (pointer) set knob that moves a bug around the periphery of the azimuth card.
   g. Lubber line -- shows the current heading
   h. Course deviation bar -- indicates the direction you would have to turn to intercept the desired radial if you were on the approximate heading of the OBS selection
   i. The airplane symbol -- a fixed symbol that shows the airplane relative to the selected course as though you were above the airplane looking down
   j. The tail of the course indicating arrow -- shows the reciprocal of the OBS heading
   k. The course setting knob -- used to adjust the OBS

2. Airplane displacement from a course is approximately 200 ft. per dot per NM on VORs.
   a. At 30 NM out, one dot is 1 NM displacement, two dots 2 NM.
   b. At 60 NM out, one dot is 2 NM displacement, two dots 4 NM.
3. A full-scale deflection of a VOR CDI indicates a 10° deviation from the course centerline.
   a. About 10° to 12° of change of the OBS setting should deflect the CDI from the center to the last dot.
   b. With the CDI centered, rotate the OBS 180° to change the ambiguity (TO/FROM) indication.
4. A few of the questions on the ATP knowledge test require you to identify the position of your airplane relative to a VOR given an HSI presentation.
   a. First, remember that the CDI needle does not point to the VOR. It indicates the position of the airplane relative to VOR radials.
      1) Irrespective of your direction of flight, the CDI needle always points toward the imaginary course line through the VOR determined by your omnibearing selector.
         a) This general rule applies assuming that you are on a heading in the general direction of your omnibearing course.
         b) If you are heading opposite your omnibearing course, the CDI needle will point away from the imaginary course line through the VOR determined by your omnibearing selector.
   b. The TO/FROM indicator operates independently of the direction (heading) of your airplane. It indicates which side of the VOR your airplane is on, based on the radial set on your omnibearing selector.
      1) Irrespective of your direction of flight, the TO/FROM indicator shows you whether you are before, on, or past a line 90° (perpendicular) to the course line determined by your omnibearing setting.
   c. Thus, the HSI shows only your location (not your heading) with respect to the VOR.
5. Solve all VOR problems by imagining yourself in an airplane heading in the general direction of the omnibearing setting.
6. The following diagram explains the TO/FROM indicator and the CDI needle.

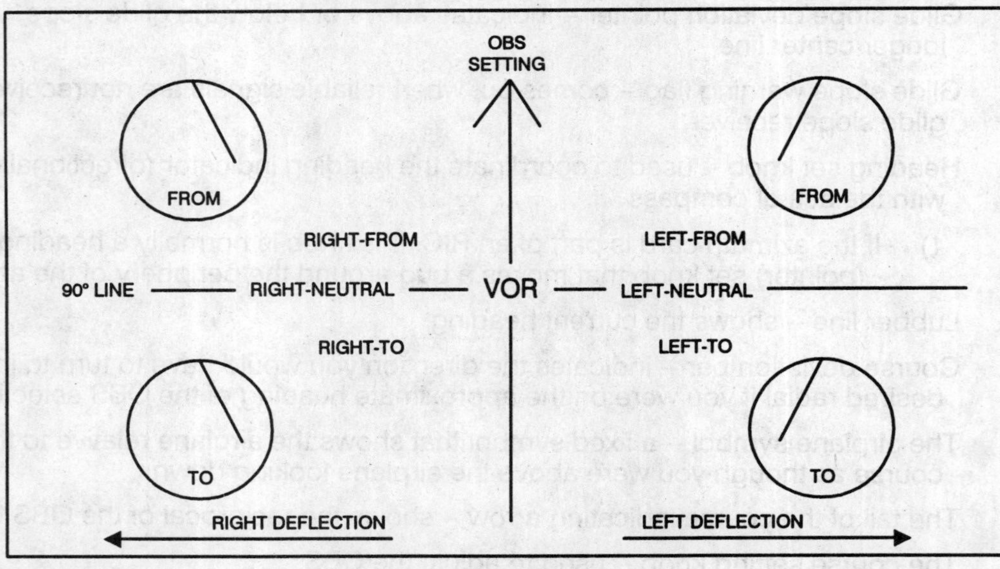

9.6 HSI/LOCALIZER (Questions 26-34)

1. When an HSI is tuned to a localizer frequency (108.10 to 111.95), the setting of the front course heading with the head of the needle will eliminate reverse sensing on back courses.
   a. Inbound on a back course, the tail of the needle will be at the top of the instrument, and you will have normal sensing.
   b. If the HSI needle is set to the front course heading, you will have normal sensing on the HSI, whether you are flying a front course or a back course approach.
   c. If the HSI needle is set to the back course heading, you will have reverse sensing on the HSI, whether you are flying a front course or a back course approach.
2. The localizer information is reported on the face of the HSI instrument just as VOR signals are.
   a. That is, it is based upon position rather than heading.
3. Similar to VORs, if you are going in the direction specified for an approach to a runway, a left deflection means you are to the right of course if you are facing in the approximate direction of the localizer.

9.7 HOLDING (Questions 35-49)

1. Holding patterns are specified by ATC to slow traffic flow. They are racetrack-shaped patterns based on a fix which is a radio navigation facility (VOR, ADF, or other NAVAID), an intersection of NAVAID bearings, radials, or a DME fix.
   a. Right turns are standard unless ATC specifies left turns.
2. Holding patterns consist of the following components (note that the fix is always at the end of the inbound leg):

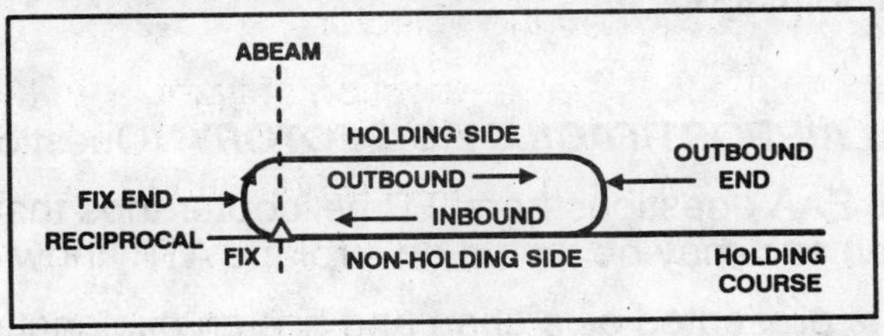

3. You enter a holding pattern using one of three procedures as illustrated in the figure below. This illustrates a standard pattern; the same concept is used in a nonstandard pattern.
   a. Parallel procedure. Fly parallel holding course as in (a). Turn left and return to holding fix or intercept holding course.
   b. Teardrop procedure. Proceed on outbound track of 30° or less to holding course; turn right to intercept holding course, as in (b).
   c. Direct entry procedure. Turn right and fly the pattern, as in (c).

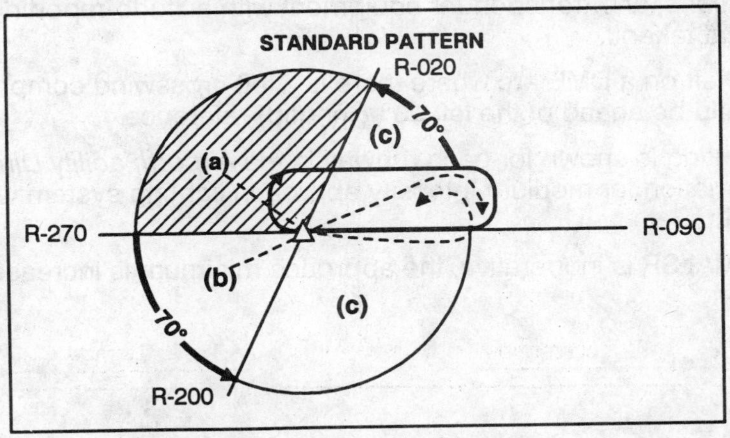

4. The best way to determine the entry method on the ATP knowledge test is to draw a holding pattern complete with the fix and inbound leg.
   a. Through the fix, draw the 70° angle such that it intersects the outbound leg at about one-third of the outbound leg length.
   b. Then slightly shade the (a) area (110°), which means parallel entry, as shown.
   c. The (b) area is the 70° angle between the 70° line and the extension of the inbound leg.
   d. EXAMPLE: In the illustration on page 271, the inbound leg to the fix is 270°.

R-200 to R-270	Teardrop
R-270 to R-020	Parallel
R-020 to R-200	Direct

5. **Maximum Holding Pattern Indicated Airspeeds (all aircraft)**
   a. From the minimum holding altitude (MHA) to 6,000 ft. MSL -- 200 kt.
   b. From 6,001 ft. MSL to 14,000 ft. MSL -- 230 kt.
   c. From 14,001 ft. MSL and above -- 265 kt.
6. In a holding pattern, using a flight director system, the rate of turn or bank angle should be 3° per second or 25° bank, whichever is less.
7. When entering a holding pattern above 14,000 ft. MSL, the initial outbound leg should not exceed 1½ min.
8. When holding at an NDB, the timing to begin at the second leg outbound should be when abeam the holding fix.

9.8 IFR CHARTS AND *AIRPORT/FACILITY DIRECTORY* (Questions 50-75)

1. There are 26 FAA questions from IFR helicopter trips that are not helicopter-specific; i.e., they can and may be tested on airplane ATP knowledge tests.
2. Each STAR is presented as a chart and has an explanation of the arrival route and the transitions from the en route fixes to the arrival route.
   a. A STAR ends at the last fix as described in the explanation, as well as at the point where the last heavy arrow appears on the chart.
3. If radio communications are lost during a STAR, you should complete the STAR then as filed, continue to the appropriate initial approach fix, and continue the approach procedure.
4. VOR/DME approaches at airports in Class B airspace require VOR, DME, VHF communications, and transponder equipment with altitude-reporting capability to be operational at takeoff.
5. When arcing left on a DME arc where there is a left crosswind component, the bearing pointer should be ahead of the left 90° (wingtip) reference.
6. Approach lighting is shown for each runway in the *Airport/Facility Directory (A/FD)*. MALSR is the abbreviation for medium-intensity approach lighting system with runway alignment indicator lights.
   a. When MALSR is inoperative, the approach minimum is increased ½ SM or RVR of 2,400 ft.

7. The **visual descent point (VDP)** is marked on the profile view of the IAP with a bold **V**.
   a. At the VDP, a descent from the MDA may begin if the runway environment is visible.
8. The **missed approach point (MAP)** on the profile view of the IAP is indicated by the end of the solid line.
   a. The missed approach procedure must be initiated at the MAP if still in IMC.
9. The **changeover point** on a VICTOR airway between two VORTAC stations is the midpoint or is indicated by "ʃ."
10. A flag with an "X" marks a minimum crossing altitude (MCA), and below the name of the intersection, it will show the Victor airway numbers and the altitude and direction, e.g., "Victor 210-394 9100 SW."
    a. If there is no altitude under the intersection name, the MCA is the MEA.
11. VOR communication (NAVAID) boxes on en route charts will indicate if Hazardous Inflight Weather Advisory Service (HIWAS) or Transcribed Weather Broadcast (TWEB) is available on the VOR frequency.
    a. HIWAS availability is indicated by a black square in the upper left corner of the communication box.
    b. TWEB availability is indicated by a white "T" within a black circle.
12. TWEB is also available on selected NDB frequencies and is depicted in the NDB communication box in the same manner as with a VOR except the color of the circle is brown.
    a. Availability of TWEB can be confirmed by checking the *A/FD*.
13. A series of dots that overlay an airway on the en route chart means that the airway penetrates a restricted or prohibited airspace.
14. To determine the minimum number of aircraft rescue and fire-fighting vehicles and the type and amount of fire-fighting agents that a FAR Part 139 airport is required to have, you must
    a. Look up the aircraft rescue and fire-fighting (ARFF) index for that airport in the *A/FD*.
    b. Next, use the required equipment table at the bottom of Legend 15 on page 312.
    c. EXAMPLE: An FAR Part 139 airport with an ARFF Index of A is required to have one vehicle and 500 lb. of dry chemical (DC) or HALON 1211 or 450 lb. DC plus 100 gal. of water (H_2O).
15. The amount that a runway threshold is displaced is in the **runway data** of the *A/FD*.
16. The maximum gross weight of any particular type of aircraft on a given runway will be included in the **Airport Remarks** section of the *A/FD*.
17. The highest spot elevation is shown in bold on the planview section of an NOS IAP chart.
18. Weather data source at an airport is listed in the *A/FD*.
    a. **LAWRS** means a limited aviation weather reporting station where observers report cloud height, weather, obstructions to vision, temperature, dew point, surface winds, altimeter, and pertinent remarks.
19. On a low-altitude en route chart, a LF/MF oceanic route is depicted by a thin, dark brown line.
20. An ARTCC remote communications site is depicted by a blue serrated-edged box with the discrete VHF and UHF frequencies listed in the box.

9.9 ILS APPROACHES (Questions 76-102)

1. ILS provides guidance, range, and visual information functions.
2. The ILS localizer operates within 108.10 to 111.95 MHz.
3. Compass locators, when used for the outer marker (OM) and middle marker (MM) of an ILS, transmit two-letter identification groups.
   a. The outer compass locator transmits the first two letters of the localizer identification group.
   b. The middle compass locator transmits the last two letters of the localizer identification group.
4. A back course marker, where installed, is indicated by a series of two-dot combinations and a white marker beacon light.
5. **Audible and Visual Indications on the ILS**
   a. Inner marker -- continuous dots at the rate of six per second
   b. Middle marker -- alternate dots and dashes at the rate of two per second
   c. Outer marker -- continuous dashes at the rate of two per second
6. The amount of deflection and distance from the localizer and glide slope for an ILS is presented in Fig. 138 on page 322.
7. ILS weather minimums are in the minimums section of the IAP chart.
   a. The height of the DH above touchdown zone (HAT) is the minimum ceiling height.
8. ILS final approach fix is depicted in the profile view of the IAP chart by a lightning bolt-type arrow () and is the glide slope/glide path intercept altitude.
9. Minimum equipment to execute an ILS approach is a localizer and glide slope.
10. On a 3° glide path, the general rule to approximate the rate of descent is five (5) times the groundspeed in knots.
11. The course deviation indicator (CDI) is considered to have a full-scale deflection when the CDI deflects from the center of the scale to the full-scale left or right.
12. In a Category I ILS approach, an inoperative middle marker has no effect on the straight-in minimums.
13. When simultaneous approaches are in progress, each pilot receives radar advisories on the tower frequency.
    a. Any inoperative or malfunctioning aircraft receivers should be immediately reported to approach control.
14. On a published side-step maneuver, the pilot is expected to commence the side step as soon as possible after the runway or runway environment is in sight.
15. The lowest ILS Category II minimums are DH of 100 ft. and an RVR of 1,200 ft.
16. The lowest ILS Category IIIA minimum is an RVR of 700 ft.
17. A Category II instrument approach to a decision height below 150 ft. requires TDZL (touchdown zone lighting), RCLS (runway centerline light system), and RVR.
    a. These requirements are in addition to the localizer, glide slope, marker beacons, approach lighting, and HIRL (high-intensity runway lights).
18. SDF (simplified directional facility) differs from an ILS LOC (localizer) in that the SDF is 6° or 12° wide, whereas the ILS is 3° to 6° wide.
19. The LDA (localizer-type directional aid) differs from an ILS LOC in that the LDA may not be aligned with the runway.

9.10 LORAN APPROACHES (Questions 103-112)

1. LORAN-C is based on the measurement of a chain of stations operating on the 90-110 kHz frequency band.
   a. It has been approved for IFR and VFR navigation in the 48 contiguous United States and the District of Columbia.
2. The authorized operational level of LORAN-C is documented in the airplane flight manual supplement or FAA Form 337, *Major Repair and Alteration*.
3. A LORAN-C receiver is authorized for IFR operations if so stated in the airplane flight manual supplement.
4. The maximum number of degrees between the final approach course and the runway centerline for LORAN RNAV approach to be considered a straight-in is 30°.
5. NOTAMs (D) under the identifier of "LRN" gives the latest information on LORAN-C chain or station outages.
6. To find the correct LORAN frequency to use, look to the heading section of the approach chart.
   a. Toward the center of this section appears three letters and four digits which identify the station and transmitter frequency to be used for the approach.
7. The time distance (TD) table in the legend contains the TD correction values for each airport with a published LORAN RNAV instrument approach procedure.
   a. This TD correction value must be entered into the LORAN airborne receiver prior to beginning the approach.

9.11 MICROWAVE LANDING SYSTEM (MLS) (Questions 113-122)

1. The MLS precision navigation provides
   a. Azimuth
   b. Elevation
   c. Distance information
2. In addition to navigation information, the following data are transmitted on MLS frequencies:
   a. MLS status
   b. Airport conditions
   c. Weather
3. Operational flexibility of the MLS includes
   a. Selectable glide path angles and boundaries providing obstruction clearance in the terminal area
4. The difference between front and back azimuth of the MLS is that transmissions are at a lower rate in the back azimuth.
5. MLS has expansion capabilities, including back azimuth and data transmissions.
6. A three-letter Morse code identifier preceded by the Morse code for the letter M is used to identify a specific interim standard microwave landing system.
7. The azimuth coverage of the MLS is laterally 40° each side, vertically 15° to 20,000 ft., and range 20 NM.
8. The range limits of the front and back guidance system for an MLS is 20 NM and 7 NM, respectively.

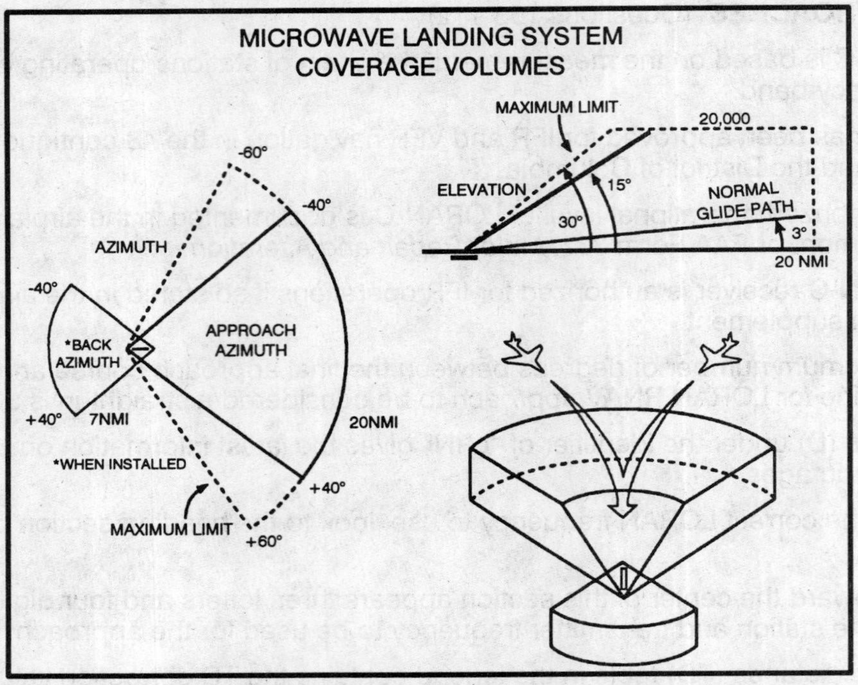

9.12 GPS APPROACHES (Questions 123-138)

1. Authorization to conduct any GPS operation under IFR requires, in part, that
   a. Procedures must be established for use in the event that the loss of receiver autonomous integrity monitoring (RAIM) capability is predicted to occur.
      1) In such an event, you must rely on other approved navigation equipment, delay departure, or cancel the flight.
   b. Air carrier and commercial operators must meet the appropriate provisions of their approved operations specifications.
   c. Aircraft navigating by GPS are considered to be RNAV-equipped aircraft and must use the appropriate equipment suffix in the flight plan.
2. GPS instrument approach operations outside the U.S. must be authorized by the appropriate sovereign authority (country or governmental unit within that country).
3. The GPS Approach Overlay Program permits pilots to use GPS avionics when IFR for flying existing IAPs, except SDF, LOC, and LDA procedures.
4. **Phases of the Approach Overlay Program**
   a. Phase I -- This phase has been completed.
   b. Phase II -- GPS avionics can be used as the IFR flight guidance system for an approach without actively monitoring the ground-based NAVAIDs which define the approach; however, these NAVAIDs must be operational.
      1) Additionally, the related avionics (i.e., VOR, ADF) must be installed but need not be turned on during the approach.
      2) Approaches must be requested and approved using the published title of the existing IAP, e.g., VOR RWY 24.

c. Phase III -- This phase begins when the IAP is retitled "GPS or VOR RWY 24." When this phase begins, ground-based NAVAIDs are not required to be operational, and the associated aircraft avionics need not be installed, operational, turned on, or monitored.

1) GPS approaches will be requested and approved using the GPS title, e.g., GPS RWY 24.

5. In each phase of the GPS Approach Overlay Program, any required alternate airport must have an approved IAP, other than GPS or LORAN-C, which is anticipated to be operational and available at the estimated time of arrival and which the airplane is equipped to fly.

6. Without RAIM capability, the accuracy of the GPS-derived altitude information should not be relied upon to determine the airplane's altitude.

a. RAIM is used to determine if a satellite is providing corrupt (bad) information. Thus, without RAIM, all GPS calculations should not be relied upon.

7. If RAIM is not available when setting up for a GPS approach, you should select another type of approach using another type of navigation aid, i.e., VOR.

8. Overriding an automatically selected CDI sensitivity during a GPS approach will cancel the approach mode annunciation.

9. If a visual descent point (VDP) is published on a GPS approach, it will not be included in the sequence of waypoints.

a. You are expected to use normal piloting techniques for beginning the visual descent.

10. When executing a GPS missed approach procedure, you must sequence the GPS receiver to "missed approach" only after passing the missed approach waypoint (MAWP).

a. Do NOT attempt to enter the "missed approach" in the GPS receiver prior to the MAWP.

11. If the missed approach procedure is not activated after passing the MAWP, the receiver will display a course that is an extension of the inbound final approach course, and the "along track distance" (ATD) will increase from the MAWP until it is manually sequenced after crossing the MAWP.

12. Missed approach routings in which the first track is via a course rather than direct to the next waypoint require you to do additional work by setting the course.

a. Example routing: Climbing right, turn to heading 180° to 5,000 ft. and then fly direct to XYZ waypoint.

13. In order to fly published IFR charted departures and SIDs, the GPS receiver must be set to terminal (± 1NM) CDI sensitivity, and the navigation routes must be in the database.

a. Remember, the database may not contain all of the transitions or departures from all runways, and some GPS receivers do not contain SIDs in the database.

QUESTIONS AND ANSWER EXPLANATIONS

All the FAA questions from the pilot knowledge test for the ATP certificate relating to IFR navigation equipment, holding, and approaches and the material outlined previously are reproduced on the following pages in the same modules as the outlines. To the immediate right of each question are the correct answer and answer explanation. You should cover these answers and answer explanations while responding to the questions. Refer to the general discussion in Chapter 1 on how to take the FAA pilot knowledge test.

9.13 INSTRUMENT APPROACH PROCEDURE CHART LEGENDS

94118

GENERAL INFO

ABBREVIATIONS

ADF	Automatic Direction Finder
ALS	Approach Light System
ALSF	Approach Light System with Sequenced Flashing Lights
APP CON	Approach Control
ARR	Arrival
ASR/PAR	Published Radar Minimums at this Airport
ATIS	Automatic Terminal Information Service
AWOS	Automated Weather Observing System
AZ	Azimuth
BC	Back Course
C	Circling
CAT	Category
CCW	Counter Clockwise
Chan	Channel
CLNC DEL	Clearance Delivery
CTAF	Common Traffic Advisory Frequency
CW	Clockwise
DH	Decision Heights
DME	Distance Measuring Equipment
DR	Dead Reckoning
ELEV	Elevation
FAF	Final Approach Fix
FM	Fan Marker
GPI	Ground Point of Interception
GPS	Global Positioning System
GS	Glide Slope
HAA	Height Above Airport
HAL	Height Above Landing
HAT	Height Above Touchdown
HIRL	High Intensity Runway Lights
IAF	Initial Approach Fix
ICAO	International Civil Aviation Organization
IM	Inner Marker
Intcp	Intercept
INT	Intersection
LDA	Localizer Type Directional Aid
Ldg	Landing
LDIN	Lead in Light System
LIRL	Low Intensity Runway Lights
LOC	Localizer
LR	Lead Radial. Provides at least 2 NM (Copter 1 NM) of lead to assist in turning onto the intermediate/final course
MALS	Medium Intensity Approach Light System
MALSR	Medium Intensity Approach Light Systems with RAIL
MAP	Missed Approach Point
MDA	Minimum Descent Altitude
MIRL	Medium Intensity Runway Lights
MLS	Microwave Landing System
MM	Middle Marker
NA	Not Authorized
NDB	Non-directional Radio Beacon
NM	Nautical Miles
NoPT	No Procedure Turn Required (Procedure Turn shall not be executed without ATC clearance)
ODALS	Omnidirectional Approach Light System
OM	Outer Marker
R	Radial
RA	Radio Altimeter setting height
Radar Required	Radar vectoring required for this approach
RAIL	Runway Alignment Indicator Lights
RBn	Radio Beacon
RCLS	Runway Centerline Light System
REIL	Runway End Identifier Lights
RNAV	Area Navigation
RPI	Runway Point of Intercept(ion)
RRL	Runway Remaining Lights
Runway Touchdown Zone	First 3000′ of Runway
Rwy	Runway
RVR	Runway Visual Range
S	Straight-in
SALS	Short Approach Light System
SSALR	Simplified Short Approach Light System with RAIL
SDF	Simplified Directional Facility
TA	Transition Altitude
TAC	TACAN
TCH	Threshold Crossing Height (height in feet Above Ground Level)
TDZ	Touchdown Zone
TDZE	Touchdown Zone Elevation
TDZ/CL	Touchdown Zone and Runway Centerline Lighting
TDZL	Touchdown Zone Lights
TLv	Transition Level
VASI	Visual Approach Slope Indicator
VDP	Visual Descent Point
WPT	Waypoint (RNAV)
X	Radar Only Frequency

PILOT CONTROLLED AIRPORT LIGHTING SYSTEMS

Available pilot controlled lighting (PCL) systems are indicated as follows:

1. Approach lighting systems that bear a system identification are symbolized using negative symbology, e.g., A1, V, ☆
2. Approach lighting systems that do not bear a system identification are indicated with a negative " ● " beside the name.

A star (*) indicates non-standard PCL, consult Directory/Supplement, e.g., ●*

To activate lights use frequency indicated in the communication section of the chart with a ● or the appropriate lighting system identification e.g., UNICOM 122.8 ●, A1, V

KEY MIKE	FUNCTION
7 times within 5 seconds	Highest intensity available
5 times within 5 seconds	Medium or lower intensity (Lower REIL or REIL-off)
3 times within 5 seconds	Lowest intensity available (Lower REIL or REIL-off)

GENERAL INFO

LEGEND 1.—General Information and Abbreviations.

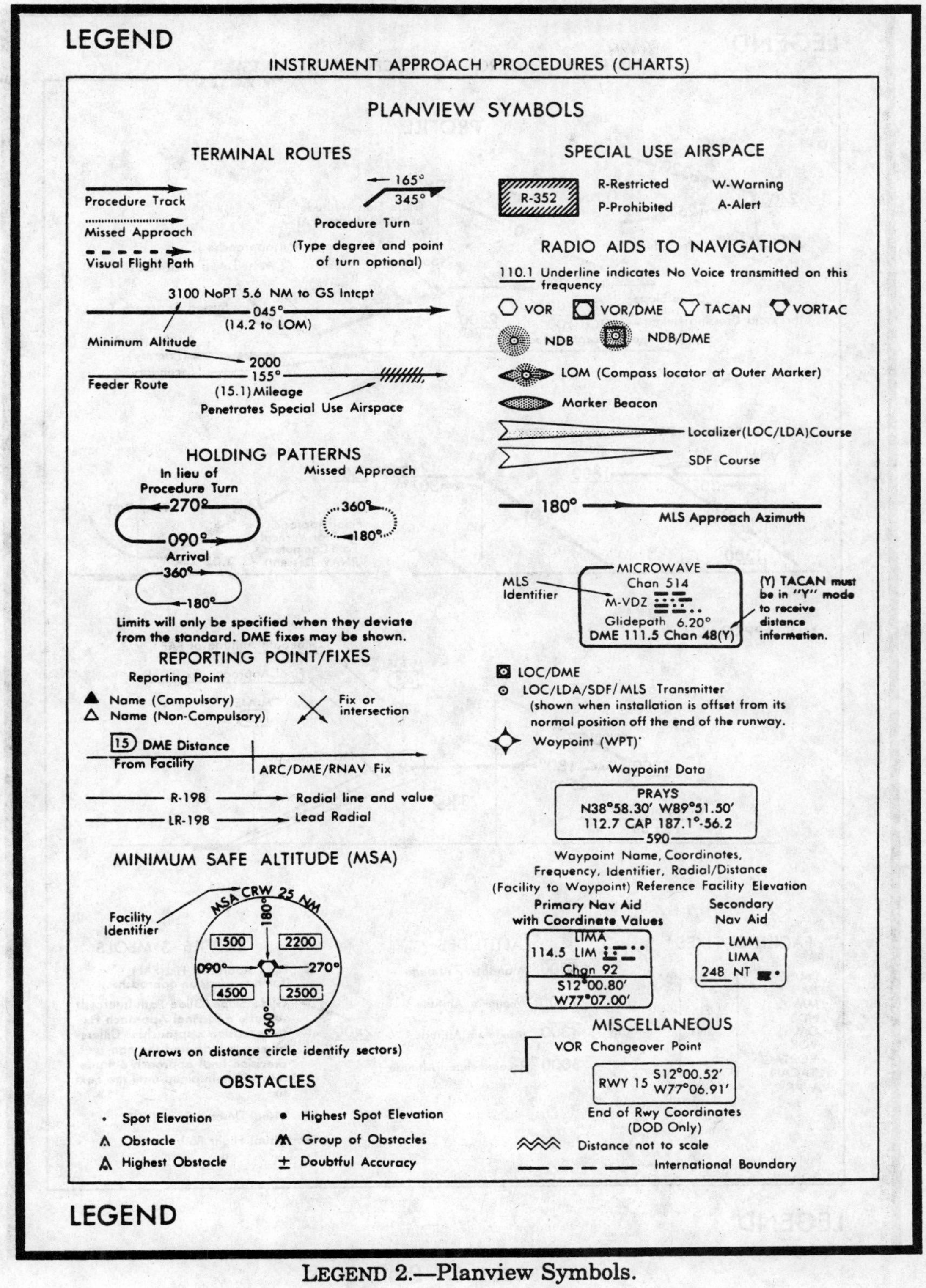

LEGEND 2.—Planview Symbols.

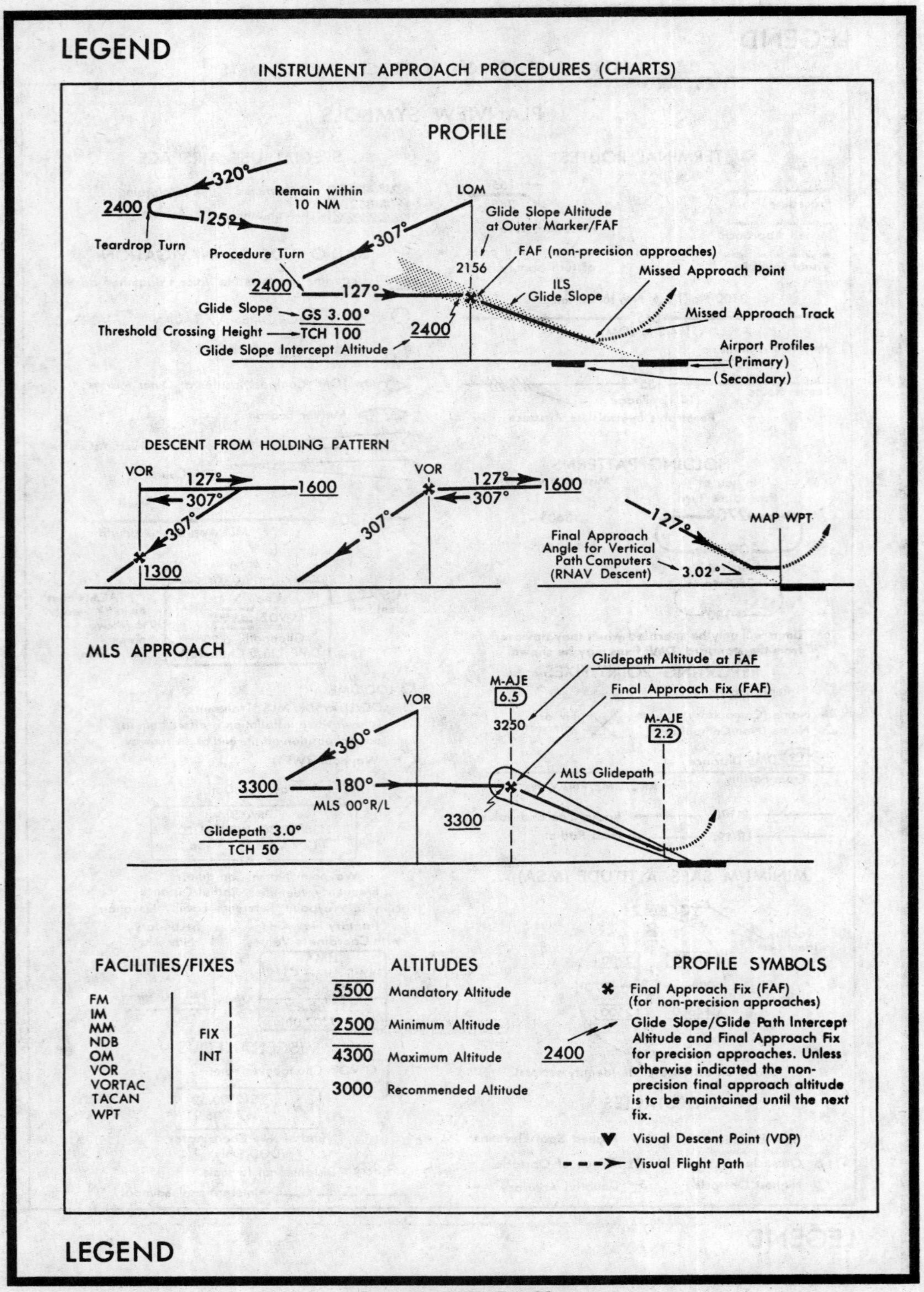

LEGEND 3.—Profile.

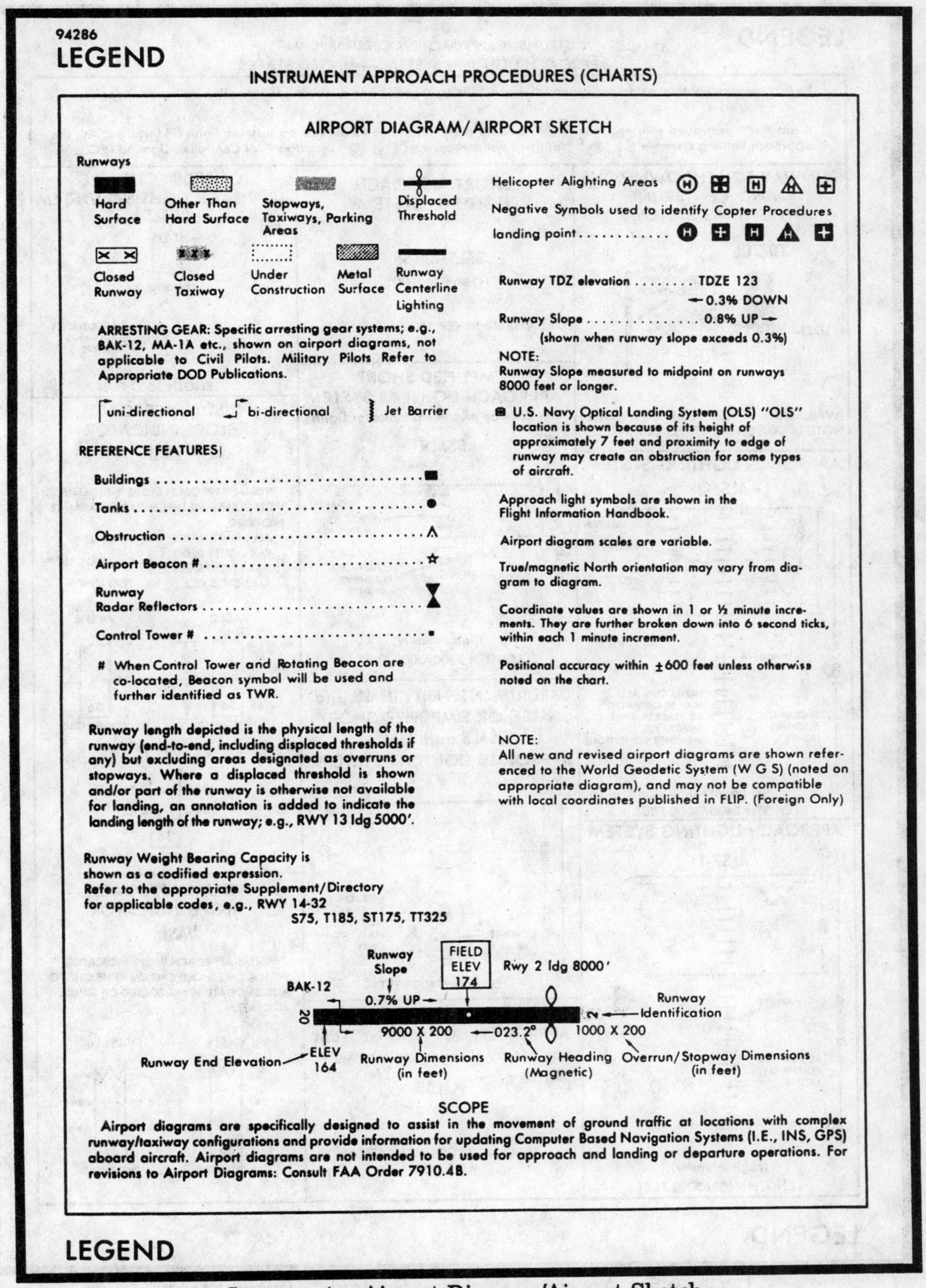

94286

LEGEND

INSTRUMENT APPROACH PROCEDURES (CHARTS)

AIRPORT DIAGRAM/AIRPORT SKETCH

Runways

Hard Surface | Other Than Hard Surface | Stopways, Taxiways, Parking Areas | Displaced Threshold

Closed Runway | Closed Taxiway | Under Construction | Metal Surface | Runway Centerline Lighting

ARRESTING GEAR: Specific arresting gear systems; e.g., BAK-12, MA-1A etc., shown on airport diagrams, not applicable to Civil Pilots. Military Pilots Refer to Appropriate DOD Publications.

uni-directional | bi-directional | Jet Barrier

REFERENCE FEATURES

Buildings ....

Tanks ....

Obstruction ....

Airport Beacon # ....

Runway Radar Reflectors ....

Control Tower # ....

When Control Tower and Rotating Beacon are co-located, Beacon symbol will be used and further identified as TWR.

Runway length depicted is the physical length of the runway (end-to-end, including displaced thresholds if any) but excluding areas designated as overruns or stopways. Where a displaced threshold is shown and/or part of the runway is otherwise not available for landing, an annotation is added to indicate the landing length of the runway; e.g., RWY 13 ldg 5000′.

Runway Weight Bearing Capacity is shown as a codified expression. Refer to the appropriate Supplement/Directory for applicable codes, e.g., RWY 14-32 S75, T185, ST175, TT325

Helicopter Alighting Areas

Negative Symbols used to identify Copter Procedures landing point ....

Runway TDZ elevation .... TDZE 123

← 0.3% DOWN

Runway Slope .... 0.8% UP →

(shown when runway slope exceeds 0.3%)

NOTE:
Runway Slope measured to midpoint on runways 8000 feet or longer.

U.S. Navy Optical Landing System (OLS) "OLS" location is shown because of its height of approximately 7 feet and proximity to edge of runway may create an obstruction for some types of aircraft.

Approach light symbols are shown in the Flight Information Handbook.

Airport diagram scales are variable.

True/magnetic North orientation may vary from diagram to diagram.

Coordinate values are shown in 1 or ½ minute increments. They are further broken down into 6 second ticks, within each 1 minute increment.

Positional accuracy within ±600 feet unless otherwise noted on the chart.

NOTE:
All new and revised airport diagrams are shown referenced to the World Geodetic System (W G S) (noted on appropriate diagram), and may not be compatible with local coordinates published in FLIP. (Foreign Only)

SCOPE

Airport diagrams are specifically designed to assist in the movement of ground traffic at locations with complex runway/taxiway configurations and provide information for updating Computer Based Navigation Systems (I.E., INS, GPS) aboard aircraft. Airport diagrams are not intended to be used for approach and landing or departure operations. For revisions to Airport Diagrams: Consult FAA Order 7910.4B.

LEGEND

LEGEND 4.—Airport Diagram/Airport Sketch.

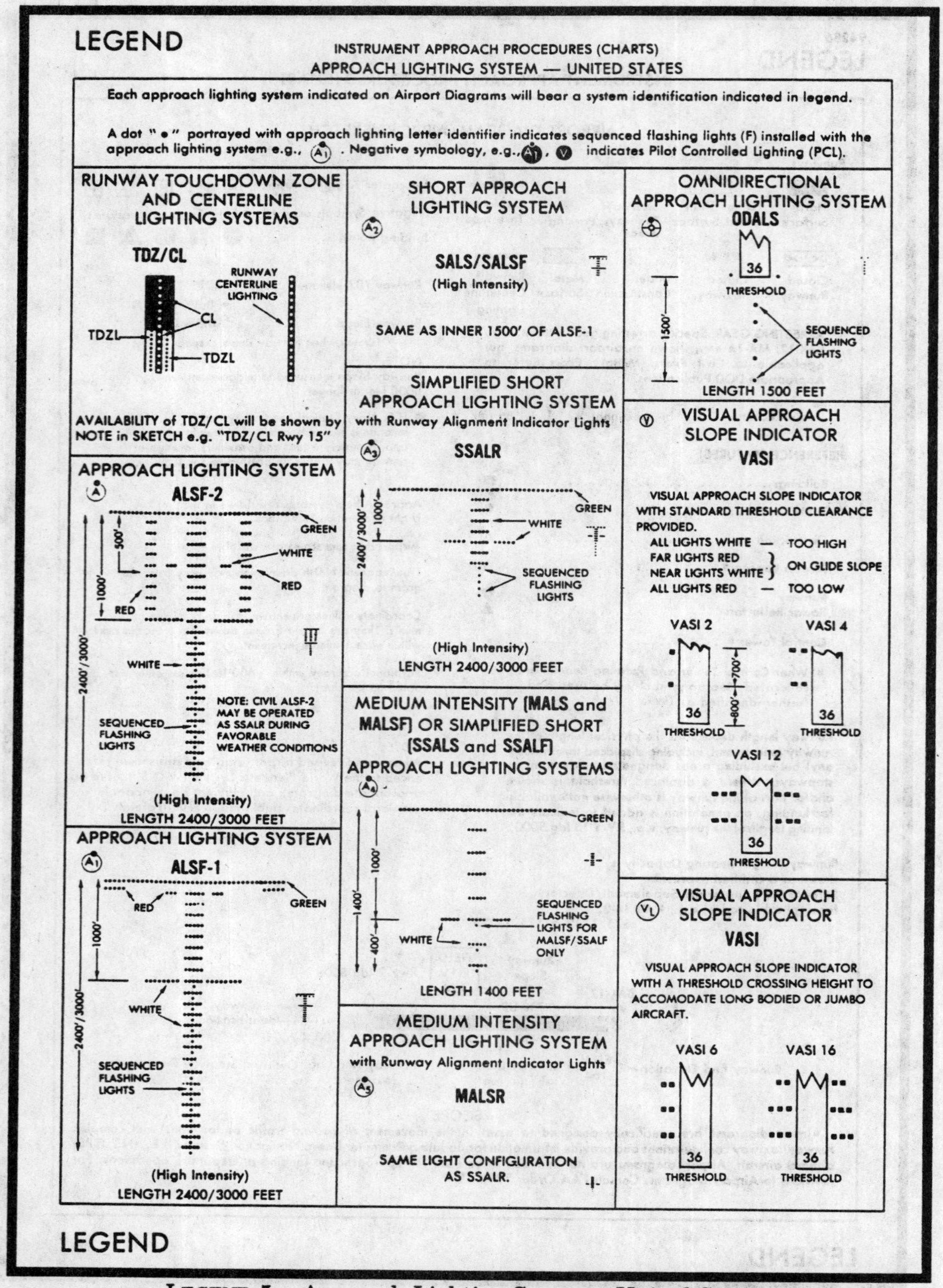

LEGEND 5.—Approach Lighting System—United States.

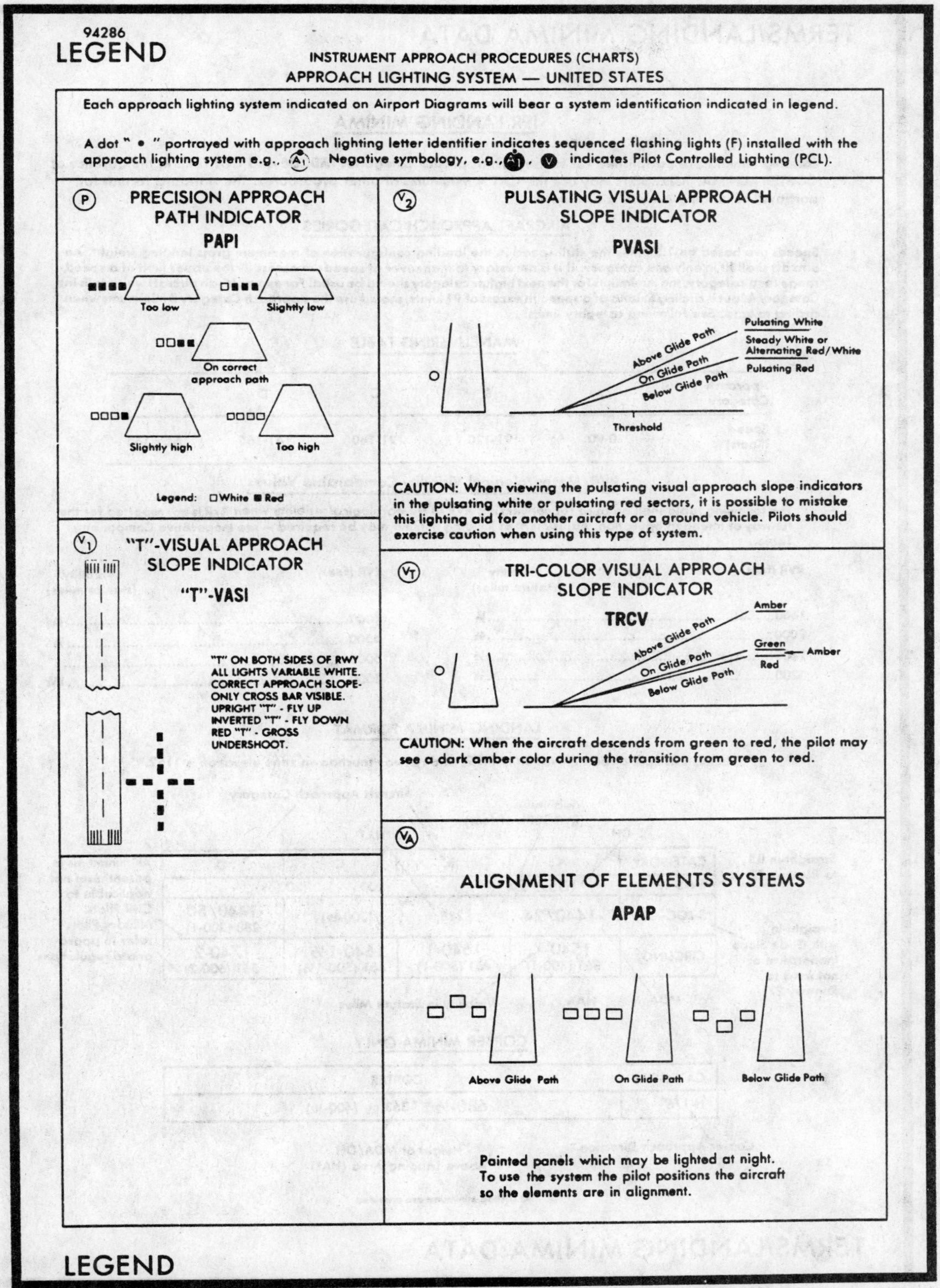

LEGEND 6.—Approach Lighting System—United States.

TERMS/LANDING MINIMA DATA

IFR LANDING MINIMA

Landing minima are established for six aircraft approach categories (ABCDE and COPTER). In the absence of COPTER MINIMA, helicopters may use the CAT A minimums of other procedures. The standard format for portrayal of landing minima is as follows:

AIRCRAFT APPROACH CATEGORIES

Speeds are based on 1.3 times the stall speed in the landing configuration of maximum gross landing weight. An aircraft shall fit in only one category. If it is necessary to maneuver at speeds in excess of the upper limit of a speed range for a category, the minimums for the next higher category should be used. For example, an aircraft which falls in Category A, but is circling to land at a speed in excess of 91 knots, should use the approach Category B minimums when circling to land. See following category limits:

MANEUVERING TABLE

Approach Category	A	B	C	D	E
Speed (Knots)	0-90	91-120	121-140	141-165	Abv 165

RVR/Meteorological Visibility Comparable Values

The following table shall be used for converting RVR to meteorological visibility when RVR is not reported for the runway of intended operation. Adjustment of landing minima may be required — see Inoperative Components Table.

RVR (feet)	Visibility (statute miles)	RVR (feet)	Visibility (statute miles)
1600	¼	4000	¾
2000	⅜	4500	⅞
2400	½	5000	1
3200	⅝	6000	1¼

LANDING MINIMA FORMAT

In this example airport elevation is 1179, and runway touchdown zone elevation is 1152.

CATEGORY	A	B	C	D
S-ILS-27	1352/24		200	(200-½)
S-LOC-27	1440/24	288	(300-½)	1440/50· 288 (300-1)
CIRCLING	1540-1 361 (400-1)	1640-1 461 (500-1)	1640-1½ 461 (500-1½)	1740-2 561 (600-2)

Visibility (RVR 100's of feet)
Aircraft Approach Category
DH
HAT
Straight-in ILS to Runway 27
Straight-in with Glide Slope Inoperative or not used to Runway 27
MDA
HAA
Visibility in Statute Miles
All minimums in parentheses not applicable to Civil Pilots. Military Pilots refer to appropriate regulations.

COPTER MINIMA ONLY

CATEGORY	COPTER
H-176°	680-½ 363 (400-½)

Copter Approach Direction
Height of MDA/DH Above Landing Area (HAL)

No circling minimums are provided

TERMS/LANDING MINIMA DATA

LEGEND 7.—IFR Landing Minima.

INOPERATIVE COMPONENTS OR VISUAL AIDS TABLE

Landing minimums published on instrument approach procedure charts are based upon full operation of all components and visual aids associated with the particular instrument approach chart being used. Higher minimums are required with inoperative components or visual aids as indicated below. If more than one component is inoperative, each minimum is raised to the highest minimum required by any single component that is inoperative. ILS glide slope inoperative minimums are published on instrument approach charts as localizer minimums. This table may be amended by notes on the approach chart. Such notes apply only to the particular approach category(ies) as stated. See legend page for description of components indicated below.

(1) ILS, MLS, and PAR

Inoperative Component or Aid	Approach Category	Increase Visibility
ALSF 1 & 2, MALSR, & SSALR	ABCD	1/4 mile

(2) ILS with visibility minimum of 1,800 RVR.

ALSF 1 & 2, MALSR, &SSALR	ABCD	To 4000 RVR
TDZI RCLS	ABCD	To 2400 RVR
RVR	ABCD	To 1/2 mile

(3) VOR, VOR/DME, VORTAC, VOR (TAC), VOR/DME (TAC), LOC, LOC/DME, LDA, LDA/DME, SDF, SDF/DME, RNAV, and ASR

Inoperative Visual Aid	Approach Category	Increase Visibility
ALSF 1 & 2, MALSR, & SSALR	ABCD	1/2 mile
SSALS, MALS, & ODALS	ABC	1/4 mile

(4) NDB

ALSF 1 & 2, MALSR & SSALR	C	1/2 mile
	ABD	1/4 mile
MALS, SSALS, ODALS	ABC	1/4 mile

LEGEND 11.—Inoperative Components or Visual Aids Table.

9.1 Navigation Systems/Miscellaneous Questions

1.
9021. When the approach procedure involves a procedure turn the maximum speed that should be observed from first overheading the course reversal IAF through the procedure turn is

A—180 knots IAS.
B—200 knots TAS.
C—200 knots IAS.

Answer (C) is correct (9021). *(AIM Para 5-4-8)*
When the approach procedure involves a procedure turn, the pilot should observe a maximum speed of not greater than 200 kt. IAS, from first overheading the course reversal IAF through completing the procedure turn maneuver, to ensure containment within the obstruction clearance area.
Answer (A) is incorrect because the maximum speed for the procedure turn maneuver is 200 kt. IAS, not 180 kt. IAS. Answer (B) is incorrect because airspeed limitations are based on indicated airspeed (IAS), not true airspeed (TAS). The maximum speed for the procedure turn maneuver is 200 kt. IAS, not 200 kt. TAS.

2.
9022. Pilots should notify controllers on initial contact that they have received the ATIS broadcast by

A—stating "Have Numbers."
B—stating "Have Weather."
C—repeating the alphabetical code word appended to the broadcast.

Answer (C) is correct (9022). *(AIM Para 4-1-13)*
Pilots should notify controllers on initial contact that they have received the ATIS broadcast by repeating the alphabetical code word appended to the broadcast.
Answer (A) is incorrect because the use of the phrase "Have Numbers" means that the pilot received only the wind, runway, and altimeter information. It does not indicate receipt of the ATIS broadcast and should never be used for this purpose. Answer (B) is incorrect because "Have Weather" does not indicate receipt of the ATIS broadcast and should never be used for this purpose.

3.
9017. During a LORAN approach the receiver must detect a lost signal, a signal blink within:

A—5 seconds of the occurrence and warn the pilot of the event.
B—10 seconds of the occurrence and warn the pilot of the event.
C—15 seconds of the occurrence and warn the pilot of the event.

Answer (B) is correct (9017). *(AIM Para 1-1-15)*
LORAN navigation for nonprecision approaches requires accurate and reliable information. During an approach, the occurrence of a signal blink or a loss of signal must be detected within 10 seconds, and the pilot must be notified.
Answer (A) is incorrect because, during a LORAN approach, a loss of signal must be detected within 10 seconds, not 5 seconds. Answer (C) is incorrect because, during a LORAN approach, a loss of signal must be detected within 10 seconds, not 15 seconds.

4.
9018. An off-route altitude which provides obstruction clearance of 1,000 feet in nonmountainous terrain areas and 2,000 feet in designated mountainous areas within the United States is called

A—Minimum Vectoring Altitude (MVA).
B—OROCA.
C—Minimum Safe/Sector Altitude (MSA).

Answer (B) is correct (9018). *(AIM Para 5-4-5)*
Off-route obstruction clearance altitude (OROCA) is an off-route altitude that provides obstruction clearance with a 1,000-ft. buffer in nonmountainous terrain areas and a 2,000-ft. buffer in designated mountainous areas within the U.S. This altitude may not provide signal coverage from ground-based navigation systems, ATC radar, or communications coverage.
Answer (A) is incorrect because MVAs in designated mountainous areas may provide only a 1,000-ft., not a 2,000-ft., obstacle clearance when required for flying terminal routes or for vectoring for an instrument approach. Answer (C) is incorrect because MSAs provide obstruction clearance of 1,000 ft., not 2,000 ft., in designated mountainous terrain.

5.
9025. What type navigation system is Inertial Navigation System (INS)? A navigation computer which provides position

A—from information by compass, airspeed, and an input of wind and variation data.
B—from radar-type sensors that measure ground speed and drift angles.
C—by signals from self-contained gyros and accelerometers.

Answer (C) is correct (9025). *(AIM Para 1-1-18)*
Inertial Navigation System (INS) is a totally self-contained system comprised of gyros, accelerometers, and a navigation computer, which provides airplane position and navigation information in response to signals resulting from inertial effects on system components, and does not require information from external sources. INS may be approved as the sole means of navigation or may be used in combination with other systems.
Answer (A) is incorrect because a Doppler radar uses the airplane's compass as a directional reference. It uses radar to detect and measure groundspeed, not airspeed, and drift angles. Answer (B) is incorrect because a Doppler radar, not INS, provides position information from radar-type sensors that measure groundspeed and drift angles.

9.2 Distance Measuring Equipment (DME)

6.
9024. Where does the DME indicator have the greatest error between the ground distance and displayed distance to the VORTAC?

A—High altitudes close to the VORTAC.
B—Low altitudes close to the VORTAC.
C—Low altitudes far from the VORTAC.

Answer (A) is correct (9024). *(IFH Chap VII)*
The mileage readout on the DME is the direct distance from the airplane to the VORTAC and is commonly referred to as slant-range distance. The difference between a measured distance on the surface and the DME slant-range is known as slant-range error and is greatest at high altitudes close to the VORTAC.
Answer (B) is incorrect because, at low altitudes close to the VORTAC, the slant-range error is less than at high altitudes close to the VORTAC. Answer (C) is incorrect because the slant-range error is at its smallest at low altitudes far from the VORTAC.

7.
9023. What DME indications should a pilot observe when directly over a VORTAC site at 12,000 feet?

A—0 DME miles.
B—2 DME miles.
C—2.3 DME miles.

Answer (B) is correct (9023). *(IFH Chap VII)*
When directly over a VORTAC site, the DME will display altitude in nautical miles (NM) above the site. 1 NM equals approximately 6,000 ft. At 12,000 ft. directly above the VORTAC, the DME will indicate 2 DME.
Answer (A) is incorrect because the DME would indicate 0 DME if the DME were sitting on top of the VORTAC site. Answer (C) is incorrect because 2.3 DME would be indicated if the airplane were at 13,800 ft. (6,000 x 2.3) above the VORTAC site.

9.3 VOR/VORTAC Identifier

8.
9019. What would be the identification when a VORTAC is undergoing routine maintenance and is considered unreliable?

A—A test signal, "TESTING", is sent every 30 seconds.
B—Identifier is preceded by "M" and an intermittent "OFF" flag would appear.
C—The identifier would be removed.

Answer (C) is correct (9019). *(AIM Para 1-1-3)*
The only positive method of identifying a VOR is by its Morse code identification or by the recorded automatic voice identification which is always indicated by the use of the word "V-O-R" following the range's name. During periods of maintenance, the facility may radiate a T-E-S-T code, or the identification code would be removed.
Answer (A) is incorrect because a facility may send a T-E-S-T code, not the test signal "TESTING," during periods of maintenance. Answer (B) is incorrect because an identifier preceded by "M" designates an identification group for the Microwave Landing System (MLS).

9.

9020. Which indication would be received when a VOR is undergoing maintenance and is considered unreliable?

A—Coded identification T-E-S-T.

B—Identifier is preceded by "M" and an intermittent "OFF" flag might appear.

C—An automatic voice recording stating the VOR is out-of-service for maintenance.

Answer (A) is correct (9020). *(AIM Para 1-1-3)*

The only positive method of identifying a VOR is by its Morse code identification or by the recorded automatic voice identification which is always indicated by the use of the word "V-O-R" following the range's name. During periods of maintenance, the facility may radiate a T-E-S-T code, or the identification code would be removed.

Answer (B) is incorrect because an identifier preceded by "M" designates an identification group for the Microwave Landing System (MLS). Answer (C) is incorrect because when a VOR is undergoing maintenance and is considered unreliable, the automatic voice recording used to identify the station is removed, not replaced with a message that the VOR is out-of-service.

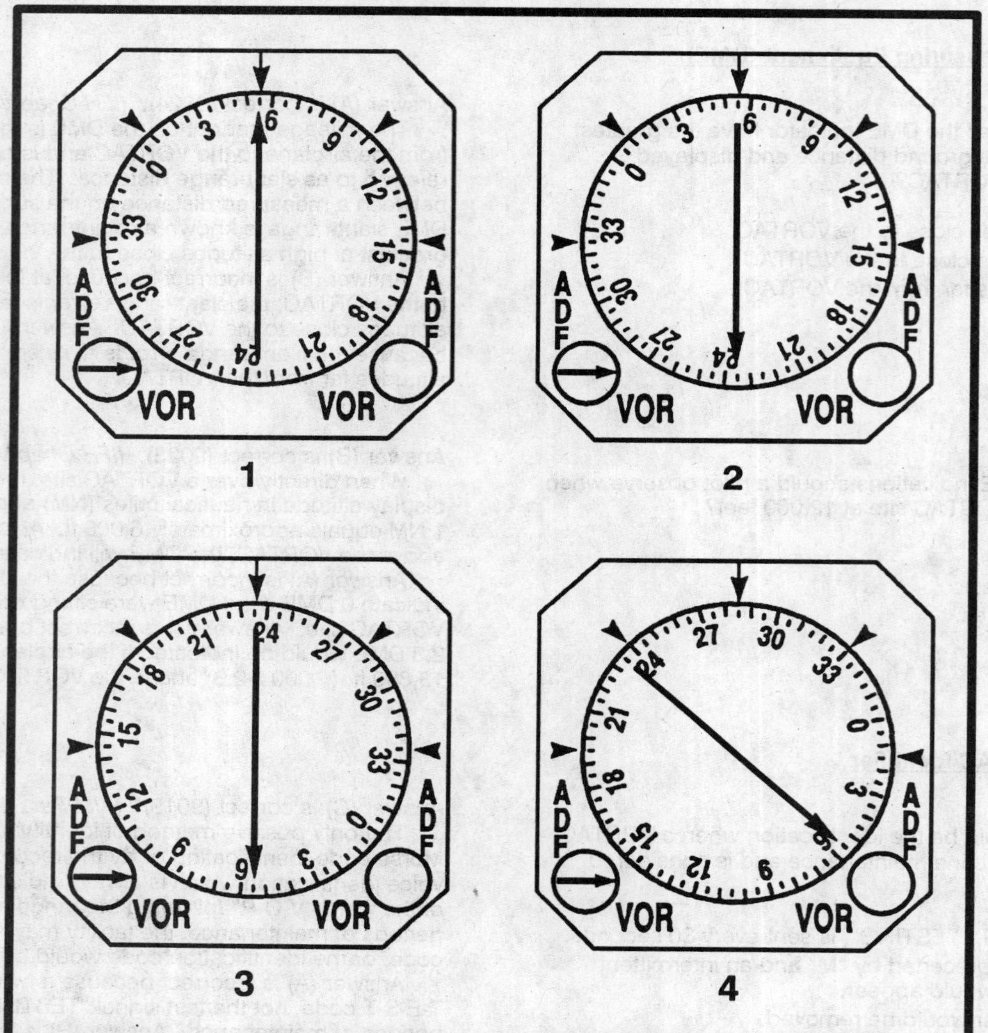

FIGURE 125.—RMI Illustrations.

9.4 RMI Interpretation

10.
8868. (Refer to figure 125 on page 288.) Which RMI illustration indicates the aircraft to be flying outbound on the magnetic bearing of 235° FROM the station? (Wind 050° at 20 knots.)

A—2.
B—3.
C—4.

Answer (B) is correct (8868). *(IFH Chap VIII)*
A radio magnetic indicator (RMI) consists of a rotating compass card which rotates as the airplane turns. The magnetic heading of the airplane is always directly under the index at the top of the instrument. The bearing pointer displays magnetic bearings to the selected station. The tail of the indicator tells you which radial you are on or the magnetic bearing from the station. Thus, a magnetic bearing of 235° from the station is indicated when the tail of the needle as in RMI 3 is on 235°. The 20-kt. wind from 050° is a direct tailwind which does not require wind correction.
Answer (A) is incorrect because illustration 2 indicates outbound on the 055° radial from the station. Answer (C) is incorrect because illustration 4 indicates a large wind correction to the right, e.g., to compensate for a strong crosswind which does not exist in this question.

11.
8869. (Refer to figure 125 on page 288.) What is the magnetic bearing TO the station as indicated by illustration 4?

A—285°.
B—055°.
C—235°.

Answer (B) is correct (8869). *(IFH Chap VIII)*
The magnetic heading of the airplane is always directly under the index at the top of the instrument. The bearing pointer displays the magnetic bearing to the selected station. In RMI 4, the needle is pointing to 055°, which is the magnetic bearing to the station.
Answer (A) is incorrect because 285° is the magnetic heading in illustration 4. Answer (C) is incorrect because 235° is the radial from the station that the airplane is crossing in illustration 4.

12.
8870. (Refer to figure 125 on page 288.) Which RMI illustration indicates the aircraft is southwest of the station and moving closer TO the station?

A—1.
B—2.
C—3.

Answer (A) is correct (8870). *(IFH Chap VIII)*
If the airplane is to the southwest of the station and moving toward it, the heading and the needle should both be indicating northeast, which is shown in RMI 1. It indicates a magnetic bearing to the station of 055°. The heading is also 055°, which means the airplane is flying to the station.
Answer (B) is incorrect because RMI 2 indicates northeast of the VOR and flying away (northeast). Answer (C) is incorrect because RMI 3 indicates flying away (to the southwest) from the station.

13.
8871. (Refer to figure 125 on page 288.) Which RMI illustration indicates the aircraft is located on the 055° radial of the station and heading away from the station?

A—1.
B—2.
C—3.

Answer (B) is correct (8871). *(IFH Chap VIII)*
The magnetic heading of the airplane is always directly under the index at the top of the instrument. The bearing pointer displays magnetic bearings to the selected station. The tail of the indicator tells you which radial you are on or the magnetic bearing from the station. Thus, a magnetic bearing of 055° from the station is indicated when the tail of the needle is on 055°, as in 2. The heading is also 055°, which means you are flying northeast, which is away from the station, and you are on the 055° radial.
Answer (A) is incorrect because illustration 1 indicates the airplane is on the 235° radial flying toward the station. Answer (C) is incorrect because illustration 3 indicates the airplane is flying away from the station on the 235° radial.

9.5 HSI Interpretation

14.
8984. (Refer to figure 139 below.) What is the lateral displacement of the aircraft in nautical miles from the radial selected on the No. 1 NAV?

A—5.0 NM.
B—7.5 NM.
C—10.0 NM.

Answer (A) is correct (8984). *(IFH Chap VIII)*

On VORs, the displacement from course is approximately 200 ft. per dot per NM. At 30 NM from the station, one dot deflection indicates approximately 1 NM displacement of the airplane from the course centerline. At 60 NM, it would be 2 NM for every dot of displacement. Since here displacement is 2½ dots, the airplane would be 5 NM from the centerline.

Answer (B) is incorrect because 7.5 NM would be indicated by a displacement of almost 4 dots. Answer (C) is incorrect because 10.0 NM would be indicated by a full deflection.

15.
8985. (Refer to figure 139 below.) On which radial is the aircraft as indicated by the No. 1 NAV?

A—R-175.
B—R-165.
C—R-345.

Answer (C) is correct (8985). *(IFH Chap VIII)*

The course selector in Fig. 139 is set on 350° with a FROM reading, indicating that, if the course deflection bar were centered, the airplane would be on R-350. Since a total deflection is approximately 10° to 12°, one-half deflection is 5° to 6°. Here, deflection is less than one-half, so it is about 5°. The course deflection bar indicates that this airplane is to the left of R-350, which would be R-345.

Answer (A) is incorrect because R-175 would require a TO indicator. Answer (B) is incorrect because R-165 would require a TO indicator and a left deflection.

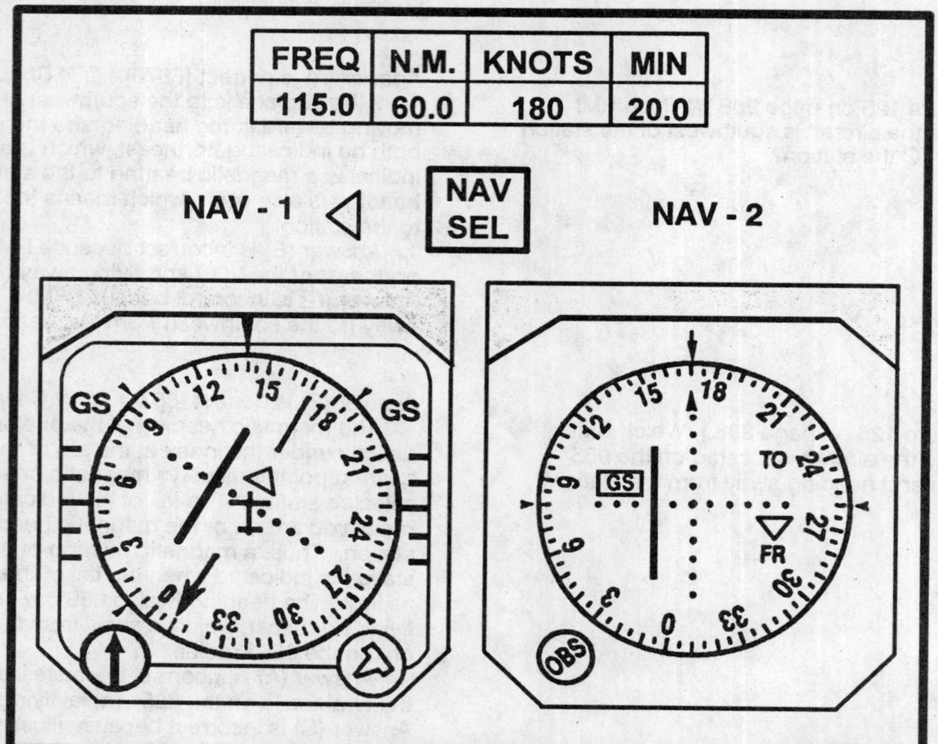

FIGURE 139.—No. 1 and No. 2 NAV Presentation.

16.
8986. (Refer to figure 139 on page 290.) Which OBS selection on the No. 1 NAV would center the CDI and change the ambiguity indication to a TO?

A—175.
B—165.
C—345.

Answer (B) is correct (8986). *(IFH Chap VIII)*
The course selector in Fig. 139 is set to 350° with a FROM indication, which means the airplane would be on R-350, if the course deviation bar were centered. However, the deviation bar indicates that the airplane is 5° (2° per dot) to the left of R-350, or R-345. Thus, to center the CDI and change the ambiguity indicator to TO, the OBS should be set to the reciprocal of 345°, which is 165° (345°-180°).
Answer (A) is incorrect because an OBS setting of 175° would change the ambiguity indication to TO, but it would not center the CDI. Answer (C) is incorrect because an OBS setting of 345° would center the CDI, but the ambiguity indication would be FROM, not TO.

17.
8987. (Refer to figure 139 on page 290.) What is the lateral displacement in degrees from the desired radial on the No. 2 NAV?

A—1°.
B—2°.
C—4°.

Answer (C) is correct (8987). *(IFH Chap VIII)*
Since on a standard 5-dot VOR indicator a full deflection of 5 dots is about 10°, 2 dots means a 4° deflection.
Answer (A) is incorrect because a 1° lateral displacement is indicated by a ½-dot displacement of the CDI. Answer (B) is incorrect because a 2° lateral displacement is indicated by a 1-dot displacement of the CDI.

18.
8988. (Refer to figure 139 on page 290.) Which OBS selection on the No. 2 NAV would center the CDI?

A—174.
B—166.
C—335.

Answer (A) is correct (8988). *(IFH Chap VIII)*
The course selector in Fig. 139 is set to 170° (it is not an HSI; it is a VOR) and the TO-FROM indicator indicates FROM, which means the airplane would be on R-170 if the course deviation bar were centered. Since the bar indicates a left deflection (2° per dot), the airplane is to the right of the radial, or on R-174.
Answer (B) is incorrect because a right, not left, deflection would indicate R-166. Answer (C) is incorrect because the TO-FROM indicator is on FROM, not TO.

19.
8989. (Refer to figure 139 on page 290.) Which OBS selection on the No. 2 NAV would center the CDI and change the ambiguity indication to a TO?

A—166.
B—346.
C—354.

Answer (C) is correct (8989). *(IFH Chap VIII)*
The course selector in Fig. 139 is set to 170° (it is not an HSI; it is a VOR) and the TO-FROM indicator indicates FROM, which means the airplane would be on R-170 if the course deviation bar were centered. Since the bar indicates a left deflection (2° per dot), the airplane is to the right of the radial, or on the 174° radial. To obtain a TO indication, one would have to change the OBS selection by 180° from 174° to 354°.
Answer (A) is incorrect because a right deflection would currently mean the airplane is on R-166. To change the ambiguity indicator to a TO, 180° must be added to the current radial. Answer (B) is incorrect because a right, not left, deflection would mean the airplane is currently on R-166.

20.
9002. (Refer to figures 142 and 143 on page 292.) To which aircraft position does HSI presentation "A" correspond?

A—1.
B—8.
C—11.

Answer (A) is correct (9002). *(IFH Chap VIII)*
On Figs. 142 and 143, HSI "A" has a VOR course selection of 090°, with a TO indication, meaning the airplane is to the left of the 360/180 radials. It has a right deflection, which means it is north of the 270/090 radials. The airplane heading is 205°, which means airplane 1 is described.
Answer (B) is incorrect because airplane 8 is to the right of the 360/180 radials, which would require a FROM indication. Answer (C) is incorrect because airplane 11 is to the right of the 360/180 radials and is south of the 270/090 radials, which would require a FROM indication and a left deviation indication.

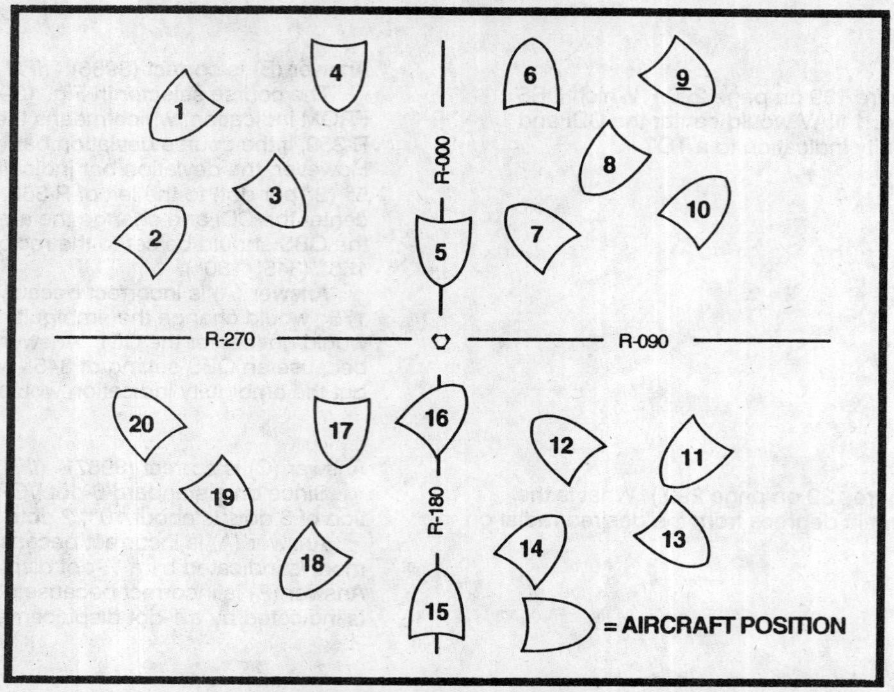

FIGURE 142.—Aircraft Position.

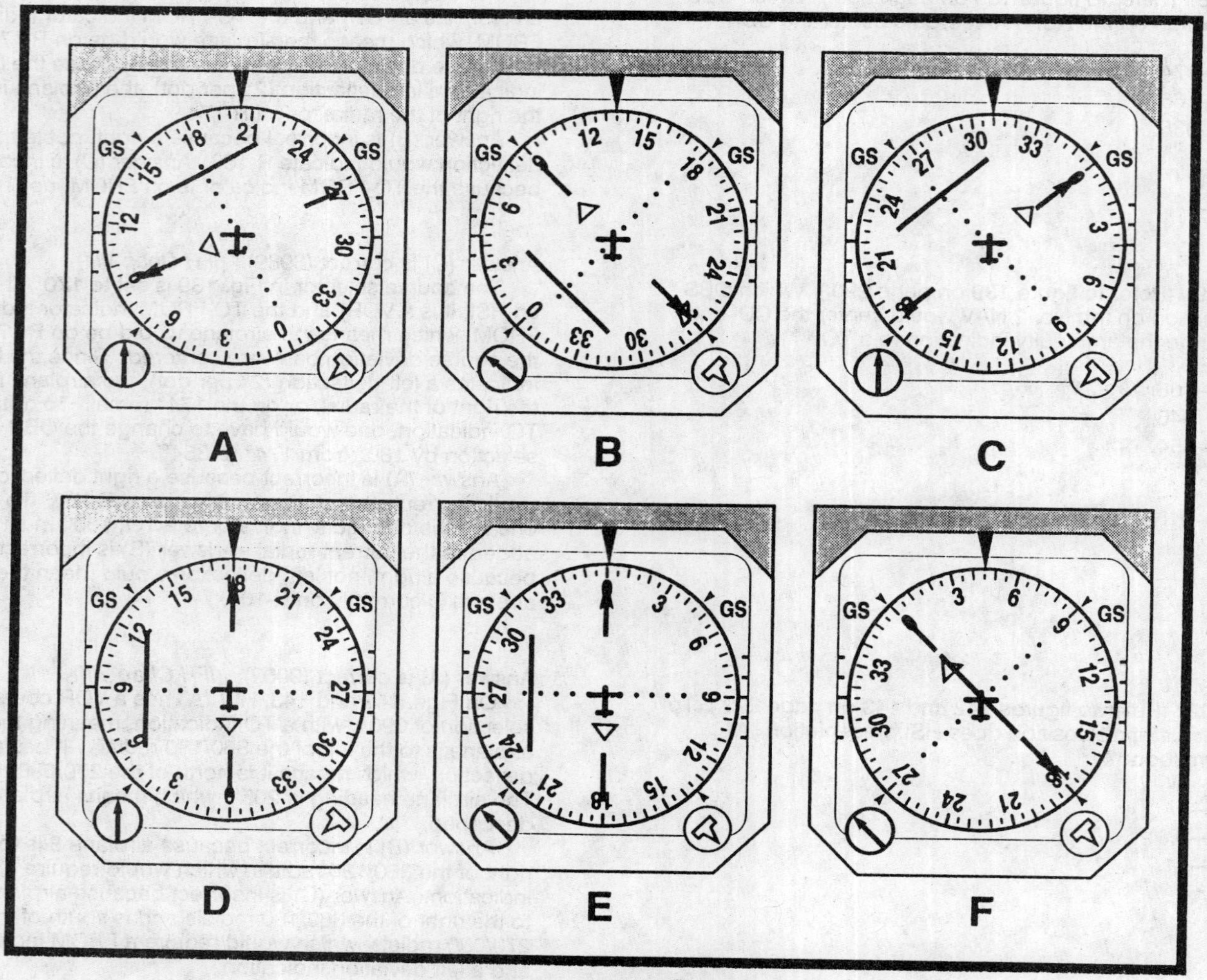

FIGURE 143.—HSI Presentation.

21.
9003. (Refer to figures 142 and 143 on page 292.) To which aircraft position does HSI presentation "B" correspond?

A—9.
B—13.
C—19.

Answer (C) is correct (9003). *(IFH Chap VIII)*
On Figs. 142 and 143, HSI "B" has a VOR course selection of 270° with a FROM indication, meaning that the airplane is to the left of the 360/180 radials. Since it has a right deflection, the airplane is south of R-270. Given a heading of 135°, airplane 19 is described.
Answer (A) is incorrect because airplane 9 would require a left, not right, course deflection bar indication and a TO indication. Answer (B) is incorrect because airplane 13 is to the right of the 360/180 radials and would require a TO indication.

22.
9004. (Refer to figures 142 and 143 on page 292.) To which aircraft position does HSI presentation "C" correspond?

A—6.
B—7.
C—12.

Answer (C) is correct (9004). *(IFH Chap VIII)*
On Figs. 142 and 143, HSI "C" has a VOR course selection of 360° with a TO indication, meaning the airplane is south of the 270/090 radials. Since the course deflection bar is to the left, the airplane is to the east of the 180° radial. Given a 310° heading, airplane 12 is described.
Answer (A) is incorrect because airplane 6 has a heading of 360° and is north of the 270/090 radials, which would require a FROM indication. Answer (B) is incorrect because airplane 7 is north of the 270/090 radials, which would require a FROM indication.

23.
8999. (Refer to figures 142 and 143 on page 292.) To which aircraft position does HSI presentation "D" correspond?

A—4.
B—15.
C—17.

Answer (C) is correct (8999). *(IFH Chap VIII)*
On Figs. 142 and 143, HSI "D" has a VOR course selection (OBS) of 180°. Its FROM indication means the airplane is south of R-270/090. Since the course deflection bar is to the left, the airplane is west of R-180. Given the heading of 180°, the position describes airplane 17.
Answer (A) is incorrect because airplane 4 is to the north of the 270/090 radials, which would require a TO indication. Answer (B) is incorrect because the course deflection bar on airplane 15 would have a centered deflection bar and a heading of 360°.

24.
9000. (Refer to figures 142 and 143 on page 292.) To which aircraft position does HSI presentation "E" correspond?

A—5.
B—6.
C—15.

Answer (B) is correct (9000). *(IFH Chap VIII)*
On Figs. 142 and 143, HSI "E" has a VOR course selection of 360°. Its FROM indication means the airplane is north of R-270/090. Given the course deflection bar to the left, the airplane is to the east of the 360° radial. Given the 360° heading, the position describes airplane 6.
Answer (A) is incorrect because airplane 5 would have a centered deflection bar and has a heading of 180°. Answer (C) is incorrect because airplane 15 is to the south of the 270/090 radials, which would require a TO indication, and the deflection bar would be centered.

25.
9001. (Refer to figures 142 and 143 on page 292.) To which aircraft position does HSI presentation "F" correspond?

A—10.
B—14.
C—16.

Answer (C) is correct (9001). *(IFH Chap VIII)*
On Figs. 142 and 143, HSI "F" has a VOR course selection of 180° with a FROM indication, meaning that the airplane is south of the 270/090 radials. Since the course deflection bar is centered, the airplane is on R-180. Given a heading of 045° (at the top of the HSI), airplane 16 is described.
Answer (A) is incorrect because airplane 10 is north of the 270/090 radials and east of the 360/180 radials, which would require a TO indication and a right course deflection. Answer (B) is incorrect because airplane 14 is to the east of R-180, which would require a right course deflection.

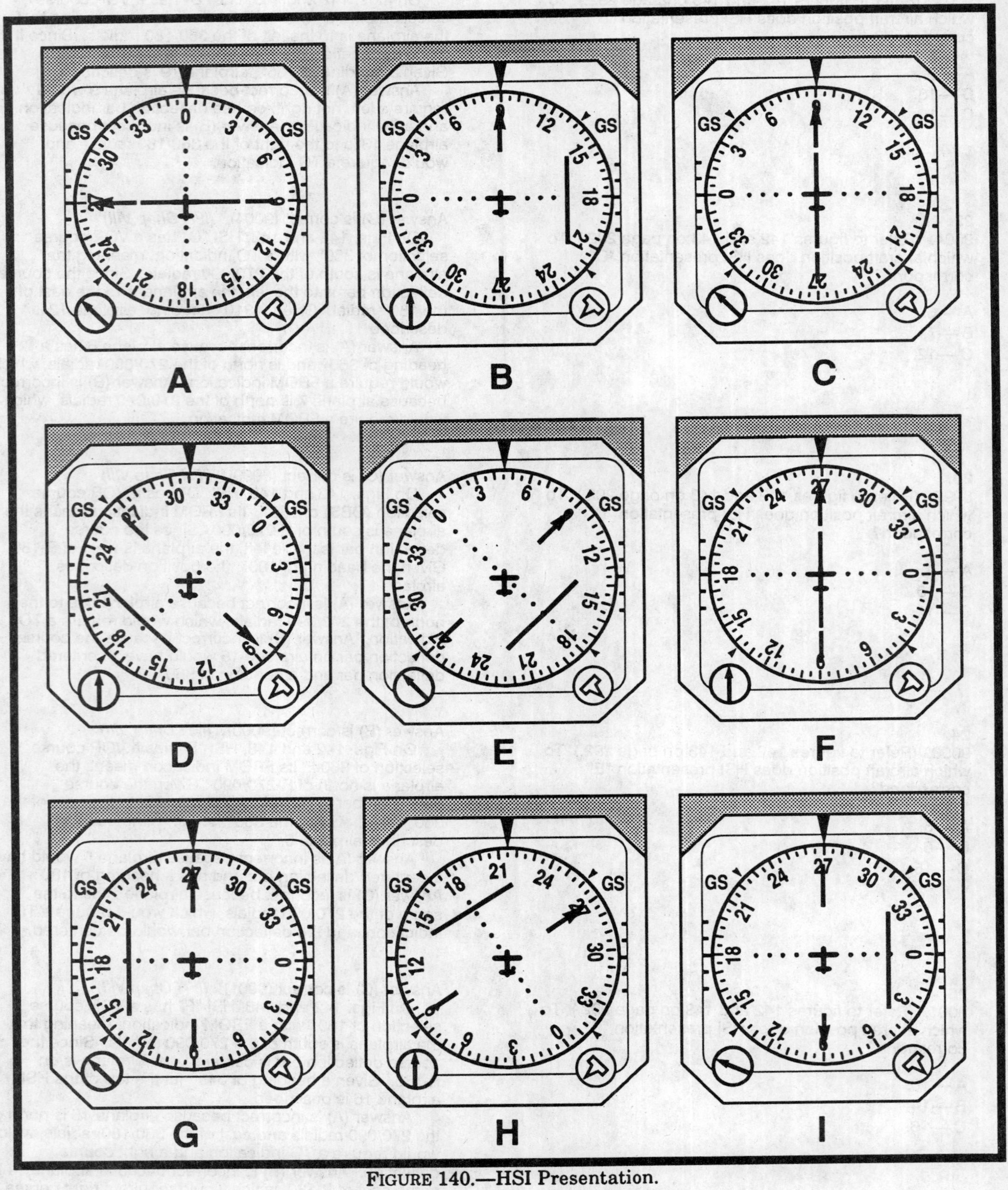

FIGURE 140.—HSI Presentation.

9.6 HSI/Localizer

NOTE: Airplanes B, C, D, E, and I have back course settings of 090°, which means there is reverse sensing irrespective of the airplane's heading.

26.
8990. (Refer to figure 140 on page 294 and figure 141 below.) To which aircraft position(s) does HSI presentation "A" correspond?

A—9 and 6.
B—9 only.
C—6 only.

Answer (A) is correct (8990). *(IFH Chap VII)*
On Figs. 140 and 141, HSI "A" has a heading of 360° with no localizer deviation, which means the airplane is on the localizer. Airplanes 6 and 9 are on the localizer with a 360° heading.

Answer (B) is incorrect because the indication will be the same on both the front course and the back course. Answer (C) is incorrect because the indication will be the same on both the front and the back course.

27.
8991. (Refer to figure 140 on page 294 and figure 141 below.) To which aircraft position(s) does HSI presentation "B" correspond?

A—11.
B—5 and 13.
C—7 and 11.

Answer (B) is correct (8991). *(IFH Chap VII)*
On Figs. 140 and 141, HSI "B" has a heading of 090°. It has a localizer setting at 090° with a right deflection, meaning the airplane is south of the localizer. Both airplanes 5 and 13 are described. Note the back course setting. If the front course 270° (instead of 90°) had been set, normal (rather than reverse) sensing would be indicated.

Answer (A) is incorrect because airplane 11 has a 270° heading. Answer (C) is incorrect because airplanes 7 and 11 have 270° headings.

28.
8992. (Refer to figure 140 on page 294 and figure 141 below.) To which aircraft position does HSI presentation "C" correspond?

A—9.
B—4.
C—12.

Answer (C) is correct (8992). *(IFH Chap VII)*
On Figs. 140 and 141, HSI "C" has a heading of 090° with a centered course deflection bar, which means the airplane is on the localizer with a 090° heading, which is airplane 12. The back course setting (090) has no effect because the deflection bar is centered.

Answer (A) is incorrect because airplane 9 has a 360° heading. Answer (B) is incorrect because airplane 4 has a 270° heading.

29.
8993. (Refer to figure 140 on page 294 and figure 141 below.) To which aircraft position does HSI presentation "D" correspond?

A—1.
B—10.
C—2.

Answer (C) is correct (8993). *(IFH Chap VII)*
On Figs. 140 and 141, HSI "D" has a heading of 310° in a back course setting (090), resulting in reverse sensing. It has a right deflection, meaning the airplane is south of the localizer. Thus, airplane 2 is described.

Note that HSI "D" incorrectly shows a course of 085 instead of 090.

Answer (A) is incorrect because airplane 1 is on a 225° heading, not a 310° heading, and is north of the localizer. Answer (B) is incorrect because airplane 10 has a 135° heading, and is north of the localizer.

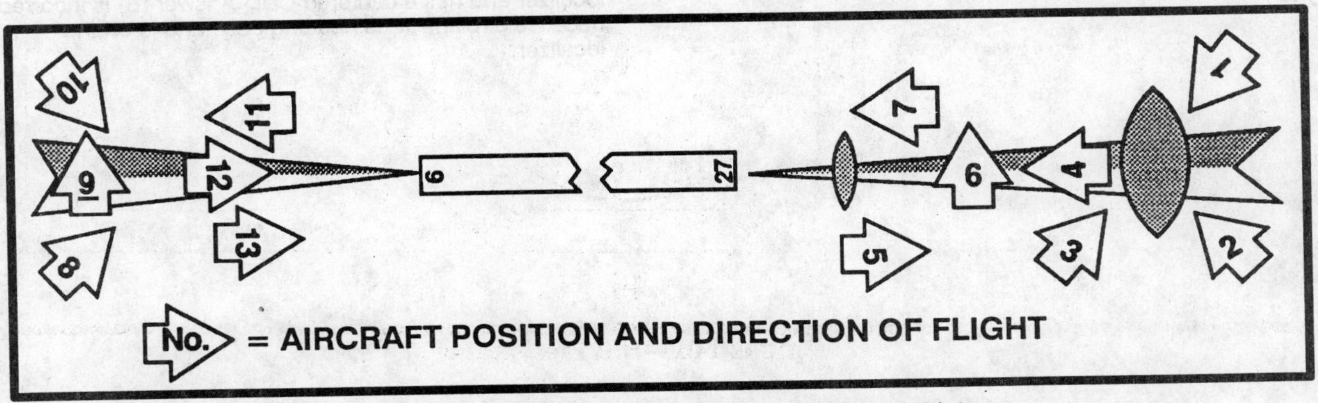

FIGURE 141.—Aircraft Position and Direction of Flight

30.
8994. (Refer to figures 140 and 141 on pages 294 and 295.) To which aircraft position(s) does HSI presentation "E" correspond?

A—8 only.
B—8 and 3.
C—3 only.

Answer (B) is correct (8994). *(IFH Chap VII)*
On Figs. 140 and 141, HSI "E" has a heading of 045°. It has a right deflection with a back course HSI setting of 090. This results in reverse sensing, meaning the airplane is south of the localizer. Thus, airplanes 3 and 8 are described.
Answer (A) is incorrect because both airplanes 8 and 3 have a 045° heading and are south of the localizer. Answer (C) is incorrect because both airplanes 8 and 3 have a 045° heading and are south of the localizer.

31.
8995. (Refer to figures 140 and 141 on pages 294 and 295.) To which aircraft position does HSI presentation "F" correspond?

A—4.
B—11.
C—5.

Answer (A) is correct (8995). *(IFH Chap VII)*
On Figs. 140 and 141, HSI "F" has a localizer setting at 270° with a centered bar and a 270° heading, which is airplane 4.
Answer (B) is incorrect because airplane 11 has a left course deviation bar. Answer (C) is incorrect because airplane 5 has a 090° heading, not 270°. It also should have a right deflection because it is south of the localizer.

32.
8996. (Refer to figures 140 and 141 on pages 294 and 295.) To which aircraft position(s) does HSI presentation "G" correspond?

A—7 only.
B—7 and 11.
C—5 and 13.

Answer (B) is correct (8996). *(IFH Chap VII)*
On Figs. 140 and 141, HSI "G" has a localizer setting at 270° with a left deviation, meaning the airplane is north of the localizer. With a 270° heading, airplanes 7 and 11 are described.
Answer (A) is incorrect because airplane 11 is also north of the localizer with a 270° heading. Answer (C) is incorrect because airplanes 5 and 13 have a 090° heading and are also south, not north, of the localizer.

33.
8997. (Refer to figures 140 and 141 on pages 294 and 295.) To which aircraft position does HSI presentation "H" correspond?

A—8.
B—1.
C—2.

Answer (B) is correct (8997). *(IFH Chap VII)*
On Figs. 140 and 141, HSI "H" has a localizer setting at 270° with a left deviation, meaning the airplane is north of the localizer. Given a heading of 215°, airplane 1 is described.
Answer (A) is incorrect because airplane 8 has a heading of 045° and is located south of the localizer. Answer (C) is incorrect because airplane 2 has a heading of 315° and is located south of the localizer.

34.
8998. (Refer to figures 140 and 141 on pages 294 and 295.) To which aircraft position does HSI presentation "I" correspond?

A—4.
B—12.
C—11.

Answer (C) is correct (8998). *(IFH Chap VII)*
On Figs. 140 and 141, HSI "I" has a left deviation with a back course HSI setting of 090 resulting in reverse sensing. Thus, the airplane is north of the localizer. Airplane 11 has a 270° heading and is north of the localizer.
Answer (A) is incorrect because airplane 4 is on the localizer and has a centered CDI. Answer (B) is incorrect because airplane 12 is heading 090° and is on the localizer.

9.7 Holding

35.
8861. (Refer to figure 123 below.) You receive this ATC clearance:

"...HOLD EAST OF THE ABC VORTAC ON THE ZERO NINER ZERO RADIAL, LEFT TURNS..."

What is the recommended procedure to enter the holding pattern?

A—Parallel only.
B—Direct only.
C—Teardrop only.

Answer (A) is correct (8861). *(AIM Para 5-3-7)*
You are cleared to hold east of the ABC VORTAC with left turns on R-090. The holding side will be south of R-090, and you are entering from the southwest on a 55° heading (see Fig. 123). Draw the 70° line through the VOR and on R-340, R-160. A parallel entry is appropriate for R-160 to R-270.

R-270 to R-340 Teardrop
R-340 to R-160 Direct
R-160 to R-270 Parallel

Answer (B) is incorrect because a direct entry would be appropriate if you were coming in on R-340 to R-160. Answer (C) is incorrect because a teardrop entry would be appropriate if you were coming in from R-270 to R-340.

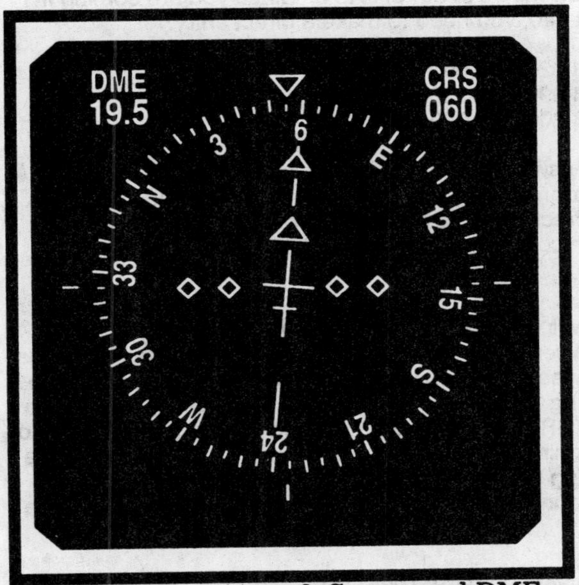

FIGURE 123.—Aircraft Course and DME Indicator.

36.
8862. (Refer to figure 123 above.) You receive this ATC clearance:

"...CLEARED TO THE ABC VORTAC. HOLD SOUTH ON THE ONE EIGHT ZERO RADIAL..."

What is the recommended procedure to enter the holding pattern?

A—Teardrop only.
B—Direct only.
C—Parallel only.

Answer (B) is correct (8862). *(AIM Para 5-3-7)*
You are cleared to hold south on the 180° radial with right turns, which means you will be to the east of R-180. Since you are coming in from the southwest (R-240), you can make a direct entry.

R-290 to R-360 Teardrop
R-360 to R-110 Parallel
R-110 to R-290 Direct

Answer (A) is incorrect because a teardrop entry would be appropriate only from R-290 to R-360. Answer (C) is incorrect because a parallel entry would be appropriate only from R-360 to R-110.

37.
8863. (Refer to figure 123 on page 297.) You receive this ATC clearance:

"...CLEARED TO THE XYZ VORTAC. HOLD NORTH ON THE THREE SIX ZERO RADIAL, LEFT TURNS..."

What is the recommended procedure to enter the holding pattern?

A—Parallel only.
B—Direct only.
C—Teardrop only.

Answer (C) is correct (8863). *(AIM Para 5-3-7)*
Holding north of the XYZ VORTAC with left turns on R-360 means you are on the east side of the radial. Since you are coming in from the southwest (R-240), you will be making a teardrop entry.

R-180 to R-250 Teardrop
R-250 to R-070 Direct
R-070 to R-180 Parallel

Answer (A) is incorrect because a parallel approach would be appropriate only if coming in between R-070 and R-180. Answer (B) is incorrect because a direct entry is appropriate only between R-250 and R-070.

38.
8864. (Refer to figure 123 on page 297.) You receive this ATC clearance:

"...CLEARED TO THE ABC VORTAC. HOLD WEST ON THE TWO SEVEN ZERO RADIAL..."

What is the recommended procedure to enter the holding pattern?

A—Parallel only.
B—Direct only.
C—Teardrop only.

Answer (B) is correct (8864). *(AIM Para 5-3-7)*
You are cleared to hold west on R-270 with right turns, so you will be south of R-270. Since you are coming in on R-240, you need to make a direct entry.

R-020 to R-090 Teardrop
R-090 to R-200 Parallel
R-200 to R-020 Direct

Answer (A) is incorrect because a parallel entry is appropriate only on R-090 to R-200. Answer (C) is incorrect because a teardrop entry is appropriate only when coming in on R-020 to R-090.

39.
8865. (Refer to figure 124 below.) A pilot receives this ATC clearance:

"...CLEARED TO THE ABC VORTAC. HOLD WEST ON THE TWO SEVEN ZERO RADIAL..."

What is the recommended procedure to enter the holding pattern?

A—Parallel or teardrop.
B—Parallel only.
C—Direct only.

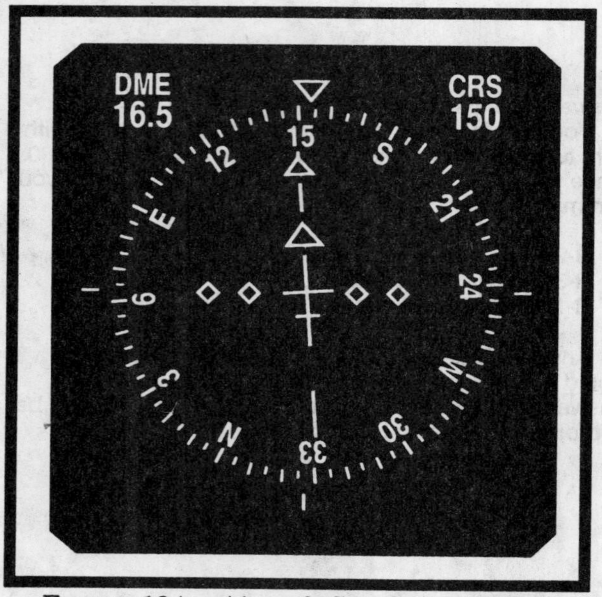

FIGURE 124.—Aircraft Course and DME Indicator.

Answer (C) is correct (8865). *(AIM Para 5-3-7)*
When holding west on the 270° radial, use right turns because left turns were not stated in the clearance. The holding pattern will be to the south of the 270° radial, so the VORTAC (the fix) is at the end of the inbound leg. To determine entry procedures, draw a 70° line through the holding fix such that the 70° line crosses through the outbound leg one-third of the leg length from abeam the fix.

R-020 to R-090 Teardrop
R-090 to R-200 Parallel
R-200 to R-020 Direct

Since you are approaching the holding fix from the northwest (R-330) on a 155° heading, you will make a direct entry.
Answer (A) is incorrect because the parallel or teardrop entries are alternatives only when approaching on R-090. Answer (B) is incorrect because the parallel entry is appropriate only when approaching on R-090 to R-200.

40.
8866. (Refer to figure 124 on page 298.) A pilot receives this ATC clearance:

"...CLEARED TO THE XYZ VORTAC. HOLD NORTH ON THE THREE SIX ZERO RADIAL, LEFT TURNS..."

What is the recommended procedure to enter the holding pattern?

A—Teardrop only.
B—Parallel only.
C—Direct.

Answer (C) is correct (8866). *(AIM Para 5-3-7)*
Visualize a 360° radial with left turns. The pattern will be to the east of the radial with the holding fix being the VORTAC. Since you are approaching from the northwest with a heading of 155° (see Fig. 124), you will be able to make a direct entry.

R-180 to R-250 Teardrop
R-250 to R-070 Direct
R-070 to R-180 Parallel

Answer (A) is incorrect because, if you were approaching on R-180 to R-250, you would make a teardrop entry. Answer (B) is incorrect because, if you were approaching on R-070 to R-180, you would fly through the VOR, parallel the holding course, turn right to the holding course, and make a parallel entry.

41.
8867. (Refer to figure 124 on page 298.) A pilot receives this ATC clearance:

"...CLEARED TO THE ABC VORTAC. HOLD SOUTH ON THE ONE EIGHT ZERO RADIAL..."

What is the recommended procedure to enter the holding pattern?

A—Teardrop only.
B—Parallel only.
C—Direct only.

Answer (A) is correct (8867). *(AIM Para 5-3-7)*
If you are holding south on the 180° radial, you will have right turns because left turns are not specified and you will be on the east side of the radial (to cross the VORTAC at the end of your inbound leg). Draw the 70° line through the VORTAC on R-110, R-290. Since you are inbound on R-330 (Fig. 124), you would make a teardrop entry.

R-290 to R-360 Teardrop
R-360 to R-110 Parallel
R-110 to R-290 Direct

Answer (B) is incorrect because a parallel entry is appropriate from R-360 to R-110. Answer (C) is incorrect because a direct entry is appropriate from R-110 to R-290.

42.
8855. The maximum speed a propeller-driven airplane may hold at is

A—265 knots.
B—230 knots.
C—156 knots.

Answer (A) is correct (8855). *(AIM Para 5-3-7)*
The maximum holding airspeed for all aircraft (including a propeller-driven airplane) is 265 kt., when holding at an altitude above 14,000 ft. MSL.
Answer (B) is incorrect because, while 230 kt. is the maximum holding airspeed from 6,001 ft. to 14,000 ft., a higher airspeed of 265 kt. is permitted when holding at an altitude above 14,000 ft. Answer (C) is incorrect because 156 kt. is not a maximum holding speed for any altitude.

43.
8856. Maximum holding speed for a turbojet airplane above 14,000 feet is

A—210 knots.
B—230 knots.
C—265 knots.

Answer (C) is correct (8856). *(AIM Para 5-3-7)*
The maximum airspeed above 14,000 ft. for holding patterns is 265 kt. for all aircraft, including a turbojet airplane. This speed limit can be increased if necessary for safety reasons through discussion with ATC.
Answer (A) is incorrect because 210 kt. is not a maximum holding speed at any altitude. Answer (B) is incorrect because 230 kt. is the maximum holding speed for all aircraft from 6,001 ft. to 14,000 ft., not above 14,000 ft.

44.
8857. Maximum holding speed for a civil turbojet aircraft at a joint use airport (civil/Navy) between 7,000 and 14,000 feet is

A—200 knots.
B—265 knots.
C—230 knots.

Answer (C) is correct (8857). *(AIM Para 5-3-7)*
The maximum holding speed for all aircraft, including a civil turbojet, from 6,001 ft. to 14,000 ft. is 230 kt. Holding speeds are based on altitudes at joint-use airports.
Answer (A) is incorrect because 200 kt. is the maximum holding speed of all aircraft from the MHA (minimum holding altitude) through 6,000 ft., not from 6,001 ft. to 14,000 ft. Answer (B) is incorrect because 265 kt. is the maximum holding speed for all aircraft from 14,001 ft. and above.

45.
9418. What is the maximum holding speed for a civil turbojet holding at a civil airport at 15,000 ft. MSL, unless a higher speed is required due to turbulence or icing and ATC is notified?

A—265 knots.
B—230 knots.
C—250 knots.

Answer (A) is correct (9418). *(AIM Para 5-3-7)*
The maximum holding speed for ali aircraft, including a civil turbojet, above 14,000 ft. MSL is 265 kt. A higher airspeed may be used if necessary due to turbulence or icing and provided ATC is notified.
Answer (B) is incorrect because 230 kt. is the maximum holding speed for any aircraft holding at an altitude between 6,001 ft. and 14,000 ft., not above 14,000 ft. Answer (C) is incorrect because 250 kt. is not a maximum holding airspeed at any altitude.

46.
9419. Civil aircraft holding at a military or joint civil/military use airports should expect to operate at which holding pattern airspeed?

A—250 knots.
B—260 knots.
C—230 knots.

Answer (C) may be graded as correct (9419). *(AIM Para 5-3-7)*
On 2/26/98, the AIM no longer classified holding patterns as civil, military, propeller-driven, or turbojet. There are three recommended maximum holding airspeeds in three altitude ranges.
Formerly, civil aircraft holding at military or joint civil/military-use airports could expect to operate at a maximum holding pattern airspeed of 230 kt.
Answer (A) is incorrect because 250 kt. is not a maximum holding airspeed at any altitude. Answer (B) is incorrect because 230 kt. is the maximum holding airspeed for all aircraft from an altitude of 6,001 ft. to 14,000 ft.

47.
8858. When using a flight director system, what rate of turn or bank angle should a pilot observe during turns in a holding pattern?

A—3° per second or 25° bank, whichever is less.
B—3° per second or 30° bank, whichever is less.
C—1-1/2° per second or 25° bank, whichever is less.

Answer (A) is correct (8858). *(AIM Para 5-3-7)*
The maximum rate of turn or bank to be used when using a flight director system should be 3° per second or 25° bank, whichever is less.
Answer (B) is incorrect because maximum bank while holding using a flight director is 25° bank, not 30° bank. Answer (C) is incorrect because maximum bank while holding using a flight director is 25° bank or 3° per second, not 1½° per second, whichever is less.

48.
8860. When entering a holding pattern above 14,000 feet, the initial outbound leg should not exceed

A—1 minute.
B—1-1/2 minutes.
C—1-1/2 minutes or 10 NM, whichever is less.

Answer (B) is correct (8860). *(AIM Para 5-3-7)*
When at an altitude greater than 14,000 ft. MSL, the initial outbound leg should not exceed 1½ minutes. Timing for subsequent outbound legs should be adjusted as necessary to achieve proper inbound leg time (1½ minutes inbound).
Answer (A) is incorrect because an initial outbound leg of 1 min. should be used only when below 14,000 ft. Answer (C) is incorrect because a DME distance is issued only by the specified controller for aircraft equipped with DME capability. A DME distance is not required unless specified by the controller.

49.
8859. When holding at an NDB, at what point should the timing begin for the second leg outbound?

A—Abeam the holding fix or when the wings are level after completing the turn to the outbound heading, whichever occurs first.
B—At the end of a 1-minute standard rate turn after station passage.
C—When abeam the holding fix.

Answer (C) is correct (8859). *(AIM Para 5-3-7)*
Outbound timing begins over or abeam the fix, whichever occurs later. On the second turn, it will be abeam the fix. Only if the abeam position cannot be determined do you start timing when the turn to outbound is complete.
Answer (A) is incorrect because only when you cannot determine position abeam the fix should you start the timing when the turn is complete. Answer (B) is incorrect because abeam the fix is preferable and should be used rather than at the completion of a standard-rate turn, especially if turn completion occurs before coming abeam the fix.

9.8 IFR Charts and *Airport/Facility Directory*

50.
8810. (Refer to figures 110 and 112 on pages 302 and 304.) How should the pilot identify the position to leave V369 for the Cugar Four Arrival?

A—Intercept R-305 of IAH.
B—21 DME miles from TNV.
C—141 DME miles from DFW.

Answer (A) is correct (8810). *(STAR)*
The textual portion in the lower portion of the STAR in Fig. 112 states that a pilot from BILEE INT on V369 (TNV R-334) will intercept and track R-305 of IAH to CUGAR INT for the Cugar Four Arrival.
Answer (B) is incorrect because the pilot should leave V369 when (s)he intercepts R-305 of IAH, not 21 DME from TNV. Answer (C) is incorrect because the pilot should have switched to TNV VORTAC for V369 course guidance before BILEE INT and should not be using DFW VORTAC for any navigational guidance.

51.
8812. (Refer to figure 112 on page 304.) The Cugar Four Arrival ends

A—at BANTY INT.
B—at IAH VORTAC.
C—when cleared to land.

Answer (A) is correct (8812). *(STAR)*
The Cugar Four Arrival is provided in Fig. 112. At the bottom of the STAR is the textual description of the STAR. From CUGAR INT, the pilot should proceed via IAH R-305 to BANTY INT. From there, the pilot should expect vectors to the final approach course. Thus, the Cugar Four Arrival ends at BANTY INT.
Answer (B) is incorrect because the Cugar Four Arrival ends at BANTY INT, not at IAH VORTAC. Answer (C) is incorrect because a clearance to land will be given during the instrument approach procedure, which is after the end of the Cugar Four Arrival.

52.
8811. (Refer to figure 112 on page 304.) What action should the pilot take if communications were lost during the Cugar Four Arrival, after turning on the 305 radial of IAH?

A—Proceed direct to IAH VORTAC, then outbound on the IAH R-125 for a procedure turn for final approach.
B—From BANTY INT, proceed to the IAF on the IAH R-290, then continue on the IAH 10 DME Arc to final approach.
C—Proceed direct to IAH VORTAC, then to either IAF on the IAH 10 DME Arc to final approach.

Answer (C) is correct (8811). *(FAR 91.185)*
Refer to Fig. 112. If radio communications were lost during the Cugar Four Arrival to IAH after turning on the R-305 of IAH, the pilot would continue to the end of the Cugar Four Arrival, which is BANTY INT. If no other information was given, the pilot should proceed to IAH VORTAC, then to either IAF on the IAH 10 DME arc to the final approach course.
Answer (A) is incorrect because no procedure turn is indicated for the VOR/DME RWY 32R approach; thus, no procedure turn can be made to reverse course.
Answer (B) is incorrect because the pilot should proceed as filed to IAH, from BANTY INT, not to the nearest IAF.

53.
9569. (Refer to figures 111 and 112 on pages 303 and 304.) In addition to VOR and DME, what other avionics equipment is required to be operational, at takeoff, to fly the VOR/DME RWY 32R approach at IAH?

A—Altitude alerting system.
B—Standby VOR and DME receivers.
C—VHF communications and transponder equipment.

Answer (C) is correct (9569). *(AIM Para 3-2-3)*
The bottom of Fig. 111 provides an *Airport/Facility Directory* excerpt for Houston Intercontinental (IAH). The line above **Radio Aids to Navigation** identifies IAH as a TCA, which is now called Class B airspace. The equipment required to be operational at takeoff are two-way VHF communications and a Mode C transponder.
Answer (A) is incorrect because an altitude alerting system is not required for the VOR/DME RWY 32R approach at IAH. Answer (B) is incorrect because additional VOR and DME receivers are not required for the VOR/DME RWY 32R approach at IAH.

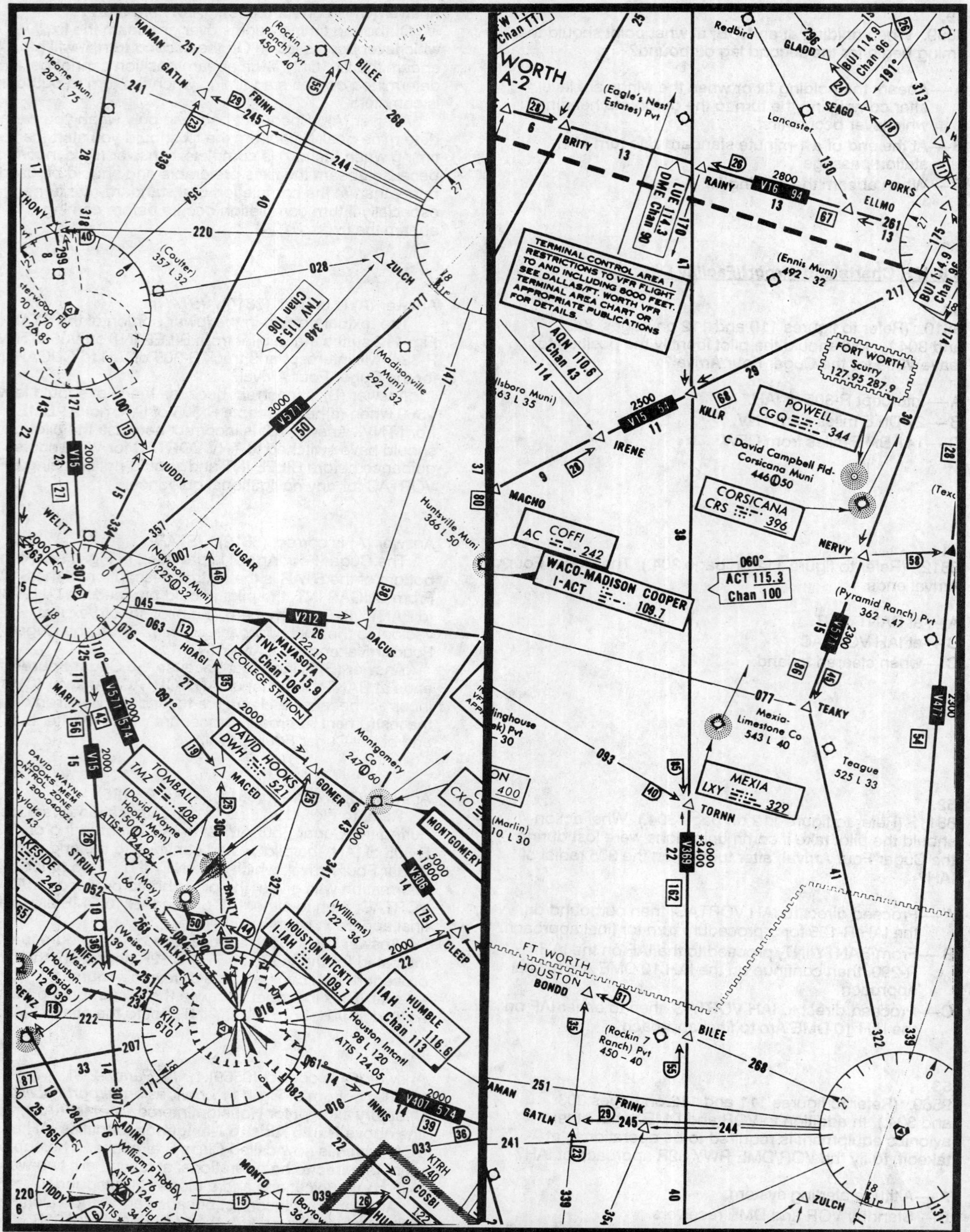

FIGURE 110.—IFR En Route Low Altitude Chart Segment.

TEXAS

§ DALLAS-FORT WORTH INTL (DFW) 12 NW UTC-6(-5DT) 32°53'47"N 97°02'28"W **DALLAS-FT. WORTH H-2K, 4F, 5B, L-13C, A IAP**
603 B **FUEL** 100LL, JET A OX 1,3 LRA CFR Index E
RWY 17L-35R: H11,388X150 (CONC-GRVD) S-120, D-200, DT-600, DDT-850 HIRL, CL
RWY 17L: ALSF2. TDZ. **RWY 35R:** MALSR. TDZ.
RWY 17R-35L: H11,388X200 (CONC-GRVD) S-120, D-200, DT-600, DDT-850 HIRL, CL
RWY 17R: SSALR TDZ. **RWY 35L:** TDZ. VASI(V6L).
RWY 18L-36R: H11,387X200 (CONC-GRVD) S-120, D-200, DT-600, DDT-850 HIRL, CL
RWY 18L: SSALR.TDZ. **RWY 36R:** TDZ. VASI(V6L).
RWY 18R-36L: H11,388X150 (CONC-GRVD) S-120, D-200, DT-600, DDT-850 HIRL, CL
RWY 18R: ALSF2. TDZ **RWY 36L:** MALSR. TDZ.
RWY 13L-31R: H9000X200 (CONC-GRVD) S-120, D-200, DT-600, DDT-850 HIRL, CL .5% up NW.
RWY 13L: TDZ. VASI(V6L)—Upper GA 3.25°TCH 93'. Lower GA 3.0°TCH 47'.
RWY 31 R: MALSR. TDZ.
RWY 13R-31L: H9300X150 (CONC-GRVD) S-120, D-220, DT-600, DDT-850 HIRL, CL
RWY 13 R: MALSR. TDZ. **RWY 31L:** TDZ.
RWY 18S-36S: H4000X100 (CONC)
AIRPORT REMARKS: Attended continuously. Prior Permission Required from arpt ops for General Aviation acft to proceed to airline terminal gate except to General Aviation Facility. Rwy 18S-36S located on taxiway G, 4000' long 100' wide restricted to prop acft 12,500 lbs. & below and stol acft daylight VFR plus IFR departures. Prior permission required from the primary tenant airlines to operate within central terminal area, CAUTION: proper minimum clearance may not be maintained within the central terminal area. Landing fee. Clearways 500x1000 each end Rwy 17L-35R, Rwy 17R-35L, Rwy 18L-36R and Rwy 18R-36L. Flight Notification Service (ADCUS) available.
WEATHER DATA SOURCES: LLWAS.
COMMUNICATIONS: ATIS 117.0 134.9 (ARR) 135.5 (DEP) **UNICOM** 122.95
FORT WORTH FSS (FTW) LC 624-8471, Toll free call, dial 1-800-WX-BRIEF. NOTAM FILE DFW
® **REGIONAL APP CON** 119.05(E) 119.4(E) 125.8(W) 132.1(W)
REGIONAL TOWER 126.55 (E) 124.15 (W) **GND CON** 121.65 133.15(E) 121.8 (W) **CLNC DEL** 128.25 127.5
® **REGIONAL DEP CON** 118.55 (E) 124.25 (WEST) 127.75 (NORTH-SOUTH)
TCA Group I: See VFR Terminal Area chart.
RADIO AIDS TO NAVIGATION: NOTAM FILE DFW.
(H) **VORTACW** 117.0 DFW Chan 117 32°51'57"N97°01'40"W at fld. 560/08E.
VOR Portion unusable 045°-050° all altitudes and distances, 350-100° beyond 30 NM below 2100'.
ISSUE NDB (LOM) 233 PK 32°47'35"N97°01'49"W 353° 5.1 NM to fld.
JIFFY NDB (LOM) 219 FL 32°59'45"N97°01'46"W 173° 5.1 NM to fld.
ILS/DME 109.5 I-LWN Chan 32 Rwy 13R
ILS/DME 109.1 I-FLQ Chan 28 Rwy 17L LOM JIFFY NDB
ILS 111.5 I-JHZ Rwy 17R LOM JIFFY NDB
ILS 111.3 I-CIX Rwy 18L
ILS/DME 111.9 I-VYN Chan 56 Rwy 18R
ILS 110.9 I-RRA Rwy 31R
ILS/DME 109.1 I-PKQ Chan 28 Rwy 35R LOM ISSUE NDB
ILS/DME 111.9 I-BXN Chan 56 Rwy 36L

§ HOUSTON INTERCONTINENTAL (IAH) 15N UTC-6(-5DT) 29°58'49"N 95°20'22"W **HOUSTON H-5B, L-17B IAP**
98 B S4 FUEL 100LL, JET A OX2 LRA CFR Index D
RWY 14L-32R: H1200X150 (CONC-GRVD) S-100, D-200, DT-400, DDT-778 HIRL, CL
RWY 14L: MALSR. VASI(V4L)—GA 3.0°TCH 54'. **RWY 32R:** MALSR.
RWY 09-27: H10000X150 (ASPH-GRVD) S-75, D-191, DT-400, DDT-850 HIRL,CL
RWY 09: MALSR. TDZ. PAPI(P4L)—GA 3.0°TCH 63'.
RWY 27: ALSF2. TDZ. PAPI(P4L)—GA 3.0°TCH 63'.
RWY 08-26: H9401X150 (CONC-GRVD) S-120, D-155, DT-265 HIRL, CL
RWY 08: MALSR. TDZ. **RWY 26:** ALSF2. TDZ. VASI(V4L)—GA 3.0°TCH 53'.
RWY 14R-32L: H6038X100 (ASPH-GRVD) S-30, D-60, DT-60 MIRL
RWY 14R: VASI(V4L)—GA 3.0°TCH 40'. Road. **RWY 32L:** VASI(V4L)—GA 3.0°TCH 45'.
AIRPORT REMARKS: Attended continuously. CAUTION: Birds on and in vicinity of arpt. CAUTION—Approach end of rwy 26 bright lgts approximately one mile from thld and 900' South of centerline. Caution—Deer on and in vicinity of arpt. Rwy 14R-32L CLOSED to acft over 140,000 lbs gross weight. Landing Fee. Flight Notification Service (ADCUS) available.
WEATHER DATA SOURCES: LLWAS
COMMUNICATIONS: ATIS 124.05 **UNICOM** 122.95
MONTGOMERY COUNTY FSS (CXO) Toll free call, dial 1-800-WX-BRIEF. NOTAM FILE IAH.
® **APP CON** 124.35 (West) 127.25 (North and East)
TOWER 118.1 (135.15 copter control) **GND CON** 121.7 **CLNC DEL** 128.1 (135.15 copter control)
® **DEP CON** 123.8 (West) 119.7 (North and East)
TCA Group II: VFR Terminal Area chart.
RADIO AIDS TO NAVIGATION: NOTAM FILE IAH.
HUMBLE (H) VORTACW 116.6 IAH Chan 113 29°57'24"N95°20'44"W at fld. 90/08E. **HIWAS.**
MARBE NDB (LOM) 379 HS 30°04'29"N 95°24'45"W 146° 5.9 NM to fld.
NIXIN NDB (LOM) 326 JY 29°59'36"N 95°12'54"W 257° 6.5 NM to fld.
ILS/DME 109.7 I-JYV Chan 34 Rwy 26 LOM NIXIN NDB
ILS 111.9 I-HSQ Rwy 14L LOM MARBE NDB
ILS/DME 109.7 I-IAH Chan 34 Rwy 08
ILS/DME 110.9 I-UYO Chan 34 Rwy 09
ILS 111.9 I-CDG Rwy 32R

FIGURE 111.—Airport / Facility Directory Excerpts.

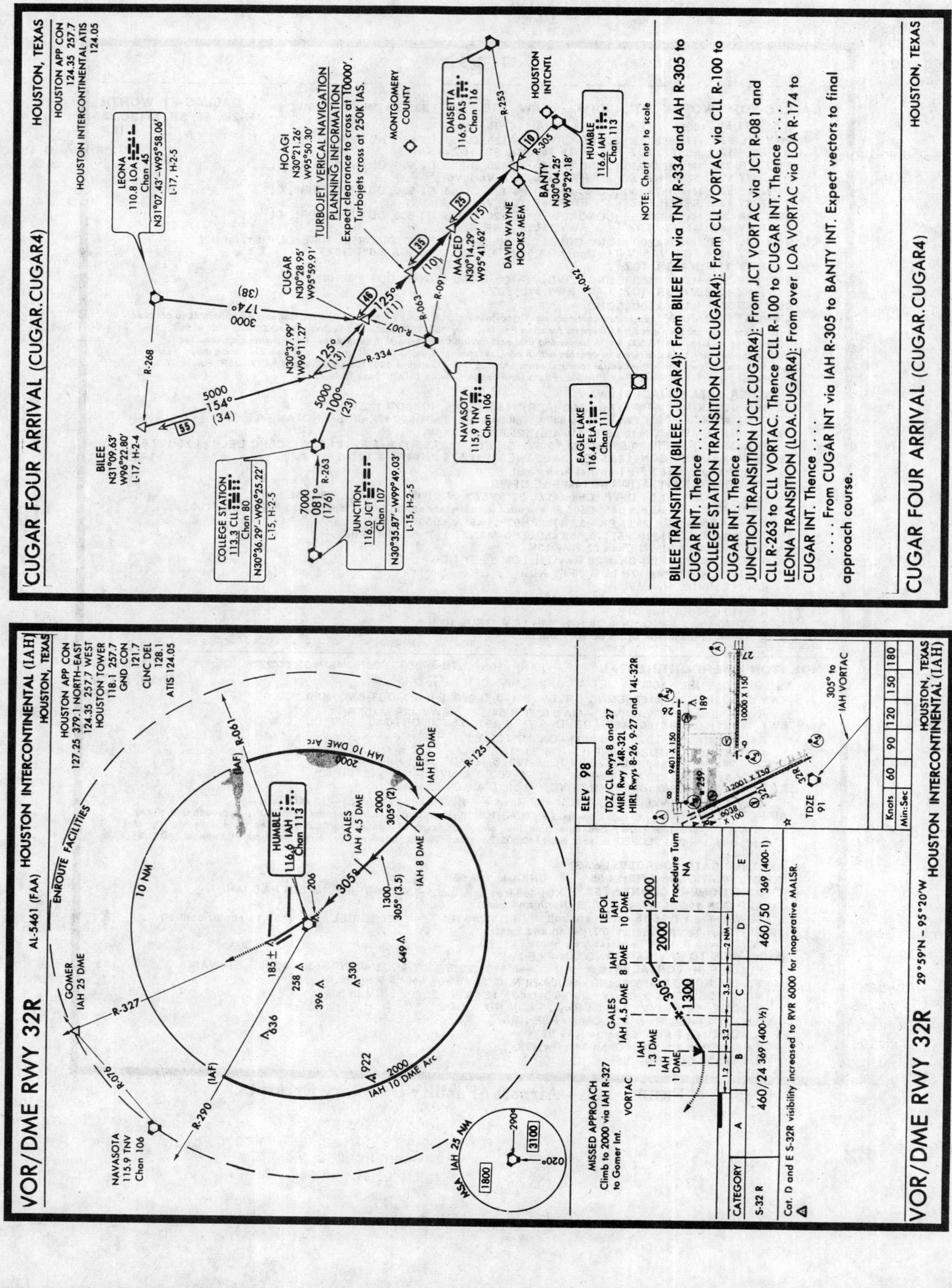

FIGURE 112.—VOR / DME RWY 32R (IAH) / Cugar Four Arrival (Cugar.Cugar4).

54.
9570. (Refer to figure 112 on page 304.) While arcing left on the IAH 10 DME Arc, the pilot experiences a left crosswind component. Where should the bearing pointer be referenced relative to the 90° (wingtip) position to maintain the 10 DME range?

A—On the left wingtip reference.
B—Behind the left wingtip reference.
C—Ahead of the left wingtip reference.

Answer (C) is correct (9570). *(IFH Chap VIII)*
While arcing left on the IAH 10 DME arc, a left crosswind component will cause the airplane to be blown away from the 10 DME arc. Thus, the airplane must be crabbed to the left to maintain the 10 DME arc, and the bearing pointer will point ahead of the left 90° wingtip reference.
Answer (A) is incorrect because the bearing pointer should be on the left wingtip reference in a calm wind, not a left crosswind. Answer (B) is incorrect because the bearing pointer should be behind the left wingtip reference when correcting for a right, not left, crosswind component.

55.
9571. (Refer to figures 111 and 112 on pages 303 and 304.) Which approach lighting is available for Rwy 32R?

A—MALSR with RAIL.
B—HIRL.
C—TDZ and CL.

Answer (A) is correct (9571). *(A/FD)*
The bottom half of Fig. 111 is the *A/FD* excerpt for Houston Intercontinental. The fourth line lists that the runway approach lighting system for RWY 32R is MALSR. MALSR is the abbreviation for medium-intensity approach lighting system (MALS) with runway alignment indicator lights (R or RAIL).
Answer (B) is incorrect because high-intensity runway lights (HIRL) are runway edge, not approach, light systems. Answer (C) is incorrect because touchdown zone (TDZ) and centerline lights (CL) are in-runway, not approach, lights and are not available on RWY 32R.

56.
8816. (Refer to figure 112 on page 304.) What effect on approach minimums, if any, does an inoperative MALSR have for an aircraft with an approach speed of 120 knots at IAH?

A—None.
B—Increases RVR to 5,000 feet.
C—Increases RVR to 6,000 feet.

Answer (B) is correct (8816). *(ACL)*
Refer to Legend 11 on page 285 for the Inoperative Components or Visual Aids Table. Item (3) is used for a VOR/DME approach. In the table, locate MALSR and move right to determine that all approach categories are affected; then move right to determine that the visibility minimum is increased ½ SM (or an RVR of 2,400 ft.). Refer to the VOR/DME RWY 32R IAP in Fig. 112 and locate the minimums section. An approach speed of 120 kt. is a Category B (91-120) airplane, and the visibility minimum is an RVR of 2,400 ft. With the MALSR inoperative, the approach minimum increases the visibility to 1 SM or an RVR of 5,000 ft.
Answer (A) is incorrect because, with an inoperative MALSR, there is no change to the MDA, but an increase of ½ mi. to the required visibility. Answer (C) is incorrect because an airplane with an approach speed of 141-165 kt. (Category D) or greater, not 120 kt., would have the visibility increased to RVR of 6,000 ft.

57.
8817. (Refer to figure 112 on page 304.) When is the earliest time the pilot may initiate a descent from 460 feet MSL to land at IAH?

A—Anytime after GALES INT if the runway environment is visible.
B—Only after the IAH 1.3 DME if the runway environment is visible.
C—Only after the IAH 1 DME if the runway environment is visible.

Answer (B) is correct (8817). *(AIM Para 5-4-5)*
Fig. 112 provides the IAP chart for the VOR/DME RWY 32R approach. In the left center of the chart is the profile view. At the IAH 1.3 DME is a bold **V**, which identifies a visual descent point (VDP). At the VDP, a normal descent from the MDA to the runway touchdown point may begin, provided the runway environment is visible. The VDP will normally be identified by DME on VOR and LOC procedures.
Answer (A) is incorrect because GALES INT is the final approach fix (FAF) which indicates the point at which a pilot may initiate a descent to, not from, the MDA. Answer (C) is incorrect because, at the IAH, 1 DME is the MAP which must be initiated if the runway environment is not in sight. The earliest time the pilot may initiate a descent from the MDA of 460 ft. MSL at IAH is at the VDP, not the MAP.

58.
8818. (Refer to figure 112 on page 304.) How should the pilot identify the MAP on the IAH VOR/DME RWY 32R?

A—After time has elapsed from FAF.
B—IAH 1.3 DME.
C—IAH 1 DME.

Answer (C) is correct (8818). *(IFH Chap X)*
Fig. 112 provides the IAP chart for the VOR/DME RWY 32R approach at IAH. The left center of the chart provides the profile view of the approach. The MAP is at the end of the solid line and is identified at IAH 1 DME. VOR/DME MAP is identified by DME.
Answer (A) is incorrect because timing from the FAF is not used on a VOR/DME approach. Answer (B) is incorrect because IAH 1.3 DME is the VDP, not MAP.

59.
9573. (Refer to figure 112 on page 304.) At what point must the missed approach be initiated on the VOR/DME RWY 32R approach at IAH, if still IMC?

A—Anytime after the FAF.
B—IAH 1.3 DME.
C—IAH 1 DME.

Answer (C) is correct (9573). *(AIM Para 5-4-19)*
A missed approach must be initiated on the VOR/DME RWY 32R approach (Fig. 112) at IAH if still IMC at the MAP or IAH 1 DME.
Answer (A) is incorrect because the missed approach procedure must be initiated at the MAP if still IMC, not at any time after the FAF. Answer (B) is incorrect because the missed approach procedure must be initiated at IAH 1 DME if still IMC, not IAH 1.3 DME (VDP).

60.
8824. (Refer to figure 114 on page 415.) The changeover point on V394 between DAG VORTAC and POM VORTAC is

A—halfway.
B—38 DME miles from DAG VORTAC.
C—64 DME miles from DAG VORTAC.

Answer (C) is correct (8824). *(AIM Para 5-3-6)*
Refer to Fig. 114. On the lower portion of the chart, locate POM VORTAC and move right to follow V394 (V210-394) to the changeover point indicated by "⌠." The number at the top is the distance to DAG VORTAC, or 64 DME.
Answer (A) is incorrect because, when the changeover point is NOT located at the midway point, aeronautical charts will depict the location and give mileage to each VORTAC. Answer (B) is incorrect because 38 DME from DAG VORTAC is APLES INT, not the changeover point.

61.
8825. (Refer to figure 114 on page 415.) The minimum crossing altitude at APLES INT southwest bound on V394 is

A—7,500 feet.
B—9,100 feet.
C—11,500 feet.

Answer (B) is correct (8825). *(En Route Chart)*
Fig. 114 provides an en route low-altitude chart. In the upper portion, locate DAG VORTAC (in the right center) and move left along V394 to APLES INT (38 DME from DAG VORTAC). The flag with an X indicates a minimum crossing altitude (MCA). Below APLES INT, it reads "V210-394 9100 SW," which means the minimum crossing altitude is 9,100 ft. when flying southwest on V394.
Answer (A) is incorrect because 7,500 ft. is the minimum en route altitude (MEA) from DAG VORTAC to APLES INT on V394, not the MCA at APLES INT. Answer (C) is incorrect because 11,500 ft. is the MEA after APLES INT, not the MCA at APLES INT.

62.
8826. (Refer to figure 114 on page 415.) What is the minimum crossing altitude at POM VORTAC when southwest bound on V210?

A—10,700 feet.
B—10,300 feet.
C—5,300 feet.

Answer (C) is correct (8826). *(En Route Chart)*
Fig. 114 provides an en route low-altitude chart. In the bottom portion, locate POM VORTAC (center). The flag with the X indicates a minimum crossing altitude (MCA). Since no MCA is given southwest bound on V210, the minimum en route altitude (MEA) is also the MCA. The MEA is to the right of the POM VORTAC symbol with an arrow pointing southwest, which is 5,300 ft.
Answer (A) is incorrect because 10,700 ft. is the MEA from MEANT INT to CALBE INT when southwest bound on V210, not the MCA at POM VORTAC. Answer (B) is incorrect because 10,300 ft. is the MCA on V210 northeast, not southwest, bound.

63.
9609. [Refer to figures 163 (not in this book), 163A, and 164 on pages 308 and 419.] When does RYAN NDB (338 RYN), which is located west of TUS, broadcast the Transcribed Weather Broadcast (TWEB), on frequency 338?

A—At 15 and 45 minutes past the hour.
B—From 1200-0500Z, when on Daylight Savings Time.
C—TWEB available 0500-2200 local time.

Answer (C) is correct (9609). *(A/FD)*
Fig. 163A is the *A/FD* excerpt for the TUS area, and the last airport listed is Ryan Field. Under **Radio Aids to Navigation**, Ryan NDB is listed on the line starting with **NDB**. At the end of that line is the statement that the TWEB is available from 1200-0500Z.

To convert from Z (or UTC) to local time, locate the time conversion factor on the first line of **RYAN FLD** to determine that you need to subtract 7 hr. from Z to get local time. Thus, the TWEB is available on the Ryan NDB from 0500 to 2200 local time.

NOTE: The FAA refers to Fig. 163, but it is not needed to answer the question, and it is not reproduced in this book.

Answer (A) is incorrect because, when the TWEB is available, it is a continuous broadcast, not only at 15 and 45 min. past the hour. Answer (B) is incorrect because this area of Arizona does not observe Daylight Savings Time, as indicated by the absence of a time conversion factor for daylight time (DT) in the *A/FD*.

64.
9623. (Refer to figure 175 on page 422.) Four airways (V298, V25, V448, and V204) near YKM have a series of dots that overlay the airway. What do these dots indicate?

A—That the airways penetrate a Prohibited and Restricted Airspace.
B—That 2 miles either side of the airway, where shaded, is a Controlled Firing Area.
C—That the airways penetrate a Military Operations Area (MOA) and a special clearance must be received from ATC.

Answer (A) is correct (9623). *(ACL)*
Yakima (YKM) VORTAC is located at the top of the right-hand chart of Fig. 175. V25 is on the 338 radial, and V298 is on the 310 radial. The series of dots that overlay these airways indicates that they penetrate prohibited and restricted airspace.

Answer (B) is incorrect because controlled firing areas are not depicted on any IFR or VFR charts. Answer (C) is incorrect because the series of dots indicates the airways have restrictions because they penetrate restricted or prohibited areas, not an MOA.

65.
9624. (Refer to figure 175 on page 422.) The NAVAID boxes at Nez Perce, Walla Walla, Pasco, and Pullman all have a black dot with a white T within the dot. What does this indicate?

A—That the frequency of the NAVAID is protected to 12,000 feet and 25 NM.
B—That the National Observatory transmits a time signal on the VOR frequency.
C—That the facility has a Transcribed Weather Broadcast (TWEB) service on the frequency.

Answer (C) is correct (9624). *(ACL)*
The left-hand chart of Fig. 175 has the communication (NAVAID) boxes at Nez Perce, Walla Walla, Pasco, and Pullman. The black dot with a white "T" within the dot indicates that each facility has a Transcribed Weather Broadcast (TWEB) service on the VOR frequency.

Answer (A) is incorrect because the white "T" within the black dot indicates TWEB service, not that each VOR has a terminal standard service volume classification. Answer (B) is incorrect because the white "T" within the black dot indicates that a TWEB, not a National Observatory time signal, is transmitted on the VOR frequency.

ARIZONA 31

TOYEI SCHOOL (See GANADO)

TUBA CITY (T03) 5W UTC–7 N36°05.57′ W111°22.96′ **LAS VEGAS**
4513 B **H-2C, L-4E,5C**
RWY 15-33: H6230X75 (ASPH) S-12.5 MIRL
RWY 15: PAPI(P2L)—GA 3.0° TCH 40′. **RWY 33:** PAPI(P2L)—GA 3.0° TCH 40′.
AIRPORT REMARKS: Unattended. Daylight operations only 1300–0100Z. Ngt operations not authorized. MIRL Rwy 15–33 out of svc indefinitely. Livestock on airport.
COMMUNICATIONS: CTAF 122.9
PRESCOTT FSS (PRC) TF 1-800-WX-BRIEF. NOTAM FILE PRC.
RCO 122.05R 113.5T (PRESCOTT FSS)
RADIO AIDS TO NAVIGATION: NOTAM FILE PRC.
(H) VORTAC 113.5 TBC Chan 82 N36°07.28′ W111°16.18′ 238° 5.8 NM to fld. 4960/15E.

TUCSON

AVRA VALLEY (E14) 13 NW UTC–7 N32°24.56′ W111°13.11′ **PHOENIX**
2031 B S3 **FUEL** 100LL, JET A **H-2C, L-4F**
RWY 12-30: H6901X100 (ASPH)
RWY 30: Road. Rgt tfc.
RWY 03-21: H4201X75 (ASPH) MIRL
RWY 03: VASI(V2L)–GA 3.0° TCH 43′. Thld dsplcd 295′. Road. Rgt tfc.
RWY 21: VASI(V2L)–GA 3.0° TCH 31′. Tree.
AIRPORT REMARKS: Attended 1400–0100Z. Parachute Jumping. Ditch apch end Rwy 21. Aerobatic activities 2–10 miles south of arpt, surface 5000′ MSL dalgt hours indefinitely. Extensive parachute training high and low levels all hours NW quadrant of arpt. ACTIVATE MIRL Rwy 03–21, VASI Rwy 03 and Rwy 21—CTAF. Note: See Special Notices—Glider Operations Northwest of Tucson, Arizona.
COMMUNICATIONS: CTAF/UNICOM 123.0
PRESCOTT FSS (PRC) TF 1–800–WX–BRIEF. NOTAM FILE PRC.
RADIO AIDS TO NAVIGATION: NOTAM FILE PRC.
TUCSON (H) VORTACW 116.0 TUS Chan 107 N32°05.71′ W110°54.89′ 309° 24.3 NM to fld. 2670/12E.
HIWAS.

- -

CASCABEL AIR PARK (05A) 35 N UTC–7 N32°18.01′ W110°21.91′ **PHOENIX**
3374
RWY 02-20: 2750X60 (DIRT)
RWY 20: Road.
AIRPORT REMARKS: Unattended. Rwy 20 10′ brush within primary surface. Rwy 02 25′ power lines 1/2 mile south of rwy. – 15′ down slope beginning at end of Rwy 02.
COMMUNICATIONS: CTAF 122.9
PRESCOTT FSS (PRC) TF 1–800 WX–BRIEF. NOTAM FILE PRC.

- -

RYAN FLD (RYN) 10 SW UTC–7 N32°08.53′ W111°10.46′ **PHOENIX**
2415 B S4 **FUEL** 80, 100LL TPA—See Remarks **H-2C, L-4F**
RWY 06R-24L: H5500X75 (ASPH) S–12.5, D–30 MIRL **IAP**
RWY 06R: REIL. Rgt tfc. **RWY 24L:** VASI(V4L)—GA 3.0° TCH 26′.
RWY 06L-24R: H4900X75 (ASPH) S–12.5, D–30
RWY 06L: Thld dsplcd 900′. Pole. **RWY 24R:** Tree. Rgt tfc.
RWY 15-33: 3547X75 (DIRT)
RWY 33: Tree.
AIRPORT REMARKS: Attended 1300–0100Z. Self svc fuel avbl 1300–0400Z. Rwy 06L–24R CLOSED 0100–1300Z. Rwy 06R preferential rwy up to 10 knot tailwind. Rwy 06L–24R paved shoulders 30′ wide both sides. TPA–3215(800), 3415(1000) when twr closed. Note: See Special Notices—Glider Operations Northwest of Tucson, Arizona.
WEATHER DATA SOURCES: AWOS–3 118.05 (602) 578–0269.
COMMUNICATIONS: CTAF 125.8
PRESCOTT FSS (PRC) TF 1–800–WX–BRIEF. NOTAM FILE PRC.
® **TUCSON APP/DEP CON** 128.5
TOWER 125.8 NFCT (Apr–Sep 1300–0300Z, Oct–Mar 1300–0100Z) **GND CON** 118.2
AIRSPACE: CLASS D svc Apr–Sep 1300–0300Z, Oct–Mar 1300–0100Z other times CLASS E.
RADIO AIDS TO NAVIGATION: NOTAM FILE PRC.
TUCSON (H) VORTACW 116.0 TUS Chan 107 N32°05.71′ W110°54.89′ 270° 13.5 NM to fld. 2670/12E.
HIWAS.
NDB (HW-SAB) 338 RYN N32°08.30′ W111°09.69′ at fld. TWEB avbl 1200–0500Z.
ILS 111.1 I–IVI Rwy 06R. Unmonitored.

- -

FIGURE 163A.—Excerpt from Airport/Facilities Directory.

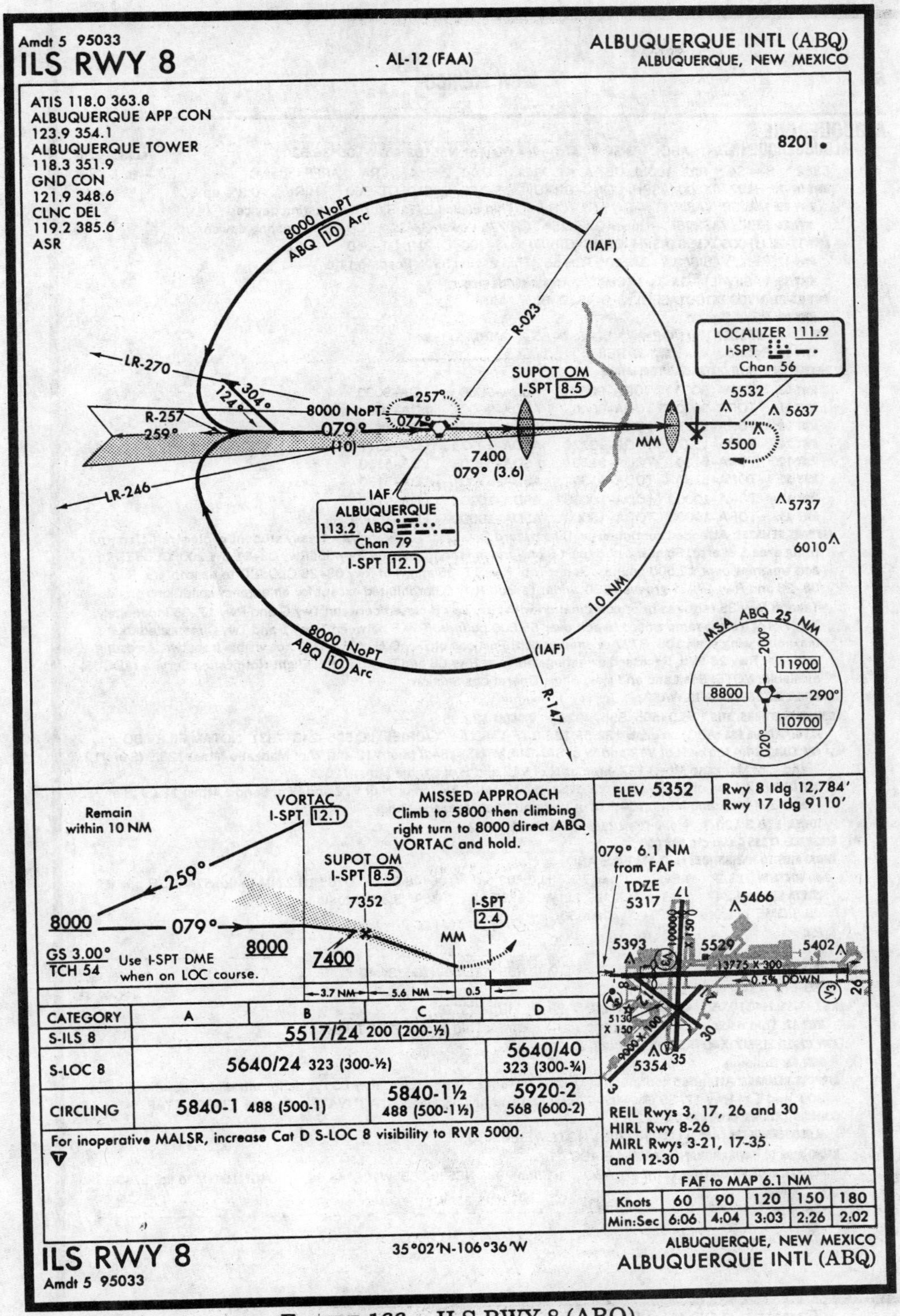

FIGURE 166.—ILS RWY 8 (ABQ).

68 **NEW MEXICO**

ALBUQUERQUE

ALBUQUERQUE INTL (ABQ) 3 SE UTC–7(–6DT) N35°02.45′ W106°36.52′ **ALBUQUERQUE**

5352 B S4 **FUEL** 100LL, JET A, A1, A1 + OX 1, 2, 3, 4 LRA ARFF Index C **H-2D, L-4G, 6E**

RWY 08-26: H13775X300 (ASPH-CONC-GRVD) S-100, D-210, DT-360 HIRL 0.3% up E **IAP**

RWY 08: MALSR. VASI(V6L)—GA 3.0° TCH 54′. Thld dsplcd 991′. Rgt tfc. Arresting device.

RWY 26: REIL. VASI(V6L)—Upper GA 3.25° TCH 77′. Lower GA 3.0° TCH 47′. Arresting device.

RWY 17-35: H10000X150 (ASPH-CONC-GRVD) S-100, D-210, DT-360 MIRL

RWY 17: REIL. VASI(V4L)—GA 3.0° TCH 53′. Thld dsplcd 890′. Road. Rgt tfc.

RWY 35: VASI(V4L)—GA 3.0° TCH 55′. Arresting device.

RWY 03-21: H9000X100 (ASPH) S-45, D-65 MIRL

RWY 03: REIL. Rgt tfc.

RWY 12-30: H5130X150 (ASPH) S-45, D-65 MIRL

RWY 12: Rgt tfc. **RWY 30:** REIL.

RUNWAY DECLARED DISTANCE INFORMATION

RWY 03:	TORA-9000	TODA-9000	ASDA-9000	LDA-9000
RWY 21:	TORA-9000	TODA-9000	ASDA-9000	LDA-9000
RWY 08:	TORA-13775	TODA-13775	ASDA-13775	LDA-12784
RWY 26:	TORA-13775	TODA-13775	ASDA-13775	LDA-13775
RWY 12:	TORA-5130	TODA-5130	ASDA-5130	LDA-5130
RWY 30:	TORA-5130	TODA-5130	ASDA-5130	LDA-5130
RWY 17:	TORA-10000	TODA-10000	ASDA-10000	LDA-9110
RWY 35:	TORA-10000	TODA-10000	ASDA-10000	LDA-10000

AIRPORT REMARKS: Attended continuously. Bird hazard Oct–Dec, and Mar–May. Heavy student copter traffic, control firing area S of arpt. Fighter acft depart S only, no military depart on Rwy 35. Rwy 03–21 SW 200′ CLOSED to acft weighing over 12,500 pounds. Ramp W of Rwy 17–35 and N of Rwy 08–26 CLOSED to helicopters. Rwy 08–26 and Rwy 17–35 grooved 130′ wide. Takeoff Rwy 03 prohibited except for emergency conditions on fld. Takeoff Rwy 35 requires prior coordination with twr. Twy H closed between Twy G and Rwy 17–35 indefinitely. Twy F S of freight ramp closed to acft over 65,000 pounds. Twy F between Twy F1 and Twy C restricted to maximum wing span 108′ B727 or smaller acft. Portions of Twy D N of Twy D-3 not visible from twr. Arresting cables at Rwy 26 thld. Recessed arresting cables at Rwy 08 and Rwy 35 thld. Flight Notification Service (ADCUS) available. NOTE: See Land and Hold Short Operations Section.

WEATHER DATA SOURCES: LLWAS.

COMMUNICATIONS: ATIS 118.0 (505) 856-4928 **UNICOM** 122.95

ALBUQUERQUE FSS (ABQ) on arpt. 122.55 122.3 TF 1-800-WX-BRIEF. LC 505-243-7831. NOTAM FILE ABQ.

® **APP CON** 124.4 (on or N of V12 and W of SANDIA MTNS) 134.8 (S of V12 and W of Manzano Mtns) 123.9 (S of V12 and E of Manzano Mtns) 127.4 (on or N of V12 and E of Sandia Mtns) 126.3

® **DEP CON** 127.4 (on or N of V12 and E of Sandia Mtns) 124.4 (on or N of V12 and W of Sandia Mtns) 123.9 (S of V12 and E of Manzano Mtns) 134.8 (S of V12 and W of Manzano Mtns)

TOWER 118.3 120.3 **GND CON** 121.9 **CLNC DEL** 119.2

AIRSPACE: CLASS C svc ctc **APP CON**

RADIO AIDS TO NAVIGATION: NOTAM FILE ABQ.

(H) VORTACW 113.2 ABQ Chan 79 N35°02.63′ W106°48.98′ 078° 10.2 NM to fld. 5740/13E. **HIWAS.**

ISLETA NDB (HW) 247 ILT N34°59.22′ W106°37.22′ 359° 3.3 NM to fld.

ILS/DME 111.9 I-SPT Chan 56 Rwy 08.

ASR

CORONADO (4AC) 6 NE UTC–7(–6DT) N35°11.75′ W106°34.40′ **ALBUQUERQUE**

5280 B S4 **FUEL** 100LL OX 3 **L-4G, 6E**

RWY 17-35: H4010X60 (ASPH) S-22, D-28 LIRL (NSTD)

RWY 17: Thld dsplcd 200′. Hill. Rgt tfc. **RWY 35:** Thld dsplcd 200′. Trees.

RWY 03-21: H3500X40 (ASPH) S-22, D-28

RWY 03: Building.

AIRPORT REMARKS: Attended continuously. Rising terrain East of airport. Rwy 03 rgt tfc for ultralight operations below 300′ and E of Rwy 17–35. Rwy 03–21 cracked and heavily weeded. ACTIVATE LIRL Rwy 17–35—CTAF.

COMMUNICATIONS: CTAF/UNICOM 122.8

ALBUQUERQUE FSS (ABQ) LC 243-7831 NOTAM FILE ABQ.

RADIO AIDS TO NAVIGATION: NOTAM FILE ABQ.

ALBUQUERQUE (H) VORTACW 113.2 ABQ Chan 79 N35°02.63′ W106°48.98′ 040° 15 NM to fld. 5740/13E. **HIWAS.**

FIGURE 166A.—Excerpt from Airport/Facilities Directory.

66.
9625. (Refer to figure 177 below and legend 15 on page 312.) Lewiston-Nez Perce Co. is a FAR Part 139 airport. What is the minimum number of aircraft rescue and fire fighting vehicles, and the type and amount of fire fighting agents that the airport should have?

A—Two vehicles and 600 pounds dry chemical (DC) or Halon 1211 or 500 pounds of DC plus 100 gallons of water.
B—One vehicle and 500 pounds of dry chemical (DC) or Halon 1211 or 450 pounds DC plus 100 gallons of water.
C—One vehicle and 500 pounds of dry chemical (DC) or Halon 1211 or 350 pounds DC and 1,000 gallons of water.

Answer (B) is correct (9625). *(A/FD)*

Fig. 177 is the *A/FD* excerpt for Lewiston-Nez Perce Co. (LWS). First, look for the aircraft rescue and fire-fighting (ARFF) index on the second line, which is **ARFF Index A**. Next, Legend 15 is an *A/FD* legend. Look at the table under item 16. Find the airport index, A, to determine that the minimum number of vehicles is one and that the airport is required to have at least 500 lb. of dry chemical (DC) or HALON 1211 or 450 lb. of DC plus 100 gal. of water (H_2O).

Answer (A) is incorrect because the airport is required to have only one, not two, vehicles. Answer (C) is incorrect because the airport is required to have 450 lb. DC plus 100 gal. of water, not 350 lb. DC and 1,000 gal. of water.

26 **IDAHO**

LEENY N47°44.57′ W116°57.66′. NOTAM FILE COE. **GREAT FALLS**
NDB (LOM) 347 CO 053° 6.0 NM to Coeur D'Alene Air Terminal.

LEE WILLIAMS MEM (See MIDVALE)

LEMHI CO (See SALMON)

LEWISTON
LEWISTON-NEZ PERCE CO (LWS) 2 S UTC–8(–7DT) N46°22.47′ W117°00.92′ **SEATTLE**
1438 B S4 **FUEL** 100, 100LL, JET A TPA—See Remarks ARFF Index A **H-1B, L-9A**
RWY 08-26: H6512X150 (ASPH-PFC) S-150, D-180, DT-400 HIRL **IAP**
RWY 08: REIL. VASI(V4R)—GA 3.0° TCH 45′. Antenna. Rgt tfc. **RWY 26:** MALSR. Tree.
RWY 11-29: H5001X100 (ASPH) S-70, D-94, DT-150 MIRL
RWY 11: REIL. Rgt tfc. **RWY 29:** VASI(V4R)—GA 3.0° TCH 47′.
AIRPORT REMARKS: Attended 1330–0500Z‡. CLOSED to unscheduled air carrier ops with more than 30 passenger seats 1500–0100Z‡ except PPR call arpt manager 208–746–7962 other times call station number 4 208–743–0172. TPA—turbine powered heavy acft 3000 (1562) all others 2500 (1062). When twr clsd ACTIVATE MALSR Rwy 26, REIL Rwy 08 and Rwy 11—CTAF.
WEATHER DATA SOURCES: LAWRS.
COMMUNICATIONS: CTAF 119.4 **UNICOM** 122.95
BOISE FSS (BOI) TF 1-800-WX-BRIEF. NOTAM FILE LWS.
RCO 122.35 (BOISE FSS)
SEATTLE CENTER APP/DEP CON 120.05
TOWER 119.4 (1400–0600Z‡) **GND CON** 121.9
AIRSPACE: CLASS D svc effective 1400–0600Z‡ other times CLASS G.
RADIO AIDS TO NAVIGATION: NOTAM FILE LWS.
NEZ PERCE (L) VORW/DME 108.2 MQG Chan 19 N46°22.89′ W116°52.17′ 246° 6.1 NM to fld. 1720/20E.
ILS 109.7 I-LWS Rwy 26. ILS unmonitored when tower closed.

WASHINGTON 105

HOQUIAM
BOWERMAN (HQM) 2 W UTC–8(–7DT) N46°58.27′ W123°56.19′ **SEATTLE**
14 B S4 **FUEL** 80, 100LL, JET A1 + LRA **L-1C**
RWY 06-24: H4999X150 (ASPH) S-30, D-40, DT-80 HIRL **IAP**
RWY 06: MALSR. REIL. VASI(V4L)—GA 3.0° TCH 52′. Antenna. Rgt tfc.
RWY 24: VASI(V4L)—GA 3.0° TCH 50′. Sign.
AIRPORT REMARKS: Attended 1600–0200Z‡. Fuel avbl between 0100–1700Z‡, call 533-6655, call-out fee required. CAUTION—Flocks of waterfowl on and in vicinity of arpt. Service road south of rwy in primary surface. Ultralights prohibited without written permission from arpt manager. ACTIVATE HIRL Rwy 06-24 and REIL Rwy 06—CTAF.
COMMUNICATIONS: CTAF/UNICOM 122.7
SEATTLE FSS (SEA) TF 1-800-WX-BRIEF. NOTAM FILE HQM.
RCO 122.2 (SEATTLE FSS)
AIRSPACE: CLASS E svc effective 1400–0600Z‡ other times CLASS G.
RADIO AIDS TO NAVIGATION: NOTAM FILE HQM. VHF/DF ctc FSS.
HOQUIAM (H) VORTACW 117.7 HQM Chan 124 N46°56.82′ W124°08.96′ 062° 8.9 NM to fld. 10/19E. **HIWAS.**
ABERN NDB (LOM) 414 HQ N46°59.26′ W123°47.86′ 241° 5.8 NM to fld. Unmonitored 0600–1400Z‡. Out of service indefinitely.
ILS/DME 108.7 I-HQM Chan 24 Rwy 24 LOM ABERN NDB. LOM out of service indefinitely. LOC/LOM/DME unmonitored 0600–1400Z‡.

FIGURE 177.—Excerpt from Airport/Facilities Directory.

4

DIRECTORY LEGEND

⑫ FUEL

CODE	FUEL
80	Grade 80 gasoline (Red)
100	Grade 100 gasoline (Green)
100LL	100LL gasoline (low lead) (Blue)
115	Grade 115 gasoline
A	Jet A—Kerosene freeze point-40° C.
A1	Jet A-1—Kerosene freeze point-50°C.
A1 +	Jet A-1—Kerosene with icing inhibitor, freeze point-50° C.
B	Jet B—Wide-cut turbine fuel, freeze point-50° C.
B+	Jet B—Wide-cut turbine fuel with icing inhibitor, freeze point-50° C.
MOGAS	Automobile gasoline which is to be used as aircraft fuel.

NOTE: Automobile Gasoline. Certain automobile gasoline may be used in specific aircraft engines if a FAA supplemental type certificate has been obtained. Automobile gasoline which is to be used in aircraft engines will be identified as "MOGAS", however, the grade/type and other octane rating will not be published.

Data shown on fuel availability represents the most recent information the publisher has been able to acquire. Because of a variety of factors, the fuel listed may not always be obtainable by transient civil pilots. Confirmation of availability of fuel should be made directly with fuel dispensers at locations where refueling is planned.

⑬ OXYGEN

OX 1 High Pressure
OX 2 Low Pressure
OX 3 High Pressure—Replacement Bottles
OX 4 Low Pressure—Replacement Bottles

⑭ TRAFFIC PATTERN ALTITUDE

Traffic Pattern Altitude (TPA)—The first figure shown is TPA above mean sea level. The second figure in parentheses is TPA above airport elevation.

⑮ AIRPORT OF ENTRY, LANDING RIGHTS, AND CUSTOMS USER FEE AIRPORTS

U.S. CUSTOMS USER FEE AIRPORT—Private Aircraft operators are frequently required to pay the costs associated with customs processing.

AOE—Airport of Entry—A customs Airport of Entry where permission from U.S. Customs is not required, however, at least one hour advance notice of arrival must be furnished.

LRA—Landing Rights Airport—Application for permission to land must be submitted in advance to U.S. Customs. At least one hour advance notice of arrival must be furnished.

NOTE: Advance notice of arrival at both an AOE and LRA airport may be included in the flight plan when filed in Canada or Mexico, where Flight Notification Service (ADCUS) is available the airport remark will indicate this service. This notice will also be treated as an application for permission to land in the case of an LRA. Although advance notice of arrival may be relayed to Customs through Mexico, Canadian, and U.S. Communications facilities by flight plan, the aircraft operator is solely responsible for insuring that Customs receives the notification. (See Customs, Immigration and Naturalization, Public Health and Agriculture Department requirements in the International Flight Information Manual for further details.)

⑯ CERTIFICATED AIRPORT (FAR 139)

Airports serving Department of Transportation certified carriers and certified under FAR, Part 139, are indicated by the ARFF index; i.e., ARFF Index A, which relates to the availability of crash, fire, rescue equipment.

FAR-PART 139 CERTIFICATED AIRPORTS

INDICES AND AIRCRAFT RESCUE AND FIRE FIGHTING EQUIPMENT REQUIREMENTS

Airport Index	*Required No. Vehicles*	*Aircraft Length*	*Scheduled Departures*	*Agent + Water for Foam*
A	1	<90′	≥1	500#DC or HALON 1211 or 450#DC + 100 gal H_2O
B	1 or 2	≥90′, <126′	≥5	Index A + 1500 gal H_2O
		≥126′, <159′	<5	
C	2 or 3	≥126′, <159′	≥5	Index A + 3000 gal H_2O
		≥159′, <200′	<5	
D	3	≥159′, <200′	≥5	Index A + 4000 gal H_2O
		>200′	<5	
E	3	≥200′	≥5	Index A + 6000 gal H_2O

> Greater Than; < Less Than; ≥ Equal or Greater Than; ≤ Equal or Less Than; H_2O–Water; DC–Dry Chemical.

LEGEND 15.—Directory Legend.

67.
9668. (Refer to legend 15 and figure 185A on pages 312 and 314.) McCarran Intl (LAS) is an FAR Part 139 airport. What is the minimum number of aircraft rescue and fire fighting vehicles and the type and amount of fire fighting agents that the airport should have?

A—Three vehicles and 500 pounds of dry chemical (DC) or Halon 1211 or 450 pounds DC and 4,000 gallons of water.
B—Two vehicles and 600 pounds dry chemical (DC) or Halon 1211 or 500 pounds of DC plus 4,000 gallons of water.
C—Three vehicles and 500 pounds of dry chemical (DC) or Halon 1211 or 450 pounds DC plus 3,000 gallons of water.

Answer (A) is correct (9668). *(A/FD)*
Fig. 185A is the *A/FD* excerpt for LAS. First, look for the aircraft rescue and fire-fighting (ARFF) index on the second line, which is **ARFF Index D**. Next, Legend 15 is an *A/FD* legend. Look at the table under item 16. Find the airport index, D, to determine that the minimum number of vehicles is three and that the airport is required to have at least 500 lb. of dry chemical (DC) or HALON 1211, or 450 lb. DC and 4,000 gal. of water (H_2O).
Answer (B) is incorrect because LAS is required to have at least three, not two, vehicles. Answer (C) is incorrect because LAS is required to have at least 4,000 gal., not 3,000 gal., of water.

68.
9659. (Refer to figures 185 and 185A on page 314.) The threshold of RWY 07L at McCarran Intl is displaced

A—874 feet, due to a pole.
B—2,133 feet, due to a hangar.
C—1,659 feet, due to a pole.

Answer (B) is correct (9659). *(A/FD)*
Refer to Fig. 185A. Locate the fourth line down from the top, which begins with **RWY 07L**. Move to the right of that line, which states that the threshold is displaced 2,133 ft. due to a hangar.
Answer (A) is incorrect because RWY 19L, not 07L, threshold is displaced 874 ft. due to a pole. Answer (C) is incorrect because RWY 07L threshold is displaced 2,133 ft., not 1,659 ft., due to a hangar, not a pole.

69.
9658. (Refer to figure 185A on page 314.) The maximum gross weight that an L1011 can be operated on RWY 07R/25L at McCarran Intl is

A—521,000 pounds.
B—633,000 pounds.
C—620,000 pounds.

Answer (A) is correct (9658). *(A/FD)*
The top portion of Fig. 185A is the *A/FD* excerpt for McCarran Intl. (LAS). Locate the **Airport Remarks** and go down seven lines. The maximum gross weight that an L-1011 can be operated on RWY 07R-25L is 521,000 lb.
Answer (B) is incorrect because 633,000 lb. is the maximum gross weight for an MD-11, not an L-1011, to operate on RWY 07R-25L. Answer (C) is incorrect because 620,000 lb. is the maximum gross weight for a DC-10, not a L-1011, to operate on RWY 07R-25L.

70.
9641. (Refer to figure 186 on page 425.) The NAVAID box at Mormon Mesa (MMM) has a black square in the upper left corner. What does this indicate?

A—That Hazardous Inflight Weather Advisory Service is available.
B—That the National Observatory transmits a time signal on the VOR frequency.
C—That the facility has a Transcribed Weather Broadcast (TWEB) service on the frequency.

Answer (A) is correct (9641). *(ACL)*
Mormon Mesa communication (NAVAID) box is located at the center of the left-hand chart of Fig. 186. The black box in the upper left corner of the box indicates that Hazardous Inflight Weather Advisory Service (HIWAS) is available on the VOR frequency.
Answer (B) is incorrect because HIWAS, not the National Observatory, transmits on the VOR frequency. Answer (C) is incorrect because TWEB service would be indicated by a white "T" inside a black circle, not a black square, in the upper right, not left, corner of the communication box.

71.
9654. (Refer to figure 198A on page 315.) The highest terrain shown in the planview section of the LOC-B approach to Eagle County Regional is

A—11,275 feet.
B—11,573 feet.
C—12,354 feet.

Answer (C) is correct (9654). *(IAP)*
The highest spot elevation (terrain) shown in the planview section of an IAP chart is indicated by a bold dot. The highest terrain shown in the planview section of the LOC-B IAP to Eagle County Regional is 12,354 ft., which is located in the upper left corner (above Denver Center).
Answer (A) is incorrect because 11,275 ft. is the highest terrain shown within 10 NM of KEEKY Int., not the entire planview section. Answer (B) is incorrect because 11,573 ft. is the spot elevation located to the right of R-184 of RLG VORTAC, but not the highest terrain elevation since the dot is not bold.

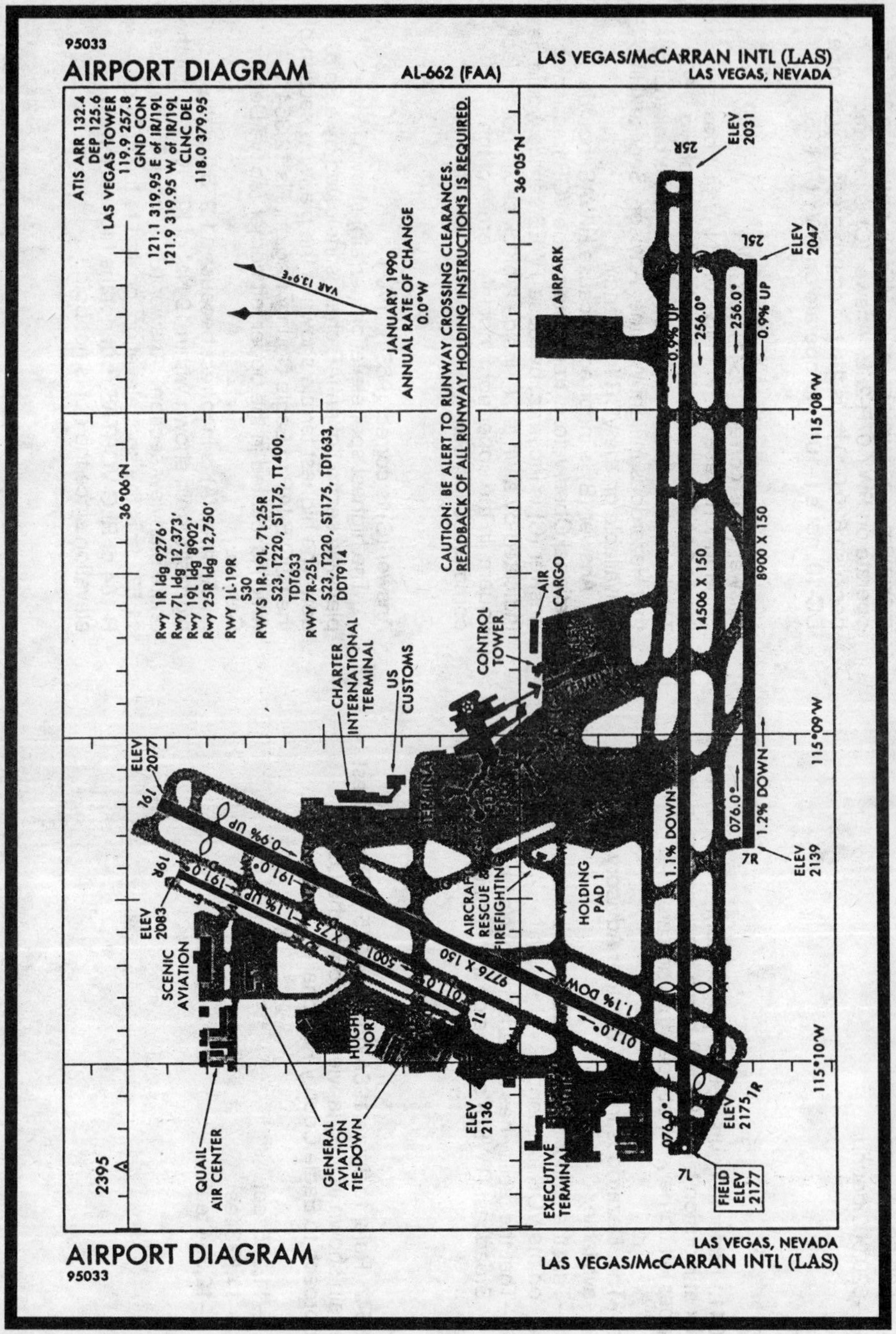

Figure 185.—Airport Diagram.

NEVADA 159

McCARRAN INTL (LAS) 5 S UTC–8(–7DT) N36°04.82' W115°09.02' — LAS VEGAS H-2B, L-5B IAP
2177 B S4 **FUEL** 100, 100LL, JET A1 + OX 1, 2, 3 LRA ARFF Index D
RWY 07L-25R: H14506X150 (ASPH-PFC) S-23, D-220, DT-633 HIRL 1.0% up W
RWY 07L: VASI(V6L)—Upper GA 3.25° TCH 94'. Lower GA 3.0° TCH 47'. Thld dsplcd 2133'. Hangar.
RWY 25R: MALSR. Thld dsplcd 1400'.
RWY 01R-19L: H9776X150 (ASPH-PFC) S-23, D-220, DT-633 MIRL 1.0% up S
RWY 01R: VASI(V4L)—GA 3.0° TCH 50'. Thld dsplcd 500'. Railroad. Rgt tfc.
RWY 19L: VASI(V6L)—Upper GA 3.25° TCH 66'. Lower GA 3.0° TCH 35'. Thld dsplcd 874'. Pole.
RWY 07R-25L: H8900X150 (ASPH-PFC) S-23, D-220, DT-633, DDT-914 HIRL
RWY 07R: REIL. Pole. **RWY 25L:** MALSF.
RWY 01L-19R: H5001X75 (ASPH) S-30 MIRL 1.1% up S
RWY 01L: REIL. VASI(V4L)—GA 3.0° TCH 35'. Antenna.
RWY 19R: REIL. VASI(V4L)—GA 3.0° TCH 60'. Pole. Rgt tfc.
AIRPORT REMARKS: Attended continuously. Rwy 19R CLOSED arrival, Rwy 01L CLOSED departure Mon–Fri 1500–2300Z‡. Extensive glider/soaring operations weekends and holidays. Sunrise to sunset, LAS 187020, altitudes up to but not including FL180. Gliders remain clear of the CLASS B airspace but otherwise operate within the entire SW quadrant of the CLASS B airspace Veil. Lgtd crane 950' AGL 4 miles N of arpt. Rotating bcn not visible 115°—240° NE to SW from McCarran Twr. Acft may experience reflection of sun from glass pyramid located NW of arpt. Reflection may occur at various altitudes, headings and distances from arpt. Rwy 07R–25L DDT GWT 521,000 lbs for L-1011, 620,000 lbs for DC-10, 633,000 lbs for MD-11. PAEW between Rwy 01R–19L and Twy D north of Twy N. PAEW west of Rwy 01L–19R. PAEW west of Twy D. Twy E clsd between Twy Q and Twy R. Twy N, Twy S and Twy T clsd between Rwy 01L–19R and Twy D. Twy Y acft be alert keep nosewheel on centerline and acft with wing span greater than 70' prohibited north of New Quail Gate. Twy D clsd to B747 and clsd to all acft with wingspan 171' or greater north of Rwy 07L–25R. All non-standard rwy operations PPR from Department of Aviation. Turbojet operations not permitted Rwy 01R–19L and Rwy 01L–19R between 0400–1600Z‡. Exceptions will be made due to weather. Rwy 07L VASI out of svc indefinitely. Rwy 25 MALSR out of svc indefinitely. Tiedown fee. Flight Notification Service (ADCUS) available. NOTE: See Land and Hold Short Operations Section.
WEATHER DATA SOURCES: LLWAS.
COMMUNICATIONS: ATIS 132.4 (ARR) 125.6 (DEP) **UNICOM** 122.95
RENO FSS (RNO) TF 1-800-WX-BRIEF. NOTAM FILE LAS.
Ⓡ **LAS VEGAS APP CON** 127.15
Ⓡ **LAS VEGAS DEP CON** 133.95 (North) 125.9 (South)
LAS VEGAS TOWER 119.9 **GND CON** 121.9 (West of Rwy 01R–19L) 121.1 (East of Rwy 01R–19L) **CLNC DEL** 118.0
AIRSPACE: CLASS B See VFR Terminal Area Chart.
RADIO AIDS TO NAVIGATION: NOTAM FILE LAS.
LAS VEGAS (H) VORTACW 116.9 LAS Chan 116 N36°04.78' W115°09.59' at fld. 2140/15E.
ILS 110.3 I-LAS Rwy 25R.
ILS 111.75 I-RLE Rwy 25L. Loc unusable byd 19° South of course.

NORTH LAS VEGAS AIR TERMINAL (VGT) 3 NW UTC–8(–7DT) — LAS VEGAS H-2B, L-5B
N36°12.75' W115°11.82'
2207 B S4 **FUEL** 100LL, JET A OX 2 TPA—3007(800)
RWY 07-25: H5005X75 (ASPH) S-30 MIRL
RWY 07: PAPI(P4L)—GA 3.0° TCH 37'. Pole. **RWY 25:** PAPI(P4L)—GA 3.0° TCH 36'.
RWY 12-30: H5000X75 (ASPH) S-30 MIRL
RWY 12: PAPI(P4L)—GA 3.0° TCH 25'.
RWY 30: MIRL. PAPI(P4L)—GA 3.0° TCH 45'. Thld dsplcd 290'. P-line.
AIRPORT REMARKS: Attended 1400–0630Z‡. Rwy 30 PAPI OTS indef. When twr clsd ACTIVATE MIRL Rwy 07–25 and Rwy 12–30—CTAF. NOTE: See Land and Hold Short Operations Section.
COMMUNICATIONS: CTAF 125.7 **ATIS** 118.05 (1400–0400Z‡) **UNICOM** 122.95
RENO FSS (RNO) TF 1-800-WX-BRIEF. NOTAM FILE RNO.
TOWER 125.7 (1400–0400Z‡) **GND CON** 121.7
AIRSPACE: CLASS D svc effective 1400–0400Z‡ other times CLASS G.
RADIO AIDS TO NAVIGATION: NOTAM FILE LAS.
LAS VEGAS (H) VORTACW 116.9 LAS Chan 116 N36°04.78' W115°09.59' 332° 8.2 NM to fld. 2140/15E.

LIDA JUNCTION (See GOLDFIELD)

LINCOLN CO (See PANACA)

Figure 185A.—Excerpt from Airport/Facilities Directory.

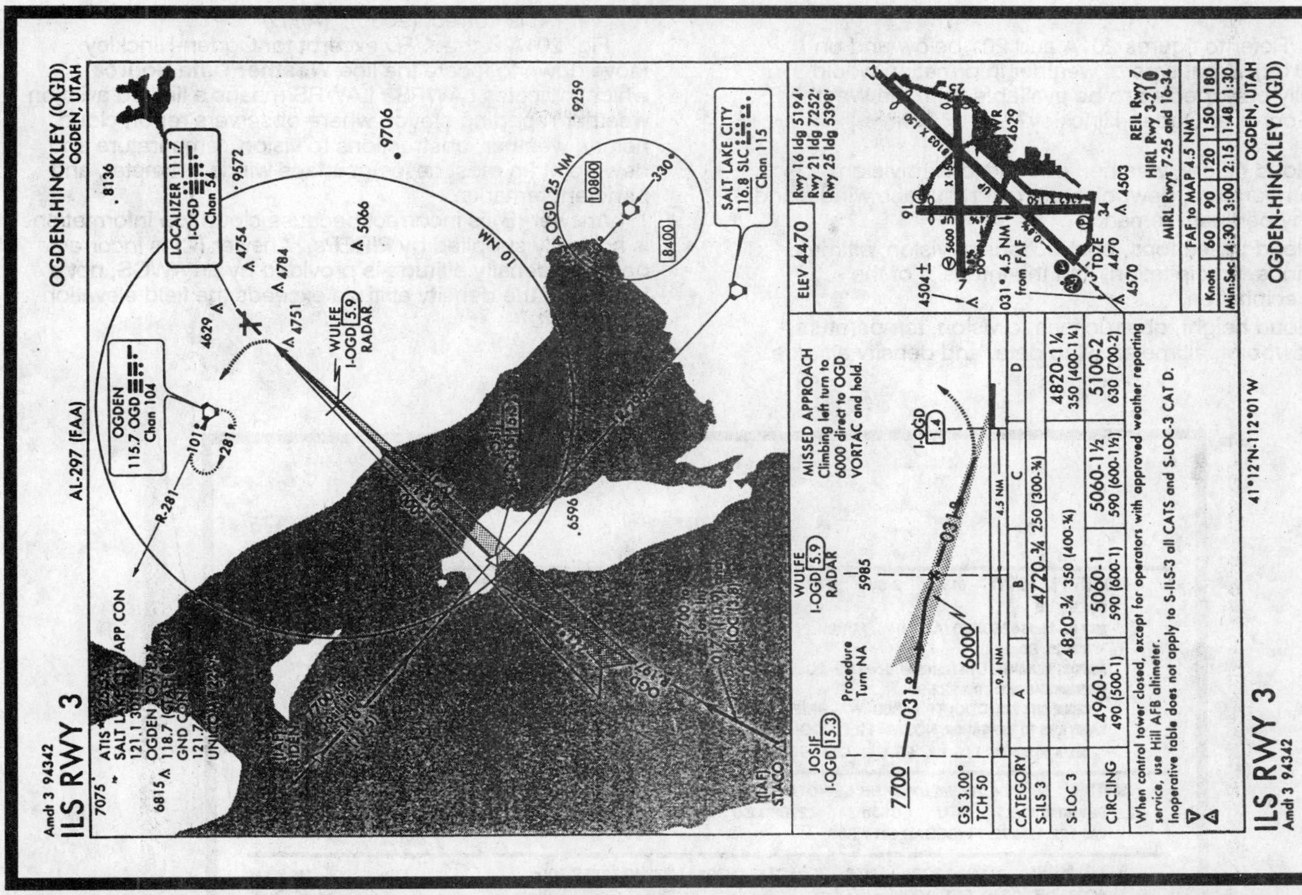

Figure 201.—ILS RWY 3 (OGD).

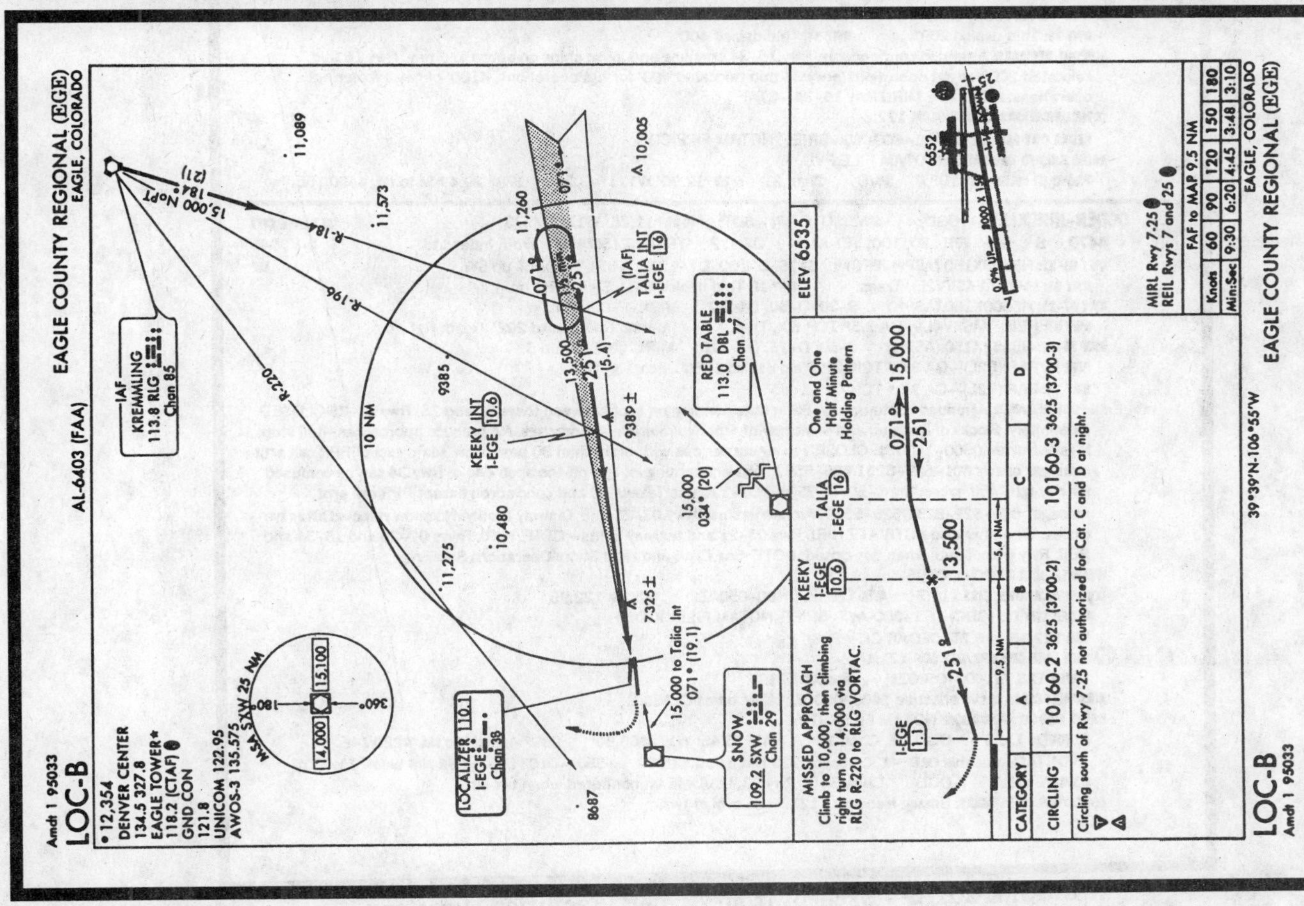

Figure 198A.—LOC-B (EGE).

72.
9655. (Refer to figures 201A and 201 below and on page 315.) What type of weather information would normally be expected to be available from the Weather Data Source at Ogden-Hinckley?

A—Cloud height, weather, obstructions to vision, temperature, dewpoint, altimeter, surface winds, and any pertinent remarks.
B—Cloud bases/tops, obstructions to vision, altimeter, winds, precipitation, and the intensity of the precipitation.
C—Cloud height, obstructions to vision, temperature, dewpoint, altimeter, wind data, and density altitude.

Answer (A) is correct (9655). *(A/FD)*
Fig. 201A is the *A/FD* excerpt for Ogden-Hinckley. Move down to locate the line **Weather Data Source**, which indicates LAWRS. LAWRS means a limited aviation weather reporting station where observers report cloud height, weather, obstructions to vision, temperature and dew point (in most cases), surface winds, altimeter, and pertinent remarks.
Answer (B) is incorrect because cloud top information is normally supplied by PIREPs. Answer (C) is incorrect because density altitude is provided by an AWOS, not a LAWRS, if the density altitude exceeds the field elevation by 1,000 ft.

UTAH 175

MOUNT PLEASANT (43U) 2 SW UTC–7(–6DT) N39°31.48′ W111°28.51′ LAS VEGAS
5829 B L-5C
RWY 02-20: H4260X60 (ASPH) MIRL
RWY 20: Road.
AIRPORT REMARKS: Unattended. Rwy 02–20 marked by stripes. For runway lights key 122.8 7 times.
COMMUNICATIONS: CTAF 122.9
CEDAR CITY FSS (CDC) TF 1-800-WX-BRIEF. NOTAM FILE CDC.
RADIO AIDS TO NAVIGATION: NOTAM FILE CDC.
DELTA (H) VORTAC 116.1 DTA Chan 108 N39°18.14′ W112°30.33′ 058° 49.7 NM to fld. 4600/16E.

MYTON N40°08.70′ W110°07.66′ NOTAM FILE CDC. SALT LAKE CITY
(H) VORTAC 112.7 MTU Chan 74 270° 12.0 NM to Duchesne Muni. 5332/14E. H-2C, L-5C, 8E
RCO 122.1R 112.7T (CEDAR CITY FSS)

NEPHI MUNI (U14) 3 NW UTC–7(–6DT) N39°44.33′ W111°52.30′ LAS VEGAS
5009 B S4 FUEL 100LL, JET A L-5C, 7D, 8E
RWY 16-34: H4700X75 (ASPH) S-21 MIRL
RWY 16: Thld dsplcd 200′. RWY 34: Thld dsplcd 400′.
AIRPORT REMARKS: Attended continuously. Rwy 16–34 cracking and loose chips on apron and rwy. Rwy 16 thld relocated 200′ for ngt operations, Rwy 34 thld relocated 400′ for ngt operations, 4100′ of rwy avbl for ngt operations. ACTIVATE MIRL Rwy 16–34—CTAF.
COMMUNICATIONS: CTAF/UNICOM 122.8
CEDAR CITY FSS (CDC) TF 1-800-WX-BRIEF. NOTAM FILE CDC.
RADIO AIDS TO NAVIGATION: NOTAM FILE PVU.
PROVO (T) VORW/DME 108.4 PVU Chan 21 N40°12.90′ W111°43.28′ 179° 29.4 NM to fld. 4490/15E.

OGDEN-HINCKLEY (OGD) 3 SW UTC–7(–6DT) N41°11.76′ W112°00.73′ SALT LAKE CITY
4470 B S4 FUEL 80, 100, JET A1 + OX 1, 2 TPA—5215(745) ARFF Index Ltd. H-1C, L-7D
RWY 03-21: H8103X150 (ASPH-PFC) S-75, D-100, DT-170 HIRL 0.8% up SW IAP
RWY 03: MALS. VASI(V2L). Trees. RWY 21: Thld dsplcd 851′. Signs. Rgt tfc.
RWY 07-25: H5600X150 (ASPH) S-20, D-50, DT-70 MIRL 0.3% up W
RWY 07: REIL. VASI(V4L)—GA 3.5° TCH 50′. Tree. RWY 25: Thld dsplcd 202′. Road. Rgt tfc.
RWY 16-34: H5352X150 (ASPH) S-50, D-75, DT-120 MIRL 0.4% up S
RWY 16: PAPI(P2L)—GA 3.0° TCH 40′. Thld dsplcd 158′. Ditch. Rgt tfc.
RWY 34: PAPI(P2L)—GA 3.0° TCH 40′. Sign.
AIRPORT REMARKS: Attended continuously. Parachute jumping on arpt between Rwys 21 and 25. Rwy 07–25 CLOSED indefinitely. Flocks of birds on and in vicinity of arpt. No multiple approaches. No practice approaches—full stop ldgs only from 0500–1400Z‡. CLOSED to air carrier ops with more than 30 passenger seats except PPR call arpt manager or twr 801-629-8251/625-5569. Be alert parking lot lgts off the apch end of Rwy 34 can be confused for rwy lgts. Acft exceeding S-50, D-75 and DT-120 use Taxiway C and conc apron except PPR call arpt manager 801-629-8251/625-5569. Air carriers use Rwy 03–21 and Taxiway C only. No snow removal after twr closes. When twr clsd ACTIVATE HIRL Rwy 03–21 and taxiway lights—CTAF. MIRL Rwys 07–25 and 16–34 and REIL Rwy 07 not avbl when twr closed. NOTE: See Land and Hold Short Operations Section.
WEATHER DATA SOURCE: LAWRS.
COMMUNICATIONS: CTAF 118.7 ATIS 125.55 (1400–0500Z‡) UNICOM 122.95
CEDAR CITY FSS (CDC) TF 1-800-WX-BRIEF. NOTAM FILE OGD.
RCO 122.1R 115.7T (CEDAR CITY FSS)
Ⓡ SALT LAKE CITY APP/DEP CON 121.1
TOWER 118.7 (1400–0500Z‡) GND CON 121.7
AIRSPACE: CLASS D svc effective 1400–0500Z‡ other times CLASS G.
RADIO AIDS TO NAVIGATION: NOTAM FILE OGD.
(L) VORTAC 115.7 OGD Chan 104 N41°13.45′ W112°05.90′ 099° 4.3 NM to fld. 4220/14E.
VORTAC unusable 010°–130° beyond 25 NM below 11,300′ 350°–010° beyond 38 NM below 11,000′
ILS/DME 111.7 I-OGD Chan 54 Rwy 03. ILS/DME unmonitored when twr clsd.
COMM/NAVAID REMARKS: Emerg frequency 121.5 not avbl at twr.

FIGURE 201A.—Excerpt from Airport/Facilities Directory.

73.
9670. (Refer to figure 210 on page 431.) The route between FIS (near Key West) and MTH, which is labeled B646, is an example of a

A—LF/MF Airway.
B—LF/MF Oceanic Route.
C—Military Training Route.

Answer (B) is correct (9670). *(ACL)*
The route labeled B646 from FIS to MTH is a thin, dark brown line which indicates a LF/MF oceanic route.
Answer (A) is incorrect because a LF/MF airway would be indicated by a wider brown line, not a thin brown line. Answer (C) is incorrect because a MTR is indicated by a thin, light brown line such as IR-53 to the south of B646.

74.
9674. (Refer to figures 210 and 211 on pages 431 and 432.) The Miami Flight Service Station has

A—Hazardous Inflight Weather Advisory Service (HIWAS).
B—Remote Communications Outlet (RCO) northeast of MIA which operates on 122.3.
C—Transcribed Weather Broadcast.

Answer (A) is correct (9674). *(ACL)*
The Miami VORTAC communication box is shown on the left chart of Fig. 210. The black square in the upper left corner indicates Hazardous Inflight Weather Advisory Service (HIWAS).
Answer (B) is incorrect because the RCO northeast of MIA VORTAC operates on 126.7, not 122.3. Answer (C) is incorrect because TWEB would be indicated by a white "T" inside of a black circle, not a black square, in the MIA VORTAC box.

75.
9675. (Refer to figure 210 on page 431.) The Miami ARTCC remote site located near Pahokee has a discrete VHF frequency of

A—123.45.
B—133.55.
C—135.35.

Answer (B) is correct (9675). *(En Route Chart)*
Pahokee is on the chart on the right side of Fig. 210 about one-third up from the bottom and near the center. To the southwest of PHK VORTAC is a blue serrated-edged box which indicates an ARTCC remote site with a discrete VHF frequency of 133.55.
Answer (A) is incorrect because the Miami ARTCC remote site located near Pahokee has a discrete VHF frequency of 133.55, not 123.45. Answer (C) is incorrect because the Miami ARTCC remote site located near Pahokee has a discrete VHF frequency of 133.55, not 135.35.

9.9 ILS Approaches

76.
8966. What functions are provided by ILS?

A—Azimuth, distance, and vertical angle.
B—Azimuth, range, and vertical angle.
C—Guidance, range, and visual information.

Answer (C) is correct (8966). *(AIM Para 1-1-9)*
The ILS system may be divided functionally into three parts:

1. Guidance information--localizer, glide slope
2. Range information--marker beacon, DME
3. Visual information--approach lights, runway lights

Answer (A) is incorrect because azimuth and distance information are provided by a TACAN. Answer (B) is incorrect because a localizer/DME approach provides azimuth and range information.

77.
8961. Within what frequency range does the localizer transmitter of the ILS operate?

A—108.10 to 118.10 MHz.
B—108.10 to 111.95 MHz.
C—108.10 to 117.95 MHz.

Answer (B) is correct (8961). *(AIM Para 1-1-9)*
The frequencies assigned for localizer transmission are from 108.10 to 111.95 MHz.
Answer (A) is incorrect because communications frequencies are above 117.95 MHz. Answer (C) is incorrect because 108.10 to 117.95 MHz is the frequency band in which VORs operate.

78.
8957. Which component associated with the ILS is identified by the first two letters of the localizer identification group?

A—Inner marker.
B—Middle compass locator.
C—Outer compass locator.

Answer (C) is correct (8957). *(AIM Para 1-1-9)*
The outer compass locator is identified by the first two letters of the coded localizer identification group.
Answer (A) is incorrect because marker beacons are not identified by letters; only compass locators are so identified. Answer (B) is incorrect because a middle compass locator is identified by the last two letters of the localizer identification group, not the first two letters.

79.
8956. Which component associated with the ILS is identified by the last two letters of the localizer group?

A—Inner marker.
B—Middle compass locator.
C—Outer compass locator.

Answer (B) is correct (8956). *(AIM Para 1-1-9)*
Compass locators transmit two-letter identification groups. The outer locator transmits the first two letters of the localizer identification group, and the middle locator transmits the last two letters of the localizer identification group. Thus, the middle compass locator is identified by the last two letters of the localizer identification group.
Answer (A) is incorrect because a simple marker beacon is not identified by letters; only compass locators are so identified. Answer (C) is incorrect because an outer compass locator is identified by the first two letters of the localizer identification group, not the last two letters.

80.
8962. If installed, what aural and visual indications should be observed over the ILS back course marker?

A—A series of two dot combinations and a white marker beacon light.
B—Continuous dashes at the rate of one per second and a white marker beacon light.
C—A series of two dash combinations and a white marker beacon light.

Answer (A) is correct (8962). *(AIM Para 1-1-9)*
The back course marker (BCM), where installed, indicates the back course final approach fix. The BCM is modulated at 3000 Hz and identified with two dots at a rate of 72 to 75 two-dot combinations per min. and a white marker beacon light.
Answer (B) is incorrect because this is a nonsense indication. This description most closely resembles an ILS outer marker which has continuous dashes at the rate of two per second. Answer (C) is incorrect because this is not a marker indication of any type. This description most closely resembles an ILS middle marker which is identified by alternate dot/dash combinations at the rate of two per second.

81.
8958. What aural and visual indications should be observed over an ILS inner marker?

A—Continuous dots at the rate of six per second.
B—Continuous dashes at the rate of two per second.
C—Alternate dots and dashes at the rate of two per second.

Answer (A) is correct (8958). *(AIM Para 1-1-9)*
The inner marker indicates a point at which an airplane is at a designated decision height on the glide slope between the middle marker and the landing threshold during a Category II ILS approach. It is identified with continuous dots keyed at the rate of six dots per second and a white marker beacon.
Answer (B) is incorrect because continuous dashes at the rate of two per second indicate the ILS outer marker, not inner marker. Answer (C) is incorrect because alternate dots and dashes at the rate of two per second indicate the ILS middle marker, not inner marker.

82.
8959. What aural and visual indications should be observed over an ILS middle marker?

A—Continuous dots at the rate of six per second.
B—Continuous dashes at the rate of two per second.
C—Alternate dots and dashes at the rate of two per second.

Answer (C) is correct (8959). *(AIM Para 1-1-9)*
The middle marker indicates a position approximately 3,500 ft. from the landing threshold and has an aural signal of alternating dots and dashes at two per second.
Answer (A) is incorrect because continuous dots at the rate of six per second indicate an ILS inner marker. Answer (B) is incorrect because continuous dashes at the rate of two per second indicate an ILS outer marker.

83.
8960. What aural and visual indications should be observed over an ILS outer marker?

A—Continuous dots at the rate of six per second.
B—Continuous dashes at the rate of two per second.
C—Alternate dots and dashes at the rate of two per second.

Answer (B) is correct (8960). *(AIM Para 1-1-9)*
An ILS outer marker is identified by continuous dashes at the rate of two per second.
Answer (A) is incorrect because continuous dots at the rate of six per second indicate an ILS inner marker. Answer (C) is incorrect because alternating dots and dashes at the rate of two per second indicate an ILS middle marker.

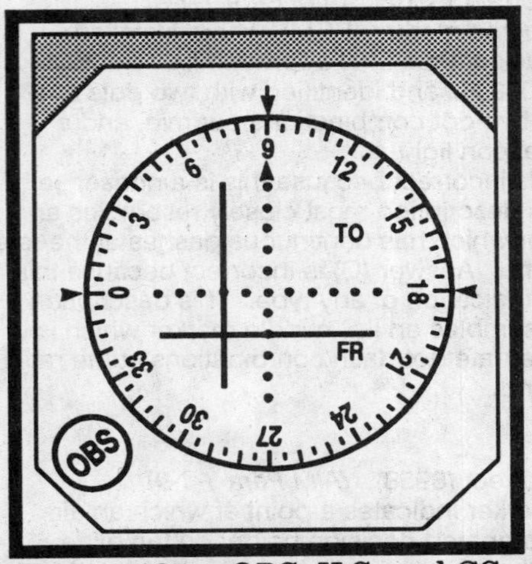

FIGURE 135.—OBS, ILS, and GS Displacement.

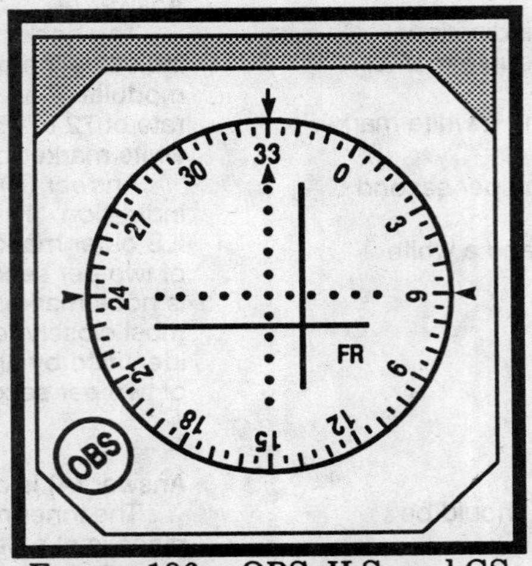

FIGURE 136.—OBS, ILS, and GS Displacement.

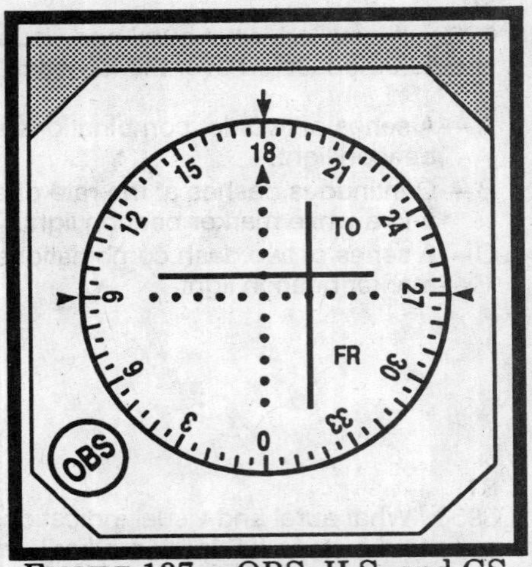

FIGURE 137.—OBS, ILS, and GS Displacement.

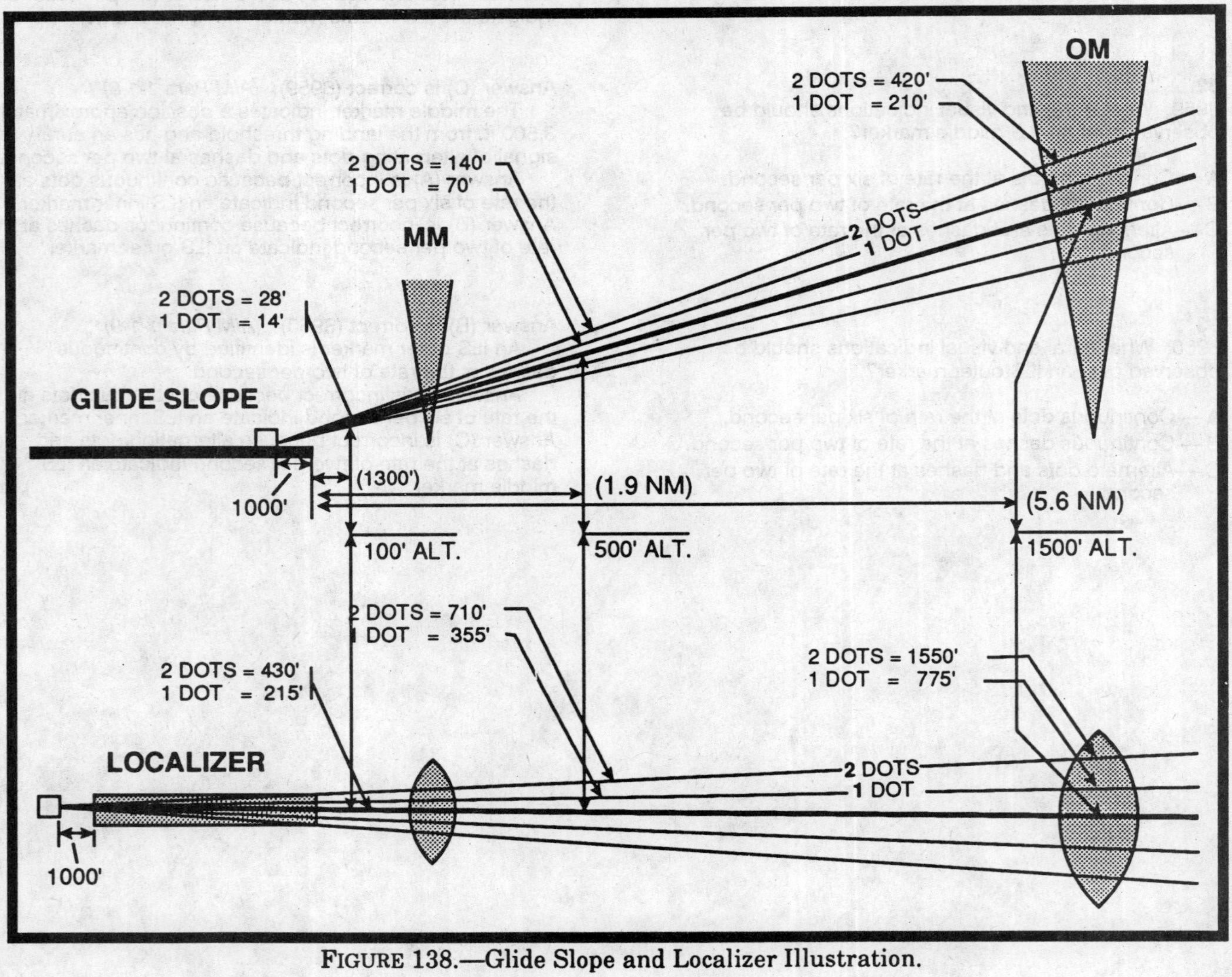

FIGURE 138.—Glide Slope and Localizer Illustration.

84.
8971. (Refer to figures 135 and 138 on page 320.) Which displacement from the localizer and glide slope at the 1.9 NM point is indicated?

A—710 feet to the left of the localizer centerline and 140 feet below the glide slope.
B—710 feet to the right of the localizer centerline and 140 feet above the glide slope.
C—430 feet to the right of the localizer centerline and 28 feet above the glide slope.

Answer (B) is correct (8971). *(AIM Para 1-1-9)*
The airplane is to the right of the localizer and above the glide slope each by two dots at 1.9 NM. Per Fig. 138, two dots at 1.9 NM indicate 140 ft. above the glide slope and 710 ft. to the right of the localizer.
Answer (A) is incorrect because the airplane is to the right, not left, of the localizer and above, not below, the glide slope. Answer (C) is incorrect because the 430-ft. and 28-ft. deviations are at 1,300 ft., not 1.9 NM.

85.
8972. (Refer to figures 136 and 138 on page 320.) Which displacement from the localizer centerline and glide slope at the 1,300-foot point from the runway is indicated?

A—21 feet below the glide slope and approximately 320 feet to the right of the runway centerline.
B—28 feet above the glide slope and approximately 250 feet to the left of the runway centerline.
C—21 feet above the glide slope and approximately 320 feet to the left of the runway centerline.

Answer (C) is correct (8972). *(AIM Para 1-1-9)*
The airplane is above the glide slope and to the left of the localizer at 1,300 ft. by one and a half dots each. By extrapolation and Fig. 138, displacement is 21 ft. above the glide slope and about 320 ft. to the left of the localizer.
Answer (A) is incorrect because the airplane is above, not below, the glide slope and to the left, not right, of the localizer. Answer (B) is incorrect because 28 ft. is two dots, and 250 ft. is less than one and one-fourth dots.

86.
8973. (Refer to figures 137 and 138 on page 320.) Which displacement from the localizer and glide slope at the outer marker is indicated?

A—1,550 feet to the left of the localizer centerline and 210 feet below the glide slope.
B—1,550 feet to the right of the localizer centerline and 210 feet above the glide slope.
C—775 feet to the left of the localizer centerline and 420 feet below the glide slope.

Answer (A) is correct (8973). *(AIM Para 1-1-9)*
The airplane is below the glide slope by one dot and to the left of the localizer by two dots at the outer marker. According to Fig. 138, one dot on the glide slope is 210 ft. at the outer marker. Two dots on the localizer mean 1,550 ft.
Answer (B) is incorrect because the airplane is to the left, not right, of the localizer and below, not above, the glide slope. Answer (C) is incorrect because, at the OM, 775 ft. is one dot on the localizer, not the glide slope, and 420 ft. is two dots on the glide slope, not the localizer.

87.
8969. Which “rule-of-thumb” may be used to approximate the rate of descent required for a 3° glidepath?

A—5 times groundspeed in knots.
B—8 times groundspeed in knots.
C—10 times groundspeed in knots.

Answer (A) is correct (8969). *(FAA-P-8740-48)*
As a general rule, you can calculate the approximate rate of descent required for a 3° glide slope by multiplying your groundspeed (in knots) by 5.
Answer (B) is incorrect because 8 times the groundspeed would be used to calculate the rate of descent required for a 4.5°, not a 3°, glide slope. Answer (C) is incorrect because 10 times the groundspeed would be used to calculate the rate of descent required for a 6°, not a 3°, glide slope.

88.
8968. When is the course deviation indicator (CDI) considered to have a full-scale deflection?

A—When the CDI deflects from full-scale left to full-scale right, or vice versa.
B—When the CDI deflects from the center of the scale to full-scale left or right.
C—When the CDI deflects from half-scale left to half-scale right, or vice versa.

Answer (B) is correct (8968). *(IFH Chap X)*
A full-scale CDI deflection occurs when the CDI moves full left or right, i.e., is fully deflected to one side or the other.
Answer (A) is incorrect because when the CDI deflects full-scale left to full-scale right (or vice versa), you have two full-scale deflections. Answer (C) is incorrect because a deflection from half-scale left to half-scale right (or vice versa) is two half-scale deflections, not a full-scale deflection.

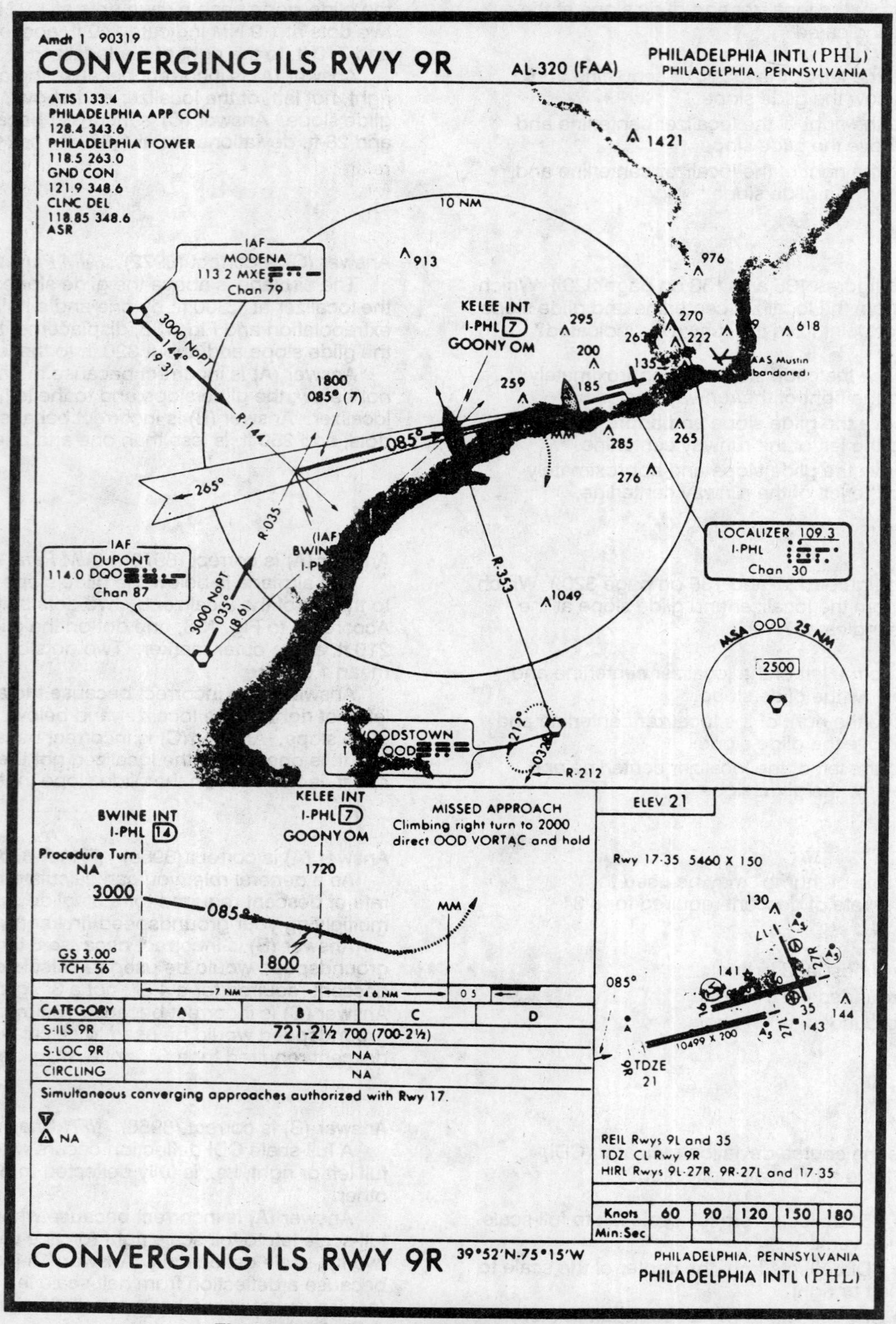

Figure 134.--Converging ILS RWY 9R (PHL)

89.
8950. (Refer to figure 134 on page 322.) What are the required weather minimums to execute the CONVERGING ILS RWY 9R approach procedure?

A—Ceiling 700 feet and 2-1/2 miles visibility.
B—At least 1,000 feet and 3 miles visibility.
C—Ceiling 800 feet and 2 miles visibility.

Answer (A) is correct (8950). *(IAP)*
In order to execute an instrument approach under Part 121 or 135, the conditions at the airport of landing must be at or above landing minimums. By referring to the minimums section of the approach chart for Fig. 134, you can see that, for the converging ILS RWY 9R approach, the decision height will be 721 ft. with visibility of 2½ SM and a HAT of 700 ft. Since ATIS broadcasts ceiling in relation to AGL, not MSL, a ceiling of 700 ft. is related to the HAT figure on the approach chart. Therefore, if the ATIS broadcasts a ceiling at or above 700 ft. and a visibility of at least 2½ SM, you will be at or above the required minimums to execute this approach.
Answer (B) is incorrect because 1,000 ft. and 3 SM visibility define the minimums required to land while operating under VFR, not the IFR minimums to execute the converging ILS RWY 9R instrument approach. Answer (C) is incorrect because 800 ft. and 2 SM visibility define the minimums required to file a specific airport with a nonprecision approach as an alternate and not required minimums to execute the converging ILS RWY 9R instrument approach.

90.
8951. (Refer to figure 134 on page 322.) What is the final approach fix for the CONVERGING ILS RWY 9R approach procedure?

A—BWINE INT and 3,000 feet MSL.
B—KELEE INT.
C—1,800 feet MSL and glide slope interception.

Answer (C) is correct (8951). *(IAP)*
For precision approaches, the glide slope intercept altitude depicted with a lightning bolt-type arrow indicates the final approach fix.
Answer (A) is incorrect because, by looking at the planview of the chart (Fig. 134), BWINE intersection is labeled as an IAF or initial approach fix, not a final approach fix. Answer (B) is incorrect because KELEE intersection identifies only the outer marker. Note that the lightning bolt arrow is depicted just prior to KELEE intersection.

91.
8952. (Refer to figure 134 on page 322.) What is the MINIMUM airborne equipment required to execute the CONVERGING ILS RWY 9R approach procedure?

A—Localizer and DME.
B—Localizer and glide slope.
C—Localizer only.

Answer (B) is correct (8952). *(IAP)*
In order to execute an ILS approach which provides both lateral and vertical guidance, an aircraft requires both a localizer and a glide slope.
Answer (A) is incorrect because the heading section of this chart does not include DME; therefore, DME is not required. Answer (C) is incorrect because, in the minimums section of the chart, the initials NA are labeled in the straight-in localizer box; therefore, a localizer-only approach is not authorized.

92.
8970. What facilities may be substituted for an inoperative middle marker during a Category I ILS approach?

A—ASR and PAR.
B—The middle marker has no effect on straight-in minimums.
C—Compass locator, PAR, and ASR.

Answer (B) is correct (8970). *(FAR 91.175)*
A compass locator or precision radar (PAR) may be substituted for the middle marker. Since an inoperative middle marker does not affect the straight-in minimums of an ILS approach, no substitution is required.
Answer (A) is incorrect because surveillance radar (ASR) can be substituted for the outer marker, not the middle marker. Answer (C) is incorrect because surveillance radar (ASR) can be substituted for the outer marker, not the middle marker.

93.
8953. When simultaneous approaches are in progress, how does each pilot receive radar advisories?

A—On tower frequency.
B—On approach control frequency.
C—One pilot on tower frequency and the other on approach control frequency.

Answer (A) is correct (8953). *(AIM Para 5-4-14)*
Whenever simultaneous approaches are in progress, radar advisories will be provided on the tower frequency.
Answer (B) is incorrect because pilots will be advised to monitor the tower, not approach control, frequency to receive radar advisories and instructions. Answer (C) is incorrect because both pilots will receive radar advisories on the tower frequency.

94.
8955. When simultaneous ILS approaches are in progress, which of the following should approach control be advised of immediately?

A—Any inoperative or malfunctioning aircraft receivers.
B—If a simultaneous ILS approach is desired.
C—If radar monitoring is desired to confirm lateral separation.

Answer (A) is correct (8955). *(AIM Para 5-4-12)*
When advised that simultaneous ILS approaches are in progress, pilots shall advise approach control immediately if receivers are malfunctioning or inoperative or if simultaneous approach is not desired.
Answer (B) is incorrect because simultaneous approaches are issued at any time according to ATC needs, and it is not the responsibility of the pilot to request such an approach. Answer (C) is incorrect because radar monitoring is always provided during simultaneous approaches.

95.
8954. When cleared to execute a published side-step maneuver, at what point is the pilot expected to commence this maneuver?

A—At the published DH.
B—At the MDA published or a circling approach.
C—As soon as possible after the runway environment is in sight.

Answer (C) is correct (8954). *(AIM Para 5-4-17)*
Pilots are expected to commence the side-step maneuver as soon as possible after the runway or runway environment is in sight.
Answer (A) is incorrect because the side-step maneuver can only be performed and should be performed as soon as possible after the runway or runway environment is in sight. Answer (B) is incorrect because the side-step maneuver can only be performed and should be performed as soon as possible after the runway or runway environment is in sight.

96.
9438. When cleared to execute a published sidestep maneuver for a specific approach and landing on the parallel runway, at what point is the pilot expected to commence this maneuver?

A—At the published minimum altitude for a circling approach.
B—As soon as possible after the runway or runway environment is in sight.
C—At the localizer MDA minimums and when the runway is in sight.

Answer (B) is correct (9438). *(AIM Para 5-4-17)*
Pilots are expected to commence the side-step maneuver as soon as possible after the runway or runway environment is in sight.
Answer (A) is incorrect because the side-step maneuver can only be performed and should be performed as soon as possible after the runway or runway environment is in sight, which may be below the published minimum altitude for a circling approach. Answer (C) is incorrect because the side-step maneuver should be performed as soon as possible after the runway or runway environment is in sight, which should be before the localizer MDA minimums.

97.
8963. The lowest ILS Category II minimums are

A—DH 50 feet and RVR 1,200 feet.
B—DH 100 feet and RVR 1,200 feet.
C—DH 150 feet and RVR 1,500 feet.

Answer (B) is correct (8963). *(AIM Para 1-1-9)*
The pilot-in-command minimums for the lowest Category II minimums are a DH of 100 ft. and an RVR of 1,200 ft.
Answer (A) is incorrect because a DH of 50 ft. is for Category III operations, not Category II. Answer (C) is incorrect because a DH of 150 ft. is for a pilot's initial Category II authorization (for the initial 6-month period) only and is not the lowest DH for Category II operations.

98.
8964. What is the lowest Category IIIA minimum?

A—DH 50 feet and RVR 1,200 feet.
B—RVR 1,000 feet.
C—RVR 700 feet.

Answer (C) is correct (8964). *(AIM Para 1-1-9)*
The lowest Category IIIA authorization is for no DH and an RVR of not less than 700 ft.
Answer (A) is incorrect because a DH of 50 ft. is for some Category III operations, and an RVR of 1,200 ft. is for Category II operations. Answer (B) is incorrect because an RVR of 1,000 ft. does not exist for any category approach.

99.
8965. How does the SDF differ from an ILS LOC?

A—SDF - 6° or 12° wide, ILS - 3° to 6°.
B—SDF - offset from runway plus 3°, ILS - aligned with runway.
C—SDF - 15° usable off course indications, ILS - 35°.

Answer (A) is correct (8965). *(AIM Para 1-1-10)*
The course width for an ILS localizer is from 3° to 6°, whereas the SDF is either 6° or 12° wide.
Answer (B) is incorrect because an SDF may not be aligned with the centerline of the runway. Answer (C) is incorrect because the usable off-course indications are limited to 35° for both types of approaches.

100.
9413. In addition to the localizer, glide slope, marker beacons, approach lighting, and HIRL, which ground components are required to be operative for a Category II instrument approach to a DH below 150 feet AGL?

A—RCLS and REIL.
B—Radar and RVR.
C—TDZL, RCLS, and RVR.

Answer (C) is correct (9413). *(FAR 91.175)*
Category II ILS operations require the following ground components to be operative to allow a Category II approach to a DH below 150 ft. AGL: localizer, glide slope, marker beacons, approach lighting, HIRL, touchdown zone lighting (TDZL), runway centerline lighting system (RCLS), and reporting of runway visual range (RVR).
Answer (A) is incorrect because runway end identifier lights (REIL) are used to provide rapid identification of the approach end of a runway and are not a required ground component for Category II ILS operations. Answer (B) is incorrect because radar is not a required ground component for Category II ILS operations.

101.
9411. Which ground components are required to be operative for a Category II approach in addition to LOC, glide slope, marker beacons, and approach lights?

A—Radar and RVR.
B—RCLS and REIL.
C—HIRL, TDZL, RCLS, and RVR.

Answer (C) is correct (9411). *(FAR 91.175)*
Category II ILS operations require these ground components to be operative: LOC, glide slope, marker beacons, approach lights, high-intensity runway lights (HIRL), touchdown zone lights (TDZL), runway centerline lighting system (RCLS), and runway visual range (RVR). If any of these is inoperative, an increase in DH and/or visibility may be required.
Answer (A) is incorrect because radar is not a required Category II ILS ground component. Answer (B) is incorrect because runway end identifier lights (REIL) are used to provide rapid identification of the approach end of a runway. They are not a required ground component for Category II ILS.

102.
8967. How does the LDA differ from an ILS LOC?

A—LDA - 6° or 12° wide, ILS - 3° to 6°.
B—LDA - offset from runway plus 3°, ILS - aligned with runway.
C—LDA - 15° usable off course indications, ILS - 35°.

Answer (B) is correct (8967). *(AIM Para 1-1-9)*
The localizer-type directional aid (LDA) is of comparable utility and accuracy to a localizer but is not part of a complete ILS. The LDA does not have to be aligned with the runway. The straight-in minimum may be published if alignment does not exceed 30° between the course and the runway. ILS localizers are aligned with the runway.
Answer (A) is incorrect because an SDF, not LDA, is fixed at either 6° or 12° wide. Answer (C) is incorrect because the usable off-course indications are limited to 35° for both types of approaches within 10 NM.

9.10 LORAN Approaches

103.
8947. LORAN-C is based upon measurements of the difference in time arrival of pulses generated by what type radio stations?

A—A group of stations operating on the 108-115 MHz frequency band.
B—Two stations operating on the 90-110 MHz frequency band.
C—A chain of stations operating on the 90-110 kHz frequency band.

Answer (C) is correct (8947). *(AIM Para 1-1-15)*
LORAN-C is a pulsed, hyperbolic system radiated by a chain of stations operating in the 90-110 kHz frequency band.
Answer (A) is incorrect because the types of stations operating within these frequency bands are localizers and VORs. Answer (B) is incorrect because no known navigational aids or communications operate within 90-110 MHz.

104.
8948. For what service has LORAN-C been approved?

A—IFR navigation in U.S. coastal areas and nonprecision approaches.
B—VFR navigation in the 48 contiguous United States and District of Columbia.
C—IFR and VFR navigation in the 48 contiguous United States and District of Columbia.

Answer (C) is correct (8948). *(AIM Para 1-1-15)*
LORAN-C has been approved to meet the requirements for VFR and IFR en route and nonprecision instrument approaches.
Answer (A) is incorrect because LORAN-C has been approved for both IFR and VFR in the 48 contiguous states, not only in the U.S. coastal areas. Answer (B) is incorrect because LORAN-C has been approved for both VFR and IFR en route navigation, not just VFR.

105.
8946. What documents the authorized operational level of LORAN-C?

A—A placard stating "KIRAB-C APPROVED FOR IFR."
B—The Airplane Flight Manual Supplement or FAA Form 337, Major Repair and Alteration.
C—An entry in the aircraft maintenance logbook giving place, date, and signature of authorizing official.

Answer (B) is correct (8946). *(AC 20-121)*
A pilot must be aware of the authorized operational approval level of the receiver installed in his/her aircraft. This information is contained in the airplane flight manual supplement or FAA Form 337, as appropriate. These documents are the only reliable means of determining FAA-approved LORAN-C operations.
Answer (A) is incorrect because a placard is needed only when a LORAN-C receiver is not approved for IFR. Answer (C) is incorrect because no entry in the maintenance log is needed for approved operations using LORAN-C as referenced to the airplane flight manual or FAA Form 337.

106.
8945. How may a pilot determine if a LORAN-C receiver is authorized for IFR operations?

A—Consult the Airplane Flight Manual Supplement.
B—A placard stating, "LORAN-C APPROVED FOR IFR EN ROUTE, TERMINAL AND APPROACH SEGMENTS."
C—An airframe logbook entry that the LORAN-C receiver has been checked within the previous 30-calendar days.

Answer (A) is correct (8945). *(AC 20-121)*
A pilot must be aware of the authorized operational approval level of the receiver installed in his/her aircraft. This information is contained in the airplane flight manual supplement or FAA Form 337, as appropriate. These documents are the only reliable means of determining FAA-approved LORAN-C operations.
Answer (B) is incorrect because LORAN-C is not approved for instrument approach segments, and placarding is required for receivers not approved for IFR. Answer (C) is incorrect because LORAN-C receivers do not require operational accuracy checks (generally internal self-checking routines are built into LORAN-C receivers).

107.
8942. What is the maximum number of degrees between the final approach course and the runway centerline for a LORAN RNAV approach to be considered a straight-in approach?

A—5°.
B—10°.
C—30°.

Answer (C) is correct (8942). *(AIM Para 5-4-18)*
Straight-in minimums are shown on the IAP when the final approach course is within 30° of the runway alignment and a normal descent can be made from the IFR altitude shown on the IAP to the runway surface. When either the normal rate of descent or the runway alignment factor of 30° is exceeded, a circling minimum applies.
Answer (A) is incorrect because 5° is within the 3°-to-6° width of the localizer. Answer (B) is incorrect because 10° is the normal limit (i.e., a full deflection) from the centerline of a localizer from 10 NM to 18 NM from the antenna.

108.
8949. Which class of NOTAM gives the latest information on LORAN-C chain or station outages?

A—NOTAM (L)'s under the identifier "LORAN-C."
B—NOTAM (D)'s under the identifier "LRN."
C—Class II NOTAM's published every 14 days.

Answer (B) is correct (8949). *(AIM Para 1-1-15)*
Notices to Airmen (NOTAMS) are issued for LORAN-C chain or station outages. LORAN NOTAMs (D) are issued under the identifier "LRN." Pilots may obtain these NOTAMs from FSS briefers upon request.
Answer (A) is incorrect because NOTAM (L) information is distributed locally only and is maintained at each FSS for facilities in the area. Information such as taxiway closure and rotating beacon outages is included, but not information relating to LORAN-C stations. Answer (C) is incorrect because the *Notices to Airmen Publication* (formerly called Class II NOTAMs) contains published NOTAMs and is published every 28 days, not 14 days. Additionally, the *Notices to Airmen Publication* does not contain the latest information on LORAN status.

109.
8940. (Refer to figure 132 on page 329 and legend 22 on page 331.) Which navigation frequency must be used for the LORAN RNAV RWY 10R to Portland Intl Airport?

A—MWX 9940.
B—104.3 MHz.
C—133.0 MHz.

Answer (A) is correct (8940). *(IAP)*
To find the correct LORAN frequency (chain) to use, look to the heading section of the approach chart. Toward the center of this section appears MWX 9940, which identifies the stations and the group repetition interval (GRI) to identify the LORAN chain to be used for the approach.
Answer (B) is incorrect because nowhere on Fig. 132 does frequency 104.3 appear. Answer (C) is incorrect because 133.0 MHz identifies the approach control facility to be used, as indicated in the communications frequency section of the chart (upper left corner).

110.
8941. (Refer to figure 132 on page 329 and legend 22 on page 331.) To which stations, if any, must TD corrections be made to the aircraft LORAN receiver before executing the LORAN RNAV RWY 10R approach to Portland Intl Airport?

A—No corrections are necessary.
B—Stations M and W.
C—Stations W and X.

Answer (C) is correct (8941). *(IAP)*
The time distance (TD) table in the legend contains the TD correction values for each airport with a published LORAN RNAV instrument approach procedure. This TD correction value must be entered into the LORAN airborne receiver prior to beginning the approach. Note that for the city of Portland the only two TD correction values shown are for the W and X locations.
Answer (A) is incorrect because TD corrections are needed for all airports using LORAN RNAV instrument approach procedures. Answer (B) is incorrect because a TD correction value for M does not exist. M stands for the master station and does not change value because the secondary stations are synchronized with the master station.

111.
8943. (Refer to figure 133 on page 330 and legend 22 on page 331.) To which stations, if any, must TD corrections be made to the aircraft LORAN receiver before executing the LORAN RNAV RWY 15 approach to the Burlington Intl Airport?

A—Correct stations X and Y.
B—Correct stations W and X.
C—No corrections are required.

Answer (B) is correct (8943). *(IAP)*
The time distance (TD) table in the legend contains the TD correction values for each airport with a published LORAN RNAV instrument approach procedure. This TD correction value must be entered into the LORAN airborne receiver prior to beginning the approach. Note that for the city of Burlington the only two TD correction values shown are for the W and X stations.
Answer (A) is incorrect because the Y station TD correction is needed only for the cities of Orlando and Columbus. Answer (C) is incorrect because TD corrections are needed for all airports using LORAN RNAV instrument approach procedures.

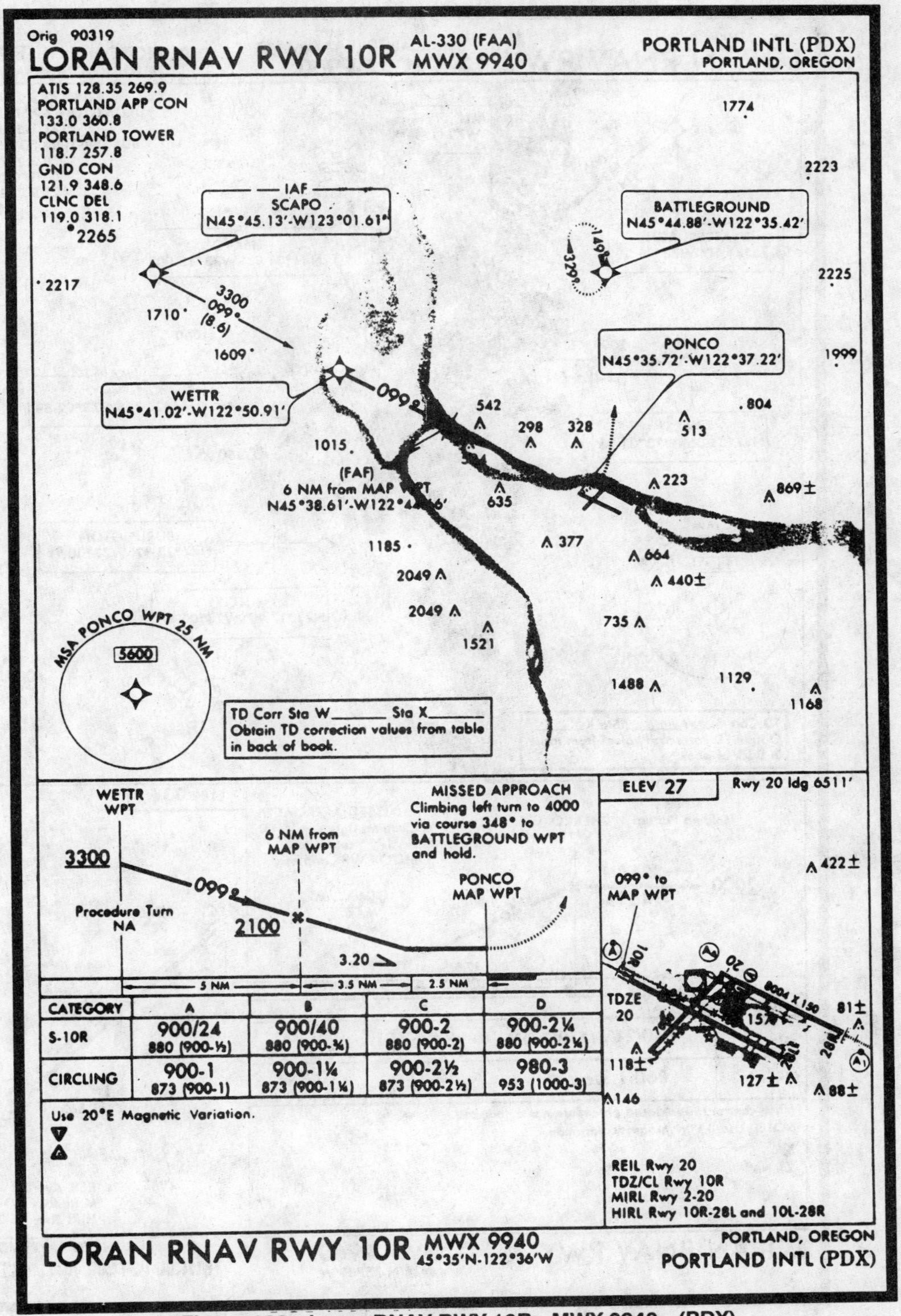

Figure 132.--Loran RNAV RWY 10R - MWX 9940 - (PDX)

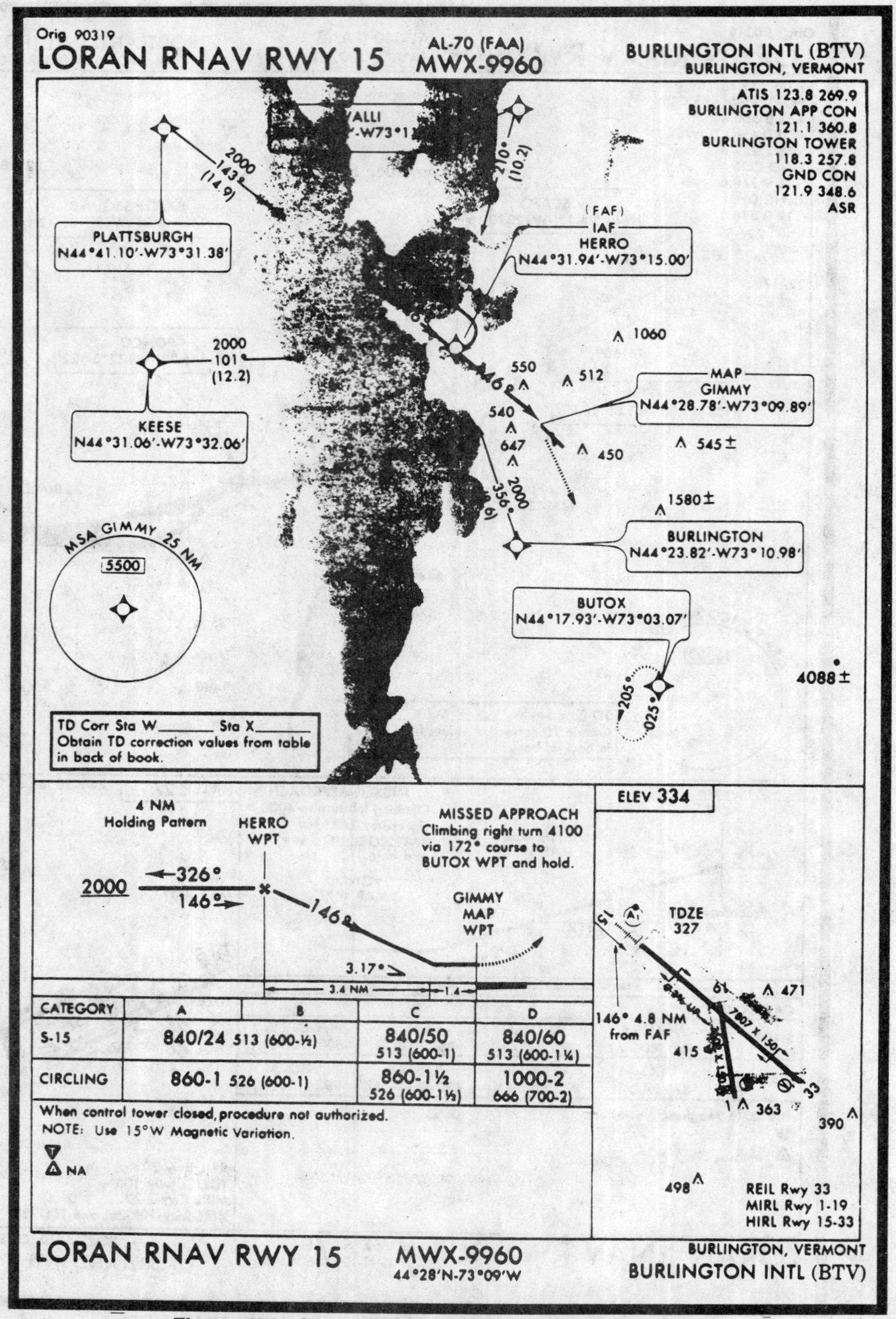

Figure 133.--Loran RNAV RWY 15 - MWX-9960 - (BTV)

AIRPORT LORAN TD CORRECTION TABLE

The following LORAN - C time difference (TD) table contains the TD correction values for each airport with a published LORAN RNAV instrument approach procedure. This TD correction value must be entered into the LORAN airborne receiver prior to beginning the approach. TD values from this table should be transferred to the TD correction box shown in the plan view of the LORAN RNAV approach for the destination airport.

Pilots are advised to check LORAN (LRN) NOTAM's to obtain the status of the LORAN chain or group repetition interval (GRI) and NOTAM's for the LORAN monitor location identifier (MLID) at their destination and alternate airport.

	AIRPORT										
CITY	ST	NAME	LID	MLID	GRI	TRI	V	W	X	Y	Z
BURLINGTON	VT	BURLINGTON INTL	BTV	BTV	9960	MWX		10.0	09.8		
COLUMBUS	OH	OHIO STATE UNIV.	OSU	OSU	9960	MYZ				08.6	11.6
NEW ORLEANS	LA	LAKEFRONT	NEW	NEW	7980	MWX		11.5	11.2		
ORLANDO	FL	ORLANDO EXEC.	ORL	ORL	7980	MYZ				11.3	11.7
PORTLAND	OR	PORTLAND INTL.	PDX	PDX	9940	MWX		11.7	09.4		
VENICE	LA	CHEVRON	8LA5	NEW	7980	MWX		11.5	11.2		

Legend 22.--Airport Loran TD Correction Table

112.
8944. (Refer to figure 133 on page 330 and legend 22 above.) Which navigation frequency must be used for the LORAN RNAV RWY 15 to the Burlington Intl Airport?

A—W=10.0; X=09.8.
B—BTV9960.
C—MWX9960.

Answer (C) is correct (8944). *(IAP)*

To find the correct LORAN frequency (chain) to use, look to the heading section of the approach chart. Toward the center of this section appears MWX-9960, which identifies the stations and the group repetition interval (GRI) to identify the LORAN chain to be used for the approach.

Answer (A) is incorrect because W=10.0 and X=09.8 are the time difference correction values for this approach. Answer (B) is incorrect because BTV is the identifier for Burlington International, not the LORAN stations.

9.11 Microwave Landing Systems (MLS)

113.
8978. What information is provided by the Microwave Landing System (MLS) precision navigation system?

A—Azimuth, elevation, and distance information.
B—Azimuth, elevation, and three-letter identification.
C—Range, elevation, and ISMLS readouts.

Answer (A) is correct (8978). *(AIM Para 1-1-11)*
The MLS (microwave landing system) provides precision navigation guidance for exact alignment and descent of aircraft on approach to a runway. It provides azimuth, elevation, and distance information.
Answer (B) is incorrect because distance information is omitted, and MLS contains a four-, not three-, letter identification. Answer (C) is incorrect because distance information is omitted and ISMLS (interim standard microwave landing system) does not provide the same information that MLS does.

114.
8982. In addition to navigation information, what data is transmitted on the Microwave Landing System (MLS) frequencies?

A—MLS status, missed approach procedure, and airport conditions.
B—ATC clearances, missed approach procedures, and airport conditions.
C—MLS status, airport conditions, and weather.

Answer (C) is correct (8982). *(AIM Para 1-1-11)*
MLS provides data including meteorological information, runway status, MLS status, waypoint coordinates, ground equipment performance level, and airport conditions.
Answer (A) is incorrect because, while MLS status and airport conditions are transmitted, missed approach procedures are not broadcast. Answer (B) is incorrect because ATC clearances and missed approach procedures are not broadcast on MLS frequencies.

115.
8983. What does operational flexibility of the Microwave Landing System (MLS) include?

A—Selectable glidepath angles and boundaries providing obstruction clearance in the terminal area.
B—An azimuth of 40° in width providing obstacle clearance within 22 NM of the airport.
C—Curved and segmented approaches collocated with a fixed glidepath angle.

Answer (A) is correct (8983). *(AIM Para 1-1-11)*
The MLS has the capability to meet a variety of needs; for example, curved and segmented approaches, selectable glide path angles, accurate three-dimensional positioning of aircraft in space, and the establishment of boundaries to ensure clearance of obstructions in the terminal area.
Answer (B) is incorrect because, while azimuth is provided to 40° on either side of the centerline, elevation coverage is provided to 20 NM, not 22 NM. Answer (C) is incorrect because curved and segmented approaches are dependent upon the particular capabilities of the airborne equipment.

116.
8981. What is the difference, if any, between the front and back azimuth of the Microwave Landing System (MLS)?

A—None, except indicator reversal.
B—Transmissions are at a lower rate.
C—Back azimuth has no DME/P.

Answer (B) is correct (8981). *(AIM Para 1-1-11)*
The back azimuth transmitter is essentially the same as the approach azimuth transmitter. However, the equipment transmits at a lower data rate, and the guidance accuracy requirements are not as stringent.
Answer (A) is incorrect because the guidance accuracy requirements are not as stringent as for the landing approach, and there is no indicator reversal on the back azimuth. Answer (C) is incorrect because both the front and the back MLS azimuths have DME/P (precision distance measuring equipment). MLS range information can be read out on existing DME indicators.

117.
8979. In addition to basic information, what expansion capabilities does the Microwave Landing System (MLS) have?

A—Back azimuth glide slope.
B—Back azimuth and data transmissions.
C—Variable front and back azimuth upon request.

Answer (B) is correct (8979). *(AIM Para 1-1-11)*
The standard MLS capabilities can be expanded to include back azimuth, auxiliary data transmissions (including refined airborne positioning, meteorological information, etc.), and larger proportional guidance (wider azimuth and steeper approach elevation).
Answer (A) is incorrect because back azimuth glide slope is not available on MLS (back azimuth is for departure and missed approach navigation). Answer (C) is incorrect because the variability of front and back azimuth information is dependent upon the aircraft's navigation equipment.

118.
8974. What international Morse Code identifier is used to identify a specific interim standard Microwave Landing System (MLS)?

A—A two letter Morse Code identifier preceded by the Morse Code for the letters "IM."
B—A three letter Morse Code identifier preceded by the Morse Code for the letter "M."
C—A three letter Morse Code identifier preceded by the Morse Code for the letters "ML."

Answer (B) is correct (8974). *(AIM Para 1-1-11)*
MLS identification consists of a three-letter Morse code identifier preceded by the Morse code for "M."
Answer (A) is incorrect because an MLS is identified by a three-, not two-, letter Morse code identifier preceded by the Morse code for "M." Answer (C) is incorrect because an MLS identifier is a three-letter designation preceded by the letter "M," not "ML."

119.
8980. What azimuth coverage of the Microwave Landing System (MLS) can be expected?

A—Laterally 20° each side, vertically 15° to 20,000 feet, and range 50 NM.
B—Laterally 40° each side, vertically 15° to 20,000 feet, and range 20 NM.
C—Laterally 15° each side, vertically 6° to 20,000 feet, and range 20 NM.

Answer (B) is correct (8980). *(AIM Para 1-1-11)*
The MLS provides precision navigation guidance for exact alignment and descent of aircraft on approach to a runway. It provides azimuth coverage laterally 40° each side, vertically 15° to 20,000 ft., and a range of 20 NM.
Answer (A) is incorrect because azimuth coverage is laterally to 40°, not 15°, each side and a range of 20 NM, not 50 NM. Answer (C) is incorrect because azimuth coverage is laterally to 40°, not 15°, each side and vertically to 15°, not 6°.

120.
8975. To at least which altitude AGL is the approach azimuth guidance angle coverage of a Microwave Landing System (MLS)?

A—20,000 feet.
B—10,000 feet.
C—8,000 feet.

Answer (A) is correct (8975). *(AIM Para 1-1-11)*
The approach azimuth guidance angle coverage of an MLS extends in elevation to an angle of 15° and to at least 20,000 feet.
Answer (B) is incorrect because the azimuth coverage of an MLS extends to at least 20,000 ft. Answer (C) is incorrect because the azimuth coverage of an MLS extends to at least 20,000 ft.

121.
8976. What are the lateral approach azimuth angle limits, referenced to either side of the landing runway, of a Microwave Landing System (MLS)?

A—At least 15°.
B—20°.
C—At least 40°.

Answer (C) is correct (8976). *(AIM Para 1-1-11)*
The lateral approach azimuth angle limits are at least 40° on each side of the runway.
Answer (A) is incorrect because lateral azimuth limits extend to at least 40° on either side of the runway, not 15°. Answer (B) is incorrect because lateral azimuth limits extend to at least 40° on either side of the runway, not 20°.

122.
8977. What are the respective range limits for the front and back guidance of a Microwave Landing System (MLS)?

A—10 NM and 10 NM.
B—15 NM and 10 NM.
C—20 NM and 7 NM.

Answer (C) is correct (8977). *(AIM Para 1-1-11)*
The range limit for the front (approach) azimuth angle guidance of an MLS is at least 20 NM. The range limit for the back azimuth angle guidance is at least 7 NM.
Answer (A) is incorrect because the front guidance extends out to 20 NM, not 10 NM, and the back course guidance is limited to 7 NM, not 10 NM. Answer (B) is incorrect because the front course guidance extends out to 20 NM, not 15 NM, and the back course guidance is limited to 7 NM, not 10 NM.

9.12 GPS Approaches

123.
9692. Aircraft navigating by GPS are considered, on the flight plan, to be

A—RNAV equipped.
B—Astrotracker equipped.
C—FMS/EFIS equipped.

Answer (A) is correct (9692). *(AIM Para 1-1-11)*
Aircraft navigating by GPS are considered to be RNAV-equipped aircraft; thus the appropriate equipment suffix must be included on the flight plan.
Answer (B) is incorrect because aircraft navigating by GPS are considered to be RNAV, not astrotracker, equipped. Answer (C) is incorrect because aircraft navigating by GPS are considered to be RNAV, not FMS/EFIS, equipped.

124.
9691. The GPS Approach Overlay Program permits pilots to use GPS avionics when IFR for flying existing instrument approach procedures, except

A—LOC, LDA and ADF.
B—LDA, TAC and SDF.
C—SDF, LOC and LDA.

Answer (C) is correct (9691). *(AIM Para 1-1-21)*
The GPS Approach Overlay Program permits pilots to use GPS avionics under IFR for flying existing IAPs, except SDF, LOC, and LDA procedures.
Answer (A) is incorrect because the GPS Approach Overlay Program permits pilots to use GPS avionics under IFR for flying existing IAPs except SDF, not ADF, procedures. Answer (B) is incorrect because the GPS Approach Overlay Program permits pilots to use GPS avionics under IFR for flying existing IAPs except LOC, not TACAN, procedures.

125.
9693. The Instrument Approach Procedure Chart top margin identification is VOR or GPS RWY 25, AL-5672 (FAA), LUKACHUKAI, ARIZONA. In what phase of the approach overlay program is this GPS approach?

A—Phase I.
B—Phase III.
C—Phase II.

Answer (B) is correct (9693). *(AIM Para 1-1-21)*
Phase III of the GPS Approach Overlay Program begins when IAPs are retitled, such as "VOR or GPS RWY 25." In this phase, ground-based NAVAIDs are not required to be operational, and the associated aircraft avionics (e.g., VOR) need not be installed, operational, turned on, or monitored. GPS approaches will be requested and approved using the GPS title, such as "GPS RWY 25."
Answer (A) is incorrect because, under Phase I, the IAP chart title would be VOR RWY 25, not VOR or GPS RWY 25. Answer (C) is incorrect because, under Phase II, the IAP chart title would be VOR RWY 25.

126.
9694. The weather forecast requires an alternate for LUKACHUKAI (GPS RWY 25) ARIZONA. The alternate airport must have an approved instrument approach procedure, which is anticipated to be operational and available at the estimated time of arrival, other than

A—GPS or VOR.
B—ILS or GPS.
C—GPS or Loran C.

Answer (C) is correct (9694). *(AIM Para 1-1-21)*
In each phase of the GPS Approach Overlay Program, any required alternate airport must have an approved IAP, other than GPS or LORAN-C, which is anticipated to be operational and available at the estimated time of arrival.
Answer (A) is incorrect because the alternate airport must have an approved IAP other than GPS or LORAN-C, not VOR. Answer (B) is incorrect because the alternate airport must have an approved IAP other than GPS or LORAN-C, not ILS.

127.
9430. Without Receiver Autonomous Integrity Monitoring (RAIM) capability, the accuracy of the GPS derived

A—altitude information should not be relied upon to determine aircraft altitude.
B—position is not affected.
C—velocity information should be relied upon to determine aircraft groundspeed.

Answer (A) is correct (9430). *(AIM Para 1-1-21)*
RAIM is used to determine if a satellite is providing corrupted information. Without RAIM capability, the accuracy of the GPS-derived altitude information should not be relied upon to determine aircraft altitude since the vertical error can be quite large.
Answer (B) is incorrect because RAIM is used to determine if a satellite is providing corrupted information. Without RAIM, the GPS position should NOT be relied upon since the position solution can be greatly affected. Answer (C) is incorrect because RAIM is used to determine if a satellite is providing corrupted information.

128.
9431. Overriding an automatically selected sensitivity during a GPS approach will

A—cancel the approach mode annunciation.
B—require flying point-to-point on the approach to comply with the published approach procedure.
C—have no effect if the approach is flown manually.

Answer (A) is correct (9431). *(AIM Para 1-1-21)*
When within 2 NM of the final approach waypoint with the approach mode armed, the approach mode will switch to active, which results in RAIM changing to approach sensitivity and a change in CDI sensitivity. Overriding an automatically selected sensitivity during an approach will cancel the approach mode annunciation.
Answer (B) is incorrect because flying point-to-point on the approach does NOT assure compliance with the published approach procedure. Answer (C) is incorrect because manually setting CDI sensitivity does not automatically change RAIM sensitivity on some GPS receivers.

129.
9432. If a visual descent point (VDP) is published on a GPS approach, it

A—will not be included in the sequence of waypoints.
B—will be coded in the waypoint sequence and identified using ATD.
C—must be included in the normal waypoints.

Answer (A) is correct (9432). *(AIM Para 1-1-21)*
If a visual descent point (VDP) is published on a GPS approach, it will not be included in the sequence of waypoints. Pilots are expected to use normal piloting techniques for beginning the visual descent.
Answer (B) is incorrect because a VDP will NOT be included in the waypoint sequence. Answer (C) is incorrect because, if a VDP is published on a GPS approach, it will NOT be included in the normal waypoint sequence.

130.
9723. Authorization to conduct any GPS operation under IFR requires that

A—the equipment be approved in accordance with TSO C-115a.
B—the pilot must review appropriate weather, aircraft flight manual (AFM), and operation of the particular receiver.
C—procedures must be established for use in the event that the loss of RAIM capability is predicted to occur.

Answer (C) is correct (9723). *(AIM Para 1-1-21)*
Authorization to conduct any GPS operation under IFR requires, among others, that procedures be established for use in the event that the loss of RAIM capability is predicted to occur. In situations in which this event is encountered, the pilot must rely on other approved equipment, delay departure, or cancel the flight.
Answer (A) is incorrect because, to conduct any GPS operation under IFR, the equipment must be approved in accordance with TSO C-129 or equivalent. TSO C-115a does not meet the requirements of TSO C-129.
Answer (B) is incorrect because, before conducting any GPS operation under IFR, the pilot must be thoroughly familiar with, not just review, the GPS equipment installed, the GPS operation manual, and the aircraft flight manual. Additionally, prior to any GPS IFR operation, the pilot must review the appropriate NOTAMs, not only the weather.

131.
9724. Authorization to conduct any GPS operation under IFR requires that

A—the pilot review appropriate weather, aircraft flight manual (AFM), and operation of the particular GPS receiver.
B—air carrier and commercial operators must meet the appropriate provisions of their approved operations specifications.
C—the equipment be approved in accordance with TSO C-115a.

Answer (B) is correct (9724). *(AIM Para 1-1-21)*
Authorization to conduct any GPS operation under IFR requires that, among others, air carriers and commercial operators meet the appropriate provisions of their approved operations specifications.
Answer (A) is incorrect because, before conducting any GPS operation under IFR, the pilot must be thoroughly familiar with, not just review, the GPS equipment installed, the GPS operation manual, and the aircraft flight manual. Additionally, prior to any GPS IFR operation, the pilot must review the appropriate NOTAMs, not only the weather. Answer (C) is incorrect because, to conduct any GPS operation under IFR, the equipment must be approved in accordance with TSO C-129 or equivalent. TSO C-115a does not meet the requirements of TSO C-129.

132.
9722. GPS instrument approach operations, outside the United States, must be authorized by

A—the FAA-approved aircraft flight manual (AFM) or flight manual supplement.
B—a sovereign country or governmental unit.
C—the FAA Administrator only.

Answer (B) is correct (9722). *(AIM Para 1-1-21)*
GPS instrument approach operations outside the U.S. must be authorized by the appropriate sovereign authority.
Answer (A) is incorrect because the aircraft flight manual or the supplement explains how to operate the GPS system installed in the airplane; it does not authorize that GPS be used for any type of GPS operation. Answer (C) is incorrect because GPS instrument approach operations inside, not outside, the U.S. must be authorized by the FAA Administrator.

133.
9725. When using GPS for navigation and instrument approaches, a required alternate airport must have

A—an approved instrument approach procedure, besides GPS, that is expected to be operational and available at the ETA.
B—a GPS approach that is expected to be operational and available at the ETA.
C—authorization to fly approaches under IFR using GPS avionics.

Answer (A) is correct (9725). *(AIM Para 1-1-21)*
When using GPS for navigation and instrument approaches, any required alternate airport must have an approved instrument approach procedure, other than GPS, that is expected to be operational and available at the ETA and that the airplane is equipped to fly.
Answer (B) is incorrect because, when using GPS for navigation and instrument approaches, any required alternate must have an approved instrument approach procedure, other than a GPS approach, that is expected to be operational and available at the ETA. Answer (C) is incorrect because, when using GPS for navigation and instrument approaches, any required alternate airport must have an approved instrument approach procedure, other than GPS, that is expected to be operational and available at the ETA. The alternate airport is not required to have an approved GPS approach.

134.
9429. If Receiver Autonomous Integrity Monitoring (RAIM) is not available when setting up for GPS approach, the pilot should

A—continue to the MAP and hold until the satellites are recaptured.
B—proceed as cleared to the IAF and hold until satellite reception is satisfactory.
C—select another type of approach using another type of navigation aid.

Answer (C) is correct (9429). *(AIM Para 1-1-21)*
If RAIM is not available when setting up for a GPS approach, you should inform ATC and select another type of approach using another type of navigation aid.
Answer (A) is incorrect because, if a RAIM failure occurs prior to the final approach waypoint (FAWP), not when setting up for a GPS approach, you should proceed to the missed approach waypoint via the FAWP, perform the missed approach, and contact ATC as soon as possible, not hold until satellites are recaptured. Answer (B) is incorrect because if RAIM is not available when setting up for a GPS approach, you should advise ATC and select another type of approach using another type of navigation aid, not proceed to the IAF and hold until satellite reception is satisfactory.

135.
9727. A GPS missed approach requires that the pilot take action to sequence the receiver

A—over the MAWP.
B—after the MAWP.
C—just prior to the MAWP.

Answer (B) is correct (9727). *(AIM Para 1-1-21)*
A GPS missed approach requires that you take action to sequence the receiver past the missed approach waypoint (MAWP) to the missed approach portion of the procedure. You must be thoroughly familiar with the activation procedure for the particular GPS receiver installed in the airplane and must initiate appropriate action after the MAWP.
Answer (A) is incorrect because a GPS missed approach requires that you take action to sequence the receiver after, not over, the MAWP. Answer (C) is incorrect because activating the missed approach prior to the MAWP will cause the CDI sensitivity to change to terminal (± 1 NM) immediately, and the receiver will continue to navigate to the MAWP but not sequence past the MAWP. Thus, you should sequence the receiver after, not prior to, the MAWP.

136.
9728. If the missed approach is not activated, the GPS receiver will display

A—an extension of the outbound final approach course, and the ATD will increase from the MAWP.
B—an extension of the outbound final approach course.
C—an extension of the inbound final approach course.

Answer (C) is correct (9728). *(AIM Para 1-1-21)*
If the missed approach is not activated, the GPS receiver will display an extension of the inbound final approach course, and the along track distance (ATD) will increase from the MAWP until it is manually sequenced after crossing the MAWP.
Answer (A) is incorrect because, if the missed approach is not activated, the GPS receiver will display an extension of the inbound, not outbound, final approach course, and the ATD will increase from the MAWP. Answer (B) is incorrect because, if the missed approach is not activated, the GPS receiver will display an extension of the inbound, not outbound, final approach course, and the ATD will increase from the MAWP.

137.
9730. Missed approach routing in which the first track is via a course rather than direct to the next waypoint requires

A—that the GPS receiver be sequenced to the missed approach portion of the procedure.
B—manual intervention by the pilot, but will not be required, if RAIM is available.
C—additional action by the operator to set the course.

Answer (C) is correct (9730). *(AIM Para 1-1-21)*
Missed approach routings in which the first track is via a course rather than direct to the next waypoint require additional action by the pilot to set the course. Being familiar with all of the inputs required is especially critical during this phase of flight.
Answer (A) is incorrect because missed approach routings in which the first track is via a course rather than direct to the next waypoint requires that the pilot take additional action to set the course, not that the GPS receiver be sequenced to the missed approach portion of the procedure. Answer (B) is incorrect because missed approach routings in which the first track is via a course rather than direct to a waypoint requires additional action by the pilot to set the course, even if RAIM is available.

138.
9729. If flying a published GPS departure,

A—the data base will contain all of the transition or departures from all runways.
B—and if RAIM is available, manual intervention by the pilot should not be required.
C—the GPS receiver must be set to terminal course deviation indicator sensitivity.

Answer (C) is correct (9729). *(AIM Para 1-1-21)*
The GPS receiver must be set to terminal (± 1 NM) CDI sensitivity, and the navigation routes must be contained in the database in order to fly published IFR charted departures and SIDs.
Answer (A) is incorrect because the database may not contain all of the transitions or departures from all runways, and some GPS receivers do not contain SIDs in the database. Answer (B) is incorrect because certain segments of a SID may require some manual intervention by the pilot, even if RAIM is available, especially when radar vectored to a course or required to intercept a specific course to a waypoint.

CHAPTER TEN
IFR FLIGHTS

This chapter contains 130 FAA test questions and answers regarding 11 IFR flights and an explanation of each answer. The individual trips within this chapter are listed above, followed in parentheses by the number of corresponding questions from the FAA pilot knowledge test and the page on which the trip begins.

The following table provides you with a list of the 11 IFR trips, which are divided for the ATP Part 135 and ATP Part 121 knowledge tests. The departure and destination airports are listed, followed by the airplane used for the trip and then the question numbers that relate to that trip.

Part 135	Airplane	Questions
Chicago Midway to Greater Buffalo	C-208	1-10
Dallas/Ft. Worth to Houston Intercontinental	BE-90	11-19
Tucson to Los Angeles (LAX)	BE-1900	20-39
Pal-Waukee to Greater Buffalo	BE-1900	40-50
Williamsburg to Philadelphia	BE-1900	51-61
St. Louis to La Guardia	G-1159	62-69
Part 121		
Los Angeles (LAX) to Phoenix	B-727	70-86
Greater Buffalo to Chicago O'Hare	B-727	87-96
Minneapolis-St. Paul to Denver	B-767	97-104
Las Vegas to San Francisco	B-747	105-115
Bradley to Philadelphia	MD-90	116-130

Each trip provides you with the following types of data:

1. Partially completed IFR flight plan
2. Partially completed flight log
3. SIDs and STARs
4. Appropriate *Airport/Facility Directory* excerpts
5. Instrument approach chart(s)
6. En Route IFR Chart

The general sequence of questions includes

1. Estimated time en route
2. Fuel requirements for trip
   a. Some fuel questions will ask for the fuel required to complete the trip. This amount includes the fuel required to fly to the destination, then to the alternate, and then for 45 min. (IFR reserves).
      1) In the flight log, the FAA also provides the fuel required for a missed approach. While this should be included as a practical matter, it is not required by the FARs and is not included to calculate the answer.
   b. Other fuel questions will ask for the fuel usage to the destination. This amount is the fuel required to fly to the destination only.
3. TAS required to arrive at a specified point in a certain time
4. Required climb rates
5. Lost communications procedures at a given point and required radio frequencies
6. IFR chart interpretation
7. IFR approach procedures
8. *A/FD* interpretation

CAUTION: The **sole purpose** of this book is to expedite your passing the FAA pilot knowledge test for the ATP certificate. Topics or regulations not directly tested on the FAA pilot knowledge test are omitted. Much more information and knowledge are necessary to fly safely. This additional material is presented in Gleim's other pilot training books (see the order form on page 818) and in many FAA books and circulars, as well as in airplane *POH*s and other commercial textbooks.

QUESTIONS AND ANSWER EXPLANATIONS

All the FAA questions from the pilot knowledge test for the ATP certificate relating to IFR flights are reproduced on the following pages. To the immediate right of each question are the correct answer and answer explanation. You should cover these answers and answer explanations while responding to the questions. Refer to the general discussion in Chapter 1 on how to take the FAA pilot knowledge test.

Remember that the questions from the FAA pilot knowledge test bank have been reordered by topic, and the topics are organized into a meaningful sequence. Accordingly, the first line of the answer explanation gives the FAA question number and the citation of the authoritative source for the answer.

10.1 C-208 MDW TO BUF (Questions 1-10)

Questions 1 through 10 pertain to an IFR flight from Chicago Midway Airport, Chicago, Illinois to the Greater Buffalo International Airport, Buffalo, New York.

The route of flight is given in block 8 on the flight plan portion of Fig. 94 on page 343. The partially completed flight planning log is given on the bottom portion of Fig. 94.

The following figures are used to answer the 10 questions concerning this flight.

Fig.	Page	Title
94	343	Flight Plan/Flight Log
95	344	Midway Four Departure (Vector)
95A	345	Excerpt (MDW)
96	414	IFR En Route High Altitude Chart Segment
97	346	RNAV or GPS RWY 32 (BUF)
97A	347	ILS RWY 28 (ROC)
97B	348	IFR Alternate Minimums
97C	349	IFR Alternate Minimums

10.1 C-208 MDW to BUF

1.
9546. (Refer to figures 94, 95, and 96 on pages 343, 344, and 414.) What is the ETE from Chicago Midway Airport to Greater Buffalo Intl?

A—2 hours 12 minutes.
B—2 hours 15 minutes.
C—2 hours 18 minutes.

Answer (A) is correct (9546). *(IFH Chap XIII)*

To determine the ETE from Chicago Midway Airport to Greater Buffalo Intl., you must complete the flight log in Fig. 94. In the remarks box of the flight plan, the magnetic variation is given at GIJ (1°W), CRL (3°W), YXU (6°W), and BUF (8°W). This information is used to convert the true wind direction to magnetic direction. Also given is the level-off point, which is GIJ R-270 at 19 NM.

Our flight log below has been expanded to provide more detail. To convert the wind direction from true to magnetic, we use 1°W to the GIJ/CRL COP; 3°W to the CRL/YXU COP; 6°W to the YXU/BUF COP; 8°W to BUF R-282/30.

	Distance	MC	Wind (mag)	Ground-speed	Time
Level-off	49G	X	X	X	0:19:00G
GIJ	19	090	231/51	196	0:05:48
GIJ/CRL COP	64.5	082	231/51	202	0:19:12
CRL	64.5	087	233/51	200	0:19:22
CRL/YXU COP	59	062	243/59	219	0:16:10
YXU	59	069	246/59	219	0:16:10
YXU/BUF COP	55	101	256/62	214	0:15:25
BUF R-282/30	25	102	258/62	215	0:06:59
Descent and approach	30G	X	X	X	0:14:00G
					2:12:06

G = Given

Answer (B) is incorrect because an ETE of 2 hr. 15 min. requires a TAS of approximately 155 kt., not 160 kt. Answer (C) is incorrect because an ETE of 2 hr. 18 min. requires a TAS of approximately 150 kt., not 160 kt.

2.
9547. (Refer to figures 94, 95, and 96 on pages 343, 344, and 414.) What are the fuel requirements from Chicago Midway Airport to Greater Buffalo Intl?

A—2,224 pounds.
B—1,987 pounds.
C—1,454 pounds.

Answer (A) is correct (9547). ***(IFH Chap XIII)***

To determine the fuel requirements from Chicago Midway to Greater Buffalo, you must complete the fuel portion of the flight log on Fig. 94. Use 610 PPH fuel flow from level-off to start of descent and 710 PPH fuel flow for the flight to the alternate (ROC) and the reserve requirements.

	Time	Fuel (lb.)
Level-off	0:19:00G	327.0G
GIJ	0:05:48	59.0
GIJ/CRL COP	0:19:12	195.2
CRL	0:19:22	196.9
CRL/YXU COP	0:16:10	164.4
YXU	0:16:10	164.4
YXU/BUF COP	0:15:25	156.7
BUF R-282/30	0:06:59	71.0
Descent and approach	0:14:00G	121.5G
ROC	0:20:00G	236.7
Reserve	0:45:00	532.5
		2,225.3

G = Given

Answer (B) is incorrect because 1,987 lb. does not include the fuel required to fly to the alternate airport (ROC). Answer (C) is incorrect because 1,454 lb. does not include the alternate and reserve fuel requirements.

3.
9548. (Refer to figures 94, 95, and 96 on pages 343, 344, and 414.) What TAS should be maintained to arrive over CRL VORTAC 42 minutes after level-off?

A—166 knots.
B—168 knots.
C—171 knots.

Answer (C) is correct (9548). ***(IFH Chap XIII)***

To determine the required TAS to arrive over CRL VORTAC 42 min. after level-off, you need to determine the required groundspeed. The distance is 19 NM (L/O to GIJ) + 129 NM (GIJ to CRL) = 148 NM. The required groundspeed is 211 kt. [148 ÷ (42/60)]. Next, compute the TAS on the wind side of your computer:

1. **Set the average magnetic wind direction of 232° (231° to GIJ and 233° to CRL) under the true index, and place a pencil mark at 51 kt. (windspeed) up from the grommet.**
2. **Place the average MC of 086° (090° to GIJ, 082° to GIJ/CRL COP, and 087° to CRL) under the true index.**
3. **Slide the grid so the groundspeed of 211 kt. is under the grommet.**
4. **Read the TAS of 171 kt. under the pencil mark.**

Answer (A) is incorrect because 166 kt. TAS would be required if the wind speed were 59 kt., not 51 kt. Answer (B) is incorrect because 168 kt. TAS would be required if the wind speed were 55 kt., not 51 kt.

4.
9549. (Refer to figures 94, 95, and 96 on pages 343, 344, and 414.) What action should be taken by the pilot, if communications are lost, while IMC, after takeoff on RWY 13L at Chicago Midway Airport?

A—Return and land immediately at Chicago Midway Airport.
B—Complete initially assigned turn south of DPA R-096, maintain 3,000 feet or lower if assigned. Then 10 minutes after departure, climb to FL 190, direct to GIJ, then flight plan route.
C—Complete initially assigned turn within 4 DME of Midway and maintain 3,000 feet or lower, if assigned. Then 10 minutes after departure, climb to FL 190, direct to GIJ, and then flight plan route.

Answer (C) is correct (9549). *(SID)*
In the event of a two-way communication failure, ATC service will be provided on the basis that the pilot is operating in accordance with FAR 91.185. If the failure occurs after takeoff on RWY 13L at Chicago Midway, while in IMC, the pilot should follow the departure route description for the Midway Four Departure. The flight plan in Fig. 94 indicates the airplane is RNAV equipped (/R); thus it has DME. The pilot should complete the initially assigned turn within 4 DME of Midway and maintain 3,000 ft. or an assigned lower altitude. Then 10 min. after departure, (s)he should climb to FL 190, direct to GIJ VORTAC, and follow the flight plan route.
Answer (A) is incorrect because to return and land immediately at Chicago Midway would mean that the pilot has also declared an emergency along with the loss of communications. A loss of communications is not an emergency in itself. Answer (B) is incorrect because a pilot would complete the initially assigned turn south of DPA R-096 if the airplane was not DME equipped. N60JB is DME equipped as indicated in the flight plan with the equipment suffix of "/R."

5.
9552. (Refer to figure 97 on page 346.) How can the FAF on the RNAV RWY 32 approach at BUF be identified?

A—The RNAV receiver will indicate 175.1° and 2.5 DME miles from BUF VORTAC.
B—The RNAV receiver will indicate a change from TO to FROM and 0 deflection of the course needle.
C—Two flashes/second on the OM beacon light.

Answer (B) is correct (9552). *(IAP)*
The pilot will input the waypoint location of the FAF by use of degree-distance fix based on navigational aids or by latitude/longitude coordinates. The waypoint crossing is noted similar to that of crossing a VORTAC station. The RNAV receiver will indicate a change from TO to FROM, and there should be no deflection of the course needle.
Answer (A) is incorrect because the waypoint is defined to the RNAV computer as 175.1° and 2.5 DME from BUF VORTAC. Answer (C) is incorrect because the OM is part of a precision approach and is a radio transmitter. An RNAV approach is a nonprecision approach, and the FAF on the RNAV RWY 32 approach to Buffalo is a waypoint.

6.
9550. (Refer to figure 97 on page 346.) In the profile view of the RNAV or GPS RWY 32 approach to Buffalo Intl, between CYUGA and the MAP, the following appears: ∠2.91°. What is it?

A—The required pitch attitude change at CYUGA, to ensure arriving at 1,220 feet and 1.5 miles at the same time.
B—It indicates that 2.91° below level is recommended on the attitude indicator.
C—The Final Approach Angle for Vertical Path Computers.

Answer (C) is correct (9550). *(IAP)*
The symbol ∠2.91° on the profile view of the IAP chart indicates the final approach angle for RNAV vertical path computers, which is 2.91° for the RNAV or GPS RWY 32 IAP.
Answer (A) is incorrect because the symbol ∠2.91° indicates the final approach angle for vertical path computers, not the required pitch attitude change. Answer (B) is incorrect because the symbol ∠2.91° indicates the final approach angle for vertical path computers, not the pitch down attitude on an attitude indicator.

7.
9553. (Refer to figure 97 on page 346.) Which of the following will define the position of the RNAV MAP for Greater Buffalo Intl.?

A—116.4 BUF 286.9°, -3.5 NM.
B—42°56.44' N - 78°38.48' W.
C—42°56.26' N - 78°43.57' W.

Answer (A) is correct (9553). *(IAP)*
The RNAV coordinates (degree-distance fix) for the RNAV RWY 32 MAP at Greater Buffalo Intl. are 116.4 BUF 286.9°, 3.5 NM.
Answer (B) is incorrect because 42°56.44' N -- 78°38.48' W are close to the coordinates of the BUF VORTAC, which is 42°55.74' N -- 78°38.78' W. Answer (C) is incorrect because 42°56.26' N -- 78°43.57' W are the coordinates of Greater Buffalo Intl. itself, not the MAP.

8.
9554. (Refer to figure 97 on page 346.) What is the procedure for initiating the missed approach on the RNAV RWY 32 approach at BUF?

A—Climbing left turn, select GANIS Waypoint and establish a direct course, climbing to 2,800 feet.
B—Select and maintain R-302 of BUF VORTAC climbing to 2,800 feet.
C—Establish and maintain R-286.9 of BUF VORTAC climbing to 2,800 feet.

Answer (A) is correct (8776). *(IAP)*
The missed approach procedure is described in the profile section of the RNAV RWY 32 approach. At the MAP, the pilot should begin a climbing left turn, select GANIS waypoint, and establish a direct course, while climbing to 2,800 ft.
Answer (B) is incorrect because the missed approach procedure is a climbing left turn to 2,800 ft. direct to GANIS waypoint, not BUF VORTAC. GANIS waypoint is located on the R-302 and 12.1 DME from BUF VORTAC. Answer (C) is incorrect because the missed approach procedure is a climbing left turn to 2,800 ft. direct to GANIS waypoint, not a track along R-286.9 of BUF VORTAC. The MAP is located on R-286.9 and 3.5 DME from BUF VORTAC.

9.
9555. (Refer to figures 97A, 97B, and 97C on pages 347, 348, and 349.) N60JB desired to list ROC as an alternate for BUF. The active RWY at ROC was expected to be RWY 28. What weather forecast was required at Greater Rochester Intl, for N60JB to list it as an alternate?

A—Nonprecision approach 800-2, precision approach 800-2.
B—Nonprecision approach 800-2, precision approach 600-2.
C—Nonprecision approach 800-2¼, precision approach 600-2.

Answer (A) is correct (9555). *(IAP)*
Fig. 97C lists the alternate minimums for Rochester, NY (ROC). For the ILS RWY 28 (precision approach), the alternate minimums for Cat. A and B aircraft is 800-2. Standard alternate minimums of 800-2 for nonprecision approach can be used since there is no listing for the LOC RWY 28 at ROC. Thus, to list ROC as an alternate, the weather forecast must be 800-2 for both precision and nonprecision approaches.
Answer (B) is incorrect because, while 600-2 are the standard alternate minimums for a precision approach, ROC has nonstandard alternate minimums for the ILS RWY 28, which is 800-2 for Cat. A and B aircraft. Answer (C) is incorrect because, while 600-2 are the standard alternate minimums for a precision approach, ROC has nonstandard alternate minimums for the ILS RWY 28, which is 800-2 for Cat. A and B aircraft. Since LOC RWY 28 is not listed, the standard alternate minimums of 800-2, not 800-2¼, can be used.

10.
9551. (Refer to figure 97A on page 347.) Greater Buffalo Intl was closed upon N60JB's arrival and was not expected to be open for 4 hours, for snow removal. N60JB received clearance to ROC. Upon arrival at ROC, the flight was cleared for the ILS RWY 28. To fly the ILS RWY 28 at ROC, the aircraft must have the following navigation equipment:

A—Radar and VOR/DME.
B—VOR/DME and ADF.
C—Radar and VOR/ILS/DME.

Answer (B) may be correct (9551). *(IAP)*
Fig. 97A is the ILS RWY 28 IAP at ROC. In the lower left corner of the chart (below the minimums section), there is a statement that an ADF is required. There is no mention that DME is required. Thus, to fly the ILS RWY 28 approach, you must have a VOR/ILS and an ADF.
Answer (A) is incorrect because radar and DME are not required to fly the ILS RWY 28 approach. Answer (C) is incorrect because an ADF and a VOR with a glide slope indicator, not a radar or DME, are required to fly the ILS RWY 28 approach.

NOT WORTH MARK !

Form Approved: OMB No. 2120-0034

U.S. DEPARTMENT OF TRANSPORTATION FEDERAL AVIATION ADMINISTRATION **FLIGHT PLAN**	(FAA USE ONLY) ☐ PILOT BRIEFING ☐ VNR ☐ STOPOVER	TIME STARTED	SPECIALIST INITIALS

1. TYPE	2. AIRCRAFT IDENTIFICATION	3. AIRCRAFT TYPE/ SPECIAL EQUIPMENT	4. TRUE AIRSPEED	5. DEPARTURE POINT	6. DEPARTURE TIME PROPOSED (Z)	ACTUAL (Z)	7. CRUISING ALTITUDE
VFR X IFR DVFR	N60JB	C208/R	160 KTS	MDW Chicago Midway			FL190

8. ROUTE OF FLIGHT
Midway Four Dep. GIJ, J554 CRL, J586 YXU, J547 BUF

9. DESTINATION (Name of airport and city)	10. EST. TIME ENROUTE HOURS	MINUTES	11. REMARKS
BUF Greater Buffalo Int'l. Buffalo			L/O = Level off. PPH = Pounds Per Hour L/O R-270/19 GIJ Variation: GIJ 1W, CRL 3W, YXU 6W, BUF 8W.

12. FUEL ON BOARD HOURS	MINUTES	13. ALTERNATE AIRPORT(S)	14. PILOT'S NAME, ADDRESS & TELEPHONE NUMBER & AIRCRAFT HOME BASE / 17. DESTINATION CONTACT/TELEPHONE (OPTIONAL)	15. NUMBER ABOARD
3	20	ROC Rochester		2

16. COLOR OF AIRCRAFT
Brown/Tan

CIVIL AIRCRAFT PILOTS. FAR Part 91 requires you file an IFR flight plan to operate under instrument flight rules in controlled airspace. Failure to file could result in a civil penalty not to exceed $1,000 for each violation (Section 901 of the Federal Aviation Act of 1958, as amended). Filing of a VFR flight plan is recommended as a good operating practice. See also Part 99 for requirements concerning DVFR flight plans.

FAA Form 7233-1 (8-82)

CLOSE VFR FLIGHT PLAN WITH ____________ FSS ON ARRIVAL

FLIGHT LOG

CHECK POINTS FROM	TO	ROUTE ALTITUDE	COURSE	WIND TEMP	SPEED-KTS TAS	GS	DIST NM	TIME LEG	TOT	FUEL LEG	TOT
MDW	L/O GIJ R-270/19	MDW 4 Climb					49		:19:00		327*
R-270/19 GIJ	GIJ	Direct FL190		230/51 ISA							
GIJ	CRL	J554 FL190									
CRL	YXU	J586 FL190		240/59 ISA							
YXU	BUF R-282/30	J547 FL190		250/62 ISA							
BUF R-282/30	BUF	Descent & Approach					30	:14:00		121.5	
BUF	ROC	V2 7000			150		44	:20:00			

OTHER DATA: * Includes Taxi Fuel
NOTE: Use 610 PPH Total Fuel Flow From L/O To Start Of Descent.
Use 710 PPH Total Fuel Flow For Reserve And Alternate Requirements.
A Missed Approach Requires 81# of Fuel.

TIME and FUEL: As required by FARs.

TIME	FUEL (LB)	
		EN ROUTE
		RESERVE
		ALTERNATE
		TOTAL

FIGURE 94.—Flight Plan / Flight Log.

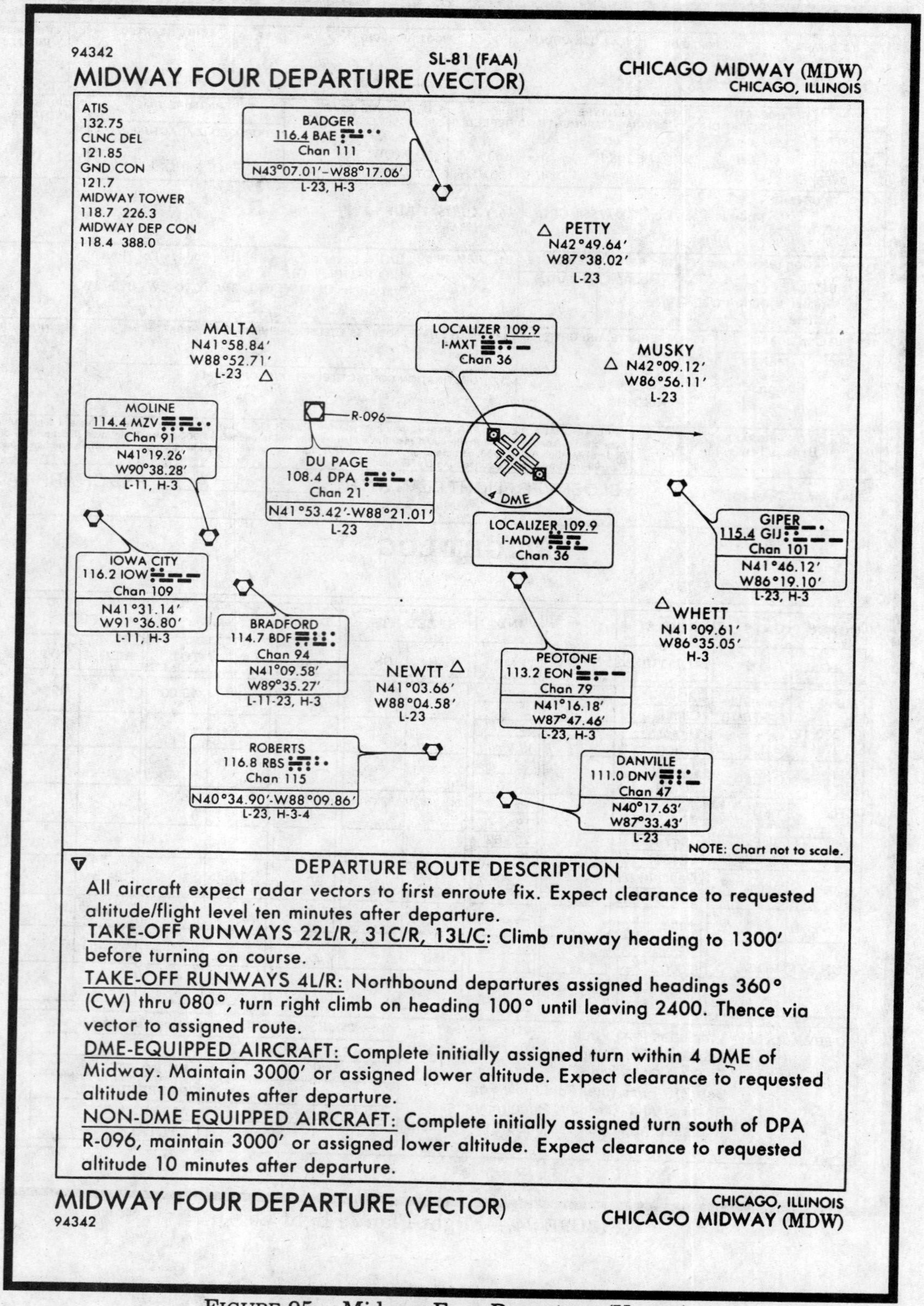

FIGURE 95.—Midway Four Departure (Vector).

16 **ILLINOIS**

CHAMPAIGN (URBANA)
UNIVERSITY OF ILLINOIS-WILLARD (CMI) 5 SW UTC-6(-5DT) N40°02.36′ W88°16.68′ — CHICAGO H-4H, L-23A IAP
754 B S4 **FUEL** 100LL, JET A1 + OX 1 ARFF Index A
RWY 14R-32L: H8100X150 (CONC-GRVD) S-100, D-180, DT-260 HIRL
RWY 14R: VASI(V4L)—GA 3.0° TCH 31′. **RWY 32L:** MALSR. VASI(V4L)—GA 3.0° TCH 54′.
RWY 04L-22R: H6500X150 (CONC-GRVD) S-100, D-180, DT-260 MIRL
RWY 04L: VASI(V4L)—GA 3.0° TCH 45′. **RWY 22R:** VASI(V4L)—GA 3.0° TCH 41′. Tree.
RWY 18-36: H5299X150 (CONC) S-40, D-50, DT-90 MIRL
RWY 36: VASI(V4L)—GA 3.0° TCH 40′. Tree.
AIRPORT REMARKS: Attended continuously. Rwy 18-36 CLOSED 0600-1200Z‡ indefinitely. PPR for unscheduled air carrier operations with more than 30 passenger seats between 0400-1200Z‡, call arpt manager 217-244-8604. Rwy 04R-22L and Rwy 14L-32R VFR day only, restricted to authorized Flight Schools only. When twr clsd HIRL Rwy 14R-32L preset low ints, to increase ints and ACTIVATE MIRL Rwys 04L-22R MALSR Rwy 32L—CTAF. Itinerant parking on southeast ramp only. Taxiway D not available for air carrier ops with more than 30 passenger seats. NOTE: See Land and Hold Short Operations Section.
COMMUNICATIONS: CTAF 120.4 **ATIS** 124.85 **UNICOM** 122.95
ST LOUIS FSS (STL) TF 1-800-WX-BRIEF. NOTAM FILE CMI.
CHAMPAIGN RCO 122.1R 110.0T (KANKAKEE FSS)
CHAMPAIGN (URBANA) RCO 122.45 (ST LOUIS FSS)
Ⓡ **CHAMPAIGN APP/DEP CON** 132.85 (134°-312°) 121.35 (313°-133°) 118.25 (1200-0600Z‡)
CHICAGO CENTER APP/DEP CON 121.35 (0600-1200Z‡)
CHAMPAIGN TOWER 120.4 (1200-0600Z‡) **GND CON** 121.8 **CLNC DEL** 128.75
AIRSPACE: CLASS C svc 1200-0600Z‡ ctc **APP CON** other times CLASS G.
RADIO AIDS TO NAVIGATION: NOTAM FILE CMI.
CHAMPAIGN (L) VORTAC 110.0 CMI Chan 37 N40°02.07′ W88°16.56′ at fld. 750/3E.
VEALS NDB (LOM) 407 CM N39°57.97′ W88°10.95′ 315°6.2 NM to fld.
ILS 109.1 I-CMI Rwy 32L. LOM VEALS NDB. ILS unmonitored when twr clsd.
ASR

CHICAGO
CHICAGO MIDWAY (MDW) 9SW UTC-6(-5DT) N41°47.16′ W87°45.15′ — CHICAGO COPTER H-3H, L-23A, A IAP
620 B S4 **FUEL** 100LL, JET A1 + OX 2, 4 AOE ARFF Index C
RWY 13C-31C: H6522X150 (CONC-GRVD) S-95, D-165, DT-250 HIRL
RWY 13C: ALSF1. PAPI (P4L)—GA 3.0° TCH 47′. Thld dsplcd 462′. Pole.
RWY 31C: LDIN. REIL. VASI(V4L)—GA 3.0° TCH 52′. Thld dsplcd 696′. Tree.
RWY 04R-22L: H6446X150 (CONC-ASPH-GRVD) S-95, D-165, DT-250 HIRL
RWY 04R: REIL. VASI(V4R)—GA 3.4° TCH 64. Thld dsplcd 518′. Building.
RWY 22L: REIL. VASI(V4R)—GA 3.0° TCH 53′. Thld dsplcd 634′. Pole.
RWY 04L-22R: H5509X150 (ASPH) S-30, D-40 MIRL
RWY 04L: VASI(V4R). Thld dsplcd 758′. Tree. **RWY 22R:** VASI(V4L). Building.
RWY 13L-31R: H5412X150 (ASPH) S-30, D-40 MIRL
RWY 13L: Thld dsplcd 753′. Tree. **RWY 31R:** Pole.
Rwy 13R-31L: H3859X60 (CONC) S-12.5 MIRL
RWY 13R: Pole. **RWY 31L:** Tree.
AIRPORT REMARKS: Attended continuously. Landing fee. Arpt CLOSED to solo student training. Birds on and in vicinity of arpt. Noise abatement procedures: All departures are requested to expedite climb through 1500 ft MSL 0400-1200Z‡. Rwys 13L-31R and 04R-22R not avbl for air carrier ops with more than 30 passenger seats. Rwy 13C PAPI and RVR out of svc indefinitely. Flight Notification Service (ADCUS) available.
WEATHER DATA SOURCES: LAWRS.
COMMUNICATIONS: ATIS 132.75 **UNICOM** 122.95
KANKAKEE FSS (IKK) TF 1-800-WX-BRIEF. NOTAM FILE MDW.
Ⓡ **APP/DEP CON** 118.4 126.05
MIDWAY TOWER 118.7 135.2 (helicopter ops) **GND CON** 121.7 **CLNC DEL** 121.85 **PRE TAXI CLNC** 121.85
AIRSPACE: CLASS C svc continuous ctc **MIDWAY RADAR** 119.45
RADIO AIDS TO NAVIGATION: NOTAM FILE IKK.
CHICAGO HEIGHTS (L) VORTAC 114.2 CGT Chan 89 N41°30.60′ W87°34.29′ 332° 18.5 NM to fld. 630/2E.
ERMIN NDB (MHW/LOM) 332 HK N41°43.14′ W87°50.19′ 044° 5.5 NM to fld. NOTAM FILE MDW.
KEDZI NDB (MHW/LOM) 248 MX N41°44.49′ W87°41.38′ 315° 3.9 NM to fld. NOTAM FILE MDW.
ILS/DME 109.9 I-MDW Chan 36 Rwy 13C.
ILS 111.5 I-HKH Rwy 04R. LOM ERMIN NDB.
ILS/DME 109.9 I-MXT Chan 36 Rwy 31C. LOM KEDZI NDB.
MLS Chan 660 Rwy 22L. MLS unusable 246°-262° byd 10NM blo 3500′; unusable clockwise byd 262°; elevation unusable clockwise beyond 226° blo 2.0°; elevation unusable counterclockwise byd 222° blo 2.0°. Disregard guidance signals found clockwise byd 314°. Disregard guidance signals found counterclockwise byd 184°.

FIGURE 95A.—Excerpt (MDW).

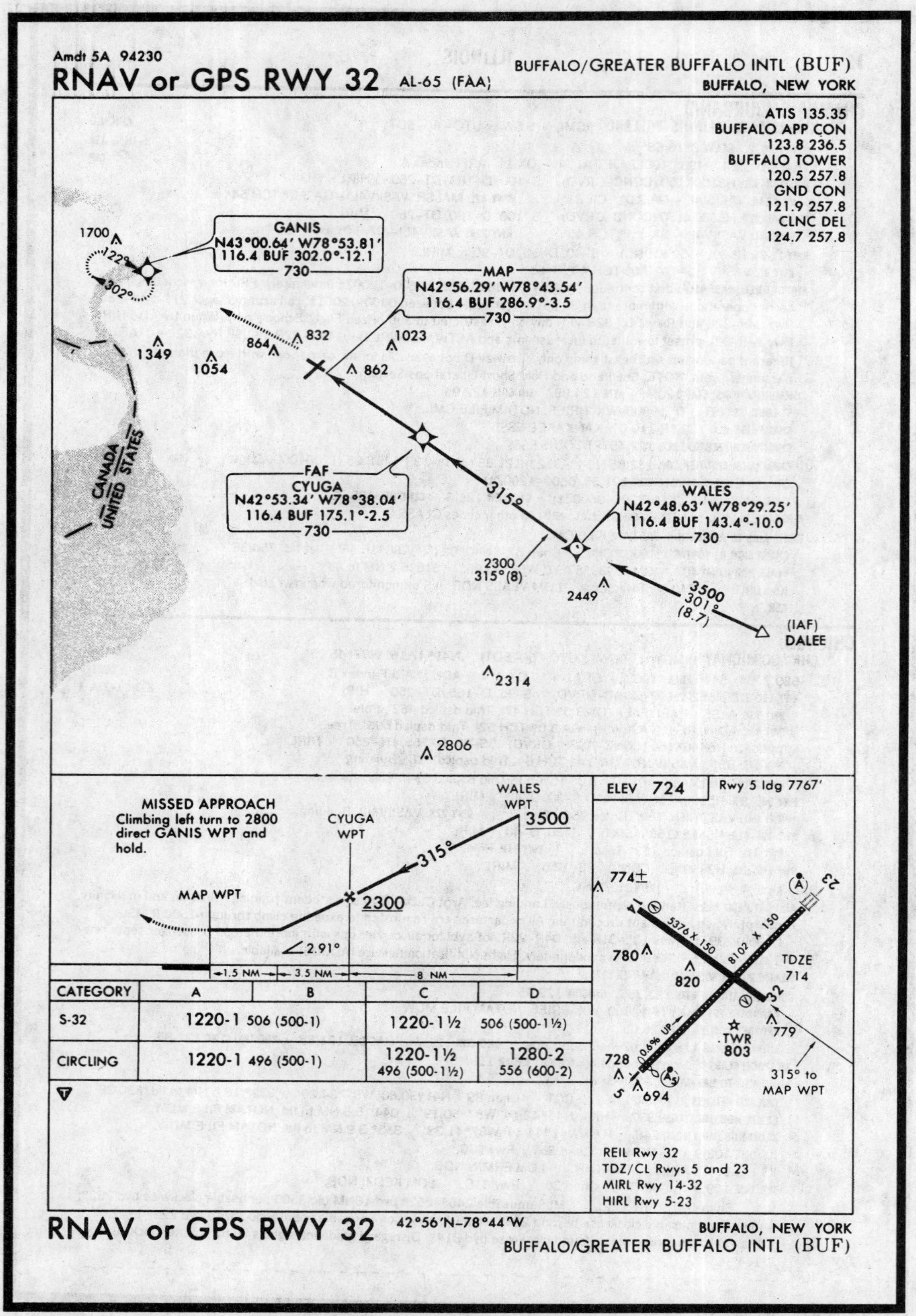

CATEGORY	A	B	C	D
S-32	1220-1 506 (500-1)		1220-1½ 506 (500-1½)	
CIRCLING	1220-1 496 (500-1)		1220-1½ 496 (500-1½)	1280-2 556 (600-2)

FIGURE 97.—RNAV or GPS RWY 32 (BUF).

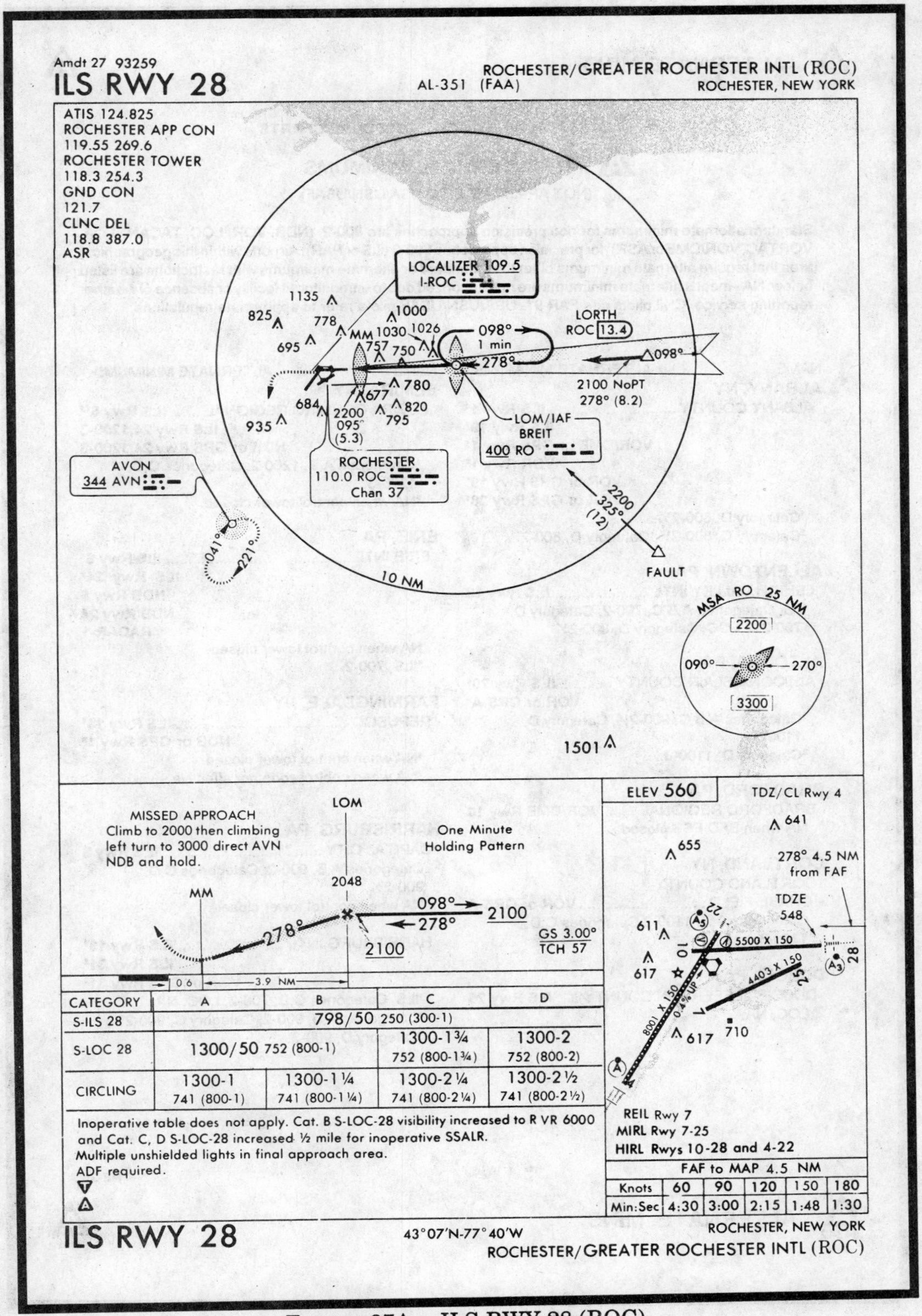

FIGURE 97A.—ILS RWY 28 (ROC).

A ALTERNATE MINS A

94342

INSTRUMENT APPROACH PROCEDURE CHARTS

A IFR ALTERNATE MINIMUMS

(NOT APPLICABLE TO USA/USN/USAF)

Standard alternate minimums for non precision approaches are 800-2 (NDB, VOR, LOC, TACAN, LDA, VORTAC, VOR/DME or ASR); for precision approaches 600-2 (ILS or PAR). Airports within this geographical area that require alternate minimums other than standard or alternate minimums with restrictions are listed below. NA - means alternate minimums are not authorized due to unmonitored facility or absence of weather reporting service. Civil pilots see FAR 91. USA/USN/USAF pilots refer to appropriate regulations.

NAME — ALTERNATE MINIMUMS

ALBANY, NY
ALBANY COUNTY .... **ILS Rwy 1[1]**
ILS Rwy 19[1]
VOR/DME or GPS Rwy 1[1]
VOR Rwy 1[2]
VOR or GPS Rwy 19[1]
VOR or GPS Rwy 28[1]
[1]Category D, 800-2½.
[2]Category C, 800-2¼; Category D, 800-2½.

ALLENTOWN, PA
LEHIGH VALLEY INTL .... **ILS Rwy 13**
ILS, Categories A,B,C, 700-2; Category D, 700-2¼. LOC, Category D, 800-2¼.

ALTOONA, PA
ALTOONA-BLAIR COUNTY .... **ILS Rwy 20[1]**
VOR or GPS-A[2]
[1]Categories A,B,C, 900-2½, Category D, 1100-3.
[2]Category D, 1100-3.

BRADFORD, PA
BRADFORD REGIONAL .... **VOR/DME Rwy 14**
NA when BFD FSS closed.

CORTLAND, NY
CORTLAND COUNTY-CHASE FIELD .... **VOR or GPS-A**
Categories A,B, 1100-2,Categories C,D, 1100-3.

DUBOIS, PA
DUBOIS-JEFFERSON COUNTY ..... **ILS Rwy 25**
LOC, NA.

NAME — ALTERNATE MINIMUMS

ELMIRA, NY
ELMIRA/CORNING REGIONAL .... **ILS Rwy 6[1,2]**
ILS Rwy 24,1200-3
NDB or GPS Rwy 24,1200-3
[1]Categories A,B, 1200-2; Categories C,D, 1200-3.
[2]NA when control tower closed.

ERIE, PA
ERIE INTL .... **ILS Rwy 6[1]**
ILS Rwy 24[1]
NDB Rwy 6
NDB Rwy 24
RADAR-1
NA when control tower closed.
[1]ILS, 700-2.

FARMINGDALE, NY
REPUBLIC .... **ILS Rwy 14[1]**
NDB or GPS Rwy 1[2]
[1]NA when control tower closed.
[2]NA when control zone not effective.

HARRISBURG, PA
CAPITAL CITY .... **ILS Rwy 8**
Categories A,B, 900-2; Categories C,D, 900-2¾.
NA when control tower closed.

HARRISBURG INTL .... **ILS Rwy 13[1]**
ILS Rwy 31[1]
VOR or GPS Rwy 31[2]
[1]ILS, Categories C,D, 700-2. LOC, NA.
[2]Categories A,B, 900-2, Category C, 900-2¾, Category D, 900-3.

NE-2

A ALTERNATE MINS A

94342

FIGURE 97B.—IFR Alternate Minimums.

A 94342 **ALTERNATE MINS** **A**

NAME — ALTERNATE MINIMUMS

PHILADELPHIA, PA(CON'T)
PHILADELPHIA INTL .... **ILS Rwy 9L[1]**
ILS Rwy 9R[2]
ILS Rwy 17[3]
ILS Rwy 27L[2]
ILS Rwy 27R[2]
NDB or GPS Rwy 27L#
RNAV or GPS Rwy 17*

[1]ILS, Category D, 700-2.
[2]ILS, 700-2.
[3]ILS, Categories A,B,C, 700-2; Category D, 700-2¼. LOC, Category D,800-2¼.
#Category C, 800-2¼; Category D, 800-2½.
*Category D, 800-2¼.

PHILIPSBURG, PA
MID-STATE .... **ILS Rwy 16[1]**
NDB Rwy 16[2]
VOR Rwy 24[3]

[1]ILS, Category C, 700-2; Category D, 700-2¼. LOC, Category D, 800-2¼.
[2]Category D, 800-2¼.
[3]Categories A,B, 900-2; Category C, 900-2¼; Category D, 900-2½.

PITTSBURGH, PA
PITTSBURGH INTL .... **ILS Rwy 10L[1]**
ILS Rwy 10R[1]
ILS Rwy 28L[1]
ILS Rwy 28R[1]
ILS Rwy 32[1]
VOR or TACAN Rwy 28L/C[2]

[1]ILS, Category E, 700-2¼. LOC, Category E, 800-2¼.
[2]Category E, 800-2¼.

POUGHKEEPSIE, NY
DUTCHESS COUNTY .... **ILS Rwy 6**
ILS, Categories B,C,D, 700-2.

READING, PA
READING REGIONAL/CARL A.
SPAATZ FIELD .... **ILS Rwy 36[1]#**
NDB Rwy 36[2]#
RNAV or GPS Rwy 13[2]*
RNAV or GPS Rwy 18[3]*

[1]ILS, Categories A,B,C, 700-2; Category D, 800-2½. LOC, Category D, 800-2½.
[2]Category D, 800-2½.
[3]Category C, 800-2¼; Category D, 800-2½.
#NA when control tower closed.
*NA when control zone not in effect.

NAME — ALTERNATE MINIMUMS

REEDSVILLE, PA
MIFFLIN COUNTY .... **LOC Rwy 6**
NA when airport unattended.
Category D, 1500-3.

ROCHESTER, NY
GREATER ROCHESTER INTL .... **ILS Rwy 4[1]**
ILS Rwy 22[1]
ILS Rwy 28[2]
NDB or GPS Rwy 28[3]
RADAR-1#
VOR/DME or GPS Rwy 4#
VOR Rwy 4#

[1]ILS, Category D, 700-2¼. LOC, Category D, 800-2¼.
[2]Categories A,B, 800-2; Category C, 800-2¼; Category D, 800-2½.
[3]Category C, 800-2¼; Category D, 800-2½.
#Category D, 800-2¼.

SARANAC LAKE, NY
ADIRONDACK
REGIONAL .... **VOR/DME or GPS Rwy 5[1]**
VOR or GPS Rwy 9[2,3]

[1]NA except Categories A,B, 1200-2; Categories C,D, 1200-3, for operators with approved weather reporting service.
[2]Category A, 1000-2; Category B, 1100-2; Categories C,D, 1100-3.
[3]NA except for operators with approved weather reporting service.

STATE COLLEGE, PA
UNIVERSITY PARK .... **ILS Rwy 24[1,2]**
VOR/DME RNAV or GPS Rwy 6[1]
VOR or GPS-B,1300-3

[1]Category D, 900-2¾.
[2]NA when airport unattended.

UTICA, NY
ONEIDA COUNTY .... **NDB Rwy 33**
Category D, 800-2¼.

WATERTOWN, NY
WATERTOWN INTL .... **ILS Rwy 7**
LOC, NA.

WESTHAMPTON BEACH, NY
THE FRANCIS S. GABRESKI .... **ILS Rwy 24**
NDB Rwy 24
NA when control zone not in effect.

NE-2

A 94342 **ALTERNATE MINS** **A**

FIGURE 97C.—IFR Alternate Minimums.

10.2 BE-90 DFW TO IAH (Questions 11-19)

Questions 11 through 19 pertain to an IFR flight from Dallas-Ft. Worth International Airport, Dallas-Ft. Worth, Texas to the Houston Intercontinental Airport, Houston, Texas.

The route of flight is given in block 8 on the flight plan portion of Fig. 98 on page 354. The partially completed flight planning log is given on the bottom portion of Fig. 98.

The following figures are used to answer the nine questions concerning this flight.

Fig.	Page	Title
98	354	Flight Plan/Flight Log
99	355	IFR Area Chart Segment
100	356	IFR En Route Low Altitude Chart Segment
101	357	*Airport/Facility Directory* Excerpts
102	358	VOR/DME RWY 32R (IAH)/Cugar Four Arrival (Cugar.Cugar4)

10.2 BE-90 DFW to IAH

11.
9556. (Refer to figures 98, 99, 100, and 102 on pages 354, 355, 356, and 358.) What is the ETE from DFW Intl to IAH?

A—1 hour 2 minutes.
B—1 hour 4 minutes.
C—1 hour 6 minutes.

Answer (B) is correct (9556). *(IFH Chap XIII)*

To determine the estimated time en route, you must complete the flight log in Fig. 98. Our flight log below has been expanded to provide more detail. Convert the true wind direction to magnetic. Refer to Fig. 101 on page 357 under the **Radio Aids to Navigation** for both DFW and IAH at the right side of the top line. You will see that magnetic variation is given as "/08E," which is magnetic variation of 8°E, which is subtracted from the true wind direction of 230° to determine the magnetic wind direction of 222° at 42 kt.

	Distance	MC	Ground-speed	Time
Level-off	27G	X	X	0:12:00G
BILEE INT	80	154	229	0:20:56
IAH R-305	34	154	229	0:08:54
CUGAR INT	13	125	250	0:03:07
Start descent	21	125	250	0:05:02
Descent and approach	25G	X	X	0:14:00G
				1:03:59

G = Given

Answer (A) is incorrect because 1 hr. 2 min. would require a TAS of 261 kt., not 248 kt. Answer (C) is incorrect because 1 hr. 6 min. would require a TAS of 236 kt., not 248 kt.

12.
9557. (Refer to figures 98, 99, 100, and 102 on pages 354, 355, 356, and 358.) What is the total fuel required from DFW Intl to IAH?

A—1,555 pounds.
B—1,863 pounds.
C—1,941 pounds.

Answer (B) is correct (9557). ***(IFH Chap XIII)***

To determine the total fuel required to be on board for the flight from DFW Intl. to IAH, you must complete the fuel portion of the flight log in Fig. 98. Use 850 PPH total fuel flow from level-off to descent. Use 880 PPH total fuel flow for reserve and alternate requirements.

	Time	Fuel (lb.)
Level-off	:12:00G	231.0G
BILEE INT	:20:56	296.6
IAH R-305	:08:54	126.1
CUGAR INT	:03:07	44.2
Start descent	:05:02	71.3
Descent and approach	:14:00G	132.0G
IAH to BPT	:21:01	308.5
Reserve	:45:00	660.0
		1,869.2

G = Given

Answer (A) is incorrect because 1,555 lb. does not include the fuel required for the flight to the alternate, i.e., from IAH to BPT. Answer (C) is incorrect because 1,941 lb. includes the fuel required for a missed approach. While this should be included as a practical matter, it is not required by the FARs.

13.
9558. (Refer to figures 98, 99, 100, and 102 on pages 354, 355, 356, and 358.) Determine the TAS required to arrive at CUGAR, 31 minutes after level-off.

A—269 knots.
B—264 knots.
C—258 knots.

Answer (B) is correct (9558). ***(IFH Chap XIII)***

To determine the required TAS to arrive at CUGAR INT 31 min. after level-off, you need to determine the required groundspeed. The distance is 114 NM (L/O to IAH R-305) + 13 NM (turn-off to CUGAR) = 127 NM. Average groundspeed required is 246 kt. [127 ÷ (31/60)]. Then compute the TAS on the wind side of your computer:

1. **Set the magnetic wind direction of 222° under the true index and place a pencil mark at 42 kt. (wind speed) up from the grommet.**
2. **Place MC of 154° (V369) under true index. (Because the MC of the last 13 NM of this leg differs, we will check our answer at the end using the MC of each leg.)**
3. **Slide the grid so the groundspeed of 246 kt. is under the grommet.**
4. **Read the TAS of 264 kt. under the pencil mark.**
5. **Using a TAS of 264 kt., the groundspeed for the first leg is 245 kt., and the second leg is 266 kt.**
6. **Time for the first leg is 28 min., and for the second leg is 3 min., for a total of 31 min.**

Answer (A) is incorrect because 269 kt. TAS would make the arrival at CUGAR approximately 30 min., not 31 min., after level-off. Answer (C) is incorrect because 258 kt. TAS would make the arrival at CUGAR 32 min., not 31 min., after level-off.

14.
9559. (Refer to figures 98, 99, 100, and 102 on pages 354, 355, 356, and 358.) Determine the TAS required to arrive at CUGAR, 29 minutes after level-off.

A—285 knots.
B—290 knots.
C—295 knots.

Answer (A) is the best answer (9559). *(IFH Chap XIII)*

To determine the required TAS to arrive at CUGAR INT 29 min. after level-off, you need to determine the required groundspeed. The distance is 114 NM (L/O to turn-off) + 13 NM (turn-off to CUGAR) = 127 NM. Average groundspeed required is 263 kt. [127 ÷ (29/60)]. Then compute the TAS on the wind side of your computer:

1. Set the magnetic wind direction of 222° under the true index and place a pencil mark at 42 kt. (wind speed) up from the grommet.
2. Place MC of 154° (V369) under true index. (Because the MC of the last 13 NM of this leg differs, we will check our answer at the end using the MC of each leg.)
3. Slide the grid so the groundspeed of 263 kt. is under the grommet.
4. Read the TAS of 281 kt. under the pencil mark.
5. The closest answer is 285 kt.
6. Using a TAS of 285 kt., the groundspeed for the first leg is 267 kt., and for the second leg is 287 kt.
7. Time for the first leg is 25.6 min., and the second leg is 2.7 min., for a total of 28.3 min.

Answer (B) is incorrect because a TAS of 290 kt. would complete the trip from level-off to CUGAR in approximately 28 min., not 29 min. Answer (C) is incorrect because a TAS of 291 kt. would complete the trip from level-off to CUGAR in approximately 27 min., not 29 min.

15.
8782. (Refer to figures 99 and 101 on pages 355 and 357.) Which frequency should be selected to check airport conditions and weather prior to departure at DFW Intl?

A—117.0 MHz.
B—134.9 MHz.
C—135.5 MHz.

Answer (C) is correct (8782). *(A/FD)*

The Automatic Terminal Information Service (ATIS) provides airport noncontrol and weather information. On Fig. 99, the ATIS information is depicted with the Dallas-Ft. Worth airport information to the left center of the chart. The *A/FD* on Fig. 101 for Dallas-Ft. Worth lists the ATIS frequencies under **Communications**. The ATIS frequency for departing airplanes is 135.5 MHz.

Answer (A) is incorrect because 117.0 MHz is the listed ATIS frequency for arriving, not departing, airplanes. Answer (B) is incorrect because 134.9 MHz is also a listed ATIS frequency for arriving, not departing, airplanes.

16.
8783. (Refer to figures 99, 100, and 101 on pages 355, 356, and 357.) The frequency change from departure control to ARTCC after departing DFW Intl for IAH is

A—135.5 to 126.0 MHz.
B—118.55 to 127.95 MHz.
C—127.75 to 127.95 MHz.

Answer (C) is correct (8783). *(En Route Chart)*

The departure control frequency is listed in the *A/FD* on Fig. 101 under **Communications**. The regional departure control frequency for a flight from DFW Intl. south to IAH is 127.75. The ARTCC frequency is found on Fig. 100 on the upper right-hand side. It is in a jagged-edged box that identifies that it is an ARTCC remote site with the discrete VHF and UHF frequencies. This is Ft. Worth Scurry on 127.95 MHz.

Answer (A) is incorrect because 135.5 MHz is the ATIS frequency for departing airplanes, and 126.0 MHz is the ARTCC discrete frequency for northwest of DFW. Answer (B) is incorrect because 118.55 MHz is the departure control frequency for eastbound traffic from DFW.

17.
8784. (Refer to figure 100 on page 356.) Where is the VOR changeover point on V369 between DFW Intl and TNV?

A—Ft. Worth/Houston ARTCC boundary.
B—81 NM from DFW Intl.
C—TORNN Int.

Answer (B) is correct (8784). *(AIM Para 5-3-6)*
The changeover point (COP) is located midway between the navigation facilities for straight route segments, or at the intersection of radials or courses forming a dogleg. When the COP is not located at the midway point, the chart will depict the COP location and give the mileage to the radio aids. According to the *A/FD*, the DFW VORTAC is located on the field at DFW International and the distance to TNV VORTAC is 162 NM; thus the COP is halfway at 81 NM.
Answer (A) is incorrect because the Ft. Worth/Houston ARTCC boundary would indicate a radio communication frequency change, not a navigational frequency change. Answer (C) is incorrect because TORNN intersection is 85 NM from DFW VORTAC. Even though a DME distance fix is shown for TORNN, there is no special VOR changeover indicator that designates TORNN as a COP; thus the midway point (81 NM) should be used.

18.
8785. (Refer to figure 100 or 101 on pages 356 or 357.) What is the magnetic variation at both DFW Intl and IAH?

A—08 E.
B—0.
C—08 W.

Answer (A) is correct (8785). *(A/FD)*
The magnetic variation is found at the end of the VORTAC information line for both DFW Intl. and IAH. Both locations indicate "08E," which is a magnetic variation of 08°E.
Answer (B) is incorrect because 0° magnetic variation is the Agonic line, the line where the variation between magnetic and true north is zero, which is well east of Texas. Answer (C) is incorrect because the magnetic variation is 08°E (not west).

19.
8786. (Refer to figures 100 and 102 on pages 356 and 358.) How should the pilot identify the position to leave V369 for the Cugar Four Arrival?

A—Intercept R-305 of IAH.
B—21 DME miles from TNV.
C—141 DME miles from DFW.

Answer (A) is correct (8786). *(STAR)*
The BILEE transition indicates that from BILEE INT the pilot should maintain the R-334 of TNV VORTAC, then intercept and track inbound on the R-305 of IAH VORTAC to CUGAR intersection for the Cugar Four Arrival.
Answer (B) is incorrect because there is no DME fix for 21 NM from TNV VORTAC on either the STAR or the IFR En Route Chart. Answer (C) is incorrect because a pilot should have changed over to TNV VORTAC, and there is no 141 DME fix from DFW on V369.

Form Approved: OMB No. 2120-0034

U.S. DEPARTMENT OF TRANSPORTATION FEDERAL AVIATION ADMINISTRATION **FLIGHT PLAN**	(FAA USE ONLY) ☐ PILOT BRIEFING ☐ VNR ☐ STOPOVER	TIME STARTED	SPECIALIST INITIALS

1. TYPE	2. AIRCRAFT IDENTIFICATION	3. AIRCRAFT TYPE/ SPECIAL EQUIPMENT	4. TRUE AIRSPEED	5. DEPARTURE POINT	6. DEPARTURE TIME PROPOSED (Z)	ACTUAL (Z)	7. CRUISING ALTITUDE
VFR X IFR DVFR	N55JB	BE90/A	248 KTS	DFW Dallas Ft. Worth			15,000

8. ROUTE OF FLIGHT
DFW V369 BILEE, CUGAR 4 IAH

9. DESTINATION (Name of airport and city)	10. EST. TIME ENROUTE HOURS	MINUTES	11. REMARKS
IAH Houston Intercontinental Houston			L/O = Level off. PPH = Pounds Per Hour

12. FUEL ON BOARD HOURS	MINUTES	13. ALTERNATE AIRPORT(S)	14. PILOT'S NAME, ADDRESS & TELEPHONE NUMBER & AIRCRAFT HOME BASE	15. NUMBER ABOARD
		BPT Beaumont-Port Arthur Jefferson County	17. DESTINATION CONTACT/TELEPHONE (OPTIONAL)	4

16. COLOR OF AIRCRAFT
BLUE/YELLOW

CIVIL AIRCRAFT PILOTS. FAR Part 91 requires you file an IFR flight plan to operate under instrument flight rules in controlled airspace. Failure to file could result in a civil penalty not to exceed $1,000 for each violation (Section 901 of the Federal Aviation Act of 1958, as amended). Filing of a VFR flight plan is recommended as a good operating practice. See also Part 99 for requirements concerning DVFR flight plans.

FAA Form 7233-1 (8-82) CLOSE VFR FLIGHT PLAN WITH ______________ FSS ON ARRIVAL

FLIGHT LOG

CHECK POINTS FROM	TO	ROUTE ALTITUDE	COURSE	WIND TEMP	SPEED-KTS TAS	GS	DIST NM	TIME LEG	TOT	FUEL LEG	TOT
DFW	L/O	V369 Climb					27		:12:00		231*
L/O	Bilee	V369 15,000		230/42 ISA							
Bilee	Cugar	Cugar 4 15,000									
Cugar	Start Descent	Cugar 4 15,000		230/42 ISA							
Start Descent	IAH	Descent & Approach					25	:14:00		132	
IAH	BPT	Vectors 3000				194	68				

OTHER DATA: * Includes Taxi Fuel
NOTE: Use 850 PPH Total Fuel Flow From L/O To Start Of Descent.
Use 880 PPH Total Fuel Flow For Reserve And Alternate Requirements.
A Missed Approach Requires 82# of Fuel.

TIME and FUEL: As required by FARs.

TIME	FUEL (LB)	
		EN ROUTE
		RESERVE
		ALTERNATE
		TOTAL

FIGURE 98.—Flight Plan / Flight Log.

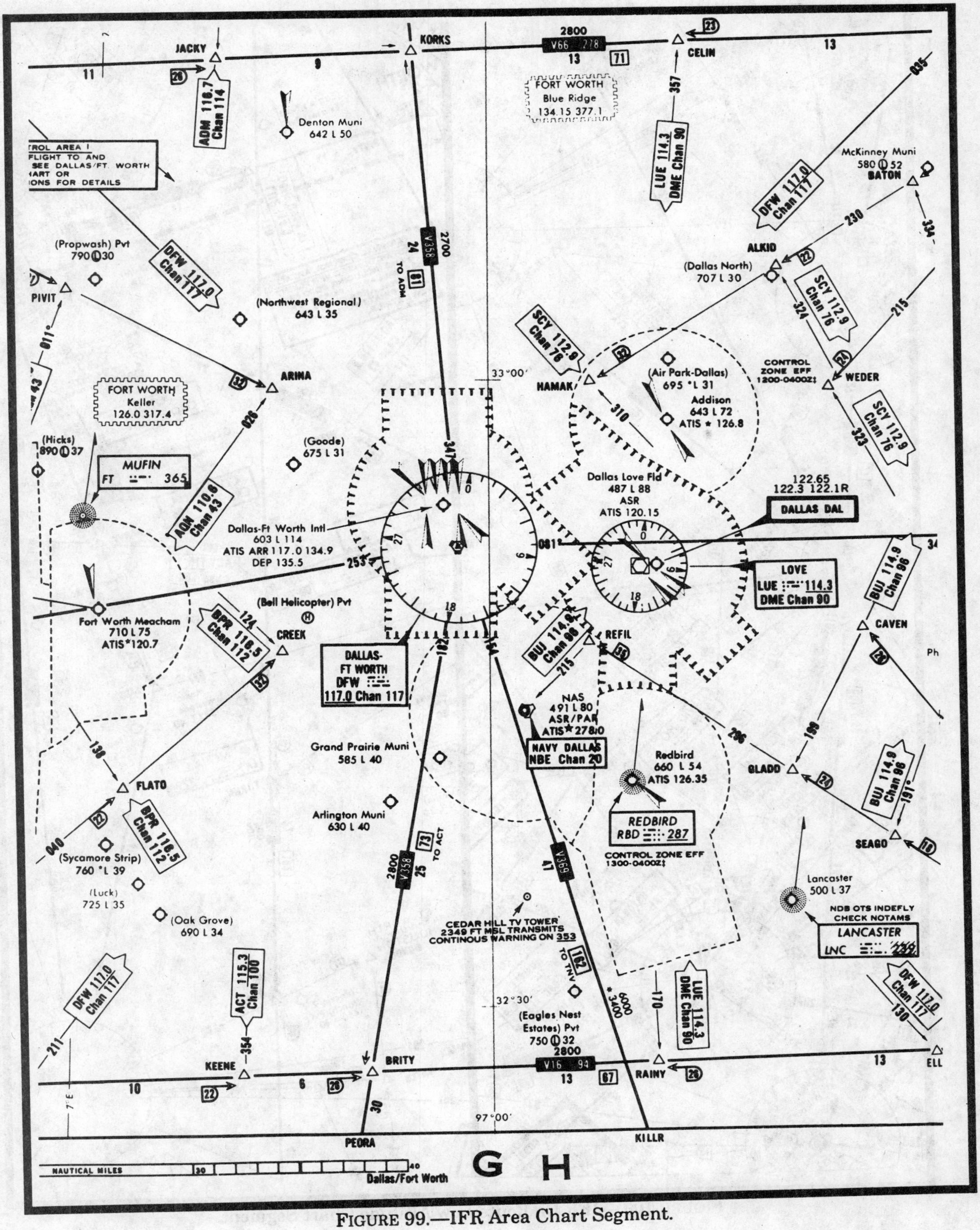

FIGURE 99.—IFR Area Chart Segment.

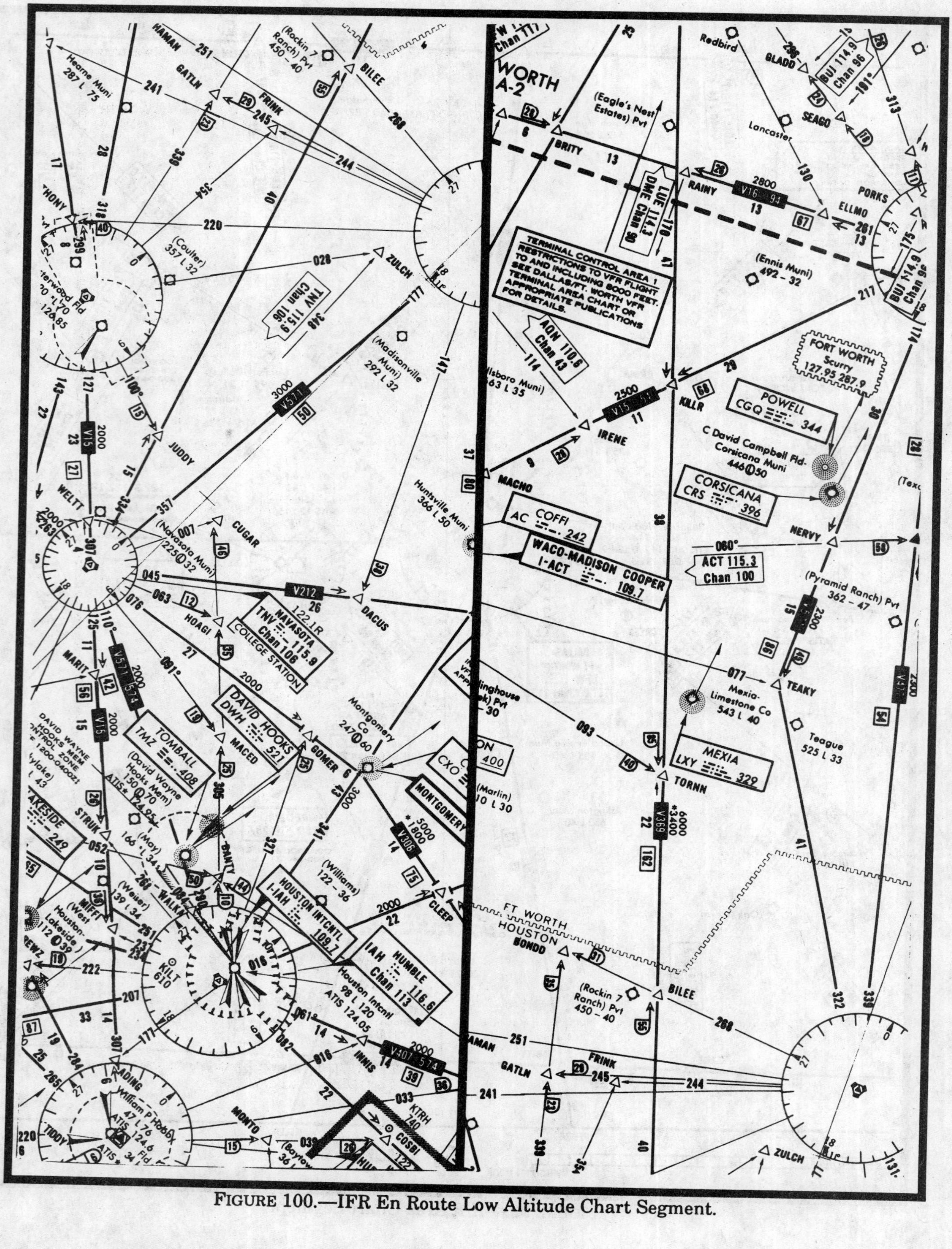

FIGURE 100.—IFR En Route Low Altitude Chart Segment.

TEXAS

§ DALLAS-FORT WORTH INTL (DFW) 12 NW UTC-6(-5DT) 32°53'47"N 97°02'28"W **DALLAS-FT. WORTH H-2K, 4F, 5B, L-13C, A IAP**

603 B FUEL 100LL, JET A OX 1,3 LRA CFR Index E

RWY 17L-35R: H11,388X150 (CONC-GRVD) S-120, D-200, DT-600, DDT-850 HIRL, CL
RWY 17L: ALSF2. TDZ. **RWY 35R:** MALSR. TDZ.
RWY 17R-35L: H11,388X200 (CONC-GRVD) S-120, D-200, DT-600, DDT-850 HIRL, CL
RWY 17R: SSALR TDZ. **RWY 35L:** TDZ. VASI(V6L).
RWY 18L-36R: H11,387X200 (CONC-GRVD) S-120, D-200, DT-600, DDT-850 HIRL, CL
RWY 18L: SSALR.TDZ. **RWY 36R:** TDZ. VASI(V6L).
RWY 18R-36L: H11,388X150 (CONC-GRVD) S-120, D-200, DT-600, DDT-850 HIRL, CL
RWY 18R: ALSF2. TDZ **RWY 36L:** MALSR. TDZ.
RWY 13L-31R: H9000X200 (CONC-GRVD) S-120, D-200, DT-600, DDT-850 HIRL, CL .5% up NW.
RWY 13L: TDZ. VASI(V6L)—Upper GA 3.25°TCH 93'. Lower GA 3.0°TCH 47'.
RWY 31 R: MALSR. TDZ.
RWY 13R-31L: H9300X150 (CONC-GRVD) S-120, D-220, DT-600, DDT-850 HIRL, CL
RWY 13 R: MALSR. TDZ. **RWY 31L:** TDZ.
RWY 18S-36S: H4000X100 (CONC)

AIRPORT REMARKS: Attended continuously. Prior Permission Required from arpt ops for General Aviation acft to proceed to airline terminal gate except to General Aviation Facility. Rwy 18S-36S located on taxiway G, 4000' long 100' wide restricted to prop acft 12,500 lbs. & below and stol acft daylight VFR plus IFR departures. Prior permission required from the primary tenant airlines to operate within central terminal area, CAUTION: proper minimum clearance may not be maintained within the central terminal area. Landing fee. Clearways 500x1000 each end Rwy 17L-35R, Rwy 17R-35L, Rwy 18L-36R and Rwy 18R-36L. Flight Notification Service (ADCUS) available.

WEATHER DATA SOURCES: LLWAS.
COMMUNICATIONS: ATIS 117.0 134.9 (ARR) 135.5 (DEP) **UNICOM** 122.95
FORT WORTH FSS (FTW) LC 624-8471, Toll free call, dial 1-800-WX-BRIEF. NOTAM FILE DFW
® **REGIONAL APP CON** 119.05(E) 119.4(E) 125.8(W) 132.1(W)
REGIONAL TOWER 126.55 (E) 124.15 (W) **GND CON** 121.65 133.15(E) 121.8 (W) **CLNC DEL** 128.25 127.5
® **REGIONAL DEP CON** 118.55 (E) 124.25 (WEST) 127.75 (NORTH-SOUTH)
TCA Group I: See VFR Terminal Area chart.
RADIO AIDS TO NAVIGATION: NOTAM FILE DFW.
(H) **VORTACW** 117.0 DFW Chan 117 32°51'57"N97°01'40"W at fld. 560/08E.
VOR Portion unusable 045°-050° all altitudes and distances, 350-100° beyond 30 NM below 2100'.
ISSUE NDB (LOM) 233 PK 32°47'35"N97°01'49"W 353° 5.1 NM to fld.
JIFFY NDB (LOM) 219 FL 32°59'45"N97°01'46"W 173° 5.1 NM to fld.
ILS/DME 109.5 I-LWN Chan 32 Rwy 13R
ILS/DME 109.1 I-FLQ Chan 28 Rwy 17L LOM JIFFY NDB
ILS 111.5 I-JHZ Rwy 17R LOM JIFFY NDB
ILS 111.3 I-CIX Rwy 18L
ILS/DME 111.9 I-VYN Chan 56 Rwy 18R
ILS 110.9 I-RRA Rwy 31R
ILS/DME 109.1 I-PKQ Chan 28 Rwy 35R LOM ISSUE NDB
ILS/DME 111.9 I-BXN Chan 56 Rwy 36L

§ HOUSTON INTERCONTINENTAL (IAH) 15N UTC-6(-5DT) 29°58'49"N 95°20'22"W **HOUSTON H-5B, L-17B IAP**

98 B S4 FUEL 100LL, JET A OX2 LRA CFR Index D

RWY 14L-32R: H1200X150 (CONC-GRVD) S-100, D-200, DT-400, DDT-778 HIRL, CL
RWY 14L: MALSR. VASI(V4L)—GA 3.0°TCH 54'. **RWY 32R:** MALSR.
RWY 09-27: H10000X150 (ASPH-GRVD) S-75, D-191, DT-400, DDT-850 HIRL,CL
RWY 09: MALSR. TDZ. PAPI(P4L)—GA 3.0°TCH 63'.
RWY 27: ALSF2. TDZ. PAPI(P4L)—GA 3.0°TCH 63'.
RWY 08-26: H9401X150 (CONC-GRVD) S-120, D-155, DT-265 HIRL, CL
RWY 08: MALSR. TDZ. **RWY 26:** ALSF2. TDZ. VASI(V4L)—GA 3.0°TCH 53'.
RWY 14R-32L: H6038X100 (ASPH-GRVD) S-30, D-60, DT-60 MIRL
RWY 14R: VASI(V4L)—GA 3.0°TCH 40'. Road. **RWY 32L:** VASI(V4L)—GA 3.0°TCH 45'.

AIRPORT REMARKS: Attended continuously. CAUTION: Birds on and in vicinity of arpt. CAUTION—Approach end of rwy 26 bright lgts approximately one mile from thld and 900' South of centerline. Caution—Deer on and in vicinity of arpt. Rwy 14R-32L CLOSED to acft over 140,000 lbs gross weight. Landing Fee. Flight Notification Service (ADCUS) available.

WEATHER DATA SOURCES: LLWAS
COMMUNICATIONS: ATIS 124.05 **UNICOM** 122.95
MONTGOMERY COUNTY FSS (CXO) Toll free call, dial 1-800-WX-BRIEF. NOTAM FILE IAH.
® **APP CON** 124.35 (West) 127.25 (North and East)
TOWER 118.1 (135.15 copter control) **GND CON** 121.7 **CLNC DEL** 128.1 (135.15 copter control)
® **DEP CON** 123.8 (West) 119.7 (North and East)
TCA Group II: VFR Terminal Area chart.
RADIO AIDS TO NAVIGATION: NOTAM FILE IAH.
HUMBLE (H) VORTACW 116.6 IAH Chan 113 29°57'24"N95°20'44"W at fld. 90/08E. **HIWAS.**
MARBE NDB (LOM) 379 HS 30°04'29"N 95°24'45"W 146° 5.9 NM to fld.
NIXIN NDB (LOM) 326 JY 29°59'36"N 95°12'54"W 257° 6.5 NM to fld.
ILS/DME 109.7 I-JYV Chan 34 Rwy 26 LOM NIXIN NDB
ILS 111.9 I-HSQ Rwy 14L LOM MARBE NDB
ILS/DME 109.7 I-IAH Chan 34 Rwy 08
ILS/DME 110.9 I-UYO Chan 34 Rwy 09
ILS 111.9 I-CDG Rwy 32R

FIGURE 101.—Airport / Facility Directory Excerpts.

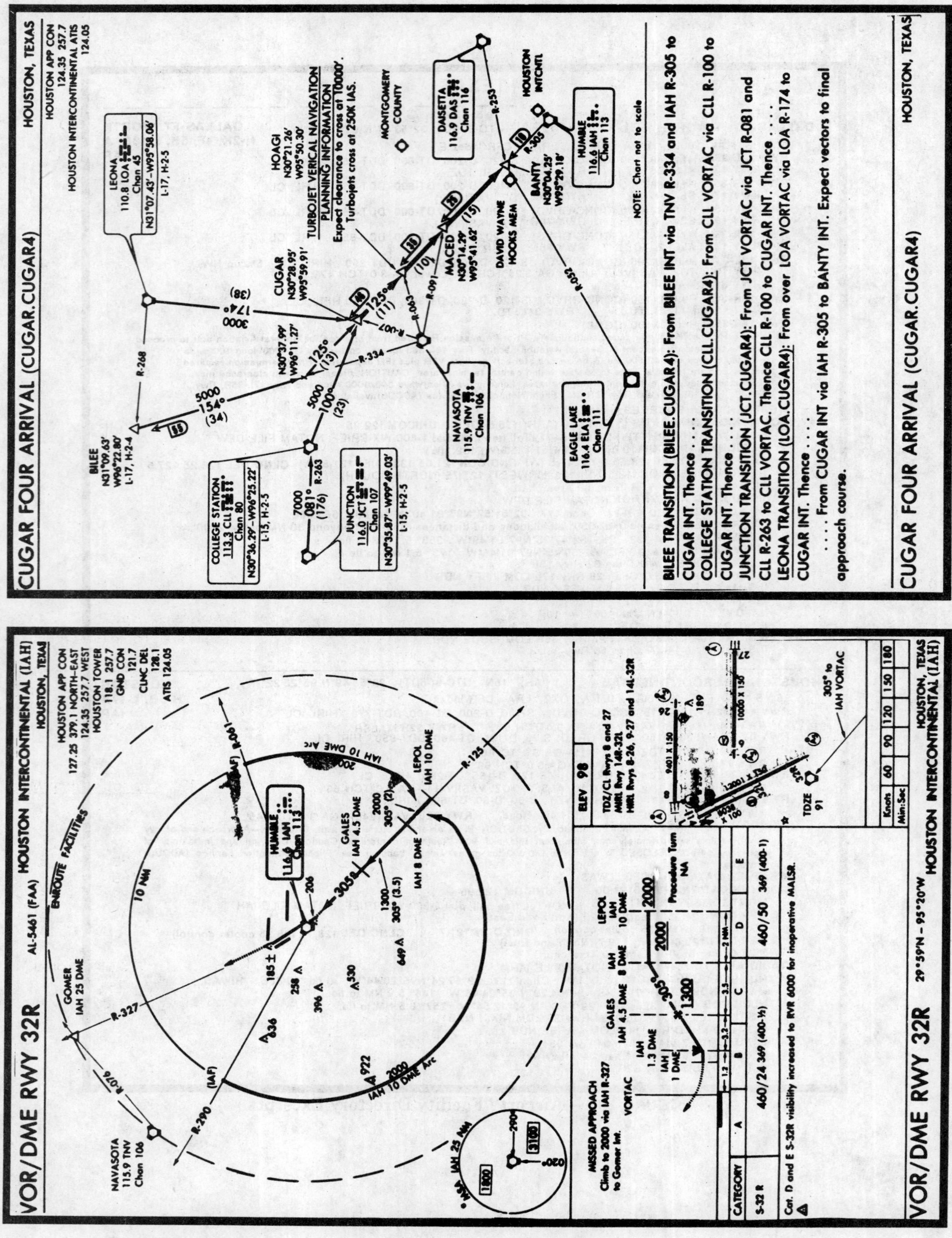

FIGURE 102.—VOR/DME RWY 32R (IAH) / Cugar Four Arrival (Cugar.Cugar4).

10.3 BE-1900 TUS TO LAX (Questions 20-39)

Questions 20 through 39 pertain to an IFR flight from Tucson International Airport, Tucson, Arizona to the Los Angeles International Airport, Los Angeles, California.

The route of flight is given in block 8 on the top portion of Fig. 103 on page 365. The partially completed flight planning log is given on the bottom portion of Fig. 103.

The following figures are used to answer the 20 questions concerning this flight.

Fig.	Page	Title
103	365	Flight Plan/Flight Log
104	366	Tucson Three Departure (Pilot Nav) (TUS3.TUS)
105	369	IFR En Route High Altitude Chart Segment
106	370	Downe Three Arrival (Downe.Downe3)
107	372	ILS RWY 25L (CAT II) - LAX
Legend 10	368	Rate-of-Climb Table
Legend 43	374	Tower Enroute Control (SW)
Legend 43A	375	Tower Enroute Control Continued

10.3 BE-1900 TUS to LAX

20.
9561. (Refer to figures 103, 104, 105, and 106 on pages 365 through 369.) Determine the ETE for the flight from Tucson Intl to Los Angeles Intl.

A—2 hours 10 minutes.
B—2 hours 15 minutes.
C—2 hours 19 minutes.

Answer (B) is correct (8787). *(IFH Chap XIII)*
To determine the estimated time en route, you must complete the flight log in Fig. 103. Convert the true wind direction to magnetic. On Fig. 104, the *A/FD* excerpt for Tucson Intl. indicates a magnetic variation of 12°E (listed under **Radio Aids to Navigation**). On Fig. 107 for Los Angeles, the magnetic variation is listed as 15°E. Easterly variation is subtracted from true headings.

	Distance	MC	Ground-speed	Time/Min.
Level-off	73G	X	X	:25G
GBN	31	289	189	:10
Int. J104	76	298	192	:24
PKE	47	277	188	:15
TNP	54	256	188	:17
Start descent	81	248	189	:26
Downe 3 LAX	52G	X	X	:18G
				2:15

G = Given

Answer (A) is incorrect because 2 hr. 10 min. would require a TAS of approximately 240 kt., not 233 kt. Answer (C) is incorrect because 2 hr. 19 min. would require a TAS of approximately 225 kt., not 233 kt.

21.
9560. (Refer to figures 103, 104, 105, and 106 on pages 365 through 369.) Estimate the total fuel required to be on the aircraft, prior to taxi at Tucson Intl.

A—2,223 pounds.
B—2,327 pounds.
C—2,447 pounds.

Answer (B) is correct (9560). *(IFH Chap XIII)*
To determine the total fuel required from Tucson Intl. to Los Angeles Intl., you must complete the fuel portion of the flight log on Fig. 103. Use 676 PPH total fuel flow from level-off to start of descent. Use 726 PPH total fuel flow for reserve and alternate requirements.

	Time	Fuel (lb.)
Level-off	:25G	350G
GBN	:10	113
Int. J104	:24	270
PKE	:15	169
TNP	:17	192
Start descent	:26	293
Descent and approach	:18G	170G
BUR	:19G	230
Reserve	:45	545
	Total	2,332

G = Given

Answer (A) is incorrect because 2,223 lb. includes the fuel required for a missed approach, not the fuel required to fly to the alternate airport (BUR). Answer (C) is incorrect because 2,447 lb. includes the fuel required for a missed approach. While this should be included as a practical matter, it is not required by the FARs.

22.
9563. (Refer to figure 104 on page 366.) If communications are lost soon after takeoff on RWY 11R at Tucson Intl, what altitude restrictions apply, in IMC conditions?

A—Fly assigned heading for vectors to intercept appropriate transition, maintain 17,000 feet to GBN, then climb to assigned altitude.
B—Fly assigned heading for vectors to intercept the Gila Bend transition; climb to 17,000 feet or lower assigned altitude; climb to FL 220, 10 minutes after departure.
C—Fly assigned heading for vectors to intercept the Gila Bend transition; climb to 17,000 feet; 10 minutes after departure, climb to FL 220.

Answer (B) is correct (9563). *(SID)*
If communications are lost soon after takeoff on RWY 11R at TUS in IMC conditions, you must fly the Tucson Three Departure as described in Fig. 104. Fly the assigned heading for vectors to intercept the Gila Bend transition. Climb to maintain 17,000 ft. or lower assigned altitude. Next, climb to FL 220, 10 min. after departure.
Answer (A) is incorrect because you must maintain 17,000 ft. or an assigned lower altitude, and you can climb to FL 220, 10 min. after departure, not only after you reach GBN VORTAC. Answer (C) is incorrect because you must climb to maintain 17,000 ft. or an assigned lower altitude.

23.
9564. (Refer to figure 104 on page 366.) What are the takeoff minimums for RWY 11R at Tucson Intl that apply to N91JB?

A—1 SM.
B—800/1.
C—4,000/3.

Answer (A) is correct (9564). *(SID)*
Fig. 104 provides the excerpt for the takeoff minimums for RWY 11R at Tucson Intl., which require a ceiling of 4,000 ft. and 3 SM visibility or standard with a minimum climb of 250 ft. per NM to 6,500 ft. The standard takeoff minimum for an airplane having two engines (e.g., BE 1900) or less is 1 SM visibility. This is the lower minimum provided the minimum climb (250 ft./NM) can be performed, as it can by the BE-1900.
Answer (B) is incorrect because an 800-ft. ceiling is required to list an airport as an alternate with a nonprecision approach. Answer (C) is incorrect because, while 4,000/3 is the takeoff minimum, a lower minimum of 1 SM is available if the airplane has a climb performance of 250 ft. per NM to 6,500 ft., as does the BE-1900.

24.
8793. (Refer to figure 104 on page 366.) Determine the DEP CON frequency for the TUS3.GBN SID after takeoff from RWY 11R at Tucson Intl.

A—125.1 MHz.
B—118.5 MHz.
C—119.0 MHz.

Answer (A) is correct (8793). *(SID, A/FD)*
In the TUS3.GBN SID, the pilot would be vectored to track outbound on the R-280 from TUS. The communication section of the *A/FD* indicates that DEP CON frequency after takeoff from RWY 11R and heading 280° will be 125.1 MHz.
Answer (B) is incorrect because 118.5 MHz is for departures from RWY 11 with a departure heading between 286° to 089°. Answer (C) is incorrect because 119.0 MHz is listed as a tower frequency for Tucson International.

25.
8794. (Refer to figure 104 on page 366.) Using an average groundspeed of 140 knots, what minimum indicated rate of climb must be maintained to meet the required climb rate (feet per NM) to 9,000 as specified on the SID?

A—349 ft/min.
B—560 ft/min.
C—584 ft/min.

Answer (C) is correct (8794). *(SID)*
The SID in Fig. 104 has a note which indicates, "Gila Bend transition requires a minimum climb of 250 ft. per NM to 9,000 ft." Refer to the Rate-of-Climb Table in Legend 10, on page 368, to determine the rate-of-climb (in ft./min.) in order to climb at 250 ft. per NM. In the right-hand column, move down to 250 ft. per NM and then move left to the 140 kt. groundspeed column to determine a rate-of-climb of 583 ft./min.
Answer (A) is incorrect because a climb rate of 349 ft./min. would be required if the average groundspeed were approximately 84 kt. Answer (B) is incorrect because a climb rate of 560 ft./min. would be required if the average groundspeed were approximately 135 kt.

26.
8795. (Refer to figure 103 on page 365.) What CAS should be used to maintain the fixed TAS at the proposed altitude?

A—157 knots.
B—167 knots.
C—172 knots.

Answer (B) is correct (8795). *(IFH Chap XIII)*
The outside air temperature is on Fig. 103 below the wind speed and direction on the flight log. The temperature is indicated as ISA −3, which is International Standard Atmosphere temperature −3°C. The ISA temperature for FL 220 is calculated by subtracting the standard lapse rate (2°C/1,000 ft.) from standard sea-level temperature of 15°C. The OAT is −32°C [15 − (22 x 2) − 3]. In the center of the computer side of the flight computer, on the right side, put the air temperature of −32°C over the pressure altitude of 22,000 ft. (given in block 7 of the flight plan). On the outer scale, find TAS of 233 kt. (from block 4), which is over calibrated airspeed (CAS) on the inner scale of 167 KCAS.
Answer (A) is incorrect because 157 KCAS will maintain the fixed TAS if the OAT is −3°C, not −32°C. Answer (C) is incorrect because 172 KCAS will maintain the fixed TAS if the OAT is −50°C, not −32°C.

27.
8796. (Refer to figure 104 on page 366.) How can the pilot receive the latest NOTAM's for the TUS-LAX flight?

A—Monitor ATIS on 123.8 MHz.
B—Contact the FSS on 122.2 MHz.
C—Request ADCUS on any FSS or Tower frequency.

Answer (B) is correct (8796). *(A/FD)*
Pilots can receive the latest NOTAMs for their flight by contacting the nearest FSS in person, telephoning, or contacting on radio. For the latest information from TUS-LAX, the pilot should contact FSS on 122.2 MHz, as listed in the *Airport/Facility Directory* on Fig. 104.
Answer (A) is incorrect because ATIS provides noncontrol airport traffic and weather information, not NOTAMs. Answer (C) is incorrect because ADCUS means to "advise customs" of an international flight and is handled by an FSS, not by a tower.

28.
8797. (Refer to figure 104 on page 366.) What distance is available for takeoff on RWY 11R at Tucson Intl?

A—7,000 feet.
B—9,129 feet.
C—10,994 feet.

Answer (B) is correct (8797). *(A/FD)*
Runway information is shown on two lines. Information common to the entire runway is shown on the first line while information concerning the runway ends is shown on the second or following line. On Fig. 104, the runway length of RWY 11R-29L is 9,129 ft., which is the distance available for takeoff on RWY 11R.
Answer (A) is incorrect because 7,000 ft. is the length of RWY 03-21. Answer (C) is incorrect because 10,994 ft. is the length of RWY 11L, not RWY 11R.

29.
8798. (Refer to figure 104 on page 366.) What effect on the takeoff run can be expected on RWY 11R at Tucson Intl?

A—Takeoff length shortened to 6,986 feet by displaced threshold.
B—Takeoff run shortened by 0.6 percent runway slope to the SE.
C—Takeoff run will be lengthened by the 0.6 percent upslope of the runway.

Answer (C) is correct (8798). *(A/FD)*
The first line of runway information provides information common to the entire runway. At the end of RWY 11R-29L on Fig. 104, the information states, "0.6% up SE." That indicates there is a 0.6% upslope grade on the runway heading SE (an upslope for RWY 11R). An upslope runway will increase the distance required for the takeoff run.
Answer (A) is incorrect because a displaced threshold will shorten the usable runway for landing, not for takeoff. Answer (B) is incorrect because the takeoff run is lengthened, not shortened, due to the 0.6% upslope to the SE.

30.
8799. (Refer to figures 106 and 107 on pages 370 and 372.) Which approach control frequency is indicated for the TNP.DOWNE3 Arrival with LAX as the destination?

A—128.5 MHz.
B—124.9 MHz.
C—124.5 MHz.

Answer (C) is correct (8799). *(STAR)*
The Downe Three Arrival on Fig. 106 indicates in the northwest corner of the chart the approach control and ATIS frequencies. The approach control frequency is 124.5 MHz.
Answer (A) is incorrect because 128.5 MHz is used for arrivals from 045° – 089°, and the TNP.DOWNE3 arrival approaches LAX from the NW from WAKER INT. Answer (B) is incorrect because 124.9 MHz is used for arrivals from 090° – 224°, and the TNP.DOWNE3 arrival approaches LAX from the NW from WAKER INT.

31.
8800. (Refer to figures 106 and 107 on pages 370 and 372.) At what point does the flight enter the final approach phase of the ILS RWY 25L at LAX?

A—FUELR INT.
B—HUNDA INT.
C—Intercept of glide slope.

Answer (C) is correct (8800). *(IAP)*
The FAA question refers you to Fig. 106, which is the STAR. To answer this question, you should refer to the IAP chart, Fig. 107.
The final approach phase for a precision approach begins with the intercept of the glide slope, at which time a descent may begin on the glide slope to the decision height. Thus, for a precision approach, the final approach fix is the intercept of the glide slope.
Answer (A) is incorrect because FUELR INT is an initial approach fix (IAF) and does not mark the point at which the flight enters the final approach phase. Answer (B) is incorrect because HUNDA INT is a fix at which the pilot should intercept the glide slope, but the intersection itself does not mark the point at which the airplane enters the final approach phase.

32.
8801. (Refer to figures 106 and 107 on pages 370 and 372.) What is the DH for the ILS RWY 25L at LAX if the pilot has completed the initial Category II certification within the preceding 6 months, but has flown no CAT II approaches?

A—201 feet.
B—251 feet.
C—301 feet.

Answer (B) is correct (8801). *(FAR 61.13)*

The FAA question refers you to Fig. 106, which is the STAR. To answer this question, you should refer to the IAP chart, Fig. 107.

Upon initial Category II certification, the authorization contains a limitation for Category II operations of 1,600 ft. RVR and a 150-ft. DH. The limitation is removed when the pilot shows that since the beginning of the sixth month (s)he has made three Category II ILS approaches with a 150-ft. DH. The first line of the minima section in Fig. 107 indicates the 150-ft. DH. Thus, the DH for the ILS RWY 25L at LAX is 251 ft.

Answer (A) is incorrect because a DH of 201 ft. is available once the initial Category II limitation is removed. Answer (C) is incorrect because a DH of 150 ft., not 200 ft., is the limitation placed upon an original issue for Category II operations.

33.
8802. (Refer to figures 106 and 107 on pages 370 and 372.) The radio altimeter indication for the DH at the inner marker on the ILS RWY 25L approach at LAX is

A—101.
B—111.
C—201.

Answer (B) is correct (8802). *(IAP)*

The FAA question refers you to Fig. 106, which is the STAR. To answer this question, you should refer to the IAP chart, Fig. 107.

The radio altimeter indication for the DH at the inner marker on the ILS RWY 25L approach is indicated by "RA" followed by the appropriate indication within parentheses in the minima section. In this approach, the RA is 111 ft.

Answer (A) is incorrect because 101 ft. is the touchdown zone elevation (TDZE). Answer (C) is incorrect because 201 ft. is the decision height, expressed in MSL.

34.
8803. (Refer to figures 106 and 107 on pages 370 and 372.) If the glide slope indication is lost upon passing HUNDA INT on the ILS RWY 25L approach at LAX, what action should the pilot take?

A—Continue the approach as an LOC and add 100 feet to the DH.
B—Immediately start the missed approach direct to INISH INT.
C—Continue to the MAP and execute the missed approach as indicated.

Answer (C) is correct (8803). *(IAP)*

The FAA question refers you to Fig. 106, which is the STAR. To answer this question, you should refer to the IAP chart, Fig. 107.

Note that there are no LOC minimums for this approach. Thus, if the glide slope indication is lost on the ILS RWY 25L approach at LAX, the pilot should continue to the MAP at or above the DH and then execute the missed approach as indicated.

Answer (A) is incorrect because there are no LOC minimums for this approach. A pilot must have a glide slope indication or execute the missed approach procedure. Answer (B) is incorrect because protected obstacle clearance areas for missed approaches are made on the assumption that the missed approach procedure is started at the MAP. No consideration is made for an abnormally early turn, unless otherwise directed by ATC.

35.
8804. (Refer to figures 106 and 107 on pages 370 and 372.) What approach lights are available for the ILS RWY 25L approach at LAX?

A—ALSF-2 with sequenced flashing lights.
B—MALSR with a displayed threshold.
C—HIRL and TDZ/CL.

Answer (A) is correct (8804). *(A/FD)*

The FAA question refers you to Fig. 106, which is the STAR. To answer this question, you should refer to the *A/FD* excerpt, Fig. 107.

Refer to the *A/FD* excerpt and locate the runway data for **RWY 07R-25L**. The first line has information common to the runway. The second line contains specific information about the runway ends. **RWY 25L** indicates "ALSF2" which translates to high-intensity approach lighting system with sequenced flashing lights, Category II configuration.

Answer (B) is incorrect because RWY 25R has an out-of-service (see **Airport Remarks**) MALSR and a displaced (not displayed) threshold. Answer (C) is incorrect because high-intensity runway lights (HIRL), touchdown zone lights (TDZ), and centerline lights (CL) are runway, not approach, lighting systems.

36.
8805. (Refer to figures 106 and 107 on pages 370 and 372.) How can DOWNE INT be identified?

A—ILAX 15 DME.
B—LAX 15 DME.
C—LAX R-249 and SLI R-327.

Answer (A) is correct (8805). *(STAR, IAP)*
Refer to Fig. 106 or 107. Downe intersection is a DME fix which is 15 DME from I-LAX. The DME is installed with the ILS and established fixes on the localizer course. ILS is identified by three letters preceded by the letter "I."
Answer (B) is incorrect because LAX 15 DME defines a circle, not an intersection. The correct answer would be LAX R-068, 15 DME. Answer (C) is incorrect because LAX R-249 and SLI R-327 do not intersect. DOWNE INT can be identified by LAX R-068 and SLI R-327.

37.
8806. (Refer to figure 107 on page 372.) How should the IFR flight plan be closed upon landing at LAX?

A—Contact Hawthorne FSS on 123.6 MHz.
B—Phone Hawthorne FSS on 644-1020.
C—LAX tower will close it automatically.

Answer (C) is correct (8806). *(AIM Para 5-1-13)*
When operating on an IFR flight plan to an airport with a functioning control tower, the flight plan is automatically closed upon landing. In this case, LAX tower will close the IFR flight plan automatically.
Answer (A) is incorrect because an IFR flight plan is closed with a flight service station only if there is no operating tower. Answer (B) is incorrect because an IFR flight plan is closed with an FSS only if there is no operating tower.

38.
9562. (Refer to legends 43 and 43A on pages 374 and 375.) The filed flight plan, for N91JB, block 13, indicates that BUR is the alternate, for LAX. The RWYs at LAX are closed and expected to remain closed for 2 hours when N91JB arrives. N91JB requests 4,000 feet, Tower Enroute Control (TEC) with radar vectors to BUR. If radar vectors are not available, what route can be expected from LAX to BUR?

A—Direct SMO, VNY, BUR.
B—LAX LAX316 SILEX.
C—Direct SMO, UR, SILEX BUR.

Answer (B) is correct (9562). *(A/FD)*
Legend 43A is the listing of city (airport) pairs for TEC. Locate **Coast TRACON** (center left of legend) and move down to the first line of airports where you will see BUR VNY WHP listed; the route is listed in the third column. If radar vectors are not available, the expected TEC route from LAX to BUR is LAX LAX316 SILEX.
Answer (A) is incorrect because the TEC route from LAX to BUR is LAX LAX316 SILEX, not direct SMO VNY BUR. Answer (C) is incorrect because the TEC route from LAX to BUR is LAX LAX316 SILEX, not SMO UR.

39.
9565. (Refer to figure 103 and legends 43 and 43A on pages 365, 374, and 375.) The RWYs at LAX are closed and expected to remain closed for 2 hours when N91JB arrives. N91JB requests 4,000 feet, Tower Enroute Control (TEC) with radar vectors to BUR. What altitude can N91JB expect based upon the type aircraft?

A—4,000 feet.
B—5,000 feet.
C—6,000 feet.

Answer (C) is correct (9565). *(A/FD)*
Legend 43 is a TEC legend. At the bottom of Legend 43 is a table titled **Aircraft Classification**. The BE 1900 is a turboprop; thus it has an (M) classification.
Legend 43A lists the TEC city pairs. Locate Coast TRACON (center left) and then the first line of airports, BUR VNY WHP. Move over to the column on the right margin (Altitude); the altitude for (M) class aircraft is 6,000 ft.
Answer (A) is incorrect because 4,000 ft. is the altitude for non-jet, not turboprop, aircraft. Answer (B) is incorrect because 5,000 ft. is not an altitude for any type of aircraft for this TEC route.

Form Approved: OMB No. 2120-0034

U.S. DEPARTMENT OF TRANSPORTATION FEDERAL AVIATION ADMINISTRATION **FLIGHT PLAN**	(FAA USE ONLY) ☐ PILOT BRIEFING ☐ VNR ☐ STOPOVER	TIME STARTED	SPECIALIST INITIALS

1. TYPE	2. AIRCRAFT IDENTIFICATION	3. AIRCRAFT TYPE/ SPECIAL EQUIPMENT	4. TRUE AIRSPEED	5. DEPARTURE POINT	6. DEPARTURE TIME PROPOSED (Z)	ACTUAL (Z)	7. CRUISING ALTITUDE
VFR X IFR DVFR	N91JB	BE1900/A	233 KTS	TUS TUCSON			FL220

8. ROUTE OF FLIGHT
TUS TUS3.GBN, J104TNP, TNP.DOWNE 3 LAX

9. DESTINATION (Name of airport and city)	10. EST. TIME ENROUTE HOURS	MINUTES	11. REMARKS
LAX LOS ANGELES INT'L Los Angeles			L/O = Level Off PPH = Pounds Per Hour TEC = Tower Enroute Control This flight is operating under FAR 135.

12. FUEL ON BOARD HOURS	MINUTES	13. ALTERNATE AIRPORT(S)	14. PILOT'S NAME, ADDRESS & TELEPHONE NUMBER & AIRCRAFT HOME BASE / 17. DESTINATION CONTACT/TELEPHONE (OPTIONAL)	15. NUMBER ABOARD
		BUR Burbank-Glendale- Pasadena		18

16. COLOR OF AIRCRAFT
Maroon/White

CIVIL AIRCRAFT PILOTS. FAR Part 91 requires you file an IFR flight plan to operate under instrument flight rules in controlled airspace. Failure to file could result in a civil penalty not to exceed $1,000 for each violation (Section 901 of the Federal Aviation Act of 1958, as amended). Filing of a VFR flight plan is recommended as a good operating practice. See also Part 99 for requirements concerning DVFR flight plans.

FAA Form 7233-1 (8-82) CLOSE VFR FLIGHT PLAN WITH ______________ FSS ON ARRIVAL

FLIGHT LOG

CHECK POINTS FROM	TO	ROUTE ALTITUDE	COURSE	WIND TEMP	SPEED-KTS TAS	GS	DIST NM	TIME LEG	TOT	FUEL LEG	TOT
TUS	L/O	TUS3.GBN Climb					73		:25:00		350*
L/O	GBN	TUS3.GBN FL220		280/46 ISA-3							
GBN	INT. J104	J104 FL220									
INT J104	PKE			280/46 ISA-3							
PKE	TNP										
TNP	Start Descent										
Start Descent	Downe 3 LAX	Descent & Approach					52	:18:00		170	
LAX	BUR	TEC 3000					31	:19:00			

OTHER DATA: * Includes Taxi Fuel
NOTE: Use 676 PPH Total Fuel Flow From L/O To Start Of Descent.
Use 726 PPH Total Fuel Flow For Reserve And Alternate Requirements.
A Missed Approach Requires 120# of Fuel.

TIME and FUEL: As required by FARs.

TIME	FUEL (LB)	
		EN ROUTE
		RESERVE
		ALTERNATE
		TOTAL

FIGURE 103.—Flight Plan / Flight Log.

(PILOT NAV) (TUS3.TUS) 90347

TUCSON THREE DEPARTURE

SL-430 (FAA)

TUCSON INTL
TUCSON, ARIZONA

CLNC DEL
126.65 326.2
ATIS 123.8 320.1

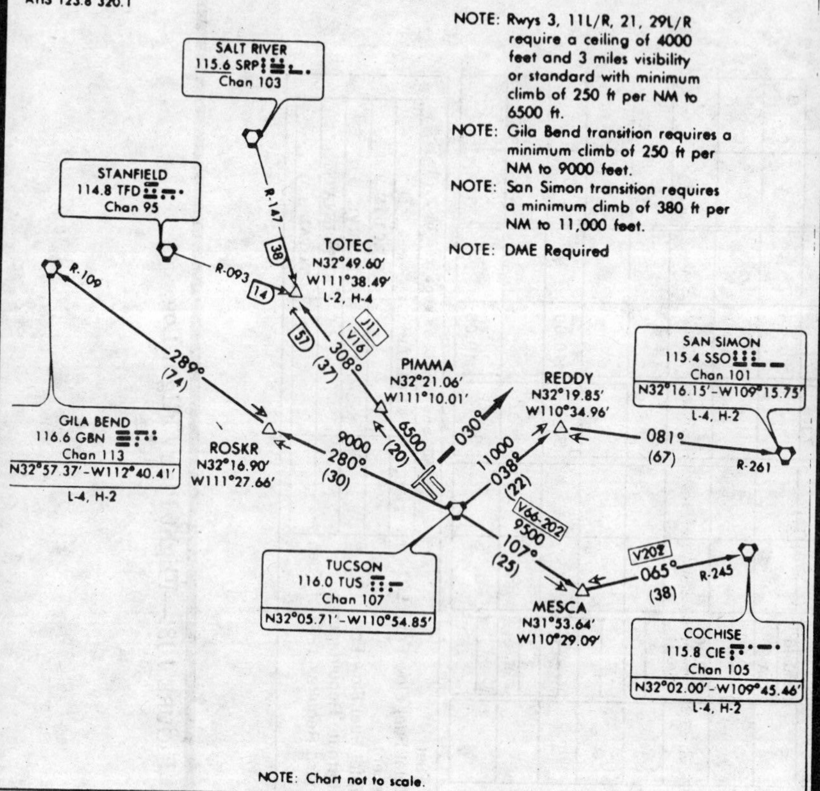

DEPARTURE ROUTE DESCRIPTION

TAKE-OFF RUNWAY 3: Fly heading 030° for vector to appropriate transition. Maintain 17,000 feet or assigned lower altitude. Expect clearance to filed flight level 10 minutes after departure.

TAKE-OFF RUNWAYS 11L/R, 21, 29L/R: Fly assigned heading for vector to intercept appropriate transition. Maintain 17,000 feet, or assigned lower altitude. Expect clearance to filed flight level 10 minutes after departure.

COCHISE TRANSITION (TUS3.CIE): Via TUS R-107 and CIE R-245 to CIE VORTAC.

GILA BEND TRANSITION (TUS3.GBN): Via TUS R-280 and GBN R-109 to GBN VORTAC.

SAN SIMON TRANSITION (TUS3.SSO): Via TUS R-038 and SSO R-261 to SSO VORTAC.

TOTEC TRANSITION (TUS3.TOTEC): Via TUS R-308 to TOTEC INT.

TUCSON THREE DEPARTURE
(PILOT NAV) (TUS3.TUS)

TUCSON, ARIZONA
TUCSON INTL

ARIZONA

TUCSON INTL (TUS) 6 S UTC-7 32°06′58″N 110°56′26″W — **PHOENIX H-2H, L-4F IAP**
2641 B S4 **FUEL** 100, 100LL, JET A OX 1, 2, 3, 4 TPA—See Remarks
AOE ARFF Index D

RWY 11L-29R: H10994X150 (ASPH-PFC) S-160, D-200, DT-350, DDT-585 HIRL 0.6% up SE
RWY 11L: MALSR. REIL. PAPI (P4L)—GA 3.0° TCH 55′. Rgt tfc. Arresting device.
RWY 29R: REIL. VASI(V6L)—Upper GA 3.25°TCH 94′. Lower GA 3.0°TCH 50′. Arresting device.
RWY 11R-29L: H9129X75 (ASPH) S-120, D-140, DT-220 MIRL 0.6% up SE
RWY 11R: REIL. Thld dsplcd 2109′. Pole. Rgt tfc. **RWY 29L:** REIL. Pole.
RWY 03-21: H7000X150 (ASPH-PFC) S-105, D-137, DT-230, DDT-500 MIRL
RWY 03: Thld dsplcd 841′. Railroad.
RWY 21: REIL. VASI(V4L)—GA 3.0°TCH 50′.Tree. Rgt tfc. Arresting device.

AIRPORT REMARKS: Attended continuously. Commercial ldg fee and tiedown fee. Acft departing Rwy 11R reqd to attain at least 400′AGL prior to starting turn. Rwy 11L-29R has distance remaining markers on both sides. Rwy 03-21 has distance remaining markers on east side. Rwy 11R dsplcd thld not lgtd. No B-747 training except PPR; No flight training 0500-1300Z except PPR; call manager aviation svc 602-573-8152. Rwy 11L-29R gross weight limit DC-10-10 315,000 lbs, DC-10-30/40 400,000 lbs, L-1011-1 325,000 lbs, L-1011-100/200 340,000 lbs, Rwy 03-21 gross weight limit DC-10-10 300,000 lbs, DC-10-30/40 375,000 lbs, L-1011-01 310,000 lbs, L-1011-100/200 315,000 lbs. TPA-3441 (800) small acft, 4041 (1400) large/heavy turbojet acft. Portions of Taxiways C and 9 not visible from the twr due to vegetation; portions of Taxiway 2 not visible from the twr due to hangars. Note: See Special Notices—Glider Operations Northwest of Tucson, Arizona. Flight Notification Service (ADCUS) available.

WEATHER DATA SOURCES: LLWAS.

COMMUNICATIONS: ATIS 123.8 (602) 741-1177 **UNICOM** 122.95
TUCSON FSS (TUS) on arpt. 122.2 LC 889-9689. NOTAM FILE TUS.
MOUNT LEMMON RCO 122.4 (TUCSON FSS)
Ⓡ **APP/DEP CON** 125.1 (Rwy 11 090°-285°) (Rwy 29 275°-065°) 118.5 (Rwy 11 286°-089°) (Rwy 29 066°-274°)128.5
TOWER 118.3 119.0 **GND CON** 124.4 **CLNC DEL** 126.65

RADIO AIDS TO NAVIGATION: NOTAM FILE TUS. VHF/DF ctc FSS.
(H) **VORTAC** 116.0 TUS Chan 107 32°05′42″N 110°54′51″W 301° 1.8 NM to fld. 2670/12E.
VORTAC unusable 050°-080°beyond 30 NM below 10,500′ 350°-005°beyond 30 NM below 11,200′
ILS/DME 108.5 I-TUS Chan 22 Rwy 11L.

▼ TAKE-OFF MINS

TUCSON, AZ

RYAN FIELD

DEPARTURE PROCEDURE: **Rwy 6**, turn right; **Rwy 24**, turn left direct to Ryan NDB. Continue climb in holding pattern (W, right turn 090° inbound) to 5000 before proceeding on course.

TUCSON INTL

TAKE-OFF MINIMUMS: **Rwys 3, 11L/R, 21, 29L/R**, 4000-3 or std. with min. climb of 250′ per NM to 6500.
DEPARTURE PROCEDURE: Comply with SID or radar vectors; or turn left or right as assigned by ATC direct TUS VORTAC, climb in holding pattern (NW, right turn, 128 inbound) to depart TUS VORTAC at or above MCA or MEA for assigned airway.

FIGURE 104.—Tucson Three Departure (Pilot Nav) (TUS3.TUS).

This page is intentionally blank because the FAA deleted a figure.

INSTRUMENT TAKEOFF PROCEDURE CHARTS

RATE OF CLIMB TABLE

(ft. per min.)

A rate of climb table is provided for use in planning and executing takeoff procedures under known or approximate ground speed conditions.

REQUIRED CLIMB RATE (ft. per NM)	GROUND SPEED (KNOTS)						
	30	60	80	90	100	120	140
200	100	200	267	300	333	400	467
250	125	250	333	375	417	500	583
300	150	300	400	450	500	600	700
350	175	350	467	525	583	700	816
400	200	400	533	600	667	800	933
450	225	450	600	675	750	900	1050
500	250	500	667	750	833	1000	1167
550	275	550	733	825	917	1100	1283
600	300	600	800	900	1000	1200	1400
650	325	650	867	975	1083	1300	1516
700	350	700	933	1050	1167	1400	1633

REQUIRED CLIMB RATE (ft. per NM)	GROUND SPEED (KNOTS)					
	150	180	210	240	270	300
200	500	600	700	800	900	1000
250	625	750	875	1000	1125	1250
300	750	900	1050	1200	1350	1500
350	875	1050	1225	1400	1575	1750
400	1000	1200	1400	1600	1700	2000
450	1125	1350	1575	1800	2025	2250
500	1250	1500	1750	2000	2250	2500
550	1375	1650	1925	2200	2475	2750
600	1500	1800	2100	2400	2700	3000
650	1625	1950	2275	2600	2925	3250
700	1750	2100	2450	2800	3150	3500

LEGEND 10.—Rate-of-Climb Table.

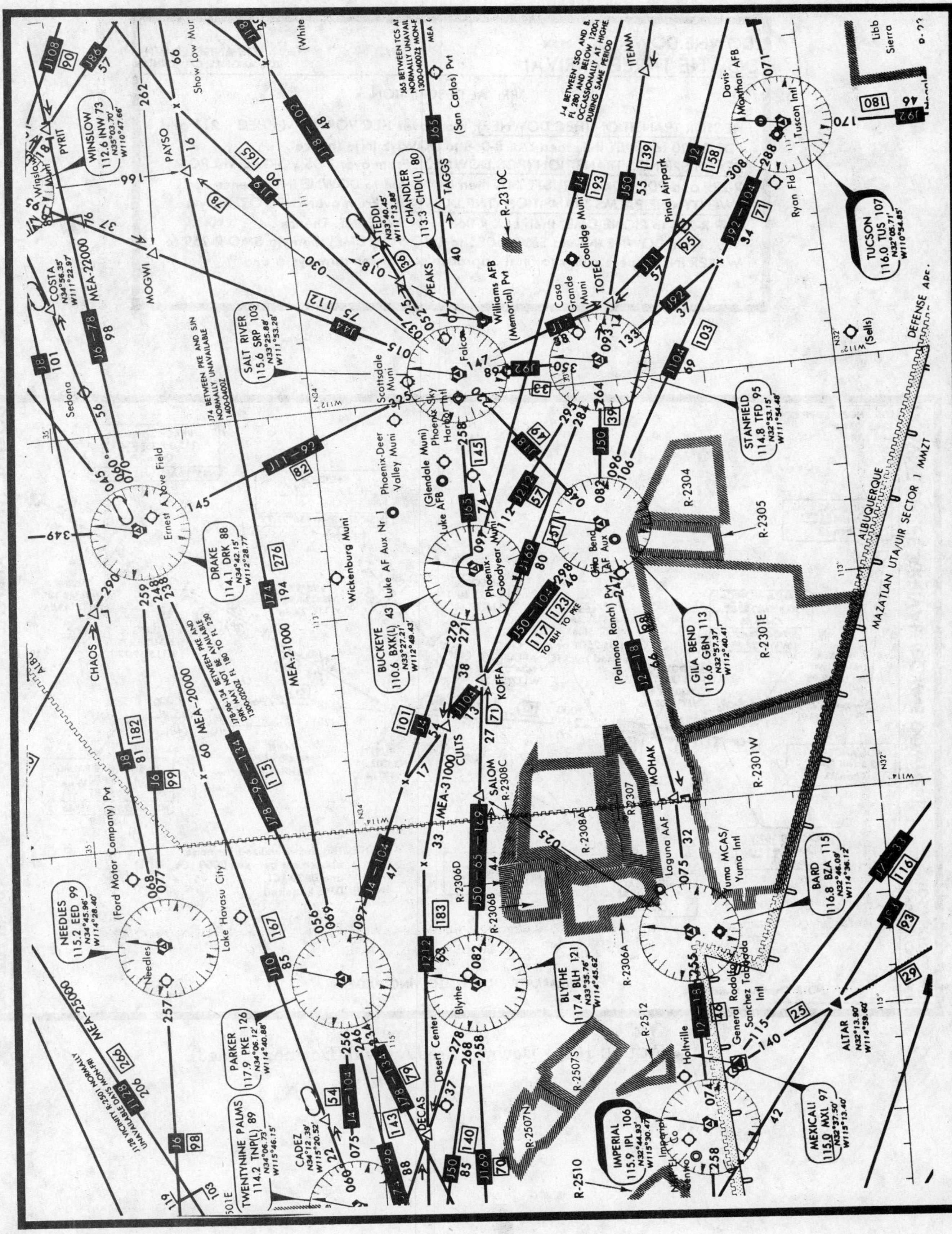

FIGURE 105.—IFR En Route High Altitude Chart Segment.

(DOWNE.DOWNE3) 89208

DOWNE THREE ARRIVAL

LOS ANGELES INTL
LOS ANGELES, CALIFORNIA

ARRIVAL DESCRIPTION

HECTOR TRANSITION (HEC.DOWNE3): From over HEC VORTAC via HEC R-211 and PDZ R-030 to CIVET INT, then LAX R-068 to DOWNE INT. Thence . . . .
PEACH SPRINGS TRANSITION (PGS.DOWNE3): From over PGS VORTAC via PGS R-229 and PDZ R-046 to RUSTT INT, then LAX R-068 to DOWNE INT. Thence . . . .
TWENTYNINE PALMS TRANSITION (TNP.DOWNE3): From over TNP VORTAC via TNP R-254 to PIONE DME, then LAX R-068 to DOWNE INT. Thence . . . .
. . . . From DOWNE INT via SMO R-085 to SMO VOR/DME, then via SMO R-259 to WAKER INT, expect vector to final approach course for runways 6 and 7.

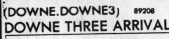

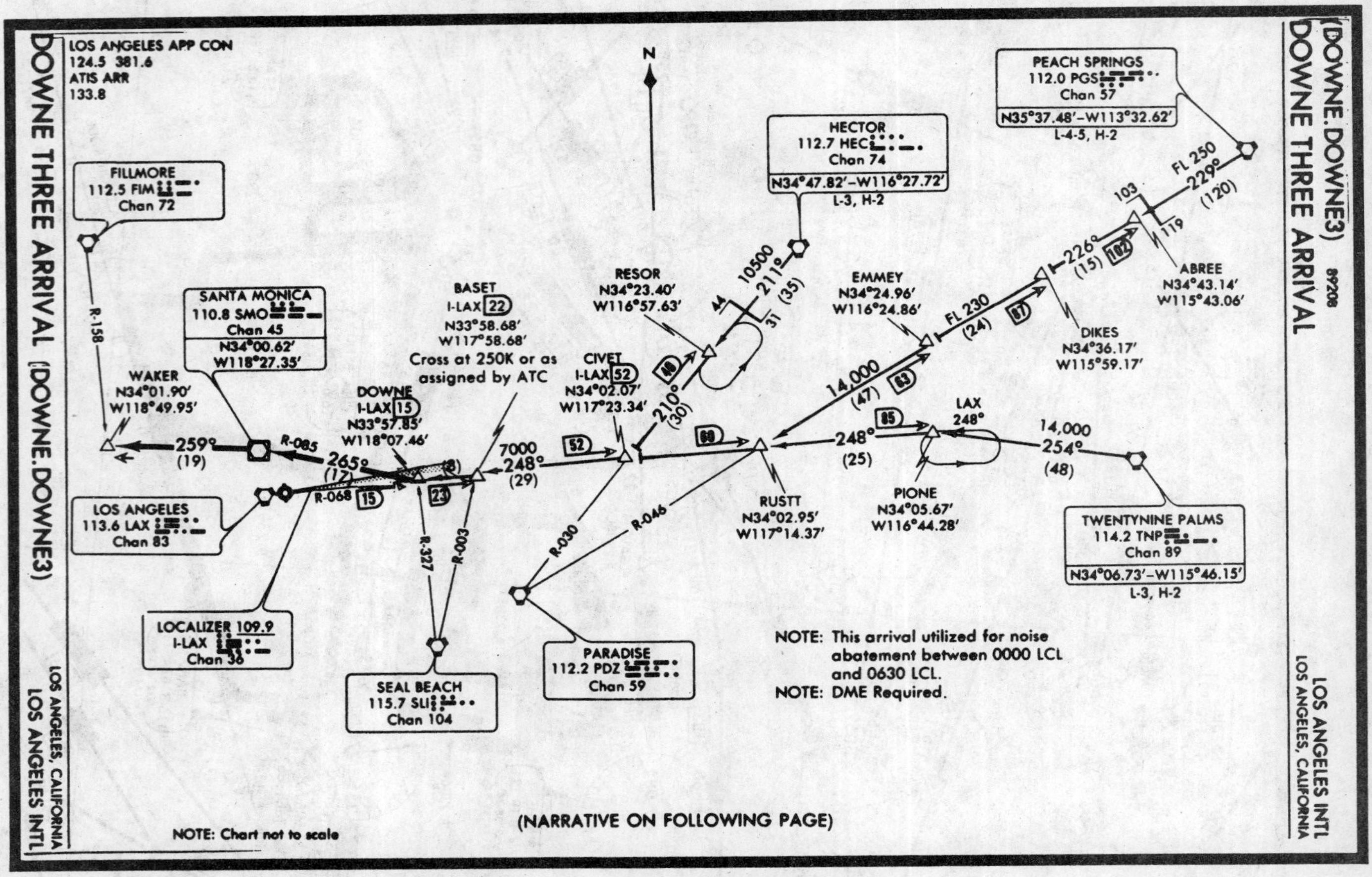

FIGURE 106.—Downe Three Arrival (Downe.Downe3).

This page is intentionally blank because the FAA deleted a figure.

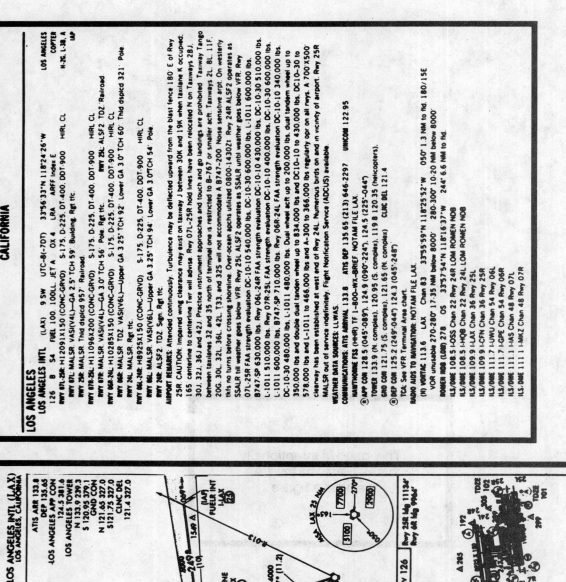

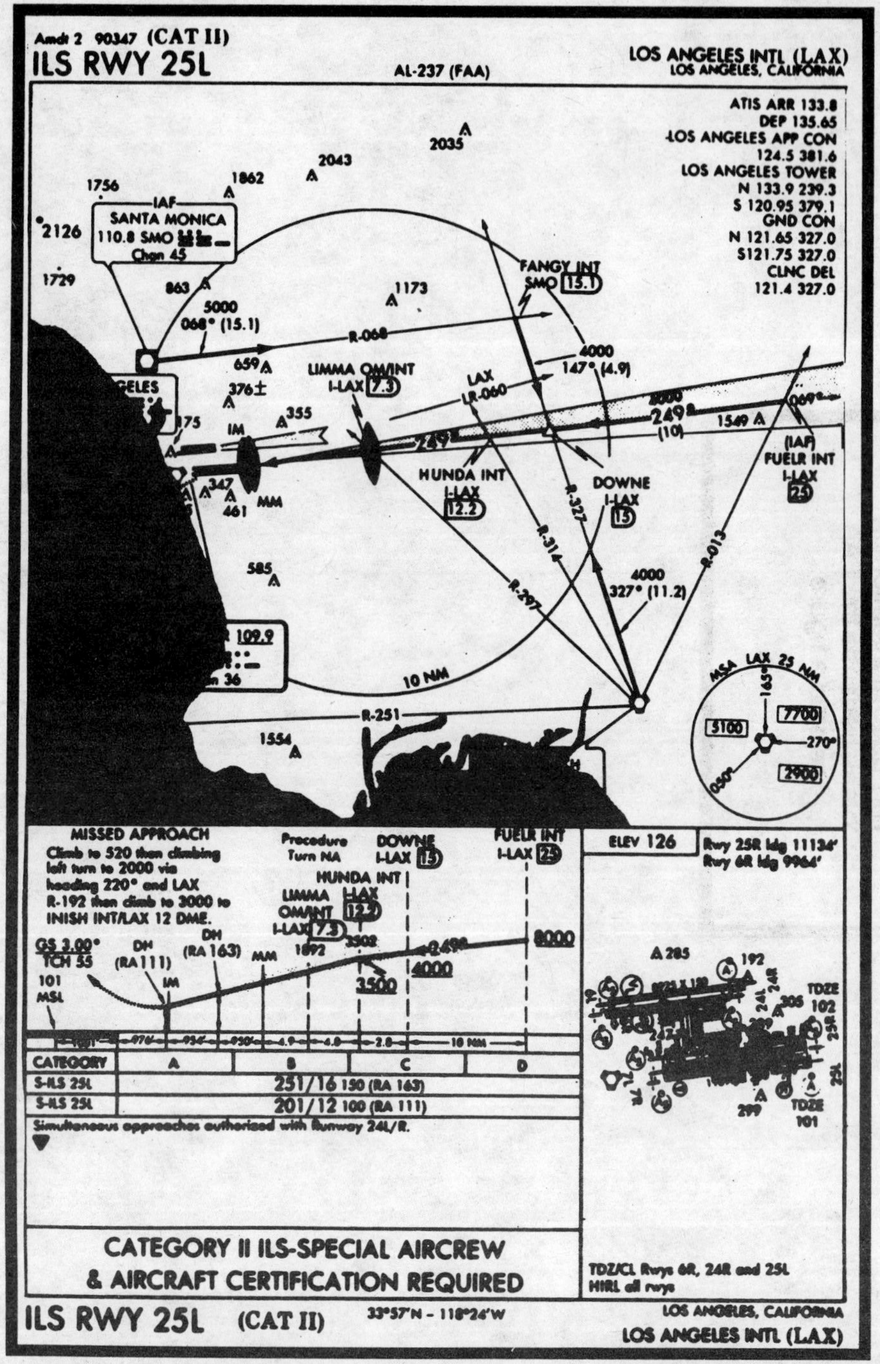

CALIFORNIA

LOS ANGELES

LOS ANGELES INTL (LAX) 9 SW UTC–8(–7DT) 33°56'33"N 118°24'26"W — LOS ANGELES COPTER H-2G, L-3B, A IAP

126 B S4 FUEL 100, 100LL, JET A OX 4 LRA ARFF Index E

RWY 07L-25R: H12091X150 (CONC-GRVD) S-175, D-225, DT-400, DDT-900 HIRL CL

RWY 07L: MALSR. VASI(V4L)—GA 2.5° TCH 59'. Building. Rgt tfc.

RWY 25R: MALSR. Thld dsplcd 957'. Railroad.

RWY 07R-25L: H11096X200 (CONC-GRVD) S-175, D-225, DT-400, DDT-900 HIRL CL

RWY 07R: MALSR. VASI(V4L)—GA 3.0° TCH 56'. Pole. Rgt tfc. **RWY 25L:** ALSF2. TDZ. Railroad.

RWY 06R-24L: H10285X150 (CONC-GRVD) S-175, D-225, DT-400, DDT-900 HIRL CL

RWY 06R: MALSR. TDZ. VASI(V6L)—Upper GA 3.25° TCH 92'. Lower GA 3.0° TCH 60'. Thld dsplcd 321'. Pole.

RWY 24L: MALSR. Rgt tfc.

RWY 06L-24R: H8925X150 (CONC-GRVD) S-175, D-225, DT-400, DDT-900 HIRL CL

RWY 06L: MALSR. VASI(V6L)—Upper GA 3.25° TCH 94'. Lower GA 3.0°TCH 54'. Pole.

RWY 24R: ALSF2. TDZ. Sign. Rgt tfc.

AIRPORT REMARKS: Attended continuously. Turbulence may be deflected upward from the blast fence 180' E of Rwy 25R. CAUTION: Impaired wing clearance may exist on taxiway J between 30K and 19K when taxilane K occupied; 165 centerline to centerline Twr will advise. Rwy 07L–25R hold lines have been relocated N on Taxiways 28J, 30J, 32J, 36J and 42J. Practice instrument approaches and touch and go landings are prohibited. Taxiway Tango between taxilanes 32 and 35 north of terminal one is restricted to B-767 or smaller acft. Taxiways 2L, 8L, 11F, 20G, 30L, 32L, 36L, 42L, T33, and 32S will not accommodate A B747-200. Noise sensitive arpt. On westerly tkfs no turns before crossing shoreline. Over-ocean apchs utilized 0800-1430Z‡. Rwy 24R ALSF2 operates as SSALR till weather goes below VFR. Rwy 25L ALSF2 operates as SSALR until weather goes below VFR. Rwy 07L-25R FAA strength evaluation DC-10-10 540,000 lbs, DC-10-30 600,000 lbs, L-1011 600,000 lbs, B747-SP 630,000 lbs. Rwy 06L-24R FAA strength evaluation DC-10-10 430,000 lbs, DC-10-30 510,000 lbs, L-1011 510,000 lbs. Rwy 07R-25L FAA strength evaluation DC-10-10 400,000 lbs, DC-10-30 600,000 lbs, L-1011 600,000 lbs, B747-SP 710,000 lbs. Rwy 06R-24L FAA strength evaluation DC-10-10 340,000 lbs, DC-10-30 480,000 lbs, L-1011 480,000 lbs. Dual wheel acft up to 200,000 lbs, dual tandem wheel up to 350,000 lbs and double dual tanden wheel up to 834,000 lbs and DC10–10 to 430,000 lbs, DC10–30 to 578,000 lbs and L-1011 to 466,000 lbs and A-300 to 366,000 lbs regularly opr on all rwys. A 700'X500' clearway has been established at west end of Rwy 24L. Numerous birds on and in vicinity of airport. Rwy 25R MALSR out of service indefinitely. Flight Notification Service (ADCUS) available.

WEATHER DATA SOURCES: LLWAS.

COMMUNICATIONS: ATIS ARRIVAL 133.8 **ATIS DEP** 135.65 (213) 646-2297 **UNICOM** 122.95

HAWTHORNE FSS (HHR) TF 1–800–WX–BRIEF. NOTAM FILE LAX.

Ⓡ **APP CON** 128.5 (045°-089°), 124.9 (090°-224°), 124.5 (225°-044°)

TOWER 133.9 (N. complex), 120.95 (S. complex), 119.8 120.35 (helicopters).

GND CON 121.75 (S. complex), 121.65 (N. complex) **CLNC DEL** 121.4

Ⓡ **DEP CON** 125.2 (249°-044°) 124.3 (045°-248°)

TCA: See VFR Terminal Area chart.

RADIO AIDS TO NAVIGATION: NOTAM FILE LAX.

(H) **VORTAC** 113.6 LAX Chan 83 33°55'59"N 118°25'52"W 050° 1.3 NM to fld. 180/15E

VOR unusable 270-280° 17-35 NM below 8000' 280-300° 10-20 NM below 8000'

ROMEN NDB (LOM) 278 OS 33°57'54"N 118°16'37"W 244° 6.6 NM to fld.

ILS/DME 108.5 I-OSS Chan 22 Rwy 24R LOM ROMEN NDB

ILS/DME 108.5 I-HQB Chan 22 Rwy 24L LOM ROMEN NDB

ILS/DME 109.9 I-LAX Chan 36 Rwy 25L

ILS/DME 109.9 I-CFN Chan 36 Rwy 25R

ILS/DME 111.7 I-UWU Chan 54 Rwy 06L

ILS/DME 111.7 I-GPE Chan 54 Rwy 06R

ILS/DME 111.1 I-IAS Chan 48 Rwy 07L

ILS/DME 111.1 I-MKZ Chan 48 Rwy 07R

FIGURE 107.—ILS RWY 25L (CAT II) – LAX.

This page is intentionally blank because the FAA deleted a figure.

TOWER ENROUTE CONTROL (TEC)

235

Within the national airspace system it is possible for a pilot to fly IFR from one point to another without leaving approach control airspace. This is referred to as "Tower Enroute" which allows flight beneath the enroute structure. The tower enroute concept has been expanded (where practical) by reallocating airspace vertically/geographically to allow flight planning between city pairs while remaining within approach control airspace. Pilots are encouraged to use the TEC route descriptions provided in the Southwest U.S. Airport/Facility Directory when filing flight plans. Other airways which appear to be more direct between two points may take the aircraft out of approach control airspace thereby resulting in additional delays or other complications. All published TEC routes are designed to avoid enroute airspace and the majority are within radar coverage. The following items should be noted before using the graphics and route descriptions.

1. The graphic is not to be used for navigation nor detailed flight planning. Not all city pairs are depicted. It is intended to show geographic areas connected by tower enroute control. Pilots should refer to route descriptions for specific flight planning.

2. The route description contains four colums of information after approach control area listed in the heading, where the departure airport is located; i.e., the airport/airports of intended landing using FAA three letter/letter-two number identifiers, the coded route number (this should be used when filing the flight plan and will be used by ATC in lieu of reading out the full route description), the specific route (airway, radial, etc.), the altitude allowed for type of aircraft and the routes.

3. The word "DIRECT" will appear as the route when radar vectors will be used or no airway exists. Also this indicates that a Standard Instrument Departure (SID) or Standard Terminal Arrival (STAR) may be applied by ATC.

4. When a NAVAID or intersection identifier appears with no airway immediately preceding or following the identifier, the routing is understood to be DIRECT to or from that point unless otherwise cleared by ATC or radials are listed (See item 5).

5. Routes beginning and ending with an airway indicate that the airway essentially overflies the airport or radar vectors will be applied.

6. Where more than one route is listed to the same destination, ensure you file correct route for type of aircraft which are denoted after the route in the altitude column using J,M,P, or Q. These are listed after item 10 under Aircraft Classification.

7. Although all airports are not listed under the destination column, IFR flight may be planned to satellite airports in the proximity to major airports via the same routing.

8. Los Angeles International Airport (LAX) and four other airports (ONT-SAN-TOA-SNA) have two options due to winds and these affect the traffic flows and runways in use. To indicate the difference the following symbols are used after the airport: Runway Number, W for west indicating normal conditions, E for East and N for North indicating other than normal operation. If nothing follows the airport use this route on either West, East or North plan. Other destinations have different arrivals due to LAX being East and they have the notation "(LAXE)." Torrance Airport is also unique in that the airport is split between Los Angeles and Coast TRACON, for Runway 11 departures use Coast TRACON routings and for Runway 29 departures use LAX TRACON routings.

9. When filing flight plans, the coded route identifier i.e. SANJ2, VTUJ4, POMJ3 may be used in lieu of the route of flight.

10. Aircraft types i.e. J, M, P, and Q are listed at the beginning of the altitude and should be used with the route of flight filed. (See Aircraft Classification below). The altitudes shown are to be used for the route. This allows for separation of various arrival routes, departure routes, and overflights to, from, and over all airports in the Southern California area.

LEGENDS

AIRCRAFT CLASSIFICATION

(J) = Jet powered
(M) = Turbo Props/Special (cruise speed 190 knots or greater)
(P) = Non-jet (cruise speed 190 knots or greater)
(Q) = Non-jet (cruise speed 189 knots or less)

LEGEND 43.—Tower Enroute Control (SW).

236 TOWER ENROUTE CONTROL

BURBANK TRACON
FROM: BUR VNY WHP

TO:	ROUTE ID	ROUTE	ALTITUDE
FUL LGB SLI TOA (RWY 29)	BURJ1	V186 V394 SLI	MPQ50
LAX	BURJ2	V186 PURMS	JMPQ40
LAX (LAXE)	BURJ3	VNY SMO	JM50PQ40
TOA (RWY 11)	BURJ4	VNY VNY095 DARTS SMO	JMPQ40
SMO	BURJ5	V186 DARTS	JMPQ30
CCB CNO EMT HMT L12 L65 L66 L67 F70 ONT POC RAL RIR RIV SBD	BURJ6	V186 PDZ	JM70PQ50
CRQ NFG NKX L39 L32	BURJ7	V186 V363 V23 OCN	JM70PQ50
MYF NRS NZY SAN SDM SEE	BURJ8	V186 V363 V23 MZB	PQ50
MYF NRS NZY SAN SDM SEE	BURJ9	V186 POM164 V208 MZB320 MZB	JM70
OXR CMA	BURJ10	VNY	JMPQ40
SBA	BURJ11	FIM V186 V27 KWANG	JMPQ60
SNA	BURJ12	V186 V363 V8 SLI	JMPQ50
SAN (SANE)	BURJ13	V186 V363 V23 V165 SARGS	PQ50
SAN (SANE)	BURJ14	V186 POM164 V25 V165 SARGS	JM70
NZJ NTK	BURJ15	V186 V363 V23 DAMPS	JM70PQ50
AVX	BURJ16	V186 V363 KRAUZ SXC	JM70PQ50
HHR	BURJ17	V186 ELMOO	JMPQ40
LGB	BURJ18	V186 V363 V23 SLI	J70

COAST TRACON
FROM: FUL LGB SLI SNA TOA (RWY 11) NTK NZJ

TO:	ROUTE ID	ROUTE	ALTITUDE
BUR VNY WHP	CSTJ1	SLI V23 LAX LAX316 SILEX	JM60PQ40
BUR VNY WHP (LAXE)	CSTJ2	SLI SLI333 V186 VNY	JM50PQ40
CMA OXR (LAXE)	CSTJ3	SLI SLI333 V186 FIM	JM50PQ40
LAX	CSTJ4	SLI	JM70PQ40
LAX (LAXE)	CSTJ5	SLI V8 TANDY	JM50PQ40
SMO	CSTJ6	SLI V23 LAX LAX046 ELMOO	JM70PQ40
SMO (LAXE)	CSTJ7	SLI SLI333 V186 DARTS	JM50PQ40
CCB EMT POC	CSTJ8	SLI V8 V363 POM	JMPQ50
CNO HMT L12 L65 L66 L67 F70 ONT RAL RIR RIV SBD	CSTJ9	SLI V8 PDZ (SNA RWY 19 ONLY)	JM60
CNO HMT L12 L65 L66 L67 F70 ONT RAL RIR RIV SBD	CSTJ10	SLI V8 PDZ	JMPQ50
CRQ L39 NFG NKX L32	CSTJ12	V25 V208 OCN	JM70
MYF NRS NZY SAN SDM SEE	CSTJ14	V25 V208 MZB320 MZB	J110M90
OXR CMA	CSTJ15	SLI V23 LAX VNY	M50PQ40
OXR CMA	CSTJ16	SXC SXC295 VTU160 VTU	J80
SBA	CSTJ17	SLI V23 LAX VTU KWANG	PQ40
SBA (LAXE)	CSTJ18	SLI SLI333 V186 V27 KWANG	M50PQ40
SBA	CSTJ19	SXC SXC295 VTU160 VTU KWANG	JM80
SAN (SANE)	CSTJ21	V25 V165 SARGS	J110M90
HHR	CSTJ26	SLI SLI340 WELLZ LOC	JM70PQ40

FROM: SNA NTK NZJ and when SNAN FUL LGB SLI TOA RWY 11

TO:	ROUTE ID	ROUTE	ALTITUDE
CRQ L39 NFG NKX L32	CSTJ11	V23 OCN	PQ50
MYF NRS NZY SAN SDM SEE	CSTJ13	V23 MZB	PQ50
SAN (SANE)	CSTJ20	V23 V165 SARGS	PQ50

FROM: AVX (DEPARTURES ONLY)

TO:	ROUTE ID	ROUTE	ALTITUDE
CRQ L39 NFG NKX L32	CSTJ22	SXC V208 OCN	JMPQ50
MYF NRS NZY SAN SDM SEE	CSTJ23	SXC V208 MZB320 MZB	J110M90
MYF NRS NZY SAN SDM SEE (SANE)	CSTJ24	SXC V208 OCN V165 SARGS	PQ50
MYF NRS NZY SAN SDM SEE	CSTJ25	SXC V208 OCN V23 MZB	PQ50

LEGEND 43A.—Tower Enroute Control Continued.

10.4 BE-1900 PWK TO BUF (Questions 40-50)

Questions 40 through 50 pertain to an IFR flight from Pal-Waukee Municipal Airport, Chicago (Wheeling), Illinois to Greater Buffalo International Airport, Buffalo, New York.

The route is given in block 8 on the flight plan portion of Fig. 168 on page 380. The partially completed flight planning log is given on the bottom portion of Fig. 168.

The following figures are used to answer the 11 questions concerning this flight.

10.4 BE-1900 PWK to BUF

40.
9610. (Refer to figures 168, 169, 169A, 171, and 172 on pages 380, 381, 382, 421, and 385.) What is the ETE for PTZ 70 from Chicago Pal-Waukee Airport to Greater Buffalo International Airport?

A—2 hours 15 minutes.
B—2 hours 18 minutes.
C—2 hours 21 minutes.

Answer (B) is correct (9610). *(IFH Chap XIII)*

To determine the ETE from Chicago Pal-Waukee (PWK) to Greater Buffalo (BUF), you must complete the flight log in Fig. 168. In the remarks box of the flight plan, the magnetic variation at PWK (1° W), FNT (3° W), and BUF (8° W) are given. This information is used to convert the true wind direction to magnetic direction. Also given is the level-off point, which is PMM R-261 at 47 NM.

Our flight log below has been expanded to provide more detail. To convert the wind direction from true to magnetic, we used 1° W variation to PMM; 3° W variation from PMM to YXU, and 8° W variation from YXU to BUF.

	Distance	MC	Wind (mag)	Ground-speed	Time
Level-off	49G	X	X	X	0:24:00G
PMM	47	081	021/61	211	0:13:21
PMM/FNT COP	54.5	073	023/61	203	0:16:06
FNT	54.5	078	023/61	207	0:15:47
FNT/YXU COP	57	090	023/61	217	0:15:45
YXU	57	097	023/61	223	0:15:20
BUF R-282/40	70	101	028/61	222	0:18:55
BUF	40G	X	X	X	0:19:00G
					2:18:14

G = Given

Answer (A) is incorrect because 2 hr. 15 min. is the approximate ETE if the true wind direction is not converted to magnetic direction. Answer (C) is incorrect because an ETE of 2 hr. 21 min. would require a TAS of 240 kt., not 247 kt.

41.
9611. (Refer to figures 168, 169, 169A, 171, and 172 on pages 380, 381, 382, 421, and 385.) What is the computed fuel usage for PTZ 70 from start of taxi at Chicago Pal-Waukee to landing at Greater Buffalo Intl?

A—1,642 pounds.
B—2,005 pounds.
C—2,550 pounds.

Answer (A) is correct (9611). *(IFH Chap XIII)*
To determine the fuel usage from start of taxi at Chicago Pal-Waukee to landing at Greater Buffalo, you must complete the fuel portion of the flight log in Fig. 168. The 410 lb. of fuel given in the log to level-off includes taxi fuel. Use 676 PPH from level-off to the start of the descent.

	Time	Fuel (lb.)
Level-off	0:24:00G	410.0G
PMM	0:13:21	150.4
PMM/FNT COP	0:16:06	181.4
FNT	0:15:47	177.8
FNT/YXU COP	0:15:45	177.5
YXU	0:15:20	172.8
BUF R-282/40	0:18:55	213.1
BUF	0:19:00G	163.0G
		1,646.0

G = Given

Answer (B) is incorrect because 2,005 lb. of fuel includes the fuel required to fly from BUF to SYR. Answer (C) is incorrect because 2,550 lb. includes the fuel required to fly from BUF to SYR and the 45 min. of fuel reserve requirement.

42.
9612. (Refer to figures 168, 171, 172, and 173 on pages 380, 421, 385, and 387.) What TAS should PTZ 70 maintain to arrive at FNT 30 minutes after passing PMM?

A—255 knots.
B—265 knots.
C—260 knots.

Answer (C) is correct (9612). *(IFH Chap XIII)*
To determine the required TAS to arrive at FNT 30 min. after passing PMM, you need to determine the required groundspeed. The distance is 109 NM; thus the groundspeed required is 218 kt. (109 NM ÷ 0.5 hr.). Next, compute the TAS on the wind side of your computer:

1. Set the magnetic wind direction of 023° under the true index, and place a pencil mark at 61 kt. (windspeed) up from the grommet.
2. Place the average MC of 075° (J547) under the true index.
3. Slide the grid so the groundspeed of 218 kt. is under the grommet.
4. Read the TAS of 260 kt. under the pencil mark.

Answer (A) is incorrect because a TAS of 255 kt. would complete the trip from PMM to FNT in approximately 31 min., not 30 min. Answer (B) is incorrect because a TAS of 265 kt. would complete the trip from PMM to FNT in approximately 29 min., not 30 min.

43.
9613. (Refer to figures 168, 169, and 169A on pages 380, 381, and 382.) What action should be taken by the pilot if communications are lost after departure from RWY 16 at PWK if VMC?

A—Continue the flight under VMC and land as soon as practicable.
B—Climb to 3,000 feet; after 3 minutes, turn direct to PMM and climb to FL 190.
C—Start right turn within 1 mile of the departure end of RWY, remain east of ORD VOR/DME R-345, and maintain 3,000 feet; 3 minutes after departure, turn direct to PMM, and climb to FL 190.

Answer (A) is correct (9613). *(FAR 91.185)*
If two-way radio communication failure occurs in VMC, you should continue the flight under VFR and land as soon as practicable.

Answer (B) is incorrect because, if radio communication failure occurs while you are in, or when you encounter, VMC, you must continue the flight under VFR and land as soon as practicable. Answer (C) is incorrect because, while you should follow the SID instructions to ensure separation from approaches to RWY 14R at O'Hare, you must continue the flight under VFR. You should follow the routing and altitude restrictions if you lose communications in IMC, not VMC.

44.
9614. (Refer to figure 169A on page 382.) The PIC of PTZ 70 will use 25° of bank during the turn after departing RWY 16 at PWK. What is the maximum TAS that the aircraft may maintain during the turn and remain east of the ORD VOR/DME R-345 under a no wind condition?

A—160 knots.
B—162 knots.
C—164 knots.

Answer (B) is correct (9614). *(SID)*

The table at the top of the Pal-Waukee Two Departure (Fig. 169A) provides the maximum TAS for a given bank angle required during the turn after takeoff to remain east of the ORD VOR/DME R-345 under a no wind condition. Under a bank angle of 25° is the maximum TAS of 162 kt.

Answer (A) is incorrect because 160 kt. would be the maximum TAS if you were to use a bank angle of slightly less than 25°, not 25°. Answer (C) is incorrect because 164 kt. would be the maximum TAS if you were to use a bank angle slightly greater than 25°, not 25°.

45.
9615. (Refer to figure 169A on page 382.) To remain east of the ORD VOR/DME R-345, while flying the PAL-WAUKEE TWO DEPARTURE, requires a turn radius of

A—over 5,000 feet.
B—5,000 feet.
C—less than 5,000 feet.

Answer (C) is correct (9615). *(SID)*

To remain east of the ORD VOR/DME R-345 while flying the Pal-Waukee Two Departure after a takeoff on RWY 16 requires a turn radius of less than 5,000 ft. This information is found as a note on the left side of the chart, above the departure route description.

Answer (A) is incorrect because a turn radius of less than 5,000 ft., not over 5,000 ft., is required by the SID. Answer (B) is incorrect because a turn radius of less than 5,000 ft., not 5,000 ft., is required by the SID.

46.
9616. (Refer to figure 169A on page 382.) What action should be taken by the PIC of PTZ 70 if the communication radios fail after takeoff from RWY 16 at PWK while in IMC conditions?

A—Climb to 3,000 feet on RWY heading; after 3 minutes, turn direct to PMM and climb to FL 190.
B—Start right turn within 1 mile of the departure end of RWY 16 and remain east of the 345 radial of the ORD VOR/DME while climbing to 3,000 feet; after 3 minutes, turn direct to PMM and climb to FL 190.
C—Set 7600 in Mode 3 of the transponder, turn direct to Northbrook (the IAF), climb to 2,700 feet, and fly the ILS RWY 16 to land at PWK.

Answer (B) is correct (9616). *(FAR 91.185)*

If radio communication failure occurs after takeoff from RWY 16 at PWK while in IMC and you have been cleared for the Pal-Waukee Two Departure, you should fly the SID as described in the narrative. Thus, you should start a right turn within 1 NM of the departure end of RWY 16 to remain east of the ORD VOR/DME R-345 while climbing to 3,000 ft. or assigned altitude. Next, proceed direct to PMM and, 3 min. after departure, climb to FL190.

Answer (A) is incorrect because, when departing RWY 16, you must make a right turn within 1 NM of the departure end, not maintain runway heading. Answer (C) is incorrect because, while you would squawk 7600, your routing clearance is the Pal-Waukee Two Departure, not a direct turn to OBK VORTAC to execute the ILS RWY 16 approach to land at PWK.

47.
9617. (Refer to figure 172A on page 386.) The airport diagram of Greater Buffalo Intl Airport has a symbol (appears to be a triangle balanced on top of another triangle) located close to the end of RWYs 14 and 32. What do these symbols indicate?

A—Helicopter landing areas.
B—That special takeoff and landing minimums apply to RWYs 14 and 32.
C—RWY radar reflectors.

Answer (C) is correct (9617). *(IAP Chart Legend)*

The symbol that appears to be a triangle balanced on top of another triangle located at the approach end of both runways 14 and 32 in the Greater Buffalo airport diagram indicates runway radar reflectors.

Answer (A) is incorrect because helicopter landing areas are indicated by a circle, square, or triangle that has a black background and either a white "+" or an "H" in the center, not by one triangle on top of another triangle. Answer (B) is incorrect because nonstandard takeoff minimums and alternate, not landing, minimums are depicted on the IAP chart, not the airport diagram chart.

48.
9618. (Refer to figures 173 and 173A on pages 387 and 388.) The PIC of PTZ 70 has less than 100 hours of PIC time in the BE 1900. Due to BUF weather being 100 feet, ¼ mile in blowing snow, which is below landing minimums, the PIC requested and received clearance to SYR, the filed alternate. Under Part 135, what are the PIC's minimums at SYR for the ILS RWY 10?

A—671/40.
B—771/64.
C—800/2.

Answer (B) is correct (9618). *(FAR 135.225)*

FAR 135.225 requires that, if the PIC has less than 100 hr. of PIC time in that type of turbine-powered airplane (i.e., BE 1900), the MDA or DH is increased by 100 ft., and the visibility is increased ½ SM (or 2,400 ft. RVR). Thus, the PIC's minimums at SYR for the straight-in ILS RWY 10 approach are 771/64.

Answer (A) is incorrect because 671/40 are the straight-in minimums if the PIC has at least, not less than, 100 hr. of PIC time in the BE 1900. Answer (C) is incorrect because 800/2 are the standard alternate weather minimums for selecting an airport as an alternate with a nonprecision approach, not the actual minimums when conducting the approach at the alternate airport.

49.
9619. (Refer to figure 173A on page 388.) During the approach (ILS RWY 10 at SYR) while maintaining an on glide slope indication with a groundspeed of 110 knots, what was the approximate rate of descent for PTZ 70?

A—475 feet per minute.
B—585 feet per minute.
C—690 feet per minute.

Answer (B) is correct (9619). *(IAP)*

Fig. 173A provides the IAP chart for the ILS RWY 10 approach at SYR. In the lower left corner of the profile view is GS 3.00°, or a 3° glide slope.

Refer to the Rate-of-Descent Table in Legend 9, on page 389, to determine the rate of descent to maintain a 3° glide slope with a groundspeed of 110 kt. Since a groundspeed of 110 kt. is not shown on the table, you must interpolate. Find 3° in the angle-of-descent column, and move right to a groundspeed of 105 kt. to determine a rate of descent of 555 fpm. For a groundspeed of 120 kt., the rate of descent is 635 fpm. Interpolate for 110 kt. to determine a rate of descent of approximately 585 fpm.

Answer (A) is incorrect because 475 fpm is the approximate rate of descent with a groundspeed of 110 kt. while maintaining a 2.5°, not 3°, glide slope. Answer (C) is incorrect because 690 fpm is the approximate rate of descent with a groundspeed of 110 kt. while maintaining a 3.5°, not 3°, glide slope.

50.
9620. (Refer to figure 171 on page 421.) The facility (Kankakee) that is located 9 miles NE of Chicago Midway or 27 miles SSE of Northbrook (OBK) is a/an

A—Aeronautical Radio Inc. (AIRINC) transmitter.
B—Automated Weather Observing System (AWOS-ASOS) with frequency.
C—Flight Service, Remote Communications Outlet.

Answer (C) is correct (9620). *(En Route Chart Legend)*

The facility labeled Kankakee that is located southeast of OBK VORTAC is an FSS remote communications outlet (RCO).

Answer (A) is incorrect because AIRINC transmitter/frequencies are not shown on en route charts. Answer (B) is incorrect because AWOS-ASOS frequencies are not shown on high-altitude en route charts.

Form Approved: OMB No. 2120-0034

U.S. DEPARTMENT OF TRANSPORTATION
FEDERAL AVIATION ADMINISTRATION

FLIGHT PLAN

(FAA USE ONLY) ☐ PILOT BRIEFING ☐ VNR ☐ STOPOVER | TIME STARTED | SPECIALIST INITIALS

1. TYPE	2. AIRCRAFT IDENTIFICATION	3. AIRCRAFT TYPE/ SPECIAL EQUIPMENT	4. TRUE AIRSPEED	5. DEPARTURE POINT	6. DEPARTURE TIME PROPOSED (Z)	ACTUAL (Z)	7. CRUISING ALTITUDE
VFR / X IFR / DVFR	PTZ 70	BE 1900/R	247 KTS	KPWK CHICAGO/ PAL-WAUKEE			FL190

8. ROUTE OF FLIGHT
PAL-WAUKEE TWO DEPARTURE, PMM J547 BUF

9. DESTINATION (Name of airport and city)	10. EST. TIME ENROUTE HOURS	MINUTES	11. REMARKS
BUF GREATER BUFFALO INT'L BUFFALO			L/O = LEVEL OFF PPH = POUNDS PER HOUR L/O PMM R-261/47 VARIATION: PWK 1W, FNT 3W, BUF 8W

12. FUEL ON BOARD HOURS	MINUTES	13. ALTERNATE AIRPORT(S)	14. PILOT'S NAME, ADDRESS & TELEPHONE NUMBER & AIRCRAFT HOME BASE	15. NUMBER ABOARD
3	35	SYR SYRACUSE HANCOCK INT'L	17. DESTINATION CONTACT/TELEPHONE (OPTIONAL)	13

16. COLOR OF AIRCRAFT
WHITE/BLACK

CIVIL AIRCRAFT PILOTS. FAR Part 91 requires you file an IFR flight plan to operate under instrument flight rules in controlled airspace. Failure to file could result in a civil penalty not to exceed $1,000 for each violation (Section 901 of the Federal Aviation Act of 1958, as amended). Filing of a VFR flight plan is recommended as a good operating practice. See also Part 99 for requirements concerning DVFR flight plans.

FAA Form 7233-1 (8-82)

CLOSE VFR FLIGHT PLAN WITH ____________ FSS ON ARRIVAL

FLIGHT LOG

CHECK POINTS FROM	TO	ROUTE ALTITUDE	COURSE	WIND TEMP	SPEED-KTS TAS	GS	DIST NM	TIME LEG	TIME TOT	FUEL LEG	FUEL TOT
PWK	L/O	VECTORS CLIMB					49		:24:00		410*
L/O	PMM	J547 FL190		020/61 ISA							
PMM	FNT										
FNT	YXU										
YXU	BUF R-282/40										
BUF R-282/40	BUF	J547 DESCENT					40	:19:00		163	
BUF	SYR	VECTORS 4000					112	:30:00			

OTHER DATA: * Includes Taxi Fuel
NOTE: Use 676 PPH Total Fuel Flow From L/O To Start Of Descent.
Use 726 PPH Total Fuel Flow for Reserve And Alternate Requirements.

A Missed Approach Requires 76# of Fuel.

TIME and FUEL: As required by FARs.

TIME	FUEL (LB)	
		EN ROUTE
		RESERVE
		ALTERNATE
		TOTAL

FIGURE 168.—Flight Plan/Flight Log.

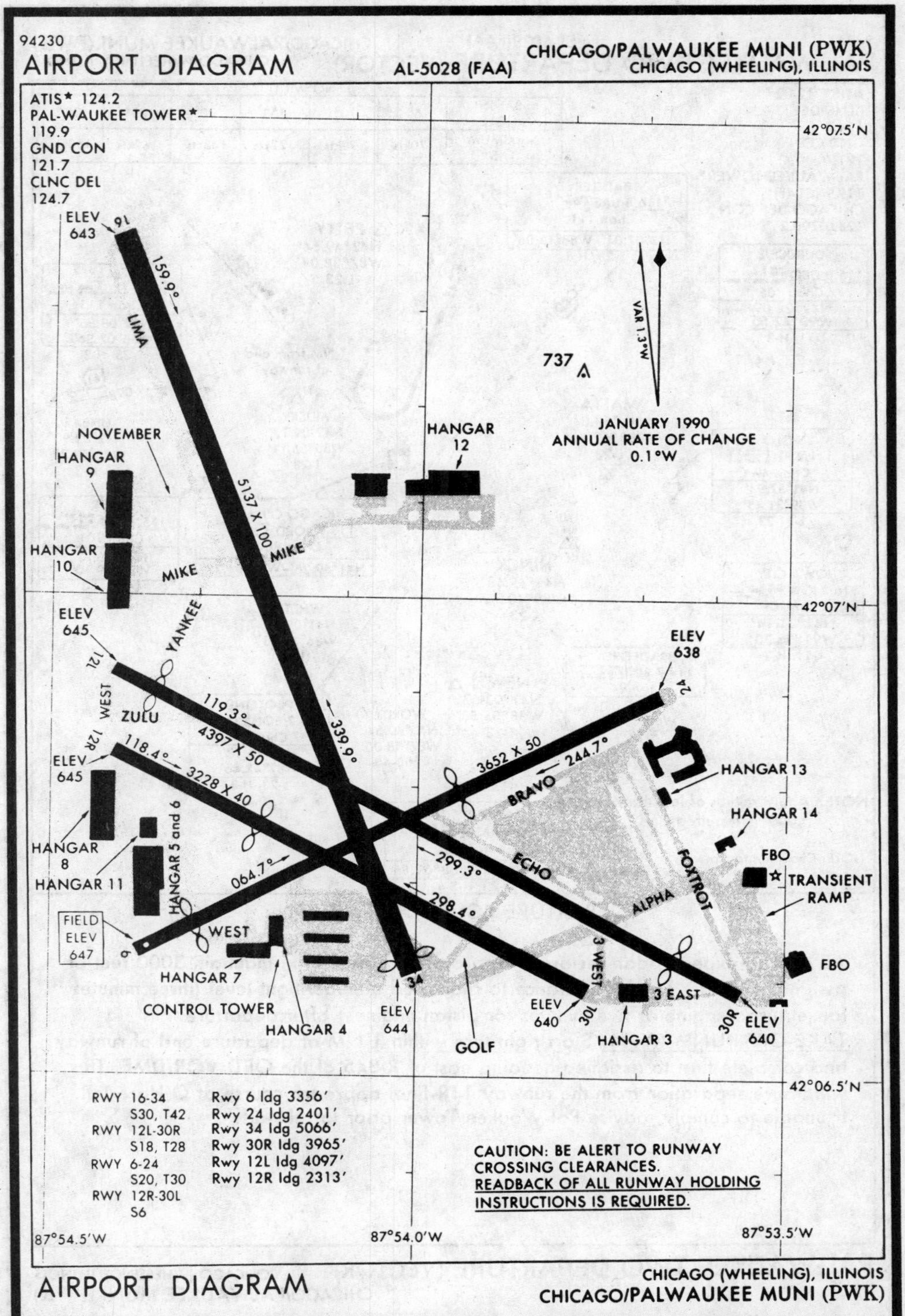

FIGURE 169.—AIRPORT DIAGRAM (PWK).

94342 SL-5028(FAA) CHICAGO/PALWAUKEE MUNI (PWK)

PAL-WAUKEE TWO DEPARTURE (VECTOR)

CHICAGO (WHEELING), ILLINOIS

ATIS* 124.2
CLNC DEL
124.7
GND CON
121.7
PAL-WAUKEE TOWER*
119.9 (CTAF)
CHICAGO DEP CON
125.0 290.2

NO WIND

BANK ANGLE	5°	10°	15°	20°	25°	30°
MAXIMUM TAS	70kts	99kts	122kts	143kts	162kts	180kts

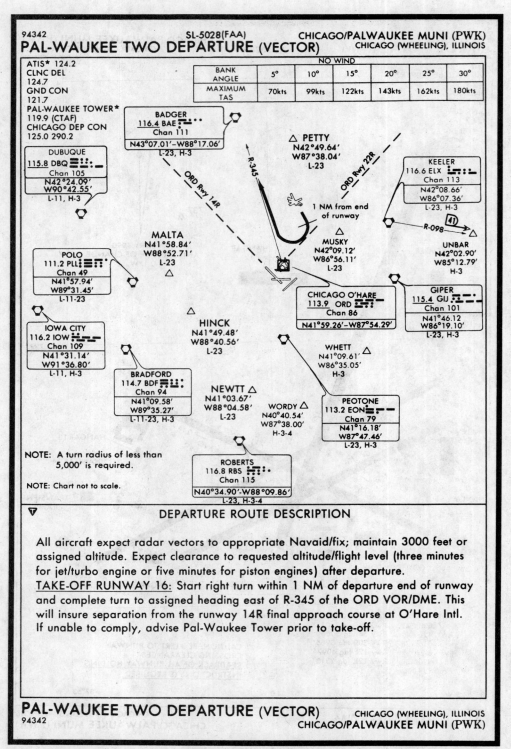

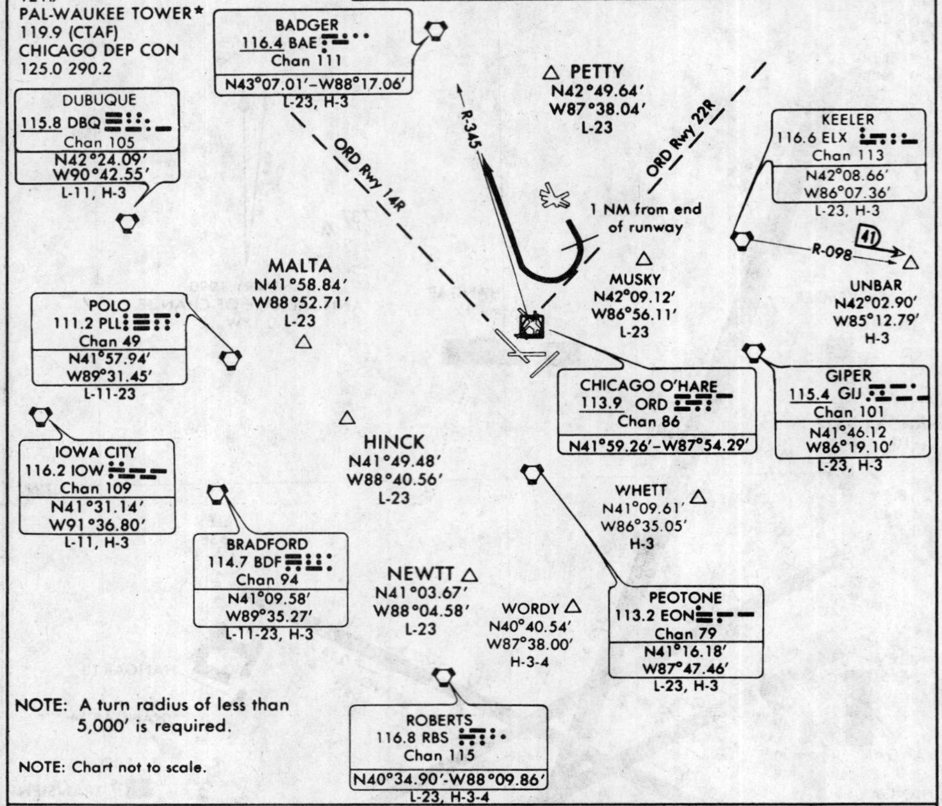

DEPARTURE ROUTE DESCRIPTION

All aircraft expect radar vectors to appropriate Navaid/fix; maintain 3000 feet or assigned altitude. Expect clearance to requested altitude/flight level (three minutes for jet/turbo engine or five minutes for piston engines) after departure.

TAKE-OFF RUNWAY 16: Start right turn within 1 NM of departure end of runway and complete turn to assigned heading east of R-345 of the ORD VOR/DME. This will insure separation from the runway 14R final approach course at O'Hare Intl. If unable to comply, advise Pal-Waukee Tower prior to take-off.

PAL-WAUKEE TWO DEPARTURE (VECTOR) CHICAGO (WHEELING), ILLINOIS
94342 CHICAGO/PALWAUKEE MUNI (PWK)

FIGURE 169A.—PAL-WAUKEE TWO DEPARTURE (VECTOR) (PWK).

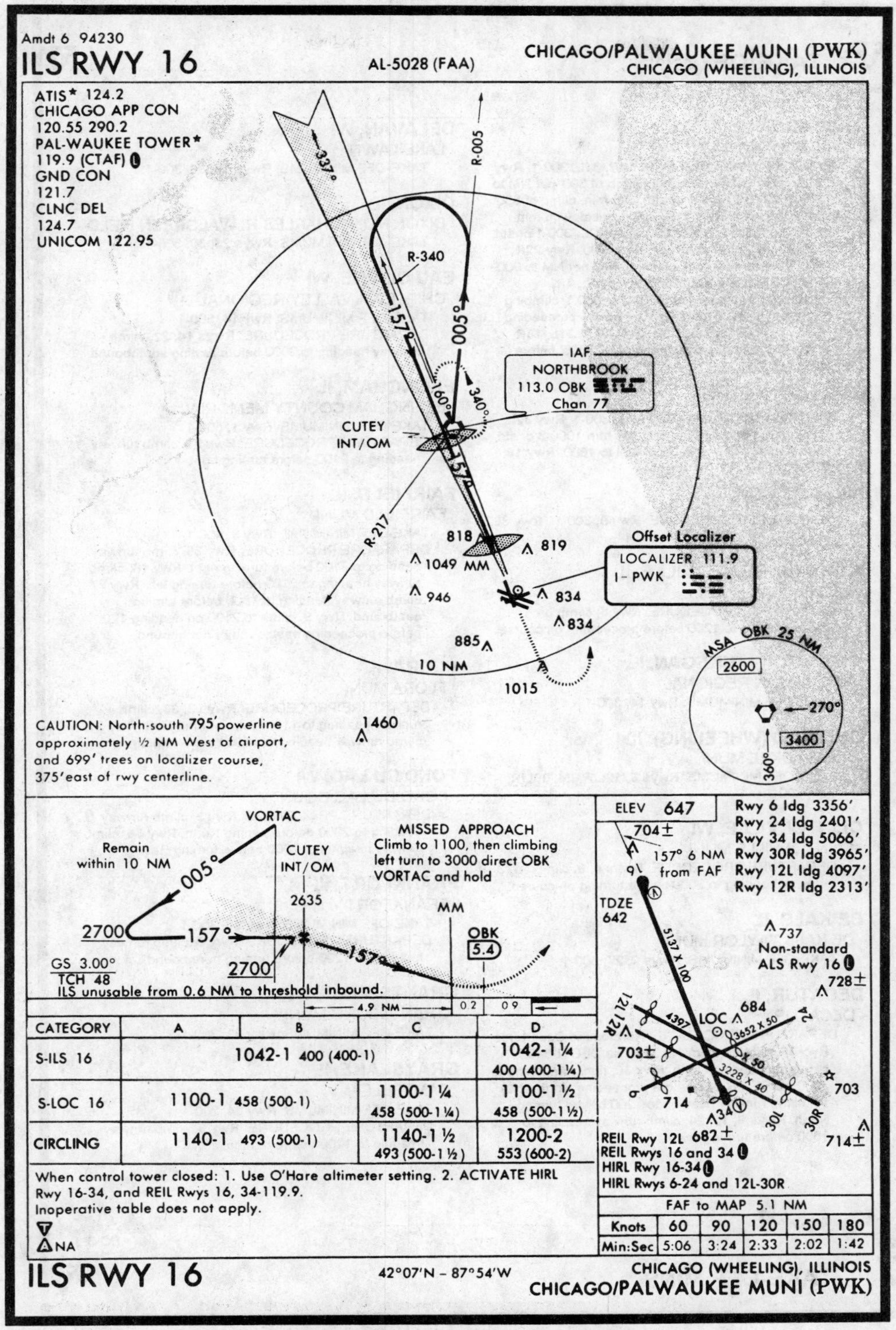

FIGURE 170.—ILS RWY 16 (PWK).

TAKE-OFF MINS

94286

CHICAGO, IL

CHICAGO MIDWAY

TAKE-OFF MINIMUMS: **Rwys 13R, 31L,** 300-1. **Rwy 13L,** 300-1 or std. with min. climb of 300' per NM to 900. **Rwy 31C,** 300-1 or std. with min. climb of 330' per NM to 900. **Rwy 31R,** 300-1 or std. with min. climb of 225' per NM to 900. **Rwy 22L,** 300-1 or std. with min. climb of 400' per NM to 900. **Rwy 22R,** 300-1 or std. with min. climb of 340' per NM to 900.

DEPARTURE PROCEDURE: **Rwys 4L, 4R,** Northbound Departures (360° CW 080°), climbing right turn to 2400 heading 100° before proceeding on course. **Rwys 22L, 22R, 31C, 31R, 31L, 13R, 13L, 13C,** climb runway heading to 1300' before turning.

CHICAGO-O'HARE INTL

TAKE-OFF MINIMUMS: **Rwy 22R,** 300-1. **Rwy 32L,** straight out or right turn, std.; left turn 1000-3 or std. with a min. climb of 240' per NM to 1800. **Rwy 18,** NA. **Rwy 36,** 500-1.

LANSING MUNI

DEPARTURE PROCEDURE: **Rwy 9,** 300-1. **Rwy 36,** 400-1.

CHICAGO/ROMEOVILLE, IL

LEWIS UNIVERSITY

DEPARTURE PROCEDURE: **Rwy 6,** climb on heading 065° to 1200 before proceeding on course.

CHICAGO/WAUKEGAN, IL

WAUKEGAN REGIONAL

TAKE-OFF MINIMUMS: **Rwy 14,** 300-1.

CHICAGO (WHEELING), IL

PALWAUKEE MUNI

TAKE-OFF MINIMUMS: **Rwys 6, 12L/R, 24, 30L/R, 34,** 300-1.

CLINTONVILLE, WI

CLINTONVILLE MUNI

DEPARTURE PROCEDURE: **Rwys 4, 9,** climb on runway heading to 2000 before turning on course.

DE KALB, IL

DE KALB TAYLOR MUNI

TAKE-OFF MINIMUMS: **Rwys 9, 27,** 300-1.

DECATUR, IL

DECATUR

DEPARTURE PROCEDURE: Northbound Departures; **Rwy 36,** left turn, climb to 3000 via DEC R-340 before proceeding North. **Rwy 30,** right turn, climb to 3000 via DEC R-340 before proceeding North. **Rwy 18,** climb runway heading to 1200 before turning North. **Rwys 6, 12, 24,** climb runway heading to 1600 before turning North.

DELAVAN, WI

LAKE LAWN

TAKE-OFF MINIMUMS: **Rwys 18, 36,** 300-1.

DIXON, IL

DIXON MUNI-CHARLES R. WALGREEN FIELD

TAKE-OFF MINIMUMS: **Rwys 26, 30,** 300-1.

EAU CLAIRE, WI

CHIPPEWA VALLEY REGIONAL

TAKE-OFF MINIMUMS: **Rwy 14,** 500-1.

DEPARTURE PROCEDURE: **Rwys 14, 22,** climb runway heading to 2500 before turning southbound.

EFFINGHAM, IL

EFFINGHAM COUNTY MEMORIAL

TAKE-OFF MINIMUMS: **Rwy 1,** 500-1.

DEPARTURE PROCEDURE: **Rwy 29,** climb runway heading to 2100 before turning right.

FAIRFIELD, IL

FAIRFIELD MUNI

TAKE-OFF MINIMUMS: **Rwy 9,** 400-1.

DEPARTURE PROCEDURE: **Rwy 36,** climb runway heading to 2100 before turning right. **Rwy 18,** climb runway heading to 2100 before turning left. **Rwy 27,** climb runway heading to 1500 before turning eastbound. **Rwy 9,** climb to 2100 on heading 120° before proceeding eastbound or northbound.

FLORA, IL

FLORA MUNI

DEPARTURE PROCEDURE: **Rwys 3, 33,** climb runway heading to 1100' before turning left. **Rwy 21,** climb runway heading to 1100 before turning right.

FOND DU LAC, WI

FOND DU LAC COUNTY

DEPARTURE PROCEDURE: **Rwy 9,** climb runway heading to 2000 before turning North. **Rwy 36,** climb runway heading to 2000 before turning East.

FRANKFORT, IL

FRANKFORT

TAKE-OFF MINIMUMS: **Rwy 27,** 300-1.

DEPARTURE PROCEDURE: **Rwy 9,** climb runway heading to 1200 before turning northbound.

GRANTSBURG, WI

GRANTSBURG MUNI

TAKE-OFF MINIMUMS: **Rwy 23,** 300-1.

GRAYSLAKE, IL

CAMPBELL

TAKE-OFF MINIMUMS: **Rwy 24,** 300-1.

DEPARTURE PROCEDURE: **Rwy 9,** climb runway heading to 1200 before turning.

94286 EC-3

TAKE-OFF MINS

FIGURE 170A.—TAKE-OFF MINS.

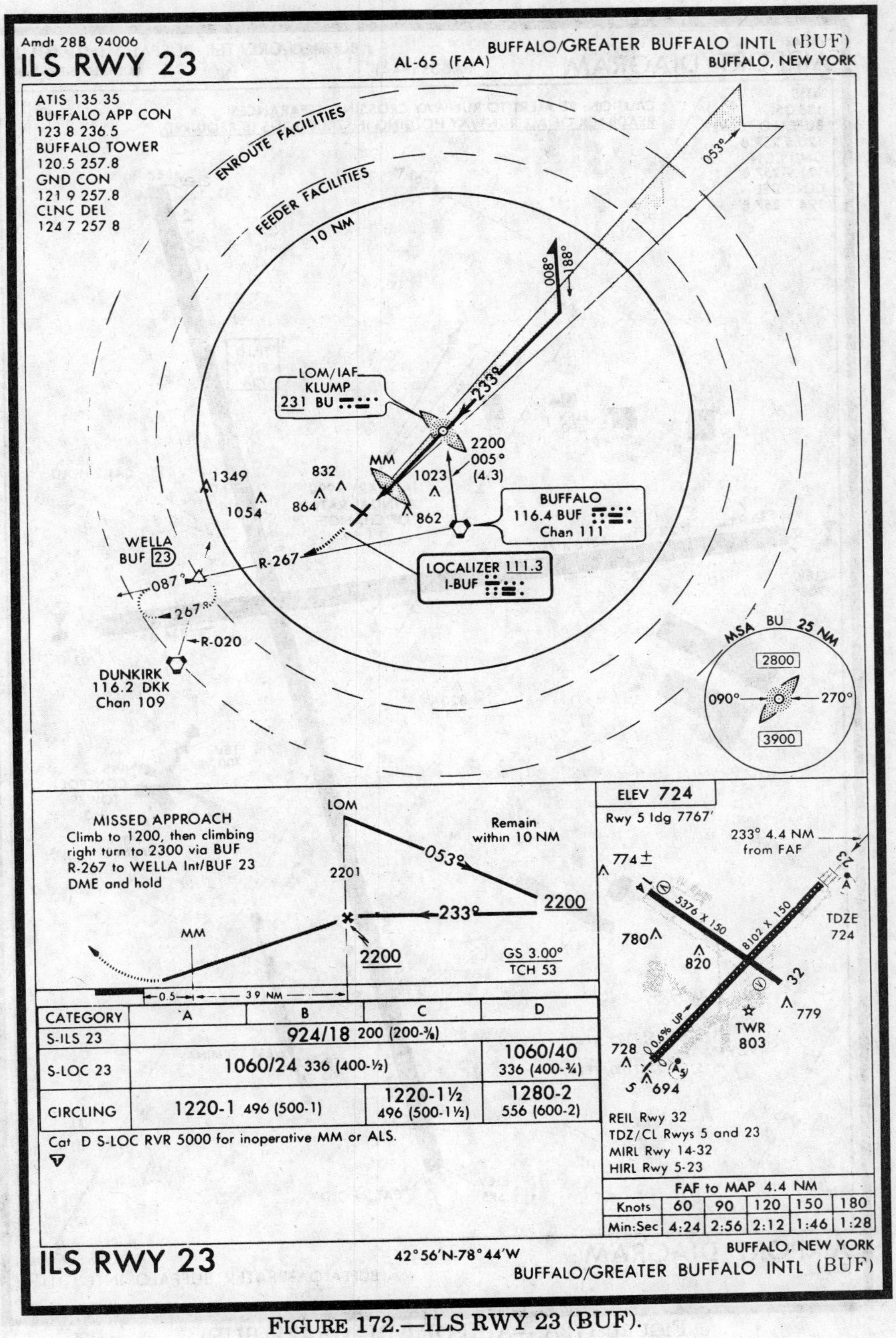

FIGURE 172.—ILS RWY 23 (BUF).

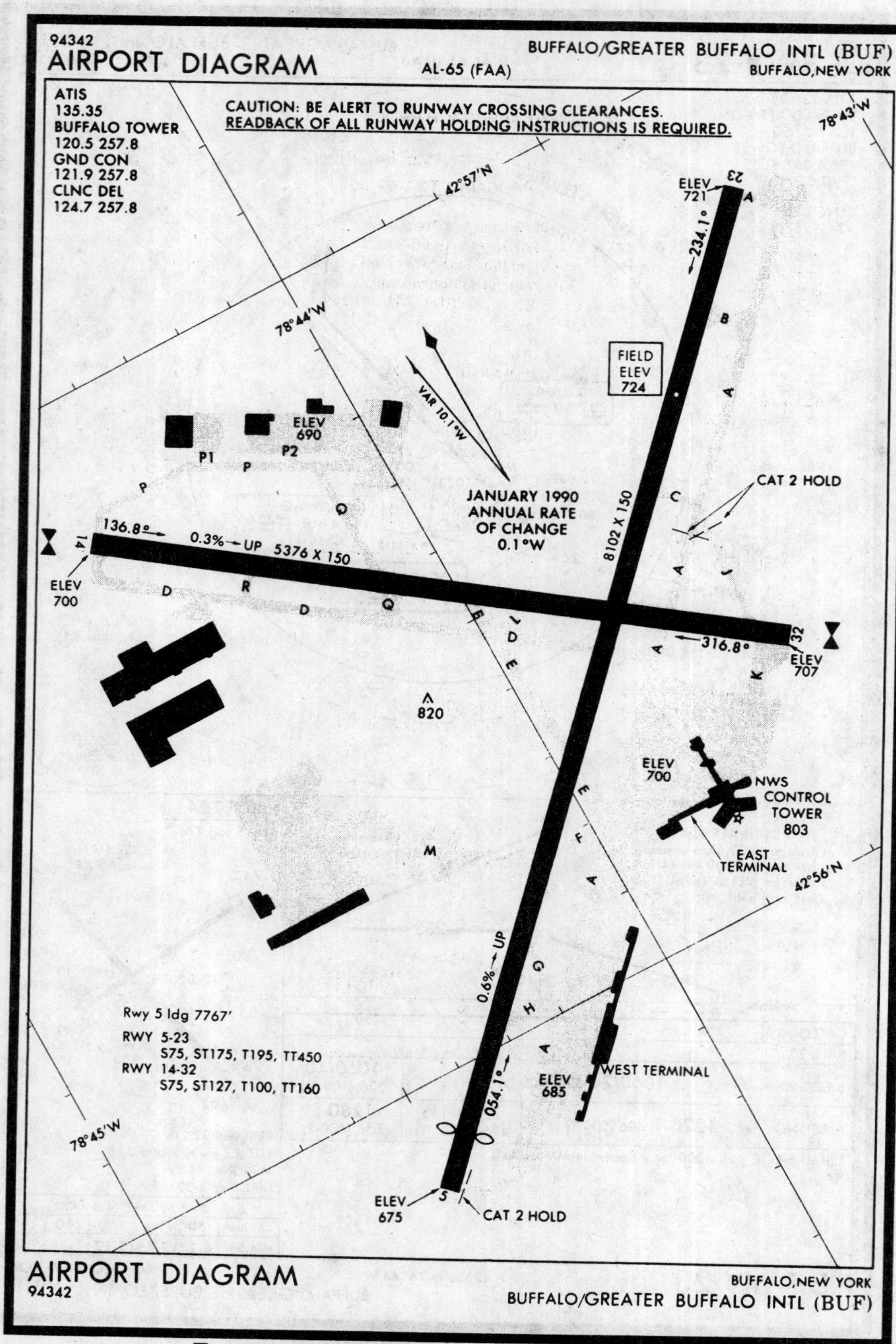

FIGURE 172A.—AIRPORT DIAGRAM (BUF).

ALTERNATE MINS

95033

INSTRUMENT APPROACH PROCEDURE CHARTS

IFR ALTERNATE MINIMUMS

(NOT APPLICABLE TO USA/USN/USAF)

Standard alternate minimums for non precision approaches are 800-2 (NDB, VOR, LOC, TACAN, LDA, VORTAC, VOR/DME or ASR); for precision approaches 600-2 (ILS or PAR). Airports within this geographical area that require alternate minimums other than standard or alternate minimums with restrictions are listed below. NA - means alternate minimums are not authorized due to unmonitored facility or absence of weather reporting service. Civil pilots see FAR 91. USA/USN/USAF pilots refer to appropriate regulations.

NAME — ALTERNATE MINIMUMS

ALBANY, NY
ALBANY COUNTY .... ILS Rwy 1[1]
ILS Rwy 19[1]
VOR/DME or GPS Rwy 1[1]
VOR Rwy 1[2]
VOR or GPS Rwy 19[1]
VOR or GPS Rwy 28[1]
[1]Category D, 800-2½.
[2]Category C, 800-2¼; Category D, 800-2½.

ALLENTOWN, PA
LEHIGH VALLEY INTL .... ILS Rwy 13
ILS, Categories A,B,C, 700-2; Category D, 700-2¼. LOC, Category D, 800-2¼.

ALTOONA, PA
ALTOONA-BLAIR COUNTY .... ILS Rwy 20[1]
VOR or GPS-A[2]
[1]Categories A,B,C, 900-2½, Category D, 1100-3.
[2]Category D, 1100-3.

BRADFORD, PA
BRADFORD REGIONAL .... VOR/DME or GPS Rwy 14
NA when BFD FSS closed.

CORTLAND, NY
CORTLAND COUNTY-CHASE FIELD .... VOR or GPS-A
Categories A,B, 1100-2, Categories C,D, 1100-3.

DUBOIS, PA
DUBOIS-JEFFERSON COUNTY ..... ILS Rwy 25
LOC, NA.

NAME — ALTERNATE MINIMUMS

ELMIRA, NY
ELMIRA/CORNING REGIONAL .... ILS Rwy 6[12]
ILS Rwy 24, 1200-3
NDB or GPS Rwy 24, 1200-3
[1]Categories A,B, 1200-2; Categories C,D, 1200-3.
[2]NA when control tower closed.

ERIE, PA
ERIE INTL .... ILS Rwy 6[1]
ILS Rwy 24[1]
NDB Rwy 6
NDB Rwy 24
RADAR-1
NA when control tower closed.
[1]ILS, 700-2.

FARMINGDALE, NY
REPUBLIC .... ILS Rwy 14[1]
NDB or GPS Rwy 1[2]
[1]NA when control tower closed.
[2]NA when control zone not effective.

HARRISBURG, PA
CAPITAL CITY .... ILS Rwy 8
Categories A,B, 900-2; Categories C,D, 900-2¾.
NA when control tower closed.

HARRISBURG INTL .... ILS Rwy 13[1]
ILS Rwy 31[1]
VOR or GPS Rwy 31[2]
[1]ILS, Categories C,D, 700-2. LOC, NA.
[2]Categories A,B, 900-2, Category C, 900-2¾, Category D, 900-3.

NE-2

ALTERNATE MINS

95033

FIGURE 173.—IFR ALTERNATE MINIMUMS.

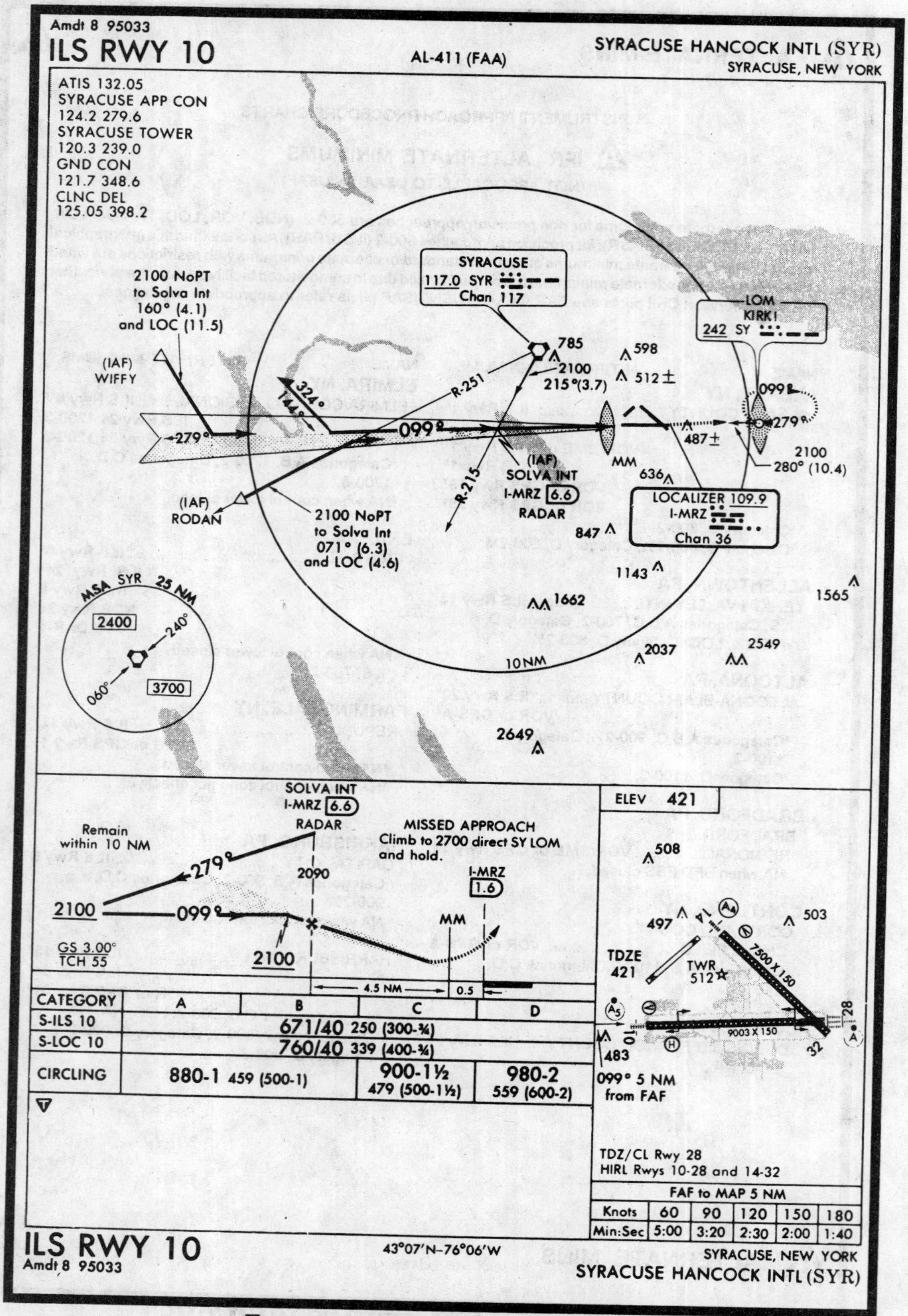

CATEGORY	A	B	C	D
S-ILS 10	671/40 250 (300-¾)			
S-LOC 10	760/40 339 (400-¾)			
CIRCLING	880-1 459 (500-1)		900-1½ 479 (500-1½)	980-2 559 (600-2)

FAF to MAP 5 NM					
Knots	60	90	120	150	180
Min:Sec	5:00	3:20	2:30	2:00	1:40

FIGURE 173A.—ILS RWY 10 (SYR).

INSTRUMENT APPROACH PROCEDURE CHARTS
RATE OF DESCENT TABLE
(ft. per min.)

A rate of descent table is provided for use in planning and executing precision descents under known or approximate ground speed conditions. It will be especially useful for approaches when the localizer only is used for course guidance. A best speed, power, attitude combination can be programmed which will result in a stable glide rate and attitude favorable for executing a landing if minimums exist upon breakout. Care should always be exercised so that the minimum descent altitude and missed approach point are not exceeded.

ANGLE OF DESCENT (degrees and tenths)	GROUND SPEED (knots)										
	30	45	60	75	90	105	120	135	150	165	180
2.0	105	160	210	265	320	370	425	475	530	585	635
2.5	130	200	265	330	395	465	530	595	665	730	795
3.0	160	240	320	395	480	555	635	715	795	875	955
3.5	185	280	370	465	555	650	740	835	925	1020	1110
4.0	210	315	425	530	635	740	845	955	1060	1165	1270
4.5	240	355	475	595	715	835	955	1075	1190	1310	1430
5.0	265	395	530	660	795	925	1060	1190	1325	1455	1590
5.5	290	435	580	730	875	1020	1165	1310	1455	1600	1745
6.0	315	475	635	795	955	1110	1270	1430	1590	1745	1905
6.5	345	515	690	860	1030	1205	1375	1550	1720	1890	2065
7.0	370	555	740	925	1110	1295	1480	1665	1850	2035	2220
7.5	395	595	795	990	1190	1390	1585	1785	1985	2180	2380
8.0	425	635	845	1055	1270	1480	1690	1905	2115	2325	2540
8.5	450	675	900	1120	1345	1570	1795	2020	2245	2470	2695
9.0	475	715	950	1190	1425	1665	1900	2140	2375	2615	2855
9.5	500	750	1005	1255	1505	1755	2005	2255	2510	2760	3010
10.0	530	790	1055	1320	1585	1845	2110	2375	2640	2900	3165
10.5	555	830	1105	1385	1660	1940	2215	2490	2770	3045	3320
11.0	580	870	1160	1450	1740	2030	2320	2610	2900	3190	3480
11.5	605	910	1210	1515	1820	2120	2425	2725	3030	3335	3635
12.0	630	945	1260	1575	1890	2205	2520	2835	3150	3465	3780

LEGEND 9.—Rate-of-Descent Table.

10.5 BE-1900 PHF TO PHL (Questions 51-61)

Questions 51 through 61 pertain to an IFR flight from Williamsburg International Airport, Newport News, Virginia to Philadelphia International Airport, Philadelphia, Pennsylvania.

The route is given in block 8 on the flight plan portion of Fig. 179 on page 395. The partially completed flight planning log is given on the bottom portion of Fig. 179.

The following figures are used to answer the 11 questions concerning this flight.

Fig.	Page	Title
179	395	Flight Plan/Flight Log
180	396	ILS RWY 7 (PHF)
180A	397	Henry One Departure (Vector) (PHF)
181	424	High Altitude Airways
182	398	Cedar Lake Five Arrival (VCN.VCN5)
182A	399	ILS RWY 9R (PHL)
183	400	IFR Alternate Minimums
183A	401	ILS RWY 13 (ACY)
Legend 15	402	Directory Legend

10.5 BE-1900 PHF to PHL

51.
9626. (Refer to figures 179, 180A, 181, 182, and 182A on pages 395, 397, 424, 398, and 399.) The time enroute from Newport News/Williamsburg Intl to Philadelphia Intl via the flight plan of EAB 90 is

A—1 hour 27 minutes.
B—1 hour 29 minutes.
C—1 hour 31 minutes.

Answer (C) is correct (9626). *(IFH Chap XIII)*

To determine the ETE from PHF to PHL, you must complete the flight log in Fig. 179. In the remarks box of the flight plan, the magnetic variation at PHF (7° W) and PHL (10° W) are given. This information is used to convert the true wind direction to magnetic direction.

Our flight log has been expanded to provide more detail. To convert wind direction from true to magnetic, we used 7°W to SWL and 10°W to PHL.

	Distance	MC	Wind (mag)	Ground-speed	Time
ORF	40G	X	X	X	0:19:00G
SAWED	42	030	307/70	217	0:11:36
SWL	37	039	307/70	228	0:09:44
SWL/SIE COP	20	034	310/70	218	0:05:30
SIE	50	036	310/70	221	0:13:34
VCN	28	353	310/70	180	0:09:20
OOD	17	301	310/70	167	0:06:06
PHL	30G	X	X	X	0:16:00G
					1:30:50

G = Given

Answer (A) is incorrect because an ETE of 1 hr. 27 min. would require a TAS of approximately 245 kt., not 236 kt. Answer (B) is incorrect because an ETE of 1 hr. 29 min. would require a TAS of 240 kt., not 236 kt.

52.
9627. (Refer to figures 179, 180, 181, 182, and 182A on pages 395, 396, 424, 398, and 399.) The planned fuel usage from Newport News/Williamsburg Intl to Philadelphia Intl for EAB 90 is

A—1,132 pounds.
B—1,107 pounds.
C—1,084 pounds.

Answer (A) is correct (9627). *(IFH Chap XIII)*

To determine the planned fuel usage from PHF to PHL, you must complete the fuel portion of the flight log on Fig. 179. Use 689 PPH total fuel flow from level-off (ORF) to start of descent (OOD).

	Time	Fuel (lb.)
ORF	0:19:00G	312.0G
SAWED	0:11:36	133.2
SWL	0:09:44	111.8
SWL/SIE COP	0:05:30	63.2
SIE	0:13:34	155.8
VCN	0:09:20	107.2
OOD	0:06:06	70.0
PHL	0:16:00G	177.0G
		1,130.2

G = Given

Answer (B) is incorrect because 1,107 lb. would be the fuel usage between PHF and PHL if the time from level-off to start of descent was 54 min., not 56 min. Answer (C) is incorrect because 1,084 lb. would be the fuel usage between PHF and PHL if the time from level-off to start of descent was 52 min., not 56 min.

53.
9628. (Refer to figures 179, 180, 181, 182, and 183 on pages 395, 396, 424, 398, and 400.) The required fuel from Newport News/Williamsburg Intl to Philadelphia Intl for EAB 90 is

A—1,860 pounds.
B—1,908 pounds.
C—2,003 pounds.

Answer (B) is correct (9628). *(IFH Chap XIII)*

To determine the fuel required from PHF to PHL, you must complete the fuel portion of the flight log on Fig. 179. Use 689 PPH total fuel flow from level-off (ORF) to start of descent (OOD) and 739 PPH total fuel flow for alternate and reserves requirements.

	Time	Fuel (lb.)
ORF	0:19:00G	312.0G
SAWED	0:11:36	133.2
SWL	0:09:44	111.8
SWL/SIE COP	0:05:30	63.2
SIE	0:13:34	155.8
VCN	0:09:20	107.2
OOD	0:06:06	70.0
PHL	0:16:00G	177.0G
ACY	0:18:00G	221.7
Reserves	0:45:00	554.3
		1,906.2

G = Given

Answer (A) is incorrect because 1,860 lb. is the required fuel from using a fuel flow of 689 PPH, not 739 PPH, for the alternate and reserve requirements. Answer (C) is incorrect because 2,003 lb. includes the 95 lb. required for a missed approach. While this should be included as a practical matter, it is not required by the FARs.

54.
9635. (Refer to figures 179, 180, 181, 182, and 183 on pages 395, 396, 424, 398, and 400.) What TAS would EAB 90 need to maintain from SWL to SIE in an attempt to cut 3 minutes off of the flight plan (SWL-SIE) ETE?

A—276.
B—280.
C—284.

Answer (A) is correct (9635). *(IFH Chap XIII)*

First you must calculate the ETE from SWL to SIE using the current flight plan on Fig. 179. The magnetic variation at PHF is 7°W and at PHL is 10°W. From SWL to SIE, we will use a magnetic variation of 10°W to convert the true wind direction to magnetic wind.

	Distance	MC	Wind (mag)	Groundspeed	Time
SWL to COP	20	034	310/70	218	0:05:30
COP to SIE	50	036	310/70	221	0:13:34
					0:19:04

Thus, to cut 3 min. off the flight, we must arrive at SIE 16 min. after passing SWL. To determine our required groundspeed, the distance is 70 NM; thus the groundspeed required is 262 kt. [70 ÷ (16/60)]. Next, compute TAS on the wind side of your computer:

1. Set the magnetic wind direction of 310° under the true index, and place a pencil mark at 70 kt. (wind speed) up from the grommet.
2. Place the MC of 036° under the true index. (Note: We use the inbound course to SIE since this is the heading that will be affected by the wind longer.)
3. Slide the grid so the groundspeed of 262 kt. is under the grommet.
4. Read the TAS of 276 kt. under the pencil mark.

Answer (B) is incorrect because a TAS of 280 kt. would cut approximately 3 min. 15 sec., not 3 min., off the flight plan ETE from SWL to SIE. Answer (C) is incorrect because a TAS of 284 kt. would cut approximately 3.5 min., not 3 min., off the flight plan ETE from SWL to SIE.

55.
9629. (Refer to figure 182A on page 399.) EAB 90 is a CAT B aircraft and received a clearance to fly the LOC RWY 09R approach, to circle to land RWY 27R. The Baldn fix was received. What are the minimums?

A—540-1.
B—600-1.
C—680-1.

Answer (B) is correct (9629). *(IAP)*

Fig. 182A is the ILS RWY 9R IAP at PHL. The BALDN fix minimums for circling are listed in the upper right corner of the planview section. For a Cat. B aircraft that received the BALDN fix, the circling minimums are 600-1.

Answer (A) is incorrect because 540-1 are the circling minimums with the BALDN fix received for a Cat. A, not Cat. B, aircraft. Answer (C) is incorrect because 680-1 are the circling minimums without, not with, the BALDN fix identified.

56.
9630. (Refer to figure 182A on page 399.) EAB 90 is a CAT B aircraft and received a clearance to fly the LOC RWY 09R, to land RWY 09R. The Baldn fix was received. What are the minimums?

A—520/24.
B—600/24.
C—680/24.

Answer (A) is correct (9630). *(IAP)*

Fig. 182A is the ILS RWY 9R IAP at PHL. The BALDN fix minimums are located at the top center of the planview section. A clearance to fly the LOC RWY 09R, to land RWY 09R, means a straight-in approach. For a Cat. B aircraft that received the BALDN fix, the S-LOC 9R minimums are 520/24.

Answer (B) is incorrect because the MDA for a S-LOC 9R approach with the BALDN fix received is 520 ft., not 600 ft. Answer (C) is incorrect because 680/24 are the minimums without, not with, the BALDN fix received for a S-LOC 9R approach.

57.
9631. (Refer to figure 182A on page 399.) EAB 90 is a CAT B aircraft and received a clearance to fly the LOC RWY 09R to sidestep and land RWY 09L. The Baldn fix was received. What are the minimums?

A—680-1.
B—520/24.
C—600-1.

Answer (C) is correct (9631). *(IAP)*
Fig. 182A is the ILS RWY 9R IAP for PHL. The BALDN fix minimums for a side step to RWY 9L are listed in the top center of the planview section below the S-LOC 9R minimums. The minimums for a Cat. B aircraft to fly the LOC RWY 9R and sidestep to land on RWY 9L with the BALDN fix received are 600-1.
Answer (A) is incorrect because 680-1 are the minimums without, not with, the BALDN fix received for a side-step RWY 9L approach. Answer (B) is incorrect because 520/24 are the minimums for a S-LOC 9R, not a side-step 9L, approach with the BALDN fix received.

58.
9632. (Refer to figure 182A on page 399.) The PIC on EAB 90 has not flown 100 hours as PIC in the BE 1900 (CAT B aircraft). What are the minimums for the PIC when flying the ILS RWY 09R, at PHL?

A—321/42.
B—221/18.
C—321/36.

Answer (A) is correct (9632). *(FAR 135.225)*
FAR 135.225 requires that, if the PIC of a turbine-powered airplane has less than 100 hr. as PIC in that type of airplane (i.e., BE 1900), the MDA or DH is increased by 100 ft., and the visibility by ½ SM (or 2,400 ft. RVR). Thus, the PIC's minimums when flying the ILS RWY 09R approach at PHL are 321/42.
Answer (B) is incorrect because 221/18 are the minimums if the PIC has at least, not less than, 100 hr. as PIC in the BE 1900. Answer (C) is incorrect because the visibility increases by ½ SM, or 2,400 ft. RVR, not 1,800 ft. RVR, if the PIC has less than 100 hr. as PIC in the BE 1900.

59.
9633. (Refer to figure 182A on page 399.) The PIC of EAB 90 has 89 hours and 29 landings as PIC in the BE 1900, while operating under Part 135. The PIC has 1,234 hours and 579 landings as PIC in the DC-3 while operating under Part 135. What are the minimums for the ILS RWY 9R approach at PHL, for this PIC?

A—221/18.
B—321/24.
C—321/42.

Answer (C) is correct (9633). *(FAR 135.225)*
FAR 135.225 requires that, if the PIC of a turbine-powered airplane has less than 100 hr. as PIC in that type of airplane (i.e., BE 1900), the MDA or DH is increased by 100 ft., and the visibility is increased by ½ SM (or 2,400 ft. RVR). Thus, the PIC's minimums when flying the ILS RWY 9R approach at PHL are 321/42. The DC-3 time does not count toward the 100-hr. requirement because it is a different type of airplane.
Answer (A) is incorrect because 221/18 are the minimums if the PIC has at least, not less than, 100 hr. as PIC in the BE 1900. Answer (B) is incorrect because visibility increases by 2,400 ft. RVR (½ SM), not 600 ft. RVR, if the PIC has less than 100 hr. as PIC in the BE 1900.

60.
9634. (Refer to figures 183 and 183A on pages 400 and 401.) When the weather at PHL goes below the PIC's minimums, the flight diverts to ACY. Upon arrival at ACY, EAB 90 is cleared for the ILS RWY 13 approach. The PIC has 89 hours of PIC time in the BE 1900. What are the PIC's minimums?

A—700-2.
B—276/18.
C—376/42.

Answer (C) is correct (9634). *(FAR 135.225)*
FAR 135.225 requires that, if the PIC of a turbine-powered airplane has less than 100 hr. as PIC in that type of airplane (i.e., BE 1900), the MDA or DH is increased by 100 ft. and the visibility is increased by ½ SM (or 2,400 ft. RVR), but not to exceed the ceiling and visibility minimums when used as an alternate airport. Thus, the PIC's minimums for the ILS RWY 13 approach at ACY are 376/42.
Answer (A) is incorrect because 700-2 are the alternate minimums for the ILS RWY 13 to list the airport as an alternate, not to fly the approach, for Cat. D, not Cat. B, aircraft. Answer (B) is incorrect because 276/18 are the minimums if the PIC has at least, not less than, 100 hr. as PIC in the BE 1900.

61.
9636. (Refer to legend 15 on page 402.) Newport News/Williamsburg Intl is an FAR Part 139 airport. The Airport/Facility Directory contains the following entry: ARFF Index A. What is the minimum number of aircraft rescue and fire fighting vehicles, and the type and amount of fire fighting agents that the airport should have?

A—Two vehicles and 600 pounds dry chemical (DC) or Halon 1211 or 500 pounds of DC plus 100 gallons of water.
B—One vehicle and 500 pounds of dry chemical (DC) or Halon 1211 or 450 pounds DC plus 100 gallons of water.
C—One vehicle and 500 pounds of dry chemical (DC) or Halon 1211 or 350 pounds DC and 1,000 gallons of water.

Answer (B) is correct (9636). *(A/FD)*

Legend 15 is an *A/FD* legend. Look at the table under item 16 and find the airport index, A, on the left margin. The minimum number of vehicles is one, and the type and amount of fire-fighting agents are 500 lb. of dry chemical (DC) or HALON 1211 or 450 lb. DC plus 100 gal. of water (H_2O).

Answer (A) is incorrect because an airport having an ARFF Index C, not A, is required to have at least two vehicles. Answer (C) is incorrect because an airport having an ARFF Index A is required to have one vehicle and 500 lb. DC or HALON 1211 or 450 lb., not 350 lb., DC and 100 gal., not 1,000 gal., of water.

Form Approved: OMB No. 2120-0034

U.S. DEPARTMENT OF TRANSPORTATION FEDERAL AVIATION ADMINISTRATION **FLIGHT PLAN**	(FAA USE ONLY)	☐ PILOT BRIEFING ☐ STOPOVER	☐ VNR	TIME STARTED	SPECIALIST INITIALS

1. TYPE	2. AIRCRAFT IDENTIFICATION	3. AIRCRAFT TYPE/ SPECIAL EQUIPMENT	4. TRUE AIRSPEED	5. DEPARTURE POINT	6. DEPARTURE TIME PROPOSED (Z)	6. DEPARTURE TIME ACTUAL (Z)	7. CRUISING ALTITUDE
VFR X IFR DVFR	EAB 90	BE1900/A	236 KTS	KPHF NEWPORT NEWS, VA			FL190

8. ROUTE OF FLIGHT HENRY ONE ORF, J121 SIE, SIE. VCN5 PHL

9. DESTINATION (Name of airport and city)	10. EST. TIME ENROUTE HOURS	MINUTES	11. REMARKS
KPHL PHILADELPHIA INT'L PHILADELPHIA			VARIATION: PHF 7°W, PHL 10°W. TEC = TOWER ENROUTE CONTROL PPH = Pounds Per Hour

12. FUEL ON BOARD HOURS	MINUTES	13. ALTERNATE AIRPORT(S)	14. PILOT'S NAME, ADDRESS & TELEPHONE NUMBER & AIRCRAFT HOME BASE / 17. DESTINATION CONTACT/TELEPHONE (OPTIONAL)	15. NUMBER ABOARD
2	45	KACY ATLANTIC CITY INT'L		13

16. COLOR OF AIRCRAFT BLUE/RED

CIVIL AIRCRAFT PILOTS. FAR Part 91 requires you file an IFR flight plan to operate under instrument flight rules in controlled airspace. Failure to file could result in a civil penalty not to exceed $1,000 for each violation (Section 901 of the Federal Aviation Act of 1958, as amended). Filing of a VFR flight plan is recommended as a good operating practice. See also Part 99 for requirements concerning DVFR flight plans.

FAA Form 7233-1 (8-82) CLOSE VFR FLIGHT PLAN WITH ________________ FSS ON ARRIVAL

FLIGHT LOG

CHECK POINTS FROM	TO	ROUTE ALTITUDE	COURSE	WIND TEMP	SPEED-KTS TAS	GS	DIST NM	TIME LEG	TOT	FUEL LEG	TOT
PHF	ORF	VECTORS CLIMB					40		:19:00		312*
ORF	SAWED	J/21 FL190		300/70 ISA+5							
SAWED	SWL										
SWL	SIE										
SIE	VCN										
VCN	OOD										
OOD	PHL	DESCENT & APPROACH					30	:16:00		177	
PHL	ACY	TEC 3000					46	:18:00			

OTHER DATA: * Includes Taxi Fuel
NOTE: Use 689 PPH Total Fuel Flow From L/O To Start Of Descent.
Use 739 PPH Total Fuel Flow For Reserve And Alternate Requirements.

A Missed Approach Requires 95# of Fuel.

TIME and FUEL: As required by FARs.

TIME	FUEL (LB)	
		EN ROUTE
		RESERVE
		ALTERNATE
		TOTAL

FIGURE 179.—Flight Plan/Flight Log.

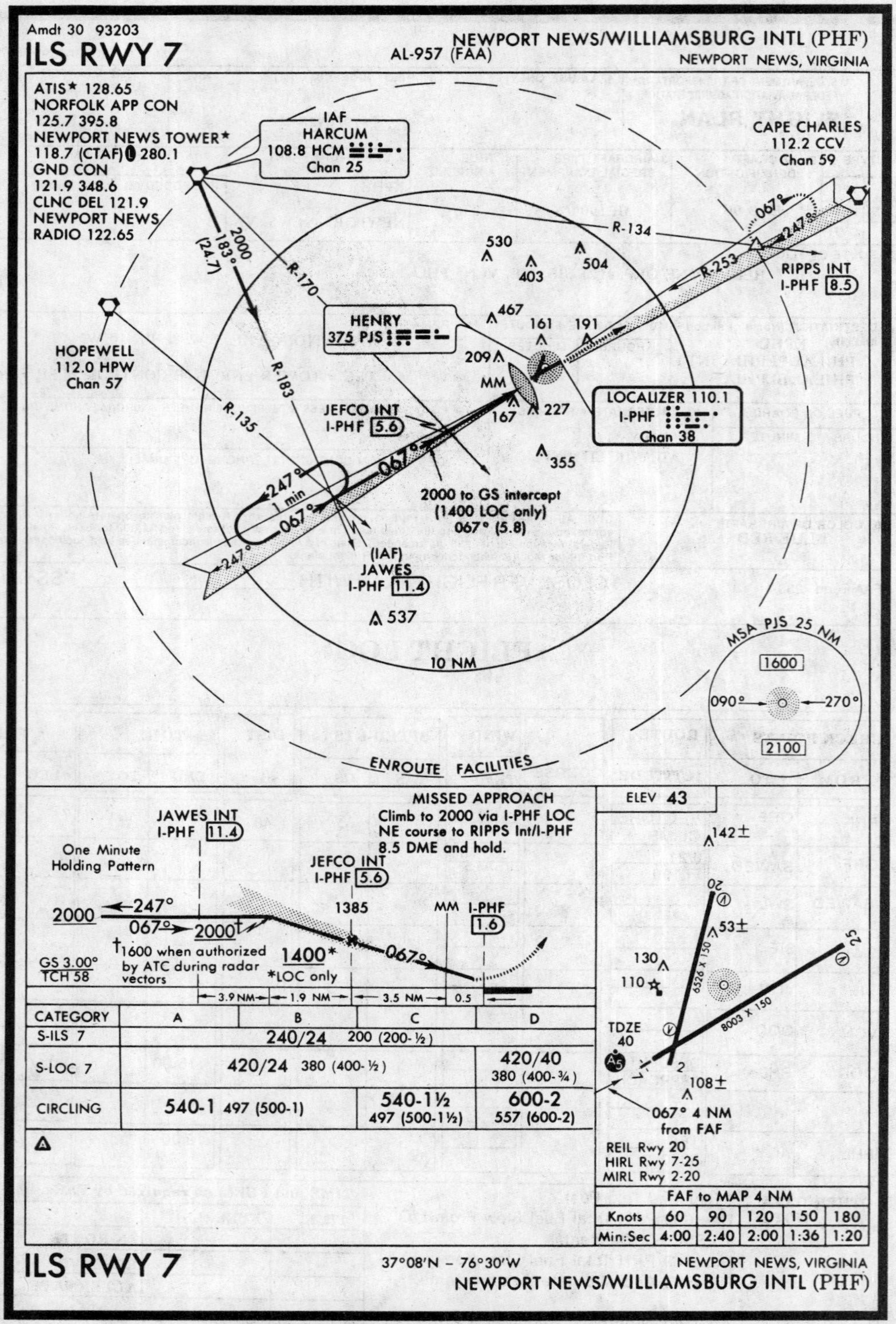

FIGURE 180.—ILS RWY 7 (PHF).

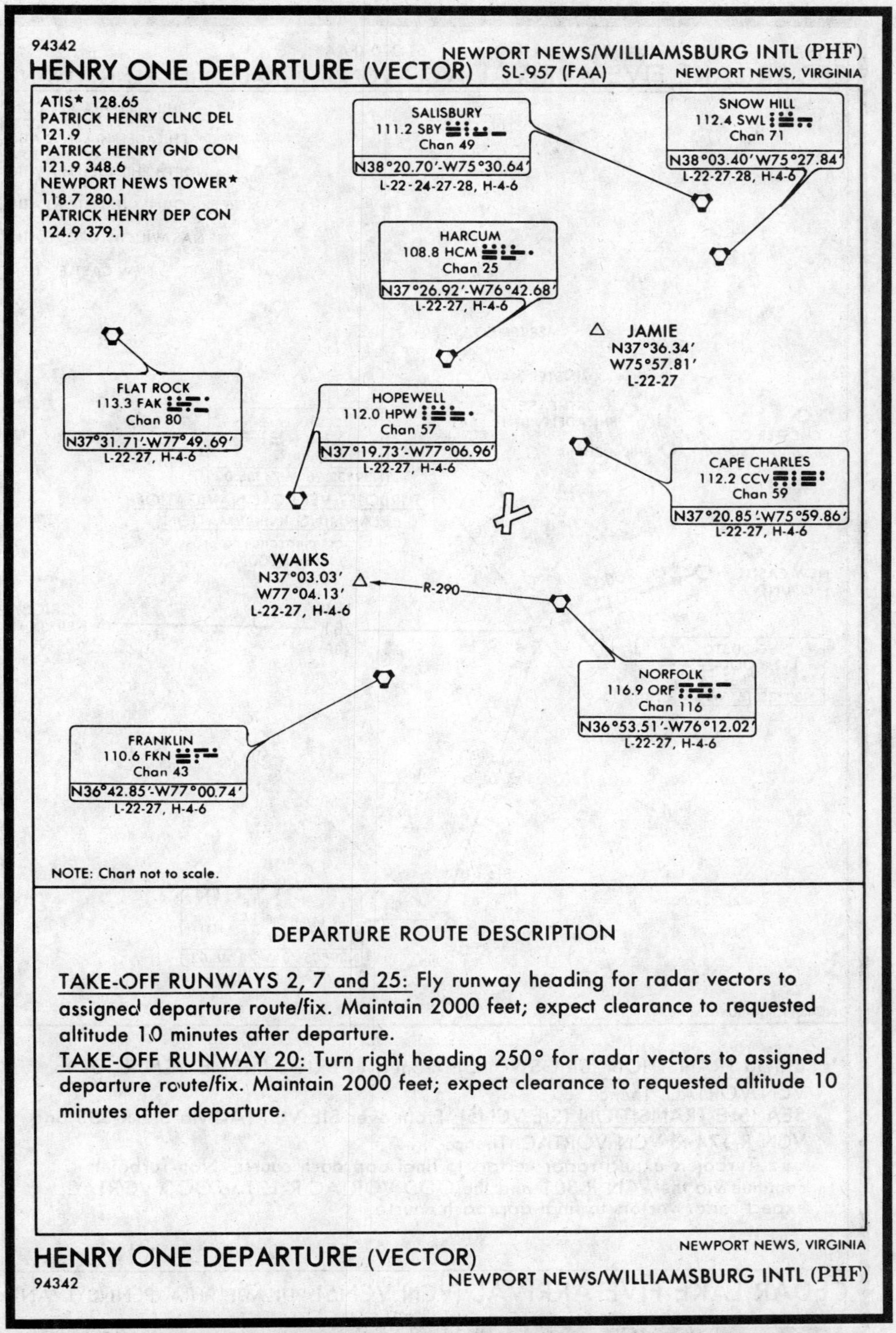

FIGURE 180A.—HENRY ONE DEPARTURE (VECTOR) (PHF).

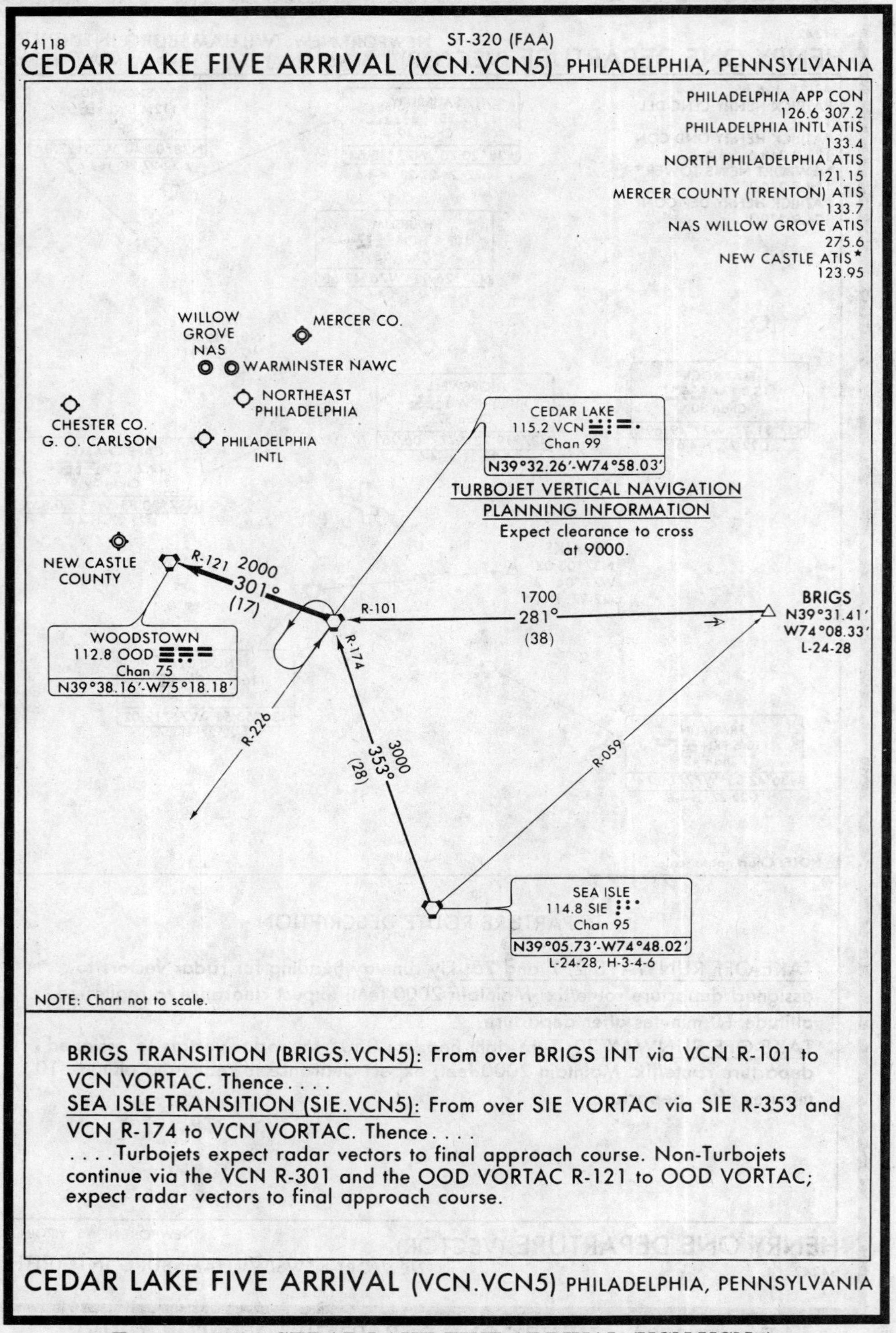

FIGURE 182.—CEDAR LAKE FIVE ARRIVAL (VCN.VCN5).

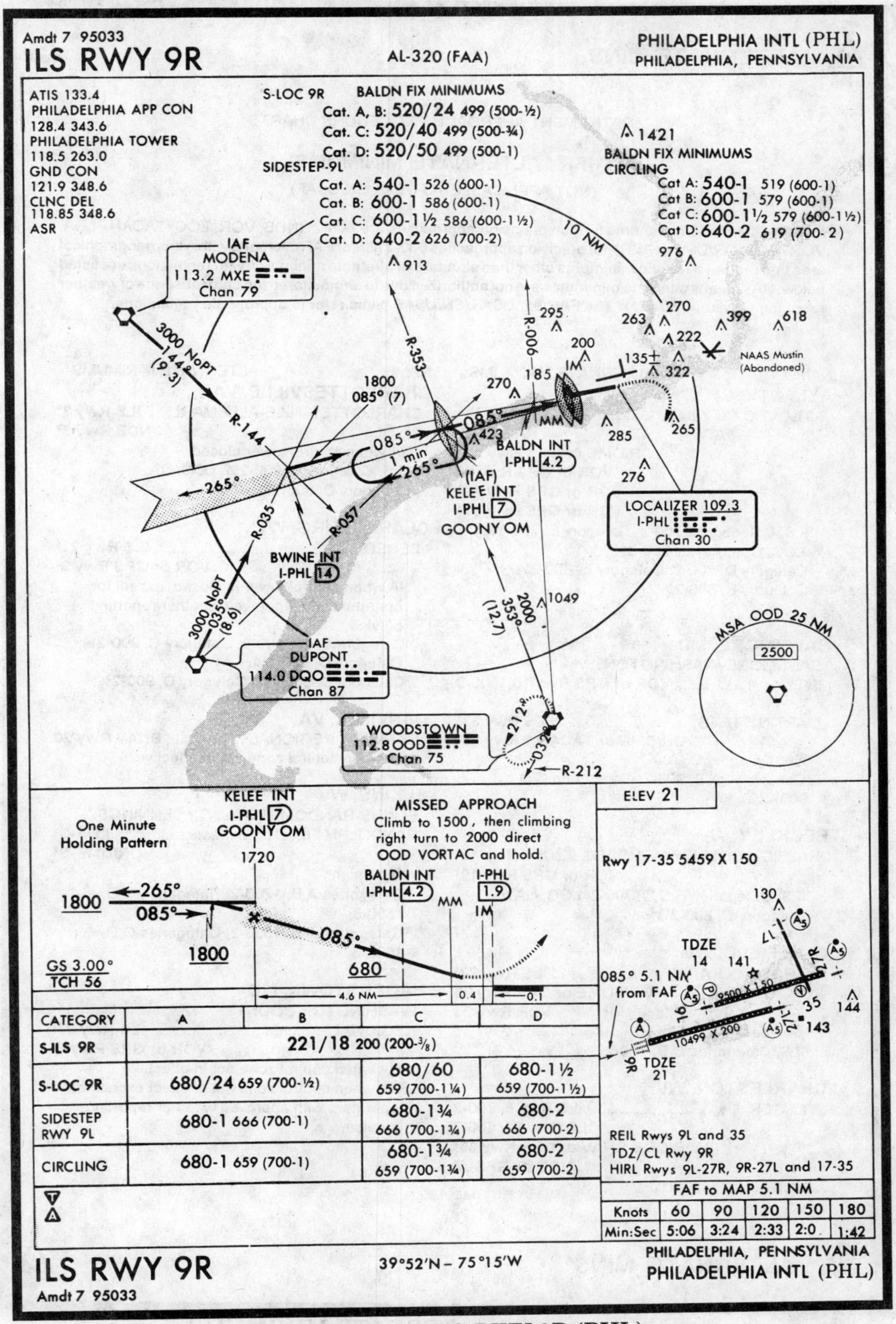

FIGURE 182A.—ILS RWY 9R (PHL).

ALTERNATE MINS

94342

INSTRUMENT APPROACH PROCEDURE CHARTS

IFR ALTERNATE MINIMUMS

(NOT APPLICABLE TO USA/USN/USAF)

Standard alternate minimums for non precision approaches are 800-2 (NDB, VOR, LOC, TACAN, LDA, VORTAC, VOR/DME or ASR); for precision approaches 600-2 (ILS or PAR). Airports within this geographical area that require alternate minimums other than standard or alternate minimums with restrictions are listed below. NA - means alternate minimums are not authorized due to unmonitored facility or absence of weather reporting service. Civil pilots see FAR 91. USA/USN/USAF pilots refer to appropriate regulations.

NAME ALTERNATE MINIMUMS

ATLANTIC CITY, NJ

ATLANTIC CITY INTL .... **ILS Rwy 13[1]**
RADAR-1[2]
VOR/DME or GPS Rwy 22[3]
VOR or GPS Rwy 4[3]
VOR or GPS Rwy 13[3]
VOR or GPS Rwy 31[3]

[1]ILS, Category D, 700-2; Category E, 700-2½. LOC, Category E, 800-2½.
[2]Category D, 700-2; Category E, 800-2½.
[3]Category E, 800-2½.

BALTIMORE, MD

BALTIMORE-WASHINGTON INTL .... **VOR or GPS Rwy 10,1000-3**

MARTIN STATE .... **ILS Rwy 33[1]**
VOR/DME or TACAN 1 Rwy 15[2]

[1]ILS, Category D, 700-2.
[2]Categories A,B, 900-2; Categories C,D, 900-2¾.

BECKLEY, WV

RALEIGH COUNTY MEMORIAL ..... **ILS Rwy 19[1]**
VOR or GPS Rwy 19[2]

[1]ILS, Categories B,C,D, 700-2. LOC, NA.
[2]Category D, 800-2¼.

BLUEFIELD, WV

MERCER COUNTY .... **ILS Rwy 23[1]**
VOR/DME or GPS Rwy 23
VOR Rwy 23

NA when FSS is closed.
[1]ILS, Categories C,D, 700-2.

CHARLESTON, WV

YEAGER .... **ILS Rwy 5, 700-2**
ILS Rwy 23, 700-2
VOR/DME RNAV or GPS Rwy 33[1]
VOR or GPS-A[1]

[1]Category D, 800-2¼.

NAME ALTERNATE MINIMUMS

CHARLOTTESVILLE, VA

CHARLOTTESVILLE-ALBEMARLE .. **ILS Rwy 3[1]**
NDB Rwy 3[2]

NA when control tower closed.
[1]ILS, Category D, 900-2¾. LOC, NA.
[2]Category D, 900-2¾.

CLARKSBURG, WV

BENEDUM .... **ILS Rwy 21[1]**
VOR or GPS Rwy 3[2]

NA when control tower is closed, except for operators with approved weather reporting service.
[1]Categories A,B, 800-2; Category C, 900-2½; Category D, 900-2¾.
[2]Category C, 900-2½; Category D, 900-2¾.

DANVILLE, VA

DANVILLE REGIONAL .... **RNAV Rwy 20**

NA when control zone not in effective.

ELKINS, WV

ELKINS-RANDOLPH COUNTY JENNINGS-RANDOLPH FIELD .... **LDA-C[1]**
VOR/DME-B[2]

NA at night.
[1]Categories A,B, 1200-2; Categories C,D, 1500-3.
[2]Categories A,B, 1500-2; Categories C,D, 1500-3.

HAGERSTOWN, MD

WASHINGTON COUNTY REGIONAL .... **ILS Rwy 27[1]**
VOR or GPS Rwy 9[2]

[1]NA when control zone not in effect.
[2]NA when control zone not in effect except for operators with approved weather reporting service.

NE-3

ALTERNATE MINS

94342

FIGURE 183.—IFR ALTERNATE MINIMUMS.

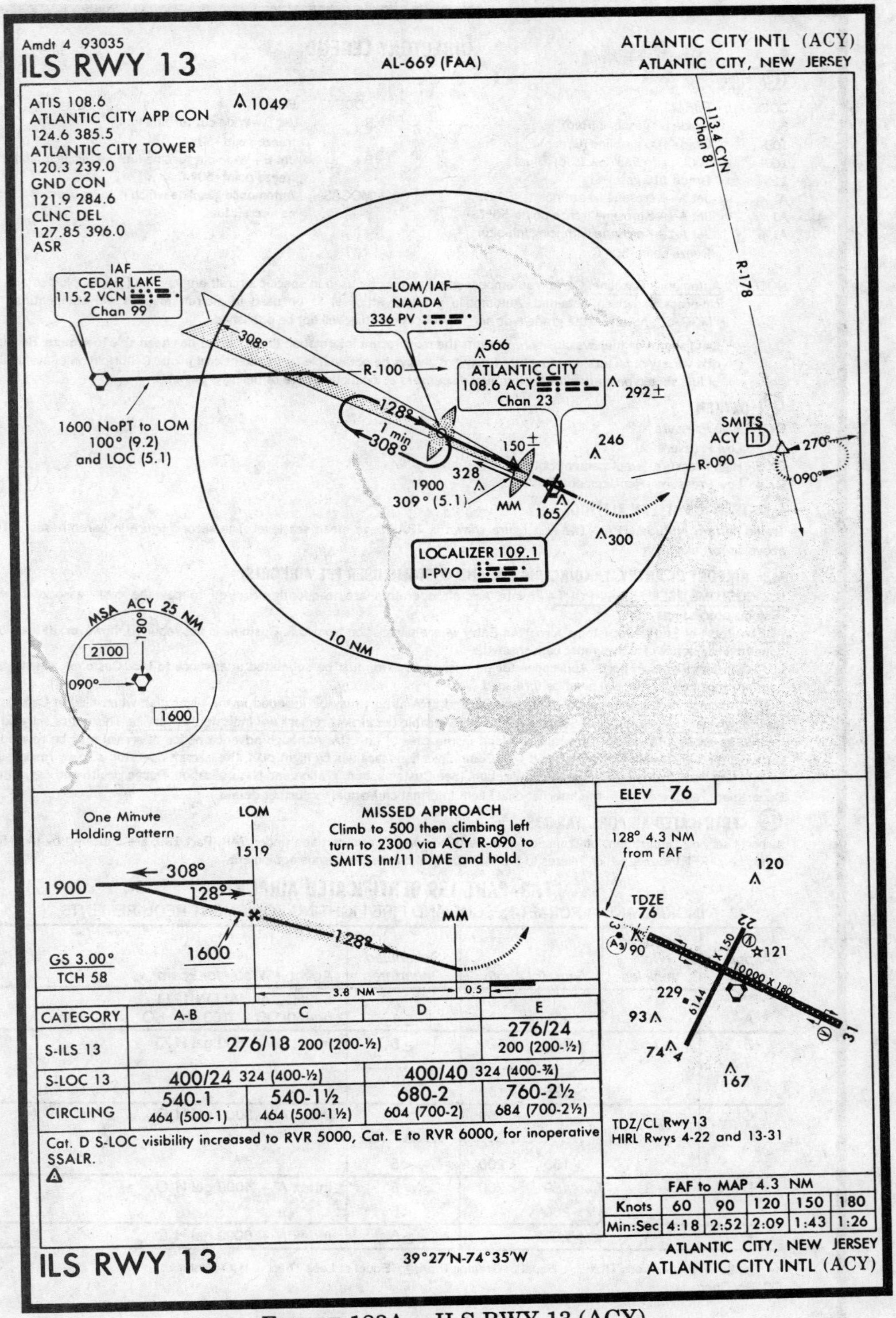

FIGURE 183A.—ILS RWY 13 (ACY).

4

DIRECTORY LEGEND

⑫ FUEL

CODE	FUEL
80	Grade 80 gasoline (Red)
100	Grade 100 gasoline (Green)
100LL	100LL gasoline (low lead) (Blue)
115	Grade 115 gasoline
A	Jet A—Kerosene freeze point-40° C.
A1	Jet A-1—Kerosene freeze point-50°C.
A1 +	Jet A-1—Kerosene with icing inhibitor, freeze point-50° C.
B	Jet B—Wide-cut turbine fuel, freeze point-50° C.
B+	Jet B—Wide-cut turbine fuel with icing inhibitor, freeze point-50° C.
MOGAS	Automobile gasoline which is to be used as aircraft fuel.

NOTE: Automobile Gasoline. Certain automobile gasoline may be used in specific aircraft engines if a FAA supplemental type certificate has been obtained. Automobile gasoline which is to be used in aircraft engines will be identified as "MOGAS", however, the grade/type and other octane rating will not be published.

Data shown on fuel availability represents the most recent information the publisher has been able to acquire. Because of a variety of factors, the fuel listed may not always be obtainable by transient civil pilots. Confirmation of availability of fuel should be made directly with fuel dispensers at locations where refueling is planned.

⑬ OXYGEN

OX 1 High Pressure
OX 2 Low Pressure
OX 3 High Pressure—Replacement Bottles
OX 4 Low Pressure—Replacement Bottles

⑭ TRAFFIC PATTERN ALTITUDE

Traffic Pattern Altitude (TPA)—The first figure shown is TPA above mean sea level. The second figure in parentheses is TPA above airport elevation.

⑮ AIRPORT OF ENTRY, LANDING RIGHTS, AND CUSTOMS USER FEE AIRPORTS

U.S. CUSTOMS USER FEE AIRPORT—Private Aircraft operators are frequently required to pay the costs associated with customs processing.

AOE—Airport of Entry—A customs Airport of Entry where permission from U.S. Customs is not required, however, at least one hour advance notice of arrival must be furnished.

LRA—Landing Rights Airport—Application for permission to land must be submitted in advance to U.S. Customs. At least one hour advance notice of arrival must be furnished.

NOTE: Advance notice of arrival at both an AOE and LRA airport may be included in the flight plan when filed in Canada or Mexico, where Flight Notification Service (ADCUS) is available the airport remark will indicate this service. This notice will also be treated as an application for permission to land in the case of an LRA. Although advance notice of arrival may be relayed to Customs through Mexico, Canadian, and U.S. Communications facilities by flight plan, the aircraft operator is solely responsible for insuring that Customs receives the notification. (See Customs, Immigration and Naturalization, Public Health and Agriculture Department requirements in the International Flight Information Manual for further details.)

⑯ CERTIFICATED AIRPORT (FAR 139)

Airports serving Department of Transportation certified carriers and certified under FAR, Part 139, are indicated by the ARFF index; i.e., ARFF Index A, which relates to the availability of crash, fire, rescue equipment.

FAR-PART 139 CERTIFICATED AIRPORTS

INDICES AND AIRCRAFT RESCUE AND FIRE FIGHTING EQUIPMENT REQUIREMENTS

Airport Index	*Required No. Vehicles*	*Aircraft Length*	*Scheduled Departures*	*Agent + Water for Foam*
A	1	<90′	≥1	500#DC or HALON 1211 or 450#DC + 100 gal H_2O
B	1 or 2	≥90′, <126′	≥5	Index A + 1500 gal H_2O
		≥126′, <159′	<5	
C	2 or 3	≥126′, <159′	≥5	Index A + 3000 gal H_2O
		≥159′, <200′	<5	
D	3	≥159′, <200′	≥5	Index A + 4000 gal H_2O
		>200′	<5	
E	3	≥200′	≥5	Index A + 6000 gal H_2O

> Greater Than; < Less Than; ≥ Equal or Greater Than; ≤ Equal or Less Than; H_2O–Water; DC–Dry Chemical.

LEGEND 15.—Directory Legend.

10.6 G-1159 STL TO LGA (Questions 62-69)

Questions 62 through 69 pertain to an IFR flight from St. Louis International Airport, St. Louis, Missouri to La Guardia International Airport, New York, New York.

The route is given in block 8 of the flight plan portion of Fig. 158 on page 406. The partially completed flight planning log is given on the bottom portion of Fig. 158.

The following figures are used to answer the eight questions concerning this flight.

Fig.	Page	Title
158	406	Flight Plan/Flight Log
159	418	High Altitude Airways
160	407	Gateway Two Departure (STL)
160A	408	Milton Eight Arrival (MIP.MIP8)
161	409	ILS/DME RWY 13 (LGA)
161A	410	VOR or GPS RWY 13L/13R (JFK)

10.6 G-1159 STL to LGA

62.
9597. (Refer to figures 158, 159, 160, 160A, and 161 on pages 406, 418, 407, 408, and 409.) The estimated time enroute from STL to LGA for N711JB is

A—1 hour 46 minutes.
B—1 hour 50 minutes.
C—1 hour 54 minutes.

Answer (C) is correct (9597). *(IFH Chap XIII)*

To determine the ETE from STL to LGA, you must complete the flight log in Fig. 158. In the remarks box of the flight plan, the magnetic variation is given at BIB (1°E), ROD (1°W), DJB (5°W), PSB (8°W), MIP (11°W), SBJ (11°W), and LGA (12°W). This information is used to convert the true wind direction to magnetic direction.

Our flight log below has been expanded to provide more detail. To convert the wind direction from true to magnetic, we use 1°E to SHB; 1°W to the ROD/DJB COP; 5°W to the DJB/PSB COP; 8°W to PSB; and 11°W to SBJ.

	Dist.	MC	Wind (mag.)	Ground-speed	Time
BIB	95G	X	X	X	0:16:00G
BIB/SHB COP	65.5	067	349/96	477	0:08:14
SHB	65.5	071	349/96	484	0:08:07
SHB/ROD COP	45.5	063	351/96	468	0:05:50
ROD	45.5	070	351/96	479	0:05:42
ROD/DJB COP	53.5	054	351/96	455	0:07:03
DJB	53.5	059	355/96	457	0:07:01
DJB/PSB COP	95.5	102	355/96	526	0:10:53
PSB	95.5	109	358/96	532	0:10:46
MIP	61.0	093	361/96	500	0:07:19
MIP/FJC COP	29.0	117	361/96	541	0:03:13
FJC	29.0	118	361/96	542	0:03:12
SBJ	34.0	115	361/96	537	0:03:47
LGA	52G	X	X	X	0:16:26G
					1:53:33

G = Given

Answer (A) is incorrect because an ETE of 1 hr. 46 min. would require a TAS of approximately 550 kt., not 506 kt. Answer (B) is incorrect because an ETE of 1 hr. 50 min. would require a TAS of 525 kt., not 506 kt.

63.
9598. (Refer to figures 158, 159, 160, 160A, and 161 on pages 406, 418, 407, 408, and 409.) The required amount of fuel (in pounds) to be on N711JB at STL, prior to taxi, is

A—5,933 pounds.
B—6,408 pounds.
C—6,641 pounds.

Answer (B) is correct (9598). ***(IFH Chap XIII)***
To determine the required amount of fuel to be on N711JB at STL prior to taxi, you must complete the fuel portion of the flight log on Fig. 158. Use 2,389 PPH total fuel flow from BIB to SBJ and 1,898 PPH total fuel flow for reserve and alternate requirements.

	Time	Fuel (lb.)
BIB	0:16:00G	987.0G
BIB/SHB COP	0:08:14	327.8
SHB	0:08:07	323.2
SHB/ROD COP	0:05:50	232.3
ROD	0:05:42	227.0
ROD/DJB COP	0:07:03	280.7
DJB	0:07:01	279.4
DJB/PSB COP	0:10:53	433.3
PSB	0:10:46	428.7
MIP	0:07:19	291.3
MIP/FJC COP	0:03:13	128.1
FJC	0:03:12	127.4
SBJ	0:03:47	150.6
LGA	0:16:26G	269.0G
JFK	0:15:00G	474.5
Reserves	0:45:00	1,423.5
		6,383.8

G = Given

Answer (A) is incorrect because 5,933 lb. does not include the 475 lb. required to fly to the alternate (JFK). Answer (C) is incorrect because 6,641 lb. includes the 233 lb. required for a missed approach. While this should be included as a practical matter, it is not required by the FARs.

64.
9599. (Refer to figure 161 on page 409.) To receive the DME information from the facility labeled "DME Chan 22" at La Guardia requires that

A—N711JB be equipped with a UHF NAV radio, which is tuned to channel 22.
B—a military TACAN be tuned to channel 22.
C—the VHF NAV radio be tuned to the ILS (108.5) frequency.

Answer (C) is correct (9599). ***(AIM Para 1-1-7)***
ILS/DME facilities provide course and distance information from collocated components under a frequency pairing program. Thus, to receive DME information requires that the DME receiver be tuned to the ILS frequency of 108.5.
Answer (A) is incorrect because channel 22 refers to a TACAN receiver, which is used by military, not civilian, aircraft. Answer (B) is incorrect because a military aircraft would select channel 22 on TACAN for DME information, but a civilian aircraft would use the ILS frequency of 108.5 to receive the DME.

65.
9600. (Refer to figure 161A on page 410.) The La Guardia weather goes below minimums and New York Approach Control issues a clearance to N711JB, via radar vectors, to ASALT Intersection. As N711JB is approaching ASALT, Approach Control clears the aircraft to fly the VOR RWY 13L/13R approach. What is the distance from ASALT Intersection to RWY 13L?

A—12.3 NM.
B—12.4 NM.
C—13.3 NM.

Answer (B) is correct (9600). ***(IAP)***
Fig. 161A is the VOR or GPS RWY 13L/13R IAP at JFK. In the lower left-hand corner of the planview is ASALT Int. From ASALT to CRI is 6 NM. Continue along the approach course to a circle, which is the symbol for the lead-in lights, and read the note. The distance from CRI to the lead-in lights is 1.7 NM, and the arc distance from the lights to RWY 13L is 4.7 NM. Thus, the distance from ASALT to RWY 13L is 12.4 NM (6 + 1.7 + 4.7).
Answer (A) is incorrect because the distance from ASALT to RWY 13L is 12.4 NM, not 12.3 NM. Answer (C) is incorrect because 13.3 NM is the distance to RWY 13L if the arc distance of 4.7 NM is added to the distance from CRI to the MAP, not from CRI to the first cluster of lead-in lights.

66.
9601. (Refer to figure 161A on page 410.) The La Guardia Weather goes below minimums and New York Approach Control issues a clearance to N711JB, via radar vectors, to ASALT Intersection. What is the lowest altitude that Approach Control may clear N711JB to cross ASALT Intersection?

A—3,000 feet.
B—2,500 feet.
C—2,000 feet.

Answer (C) is correct (9601). *(IAP)*

Fig. 161A is the VOR or GPS RWY 13L/13R IAP at JFK. Look at the profile view and locate ASALT Int. at the top left corner. Next to ASALT is 3000 with a line above and below the number which means a mandatory altitude. To the left is a cross to reference a footnote, which is just below. The note states that, at ASALT Int., 3,000 ft. is a mandatory altitude unless advised otherwise by ATC, and 2,000 ft. is the minimum altitude.

Answer (A) is incorrect because 3,000 ft. is the mandatory altitude to cross ASALT, unless advised otherwise by ATC, which may use 2,000 ft. as the lowest altitude. Answer (B) is incorrect because the lowest altitude at which ATC may clear an aircraft to cross ASALT is 2,000 ft., not 2,500 ft.

67.
9604. (Refer to figure 161A on page 410.) The distance from Canarsie (CRI) to RWY 13R at JFK is

A—5.4 NM.
B—6.3 NM.
C—7.3 NM.

Answer (A) is correct (9604). *(IAP)*

Fig. 161A is the VOR or GPS RWY 13L/13R IAP at JFK. Look at the profile view and locate CRI. Follow the approach course to the circle (which is a symbol for lead-in light clusters) and read the note. The distance from CRI to the lead-in lights is 1.7 NM. The arc distance via the lead-in lights to RWY 13R is 3.7 NM. Thus, the distance from CRI to RWY 13R is 5.4 NM (1.7 + 3.7).

Answer (B) is incorrect because 6.3 NM is the distance to RWY 13R if the arc distance of 3.7 NM is added to the distance from CRI to the MAP, not from CRI to the first cluster of lead-in lights. Answer (C) is incorrect because 7.3 NM is the distance to RWY 13L, not RWY 13R, if the arc distance of 4.7 NM is added to the distance from CRI to the MAP, not from CRI to the first cluster of lead-in lights.

68.
9603. (Refer to figure 161A on page 410.) What must be operational for N711JB to execute the VOR RWY 13L/13R approach to JFK?

A—Radar and DME.
B—LDIN and VOR.
C—Lead-in Light System, VOR and Radar.

Answer (C) is correct (9603). *(IAP)*

Fig. 161A is the VOR or GPS RWY 13L/13R IAP at JFK. To execute the approach, the navigation equipment listed in the title must be operational (VOR). Additionally, the planview section in bold letters states that radar is required, and a note in the box in the lower left corner of the chart states that the lead-in light system must be operational.

Answer (A) is incorrect because DME is not required for the VOR RWY 13L/13R approach to JFK. Answer (B) is incorrect because radar, in addition to LDIN and VOR, is required to be operational to execute the VOR RWY 13L/13R IAP at JFK.

69.
9602. (Refer to figure 161A on page 410.) For landing on RWY 31L at JFK, how much RWY is available?

A—11,248 feet.
B—11,966 feet.
C—14,572 feet.

Answer (A) is correct (9602). *(IAP)*

Fig. 161A is the VOR or GPS RWY 13L/13R IAP at JFK. The airport diagram is at the lower right corner of the chart. At the top portion are the available landing distances for various runways at JFK. For a landing on RWY 31L, there is 11,248 ft. of available runway.

Answer (B) is incorrect because 11,966 ft. is the available landing distance for RWY 13R, not RWY 31L. Answer (C) is incorrect because 14,572 ft. is the total runway length, not the landing distance available, for RWY 31L.

Form Approved: OMB No. 2120-0034

U.S. DEPARTMENT OF TRANSPORTATION FEDERAL AVIATION ADMINISTRATION **FLIGHT PLAN**	(FAA USE ONLY) ☐ PILOT BRIEFING ☐ VNR ☐ STOPOVER	TIME STARTED	SPECIALIST INITIALS

1. TYPE	2. AIRCRAFT IDENTIFICATION	3. AIRCRAFT TYPE/ SPECIAL EQUIPMENT	4. TRUE AIRSPEED	5. DEPARTURE POINT	6. DEPARTURE TIME PROPOSED (Z)	ACTUAL (Z)	7. CRUISING ALTITUDE
VFR							
X IFR	N711JB	G1159/A	506 KTS	STL ST LOUIS, MO			FL370
DVFR							

8. ROUTE OF FLIGHT: STL, GATWAY2.ROD, J29 DJB, J60 PSB, PSB.MIP8, LGA

9. DESTINATION (Name of airport and city)	10. EST. TIME ENROUTE HOURS	MINUTES	11. REMARKS
LGA LA GAURDIA NEW YORK, NY			L/O = LEVEL OFF PPH = POUNDS PER HOUR TEC = TOWER ENROUTE CONTROL VARIATION: BIB IE, ROD 1W, DJB 5W, PSB 8W, MIP 11W, SBJ 11W, LGA 12W

12. FUEL ON BOARD HOURS	MINUTES	13. ALTERNATE AIRPORT(S)	14. PILOT'S NAME, ADDRESS & TELEPHONE NUMBER & AIRCRAFT HOME BASE	15. NUMBER ABOARD
4	00	JFK NEW YORK, NY	17. DESTINATION CONTACT/TELEPHONE (OPTIONAL)	12

16. COLOR OF AIRCRAFT	
BLACK/RED	CIVIL AIRCRAFT PILOTS. FAR Part 91 requires you file an IFR flight plan to operate under instrument flight rules in controlled airspace. Failure to file could result in a civil penalty not to exceed $1,000 for each violation (Section 901 of the Federal Aviation Act of 1958, as amended). Filing of a VFR flight plan is recommended as a good operating practice. See also Part 99 for requirements concerning DVFR flight plans.

FAA Form 7233-1 (8-82) CLOSE VFR FLIGHT PLAN WITH ____________ FSS ON ARRIVAL

FLIGHT LOG

CHECK POINTS FROM	TO	ROUTE ALTITUDE	COURSE	WIND TEMP	SPEED-KTS TAS	GS	DIST NM	TIME LEG	TOT	FUEL LEG	TOT
STL	BIB	GATWAY 2.ROD CLIMB					95	:16:00			987*
BIB	ROD	GATWAY2.ROD FL370		350/96 ISA-1							
ROD	DJB	J29 FL370									
DJB	PSB	J60 FL370									
PSB	MIP	PSB.MIP8 FL370									
MIP	SBJ										
SBJ	LGA	DESCENT					52	:16:26		269	
LGA	JFK	TEC 4000			260			:15:00			

OTHER DATA: * Includes Taxi Fuel
NOTE: Use 2389 PPH Total Fuel Flow From L/O To Start Of Descent.
Use 1898 PPH Total Fuel Flow For Reserve And Alternate Requirements.
A Missed Approach Requires 233# of Fuel.

TIME and FUEL: As required by FARs.

TIME	FUEL (LB)	
		EN ROUTE
		RESERVE
		ALTERNATE
		TOTAL

FIGURE 158.—Flight Plan/Flight Log.

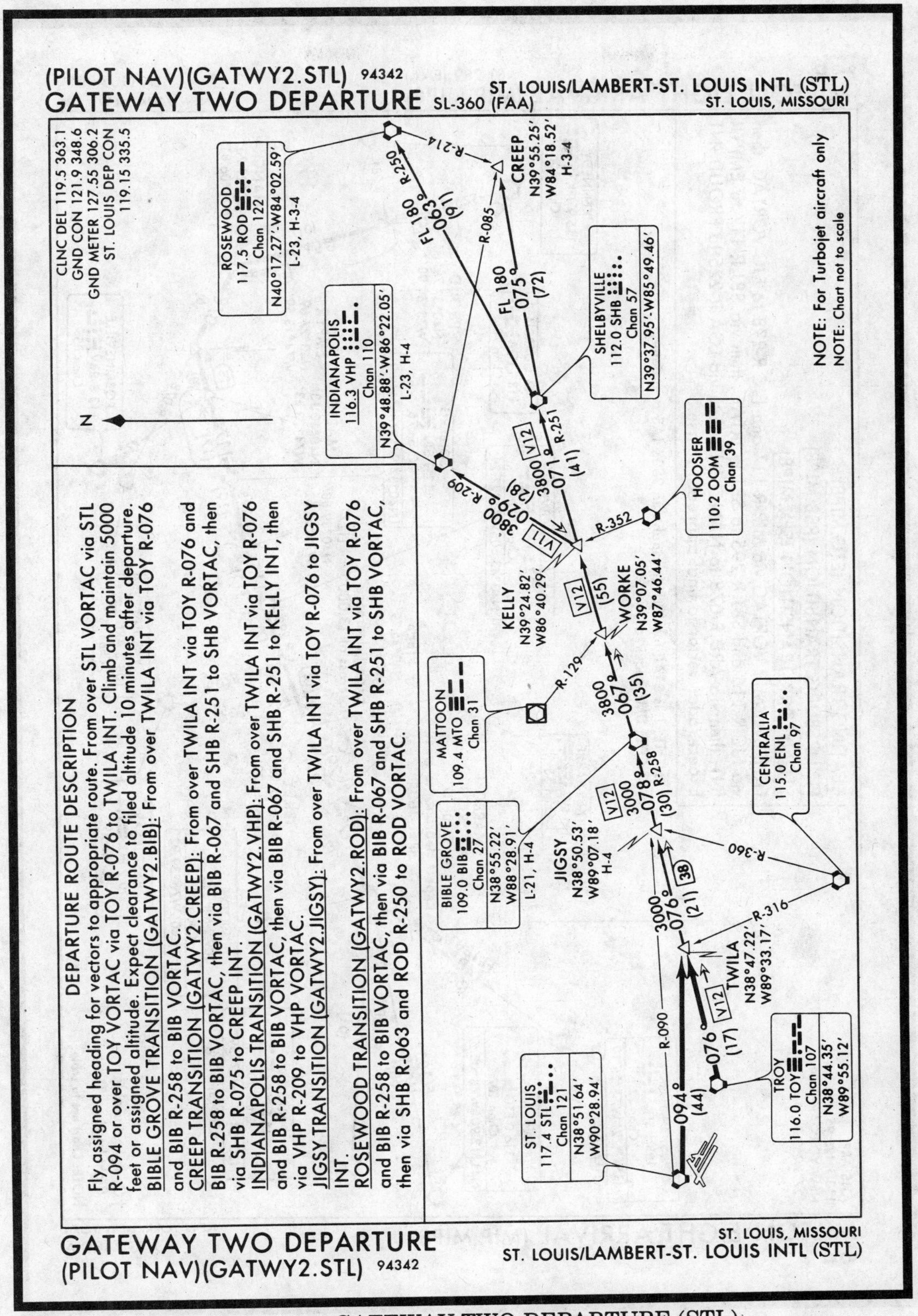

FIGURE 160.—GATEWAY TWO DEPARTURE (STL).

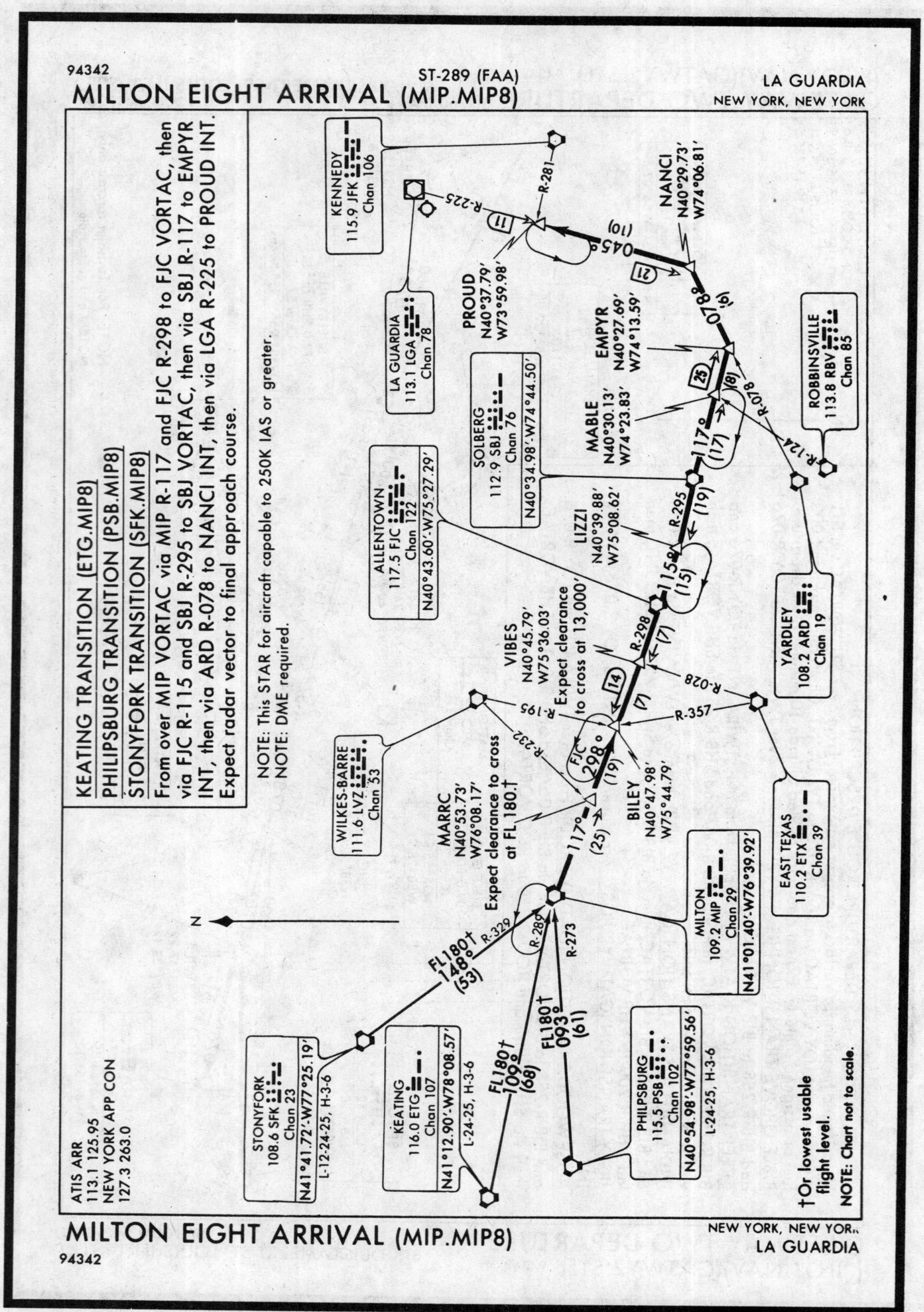

FIGURE 160A.—MILTON EIGHT ARRIVAL (MIP.MIP8).

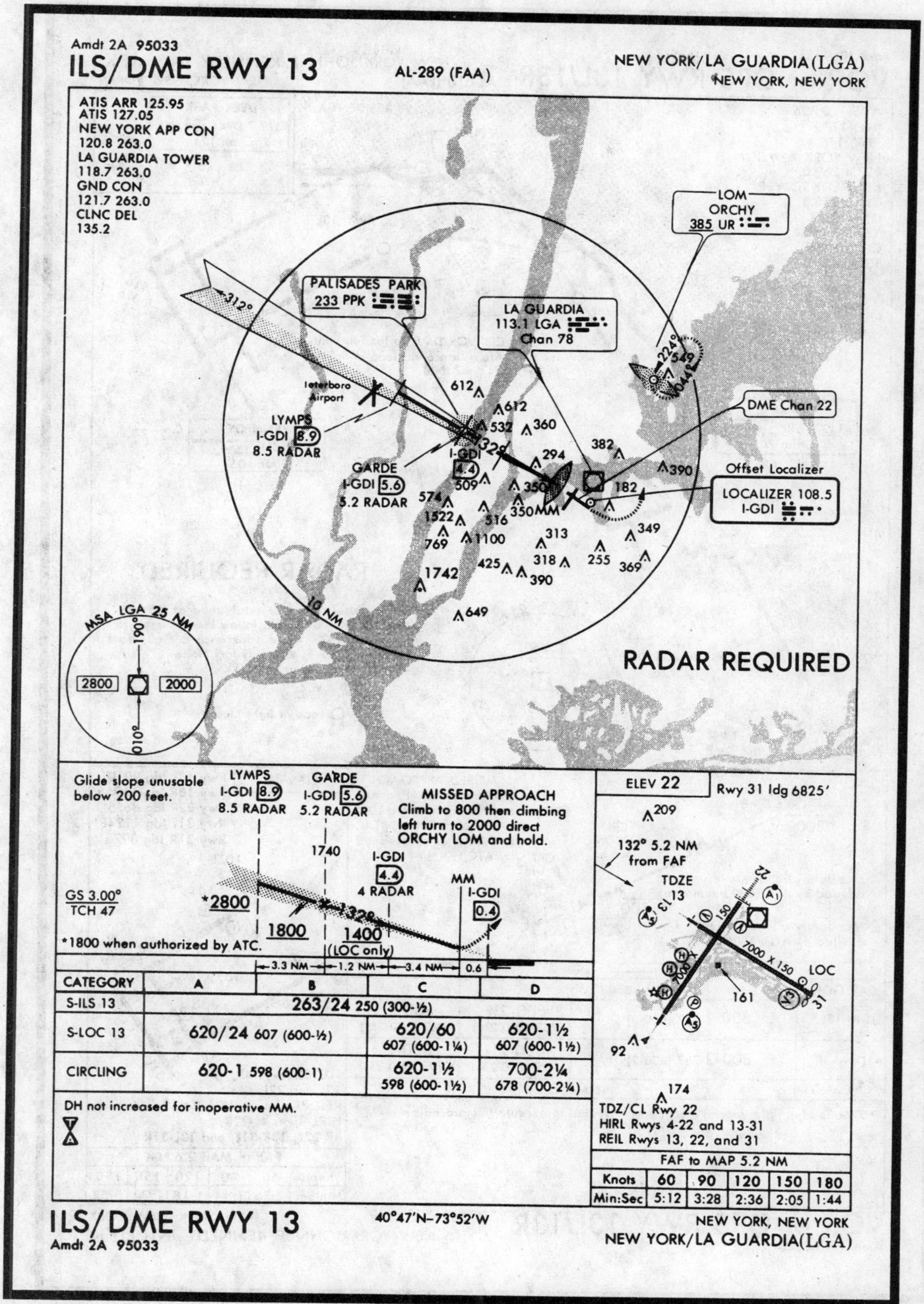

FIGURE 161.—ILS/DME RWY 13 (LGA).

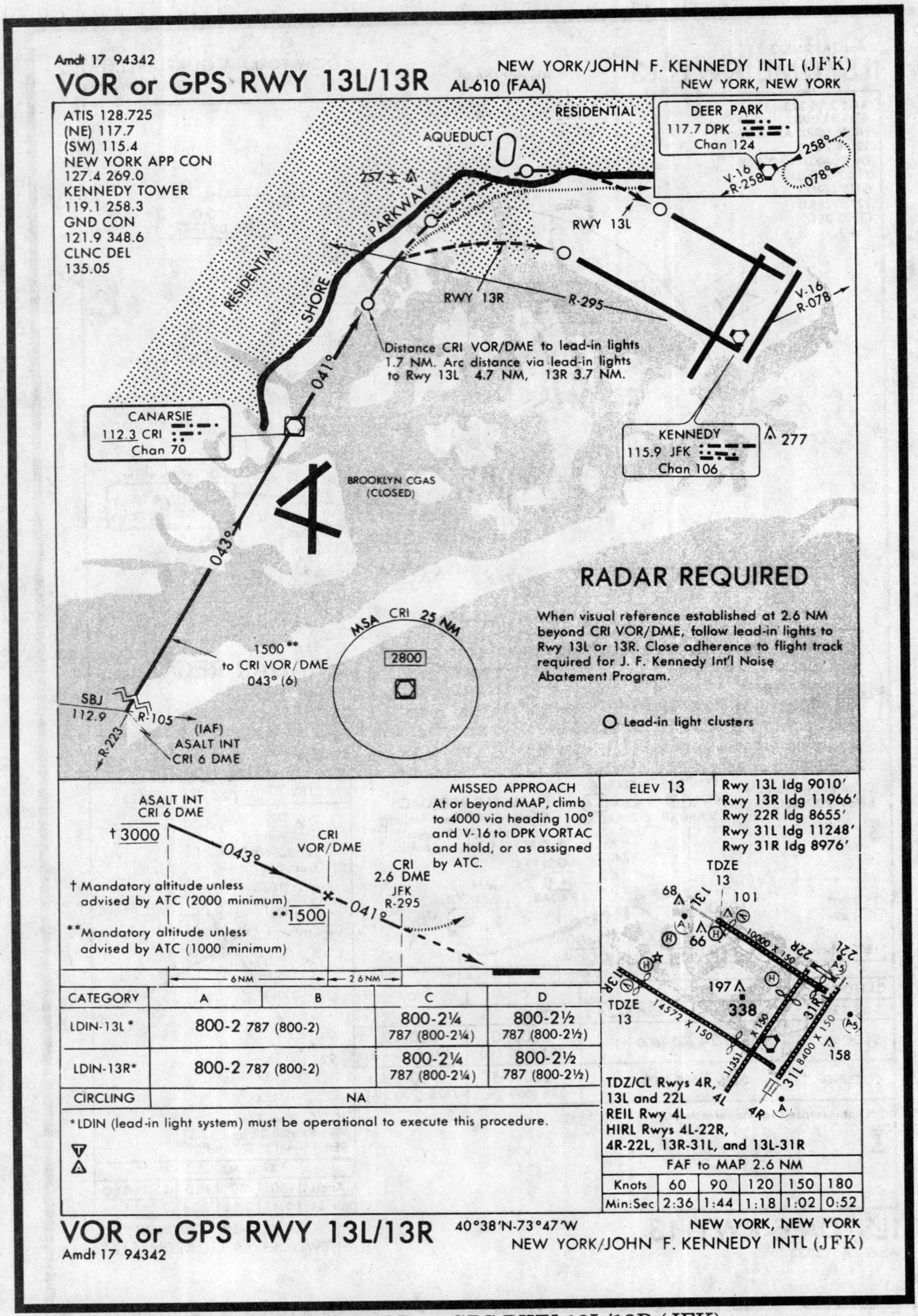

FIGURE 161A.—VOR or GPS RWY 13L/13R (JFK).

COLOR FIGURES AND LEGENDS

On the next 23 pages, we have reproduced the color FAA figures and legends listed below to assist you in studying for the pilot knowledge test.

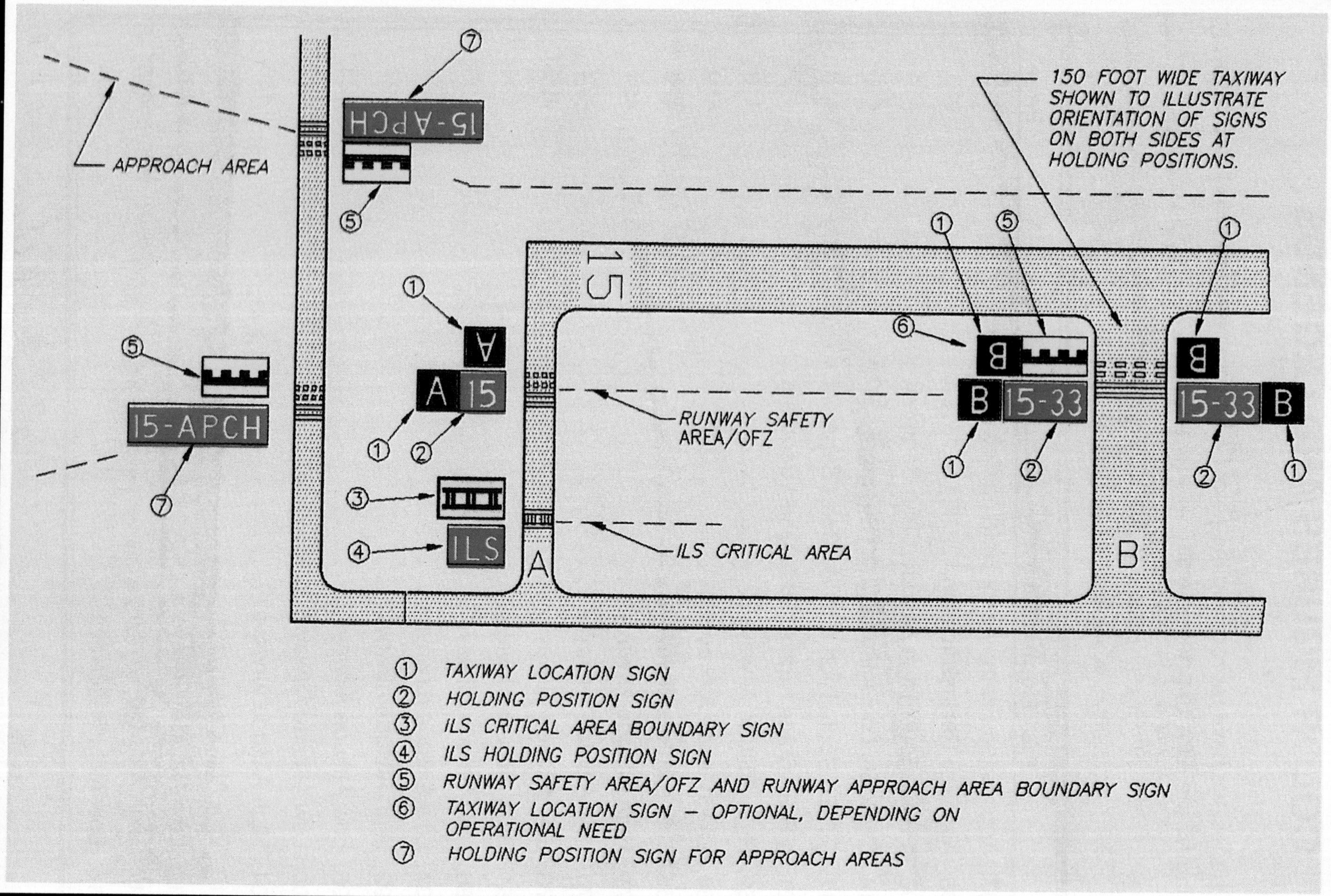

LEGEND 37.—Application Examples for Holding Position Signs.

Airspace Reclassification at a Glance

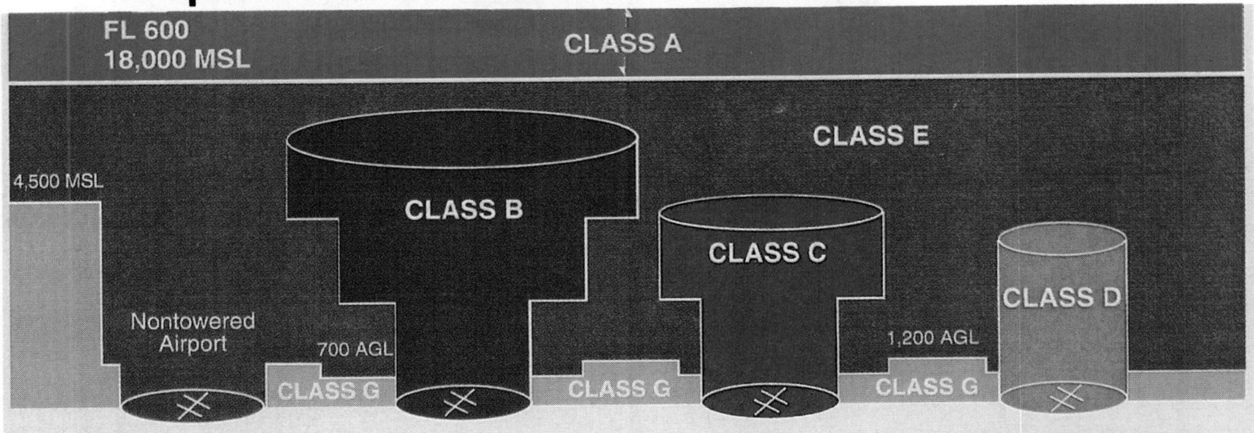

AGL - above ground level FL - flight level MSL - mean sea level

Effective September 16, 1993

And an Easy-to-Read Chart

Airspace Features	Class A	Class B	Class C	Class D	Class E	Class G
Former Airspace Equivalent	Positive Control Area (PCA)	Terminal Control Area (TCA)	Airport Radar Service Area (ARSA)	Airport Traffic Area (ATA) and Control Zone (CZ)	General Controlled Airspace	Uncontrolled Airspace
Operations Permitted	IFR	IFR and VFR	IFR and VFR	IFR and VFR	IFR and VFR	IFR and VFR
Entry Requirements	ATC clearance	ATC clearance	ATC clearance for IFR. All require radio contact.	ATC clearance for IFR. All require radio contact.	ATC clearance for IFR. All IFR require radio contact.	None
Minimum Pilot Qualifications	Instrument Rating	Private or student certificate	Student certificate	Student certificate	Student certificate	Student certificate
Two-way Radio Communications	Yes	Yes	Yes	Yes	Yes for IFR	No
VFR Minimum Visibility	N/A	3 statute miles	3 statute miles	3 statute miles	[1]3 statute miles	[2]1 statute mile
VFR Minimum Distance from Clouds	N/A	Clear of clouds	500' below, 1,000' above, and 2,000' horizontal	500' below, 1,000' above, and 2,000' horizontal	[1]500' below, 1,000' above, and 2,000' horizontal	Clear of clouds
Aircraft Separation	All	All	IFR, SVFR, and runway operations	IFR, SVFR, and runway operations	IFR and SVFR	None
Conflict Resolution	N/A	N/A	Between IFR and VFR ops	No	No	No
Traffic Advisories	N/A	N/A	Yes	Workload permitting	Workload permitting	Workload permitting
Safety Advisories	Yes	Yes	Yes	Yes	Yes	Yes
Differs from ICAO	No	[3]Yes	[3, 4]Yes	[4]Yes for VFR	No	[5]Yes for VFR
Changes the Existing Rule	No	[6]Yes for VFR	No	[7, 8, 9]Yes	No	No

[1] Different visibility minima and distance from cloud requirements exist for operations above 10,000 feet MSL

[2] Different visibility minima and distance from cloud requirements exist for night operations above 10,000 feet MSL, and operations below 1,200 feet AGL

[3] ICAO does not have speed restrictions in this class - U.S. will retain the 250 KIAS rule

[4] ICAO requires an ATC clearance for VFR

[5] ICAO requires 3 statute miles visibility

[6] Reduces the cloud clearance distance from standard to clear of clouds

[7] Generally, the upper limits of the Control Zone have been lowered from 14,500 MSL to 2,500 feet AGL

[8] Generally, the upper limits of the Airport Traffic Area has been lowered from 2,999 feet AGL to 2,500 feet AGL

[9] The requirement for two-way communications for Airport Traffic Areas has been retained

LEGEND 38.—Airspace Reclassification.

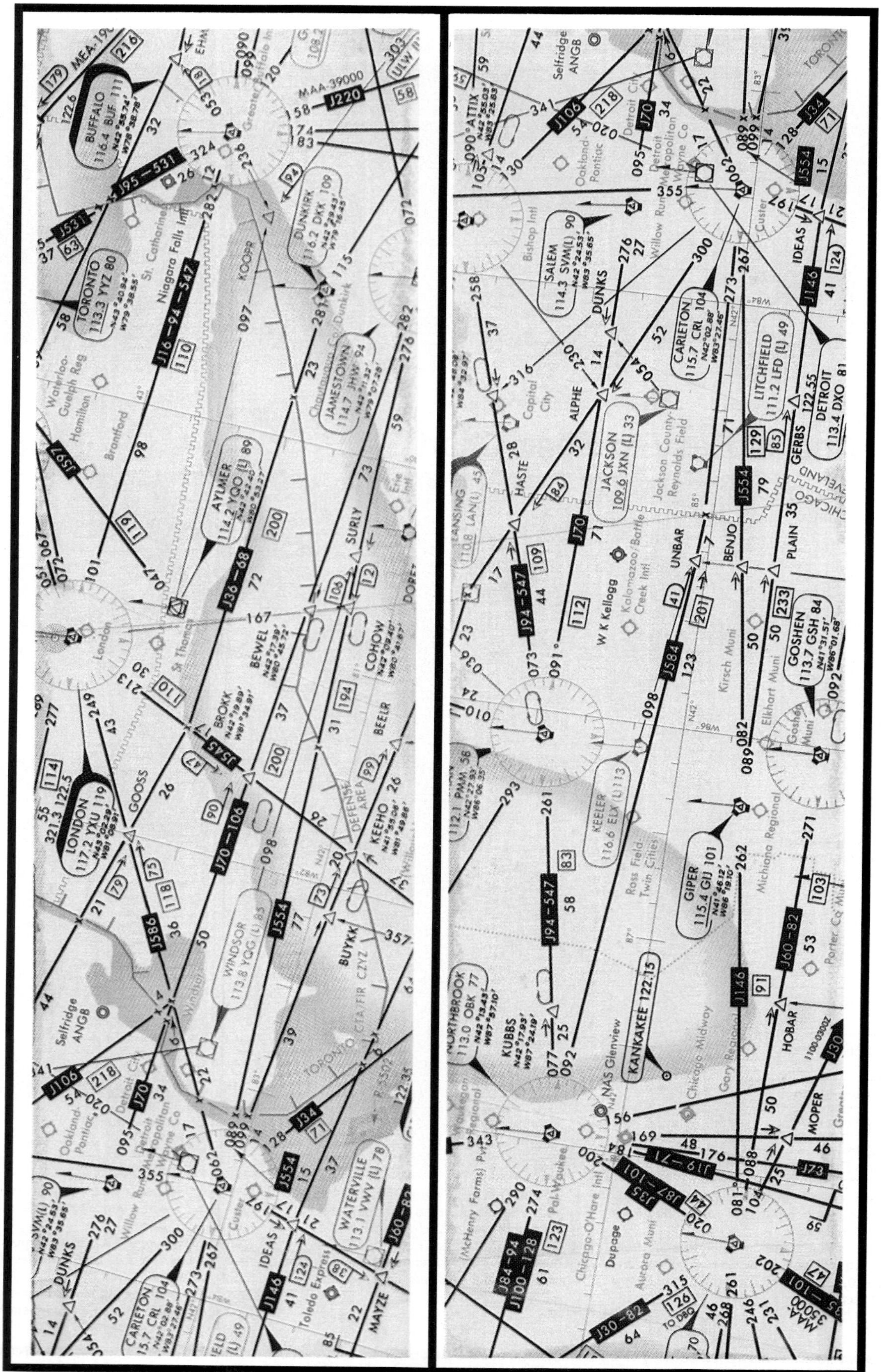

FIGURE 96.—IFR En Route High Altitude Chart Segment.

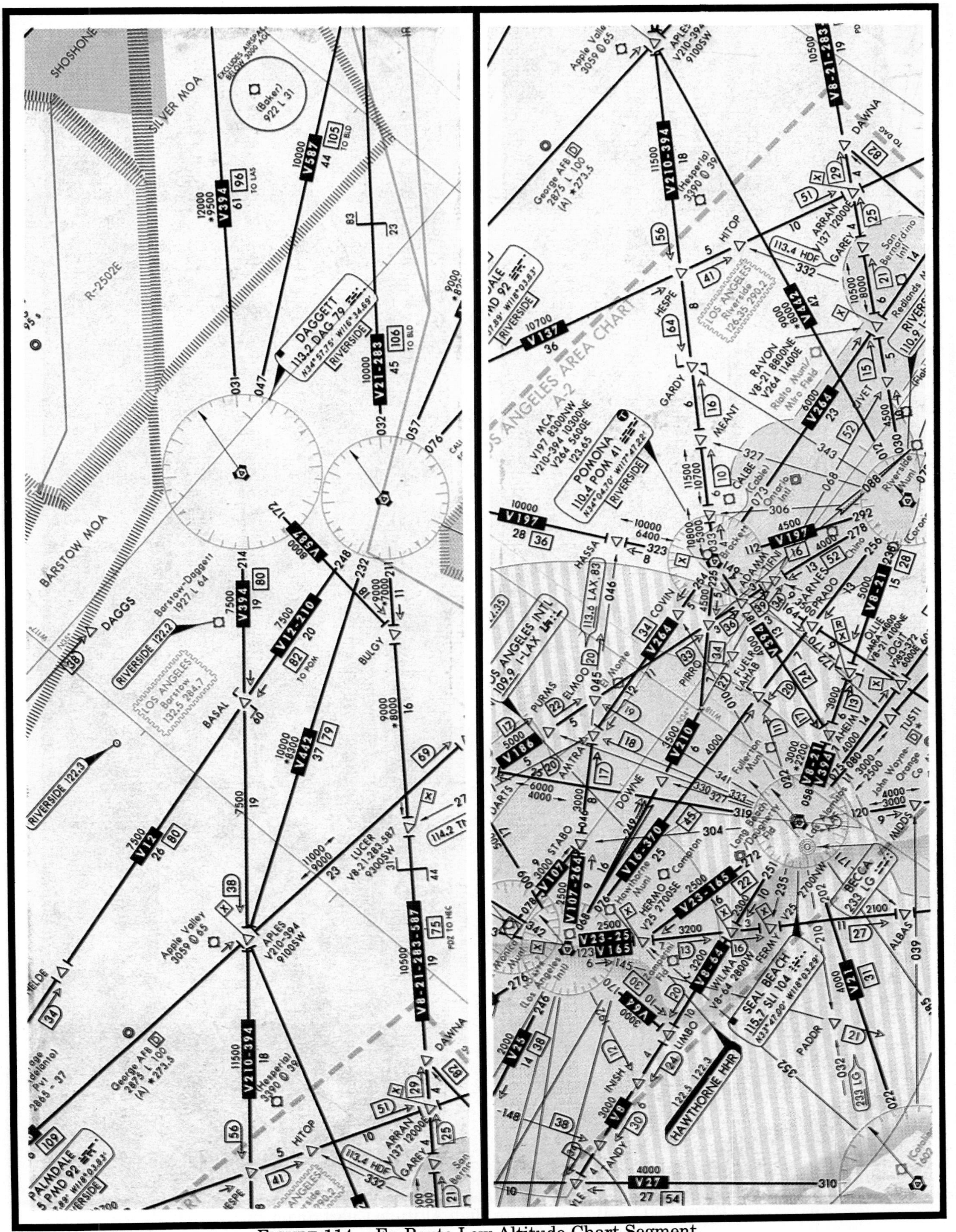

FIGURE 114.—En Route Low Altitude Chart Segment.

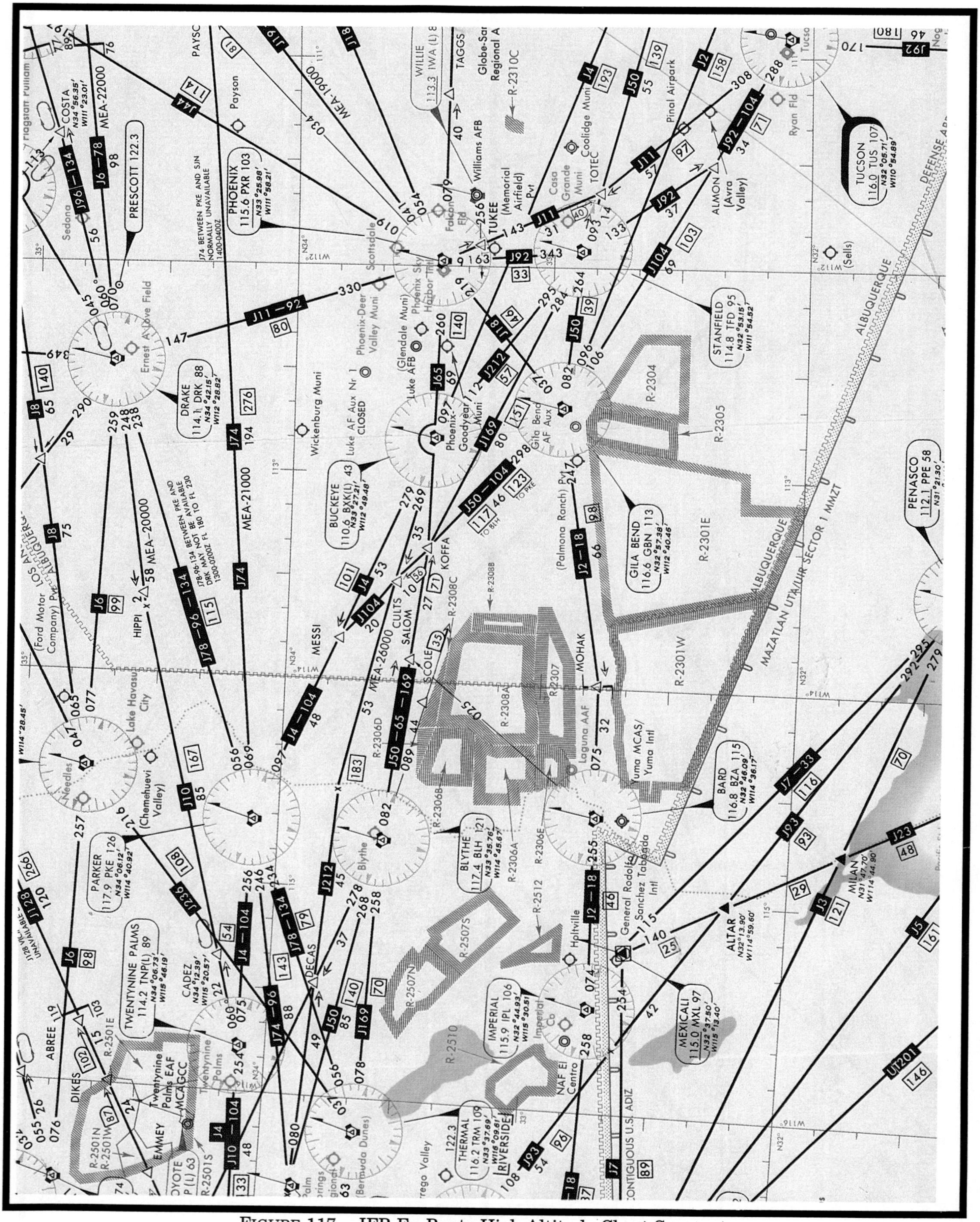

FIGURE 117.—IFR En Route High Altitude Chart Segment.

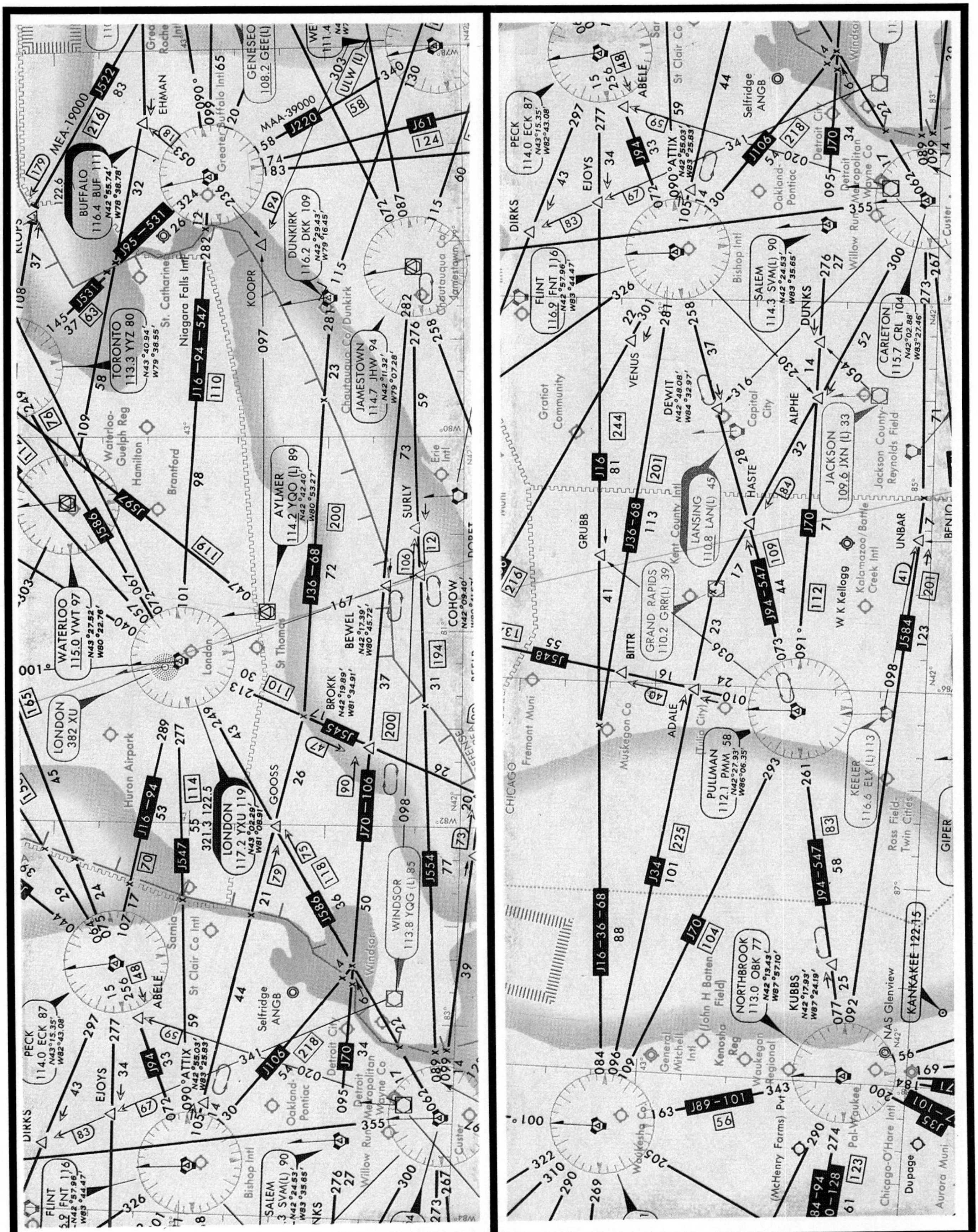

FIGURE 121.—IFR En Route High Altitude Chart Segment.

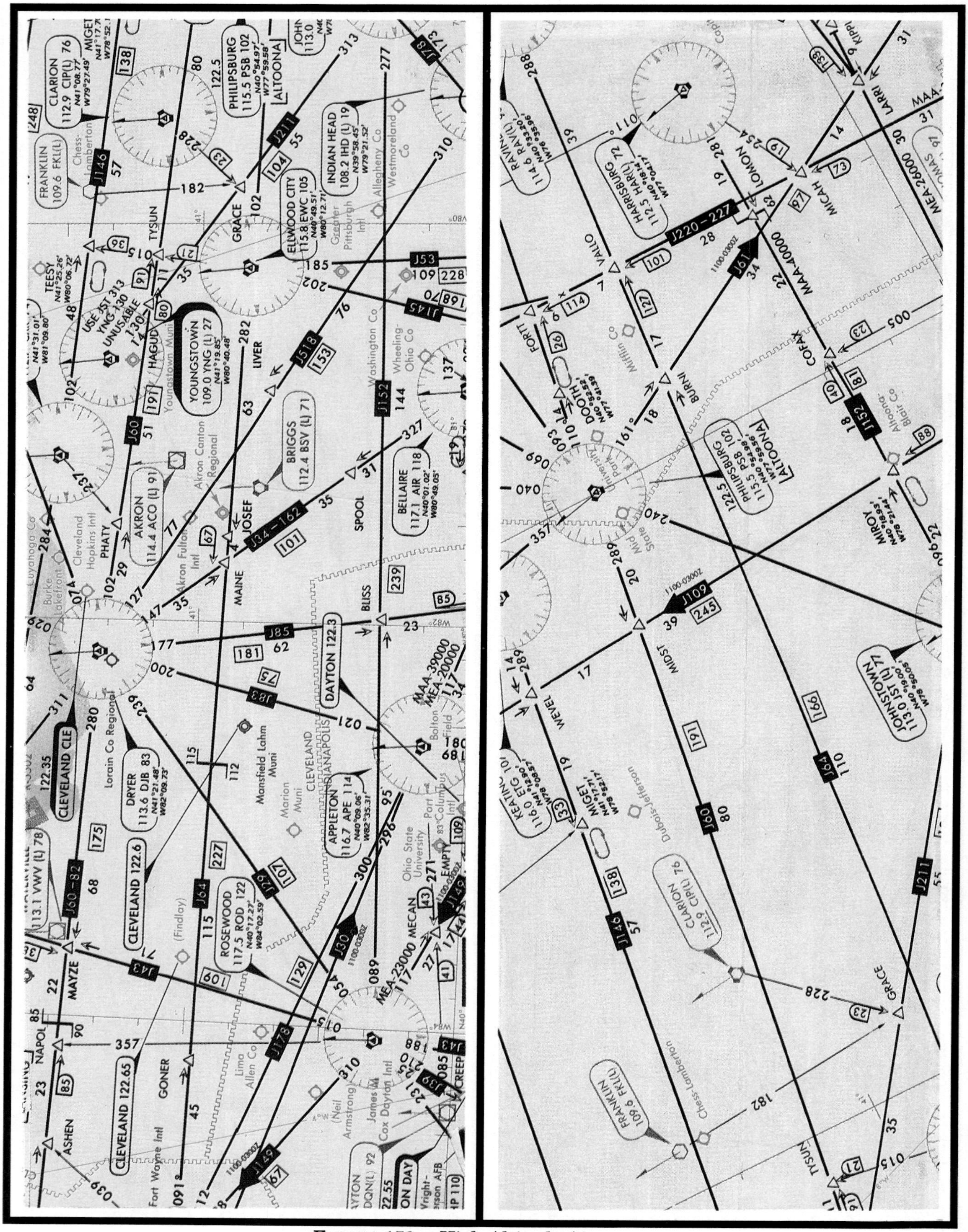

FIGURE 159.—High Altitude Airways.

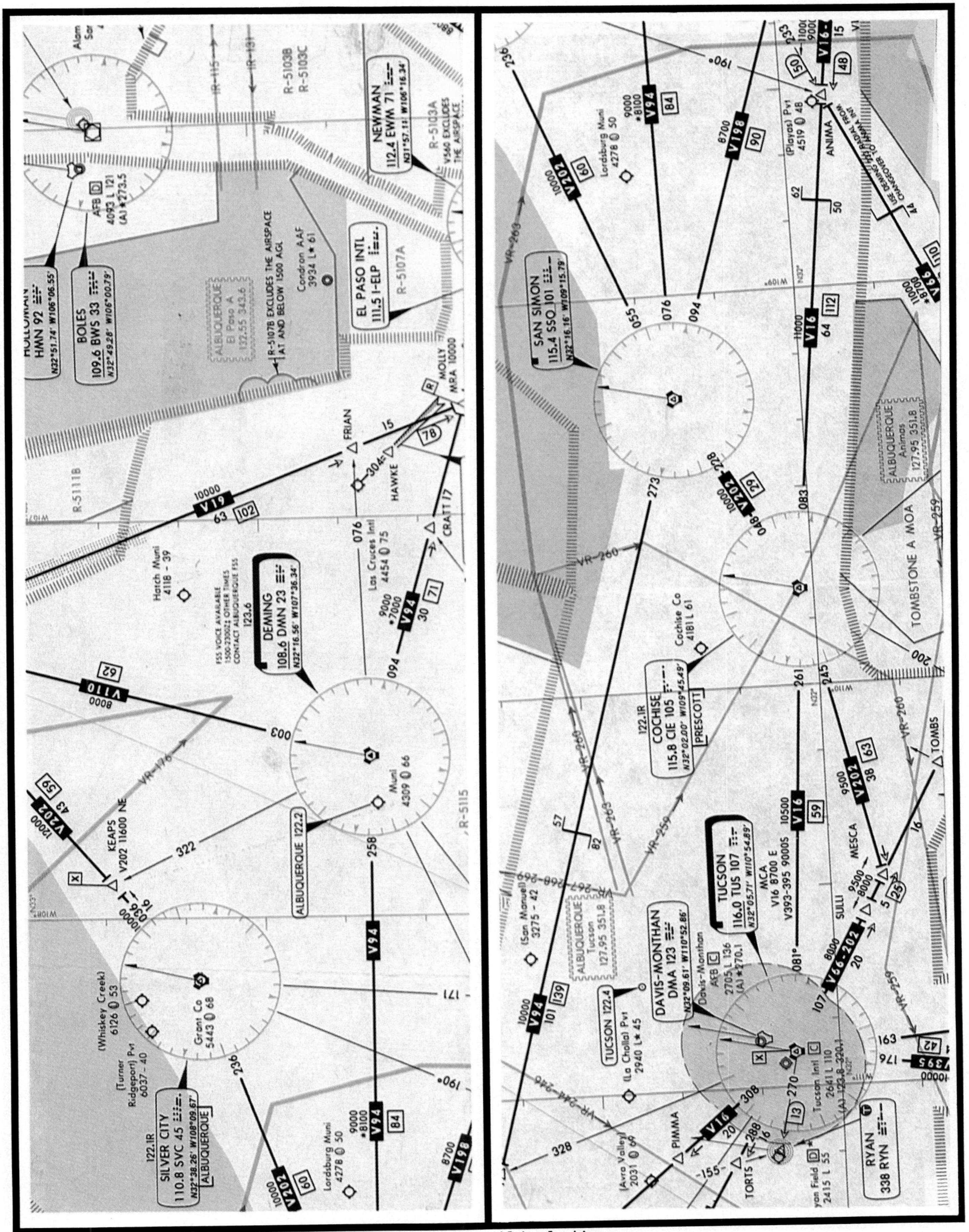

FIGURE 164.—Low Altitude Airways.

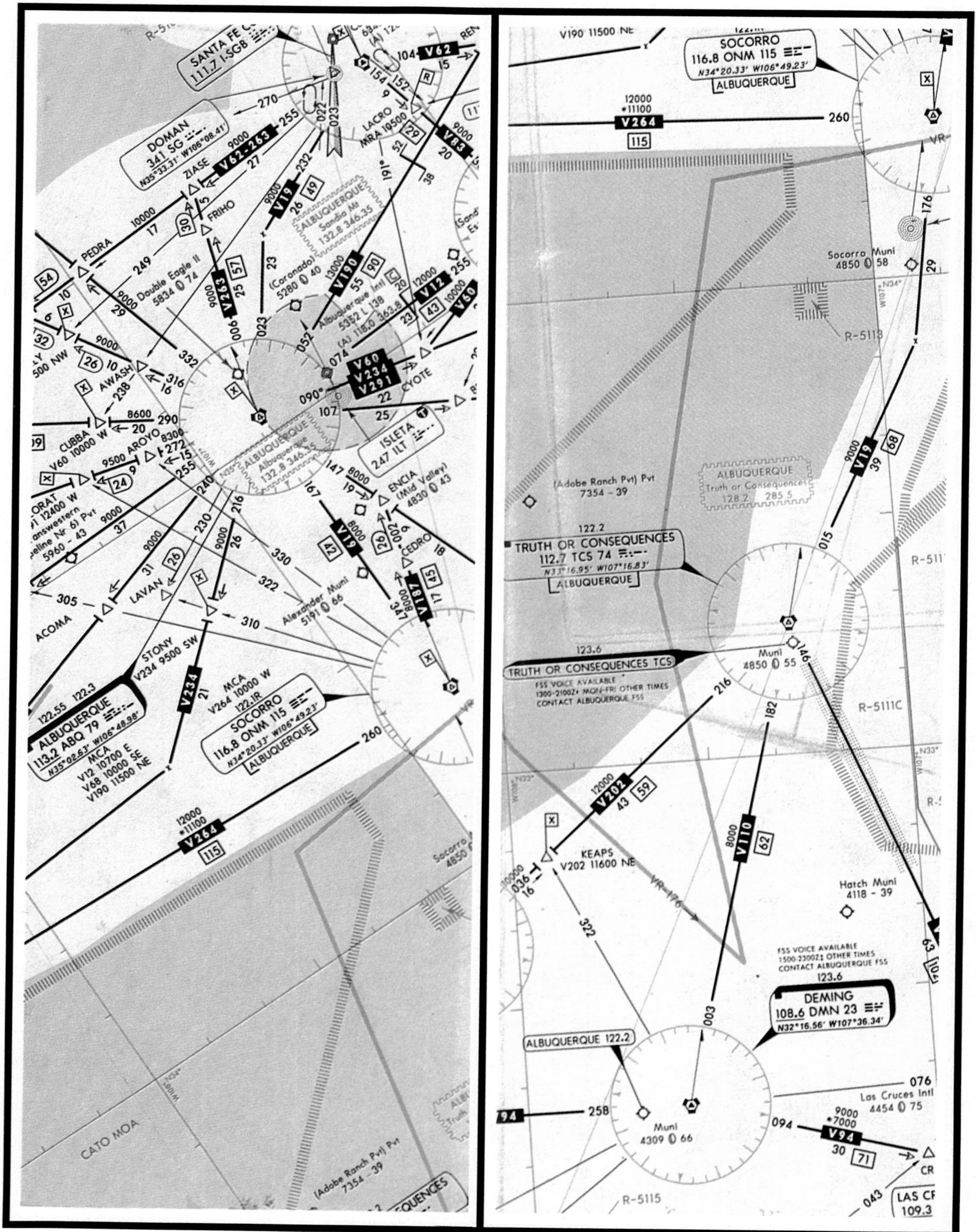

FIGURE 165.—Low Altitude Airways.

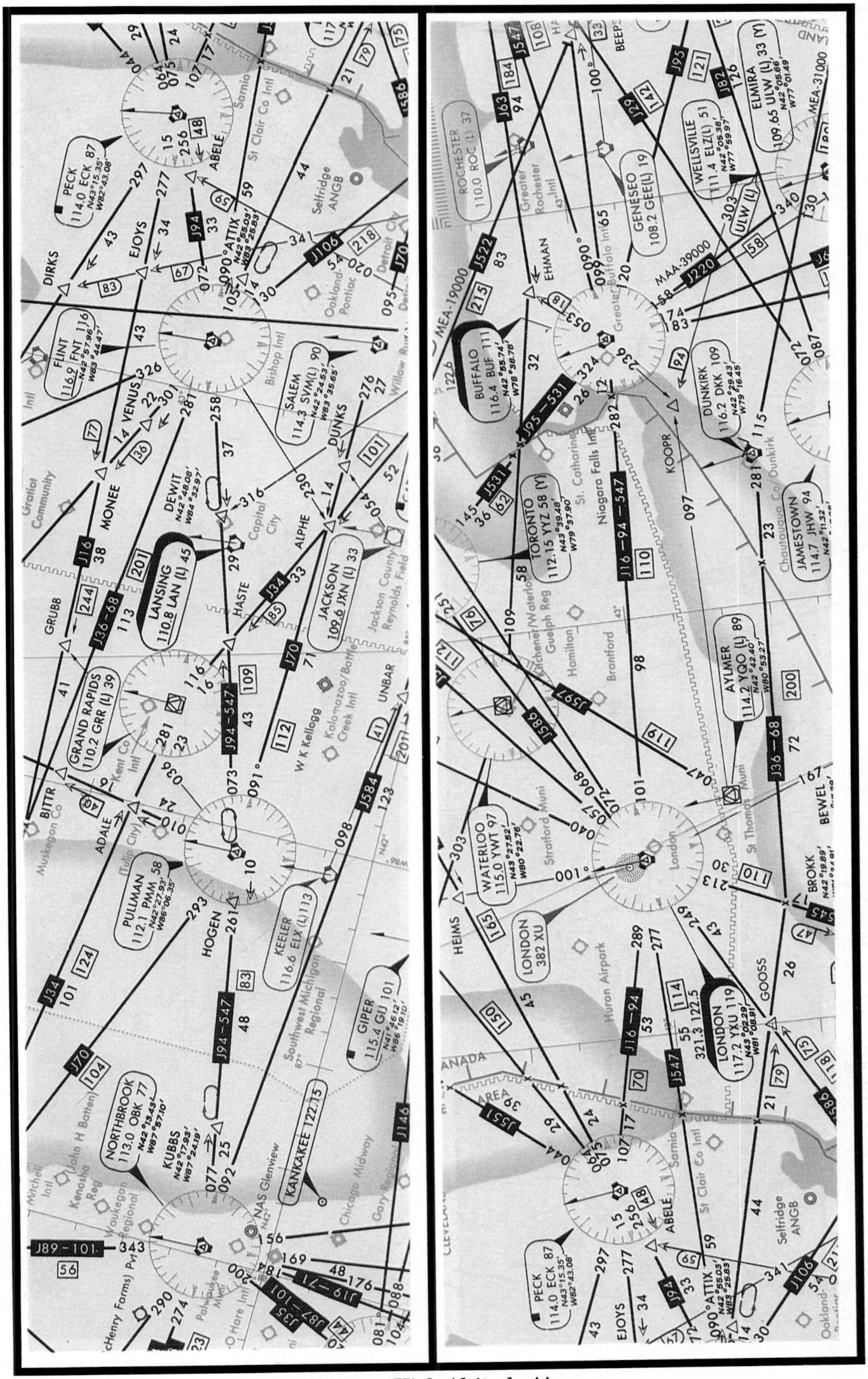

FIGURE 171.—High Altitude Airways.

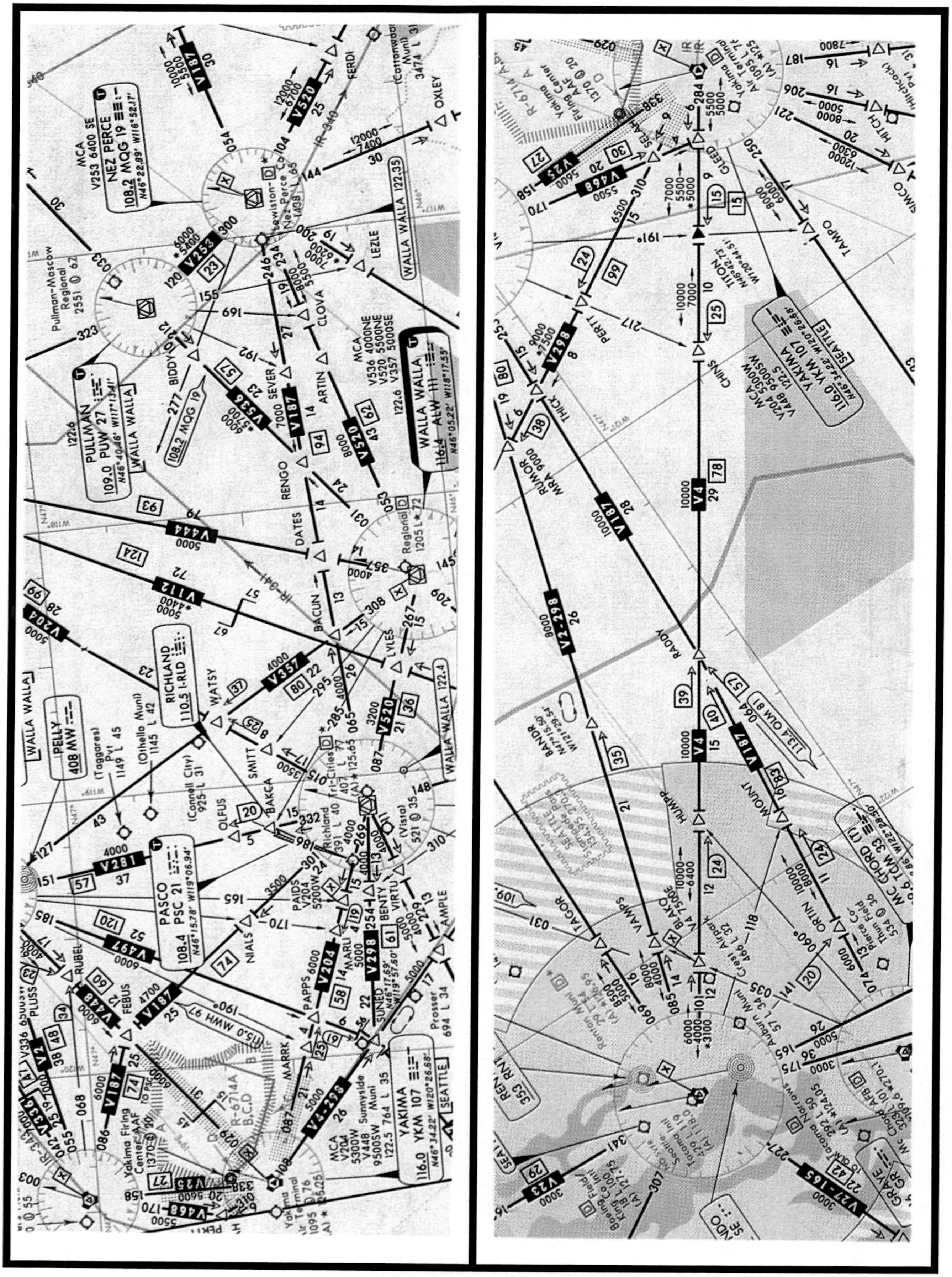

FIGURE 175.—Low Altitude Airways.

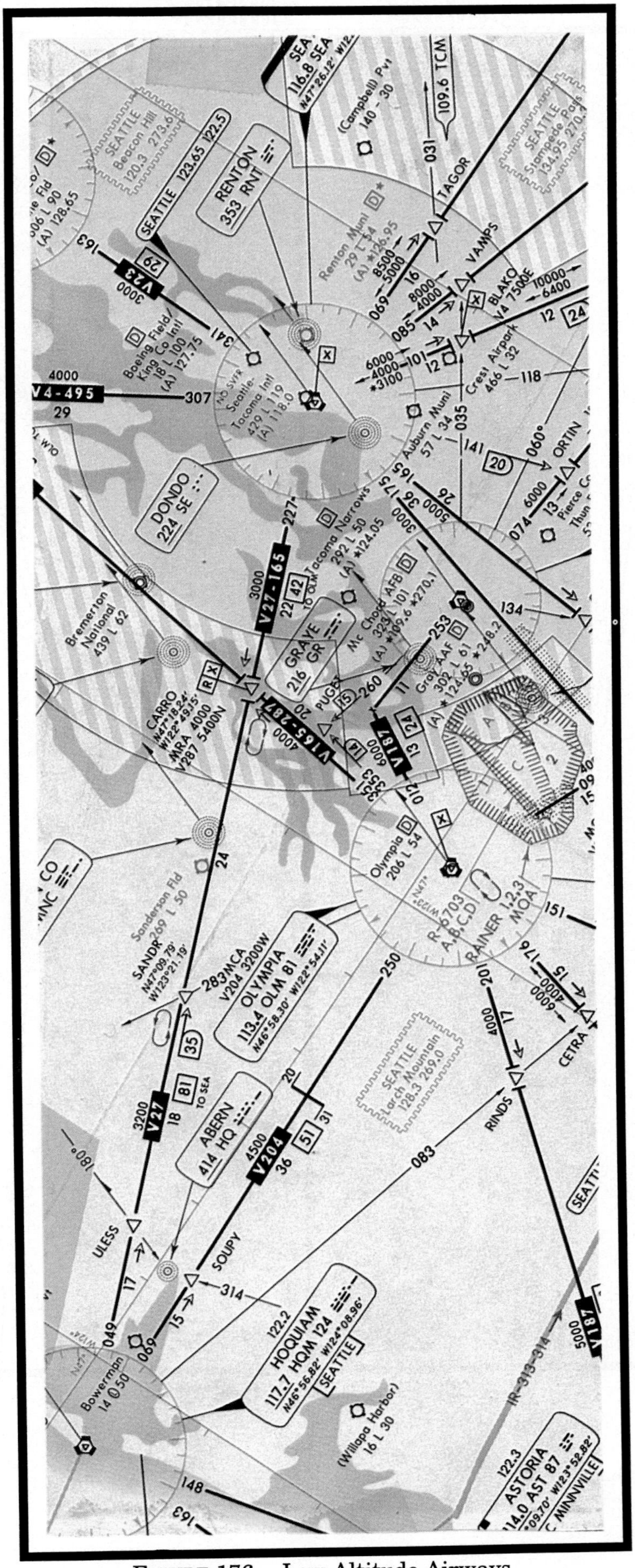

FIGURE 176.—Low Altitude Airways.

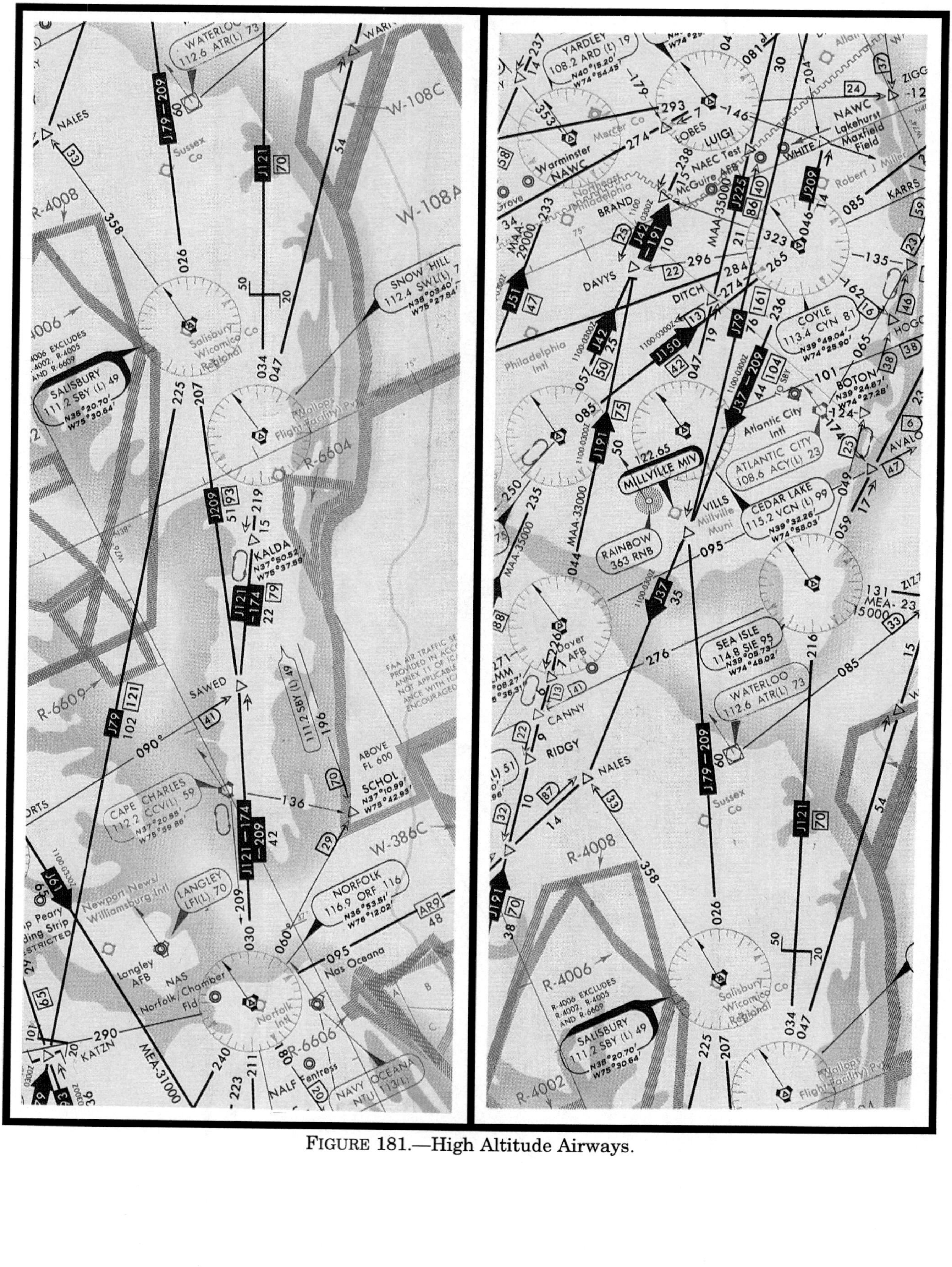

FIGURE 181.—High Altitude Airways.

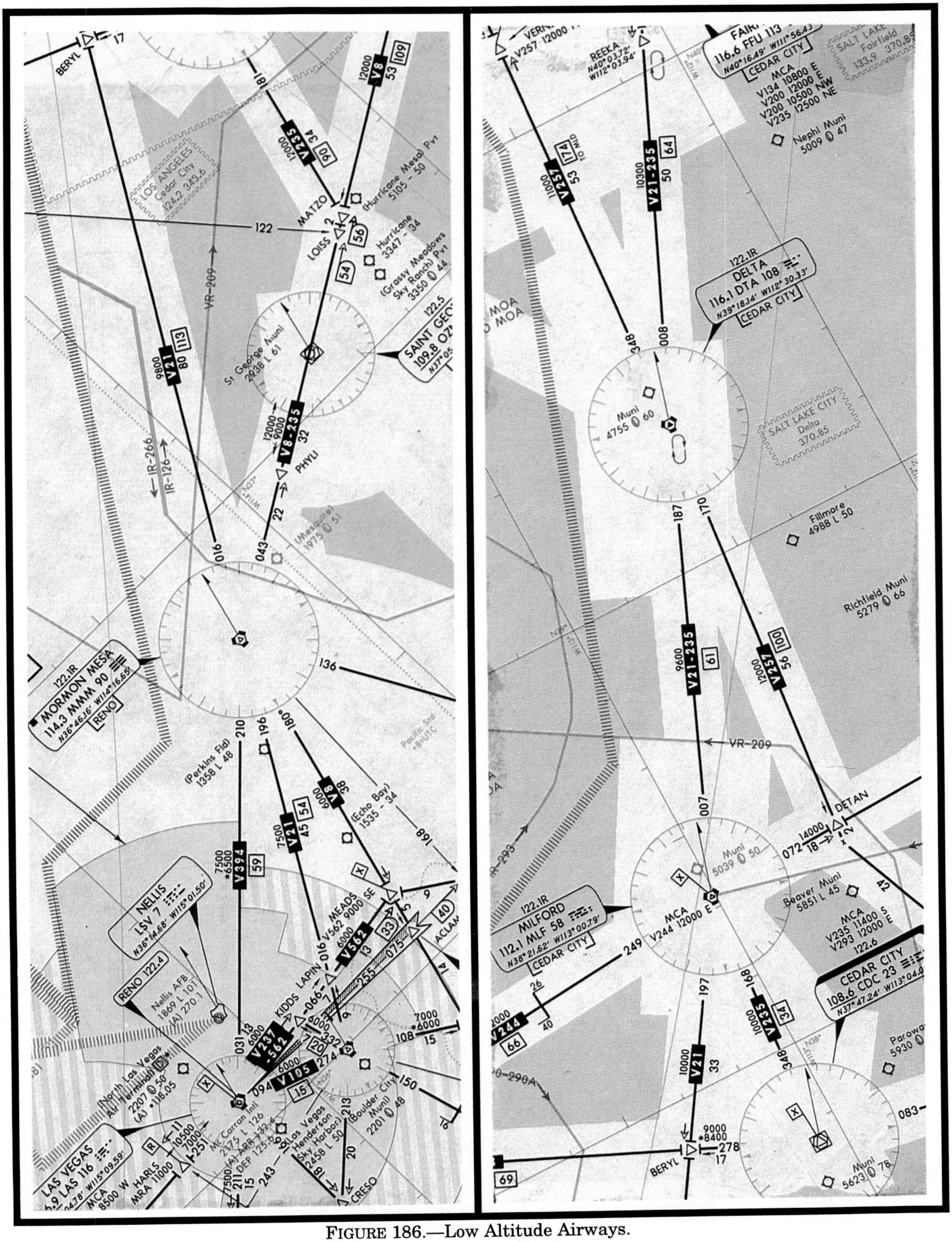

FIGURE 186.—Low Altitude Airways.

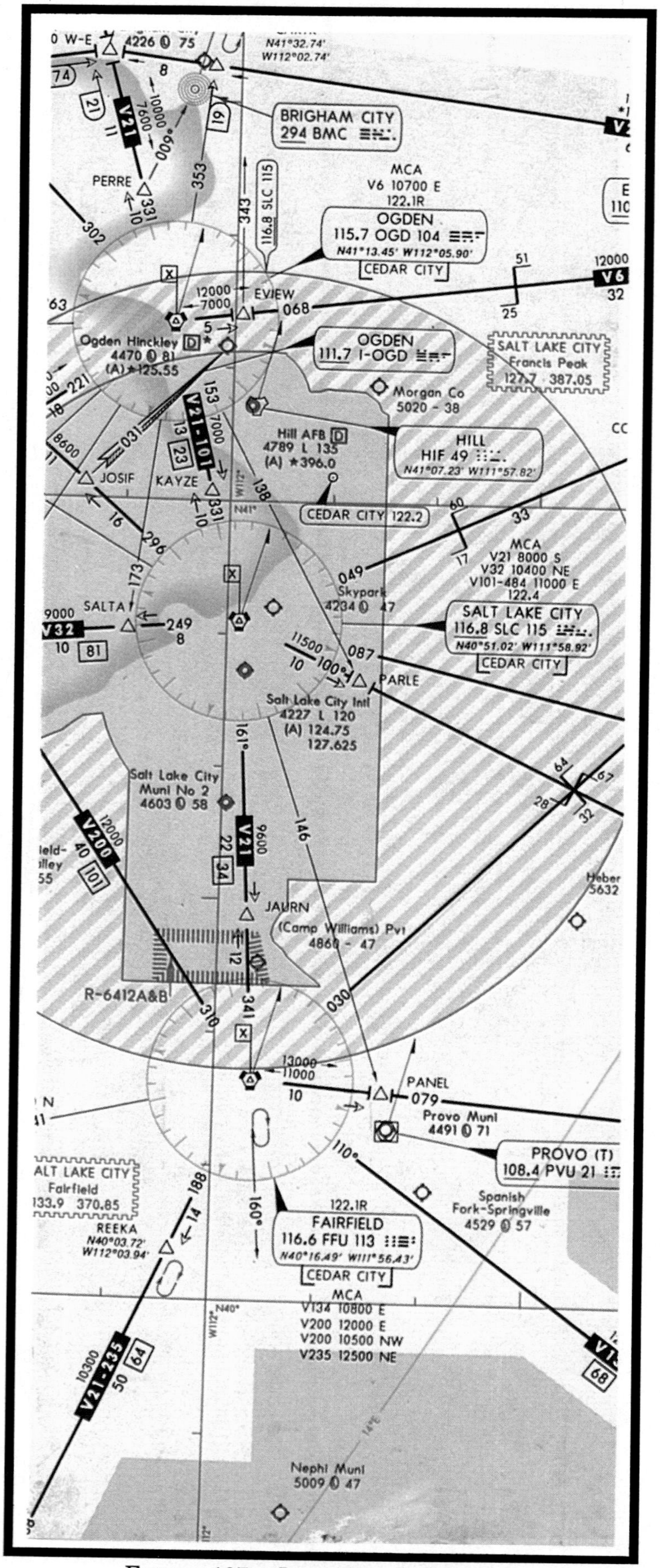

FIGURE 187.—Low Altitude Airways.

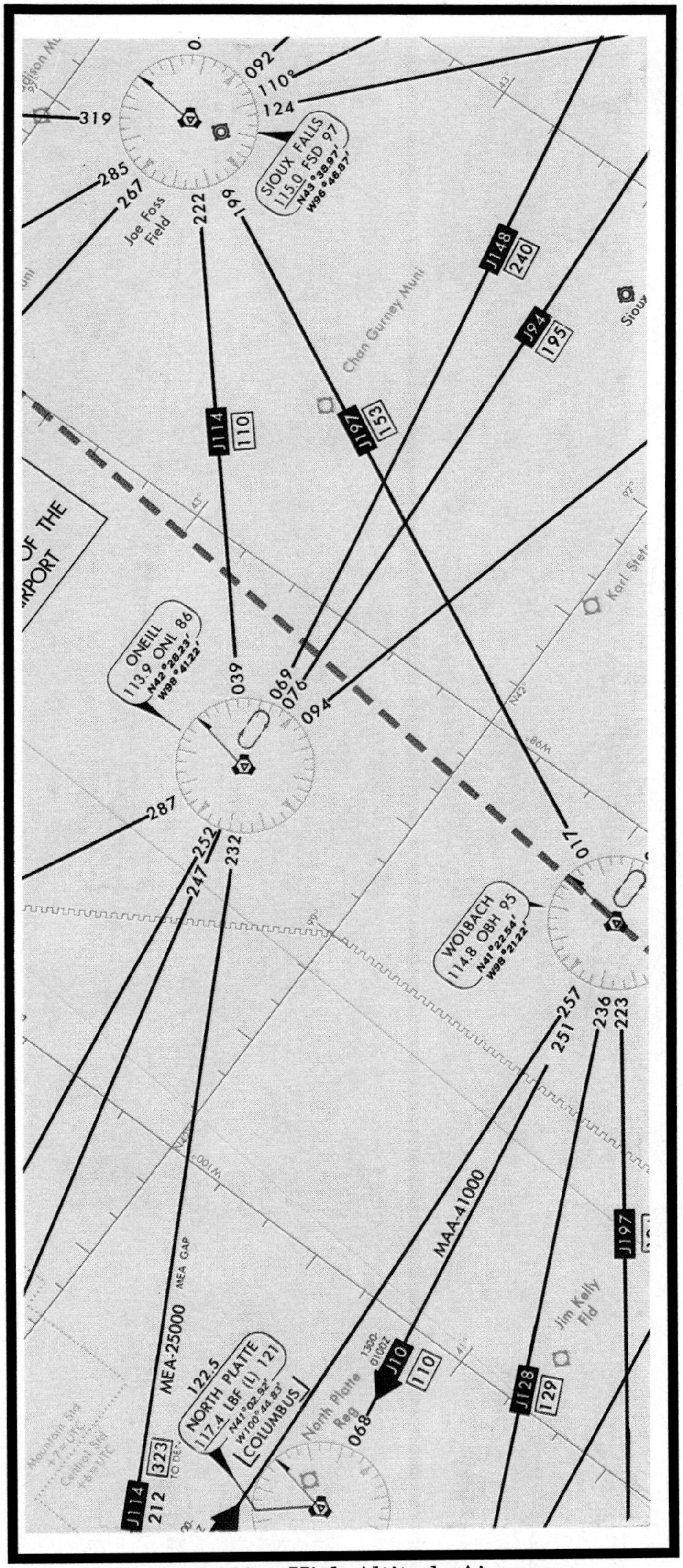

FIGURE 192.—High Altitude Airways.

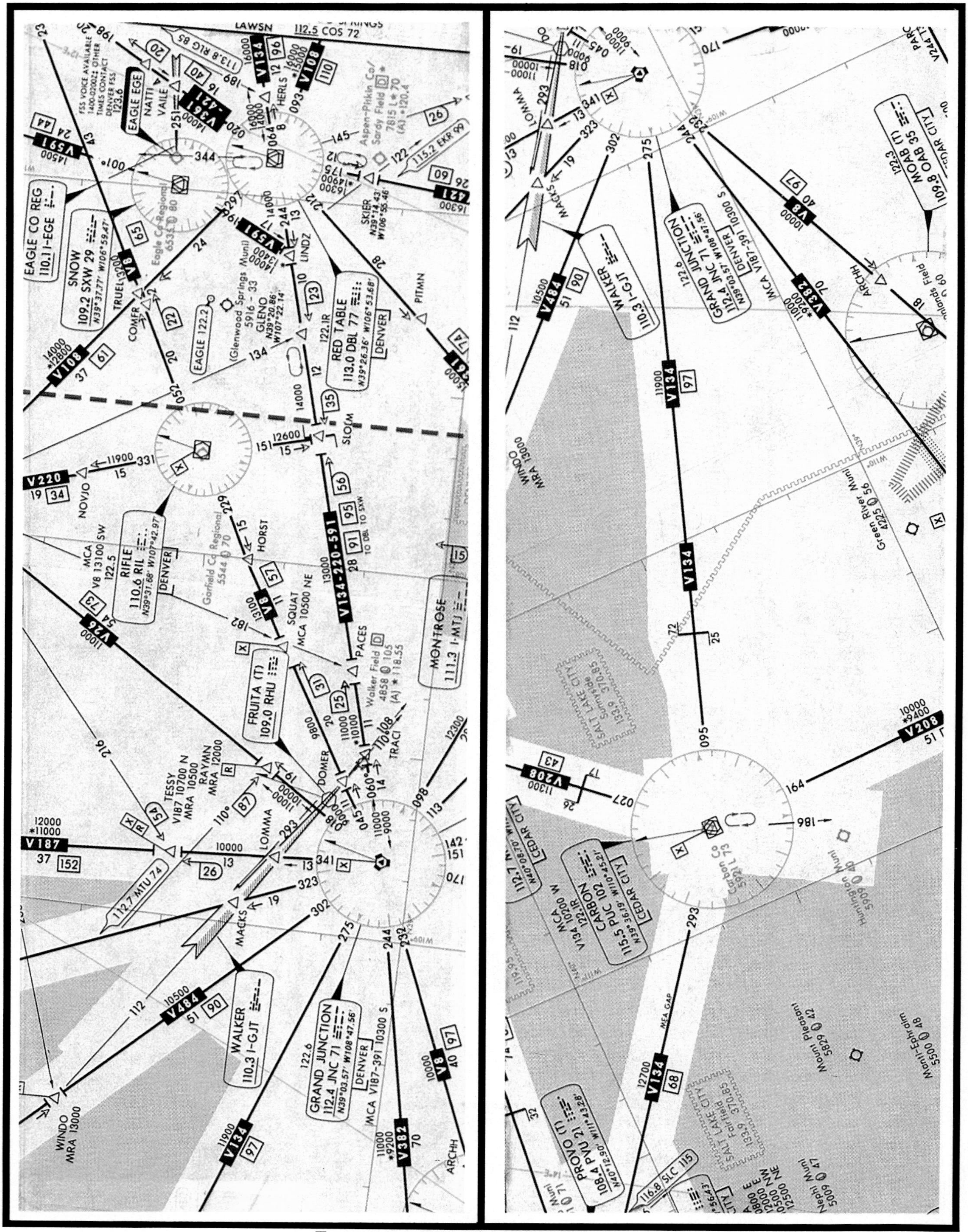

FIGURE 199.—Low Altitude Airways.

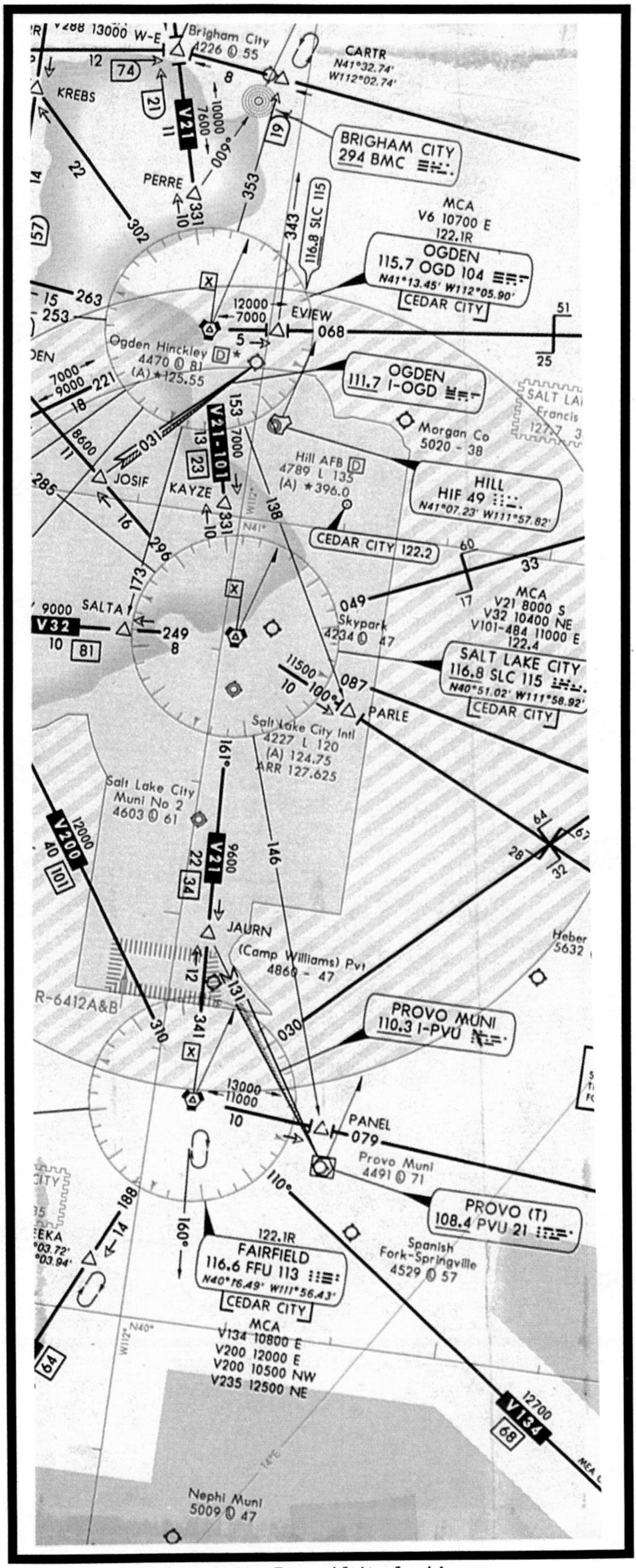

FIGURE 200.—Low Altitude Airways.

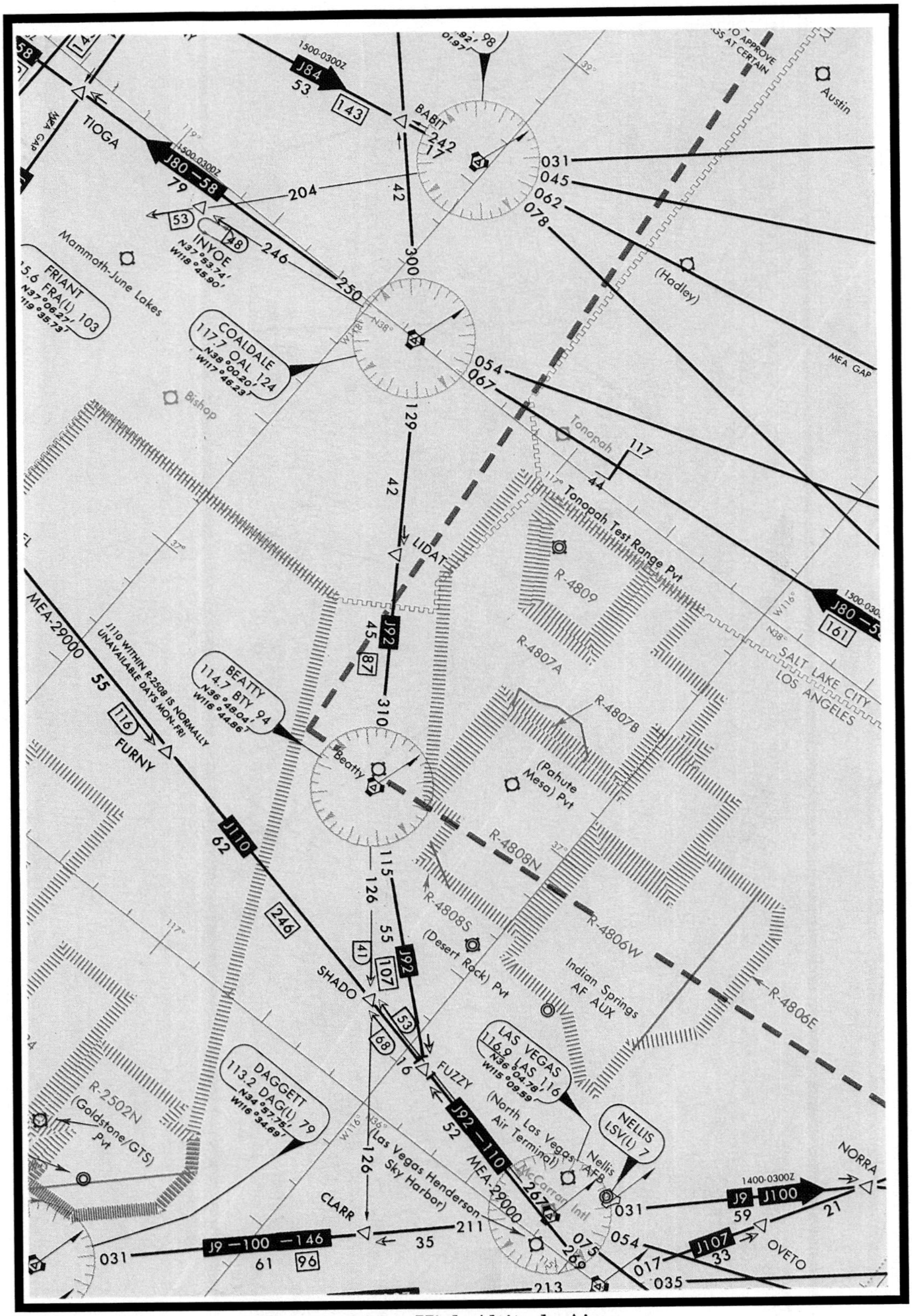

FIGURE 204.—High Altitude Airways.

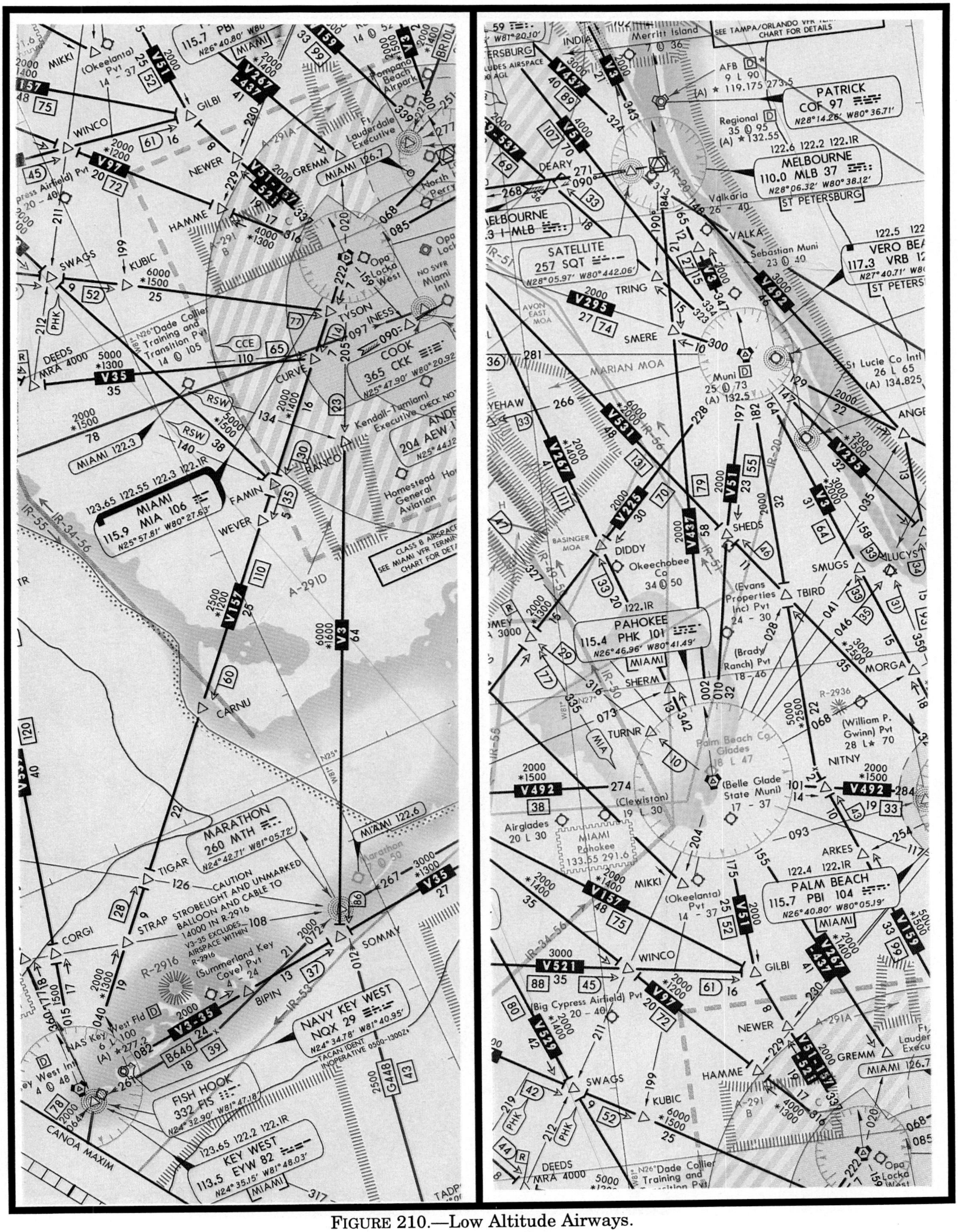

FIGURE 210.—Low Altitude Airways.

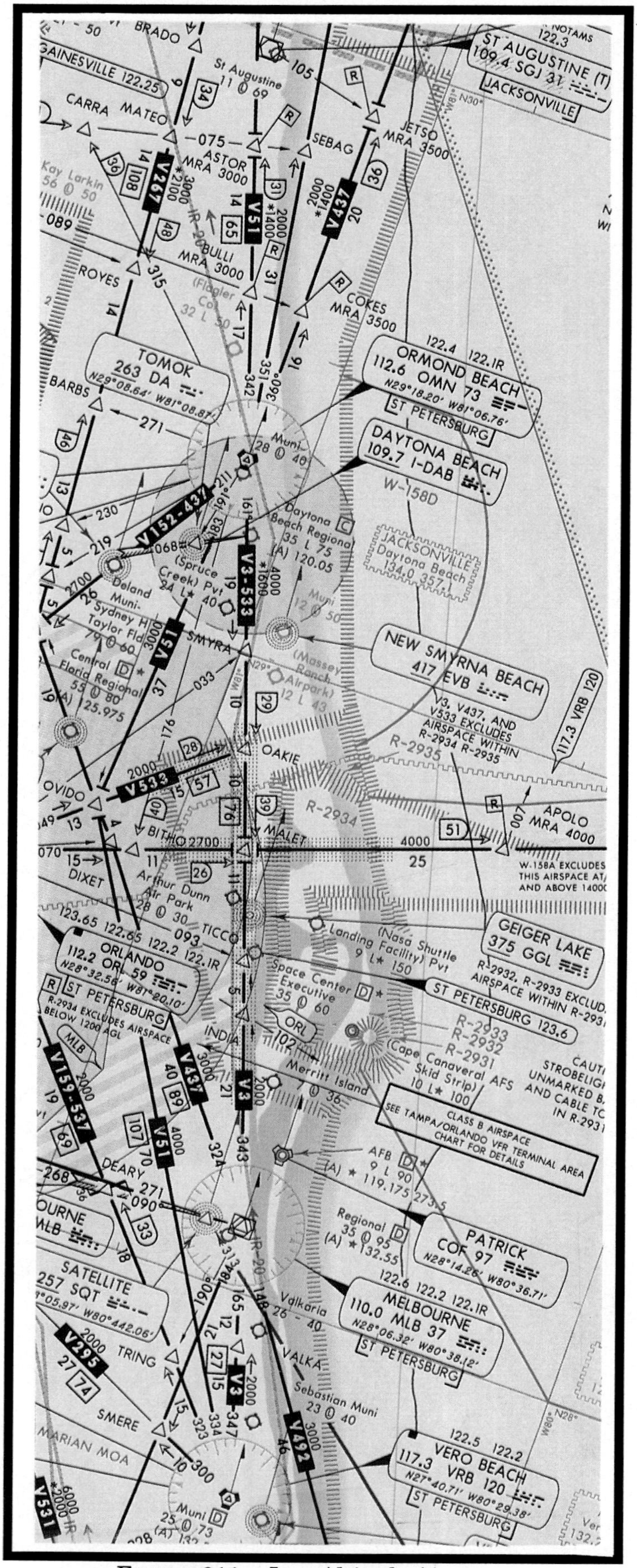

FIGURE 211.—Low Altitude Airways.

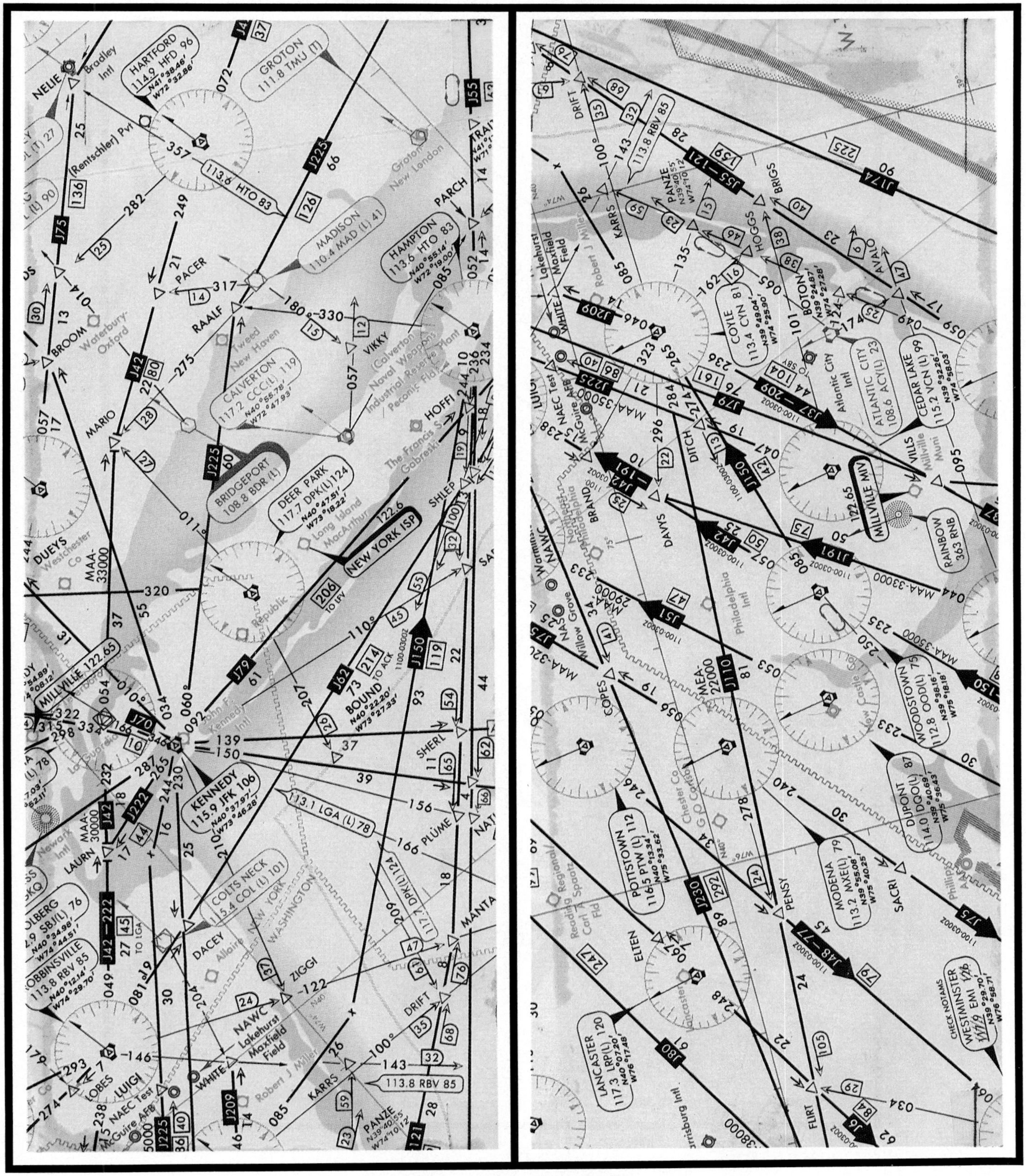

FIGURE 217.—High Altitude Airways.

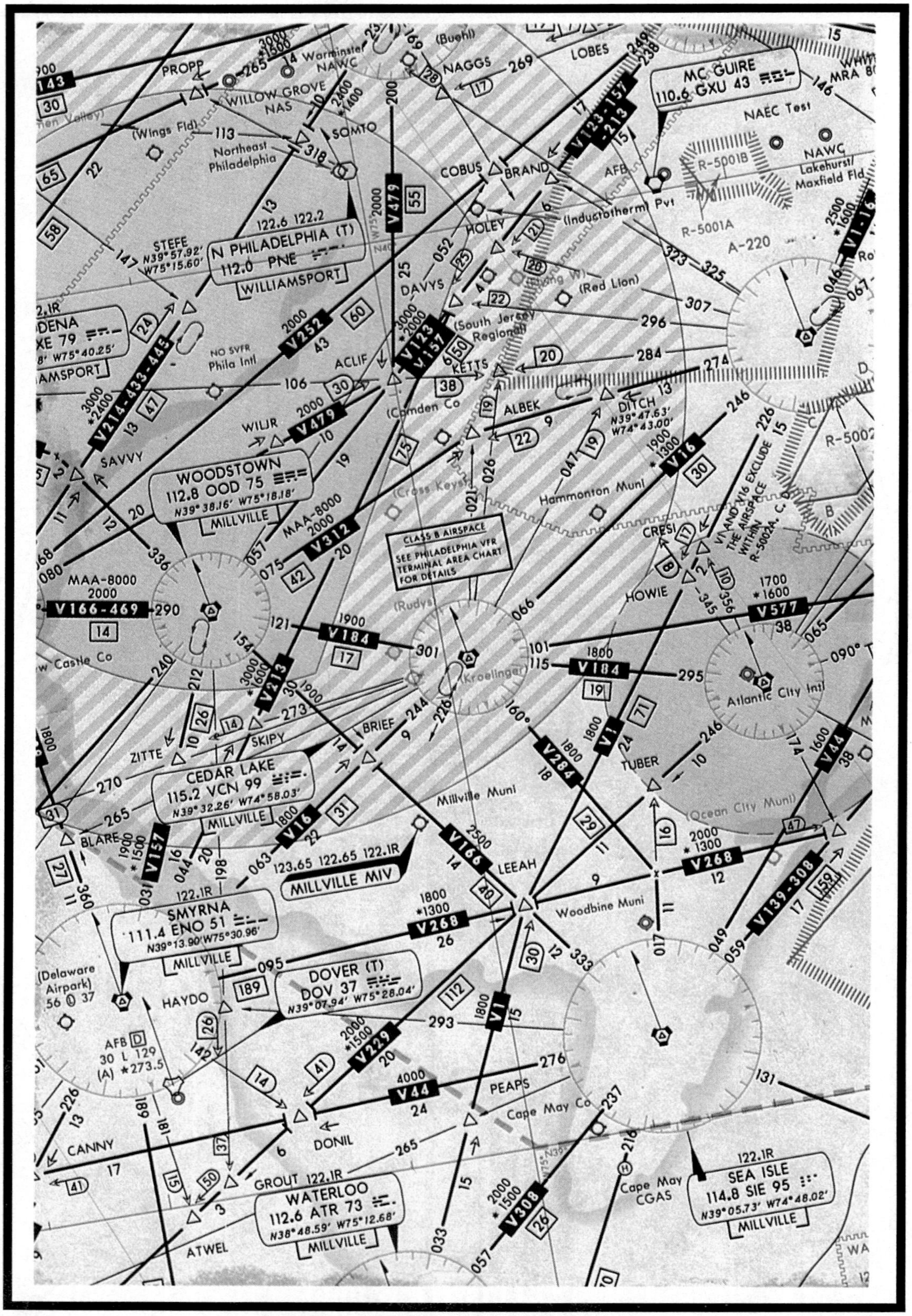

FIGURE 218.—Low Altitude Airways.

10.7 B-727 LAX TO PHX (Questions 70-86)

Questions 70 through 86 pertain to an IFR flight from Los Angeles International Airport, Los Angeles, California to the Phoenix Sky Harbor Airport, Phoenix, Arizona.

The route of flight is given in block 8 on the flight plan portion of Fig. 115 on page 442. The partially completed flight planning log is given on the bottom portion of Fig. 115.

The following figures are used to answer the 17 questions concerning this flight.

Fig.	Page	Title
107	372	ILS RWY 25L (CAT II) - LAX
115	442	Flight Plan/Flight Log
116	443	Imperial Three Departure (IPL3.IPL) (PILOT NAV)
117	416	IFR En Route High Altitude Chart Segment
118	444	Arlin Nine Arrival (ARLIN.ARLIN9)
118A	445	LOC BC RWY 26L (PHX)
118B	446	VOR or TACAN or GPS RWY 11L (TUS)
118C	447	Excerpt from *Airport/Facility Directory*

10.7 B-727 LAX to PHX

70.
9578. (Refer to figures 107, 115, 116, 117, 118, and 118C on pages 372, 442, 443, 416, 444, and 447.) What is the ETE at .78 Mach?

A—1 hour 08 minutes.
B—1 hour 02 minutes.
C—1 hour 05 minutes.

Answer (A) is correct (9578). *(IFH Chap XIII)*

To determine the estimated time en route (ETE) from Los Angeles to Phoenix Sky Harbor, you must complete the flight log in Fig. 115. The variation at LAX is 15°E (Fig. 107) and the variation at PHX is 12°E (Fig. 118C). The average variation is approximately 13°E, which is subtracted from the true wind direction of 300° to determine the magnetic wind direction of 287° at 43 kt. The temperature (ISA) at FL 270 is –39°C [15°C – (27 x 2)]; thus ISA –2 is –41°C.

To obtain TAS from .78 Mach, use the calculator side of your flight computer and set OAT at –41°C over the Mach index. Find the Mach number on the "minutes" scale, and read TAS above on "miles" scale, or 463 kt.

The flight log below has been expanded to provide more detail.

	Distance	MC	Ground-speed	Time
Level-off	43G	X	X	0:19:00G
OCN	50	090	504	0:05:57
JLI	42	083	502	0:05:01
KUMBA	35	115	506	0:04:09
IPL	27	078	500	0:03:14
BZA	46	074	498	0:05:32
MOHAK	32	075	499	0:03:50
BXK R-215	15	067	495	0:01:49
HYDRR	42	035	474	0:05:19
ARLIN	19	076	499	0:02:17
PHX	X	X	X	0:12:00G
				1:08:08

G = Given

Answer (B) is incorrect because an ETE of 1 hr. 2 min. would require a TAS of approximately .92 Mach, not .78 Mach. Answer (C) is incorrect because an ETE of 1 hr. 5 min. would require a TAS of Mach .84, not Mach .78.

71.
9579. (Refer to figures 115, 116, 117, 118, and 118C on pages 442, 443, 416, 444, and 447.) What is the total fuel required at .78 Mach?

A—22,140 pounds.
B—22,556 pounds.
C—22,972 pounds.

Answer (B) is correct (9579). *(IFH Chap XIII)*
To determine fuel requirements from Los Angeles to Phoenix Sky Harbor at .78 Mach, complete the fuel portion of the flight log in Fig. 115. Use 9,600 PPH fuel flow from level-off to ARLIN INT and 9,250 PPH fuel flow for the reserve and alternate requirements.

	Time	Fuel (lb.)
Level-off	0:19:00G	4,510.0G
OCN	0:05:57	952.0
JLI	0:05:01	802.7
KUMBA	0:04:09	664.0
IPL	0:03:14	517.3
BZA	0:05:32	885.3
MOHAK	0:03:50	613.3
BXK R-215	0:01:49	290.7
HYDRR	0:05:19	850.7
ARLIN	0:02:16	362.7
Descent and approach	0:12:00G	1,140.0G
Flight to TUS	0:26:00G	4,008.3
Reserve	0:45:00	6,937.5
G = Given		22,534.5

Answer (A) is incorrect because 22,140 lb. requires a cruise fuel flow of approximately 8,273, not 9,600 PPH. Answer (C) is incorrect because 22,972 lb. includes the 416 lb. of fuel required for a missed approach. While this should be included as a practical matter, it is not required by the FARs.

72.
9580. (Refer to figures 115, 116, 117, 118, and 118C on pages 442, 443, 416, 444, and 447.) What is the specific range in nautical miles per 1,000 pounds of fuel from level-off to the ARLIN Intersection using .78 Mach?

A—46.1 NAM/1,000 pounds.
B—48.2 NAM/1,000 pounds.
C—50.0 NAM/1,000 pounds.

Answer (B) is correct (9580). *(FTP Chap 6)*
The following formula is used to determine the specific range in nautical air miles (NAM) per 1,000 lb. of fuel.

$$\textit{Specific range (NAM/1,000)} = \frac{\textit{True airspeed (TAS)}}{\textit{Fuel flow (PPH)} \div 1{,}000}$$

The flight log in Fig. 115 provides information to determine the TAS and cruise fuel flow. First, the temperature (ISA) at cruise (FL 270) is –39°C [15 – (27 x 2)]; thus ISA –2 is –41°C (–39 –2). To obtain TAS from .78 Mach, use the calculator side of the flight computer and set OAT of –41°C over the Mach number index. Find the Mach number (.78) on the "minutes" scale, and read TAS above on the "miles" scale, which is 463 kt. Next, at the bottom of the flight log is a note indicating that the fuel flow from level-off to start of descent is 9,600 PPH. Thus,

$$\textit{Specific range (NAM/1,000)} = \frac{463}{9{,}600 \div 1{,}000}$$

$$= 48.2 \textit{ NAM/1,000}$$

Answer (A) is incorrect because a specific range of 46.1 NAM/1,000 is determined by using a TAS of 443 kt., not 463 kt. Answer (C) is incorrect because a specific range of 50.0 NAM/1,000 is determined by using a TAS of 480 kt., not 463 kt.

73.
9581. (Refer to figures 107, 115, 116, 117, 118, and 118C on pages 372, 442, 443, 416, 444, and 447.) What is the ETE at .80 Mach?

A—1 hour 02 minutes.
B—1 hour 04 minutes.
C—1 hour 07 minutes.

Answer (C) is correct (9581). *(IFH Chap XIII)*

To determine the estimated time en route (ETE) from Los Angeles to Phoenix Sky Harbor, you must complete the flight log in Fig. 115. Variation at LAX is 15°E (Fig. 107) and the variation at PHX is 12°E (Fig. 118C). The average variation is approximately 13°E, which is subtracted from the true wind direction of 300° to determine the magnetic wind direction of 287° at 43 kt. The temperature (ISA) at FL 270 is −39°C [15°C − (27 x 2)]; thus ISA −2 is −41°C.

To obtain TAS from .80 Mach, use the calculator side of your flight computer and set OAT of −41°C over the Mach index. Find the Mach number on the "minutes" scale, and read TAS above on "miles" scale, or 475 kt.

The flight log below has been expanded to provide more detail.

	Distance	MC	Ground-speed	Time
Level-off	43G	X	X	0:19:00G
OCN	50	090	516	0:05:48
JLI	42	083	514	0:04:54
KUMBA	35	115	518	0:04:03
IPL	27	078	512	0:03:09
BZA	46	074	510	0:05:24
MOHAK	32	075	511	0:03:45
BXK R-215	15	067	507	0:01:46
HYDRR	42	035	487	0:05:10
ARLIN	19	076	511	0:02:13
PHX	X	X	X	0:12:00G
				1:07:12

G = Given

Answer (A) is incorrect because an ETE of 1 hr. 2 min. would require a TAS of approximately .92 Mach, not .80 Mach. Answer (B) is incorrect because an ETE of 1 hr. 4 min. would require a TAS of approximately .89 Mach, not .80 Mach.

74.
9582. (Refer to figures 115, 116, 117, 118, and 118C on pages 442, 443, 416, 444, and 447.) What is the total fuel required at .80 Mach?

A—22,836 pounds.
B—22,420 pounds.
C—22,556 pounds.

Answer (B) is correct (9582). *(IFH Chap XIII)*

To determine fuel requirements from Los Angeles to Phoenix Sky Harbor at .80 Mach, complete the fuel portion of the flight log in Fig. 115. Use 9,600 PPH fuel flow from level-off to ARLIN INT and 9,250 PPH fuel flow for the reserve and alternate requirement.

	Time	Fuel (lb.)
Level-off	0:19:00G	4,510.0G
OCN	0:05:48	928.0
JLI	0:04:54	784.0
KUMBA	0:04:03	648.0
IPL	0:03:09	504.0
BZA	0:05:24	864.0
MOHAK	0:03:45	600.0
BXK R-215	0:01:46	282.7
HYDRR	0:05:11	829.3
ARLIN	0:02:13	354.7
Descent and approach	0:12:00G	1,140.0G
Flight to TUS	0:26:00G	4,008.3
Reserve	0:45:00	6,937.5
		22,390.5

G = Given

Answer (A) is incorrect because 22,836 lb. includes the 416 lb. of fuel required for a missed approach. While this should be included as a practical matter, it is not required by the FARs. Answer (C) is incorrect because 22,556 lb. requires a cruise fuel flow of 9,138 PPH, not 9,600 PPH.

75.
9584. (Refer to figures 107, 115, 116, 117, 118, and 118C on pages 372, 442, 443, 416, 444, and 447.) What is the ETE at .82 Mach?

A—1 hour 05 minutes.
B—1 hour 07 minutes.
C—1 hour 03 minutes.

Answer (B) is correct (9584). *(IFH Chap XIII)*

To determine the estimated time en route (ETE) from Los Angeles to Phoenix Sky Harbor, you must complete the flight log in Fig. 115. Variation at LAX is 15°E (Fig. 107) and the variation at PHX is 12°E (Fig. 118C). The average variation is approximately 13°E, which is subtracted from the true wind direction of 300° to determine the magnetic wind direction of 287° at 43 kt. The temperature (ISA) at FL 270 is –39°C [15°C – (27 x 2)]; thus ISA –2 is –41°C.

To obtain TAS from .82 Mach, use the calculator side of your flight computer and set OAT of –41°C over the Mach index. Find the Mach number on the "minutes" scale, and read TAS above on "miles" scale, or 487 kt.

The flight log below has been expanded to provide more detail.

	Distance	MC	Ground-speed	Time
Level-off	43G	X	X	0:19:00G
OCN	50	090	528	0:05:40
JLI	42	083	526	0:04:47
KUMBA	35	115	530	0:03:57
IPL	27	078	524	0:03:05
BZA	46	074	522	0:05:17
MOHAK	32	075	523	0:03:40
BXK R-215	15	067	519	0:01:44
HYDRR	42	035	499	0:05:03
ARLIN	19	076	523	0:02:10
PHX	X	X	X	0:12:00G
				1:06:23

G = Given

Answer (A) is incorrect because an ETE of 1 hr. 5 min. would require a TAS of approximately .84 Mach, not .82 Mach. Answer (C) is incorrect because an ETE of 1 hr. 3 min. would require a TAS of .91 Mach, not .82 Mach.

76.
9585. (Refer to figures 115, 116, 117, 118, and 118C on pages 442, 443, 416, 444, and 447.) What is the total fuel required at .82 Mach?

A—22,420 pounds.
B—22,284 pounds.
C—22,700 pounds.

Answer (B) is correct (9585). *(IFH Chap XIII)*

To determine the fuel requirements from Los Angeles to Phoenix Sky Harbor at .82 Mach, complete the fuel portion of the flight log in Fig. 115. Use 9,600 PPH fuel flow from level-off to ARLIN INT and 9,250 PPH fuel flow for the reserve requirement.

	Time	Fuel (lb.)
Level-off	0:19:00G	4,510.0G
OCN	0:05:40	906.7
JLI	0:04:47	765.3
KUMBA	0:03:57	632.0
IPL	0:03:05	494.7
BZA	0:05:17	845.3
MOHAK	0:03:40	586.7
BXK R-215	0:01:44	277.3
HYDRR	0:05:03	808.0
ARLIN	0:02:10	346.7
Descent and approach	0:12:00G	1,140.0G
Flight to TUS	0:26:00G	4,008.3
Reserve	0:45:00	6,937.5
		22,258.5

G = Given

Answer (A) is incorrect because 22,420 lb. requires a cruise fuel flow of 9,138 PPH, not 9,600 PPH. Answer (C) is incorrect because 22,700 lb. includes the 416 lb. of fuel required for a missed approach. While this should be included as a practical matter, it is not required by the FARs.

77.
9583. (Refer to figures 115, 116, 117, and 118C on pages 442, 443, 416, and 447.) What approximate indicated Mach should be maintained to arrive over the BZA VORTAC 6 minutes after passing IPL VORTAC?

A—.73 Mach.
B—.74 Mach.
C—.715 Mach.

Answer (C) is correct (9583). *(IFH Chap XIII)*

Fig. 117 provides an en route chart to determine the distance from IPL VORTAC to BZA VORTAC of 46 NM. On the calculator side of the flight computer, set 46 NM over 6 min. to determine a groundspeed of 460 kt.

Determine the magnetic variation of 12°E by referring to the PHX *A/FD* excerpt. Magnetic variation is found under the **Radio Aids to Navigation**. Adjust the winds aloft (Fig. 115) from a true course of 300° to a magnetic course of 288° (300 – 12). The temperature (ISA) at FL 270 is –39°C [15 – (27 x 2)]. Thus, ISA –2 is –41°C (–39 – 2).

On the wind side of the flight computer, set the wind direction of 288° under the true index, and mark the wind dot 43 kt. up from the grommet. Next, place the MC of 074° under the true index, and slide the grommet over the groundspeed of 460 kt. Under the wind dot, determine TAS of 425 kt.

On the calculator side, place the Mach number index under the OAT of –41°C in the True Airspeed and Density Altitude window. Read TAS of 425 kt. on the "miles" scale over the Mach number of .715 on the "minutes" scale.

Answer (A) is incorrect because .73 Mach is required with a magnetic wind direction of 300°, not 286°. Answer (B) is incorrect because at .74 Mach it would take approximately 5 min. 45 sec., not 6 min., to travel from the IPL VORTAC to the BZA VORTAC.

78.
8835. (Refer to figures 115, 116, and 117 on pages 442, 443, and 416.) Due to traffic LAX Center radar vectored PTL 130 to TRM. Then cleared the flight to PHX via J169 BLH, direct to Arlin Intersection. What approximate indicated Mach should be maintained to arrive over the BLH VORTAC 8 minutes after passing TRM VORTAC?

A—.84 Mach.
B—.82 Mach.
C—.86 Mach.

Answer (B) is correct (8835). *(IFH Chap XIII)*

Fig. 117 provides an en route chart to determine the distance from TRM VORTAC (left center of chart) to BLH VORTAC (center of chart) of 70 NM. On the calculator side of the flight computer, set 70 NM over 8 min. to determine a groundspeed of 525 kt.

Determine the magnetic variation to be 12°E by referring to the *A/FD* in Fig. 118C. Magnetic variation is found under the **Radio Aids to Navigation**. Adjust the winds aloft (Fig. 115) from a true course of 300° to a magnetic course of 288° (300 – 12). The temperature (ISA) at FL 270 is –39°C [15 – (27 x 2)]. Thus ISA –2 is –41°C (–39 – 2).

On the wind side of the flight computer, set the wind direction of 288° under the true index and mark the wind dot 43 kt. up from the grommet. Next, place the MC of 078° under the true index and slide the grommet over the groundspeed of 525 kt. Under the wind dot, read the TAS of 488 kt.

On the calculator side, place the Mach number index under the OAT of –41°C in the True Airspeed and Density Altitude window. Read TAS of 488 kt. on the "miles" scale over the Mach number of .82 on the "minutes" scale.

Answer (A) is incorrect because .84 Mach is required with a magnetic wind of 300°, not 288°. Answer (C) is incorrect because at .86 Mach it would take approximately 7 min. 40 sec., not 8 min., to travel from the TRM VORTAC to the BLH VORTAC.

79.
8837. (Refer to figure 118A on page 445.) How is course reversal accomplished when outbound on the LOC BC RWY 26L approach at Phoenix Sky Harbor Intl?

A—Radar vector only.
B—Procedure turn beyond 10 NM.
C—Holding pattern entry beyond 10 NM.

Answer (A) is correct (8837). *(IAP)*
Fig. 118A provides the IAP chart for the LOC BC RWY 26L approach at Phoenix Sky Harbor Intl. The plan view (top center of chart) provides information for the initial approach segment, including procedure turns. At the lower left of the plan view is RADAR REQUIRED which means that radar vectoring is provided to the final approach course and any course reversal is accomplished by radar vectors only.
Answer (B) is incorrect because no procedure turn is depicted on the IAP chart, and when radar is used for vectoring, no pilot may make a procedure turn unless (s)he requests and is issued a clearance by ATC. Answer (C) is incorrect because no holding pattern is depicted on the IAP chart, and it may not be used as a course reversal.

80.
8839. (Refer to figure 118A on page 445.) Identify the final approach fix on the LOC BC RWY 26L approach at Phoenix Sky Harbor Intl.

A—Upon intercepting the glide slope beyond I-PHX 5 DME.
B—When crossing I-PHX 5 DME at 3,000 feet.
C—When crossing the SRP VORTAC on the glide slope.

Answer (B) is correct (8839). *(IAP)*
Fig. 118A is the IAP for the LOC BC RWY 26L approach to Phoenix Sky Harbor Intl. The profile view (lower-left center) provides information of the location of the final approach fix and the prescribed altitude. The Maltese cross depicts the final approach fix on a nonprecision approach, which here is identified as 5 DME from I-PHX at 3,000 ft.
Answer (A) is incorrect because an LOC approach is a nonprecision approach that does not provide glide slope information. On the back course, a glide slope indication may be indicated, but it must be ignored. The final approach fix is at, not before, the I-PHX 5 DME. Answer (C) is incorrect because an LOC approach is a nonprecision approach that does not provide glide slope information. On the back course, a glide slope indication may be indicated, but it must be ignored, as stated in the lower right corner of the profile view.

81.
8836. (Refer to figure 118A on page 445.) Straight-in minimums for a Category B aircraft equipped with DME on the LOC BC RWY 26L approach are

A—1,800/1.
B—700/1.
C—1,640/1.

Answer (C) is correct (8836). *(IAP)*
Fig. 118A provides the IAP chart for the LOC BC RWY 26L approach. The lower left of the IAP chart is the minimums section. Under Category B and HADEN DME MINIMUMS the straight-in (S-26L) minimums are 1,640 ft. and 1 SM.
Answer (A) is incorrect because 1,800/1 are the straight-in minimums without, not with, DME. Answer (B) is incorrect because 700/1 are military, not civilian, minimums without, not with, DME.

82.
9590. (Refer to figure 118A on page 445.) What is the HAT a Category B aircraft may descend to if the pilot has identified HADEN INT on the LOC BC RWY 26L approach at Phoenix Sky Harbor Intl?

A—510 feet.
B—667 feet.
C—670 feet.

Answer (A) is correct (9590). *(IAP)*
Fig. 118A provides the IAP for the LOC BC RWY 26L approach at Phoenix Sky Harbor Intl. The height above touchdown (HAT) is located in the minimums section (lower left side) of the chart. HADEN INT has been identified, which indicates that the DME minimums apply. The HAT, which is 510 ft. for a Category B aircraft on a straight-in approach, is indicated after the MDA/flight visibility minimums.
Answer (B) is incorrect because 667 ft. is the HAA, not HAT, for a Category B aircraft conducting a circling approach without, not with, DME. Answer (C) is incorrect because 670 ft. is the approximate circling HAT for a Category B aircraft without, not with, DME.

83.
9589. (Refer to figure 118A on page 445.) Determine the FAR Part 121 landing minimums for the LOC BC RWY 26L approach at Phoenix Sky Harbor Intl.

PIC time .... 94 hours
Airplane V_{SO} maximum
certificated weight .... 105 knots
V_{REF} approach speed .... 140 knots
DME NOTAMed OTS

A—1,800/1-3/4.
B—1,900/2-1/4.
C—1,900/2-1/2.

Answer (B) is correct (9589). *(FAR 121.652)*

Fig. 118A provides the IAP for the LOC BC RWY 26L approach at Phoenix Sky Harbor Intl. The minimums section is at the lower left of the chart.

Determine the aircraft category by using the higher of 1.3 V_{SO} or V_{REF}, which is the approach speed based on the airplane's landing weight. 1.3 V_{SO} is 136.5 kt. (1.3 x 105) and V_{REF} of 140 kt. is higher, which is Category C.

The NOTAM refers to the DME out of service. The landing minimums for a Category C airplane are 1,800/1¾.

FAR 121.652 requires that, if the pilot has less than 100 hr. as PIC, the MDA or DH is increased by 100 ft. and the visibility is increased ½ SM (or 2,400 RVR).

Thus, the FAR Part 121 landing minimums are 1,900/2¼.

Answer (A) is incorrect because 1,800/1¾ are the FAR Part 121 minimums for a pilot with 100 hr. or more, not less, of PIC time. Answer (C) is incorrect because 1,900/2½ would be the landing minimums for a Category D, not Category C, aircraft.

84.
9587. (Refer to figure 118C on page 447.) What instrument approach light system or RWY lighting system is available for the LOC BC RWY 26L approach at Phoenix Sky Harbor Intl?

A—HIRL and REIL.
B—MALS and REIL.
C—SALS and ODALS.

Answer (A) is correct (9587). *(A/FD)*

Fig. 118C is the *A/FD* excerpt for Phoenix Sky Harbor Intl. Look for the runway information line titled **RWY 08R-26L**; at the end of that line is "HIRL." HIRL means high-intensity runway lights. Two lines down is the **RWY 26L** information, which indicates that REIL (runway end identifier lights) and VASI (visual approach slope indicator) are available on RWY 26L at PHX.

Answer (B) is incorrect because MALSR (medium-intensity approach lighting system with runway alignment indicator lights) is available on RWY 08R, not RWY 26L. Answer (C) is incorrect because SALS (short approach light system) and ODALS (omnidirectional approach lighting system) are not available on any runway at PHX.

85.
9588. (Refer to figure 118A on page 445.) The touchdown zone elevation of the LOC BC RWY 26L approach at Phoenix Sky Harbor Intl is

A—1,132 feet.
B—1,130 feet.
C—1,131 feet.

Answer (B) is correct (9588). *(IAP)*

Fig. 118A provides the IAP for the LOC BC RWY 26L approach at Phoenix Sky Harbor Intl. The aerodrome sketch (lower right-hand corner) provides airport information. The touchdown zone elevation (TDZE) is depicted below 26L as 1,130 ft.

Answer (A) is incorrect because 1,132 ft. is approximately the airport, not touchdown zone, elevation. Answer (C) is incorrect because the TDZE is 1,130 ft., not 1,131 ft.

86.
9586. (Refer to figures 115, 116, 117, 118, 118A, 118B, and 118C on pages 442, 443, 416, 444, 445, 446, and 447.) At ARLIN Intersection, PTL 130 is notified that the Phoenix Sky Harbor Airport is closed. PTL 130 is told to proceed to Tucson. PTL 130 is operating under FAR Part 121. The PIC on PTL 130 has less than 100 hours as PIC in the B-727 (approach category C). What are the PIC's minimums for the VOR RWY 11L approach at Tucson Intl Airport?

A—2,860-1/2.
B—2,900-1.
C—2,960-1.

Answer (B) is correct (9586). *(FAR 121.652)*

FAR 121.652 states that, at an alternate airport, the MDA or DH and visibility minimums need not be increased above those applicable for the airport, but in no event may the landing minimums be less than 300-1 if the PIC has less than 100 hr. as PIC in the type of airplane.

The TDZE for RWY 11L at TUS is 2,596 ft. Since the pilot has less than 100 hr. as PIC in the B-727, the minimums are 2,900 ft. (2,596 + 300) and 1 SM.

Answer (A) is incorrect because 2,860-½ are the landing minimums for a Category C airplane if the PIC has 100 hr. or more, not less, as PIC in the B-727. Answer (C) is incorrect because 2,960-1 would be the landing minimums for the PIC if TUS were the destination, not alternate, airport.

Form Approved: OMB No. 2120-0034

U.S. DEPARTMENT OF TRANSPORTATION FEDERAL AVIATION ADMINISTRATION **FLIGHT PLAN**	(FAA USE ONLY)	☐ PILOT BRIEFING ☐ STOPOVER	☐ VNR	TIME STARTED	SPECIALIST INITIALS

1. TYPE	2. AIRCRAFT IDENTIFICATION	3. AIRCRAFT TYPE/ SPECIAL EQUIPMENT	4. TRUE AIRSPEED	5. DEPARTURE POINT	6. DEPARTURE TIME PROPOSED (Z)	ACTUAL (Z)	7. CRUISING ALTITUDE
VFR X IFR DVFR	PTL 130	B727/R	*** KTS	LAX			FL270

8. ROUTE OF FLIGHT
LAX INP3.IPL, J2 MOHAK, ARLIN 9 PHX

9. DESTINATION (Name of airport and city)	10. EST. TIME ENROUTE HOURS	MINUTES	11. REMARKS
PHX PHOENIX SKY HARBOR PHOENIX			L/O = Level Off PPH = Pounds Per Hour ** L/O at OCN R-270/50 *** MACH .78

12. FUEL ON BOARD HOURS	MINUTES	13. ALTERNATE AIRPORT(S)	14. PILOT'S NAME, ADDRESS & TELEPHONE NUMBER & AIRCRAFT HOME BASE / 17. DESTINATION CONTACT/TELEPHONE (OPTIONAL)	15. NUMBER ABOARD
		TUS TUCSON INT'L		83

16. COLOR OF AIRCRAFT
RED/BLACK

CIVIL AIRCRAFT PILOTS. FAR Part 91 requires you file an IFR flight plan to operate under instrument flight rules in controlled airspace. Failure to file could result in a civil penalty not to exceed $1,000 for each violation (Section 901 of the Federal Aviation Act of 1958, as amended). Filing of a VFR flight plan is recommended as a good operating practice. See also Part 99 for requirements concerning DVFR flight plans.

FAA Form 7233-1 (8-82) CLOSE VFR FLIGHT PLAN WITH ______ FSS ON ARRIVAL

FLIGHT LOG

CHECK POINTS FROM	TO	ROUTE ALTITUDE	COURSE	WIND TEMP	SPEED-KTS TAS	GS	DIST NM	TIME LEG	TOT	FUEL LEG	TOT
LAX	L/O**	IPL3.IPL Climb					43		:19:00		4510*
L/O	IPL	IPL3.IPL FL270		300/43 ISA-2							
IPL	BZA	J2 FL270									
BZA	Mohak Int	J2 FL270		300/43 ISA-2							
Mohak	Arlin Int	Arlin 9 FL270									
Arlin	PHX	Radar Vec DES/APP						:12:00		1140	
PHX	TUS	Radar V FL190					97	:26:00			

OTHER DATA: * Includes Taxi Fuel
NOTE: Use 9600 PPH Total Fuel Flow From L/O To Start Of Descent.
Use 9250 PPH Total Fuel Flow For Reserve And Alternate Requirements.
A Missed Approach Requires 416# of Fuel.

TIME and FUEL: As required by FARs.

TIME	FUEL (LB)	
		EN ROUTE
		RESERVE
		ALTERNATE
		TOTAL

FIGURE 115.—Flight Plan / Flight Log.

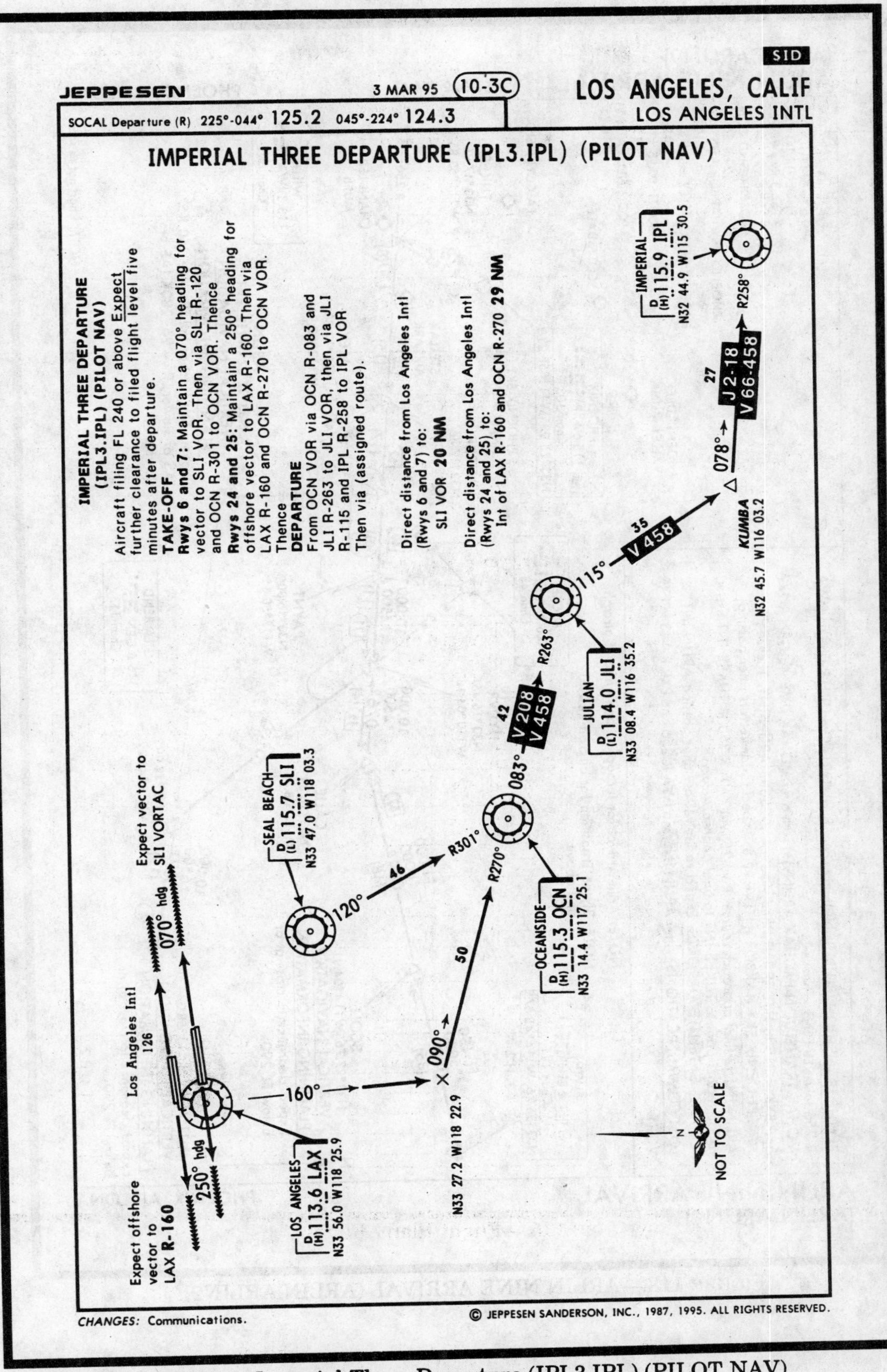

FIGURE 116.—Imperial Three Departure (IPL3.IPL) (PILOT NAV).

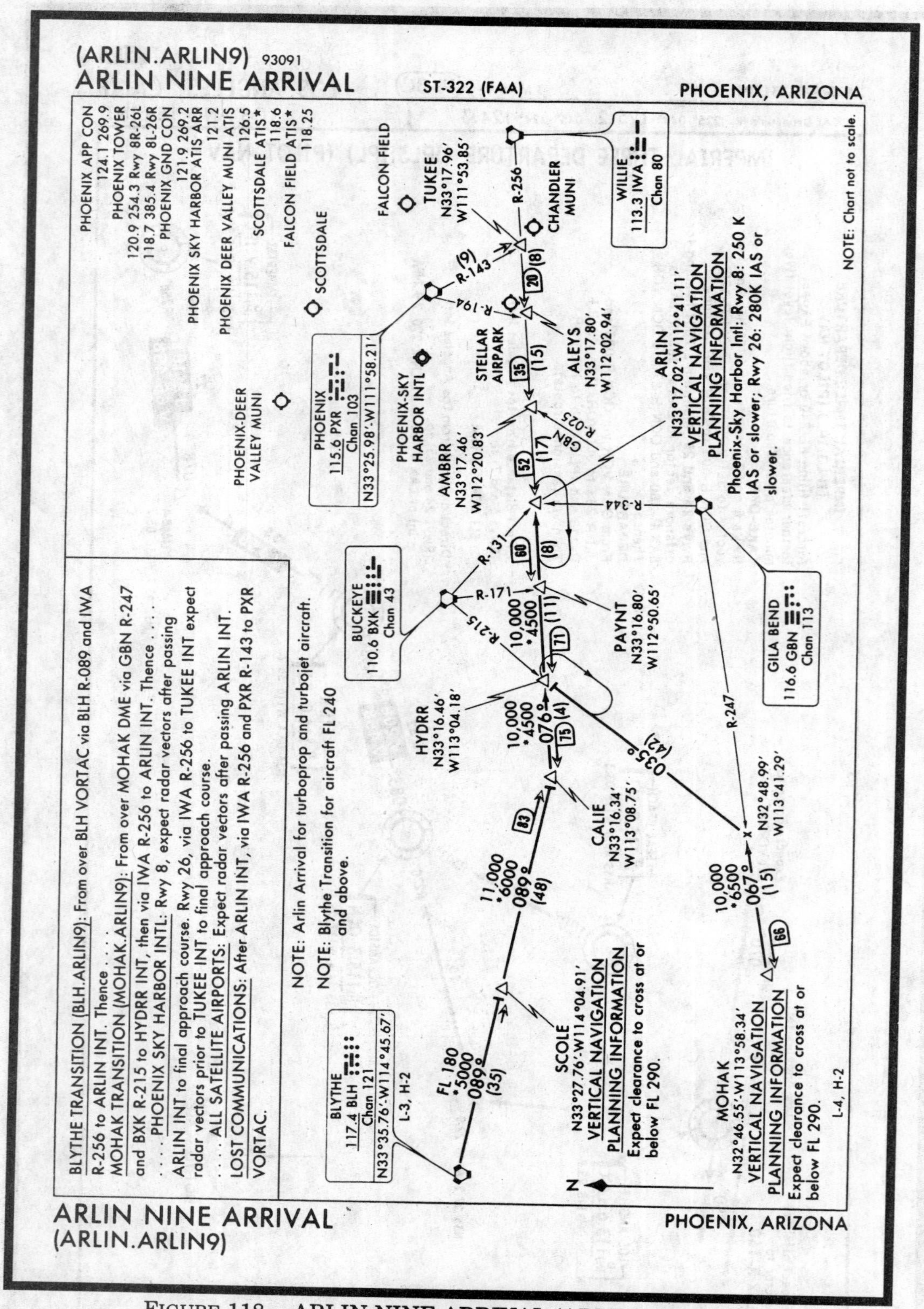

FIGURE 118.—ARLIN NINE ARRIVAL (ARLIN.ARLIN9).

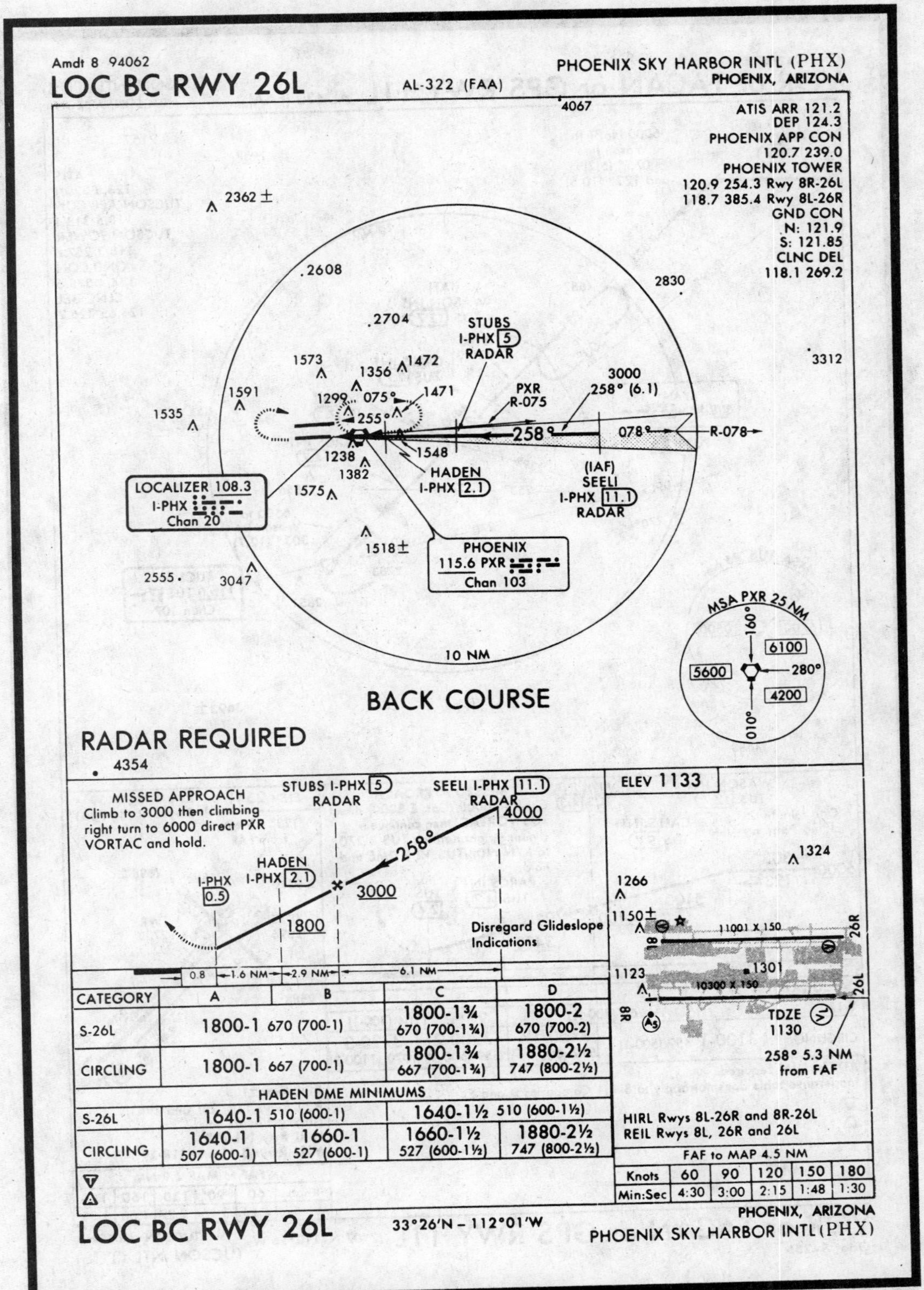

FIGURE 118A.—LOC BC RWY 26L (PHX).

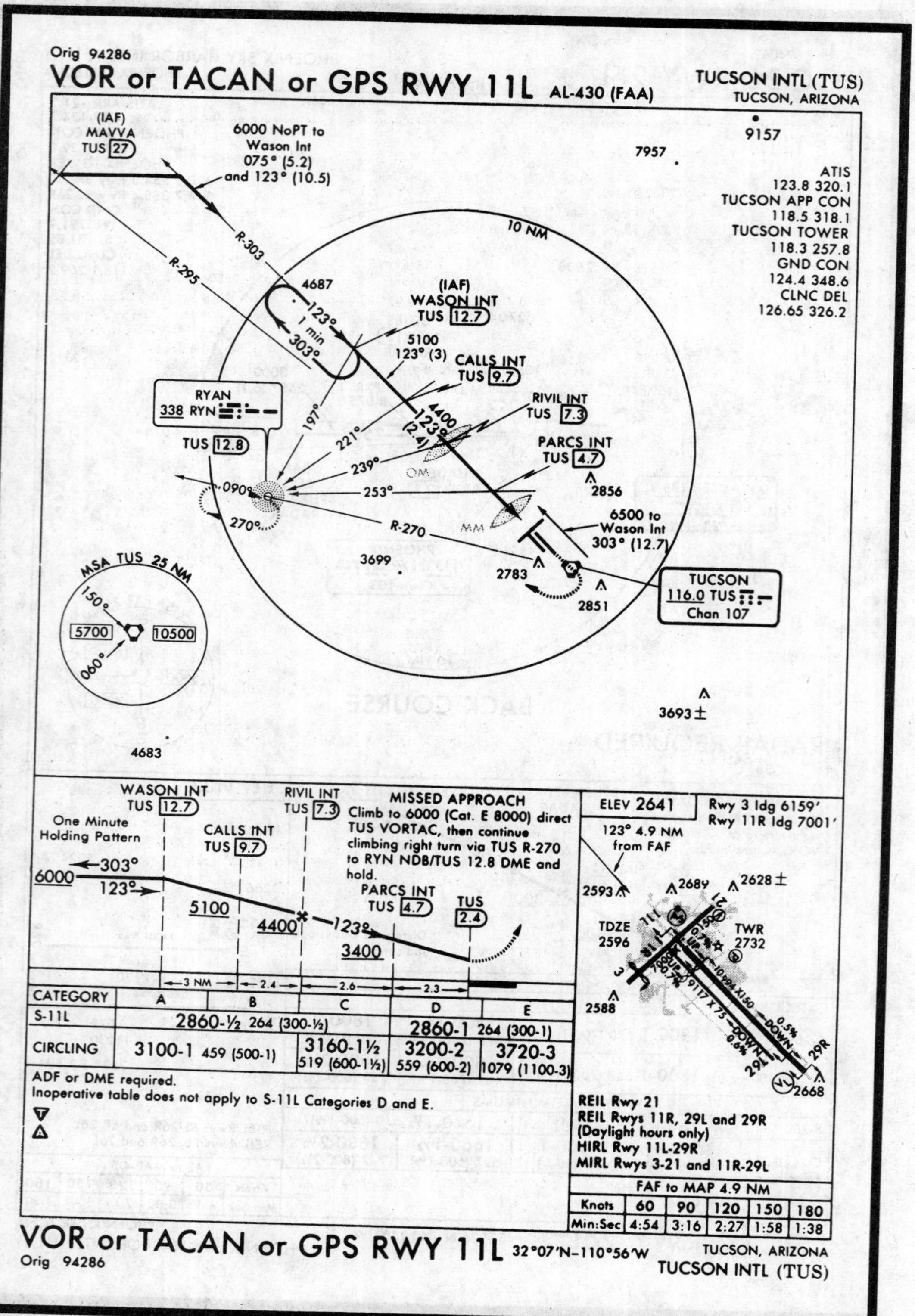

CATEGORY	A	B	C	D	E
S-11L	2860-½ 264 (300-½)			2860-1 264 (300-1)	
CIRCLING	3100-1 459 (500-1)		3160-1½ 519 (600-1½)	3200-2 559 (600-2)	3720-3 1079 (1100-3)

ADF or DME required.
Inoperative table does not apply to S-11L Categories D and E.

REIL Rwy 21
REIL Rwys 11R, 29L and 29R (Daylight hours only)
HIRL Rwy 11L-29R
MIRL Rwys 3-21 and 11R-29L

FAF to MAP 4.9 NM					
Knots	60	90	120	150	180
Min:Sec	4:54	3:16	2:27	1:58	1:38

VOR or TACAN or GPS RWY 11L 32°07'N-110°56'W
Orig 94286
TUCSON, ARIZONA
TUCSON INTL (TUS)

FIGURE 118B.—VOR or TACAN or GPS RWY 11L (TUS).

PHOENIX

PHOENIX-DEER VALLEY MUNI (DVT) 15 N UTC–7 N33°41.30′ W112°04.93′ **PHOENIX**
1476 B S4 **FUEL** 80, 100LL, JET A OX 1, 3 TPA—See Remarks **H-2C, L-4E**
RWY 07R-25L: H8200X100 (ASPH) S-40, D-50, DT-80 MIRL **IAP**
RWY 07R: REIL. VASI(V2L)—GA 3.0° Thld dsplcd 900′. Rgt tfc.
RWY 25L: REIL. VASI(V2L)—GA 3.0° Thld dsplcd 920′.
RWY 07L-25R: H4500X75 (ASPH) S-20 MIRL
RWY 07L: REIL. PVASI(PSIL)—GA 3.0° TCH 40′. **RWY 25R:** REIL. PVASI(PSIL)—GA 3.5° TCH 47′. Hill. Rgt tfc.
AIRPORT REMARKS: Attended 1300–0400Z. Fuel avbl only during hours 1400–0300Z 7 days. Lgtd hills NE, E, SE and W. Hot air balloon ops fall, winter, and spring months and ultralight opr South and West of arpt. Rwy 07L–25R is designated training rwy. Aerobatic practice area approximately 8½ miles northwest of the Deer Valley Arpt from the surface to 6000′ MSL. Parallel taxiway north and close proximity to Rwy 07L–25R. Rwy 07R VASI and REIL, Rwy 25L VASI and REIL, Rwy 07L PVASI and Rwy 25R PVASI on when twr clsd. Fee for all charters; travel clubs and certain revenue producing acft. TPA–2501(1025) single engine and 3001(1525) multi engine.
COMMUNICATIONS: CTAF 118.4 **ATIS** 126.5 **UNICOM** 122.95
PRESCOTT FSS (PRC) TF 1-800-992-7433. NOTAM FILE DVT.
PHOENIX RCO 122.6 122.2 (PRESCOTT FSS)
Ⓡ **PHOENIX APP/DEP CON** 120.7
DEER VALLEY TOWER 118.4 (Rwy 07R–25L) 120.2 (Rwy 07L–25R) (1300–0400Z) **GND CON** 121.8
CLNC DEL 119.5
AIRSPACE: CLASS D svc effective 1300–0400Z other times CLASS G.
RADIO AIDS TO NAVIGATION: NOTAM FILE PRC.
PHOENIX (H) VORTACW 115.6 PXR Chan 103 N33°25.98′ W111°58.21′ 328° 16.3 NM to fld. 1180/12E.
HIWAS.
SCOTTSDALE NDB (MHW) 224 SDL N33°37.75′ W111°54.47′ 279° 9.4 NM to fld. NOTAM FILE SDL.
Unmonitored when twr closed.
COMM/NAVAID REMARKS: Emerg frequency 121.5 not available at twr.

PHOENIX SKY HARBOR INTL (PHX) 3 E UTC–7 N33°26.17′ W112°00.57′ **PHOENIX**
1133 B S4 **FUEL** 100LL, JET A OX 1, 2, 3, 4 TPA—See Remarks **H-2C, L-4E**
LRA ARFF Index D **IAP**
RWY 08L-26R: H11001X150 (ASPH-GRVD) S-30, D-170, DT-280, DDT-620 HIRL
RWY 08L: REIL. VASI(V4L)—GA 3.0° TCH 55′. Building.
RWY 26R: REIL. VASI(V4L)—GA 3.0° TCH 60′. Road. Rgt tfc.
RWY 08R-26L: H10300X150 (ASPH-GRVD) S-30, D-200, DT-400, DDT-620 HIRL
RWY 08R: MALSR. Pole. Rgt tfc.
RWY 26L: REIL. VASI(V6L)—Upper GA 3.25° TCH 90′. Lower GA 3.0° TCH 53′. Antenna.
AIRPORT REMARKS: Attended continuously. Training by civil turbojet acft prohibited except PPR. TPA—2133(1000) lgt acft and non-turbo jets; 2633(1500) heavy acft and turbojets. Unless advised by ATC all turbine acft and acft 12,500 lbs and over remain at or above 3000′ MSL until established on final. Fly base leg at least 5 mile from arpt. Overnight parking fee. Fee for all charters; travel clubs and certain revenue producing aircraft. Taxiway A-6 limited to 68,000 GWT. Rwy 08L-26R FAA strength evaluation DC-10-10 505,000 pounds, DC-10-30/40 500,000 pounds, L-1011-1 450,000 pounds, aircraft up to DDTW 620,000 pounds, DC-10-10 505,000 pounds, DC-10-30/40 540,000 pounds, L-1011-1 450,000 pounds regularly operate on rwy. Rwy 08R-26L gross weight limit DC-10-10 430,000 pounds, DC-10-30/40 540,000 pounds, L-1011-1 430,000 pounds. Flight Notification Service (ADCUS) available.
WEATHER DATA SOURCES: ASOS (602) 231-8557. LLWAS.
COMMUNICATIONS: ATIS ARR 121.2 DEP 124.3 (602) 244-0963 **UNICOM** 122.95
PRESCOTT FSS (PRC) TF 1-800-992-7433. NOTAM FILE PHX.
RCO 122.6 122.2 (PRESCOTT FSS)
Ⓡ **APP/DEP CON** 126.8 (259°–309°) 124.9 (053°–146°) 124.1(147°–258° above 5500′) 123.7 (147°–258° 5500′ and below) 120.7 120.4 (Rwy 08L 275°–290° blo 6000′, Rwy 26R 030°–080°) (310°–052° 5500′ and below) 119.2 (310°–052° above 5500′)
TOWER 118.7 (Rwy 08L–26R) 120.9 (Rwy 08R–26L) **GND CON** 121.9 (North) 121.85 (South) **CLNC DEL** 118.1
AIRSPACE: CLASS B See VFR Terminal Area Chart.
RADIO AIDS TO NAVIGATION: NOTAM FILE PRC.
PHOENIX (H) VORTACW 115.6 PXR Chan 103 N33°25.98′ W111°58.21′ 263° 2.0 NM to fld. 1180/12E.
HIWAS.
ILS 111.75 I-PZZ Rwy 26R (LOC only).
ILS/DME 108.3 I-PHX Chan 20 Rwy 08R. GS unusable below 1280′. LOC back course unusable beyond 20° south of course.

FIGURE 118C.—Excerpt from Airport/Facilities Directory.

10.8 B-727 BUF TO ORD (Questions 87-96)

Questions 87 through 96 pertain to an IFR flight from Greater Buffalo International Airport, Buffalo, New York to the O'Hare International Airport, Chicago, Illinois.

The route of flight is given in block 8 on the flight plan portion of Fig. 119 on page 452. The partially completed flight planning log is given on the bottom portion of Fig. 119.

The following figures are used to answer the 10 questions concerning this flight.

Fig.	Page	Title
119	452	Flight Plan/Flight Log
120	453	Buffalo One Departure (Vector)
121	417	IFR En Route High Altitude Chart Segment
122	454	ILS RWY 32L (ORD)/Pullman Two Arrival (PMM.PMM2)
Legend 9	455	Rate-of-Descent Table

10.8 B-727 BUF to ORD

87.
9591. (Refer to figures 119, 120, 121, and 122 on pages 452, 453, 417, and 454.) What is the ETE from BUF to ORD using .78 Mach?

A—1 hour 09 minutes.
B—1 hour 07 minutes.
C—1 hour 05 minutes.

Answer (C) is correct (9591). *(IFH Chap XIII)*

To determine the ETE from Greater Buffalo (BUF) to Chicago-O'Hare (ORD), you must complete the flight log in Fig. 119. In the remarks box of the flight plan, the variations at BUF (8°W), FNT (3°W), and ORD (2°E) are given. This information is used to convert the true wind direction to magnetic direction. The temperature (ISA) at FL 310 is –47°C [15°C – (31 x 2)]; thus ISA-6 is –53°C.

To obtain TAS from .78 Mach, use the calculator side of your flight computer and set OAT (FL 310) at –53°C over the Mach index. Find the Mach number on the "minutes" scale, and read TAS above on the "miles" scale, which is 451 kt.

Our flight log below has been expanded to provide more detail. The distance from level-off (L/O) to YXU is calculated by subtracting the 70 NM for the climb from 110 NM (distance between BUF and YXU). To convert the wind direction from true to magnetic, we used 8°W variation to YXU; 3°W variation from YXU to the FNT/PMM VOR COP; and 2°E variation from the COP to PMM R-073/15.

	Distance	MC	Wind (Mag)	Ground-speed	Time
Level-off	70G	X	X	X	0:16:00G
YXU	40	281	338/39	429	0:05:35
YXU/FNT COP	57	277	333/39	428	0:07:59
FNT	57	270	333/39	432	0:07:55
FNT/PMM COP	54	258	333/39	439	0:07:22
PMM R-073/15	40	253	328/39	439	0:05:28
PMM	15G	253G	X	X	0:02:00G
ORD	89G	X	X	X	0:13:00G
					1:05:19

G = Given

Answer (A) is incorrect because an ETE of 1 hr. 9 min. requires a TAS of .71 Mach, not .78 Mach. Answer (B) is incorrect because an ETE of 1 hr. 7 min. requires a TAS of approximately .74 Mach, not .78 Mach.

88.
9592. (Refer to figures 119, 120, 121, and 122 on pages 452, 453, 417, and 454.) What is the total fuel required for the flight from BUF to ORD using .78 Mach?

A—19,033 pounds.
B—21,739 pounds.
C—22,189 pounds.

Answer (B) is correct (9592). *(IFH Chap XIII)*
To determine the fuel requirements from BUF to ORD, you must complete the fuel portion of the flight log in Fig. 119. Use 9,300 PPH from level-off to start of descent and 9,550 PPH for the fuel flow for the 45 min. reserve and alternate requirement.

	Time	Fuel (lb.)
Level-off	0:16:00G	4,960.0G
YXU	0:05:35	865.4
YXU/FNT COP	0:07:39	1,185.7
FNT	0:07:55	1,227.1
FNT/PMM COP	0:07:22	1,141.8
PMM R-073/15	0:05:28	847.3
PMM	0:02:00G	216.7G
ORD	0:13:00G	1,408.3G
Flight to RFD	0:17:00G	2,705.8
Reserve	0:45:00	7,162.5
		21,720.6

G = Given

Answer (A) is incorrect because 19,033 lb. does not include the 2,706 lb. required to fly to the alternate, i.e., from ORD to RFD. Answer (C) is incorrect because 22,189 lb. includes the 450 lb. of fuel required for a missed approach. While this should be included as a practical matter, it is not required by the FARs.

89.
9593. (Refer to figures 119, 120, 121, and 122 on pages 452, 453, 417, and 454.) What is the specific range in nautical air miles per 1,000 pounds of fuel from level-off to start of descent using .78 Mach?

A—48.8 NAM/1000.
B—52.5 NAM/1000.
C—55.9 NAM/1000.

Answer (A) is correct (9593). *(FTP Chap 6)*
The following formula is used to determine the specific range in nautical air miles (NAM) per 1,000 lb. of fuel.

$$\text{Specific range } (NAM/1{,}000) = \frac{\text{True airspeed } (TAS)}{\text{Fuel flow } (PPH)/1{,}000}$$

The flight log in Fig. 119 provides information to determine the TAS and cruise fuel flow. First, the temperature (ISA) at cruise (FL 310) is –47°C [15° – (31 x 2)]; thus ISA – 6 is –53°C (–47 – 6). To obtain TAS from .78 Mach, use the calculator side of the flight computer and set OAT of –53°C over the Mach index. Find the Mach number (.78) on the "minutes" scale and read TAS above on the "miles" scale, which is 451 kt. Next, at the bottom of the flight log is a note indicating that the fuel flow from level-off to start of descent is 9,300 PPH. Thus,

$$\text{Specific range } (NAM/1{,}000) = \frac{451 \text{ kt.}}{9{,}300 \; PPH/1{,}000}$$

$$= 48.5 \; NAM/1{,}000$$

Answer (B) is incorrect because a 52.5 NAM/1,000 is determined by using a TAS of 490 kt., not 451 kt. Answer (C) is incorrect because a 55.9 NAM/1,000 is determined by using fuel flow of 8,068 PPH, not 9,300 PPH.

90.
9594. (Refer to figures 119, 120, 121, and 122 on pages 452, 453, 417, and 454.) What is the ETE from BUF to ORD using .80 Mach?

A—1 hour 01 minutes.
B—1 hour 04 minutes.
C—1 hour 08 minutes.

Answer (B) is correct (9594). *(IFH Chap XIII)*
To determine the ETE from Greater Buffalo (BUF) to Chicago-O'Hare (ORD), you must complete the flight log in Fig. 119. In the remarks box of the flight plan, the variations at BUF (8°W), FNT (3°W), and ORD (2°E) are given. This information is used to convert the true wind direction to magnetic direction. The temperature (ISA) at FL 310 is –47°C [15°C – (31 x 2)]; thus ISA-6 is –53°C.

To obtain TAS from .80 Mach, use the calculator side of your flight computer and set OAT (FL 310) at –53°C over the Mach index. Find the Mach number on the "minutes" scale, and read TAS above on the "miles" scale, which is 463 kt.

Our flight log below has been expanded to provide more detail. The distance from level-off (L/O) to YXU is calculated by subtracting the 70 NM for the climb from 110 NM (distance between BUF and YXU). To convert the wind direction from true to magnetic, we used 8°W variation to YXU; 3°W variation from YXU to the FNT/PMM VOR COP; and 2°E variation from the COP to PMM R-073/15.

	Distance	MC	Wind (Mag)	Ground-speed	Time
Level-off	70G	X	X	X	0:16:00G
YXU	40	281	338/39	441	0:05:26
YXU/FNT COP	57	277	333/39	440	0:07:46
FNT	57	270	333/39	444	0:07:42
FNT/PMM COP	54	258	333/39	451	0:07:11
PMM R-073/15	40	253	328/39	451	0:05:19
PMM	15G	253G	X	X	0:02:00G
ORD	89G	X	X	X	0:13:00G
G = Given					1:04:24

Answer (A) is incorrect because an ETE of 1 hr. 1 min. requires a TAS of .88 Mach, not .80 Mach. Answer (C) is incorrect because an ETE of 1 hr. 8 min. requires a TAS of .73 Mach, not .80 Mach.

91.
9595. (Refer to figures 119, 120, 121, and 122 on pages 452, 453, 417, and 454.) What is the total fuel required for the flight from BUF to ORD using .80 Mach?

A—19,388 pounds.
B—22,094 pounds.
C—21,644 pounds.

Answer (C) is correct (9595). *(IFH Chap XIII)*
To determine the fuel requirements from Greater Buffalo Intl. to Chicago-O'Hare Intl., you must complete the fuel portion of the flight log in Fig. 119. Use 9,300 PPH from level-off to start of descent and 9,550 PPH for the fuel flow for the 45 min. reserve and alternate requirement.

	Time	Fuel (lb.)
Level-off	0:16:00G	4,960.0G
YXU	0:05:26	842.2
YXU/FNT COP	0:07:46	1,203.8
FNT	0:07:42	1,193.5
FNT/PMM COP	0:07:11	1,113.4
PMM R-073/15	0:05:19	824.1
PMM	0:02:00G	216.7G
ORD	0:13:00G	1,408.3G
Flight to RFD	0:17:00G	2,705.8
Reserve	0:45:00	7,162.5
G = Given		21,630.3

Answer (A) is incorrect because 19,388 lb. does not include the fuel required to fly to the alternate airport (RFD). Answer (B) is incorrect because 22,094 lb. includes the 450 lb. of fuel required for the missed approach. While this should be included as a practical matter, it is not required by the FARs.

92.
9596. (Refer to figure 121 on page 417.) On the airway J220 (BUF R-158) SE of Buffalo, the MAA is 39,000 feet. What is the MAA on J547 between BUF and PMM?

A—60,000 feet.
B—43,000 feet.
C—45,000 feet.

Answer (C) is correct (9596). *(AIM Para 5-3-4)*
The jet route system consists of routes established from 18,000 ft. MSL to 45,000 ft. MSL inclusive. Jet routes are identified by the letter "J" followed by the airway number. Since there is no lower MAA established for J547 between BUF and PMM, the MAA is the upper limit of the jet route.
Answer (A) is incorrect because 60,000 ft. MSL is the upper limit of Class A airspace, not a jet route. Answer (B) is incorrect because the upper limit of a jet route is 45,000 ft. MSL, not 43,000 ft. MSL.

93.
8851. (Refer to figure 122 on page 454.) At what altitude and indicated airspeed would you expect to cross PIVOT INT on the approach to ORD?

A—FL 200 and 300 KIAS.
B—10,000 feet and 250 KIAS.
C—12,000 feet and 200 KIAS.

Answer (B) is correct (8851). *(STAR)*
Fig. 122 provides the Pullman Two Arrival (right-hand chart) to ORD. The Vertical Navigation Planning Information indicates that a turbojet arrival should expect a clearance to cross PIVOT INT at 10,000 ft. and 250 KIAS.
Answer (A) is incorrect because turbojet arrivals should expect a clearance to cross PMM VORTAC, not PIVOT INT, at FL 200. Answer (C) is incorrect because 12,000 ft. and 200 KIAS is not an expected clearance for either a turbojet or turboprop aircraft using the Pullman Two Arrival to ORD.

94.
8849. (Refer to figure 122 on page 454.) What is the lowest altitude at which the glide slope may be intercepted when authorized by ATC?

A—2,500 feet.
B—3,000 feet.
C—4,000 feet.

Answer (A) is correct (8849). *(IAP)*
The left-hand chart in Fig. 122 provides the IAP chart for the ILS RWY 32L approach to ORD. The note in the profile view indicates that the glide slope may be intercepted at 2,500 ft. when authorized by ATC.
Answer (B) is incorrect because 3,000 ft. is the minimum altitude at GRETI and is marked by an asterisk, which indicates that 2,500 ft. may be used if authorized by ATC. Answer (C) is incorrect because 4,000 ft. is the minimum altitude at KITTS and is marked by an asterisk, which indicates that 2,500 ft. may be used if authorized by ATC.

95.
8850. (Refer to figure 122 on page 454.) What would be the DME reading at the lowest altitude at which the glide slope may be intercepted when authorized by ATC?

A—12.4 miles.
B—9.4 miles.
C—7.7 miles.

Answer (C) is correct (8850). *(IAP)*
The left-hand chart in Fig. 122 provides the IAP chart for the ILS RWY 32L approach to ORD. The lowest altitude at which the glide slope may be intercepted when authorized by ATC is 2,500 ft., which is at JOCKY LOM/INT, and the DME would read 7.7 NM to I-RVG.
Answer (A) is incorrect because 12.4 NM is the DME reading at KITTS, not JOCKY. Answer (B) is incorrect because 9.4 NM is the DME reading at GRETI, not JOCKY.

96.
8852. (Refer to figure 122 on page 454.) What is the approximate rate of descent required (for planning purposes) to maintain the electronic glide slope at 120 KIAS with a reported headwind component of 15 knots?

A—555 ft/min.
B—635 ft/min.
C—650 ft/min.

Answer (A) is correct (8852). *(IAP)*
The left-hand chart in Fig. 122 provides the IAP chart for the ILS RWY 32L approach to ORD. In the lower right corner of the profile view is GS 3.00°, or a 3° glide slope.
Refer to the Rate-of-Descent Table in Legend 9, on page 455, to determine the rate of descent to maintain a 3° glide slope. With an airspeed of 120 KIAS and a 15-kt. headwind component, the groundspeed is 105 kt. (120 – 15). Find 3.0° in the angle-of-descent column and move right to a groundspeed of 105 kt. to determine a rate of descent of 555 ft./min.
Answer (B) is incorrect because a rate of descent of 635 ft./min. is appropriate for the indicated airspeed, not groundspeed, of 120 kt. Answer (C) is incorrect because a rate of descent of 650 ft./min. is appropriate for a 3.5°, not 3.0°, glide slope angle.

Form Approved: OMB No. 2120-0034

U.S. DEPARTMENT OF TRANSPORTATION
FEDERAL AVIATION ADMINISTRATION

FLIGHT PLAN

(FAA USE ONLY) ☐ PILOT BRIEFING ☐ VNR ☐ STOPOVER | TIME STARTED | SPECIALIST INITIALS

1. TYPE	2. AIRCRAFT IDENTIFICATION	3. AIRCRAFT TYPE/ SPECIAL EQUIPMENT	4. TRUE AIRSPEED	5. DEPARTURE POINT	6. DEPARTURE TIME PROPOSED (Z)	ACTUAL (Z)	7. CRUISING ALTITUDE
VFR X IFR DVFR	N130JB	B727/A	** KTS	BUF Greater Buffalo Int'l			FL310

8. ROUTE OF FLIGHT
Buffalo One Dep. J547 FNT, FNT.PMM 2 ORD

9. DESTINATION (Name of airport and city)
ORD
Chicago-Ohare Int'l
Chicago

10. EST. TIME ENROUTE HOURS MINUTES

11. REMARKS
L/O = Level Off PPH = Pounds Per Hour
** MACH .78 Variation: BUF 8W, FNT 3W, ORD 2E
ATC cleared N130JB to maintain FL310 until PMM R-073/15
cross PMM at FL200, cross Pivot at 10,000 feet.

12. FUEL ON BOARD HOURS MINUTES

13. ALTERNATE AIRPORT(S)
RFD
Greater Rockford
Rockford, Ill

14. PILOT'S NAME, ADDRESS & TELEPHONE NUMBER & AIRCRAFT HOME BASE

15. NUMBER ABOARD
101

17. DESTINATION CONTACT/TELEPHONE (OPTIONAL)

16. COLOR OF AIRCRAFT
RED/WHITE/BLUE

CIVIL AIRCRAFT PILOTS. FAR Part 91 requires you file an IFR flight plan to operate under instrument flight rules in controlled airspace. Failure to file could result in a civil penalty not to exceed $1,000 for each violation (Section 901 of the Federal Aviation Act of 1958, as amended). Filing of a VFR flight plan is recommended as a good operating practice. See also Part 99 for requirements concerning DVFR flight plans.

FAA Form 7233-1 (8-82) CLOSE VFR FLIGHT PLAN WITH ______ FSS ON ARRIVAL

FLIGHT LOG

CHECK POINTS FROM	TO	ROUTE ALTITUDE	COURSE	WIND TEMP	SPEED-KTS TAS	GS	DIST NM	TIME LEG	TOT	FUEL LEG	TOT
BUF	L/O	Buffalo 1 Climb					70		:16:00		4960*
L/O	YXU	J547 FL310		330/39 ISA-6							
YXU	FNT										
FNT	R-073/15 PMM	FNT.PMM2		330/39 ISA-6							
R-073/15 PMM	PMM	FNT.PMM2 Descent	253				15	:02:00		216.7	
PMM	ORD	FNT.PMM2 Descent & Approach	261/216				89	:13:00		1408.3	
ORD	RFD	Radar V 10,000					97	:17:00			

OTHER DATA: * Includes Taxi Fuel
NOTE: Use 9300 PPH Total Fuel Flow From L/O To Start Of Descent.
Use 9550 PPH Total Fuel Flow For Reserve And Alternate Requirements.
A Missed Approach Requires 450# of Fuel.

TIME and FUEL: As required by FARs.

TIME	FUEL (LB)	
		EN ROUTE
		RESERVE
		ALTERNATE
		TOTAL

FIGURE 119.—Flight Plan/Flight Log.

90347 SL-65 (FAA) BUFFALO/GREATER BUFFALO INTL

BUFFALO ONE DEPARTURE (VECTOR)

BUFFALO, NEW YORK

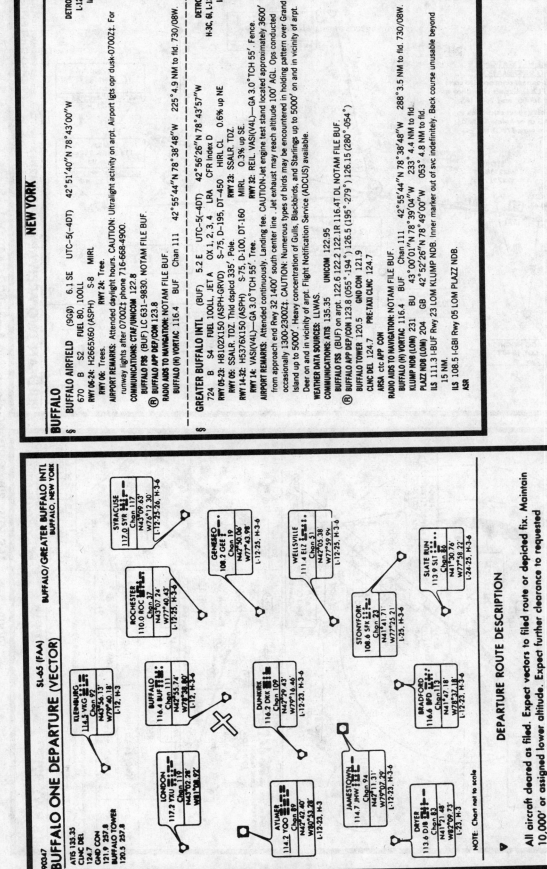

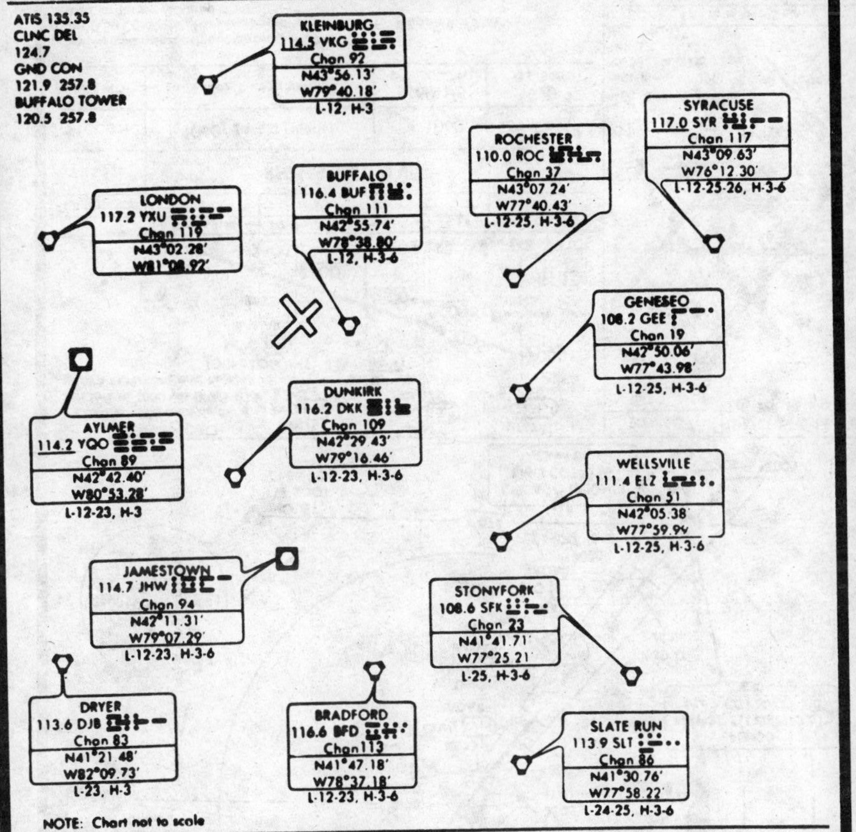

DEPARTURE ROUTE DESCRIPTION

▼

All aircraft cleared as filed. Expect vectors to filed route or depicted fix. Maintain 10,000′ or assigned lower altitude. Expect further clearance to requested altitude/flight level ten minutes after departure.

<u>All Runways:</u> Maintain runway heading for vectors.

BUFFALO ONE DEPARTURE (VECTOR) BUFFALO, NEW YORK BUFFALO/GREATER BUFFALO INTL

NEW YORK

BUFFALO

§ **BUFFALO AIRFIELD** (9G0) 6.1 SE UTC–5(–4DT) 42°51′40″N 78°43′00″W DETROIT L-12H IAP
670 B S2 **FUEL** 80, 100LL
RWY 06-24: H2665X60 (ASPH) S-8 MIRL
RWY 06: Trees. **RWY 24:** Tree.
AIRPORT REMARKS: Attended daylight hours. CAUTION: Ultralight activity on arpt. Airport lgts opr dusk-0700Z‡. For runway lights after 0700Z‡ phone 716-668-4900.
COMMUNICATIONS: CTAF/UNICOM 122.8
BUFFALO FSS (BUF) LC 631–9830. NOTAM FILE BUF.
Ⓡ **BUFFALO APP DEP/CON** 123.8
RADIO AIDS TO NAVIGATION: NOTAM FILE BUF.
BUFFALO (H) VORTAC 116.4 BUF Chan 111 42°55′44″N 78°38′48″W 225°4.9 NM to fld. 730/08W.

---

§ **GREATER BUFFALO INTL** (BUF) 5.2 E UTC–5(–4DT) 42°56′26″N 78°43′57″W DETROIT H-3C, 6I, L-12H IAP
724 B S4 **FUEL** 100LL, JET A OX 1, 2, 3, 4 LRA CFR Index D
RWY 05-23: H8102X150 (ASPH-GRVD) S–75, D–195, DT–450 HIRL CL 0.6% up NE
RWY 05: SSALR. TDZ. Thld dsplcd 335′. Pole. **RWY 23:** SSALR. TDZ.
RWY 14-32: H5376X150 (ASPH) S-75, D-100, DT-160 MIRL 0.3% up SE.
RWY 14: VASI(V4L)—GA 3.0°TCH 55′. Tree. **RWY 32:** REIL. VASI(V4L)—GA 3.0°TCH 55′. Fence.
AIRPORT REMARKS: Attended continuously. Landing fee. CAUTION-Jet engine test stand located approximately 3600′ from approach end Rwy 32 1400′ south center line . Jet exhaust may reach altitude 100′ AGL. Ops conducted occasionally 1300-2300Z‡. CAUTION: Numerous types of birds may be encountered in holding pattern over Grand Island up to 5000′. Heavy concentration of Gulls, Blackbirds, and Starlings up to 5000′ on and in vicinity of arpt. Deer on and in vicinity of arpt. Flight Notification Service (ADCUS) available.
WEATHER DATA SOURCES: LLWAS.
COMMUNICATIONS: ATIS 135.35 **UNICOM** 122.95
BUFFALO FSS (BUF) on arpt. 122.6 122.2 122.1R 116.4T DL NOTAM FILE BUF.
Ⓡ **BUFFALO APP DEP/CON** 123.8 (055°-194°) 126.5 (195°-279°) 126.15 (280°-054°)
BUFFALO TOWER 120.5 **GND CON** 121.9
CLNC DEL 124.7 **PRE-TAXI CLNC** 124.7
ARSA ctc **APP CON**
RADIO AIDS TO NAVIGATION: NOTAM FILE BUF.
BUFFALO (H) VORTAC 116.4 BUF Chan 111 42°55′44″N 78°38′48″W 288°3.5 NM to fld. 730/08W.
KLUMP NDB (LOM) 231 BU 43°00′01″N 78°39′04″W 233° 4.4 NM to fld.
PLAZZ NDB (LOM) 204 GB 42°52′26″N 78°49′00″W 053° 4.8 NM to fld.
ILS 111.3 I-BUF Rwy 23 LOM KLUMP NDB. Inner marker out of svc indefinitely. Back course unusable beyond 15 NM.
ILS 108.5 I-GBI Rwy 05 LOM PLAZZ NDB.
ASR

FIGURE 120.—Buffalo One Departure (Vector).

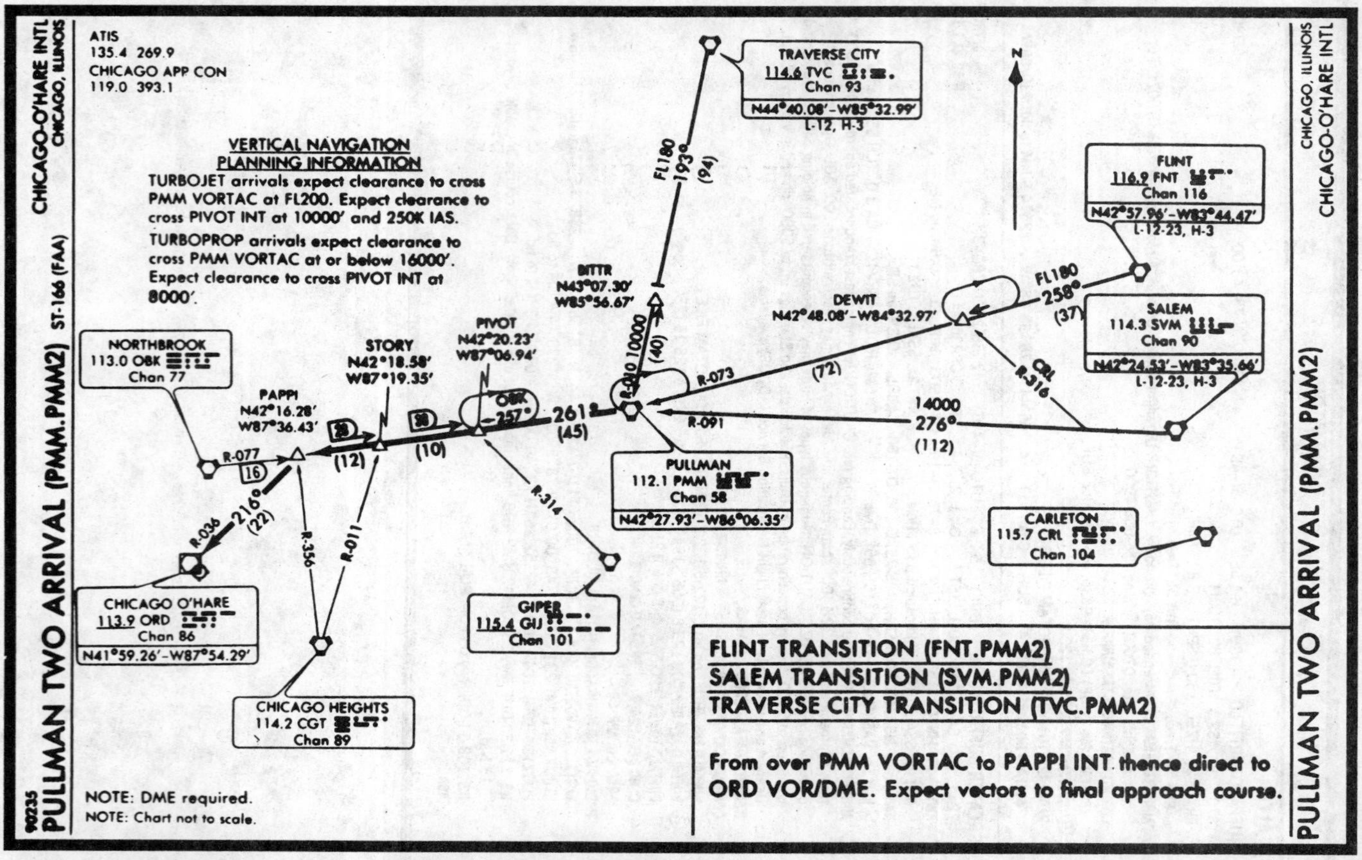

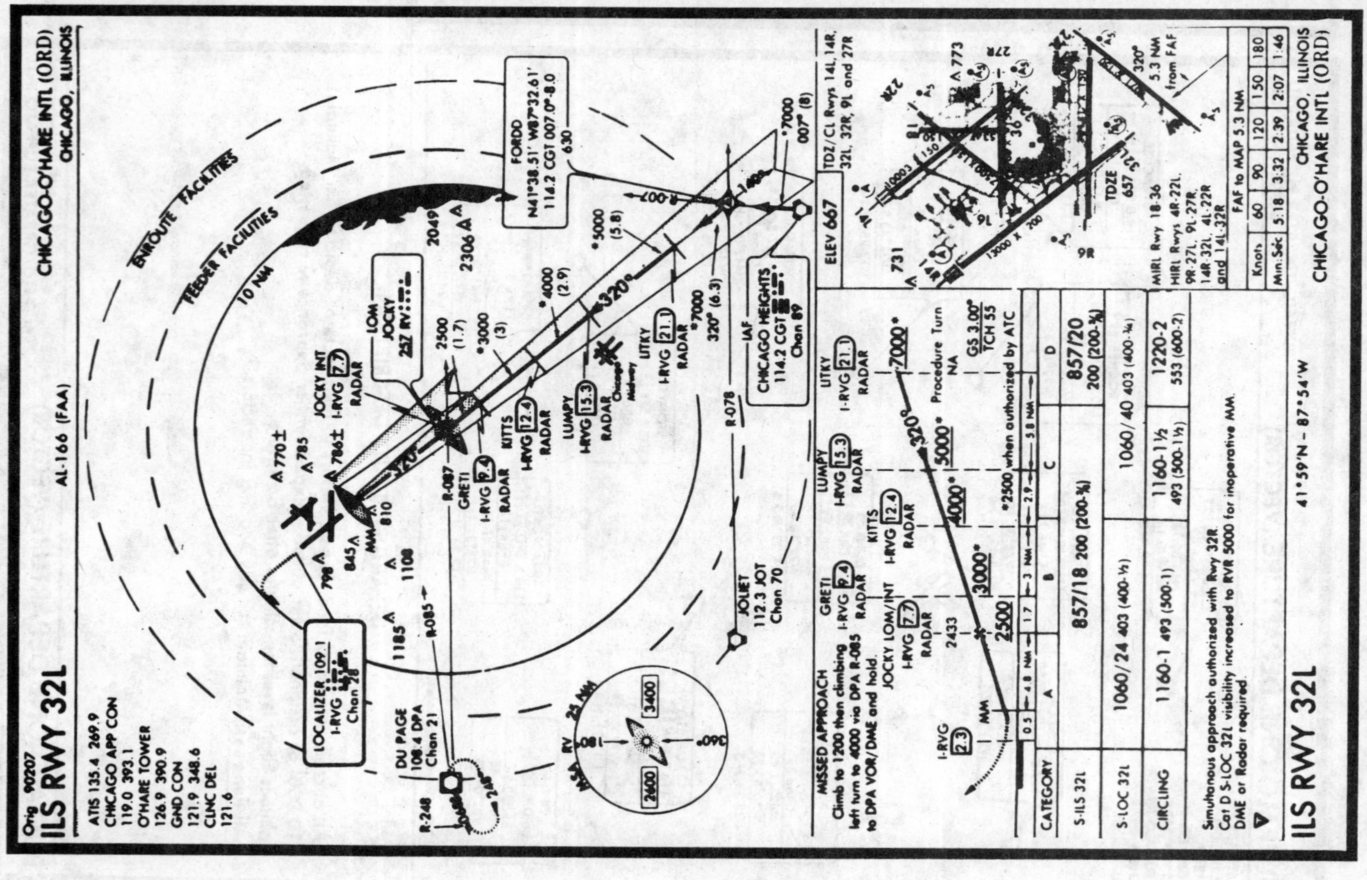

FIGURE 122.—ILS RWY 32L (ORD) / Pullman Two Arrival (PMM.PMM2).

INSTRUMENT APPROACH PROCEDURE CHARTS
RATE OF DESCENT TABLE
(ft. per min.)

A rate of descent table is provided for use in planning and executing precision descents under known or approximate ground speed conditions. It will be especially useful for approaches when the localizer only is used for course guidance. A best speed, power, attitude combination can be programmed which will result in a stable glide rate and attitude favorable for executing a landing if minimums exist upon breakout. Care should always be exercised so that the minimum descent altitude and missed approach point are not exceeded.

ANGLE OF DESCENT (degrees and tenths)	GROUND SPEED (knots)										
	30	45	60	75	90	105	120	135	150	165	180
2.0	105	160	210	265	320	370	425	475	530	585	635
2.5	130	200	265	330	395	465	530	595	665	730	795
3.0	160	240	320	395	480	555	635	715	795	875	955
3.5	185	280	370	465	555	650	740	835	925	1020	1110
4.0	210	315	425	530	635	740	845	955	1060	1165	1270
4.5	240	355	475	595	715	835	955	1075	1190	1310	1430
5.0	265	395	530	660	795	925	1060	1190	1325	1455	1590
5.5	290	435	580	730	875	1020	1165	1310	1455	1600	1745
6.0	315	475	635	795	955	1110	1270	1430	1590	1745	1905
6.5	345	515	690	860	1030	1205	1375	1550	1720	1890	2065
7.0	370	555	740	925	1110	1295	1480	1665	1850	2035	2220
7.5	395	595	795	990	1190	1390	1585	1785	1985	2180	2380
8.0	425	635	845	1055	1270	1480	1690	1905	2115	2325	2540
8.5	450	675	900	1120	1345	1570	1795	2020	2245	2470	2695
9.0	475	715	950	1190	1425	1665	1900	2140	2375	2615	2855
9.5	500	750	1005	1255	1505	1755	2005	2255	2510	2760	3010
10.0	530	790	1055	1320	1585	1845	2110	2375	2640	2900	3165
10.5	555	830	1105	1385	1660	1940	2215	2490	2770	3045	3320
11.0	580	870	1160	1450	1740	2030	2320	2610	2900	3190	3480
11.5	605	910	1210	1515	1820	2120	2425	2725	3030	3335	3635
12.0	630	945	1260	1575	1890	2205	2520	2835	3150	3465	3780

LEGEND 9.—Rate-of-Descent Table.

10.9 B-767 MSP TO DEN (Questions 97-104)

Questions 97 through 104 pertain to an IFR flight from Minneapolis-St. Paul International Airport, Minneapolis, Minnesota to Denver International Airport, Denver, Colorado.

The route is given in block 8 of the flight plan portion of Fig. 190 on page 459. The partially completed flight planning log is given on the bottom portion of Fig. 190.

The following figures are used to answer the eight questions concerning this flight.

Fig.	Page	Title
190	459	Flight Plan/Flight Log
191	460	Minneapolis Four Departure (MSP)
191A	461	Excerpt from *Airport/Facility Directory*
192	427	High Altitude Airways
193	462	Sayge One Arrival (SAYGE.SAYGE1)
193A	463	Sayge One Arrival (SAYGE.SAYGE1)
194	464	Landr One Arrival/Sayge One Arrival
195	465	ILS/DME RWY 35R
195A	466	ILS/DME RWY 35R (DEN)
196	467	Airport Diagram
196A	468	Excerpt from *Airport/Facility Directory*

10.9 B-767 MSP to DEN

97.
9642. (Refer to figures 190, 191, 192, 193, 193A, 194, 195, and 195A on pages 459, 460, 427, 462, 463, 464, 465, and 466.) The estimated time enroute from MSP to DEN for PIL 10 is

A—1 hour 54 minutes.
B—1 hour 57 minutes.
C—2 hours 00 minutes.

Answer (A) is correct (9642). *(IFH Chap XIII)*

To determine the ETE from MSP to DEN, you must complete the flight log in Fig. 190. In the remarks box of the flight plan, the level-off (L/O) point is FSD R-048 at 90 NM. Additionally, the magnetic variation is given at MSP (3°E), FSD (9°E), and LBF (10°E). This information is used to convert the true wind direction to magnetic direction.

Our flight log below has been expanded to provide more detail. To convert the wind direction from true to magnetic, we use 9°E from L/O to OBH and 10°E to AMWAY. Note that the wind direction and speed change after OBH.

	Distance	MC	Wind (mag)	Ground-speed	Time
Level-off	90G	X	X	X	0:19:00G
FSD	90	228	281/89	397	0:13:36
FSD/OBH COP	76.5	199	281/89	435	0:10:33
OBH	76.5	197	281/89	438	0:10:28
OBH/LBF COP	55	251	290/83	389	0:08:29
LBF	55	248	290/83	391	0:08:26
MODES	104	250	290/83	389	0:16:02
AMWAY	11	218	290/83	423	0:01:33
DEN	97G	X	X	X	0:25:00G
					1:53:07

G = Given

Answer (B) is incorrect because an ETE of 1 hr. 57 min. requires a TAS of 435 kt., not 456 kt. Answer (C) is incorrect because an ETE of 2 hr. requires a TAS of 420 kt., not 456 kt.

98.
9643. (Refer to figures 190, 191, 192, 193, 193A, 194, 195, and 195A on pages 459, 460, 427, 462, 463, 464, 465, and 466.) The required fuel that should be onboard PIL 10 at MSP is

A—28,053 pounds.
B—29,057 pounds.
C—29,960 pounds.

Answer (A) is correct (9643). *(IFH Chap XIII)*

To determine the required fuel that should be on board PIL 10 at MSP, you must complete the fuel portion of the flight log on Fig. 190. Use 9,026 PPH total fuel flow from level-off to start of descent and 7,688 PPH total fuel flow for reserve and alternate requirements.

	Time	Fuel (lb.)
Level-off	0:19:00G	4,170.0G
FSD	0:13:36	2,045.9
FSD/OBH COP	0:10:33	1,587.1
OBH	0:10:28	1,574.5
OBH/LBF COP	0:08:29	1,276.2
LBF	0:08:26	1,268.7
MODES	0:16:02	2,411.9
AMWAY	0:01:33	233.2
DEN	0:25:00G	3,107.0G
ABQ	0:36:00G	4,612.8
Reserves	0:45:00	5,766.0
		28,053.3

G = Given

Answer (B) is incorrect because 29,057 lb. includes the approximate fuel required for a missed approach. While this should be included as a practical matter, it is not required by the FARs. Answer (C) is incorrect because 29,960 lb. is the required fuel if 9,026 PPH, not 7,688 PPH, is used for the reserve and alternate requirements.

99.
9644. (Refer to figure 192 on page 427.) On the airway J10 between OBH and LBF, the MAA is 41,000 feet. What is the MAA on J197 between FSD and OBH?

A—43,000 feet.
B—45,000 feet.
C—60,000 feet.

Answer (B) is correct (9644). *(AIM Para 5-3-4)*

The jet route system consists of routes established from 18,000 ft. MSL to 45,000 ft. MSL inclusive. Jet routes are identified by the letter "J" followed by the airway number. Since there is no lower MAA established for J197 between FSD and OBH, the MAA is the upper limit of the jet route.

Answer (A) is incorrect because the upper limit of a jet route is 45,000 ft. MSL, not 43,000 ft. MSL. Answer (C) is incorrect because 60,000 ft. MSL is the upper limit of Class A airspace, not a jet route.

100.
9647. (Refer to figures 193, 193A, and 194 on pages 462, 463, and 464.) The entry points for the (NORTHEAST GATE) LANDR ONE and SAYGE ONE arrivals are approximately

A—11 NM apart.
B—12 NM apart.
C—13 NM apart.

Answer (B) is correct (9647). *(STAR)*

Fig. 194 is JEPP LANDR ONE and SAYGE ONE STAR chart. In the upper left corner is a box titled "Arrival Overview." At the bottom of that box is a note that states the entry points for parallel arrivals (e.g., northeast gate LANDR ONE and SAYGE ONE) are approximately 12 NM apart.

Answer (A) is incorrect because the entry points for the northeast gate LANDR ONE and SAYGE ONE arrivals are approximately 12 NM, not 11 NM, apart. Answer (C) is incorrect because the entry points for the northeast gate LANDR ONE and SAYGE ONE arrivals are approximately 12 NM, not 13 NM, apart.

101.
9645. (Refer to figures 193, 193A, 194, 195, 195A, 196, and 196A on pages 462 through 468.) While being radar vectored for the ILS/DME RWY 35R, Denver Approach Control tells PIL 10 to contact the tower, without giving the frequency. What frequency should PIL 10 use for tower?

A—121.85.
B—132.35.
C—124.3.

Answer (C) is correct (9645). *(IAP)*
Fig. 195 (JEPP) and Fig. 195A (NOS) are the IAP charts for the ILS/DME RWY 35R approach at DEN. In both charts, the communication frequencies are shown in the upper left corner. Under Denver Tower is the frequency 124.3.
Answer (A) is incorrect because 121.85 is the ground control, not tower, frequency for RWY 35R. Answer (B) is incorrect because 132.35 is the tower frequency for RWY 35L, not RWY 35R.

102.
9646. (Refer to figures 190, 195, 195A, 196 and 196A on pages 459, 465, 466, 467, and 468.) The PIC of PIL 10 has 87.5 hours and 26 landings as PIC in the B-767, while operating under Part 121. The PIC has 1,876 hours and 298 landings, as PIC in the L-1011 while operating under Part 121. What are the minimums for the ILS/DME RWY 35R approach at DEN for the PIC?

A—5567/18.
B—5667/42.
C—5631/20.

Answer (A) is correct (9646). *(FAR 121.652)*
If the PIC has not served 100 hr. as PIC in the type of airplane (s)he is operating under Part 121, the MDA or DH must be increased by 100 ft., and the visibility by ½ SM (or 2,400 ft. RVR). However, the PIC time requirement may be reduced (not more than 50%) by substituting one landing in that type of airplane, while operating under Part 121, for one required hour of PIC time, if the PIC has at least 100 hr. as PIC in another type of airplane while operating under Part 121.
Since the PIC has over 100 hr. as PIC in the L-1011 while operating under Part 121, (s)he can substitute each landing in the B-767 for one required hour of PIC time. Thus, the PIC meets the 100-hr. PIC requirement and can use the published minimums of 5567/18 for the ILS/DME RWY 35R approach at DEN.
Answer (B) is incorrect because 5667/42 would be the PIC minimums for the ILS/DME RWY 35R approach at DEN if the PIC had less than, not more than, 100 hr. as PIC in the L-1011. Answer (C) is incorrect because 5631/20 are not minimums for the ILS/DME RWY 35R approach at DEN for a PIC with or without 100 hr. as PIC in the B-767 under Part 121.

103.
9648. (Refer to figures 195, 195A, 196, and 196A on pages 465, 466, 467, and 468.) When PIL 10 becomes visual, at 3.8 NM from the end of Runway 35R, if the aircraft is on glide slope and on course what should the pilot see for a Visual Glideslope Indicator?

A—Two white and two red lights on the left side of the runway, in a row.
B—One white and one red light on the left or right side of the runway, in a row.
C—Two red and two white lights, in a row, on the right side of the runway.

Answer (C) is correct (9648). *(A/FD)*
Fig. 196A is the *A/FD* excerpt for Denver Intl. The runway data begin on the line titled **RWY 17L-35R**. Go down one line to **RWY 35R**, which has information concerning the approach end of the runway. The visual glideslope indicator is given as PAPI (P4R), which means that the PAPI is a four-light system installed on the right side of the runway. Thus, when on the glide slope, the pilot will see two red and two white lights, in a row, on the right side of the runway.
Answer (A) is incorrect because the PAPI on RWY 35R is on the right, not left, side of the runway. Answer (B) is incorrect because RWY 35R has a four-light, not a two-light, PAPI system.

104.
9649. (Refer to figures 195, 195A, 196, and 196A on pages 465, 466, 467, and 468.) All of the runways at Denver Intl have what type of Visual Glideslope Indicators?

A—PVASI.
B—PAPI.
C—APAP.

Answer (B) is correct (9649). *(A/FD)*
Fig. 196A is the *A/FD* excerpt for DEN. Look at the second line of each runway data line for the runway end data which list lighting systems for each runway end. Note that all runways at DEN have PAPI (precision approach path indicator) type of visual glideslope indicators.
Answer (A) is incorrect because all runways at DEN are equipped with PAPI, not PVASI (pulsating/steady burning visual approach slope indicator), type of visual glideslope indicators. Answer (C) is incorrect because all runways at DEN are equipped with PAPI, not APAP (alignment of panels on approach path), type of visual glideslope indicators.

Form Approved: OMB No. 2120-0034

U.S. DEPARTMENT OF TRANSPORTATION FEDERAL AVIATION ADMINISTRATION **FLIGHT PLAN**	(FAA USE ONLY) ☐ PILOT BRIEFING ☐ VNR ☐ STOPOVER	TIME STARTED	SPECIALIST INITIALS

1. TYPE	2. AIRCRAFT IDENTIFICATION	3. AIRCRAFT TYPE/ SPECIAL EQUIPMENT	4. TRUE AIRSPEED	5. DEPARTURE POINT	6. DEPARTURE TIME PROPOSED (Z)	ACTUAL (Z)	7. CRUISING ALTITUDE
VFR X IFR DVFR	PIL 10	B767/G	456 KTS	MSP			FL430

8. ROUTE OF FLIGHT
MINNEAPOLIS FOUR DEPARTURE FSD, J197 OBH, J10 LBF, SAYGE.SAYGE1

9. DESTINATION (Name of airport and city)	10. EST. TIME ENROUTE HOURS	MINUTES	11. REMARKS
DEN			L/O = LEVEL OFF PPH = POUNDS PER HOUR L/O FSD R-048/90 VARIATION: FSD 9E, LBF 10E, MSP 3E

12. FUEL ON BOARD HOURS	MINUTES	13. ALTERNATE AIRPORT(S)	14. PILOT'S NAME, ADDRESS & TELEPHONE NUMBER & AIRCRAFT HOME BASE	15. NUMBER ABOARD
		ABQ ALBUQUERQUE	17. DESTINATION CONTACT/TELEPHONE (OPTIONAL)	190

16. COLOR OF AIRCRAFT	
SILVER/RED	CIVIL AIRCRAFT PILOTS. FAR Part 91 requires you file an IFR flight plan to operate under instrument flight rules in controlled airspace. Failure to file could result in a civil penalty not to exceed $1,000 for each violation (Section 901 of the Federal Aviation Act of 1958, as amended). Filing of a VFR flight plan is recommended as a good operating practice. See also Part 99 for requirements concerning DVFR flight plans.

FAA Form 7233-1 (8-82) CLOSE VFR FLIGHT PLAN WITH ________________ FSS ON ARRIVAL

FLIGHT LOG

CHECK POINTS FROM	TO	ROUTE ALTITUDE	COURSE	WIND TEMP	SPEED-KTS TAS	GS	DIST NM	TIME LEG	TOT	FUEL LEG	TOT
MSP	FSD R-048/90	VECTORS CLIMB					90		:19:00		4170*
FSD R-048/90	FSD	DIRECT FL430		290/89 ISA-6							
FSD	OBH	J197 FL430									
OBH	LBF	J10 FL410		300/83 ISA-5							
LBF	MODES	SAUGE.SAUGE.1 FL410									
MODES	AMWAY	SAUGE.SAUGE.1 FL410									
AMWAY	DEN	DESCENT & APPROACH					97	:25:00		3107	
DEN	ABQ	VECTORS FL410						:36:00			

OTHER DATA: * Includes Taxi Fuel
NOTE: Use 9026 PPH Total Fuel Flow From L/O To Start Of Descent.
Use 7688 PPH Total Fuel Flow For Reserve And Alternate Requirements.
A Missed Approach Requires 1050# of Fuel.

TIME and FUEL: As required by FARs.

TIME	FUEL (LB)	
		EN ROUTE
		RESERVE
		ALTERNATE
		TOTAL

FIGURE 190.—Flight Plan/Flight Log.

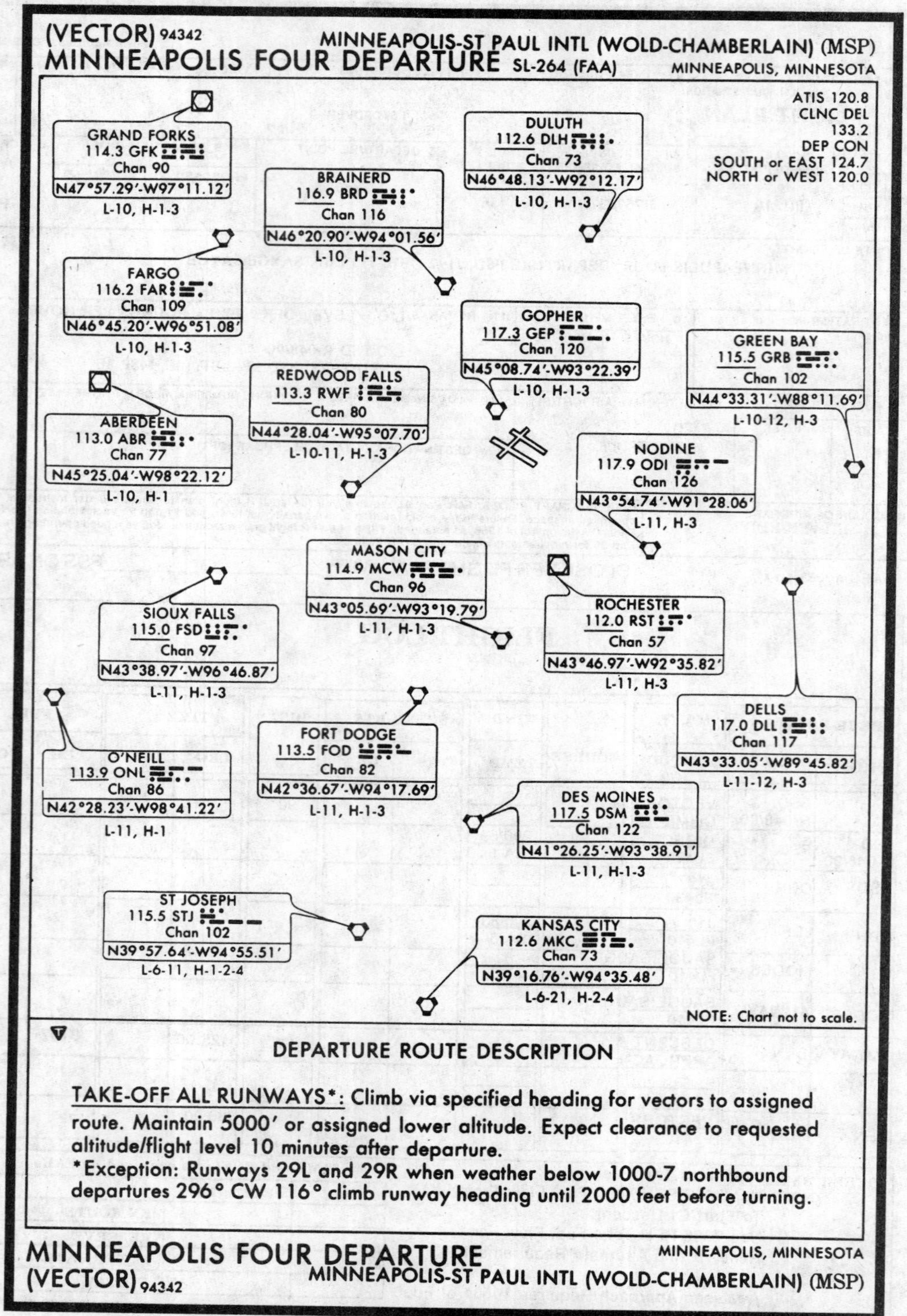

FIGURE 191.—MINNEAPOLIS FOUR DEPARTURE (MSP).

FLYING CLOUD (FCM) 11 SW UTC-6(-5DT) N44°49.63′ W93°27.43′ **TWIN CITIES**
906 B S4 **FUEL** 100, 100LL, JET A OX 3, 4 TPA-1906(1000) **L-10G, A**
RWY 09R-27L: H3909X75 (ASPH) S-30 HIRL **IAP**
RWY 09R: MALSR. VASI(V4L)—GA 3.0° TCH 41′ Rgt tfc.
RWY 27L: REIL. VASI(V4L)—GA 3.0° TCH 45′. Thld dsplcd 200′. Road.
RWY 09L-27R: H3599X75 (ASPH) S-30
RWY 27R: Road. Rgt tfc.
RWY 18-36: H2691X75 (ASPH) S-23 MIRL
RWY 18: VASI(V4L)—GA 3.0° TCH 37′. Barn. **RWY 36:** REIL. VASI(V4L)—GA 3.0° TCH 31′. Road.
AIRPORT REMARKS: Attended 1300-0400Z‡. Rwy 09L-27R CLOSED when twr clsd. Arpt CLOSED to jet acft not meeting FAR 36, jet training and jet acft over 20,000 lbs. Deer and waterfowl on and in vicinity of arpt. Rwy 09R and Rwy 27R rgt tfc during twr hours only. When twr clsd ACTIVATE VASI Rwy 09R, VASI Rwy 18, MALSR Rwy 09R, HIRL Rwy 09R-27L and MIRL Rwy 18-36—118.1.
WEATHER DATA SOURCES: LAWRS
COMMUNICATIONS: CTAF 118.1 **ATIS** 124.9 (612) 944-2970 **UNICOM** 122.95
PRINCETON FSS (PNM) TF 1-800-WX-BRIEF. NOTAM FILE FCM
® **MINNEAPOLIS APP/DEP CON** 125.0
MINNEAPOLIS CLNC DEL 121.7 (When twr closed)
TOWER 118.1 125.2 (Apr-Oct 1300-0400Z‡, Nov-Mar 1300-0300Z‡) **GND CON** 121.7 **CLNC DEL** 121.7
AIRSPACE: CLASS D svc effective Apr-Oct 1300-0400Z‡ Nov-Mar 1300-0300Z‡ other times CLASS G.
RADIO AIDS TO NAVIGATION: NOTAM FILE FCM.
(L) ABVORW/DME 111.8 FCM Chan 55 N44°49.54′ W93°27.41′ at fld. 900/6E.
Route forecast only on TWEB 0400-1100Z‡.
ILS 109.7 I-FCM RWY 09R. LOC unusable byd 30 degrees either side of centerline. GS unusable byd 5 degrees left of course.

MINNEAPOLIS-ST PAUL INTL (WOLD-CHAMBERLAIN) (MSP) 6 SW UTC-6(-5DT) **TWIN CITIES**
N44°53.05′ W93°12.90′ **H-1E, 3G, L-10G, A**
841 B S4 **FUEL** 100, JET A, A1 + OX 1, 2, 3, 4 LRA ARFF Index E **IAP**
RWY 11R-29L: H10000X200 (ASPH-CONC-GRVD) S-65, D-85, DT-145 HIRL CL 0.3% up W
RWY 11R: MALSR. PAPI(P4L)—GA 3.0° TCH 65′. Tree.
RWY 29L: ALSF1. TDZ. PAPI(P4L)—GA 3.0° TCH 73′. Pole.
RWY 04-22: H8256X150 (CONC-GRVD) S-65, D-85, DT-145 HIRL
RWY 04: SSALR. PAPI(P4L)—GA 3.0° TCH 76′.
RWY 22: MALSR. PAPI(P4L)—GA 3.0° TCH 42′. Thld dsplcd 988′. Fence.
RWY 11L-29R: H8200X150 (ASPH-CONC-GRVD) S-100, D-125, DT-210 HIRL
RWY 11L: MALSR. PAPI(P4L)—GA 3.0° TCH 75′. Tree. 0.3% down.
RWY 29R: REIL. PAPI(P4L)—GA 3.0° TCH 73′.
AIRPORT REMARKS: Attended continuously. Birds on and in vicinity of arpt. Training prohibited. Only Initial departure and full stop termination training flights permitted. PPR for noise abatement procedures —call 612-726-9411. No stage 1 noise Category Civil acft. Landing fee. Flight Notification Service (ADCUS) available. NOTE: See Land and Hold Short Operations Section.
WEATHER DATA SOURCES: LLWAS.
COMMUNICATIONS: ATIS 135.35 (612) 726-9240. 120.8 (TCA ARR INFO) **UNICOM** 122.95
PRINCETON FSS (PNM) TF 1-800-WX-BRIEF. NOTAM FILE MSP.
RCO 122.55 122.3 (PRINCETON FSS) **RCO** 122.1R 115.3T (PRINCETON FSS)
® **APP CON** 119.3 (N or E of arrival rwy) 126.95 (S or W of arrival rwy and Rwys 04, 11R and 29L)
TOWER 126.7 (Rwys 11R-29L and 04-22) 123.95 (Rwy 11L-29R) **GND CON** 121.9 (S) 121.8 (N) **CLNC DEL** 133.2
® **DEP CON** 127.925 (N or E of arrival rwy) 124.7 (S or W of arrival rwy)
AIRSPACE: CLASS B: See VFR Terminal Area Chart.
RADIO AIDS TO NAVIGATION: NOTAM FILE MSP.
(H) VORTAC 115.3 MSP Chan 100 N44°52.92′ W93°13.99′ at fld. 850/3E.
VOR portion unusable below 3000′, beyond 20 NM below 4000′, 205°-235°/265°-025° all distances and altitudes, 235°-265° below 7000′.
NARCO NDB (MH-SAB/LOM) 266 MS N44°49.55′ W93°05.48′ 299° 6.3 NM to fld.
Route forecast only on TWEB 0400-1100Z‡.
VAGEY NDB (LOM) 338 AP N44°49.45′ W93°18.36′ 042° 5.3 NM to fld. Unmonitored.
ILS 109.9 I-INN Rwy 29R
ILS/DME 110.3 I-MSP Chan 40 Rwy 29L LOM NARCO NDB.
ILS 109.3 I-APL Rwy 04 LOM VAGEY NDB. Glide slope unusable for coupled approaches below 1085.
ILS/DME 110.3 I-HKZ Chan 40 Rwy 11R.
ILS 110.7 I-PJL Rwy 11L.
ILS 110.5 I-SIJ Rwy 22.

MOBERG AIR BASE SPB (See BEMIDJI)

FIGURE 191A.—Excerpt from Airport/Facilities Directory.

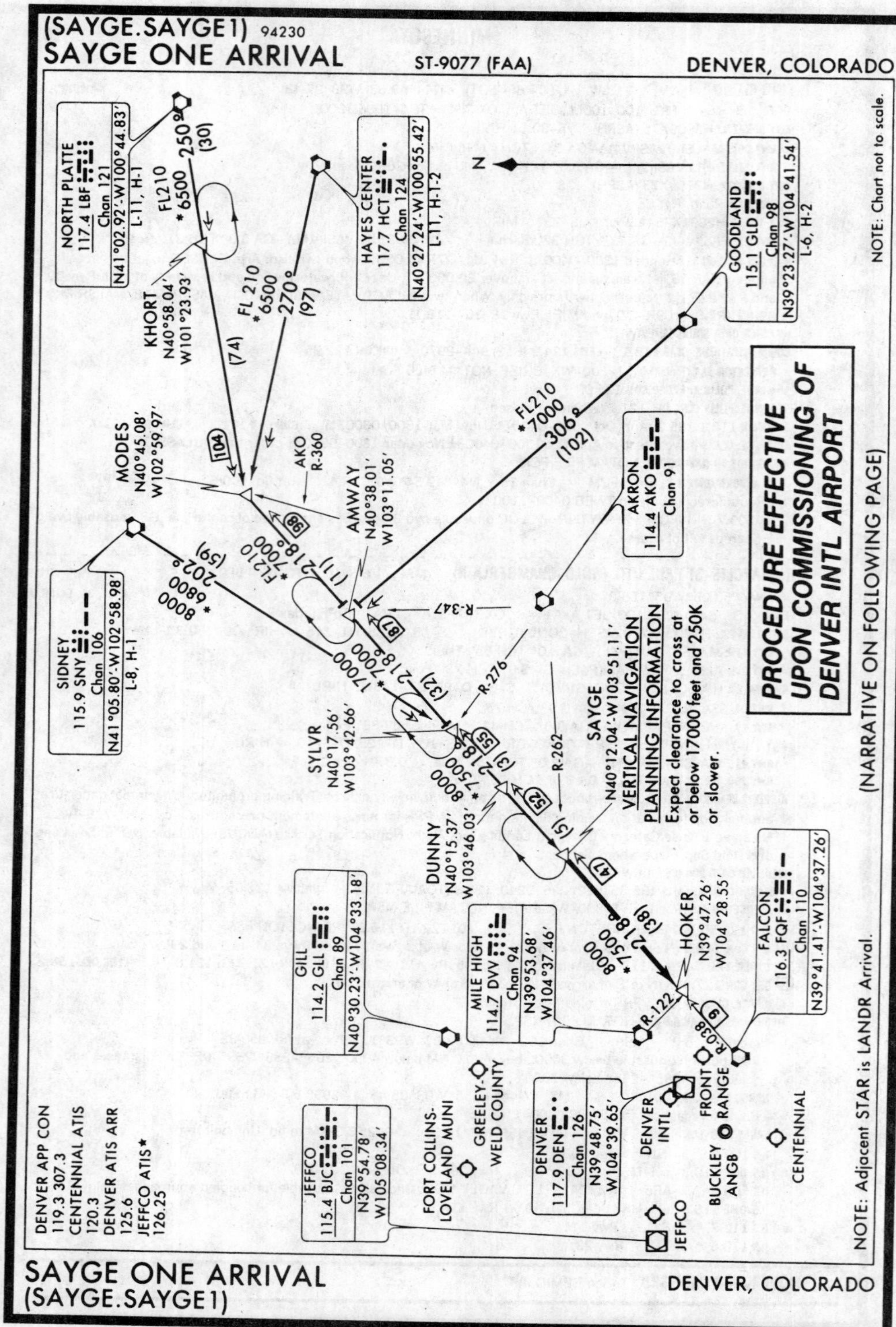

FIGURE 193.—SAYGE ONE ARRIVAL (SAYGE.SAYGE1).

(SAYGE.SAYGE1) 93315

SAYGE ONE ARRIVAL ST-9077 (FAA) DENVER, COLORADO

ARRIVAL DESCRIPTION

GOODLAND TRANSITION (GLD.SAYGE1): From over GLD VORTAC via GLD R-306 and FQF R-038 to SAYGE INT. Thence . . . .

HAYES CENTER TRANSITION (HCT.SAYGE1): From over HCT VORTAC via HCT R-270 and FQF R-038 to SAYGE INT. Thence . . . .

NORTH PLATTE TRANSITION (LBF.SAYGE1): From over LBF VORTAC via LBF R-250 and FQF R-038 to SAYGE INT. Thence . . . .

SIDNEY TRANSITION (SNY.SAYGE1): From over SNY VORTAC via SNY R-202 and FQF R-038 to SAYGE INT. Thence . . . .

. . . . From over SAYGE INT via FQF R-038 to HOKER INT. Expect radar vectors to the final approach course at or before HOKER INT.

PROCEDURE EFFECTIVE UPON COMMISSIONING OF DENVER INTL AIRPORT

SAYGE ONE ARRIVAL DENVER, COLORADO
(SAYGE.SAYGE1)

FIGURE 193A.—SAYGE ONE ARRIVAL (SAYGE.SAYGE1).

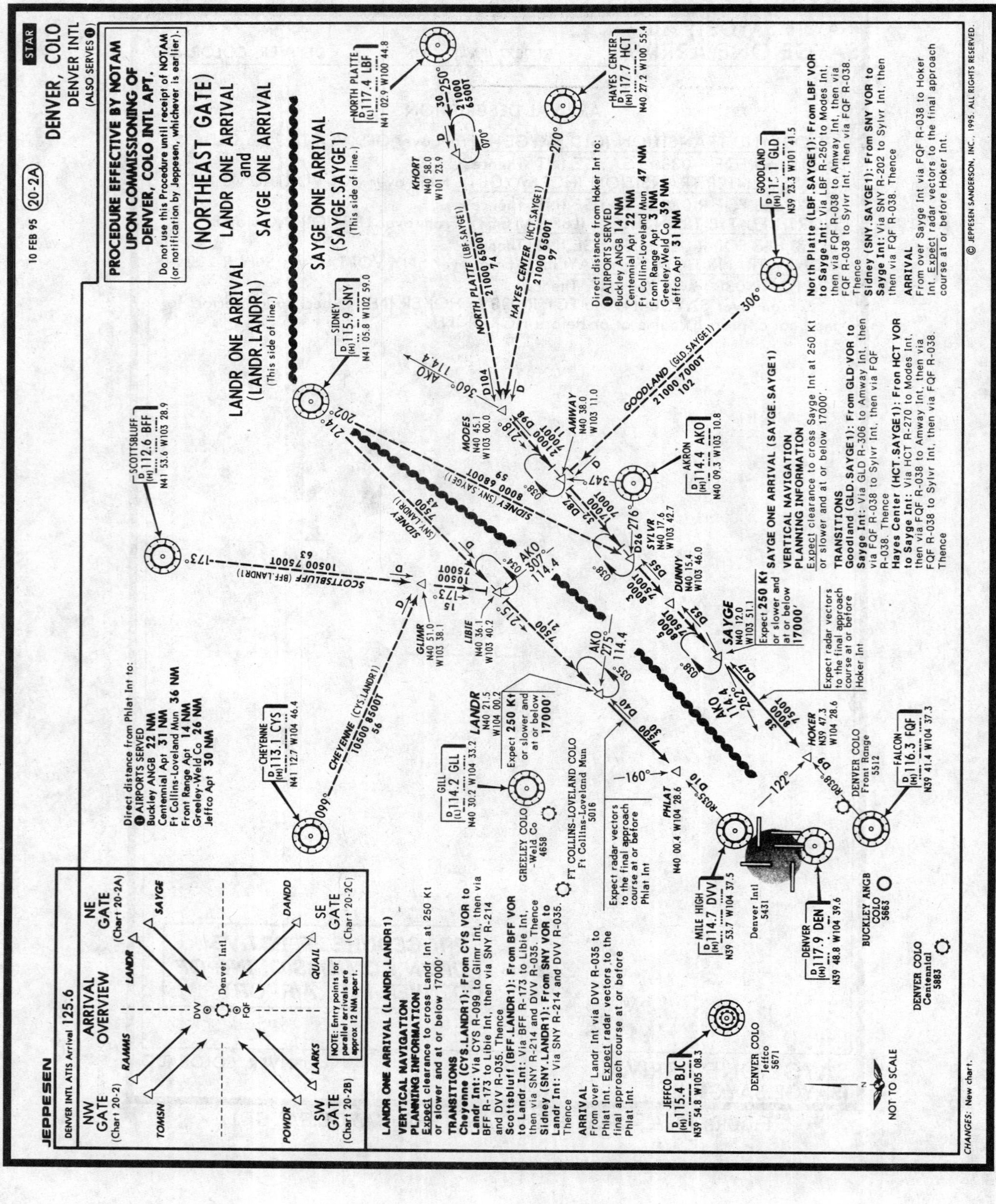

FIGURE 194.—Landr One Arrival/Sayge One Arrival.

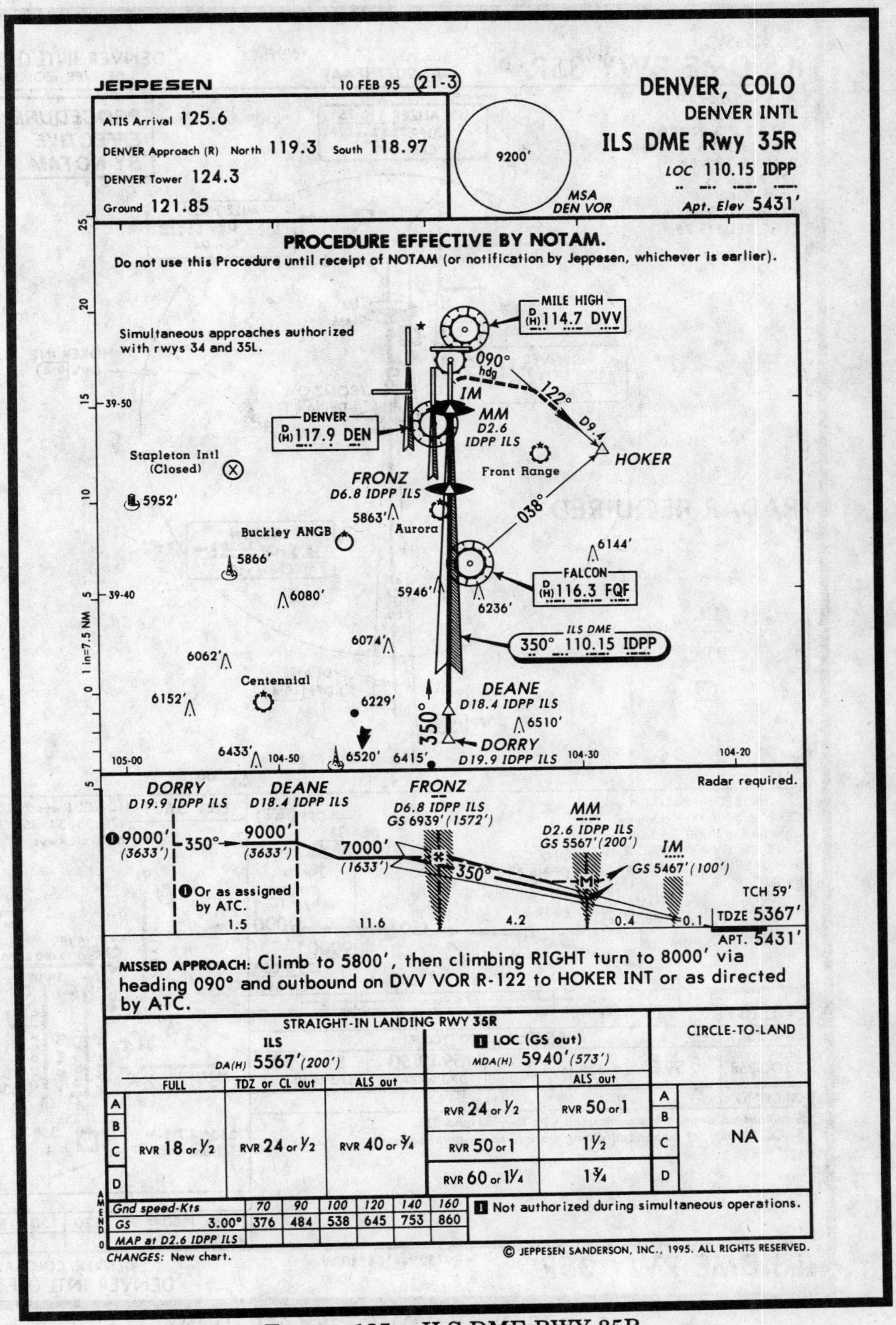

FIGURE 195.—ILS DME RWY 35R.

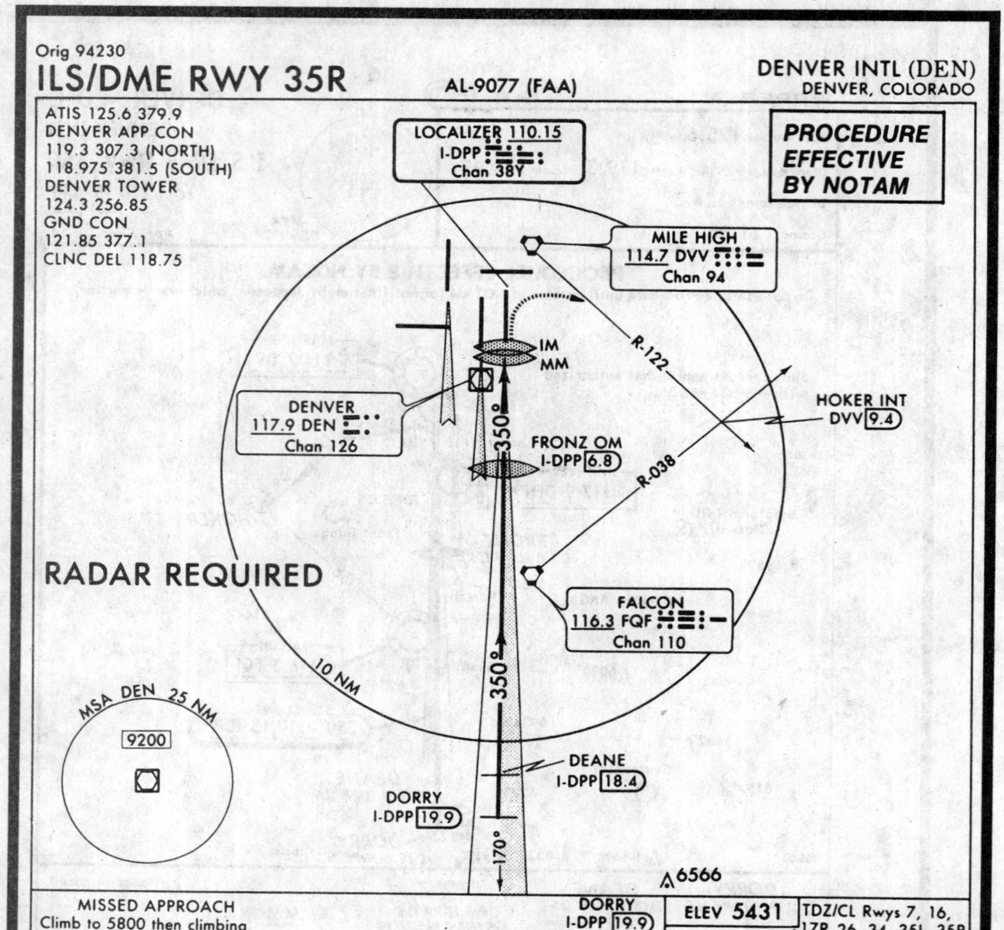

CATEGORY	A	B	C	D
S-ILS 35R	5567/18 200 (200-⅜)			
S-LOC 35R	5940/24 573 (600-½)		5940/50 573 (600-1)	5940/60 573 (600-1¼)
CIRCLING	NA			

Simultaneous approaches authorized with Rwy 34 and 35L.
S-LOC minima not authorized during simultaneous operations.

Knots	60	90	120	150	180
Min:Sec					

FIGURE 195A.—ILS/DME RWY 35R (DEN).

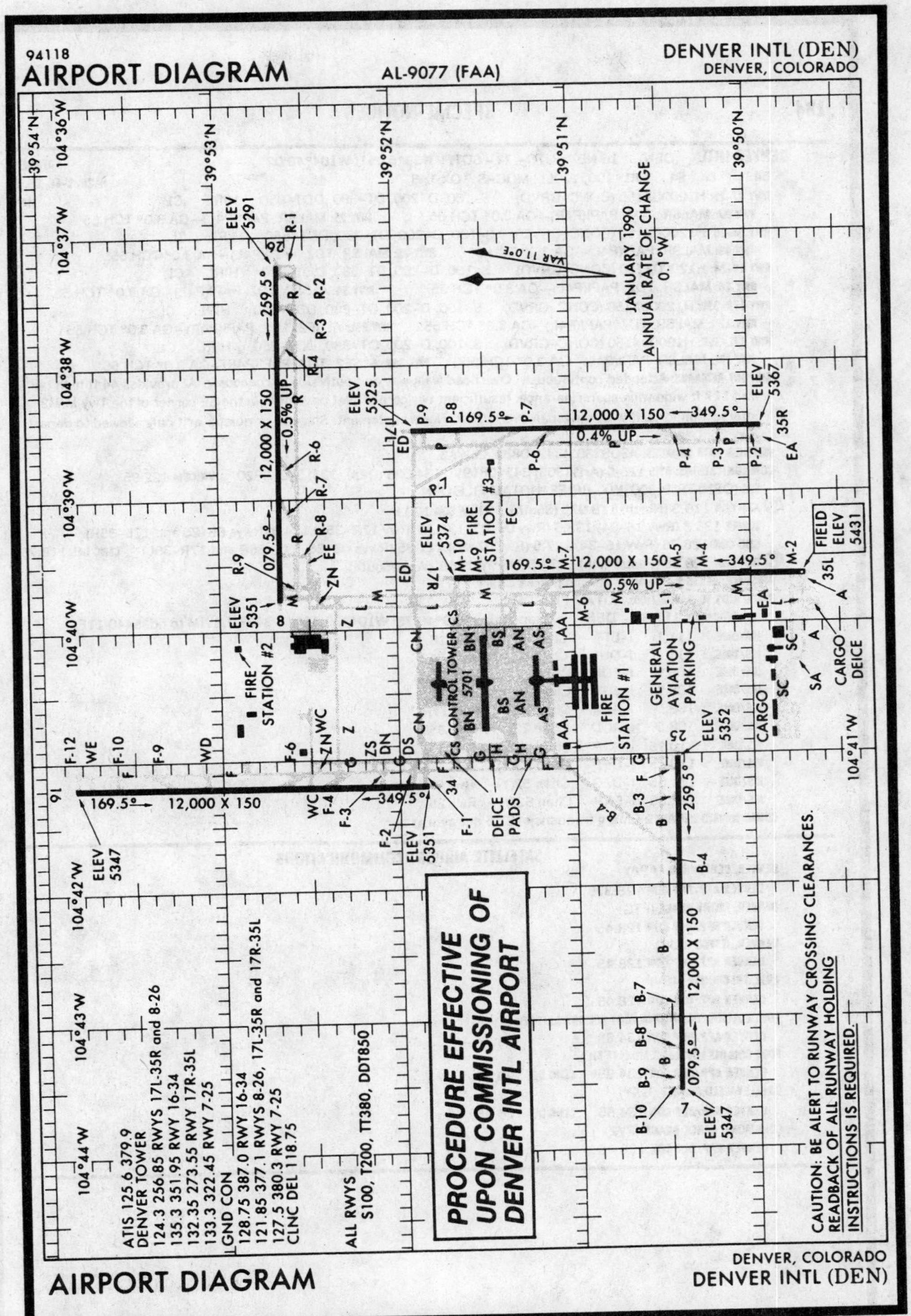

FIGURE 196.—AIRPORT DIAGRAM.

184 **SPECIAL NOTICES**

DENVER INTL (DEN) 16 NE UTC–7(–6DT) N39°51.51′ W104°40.02′ **DENVER**
5431 B S4 **FUEL** 100, 100LL, MOGAS OX 1, 3 **H-2D, L-6E, 8G, A**
RWY 07-25: H12000X150 (CONC-GRVD) S-100, D-200, DT-380, DDT-850 HIRL CL **IAP**
RWY 07: MALSR. TDZ. PAPI(P4R)—GA 3.0° TCH 55.′ **RWY 25:** MALSR. PAPI(P4L)—GA 3.0° TCH 55′.
RWY 08-26: H12000X150 (CONC-GRVD) S-100, D-200, DT-380, DDT-850 HIRL CL
RWY 08: MALSR. PAPI(P4L)—GA 3.0° TCH 55′. **RWY 26:** MALSR. TDZ. PAPI(P4L)—GA 3.0° TCH 55′.
RWY 16-34: H12000X150 (CONC-GRVD) S-100, D-200, DT-380, DDT-850 HIRL CL
RWY 16: MALSR. TDZ. PAPI(P4L)—GA 3.0° TCH 55.′ **RWY 34:** ALSF2. TDZ. PAPI(P4L)—GA 3.0° TCH 55′.
RWY 17R-35L: H12000X150 (CONC-GRVD) S-100, D-200, DT-380, DDT-850 HIRL CL
RWY 17R: MALSR. TDZ. PAPI(P4L)—GA 3.0° TCH 55′. **RWY 35L:** ALSF2. TDZ. PAPI(P4R)—GA 3.0° TCH 55′.
RWY 17L-35R: H12000X150 (CONC-GRVD) S-100, D-200, DT-380, DDT-850 HIRL CL
RWY 17L: MALSR. PAPI(P4L)—GA 3.0° TCH 55′. **RWY 35R:** ALSF2. TDZ. PAPI(P4R)—GA 3.0° TCH 55′.
AIRPORT REMARKS: Attended continuously. Overhead walk-way on South side of concourse 'A' provides 44 ft high tail and 117 ft wide wing span clearance. Insufficient twy corner fillet pavement in the SE corner of the Twy M/M2 intersection for acft with wingspan over 107 ft. Noise abatement: Stage III or quieter acft only allowed to depart Rwy 25. Ldg fee.
WEATHER DATA SOURCES: ASOS (303)342-0838. LLWAS.
COMMUNICATIONS: ATIS 125.6 (Arr) (303) 342-0819 134.025 (Dep) (303) 342-0820 **UNICOM** 122.95
FSS (DEN) TF 1-800-WX-BRIEF. NOTAM FILE DEN.
® **APP CON** 119.3 (North) 118.975 (South) **FINAL CON** 120.8
TOWER 135.3 (Rwy 16-34) 133.3 (Rwy 07-25) 132.35 (Rwy 17R-35L) 124.3 (Rwys 08-26 and 17L-35R)
GND CON 128.75 (Rwy 16-34) 127.5 (Rwy 07-25) 121.85 (Rwys 08-26, 17L-35R and 17R-35L) **CLNC DEL** 118.75
® **DEP CON** 128.25 (East/South) 127.05 (North) 126.1 (West/South)
AIRSPACE: CLASS B See VFR Terminal Area Chart.
RADIO AIDS TO NAVIGATION: NOTAM FILE DEN.
(H) VORW/DME 117.9 DEN Chan 126 N39°48.75′ W104°39.65′ 343° 2.8 NM to fld. 5440/11E.

ILS/DME	111.1	I-LTT	Chan 48	Rwy 16.
ILS/DME	111.1	I-OUF	Chan 48	Rwy 34.
ILS/DME	108.9	I-FUI	Chan 26	Rwy 08.
ILS/DME	108.9	I-JOY	Chan 26	Rwy 26.
ILS/DME	108.5	I-ACX	Chan 22	Rwy 17R.
ILS/DME	108.5	I-AQD	Chan 22	Rwy 35L.
ILS/DME	110.15	I-BXP	Chan 38(Y)	Rwy 17L.
ILS/DME	110.15	I-DPP	Chan 38(Y)	Rwy 35R.
ILS/DME	111.55	I-DZG	Chan 52(Y)	Rwy 07.
ILS/DME	111.55	I-ERP	Chan 52(Y)	Rwy 25.

COMM/NAVAID REMARKS: Emerg frequency 121.5 not avbl at twr.

SATELLITE AIRPORT COMMUNICATIONS

DENVER, CENTENNIAL (APA)
DENVER APP/DEP CON 126.375
DENVER, FRONT RANGE (FTG)
DENVER APP/DEP CON 128.45
DENVER, JEFFCO (BJC)
DENVER APP/DEP CON 128.45
ERIE, TRI-COUNTY (48V)
DENVER APP/DEP CON 128.45
FORT COLLINS, DOWNTOWN FORT COLLINS AIRPARK (3V5)
DENVER APP/DEP CON 134.85
FORT COLLINS-LOVELAND MUNI (FNL)
DENVER APP/DEP CON 134.85 **CLNC DEL** 120.25
GREELEY-WELD COUNTY (GXY)
DENVER APP/DEP CON 134.85 **CLNC DEL** 126.65
LONGMONT, VANCE BRAND (2V2)
DENVER APP/DEP CON 128.45

FIGURE 196A.—Excerpt from Airport/Facilities Directory.

10.10 B-747 LAS TO SFO (Questions 105-115)

Questions 105 through 115 pertain to an IFR flight from McCarran International Airport, Las Vegas, Nevada to San Francisco International, San Francisco, California.

The route is given in block 8 of the flight plan portion of Fig. 202 on page 473. The partially completed flight planning log is given on the bottom portion of Fig. 202.

The following figures are used to answer the 11 questions concerning this flight.

Fig.	Page	Title
202	473	Flight Plan/Flight Log
185A	474	Excerpt from *Airport/Facility Directory*
203	475	Oasis Eight Departure (LAS)
203A	476	Oasis Eight Departure (Departure Route Descriptions)
204	430	High Altitude Airways
205	477	Excerpt from *Airport/Facility Directory*
205A	478	Locke One Arrival (MOD.LOCKE1)
206	479	ILS RWY 19L (SFO)
206A	480	Airport Diagram
207	481	ILS RWY 11 (OAK)
207A	482	Excerpt from *Airport/Facility Directory*
Legend 15	483	Directory Legend

10.10 B-747 LAS to SFO

105.
9664. (Refer to figure 202 on page 473.) In block 3 of the flight plan, there is the following entry: B/B747/R. What does the prefix "B" indicate?

A—Foreign air carrier (Brazil).
B—TCAS and heavy.
C—DME and transponder but no altitude encoding capability.

Answer (B) is correct (9664). *(AIM Para 5-1-7)*

In a flight plan, a prefix "B" before the airplane type in block 3 indicates that the airplane is TCAS equipped and heavy.

Answer (A) is incorrect because block 2 (aircraft identification), not block 3 (aircraft type), lists the identifier for Brazil before the airplane number. Answer (C) is incorrect because the presence of a DME and a transponder without altitude-reporting capability is indicated by a "/B" after, not before, the airplane type.

106.
9665. (Refer to figure 202 on page 473.) In block 3 of the flight plan, there is the following entry: B/B747/R. What does the suffix "/R" indicate?

A—RNAV/Transponder/altitude encoding capability.
B—That the flight plan contains an RNAV route.
C—RNAV/TCAS/Transponder/altitude encoding capability.

Answer (A) is correct (9665). *(AIM Para 5-1-7)*

The suffix "/R" to the airplane type indicates that the airplane has RNAV (area navigation) and a transponder with altitude-encoding capability.

Answer (B) is incorrect because block 3 contains information on the aircraft equipment (i.e., RNAV and a transponder with altitude encoding), not routing information. Answer (C) is incorrect because "B/," not "/R," indicates the airplane is TCAS equipped and the airplane is heavy.

107.
9657. (Refer to figures 185A, 202, 203, 203A, 204, 205A, and 206 on pages 474, 473, 475, 476, 430, 478, and 479.) The ETE on this flight (PTL 55 LAS-SFO) is

A—1 hour 25 minutes.
B—1 hour 27 minutes.
C—1 hour 29 minutes.

Answer (C) is correct (9657). ***(IFH Chap XIII)***

To determine the ETE from LAS to SFO, you must complete the flight log in Fig. 202. The level-off point is determined by following the Oasis Eight Departure (Fig. 203) for 65 NM from LAS, which is SHADO intersection. Magnetic variation at LAS is 15°E (Fig. 185A), and at SFO, it is 17°E (Fig. 205). This information is used to convert the true wind direction to magnetic direction.

Our flight log below has been expanded to provide more detail. To convert the wind direction from true to magnetic, we use 15°E from L/O (SHADO) to OAL and 17°E to GROAN.

	Distance	MC	Wind (mag)	Ground-speed	Time
Level-off	65G	X	X	X	0:21:00G
BTY	41	306	325/53	410	0:06:00
BTY/OAL COP	43.5	310	325/53	409	0:06:22
OAL	43.5	309	325/53	409	0:06:22
OAL/MOD COP	77	246	323/53	445	0:10:22
MOD	77	244	323/53	447	0:10:20
GROAN	16	245	323/53	446	0:02:09
SFO	75G	X	X	X	0:26:00G
					1:28:35

G = Given

Answer (A) is incorrect because an ETE of 1 hr. 25 min. requires a TAS of approximately 480 kt., not 460 kt. Answer (B) is incorrect because 1 hr. 27 min. is the ETE from LAS to SFO if true, not magnetic, wind direction is used.

108.
9656. (Refer to figures 185A, 202, 203, 203A, 204, 205A, and 206 on pages 474, 473, 475, 476, 430, 478, and 479.) For PTL 55 to be dispatched on this flight plan (LAS-SFO), how much fuel is required to be onboard at the start of taxi?

A—27,800 pounds.
B—28,317 pounds.
C—29,450 pounds.

Answer (B) is correct (9656). ***(IFH Chap XIII)***

To determine how much fuel is required to be on board PTL 55 at the start of taxi at LAS, you must complete the fuel portion of the flight log on Fig. 202. Use 12,000 PPH total fuel flow from level-off to start of descent and 11,000 PPH total fuel flow for reserve and alternate requirements.

	Time	Fuel (lb.)
Level-off	0:21:00G	5,600.0G
BTY	0:06:00	1,200.0
BTY/OAL COP	0:06:22	1,273.3
OAL	0:06:22	1,273.3
OAL/MOD COP	0:10:22	2,073.3
MOD	0:10:20	2,066.7
GROAN	0:02:09	430.0
SFO	0:26:00G	4,500.0G
OAK	0:09:00G	1,650.0
Reserves	0:45:00	8,250.0
		28,316.6

G = Given

Answer (A) is incorrect because 27,000 lb. is the approximate fuel required if 11,000 PPH, not 12,000 PPH, total fuel flow is used from level-off to start of descent. Answer (C) is incorrect because 29,450 lb. includes the 1,133 lb. of fuel required for a missed approach. While this should be included as a practical matter, it is not required by the FARs.

109.
9660. (Refer to figures 203 and 203A on pages 475 and 476.) PTL 55 will be unable to cross the Oasis Intersection at 9,500 feet. What should the crew do?

A—Enter holding on R-211 LAS at 15 DME, right-hand turns, advise Departure Control, climb to 9,500 prior to Oasis.
B—Advise Las Vegas Departure Control and request radar vectors.
C—Continue the climb on LAS R-211 to 9,500 feet, then turn right to 260°.

Answer (C) is correct (9660). *(SID)*
Fig. 203 is the SID chart. At the top center of the chart are five notes concerning the SID. PTL 55 has filed the Beatty transition. The first note is about the Beatty transition. The note states that aircraft unable to cross OASIS at 9,500 ft. should continue the climb on LAS R-211 to 9,500 ft., then turn right to 260°.
Answer (A) is incorrect because the SID states that aircraft unable to cross OASIS at 9,500 ft. should continue the climb on LAS R-211, not enter a holding pattern at OASIS while climbing to 9,500 ft. Answer (B) is incorrect because the SID states that aircraft unable to cross OASIS at 9,500 ft. should continue the climb on LAS R-211 to 9,500 ft., then turn to 260°, not request radar vectors from Las Vegas Departure.

110.
9662. (Refer to figures 202 and 206 on pages 473 and 479.) PTL 55 received the following clearance from SFO Approach Control. PTL 55 is cleared ILS RWY 19L at SFO, sidestep to RWY 19R. 1.3 times the V_{S0} speed, of PTL 55, is 165 knots. What is the lowest minimum descent altitude (MDA) and the lowest visibility that PTL 55 may accomplish the sidestep?

A—340-1.
B—340-1-½.
C—340-2.

Answer (C) is correct (9662). *(IAP)*
Fig. 206 is the IAP chart for the ILS RWY 19L at SFO. Look at the minimums section at the lower left portion of the chart. On the left side of the table, locate the SIDESTEP RWY 19R row. Since PTL 55 has a speed of 1.3 V_{S0} of 165 kt., it is an approach category D airplane (i.e., 1.3 V_{S0} of 141 kt. or more, but less than 166 kt.). The minimums for a Cat. D airplane for the side step to RWY 19R approach are 340-2.
Answer (A) is incorrect because 340-1 (note that 1 SM is equivalent to an RVR of 5,000 ft.) are the minimums for Cat. A and B, not Cat. D, aircraft for the side step to RWY 19R approach. Answer (B) is incorrect because 340-1½ are the minimums for a Cat. C, not Cat. D, aircraft for the side step to RWY 19R approach.

111.
9663. (Refer to figure 206 on page 479.) The PIC of PTL 55 has 75 hours and 30 landings as PIC in the B-747, while operating under Part 121. The PIC has 759 hours and 312 landings, as PIC, in the B-767 while operating under Part 121. What are the minimums for the ILS RWY 19L approach at SFO, for the PIC?

A—308/64.
B—208/40.
C—308-1.

Answer (B) is correct (9663). *(FAR 121.652)*
If the PIC has not served 100 hr. as PIC in the type of airplane (s)he is operating under Part 121, the MDA or DH must be increased by 100 ft. and the visibility by ½ SM (or 2,400 ft. RVR). However, the PIC time requirement may be reduced (not more than 50%) by substituting one landing in that type of airplane, while operating under Part 121, for one required hour of PIC time if the PIC has at least 100 hr. as PIC in another type of airplane while operating under Part 121.
Since the PIC has over 100 hr. as PIC in the B-767 while operating under Part 121, (s)he can substitute each landing in the B-747 for one hour of required PIC time. Thus, the PIC meets the 100-hr. PIC requirement and can use the published minimums of 208/40 for the ILS RWY 19L approach at SFO.
Answer (A) is incorrect because 308/64 would be the minimums for the PIC if (s)he had less than, not more than, 100 hr. as PIC in another type of airplane while operating under Part 121. Answer (C) is incorrect because 308-1 would be the minimums if SFO was used as the alternate, not destination, and the PIC had less than, not more than, 100 hr. as PIC in another type of airplane while operating under Part 121.

112.
9669. (Refer to legend 15 and figure 205 on pages 483 and 477.) San Francisco Intl (SFO) is an FAR Part 139 airport. What is the minimum number of aircraft rescue and fire fighting vehicles, and the type and amount of fire fighting agents that the airport should have?

A—Three vehicles and 500 pounds of dry chemical (DC) or Halon 1211 or 450 pounds DC and 4,000 gallons of water.
B—Three vehicles and 500 pounds of dry chemical (DC) or Halon 1211 or 500 pounds of DC plus 5,000 gallons of water.
C—Three vehicles and 500 pounds of dry chemical (DC) or Halon 1211 or 450 pounds DC plus 6,000 gallons of water.

Answer (C) is correct (9669). *(A/FD)*

Fig. 205 is the *A/FD* excerpt for SFO. First, look for the aircraft rescue and fire-fighting (ARFF) index on the second line, which is ARFF Index E.

Next, Legend 15 is an *A/FD* legend. Look at the table under item 16. Locate the Airport Index column on the left side and move down to Index E. The minimum number of vehicles is three, and the airport is required to have at least 500 lb. of dry chemical (DC) or HALON 1211 or 450 lb. DC plus 6,000 gal. of water (H_2O).

Answer (A) is incorrect because three vehicles and 500 lb. DC or HALON 1211 or 450 lb. DC and 4,000 gal. of water are required at OAK (ARFF Index D), not SFO (ARFF Index E). Answer (B) is incorrect because an airport with an ARFF Index E is required to have three vehicles and 500 lb. DC or HALON 1211 or 450 lb., not 500 lb., DC plus 6,000 gal., not 5,000 gal., of water.

113.
9666. (Refer to figures 205 and 206A on pages 477 and 480.) At San Francisco Intl (SFO), the runway hold position signs are

A—all on the left-hand side of the taxiways.
B—all on the right-hand side of the taxiways.
C—on either side of the taxiways.

Answer (C) is correct (9666). *(IAP)*

Fig. 206A is the airport diagram for SFO. On the right side of the diagram, you will find a note that states, "Several runway hold position signs are on the right rather than the left side of the taxiways."

Answer (A) is incorrect because, while normally runway hold position signs are on the left side of the taxiways, SFO has some on the right side, as noted in the *A/FD*. Answer (B) is incorrect because several, not all, runway hold position signs are on the right rather than the left side of the taxiways.

114.
9661. (Refer to figures 205 and 206 on pages 477 and 479.) What is the maximum weight that PTL 55 may weigh for landing at San Francisco Intl (SFO)?

A—710,000 pounds.
B—715,000 pounds.
C—720,000 pounds.

Answer (A) is correct (9661). *(A/FD)*

Fig. 206 is the ILS RWY 19L approach to SFO; thus we assume that PTL 55 will be landing on RWY 19L. Fig. 205 is the *A/FD* excerpt for SFO. Look for the section titled **Airport Remarks** and go to the 10th line. There, RWY 01R-19L (among others) is listed along with aircraft and maximum weight. The maximum weight for a B-747 is 710,000 lb.

Answer (B) is incorrect because the maximum weight for a B-747 on RWY 19L at SFO is 710,000 lb., not 715,000 lb. Answer (C) is incorrect because the maximum weight for a B-747 on RWY 19L at SFO is 710,000 lb., not 720,000 lb.

115.
9667. (Refer to figures 207 and 207A on pages 481 and 482.) Due to weather PTL 55 was unable to land at SFO. PTL 55 was given radar vectors to COMMO Intersection and clearance to fly the ILS RWY 11 approach at Oakland Intl. What frequencies will PTL 55 use for Oakland Tower and Oakland Ground Control?

A—118.3 and 121.75.
B—127.2 and 121.75.
C—127.2 and 121.9.

Answer (B) is correct (9667). *(IAP)*

Fig. 207 is the IAP chart for the ILS RWY 11 approach at OAK. The communication frequencies are listed in the upper right corner of the planview section. Look for RWY 11-29. The tower control frequency is 127.2, and the ground control frequency of 121.75 is given on the next line.

Answer (A) is incorrect because 118.3 is the tower frequency for RWY 9-27 and RWY 15-33, not RWY 11-29. Answer (C) is incorrect because 121.9 is the ground control frequency for RWY 9-27 and RWY 15-33, not RWY 11-29.

Form Approved: OMB No. 2120-0034

U.S. DEPARTMENT OF TRANSPORTATION FEDERAL AVIATION ADMINISTRATION **FLIGHT PLAN**	(FAA USE ONLY)	☐ PILOT BRIEFING ☐ STOPOVER	☐ VNR	TIME STARTED	SPECIALIST INITIALS

1. TYPE	2. AIRCRAFT IDENTIFICATION	3. AIRCRAFT TYPE/ SPECIAL EQUIPMENT	4. TRUE AIRSPEED	5. DEPARTURE POINT	6. DEPARTURE TIME PROPOSED (Z)	ACTUAL (Z)	7. CRUISING ALTITUDE
VFR X IFR DVFR	PTL 55	B/B747/R	460 KTS	LAS LAS VEGAS			FL390

8. ROUTE OF FLIGHT
LAS OASIS8.BTY, J92 OAL, OAL.LOCKE SFO

9. DESTINATION (Name of airport and city)	10. EST. TIME ENROUTE HOURS	MINUTES	11. REMARKS
SFO SAN FRANCISCO INT'L.			L/O = LEVEL OFF PPH = POUNDS PER HOUR

12. FUEL ON BOARD HOURS	MINUTES	13. ALTERNATE AIRPORT(S)	14. PILOT'S NAME, ADDRESS & TELEPHONE NUMBER & AIRCRAFT HOME BASE 17. DESTINATION CONTACT/TELEPHONE (OPTIONAL)	15. NUMBER ABOARD
4	30	OAK METROPOLITAN OAKLAND INT'L		339

16. COLOR OF AIRCRAFT
WHITE/GREEN

CIVIL AIRCRAFT PILOTS. FAR Part 91 requires you file an IFR flight plan to operate under instrument flight rules in controlled airspace. Failure to file could result in a civil penalty not to exceed $1,000 for each violation (Section 901 of the Federal Aviation Act of 1958, as amended). Filing of a VFR flight plan is recommended as a good operating practice. See also Part 99 for requirements concerning DVFR flight plans.

FAA Form 7233-1 (8-82) CLOSE VFR FLIGHT PLAN WITH FSS ON ARRIVAL

FLIGHT LOG

CHECK POINTS FROM	TO	ROUTE ALTITUDE	COURSE	WIND TEMP	SPEED-KTS TAS	GS	DIST NM	TIME LEG	TOT	FUEL LEG	TOT
LAS	L/O	OASIS8.BTY CLIMB					65		:21:00		5600*
L/O	BTY	BTY R-126 FL390		340/53 ISA+4							
BTY	OAL	J92 FL390									
OAL	GROAN	OAL LOCKE.1 FL390									
GROAN	SFO	DESCENT					75	:26:00		4500	
SFO	OAK	VECTORS 3000					29	:09:00			

OTHER DATA:
NOTE: * Includes Taxi Fuel
Use 12,000 PPH Total Fuel Flow From L/O To Start Of Descent.
Use 11,000 PPH Total Fuel Flow For Reserve/Alternate Requirements.

A Missed Approach Requires 1133# of Fuel

TIME and FUEL: As required by FARs.

TIME	FUEL (LB)	
		EN ROUTE
		RESERVE
		ALTERNATE
		TOTAL

FIGURE 202.—Flight Plan/Flight Log.

NEVADA 159

McCARRAN INTL (LAS) 5 S UTC–8(–7DT) N36°04.82′ W115°09.02′ **LAS VEGAS**
2177 B S4 **FUEL** 100, 100LL, JET A1 + OX 1, 2, 3 LRA ARFF Index D **H-2B, L-5B**
RWY 07L-25R: H14506X150 (ASPH-PFC) S-23, D-220, DT-633 HIRL 1.0% up W **IAP**
RWY 07L: VASI(V6L)—Upper GA 3.25° TCH 94′. Lower GA 3.0° TCH 47′. Thld dsplcd 2133′. Hangar.
RWY 25R: MALSR. Thld dsplcd 1400′.
RWY 01R-19L: H9776X150 (ASPH-PFC) S-23, D-220, DT-633 MIRL 1.0% up S
RWY 01R: VASI(V4L)—GA 3.0° TCH 50′. Thld dsplcd 500′. Railroad. Rgt tfc.
RWY 19L: VASI(V6L)—Upper GA 3.25° TCH 66′. Lower GA 3.0° TCH 35′. Thld dsplcd 874′. Pole.
RWY 07R-25L: H8900X150 (ASPH-PFC) S-23, D-220, DT-633, DDT-914 HIRL
RWY 07R: REIL. Pole. **RWY 25L:** MALSF.
RWY 01L-19R: H5001X75 (ASPH) S-30 MIRL 1.1% up S
RWY 01L: REIL. VASI(V4L)—GA 3.0° TCH 35′. Antenna.
RWY 19R: REIL. VASI(V4L)—GA 3.0° TCH 60′. Pole. Rgt tfc.
AIRPORT REMARKS: Attended continuously. Rwy 19R CLOSED arrival, Rwy 01L CLOSED departure Mon–Fri 1500–2300Z‡. Extensive glider/soaring operations weekends and holidays. Sunrise to sunset, LAS 187020, altitudes up to but not including FL180. Gliders remain clear of the CLASS B airspace but otherwise operate within the entire SW quadrant of the CLASS B airspace Veil. Lgtd crane 950′ AGL 4 miles N of arpt. Rotating bcn not visible 115°—240° NE to SW from McCarran Twr. Acft may experience reflection of sun from glass pyramid located NW of arpt. Reflection may occur at various altitudes, headings and distances from arpt. Rwy 07R-25L DDT GWT 521,000 lbs for L-1011, 620,000 lbs for DC-10, 633,000 lbs for MD-11. PAEW between Rwy 01R-19L and Twy D north of Twy N. PAEW west of Rwy 01L-19R. PAEW west of Twy D. Twy E clsd between Twy Q and Twy R. Twy N, Twy S and Twy T clsd between Rwy 01L-19R and Twy D. Twy Y acft be alert keep nosewheel on centerline and acft with wing span greater than 70′ prohibited north of New Quail Gate. Twy D clsd to B747 and clsd to all acft with wingspan 171′ or greater north of Rwy 07L-25R. All non-standard rwy operations PPR from Department of Aviation. Turbojet operations not permitted Rwy 01R-19L and Rwy 01L-19R between 0400–1600Z‡. Exceptions will be made due to weather. Rwy 07L VASI out of svc indefinitely. Rwy 25 MALSR out of svc indefinitely. Tiedown fee. Flight Notification Service (ADCUS) available. NOTE: See Land and Hold Short Operations Section.
WEATHER DATA SOURCES: LLWAS.
COMMUNICATIONS: ATIS 132.4 (ARR) 125.6 (DEP) **UNICOM** 122.95
RENO FSS (RNO) TF 1-800-WX-BRIEF. NOTAM FILE LAS.
Ⓡ **LAS VEGAS APP CON** 127.15
Ⓡ **LAS VEGAS DEP CON** 133.95 (North) 125.9 (South)
LAS VEGAS TOWER 119.9 **GND CON** 121.9 (West of Rwy 01R-19L) 121.1 (East of Rwy 01R-19L) **CLNC DEL** 118.0
AIRSPACE: CLASS B See VFR Terminal Area Chart.
RADIO AIDS TO NAVIGATION: NOTAM FILE LAS.
LAS VEGAS (H) VORTACW 116.9 LAS Chan 116 N36°04.78′ W115°09.59′ at fld. 2140/15E.
ILS 110.3 I-LAS Rwy 25R.
ILS 111.75 I-RLE Rwy 25L. Loc unusable byd 19° South of course.

NORTH LAS VEGAS AIR TERMINAL (VGT) 3 NW UTC–8(–7DT) **LAS VEGAS**
N36°12.75′ W115°11.82′ **H-2B, L-5B**
2207 B S4 **FUEL** 100LL, JET A OX 2 TPA—3007(800)
RWY 07-25: H5005X75 (ASPH) S-30 MIRL
RWY 07: PAPI(P4L)—GA 3.0° TCH 37′. Pole. **RWY 25:** PAPI(P4L)—GA 3.0° TCH 36′.
RWY 12-30: H5000X75 (ASPH) S-30 MIRL
RWY 12: PAPI(P4L)—GA 3.0° TCH 25′.
RWY 30: MIRL. PAPI(P4L)—GA 3.0° TCH 45′. Thld dsplcd 290′. P-line.
AIRPORT REMARKS: Attended 1400–0630Z‡. Rwy 30 PAPI OTS indef. When twr clsd ACTIVATE MIRL Rwy 07-25 and Rwy 12-30—CTAF. NOTE: See Land and Hold Short Operations Section.
COMMUNICATIONS: CTAF 125.7 **ATIS** 118.05 (1400–0400Z‡) **UNICOM** 122.95
RENO FSS (RNO) TF 1-800-WX-BRIEF. NOTAM FILE RNO.
TOWER 125.7 (1400–0400Z‡) **GND CON** 121.7
AIRSPACE: CLASS D svc effective 1400–0400Z‡ other times CLASS G.
RADIO AIDS TO NAVIGATION: NOTAM FILE LAS.
LAS VEGAS (H) VORTACW 116.9 LAS Chan 116 N36°04.78′ W115°09.59′ 332° 8.2 NM to fld. 2140/15E.

LIDA JUNCTION (See GOLDFIELD)

LINCOLN CO (See PANACA)

FIGURE 185A.—Excerpt from Airport/Facilities Directory.

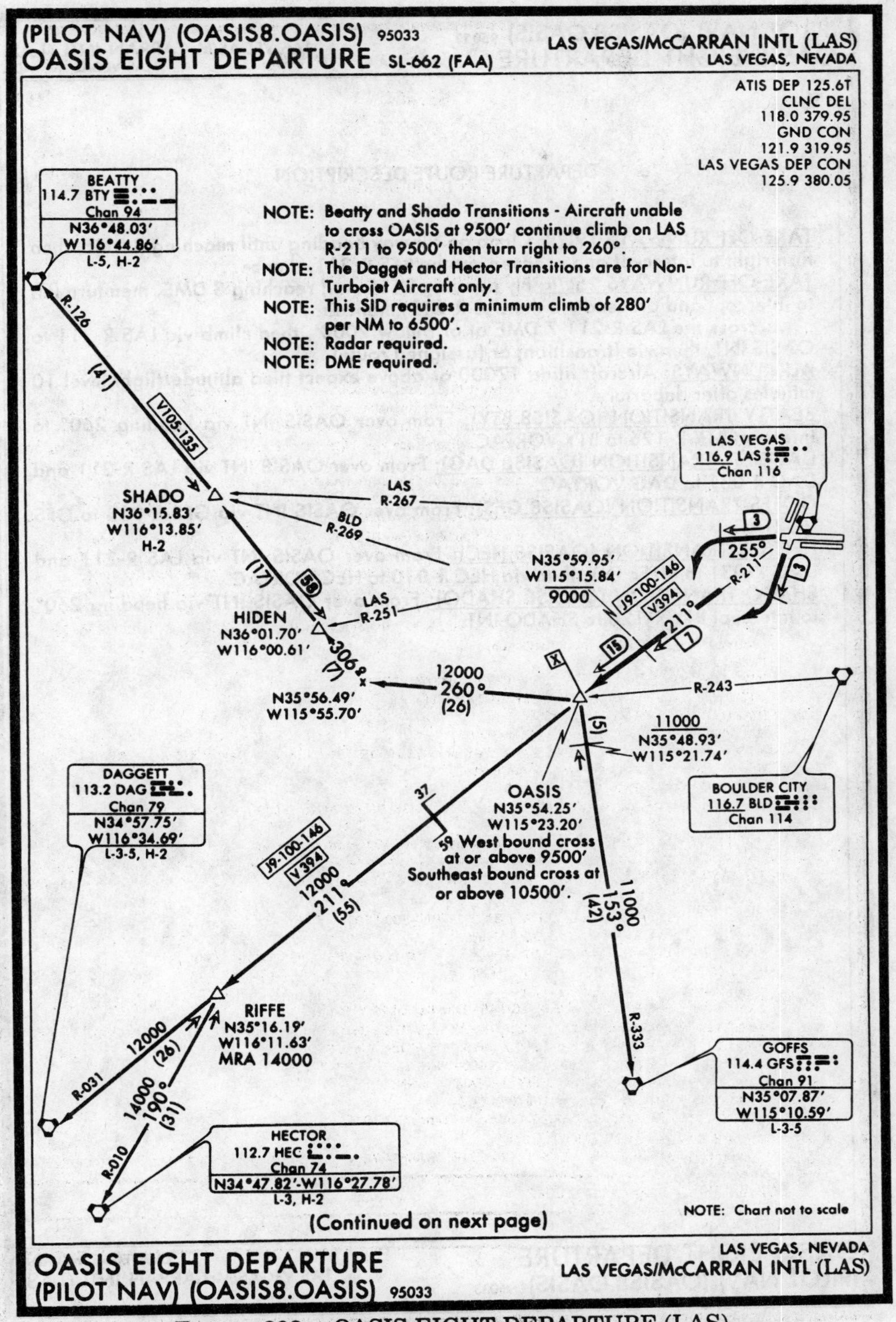

FIGURE 203.—OASIS EIGHT DEPARTURE (LAS).

(PILOT NAV) (OASIS8.OASIS) 95033
OASIS EIGHT DEPARTURE SL-662 (FAA)
LAS VEGAS/McCARRAN INTL (LAS)
LAS VEGAS, NEVADA

▽

DEPARTURE ROUTE DESCRIPTION

TAKE-OFF RUNWAYS 19L/R: Climb on runway heading until reaching 3 DME, then turn right to intercept and proceed via the LAS R-211, thence. . . .
TAKE-OFF RUNWAYS 25L/R: Fly heading 255° until reaching 3 DME, then turn left to intercept and proceed via the LAS R-211, thence. . . .
. . . . cross the LAS R-211 7 DME at or below 9000′, then climb via LAS R-211 to OASIS INT, then via (transition) or (assigned route).
ALL RUNWAYS: Aircraft filing 17000 or above expect filed altitude/flight level 10 minutes after departure.
BEATTY TRANSITION (OASIS8.BTY): From over OASIS INT via heading 260° to intercept BTY R-126 to BTY VORTAC.
DAGGETT TRANSITION (OASIS8.DAG): From over OASIS INT via LAS R-211 and DAG R-031 to DAG VORTAC.
GOFFS TRANSITION (OASIS8.GFS): From over OASIS INT via GFS R-333 to GFS VORTAC.
HECTOR TRANSITION (OASIS8.HEC): From over OASIS INT via LAS R-211 and DAG R-031 to RIFFE INT, then via HEC R-010 to HEC VORTAC.
SHADO TRANSITION (OASIS8.SHADO): From over OASIS INT via heading 260° to intercept BTY R-126 to SHADO INT.

OASIS EIGHT DEPARTURE
(PILOT NAV) (OASIS8.OASIS) 95033
LAS VEGAS, NEVADA
LAS VEGAS/McCARRAN INTL (LAS)

FIGURE 203A.—OASIS EIGHT DEPARTURE (DEPARTURE ROUTE DESCRIPTIONS).

CALIFORNIA **103**

SAN FRANCISCO INTL (SFO) 8 SE UTC–8(–7DT) N37°37.14′ W122°22.49′ **SAN FRANCISCO**
11 B S4 **FUEL** 100, 100LL OX 1, 2, 3, 4 ARFF Index E **H-2A, L-2F, A**
RWY 10L-28R: H11870X200 (ASPH-GRVD) S-60, D-200, DT-355, DDT-710 HIRL CL **IAP**
RWY 10L: REIL. VASI(V6L)—Upper GA 3.25° TCH 109′, Lower GA 3.0° TCH 69′. Transmission twr.
RWY 28R: ALSF2. TDZ. PAPI(P4L)—GA 3.0° TCH 51′. Rgt tfc.
RWY 10R-28L: H10600X200 (ASPH-GRVD) S-60, D-200, DT-355, DDT-710 HIRL CL
RWY 10R: VASI(V6L)—Upper GA 3.25° TCH 101′, Lower GA 3.0° TCH 60′. Transmission twr. Rgt tfc.
RWY 28L: SSALR.
RWY 01R-19L: H8901X200 (ASPH-GRVD) S-60, D-195, DT-325, DDT-710 HIRL CL
RWY 01R: REIL. Thld dsplcd 492′. Blast fence. **RWY 19L:** SSALS. TDZ.
RWY 01L-19R: H7001X200 (ASPH) S-60, D-170, DT-270, DDT-710 HIRL
RWY 01L: REIL. Trees. **RWY 19R:** VASI(V6L)—Upper GA 3.25° TCH 79′, Lower GA 3.0° TCH 47′.
AIRPORT REMARKS: Attended continuously. Rwy 19L SALSF are only 1100′ long with only one flasher on the last light station. Flocks of birds feeding along shoreline adjacent to arpt; on occasions fly across various parts of arpt. Noise sensitive arpt. For noise abatement procedures ctc arpt noise office Monday–Friday 1600–0100Z‡ by calling 415–876–2220. Ldg fee. Rubber accumulated on first 3000 feet of Rwys 28L–28R. No grooving exists at arpt rwy intersections. Rwy 01R–19L is grooved full length except area between Rwys 28L and 28R and 535′ from Taxiway Charlie north. Rwy 10L–28R grooved full length except from Taxiway Tango to Rwy 10L thld. Rwy 10R–28L grooved full length except from east edge of Rwy 01R–19L to Taxiway Kilo. Rwy 01L–19R grooved full length except from south edge of Taxiway Foxtrot to north edge of Rwy 10L–28R. Widebody acft restricted on Taxiway M west of Taxiway A. Several rwy hold position signs are on the right rather than the left side of the taxiways. Rwys 01L–19R, 01R–19L, 10L–28R and 10R–28L gross weight limit DC–10–10 430,000 pounds, DC–10–30 555,000 pounds, L–1011–100 450,000 pounds, L–1011–200 466,000 pounds, B–747 710,000 pounds. 747–400's shall taxi at a speed of less than 10 miles per hour on all non-restricted taxiways on the terminal side of the intersecting rwys. Movement speed of not more than 5 miles per hour is required when two 747–400's pass or overtake each other on parallel taxiways A and B. 747–400 are restricted from using Twy E to or from Twy B. Airline pilots shall strictly follow the painted nose–gear lines and no oversteering adjustment is permitted. Acft with wingspan of 140–156′ must be under tow with wing walkers on Twy R southwest of the fix–base operator, acft with wingspan exceeding 156′ are prohibited. B747 and larger acft are prohibited from using Twy A between Twy S and the United Airline Freedom area. Twy M clsd west of Gate 16 to acft exceeding a wingspan of 125′. Flight Notification Service (ADCUS) available. NOTE: See Land and Hold Short Operations Section.
WEATHER DATA SOURCES: AWOS–1 118.05 (San Bruno Hill). LLWAS.
COMMUNICATIONS: ATIS (ARR) 118.85 113.7 108.9 (415) 877–3585 **(DEP)** 135.45 (415) 877–8422/8423
UNICOM 122.95
OAKLAND FSS (OAK) TF 1–800–WX–BRIEF. NOTAM FILE SFO.
Ⓡ **BAY APP CON** 134.5 132.55 135.65
Ⓡ **BAY DEP CON** 135.1 (SE–W) 120.9 (NW–E)
TOWER 120.5 **GND CON** 121.8 (Gates 53–90 W side) 124.25 (Gates 1–52 E side) **CLNC DEL** 118.2
PRE TAXI CLNC 118.2
AIRSPACE: CLASS B See VFR Terminal Area Chart.
RADIO AIDS TO NAVIGATION: NOTAM FILE SFO.
(L) VORW/DME 115.8 SFO Chan 105 N37°37.17′ W122°22.43′ at fld. 10/17E.
VOR/DME unusable:
035–055° beyond 15 NM below 6500′
025–065° beyond 30 NM
150–190° beyond 25 NM below 4500′
190–260° beyond 10 NM below 4500′
260–295° beyond 35 NM below 3000′
295–330° beyond 20 NM below 4000′
BRIJJ NDB (LOM) 379 SF N37°34.33′ W122°15.59′ 280° 6.2 NM to fld.
Unusable 160°–195° byd 6 NM all altitudes.
ILS/DME 109.55 I–SFO Chan 32Y Rwy 28L. LOM BRIJJ NDB. LOM unusable 160°–195° byd 6 NM all altitudes.
ILS/DME 111.7 I–GWQ Chan 54 Rwy 28R. LOM BRIJJ NDB. LOM unusable 160°–195° byd 6 NM all altitudes.
ILS/DME 108.9 I–SIA Chan 26 Rwy 19L.
LDA/DME 110.75 Chan 44(Y) Rwy 28R.
COMM/NAVID REMARKS: ILS Rwy 19L–pilots be alert for momentary LOC course excursions due to large acft opr in vicinity of LOC antenna. ATIS frequency 108.9 avbl when SFO VOR out of service 415–877–3585.

SAN JACINTO N33°47.70′ W116°59.96′ NOTAM FILE RAL. **LOS ANGELES**
NDB (MHW) 227 SJY 184° 3.8 NM to Hemet–Ryan. NDB unmonitored. **L-3C**

FIGURE 205.—Excerpt from Airport/Facilities Directory.

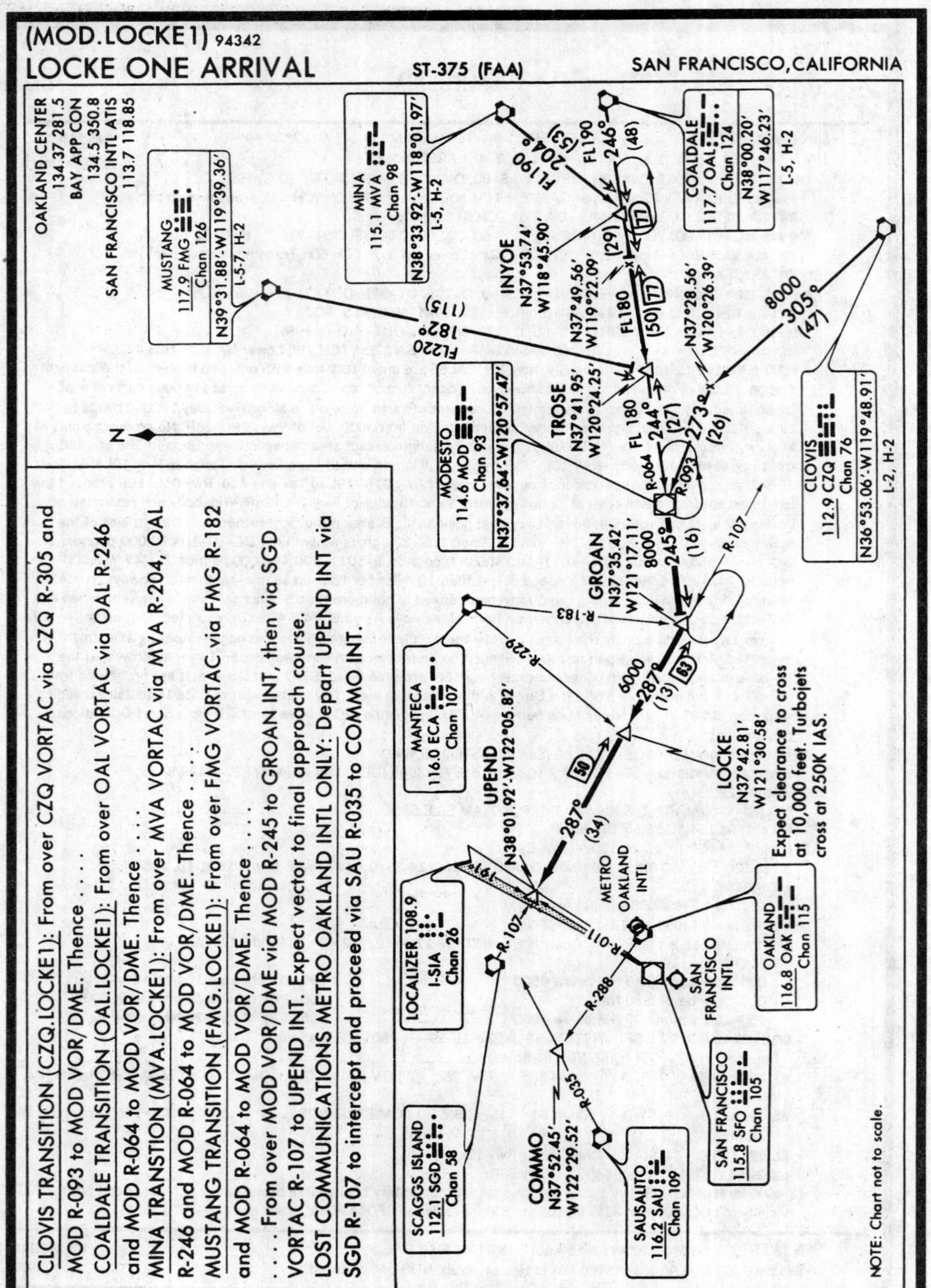

FIGURE 205A.—LOCKE ONE ARRIVAL (MOD.LOCKE1).

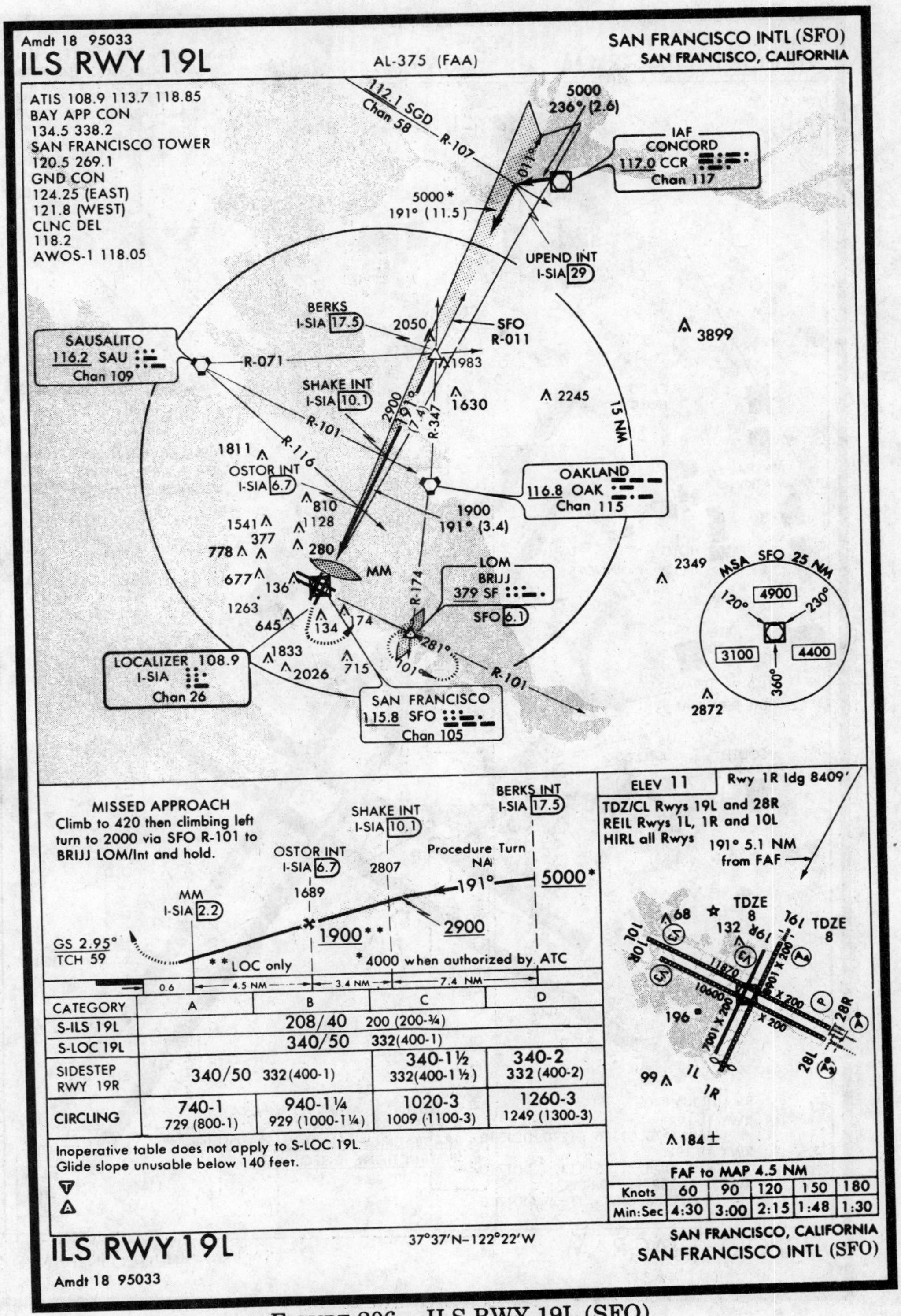

FIGURE 206.—ILS RWY 19L (SFO).

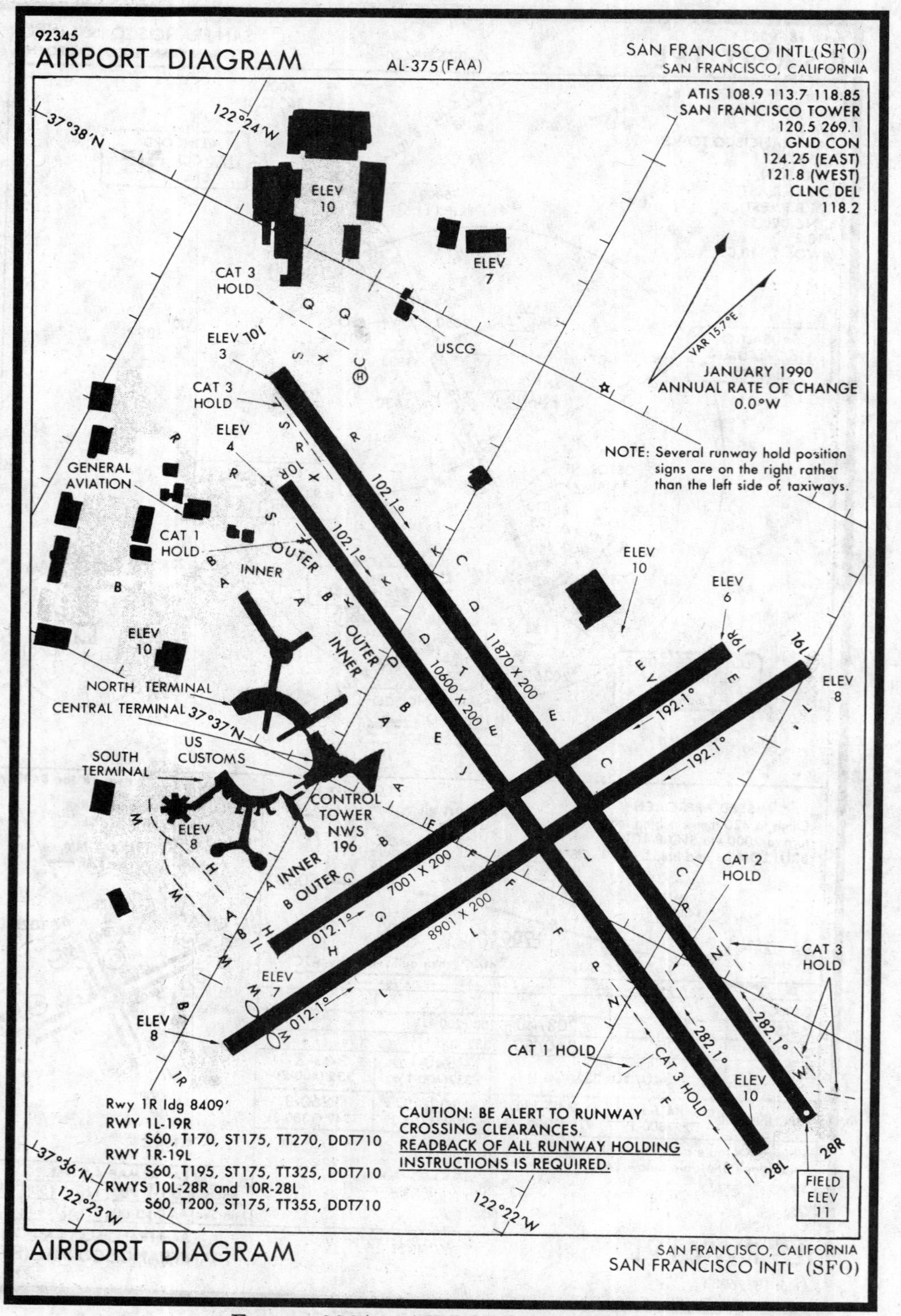

FIGURE 206A.—AIRPORT DIAGRAM.

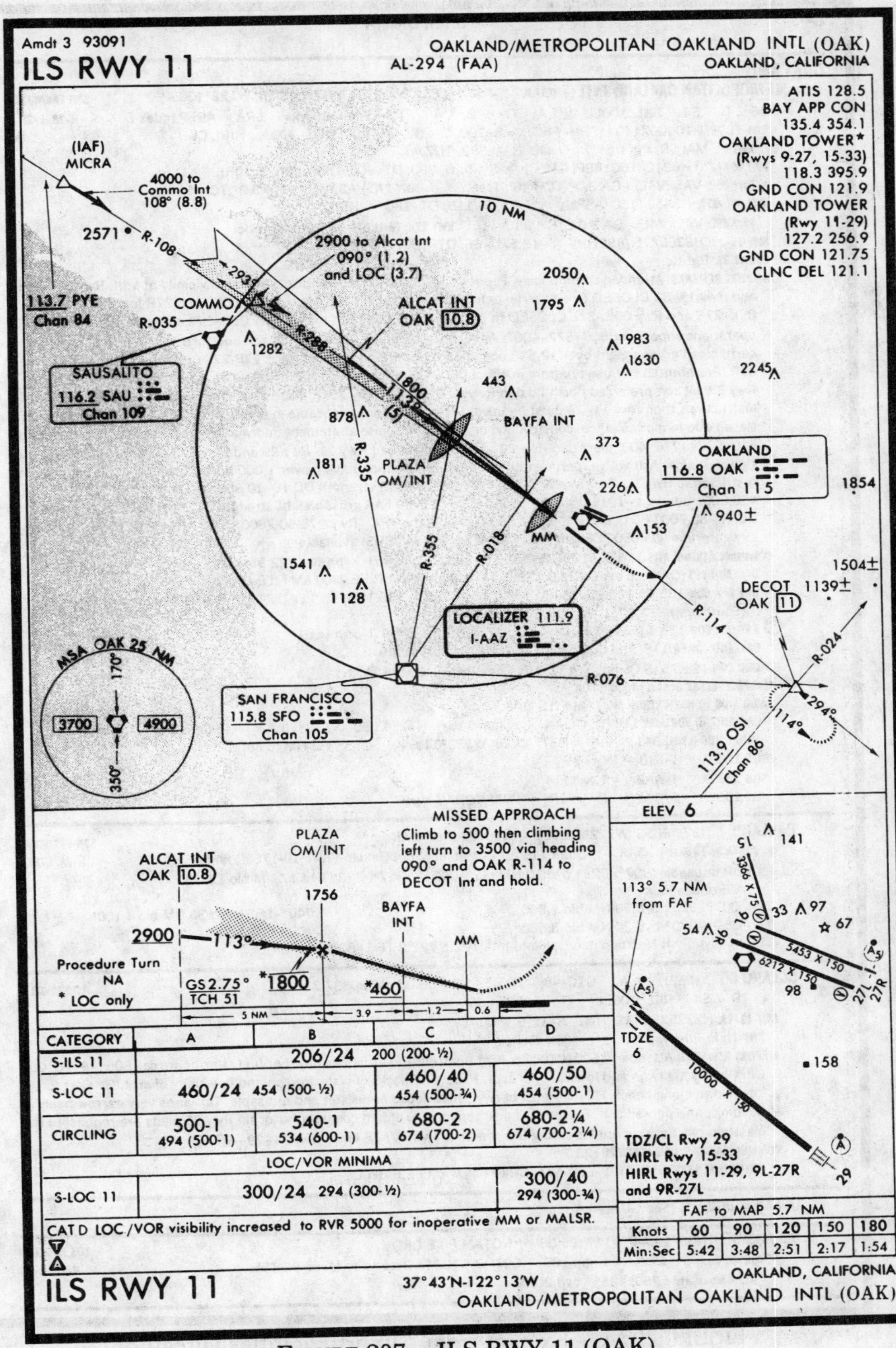

FIGURE 207.—ILS RWY 11 (OAK).

84 CALIFORNIA

OAKLAND

METROPOLITAN OAKLAND INTL (OAK) 4 S UTC–8(–7DT) N37°43.28′ W122°13.24′ **SAN FRANCISCO**
06 B S4 **FUEL** 100LL, JET A OX 1, 2, 3, 4 TPA—See Remarks LRA ARFF Index D **H-2A, L-2F, A**
RWY 11-29: H10000X150 (ASPH-PFC) S-200, D-200, DT-400, DDT-900 HIRL CL **IAP**
RWY 11: MALSR. Rgt tfc. **RWY 29:** ALSF2. TDZ.
RWY 09R-27L: H6212X150 (ASPH-PFC) S-75, D-200, DT-400, DDT-800 HIRL
RWY 09R: VASI(V4L)—GA 3.0° TCH 46′. Tree. **RWY 27L:** VASI(V4L)—GA 3.0° TCH 55′.
RWY 09L-27R: H5453X150 (ASPH) S-75, D-115, DT-180 HIRL
RWY 09L: VASI(V4L)—GA 3.0° TCH 38′. **RWY 27R:** MALSR. Building. Rgt tfc.
RWY 15-33: H3366X75 (ASPH) S-12.5, D-65, DT-100 MIRL
RWY 33: Rgt tfc.
AIRPORT REMARKS: Attended continuously. Fee Rwy 11-29 and tiedown. Birds on and in vicinity of arpt. Rwy 09L-27R and Rwy 15-33 CLOSED to air carrier acft, except air carrier acft may use Rwy 09L and 27R for taxiing. Rwy 09L-27R and Rwy 09R-27L CLOSED to 4 engine wide body acft except Rwy 09R-27L operations avbl PPR call operations supervisor 510-577-4067. All turbo-jet/fan acft, all 4-engine acft and turbo-prop acft with certificated gross weight over 12,500 pounds are prohibited from tkf Rwys 27R/27L or ldg Rwy 09L and Rwy 09R. Preferential rwy use program in effect 0600-1400Z‡: All acft preferred north fld arrive Rwys 27R/27L or Rwy 33; all acft preferred north fld dep Rwys 09R/09L or Rwy 15. If these rwys unacceptable for safety or ATC instructions then Rwy 11-29 must be used. Prohibitions not applicable in emerg or whenever Rwy 11-29 is closed due to maintenance, construction or safety. For noise abatement information ctc noise abatement office at 510-577-4276. 400′ blast pad Rwy 29 and 500′ blast pad Rwy 11. Rwy 29 and Rwy 27L distance remaining signs left side. Acft with experimental or limited certification having over 1,000 horsepower or 4,000 pounds are restricted to Rwy 11-29. Rwy 09R-27L FAA gross weight strength DC 10-10 350,000 pounds, DC 10-30 450,000 pounds, L-1011 350,000 pounds. Rwy 11-29 FAA gross weight strength DC 10-10 600,000 pounds, DC 10-30 700,000 pounds, L-1011 600,000 pounds. TPA—Rwy 27L 606(600), TPA—Rwy 27R 1006(1000). Rwy 29 centerline lgts 6500′. Flight Notification Service (ADCUS) available.
COMMUNICATIONS: **ATIS** 128.5 (510) 635-5850 (N and S Complex) **UNICOM** 122.95
OAKLAND FSS (OAK) on arpt. 122.5 122.2. TF 1-800-WX-BRIEF. NOTAM FILE OAK.
® **BAY APP CON** 135.65 133.95 (South) 135.4 134.5 (East) 135.1 (West) 127.0 (North) 120.9 (Northwest) 120.1 (Southeast)
® **BAY DEP CON** 135.4 (East) 135.1 (West) 127.0 (North) 120.9 (Northwest)
OAKLAND TOWER 118.3 (N Complex) 127.2 (S Complex) 124.9
GND CON 121.75 (S Complex) 121.9 (N Complex) **CLNC DEL** 121.1
AIRSPACE: CLASS C svc ctc **APP CON**
RADIO AIDS TO NAVIGATION: NOTAM FILE OAK.
OAKLAND (H) VORTACW 116.8 OAK Chan 115 N37°43.55′ W122°13.42′ at fld. 10/17E. **HIWAS.**
RORAY NDB (LMM) 341 AK N37°43.28′ W122°11.65′ 253° 1.3 NM to fld.
ILS 108.7 I-INB Rwy 29
ILS 111.9 I-AAZ Rwy 11
ILS 109.9 I-OAK Rwy 27R LMM RORAY NDB.

OAKLAND N37°43.56′ W122°13.42′ NOTAM FILE OAK. **SAN FRANCISCO**
(H) VORTACW 116.8 OAK Chan 115 at Metropolitan Oakland Intl. 10/17E. **HIWAS.** **H-2A, L-2F, A**
VOR unusable: 307°-323° byd 10 NM blo 5,000′ 307°-323° byd 17 NM blo 12,500′
DME unusable:
307°-323° byd 30 NM blo 1,500′ 040°-065° byd 30 NM blo 4,100′
350°-030° byd 20 NM blo 3,500′
FSS (OAK) at Metropolitan Oakland Intl. 122.5 122.2 TF 1-800-WX-BRIEF.

OCEANO CO (L52) 1 W UTC–8(–7DT) N35°06.08′ W120°37.33′ **LOS ANGELES**
14 B S4 **FUEL** 100LL TPA—1000(986)
RWY 11-29: H2325X50 (ASPH) S-12.5 MIRL
RWY 11: P-line. Rgt tfc. **RWY 29:** Pole.
AIRPORT REMARKS: Attended 1600-0100Z‡. Arpt unattended Christmas day. For fuel after hours call 805-481-6100. Ultralight activity on and in vicinity of arpt. Recurring flocks of waterfowl on and in vicinity of arpt. Be alert for kites flown along beach 1/2 mile west of rwy. Unsurfaced areas soft and unusable. Taxilanes very narrow near buildings and parked acft. Extremely noise sensitive arpt and community, for tkf Rwy 29 pilots are requested to maintain rwy heading until crossing the shoreline. ACTIVATE MIRL Rwy 11-29—CTAF.
COMMUNICATIONS: CTAF/UNICOM 122.7
HAWTHORNE FSS (HHR) TF 1-800-WX-BRIEF. NOTAM FILE HHR.

OCEAN RIDGE (See GUALALA)

OCEANSIDE N33°14.44′ W117°25.06′ NOTAM FILE CRQ. **LOS ANGELES**
(H) VORTAC 115.3 OCN Chan 100 097° 3.6 NM to Oceanside Muni. 90/15E. **H-2B, L-3C**
VOR unusable 260°-265° byd 20NM.

FIGURE 207A -- Excerpt from Airport/Facilities Directory.

4 **DIRECTORY LEGEND**

⑫ FUEL

CODE	FUEL
80	Grade 80 gasoline (Red)
100	Grade 100 gasoline (Green)
100LL	100LL gasoline (low lead) (Blue)
115	Grade 115 gasoline
A	Jet A—Kerosene freeze point-40° C.
A1	Jet A-1—Kerosene freeze point-50°C.
A1 +	Jet A-1—Kerosene with icing inhibitor, freeze point-50° C.
B	Jet B—Wide-cut turbine fuel, freeze point-50° C.
B +	Jet B—Wide-cut turbine fuel with icing inhibitor, freeze point-50° C.
MOGAS	Automobile gasoline which is to be used as aircraft fuel.

NOTE: Automobile Gasoline. Certain automobile gasoline may be used in specific aircraft engines if a FAA supplemental type cetificate has been obtained. Automobile gasoline which is to be used in aircraft engines will be identified as "MOGAS", however, the grade/type and other octane rating will not be published.

Data shown on fuel availability represents the most recent information the publisher has been able to acquire. Because of a variety of factors, the fuel listed may not always be obtainable by transient civil pilots. Confirmation of availability of fuel should be made directly with fuel dispensers at locations where refueling is planned.

⑬ OXYGEN

OX 1 High Pressure
OX 2 Low Pressure
OX 3 High Pressure—Replacement Bottles
OX 4 Low Pressure—Replacement Bottles

⑭ TRAFFIC PATTERN ALTITUDE

Traffic Pattern Altitude (TPA)—The first figure shown is TPA above mean sea level. The second figure in parentheses is TPA above airport elevation.

⑮ AIRPORT OF ENTRY, LANDING RIGHTS, AND CUSTOMS USER FEE AIRPORTS

U.S. CUSTOMS USER FEE AIRPORT—Private Aircraft operators are frequently required to pay the costs associated with customs processing.

AOE—Airport of Entry—A customs Airport of Entry where permission from U.S. Customs is not required, however, at least one hour advance notice of arrival must be furnished.

LRA—Landing Rights Airport—Application for permission to land must be submitted in advance to U.S. Customs. At least one hour advance notice of arrival must be furnished.

NOTE: Advance notice of arrival at both an AOE and LRA airport may be included in the flight plan when filed in Canada or Mexico, where Flight Notification Service (ADCUS) is available the airport remark will indicate this service. This notice will also be treated as an application for permission to land in the case of an LRA. Although advance notice of arrival may be relayed to Customs through Mexico, Canadian, and U.S. Communications facilities by flight plan, the aircraft operator is solely responsible for insuring that Customs receives the notification. (See Customs, Immigration and Naturalization, Public Health and Agriculture Department requirements in the International Flight Information Manual for further details.)

⑯ CERTIFICATED AIRPORT (FAR 139)

Airports serving Department of Transportation certified carriers and certified under FAR, Part 139, are indicated by the ARFF index; i.e., ARFF Index A, which relates to the availability of crash, fire, rescue equipment.

FAR-PART 139 CERTIFICATED AIRPORTS

INDICES AND AIRCRAFT RESCUE AND FIRE FIGHTING EQUIPMENT REQUIREMENTS

Airport Index	*Required No. Vehicles*	*Aircraft Length*	*Scheduled Departures*	*Agent + Water for Foam*
A	1	<90′	≥1	500#DC or HALON 1211 or 450#DC + 100 gal H_2O
B	1 or 2	≥90′, <126′	≥5	Index A + 1500 gal H_2O
		≥126′, <159′	<5	
C	2 or 3	≥126′, <159′	≥5	Index A + 3000 gal H_2O
		≥159′, <200′	<5	
D	3	≥159′, <200′	≥5	Index A + 4000 gal H_2O
		>200′	<5	
E	3	≥200′	≥5	Index A + 6000 gal H_2O

> Greater Than; < Less Than; ≥ Equal or Greater Than; ≤ Equal or Less Than; H_2O–Water; DC–Dry Chemical.

LEGEND 15.—Directory Legend.

10.11 MD-90 BDL TO PHL (Questions 116-130)

Questions 116 through 130 pertain to an IFR flight from Bradley International Airport, Windsor Locks, Connecticut to Philadelphia International Airport, Philadelphia, Pennsylvania.

The route is given in block 8 of the flight plan portion of Fig. 214 on page 490. The partially completed flight planning log is given on the bottom portion of Fig. 214.

The following figures are used to answer the 15 questions concerning this flight.

Fig.	Page	Title
214	490	Flight Plan/Flight Log
215	491	Excerpts from *Airport/Facility Directory*
215A	492	Airport Diagram
216	493	Coastal (HI) Departure (BDL)
216A	494	Departure Route Description
217	433	High Altitude Airways
218	434	Low Altitude Airways
182	398	Cedar Lake Five Arrival (VCN.VCN5)
182A	495	ILS RWY 9R (PHL)
183	496	IFR Alternate Minimums
183A	497	ILS RWY 13 (ACY)
Legend 15	498	Directory Legend
Legend 42	499	Tower Enroute Control (NE)
Legend 42A	500	Tower Enroute Control Continued
Legend 42B	501	Tower Enroute Control Continued

10.11 MD-90 BDL to PHL

116.
9676. (Refer to figure 214 on page 490.) In block 3 of the flight plan, the G following MD90/ indicates the aircraft is equipped with

A—GPS/GNSS that has oceanic, en route, terminal, and GPS approach capability.
B—Traffic Alert and Collision Avoidance System (TCAS) with /R capability.
C—Electronic Flight Instrument System (EFIS).

Answer (A) is correct (9676). *(AIM Para 5-1-7))*

In block 3 of the flight plan, the aircraft type followed by a "/G" means that the airplane is equipped with a Global Positioning System (GPS)/Global Navigation Satellite System (GNSS) that has oceanic, en route, terminal, and GPS approach capability.

Answer (B) is incorrect because TCAS is indicated by a "T/" prefix to the aircraft type, not a "/G" suffix. Answer (C) is incorrect because in Oct. 1996 the equipment suffix "/G" was changed from EFIS with /R capability to GPS/GNSS with oceanic, en route, terminal, and GPS approach capability. Currently, there is no equipment suffix specifically for EFIS-equipped aircraft.

117.
9677. (Refer to figures 182, 214, 216, 216A, 217, and 218 on pages 398, 490, 493, 494, 433, and 434.) The time enroute between BDL and PHL for TNA 90 is

A—54 minutes.
B—52 minutes.
C—50 minutes.

Answer (B) is correct (9677). *(IFH Chap XIII)*

To determine the ETE from BDL to PHL, you must complete the flight log in Fig. 214. In the remarks box of the flight plan, the magnetic variation is given at BDL (14°W) and PHL (10°W). This information is used to convert the true wind direction to magnetic direction.

Our flight log below has been expanded to provide more detail. To convert the wind direction from true to magnetic, we use 14°W to SHERL Int. and 10°W to PHL.

	Distance	MC	Wind (mag)	Ground-speed	Time
YODER	45G	X	X	X	0:15:00G
CCC	30	237	354/55	462	0:03:53
SHERL	43	213	354/55	481	0:05:21
MANTA	29	236	350/55	460	0:03:47
BRIGS	36	239	350/55	457	0:04:43
VCN	38	281	350/55	417	0:05:28
PHL	46G	X	X	X	0:14:00G
					0:52:12

G = Given

Answer (A) is incorrect because an ETE of 54 min. requires a TAS of approximately 410 kt., not 440 kt. Answer (C) is incorrect because an ETE of 50 min. requires a TAS of approximately 480 kt., not 440 kt.

118.
9678. (Refer to figures 214, 216, 216A, 217, and 218 on pages 490, 493, 494, 433, and 434.) The total fuel required to be onboard TNA 90 before starting to taxi at BDL is

A—11,979 pounds.
B—11,735 pounds.
C—11,851 pounds.

Answer (B) is correct (9678). *(IFH Chap XIII)*

To determine the total fuel required to be on board TNA 90 before starting to taxi at BDL, you must complete the fuel portion of the flight log on Fig. 214. Use 6,150 PPH total fuel flow from level-off (YODER) to start of descent (VCN) and 5,900 PPH total fuel flow for reserve and alternate requirements.

	Time	Fuel (lb.)
YODER	0:15:00G	2,560.0G
CCC	0:03:53	398.0
SHERL	0:05:21	548.4
MANTA	0:03:47	387.8
BRIGS	0:04:43	483.5
VCN	0:05:28	560.3
PHL	0:14:00G	1,190.0G
ACY	0:12:00G	1,180.0
Reserves	0:45:00	4,425.0
		11,733.0

G = Given

Answer (A) is incorrect because 11,979 lb. includes the 244 lb. of fuel required for a missed approach. While this should be included as a practical matter, it is not required by the FARs. Answer (C) is incorrect because 11,851 lb. is the approximate fuel needed if a fuel flow of 6,510 PPH, not 6,150 PPH, is used from YODER to VCN.

119.
9679. (Refer to figures 214, 216, 216A, 217, and 218 on pages 490, 493, 494, 433, and 434.) The estimated fuel usage between BDL and PHL for TNA 90 is

A—10,555 pounds.
B—10,799 pounds.
C—6,130 pounds.

Answer (C) is correct (9679). *(IFH Chap XIII)*
To determine the estimated fuel to be used between BDL and PHL, you must complete the fuel portion of the flight log on Fig. 214. Use 6,150 PPH fuel flow rate from level-off (YODER) to start of descent (VCN).

	Time	Fuel (lb.)
YODER	0:15:00G	2,560.0G
CCC	0:03:53	398.0
SHERL	0:05:21	548.4
MANTA	0:03:47	387.8
BRIGS	0:04:43	483.5
VCN	0:05:28	560.3
PHL	0:14:00G	1,190.0G
		6,128.0

G = Given

Answer (A) is incorrect because 10,555 lb. includes the 45 min. reserve fuel requirement. Reserve fuel should not be included when calculating only the fuel to be used from BDL to PHL. Answer (B) is incorrect because 10,799 lb. includes the fuel required for the missed approach and the 45 min. reserve. These requirements are not included when calculating only the fuel to be used from BDL to PHL.

120.
9686. (Refer to figure 215A on page 492.) The airport diagram of Bradley Intl Airport has a symbol (appears to be a triangle balanced on top of another triangle) located close to the approach end of RWY 19. What does this symbol indicate?

A—Runway Radar Reflectors.
B—Practice hover area for the Army National Guard helicopters.
C—Two course lights, back to back, which flash beams of light along the course of an airway.

Answer (A) is correct (9686). *(IAP)*
Fig. 215A is the airport diagram for BDL. The symbol that appears to be one triangle on top of another triangle located off the approach end of RWY 19 indicates that runway radar reflectors are at that position.
Answer (B) is incorrect because symbols are not used to indicate a practice hover area for helicopters. Answer (C) is incorrect because two course lights, back to back, which flash beams of light along the course of an airway are used to mark airway segments in a few remote mountainous areas, not at an airport.

121.
9690. (Refer to legend 15 and figure 215 on pages 498 and 491.) Windsor Locks/Bradley Intl, is an FAR Part 139 airport. What is the minimum number of aircraft rescue and fire-fighting vehicles, and what type and amount of fire-fighting agents should the airport have?

A—Two vehicles and 600 pounds dry chemical (DC), or Halon 1211 or 500 pounds of DC plus 4,000 gallons of water.
B—Three vehicles and 500 pounds of dry chemical (DC), or Halon 1211 or 450 pounds DC plus 3,000 gallons of water.
C—Three vehicles and 500 pounds of dry chemical (DC), or Halon 1211 or 450 pounds DC and 4,000 gallons of water.

Answer (C) is correct (9690). *(A/FD)*
Fig. 215 is the *A/FD* excerpt for BDL. First, look at the aircraft rescue and fire-fighting (ARFF) index on the third line, which is ARFF Index D.
Next, Legend 15 is an *A/FD* legend. Look at the table under item 16. Locate the Airport Index column on the left side and move down to Index D. The minimum number of vehicles is three, and the airport is required to have at least 500 lb. of dry chemical (DC) or HALON 1211 or 450 lb. DC plus 4,000 gal. of water (H_2O).
Answer (A) is incorrect because BDL is required to have three, not two, vehicles. Answer (B) is incorrect because three vehicles and 500 lb. DC or HALON 1211 or 450 lb. DC plus 3,000 gal. of water are required for an airport with an ARFF Index C, not ARFF Index D.

122.
9681. (Refer to figures 214 and 182A on pages 490 and 495.) TNA 90 is a CAT C aircraft and has received a clearance to fly the ILS 9R approach and sidestep to RWY 9L at PHL. What are the minimums?

A—520/40.
B—600/1-½.
C—680/1-¾.

Answer (C) is correct (9681). *(IAP)*

Fig 182A is the IAP chart for the ILS RWY 9R approach at PHL. The minimums section is located below the profile view near the bottom of the chart. Locate the row titled SIDESTEP RWY 9L and move right to the Cat. C column. The minimums are listed as 680/1¾. BALDN fix minimums are not used since the FAA's question did not specify "BALDN fix is received," as in our questions 123 and 124 (FAA questions 9682 and 9683).

Answer (A) is incorrect because 520/40 are the Cat. C minimums for the S-LOC RWY 9R with the BALDN fix identified, not the SIDESTEP RWY 9L without BALDN fix identified. Answer (B) is incorrect because 680/1½ are Cat. C minimums for the SIDESTEP RWY 9L with, not without, the BALDN fix identified.

123.
9682. (Refer to figures 214 and 182A on pages 490 and 495.) TNA 90 is a CAT C aircraft and has received clearance to fly the LOC RWY 09R and circle to land RWY 27R. Baldn fix is received. What are the minimums?

A—640/2.
B—600/1-½.
C—680/1-¾.

Answer (B) is correct (9682). *(IAP)*

Fig. 182A is the IAP chart for the ILS RWY 9R approach at PHL. The BALDN fix minimums for a circling approach are listed in the upper right corner of the planview section. The Cat. C minimums for an aircraft cleared to fly the LOC RWY 09R and circle to land on RWY 27R are 600/1½.

Answer (A) is incorrect because 640/2 are the circling minimums with BALDN fix identified for a Cat. D, not Cat. C, airplane. Answer (C) is incorrect because 680/1¾ are the circling minimums if BALDN fix cannot be identified, not if BALDN fix is identified.

124.
9683. (Refer to figures 214 and 182A on pages 490 and 495.) TNA 90 is a CAT C aircraft and has received a clearance to fly the LOC RWY 09R; Baldn fix is received and TNA 90 is cleared to land 09R. What are the minimums?

A—520/40.
B—680/60.
C—600/1-½.

Answer (A) is correct (9683). *(IAP)*

Fig. 182A is the IAP chart for the ILS RWY 9R approach at PHL. The BALDN fix minimums for the S-LOC 9R approach are listed in the top center of the planview section. For a Cat. C airplane, the BALDN fix minimums for a S-LOC 9R are 520/40.

Answer (B) is incorrect because 680/60 are the minimums for a Cat. C airplane if BALDN fix cannot be identified, not if BALDN fix is identified. Answer (C) is incorrect because 600/1½ are the BALDN fix minimums for a Cat. C airplane conducting a side step to RWY 9L or a circling approach, not an S-LOC 9R approach.

125.
9680. (Refer to figures 214 and 182A on pages 490 and 495.) The PIC of TNA 90 has 49 hours and 102 landings as PIC in the MD-90 while operating under Part 121. The PIC also has 959 hours and 246 landings, as PIC, in the B-727 while operating under Part 121. What are the minimums for the ILS RWY 9R approach at PHL, for this PIC?

A—221/18.
B—321/42.
C—321/24.

Answer (B) is correct (9680). *(FAR 121.652)*

If the PIC has not served 100 hr. as PIC in the type of airplane (s)he is operating under Part 121, the MDA or DH must be increased by 100 ft., and the visibility by ½ SM (or 2,400 ft. RVR). However, the PIC time requirement may be reduced (not more than 50%) by substituting one landing in that type of airplane, while operating under Part 121, for one required hour of PIC time if the PIC has at least 100 hr. as PIC in another type of airplane while operating under Part 121.

Since the PIC has over 100 hr. as PIC in the B-727 while operating under Part 121, (s)he can substitute each of only 50 landings (i.e., 50% of required time) in the MD-90 for one hour of required PIC time. This will give the PIC only 99 hr., which means the PIC minimums are raised for the ILS RWY 9R approach at PHL. The PIC minimums are 321/42.

Answer (A) is incorrect because 221/18 are the published minimums, which can be used only if the PIC has 100 hr. or more, not less than 100 hr., as PIC in the MD-90. Answer (C) is incorrect because RVR visibility is increased by 2,400 ft., not 600 ft.

126.
9684. (Refer to figures 214 and 182A on pages 490 and 495.) The PIC on TNA 90 (CAT C aircraft operated under FAR Part 121) has not flown 100 hours as PIC in the MD-90. What are the minimums while flying the ILS RWY 9R to land 09R at PHL?

A—321/30.
B—321/36.
C—321/42.

Answer (C) is correct (9684). *(FAR 121.652)*

Fig. 182A is the IAP chart for the ILS RWY 9R approach at PHL.

If the PIC has not served 100 hr. as PIC in the type of airplane (s)he is operating under Part 121, the MDA or DH must be increased by 100 ft., and the visibility by ½ SM (or 2,400 ft. RVR).

Thus, if the PIC of TNA 90 has not flown 100 hr. as PIC in the MD-90, the minimums to conduct the ILS RWY 9R at PHL are 321/42.

Answer (A) is incorrect because, if the PIC has less than 100 hr. as PIC in the MD-90, the RVR visibility must be increased by 2,400 ft., not 1,200 ft. Answer (B) is incorrect because, if the PIC has less than 100 hr. as PIC in the MD-90, the RVR visibility must be increased by 2,400 ft., not 1,800 ft.

127.
9688. (Refer to figure 214 and legends 42 and 42B on pages 490, 499, and 501.) The filed flight plan for TNA 90 indicates, if it becomes necessary to divert to the alternate, that tower enroute (TEC), radar vectors, and 3,000 feet are requested to ACY. If radar vectors are not available, what route can be expected from PHL to ACY?

A—Direct SAVVY Intersection, V166 OOD, V184 ACY.
B—Direct WILJR Intersection, VCN, V184 ACY.
C—OOD VCN V184 ACY.

Answer (C) is correct (9688). *(A/FD)*

The TEC city pairs for PHL are shown in Legend 42B. Locate Philadelphia on the left margin; then locate Atlantic City (ACY) under the destination column on the right margin, which is the second line under PHL. The route listed is OOD VCN V184 ACY, which is the expected route if radar vectors are not available.

Answer (A) is incorrect because the TEC routing from PHL to ACY without radar vectors is direct OOD, not direct SAVVY V166 OOD. Answer (B) is incorrect because the TEC routing from PHL to ACY without radar vectors is direct OOD, not direct WILJR.

128.
9689. (Refer to figure 214 and legends 42 and 42B on pages 490, 499, and 501.) The filed flight plan for TNA 90 indicates, if it becomes necessary to divert to the alternate, that tower enroute (TEC), radar vectors, and 3,000 feet are requested to ACY. What is the maximum altitude that TNA 90 may be cleared to under TEC?

A—2,000 feet.
B—3,000 feet.
C—4,000 feet.

Answer (B) is correct (9689). *(A/FD)*
The TEC city pairs for PHL are shown in Legend 42B. Locate Philadelphia on the left margin and then locate Atlantic City on the right margin (destination), which is the second line under PHL. The highest altitude for the TEC route is 3,000 ft.
Answer (A) is incorrect because the highest altitude for the TEC route from PHL to ACY is 3,000 ft., not 2,000 ft. Answer (C) is incorrect because the highest altitude for the TEC route from Philadelphia to Allentown, not Atlantic City, is 4,000 ft.

129.
9687. (Refer to figures 214, 183, and 183A on pages 490, 496, and 497.) The PIC, of TNA 90, has 75 hours as PIC of this type airplane. The MD-90 is a Category C aircraft. What is the lowest ceiling/visibility that may be forecast to use ACY as an alternate on the flight plan, and what is the lowest visibility that may exist at ACY prior to the final approach segment to continue the ILS RWY 13 approach?

A—600-2 and 2 miles.
B—600-2 and 50 RVR.
C—700-2 and 18 RVR.

Answer (B) is correct (9687). *(IAP, FAR 121.652)*
Fig. 183A is the IAP chart for the ILS RWY 13 approach at ACY. Below the minimums section (lower left corner), there is a black triangle with a white "A" inside which indicates nonstandard alternate minimums. Fig. 183 lists the nonstandard alternate minimums for ACY. Since the nonstandard alternate minimums for the ILS RWY 13 apply to Cat. D and E aircraft only, a Cat. C aircraft can use the standard alternate minimums for a precision approach of 600-2.
If the PIC has not served 100 hr. as PIC in that type of airplane, the minimum landing visibility at an alternate airport cannot be less than 1 SM (or 5,000 ft. RVR).
Answer (A) is incorrect because the lowest visibility that may exist at ACY prior to the final approach segment to continue to ILS RWY 13 approach is 1 SM, not 2 SM. Answer (C) is incorrect because 700-2 is the minimum ceiling/visibility that may be forecast to use ACY as an alternate on a flight plan for a Cat. D, not Cat. C, airplane; the minimum RVR visibility must be 5,000 ft., not 1,800 ft.

130.
9685. (Refer to figures 214, 183, and 183A on pages 490, 496, and 497.) The weather at PHL goes below the PIC's minimums and TNA 90 (a CAT C aircraft operating under FAR Part 121) diverts to the alternate ACY. Upon arrival at ACY, TNA 90 is cleared for an ILS RWY 13 approach. The PIC has less than 100 hours of PIC time in the MD-90. What are the landing minimums?

A—376/18.
B—376/50.
C—376/42.

Answer (B) is correct (9685). *(FAR 121.652)*
If the PIC has not served 100 hr. as PIC in the type of airplane (s)he is operating under Part 121, the MDA or DH and visibility need not be increased above those applicable to the airport when used as an alternate, but in no event may the landing minimums be less than 300 ft. and 1 SM (or 5,000 ft. RVR).
Fig. 183A is the IAP chart for the ILS RWY 13 approach at ACY. The TDZE for RWY 13 is found in the airport diagram at the lower right of the chart. The TDZE for RWY 13 is 76 ft. Thus, the landing minimums for the PIC of TNA 90 for the ILS RWY 13 approach are 376/50.
Answer (A) is incorrect because the RVR visibility must be at least 5,000 ft., not remain the same. Answer (C) is incorrect because an RVR visibility of 4,200 ft. would be required if ACY were the destination, not the alternate, airport.

Form Approved: OMB No. 2120-0034

U.S. DEPARTMENT OF TRANSPORTATION FEDERAL AVIATION ADMINISTRATION **FLIGHT PLAN**	(FAA USE ONLY) ☐ PILOT BRIEFING ☐ VNR ☐ STOPOVER	TIME STARTED	SPECIALIST INITIALS

1. TYPE	2. AIRCRAFT IDENTIFICATION	3. AIRCRAFT TYPE/ SPECIAL EQUIPMENT	4. TRUE AIRSPEED	5. DEPARTURE POINT	6. DEPARTURE TIME PROPOSED (Z)	ACTUAL (Z)	7. CRUISING ALTITUDE
VFR X IFR DVFR	TNA 90	MD90/G	440 KTS	KBDL Bradley Int'l			FL330

8. ROUTE OF FLIGHT

CSTL.SHERL, J121 BRIGS, BRIGS.VCN 5 PHL

9. DESTINATION (Name of airport and city)	10. EST. TIME ENROUTE HOURS	MINUTES	11. REMARKS
KPHL PHILADELPHIA INT'L PHILADELPHIA			L/O = Level Off PPH = Pounds Per Hour TEC = Tower to Tower Variation: BDL 14W, PHL 10W

12. FUEL ON BOARD HOURS	MINUTES	13. ALTERNATE AIRPORT(S)	14. PILOT'S NAME, ADDRESS & TELEPHONE NUMBER & AIRCRAFT HOME BASE	15. NUMBER ABOARD
2	20	KACY ATLANTIC CITY INT'L	17. DESTINATION CONTACT/TELEPHONE (OPTIONAL)	99

16. COLOR OF AIRCRAFT	
BLACK/RED	CIVIL AIRCRAFT PILOTS. FAR Part 91 requires you file an IFR flight plan to operate under instrument flight rules in controlled airspace. Failure to file could result in a civil penalty not to exceed $1,000 for each violation (Section 901 of the Federal Aviation Act of 1958, as amended). Filing of a VFR flight plan is recommended as a good operating practice. See also Part 99 for requirements concerning DVFR flight plans.

FAA Form 7233-1 (8-82) CLOSE VFR FLIGHT PLAN WITH ______________ FSS ON ARRIVAL

FLIGHT LOG

CHECK POINTS FROM	TO	ROUTE ALTITUDE	COURSE	WIND TEMP	SPEED-KTS TAS	GS	DIST NM	TIME LEG	TOT	FUEL LEG	TOT
BDL	YODER INTER	CSTL1.SHERL CLIMB					45		:15:00		2560*
Yoder Inter	SHERL INTER	CSTL1.SHERL FL330		340/55 ISA							
Sherl Inter	BRIGS INTER	J121 FL330									
Brigs Inter	VCN	BRIGS.VCN5 FL300									
VCN	PHL	BRIGS.VCN5 DESCENT & APPROACH					46	:14:00		1190	
PHL	ACY	TEC 3000					44	:12:00			

OTHER DATA: * Includes Taxi Fuel

NOTE: Use 6150 PPH Total Fuel Flow From L/O To Start Of Descent.
Use 5900 PPH Total Fuel Flow For Reserve And Alternate Requirements.

A Missed Approach Requires 244# of Fuel.

TIME and FUEL: As required by FARs.

TIME	FUEL (LB)	
		EN ROUTE
		RESERVE
		ALTERNATE
		TOTAL

FIGURE 214.—Flight Plan/Flight Log.

20 **CONNECTICUT**

WINDSOR LOCKS

BRADLEY INTL (BDL) 3 W UTC–5(–4DT) N41°56.33′ W72°40.99′ **NEW YORK**

174 B S4 **FUEL** 100LL, JET A OX 1, 2, 3, 4 TPA—See Remarks **H-3J, 6J, L-25C, 28I**

LRA ARFF Index D **IAP**

RWY 06-24: H9502X200 (ASPH-GRVD) S-200, D-200, DT-350,DDT-710 HIRL CL

RWY 06: ALSF2 TDZ. **RWY 24:** MALSR. VASI(V4L)—GA 3.0°TCH 56′. Trees.

RWY 15-33: H6846X150 (ASPH-GRVD) S-200, D-200, DT-350 HIRL

RWY 15: REIL. VASI(V4L)—GA 3.5°TCH 59′. Trees. **RWY 33:** MALSF. VASI(V4R)—GA 3.0°TCH 59′. Trees.

RWY 01-19: H5145X100 (ASPH) S-60, D-190, DT-328 MIRL

RWY 01: Building. **RWY 19:** Trees.

AIRPORT REMARKS: Attended continuously. Numerous birds frequently on or in vicinity or arpt. TPA—1174(1000) light acft, 1874(1700) heavy acft. Landing fee for business, corporate and revenue producing aircraft. Flight Notification Service (ADCUS) available. NOTE: See Land and Hold Short Operations Section.

WEATHER DATA SOURCES: LLWAS.

COMMUNICATIONS: ATIS 118.15 (203–627–3423) **UNICOM** 122.95

BRIDGEPORT FSS (BDR) TF 1-800-WX-BRIEF. NOTAM FILE BDL.

WINDSOR LOCKS RCO 122.3 (BRIDGEPORT FSS)

® **BRADLEY APP CON** 125.8 (within 20 miles)

® **BRADLEY DEP CON** 127.8 (South) 125.35 (North and West) 123.95 (Northeast)

TOWER 120.3 **GND CON** 121.9 **CLNC DEL** 121.75

AIRSPACE: CLASS C svc continuous ctc **APP CON**

RADIO AIDS TO NAVIGATION: NOTAM FILE BDL.

(T) VORTACW 109.0 BDL Chan 27 N41°56.45′ W72°41.32′ at fld. 160/14W.

VOR portion unusable:

093°–103° byd 24 NM blo 5000′

104°–139° byd 10 NM blo 6000′

140°–170° byd 15 NM blo 6000′

260°–290° byd 15 NM blo 6000′

DME unusable 250°–290° byd 18 NN blo 6000′.

CHUPP NDB (LOM) 388 BD N41°52.64′ W72°45.98′ 059° 5.2 NM to fld.

ILS/DME 111.1 I-BDL Chan 48 Rwy 06. LOM CHUPP NDB.

ILS/DME 108.55 I-IKX Chan 22Y Rwy 33.

ILS/DME 111.1 I-MYQ Chan 48 Rwy 24.

TAKE-OFF MINS

94286

INSTRUMENT APPROACH PROCEDURE CHARTS

IFR TAKE-OFF MINIMUMS AND DEPARTURE PROCEDURES

Civil Airports and Selected Military Airports

CIVIL USERS: FAR 91 prescribes take-off rules and establishes take-off minimums for certain operators as follows: (1) Aircraft having two engines or less - one statute mile. (2) Aircraft having more than two engines - one-half statute mile. Airports with IFR take-off minimums other than standard are listed below. Departure procedures and/or ceiling visibility minimums are established to assist all pilots conducting IFR flight in avoiding obstacles during climb to the minimum enroute altitude. Take-off minimums and departures apply to all runways unless otherwise specified. Altitudes, unless otherwise indicated, are minimum altitudes in feet MSL.

MILITARY USERS: Special IFR departures not published as Standard Instrument Departure (SIDS) and civil take-off minima are included below and are established to assist pilots in obstacle avoidance. Refer to appropriate service directives for take-off minimums

WINDSOR LOCKS, CT

BRADLEY INTL

TAKE-OFF MINIMUMS: Rwy 15, 300-1 or std. with a min. climb of 350′ per NM to 300. Rwy 33, 700-1 or std. with a min. climb of 300′ per NM to 1000.

DEPARTURE PROCEDURE: Rwy 1, climb to 1000 via runway heading before turning westbound

FIGURE 215.—Excerpts from Airport/Facilities Directory.

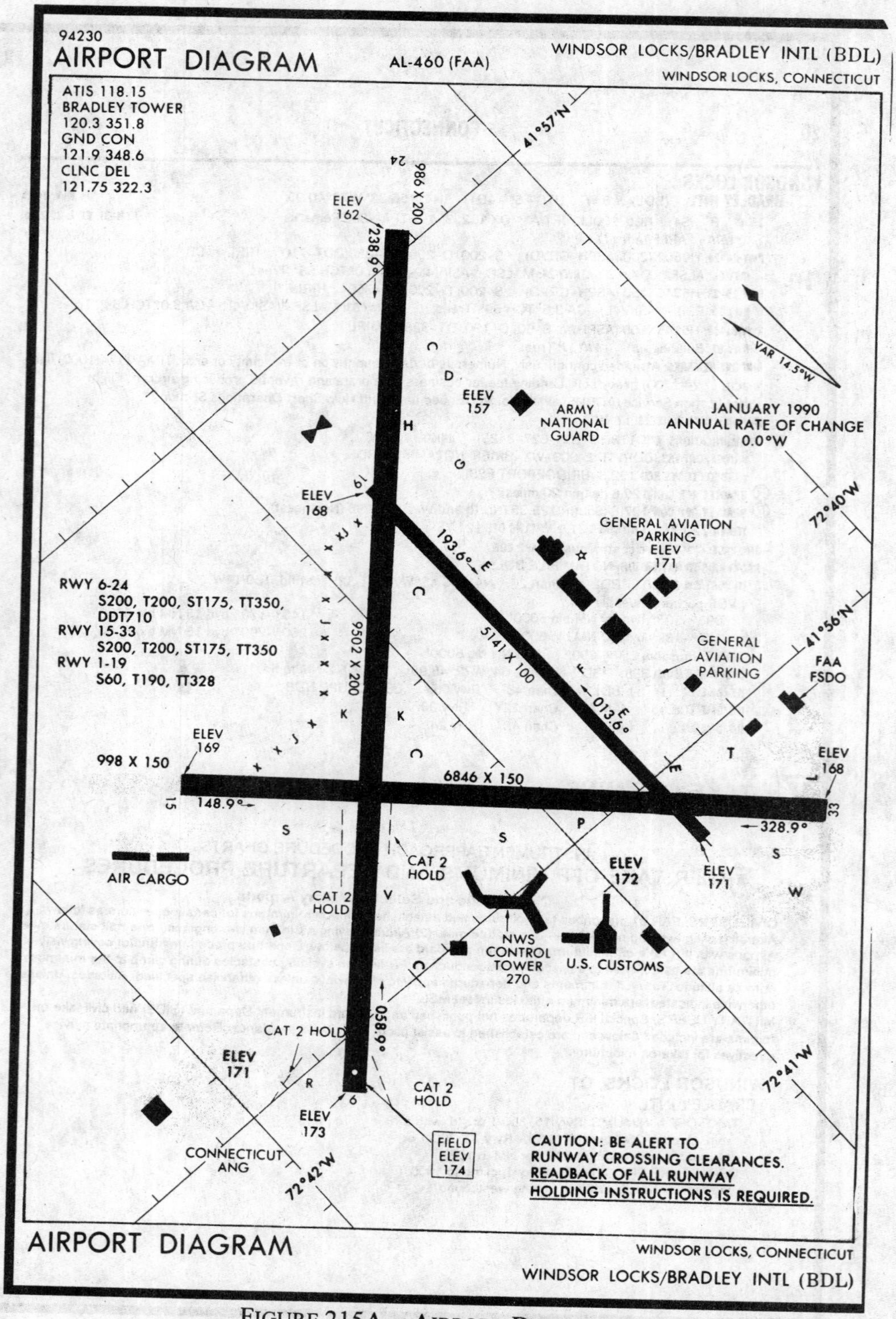

FIGURE 215A -- AIRPORT DIAGRAM.

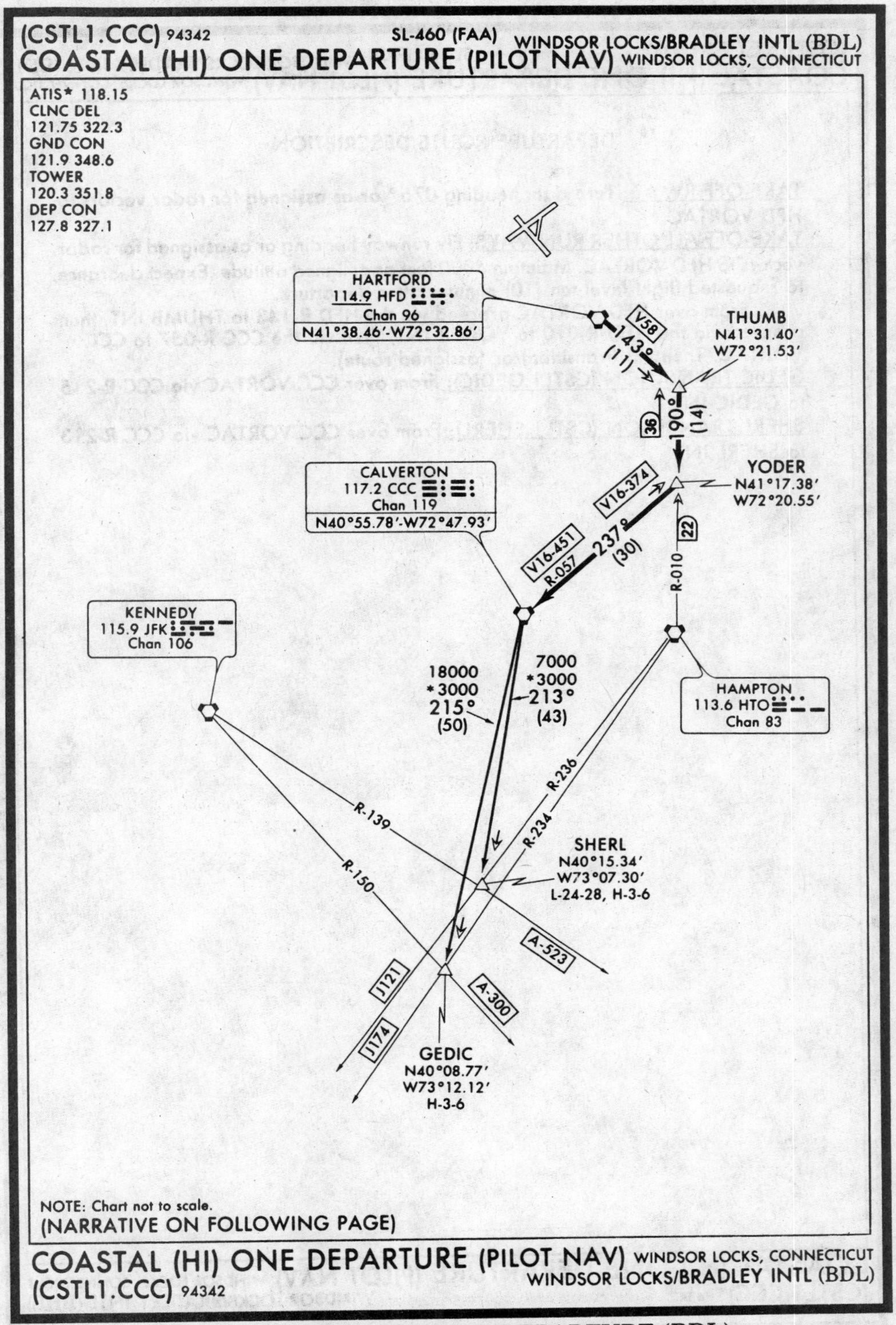

FIGURE 216.—COASTAL (HI) DEPARTURE (BDL).

(CSTL1.CCC) 94342 SL-460 (FAA) WINDSOR LOCKS/BRADLEY INTL (BDL)

COASTAL (HI) ONE DEPARTURE (PILOT NAV) WINDSOR LOCKS, CONNECTICUT

DEPARTURE ROUTE DESCRIPTION

TAKE-OFF RWY 6: Turn right heading 075° or as assigned for radar vectors to HFD VORTAC.

TAKE-OFF ALL OTHER RUNWAYS: Fly runway heading or as assigned for radar vectors to HFD VORTAC. Maintain 4000 feet or assigned altitude. Expect clearance to requested flight level ten (10) minutes after departure.

. . . . From over HFD VORTAC proceed via the HFD R-143 to THUMB INT, then proceed via the HTO R-010 to YODER INT, then via the CCC R-057 to CCC VORTAC. Then via (transition) or (assigned route).

GEDIC TRANSITION (CSTL1.GEDIC): From over CCC VORTAC via CCC R-215 to GEDIC INT.

SHERL TRANSITION (CSTL1.SHERL): From over CCC VORTAC via CCC R-213 to SHERL INT.

COASTAL (HI) ONE DEPARTURE (PILOT NAV) WINDSOR LOCKS, CONNECTICUT

(CSTL1.CCC) 94342 WINDSOR LOCKS/BRADLEY INTL (BDL)

FIGURE 216A.—Departure Route Description.

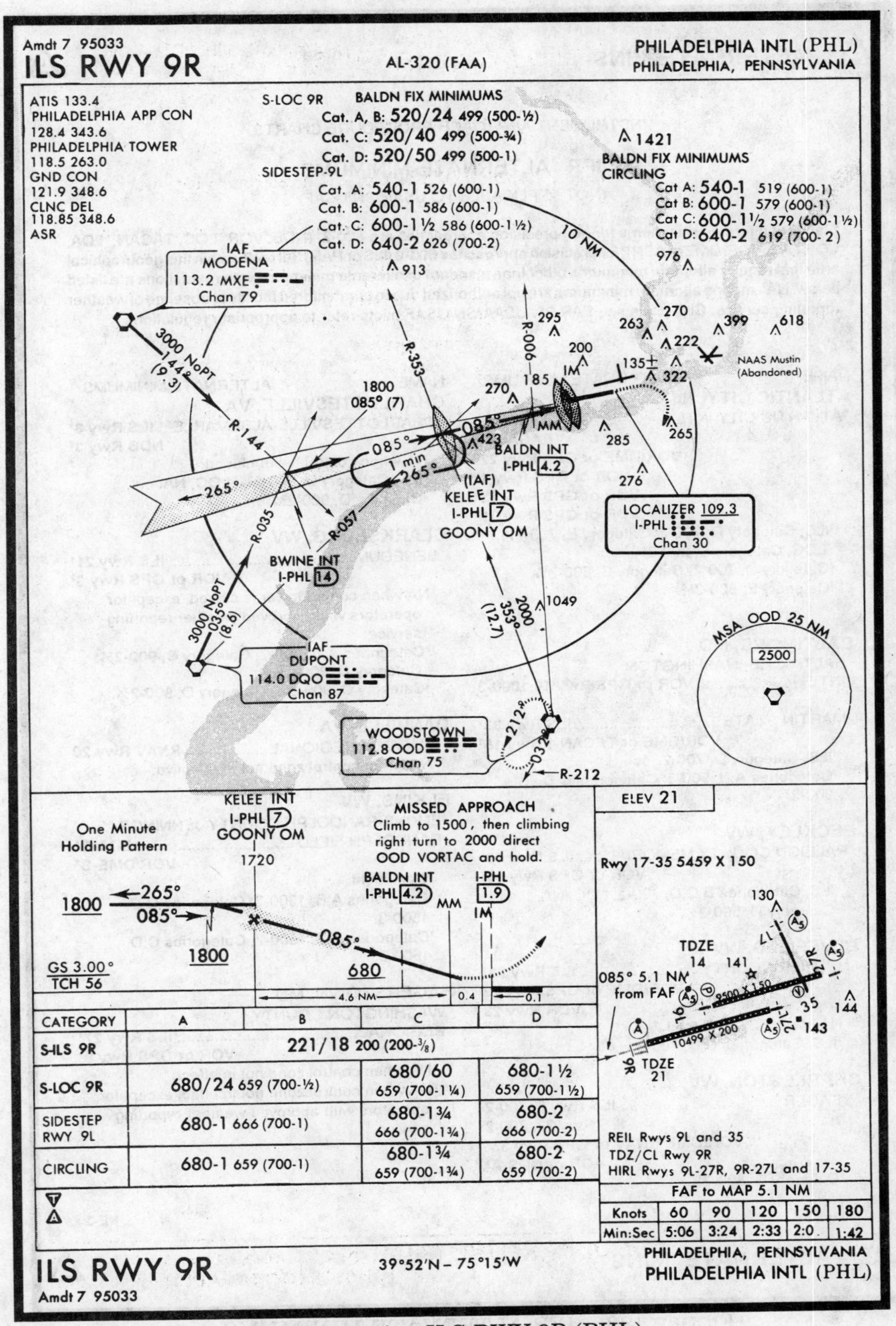

FIGURE 182A.—ILS RWY 9R (PHL).

ALTERNATE MINS

94342

INSTRUMENT APPROACH PROCEDURE CHARTS

IFR ALTERNATE MINIMUMS

(NOT APPLICABLE TO USA/USN/USAF)

Standard alternate minimums for non precision approaches are 800-2 (NDB, VOR, LOC, TACAN, LDA, VORTAC, VOR/DME or ASR); for precision approaches 600-2 (ILS or PAR). Airports within this geographical area that require alternate minimums other than standard or alternate minimums with restrictions are listed below. NA - means alternate minimums are not authorized due to unmonitored facility or absence of weather reporting service. Civil pilots see FAR 91. USA/USN/USAF pilots refer to appropriate regulations.

NAME — ALTERNATE MINIMUMS

ATLANTIC CITY, NJ

ATLANTIC CITY INTL .... ILS Rwy 13[1]
RADAR-1[2]
VOR/DME or GPS Rwy 22[3]
VOR or GPS Rwy 4[3]
VOR or GPS Rwy 13[3]
VOR or GPS Rwy 31[3]

[1]ILS, Category D, 700-2; Category E, 700-2½. LOC, Category E, 800-2½.
[2]Category D, 700-2; Category E, 800-2½.
[3]Category E, 800-2½.

BALTIMORE, MD

BALTIMORE-WASHINGTON INTL .... VOR or GPS Rwy 10,1000-3

MARTIN STATE .... ILS Rwy 33[1]
VOR/DME or TACAN 1 Rwy 15[2]

[1]ILS, Category D, 700-2.
[2]Categories A,B, 900-2; Categories C,D, 900-2¾.

BECKLEY, WV

RALEIGH COUNTY MEMORIAL ..... ILS Rwy 19[1]
VOR or GPS Rwy 19[2]

[1]ILS, Categories B,C,D, 700-2. LOC, NA.
[2]Category D, 800-2¼.

BLUEFIELD, WV

MERCER COUNTY .... ILS Rwy 23[1]
VOR/DME or GPS Rwy 23
VOR Rwy 23

NA when FSS is closed.
[1]ILS, Categories C,D, 700-2.

CHARLESTON, WV

YEAGER .... ILS Rwy 5, 700-2
ILS Rwy 23, 700-2
VOR/DME RNAV or GPS Rwy 33[1]
VOR or GPS-A[1]

[1]Category D, 800-2¼.

NAME — ALTERNATE MINIMUMS

CHARLOTTESVILLE, VA

CHARLOTTESVILLE-ALBEMARLE .. ILS Rwy 3[1]
NDB Rwy 3[2]

NA when control tower closed.
[1]ILS, Category D, 900-2¾. LOC, NA.
[2]Category D, 900-2¾.

CLARKSBURG, WV

BENEDUM .... ILS Rwy 21[1]
VOR or GPS Rwy 3[2]

NA when control tower is closed, except for operators with approved weather reporting service.
[1]Categories A,B, 800-2; Category C, 900-2½; Category D, 900-2¾.
[2]Category C, 900-2½; Category D, 900-2¾.

DANVILLE, VA

DANVILLE REGIONAL .... RNAV Rwy 20

NA when control zone not in effective.

ELKINS, WV

ELKINS-RANDOLPH COUNTY JENNINGS-RANDOLPH FIELD .... LDA-C[1]
VOR/DME-B[2]

NA at night.
[1]Categories A,B, 1200-2; Categories C,D, 1500-3.
[2]Categories A,B, 1500-2; Categories C,D, 1500-3.

HAGERSTOWN, MD

WASHINGTON COUNTY REGIONAL .... ILS Rwy 27[1]
VOR or GPS Rwy 9[2]

[1]NA when control zone not in effect.
[2]NA when control zone not in effect except for operators with approved weather reporting service.

NE-3

ALTERNATE MINS

94342

FIGURE 183.—IFR ALTERNATE MINIMUMS.

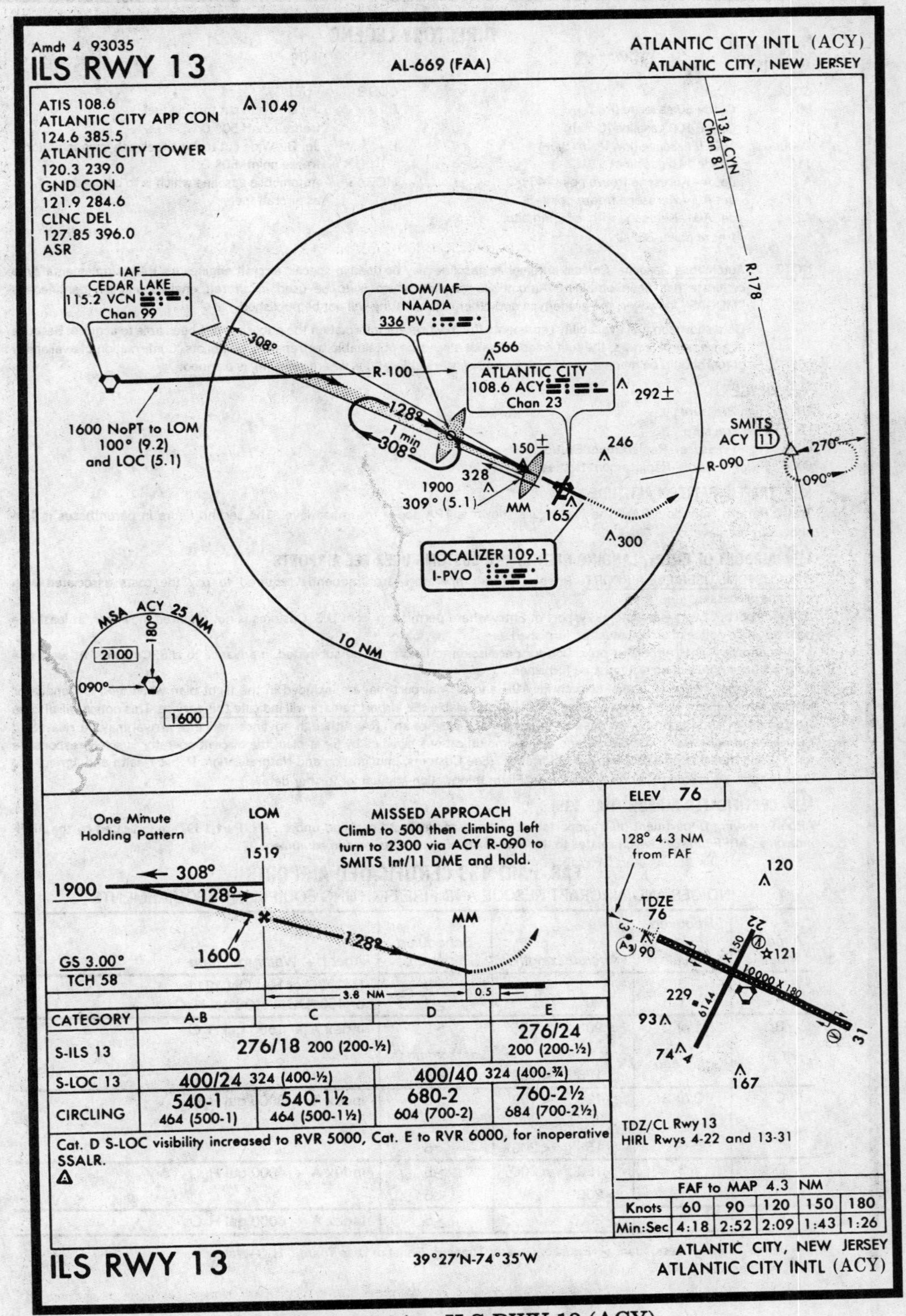

FIGURE 183A.—ILS RWY 13 (ACY).

4

DIRECTORY LEGEND

⑫ FUEL

CODE	FUEL	CODE	FUEL
80	Grade 80 gasoline (Red)	B	Jet B—Wide-cut turbine fuel, freeze point-50° C.
100	Grade 100 gasoline (Green)	B +	Jet B—Wide-cut turbine fuel with icing inhibitor, freeze point-50° C.
100LL	100LL gasoline (low lead) (Blue)	MOGAS	Automobile gasoline which is to be used as aircraft fuel.
115	Grade 115 gasoline		
A	Jet A—Kerosene freeze point-40° C.		
A1	Jet A-1—Kerosene freeze point-50°C.		
A1 +	Jet A-1—Kerosene with icing inhibitor, freeze point-50° C.		

NOTE: Automobile Gasoline. Certain automobile gasoline may be used in specific aircraft engines if a FAA supplemental type cetificate has been obtained. Automobile gasoline which is to be used in aircraft engines will be identified as "MOGAS", however, the grade/type and other octane rating will not be published.

Data shown on fuel availability represents the most recent information the publisher has been able to acquire. Because of a variety of factors, the fuel listed may not always be obtainable by transient civil pilots. Confirmation of availability of fuel should be made directly with fuel dispensers at locations where refueling is planned.

⑬ OXYGEN

OX 1 High Pressure
OX 2 Low Pressure
OX 3 High Pressure—Replacement Bottles
OX 4 Low Pressure—Replacement Bottles

⑭ TRAFFIC PATTERN ALTITUDE

Traffic Pattern Altitude (TPA)—The first figure shown is TPA above mean sea level. The second figure in parentheses is TPA above airport elevation.

⑮ AIRPORT OF ENTRY, LANDING RIGHTS, AND CUSTOMS USER FEE AIRPORTS

U.S. CUSTOMS USER FEE AIRPORT—Private Aircraft operators are frequently required to pay the costs associated with customs processing.

AOE—Airport of Entry—A customs Airport of Entry where permission from U.S. Customs is not required, however, at least one hour advance notice of arrival must be furnished.

LRA—Landing Rights Airport—Application for permission to land must be submitted in advance to U.S. Customs. At least one hour advance notice of arrival must be furnished.

NOTE: Advance notice of arrival at both an AOE and LRA airport may be included in the flight plan when filed in Canada or Mexico, where Flight Notification Service (ADCUS) is available the airport remark will indicate this service. This notice will also be treated as an application for permission to land in the case of an LRA. Although advance notice of arrival may be relayed to Customs through Mexico, Canadian, and U.S. Communications facilities by flight plan, the aircraft operator is solely responsible for insuring that Customs receives the notification. (See Customs, Immigration and Naturalization, Public Health and Agriculture Department requirements in the International Flight Information Manual for further details.)

⑯ CERTIFICATED AIRPORT (FAR 139)

Airports serving Department of Transportation certified carriers and certified under FAR, Part 139, are indicated by the ARFF index; i.e., ARFF Index A, which relates to the availability of crash, fire, rescue equipment.

FAR-PART 139 CERTIFICATED AIRPORTS

INDICES AND AIRCRAFT RESCUE AND FIRE FIGHTING EQUIPMENT REQUIREMENTS

Airport Index	*Required No. Vehicles*	*Aircraft Length*	*Scheduled Departures*	*Agent + Water for Foam*
A	1	<90′	≥1	500#DC or HALON 1211 or 450#DC + 100 gal H_2O
B	1 or 2	≥90′, <126′	≥5	Index A + 1500 gal H_2O
		≥126′, <159′	<5	
C	2 or 3	≥126′, <159′	≥5	Index A + 3000 gal H_2O
		≥159′, <200′	<5	
D	3	≥159′, <200′	≥5	Index A + 4000 gal H_2O
		>200′	<5	
E	3	≥200′	≥5	Index A + 6000 gal H_2O

> Greater Than; < Less Than; ≥ Equal or Greater Than; ≤ Equal or Less Than; H_2O–Water; DC–Dry Chemical.

LEGEND 15.—Directory Legend.

332

TOWER ENROUTE CONTROL (TEC)

Within the national airspace system it is possible for a pilot to fly IFR from one point to another without leaving approach control airspace. This is referred to as "tower enroute" which allows flight beneath the enroute structure. The tower enroute concept has been expanded (where practical) by reallocating airspace vertically/geographically to allow flight planning between city pairs while remaining within approach control airspace. Pilots are encouraged to solicit tower enroute information from FSS's and to use the route descriptions provided in this directory when filing flight plans. Other airways which appear to be more direct between two points may take the aircraft out of approach control airspace thereby resulting in additional delays or other complications. All published TEC routes are designed to avoid enroute airspace and the majority are within radar coverage. Additional routes and other changes will appear in forthcoming editions as necessary. The acronym "TEC" should be included in the remarks section of the flight plan. This will advise ATC that the pilot intends to remain within approach control airspace for the entire flight. The following items should be noted before using the graphics and route descriptions:

1. The graphic is not to be used for navigation nor detailed flight planning. Not all city pairs are depicted. It is intended to show general geographic areas connected by tower enroute control. Pilots should refer to route descriptions for specific flight planning.
2. The route description contains four columns of information; i.e., the approach control area (listed alphabetically) within which the departure airport is located (check appropriate flight information publications), the specific route (airway, radial, etc.), the highest altitude allowed for the route, and the destination airport (listed alphabetically).
3. The word "DIRECT" will appear as the route when radar vectors will be used or no airway exists. Also, this indicates that a Standard Instrument Departure (SID) or Standard Terminal Arrival Route (STAR) may be applied by ATC.
4. When a NAVAID or intersection identifier appears with no airway immediately preceding or following the identifier, the routing is understood to be DIRECT to or from that point unless otherwise cleared by ATC.
5. Routes beginning or ending with an airway indicate that the airway essentially overflies the airport or radar vectors will be applied.
6. Where more than one route is listed to the same destination, the pilot may select which route is desired. Unless otherwise stated, all routes may be flown in either direction.
7. Routes are effective only during each respective terminal facility's normal operating hours. Pilots are cautioned to check NOTAMS to ensure appropriate terminal facilities will be operating for the planned flight time.
8. All identifiers used for NAVAIDS, airports, and intersections are official identifiers.
9. Altitudes are listed in thousands of feet. ATC may require altitude changes to maintain flight within approach control airspace. ATC will provide radar monitoring and, if necessary, course guidance if the highest altitude assigned by ATC is below the Minimum Enroute Altitude (MEA).
10. Although all airports are not listed under the destination column, IFR flight may be planned to satellite airports in proximity to major airports via the same routing.
11. Flight plans should be filed with a Flight Service Station (FSS).

TOWER ENROUTE CONTROL CITY PAIRS

(1) Single Engine only.
(2) Props less than 210 KT IAS.
(3) Props less than 250 KT IAS.
(4) Jets and Props greater than 210 KT IAS.

Boston—NO SATS = BED/LWM/BVY/AYE/FIT/B09/6B6/2B2
SO SATS = BOS/OWD/NZW/1B9/3B2

Approach Control Area (Including Satellites)	Route	Highest Altitude	Destination
Albany	V14 V428 V29	6000	Binghamton
	V130	7000	Bradley
	V14	10,000	Buffalo
	V14 V428	8000	Elmira
	V14 V428	8000	Ithaca
	V2	10,000	Rochester
	V14 BEEPS	10,000	Rochester
	V2	10,000	Utica/Rome
Allentown	FJC V149 LHY	8000	Albany
	ETX LHY	8000	Albany
	FJC ARD V276 DIXIE V229	5000 (only)	Atlantic City
	V93 LRP	8000	Baltimore
	ETX V162 DUMMR V93 LRP	6000	Baltimore
	V39 LRP	8000 (only)	Baltimore
	FJC BWZ	5000 (only)	Caldwell, NJ
	(2) ETX V30 SBJ	5000 (only)	Farmingdale, NY
	(2) FJC V6 SBJ	5000 (only)	Farmingdale, NY
	ETX V162 HAR	8000	Harrisburg
	ETX ETX004 WEISS	4000 (only)	Hazleton
	ETX V39	4000	Lancaster
	(2) ETX V30 SBJ	5000 (only)	Newark

LEGEND 42.—Tower Enroute Control (NE).

TOWER ENROUTE CONTROL

343

Approach Control Area (Including Satellites)	Route	Highest Altitude	Destination
New York /Kennedy	SAX V249 SBJ V30 ETX (Non jet/Non turboprop)	8000	Allentown
	DIXIE V229 ACY (Props only)	6000	Atlantic City
	DIXIE V1 HOWIE (Jets only)	8000	Atlantic City
	DIXIE V1 V308 OTT (Props only)	6000	Andrews AFB
	DIXIE V16 ENO V268 SWANN (Props only)	6000	Baltimore
	COL	2000	Belmar
	BDR MAD V475 V188 TMU	9000	Block Island
	BDR V229 HFD V3 WOONS	9000	Boston
	BDR V229 HFD HFD053 DREEM	9000	Boston (North)
	BDR BDR014 JUDDS V419 BRISS	9000	Bradley
	BDR BDR014 JUDDS V419 BRISS (Jets only)	10000	Bradley
	BDR	3000	Bridgeport
	SAX V249 SBJ V30 ETX V162 HAR (Non jet/Non turboprop)	8000	Capital City
	DIXIE V1 LEEAH V268 BAL BAL291 KROLL AML (Non-pressurized aircraft only)	6000	Dulles
	BDR MAD MAD126 MONDI	9000	Groton
	R/V CCC 232 CCC HTO	3000	Hampton
	BDR V229 HFD	9000	Hartford
	BDR V229 HFD V167 PVD V151 GAILS	9000	Hyannis
	R/V ILS 6 LOC (Text Info)	3000	Islip
	R/V CCC232 CCC	3000	Islip
	Direct	2000	LaGuardia
	SAX V249 SBJ V30 ETX V162 V93 LRP (Props only)	8000	Lancaster
	DIXIE V16 CYN	6000	McGuire
	BDR MAD V475 V188 TMU V374 MVY	9000	Martha's Vineyard
	BDR MAD	3000	Meriden Markham
	DIXIE V16 VCN (Props only)	6000	Millville
	BDR MAD V475 V188 TMU V374 MVY	9000	Nantucket
	COL V232 SBJ	3000	Newark
	BDR MAD V475 V188 TMU V374 MINNK	9000	New Bedford
	DIXIE V1 (Props only)	6000	Norfolk
	DIXIE V276 ARD	4000	N. Philadelphia
	DIXIE V16 CYN V312 OOD (Props only)	6000	Philadelphia
	DIXIE V16 CYN V312 OOD (Jets only)	8000	Philadelphia
	BDR MAD V475 V188 TMU (210 kts +)	9000	Providence
	BDR MAD V475 V188 TMU	9000	Quonset
	SAX V249 SBJ V30 ETX V39 FLOAT (Non jet/Non turboprop only)	8000	Reading
	DIXIE V16 (Props only)	6000	Richmond
	DIXIE V1 (Props only)	6000	Salisbury
	DIXIE V1 V308 OTT (Props only)	6000	Washington
	DPK V483 CMK	2000	Westchester Co
	BDR MAD V475 V188 TMU	9000	Westerly
	DIXIE V229 PANZE V44 SIE (Props only)	6000	Wildwood
	DIXIE V1 HOWIE (Jets only)	8000	Wildwood
	BDR MAD V1 GRAYM	9000	Worcester
New York/ LaGuardia	SAX V249 SBJ V30 ETX	8000	Allentown
	DIXIE V229 ACY (Props only)	6000	Atlantic City
	DIXIE V1 HOWIE (Jets only)	8000	Atlantic City
	ABBYS V403 GLOMO V408 V93 BAL (Props only)	7000	Andrews AFB
	ABBYS V403 BELAY V378 BAL (Props only)	7000	Baltimore
	JFK COL	6000	Belmar
	BDR MAD V475 V188 TMU	9000	Block Island
	BDR V229 HFD V3 WOONS	9000	Boston
	BDR V229 HFD HFD053 DREEM	9000	Boston (North)
	BDR BDR014 JUDDS V419 BRISS (Props only)	9000	Bradley
	BDR BDR014 JUDDS V419 BRISS (Jets only)	10000	Bradley
	BDR 248 CCC285 PUGGS V229 BDR	5000	Bridgeport
	R/V BDR248 BDR. . .(Helicopter Route)	5000	Bridgeport (Points NE)
	SAX V249 SBJ V30 ETX V162 HAR	8000	Capital City
	SAX V249 SBJ V30 ETX V162 V93 V143 ROBRT AML (Props only)	8000	Dulles

LEGEND 42A—Tower Enroute Control Continued.

346 **TOWER ENROUTE CONTROL**

Approach Control Area (Including Satellites)	Route	Highest Altitude	Destination
	ABBYS V403 GLOMO V408 V93 BAL (Props only)	7000	Washington
	DIXIE V229 PANZE V44 SIE (Props only)	6000	Wildwood
	DIXIE V1 HOWIE (Jets only)	8000	Wildwood
	CMK V3 HFD V1 GRAYM	9000	Worcester
Norfolk	CCV CCV345 PXT175 PXT	5000	Patuxent River
	HPW V260 RIC (West-bound only)	9000	Richmond
	CCV V1 SBY	5000	Salisbury
	CCV V139 SWL (Northeast-bound only)	5000	Snow Hill
	HCM HCM330 SVILL	7000	Washington
Patuxent	SWL V139	5000	Atlantic City
	PXT V16 V44	5000	Atlantic City
	SBY V1 V44	5000	Atlantic City
	SBY332 BAL130	4000	Baltimore
	PXT V93	5000	Baltimore
	SBY V29 ENO	5000	Dover AFB
	PXT V16 ENO	5000	Dover AFB
	PXT V16	5000	Dover AFB
	SBY VI ATR	5000	Dover AFB
	PXT V213 V286 FLUKY	6000	Dulles
	COLIN V33 HCM	6000	Newport News
	SBY V1 CCV	6000	Norfolk
	SWL V139 CCV	6000	Norfolk
	WHINO V33 V286 STEIN	5000	Norfolk
	PXT V213 ENO V29 DQO	5000	Philadelphia
	SBY V29 DQO	5000	Philadelphia
	PXT V16	6000	Richmond
	SBY V1 JAMIE HCM	6000	Richmond
	COLIN V33 HCM	6000	Richmond
	PXT V31 OTT (No Overflight of D.C. Area)	4000	Washington
	SBY CHURK OTT (No Overflight of D.C. Area)	4000	Washington
Pease	RAYMY LWM	8000	Boston
	EXALT V139 V141 GAILS	10000	Hyannis
	V106 GDM V14 ORW V16 CCC	10000	Islip
	V106 GDM V14 ORW V16 DPK	10000	Kennedy
	EXALT V139 BURDY	10000	Providence
Philadelphia	RV FJC180 FJC	4000	Allentown
	OOD VCN V184 ACY	3000	Atlantic City
	MXE V378 BAL	6000	Baltimore
	DQO V166 V378 BAL	6000	Baltimore
	OOD V157 ENO	4000	Dover AFB
	DQO V29 ENO	4000	Dover AFB
	MXE V408 ROBRT AML	8000	Dulles
	MXE V184 MXE283027 V469 HAR	6000	Harrisburg
	PNE PNE090 ARD126 V16 DIXIE (Direct) (Single Engine only)	5000	Kennedy
	PNE PNE090 ARD126 V16 V276 ZIGGI (Direct) (No Single Engine)	5000	Kennedy
	RBV V123 PROUD	7000	LaGuardia
	MXE MXE295 HABER LRP137 LRP	4000	Lancaster
	ARD V214 METRO (Non Turbojets only)	5000	Newark
	RBV V213 WARRD (Turbojets only)	7000	Newark
	MXE MXE334 HUMEL	4000	Reading
	ARD V214 METRO	5000	Teterboro
	MXE V408 VINNY V93 BAL	8000	Washington
	DQO V166 V93 BAL	8000	Washington
	RV FJC180 FJC BWZ SAX V39 BREZY	5000	Westchester Co.
	RV FJC180 FJC V149 RITTY	5000	Wilkes Barre/Scranton
Pittsburgh	BSV (Westbound only)	8000	Akron-Canton
	V37 (Southbound only)	8000	Clarksburg
	EWC V37 (Northbound only)	8000	Erie

LEGEND 42B.—Tower Enroute Control Continued.

END OF CHAPTER

CHAPTER ELEVEN
BEECHCRAFT 1900 OPERATING/PERFORMANCE DATA

This chapter contains outlines of major concepts tested, all FAA test questions and answers regarding Beechcraft 1900 operating/performance data, and an explanation of each answer. Each module is listed above with the number of questions from the FAA pilot knowledge test pertaining to that particular module. For each module, the first number following the parentheses is the page number on which the outline begins, and the next number is the page number on which the questions begin.

There are 79 questions in this chapter. We separate and organize the FAA ATP questions into meaningful study units, i.e., chapters and modules. As an analogy, it is easier to deal with the "trees" if you understand the "forest." In this context, "trees" are individual FAA questions and the "forest" is the ATP knowledge test. The organizational units between the overall ATP test and individual ATP test questions are chapters and modules in this book.

CAUTION: The **sole purpose** of this book is to expedite your passing the FAA pilot knowledge test for the ATP certificate. Topics or regulations not directly tested on the FAA pilot knowledge test are omitted. Much more information and knowledge are necessary to fly safely. This additional material is presented in Gleim's other pilot training books (see the order form on page 818) and in many FAA books and circulars, as well as in airplane *POH*s and other commercial textbooks.

11.1 CG COMPUTATION (Questions 1-10)

1. These questions (as well as Questions 11-25 under the next two sections) are based on the following figures:

Fig.	Page	Description
3	515	Beech 1900 -- Loading Passenger Configuration
4	515	Beech 1900 -- Loading Cargo Configuration
5	516	Beech 1900 -- Loading Limitations
6	516	Airplane -- Loading Data
7	517	Beech 1900 -- CG Envelope and Cargo Loading Data
8	518	Airplane --Weights and Moments -- Baggage
9	519	Beech 1900 --Weights and Moments -- Occupants
10	520	Density Variation of Aviation Fuel
11	521	Beech 1900 -- Weights and Moments -- Usable Fuel

2. Given a specific loading configuration, set up a two-column table to determine the total weight and total moment.
3. EXAMPLE: Calculate the CG given the loading conditions of BE-1 (see Fig. 3 on page 515).
   a. Note that the basic empty weight and moment in the passenger configuration are provided in Fig. 6 on page 516.
      1) In the cargo configuration, a basic operating weight is given at the bottom of Fig. 4 on page 515.
         a) **Basic operating weight** is the weight of the airplane, including the crew, ready for flight but without payload and fuel.
   b. Determine the moments for the crew and passengers by using Fig. 9 on page 519 and for the baggage by using Fig. 8 on page 518.
   c. Determine the specific weight of the fuel by using Fig. 10 on page 520.
      1) Enter the graph at the bottom of the chart at the given temperature and move up to the heavy line that is marked with the appropriate type of fuel. Then, move horizontally to the left margin to determine the specific weight of the fuel.
      2) EXAMPLE: The specific weight for Jet B fuel at +5° is 6.6 lb./gal.
   d. Determine the weight and the moment for the fuel by using Fig. 11 on page 521.

Item	Weight (lb.)	Mom./100
Basic empty weight	9,226	25,823
Crew	360	464
Passengers		
Row 1	350	700
Row 2	260	598
Row 3	200	520
Row 4	340	986
Row 5	120	384
Row 6	400	1,400
Row 7	120	456
Row 8	250	1,025
Row 9	--	--
Baggage		
Nose	60	39
Forward cabin	250	409
Aft (fwd. sec.)	500	2,418
Aft (aft sec.)	--	--
Fuel: 370 gal. Jet B at +5°C	2,442	7,299
Total	14,878	42,521

   e. Calculate CG by dividing the sum of the individual moments by the sum of the individual weights.

$$CG = \frac{42{,}521}{14{,}878} \times 100 = 285.8$$

11.2 CG SHIFT (Questions 11-20)

1. In a CG shift problem, use the following formula:

$$CG = \frac{M_1 \pm \Delta M}{W_1 \pm \Delta W}$$

If M_1 = original moment and W_1 = original weight.

2. On a CG shift if there is no gross weight change and the original CG is not known, you can define the datum point as the old CG, thus making $M_1 = 0$. Since there is no gross weight change, $\Delta W = 0$. Thus,

$$CG\ shift = \frac{\Delta M}{W_1}$$

3. Set up a schedule as illustrated in the example below, and determine the gross weight and the arms of the weight shifts.

   a. EXAMPLE: What is the CG shift if the passengers in row 1 are moved to seats in row 9 under Loading Conditions BE-1?

      1) Fig. 3 on page 515 provides loading conditions for BE-1, which are used in the schedule below to provide the gross weight. Fig. 6 on page 516 provides loading data for the BE-1900. Note that the passengers in row 1 are moving to row 9; i.e., their arm changes from 200 to 440. The weight in row 1 (350 lb.) will move aft 240 in. (440 in. – 200 in.).

Item	Weight	Arm
Crew	360	
Passengers		
Row 1	350	200
Row 2	260	
Row 3	200	
Row 4	340	
Row 5	120	
Row 6	400	
Row 7	120	
Row 8	250	
Row 9	--	440
Baggage		
Nose	60	
Forward cabin	250	
Aft (fwd. sec.)	500	
Aft (aft sec.)	--	
Fuel (370 gal. Jet B at +5°C)	2,442	
Basic empty weight	9,226	
Gross weight	14,878	

$$CG\ shift = \frac{\Delta M}{W_1} = \frac{350 \times 240}{14{,}878} = \frac{84{,}000}{14{,}878} = 5.6\ in.$$

      2) The direction of CG shift corresponds directly to the direction of the weight shift. Thus, the CG is shifted 5.6 in. aft.

4. **Total Weight Changes**. Use the following formula:

$$New\ CG = \frac{M_1 \pm \Delta M}{W_1 \pm \Delta W}$$

   a. You have to go through the entire weight and balance procedure to determine the weight and CG.

   b. An example of this calculation is question 14 on page 523.

11.3 CG AND WEIGHT LIMITS EXCEEDED (Questions 21-25)

1. For each of these questions, you need to compute the zero fuel weight (ZFW), takeoff weight, CG at takeoff, and CG at landing.
   a. Add the basic empty weight + crew + passengers and baggage to determine ZFW, and compare it to the maximum of 14,000 lb.
   b. Add the ZFW + ramp load of fuel (lb.) – fuel used during engine start and taxi to determine takeoff weight and compare it to the maximum of 16,600 lb.
   c. Compute the CG at takeoff by dividing total moments by total weight.
   d. Compute the CG at landing by recomputing the CG after fuel usage.
2. EXAMPLE: See question 21 on page 527.

11.4 MINIMUM TAKEOFF TORQUE (Questions 26-30)

1. Fig. 12 on page 530 provides minimum takeoff power at 1700 RPM with ice vanes extended or retracted.
   a. Ice vanes are used to keep ice from being ingested into the engine. They reduce the air flow into the engine and, accordingly, reduce available power.
2. The horizontal axis of the chart is outside air temperature (OAT), and the vertical axis is engine torque.
   a. Choose the chart for ice vanes extended or the chart for ice vanes retracted.
   b. Find the OAT at the bottom of the chart.
   c. Move up vertically to the pressure altitude line.
   d. From the point of intersection, move horizontally to the left edge of the chart to determine engine torque.
   e. EXAMPLE: Ice vanes are extended at a pressure altitude of 9,000 ft. with an OAT of +3°C. Fig. 12 on page 530 is a "Minimum Takeoff Power at 1700 RPM" graph. Use the graph on the left for ice vanes extended. Find +3°C at the bottom and go up vertically to 9,000 ft. pressure altitude. From that intersection, go horizontally to the left side of the graph which indicates 3,100 ft.-lb. of torque.

11.5 TAKEOFF DISTANCE (Questions 31-35)

1. Fig. 13 on page 532 is a takeoff distance chart that takes into account
   a. Outside air temperature (OAT)
   b. Pressure altitude
   c. Weight
   d. Wind component
   e. Obstacle height
2. On the graph, there is an example for an OAT of +15°C, 3,500 ft. pressure altitude; 15,000 lb. weight; 10-kt. headwind; and either no obstacle or a 50-ft. obstacle.
   a. Start in the left portion of the chart.
   b. From the OAT found at the bottom, move up vertically to the appropriate pressure altitude line.
      1) If the ice vanes are extended, add 5°C to the actual OAT before entering the graph, as stated in the note above the left portion of the graph.
   c. From the point of intersection, move over to the first reference line.

d. As appropriate, move to the right and down, parallel to the guide lines, to the weight of the aircraft.

e. From that point, move to the right horizontally to the second reference line.

f. From the second reference line, move to the right and down, parallel to the guide lines for a headwind (or up, parallel to the guide lines for a tailwind), to the wind velocity.

g. From that point, move to the right horizontally to the third reference line.

h. From the third reference line, move horizontally to the right side of the graph for the ground roll.

1) For obstacles, move to the right and up, parallel to the guide lines, to the obstacle height of 50 ft., which is at the right margin of the graph.

3. In the upper right-hand corner of Fig. 13 is a takeoff speed/weight conversion table.

a. V_1 is the takeoff decision speed and will be determined by aircraft weight.

b. Find the takeoff weight in the left column and move to the center column to determine V_1 at that weight.

c. If the takeoff weight falls between the weights shown, you will need to interpolate.

11.6 ACCELERATE-STOP FIELD LENGTH (Questions 36-40)

1. Fig. 14 on page 535 has the accelerate-stop distance.

2. An example is provided for +15°C OAT, 3,800 ft. pressure altitude, 15,000 lb. weight, and a 10-kt. headwind, resulting in a 3,800-ft. accelerate-stop distance.

a. At the lower left, find +15°C and move up vertically to pressure altitude of 3,800 ft.

1) If the ice vanes are extended, add 3°C to the actual OAT before entering the graph, as stated in the note above the left portion of the graph.

b. Move to the right horizontally to the first reference line and then down and to the right (parallel to the guide lines) to 15,000 lb.

c. Move to the right horizontally to the second reference line and then down and to the right (parallel to the guide lines) to 10 kt. headwind.

1) For a tailwind, follow the guide lines up and to the right.

d. Move horizontally to the right edge of the chart and find 3,800 ft. as the accelerate-stop distance.

11.7 RATE OF CLIMB (Questions 41-45)

1. Rate-of-climb performance is provided in two similar charts: one for two engines and one for one engine inoperative.

2. On Fig. 16 (two engines) on page 539, the example shows −4°C OAT and a pressure altitude of 9,000 ft. with a weight of 14,500 lb., providing a rate of climb of 2,500 fpm.

a. On Fig. 17 (one engine inoperative), on page 540, the example uses the same situation as described just above except the rate of climb is 450 fpm.

b. A note on each chart indicates that, during operation with ice vanes extended, rate of climb will be reduced a specified amount, depending on the chart.

3. Note that just to the right of the rate of climb in feet per minute is a climb gradient as a percentage. Thus, if you extend over from the right side of the rate-of-climb chart, you can get a climb gradient.

a. The climb gradient in the two-engine airplane example is 14.7%, and in the single-engine example, it is 3.1%.

11.8 TIME, FUEL, AND DISTANCE TO CLIMB (Questions 46-50)

1. Fig. 18 on page 542 shows a "Time, Fuel, and Distance to Cruise Climb" graph.
   a. An example is provided in the upper right-hand corner.

OAT at takeoff	15°C
OAT at cruise	–10°C
Airport pressure altitude	3,499 ft.
Cruise altitude	11,000 ft.
Initial climb weight	15,000 lb.

2. Given the altitude and temperature at the departure airport and the cruise level, as well as the initial weight, you compute two times, two fuel usages, and two distances, and then compute the difference for each.

11.9 SINGLE ENGINE SERVICE CEILING (Questions 51-55)

1. Fig. 20 on page 547 has a "Service Ceiling with One Engine Inoperative" graph.
   a. The OAT is on the horizontal axis.
   b. The pressure altitude of the single-engine service ceiling is on the vertical axis.
   c. Two graphs are provided: one with bleed air ON and one with bleed air OFF.
2. On Fig. 20 on page 547, the example is –4°C and 14,500 lb., resulting in a single-engine service ceiling of 13,800 with bleed air on and a 15,400 service ceiling with bleed air off.

11.10 EN ROUTE CRUISE TIME AND FUEL (Questions 56-65)

1. Recommended cruise power at 1550 RPM is provided on Figs. 23, 24, and 25 on pages 554, 555, and 556. (ISA = International standard atmosphere, which is +15°C at sea level and decreases 2°C for every 1,000 ft. of altitude.)
   a. ISA –10°C
   b. ISA, i.e., standard temperature
   c. ISA +10°C
2. Determine the ISA temperature at the given pressure altitude and then compare the ISA temperature with the OAT as given.
   a. Select the appropriate figure: 23, 24, or 25, depending upon the OAT relative to ISA.
3. Under the pressure altitude column, on the left side of the appropriate chart, find the pressure altitude given, or interpolate.
   a. Move right horizontally to determine the true airspeed for the appropriate weight, or interpolate.
4. Given the true airspeed, compute the time en route, given
   a. True course
   b. Wind
   c. Cruise distance
5. EXAMPLE: Fig. 21 on page 553 provides the operating conditions for BE-31.

Weight	15,000 lb.
Pressure altitude	22,000 ft.
Temperature (OAT)	–19°C
True course	110°
Wind	180°/30 kt.
Cruise distance	280 NM

a. Determine the standard (ISA) temperature at 22,000 ft. to be –29°C, which is equal to 15°C – (22 x 2). An OAT of –19°C is ISA +10°C. Fig. 23 on page 554 provides cruise data for ISA +10°C.

b. Find 22,000 ft. under the pressure altitude column on the left edge of the chart, and move right horizontally to determine the TAS for both 16,000 lb. (221 kt.) and 14,000 lb. (235 kt.). Interpolate for 15,000 lb. to determine a TAS of 228 kt.

c. On the wind side of the flight computer, set the wind direction of 180° under the true index and place a mark (wind dot) 30 kt. above the grommet. Set true course (110°) under the true index and slide the wind dot under TAS of 228 kt. Ground speed is read under the grommet as 216 kt. On the calculator side, set the ground speed under the solid pointer triangle and locate 280 NM on the outer scale. Below that, read the time en route of 77 min., or 1 hr. 17 min.

6. To determine the total fuel consumption during cruise, find the fuel flow on the appropriate cruise power chart, interpolating for altitude and weight as necessary, and multiply by the time en route in hours.

   a. EXAMPLE: In the above problem, determine the total fuel flow at 16,000 lb. (632 PPH) and 14,000 lb. (634 PPH), and interpolate for 15,000 lb. (633 PPH).

   b. Multiply the fuel flow by the time en route in hours to determine a total fuel consumption of 812 lb. [633 x (77 ÷ 60)].

11.11 TIME, FUEL, AND DISTANCE TO DESCEND (Questions 66-70)

1. Fig. 26 on page 557 gives time, fuel, and distance to descend at 200 kt., 1,500 fpm.

   a. Time, fuel, and distance are on the horizontal axis.

   b. Pressure altitude is on the vertical axis.

   c. If distance is given in nautical air miles (NAM), the distance has been adjusted for wind effect.

      1) See discussion of NAM in Chapter 12, page 569.

2. To use the chart, find the difference between the time, fuel, and distance values at your present altitude and the altitude to which you wish to descend, similarly to the use of the time, fuel, and distance to climb chart.

3. As an example, descending from 11,000 ft. to 6,000 ft. takes 3 min., 33 lb. of fuel, and 13 NM, as computed in the upper right corner of the chart.

11.12 LANDING DISTANCE (Questions 71-79)

1. Fig. 28 on page 564 shows the normal landing distance chart.

   a. Outside air temperature, gross weight, wind component, and obstacle height are on the horizontal axis.

   b. Distance in feet is on the vertical axis.

   c. There is an example in the upper right-hand corner which is drawn as an arrowed line on the chart.

2. Note that the suggested approach speeds are in the upper center based upon the weight of the aircraft.

3. This chart is used similarly to the takeoff distance chart.

4. To determine the remaining runway length when stopped after landing, subtract the landing distance from the runway length.

QUESTIONS AND ANSWER EXPLANATIONS

All the FAA questions from the pilot knowledge test for the ATP certificate relating to the BE-1900 operating/performance data and the material outlined previously are reproduced on the following pages in the same modules as the outlines. To the immediate right of, or below, each question are the correct answer and answer explanation. You should cover these answers and answer explanations while responding to the questions.

The questions from the FAA pilot knowledge test bank have been reordered by topic, and the topics are organized into a meaningful sequence. Accordingly, the first line of the answer explanation gives the FAA question number and the citation of the authoritative source for the answer.

11.1 CG Computation

1.
8434. (Refer to figures 3, 6, 8, 9, 10, and 11 on pages 515, 516, 518, 519, 520, and 521.) What is the CG in inches from datum under Loading Conditions BE-1?

A—Station 290.3.
B—Station 285.8.
C—Station 291.8.

Answer (B) is correct (8434). *(PWBH Chap 6)*

The requirement is the CG given loading conditions of BE-1. The weights from BE-1 (Fig. 3) appear below with the moments to the immediate right based on Figs. 6 (empty weight), 9 (crew and passengers), 8 (baggage), 10 (fuel density), and 11 (fuel weight).

From Fig. 10, determine the specific weight of Jet B at +5°C to be 6.6 lb./gal. From Fig. 11, determine the fuel weight of 370 gal. to be 2,442 lb. with a Mom./100 of 7,299.

Item	Weight (lb.)	Mom./100
Basic empty weight	9,226	25,823
Crew	360	464
Passengers		
Row 1	350	700
Row 2	260	598
Row 3	200	520
Row 4	340	986
Row 5	120	384
Row 6	400	1,400
Row 7	120	456
Row 8	250	1,025
Row 9	--	--
Baggage		
Nose	60	39
Forward cabin	250	409
Aft (fwd. sec.)	500	2,418
Aft (aft sec.)	--	--
Fuel: 370 gal. Jet B, +5°C	2,442	7,299
Total	14,878	42,521

$$CG = \frac{42{,}521}{14{,}878} \times 100 = 285.8$$

Answer (A) is incorrect because a CG of 290.3 would require a Mom./100 of 43,191 given a weight of 14,878 lb. Answer (C) is incorrect because a CG of 291.8 would require a Mom./100 of 43,414 given a weight of 14,878 lb.

2.
8435. (Refer to figures 3, 6, 8, 9, 10, and 11 on pages 515, 516, 518, 519, 520, and 521.) What is the CG in inches from datum under Loading Conditions BE-2?

A—Station 295.2.
B—Station 292.9.
C—Station 293.0.

Answer (B) is correct (8435). *(PWBH Chap 6)*

The requirement is the CG given loading conditions of BE-2. The weights from BE-2 (Fig. 3) appear below with the moments to the immediate right based on Figs. 6 (empty weight), 9 (crew and passengers), 8 (baggage), 10 (fuel density), and 11 (fuel weight).

From Fig. 10, determine the specific weight of Jet A at +15°C to be 6.8 lb./gal. From Fig. 11, determine the fuel weight of 390 gal. to be 2,652 lb. with a Mom./100 of 7,924.

Item	Weight (lb.)	Mom./100
Basic empty weight	9,226	25,823
Crew	340	439
Passengers		
Row 1	300	600
Row 2	250	575
Row 3	190	494
Row 4	170	493
Row 5	190	608
Row 6	340	1,190
Row 7	190	722
Row 8	--	--
Row 9	--	--
Baggage		
Nose	--	--
Forward cabin	100	164
Aft (fwd. sec.)	200	967
Aft (aft sec.)	600	3,198
Fuel: 390 gal. Jet A, +15°C	2,652	7,924
Total	14,748	43,197

$$CG = \frac{43{,}197}{14{,}748} \times 100 = 292.9$$

Answer (A) is incorrect because a CG of 295.2 would require a Mom./100 of 43,536 given a weight of 14,748 lb. Answer (C) is incorrect because a CG of 293.0 would require a Mom./100 of 43,212 given a weight of 14,478 lb.

3.
8436. (Refer to figures 3, 6, 8, 9, 10, and 11 on pages 515, 516, 518, 519, 520, and 521.) What is the CG in inches from datum under Loading Conditions BE-3?

A—Station 288.2.
B—Station 285.8.
C—Station 290.4.

Answer (A) is correct (8436). *(PWBH Chap 6)*

The requirement is the CG given loading conditions of BE-3. The weights from BE-3 (Fig. 3) appear below with the moments to the immediate right based on Figs. 6 (empty weight), 9 (crew and passengers), 8 (baggage), 10 (fuel density), and 11 (fuel weight).

From Fig. 10, determine the specific weight of Jet B at –15°C to be 6.7 lb./gal. From Fig. 11, determine the fuel weight of 400 gal. to be 2,680 lb. with a Mom./100 of 8,007.

Item	Weight (lb.)	Mom./100
Basic empty weight	9,226	25,823
Crew	350	452
Passengers		
Row 1	120	240
Row 2	340	782
Row 3	350	910
Row 4	300	870
Row 5	170	544
Row 6	--	--
Row 7	--	--
Row 8	--	--
Row 9	--	--
Baggage		
Nose	80	52
Forward cabin	120	197
Aft (fwd. sec.)	250	1,209
Aft (aft sec.)	500	2,665
Fuel: 400 gal. Jet B, –15°C	2,680	8,007
Total	14,486	41,751

$$CG = \frac{41,751}{14,486} \times 100 = 288.2$$

Answer (B) is incorrect because a CG of 285.8 would require a Mom./100 of 41,401 given a weight of 14,486 lb. Answer (C) is incorrect because a CG of 290.4 would require a Mom./100 of 42,067 given a weight of 14,486 lb.

4.
8437. (Refer to figures 3, 6, 8, 9, 10, and 11 on pages 515, 516, 518, 519, 520, and 521.) What is the CG in inches from datum under Loading Conditions BE-4?

A—Station 297.4.
B—Station 299.6.
C—Station 297.7.

Answer (C) is correct (8437). *(PWBH Chap 6)*

The requirement is the CG given loading conditions of BE-4. The weights from BE-4 (Fig. 3) appear below with the moments to the immediate right based on Figs. 6 (empty weight), 9 (crew and passengers), 8 (baggage), 10 (fuel density), and 11 (fuel weight).

From Fig. 10, determine the specific weight of Jet A at +10°C to be 6.8 lb./gal. From Fig. 11, determine the fuel weight of 290 gal. to be 1,972 with a Mom./100 of 5,912.

Item	Weight (lb.)	Mom./100
Basic empty weight	9,226	25,823
Crew	340	439
Passengers		
Row 1	--	--
Row 2	370	851
Row 3	400	1,040
Row 4	290	841
Row 5	200	640
Row 6	170	595
Row 7	210	798
Row 8	190	779
Row 9	420	1,848
Baggage		
Nose	--	--
Forward cabin	--	--
Aft (fwd. sec.)	800	3,868
Aft (aft sec.)	--	
Fuel: 290 gal. Jet A, +10°C	1,972	5,912
Total	14,588	43,434

$$CG = \frac{43,434}{14,588} \times 100 = 297.7$$

Answer (A) is incorrect because a CG of 297.4 would require a Mom./100 of 43,385 given a weight of 14,588 lb. Answer (B) is incorrect because a CG of 299.6 would require a Mom./100 of 43,706 given a weight of 14,588 lb.

5.
8438. (Refer to figures 3, 6, 8, 9, 10, and 11 on pages 515, 516, 518, 519, 520, and 521.) What is the CG in inches from datum under Loading Conditions BE-5?

A—Station 288.9.
B—Station 290.5.
C—Station 289.1.

Answer (C) is correct (8438). *(PWBH Chap 6)*
The requirement is the CG given loading conditions of BE-5. The weights from BE-5 (Fig. 3) appear below with the moments to the immediate right based on Figs. 6 (empty weight), 9 (crew and passengers), 8 (baggage), 10 (fuel density), and 11 (fuel weight).

From Fig. 10, determine the specific weight of Jet B at +25°C to be 6.5 lb./gal. From Fig. 11, determine that the fuel weight of 340 gal. is 2,210 lb. and the Mom./100 is 6,610.

Item	Weight (lb.)	Mom./100
Basic empty weight	9,226	25,823
Crew	360	465
Passengers		
Row 1	--	--
Row 2	--	--
Row 3	170	442
Row 4	200	580
Row 5	290	928
Row 6	400	1,400
Row 7	370	1,406
Row 8	340	1,394
Row 9	430	1,892
Baggage		
Nose	100	66
Forward cabin	200	328
Aft (fwd. sec.)	--	--
Aft (aft sec.)	--	--
Fuel: 340 gal. Jet B, +25°C	2,210	6,610
Total	14,296	41,334

$$CG = \frac{41{,}334}{14{,}296} \times 100 = 289.1$$

Answer (A) is incorrect because a CG of 288.9 would require a Mom./100 of 41,301 given a weight of 14,296 lb. Answer (B) is incorrect because a CG of 290.5 would require a Mom./100 of 41,530 given a weight of 14,296 lb.

6.
8444. (Refer to figures 4, 7, 9, 10, and 11 on pages 515, 517, 519, 520, and 521.) What is the CG in inches from datum under Loading Conditions BE-6?

A—Station 300.5.
B—Station 296.5.
C—Station 300.8.

Answer (A) is correct (8444). *(PWBH Chap 6)*
The requirement is the CG given loading conditions of BE-6. The weights from BE-6 (Fig. 4) appear below with the moments to the immediate right based on Figs. 7 (cargo loading data), 10 (fuel density), and 11 (fuel weight).

NOTE: By definition, the basic operating weight includes the crew weight.

From Fig. 10, determine the specific weight of Jet B at +25°C to be 6.5 lb./gal. From Fig. 11, determine that the fuel weight of 340 gal. is 2,210 lb. and the Mom./100 is 6,610.

Item	Weight (lb.)	Mom./100
Basic operating weight	9,005	25,934
Cargo section		
A	500	1,125
B	500	1,275
C	550	1,568
D	550	1,732
E	600	2,070
F	600	2,250
G	450	1,822
H	--	--
J	350	1,628
K	--	--
L	--	--
Fuel: 340 gal. Jet B, +25°C	2,210	6,610
Total	15,315	46,014

$$CG = \frac{46{,}014}{15{,}315} \times 100 = 300.5$$

Answer (B) is incorrect because a CG of 296.5 is obtained by adding the crew weight, which is not necessary since the basic operating weight includes crew weight. Answer (C) is incorrect because a CG of 300.8 requires a Mom./100 of 46,068 given a weight of 15,315 lb.

7.
8445. (Refer to figures 4, 7, 9, 10, and 11 on pages 515, 517, 519, 520, and 521.) What is the CG in inches from datum under Loading Conditions BE-7?

A—Station 296.0.
B—Station 297.8.
C—Station 299.9.

Answer (C) is correct (8445). *(PWBH Chap 6)*

The requirement is the CG given loading conditions of BE-7. The weights from BE-7 (Fig. 4) appear below with the moments to the immediate right based on Figs. 7 (cargo loading data), 10 (fuel density), and 11 (fuel weight).

NOTE: By definition, the basic operating weight includes the crew weight.

From Fig. 10, determine the specific weight of Jet B at +5°C to be 6.6 lb./gal. From Fig. 11, determine the fuel weight of 370 gal. is 2,442 lb. and a Mom./100 of 7,299.

Item	Weight (lb.)	Mom./100
Basic operating weight	9,005	25,934
Cargo section		
A	--	--
B	400	1,020
C	450	1,283
D	600	1,890
E	600	2,070
F	600	2,250
G	500	2,025
H	--	--
J	--	--
K	--	--
L	--	--
Fuel: 370 gal. Jet B, +5°C	2,442	7,299
Total	14,597	43,771

$$CG = \frac{43{,}771}{14{,}597} \times 100 = 299.9$$

Answer (A) is incorrect because a CG of 296.0 is obtained by adding the crew weight, which is not necessary since the basic operating weight includes crew weight. Answer (B) is incorrect because a CG of 297.8 would require a Mom./100 of 43,470 given a weight of 14,597 lb.

8.
8446. (Refer to figures 4, 7, 9, 10, and 11 on pages 515, 517, 519, 520, and 521.) What is the CG in inches from datum under Loading Conditions BE-8?

A—Station 297.4.
B—Station 298.1.
C—Station 302.0.

Answer (C) is correct (8446). *(PWBH Chap 6)*

The requirement is the CG given loading conditions of BE-8. The weights from BE-8 (Fig. 4) appear below with the moments to the immediate right based on Figs. 7 (cargo loading data), 10 (fuel density), and 11 (fuel weight).

NOTE: By definition, the basic operating weight includes the crew weight.

From Fig. 10, determine the specific weight of Jet A at +15°C to be 6.8 lb./gal. From Fig. 11, determine the fuel weight of 390 gal. is 2,652 lb. and a Mom./100 of 7,924.

Item	Weight (lb.)	Mom./100
Basic operating weight	9,005	25,934
Cargo section		
A	600	1,350
B	200	510
C	400	1,140
D	400	1,260
E	200	690
F	200	750
G	200	810
H	200	870
J	300	1,395
K	250	1,249
L	100	533
Fuel: 390 gal. Jet A, +15°C	2,652	7,924
Total	14,707	44,415

$$CG = \frac{44{,}415}{14{,}707} \times 100 = 302.0$$

Answer (A) is incorrect because a CG of 297.4 would require a Mom./100 of 44,739 given a weight of 14,707 lb. Answer (B) is incorrect because a CG of 298.1 is obtained by adding the crew weight, which is not necessary since the basic operating weight includes crew weight.

9.

8447. (Refer to figures 4, 7, 9, 10, and 11 on pages 515, 517, 519, 520, and 521.) What is the CG in inches from datum under Loading Conditions BE-9?

A—Station 296.7.
B—Station 297.1.
C—Station 301.2.

Answer (C) is correct (8447). *(PWBH Chap 6)*

The requirement is the CG given loading conditions of BE-9. The weights from BE-9 (Fig. 4) appear below with the moments to the immediate right based on Figs. 7 (cargo loading data), 10 (fuel density), and 11 (fuel weight).

NOTE: By definition, the basic operating weight includes the crew weight.

From Fig. 10, determine the specific weight of Jet A at +10°C to be 6.8 lb./gal. From Fig. 11, determine the fuel weight of 290 gal. is 1,972 lb. and the Mom./100 of 5,912.

Item	Weight (lb.)	Mom./100
Basic operating weight	9,005	25,934
Cargo section		
A	600	1,350
B	600	1,530
C	600	1,710
D	600	1,890
E	550	1,898
F	350	1,313
G	250	1,013
H	250	1,088
J	150	698
K	200	999
L	100	533
Fuel: 290 gal. Jet A, +10°C	1,972	5,912
Total	15,227	45,868

$$CG = \frac{45,868}{15,227} \times 100 = 301.2$$

Answer (A) is incorrect because a CG of 296.7 would require a Mom./100 of 45,178 given a weight of 15,227 lb. Answer (B) is incorrect because a CG of 297.1 is obtained by adding the crew weight, which is not necessary since the basic operating weight includes crew weight.

10.

8448. (Refer to figures 4, 7, 9, 10, and 11 on pages 515, 517, 519, 520, and 521.) What is the CG in inches from datum under Loading Conditions BE-10?

A—Station 298.4.
B—Station 298.1.
C—Station 293.9.

Answer (A) is correct (8448). *(PWBH Chap 6)*

The requirement is the CG given loading conditions of BE-10. The weights from BE-10 (Fig. 4) appear below with the moments to the immediate right based on Figs. 7 (cargo loading data), 10 (fuel density), and 11 (fuel weight).

NOTE: By definition, the basic operating weight includes the crew weight.

From Fig. 10, determine the specific weight of Jet B at –15°C to be 6.7 lb./gal. From Fig. 11, determine the fuel weight of 400 gal. is 2,680 lb. and the Mom./100 is 8,007.

Item	Weight (lb.)	Mom./100
Basic operating weight	9,005	25,934
Cargo section		
A	350	788
B	450	1,148
C	450	1,283
D	550	1,733
E	550	1,898
F	600	2,250
G	600	2,430
H	--	--
J	--	--
K	--	--
L	--	--
Fuel: 400 gal. Jet B, –15°C	2,680	8,007
Total	15,235	45,471

$$CG = \frac{45,471}{15,235} \times 100 = 298.5$$

Answer (B) is incorrect because a CG of 298.1 would require a Mom./100 of 45,416 given a weight of 15,235 lb. Answer (C) is incorrect because a CG of 293.9 is obtained by adding the crew weight, which is not necessary since the basic operating weight includes crew weight.

LOADING CONDITIONS	BE-1	BE-2	BE-3	BE-4	BE-5
CREW	360	340	350	340	360
PASSENGERS ROW 1	350	300	120	-	-
ROW 2	260	250	340	370	-
ROW 3	200	190	350	400	170
ROW 4	340	170	300	290	200
ROW 5	120	190	170	200	290
ROW 6	400	340	-	170	400
ROW 7	120	190	-	210	370
ROW 8	250	-	-	190	340
ROW 9	-	-	-	420	430
BAGGAGE NOSE	60	-	80	-	100
FWD CABIN	250	100	120	-	200
AFT (FWD SEC)	500	200	250	800	-
AFT (AFT SEC)	-	600	500	-	-
FUEL GAL	370	390	400	290	340
TYPE	JET B	JET A	JET B	JET A	JET B
TEMP	+5 °C	+15 °C	-15 °C	+10 °C	+25 °C

FIGURE 3.—Beech 1900 – Loading Passenger Configuration.

LOADING CONDITIONS	BE-6	BE-7	BE-8	BE-9	BE-10
CREW	360	340	350	370	420
CARGO SECTION A	500	-	600	600	350
B	500	400	200	600	450
C	550	450	400	600	450
D	550	600	400	600	550
E	600	600	200	550	550
F	600	600	200	350	600
G	450	500	200	250	600
H	-	-	200	250	-
J	350	-	300	150	-
K	-	-	250	200	-
L	-	-	100	100	-
FUEL GAL	340	370	390	290	400
TYPE	JET B	JET B	JET A	JET A	JET B
TEMP	+25 °C	+5 °C	+15 °C	+10 °C	-15 °C

BASIC OPERATING WEIGHT - 9,005 POUNDS, 25,934 MOM/100

FIGURE 4.—Beech 1900 – Loading Cargo Configuration.

OPERATING CONDITIONS	BE-11	BE-12	BE-13	BE-14	BE-15
BASIC EMPTY WT					
WEIGHT	9,225	9,100	9,000	8,910	9,150
MOM/100	25,820	24,990	24,710	24,570	25,240
CREW WEIGHT	340	380	360	400	370
PASS AND BAG					
WEIGHT	4,200	4,530	4,630	4,690	4,500
MOM/100	15,025	16,480	16,743	13,724	13,561
FUEL (6.8 LB/GAL)					
RAMP LOAD-GAL	360	320	340	310	410
USED START AND TAXI	20	20	10	20	30
REMAIN AT LDG	100	160	140	100	120

FIGURE 5.—Beech 1900 – Loading Limitations.

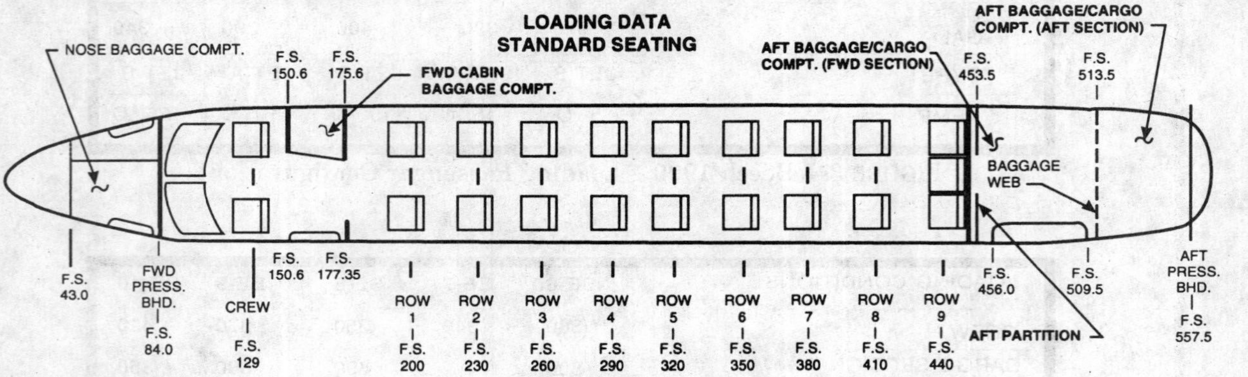

BAGGAGE/CARGO LOCATION		CAPACITY – POUNDS	CENTROID (FUSELAGE STATION)
NOSE BAGGAGE COMPARTMENT		150	65.5
FORWARD CABIN BAGGAGE COMPARTMENT (INCLUDES UP TO 100 POUNDS WHICH MAY BE SUSPENDED FROM CLOTHES ROD)		250	163.6
AFT BAGGAGE/CARGO COMPARTMENT	– FWD SECTION	880	483.5
	– AFT SECTION	630	533.0

NOTE:

1. For compartment loadings which result in only partial utilization of total compartment volume, load items must be distributed or secured in a manner to preclude shifting under normally anticipated operating conditions.

BASIC EMPTY WEIGHT 9,226 LB
BASIC MOMENT/100 25,823

FIGURE 6.—Airplane – Loading Data.

WEIGHT AND BALANCE DIAGRAM

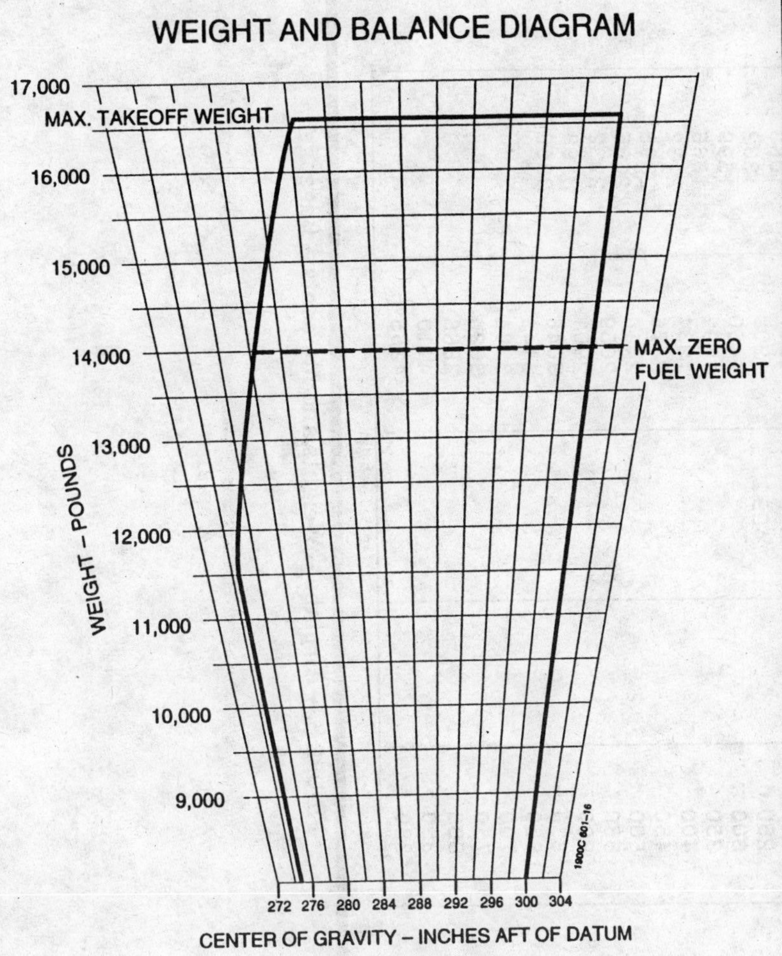

MAX TAKEOFF WEIGHT	– 16,600
MAX LANDING WEIGHT	– 16,000
MAX ZERO FUEL WEIGHT	– 14,000

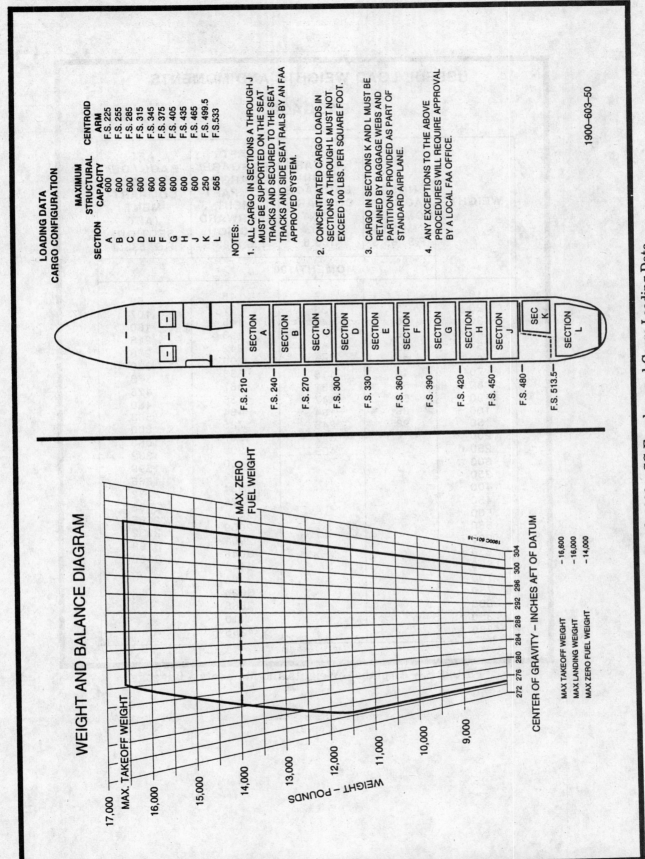

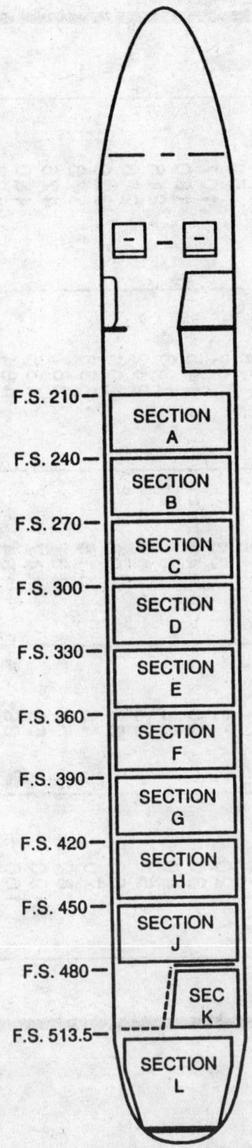

LOADING DATA
CARGO CONFIGURATION

SECTION	MAXIMUM STRUCTURAL CAPACITY	CENTROID ARM
A	600	F.S. 225
B	600	F.S. 255
C	600	F.S. 285
D	600	F.S. 315
E	600	F.S. 345
F	600	F.S. 375
G	600	F.S. 405
H	600	F.S. 435
J	600	F.S. 465
K	250	F.S. 499.5
L	565	F.S.533

NOTES:

1. ALL CARGO IN SECTIONS A THROUGH J MUST BE SUPPORTED ON THE SEAT TRACKS AND SECURED TO THE SEAT TRACKS AND SIDE SEAT RAILS BY AN FAA APPROVED SYSTEM.
2. CONCENTRATED CARGO LOADS IN SECTIONS A THROUGH L MUST NOT EXCEED 100 LBS. PER SQUARE FOOT.
3. CARGO IN SECTIONS K AND L MUST BE RETAINED BY BAGGAGE WEBS AND PARTITIONS PROVIDED AS PART OF STANDARD AIRPLANE.
4. ANY EXCEPTIONS TO THE ABOVE PROCEDURES WILL REQUIRE APPROVAL BY A LOCAL FAA OFFICE.

1900–603–50

FIGURE 7.—Beech 1900 – CG Envelope and Cargo Loading Data.

USEFUL LOAD WEIGHTS AND MOMENTS

BAGGAGE

WEIGHT	NOSE BAGGAGE COMPARTMENT F.S. 65.5	FORWARD CABIN BAGGAGE COMPARTMENT F.S. 163.6	AFT BAGGAGE/CARGO COMPARTMENT (FORWARD SECTION) F.S. 483.5	AFT BAGGAGE/CARGO COMPARTMENT (AFT SECTION) F.S. 533.0
	MOMENT/100			
10	7	16	48	53
20	13	33	97	107
30	20	49	145	160
40	26	65	193	213
50	33	82	242	266
60	39	98	290	320
70	46	115	338	373
80	52	131	387	426
90	59	147	435	480
100	66	164	484	533
150	98	245	725	800
200		327	967	1066
250		409	1209	1332
300			1450	1599
350			1692	1866
400			1934	2132
450			2176	2398
500			2418	2665
550			2659	2932
600			2901	3198
630			3046	3358
650			3143	
700			3384	
750			3626	
800			3868	
850			4110	
880			4255	

FIGURE 8.—Airplane – Weights and Moments – Baggage.

USEFUL LOAD WEIGHTS AND MOMENTS

OCCUPANTS

	CREW	CABIN SEATS								
WEIGHT	F.S. 129	F.S. 200	F.S. 230	F.S. 260	F.S. 290	F.S. 320	F.S. 350	F.S. 380	F.S. 410	F.S. 440
	MOMENT/100									
80	103	160	184	208	232	256	280	304	328	352
90	116	180	207	234	261	288	315	342	369	396
100	129	200	230	260	290	320	350	380	410	440
110	142	220	253	286	319	352	385	418	451	484
120	155	240	276	312	348	384	420	456	492	528
130	168	260	299	338	377	416	455	494	533	572
140	181	280	322	364	406	448	490	532	574	616
150	194	300	345	390	435	480	525	570	615	660
160	206	320	368	416	464	512	560	608	656	704
170	219	340	391	442	493	544	595	646	697	748
180	232	360	414	468	522	576	630	684	738	792
190	245	380	437	494	551	608	665	722	779	836
200	258	400	460	520	580	640	700	760	820	880
210	271	420	483	546	609	672	735	798	861	924
220	284	440	506	572	638	704	770	836	902	968
230	297	460	529	598	667	736	805	874	943	1012
240	310	480	552	624	696	768	840	912	984	1056
250	323	500	575	650	725	800	875	950	1025	1100

Note: Weights reflected in above table represent weight per seat.

FIGURE 9.—Beech 1900 – Weights and Moments – Occupants.

DENSITY VARIATION OF AVIATION FUEL

BASED ON AVERAGE SPECIFIC GRAVITY

FUEL	AVERAGE SPECIFIC GRAVITY AT 15 °C (59 °F)
AVIATION KEROSENE JET A AND JET A1	.812
JET B (JP-4)	.785
AV GAS GRADE 100/130	.703

NOTE: The Fuel Quantity Indicator is calibrated for correct indication when using Aviation Kerosene Jet A and Jet A1. When using other fuels, multiply the indicated fuel quantity in pounds by .99 for Jet B (JP-4) or by .98 for Aviation Gasoline (100/130) to obtain actual fuel quantity in pounds.

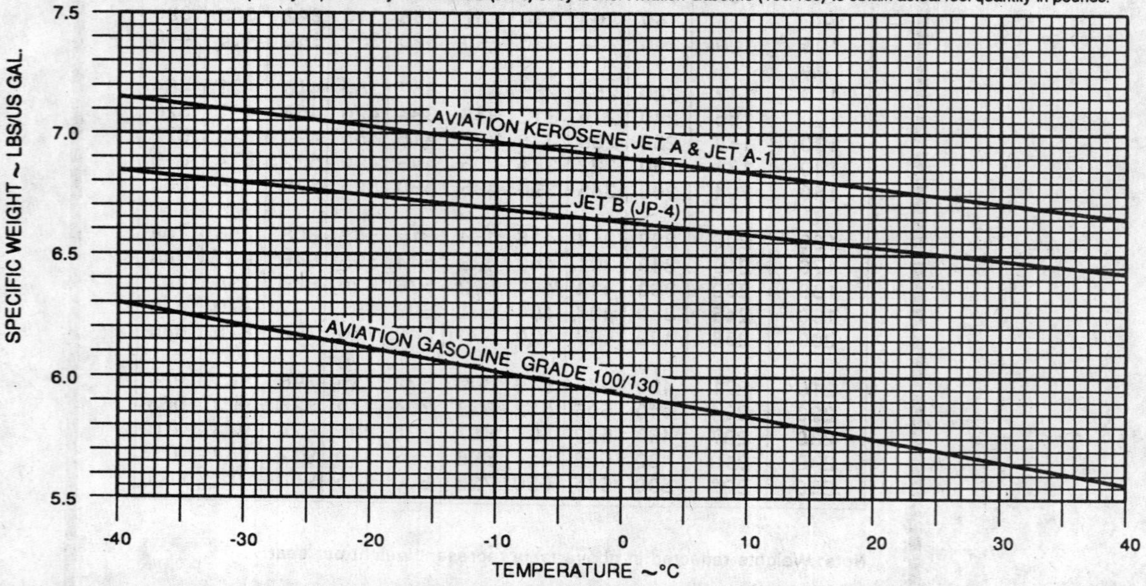

FIGURE 10.—Density Variation of Aviation Fuel.

USEFUL LOAD WEIGHTS AND MOMENTS

USABLE FUEL

GALLONS	6.5 LB/GAL		6.6 LB/GAL		6.7 LB/GAL		6.8 LB/GAL	
	WEIGHT	MOMENT/100	WEIGHT	MOMENT/100	WEIGHT	MOMENT/100	WEIGHT	MOMENT/100
10	65	197	66	200	67	203	68	206
20	130	394	132	401	134	407	136	413
30	195	592	198	601	201	610	204	619
40	260	789	264	802	268	814	272	826
50	325	987	330	1002	335	1018	340	1033
60	390	1185	396	1203	402	1222	408	1240
70	455	1383	462	1404	469	1426	476	1447
80	520	1581	528	1605	536	1630	544	1654
90	585	1779	594	1806	603	1834	612	1861
100	650	1977	660	2007	670	2038	680	2068
110	715	2175	726	2208	737	2242	748	2275
120	780	2372	792	2409	804	2445	816	2482
130	845	2569	858	2608	871	2648	884	2687
140	910	2765	924	2808	938	2850	952	2893
150	975	2962	990	3007	1005	3053	1020	3099
160	1040	3157	1056	3205	1072	3254	1088	3303
170	1105	3351	1122	3403	1139	3454	1156	3506
180	1170	3545	1188	3600	1206	3654	1224	3709
190	1235	3739	1254	3797	1273	3854	1292	3912
200	1300	3932	1320	3992	1340	4053	1360	4113
210	1365	4124	1386	4187	1407	4250	1428	4314
220	1430	4315	1452	4382	1474	4448	1496	4514
230	1495	4507	1518	4576	1541	4646	1564	4715
240	1560	4698	1584	4770	1608	4843	1632	4915
250	1625	4889	1650	4964	1675	5040	1700	5115
260	1690	5080	1716	5158	1742	5236	1768	5315
270	1755	5271	1782	5352	1809	5433	1836	5514
280	1820	5462	1848	5546	1876	5630	1904	5714
290	1885	5651	1914	5738	1943	5825	1972	5912
300	1950	5842	1980	5932	2010	6022	2040	6112
310	2015	6032	2046	6125	2077	6218	2108	6311
320	2080	6225	2112	6321	2144	6416	2176	6512
330	2145	6417	2178	6516	2211	6615	2244	6713
340	2210	6610	2244	6711	2278	6813	2312	6915
350	2275	6802	2310	6907	2345	7011	2380	7116
360	2340	6995	2376	7103	2412	7210	2448	7318
370	2405	7188	2442	7299	2479	7409	2516	7520
380	2470	7381	2508	7495	2546	7609	2584	7722
390	2535	7575	2574	7691	2613	7808	2652	7924
400	2600	7768	2640	7888	2680	8007	2720	8127
410	2665	7962	2706	8085	2747	8207	2788	8330
420	2730	8156	2772	8282	2814	8407	2856	8532
425	2763	8259	2805	8386	2848	8513	2890	8640

FIGURE 11.—Beech 1900 – Weights and Moments – Usable Fuel.

11.2 CG Shift

11.
8439. (Refer to figures 3, 6, 8, 9, 10, and 11 on pages 515, 516, 518, 519, 520, and 521.) What is the CG shift if the passengers in row 1 are moved to seats in row 9 under Loading Conditions BE-1?

A—1.5 inches aft.
B—5.6 inches aft.
C—6.2 inches aft.

Answer (B) is correct (8439). *(PWBH Chap 5)*
Fig. 3 provides loading conditions for BE-1, which is used in the schedule below to provide the gross weight. Fig. 6 provides loading data for the BE-1900. Note that the passengers in row 1 are moving to row 9; i.e., their arm changes from 200 to 440.

From Fig. 10, determine the specific fuel weight of Jet B at +5°C to be 6.6 lb./gal. Fuel weight is 2,442 lb. (6.6 x 370).

Item	Weight	Arm
Crew	360	
Passengers		
Row 1	350	200
Row 2	260	
Row 3	200	
Row 4	340	
Row 5	120	
Row 6	400	
Row 7	120	
Row 8	250	
Row 9	--	440
Baggage		
Nose	60	
Forward cabin	250	
Aft (fwd. sec.)	500	
Aft (aft sec.)	--	
Fuel: 370 gal. Jet B, +5°C	2,442	
Basic empty weight	9,226	
Gross weight	14,878	

The weight in row 1 (350 lb.) will move aft 240 in. (440 – 200).

$$CG = \frac{M_1 \pm \Delta M}{W_1 \pm \Delta W}$$

Since current CG location is unknown, $M_1 = 0$, and there is no change in weight so $\Delta W = 0$.

$$CG\ shift = \frac{\Delta M}{W_1} = \frac{(350) \times (240)}{14{,}878} = \frac{84{,}000}{14{,}878} = 5.6\ in.$$

The direction of CG shift corresponds directly to the direction of the weight shift. Thus, the CG is shifted 5.6 in. aft.

Answer (A) is incorrect because a CG shift of 1.5 in. aft would occur if the 350 lb. were moved only 66 in., not 240 in., aft of row 1. Answer (C) is incorrect because a CG shift of 6.2 in. aft would occur if the 350 lb. were moved 264 in., not 240 in., aft of row 1.

12.
8440. (Refer to figures 3, 6, 8, 9, 10, and 11 on pages 515, 516, 518, 519, 520, and 521.) What is the CG shift if the passengers in row 1 are moved to row 8, and the passengers in row 2 are moved to row 9 under Loading Conditions BE-2?

A—9.2 inches aft.
B—5.7 inches aft.
C—7.8 inches aft.

Answer (C) is correct (8440). *(PWBH Chap 5)*
Fig. 3 provides loading conditions for BE-2, which is used in the schedule below to provide the gross weight. Fig. 6 provides loading data for the BE-1900. Note that the passengers in rows 1 and 2 are moving to rows 8 and 9.

From Fig. 10, determine the specific fuel weight of Jet A at +15°C to be 6.8 lb./gal. Fuel weight is 2,652 lb. (6.8 x 390).

Item	Weight	Arm
Crew	340	
Passengers		
Row 1	300	200
Row 2	250	230
Row 3	190	
Row 4	170	
Row 5	190	
Row 6	340	
Row 7	190	
Row 8	--	410
Row 9	--	440
Baggage		
Nose	--	
Forward cabin	100	
Aft (fwd. sec.)	200	
Aft (aft sec.)	600	
Fuel: 390 gal. Jet A, +15°C	2,652	
Basic empty weight	9,226	
Gross weight	14,748	

The weight in row 1 (300 lb.) will move aft 210 in. (410 – 200). The weight in row 2 (250 lb.) will move aft 210 in. (440 – 230).

$$CG = \frac{M_1 \pm \Delta M}{W_1 \pm \Delta W}$$

Since current CG location is unknown, $M_1 = 0$, and there is no change in weight so $\Delta W = 0$.

$$CG\ shift = \frac{\Delta M}{W_1} = \frac{(210)(300) + (210)(250)}{14{,}748}$$

$$= \frac{115{,}500}{14{,}748} = 7.8\ in.$$

The direction of CG shift corresponds directly to the direction of the weight shift. Thus, the CG is shifted 7.8 in. aft.

Answer (A) is incorrect because a CG shift of 9.2 in. aft would occur if the weight in each row were moved 247 in., not 210 in., aft. Answer (B) is incorrect because a CG shift of 5.7 in. aft would occur if the weight in each row were moved only 153 in., not 210 in., aft.

13.
8441. (Refer to figures 3, 6, 8, 9, 10, and 11 on pages 515, 516, 518, 519, 520, and 521.) What is the CG shift if four passengers weighing 170 pounds each are added; two to seats in row 6 and two to seats in row 7, under Loading Conditions BE-3?

A—3.5 inches aft.
B—2.2 inches forward.
C—1.8 inches aft.

Answer (A) is correct (8441). *(PWBH Chap 5)*

The requirement is the CG shift given loading conditions BE-3. BE-3 from Fig. 3 appears below with the moments to the immediate right based on Figs. 6 (empty weight), 9 (crew and passengers), 8 (baggage), 10 (fuel density), and 11 (fuel weight).

From Fig. 10, determine the specific fuel weight of Jet B at –15°C to be 6.7 lb./gal. From Fig. 11, determine the fuel weight of 400 gal. to be 2,680 lb. with a Mom./100 of 8,007.

Item	Weight (lb.)	Mom./100
Basic empty weight	9,226	25,823
Crew	350	452
Passengers		
Row 1	120	240
Row 2	340	782
Row 3	350	910
Row 4	300	870
Row 5	170	544
Rows 6 - 9	--	--
Baggage		
Nose	80	52
Forward cabin	120	197
Aft (fwd. sec.)	250	1,209
Aft (aft sec.)	500	2,665
Fuel: 400 gal. Jet B, –15°C	2,680	8,007
Total	14,486	41,751

$$CG = \frac{41,751}{14,486} \times 100 = 288.2$$

Find the new CG with 340 lb. added to row 6 (arm 350) and 340 lb. added to row 7 (arm 380) with the following formula:

$$New\ CG = \frac{M_1 \pm \Delta M}{W_1 \pm \Delta W}$$

if M_1 = original moment and W_1 = original weight.

Calculate Mom./100 and enter the data.

$$New\ CG = \frac{41,751 + 1,190 + 1,292}{14,486 + 340 + 340} \times 100$$

$$= \frac{44,233}{15,166} \times 100 = 291.7$$

The new CG shifts 3.5 in. aft (288.2 – 291.7).

Answer (B) is incorrect because a CG shift of 2.2 in. forward would require a new CG of 286.0, not 291.7. Answer (C) is incorrect because a CG shift of 1.8 in. aft would require a new CG of 290.0, not 291.7.

14.
8442. (Refer to figures 3, 6, 8, 9, 10, and 11 on pages 515, 516, 518, 519, 520, and 521.) What is the CG shift if all passengers in rows 2 and 4 are deplaned under Loading Conditions BE-4?

A—2.5 inches aft.
B—2.5 inches forward.
C—2.0 inches aft.

Answer (C) is correct (8442). *(PWBH Chap 5)*

The requirement is the CG shift given loading conditions BE-4. BE-4 from Fig. 3 appears below with the moments to the immediate right based on Figs. 6 (empty weight), 9 (crew and passengers), 8 (baggage), 10 (fuel density), and 11 (fuel weight).

From Fig. 10, determine the specific fuel weight of Jet A at +10°C to be 6.8 lb./gal. From Fig. 11, determine the fuel weight of 290 gal. to be 1,972 lb. with a Mom./100 of 5,912.

Item	Weight (lb.)	Mom./100
Basic empty weight	9,226	25,823
Crew	340	439
Passengers		
Row 1	--	--
Row 2	370	851
Row 3	400	1,040
Row 4	290	841
Row 5	200	640
Row 6	170	595
Row 7	210	798
Row 8	190	779
Row 9	420	1,848
Baggage		
Nose	--	--
Forward cabin	--	--
Aft (fwd. sec.)	800	3,868
Aft (aft sec.)	--	--
Fuel: 290 gal. Jet A, +10°C	1,972	5,912
Total	14,588	43,434

$$CG = \frac{43,434}{14,588} \times 100 = 297.7$$

Find the new CG when the weight in rows 2 (370 lb.) and 4 (290 lb.) is removed, with the following formula:

$$New\ CG = \frac{M_1 \pm \Delta M}{W_1 \pm \Delta W}$$

if M_1 = original moment and W_1 = original weight.

$$New\ CG = \frac{43,434 - 851 - 841}{14,588 - 370 - 290} \times 100$$

$$= \frac{41,742}{13,928} \times 100 = 299.7$$

The new CG shifted 2.0 in. aft (297.7 – 299.7).

Answer (A) is incorrect because a CG shift of 2.5 in. aft would require a new CG of 300.2, not 299.7. Answer (B) is incorrect because a CG shift of 2.5 in. forward would require a new CG of 295.2, not 299.7.

15.
8443. (Refer to figures 3, 6, 8, 9, 10, and 11 on pages 515, 516, 518, 519, 520, and 521.) What is the CG shift if the passengers in row 8 are moved to row 2, and the passengers in row 7 are moved to row 1 under Loading Conditions BE-5?

A—1.0 inches forward.
B—8.9 inches forward.
C—6.5 inches forward.

Answer (B) is correct (8443). *(PWBH Chap 5)*
Fig. 3 provides loading conditions for BE-5, which is used in the schedule below to provide the gross weight. Fig. 6 provides loading data for the BE-1900. Note that the passengers in rows 7 and 8 are moving to rows 1 and 2.
From Fig. 10, determine the specific fuel weight of Jet B at +25°C to be 6.5 lb./gal. Fuel weight is 2,210 lb. (6.5 x 340).

Item	Weight	Arm
Crew	360	
Passengers		
Row 1	--	200
Row 2	--	230
Row 3	170	
Row 4	200	
Row 5	290	
Row 6	400	
Row 7	370	380
Row 8	340	410
Row 9	430	
Baggage		
Nose	100	
Forward cabin	200	
Aft (fwd. sec.)	--	
Aft (aft sec.)	--	
Fuel: 340 gal. Jet B, +25°C	2,210	
Basic empty weight	9,226	
Gross weight	14,296	

The weight in row 8 (340 lb.) will move forward 180 in. (410 – 230). The weight in row 7 (370 lb.) will move forward 180 (380 – 200).

$$CG = \frac{M_1 \pm \Delta M}{W_1 \pm \Delta W}$$

Since current CG location is unknown, $M_1 = 0$, and there is no change in weight so $\Delta W = 0$.

$$CG\ shift = \frac{\Delta M}{W_1} = \frac{(340)(180) + (370)(180)}{14{,}296}$$

$$= \frac{127{,}800}{14{,}296} = 8.9\ in.$$

The direction of CG shift corresponds directly to the direction of the weight shift. Thus, the CG is shifted 8.9 in. forward.

Answer (A) is incorrect because a CG shift of 1.0 in. forward would occur if the weight in each row were moved only 20 in., not 180 in., forward. Answer (C) is incorrect because a CG shift of 6.5 in. forward would occur if the weight in each row were moved 131 in., not 180 in., forward.

16.
8449. (Refer to figures 4, 7, 9, 10, and 11 on pages 515, 517, 519, 520, and 521.) What is the CG shift if 300 pounds of cargo in section A is moved to section H under Loading Conditions BE-6?

A—4.1 inches aft.
B—3.5 inches aft.
C—4.0 inches aft.

Answer (A) is correct (8449). *(PWBH Chap 5)*
Fig. 4 provides loading conditions for BE-6, which is used in the schedule below to provide the gross weight. Fig. 7 provides loading data for the BE-1900. Note that the cargo in section A is moving to section H; i.e., the arm changes from 225 to 435.
NOTE: By definition, basic operating weight includes crew weight.
From Fig. 10, determine the specific fuel weight of Jet B at +25°C to be 6.5 lb./gal. Fuel weight is 2,210 lb. (6.5 x 340).

Item	Weight	Arm
Basic operating weight	9,005	
Cargo section		
A	500	225
B	500	
C	550	
D	550	
E	600	
F	600	
G	450	
H	--	435
J	350	
K	--	
L	--	
Fuel: 340 gal. Jet B, +25°C	2,210	
Gross weight	15,315	

The weight in section A (300 lb.) will move aft 210 in. (435 – 225).

$$CG = \frac{M_1 \pm \Delta M}{W_1 \pm \Delta W}$$

Since current CG location is unknown, $M_1 = 0$, and there is no change in weight so $\Delta W = 0$.

$$CG\ shift = \frac{\Delta M}{W_1} = \frac{(300)(210)}{15{,}315} = \frac{63{,}000}{15{,}315} = 4.1\ in.$$

The direction of CG shift corresponds directly to the direction of the weight shift. Thus, the CG is shifted 4.1 in. aft.

Answer (B) is incorrect because a CG shift of 3.5 in. aft would occur if the 300 lb. were moved only 179 in. to the aft of section A. Answer (C) is incorrect because a CG shift of 4.0 in. aft is obtained by adding the crew weight, which is not necessary since the basic operating weight includes crew weight.

17.
8450. (Refer to figures 4, 7, 9, 10, and 11 on pages 515, 517, 519, 520, and 521.) What is the CG shift if the cargo in section F is moved to section A, and 200 pounds of the cargo in section G is added to the cargo in section B, under Loading Conditions BE-7?

A—7.5 inches forward.
B—8.0 inches forward.
C—8.2 inches forward.

Answer (C) is correct (8450). *(PWBH Chap 5)*

Fig. 4 provides loading conditions for BE-7, which is used in the schedule below to provide the gross weight. Fig. 7 provides loading data for the BE-1900. Note that the cargo in section F is moved to section A, and some cargo is moved from section G to section B.

NOTE: By definition, basic operating weight includes crew weight.

From Fig. 10, determine the specific fuel weight of Jet B at +5°C to be 6.6 lb./gal. Fuel weight is 2,442 lb. (6.6 x 370).

Item	Weight	Arm
Basic operating weight	9,005	
Cargo section		
A	--	225
B	400	255
C	450	
D	600	
E	600	
F	600	375
G	500	405
H	--	
J	--	
K	--	
L	--	
Fuel: 370 gal. Jet B, +5°C	2,442	
Gross weight	14,597	

The weight in section F (600 lb.) will move forward 150 in. (375 – 225), and 200 lb. in section G will move forward 150 in. (405 – 255).

$$CG = \frac{M_1 \pm \Delta M}{W_1 \pm \Delta W}$$

Since current CG location is unknown, $M_1 = 0$, and there is no change in weight so $\Delta W = 0$.

$$CG\ shift = \frac{\Delta M}{W_1} = \frac{(600)(150) + (200)(150)}{14{,}597}$$

$$= \frac{90{,}000 + 30{,}000}{14{,}597} = \frac{120{,}000}{14{,}597} = 8.2\ in.$$

The direction of CG shift corresponds directly to the direction of the weight shift. Thus, the CG is shifted 8.2 in. forward.

Answer (A) is incorrect because a CG shift of 7.5 in. forward would occur if the weight were moved from sections F and G only 97 in., not 150 in., forward. Answer (B) is incorrect because a CG shift of 8.0 in. forward is obtained by adding crew weight, which is not necessary since the basic operating weight includes crew weight.

18.
8451. (Refer to figures 4, 7, 9, 10, and 11 on pages 515, 517, 519, 520, and 521.) What is the CG if all cargo in sections A, B, J, K, and L are off-loaded under Loading Conditions BE-8?

A—Station 292.7.
B—Station 297.0.
C—Station 294.6.

Answer (B) is correct (8451). *(PWBH Chap 5)*

Fig. 4 provides loading conditions for BE-8. Fig. 7 provides loading data, Fig. 10 fuel density, and Fig. 11 fuel weight. This problem is a basic CG computation. In the schedule below, the weight has been removed from sections A, B, J, K, and L from loading condition BE-8.

NOTE: By definition, basic operating weight includes crew weight.

From Fig. 10, determine the specific fuel weight of Jet A at +15°C to be 6.8 lb./gal. Fuel weight is 2,652 lb. (6.8 x 390).

Item	Weight (lb.)	Mom./100
Basic operating weight	9,005	25,934
Cargo section		
A	--	--
B	--	--
C	400	1,140
D	400	1,260
E	200	690
F	200	750
G	200	810
H	200	870
J	--	--
K	--	--
L	--	--
Fuel: 390 gal. Jet A, +15°C	2,652	7,924
Total	13,257	39,378

$$CG = \frac{39{,}378}{13{,}257} \times 100 = 297.0$$

Answer (A) is incorrect because a CG of 292.7 is obtained by adding crew weight, which is not necessary since the basic operating weight includes crew weight. Answer (C) is incorrect because a CG of 294.6 would require a new Mom./100 of 39,055 given a weight of 13,257 lb.

19.

8452. (Refer to figures 4, 7, 9, 10, and 11 on pages 515, 517, 519, 520, and 521.) What is the CG if cargo is loaded to bring sections F, G, and H to maximum capacity under Loading Conditions BE-9?

A—Station 307.5.
B—Station 305.4.
C—Station 303.5.

Answer (A) is correct (8452). *(PWBH Chap 5)*

Fig. 4 provides loading conditions for BE-9. Fig. 7 provides loading data, Fig. 10 fuel density, and Fig. 11 fuel weight. Determine the CG when sections F, G, and H have a total of 600 lb. in each section. The schedule below reflects these additions:

NOTE: By definition, basic operating weight includes crew weight.

From Fig. 10, determine the specific fuel weight of Jet A at +10°C to be 6.8 lb./gal. Fuel weight is 1,972 lb. (6.8 x 290) and the Mom./100 from Fig. 11 of 5,912.

Item	Weight (lb.)	Mom./100
Basic operating weight	9,005	25,934
Cargo section		
A	600	1,350
B	600	1,530
C	600	1,710
D	600	1,890
E	550	1,898
F	600	2,250
G	600	2,430
H	600	2,610
J	150	698
K	200	999
L	100	533
Fuel: 290 gal. Jet A, +10°C	1,972	5,912
Total	16,177	49,744

$$CG = \frac{49{,}744}{16{,}177} \times 100 = 307.5$$

Answer (B) is incorrect because a CG of 305.4 would require a new Mom./100 of 49,405 given a weight of 16,177 lb. Answer (C) is incorrect because a CG of 303.4 is obtained by adding crew weight, which is not necessary since basic operating weight includes crew weight.

20.

8453. (Refer to figures 4, 7, 9, 10, and 11 on pages 515, 517, 519, 520, and 521.) What is the CG shift if the cargo in section G is moved to section J under Loading Conditions BE-10?

A—2.7 inches aft.
B—2.4 inches aft.
C—3.2 inches aft.

Answer (B) is correct (8453). *(PWBH Chap 5)*

Fig. 4 provides loading conditions for BE-10, which is used in the schedule below to provide the gross weight. Fig. 7 provides loading data for the BE-1900. Note that the cargo in section G is moved to section J; i.e., the arm changes from 405 to 465.

NOTE: By definition, basic operating weight includes crew weight.

From Fig. 10, determine the specific fuel weight of Jet B at −15°C to be 6.7 lb./gal. Fuel weight is 2,680 lb. (6.7 x 400).

Item	Weight	Arm
Basic operating weight	9,005	
Cargo section		
A	350	
B	450	
C	450	
D	550	
E	550	
F	600	
G	600	405
H	--	
J	--	465
K	--	
L	--	
Fuel: 400 gal. Jet B, −15°C	2,680	
Gross weight	15,235	

The weight in section G (600 lb.) will move aft 60 in. (465 − 405).

$$CG = \frac{M_1 \pm \Delta M}{W_1 \pm \Delta W}$$

Since current CG location is unknown, $M_1 = 0$, and there is no change in weight so $\Delta W = 0$.

$$CG\ shift = \frac{\Delta M}{W_1} = \frac{(600)(60)}{15{,}235} = \frac{36{,}000}{15{,}235} = 2.4\ in.$$

The direction of CG shift corresponds directly to the direction of the weight shift. Thus, the CG is shifted 2.4 in. aft.

Answer (A) is incorrect because a CG shift of 2.7 in. aft would occur if the 600 lb. were moved 68 in., not 60 in., aft of section G. Answer (C) is incorrect because a CG shift of 3.2 in. aft would occur if the 600 lb. were moved 81 in., not 60 in., aft of section G.

11.3 CG and Weight Limits Exceeded

21.
8454. (Refer to figures 5, 7, 9, and 11 on pages 516, 517, 519, and 521.) What limit is exceeded under Operating Conditions BE-11?

A—ZFW limit is exceeded.
B—Aft CG limit is exceeded at takeoff weight.
C—Aft CG limit is exceeded at landing weight.

Answer (C) is correct (8454). *(PWBH Chap 4)*

Fig. 5 provides the operating conditions. The information from the first column, BE-11, is used to determine weight and balance in the schedule below. Fig. 7 provides BE-1900 weight and balance diagram. Fig. 9 provides weights and moments for occupants. Fig. 11 provides BE-1900 weights and moments for usable fuel. Compute the various conditions as illustrated below.

Item	Weight	Mom./100
Basic empty weight	9,225	25,820.0
Crew	340	438.6
Passengers and baggage	4,200	15,025.0
Zero fuel weight (ZFW)	13,765	41,283.6
Fuel (6.8 lb./gal.)		
Ramp	2,448	7,318.0
Takeoff [ramp – (start + taxi)]	2,312	6,915.0
Landing	680	2,068.0

1. ZFW of 13,765 lb. is below maximum ZFW of 14,000 lb.
2. CG at takeoff:

Item	Weight	Mom./100
ZFW	13,765	41,283.6
Fuel	2,312	6,915.0
Total	16,077	48,198.6

$$CG = \frac{\textit{Total mom.}}{\textit{Total weight}} \times 100 = \frac{48{,}198.6}{16{,}077} \times 100 = 299.8$$

which is within the aft CG limit of 300.

3. CG at landing:

Item	Weight	Mom./100
ZFW	13,765	41,283.6
Fuel	680	2,068.0
Total	14,445	43,351.6

$$CG = \frac{43{,}351.6}{14{,}445} \times 100 = 300.1$$

which exceeds the aft CG limit of 300.

Answer (A) is incorrect because the 13,756 lb. ZFW weight is below the maximum ZFW of 14,000 lb. Answer (B) is incorrect because the takeoff CG of 299.8 is within the aft CG limit of 300.

22.
8455. (Refer to figures 5, 7, 9, and 11 on pages 516, 517, 519, and 521.) What limit(s) is (are) exceeded under Operating Conditions BE-12?

A—ZFW limit is exceeded.
B—Landing aft CG limit is exceeded.
C—ZFW and maximum takeoff weight limits are exceeded.

Answer (A) is correct (8455). *(PWBH Chap 4)*

Fig. 5 provides the operating conditions. The information from the second column, BE-12, is used to determine weight and balance in the schedule below. Fig. 7 provides BE-1900 weight and balance diagram. Fig. 9 provides weights and moments for occupants. Fig. 11 provides BE-1900 weights and moments for usable fuel. Compute the various conditions as illustrated below.

Item	Weight	Mom./100
Basic empty weight	9,100	24,990
Crew	380	490
Passengers and baggage	4,530	16,480
Zero fuel weight (ZFW)	14,010	41,960
Fuel (6.8 lb./gal.)		
Ramp	2,176	
Takeoff [ramp – (start + taxi)]	2,040	
Landing	1,088	3,303

1. ZFW of 14,010 lb. exceeds maximum ZFW of 14,000 lb.
2. Takeoff weight is the sum of the ZFW and the takeoff fuel, which is 16,050 lb. (14,010 + 2,040) and is below the maximum takeoff weight of 16,600 lb.
3. CG at landing:

Item	Weight	Mom./100
ZFW	14,010	41,960
Fuel	1,088	3,303
Total	15,098	45,263

$$CG = \frac{45{,}263}{15{,}098} \times 100 = 299.8$$

which is within the aft CG limit of 300.

Answer (B) is incorrect because landing CG of 299.8 is within the aft CG limit of 300. Answer (C) is incorrect because the 16,050 lb. takeoff weight is below the maximum takeoff weight of 16,600 lb.

23.
8456. (Refer to figures 5, 7, 9, and 11 on pages 516, 517, 519, and 521.) What limit, if any, is exceeded under Operating Conditions BE-13?

A—Takeoff forward CG limit is exceeded.
B—No limit is exceeded.
C—Landing aft CG limit is exceeded.

Answer (B) is correct (8456). *(PWBH Chap 4)*

Fig. 5 provides the operating conditions. The information from the third column, BE-13, is used to determine weight and balance in the schedule below. Fig. 7 provides BE-1900 weight and balance diagram. Fig. 9 provides weights and moments for occupants. Fig. 11 provides BE-1900 weights and moments for usable fuel. Compute the various conditions as illustrated below.

Item	Weight	Mom./100
Basic empty weight	9,000	24,710
Crew	360	465
Passengers and baggage	4,630	16,743
Zero fuel weight (ZFW)	13,990	41,918
Fuel (6.8 lb./gal.)		
Ramp	2,312	6,915
Takeoff [ramp – (start + taxi)]	2,244	6,713
Landing	952	2,893

1. ZFW of 13,990 lb. is below maximum ZFW of 14,000 lb.
2. CG at takeoff:

Item	Weight	Mom./100
ZFW	13,990	41,918
Fuel	2,244	6,713
Total	16,234	48,631

$$CG = \frac{Total\ mom.}{Total\ weight} \times 100 = \frac{48,631}{16,234} \times 100 = 299.6$$

which is within the forward CG limit of 281.

3. CG at landing:

Item	Weight	Mom./100
ZFW	13,990	41,918
Fuel	952	2,893
Total	14,942	44,811

$$CG = \frac{44,811}{14,942} \times 100 = 299.9$$

which is within the aft CG limit of 300.

Answer (A) is incorrect because the takeoff CG of 299.6 is within the forward CG limit of 281. Answer (C) is incorrect because the landing CG of 299.9 is within the aft CG limit of 300.

24.
8457. (Refer to figures 5, 7, 9, and 11 on pages 516, 517, 519, and 521.) What limit(s) is (are) exceeded under Operating Conditions BE-14?

A—Maximum ZFW limit is exceeded.
B—Takeoff forward CG limit is exceeded.
C—Maximum landing weight and landing forward CG limits are exceeded.

Answer (B) is correct (8457). *(PWBH Chap 4)*

Fig. 5 provides the operating conditions. The information from the fourth column, BE-14, is used to determine weight and balance in the schedule below. Fig. 7 provides BE-1900 weight and balance diagram. Fig. 9 provides weights and moments for occupants. Fig. 11 provides BE-1900 weights and moments for usable fuel. Compute the various conditions as illustrated below.

Item	Weight	Mom./100
Basic empty weight	8,910	24,570
Crew	400	516
Passengers and baggage	4,690	13,724
Zero fuel weight (ZFW)	14,000	38,810
Fuel (6.8 lb./gal.)		
Ramp	2,108	
Takeoff [ramp – (start + taxi)]	1,972	5,912
Landing	680	2,068

1. ZFW of 14,000 lb. is the maximum ZFW.
2. CG at takeoff:

Item	Weight	Mom./100
ZFW	14,000	38,810
Fuel	1,972	5,912
Total	15,972	44,722

$$CG = \frac{Total\ mom.}{Total\ weight} \times 100 = \frac{44,722}{15,972} \times 100 = 280.0$$

which exceeds the forward CG limit of 281.

3. CG at landing:

Item	Weight	Mom./100
ZFW	14,000	38,810
Fuel	680	2,068
Total	14,680	40,878

$$CG = \frac{40,878}{14,680} \times 100 = 278.5$$

which is within the aft CG limit of 300.

4. The landing weight of 14,680 lb. is below the maximum landing weight of 16,000 lb.

Answer (A) is incorrect because the 14,000 lb. ZFW is at, not above, the maximum ZFW of 14,000 lb. Answer (C) is incorrect because the landing weight of 14,680 lb. is below the maximum landing weight of 16,000 lb., and the landing CG of 278.5 is within the aft CG limit of 300.

25.
8458. (Refer to figures 5, 7, 9, and 11 on pages 516, 517, 519, and 521.) What limit(s) is (are) exceeded under Operating Conditions BE-15?

A—Maximum takeoff weight limit is exceeded.
B—Maximum ZFW and takeoff forward CG limits are exceeded.
C—Maximum takeoff weight and takeoff forward CG limits are exceeded.

Answer (A) is correct (8458). *(PWBH Chap 4)*
Fig. 5 provides the operating conditions. The information from the last column, BE-15, is used to determine weight in balance in the schedule below. Fig. 7 provides BE-1900 weight and balance diagram. Fig. 9 provides weights and moments for occupants. Fig. 11 provides BE-1900 weights and moments for usable fuel. Compute the various conditions as illustrated below.

Item	Weight	Mom./100
Basic empty weight	9,150	25,240
Crew	370	478
Passengers and baggage	4,500	13,561
Zero fuel weight (ZFW)	14,020	39,279
Fuel (6.8 lb./gal.)		
Ramp	2,788	
Takeoff [ramp – (start + taxi)]	2,584	7,722

1. ZFW of 14,020 lb. exceeds the maximum ZFW of 14,000 lb.

2. CG at takeoff:

Item	Weight	Mom./100
ZFW	14,020	39,279
Fuel	2,584	7,722
Total	16,604	47,001

$$CG = \frac{\textit{Total mom.}}{\textit{Total weight}} \times 100 = \frac{47{,}001}{16{,}604} \times 100 = 283.1$$

The takeoff weight of 16,604 lb. exceeds the maximum takeoff weight of 16,600 lb., and the CG of 283.1 is outside the CG envelope. At maximum takeoff weight of 16,600 lb., the forward CG limit is 282.1; thus the forward limit is not exceeded.

Answer (B) is incorrect because the maximum ZFW and the maximum takeoff weight have been exceeded, not the takeoff forward CG limit. Answer (C) is incorrect because the maximum ZFW and the maximum takeoff weight have been exceeded, not the takeoff forward CG limit.

11.4 Minimum Takeoff Torque

26.
8459. (Refer to figure 12 on page 530.) Given the following conditions, what is the minimum torque for takeoff?

Pressure altitude	9,000 ft
Temperature (OAT)	+3 °C
Ice vanes	Extended

A—3,100 foot-pound.
B—3,040 foot-pound.
C—3,180 foot-pound.

Answer (A) is correct (8459). *(PHAK Chap IV)*
Fig. 12 is a "Minimum Takeoff Power at 1700 RPM" graph. This question indicates the ice vanes are extended; i.e., use the graph on the left. Find +3°C at the bottom and go up vertically to 9,000 ft. pressure altitude. From that intersection, go to the left horizontally to the left side of the graph, which indicates 3,100 ft.-lb. of torque.
Answer (B) is incorrect because 3,040 ft.-lb. intersects the 9,000-ft. pressure altitude line at about +8°C. Answer (C) is incorrect because 3,180 ft.-lb. intersects the 9,000-ft. pressure altitude line at about –1°C.

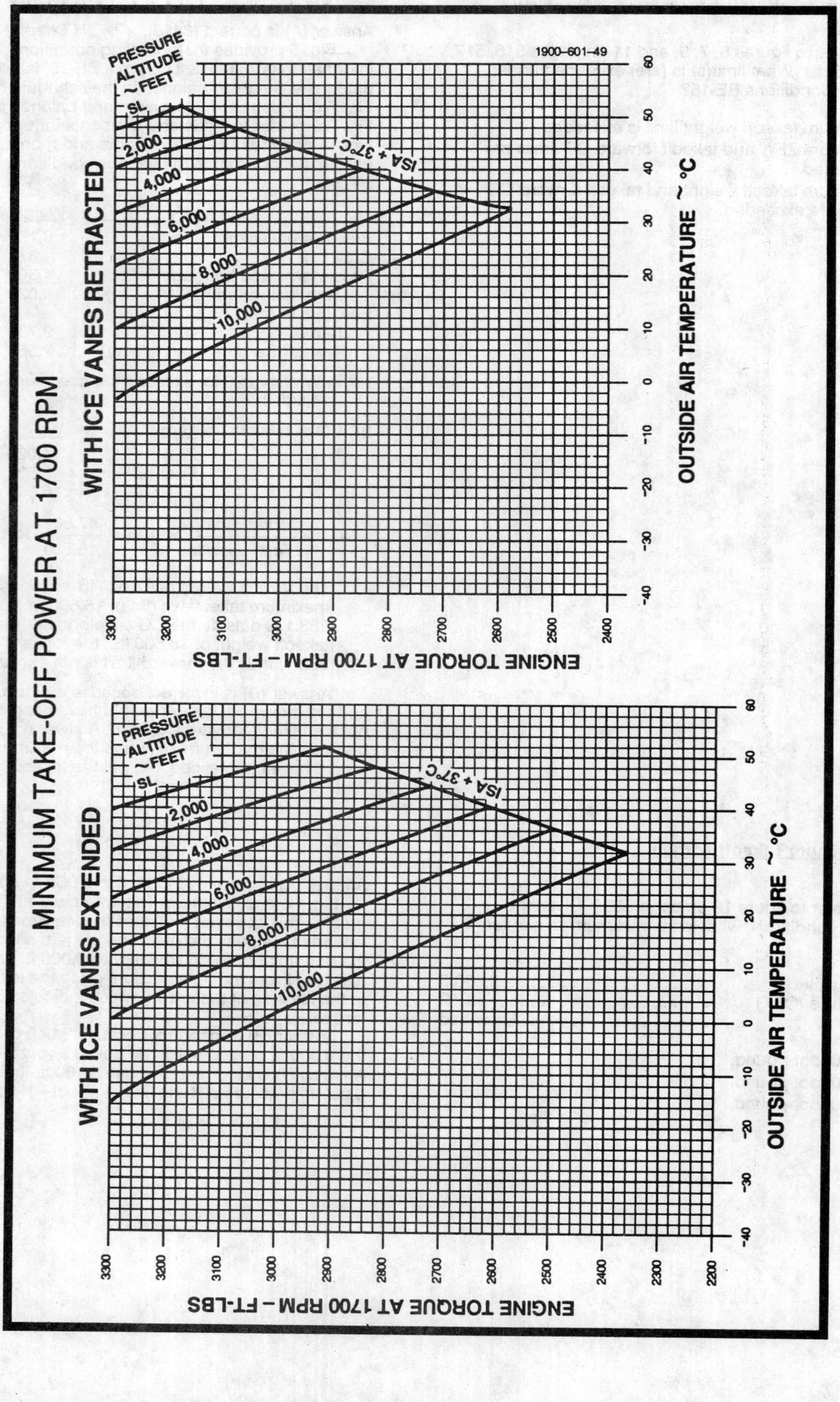

FIGURE 12.—Minimum Takeoff Power at 1700 RPM.

27.
8460. (Refer to figure 12 on page 530.) Given the following conditions, what is the minimum torque for takeoff?

Pressure altitude .... 7,500 ft
Temperature (OAT) .... +35 °C
Ice vanes .... Retracted

A—2,820 foot-pound.
B—2,880 foot-pound.
C—2,780 foot-pound.

Answer (A) is correct (8460). *(PHAK Chap IV)*

Fig. 12 is a "Minimum Take-Off Power at 1700 RPM" graph. This question indicates the ice vanes are retracted; i.e., use the graph on the right. Find +35°C at the bottom and go up vertically to 7,500 ft. pressure altitude. From that intersection, go to the left horizontally to the left side of the graph which indicates 2,820 ft.-lb. of torque.

Answer (B) is incorrect because 2,880 ft.-lb. intersects the 7,500-ft. pressure altitude line at about +32°C. Answer (C) is incorrect because 2,780 ft.-lb. intersects the 7,500-ft. pressure altitude line at about +37°C.

28.
8461. (Refer to figure 12 on page 530.) Given the following conditions, what is the minimum torque for takeoff?

Pressure altitude .... 7,500 ft
Temperature (OAT) .... +9 °C
Ice vanes .... Extended

A—3,200 foot-pound.
B—3,160 foot-pound.
C—3,300 foot-pound.

Answer (B) is correct (8461). *(PHAK Chap IV)*

Fig. 12 is a "Minimum Take-Off Power at 1700 RPM" graph. This question indicates the ice vanes are extended; i.e., use the graph on the left. Find +9°C at the bottom and go up vertically to 7,500 ft. pressure altitude. From that intersection, go to the left horizontally to the left side of the graph which indicates 3,160 ft.-lb. of torque.

Answer (A) is incorrect because 3,200 ft.-lb. intersects the 7,500-ft. pressure altitude line at about +7°C. Answer (C) is incorrect because 3,300 ft.-lb. intersects the 7,500-ft. pressure altitude line at about +3°C.

29.
8462. (Refer to figure 12 on page 530.) Given the following conditions, what is the minimum torque for takeoff?

Pressure altitude .... 3,500 ft
Temperature (OAT) .... +43 °C
Ice vanes .... Retracted

A—3,000 foot-pound.
B—3,050 foot-pound.
C—3,110 foot-pound.

Answer (B) is correct (8462). *(PHAK Chap IV)*

Fig. 12 is a "Minimum Take-Off Power at 1700 RPM" graph. This question indicates the ice vanes are retracted; i.e., use the graph on the right. Find +43°C at the bottom and go up vertically to 3,500 ft. pressure altitude. From that intersection, go to the left horizontally to the left side of the graph which indicates 3,050 ft.-lb. of torque.

Answer (A) is incorrect because 3,000 ft.-lb. intersects the 3,500-ft. pressure altitude line at about +46°C. Answer (C) is incorrect because 3,110 ft.-lb. intersects the 3,500-ft. pressure altitude line at about +41°C.

30.
8463. (Refer to figure 12 on page 530.) Given the following conditions, what is the minimum torque for takeoff?

Pressure altitude .... 5,500 ft
Temperature (OAT) .... +29 °C
Ice vanes .... Retracted

A—2,950 foot-pound.
B—3,100 foot-pound.
C—3,200 foot-pound.

Answer (C) is correct (8463). *(PHAK Chap IV)*

Fig. 12 is a "Minimum Take-Off Power at 1700 RPM" graph. This question indicates the ice vanes are retracted; i.e., use the graph on the right. Find +29°C at the bottom and go up vertically to 5,500 ft. pressure altitude. From that intersection, go to the left horizontally to the left side of the graph which indicates 3,200 ft.-lb. of torque.

Answer (A) is incorrect because 2,950 ft.-lb. intersects the 5,500-ft. pressure altitude line at about +39°C. Answer (B) is incorrect because 3,100 ft.-lb. intersects the 5,500-ft. pressure altitude line at about +32°C.

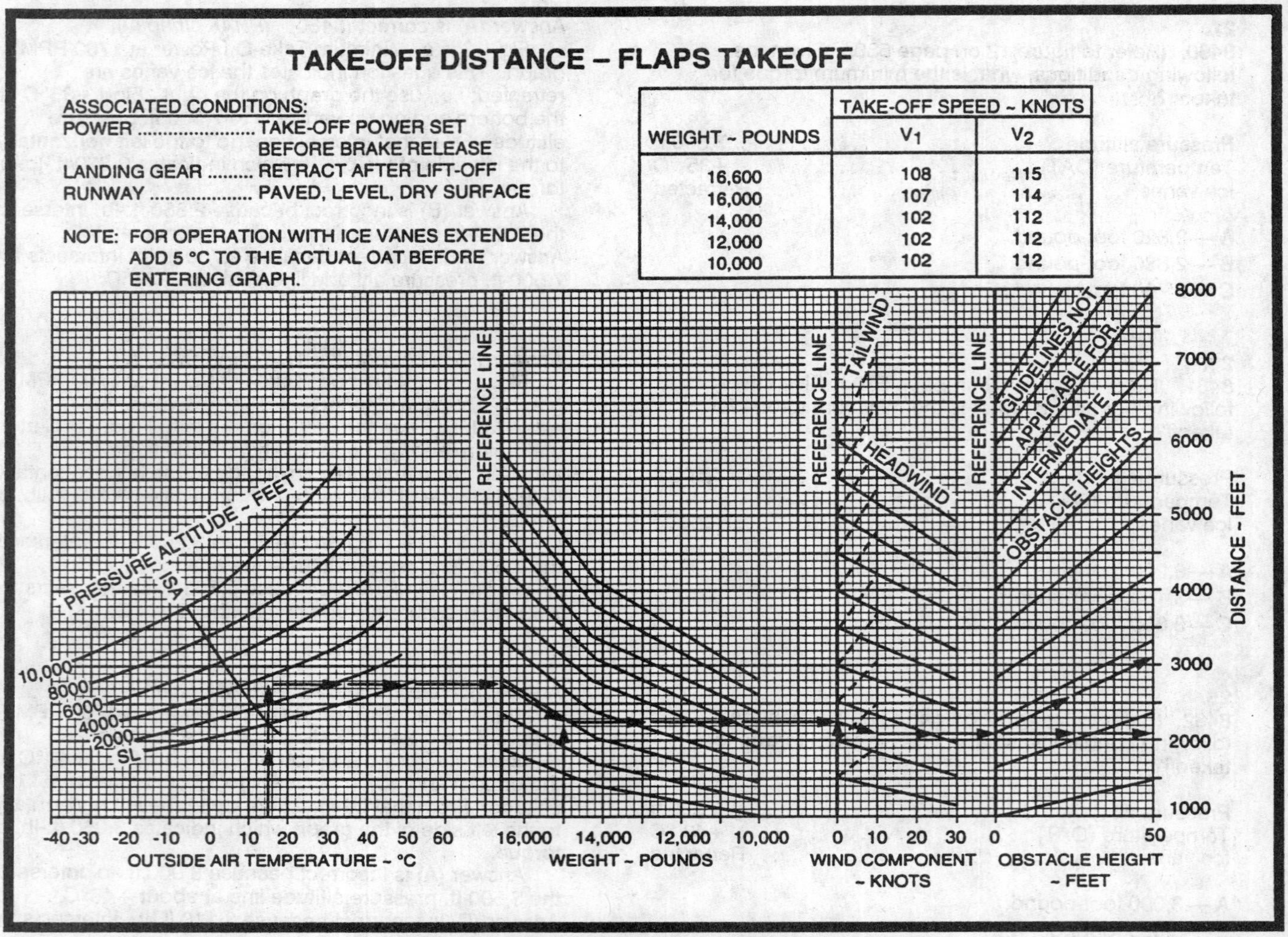

FIGURE 13.—Takeoff Distance – Flaps Takeoff.

11.5 Takeoff Distance

31.
8464. (Refer to figure 13 above.) Given the following conditions, what is the takeoff distance over a 50-foot obstacle?

Pressure altitude .... Sea Level
Temperature (OAT) .... +12 °C
Weight .... 16,000 lb
Wind component .... 16 kts HW
Ice vanes .... Retracted

A—1,750 feet.
B—2,800 feet.
C—2,550 feet.

Answer (C) is correct (8464). *(PHAK Chap IV)*
Fig. 13 presents the takeoff distance graph. To find takeoff ground roll over a 50-ft. obstacle:

1. Move up vertically from 12°C to the sea level (SL) pressure altitude line.
2. Move to the right horizontally to the first reference line.
3. Move to the right parallel to the guide line to 16,000 lb.
4. Move to the right horizontally to the second reference line.
5. Move down and to the right parallel to the guide line, for a headwind, to 16 kt.
6. Move to the right horizontally to the third reference line.
7. Move up and to the right parallel to the guide line to the obstacle height of 50 ft., which is at the right margin of the graph.
8. Read the distance at that point which is 2,550 ft.

Answer (A) is incorrect because 1,750 ft. is the takeoff distance with no obstacle. Answer (B) is incorrect because 2,800 ft. is the takeoff distance over a 50-ft. obstacle with a calm wind, not a 16-kt. HW.

32.
8466. (Refer to figure 13 on page 532.) Given the following conditions, what is the takeoff distance over a 50-foot obstacle?

Pressure altitude	2,000 ft
Temperature (OAT)	+15 °C
Weight	16,600 lb
Wind component	Calm
Ice vanes	Retracted

A—3,400 feet.
B—3,700 feet.
C—4,200 feet.

Answer (B) is correct (8466). *(PHAK Chap IV)*
Fig. 13 presents the takeoff distance graph. To find takeoff ground roll over a 50-ft. obstacle:

1. Move up vertically from 15°C to the 2,000-ft. pressure altitude line.
2. Move to the right horizontally to the first reference line, which is the weight line of 16,600 lb.
3. Move to the right horizontally to the third reference line. Note that there is a calm wind; ignore the second reference line.
4. Move up and to the right parallel to the guide line to the obstacle height of 50 ft., which is at the right margin of the graph.
5. Read the distance at that point, which is 3,700 ft.

Answer (A) is incorrect because 3,400 ft. is the distance required to clear a 50-ft. obstacle with a weight of 15,600, not 16,600, lb. The first reference line is at 16,600 lb. Answer (C) is incorrect because 4,200 ft. is the distance required to clear a 50-ft. obstacle at a pressure altitude of 3,000 ft. (as shown on the chart example).

33.
8468. (Refer to figure 13 on page 532.) Given the following conditions, what is the takeoff distance over a 50-foot obstacle?

Pressure altitude	6,000 ft
Temperature (OAT)	+35 °C
Weight	14,500 lb
Wind component	10 kts HW
Ice vanes	Retracted

A—4,150 feet.
B—4,550 feet.
C—2,600 feet.

Answer (A) is correct (8468). *(PHAK Chap IV)*
Fig. 13 presents the takeoff distance graph. To find takeoff ground roll over a 50-ft. obstacle:

1. Move up vertically from +35°C to the 6,000 ft. pressure altitude line.
2. Move to the right horizontally to the first reference line.
3. Move to the right parallel to the guide line to 14,500 lb.
4. Move to the right horizontally to the second reference line.
5. Move down and to the right parallel to the guide line, for a headwind, to 10 kt.
6. Move to the right horizontally to the third reference line.
7. Move up and to the right parallel to the guide line to the obstacle height of 50 ft., which is at the right margin of the graph.
8. Read the distance at that point, which is 4,150 ft.

Answer (B) is incorrect because 4,550 ft. is the takeoff distance over a 50-ft. obstacle with a 4-kt. tailwind, not a 10-kt. headwind. Answer (C) is incorrect because 2,600 ft. is the takeoff distance over a 50-ft. obstacle with an 18-kt., not 10-kt., headwind.

34.
8467. (Refer to figure 13 on page 532.) Given the following conditions, what is the takeoff ground roll and V_1 speed?

Pressure altitude	3,000 ft
Temperature (OAT)	–10 °C
Weight	15,000 lb
Wind component	8 kts TW
Ice vanes	Extended

A—2,200 feet, 105 knots.
B—2,000 feet, 113 knots.
C—1,900 feet, 103 knots.

Answer (A) is correct (8467). *(PHAK Chap IV)*
Fig. 13 presents the takeoff distance graph and the takeoff speeds/weight conversion table. V_1 is the takeoff decision speed and will be determined by aircraft weight. Interpolating the upper right chart between 14,000 lb. and 16,000 lb., V_1 for a 15,000-lb. airplane is 105 kt. To find takeoff ground roll, first notice the ice vanes are extended, so you must add 5°C to the actual OAT as instructed by the note at the top of the graph.

1. Add 5°C to –10°C OAT because the ice vanes are extended.
2. Move up vertically from –5°C to the 3,000-ft. pressure altitude line.
3. Move to the right horizontally to the first reference line.
4. Move to the right parallel to the guide line to 15,000 lb.
5. Move to the right horizontally to the second reference line.
6. Move up and to the right parallel to the guide line, for a tailwind, to 8 kt.
7. Move horizontally to the right to the right edge of the graph (at 2,200 ft.). Note that no obstacle height is given; ignore the third reference line and third part of the graph.

Answer (B) is incorrect because 113 kt. is the V_2, not V_1, speed for a takeoff weight of 16,300 lb., not 15,000 lb. Answer (C) is incorrect because 1,900 ft. is the takeoff ground roll with a calm wind, not an 8-kt. TW.

35.
8465. (Refer to figure 13 on page 532.) Given the following conditions, what is the takeoff ground roll and V_1 speed?

Pressure altitude	4,000 ft
Temperature (OAT)	0 °C
Weight	15,500 lb
Wind component	10 kts TW
Ice vanes	Extended

A—2,900 feet, 106 knots.
B—4,250 feet, 102 knots.
C—2,700 feet, 107 knots.

Answer (A) is correct (8465). *(PHAK Chap IV)*
Fig. 13 presents the takeoff distance graph and the takeoff speeds/weight conversion table. V_1 is the takeoff decision speed and will be determined by aircraft weight. Interpolating the upper right chart between 14,000 lb. and 16,000 lb., V_1 for a 15,500-lb. airplane is 106 kt. To find takeoff ground roll, first notice the ice vanes are extended, so you must add 5°C to the actual OAT as instructed by the note at the top of the graph.

1. Add 5°C to 0°C OAT because the ice vanes are extended.
2. Move up vertically from 5°C to the 4,000-ft. pressure altitude line.
3. Move to the right horizontally to the first reference line.
4. Move to the right parallel to the guide line to 15,500 lb.
5. Move to the right horizontally to the second reference line.
6. Move up and to the right parallel to the guide line, for a tailwind, to 10 kt.
7. Move horizontally to the right to the right side of the graph (at 2,900 ft.). Note that no obstacle height is given; ignore the third reference line and third part of the graph.

Answer (B) is incorrect because 102 kt. is V_1 for takeoff weights of 14,000 lb. and below, and 4,250 ft. is the takeoff distance over a 50-ft. obstacle, not the takeoff ground roll. Answer (C) is incorrect because 107 kt. is V_1 for a 16,000-lb. aircraft.

11.6 Accelerate-Stop Field Length

36.
8469. (Refer to figure 14 below.) Given the following conditions, what is the accelerate-stop field length?

Pressure altitude	5,000 ft
Temperature (OAT)	+20 °C
Weight	15,000 lb
Wind component	10 kts HW
Ice vanes	Retracted

A—6,300 feet.
B—4,700 feet.
C—4,300 feet.

Answer (C) is correct (8469). *(PHAK Chap IV)*
Fig. 14 provides a chart to compute accelerate-stop distance. At the lower left, find +20°C and move up vertically to pressure altitude of 5,000 ft. Move to the right horizontally to the first reference line and then down and to the right (parallel to the guide line) to 15,000 lb. Move to the right horizontally to the second reference line and then down and to the right (parallel to the guide line) to 10-kt. headwind. Move horizontally to the right edge of the chart and find 4,300 ft. as the accelerate-stop distance.

Answer (A) is incorrect because 6,300 ft. is the accelerate-stop distance using +30°C OAT, not +20°C, and a tailwind, not a headwind, of 10 kt. Answer (B) is incorrect because 4,700 ft. is the accelerate-stop distance with a calm wind, not a 10-kt. headwind.

ACCELERATE–STOP — FLAPS TAKEOFF

ASSOCIATED CONDITIONS:

POWER .... 1. TAKE-OFF POWER SET BEFORE BRAKE RELEASE
2. BOTH ENGINES IDLE AT V_1 SPEED

AUTOFEATHER .... ARMED
BRAKING .... MAXIMUM
RUNWAY .... PAVED, LEVEL, DRY SURFACE

NOTE: FOR OPERATION WITH ICE VANES EXTENDED, ADD 3 °C TO THE ACTUAL OAT BEFORE ENTERING GRAPH.

WEIGHT ~ POUNDS	V_1 ~ KNOTS
16,600	108
16,000	107
14,000	102
12,000	102
10,000	102

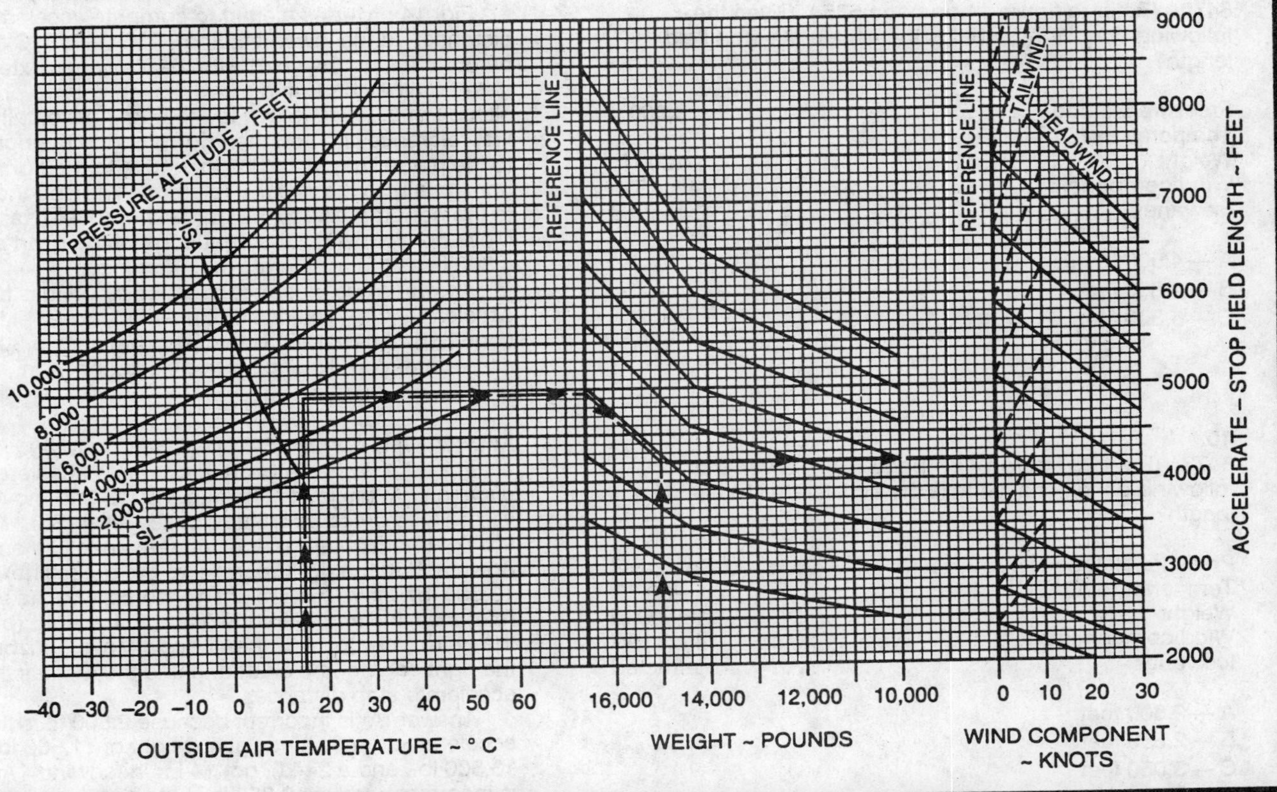

FIGURE 14.—Accelerate-Stop – Flaps Takeoff.

37.
8470. (Refer to figure 14 on page 535.) Given the following conditions, what is the accelerate-stop field length?

Pressure altitude	2,000 ft
Temperature (OAT)	–15 °C
Weight	16,000 lb
Wind component	5 kts TW
Ice vanes	Extended

A—3,750 feet.
B—4,600 feet.
C—4,250 feet.

Answer (C) is correct (8470). *(PHAK Chap IV)*
Fig. 14 provides a chart to compute accelerate-stop distance. At the lower left, find –12°C (add 3°C to the actual OAT before entering the graph with the ice vanes extended, as noted on the chart) and move up vertically to pressure altitude of 2,000 ft. Move to the right horizontally to the first reference line and then down and to the right (parallel to the guide line) to 16,000 lb. Move to the right horizontally to the second reference line and then up and to the right (parallel to the guide line) to 5-kt. tailwind. Move horizontally to the right edge of the chart and find 4,250 ft. as the accelerate-stop distance.
Answer (A) is incorrect because 3,750 ft. is the accelerate-stop distance with a calm wind, not a 5-kt. tailwind. Answer (B) is incorrect because 4,600 ft. is the accelerate-stop distance using +12°C, not –12°C.

38.
8471. (Refer to figure 14 on page 535.) Given the following conditions, what is the accelerate-stop field length?

Pressure altitude	6,000 ft
Temperature (OAT)	+10 °C
Weight	16,600 lb
Wind component	15 kts HW
Ice vanes	Retracted

A—4,950 feet.
B—4,800 feet.
C—5,300 feet.

Answer (A) is correct (8471). *(PHAK Chap IV)*
Fig. 14 provides a chart to compute accelerate-stop distance. At the lower left, find +10°C and move up vertically to pressure altitude of 6,000 ft. Move to the right horizontally to the first reference line, which is 16,600 lb. Move to the right horizontally to the second reference line and then down and to the right (parallel to the guide line) to 15-kt. headwind. Move horizontally to the right edge of the chart and find 4,950 ft. as the accelerate-stop distance.
Answer (B) is incorrect because 4,800 ft. is the accelerate-stop distance with a 20-kt., not 15-kt., headwind. Answer (C) is incorrect because 5,300 ft. is the accelerate-stop distance with a 5-kt., not 15-kt., headwind.

39.
8472. (Refer to figure 14 on page 535.) Given the following conditions, what is the accelerate-stop field length?

Pressure altitude	8,000 ft
Temperature (OAT)	–5 °C
Weight	14,000 lb
Wind component	4 kts TW
Ice vanes	Extended

A—4,500 feet.
B—4,800 feet.
C—5,300 feet.

Answer (B) is correct (8472). *(PHAK Chap IV)*
Fig. 14 provides a chart to compute accelerate-stop distance. At the lower left, find –2°C (add 3°C to the OAT before entering the chart with the ice vanes extended, as noted on the chart) and move up vertically to pressure altitude of 8,000 ft. Move to the right horizontally to the first reference line and then down and to the right (parallel to the guide line) to 14,000 lb. Move to the right horizontally to the second reference line and then up and to the right (parallel to the guide line) to 4-kt. tailwind. Move horizontally to the right edge of the chart and find 4,800 ft. as the accelerate-stop distance.
Answer (A) is incorrect because 4,500 ft. is the accelerate-stop distance in a no-wind, not a 4-kt. tailwind, condition. Answer (C) is incorrect because 5,300 ft. is the accelerate-stop distance with an 8-kt., not 4-kt., tailwind.

40.
8473. (Refer to figure 14 on page 535.) Given the following conditions, what is the accelerate-stop field length?

Pressure altitude	Sea Level
Temperature (OAT)	+30 °C
Weight	13,500 lb
Wind component	14 kts HW
Ice vanes	Retracted

A—2,500 feet.
B—2,850 feet.
C—3,050 feet.

Answer (C) is correct (8473). *(PHAK Chap IV)*
Fig. 14 provides a chart to compute accelerate-stop distance. At the lower left, find +30°C and move up vertically to pressure altitude of sea level (SL). Move to the right horizontally to the first reference line and then down and to the right (parallel to the guide line) to 13,500 lb. Move to the right horizontally to the second reference line and then down and to the right (parallel to the guide line) to 14-kt. headwind. Move horizontally to the right edge of the chart and find 3,050 ft. as the accelerate-stop distance.
Answer (A) is incorrect because 2,500 ft. is the accelerate-stop distance at a weight of 11,500 lb., not 13,500 lb., and a 24-kt., not 14-kt., headwind. Answer (B) is incorrect because 2,850 ft. is the accelerate-stop distance at a weight of 12,500 lb., not 13,500 lb.

11.7 Rate of Climb

41.
8474. (Refer to figures 15, 16, and 17 on pages 539 and 540.) What is the two-engine rate of climb after takeoff in climb configuration for Operating Conditions BE-21?

A—1,350 ft/min.
B—2,450 ft/min.
C—2,300 ft/min.

Answer (C) is correct (8474). *(PHAK Chap IV)*
Fig. 15 gives the following operating conditions for BE-21.

OAT at takeoff	+10°C
Airport pressure altitude	2,000 ft.
Initial climb weight	16,600 lb.
Ice vanes	Retracted

Fig. 16 gives the two-engine climb chart. Find +10°C OAT at the bottom left of the graph and proceed up vertically to the 2,000-ft. airport pressure altitude. From that point, move right horizontally to the aircraft weight reference line. Note 16,600 lb. is the maximum weight, so you proceed horizontally to the right side of the graph, which indicates 2,300 fpm.

Answer (A) is incorrect because 1,350 fpm is the climb rate at a pressure altitude of 16,000 ft. and OAT of –22°C. Answer (B) is incorrect because 2,450 fpm is the climb rate at 16,000 lb., not 16,600 lb.

42.
8476. (Refer to figures 15, 16, and 17 on pages 539 and 540.) What is the two-engine rate of climb after takeoff in climb configuration for Operating Conditions BE-23?

A—1,500 ft/min.
B—2,600 ft/min.
C—2,490 ft/min.

Answer (B) is correct (8476). *(PHAK Chap IV)*
Fig. 15 gives the following operating conditions for BE-23.

OAT at takeoff	+20°C
Airport pressure altitude	3,000 ft.
Initial climb weight	15,000 lb.
Ice vanes	Retracted

Fig. 16 gives the two-engine climb chart. Find +20°C OAT at the bottom left of the graph and proceed up vertically to the 3,000-ft. airport pressure altitude. From that point, move right horizontally to the aircraft weight reference line. Move up and to the right (parallel to the guide line) to 15,000 lb.; then move horizontally to the right side of the graph which indicates 2,600 fpm.

Answer (A) is incorrect because 1,500 fpm is the climb rate at a pressure altitude of 10,500 ft., not 3,000 ft. Answer (C) is incorrect because 2,490 fpm is the climb rate with an OAT of +30°C, not +20°C.

43.
8477. (Refer to figures 15, 16, and 17 on pages 539 and 540.) What is the two-engine rate of climb after takeoff in climb configuration for Operating Conditions BE-24?

A—2,100 ft/min.
B—2,400 ft/min.
C—1,500 ft/min.

Answer (A) is correct (8477). *(PHAK Chap IV)*
Fig. 15 gives the following operating conditions for BE-24.

OAT at takeoff	+25°C
Airport pressure altitude	4,000 ft.
Initial climb weight	16,000 lb.
Ice vanes	Retracted

Fig. 16 gives the two-engine climb chart. Find +25°C OAT at the bottom left of the graph and proceed up vertically to the 4,000-ft. airport pressure altitude. From that point, move right horizontally to the aircraft weight reference line. Move up and to the right (parallel to the guide line) to 16,000 lb.; then move horizontally to the right side of the graph which indicates 2,100 fpm.

Answer (B) is incorrect because 2,400 fpm is the climb rate at a pressure altitude of 3,000 ft., not 4,000 ft. Answer (C) is incorrect because 1,500 fpm is the climb rate at cruise (OAT 0°C, altitude 14,000 ft.), not at takeoff, conditions.

44.
8478. (Refer to figures 15, 16, and 17 on pages 539 and 540.) What is the single-engine rate of climb after takeoff in climb configuration for Operating Conditions BE-25?

A—385 ft/min.
B—780 ft/min.
C—665 ft/min.

Answer (C) is correct (8478). *(PHAK Chap IV)*

Fig. 15 gives the following operating conditions for BE-25.

OAT at takeoff	−10°C
Airport pressure altitude	5,000 ft.
Initial climb weight	14,000 lb.
Ice vanes	Extended

Fig. 17 gives the single-engine climb chart. Find −10°C OAT at the bottom left of the graph and proceed up vertically to the 5,000-ft. airport pressure altitude. From that point, move right horizontally to the aircraft weight reference line. Move up and to the right (parallel to the guide line) to 14,000 lb.; then move horizontally to the right side of the graph which indicates 780 fpm. Next, adjust the rate of climb for the ice vanes extended as indicated in the note above the graph. Thus, the single-engine rate of climb with ice vanes extended is 665 fpm (780 – 115).

Answer (A) is incorrect because 385 fpm is the single-engine climb rate at a weight of 16,000 lb., not 14,000 lb. Answer (B) is incorrect because 780 fpm is the single-engine climb rate before the adjustment is made for the ice vanes being extended.

45.
8475. (Refer to figures 15, 16, and 17 on pages 539 and 540.) What is the single-engine climb gradient after takeoff in climb configuration for Operating Conditions BE-22?

A—6.8 percent gradient.
B—7.5 percent gradient.
C—5.6 percent gradient.

Answer (C) is correct (8475). *(PHAK Chap IV)*

Fig. 15 gives the following operating conditions for BE-22.

OAT at takeoff	0°C
Airport pressure altitude	1,000 ft.
Initial climb weight	14,000 lb.
Ice vanes	Extended

Fig. 17 gives the single-engine climb chart. Find 0°C OAT at the bottom left of the graph and proceed up vertically to the 1,000-ft. airport pressure altitude. From that point, move right horizontally to the aircraft weight reference line. Move up and to the right (parallel to the guide line) to 14,000 lb.; then move horizontally to the right side of the graph, which indicates 870 fpm. Adjust the rate of climb for the ice vanes extended as in the note above the graph. Thus, the single-engine rate of climb with ice vanes extended is 755 fpm (870 – 115). Find 755 fpm on the right end of the chart and move right horizontally to the reference line to determine a climb gradient of 5.6%.

Answer (A) is incorrect because 6.8% is the climb gradient before the adjustment is made for the ice vanes being extended. Answer (B) is incorrect because 7.5% is the climb gradient at a weight of 13,600 lb., not 14,000 lb., with the ice vanes retracted, not extended.

OPERATING CONDITIONS	BE-21	BE-22	BE-23	BE-24	BE-25
OAT AT TAKEOFF	+10 °C	0 °C	+20 °C	+25 °C	–10 °C
OAT AT CRUISE	–20 °C	–25 °C	ISA	0 °C	–40 °C
AIRPORT PRESS ALTITUDE	2,000	1,000	3,000	4,000	5,000
CRUISE ALTITUDE	16,000	18,000	20,000	14,000	22,000
INITIAL CLIMB WEIGHT	16,600	14,000	15,000	16,000	14,000
ICE VANES	RETRACT	EXTEND	RETRACT	RETRACT	EXTEND

FIGURE 15.— Beech 1900 – Climb.

CLIMB — TWO ENGINES — FLAPS UP

ASSOCIATED CONDITIONS:

POWER .... MAXIMUM CONTINUOUS
FLAPS .... UP
LANDING GEAR .... UP

WEIGHT ~ POUNDS	CLIMB SPEED ~ KNOTS
16,600	135
16,000	134
14,000	130
12,000	125
10,000	121

NOTE: DURING OPERATION WITH ICE VANES EXTENDED, RATE OF CLIMB WILL BE REDUCED APPROXIMATELY 240 FEET PER MINUTE.

EXAMPLE:

OAT .... –4 °C
PRESSURE ALTITUDE .... 9,000 FT
WEIGHT .... 14,500 LBS
RATE OF CLIMB .... 2490 FT/MIN
CLIMB GRADIENT .... 14.7 %
CLIMB SPEED .... 131 KTS

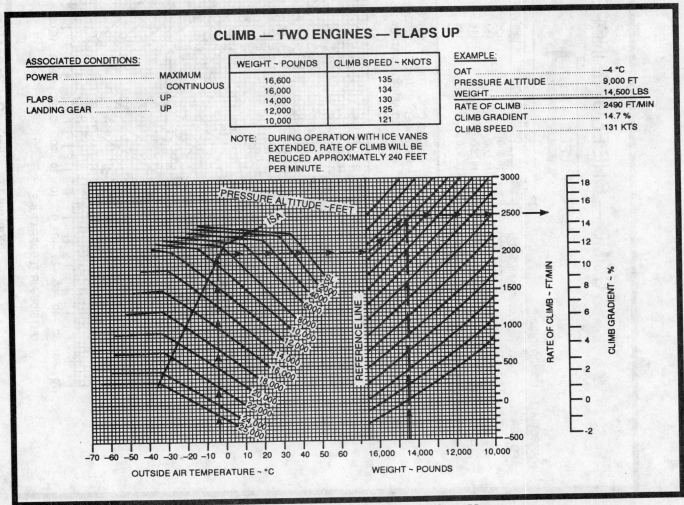

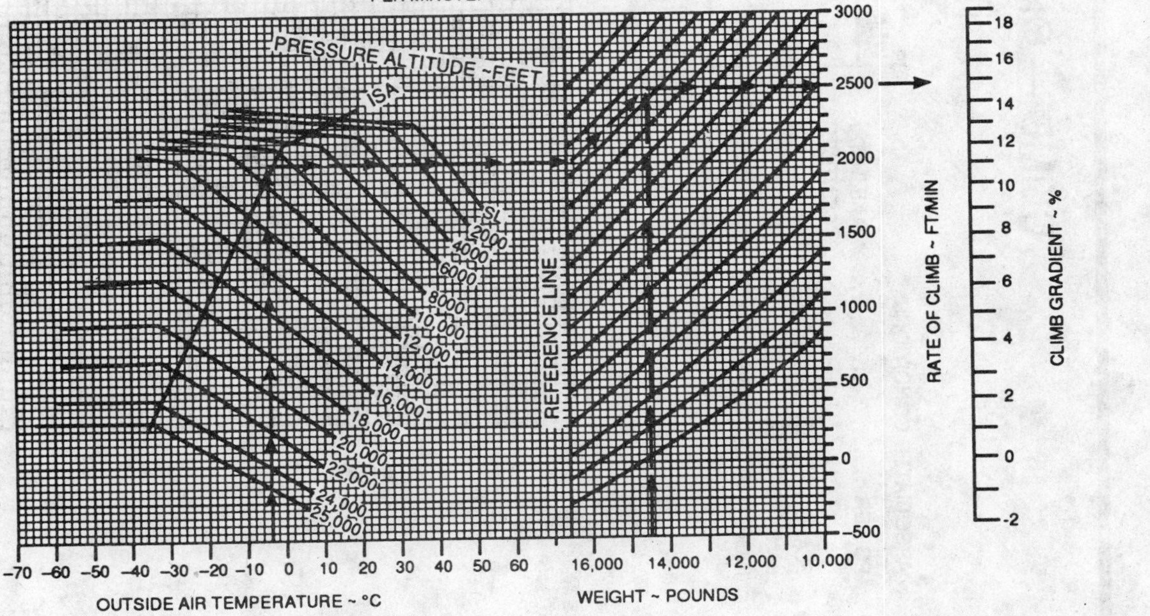

FIGURE 16.—Climb – Two Engines – Flaps Up.

CLIMB — ONE ENGINE INOPERATIVE

BLEED AIR ON

ASSOCIATED CONDITIONS:

POWER .... MAXIMUM CONTINUOUS
FLAPS .... UP
LANDING GEAR .... UP
INOPERATIVE PROPELLER .... FEATHERED

WEIGHT ~ POUNDS	CLIMB SPEED ~ KNOTS
16,600	125
16,000	124
14,000	119
12,000	116
10,000	112

NOTES: DURING OPERATION WITH ICE VANES EXTENDED, RATE OF CLIMB WILL BE REDUCED APPROXIMATELY 115 FEET PER MINUTE.

EXAMPLE:

OAT .... –4 °C
PRESSURE ALTITUDE ...... 9,000 FT
WEIGHT .... 14,500 LBS

RATE OF CLIMB .... 450 FT/MIN
CLIMB GRADIENT .... 3.1 %
CLIMB SPEED .... 120 KTS

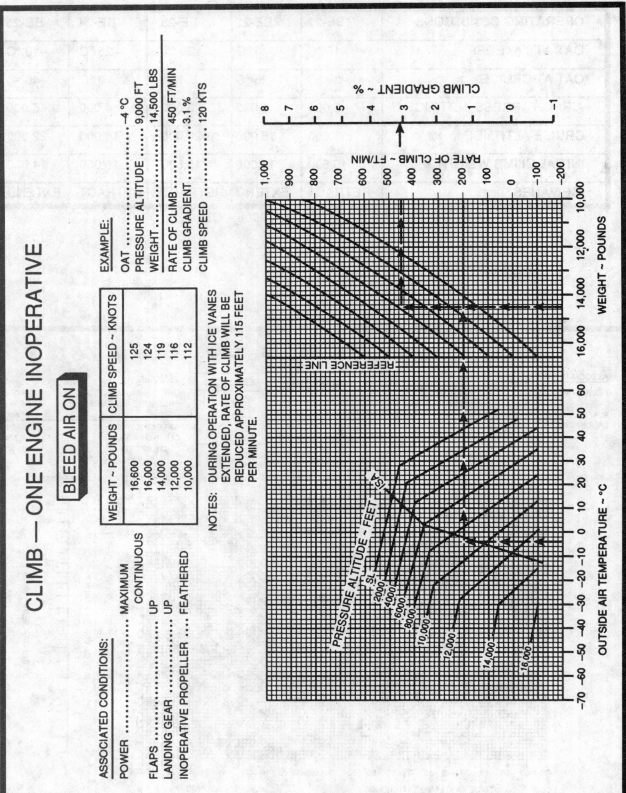

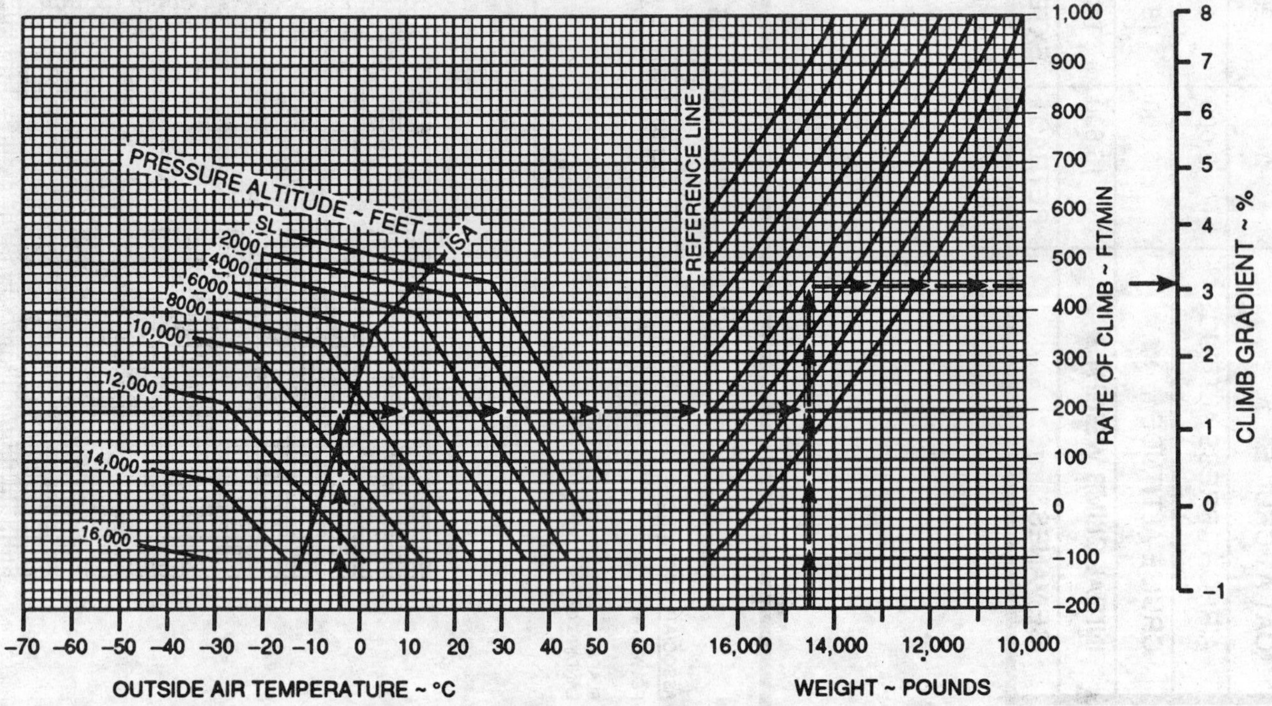

FIGURE 17.—Climb – One Engine Inoperative.

11.8 Time, Fuel, and Distance to Climb

46.
8479. (Refer to figure 15 below and figure 18 on page 542.) What are the time, fuel, and distance from the start of climb to cruise altitude for Operating Conditions BE-21?

A—10.0 minutes; 290 pounds; 35 NM.
B—10.0 minutes; 165 pounds; 30 NM.
C—11.5 minutes; 165 pounds; 30 NM.

Answer (B) is correct (8479). *(PHAK Chap IV)*

Fig. 15 provides the following operating conditions for BE-21:

OAT at takeoff	+10°C
OAT at cruise	–20°C
Airport pressure altitude	2,000 ft.
Cruise altitude	16,000 ft.
Initial climb weight	16,600 lb.
Ice vanes	Retracted

Fig. 18 provides a chart to determine time, fuel, and distance to cruise climb. At the bottom of the chart, find –20°C OAT and move up vertically to the cruise altitude of 16,000 ft. Then move right horizontally to the initial climb weight of 16,600 lb. Then move down vertically to the bottom of the graph to determine the time to climb of 11.5 min. Move down vertically to the fuel-to-climb line to determine fuel burned of 190 lb., and move down vertically to the next line to determine a distance to climb of 32 NM. Repeat this process using an OAT of +10°C and the airport pressure altitude of 2,000 ft. to determine the time to climb of 1.5 min., fuel burned of 25 lb., and a distance of 2 NM. Next subtract the results of the airport altitude from the results of the cruise altitude. Thus, from 2,000 ft. to 16,000 ft., it will take 10 min. (11.5 – 1.5), burn 165 lb. (190 – 25) of fuel, and cover a distance of 30 NM (32 – 2).

Answer (A) is incorrect because fuel burned of 290 lb. would mean that the OAT at cruise altitude is warmer than –20°C. Answer (C) is incorrect because 11.5 min. is the time to climb to 16,000 ft. before the airport altitude time has been subtracted.

OPERATING CONDITIONS	BE-21	BE-22	BE-23	BE-24	BE-25
OAT AT TAKEOFF	+10 °C	0 °C	+20 °C	+25 °C	–10 °C
OAT AT CRUISE	–20 °C	–25 °C	ISA	0 °C	–40 °C
AIRPORT PRESS ALTITUDE	2,000	1,000	3,000	4,000	5,000
CRUISE ALTITUDE	16,000	18,000	20,000	14,000	22,000
INITIAL CLIMB WEIGHT	16,600	14,000	15,000	16,000	14,000
ICE VANES	RETRACT	EXTEND	RETRACT	RETRACT	EXTEND

FIGURE 15.— Beech 1900 – Climb.

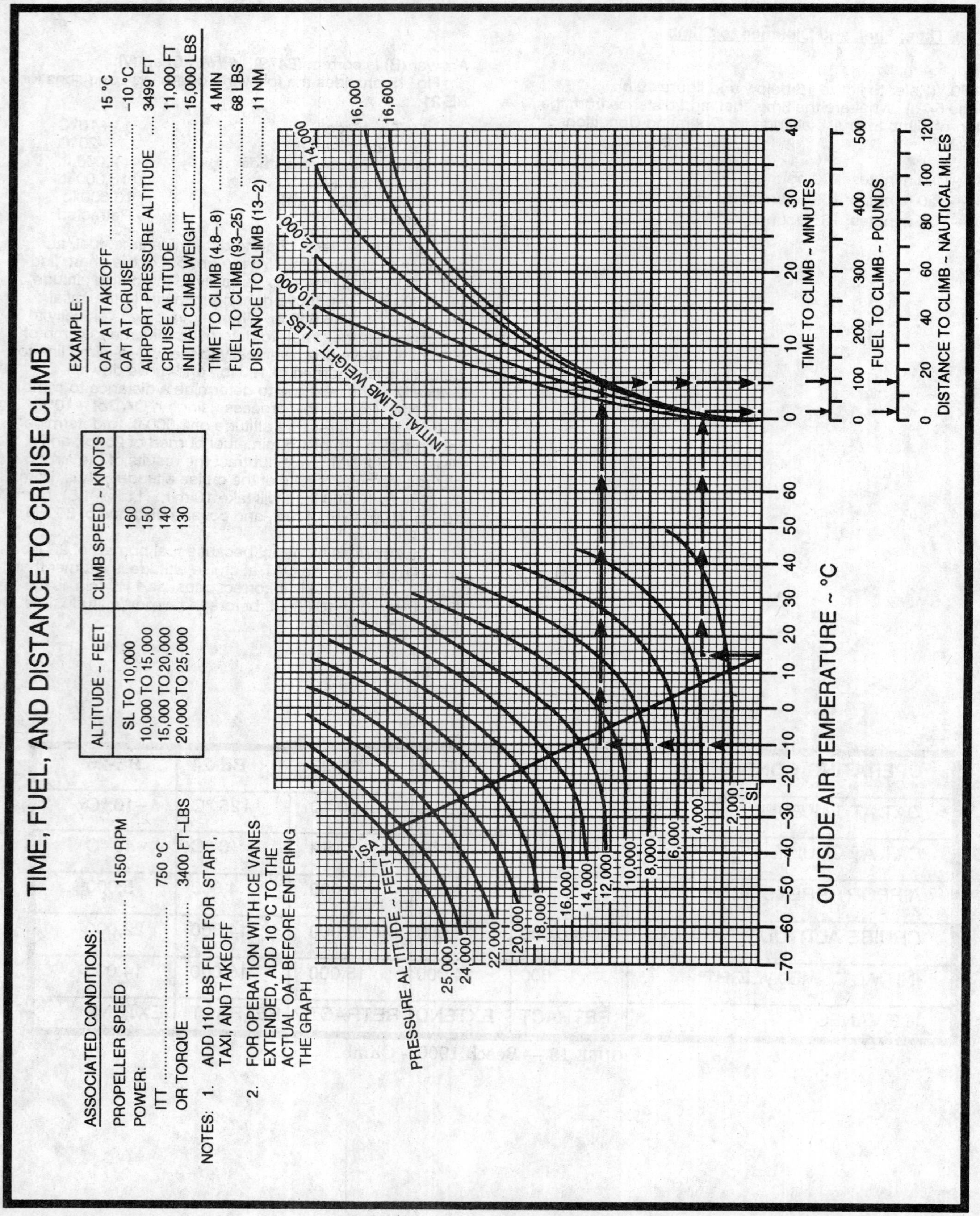

FIGURE 18.—Time, Fuel, and Distance to Cruise Climb.

47.
8480. (Refer to figures 15 and 18 on pages 541 and 542.) What are the time, fuel, and distance from the start of climb to cruise altitude for Operating Conditions BE-22?

A—12.0 minutes; 220 pounds; 40 NM.
B—11.0 minutes; 185 pounds; 37 NM.
C—10.5 minutes; 175 pounds; 32 NM.

Answer (B) is correct (8480). *(PHAK Chap IV)*
Fig. 15 provides the following operating conditions for BE-22:

OAT at takeoff	0°C
OAT at cruise	−25°C
Airport pressure altitude	1,000 ft.
Cruise altitude	18,000 ft.
Initial climb weight	14,000 lb.
Ice vanes	Extended

Fig. 18 provides a chart to determine time, fuel, and distance to cruise climb. For operation with the ice vanes extended, add 10°C to the OAT before entering chart (note 2 in Fig. 18). At the bottom of the chart, find −15°C (−25 + 10) OAT and move up vertically to the cruise altitude of 18,000 ft. Then move right horizontally to the initial climb weight of 14,000 lb. Then move down vertically to the bottom of the graph to determine the time to climb of 12 min. Move down vertically to the fuel-to-climb line to determine fuel burned of 200 lb., and move down vertically to the next line to determine a distance to climb of 37.5 NM. Repeat this process using an OAT of +10°C (0 + 10) and the airport pressure altitude of 1,000 ft. to determine the time to climb of 1 min., fuel burned of 15 lb., and a distance of 0.5 NM. Next subtract the results of the airport altitude from the results of the cruise altitude. Thus, from 1,000 ft. to 18,000 ft., it will take 11 min. (12 − 1), burn 185 lb. (200 − 15) of fuel, and cover a distance of 37 NM (37.5 − 0.5).

Answer (A) is incorrect because 12 min. is the time to climb at cruise altitude before subtracting the time to climb at the airport pressure altitude. Answer (C) is incorrect because 10.5 min. to climb to cruise altitude would require an airport pressure altitude of 3,000 ft., not 1,000 ft.

48.
8481. (Refer to figures 15 and 18 on pages 541and 542.) What are the time, fuel, and distance from the start of climb to cruise altitude for Operating Conditions BE-23?

A—13.0 minutes; 180 pounds; 35 NM.
B—14.0 minutes; 210 pounds; 40 NM.
C—15.0 minutes; 240 pounds; 46 NM.

Answer (B) is correct (8481). *(PHAK Chap IV)*
Fig. 15 provides the following operating conditions for BE-23:

OAT at takeoff	+20°C
OAT at cruise	ISA
Airport pressure altitude	3,000 ft.
Cruise altitude	20,000 ft.
Initial climb weight	15,000 lb.
Ice vanes	Retracted

Fig. 18 provides a chart to determine time, fuel, and distance to cruise climb. At the bottom of the chart, find ISA and move up and to the left on the ISA line to the cruise altitude of 20,000 ft. Then move right horizontally to the initial climb weight of 15,000 lb. Then move down vertically to the bottom of the graph to determine the time to climb of 14.5 min. Move down vertically to the fuel-to-climb line to determine fuel burned of 235 lb., and move down vertically to the next line to determine a distance to climb of 44 NM. Repeat this process using an OAT of +20°C and the airport pressure altitude of 3,000 ft. to determine the time to climb of 0.5 min., fuel burned of 25 lb., and a distance of 4 NM. Next subtract the results of the airport altitude from the results of the cruise altitude. Thus, from 3,000 ft. to 20,000 ft., it will take 14 min. (14.5 − 0.5), burn 210 lb. (235 − 25) of fuel, and cover a distance of 40 NM (44 − 4).

Answer (A) is incorrect because 180 lb. of fuel burned would require an OAT at takeoff of +40°C, not +20°C, or an OAT at cruise of −36°C, not ISA. Answer (C) is incorrect because 15.0 min. would require an OAT at cruise of −19°C, not ISA.

49.
8482. (Refer to figures 15 and 18 on pages 541 and 542.) What are the time, fuel, and distance from the start of climb to cruise altitude for Operating Conditions BE-24?

A—12.0 minutes; 220 pounds; 45 NM.
B—9.0 minutes; 185 pounds; 38 NM.
C—10.0 minutes; 170 pounds; 30 NM.

Answer (C) is correct (8482). *(PHAK Chap IV)*

Fig. 15 provides the following operating conditions for BE-24:

OAT at takeoff	+25°C
OAT at cruise	0°C
Airport pressure altitude	4,000 ft.
Cruise altitude	14,000 ft.
Initial climb weight	16,000 lb.
Ice vanes	Retracted

Fig. 18 provides a chart to determine time, fuel, and distance to cruise climb. At the bottom of the chart, find 0°C OAT and move up vertically to the cruise altitude of 14,000 ft. Then move right horizontally to the initial climb weight of 16,000 lb. Then move down vertically to the bottom of the graph to determine the time to climb of 12.8 min. Move down vertically to the fuel-to-climb line to determine fuel burned of 210 lb., and move down vertically to the next line to determine a distance to climb of 38 NM. Repeat this process using an OAT of +25°C and the airport pressure altitude of 4,000 ft. to determine the time to climb of 2.0 min., fuel burned of 40 lb., and a distance of 8 NM. Next subtract the results of the airport altitude from the results of the cruise altitude. Thus, from 4,000 ft. to 14,000 ft., it will take 10.8 min. (12.8 – 2.0), burn 170 lb. (210 – 40) of fuel, and cover a distance of 30 NM (38 – 8).

Answer (A) is incorrect because 12.0 min. to climb would require a cruise OAT of +5°C, not 0°C.
Answer (B) is incorrect because 9.0 min. to climb would require a cruise OAT of –2°C, not 0°C, or an OAT at takeoff of +34°C, not +25°C.

50.
8483. (Refer to figures 15 and 18 on pages 541 and 542.) What are the time, fuel, and distance from the start of climb to cruise altitude for Operating Conditions BE-25?

A—11.5 minutes; 170 pounds; 31 NM.
B—8.0 minutes; 270 pounds; 28 NM.
C—12.5 minutes; 195 pounds; 38 NM.

Answer (C) is correct (8483). *(PHAK Chap IV)*

Fig. 15 provides the following operating conditions for BE-25:

OAT at takeoff	–10°C
OAT at cruise	–40°C
Airport pressure altitude	5,000 ft.
Cruise altitude	22,000 ft.
Initial climb weight	14,000 lb.
Ice vanes	Extended

Fig. 18 provides a chart to determine time, fuel, and distance to cruise climb. For operation with the ice vanes extended, add 10°C to the OAT before entering chart (note 2 in Fig. 18). At the bottom of the chart, find –30°C (–40 + 10) OAT and move up vertically to the cruise altitude of 22,000 ft. Then move right horizontally to the initial climb weight of 14,000 lb. Then move down vertically to the bottom of the graph to determine the time to climb of 14.5 min. Move down vertically to the fuel-to-climb line to determine fuel burned of 235 lb., and move down vertically to the next line to determine a distance to climb of 44 NM. Repeat this process using an OAT of +0°C (–10 + 10) and the airport pressure altitude of 5,000 ft. to determine the time to climb of 2.0 min., fuel burned of 40 lb., and a distance of 6 NM. Next subtract the results of the airport altitude from the results of the cruise altitude. Thus, from 5,000 ft. to 22,000 ft., it will take 12.5 min. (14.5 – 2.0), burn 195 lb. (235 – 40) of fuel, and cover a distance of 38 NM (44 – 6).

Answer (A) is incorrect because 11.5 min. is the time to climb to a cruise altitude of 21,000 ft., not 22,000 ft.
Answer (B) is incorrect because 8.0 min. is the time to climb to a cruise altitude of 19,000 ft., not 22,000 ft.

11.9 Single Engine Service Ceiling

51.
8484. (Refer to figures 19 and 20 on page 547.) At what altitude is the service ceiling with one engine inoperative for Operating Conditions BE-26?

A—13,000 feet.
B—14,200 feet.
C—13,600 feet.

Answer (A) is correct (8484). *(PHAK Chap IV)*

Fig. 19 provides operating conditions for BE-26. Given an OAT of –8°C, weight of 15,500 lb., and the bleed air ON, determine the service ceiling with one engine inoperative. Fig. 20 provides a chart to determine the service ceiling with bleed air ON or OFF. Use the graph on the left-hand side for bleed air ON. Find OAT –8°C at the bottom of the chart and move up vertically to 15,500 lb. Then move horizontally to the left edge of the chart to determine a pressure altitude service ceiling with one engine inoperative of 13,000 ft.

Answer (B) is incorrect because a 14,200-ft. service ceiling with one engine inoperative would occur with an OAT of –18°C, not –8°C. Answer (C) is incorrect because a 13,600-ft. service ceiling with one engine inoperative would occur with an OAT of –13°C, not –8°C.

52.
8486. (Refer to figures 19 and 20 on page 547.) At what altitude is the service ceiling with one engine inoperative for Operating Conditions BE-28?

A—1,500 feet above the MEA.
B—10,400 feet.
C—11,800 feet.

Answer (C) is correct (8486). *(PHAK Chap IV)*

Fig. 19 provides operating conditions for BE-28. Given an OAT of +5°C, weight of 16,000 lb., and the bleed air OFF, determine the service ceiling with one engine inoperative. Fig. 20 provides a chart to determine the service ceiling with bleed air ON or OFF. Use the graph on the right-hand side for bleed air OFF. Find OAT +5°C at the bottom of the chart and move up vertically to 16,000 lb. Then move left horizontally to the left edge of the chart to determine a pressure altitude service ceiling with one engine inoperative of 11,800 ft., which is 2,800 ft. above the 9,000-ft. MEA.

Answer (A) is incorrect because the 11,800-ft. service ceiling with one engine inoperative is 2,800 ft., not 1,500 ft., above the route segment MEA of 9,000 ft. Answer (B) is incorrect because a 10,400-ft. service ceiling with one engine inoperative would occur with an OAT of +15°C, not +5°C.

53.
8488. (Refer to figures 19 and 20 on page 547.) At what altitude is the service ceiling with one engine inoperative for Operating Conditions BE-30?

A—9,600 feet.
B—13,200 feet.
C—2,100 feet above the MEA.

Answer (C) is correct (8488). *(PHAK Chap IV)*

Fig. 19 provides operating conditions for BE-30. Given an OAT of +22°C, weight of 14,500 lb., the bleed air OFF, and an MEA of 9,500 ft., determine the service ceiling with one engine inoperative. Fig. 20 provides a chart to determine the service ceiling with bleed air ON or OFF. Use the graph on the right-hand side for bleed air OFF. Find OAT +22°C at the bottom of the chart and move up vertically to 14,500 lb. Then move left horizontally to the left edge of the chart to determine a pressure altitude service ceiling with one engine inoperative of 11,600 ft., which is 2,100 ft. above the 9,500-ft. MEA (11,600 – 9,500).

Answer (A) is incorrect because a 9,600-ft. service ceiling with one engine inoperative would occur with the bleed air ON, not OFF. Answer (B) is incorrect because a 13,200-ft. service ceiling with one engine inoperative would occur with an OAT of +11°C, not +22°C.

54.
8485. (Refer to figures 19 and 20 on page 547.) Which statement is true regarding performance with one engine inoperative for Operating Conditions BE-27?

A—Climb rate at the MEA is more than 50 ft/min.
B—Service ceiling is below the MEA.
C—Bleed air OFF improves service ceiling by 3,000 feet.

Answer (B) is correct (8485). *(PHAK Chap IV)*

Fig. 19 provides operating conditions for BE-27. Given an OAT of +30°C, weight of 16,600 lb., the bleed air ON, and an MEA of 5,500 ft., determine the service ceiling with one engine inoperative. Fig. 20 provides a chart to determine the service ceiling with bleed air ON or OFF. Use the graph on the left-hand side for bleed air ON. Find OAT +30°C at the bottom of the chart and move up vertically to 16,600 lb. Then move horizontally to the left edge of the chart to determine a pressure altitude service ceiling (maximum altitude for 50 fpm rate of climb) with one engine inoperative of 5,000 ft. Thus, the service ceiling of 5,000 ft. is below the MEA of 5,500 ft.

Answer (A) is incorrect because a climb rate of 50 fpm would occur below the service ceiling of 5,000 ft., which is below, not at, the MEA of 5,500 ft. Answer (C) is incorrect because, using the right-hand chart in Fig. 20, the service ceiling with the bleed air OFF is 7,100 ft., which is an improvement of only 2,100 ft. (7,100 – 5,000), not 3,000 ft.

55.
8487. (Refer to figures 19 and 20 on page 547.) Which statement is true regarding performance with one engine inoperative for Operating Conditions BE-29?

A—Service ceiling is more than 100 feet above the MEA.
B—Bleed air must be OFF to obtain a rate of climb of 50 ft/min at the MEA.
C—Climb is not possible at the MEA.

Answer (A) is correct (8487). *(PHAK Chap IV)*

Fig. 19 provides operating conditions for BE-29. Given an OAT of +18°C, weight of 16,300 lb., the bleed air ON, and an MEA of 7,000 ft., determine the service ceiling with one engine inoperative. Fig. 20 provides a chart to determine the service ceiling with bleed air ON or OFF. Use the graph on the right-hand side for bleed air ON. Find OAT +18°C at the bottom of the chart and move up vertically to 16,300 lb. Then move horizontally to the left edge of the chart to determine a pressure altitude service ceiling with one engine inoperative of 7,700 ft., which is more than 100 ft. above the MEA of 7,000 ft.

Answer (B) is incorrect because the service ceiling is the maximum altitude for a rate of climb at 50 fpm, which is above the MEA of 7,000 ft. with the bleed air ON 7,700 ft. and the bleed air OFF 9,500 ft. Answer (C) is incorrect because, at the MEA of 7,000 ft., the airplane is climbing at a rate above 50 fpm.

OPERATING CONDITIONS	BE-26	BE-27	BE-28	BE-29	BE-30
OAT AT MEA	−8 °C	+30 °C	+5 °C	+18 °C	+22 °C
WEIGHT	15,500	16,600	16,000	16,300	14,500
ROUTE SEGMENT MEA	6,000	5,500	9,000	7,000	9,500
BLEED AIR	ON	ON	OFF	ON	OFF

FIGURE 19.—Beech 1900 – Service Ceiling.

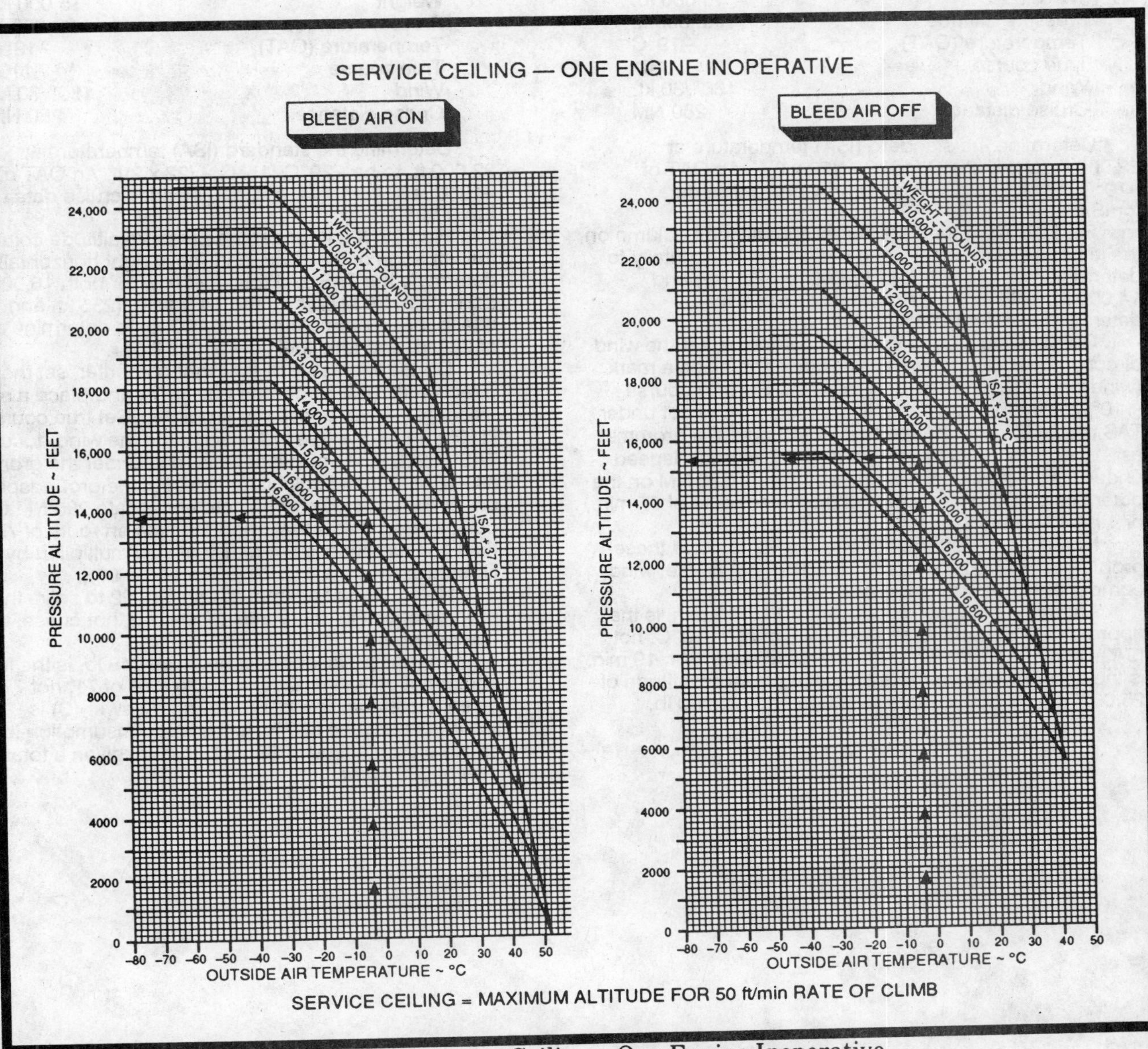

FIGURE 20.—Service Ceiling – One Engine Inoperative.

11.10 En Route Cruise Time and Fuel

56.
8489. (Refer to figures 21, 22, 23, 24, and 25 on pages 553 through 556.) What is the en route time of the cruise leg for Operating Conditions BE-31?

A—1 hour 11 minutes.
B—1 hour 17 minutes.
C—1 hour 19 minutes.

Answer (B) is correct (8489). *(PHAK Chap IV)*

Fig. 21 provides the operating conditions for BE-31.

Weight	15,000 lb.
Pressure altitude	22,000 ft.
Temperature (OAT)	−19°C
True course	110°
Wind	180°/30 kt.
Cruise distance	280 NM

Determine the standard (ISA) temperature at 22,000 ft. to be −29°C [15°C − (22 x 2)]. An OAT of −19°C is ISA +10°C. Fig. 23 provides cruise data for ISA +10°C.

Find 22,000 ft. under the pressure altitude column on the left edge of the chart, and move right horizontally to determine the TAS for both 16,000 lb. (221 kt.) and 14,000 lb. (235 kt.). Interpolate for 15,000 lb. to determine a TAS of 228 kt.

On the wind side of the flight computer, set the wind direction of 180° under the true index and place a mark (wind dot) 30 kt. above the grommet. Set true course (110°) under the true index and slide the wind dot under TAS of 228 kt. Groundspeed is read under the grommet as 216 kt. On the calculator side, set the groundspeed under the solid pointer triangle and locate 280 NM on the outer scale. Below that, read the time en route of 77 min., or 1 hr. 17 min.

Note: Do not attempt to use Fig. 22 to solve these problems, as Fig. 22 relates to landing, not cruise, wind components.

Answer (A) is incorrect because 1 hr. 11 min. is the approximate en route time at an OAT of ISA −10°C, not ISA +10°C. Answer (C) is incorrect because 1 hr. 19 min. is the approximate en route time at a pressure altitude of 25,000, not 22,000, ft. and 14,000 lb., not 15,000 lb.

57.
8494. (Refer to figures 21, 22, 23, 24, and 25 on pages 553 through 556.) What is the fuel consumption during the cruise leg for Operating Conditions BE-31?

A—812 pounds.
B—749 pounds.
C—870 pounds.

Answer (A) is correct (8494). *(PHAK Chap IV)*

Fig. 21 provides the operating conditions for BE-31.

Weight	**15,000 lb.**
Pressure altitude	**22,000 ft.**
Temperature (OAT)	**−19°C**
True course	**110°**
Wind	**180°/30 kt.**
Cruise distance	**280 NM**

Determine the standard (ISA) temperature at 22,000 ft. to be −29°C [15°C − (22 x 2)]. An OAT of −19°C is ISA +10°C. Fig. 23 provides cruise data for ISA +10°C.

Find 22,000 ft. under the pressure altitude column on the left edge of the chart, and move right horizontally to determine the TAS and total fuel flow for both 16,000 lb. (221 kt. and 632 lb./hr.) and 14,000 lb. (235 kt. and 634 lb./hr.). Interpolate for 15,000 lb. to determine a TAS of 228 kt. and total fuel flow of 633 lb./hr.

On the wind side of the flight computer, set the wind direction of 180° under the true index and place a mark (wind dot) 30 kt. above the grommet. Set true course (110°) under the true index and slide the wind dot under TAS of 228 kt. Groundspeed is read under the grommet as 216 kt. On the calculator side, set the groundspeed under the solid pointer triangle and locate 280 NM on the outer scale. Below that, read the time en route of 77 min. Fuel consumption is the total fuel flow multiplied by the time (hr.), which is 812 lb. [633 x (77 ÷ 60)].

Note: Do not attempt to use Fig. 22 to solve these problems, as Fig. 22 relates to landing, not cruise, wind components.

Answer (B) is incorrect because 749 lb. is the fuel consumption for a cruise en route time of 71, not 77, min. given a total fuel flow of 633 lb./hr. Answer (C) is incorrect because 870 lb. is the fuel consumption for a cruise en route time of 83, not 77, min. given a total fuel flow of 633 lb./hr.

58.
8490. (Refer to figures 21, 22, 23, 24, and 25 on pages 553 through 556.) What is the en route time of the cruise leg for Operating Conditions BE-32?

A—1 hour 13 minutes.
B—1 hour 15 minutes.
C—1 hour 20 minutes.

Answer (A) is correct (8490). *(PHAK Chap IV)*
Fig. 21 provides the operating conditions for BE-32.

Weight	14,000 lb.
Pressure altitude	17,000 ft.
Temperature (OAT)	−19°C
True course	270°
Wind	020°/35 kt.
Cruise distance	320 NM

Determine the standard (ISA) temperature at 17,000 ft. to be −19°C [15°C − (17 x 2)]. An OAT of −19°C is ISA. Fig. 24 provides cruise data for ISA.

Find 14,000 lb. at the top of the chart, and move down vertically to determine the TAS for both 16,000 ft. (253 kt.) and 18,000 ft. (251 kt.). Interpolate for 17,000 ft. to determine a TAS of 252 kt.

On the wind side of the flight computer, set the wind direction of 020° under the true index and place a mark (wind dot) 35 kt. above the grommet. Set true course (270°) under the true index and slide the wind dot under TAS of 252 kt. Groundspeed is read under the grommet as 262 kt. On the calculator side, set the groundspeed under the solid pointer triangle and locate 320 NM on the outer scale. Below that, read the time en route of 73 min., or 1 hr. 13 min.

Note: Do not attempt to use Fig. 22 to solve these problems, as Fig. 22 relates to landing, not cruise, wind components.

Answer (B) is incorrect because 1 hr. 15 min. is the en route time at an OAT of ISA +10°C, not ISA. Answer (C) is incorrect because 1 hr. 20 min. is the en route time at a pressure altitude of approximately 23,400 ft., not 17,000 ft., and 16,000 lb., not 14,000 lb.

59.
8495. (Refer to figures 21, 22, 23, 24, and 25 on pages 553 through 556.) What is the fuel consumption during the cruise leg for Operating Conditions BE-32?

A—1,028 pounds.
B—896 pounds.
C—977 pounds.

Answer (C) is correct (8495). *(PHAK Chap IV)*
Fig. 21 provides the operating conditions for BE-32.

Weight	14,000 lb.
Pressure altitude	17,000 ft.
Temperature (OAT)	−19°C
True course	270°
Wind	020°/35 kt.
Cruise distance	320 NM

Determine the standard (ISA) temperature at 17,000 ft. to be −19°C [15°C − (17 x 2)]. An OAT of −19°C is ISA. Fig. 24 provides cruise data for ISA.

Find 14,000 lb. at the top of the chart, and move down vertically to determine the TAS and total fuel flow for both 16,000 ft. (253 kt. and 828 lb./hr.) and 18,000 ft. (251 kt. and 778 lb./hr.). Interpolate for 17,000 ft. to determine a TAS of 252 kt. and total fuel flow of 803 lb./hr.

On the wind side of the flight computer, set the wind direction of 020° under the true index and place a mark (wind dot) 35 kt. above the grommet. Set true course (270°) under the true index and slide the wind dot under TAS of 252 kt. Groundspeed is read under the grommet as 262 kt. On the calculator side, set the groundspeed under the solid pointer triangle and locate 320 NM on the outer scale. Below that, read the time en route of 73 min. Fuel consumption is the total fuel flow multiplied by the time (hr.), which is 977 lb. [803 x (73 ÷ 60)].

Note: Do not attempt to use Fig. 22 to solve these problems, as Fig. 22 relates to landing, not cruise, wind components.

Answer (A) is incorrect because 1,028 lb. is the fuel consumption for a cruise en route time of 77, not 73, min. given a total fuel flow of 803 lb./hr. Answer (B) is incorrect because 896 lb. is the fuel consumption for a cruise en route time of 67, not 73, min. given a total fuel flow of 803 lb./hr.

60.
8491. (Refer to figures 21, 22, 23, 24, and 25 on pages 553 through 556.) What is the en route time of the cruise leg for Operating Conditions BE-33?

A—1 hour 50 minutes.
B—1 hour 36 minutes.
C—1 hour 46 minutes.

61.
8496. (Refer to figures 21, 22, 23, 24, and 25 on pages 553 through 556.) What is the fuel consumption during the cruise leg for Operating Conditions BE-33?

A—1,165 pounds.
B—1,373 pounds.
C—976 pounds.

Answer (C) is correct (8491). *(PHAK Chap IV)*
Fig. 21 provides the operating conditions for BE-33.

Weight	13,000 lb.
Pressure altitude	20,000 ft.
Temperature (OAT)	−35°C
True course	185°
Wind	135°/45 kt.
Cruise distance	400 NM

Determine the standard (ISA) temperature at 20,000 ft. to be −25°C [15°C − (20 x 2)]. An OAT of −35°C is ISA −10°C. Fig. 25 provides cruise data for ISA −10°C.

Find 20,000 ft. under the pressure altitude column on the left edge of the chart, and move right horizontally to determine the TAS for both 14,000 lb. (254 kt.) and 12,000 lb. (259 kt.). Interpolate for 13,000 lb. to determine a TAS of 257 kt.

On the wind side of the flight computer, set the wind direction of 135° under the true index and place a mark (wind dot) 45 kt. above the grommet. Set true course (185°) under the true index and slide the wind dot under TAS of 257 kt. Groundspeed is read under the grommet as 225 kt. On the calculator side, set the groundspeed under the solid pointer triangle and locate 400 NM on the outer scale. Below that, read the time en route of 106 min., or 1 hr. 46 min.

Note: Do not attempt to use Fig. 22 to solve these problems, as Fig. 22 relates to landing, not cruise, wind components.

Answer (A) is incorrect because 1 hr. 50 min. is the approximate en route time at an OAT of ISA, not ISA −10°C. Answer (B) is incorrect because 1 hr. 36 min. requires a TAS of 281 kt., which is a TAS higher than on any chart.

Answer (B) is correct (8496). *(PHAK Chap IV)*
Fig. 21 provides the operating conditions for BE-33.

Weight	13,000 lb.
Pressure altitude	20,000 ft.
Temperature (OAT)	−35°C
True course	185°
Wind	135°/45 kt.
Cruise distance	400 NM

Determine the standard (ISA) temperature at 20,000 ft. to be −25°C [15°C − (20 x 2)]. An OAT of −35°C is ISA −10°C. Fig. 25 provides cruise data for ISA −10°C.

Find 20,000 ft. under the pressure altitude column on the left edge of the chart, and move right horizontally to determine the TAS and total fuel flow for both 14,000 lb. (254 kt. and 776 lb./hr.) and 12,000 lb. (259 kt. and 778 lb./hr.). Interpolate for 13,000 lb. to determine a TAS of 257 kt. and total fuel flow of 777 lb./hr.

On the wind side of the flight computer, set the wind direction of 135° under the true index and place a mark (wind dot) 45 kt. above the grommet. Set true course (185°) under the true index and slide the wind dot under TAS of 257 kt. Groundspeed is read under the grommet as 225 kt. On the calculator side, set the groundspeed under the solid pointer triangle and locate 400 NM on the outer scale. Below that, read the time en route of 106 min. Fuel consumption is the total fuel flow multiplied by the time (hr.), which is 1,373 lb. [777 x (106 ÷ 60)].

Note: Do not attempt to use Fig. 22 to solve these problems, as Fig. 22 relates to landing, not cruise, wind components.

Answer (A) is incorrect because 1,165 lb. is the fuel consumption for a cruise en route time of 90, not 106, min. given a total fuel flow of 777 lb./hr. Answer (C) is incorrect because 976 lb. is the fuel consumption for a cruise en route time of 78, not 106, min. given a total fuel flow of 777 lb./hr.

62.
8492. (Refer to figures 21, 22, 23, 24, and 25 on pages 553 through 556.) What is the en route time of the cruise leg for Operating Conditions BE-34?

A—1 hour 6 minutes.
B—1 hour 3 minutes.
C—1 hour 11 minutes.

Answer (A) is correct (8492). *(PHAK Chap IV)*
Fig. 21 provides the operating conditions for BE-34.

Weight	16,000 lb.
Pressure altitude	23,000 ft.
Temperature (OAT)	–31°C
True course	020°
Wind	340°/25 kt.
Cruise distance	230 NM

Determine the standard (ISA) temperature at 23,000 ft. to be –31°C [15°C – (23 x 2)]. An OAT of –31°C is ISA. Fig. 24 provides cruise data for ISA.

Find 16,000 lb. at the top of the chart, and move down vertically to determine the TAS for both 22,000 ft. (233 kt.) and 24,000 ft. (223 kt.). Interpolate for 23,000 ft. to determine a TAS of 228 kt.

On the wind side of the flight computer, set the wind direction of 340° under the true index and place a mark (wind dot) 25 kt. above the grommet. Set true course (020°) under the true index and slide the wind dot under TAS of 228 kt. Groundspeed is read under the grommet as 208 kt. On the calculator side, set the groundspeed under the solid pointer triangle and locate 230 NM on the outer scale. Below that, read the time en route of 66 min., or 1 hr. 6 min.

Note: Do not attempt to use Fig. 22 to solve these problems, as Fig. 22 relates to landing, not cruise, wind components.

Answer (B) is incorrect because 1 hr. 3 min. is the en route time at an OAT of ISA –10°C, not ISA. Answer (C) is incorrect because 1 hr. 11 min. is the en route time at an OAT of ISA +10°C, not ISA.

63.
8497. (Refer to figures 21, 22, 23, 24, and 25 on pages 553 through 556.) What is the fuel consumption during the cruise leg for Operating Conditions BE-34?

A—668 pounds.
B—718 pounds.
C—737 pounds.

Answer (B) is correct (8497). *(PHAK Chap IV)*
Fig. 21 provides the operating conditions for BE-34.

Weight	16,000 lb.
Pressure altitude	23,000 ft.
Temperature (OAT)	–31°C
True course	020°
Wind	340°/25 kt.
Cruise distance	230 NM

Determine the standard (ISA) temperature at 23,000 ft. to be –31°C [15°C – (23 x 2)]. An OAT of –31°C is ISA. Fig. 24 provides cruise data for ISA.

Find 16,000 lb. at the top of the chart, and move down vertically to determine the TAS and total fuel flow for both 22,000 ft. (233 kt. and 676 lb./hr.) and 24,000 ft. (223 kt. and 630 lb./hr.). Interpolate for 23,000 ft. to determine a TAS of 228 kt. and total fuel flow of 653 lb./hr.

On the wind side of the flight computer, set the wind direction of 340° under the true index and place a mark (wind dot) 25 kt. above the grommet. Set true course (020°) under the true index and slide the wind dot under TAS of 228 kt. Groundspeed is read under the grommet as 208 kt. On the calculator side, set the groundspeed under the solid pointer triangle and locate 230 NM on the outer scale. Below that, read the time en route of 66 min. Fuel consumption is the total fuel flow multiplied by the time (hr.), which is 718 lb. [653 x (66 ÷ 60)].

Note: Do not attempt to use Fig. 22 to solve these problems, as Fig. 22 relates to landing, not cruise, wind components.

Answer (A) is incorrect because 668 lb. is the fuel consumption for a cruise en route time of 61, not 66, min. given a total fuel flow of 653 lb./hr. Answer (C) is incorrect because 737 lb. is the fuel consumption for a cruise en route time of 68, not 66, min. given a total fuel flow of 653 lb./hr.

64.
8493. (Refer to figures 21, 22, 23, 24, and 25 on pages 553 through 556.) What is the en route time of the cruise leg for Operating Conditions BE-35?

A—1 hour 6 minutes.
B—1 hour 8 minutes.
C—1 hour 10 minutes.

Answer (C) is correct (8493). *(PHAK Chap IV)*
Fig. 21 provides the operating conditions for BE-35.

Weight	11,000 lb.
Pressure altitude	14,000 ft.
Temperature (OAT)	−3°C
True course	305°
Wind	040°/50 kt.
Cruise distance	300 NM

Determine the standard (ISA) temperature at 14,000 ft. to be −13°C [15°C − (14 x 2)]. An OAT of −3°C is ISA +10°C. Fig. 23 provides cruise data for ISA +10°C.

Find 14,000 ft. under the pressure altitude column on the left edge of the chart, and move right horizontally to determine the TAS for both 12,000 lb. (251 kt.) and 10,000 lb. (255 kt.). Interpolate for 11,000 lb. to determine a TAS of 253 kt.

On the wind side of the flight computer, set the wind direction of 040° under the true index and place a mark (wind dot) 50 kt. above the grommet. Set true course under the true index and slide the wind dot under TAS of 253 kt. Groundspeed is read under the grommet as 253 kt. On the calculator side, set the groundspeed under the solid pointer triangle and locate 300 NM on the outer scale. Below that, read the time en route of 71 min., or 1 hr. 11 min.

Note: Do not attempt to use Fig. 22 to solve these problems, as Fig. 22 relates to landing, not cruise, wind components.

Answer (A) is incorrect because 1 hr. 6 min. requires a TAS of 273 kt., which is a TAS higher than on any chart provided. Answer (B) is incorrect because 1 hr. 8 min. is the en route time at an OAT of ISA −10°C, not ISA +10°C.

65.
8498. (Refer to figures 21, 22, 23, 24, and 25 on pages 553 through 556.) What is the fuel consumption during the cruise leg for Operating Conditions BE-35?

A—900 pounds.
B—1,030 pounds.
C—954 pounds.

Answer (C) is correct (8498). *(PHAK Chap IV)*
Fig. 21 provides the operating conditions for BE-35.

Weight	11,000 lb.
Pressure altitude	14,000 ft.
Temperature (OAT)	−3°C
True course	305°
Wind	040°/50 kt.
Cruise distance	300 NM

Determine the standard (ISA) temperature at 14,000 ft. to be −13°C [15°C − (14 x 2)]. An OAT of −3°C is ISA +10°C. Fig. 23 provides cruise data for ISA +10°C.

Find 14,000 ft. under the pressure altitude column on the left edge of the chart, and move right horizontally to determine the TAS and total fuel flow for both 12,000 lb. (251 kt. and 818 lb./hr.) and 10,000 lb. (255 kt. and 818 lb./hr.). Interpolate for 11,000 lb. to determine a TAS of 253 kt. and a total fuel flow of 818 lb./hr.

On the wind side of the flight computer, set the wind direction of 040° under the true index and place a mark (wind dot) 50 kt. above the grommet. Set true course (305°) under the true index and slide the wind dot under TAS of 253 kt. Groundspeed is read under the grommet as 253 kt. On the calculator side, set the groundspeed under the solid pointer triangle and locate 300 NM on the outer scale. Below that, read the time en route of 71 min. Fuel consumption is the total fuel flow multiplied by the time (hr.), which is 968 lb. [818 x (71 ÷ 60)].

Note: Do not attempt to use Fig. 22 to solve these problems, as Fig. 22 relates to landing, not cruise, wind components.

Answer (A) is incorrect because 900 lb. is the fuel consumption for a cruise en route time of 66, not 71, min. given a total fuel flow of 818 lb./hr. Answer (B) is incorrect because 1,030 lb. is the fuel consumption for a cruise en route time of 76, not 71, min. given a total fuel flow of 818 lb./hr.

OPERATING CONDITIONS	BE-31	BE-32	BE-33	BE-34	BE-35
WEIGHT	15,000	14,000	13,000	16,000	11,000
PRESSURE ALTITUDE	22,000	17,000	20,000	23,000	14,000
TEMPERATURE (OAT)	–19 °C	–19 °C	–35 °C	–31 °C	–3 °C
TRUE COURSE	110	270	185	020	305
WIND	180/30	020/35	135/45	340/25	040/50
CRUISE DISTANCE	280	320	400	230	300

FIGURE 21.—Beech 1900 – Cruise.

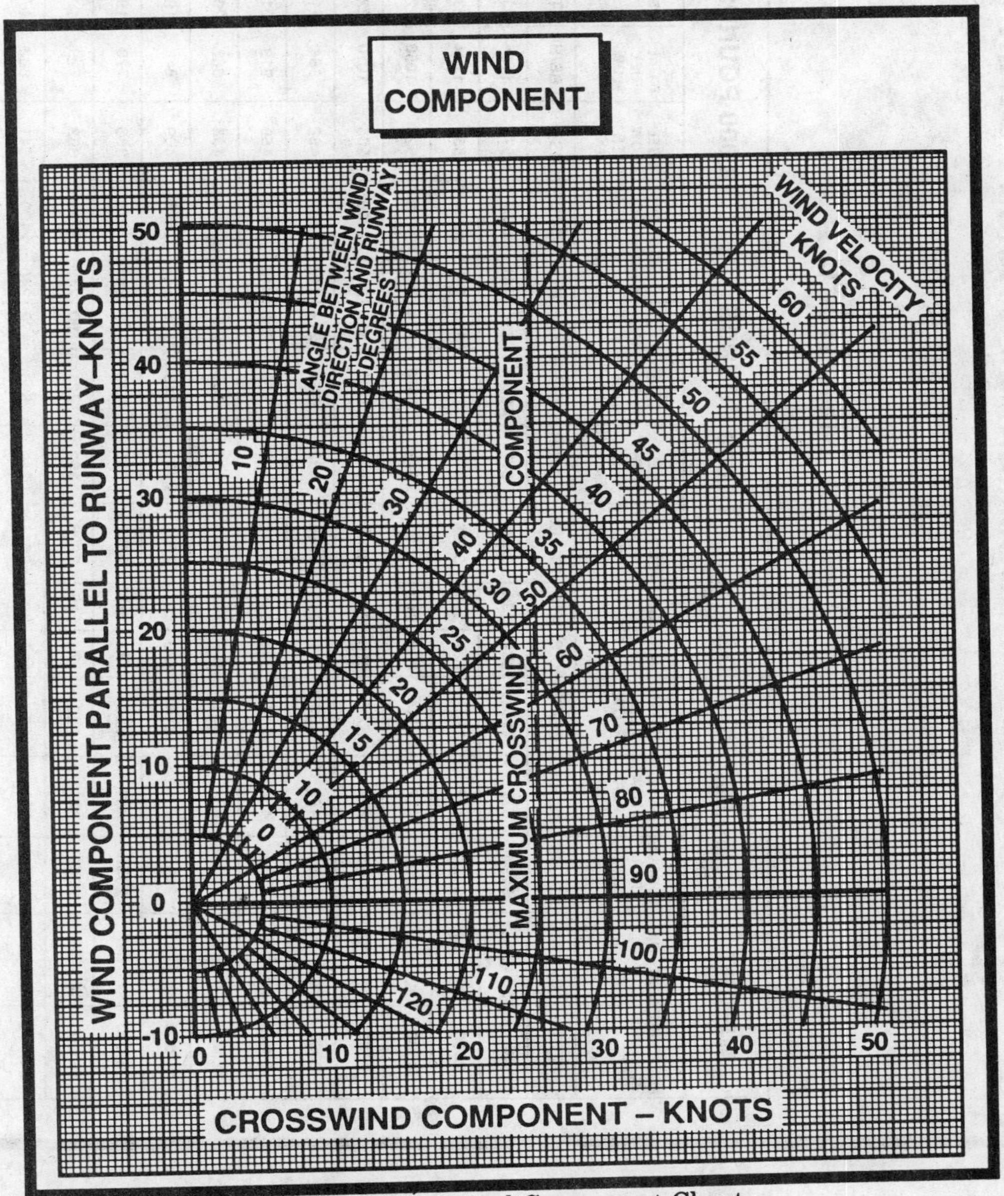

FIGURE 22.—Wind Component Chart.

RECOMMENDED CRUISE POWER

1550 RPM

ISA +10 °C

WEIGHT			16,000 POUNDS					14,000 POUNDS					12,000 POUNDS					10,000 POUNDS				
PRESSURE ALTITUDE	IOAT	OAT	TORQUE PER ENG	FUEL FLOW PER ENG	TOTAL FUEL FLOW	IAS	TAS	TORQUE PER ENG	FUEL FLOW PER ENG	TOTAL FUEL FLOW	IAS	TAS	TORQUE PER ENG	FUEL FLOW PER ENG	TOTAL FUEL FLOW	IAS	TAS	TORQUE PER ENG	FUEL FLOW PER ENG	TOTAL FUEL FLOW	IAS	TAS
FEET	°C	°C	FT-LBS	LBS/HR	LBS/HR	KTS	KTS	FT-LBS	LBS/HR	LBS/HR	KTS	KTS	FT-LBS	LBS/HR	LBS/HR	KTS	KTS	FT-LBS	LBS/HR	LBS/HR	KTS	KTS
SL	30	25	3294	577	1154	232	239	3301	577	1154	235	241	3307	577	1154	237	243	3312	577	1154	238	245
2000	26	21	3191	551	1102	227	240	3198	551	1102	230	243	3204	552	1104	232	245	3209	552	1104	233	247
4000	22	17	3092	527	1054	222	242	3100	528	1056	224	244	3106	528	1056	227	247	3111	528	1056	228	249
6000	19	13	2992	504	1008	216	243	3000	505	1010	219	246	3006	505	1010	222	249	3012	505	1010	224	251
8000	15	9	2886	481	962	211	244	2896	482	964	214	247	2903	482	964	216	250	2909	482	964	219	253
10,000	11	5	2778	458	916	205	244	2789	458	916	208	248	2797	459	918	211	252	2804	459	918	213	254
12,000	7	1	2636	432	864	198	243	2648	433	866	202	248	2657	433	866	205	252	2664	434	868	207	255
14,000	3	-3	2495	408	816	190	241	2508	409	818	195	247	2518	409	818	198	251	2525	409	818	201	255
16,000	-1	-7	2352	384	768	182	239	2367	385	770	188	246	2378	385	770	192	251	2386	386	772	195	255
18,000	-6	-11	2208	361	722	174	235	2226	362	724	180	243	2239	363	726	185	250	2248	363	726	188	254
20,000	-10	-15	2063	338	676	164	229	2085	340	680	172	240	2100	341	682	177	248	2111	341	682	181	253
22,000	-14	-19	1911	316	632	153	221	1939	317	634	163	235	1957	319	638	169	245	1969	319	638	174	252
24,000	-19	-23	1749	292	584	137	206	1790	295	590	152	229	1812	297	594	161	241	1827	298	596	167	249
25,000	-21	-25	1649	279	558	122	187	1714	284	568	147	224	1739	286	572	156	238	1756	287	574	163	248

FIGURE 23.—Recommended Cruise Power – ISA +10 °C.

RECOMMENDED CRUISE POWER

1550 RPM

ISA

WEIGHT			16,000 POUNDS					14,000 POUNDS					12,000 POUNDS					10,000 POUNDS				
PRESSURE ALTITUDE	IOAT	OAT	TORQUE PER ENG	FUEL FLOW PER ENG	TOTAL FUEL FLOW	IAS	TAS	TORQUE PER ENG	FUEL FLOW PER ENG	TOTAL FUEL FLOW	IAS	TAS	TORQUE PER ENG	FUEL FLOW PER ENG	TOTAL FUEL FLOW	IAS	TAS	TORQUE PER ENG	FUEL FLOW PER ENG	TOTAL FUEL FLOW	IAS	TAS
FEET	°C	°C	FT-LBS	LBS/HR	LBS/HR	KTS	KTS	FT-LBS	LBS/HR	LBS/HR	KTS	KTS	FT-LBS	LBS/HR	LBS/HR	KTS	KTS	FT-LBS	LBS/HR	LBS/HR	KTS	KTS
SL	20	15	3400	586	1172	237	239	3400	585	1170	239	241	3400	585	1170	241	243	3400	585	1170	242	244
2000	17	11	3400	573	1146	234	244	3400	573	1146	236	246	3400	572	1144	238	248	3400	572	1144	240	249
4000	13	7	3400	560	1120	232	248	3400	559	1118	234	250	3400	559	1118	236	252	3400	559	1118	237	254
6000	9	3	3397	548	1096	229	252	3400	548	1096	231	255	3400	547	1094	233	257	3400	547	1094	235	259
8000	5	-1	3253	521	1042	223	253	3260	522	1044	225	256	3265	522	1044	228	258	3270	522	1044	229	260
10,000	1	-5	3092	494	988	216	252	3100	494	988	219	256	3107	495	990	221	258	3112	495	990	223	261
12,000	-3	-9	2929	466	932	208	251	2937	467	934	212	255	2945	467	934	214	258	2950	467	934	217	261
14,000	-7	-13	2772	440	880	201	250	2781	441	882	205	255	2789	441	882	208	258	2795	442	884	210	261
16,000	-11	-17	2606	414	828	193	248	2618	414	828	197	253	2626	415	830	201	258	2633	415	830	203	261
18,000	-15	-21	2435	288	776	184	244	2449	389	778	189	251	2459	389	778	193	256	2467	390	780	196	260
20,000	-19	-25	2263	363	726	175	239	2282	364	728	181	248	2294	365	730	186	254	2302	365	730	189	259
22,000	-24	-29	2094	338	676	164	233	2118	340	680	172	244	2133	341	682	178	251	2144	342	684	182	257
24,000	-28	-33	1931	315	630	152	223	1960	317	634	163	238	1979	318	636	169	248	1991	319	638	174	255
25,000	-30	-35	1846	303	606	145	216	1880	305	610	157	235	1901	307	614	165	246	1915	308	616	170	253

FIGURE 24.—Recommended Cruise Power – ISA.

RECOMMENDED CRUISE POWER

1550 RPM

ISA -10 °C

WEIGHT			16,000 POUNDS					14,000 POUNDS					12,000 POUNDS					10,000 POUNDS				
PRESSURE ALTITUDE	IOAT	OAT	TORQUE PER ENG	FUEL FLOW PER ENG	TOTAL FUEL FLOW	IAS	TAS	TORQUE PER ENG	FUEL FLOW PER ENG	TOTAL FUEL FLOW	IAS	TAS	TORQUE PER ENG	FUEL FLOW PER ENG	TOTAL FUEL FLOW	IAS	TAS	TORQUE PER ENG	FUEL FLOW PER ENG	TOTAL FUEL FLOW	IAS	TAS
FEET	°C	°C	FT-LBS	LBS/HR	LBS/HR	KTS	KTS	FT-LBS	LBS/HR	LBS/HR	KTS	KTS	FT-LBS	LBS/HR	LBS/HR	KTS	KTS	FT-LBS	LBS/HR	LBS/HR	KTS	KTS
SL	10	5	3400	582	1164	238	237	3400	582	1164	240	239	3400	581	1162	242	240	3400	581	1162	243	242
2000	6	1	3400	569	1138	236	241	3400	569	1138	238	243	3400	568	1136	240	245	3400	568	1136	241	246
4000	3	-3	3400	558	1116	233	245	3400	557	1114	236	248	3400	557	1114	237	249	3400	557	1114	239	251
6000	-1	-7	3400	548	1096	231	250	3400	547	1094	233	252	3400	547	1094	235	254	3400	546	1092	236	256
8000	-5	-11	3400	538	1076	228	254	3400	538	1076	231	257	3400	538	1076	232	259	3400	537	1074	234	261
10,000	-9	-15	3400	530	1060	226	259	3400	530	1060	228	262	3400	530	1060	230	264	3400	529	1058	232	266
12,000	-13	-19	3200	499	998	218	258	3208	500	1000	221	261	3215	500	1000	223	264	3220	501	1002	225	266
14,000	-17	-23	3010	470	940	210	256	3019	471	942	213	260	3026	471	942	216	263	3032	472	944	218	266
16,000	-21	-27	2823	442	884	202	254	2833	442	884	205	258	2841	443	886	209	262	2848	443	886	211	265
18,000	-25	-31	2641	414	828	193	251	2652	415	830	198	256	2661	416	832	201	261	2668	416	832	204	264
20,000	-29	-35	2456	387	774	184	247	2471	388	776	189	254	2481	389	778	193	259	2489	390	780	196	263
22,000	-33	-39	2277	361	722	174	242	2296	363	726	181	250	2308	363	726	185	256	2318	364	728	189	261
24,000	-37	-43	2105	336	672	163	234	2128	338	676	172	246	2144	339	678	177	254	2155	340	680	181	260
25,000	-40	-45	2017	324	648	157	230	2044	326	652	167	243	2061	327	654	173	252	2073	328	656	177	258

FIGURE 25.—Recommended Cruise Power – ISA –10 °C.

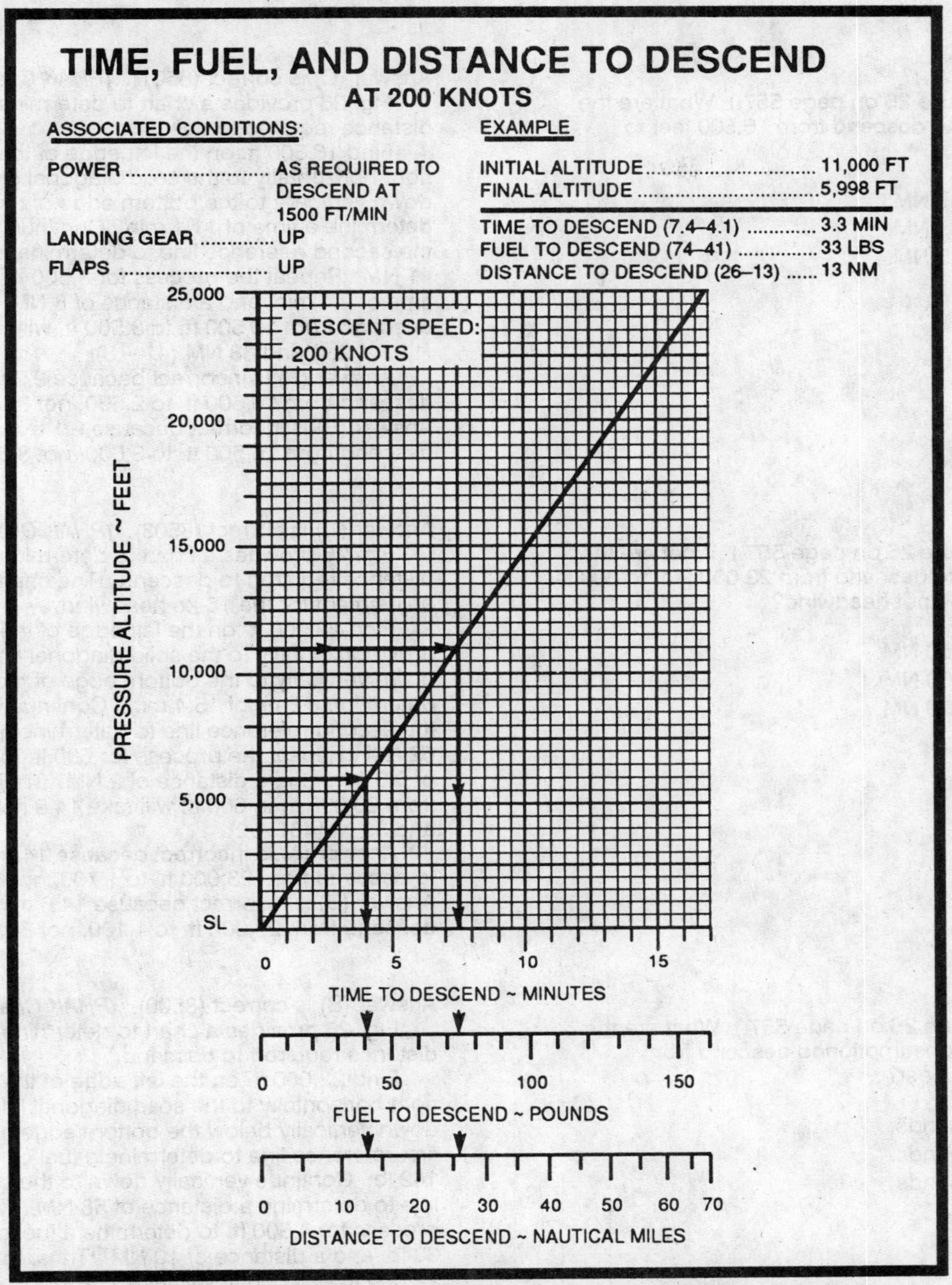

FIGURE 26.—Time, Fuel, and Distance to Descend.

11.11 Time, Fuel, and Distance to Descend

66.
8499. (Refer to figure 26 above.) What are the time and distance to descend from 18,000 feet to 2,500 feet?

A—10.3 minutes, 39 NM.
B—9.8 minutes, 33 NM.
C—10.0 minutes, 36 NM.

Answer (A) is correct (8499). *(PHAK Chap IV)*

Fig. 26 provides a chart to determine time, fuel, and distance required to descend.

Find 18,000 ft. on the left edge of the chart, and move right horizontally to the solid diagonal line; then move down vertically to the bottom edge of the chart to determine a time of 12 min. Continue vertically down to the second reference line to determine a distance of 45 NM. Repeat the process for 2,500 ft. to determine a time of 1.7 min. and a distance of 6 NM. Thus, to descend from 18,000 ft. to 2,500 ft. will take 10.3 min. (12 – 1.7) and 39 NM (45 – 6).

Answer (B) is incorrect because 9.8 min. is the time to descend from 18,000 ft. to 3,200 ft., not 2,500 ft. Answer (C) is incorrect because 10.0 min. is the time to descend from 18,000 ft. to 3,000 ft., not 2,500 ft.

67.
8501. (Refer to figure 26 on page 557.) What are the time and distance to descend from 16,500 feet to 3,500 feet?

A—9.3 minutes, 37 NM.
B—9.1 minutes, 35 NM.
C—8.7 minutes, 33 NM.

Answer (C) is correct (8501). *(PHAK Chap 4)*
Fig. 26 provides a chart to determine time, fuel, and distance required to descend.

Find 16,500 ft. on the left edge of the chart, and move right horizontally to the solid diagonal line; then move down vertically to the bottom edge of the chart to determine a time of 11.1 min. Continue vertically down to the second reference line to determine a distance of 41 NM. Repeat the process for 3,500 ft. to determine a time of 2.4 min. and a distance of 8 NM. Thus, to descend from 16,500 ft. to 3,500 ft. will take 8.7 min. (11.1 – 2.4) and 33 NM (41 – 8).

Answer (A) is incorrect because 9.3 min. is the time to descend from 16,500 ft. to 2,550, not 3,500, ft. Answer (B) is incorrect because 9.1 min. is the time to descend from 16,500 ft. to 3,000, not 3,500, ft.

68.
8503. (Refer to figure 26 on page 557.) What are the time and distance to descend from 23,000 feet to 600 feet with an average 15-knot headwind?

A—14.2 minutes, 50 NM.
B—14.6 minutes, 56 NM.
C—14.9 minutes, 59 NM.

Answer (C) is correct (8503). *(PHAK Chap 4)*
Fig. 26 provides a chart to determine time, fuel, and distance required to descend. The chart provides no adjustment for the 15-kt. headwind.

Find 23,000 ft. on the left edge of the chart, and move right horizontally to the solid diagonal line; then move down vertically to the bottom edge of the chart to determine a time of 15.4 min. Continue vertically down to the second reference line to determine a distance of 62 NM. Repeat the process for 600 ft. to determine a time of 0.5 min. and a distance of 2 NM. Thus, to descend from 23,000 ft. to 600 ft. will take 14.9 min. (15.4 – 0.5) and 59 NM (61 – 2).

Answer (A) is incorrect because 14.2 min. is the time to descend from 23,000 ft. to 1,700, not 600, ft. Answer (B) is incorrect because 14.6 min. is the time to descend from 23,000 ft. to 1,100, not 600, ft.

69.
8500. (Refer to figure 26 on page 557.) What are the distance and fuel consumption to descend from 22,000 feet to 4,500 feet?

A—44 NM, 117 pounds.
B—48 NM, 112 pounds.
C—56 NM, 125 pounds.

Answer (B) is correct (8500). *(PHAK Chap 4)*
Fig. 26 provides a chart to determine time, fuel, and distance required to descend.

Find 22,000 ft. on the left edge of the chart, and move right horizontally to the solid diagonal line; then move down vertically below the bottom edge of the chart to the first reference line to determine a fuel consumption of 142 lb. Continue vertically down to the second reference line to determine a distance of 58 NM. Repeat the process for 4,500 ft. to determine a fuel consumption of 30 lb. and a distance of 10 NM. Thus, to descend from 22,000 ft. to 4,500 ft. will take 112 lb. (142 – 30) of fuel and 48 NM (58 – 10).

Answer (A) is incorrect because 44 NM is the distance to descend from 22,000 ft. to 6,500, not 4,500, ft. Answer (C) is incorrect because 56 NM is the distance to descend from 22,000 ft. to 800, not 4,500, ft.

70.
8502. (Refer to figure 26 on page 557.) What are the distance and fuel consumption to descend from 13,500 feet to 1,500 feet?

A—30 NM, 87 pounds.
B—29 NM, 80 pounds.
C—38 NM, 100 pounds.

Answer (B) is correct (8502). *(PHAK Chap 4)*

Fig. 26 provides a chart to determine time, fuel, and distance required to descend.

Find 13,500 ft. on the left edge of the chart, and move right horizontally to the solid diagonal line; then move down vertically below the bottom edge of the chart to the first reference line to determine a fuel consumption of 90 lb. Continue vertically down to the second reference line to determine a distance of 32.5 NM. Repeat the process for 1,500 ft. to determine a fuel consumption of 10 lb. and a distance of 3.5 NM. Thus, to descend from 13,500 ft. to 1,500 ft. will take 80 lb. (90 – 10) of fuel and 29 NM (32.5 – 3.5).

Answer (A) is incorrect because 87 lb. is the fuel consumption to descend from 13,500 ft. to 350, not 1,500, ft. Answer (C) is incorrect because 38 NM is the distance to descend from 16,500, not 13,500, ft.

11.12 Landing Distance

71.
8504. (Refer to figures 27 and 28 on pages 563 and 564.) What is the landing distance over a 50-foot obstacle for Operating Conditions B-36?

A—1,900 feet.
B—1,625 feet.
C—950 feet.

Answer (A) is correct (8504). *(PHAK Chap 4)*

Fig. 27 gives the following operating conditions for B-36.

Pressure altitude (ft.)	SL
Temperature (OAT)	+30°C
Weight (lb.)	16,000
Wind component (kt.)	20 HW
Runway length (ft.)	4,000

Fig. 28 provides a chart to determine the normal landing distance. Find OAT +30°C at the bottom left of the chart and move up vertically to a pressure altitude of SL (sea level). Then move right horizontally to the first reference line. Move down and to the right (parallel to the guide line) to a weight of 16,000 lb. Move right horizontally to the second reference line and move down (headwind) and to the right (parallel to the guide line) to 20 kt. Then move right horizontally to the third reference line and move up and to the right (parallel to the guide line) to the right edge of the chart for a 50-ft. obstacle. The landing distance is 1,900 ft.

Answer (B) is incorrect because 1,625 ft. is the landing distance at a weight of 13,000 lb., not 16,000 lb. Answer (C) is incorrect because 950 ft. is the ground roll, not landing, distance over a 50-ft. obstacle.

72.
8505. (Refer to figures 27 and 28 on pages 563 and 564.) What are the approach speed and ground roll when landing under Operating Conditions B-36?

A—113 knots and 950 feet.
B—113 knots and 1,950 feet.
C—112 knots and 900 feet.

Answer (A) is correct (8505). *(PHAK Chap IV)*
Fig. 27 gives the following operating conditions for B-36.

Pressure altitude (ft.)	SL
Temperature (OAT)	+30°C
Weight (lb.)	16,000
Wind component (kt.)	20 HW
Runway length (ft.)	4,000

Fig. 28 provides a chart to determine the normal landing distance. Find OAT +30°C at the bottom left of the chart and move up vertically to a pressure altitude of SL (sea level). Then move right horizontally to the first reference line. Move down and to the right (parallel to the guide line) to a weight of 16,000 lb. Move right horizontally to the second reference line and move down (headwind) and to the right (parallel to the guide line) to 20 kt. Then move right horizontally to the edge of the chart. The ground roll distance is 950 ft.

The box above the graph in Fig. 28 provides information on approach speed. Find the approach speed for both 16,100 lb. (113 kt.) and 14,000 lb. (107 kt.). Interpolate for 16,000 lb. to determine an approach speed of 112.7 or 113 kt.

Answer (B) is incorrect because 1,950 ft. is the approximate total landing distance over a 50-ft. obstacle, not ground roll. Answer (C) is incorrect because an approach speed of 112 kt. is for a weight of 15,750, not 16,000, lb.

73.
8506. (Refer to figures 27 and 28 on pages 563 and 564.) What is the remaining runway length when stopped after landing over a 50-foot obstacle for Operating Conditions B-37?

A—2,500 feet.
B—2,000 feet.
C—2,600 feet.

Answer (B) is correct (8506). *(PHAK Chap IV)*
Fig. 27 gives the following operating conditions for B-37.

Pressure altitude (ft.)	1,000
Temperature (OAT)	+16°C
Weight (lb.)	14,500
Wind component (kt.)	10 TW
Runway length (ft.)	4,500

Fig. 28 provides a chart to determine the normal landing distance. Find OAT +16°C at the bottom left of the chart and move up vertically to a pressure altitude of 1,000 ft. Then move right horizontally to the first reference line. Move down and to the right (parallel to the guide line) to a weight of 14,500 lb. Move right horizontally to the second reference line and move up (tailwind) and to the right (parallel to the guide line) to 10 kt. Then move right horizontally to the third reference line and move up and to the right (parallel to the guide line) to the right edge of the chart for a 50-ft. obstacle. The landing distance is 2,500 ft. The remaining runway length when stopped is the runway length minus the landing distance, or 2,000 ft. (4,500 – 2,500).

Answer (A) is incorrect because 2,500 ft. is the total landing, not runway remaining, distance over a 50-ft. obstacle. Answer (C) is incorrect because 2,600 ft. is the remaining runway length with a 10-kt. headwind, not tailwind.

74.
8507. (Refer to figures 27 and 28 on pages 563 and 564.) What are the approach speed and ground roll when landing under Operating Conditions B-37?

A—108 knots and 1,400 feet.
B—109 knots and 900 feet.
C—107 knots and 1,350 feet.

Answer (A) is correct (8507). *(PHAK Chap IV)*

Fig. 27 gives the following operating conditions for B-37.

Pressure altitude (ft.)	1,000
Temperature (OAT)	+16°C
Weight (lb.)	14,500
Wind component (kt.)	10 TW
Runway length (ft.)	4,500

Fig. 28 provides a chart to determine the normal landing distance. Find OAT +16°C at the bottom left of the chart and move up vertically to a pressure altitude of 1,000 ft. Then move right horizontally to the first reference line. Move down and to the right (parallel to the guide line) to a weight of 14,500 lb. Move right horizontally to the second reference line and move up (tailwind) and to the right (parallel to the guide line) to 10 kt. Then move right horizontally to the right edge of the chart. The ground roll distance is 1,400 ft. The box above the graph in Fig. 28 provides information on approach speed. Find the approach speeds for both 16,100 lb. (113 kt.) and 14,000 lb. (107 kt.). Interpolate for 14,500 lb. to determine an approach speed of 108 kt.

Answer (B) is incorrect because 900 ft. is the ground roll with a 10-kt. headwind, not tailwind. Answer (C) is incorrect because 107 kt. is the approach speed at a weight of 14,000, not 14,500, lb.

75.
8508. (Refer to figures 27 and 28 on pages 563 and 564.) What is the landing distance over a 50-foot obstacle for Operating Conditions B-38?

A—1,850 feet.
B—1,700 feet.
C—1,800 feet.

Answer (B) is correct (8508). *(PHAK Chap IV)*

Fig. 27 gives the following operating conditions for B-38.

Pressure altitude (ft.)	2,000
Temperature (OAT)	0°C
Weight (lb.)	13,500
Wind component (kt.)	15 HW
Runway length (ft.)	3,800

Fig. 28 provides a chart to determine the normal landing distance. Find OAT 0°C at the bottom left of the chart and move up vertically to a pressure altitude of 2,000 ft. Then move right horizontally to the first reference line. Move down and to the right (parallel to the guide line) to a weight of 13,500 lb. Move right horizontally to the second reference line and move down (headwind) and to the right (parallel to the guide line) to 15 kt. Then move right horizontally to the third reference line and move up and to the right (parallel to the guide line) to the right edge of the chart for a 50-ft. obstacle. The landing distance is 1,700 ft.

Answer (A) is incorrect because 1,850 ft. is the landing distance over a 50-ft. obstacle in a calm wind, not a 15-kt. headwind. Answer (C) is incorrect because 1,800 ft. is the landing distance over a 50-ft. obstacle at a weight of 14,500, not 13,500, lb.

76.
8509. (Refer to figures 27 and 28 on pages 563 and 564.) What is the total runway used when touchdown is at the 1,000-foot marker for Operating Conditions B-38?

A—2,000 feet.
B—1,700 feet.
C—1,800 feet.

Answer (C) is correct (8509). *(PHAK Chap IV)*
Fig. 27 gives the following operating conditions for B-38.

Pressure altitude (ft.)	2,000
Temperature (OAT)	0°C
Weight (lb.)	13,500
Wind component (kt.)	15 HW
Runway length (ft.)	3,800

Fig. 28 provides a chart to determine the normal landing distance. Find OAT 0°C at the bottom left of the chart and move up vertically to a pressure altitude of 2,000 ft. Then move right horizontally to the first reference line. Move down and to the right (parallel to the guide line) to a weight of 13,500 lb. Move right horizontally to the second reference line and move down (headwind) and to the right (parallel to the guide line) to 15 kt. Then move right horizontally to the edge of the chart. The ground roll distance is 800 ft. The total runway used is the distance from the threshold of the runway to the touchdown point plus the ground roll distance or 1,800 ft. (1,000 + 800).

Answer (A) is incorrect because 2,000 ft. is the total runway used at a weight of 14,500, not 13,500, lb. and a calm wind, not a 15-kt. headwind. Answer (B) is incorrect because 1,700 ft. is the total runway used with a 20-kt., not a 15-kt., headwind.

77.
8510. (Refer to figures 27 and 28 on pages 563 and 564.) What is the remaining runway length when stopped after landing over a 50-foot obstacle for Operating Conditions B-39?

A—2,300 feet.
B—2,400 feet.
C—2,500 feet.

Answer (C) is correct (8510). *(PHAK Chap IV)*
Fig. 27 gives the following operating conditions for B-39.

Pressure altitude (ft.)	4,000
Temperature (OAT)	+20°C
Weight (lb.)	15,000
Wind component (kt.)	5 TW
Runway length (ft.)	5,000

Fig. 28 provides a chart to determine the normal landing distance. Find OAT +20°C at the bottom left of the chart and move up vertically to a pressure altitude of 4,000 ft. Then move right horizontally to the first reference line. Move down and to the right (parallel to the guide line) to a weight of 15,000 lb. Move right horizontally to the second reference line and move up (tailwind) and to the right (parallel to the guide line) to 5 kt. Then move right horizontally to the third reference line and move up and to the right (parallel to the guide line) to the right edge of the chart for a 50-ft. obstacle. The landing distance is 2,500 ft. The remaining runway length when stopped is the runway length minus the landing distance, or 2,500 ft. (5,000 – 2,500).

Answer (A) is incorrect because 2,300 ft. is the remaining runway length when stopped with a 10-kt., not a 5-kt., tailwind. Answer (B) is incorrect because 2,400 ft. is the remaining runway length when stopped at a weight of 15,500, not 15,000, lb.

78.
8511. (Refer to figure 27 below and figure 28 on page 564.) What are the approach speed and ground roll when landing under Operating Conditions B-39?

A—111 knots and 1,550 feet.
B—110 knots and 1,400 feet.
C—109 knots and 1,300 feet.

Answer (B) is correct (8511). *(PHAK Chap IV)*
Fig. 27 gives the following operating conditions for B-39.

Pressure altitude (ft.)	4,000
Temperature (OAT)	+20°C
Weight (lb.)	15,000
Wind component (kt.)	5 TW
Runway length (ft.)	5,000

Fig. 28 provides a chart to determine the normal landing distance. Find OAT +20°C at the bottom left of the chart and move up vertically to a pressure altitude of 4,000 ft. Then move right horizontally to the first reference line. Move down and to the right (parallel to the guide line) to a weight of 15,000 lb. Move right horizontally to the second reference line and move up (tailwind) and to the right (parallel to the guide line) to 5 kt. Then move right horizontally to the edge of the chart. The ground roll distance is 1,400 ft. The box above the graph in Fig. 28 provides information on approach speed. Find the approach speeds for both 16,100 lb. (113 kt.) and 14,000 lb. (107 kt.). Interpolate for 15,000 lb. to determine an approach speed of 110 kt.

Answer (A) is incorrect because 111 kt. is the approach speed at a weight of 15,400, not 15,000, lb. Answer (C) is incorrect because 109 kt. is the approach speed at a weight of 14,700, not 15,000, lb.

79.
8512. (Refer to figure 27 below and figure 28 on page 564.) What is the landing distance over a 50-foot obstacle for Operating Conditions B-40?

A—1,500 feet.
B—1,750 feet.
C—1,650 feet.

Answer (C) is correct (8512). *(PHAK Chap IV)*
Fig. 27 gives the following operating conditions for B-40.

Pressure altitude (ft.)	5,000
Temperature (OAT)	ISA
Weight (lb.)	12,500
Wind component (kt.)	25 HW
Runway length (ft.)	4,000

Fig. 28 provides a chart to determine the normal landing distance. Find the ISA (solid diagonal) line at the left side of the chart and move on the ISA line to a pressure altitude of 5,000 ft. Then move right horizontally to the first reference line. Move down and to the right (parallel to the guide line) to a weight of 12,500 lb. Move right horizontally to the second reference line and move down (headwind) and to the right (parallel to the guide line) to 25 kt. Then move right horizontally to the third reference line and move up and to the right (parallel to the guide line) to the right edge of the chart for a 50-ft. obstacle. The landing distance is 1,650 ft.

Answer (A) is incorrect because 1,500 ft. is the landing distance over a 50-ft. obstacle at a weight of 11,500, not 12,500, lb. Answer (B) is incorrect because 1,750 ft. is the landing distance over a 50-ft. obstacle at a weight of 13,500, not 12,500, lb.

OPERATING CONDITIONS	B–36	B–37	B–38	B–39	B–40
PRESSURE ALTITUDE	SL	1,000	2,000	4,000	5,000
TEMPERATURE (OAT)	+30 °C	+16 °C	0 °C	+20 °C	ISA
WEIGHT	16,000	14,500	13,500	15,000	12,500
WIND COMPONENT (KTS)	20 HW	10 TW	15 HW	5 TW	25 HW
RUNWAY LENGTH (FT)	4,000	4,500	3,800	5,000	4,000

FIGURE 27.--Beech 1900 - Landing.

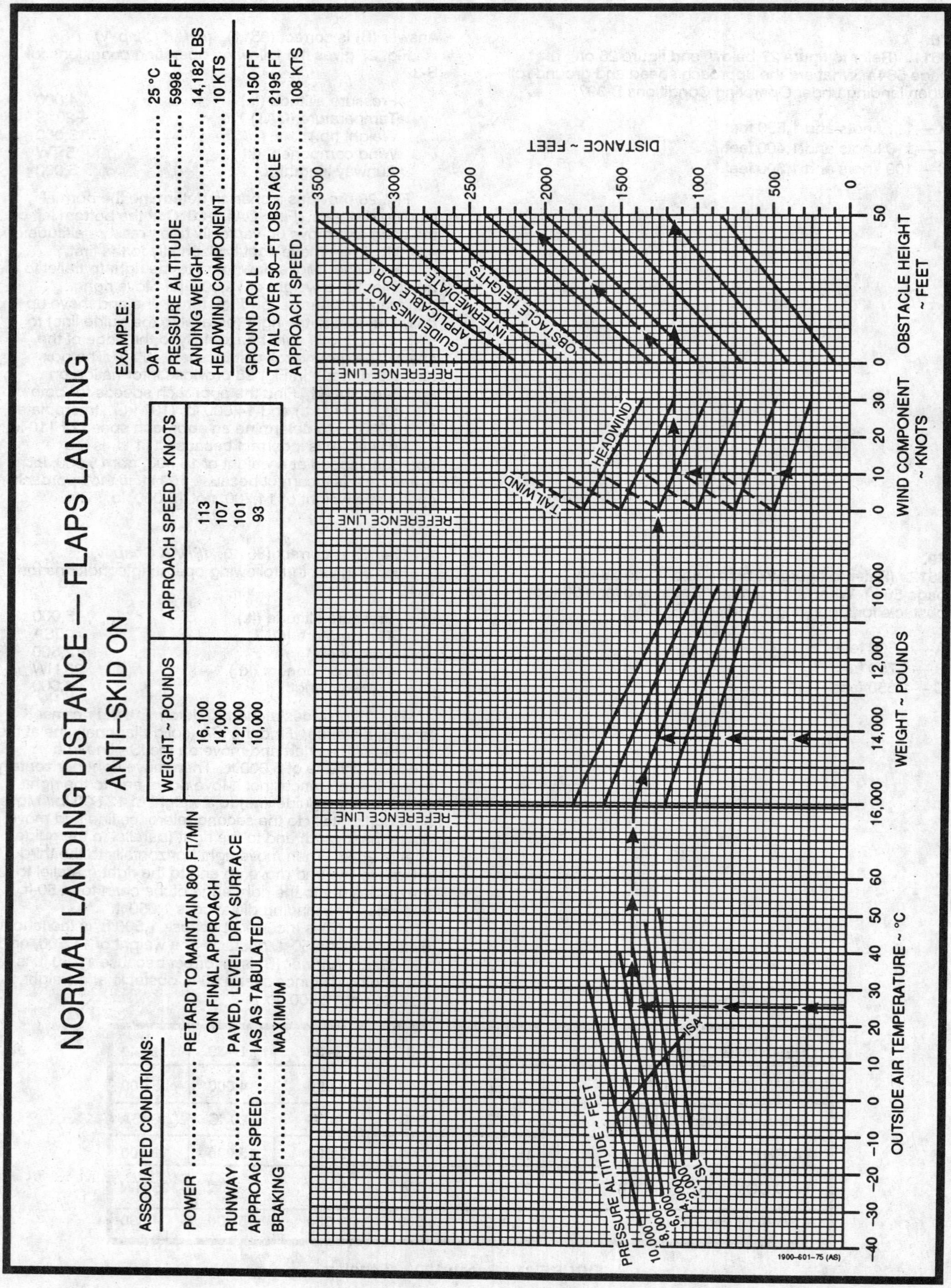

FIGURE 28.—Normal Landing Distance – Flaps Landing.

CHAPTER TWELVE
DC-9 OPERATING/PERFORMANCE DATA

This chapter contains outlines of major concepts tested, all FAA test questions and answers regarding DC-9 operating/performance data, and an explanation of each answer. Each module, or subtopic, within this chapter is listed above with the number of questions from the FAA pilot knowledge test pertaining to that particular module. For each module, the first number following the parentheses is the page number on which the outline begins, and the next number is the page number on which the questions begin.

There are 40 questions in this chapter. We separate and organize the FAA ATP questions into meaningful study units and subunits, i.e., chapters and modules. As an analogy, it is easier to deal with the "trees" if you understand the "forest." In this context, "trees" are individual FAA questions and the "forest" is the ATP knowledge test. The organizational units between the overall ATP knowledge test and individual ATP test questions are chapters and modules in this book.

CAUTION: The **sole purpose** of this book is to expedite your passing the FAA pilot knowledge test for the ATP certificate. Topics or regulations not directly tested on the FAA pilot knowledge test are omitted. Much more information and knowledge are necessary to fly safely. This additional material is presented in Gleim's other pilot training books (see the order form on page 818) and in many FAA books and circulars, as well as in airplane *POH*s and other commercial textbooks.

12.1 CG AFTER WEIGHT SHIFT (Questions 1-5)

1. Sweptwing airplanes (e.g., DC-9s and other jet transports) express CG as a "percent of MAC" as well as distance in inches from a datum.
   a. MAC is the acronym for **mean aerodynamic chord**. It relates to sweptwing planes.
   b. MAC is a distance--the width of the mean aerodynamic chord, usually given in inches.
   c. LEMAC is the leading edge of MAC, i.e., the forward edge of MAC.
2. Percent of MAC (% MAC) is the number of inches the CG is aft of the front edge of the mean aerodynamic chord divided by the total distance of MAC.
   a. EXAMPLE: If MAC is 141.5 in. and the CG is 22.5% of MAC, the CG is 31.84 in. (141.5 in. x 22.5%) aft of LEMAC (i.e., the leading edge of MAC).
   b. Conversely, if you know CG is 31.84 in. aft of LEMAC, you can compute % MAC by dividing 31.84 in. by 141.5 in., which computes to 22.5% MAC (31.84 ÷ 141.5).

3. The first four questions in this chapter provide for a weight shift after the CG has been computed as % MAC.
   a. Compute the change in CG in inches with the formula below:

$$CG\ change\ (in.) = \frac{(Wt.\ shifted) \times (Dist.\ of\ shift)}{Aircraft\ wt.}$$

   b. Compute the new CG in % MAC with the following formula:

$$\frac{(MAC)(prev.\ \%\ MAC) \pm (Net\ CG\ change\ in\ in.)}{MAC}$$

      1) Note that [(MAC)(prev. % MAC)] is the old CG in inches.

4. EXAMPLE:

Loaded weight	90,000 lb.
Loaded CG (% MAC)	22.5%
Weight shifted	2,500 lb.
FWD compartment	352.1 in.
AFT compartment	724.9 in.
MAC	141.5 in.

$$CG\ change\ (in.) = \frac{(Wt.\ shifted) \times (Dist.\ of\ shift)}{Aircraft\ wt.} = \frac{2{,}500 \times (724.9 - 352.1)}{90{,}000} =$$

$$\frac{2{,}500 \times 372.8}{90{,}000} = \frac{932{,}000}{90{,}000} = 10.36\ in.$$

Since this change is from forward to aft, the net change is positive, or +10.36 in. (the CG moves aft). To convert the change in inches to % of MAC, use the following formula:

$$\frac{(MAC)(prev.\ \%\ MAC) \pm (Net\ CG\ change\ in\ in.)}{MAC} =$$

$$\frac{(141.5)(.225) + (10.36)}{141.5} = \frac{31.84 + 10.36}{141.5} = \frac{42.2}{141.5} = .298\ or\ 29.8\%\ MAC$$

5. The fifth question deals with CG on index arm rather than % MAC. You are required to determine where the CG datum is. This determination is made using LEMAC (i.e., leading edge of mean aerodynamic chord) and its relation to the datum.

12.2 CG AFTER WEIGHT CHANGE (Questions 6-10)

1. When there is a weight change (weight added or removed), adjust the previous total weight and the previous total moments; then compute the new CG.
2. **Steps to Compute a New CG after a Weight Change**
   a. Convert previous % MAC to inches aft of LEMAC.
   b. Determine previous CG index arm by adjusting previous CG aft of LEMAC by adding (subtracting) the LEMAC index arm.

c. Compute previous airplane moment (previous weight x previous CG index arm).

d. Adjust previous weight and previous airplane moment by the weight added or removed and the index arm of the weight added or removed.

e. Compute new CG.

f. Convert the new CG in inches to distance from LEMAC (CG – LEMAC).

g. Compute % MAC: CG distance aft of LEMAC divided by MAC.

3. EXAMPLE: 2,500 lb. is removed from the forward compartment of the airplane. The forward compartment is Station 352.1. WS-1 on Fig. 44 on page 571 indicates an aircraft weight of 90,000 lb. and a loaded CG as 22.5% MAC. First convert 22.5% MAC to a station number. MAC is given as 141.5 in., and 22.5% of it is +31.83 in. Add LEMAC of 549.13 in. to get the CG of 580.96 in. (549.13 + 31.83). Then use conventional weight/balance formulas:

Item	Wt./1,000	Index Arm	Mom./1,000
Aircraft wt.	90.0	580.96	52,286.40
Cargo removed	–2.5	352.1	880.25
	87.5		51,406.15

$$CG = \frac{\textit{Total moment}}{\textit{Total wt.}} = \frac{51{,}406.15}{87.5} = 587.50 \textit{ in.}$$

Subtracting LEMAC (549.13), we can obtain the new CG of 38.37 (587.5 – 549.13). Use the following formula to obtain % MAC:

$$\% MAC = \frac{CG}{MAC} = \frac{38.37}{141.5} = 27.1\% \ MAC$$

12.3 V_1 AND V_R SPEEDS (Questions 11-15)

1. **Definitions**

a. **V_1** is the maximum speed in the takeoff at which the pilot must take the first action (e.g., apply brakes, reduce thrust, deploy speed brakes) to stop the airplane.

1) V_1 is also the minimum speed in the takeoff, following a failure of the critical engine at V_{EF}, at which the pilot can continue the takeoff and achieve the required height above the takeoff surface within the takeoff distance.

b. **V_R** is rotation speed -- when you rotate.

c. **V_2** (not tested in this series of questions) is takeoff safety speed -- airspeed necessary for climb profile.

2. Weight determines takeoff speeds for DC-9s, adjusted for

a. Pressure altitude
b. Temperature
c. Runway slope
d. Wind
e. Use or nonuse of ice protection devices

3. **Steps to Determine V_1 and V_R**
   a. Determine the unadjusted takeoff speeds based on weight using the top portion of Fig. 47 on page 581 (e.g., at 75,000 lb., V_1 and V_R are 120.5 kt. and 123 kt.).
   b. Convert field elevation into pressure altitude given the altimeter setting (see Fig. 46 on page 580). Given a field elevation of 2,500 ft. and an altimeter setting of 30.48, the correction factor is −500 ft.
   c. Using pressure altitude and temperature, determine the V_1 and V_R airspeed correction with the middle portion of Fig. 47 on page 581. Pressure altitude is on the horizontal scale, and temperature on the vertical scale. The intersection determines the density altitude (pressure altitude corrected for temperature) V_1 and V_R adjustment.
      1) EXAMPLE: At 2,000 ft. and 60°F, the adjustment is +2 kt. for both V_1 and V_R.
   d. Adjust for runway slope, either uphill or downhill, using the bottom of Fig. 47 on page 581 (e.g., add 1.5 kt. to V_1 and .9 kt. to V_R for every +1% of runway slope).
   e. Adjust for headwind or tailwind; i.e., add .3 kt. to V_1 for every 10 kt. of headwind, and subtract .8 kt. from V_1 for every 10 kt. of tailwind.
   f. Adjust for engine and airplane ice protection only if both are being used; i.e., add .8 kt. to both V_1 and V_R.

12.4 STAB TRIM SETTING (Questions 16-20)

1. The five questions for this module require STAB TRIM setting (stabilizer trim setting) given certain operating conditions.
2. The bottom line in Fig. 45 on page 579 states, "CG% MAC = STAB TRIM setting."
   a. This statement means that the trim setting at takeoff should be set to the CG.
3. Thus, you must compute CG as a percent of MAC.
4. Remember, LEMAC is the leading edge of the mean aerodynamic chord.
5. **Steps to Compute % MAC**
   a. Subtract LEMAC from the CG station to determine the CG station aft of MAC.
   b. Divide MAC into the distance that CG is aft of LEMAC.
6. EXAMPLE: MAC 141.5 in., LEMAC 549.13 in., CG station 590.2 in. Thus, the CG is 41.07 in. aft of LEMAC (590.2 – 549.13 = 41.07). Then compute percent MAC using the following formula:

$$\frac{CG}{MAC} = \frac{41.07}{141.5} = .290 \textit{ or } 29\%\ MAC$$

   Thus, the STAB TRIM setting should be 29% of MAC.

12.5 DISTANCE DURING CLIMB (Questions 21-25)

1. The five questions for this module require the ground distance during climb.
2. Two climb schedule charts are provided: long range (LR) and high speed (HS). See Figs. 49 and 50 on pages 586 and 587. Each chart has
   a. Initial weight
   b. Cruise pressure altitude

3. **Steps to Determine Ground Distance during En Route Climb**
   a. Choose either the LR or HS climb schedule chart.
   b. Find the time and distance to climb in still air based on initial weight and cruise pressure altitude.
   c. Compute the groundspeed in still air:

$$\frac{\textit{Distance (NM)}}{\textit{Time (min.)}} \times 60 = \textit{Groundspeed}$$

   d. Determine distance change caused by headwind or tailwind:

$$\textit{Dist. change} = \frac{\textit{NM} \times \textit{Wind component}}{\textit{TAS}}$$

   e. Compute ground distance covered by adjusting distance from climb schedule chart by
      1) Subtracting "dist. change" if a headwind
      2) Adding "dist. change" if a tailwind
4. EXAMPLE: Climb distance and time: 109.7 NM and 17.1 min. -- 20 kt. headwind
   a. Compute groundspeed of 385 kt. in still air [109.7 ÷ (17.1 ÷ 60)].
   b. Determine distance change due to 20-kt. headwind.

$$\frac{(109.7\ \textit{NM}) \times (20\ \textit{kts. HW})}{385\ \textit{kt. (Groundspeed)}} = 5.69\ \textit{NM}$$

   Subtract 5.69 NM from 109.7 NM to equal 104 NM.

12.6 WEIGHT AFTER CLIMB (Questions 26-30)

1. The weight after climb is the initial weight less fuel burn during climb.
2. Use the same climb schedule charts (Figs. 49 and 50) as for computing distance to climb.
3. The climb schedule charts indicate the fuel burn to altitude.
4. Subtract fuel burn from initial weight.
5. Headwind or tailwind does not affect fuel burn.

12.7 ALTERNATE PLANNING (Questions 31-35)

1. Time to fly to an alternate is based on an alternate planning chart. See Fig. 52 on page 591.
2. The alternate planning chart is based on distance to alternate. For each distance, there is a(n)
   a. Optimal attitude
   b. Time
   c. Fuel burn
   d. Optimal TAS
3. Distance is given as NAM (nautical air miles).
   a. NAM has already been determined by dividing the TAS by the GS (using wind and temperature at altitude) and multiplying this amount by the nautical ground miles (NGM), or *NAM = NGM × (TAS ÷ GS)*.
      1) Thus, NAM accounts for the wind component.
   b. You will NOT be required to do this on the test.

4. There are two notes to the chart:
   a. Fuel includes ½ climb distance en route credit, fuel to cruise remaining distance at LRC (long-range cruise) schedule, 15 min. holding at alternate, and 800 lb. for descent.
   b. Time includes ½ climb distance credit, time to cruise distance shown at LRC schedule, and 8 min. for descent. 15 min. holding is not included in time.
5. **Steps to Find the Time to Fly to the Alternate**
   a. Given the distance to the alternate, find the time by using Fig. 52.
   b. Add together
      1) Original time
      2) Holding time at alternate
6. EXAMPLE: What is the total time from starting to the alternate through completing the approach for a distance of 110 NAM and 15 min. holding time at the alternate?
   a. Locate 110 NAM on Fig. 52 and move down to determine that the time to the alternate is 29 min.
   b. Add the time to the alternate and the 15-min. holding time to determine the total time of 44 min. (29 + 15).

12.8 LANDING WEIGHT (Questions 36-40)

1. Landing weight is computed with the same alternate planning chart. See Fig. 52 on page 591.
2. Given the distance to the alternate, determine the fuel burned by using Fig. 52.
   a. Note 1 on Fig. 52 states that the fuel includes 15 min. holding at alternate.
3. To determine the landing weight, subtract the fuel burned from the weight when the airplane starts to the alternate, which is given in Fig. 51 on page 591.
4. EXAMPLE: What is the approximate landing weight at an alternate at a distance of 110 NAM and a starting weight of 85,000 lb.
   a. Locate 110 NAM on Fig. 52 and move down to determine that the fuel burned is 3,400 lb.
   b. The landing weight is 81,600 lb. (85,000 – 3,400).

QUESTIONS AND ANSWER EXPLANATIONS

All the FAA questions from the pilot knowledge test for the ATP certificate relating to the DC-9 operating/performance data and the material outlined previously are reproduced on the following pages in the same modules as the outlines. To the immediate right of, or below, each question are the correct answer and answer explanation. You should cover these answers and answer explanations while responding to the questions. Refer to the general discussion in Chapter 1 on how to take the FAA pilot knowledge test.

Remember that the questions from the FAA pilot knowledge test bank have been reordered by topic, and the topics are organized into a meaningful sequence. Accordingly, the first line of the answer explanation gives the FAA question number and the citation of the authoritative source for the answer.

12.1 CG after Weight Shift

1.
8573. (Refer to figure 44 below.) What is the new CG if the weight is shifted from the forward to the aft compartment under Loading Conditions WS-1?

A—15.2 percent MAC.
B—29.8 percent MAC.
C—30.0 percent MAC.

Answer (B) is correct (8573). *(PWBH Chap 5)*

This question presents a CG situation and requires you to compute the CG after a weight shift. Note that the weight is shifted from forward to aft. WS-1 on Fig. 44 indicates

Loaded weight	90,000 lb.
Loaded CG (% MAC)	22.5%
Weight shifted	2,500 lb.
FWD compartment	352.1 in.
AFT compartment	724.9 in.
MAC	141.5 in.

$$\textit{CG change (in.)} = \frac{(\textit{Wt. shifted}) \times (\textit{Dist. of shift})}{\textit{Aircraft wt.}} =$$

$$\frac{2{,}500 \times (724.9 - 352.1)}{90{,}000} = \frac{2{,}500 \times 372.8}{90{,}000} =$$

$$\frac{932{,}000}{90{,}000} = 10.36 \textit{ in.}$$

Since this change is from forward to aft, the net change is positive, or +10.36 in. To convert the change in inches to % of MAC, use the following formula:

$$\frac{[(\textit{MAC})(\textit{prev. \% MAC})] \pm (\textit{Net CG change in in.})}{\textit{MAC}} =$$

$$\frac{[(141.5)(.225)] + (10.36)}{141.5} = \frac{31.84 + 10.36}{141.5} =$$

$$\frac{42.2}{141.5} = .298 \textit{ or } 29.8\% \textit{ MAC}$$

Answer (A) is incorrect because 15.2% MAC is the new CG if the weight shift is forward, not aft. Answer (C) is incorrect because 30.0% MAC is the new CG if 2,561 lb., not 2,500 lb., is shifted from the forward to the aft compartment.

LOADING CONDITIONS	WS-1	WS-2	WS-3	WS-4	WS-5
LOADED WEIGHT	90,000	85,000	84,500	81,700	88,300
LOADED CG (% MAC)	22.5%	28.4%	19.8%	30.3%	25.5%
WEIGHT CHANGE (POUNDS)	2,500	1,800	3,000	2,100	3,300

FWD COMPT CENTROID – STA 352.1 AND –227.9 INDEX ARM
AFT COMPT CENTROID – STA 724.9 AND +144.9 INDEX ARM
MAC – 141.5 INCHES, LEMAC – STA 549.13, AND –30.87 INDEX ARM

FIGURE 44.—DC-9 – Weight Shift.

2.
8574. (Refer to figure 44 on page 571.) What is the new CG if the weight is shifted from the aft to the forward compartment under Loading Conditions WS-2?

A—26.1 percent MAC.
B—20.5 percent MAC.
C—22.8 percent MAC.

Answer (C) is correct (8574). *(PWBH Chap 5)*
This question presents a CG situation and requires you to compute the CG after a weight shift. Note the weight is shifted from aft to forward. WS-2 on Fig. 44 indicates

Loaded weight	85,000 lb.
Loaded CG (% MAC)	28.4%
Weight shifted from station 724.9 in. to 352.1 in.	1,800 lb.
MAC	141.5 in.
FWD compartment	352.1 in.
AFT compartment	724.9 in.

$$\textit{CG change (in.)} = \frac{\textit{(Wt. shifted)} \times \textit{(Dist. of shift)}}{\textit{Aircraft wt.}} =$$

$$\frac{1{,}800 \times (724.9 - 352.1)}{85{,}000} = \frac{1{,}800 \times 372.8}{85{,}000} =$$

$$\frac{671{,}040}{85{,}000} = 7.89 \textit{ in.}$$

Since this change is from aft to forward, the net change is negative, or −7.89 in.

To convert the change in inches to % of MAC, use the following formula:

$$\frac{[\textit{(MAC) (prev. \% MAC)}] \pm \textit{(Net CG change in in.)}}{\textit{MAC}} =$$

$$\frac{[(141.5)(.284)] - (7.89)}{141.5} = \frac{32.296}{141.5} =$$

$$.228 \textit{ or } 22.8\% \textit{ MAC}$$

Answer (A) is incorrect because 26.1% MAC is the new CG if 742 lb., not 1,800 lb., is shifted from the aft to the forward compartment. Answer (B) is incorrect because 20.5% MAC is the new CG if 2,549 lb., not 1,800 lb., is shifted from the aft to the forward compartment.

3.
8575. (Refer to figure 44 on page 571.) What is the new CG if the weight is shifted from the forward to the aft compartment under Loading Conditions WS-3?

A—29.2 percent MAC.
B—33.0 percent MAC.
C—28.6 percent MAC.

Answer (A) is correct (8575). *(PWBH Chap 5)*
This question presents a CG situation and requires you to compute the CG after a weight shift. Note that the weight is shifted from forward to aft. WS-3 on Fig. 44 indicates

Loaded weight	84,500 lb.
Loaded CG (% MAC)	19.8%
Weight shifted	3,000 lb.
FWD compartment	352.1 in.
AFT compartment	724.9 in.
MAC	141.5 in.

$$\textit{CG change (in.)} = \frac{\textit{(Wt. shifted)} \times \textit{(Dist. of shift)}}{\textit{Aircraft wt.}} =$$

$$\frac{3{,}000 \times (724.9 - 352.1)}{84{,}500} = \frac{3{,}000 \times 372.8}{84{,}500} =$$

$$\frac{1{,}118{,}400}{84{,}500} = 13.24 \textit{ in.}$$

Since this change is from forward to aft, the net change is positive, or +13.24 in. To convert the change in inches to % of MAC, use the following formula:

$$\frac{[\textit{(MAC) (prev. \% MAC)}] \pm \textit{(Net CG change in in.)}}{\textit{MAC}} =$$

$$\frac{[(141.5)(.198)] + (13.24)}{141.5} =$$

$$\frac{28.02 + 13.24}{141.5} = \frac{41.26}{141.5} =$$

$$.292 \textit{ or } 29.2\% \textit{ MAC}$$

Answer (B) is incorrect because 33.0% MAC is the new CG if 4,233 lb., not 3,000 lb., is shifted from the forward to the aft compartment. Answer (C) is incorrect because 28.6% MAC is the new CG if 2,822 lb., not 3,000 lb., is shifted from the forward to the aft compartment.

4.
8576. (Refer to figure 44 on page 571.) What is the new CG if the weight is shifted from the aft to the forward compartment under Loading Conditions WS-4?

A—37.0 percent MAC.
B—23.5 percent MAC.
C—24.1 percent MAC.

Answer (B) is correct (8576). *(PWBH Chap 5)*

This question presents a CG situation and requires you to compute the CG after a weight shift. Note that the weight is shifted from aft to forward. WS-4 on Fig. 44 indicates

Loaded weight	81,700 lb.
Loaded CG (% MAC)	30.3%
Weight shifted	2,100 lb.
MAC	141.5 in.
FWD compartment	352.1 in.
AFT compartment	724.9 in.

$$\textit{CG change (in.)} = \frac{(\textit{Wt. shifted}) \times (\textit{Dist. of shift})}{\textit{Aircraft wt.}} =$$

$$\frac{2{,}100 \times (724.9 - 352.1)}{81{,}700} = \frac{2{,}100 \times 372.8}{81{,}700} =$$

$$\frac{782{,}880}{81{,}700} = 9.58 \textit{ in.}$$

Since this change is from aft to forward, the net change is negative, or −9.58 in.

To convert the change in inches to % of MAC, use the following formula:

$$\frac{[(\textit{MAC})(\textit{prev. \% MAC})] \pm (\textit{Net CG change in in.})}{\textit{MAC}} =$$

$$\frac{[(141.5)(.303)] - (9.58)}{141.5} =$$

$$\frac{33.30}{141.5} = .235 \textit{ or } 23.5\% \textit{ MAC}$$

Answer (A) is incorrect because 37.0% MAC is the new CG if 2,100 lb. is shifted from the forward to the aft, not the aft to the forward, compartment. Answer (C) is incorrect because 24.1% MAC is the new CG if 1,923 lb., not 2,100 lb., is shifted from the aft to the forward compartment.

5.
8577. (Refer to figure 44 on page 571.) Where is the new CG if the weight is shifted from the forward to the aft compartment under Loading Conditions WS-5?

A— +19.15 index arm.
B— +13.93 index arm.
C— −97.92 index arm.

Answer (A) is correct (8577). *(PWBH Chap 5)*

This question presents a CG situation and requires you to compute the CG after a weight shift. Note that the weight is shifted from the forward to the aft compartment. WS-5 on Fig. 44 indicates

Loaded weight	88,300 lb.
Loaded CG	25.5% MAC
Weight shifted	3,300 lb.
MAC	141.5 in.
LEMAC	−30.87 index arm
FWD compartment	352.1 in.
AFT compartment	724.9 in.

Find original CG index arm:

MAC	=	141.5 in.
CG % MAC	=	x .255
CG aft of LEMAC	=	36.08 in.
LEMAC index arm	=	+(−30.87)
Orig. CG index arm	=	5.21

$$\textit{CG change (in.)} = \frac{(\textit{Wt. shifted}) \times (\textit{Dist. of shift})}{\textit{Aircraft wt.}} =$$

$$\frac{3{,}300 \times (724.9 - 352.1)}{88{,}300} = \frac{3{,}300 \times 372.8}{88{,}300} =$$

$$\frac{1{,}230{,}240}{88{,}300} = 13.93 \textit{ in.}$$

Since this change is from forward to aft, the net change is positive, or +13.93 in. Thus, the new CG is +19.14 index arm (5.21 + 13.93).

Answer (B) is incorrect because +13.93 is the net change in CG, not the new CG. Answer (C) is incorrect because, when weight is shifted aft, the CG also shifts aft, not forward.

12.2 CG after Weight Change

6.
8578. (Refer to figure 44 on page 571.) What is the new CG if the weight is removed from the forward compartment under Loading Conditions WS-1?

A—27.1 percent MAC.
B—26.8 percent MAC.
C—30.0 percent MAC.

Answer (A) is correct (8578). *(PWBH Chap 5)*

Note that 2,500 lb. is to be removed from the forward compartment. (See Fig. 44.) The forward compartment is Station 352.1. WS-1 on Fig. 44 indicates an aircraft weight of 90,000 lb. and a loaded CG as 22.5% MAC. First convert 22.5% MAC to a station number. MAC is given as 141.5 in. and 22.5% of it is +31.83 in. Add LEMAC of 549.13 to get the CG of 580.96 in. (549.13 + 31.83). Then use conventional weight/balance formulas:

Item	Wt./1,000	Index Arm	Mom./1,000
Aircraft wt.	90.0	580.96	52,286.40
Cargo removed	–2.5	352.1	–880.25
	87.5		51,406.15

$$CG = \frac{\textit{Total moment}}{\textit{Total wt.}} = \frac{51{,}406.15}{87.5} = 587.50 \textit{ in.}$$

Subtracting LEMAC (549.13), we can obtain the new CG of 38.37 in. aft of LEMAC (587.5 – 549.13). Use the following formula to obtain % MAC:

$$\% \, MAC = \frac{CG}{MAC} = \frac{38.37}{141.5} = 27.1\% \, MAC$$

Answer (B) is incorrect because CG moves farther back than 26.8% MAC. Answer (C) is incorrect because CG does not move as far back as 30.0% MAC.

7.
8579. (Refer to figure 44 on page 571.) Where is the new CG if the weight is added to the aft compartment under Loading Conditions WS-2?

A—+17.06 index arm.
B—+14.82 index arm.
C—+12.13 index arm.

Answer (C) is correct (8579). *(PWBH Chap 5)*

Note the weight is added to the aft compartment. WS-2 on Fig. 44 indicates

Loaded weight	85,000 lb.
Loaded CG (% MAC)	28.4%
Weight added to Station 724.9 in. aft cargo compartment	1,800 lb.
MAC	141.5 in.
Aft compartment arm	+144.9 index arm
LEMAC	–30.87 index arm

Find original CG index arm:

MAC	=	141.5 in.
CG % MAC	=	x .284
CG aft of LEMAC	=	40.19 in.
LEMAC index arm	=	+(–30.87)
Orig. CG index arm	=	9.32

Item	Wt./1,000	Index Arm	Mom./1,000
Aircraft wt.	85.0	9.32	792.20
Wt. added	+1.8	144.9	260.82
	86.8		1,053.02

$$New\ CG = \frac{\textit{Total moment}}{\textit{Total wt.}} = \frac{1{,}053.02}{86.8} = +12.13 \textit{ index arm}$$

Answer (A) is incorrect because CG does not move as far back as the +17.06 index arm. Answer (B) is incorrect because CG does not move as far back as the +14.82 index arm.

8.
8580. (Refer to figure 44 on page 571.) What is the new CG if the weight is added to the forward compartment under Loading Conditions WS-3?

A—11.4 percent MAC.
B—14.3 percent MAC.
C—14.5 percent MAC.

Answer (B) is correct (8580). *(PWBH Chap 5)*
Note that 3,000 lb. is to be added to the forward compartment. (See Fig. 44.) The forward compartment is Station 352.1. WS-3 on Fig. 44 indicates an aircraft weight of 84,500 lb. and a loaded CG as 19.8% MAC. First convert 19.8% MAC to a station number. MAC is given as 141.5 in., and 19.8% of it is 28.02 in. Add the LEMAC station of 549.13 in. to get the CG of 577.15 in. (549.13 + 28.02). Then use conventional weight/balance formulas:

Item	Wt./1,000	Station	Mom./1,000
Aircraft wt.	84.5	577.15	48,769.18
Weight change	3.0	352.1	1,056.30
	87.5		49,825.48

$$CG\ station = \frac{Total\ moment}{Total\ wt.} = \frac{49{,}825.48}{87.5} = 569.43\ in.$$

Subtracting the LEMAC station (549.13), we can obtain the new CG of 20.3 in. aft of LEMAC (569.43 – 549.13). Use the following formula to obtain % MAC:

$$\%\ MAC = \frac{CG}{MAC} = \frac{20.3}{141.5} = 14.3\%\ MAC$$

Answer (A) is incorrect because CG does not move as far forward as 11.4% MAC. Answer (C) is incorrect because CG moves farther forward than 14.5% MAC.

9.
8581. (Refer to figure 44 on page 571.) Where is the new CG if the weight is removed from the aft compartment under Loading Conditions WS-4?

A— +15.53 index arm.
B— +8.50 index arm.
C— -93.51 index arm.

Answer (B) is correct (8581). *(PWBH Chap 5)*
Note the weight is removed from the aft compartment. WS-4 on Fig. 44 indicates

Loaded weight	81,700 lb.
Loaded CG (% MAC)	30.3%
Weight removed from Station 724.9 in.	2,100 lb.
MAC	141.5 in.
Aft compartment	+144.9 index arm
LEMAC	–30.87 index arm

Find original CG index arm:

MAC	=	141.5 in.
CG % MAC	=	x .303
CG aft of LEMAC	=	42.87 in.
LEMAC index arm	=	+(–30.87)
Orig. CG index arm	=	12.00

Using conventional Weight x Arm = Moment formula, the index arm can be computed.

Item	Wt./1,000	Index Arm	Mom./1,000
Aircraft wt.	81.7	12.0	980.40
Wt. removed	–2.1	144.90	–304.29
	79.6		676.11

$$New\ CG = \frac{Total\ moment}{Total\ wt.} = \frac{676.11}{79.6} = +8.50\ index\ arm$$

Answer (A) is incorrect because the CG moves forward, not backward. Answer (C) is incorrect because more than 2,100 lb. would have to be removed from the aft compartment to have a new CG index arm of –3.51.

10.
8582. (Refer to figure 44 on page 571.) What is the new CG if the weight is removed from the forward compartment under Loading Conditions WS-5?

A—31.9 percent MAC.
B—19.1 percent MAC.
C—35.2 percent MAC.

Answer (A) is correct (8582). *(PWBH Chap 5)*

Note that 3,300 lb. is to be removed from the forward compartment. (See Fig. 44.) The forward compartment is Station 352.1. WS-5 on Fig. 44 indicates an aircraft weight of 88,300 lb. and a loaded CG as 25.5% MAC. First convert 25.5% MAC to a station number. MAC is given as 141.5 in. and 25.5% of it is 36.08 in. Add the LEMAC station of 549.13 in. to get the CG of 585.21 in. (549.13 + 36.08). Then use conventional weight/balance formulas:

Item	Wt./1,000	Station	Mom./1,000
Aircraft wt.	88.3	585.21	51,674.04
Weight change	–3.3	352.1	–1,161.93
	85.0		50,512.11

$$CG\ station = \frac{Total\ moment}{Total\ wt.} = \frac{50{,}512.11}{85.0} = 594.26\ in.$$

Subtracting the LEMAC station (549.13), we can obtain the new CG station of 45.13 in. aft of LEMAC (594.26 – 549.13). Use the following formula to obtain % MAC:

$$\%\ MAC = \frac{CG}{MAC} = \frac{45.13}{141.5} = 31.9\%\ MAC$$

Answer (B) is incorrect because CG moves backward, not forward. Answer (C) is incorrect because CG does not move as far backward as 35.2% MAC.

12.3 V_1 and V_R Speeds

11.
8583. (Refer to figures 45, 46, and 47 on pages 579, 580, and 581.) What are V_1 and V_R speeds for Operating Conditions A-1?

A—V_1 123.1 knots; V_R 125.2 knots.
B—V_1 120.5 knots; V_R 123.5 knots.
C—V_1 122.3 knots; V_R 124.1 knots.

Answer (A) is correct (8583). *(FTW Chap 8)*

Weight determines V_1 and V_R for DC-9s, after which you must adjust for pressure altitude and temperature, runway slope, wind, and ice protection.

A-1 of Fig. 45 indicates

Field elevation	2,500 ft.
Altimeter setting	29.40 in.
Weight (x 1,000)	75
Ambient temperature	+10°F
Runway slope %	+1%
Wind component	10 HW
Ice protection	Both

1. Adjust the field elevation of 2,500 ft. in A-1 by +500 due to the altimeter setting of 29.40 being in the 29.34-to-29.44 range on Fig. 46. Thus, the pressure altitude is 3,000 ft. (2,500 ft. + 500 ft.). Use Fig. 47 for the remaining steps.

	V_1	V_R
2. Find 75,000-lb. takeoff speeds.	120.5	123.5
3. Adjust for temperature and pressure alt. (10°F and 3,000 ft.).	0	0
4. Adjust for 1% uphill slope.	1.5	0.9
5. Adjust for 10-kt. headwind.	0.3	0
6. Adjust for ice protection.	0.8	0.8
Corrected speeds (kt.)	123.1	125.2

Answer (B) is incorrect because V_1 120.5 kt. and V_R 123.5 kt. are the takeoff speeds without any corrections applied. Answer (C) is incorrect because V_1 122.3 kt. and V_R 124.1 kt. are not corrected for engine and airplane ice protection.

12.
8584. (Refer to figure 45, 46, and 47 on pages 579, 580, and 581.) What are V_1 and V_R speeds for Operating Conditions A-2?

A—V_1 129.7 knots; V_R 134.0 knots.
B—V_1 127.2 knots; V_R 133.2 knots.
C—V_1 127.4 knots; V_R 133.6 knots.

Answer (C) is correct (8584). *(FTW Chap 8)*
Weight determines V_1 and V_R for DC-9s, after which you must adjust for pressure altitude and temperature, runway slope, wind, and ice protection.
A-2 of Fig. 45 indicates

Field elevation	600
Altimeter setting	30.50 in.
Weight (x 1,000)	85
Ambient temperature	+80°F
Runway slope %	–1.5%
Wind component	10 TW
Ice protection	None

1. Adjust the field elevation of 600 ft. in A-2 by –500 due to the altimeter setting of 30.50 being in the 30.41-to-30.52 range on Fig. 46. Thus, the pressure altitude is 100 ft. (600 ft. – 500 ft.). Use Fig. 47 for the remaining steps.

	V_1	V_R
2. Find 85,000-lb. takeoff speeds (kt.).	129.5	134.0
3. Adjust for temperature and pressure alt. (80°F and 100 ft.).	+1.0	+1.0
4. Adjust for 1.5° downhill RW slope.	–2.25	–1.35
5. Adjust for 10-kt. tailwind.	–.8	0
6. Adjust for ice protection.	NA	NA
Corrected speeds (kt.)	127.4	133.6

Answer (A) is incorrect because 134.0 kt. is V_R before any corrections have been made. Answer (B) is incorrect because 127.2 kt. is V_1 for a –1.0%, not –1.5%, runway slope.

13.
8585. (Refer to figures 45, 46, and 47 on pages 579, 580, and 581.) What are V_1 and V_R speeds for Operating Conditions A-3?

A—V_1 136.8 knots; V_R 141.8 knots.
B—V_1 134.8 knots; V_R 139.0 knots.
C—V_1 133.5 knots; V_R 141.0 knots.

Answer (A) is correct (8585). *(FTW Chap 8)*
Weight determines V_1 and V_R for DC-9s, after which you must adjust for pressure altitude and temperature, runway slope, wind, and ice protection.
A-3 of Fig. 45 indicates

Field elevation	4,200 ft.
Altimeter setting	1020 mb
Weight (x 1,000)	90
Ambient temperature	0°C
Runway slope %	0
Wind component	15 HW
Ice protection	Both

1. Adjust the field elevation of 4,200 ft. in A-3 by –200 ft. due to the altimeter setting of 1020 being in the 1019-to-1022 mb range on Fig. 46. Thus, the pressure altitude is 4,000 ft. (4,200 ft. – 200 ft.). Use Fig. 47 for the remaining steps.

	V_1	V_R
2. Find 90,000-lb. takeoff speeds (kt.).	133.5	139.0
3. Adjust for temperature and pressure alt. (0°C and 4,000 ft.).	+2.0	+2.0
4. Adjust for RW slope.	0	0
5. Adjust for 15-kt. headwind.	+.45	0
6. Adjust for ice protection.	+.8	+.8
Corrected speeds (kt.)	136.75	141.8

Answer (B) is incorrect because 139.0 kt. is V_R uncorrected. Answer (C) is incorrect because 133.5 kt. is V_1 uncorrected.

14.
8586. (Refer to figures 45, 46, and 47 on pages 579, 580, and 581.) What are V_1 and V_R speeds for Operating Conditions A-4?

A—V_1 128.0 knots; V_R 130.5 knots.
B—V_1 129.9 knots; V_R 133.4 knots.
C—V_1 128.6 knots; V_R 131.1 knots.

Answer (B) is correct (8586). *(FTW Chap 8)*
Weight determines V_1 and V_R for DC-9s, after which you must adjust for pressure altitude and temperature, runway slope, wind, and ice protection. Note that engine-only ice protection requires no correction.
A-4 of Fig. 45 indicates

Field elevation	5,100 ft.
Altimeter setting	29.35 in.
Weight (x 1,000)	80
Ambient temperature	+30°F
Runway slope %	+1.5%
Wind component	5 TW
Ice protection	Engine only

1. Adjust the field elevation of 5,100 ft. in A-4 by +500 due to the altimeter setting of 29.35 being in the 29.34-to-29.44 range on Fig. 46. Thus, the pressure altitude is 5,600 ft. (5,100 ft. + 500 ft.). Use Fig. 47 for the remaining steps.

	V_1	V_R
2. Find 80,000-lb. takeoff speeds (kt.).	125.0	129.0
3. Adjust for temperature and pressure alt. (30°F and 5,600 ft.).	+3.0	+3.0
4. Adjust for 1.5° uphill RW slope.	+2.25	+1.35
5. Adjust for 5-kt. tailwind.	–.4	0
6. Adjust for ice protection.	0	0
Corrected speeds (kt.)	129.85	133.35

Answer (A) is incorrect because 128 kt. is V_1 before runway slope and tailwind adjustments. Answer (C) is incorrect because V_1 and V_R are higher than 128.6 kt. and 131.1 kt., respectively.

15.
8587. (Refer to figures 45, 46, and 47 on pages 579, 580, and 581.) What are V_1 and V_R speeds for Operating Conditions A-5?

A—V_1 110.4 knots; V_R 110.9 knots.
B—V_1 109.6 knots; V_R 112.7 knots.
C—V_1 106.4 knots; V_R 106.4 knots.

Answer (B) is correct (8587). *(FTW Chap 8)*
Weight determines V_1 and V_R for DC-9s, after which you must adjust for pressure altitude and temperature, runway slope, wind, and ice protection.
A-5 of Fig. 45 indicates

Field elevation	2,100 ft.
Altimeter setting	1035 mb
Weight (x 1,000)	65
Ambient temperature	+20°C
Runway slope %	–2%
Wind component	20 HW
Ice protection	None

1. Adjust the field elevation of 2,100 ft. in A-5 by –600 ft. due to the altimeter setting of 1035 mb being in the 1034-to-1037 mb range on Fig. 46. Thus, the pressure altitude is 1,500 ft. (2,100 ft. – 600 ft.). Use Fig. 47 for the remaining steps.

	V_1	V_R
2. Find 65,000-lb. takeoff speeds (kt.).	110.0	112.5
3. Adjust for temperature and pressure alt. (20°C and 1,500 ft.).	+2.0	+2.0
4. Adjust for 2% downhill RW slope.	–3.0	–1.8
5. Adjust for 10-kt. headwind.	+.60	0
6. Adjust for ice protection.	0	0
Corrected speeds (kt.)	109.6	112.7

Answer (A) is incorrect because V_1 is less than 110.4 kt. and V_R is less than 110.9 kt. Answer (C) is incorrect because both V_1 and V_R are above 106.4 kt.

OPERATING CONDITIONS	A-1	A-2	A-3	A-4	A-5
FIELD ELEVATION	2,500	600	4,200	5,100	2,100
ALTIMETER SETTING	29.40"	30.50"	1020mb	29.35"	1035mb
AMBIENT TEMPERATURE	+10 °F	+80 °F	0 °C	+30 °F	+20 °C
WEIGHT (X1000)	75	85	90	80	65
FLAP POSITION	20°	20°	20°	20°	20°
RUNWAY SLOPE %	+1%	–1.5%	0	+1.5%	–2%
WIND COMPONENT	10 HW	10 TW	15 HW	5 TW	20 HW
ICE PROTECTION	BOTH	NONE	BOTH	ENGINE	NONE
CG STATION	590.2	—	580.3	—	594.4
CG INDEX ARM	—	–3.1	—	+5.9	—
INDEX ARM REF – STA 580.0, LEMAC – STA 549.13, AND –30.87 INDEX, MAC 141.5 CG % MAC = STAB TRIM SETTING					

FIGURE 45.—DC-9 – Takeoff.

ALTIMETER SETTING TO STATION PRESSURE

QFE STATION PRESSURE

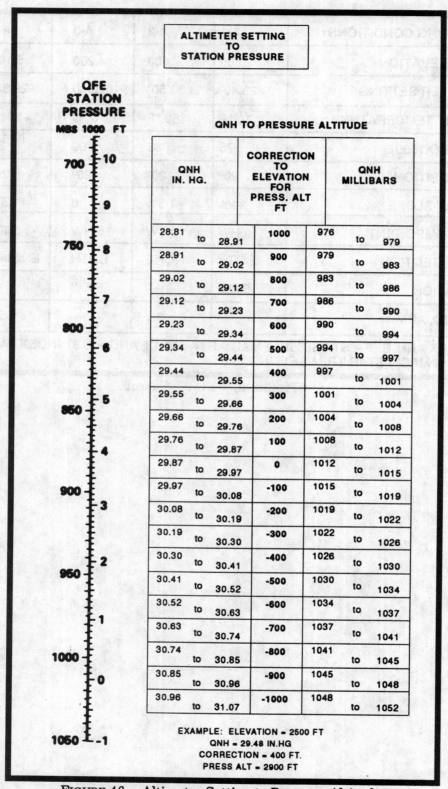

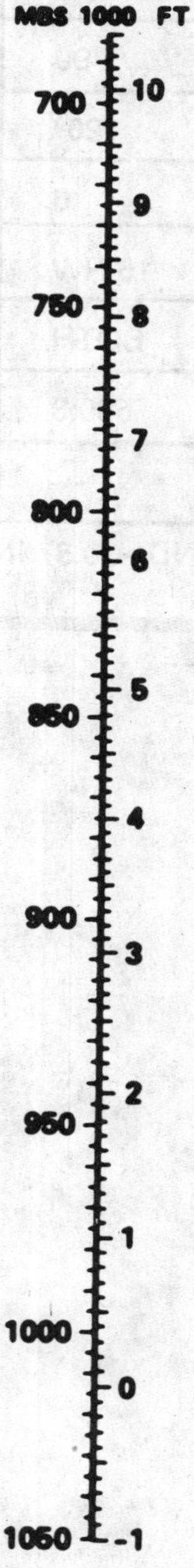

QNH TO PRESSURE ALTITUDE

QNH IN. HG.			CORRECTION TO ELEVATION FOR PRESS. ALT FT	QNH MILLIBARS		
28.81	to	28.91	1000	976	to	979
28.91	to	29.02	900	979	to	983
29.02	to	29.12	800	983	to	986
29.12	to	29.23	700	986	to	990
29.23	to	29.34	600	990	to	994
29.34	to	29.44	500	994	to	997
29.44	to	29.55	400	997	to	1001
29.55	to	29.66	300	1001	to	1004
29.66	to	29.76	200	1004	to	1008
29.76	to	29.87	100	1008	to	1012
29.87	to	29.97	0	1012	to	1015
29.97	to	30.08	-100	1015	to	1019
30.08	to	30.19	-200	1019	to	1022
30.19	to	30.30	-300	1022	to	1026
30.30	to	30.41	-400	1026	to	1030
30.41	to	30.52	-500	1030	to	1034
30.52	to	30.63	-600	1034	to	1037
30.63	to	30.74	-700	1037	to	1041
30.74	to	30.85	-800	1041	to	1045
30.85	to	30.96	-900	1045	to	1048
30.96	to	31.07	-1000	1048	to	1052

EXAMPLE: ELEVATION = 2500 FT
QNH = 29.48 IN.HG
CORRECTION = 400 FT.
PRESS ALT = 2900 FT

FIGURE 46.—Altimeter Setting to Pressure Altitude.

MODEL DC–9
TAKEOFF SPEEDS
JT8D–1 ENGINES

TAKEOFF SPEED – 20 ° FLAPS
EITHER NO ICE PROTECTION OR ENGINE ICE PROTECTION ONLY

TAKEOFF WEIGHT (1000 LB)	60	65	70	75	80	85	90	95
V_1 (KNOTS, IAS)	104.0	110.0	115.0	120.5	125.0	129.5	133.5	136.0
V_R (KNOTS, IAS)	106.5	112.5	118.0	123.5	129.0	134.0	139.0	143.5
V_2 (KNOTS, IAS)	117.0	121.5	126.5	130.5	135.0	139.0	143.0	147.0

CORRECTION TO SPEEDS

		V_1	V_R	V_2
AMBIENT TEMPERATURE AND AIRPORT PRESSURE ALTITUDE		(see chart)	(see chart)	0
SLOPE PER 1%	UPHILL	+ 1.5* KNOTS	+ 0.9 KNOTS	0
	DOWNHILL	– 1.5 KNOTS	– 0.9 KNOTS	
WIND PER 10 KNOTS	HEADWIND	+0.30* KNOTS	0 KNOTS	0
	TAILWIND	–0.8 KNOTS		
ENGINE AND AIRPLANE ICE PROTECTION		+ 0.8 KNOTS	+ 0.8 KNOTS	0

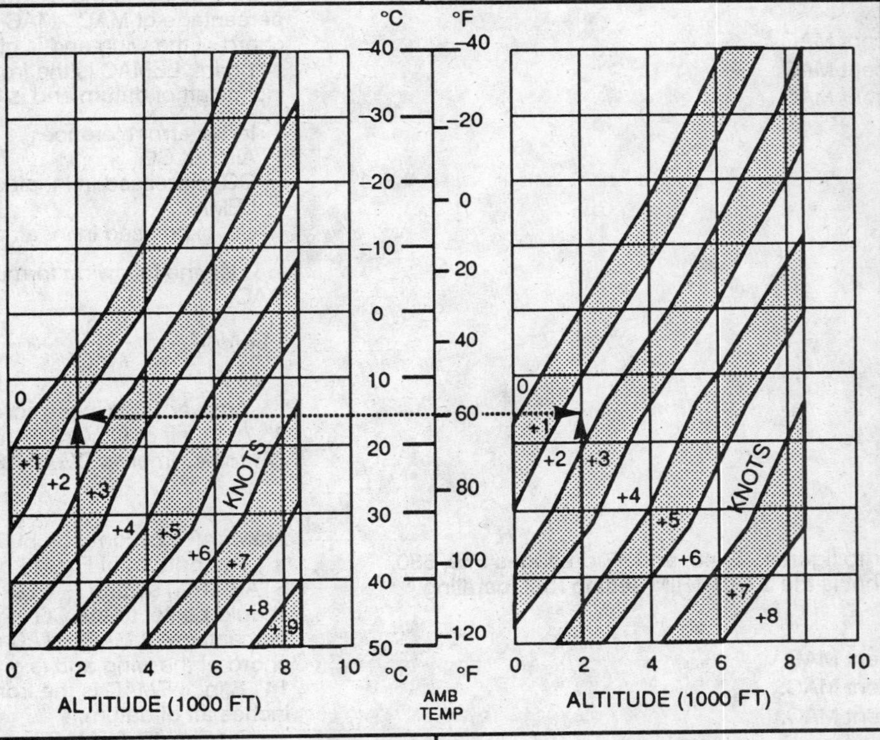

* IF V_1 EXCEEDS V_R, SET V_1 EQUAL TO V_R

FIGURE 47.—DC-9 – Takeoff Speeds.

12.4 STAB TRIM Setting

16.
8588. (Refer to figures 45, 46, and 47 on pages 579, 580, and 581.) What is the STAB TRIM setting for Operating Conditions A-1?

A—29 percent MAC.
B—32 percent MAC.
C—36 percent MAC.

Answer (A) is correct (8588). *(FTW Chap 8)*
The bottom of Fig. 45 has footnote "CG % MAC = STAB TRIM setting." This means trim setting at takeoff should be set to the CG of the wing and is given at the bottom of Fig. 45 as 141.5 in. LEMAC is the front of the wing in terms of inches aft of datum.

On Fig. 45, LEMAC is given as 549.13 in. Under A-1, the CG station is given as 590.2 in. Thus, the CG is 41.07 in. aft of LEMAC (590.2 – 549.13 = 41.07). Then compute percent MAC using the formula:

$$\frac{CG}{MAC} = \frac{41.07}{141.5} = .290 \text{ or } 29\% \text{ MAC}$$

Answer (B) is incorrect because 32% MAC requires a CG station of 45.28 in. aft of LEMAC. Answer (C) is incorrect because 36% MAC requires a CG station of 50.94 in. aft of LEMAC.

17.
8589. (Refer to figures 45, 46, and 47 on pages 579, 580, and 581.) What is the STAB TRIM setting for Operating Conditions A-2?

A—26 percent MAC.
B—20 percent MAC.
C—22 percent MAC.

Answer (B) is correct (8589). *(FTW Chap 8)*
The bottom of Fig. 45 has footnote "CG % MAC = STAB TRIM setting." This means trim setting at takeoff should be set to the CG which is expressed as a percentage of MAC. MAC refers to mean aerodynamic chord of the wing and is given at the bottom of Fig. 45 as 141.5 in. LEMAC is the front of the wing in terms of inches aft of datum and is given as 549.13 in. Given:

Index arm reference	station (in.) 580.0
Aircraft CG	–3.1
CG expressed in in. aft of datum	576.9
LEMAC	–549.13
CG expressed in in. aft of LEMAC	27.77

Use the following formula to convert from inches to % MAC:

$$\% \text{ MAC} = \frac{CG}{MAC} = \frac{27.77}{141.5} = .196 \text{ or } 20\% \text{ MAC}$$

Answer (A) is incorrect because 26% MAC implies CG 36.79 in. aft of LEMAC. Answer (C) is incorrect because 22% MAC implies CG 31.13 in. aft of LEMAC.

18.
8590. (Refer to figures 45, 46, and 47 on pages 579, 580, and 581.) What is the STAB TRIM setting for Operating Conditions A-3?

A—18 percent MAC.
B—20 percent MAC.
C—22 percent MAC.

Answer (C) is correct (8590). *(FTW Chap 8)*
The bottom of Fig. 45 has footnote "CG % MAC = STAB TRIM setting." This means trim setting at takeoff should be set to the CG which is expressed as a percentage of MAC. MAC refers to mean aerodynamic chord of the wing and is given at the bottom of Fig. 45 as 141.5 in. LEMAC is the front of the wing in terms of inches aft of datum.

On Fig. 45, LEMAC is given as 549.13 in. Under A-3, the CG station is given as 580.3. Thus, the CG aft of LEMAC is 31.17 in. (580.3 – 549.13). Then compute percent MAC using the formula:

$$\% \text{ MAC} = \frac{CG}{MAC} = \frac{31.17}{141.5} = .220 \text{ or } 22\% \text{ MAC}$$

Answer (A) is incorrect because 18% MAC requires a CG station of 25.47 in. Answer (B) is incorrect because 20% MAC requires a CG station of 28.3 in.

19.
8591. (Refer to figures 45, 46, and 47 on pages 579, 580, and 581.) What is the STAB TRIM setting for Operating Conditions A-4?

A—26 percent MAC.
B—22 percent MAC.
C—18 percent MAC.

Answer (A) is correct (8591). *(FTW Chap 8)*
The bottom of Fig. 45 has footnote "CG % MAC = STAB TRIM setting." This means trim setting at takeoff should be set to the CG which is expressed as a percentage of MAC. MAC refers to mean aerodynamic chord of the wing and is given at the bottom of Fig. 45 as 141.5 in. LEMAC is the front of the wing in terms of inches aft of datum and is given as 549.13 in.

Index reference	station (in.) 580.0
Aircraft CG	+5.9
CG expressed in in. aft of datum	585.9
LEMAC	–549.13
CG expressed in in. aft of LEMAC	36.77

Use the following formula to convert from inches to % MAC:

$$\% \, MAC = \frac{CG}{MAC} = \frac{36.77}{141.5} = .259 \text{ or } 26\% \, MAC$$

Answer (B) is incorrect because 22% MAC implies CG 31.13 in. aft of LEMAC. Answer (C) is incorrect because 18% MAC implies CG 25.47 in. aft of LEMAC.

20.
8592. (Refer to figures 45, 46, and 47 on pages 579, 580, and 581.) What is the STAB TRIM setting for Operating Conditions A-5?

A—26 percent MAC.
B—30 percent MAC.
C—32 percent MAC.

Answer (C) is correct (8592). *(FTW Chap 8)*
The bottom of Fig. 45 has footnote "CG % MAC = STAB TRIM setting." This means trim setting at takeoff should be set to the CG which is expressed as a percentage of MAC. MAC refers to mean aerodynamic chord of the wing and is given at the bottom of Fig. 45 as 141.5 in. LEMAC is the front of the wing in terms of inches aft of datum.
On Fig. 45, LEMAC is given as 549.13 in. Under A-5, the CG station is given as 594.4. Thus, the CG aft of LEMAC is 45.27 in. (594.4 – 549.13). Then compute percent MAC using the formula:

$$\% \, MAC = \frac{CG}{MAC} = \frac{45.27}{141.5} = .319 \text{ or } 32\% \, MAC$$

Answer (A) is incorrect because 26% MAC requires a CG station of 36.79 in. Answer (B) is incorrect because 30% MAC requires a CG station of 42.45 in.

12.5 Distance during Climb

21.
8593. (Refer to figures 48, 49, and 50 on pages 586 and 587.) What is the ground distance covered during en route climb for Operating Conditions W-1?

A—104.0 NM.
B—99.2 NM.
C—109.7 NM.

Answer (A) is correct (8593). *(FTW Chap 10)*
Chart W-1 on Fig. 48 indicates

Climb schedule	LR (long range)
Initial weight	84,000 lb.
Cruise pressure altitude	34,000 ft.
Headwind component	20 kt.

Fig. 50 is for long-range climb; lower right of chart is for 84,000 lb. initial weight. Under the "Dist. N. Miles" column, 109.7 NM is indicated for 34,000 ft. and time of 17.1 min. Correct for the 20-kt. HW by computing groundspeed of 385 kt. for still air [109.7 NM ÷ (17.1 min. ÷ 60 min./hr.)]. Using the formula of

$$Dist. \ change = \frac{NM \times Wind \ component}{TAS}$$

Gives:

$$\frac{(109.7 \ NM) \times (20 \ kt. \ HW)}{385 \ kt. \ (Groundspeed)} = 5.69 \ NM$$

Subtract (headwind) 5.69 NM from 109.7 NM to equal 104 NM.
Answer (B) is incorrect because 99.2 NM assumes a groundspeed of 348 kt. Answer (C) is incorrect because 109.7 NM is uncorrected for the 20-kt. headwind.

22.
8594. (Refer to figures 48, 49, and 50 on pages 586 and 587.) What is the ground distance covered during en route climb for Operating Conditions W-2?

A—85.8 NM.
B—87.8 NM.
C—79.4 NM.

Answer (C) is correct (8594). *(FTW Chap 10)*
Chart W-2 on Fig. 48 indicates

Climb schedule	HS (high speed)
Initial weight	86,000 lb.
Cruise pressure altitude	28,000 ft.
Headwind component	30 kt.

See Fig. 49. For high-speed climb, the upper left is for 86,000 lb. initial weight. Under the "Dist. N. Miles" column, 85.8 NM is indicated for 28,000 ft. and time of 12.8 min. Correct for the 30 kt. (HW) by computing groundspeed of 402 kt. for still air [85.8 NM ÷ (12.8 min. ÷ 60 min./hr.)]. Using the formula of

$$\textit{Dist. change} = \frac{\textit{NM} \times \textit{Wind component}}{\textit{TAS}}$$

Gives:

$$\frac{(85.8\ \textit{NM}) \times (30\ \textit{kts. HW})}{402\ \textit{kt. (Groundspeed)}} = 6.4\ \textit{NM}$$

Subtract (headwind) 6.4 NM from 85.8 NM to equal 79.4 NM.

Answer (A) is incorrect because 85.8 NM is uncorrected for the 30-kt. HW. Answer (B) is incorrect because 87.8 NM would require a tailwind, not a headwind, of 10 kt.

23.
8595. (Refer to figures 48, 49, and 50 on pages 586 and 587.) What is the ground distance covered during en route climb for Operating Conditions W-3?

A—86.4 NM.
B—84.2 NM.
C—85.1 NM.

Answer (A) is correct (8595). *(FTW Chap 10)*
Chart W-3 on Fig. 48 indicates

Climb schedule	LR (long range)
Initial weight	78,000 lb.
Cruise pressure altitude	32,000 ft.
Tailwind component	10 kt.

See Fig. 50. For long-range climb, the upper left is for 78,000 lb. initial weight. Under the "Dist. N. Miles" column, 84.2 NM is indicated for 32,000 ft. and time of 13.3 min. Correct for the 10 kt. (TW) by computing groundspeed of 380 kt. for still air [84.2 NM ÷ (13.3 min. ÷ 60 min./hr.)]. Using the formula of

$$\textit{Dist. change} = \frac{\textit{NM} \times \textit{Wind component}}{\textit{TAS}}$$

Gives:

$$\frac{(84.2\ \textit{NM}) \times (10\ \textit{kt. TW})}{380\ \textit{kt. (Groundspeed)}} = 2.2\ \textit{NM}$$

Add (tailwind) 2.2 NM to 84.2 NM to equal 86.4 NM.

Answer (B) is incorrect because 84.2 NM is uncorrected for the 10-kt. tailwind. Answer (C) is incorrect because 85.1 NM is the distance with a 4-kt. (not 10-kt.) tailwind.

24.
8596. (Refer to figures 48, 49, and 50 on pages 586 and 587.) What is the ground distance covered during en route climb for Operating Conditions W-4?

A—58.4 NM.
B—61.4 NM.
C—60.3 NM.

Answer (B) is correct (8596). *(FTW Chap 10)*
Chart W-4 on Fig. 48 indicates

Climb schedule	HS (high speed)
Initial weight	88,000 lb.
Cruise pressure altitude	22,000 ft.
Tailwind component	20 kt.

See Fig. 49. For high-speed climb, the lower left is for 88,000 lb. initial weight. Under the "Dist. N. Miles" column, 58.4 NM is indicated for 22,000 ft. and time of 9.1 min. Correct for the 20 kt. (TW) by computing groundspeed of 385 kt. for still air [58.4 NM ÷ (9.1 min. ÷ 60 min./hr.)]. Using the formula of

$$\textit{Dist. change} = \frac{\textit{NM} \times \textit{Wind component}}{\textit{TAS}}$$

Gives:

$$\frac{(58.4\ \textit{NM}) \times (20\ \textit{kt. TW})}{385\ \textit{kt. (Groundspeed)}} = 3.0\ \textit{NM}$$

Add (tailwind) 3.0 NM to 58.4 NM to equal 61.4 NM.
Answer (A) is incorrect because 58.4 NM is uncorrected for the 20-kt. tailwind. Answer (C) is incorrect because 60.3 NM is the distance with a tailwind of 12 (not 20) kt.

25.
8597. (Refer to figures 48, 49, and 50 on pages 586 and 587.) What is the ground distance covered during en route climb for Operating Conditions W-5?

A—68.0 NM.
B—73.9 NM.
C—66.4 NM.

Answer (C) is correct (8597). *(FTW Chap 10)*
Chart W-5 on Fig. 48 indicates

Climb schedule	HS (high speed)
Initial weight	92,000 lb.
Cruise pressure altitude	24,000 ft.
Headwind component	40 kt.

See Fig. 49. For high-speed climb, the lower right is for 92,000 lb. initial weight. Under the "Dist. N. Miles" column, 73.9 NM is indicated for 24,000 ft. and time of 11.3 min. Correct for the 40 kt. (HW) by computing groundspeed of 392 kt. for still air [73.9 NM ÷ (11.3 min. ÷ 60 min./hr.)]. Using the formula of

$$\textit{Dist. change} = \frac{\textit{NM} \times \textit{Wind component}}{\textit{TAS}}$$

Gives:

$$\frac{(73.9\ \textit{NM}) \times (40\ \textit{kt. HW})}{392\ \textit{kt. (Groundspeed)}} = 7.5\ \textit{NM}$$

Subtract (headwind) 7.5 NM from 73.9 NM to equal 66.4 NM.
Answer (A) is incorrect because 68.0 NM is the distance with a headwind of 31 kt., not 40 kt. Answer (B) is incorrect because 73.9 NM is uncorrected for the 30-kt. headwind.

OPERATING CONDITIONS	W-1	W-2	W-3	W-4	W-5
CLIMB SCHEDULE	LR	HS	LR	HS	HS
INITIAL WEIGHT (X1000)	84	86	78	88	92
CRUISE PRESS ALTITUDE	34,000	28,000	32,000	22,000	24,000
ISA TEMPERATURE	ISA	ISA	ISA	ISA	ISA
AVG WIND COMP (KTS)	20 HW	30 HW	10 TW	20 TW	40 HW

FIGURE 48.—DC-9 – En Route Climb.

TIME, FUEL, AND DISTANCE TO CLIMB
JT8D-1 ENGINES - NORMAL BLEED
DC-9 SERIES 10 - HIGH SPEED CLIMB SCHEDULE
CLIMB AT 320 KNOTS IAS TO 23500 FT ALTITUDE THEN CLIMB AT M .74

INITIAL WEIGHT = 86000. POUNDS

PRES. ALT. FEET	TIME MIN.	FUEL BURNED LB.	DIST. N. MI.
0.	0.	0.	0.
2000.	0.5	133.	2.8
4000.	1.1	267.	5.9
6000.	1.7	403.	9.3
8000.	2.3	541.	13.0
10000.	3.0	684.	17.2
12000.	3.8	830.	21.3
14000.	4.6	982.	27.0
16000.	5.5	1141.	32.9
18000.	6.4	1309.	39.6
20000.	7.6	1489.	47.4
22000.	8.8	1684.	56.6
23500.	9.9	1845.	64.7
23500.	9.9	1845.	64.7
24000.	10.2	1886.	66.8
26000.	11.4	2052.	75.9
28000.	12.8	2225.	85.8
30000.	14.3	2410.	97.1
32000.	16.2	2613.	110.3
34000.	18.4	2844.	126.3
36000.	21.4	3136.	147.8

INITIAL WEIGHT = 90000. POUNDS

PRES. ALT. FEET	TIME MIN.	FUEL BURNED LB.	DIST. N. MI.
0.	0.	0.	0.
2000.	0.6	140.	3.0
4000.	1.1	282.	6.3
6000.	1.8	426.	9.8
8000.	2.5	573.	13.8
10000.	3.2	724.	18.2
12000.	4.0	879.	23.1
14000.	4.8	1041.	28.6
16000.	5.8	1211.	34.9
18000.	6.9	1390.	42.1
20000.	8.0	1583.	50.4
22000.	9.4	1793.	60.3
23500.	10.6	1968.	69.1
23500.	10.6	1968.	69.1
24000.	10.9	2013.	71.5
26000.	12.3	2196.	81.5
28000.	13.8	2389.	92.6
30000.	15.5	2598.	105.4
32000.	17.6	2833.	120.6
34000.	20.3	3110.	139.8
36000.	24.3	3494.	168.0

INITIAL WEIGHT = 88000. POUNDS

PRES. ALT. FEET	TIME MIN.	FUEL BURNED LB.	DIST. N. MI.
0.	0.	0.	0.
2000.	0.5	136.	2.9
4000.	1.1	274.	6.1
6000.	1.7	414.	9.6
8000.	2.4	557.	13.4
10000.	3.1	703.	17.7
12000.	3.9	855.	22.5
14000.	4.7	1012.	27.8
16000.	5.6	1176.	33.9
18000.	6.6	1349.	40.8
20000.	7.8	1535.	48.9
22000.	9.1	1738.	58.4
23500.	10.3	1906.	66.9
23500.	10.3	1906.	66.9
24000.	10.6	1949.	69.1
26000.	11.9	2123.	78.6
28000.	13.3	2306.	89.1
30000.	14.9	2502.	101.2
32000.	16.9	2720.	115.3
34000.	19.3	2973.	132.8
36000.	22.7	3304.	157.2

INITIAL WEIGHT = 92000. POUNDS

PRES. ALT. FEET	TIME MIN.	FUEL BURNED LB.	DIST. N. MI.
0.	0.	0.	0.
2000.	0.6	144.	3.1
4000.	1.2	290.	6.4
6000.	1.8	438.	10.1
8000.	2.5	589.	14.2
10000.	3.3	744.	18.7
12000.	4.1	905.	23.8
14000.	5.0	1072.	29.5
16000.	6.0	1247.	36.0
18000.	7.1	1432.	43.4
20000.	8.3	1631.	52.0
22000.	9.7	1850.	62.3
23500.	11.0	2032.	71.5
23500.	11.0	2032.	71.5
24000.	11.3	2079.	73.9
26000.	12.7	2272.	84.4
28000.	14.3	2476.	96.2
30000.	16.2	2693.	109.8
32000.	18.4	2951.	126.2
34000.	21.4	3258.	147.4
36000.	26.1	3713.	181.0

FIGURE 49.—High-Speed Climb Schedule.

TIME, FUEL, AND DISTANCE TO CLIMB
JT8D-1 ENGINES - NORMAL BLEED
DC-9 SERIES 10 - LONG RANGE CLIMB SCHEDULE
CLIMB AT 290 KNOTS IAS TO 26860 FT ALTITUDE THEN CLIMB AT M .72

INITIAL WEIGHT = 78000. POUNDS

PRES. ALT. FEET	TIME MIN.	FUEL BURNED LB.	DIST. N. MI.
0.	0.	0.	0.
2000.	0.5	113.	2.2
4000.	0.9	227.	4.6
6000.	1.5	342.	7.3
8000.	2.0	457.	10.2
10000.	2.6	574.	13.3
12000.	3.2	693.	16.8
14000.	3.9	815.	20.7
16000.	4.6	941.	25.0
18000.	5.4	1070.	29.9
20000.	6.3	1205.	35.4
22000.	7.2	1347.	41.7
24000.	8.3	1498.	49.0
26000.	9.5	1661.	57.6
26860.	10.1	1736.	61.8
26860.	10.1	1736.	61.8
28000.	10.7	1813.	66.2
30000.	11.9	1953.	74.6
32000.	13.3	2102.	84.2
34000.	14.9	2267.	95.4
36000.	16.9	2456.	109.2

INITIAL WEIGHT = 82000. POUNDS

PRES. ALT. FEET	TIME MIN.	FUEL BURNED LB.	DIST. N. MI.
0.	0.	0.	0.
2000.	0.5	120.	2.4
4000.	1.0	241.	4.9
6000.	1.5	363.	7.7
8000.	2.1	486.	10.8
10000.	2.7	610.	14.2
12000.	3.4	737.	17.9
14000.	4.1	868.	22.1
16000.	4.9	1002.	26.7
18000.	5.7	1141.	31.9
20000.	6.7	1286.	37.9
22000.	7.7	1439.	44.6
24000.	8.9	1602.	52.5
26000.	10.2	1780.	61.9
26860.	10.9	1863.	66.5
26860.	10.9	1863.	66.5
28000.	11.6	1948.	71.4
30000.	12.9	2104.	80.8
32000.	14.4	2274.	91.7
34000.	16.3	2464.	104.6
36000.	18.7	2693.	121.3

INITIAL WEIGHT = 80000. POUNDS

PRES. ALT. FEET	TIME MIN.	FUEL BURNED LB.	DIST. N. MI.
0.	0.	0.	0.
2000.	0.5	117.	2.3
4000.	1.0	234.	4.8
6000.	1.5	352.	7.5
8000.	2.1	471.	10.5
10000.	2.7	592.	13.7
12000.	3.3	715.	17.4
14000.	4.0	841.	21.4
16000.	4.7	971.	25.9
18000.	5.6	1105.	30.9
20000.	6.5	1245.	36.6
22000.	7.5	1392.	43.2
24000.	8.6	1549.	50.7
26000.	9.9	1719.	59.7
26860.	10.5	1798.	64.1
26860.	10.5	1798.	64.1
28000.	11.1	1879.	68.7
30000.	12.4	2027.	77.7
32000.	13.8	2186.	87.8
34000.	15.6	2362.	99.8
36000.	17.7	2570.	114.9

INITIAL WEIGHT = 84000. POUNDS

PRES. ALT. FEET	TIME MIN.	FUEL BURNED LB.	DIST. N. MI.
0.	0.	0.	0.
2000.	0.5	124.	2.4
4000.	1.0	248.	5.1
6000.	1.6	374.	8.0
8000.	2.2	500.	11.1
10000.	2.8	629.	14.6
12000.	3.5	760.	18.5
14000.	4.2	894.	22.8
16000.	5.1	1033.	27.6
18000.	5.9	1177.	33.0
20000.	6.9	1327.	39.1
22000.	8.0	1486.	46.2
24000.	9.2	1656.	54.4
26000.	10.6	1841.	64.1
26860.	11.3	1928.	69.0
26860.	11.3	1928.	69.0
28000.	12.0	2018.	74.1
30000.	13.4	2183.	84.1
32000.	15.0	2364.	95.7
34000.	17.1	2570.	109.7
36000.	19.7	2826.	128.3

FIGURE 50.—Long-Range Climb Schedule.

12.6 Weight after Climb

26.
8598. (Refer to figures 48, 49, and 50 on pages 586 and 587.) What is the aircraft weight at the top of climb for Operating Conditions W-1?

A—81,600 pounds.
B—81,400 pounds.
C—81,550 pounds.

Answer (B) is correct (8598). *(FTW Chap 10)*
Fig. 48 gives the following operating conditions for W-1:

Climb schedule	LR (long range)
Initial weight (x 1,000)	84 lb.
Cruise pressure altitude	34,000 ft.

Find the lower right-hand block of Fig. 50 under initial weight = 84,000 lb. Follow the left-hand column "Pres. Alt. Feet" down to the cruise altitude of 34,000 ft. A fuel burn of 2,570 lb. is indicated. Subtract the fuel burn from initial weight.

84,000 lb. initial weight
– 2,570 lb. fuel burn
81,430 lb. operating weight

Answer (A) is incorrect because 81,600 lb. would be the aircraft weight after climbing to approximately FL 330, not FL 340. Answer (C) is incorrect because 81,550 lb. would be the aircraft weight after climbing to approximately FL 330, not FL 340.

27.
8599. (Refer to figures 48, 49, and 50 on pages 586 and 587.) What is the aircraft weight at the top of climb for Operating Conditions W-2?

A—82,775 pounds.
B—83,650 pounds.
C—83,800 pounds.

Answer (C) is correct (8599). *(FTW Chap 10)*
Fig. 48 gives the following operating conditions for W-2:

Climb schedule	HS (high speed)
Initial weight (x 1,000)	86 lb.
Cruise pressure altitude	28,000 ft.

On Fig. 49, see the high-speed climb schedule for initial weight 86,000 lb. (upper left). Upon reaching 28,000 ft., or FL 280, the fuel burn will be 2,225 lb. Subtract the fuel burn from the initial weight.

86,000 lb. initial weight
– 2,225 lb. fuel burned in climb
83,775 lb. aircraft operating weight

Answer (A) is incorrect because 82,775 lb. would be the aircraft weight after climbing above FL 360, not to FL 280. Answer (B) is incorrect because 83,650 lb. would be the aircraft weight after climbing to approximately FL 290, not FL 280.

28.
8600. (Refer to figures 48, 49, and 50 on pages 586 and 587.) What is the aircraft weight at the top of climb for Operating Conditions W-3?

A—75,750 pounds.
B—75,900 pounds.
C—76,100 pounds.

Answer (B) is correct (8600). *(FTW Chap 10)*
Fig. 48 gives the following conditions for W-3:

Climb schedule	LR (long range)
Initial weight (x 1,000)	78 lb.
Cruise pressure altitude	32,000 ft.

On Fig. 50, see the long-range climb schedule, with an initial weight of 78,000 lb. (upper left). Upon reaching 32,000 ft. pressure altitude, or FL 320, 2,102 lb. of fuel will be burned. Subtract the fuel burned from the initial weight.

78,000 lb. initial weight
– 2,102 lb. fuel burned
75,898 lb. aircraft weight at top of climb

Answer (A) is incorrect because 75,750 lb. would be the aircraft weight after climbing to approximately FL 340, not FL 320. Answer (C) is incorrect because 76,100 lb. would be the aircraft weight after climbing to approximately FL 290, not FL 320.

29.
8601. (Refer to figures 48, 49, and 50 on pages 586 and 587.) What is the aircraft weight at the top of climb for Operating Conditions W-4?

A—86,150 pounds.
B—86,260 pounds.
C—86,450 pounds.

Answer (B) is correct (8601). *(FTW Chap 10)*
Fig. 48 gives the following conditions for W-4:

Climb schedule	HS (high speed)
Initial weight (x 1,000)	88 lb.
Cruise pressure altitude	22,000 ft.

Fig. 49 is the high-speed climb schedule for initial weight of 88,000 lb. (lower left). Upon reaching 22,000 ft., or FL 220, the fuel burned will be 1,738 lb. Subtract the fuel burned from the initial weight.

88,000	lb. initial weight
– 1,738	lb. fuel burned in climb
86,262	lb. aircraft weight at top of climb

Answer (A) is incorrect because 86,150 lb. would be the aircraft weight after climbing to approximately FL 230, not FL 220. Answer (C) is incorrect because 86,450 lb. would be the aircraft weight after climbing to approximately FL 210, not FL 220.

30.
8602. (Refer to figures 48, 49, and 50 on pages 586 and 587.) What is the aircraft weight at the top of climb for Operating Conditions W-5?

A—89,900 pounds.
B—90,000 pounds.
C—90,100 pounds.

Answer (A) is correct (8602). *(FTW Chap 10)*
Fig. 48 gives the following conditions for W-5:

Climb schedule	HS (high speed)
Initial weight (x 1,000)	92 lb.
Cruise pressure altitude	24,000 ft.

Use the high-speed (HS) climb schedule (Fig. 49) for initial weight of 92,000 lb. (lower right). Upon reaching FL 240, the fuel burned will be 2,079 lb. Subtract the fuel burned from the initial weight.

92,000	lb. initial weight
– 2,079	lb. fuel burned in climb
89,921	lb. operating weight at top of climb

Answer (B) is incorrect because 90,000 lb. would be the aircraft weight after climbing to approximately FL 230, not FL 240. Answer (C) is incorrect because 90,100 lb. would be the aircraft weight after climbing to approximately FL 220, not FL 240.

12.7 Alternate Planning

31.
8603. (Refer to figures 51 and 52 on page 591.) What is the total time from starting to the alternate through completing the approach for Operating Conditions L-1?

A—30 minutes.
B—44 minutes.
C—29 minutes.

Answer (B) is correct (8603). *(FTW Chap 10)*
The requirement is total time to fly to an alternate given certain operating conditions. Operating conditions L-1 on Fig. 51 are

Distance (NAM)	110
Holding time at alternate	15 min.

Note the use of NAM, which means you should ignore the wind component given in the operating conditions. See explanation of NAM on pages 569 and 570.

Using the alternate planning chart (Fig. 52), under 110 NAM, the time to the alternate is 29 min. Next, add the 15-min. holding time to determine that the total time from starting to the alternate through completing the approach is 44 min. (29 + 15).

Answer (A) is incorrect because 30 min. is the time to the alternate (excluding holding) for 120 NAM, not 110 NAM. Answer (C) is incorrect because 29 min. has not been adjusted for the 15-min. holding time.

32.
8604. (Refer to figures 51 and 52 on page 591.) What is the total time from starting to the alternate through completing the approach for Operating Conditions L-2?

A—36 minutes.
B—55 minutes.
C—40 minutes.

Answer (B) is correct (8604). *(FTW Chap 10)*
The requirement is total time to fly to an alternate given certain operating conditions. Operating conditions L-2 on Fig. 51 are

Distance (NAM)	190
Holding time at alternate	15 min.

Note the use of NAM, which means you should ignore the wind component given in the operating conditions. See explanation of NAM on pages 569 and 570.
Using the alternate planning chart (Fig. 52), under 190 NAM, the time to the alternate is 40 min. Next, add the 15-min. holding time to determine that the total time from starting to the alternate through completing the approach is 55 min. (40 + 15).
Answer (A) is incorrect because 36 min. is the time to the alternate (excluding holding) for 160 NAM, not 190 NAM. Answer (C) is incorrect because 40 min. has not been adjusted for the 15 min. holding time.

33.
8605. (Refer to figures 51 and 52 on page 591.) What is the total time from starting to the alternate through completing the approach for Operating Conditions L-3?

A—1 hour.
B—1 hour 15 minutes.
C—1 hour 24 minutes.

Answer (B) is correct (8605). *(FTW Chap 10)*
The requirement is total time to land at an alternate given certain operating conditions. Operating conditions L-3 on Fig. 51 are

Distance (NAM)	330
Holding time at alternate	15 min.

Note the use of NAM, which means you should ignore the wind component given in the operating conditions. See explanation of NAM on pages 569 and 570.
Using the alternate planning chart (Fig. 52), under 330 NAM, the time to the alternate is 1 hr. Next, add the 15-min. holding time to determine that the total time from starting to the alternate through completing the approach is 1 hr. 15 min. (1 hr. + 15 min.)
Answer (A) is incorrect because 1 hr. has not been adjusted for the 15-min. holding time. Answer (C) is incorrect because 1 hr. 24 min. is the total time required to an alternate at a distance of 395 NAM, not 330 NAM.

34.
8606. (Refer to figures 51 and 52 on page 591.) What is the total time from starting to the alternate through completing the approach for Operating Conditions L-4?

A—35 minutes.
B—19 minutes.
C—20 minutes.

Answer (A) is correct (8606). *(FTW Chap 10)*
The requirement is total time to land at an alternate given certain operating conditions. Operating conditions L-4 on Fig. 51 are

Distance (NAM)	50
Holding time at alternate	15 min.

Note the use of NAM, which means you should ignore the wind component given in the operating conditions. See explanation of NAM on pages 569 and 570.
Using the alternate planning chart (Fig. 52), under 50 NAM, the time to the alternate is 20 min. Next, add the 15-min. holding time to determine that the total time from starting to the alternate through completing the approach is 35 min. (20 + 15).
Answer (B) is incorrect because 19 min. is the time to an alternate (excluding holding) for 40 NAM, not 50 NAM. Answer (C) is incorrect because 20 min. has not been adjusted for the 15-min. holding time.

OPERATING CONDITIONS	L-1	L-2	L-3	L-4	L-5
WEIGHT (START TO ALT)	85,000	70,000	86,000	76,000	82,000
DISTANCE (NAM)	110	190	330	50	240
WIND COMPONENT (KTS)	15 HW	40 TW	50 HW	20 TW	45 HW
HOLDING TIME AT ALT (MIN)	15	15	15	15	15

FIGURE 51.—DC-9 – Alternate Planning.

ALTERNATE PLANNING CHART

DIST. - NAM	20	30	40	50	60	70	80	90	100	110	120	130	140
OPTM. ALT.	2000	3000	4000	5000	6000	7000	8000	9000	10000	11000	12000	13000	14000
TIME:	:16	:17	:19	:20	:22	:23	:25	:26	:28	:29	:30	:32	:33
FUEL	2500	2600	2700	2800	2900	3000	3100	3200	3300	3400	3500	3600	3700
TAS	275	280	283	286	289	292	296	300	303	306	309	312	315
DIST. NAM	150	160	170	180	190	200	210	220	230	240	250	260	270
OPTM. ALT.	15000	16000	17000	18000	19000	20000	21000	22000	23000	24000	25000	26000	27000
TIME:	:35	:36	:38	:39	:40	:42	:43	:45	:46	:48	:49	:50	:52
FUEL	3800	3900	4000	4100	4200	4300	4400	4500	4600	4700	4800	4900	5000
TAS	319	323	326	330	334	338	341	345	349	353	357	361	365
DIST. - NAM	280	290	300	310	320	330	340	350	360	370	380	390	400
OPTM. ALT.	27000	28000	28000	29000	29000	30000	30000	31000	31000	31000	31000	31000	31000
TIME:	:53	:55	:56	:58	:59	1:00	1:02	1:03	1:04	1:05	1:07	1:08	1:10
FUEL	5150	5250	5350	5450	5600	5700	5800	5900	6050	6150	6250	6350	6500
TAS	368	372	376	380	385	388	392	397	397	397	397	397	397

NOTES:

1. Fuel includes 1/2 climb distance en route credit, fuel to cruise remaining distance at LRC schedule, 15 minutes holding at alternate, and 800 lbs. for descent.

2. Time includes 1/2 climb distance credit, time to cruise distance shown at LRC schedule and 8 minutes for descent. 15 minutes holding is not included in time.

FIGURE 52.—DC-9 – Alternate Planning Chart.

35.
8607. (Refer to figures 51 and 52 on page 591.) What is the total time from starting to the alternate through completing the approach for Operating Conditions L-5?

A—1 hour 3 minutes.
B—48 minutes.
C—55 minutes.

Answer (A) is correct (8607). *(FTW Chap 10)*
The requirement is total time to land at an alternate given certain operating conditions. Operating conditions L-5 on Fig. 51 are

Distance (NAM)	240
Holding time at alternate	15 min.

Note the use of NAM, which means you should ignore the wind component given in the operating conditions. See explanation of NAM on pages 569 and 570.

Using the alternate planning chart (Fig. 52), under 240 NAM, the time to the alternate is 48 min. Next, add the 15-min. holding time to determine that the total time from starting to the alternate through completing the approach is 63 min. (48 + 15), or 1 hr. and 3 min.

Answer (B) is incorrect because 48 min. has not been adjusted for the 15-min. holding time. Answer (C) is incorrect because 55 min. is the total time required to an alternate at a distance of 190 NAM, not 240 NAM.

12.8 Landing Weight

36.
8608. (Refer to figures 51 and 52 on page 591.) What is the approximate landing weight for Operating Conditions L-1?

A—79,000 pounds.
B—83,600 pounds.
C—81,500 pounds.

Answer (C) is correct (8608). *(FTW Chap 15)*
Landing weight is required given a starting weight and information regarding operation to approach and landing. Landing weight will be starting weight less fuel burn. Consult Fig. 51 for operating conditions L-1, which indicate 85,000 lb., 110 NAM, a 15-kt. headwind, and 15 min. holding. On Fig. 52 under 110 NAM, a fuel burn of 3,400 lb. is given, which includes 15 min. of holding time per note 1 (at the bottom of Fig. 52).

Note the use of NAM, which means you should ignore the wind component given in the operating conditions. See explanation of NAM on pages 569 and 570.

Thus, the landing weight is 81,600 lb. (85,000 – 3,400).

Answer (A) is incorrect because 79,000 lb. assumes a fuel burn of 6,000 lb., which relates to about 360 NAM, not 110 NAM. Answer (B) is incorrect because 83,600 lb. assumes a fuel burn of 2,500 lb., which relates to about 20 NAM, not 110 NAM.

37.
8609. (Refer to figures 51 and 52 on page 591.) What is the approximate landing weight for Operating Conditions L-2?

A—65,200 pounds.
B—65,800 pounds.
C—69,600 pounds.

Answer (B) is correct (8609). *(FTW Chap 15)*
Landing weight is required given a starting weight and information regarding operation to approach and landing. Landing weight will be starting weight less fuel burn. Consult Fig. 51 for operating conditions L-2, which indicate 70,000 lb., 190 NAM, a 40-kt. tailwind, and 15 min. holding. On Fig. 52 under 190 NAM, a fuel burn of 4,200 lb. is given, which includes 15 min. of holding time per note 1 (at the bottom of Fig. 52).

Note the use of NAM, which means you should ignore the wind component given in the operating conditions. See explanation of NAM on pages 569 and 570.

Thus, the landing weight is 65,800 lb. (70,000 – 4,200).

Answer (A) is incorrect because 65,200 lb. assumes a fuel burn of 4,800 lb., which relates to 250 NAM, not 190 NAM. Answer (C) is incorrect because 69,600 lb. assumes a fuel burn of 400 lb., which is unrealistic.

38.
8610. (Refer to figures 51 and 52 on page 591.) What is the approximate landing weight for Operating Conditions L-3?

A—80,300 pounds.
B—85,400 pounds.
C—77,700 pounds.

Answer (A) is correct (8610). *(FTW Chap 15)*
Landing weight is required given a starting weight and information regarding operation to approach and landing. Landing weight will be starting weight less fuel burn. Consult Fig. 51 for operating conditions L-3, which indicate 86,000 lb., 330 NAM, a 50-kt. headwind, and 15 min. holding. On Fig. 52 under 330 NAM, a fuel burn of 5,700 lb. is given, which includes 15 min. of holding time per note 1 (at the bottom of Fig. 52).

Note the use of NAM, which means you should ignore the wind component given in the operating conditions. See explanation of NAM on pages 569 and 570.

Thus, the landing weight is 80,300 lb. (86,000 – 5,700).

Answer (B) is incorrect because 85,400 lb. assumes a fuel burn of 600 lb., which is totally unrealistic for 330 NAM. Answer (C) is incorrect because 77,700 lb. assumes a fuel burn of 8,300 lb., which is for a distance greater than 400 NAM, i.e., not on the chart.

39.
8611. (Refer to figures 51 and 52 on page 591.) What is the approximate landing weight for Operating Conditions L-4?

A—73,200 pounds.
B—74,190 pounds.
C—73,500 pounds.

Answer (A) is correct (8611). *(FTW Chap 15)*
Landing weight is required given a starting weight and information regarding operation to approach and landing. Landing weight will be starting weight less fuel burn. Consult Fig. 51 for operating conditions L-4, which indicate 76,000 lb., 50 NAM, a 20-kt. tailwind, and 15 min. holding. On Fig. 52 under 50 NAM, a fuel burn of 2,800 lb. is given, which includes 15 min. of holding time per note 1 (at the bottom of Fig. 52).

Note the use of NAM, which means you should ignore the wind component given in the operating conditions. See explanation of NAM on pages 569 and 570.

Thus, the landing weight is 73,200 lb. (76,000 – 2,800).

Answer (B) is incorrect because 74,190 lb. assumes a fuel burn of 1,800 lb., which relates to a distance less than 20 NAM, not 50 NAM. Answer (C) is incorrect because 73,500 lb. assumes a fuel burn of 2,500 lb., which relates to 20 NAM, not 50 NAM.

40.
8612. (Refer to figures 51 and 52 on page 591.) What is the approximate landing weight for Operating Conditions L-5?

A—78,600 pounds.
B—77,000 pounds.
C—76,300 pounds.

Answer (B) is correct (8612). *(FTW Chap 15)*
Landing weight is required given a starting weight and information regarding operation to approach and landing. Landing weight will be starting weight less fuel burn. Consult Fig. 51 for operating conditions L-5, which indicate 82,000 lb., 240 NAM, a 45-kt. headwind, and 15 min. holding. On Fig. 52 under 240 NAM, a fuel burn of 4,700 lb. is given, which includes 15 min. of holding time per note 1 (at the bottom of Fig. 52).

Note the use of NAM, which means you should ignore the wind component given in the operating conditions. See explanation of NAM on pages 569 and 570.

Thus, the landing weight is 77,300 lb. (82,000 – 4,700).

Answer (A) is incorrect because 78,600 lb. assumes a fuel burn of 3,400 lb., which relates to 110 NAM, not 240 NAM. Answer (C) is incorrect because 76,300 lb. assumes a fuel burn of 5,700 lb., which relates to 330 NAM, not 240 NAM.

END OF CHAPTER

CHAPTER THIRTEEN
BOEING 737 OPERATING/PERFORMANCE DATA

This chapter contains outlines of major concepts tested, all FAA test questions and answers regarding Boeing 737 operating/performance data, and an explanation of each answer. Each module, or subtopic, within this chapter is listed above with the number of questions from the FAA pilot knowledge test pertaining to that particular module. For each module, the first number following the parentheses is the page number on which the outline begins, and the next number is the page number on which the questions begin.

There are 84 questions in this chapter and hundreds of questions in other chapters. We separate and organize the FAA questions into meaningful study units, i.e., chapters and modules. As an analogy, it is easier to deal with the "trees" if you understand the "forest." In this context, "trees" are individual FAA questions and the "forest" is the ATP knowledge test. The organizational units between the overall ATP knowledge test and individual ATP test questions are chapters and modules in this book.

CAUTION: The **sole purpose** of this book is to expedite passing the knowledge test. Topics or regulations not directly tested on the FAA pilot knowledge test are omitted. Much more information and knowledge are necessary to fly safely. Additional material is presented in Gleim's other pilot training books and in many FAA books and circulars, as well as in airplane *POH*s and other commercial textbooks.

13.1 TAKEOFF SPEEDS AND EPR (Questions 1-10)

1. Takeoff EPR is provided on the top of Fig. 55 on page 607, which is based on
   a. Pressure altitude
   b. Temperature
   c. Air-conditioning on or off
2. Takeoff EPR is limited to the lower of
   a. Temperature limit EPR
   b. Pressure limit EPR
3. **Steps to Determine Maximum Takeoff EPR**
   a. Determine pressure altitude using Fig. 54 on page 606, which gives an adjustment, based on altimeter setting, for field elevation.
      1) Add or subtract the adjustment as indicated to (from) your takeoff airport altitude to determine pressure altitude.

b. On Fig. 55 on page 607, determine the temperature limit EPR by finding the appropriate OAT at the top of the chart; the temperature limit EPR is just below.

c. Find the pressure limit EPR just below the temperature limit EPR figure based on your pressure altitude.

1) You must interpolate for your pressure altitude.

d. Use the lower limit EPR (temperature or pressure).

1) Then add .03 if the air-conditioning is off to get final takeoff EPR.

4. EXAMPLE: Question 1 on page 602 provides an example in which the takeoff EPR is the pressure limit EPR of 2.035, which is smaller than the temperature limit EPR of 2.04.

a. Also note that, with air-conditioning on, there is no adjustment, but you would add .03 if the air-conditioning were off.

b. Whether the engine ice is on or off makes no difference for takeoff EPR.

5. Questions 6 through 10 require you to determine takeoff airspeeds of V_1, V_R, and/or V_2.

a. **V_1** -- maximum speed in the takeoff at which the pilot must take the first action (e.g., apply brakes, reduce thrust, deploy speed brakes) to stop the airplane within the accelerate-stop distance.

1) V_1 is also the minimum speed in the takeoff, following a failure of the critical engine at V_{EF}, at which the pilot can continue the takeoff and achieve the required height above the takeoff surface within the takeoff distance.

b. **V_R** -- rotation air speed

c. **V_2** -- takeoff safety speed

6. These airspeeds are determined by

a. Pressure altitude
b. Outside air temperature
c. Flap setting
d. Gross weight
e. Wind
f. Runway slope

7. **Steps to Determine Takeoff Speeds**

a. Use Fig. 54 on page 606 to determine pressure altitude.

1) EXAMPLE: An altimeter setting of 29.35 would require you to add 500 ft. to correct field elevation for pressure altitude.

b. Enter the appropriate pressure altitude block in the upper left-hand corner of the V_1, V_R, and V_2 schedule on Fig. 55 on page 607.

c. Proceed to the right to the appropriate temperature (OAT) column.

d. Proceed downward to the appropriate flap settings, which are given for 1°, 5°, 15°, and 25° at the lower left.

e. Within the appropriate flap setting block, find the appropriate gross weight and then proceed to the right horizontally to the appropriate column, which is determined by the OAT above.

f. Interpolate for gross weight as appropriate.

g. V_1 adjustments are to

1) Add 1 kt. per 20 kt. headwind and subtract 1 kt. per 5 kt. tailwind.
2) Add 1 kt. per 1% upslope and subtract 1 kt. per 1% downslope.

h. V_1 must not exceed V_R.

13.2 STAB TRIM SETTING (Questions 11-15)

1. The STAB TRIM setting schedule is in the lower left of Fig. 55 on page 607.
   a. It is determined based on the CG as a percentage of MAC.
2. On Fig. 53, page 605, the CG station is given on the bottom line of the chart.
   a. LEMAC is given as 625.0, and MAC is given as 134.0.
3. To determine CG as a percentage of MAC, take the difference between the CG station and 625.0 and place the difference over 134.0.
   a. $\frac{\textit{CG station} - \textit{LEMAC}}{\textit{MAC}} = \%\ \textit{MAC}$
   b. EXAMPLE: CG is 635.7: $\frac{635.7 - 625.0}{134.0} = .079$ *or* 8.0% *MAC*
4. Given CG as a percentage of MAC, enter the STAB TRIM setting table on Fig. 55 on the left and find the STAB TRIM setting in ANU immediately to the right.
   a. **ANU** means airplane nose-up.
   b. EXAMPLE: The ANU for 8% MAC is 7-3/4.

13.3 EN ROUTE CLIMB DISTANCE, FUEL (Questions 16-25)

1. Figs. 57 and 58, on pages 612 and 613, provide information regarding en route climb at 280/.70 ISA (Fig. 57) and 280/.70 ISA +10°C (Fig. 58) for
   a. Time
   b. Fuel
   c. Distance
   d. True airspeed
2. To use these figures, you must know the
   a. Brake release weight in pounds
   b. Cruise pressure altitude
3. **Steps to Compute En Route Distance and Fuel**
   a. Determine whether you are to use Fig. 57 for ISA or Fig. 58 for ISA +10°C. See Fig. 56 on page 612 (next to last line).
   b. Find the appropriate brake release weight on the horizontal axis as specified on the top line of Fig. 56.
   c. Go down vertically to the appropriate cruise pressure altitude and determine
      1) Minutes
      2) Pounds
      3) Nautical miles
      4) True airspeed
   d. Note the fuel adjustment that is given at the very bottom of the charts for high altitude airports (and there is negligible effect on time and distance).
   e. Adjust the distance (but not time and fuel).
      1) Wind velocity x minutes/60
      2) Subtract for headwind; add for tailwind.
      3) EXAMPLE: A 40-kt. headwind in a 15-min. climb will result in a 10-NM adjustment (40 x 15/60). Subtract for headwind.

13.4 CLIMB AND CRUISE POWER (Questions 26-30)

1. Maximum climb and maximum continuous EPR and maximum cruise EPR are given in Fig. 60 on page 616.
   a. They are determined by pressure altitude and temperature.
2. **Steps to Determine Maximum Climb EPR**
   a. Enter the maximum climb and maximum continuous EPR chart, top of Fig. 60, page 616, using sea level (SL) to 30,000 on the top line.
   b. Move right horizontally to the appropriate total air temperature (TAT) column to determine the temperature limit EPR.
   c. At the bottom of the chart is the pressure limit EPR.
   d. Use the smaller of the two EPR limits: temperature limit EPR or pressure limit EPR.
      1) Apply the bleed air correction for engine anti-ice if it is being used by subtracting .08.
      2) Subtract wing anti-ice of .04 for two engines and .06 for one engine.
      3) Add .04 if the air-conditioning is off from sea level to 37,000 ft.
3. **Steps to Determine Maximum Continuous Climb EPR**
   a. Use the same procedures as above EXCEPT
      1) Choose between three altitude intervals for temperature EPR:
         a) SL to 1,500; 20,000 to 30,000
         b) 1,500 to 20,000
         c) 35,000 and 37,000
4. Determine maximum cruise climb EPR by using the chart MAX CRUISE EPR, which is just below MAX CLIMB and MAX CONTINUOUS EPR on Fig. 60.

13.5 FLIGHT PLANNING AT .78 MACH CRUISE (Questions 31-40)

1. Fig. 62 on page 618 provides a means of determining trip time and trip fuel.
   a. Trip distance in nautical ground miles is on the horizontal axis at the bottom.
   b. For determining trip fuel, pressure altitude lines are provided
      1) In the lower middle for 20, 22, 23, 25, 27, 29, 31, 33, 35, and 37,000
      2) In the upper left for 20, 27, 35, and 37,000
   c. The section just above the bottom of the chart contains adjustments for headwinds and tailwinds.
2. **Steps to Determine Trip Time**
   a. Find the trip distance at the bottom of the chart.
   b. Move up to the horizontal reference line, 3/8 in. from the bottom of the line.
   c. Move up and to the right for a headwind (down and to the left for a tailwind) to adjust for winds.
   d. Move up vertically to the top set of pressure altitude lines, and from the point of intersection with your pressure altitude line, move to the left to the vertical reference line of 0°C.
   e. Move up and to the right (or down and to the left) to adjust for nonstandard temperature.
   f. Move horizontally to the left to the trip time scale on the left of the chart.

3. **Steps to Determine Trip Fuel**
   a. Find the trip distance at the bottom of the chart.
   b. Move up to the horizontal reference line, 3/8 in. from the bottom of the line.
   c. Move up and to the right for a headwind (down and to the left for a tailwind) to adjust for winds.
   d. Move up vertically to the intersection with the lower set of pressure altitude lines, and from the intersection with your pressure altitude line, move to the right to the vertical reference line.
   e. Move up and to the right to the appropriate landing weight in thousands of pounds, and from that point, move horizontally to the right to determine the fuel burn in thousands of pounds.

13.6 TURBULENT AIR PENETRATION RPM (Questions 41-45)

1. Fig. 64 on page 622 determines the power setting in % N_1 RPM based on pressure altitude and gross weight.
   a. N_1 refers to percentage of turbine output.
2. **Steps to Determine Turbulent Air Penetration**
   a. Find the appropriate pressure altitude line (vertical axis) and move right horizontally to the appropriate gross weight (horizontal axis).
      1) This is %N_1 before temperature adjustment.
   b. Compare ISA TAT (total, or true, air temperature) with actual TAT (given in Fig. 63 bottom line on page 622).
      1) Adjust your % N_1 figure for the difference between standard and actual.
      2) The temperature adjustment factors are given on the right side of Fig. 64.

13.7 FLIGHT PLANNING AT .74 MACH CRUISE (Questions 46-55)

1. Fig. 67 on page 625 contains an abbreviated flight planning chart for a 280-kt. climb and a 320/340-kt. descent with a .74 Mach cruise at 24,000 ft. and above.
2. To determine trip time, find the nautical miles on the left and move horizontally to the right to determine the appropriate recommended altitude true airspeeds, air time in minutes, and fuel in pounds.
   a. Correct the time by adding for a headwind or subtracting for a tailwind with the formula below:

$$\Delta\ Time = \frac{Time \times Wind\ component}{TAS}$$

3. To determine fuel consumption, use the above procedures and adjust for fuel usage.
   a. Correct the fuel by adding for a headwind or subtracting for a tailwind with the formula below:

$$\Delta\ Fuel = \frac{Fuel \times Wind\ component}{TAS}$$

13.8 HOLDING PERFORMANCE (Questions 56-65)

1. Fig. 69 on page 630, given the gross weight of the airplane and the flight level, provides
   a. Recommended EPR setting
   b. IAS in knots
   c. Fuel flow per engine (LB/HR)
2. **Steps to Determine Recommended Holding EPR, IAS, and Fuel Flow/Engine**
   a. Find the appropriate altitude on the left side of Fig. 69.
   b. Find the gross weight at the top of the figure; the intersection of weight and pressure altitude provides EPR, IAS, and fuel flow.
   c. Interpolate as appropriate.

13.9 FUEL DUMP TIME (Questions 66-69)

1. Fig. 70 on page 635 provides the fuel dump time based on thousands of pounds of fuel dumped and the ending fuel weight in thousands of pounds.
2. EXAMPLE: If the initial weight was 180,500 lb. and the zero fuel weight is 125,500, how much time does it take to dump fuel down to 144,500 lb.
   a. The remaining fuel weight would be 19,000 lb. (144,500 – 125,000).
   b. The amount of fuel to be dumped would be 36,000 lb. (180,500 – 144,500).
   c. Enter initial fuel weight of 55,000 lb. (180,500 – 125,500).
3. The questions tell you either the fuel load desired or the total weight desired as well as initial weight and zero fuel weight.
4. **Steps to Determine Fuel Dump Time**
   a. Subtract zero fuel weight from initial weight to determine initial fuel weight.
   b. Subtract zero fuel weight from desired weight to determine ending fuel weight (i.e., after fuel dump).
      1) Or add desired fuel load to zero fuel weight.
   c. Find the initial fuel weight on the vertical axis (left side) of Fig. 70 and the ending fuel weight on the horizontal axis (at top of figure).
      1) The intersection provides the number of minutes to dump the fuel.

13.10 DRIFT-DOWN PERFORMANCE (Questions 70-74)

1. Drift-down performance provides a means of operating to the critical engine altitude to maximize range, i.e., after an engine malfunction.
2. Fig. 72 on page 638 is a drift-down performance chart. Note that there are three subcharts:
   a. Engine anti-ice off
   b. Engine anti-ice on
   c. Engine and wing anti-ice on
3. Fig. 71 on page 637 gives
   a. Weight at engine failure
   b. Temperature: ISA, +10, –10, +20, etc.
   c. Whether the following are on or off:
      1) Engine anti-ice
      2) Wing anti-ice
      3) Air-conditioning

4. **Steps to Determine Level-off Altitude**
   a. Select the correct chart on Fig. 72 regarding use of engine and/or wing anti-ice.
   b. Enter the chart at the left on the correct gross weight (vertical axis).
   c. Move horizontally to the right to the appropriate temperature (horizontal axis).

13.11 LANDING PERFORMANCE (Questions 75-84)

1. Fig. 75 on page 643 contains a landing performance chart which includes
   a. Go-around EPR
   b. Flap extension/maneuvering speed
   c. Landing speed
2. **Steps to Determine Go-Around EPR**
   a. On Fig. 75 on page 643, determine the temperature EPR based on either OAT or TAT.
      1) Enter the chart at the left and move to the right horizontally to temperature; the temperature EPR is on the bottom line.
   b. Find the pressure limit EPR, on the chart below the temperature limit EPRs, based on the pressure altitude.
      1) You must interpolate for the pressure altitude.
   c. Use the lower limit EPR (temperature or pressure).
   d. Make the appropriate EPR bleed corrections.
      1) Air-conditioning OFF: +0.03
      2) Wing anti-ice ON
         a) One-engine: –0.06
         b) Two-engine: –0.04
3. V_{REF} is landing speed and is given in the lower right of Fig. 75.
   a. Enter the chart on the left given the landing weight.
   b. Move horizontally to the right to the given flap setting.
   c. Add 1/2 of the given headwind component.
      1) The headwind component is determined by Fig. 74 on page 642.
         a) Determine the angle between the wind and the runway.
         b) Find the "angle between wind direction and runway degrees" line on Fig. 74.
         c) Find the intersection with the "wind velocity" curves.
         d) Move horizontally to the left side of the chart to determine the expected headwind component when landing.

QUESTIONS AND ANSWER EXPLANATIONS

All the FAA questions from the pilot knowledge test for the ATP certificate relating to the Boeing 737 operating/performance data and the material outlined previously are reproduced on the following pages in the same modules as the outlines. To the immediate right of each question are the correct answer and answer explanation. Cover these answers and answer explanations while responding to the questions. Refer to Chapter 1 on how to take the FAA pilot knowledge test.

The questions from the FAA pilot knowledge test bank have been reordered by topic, and the topics are organized into a meaningful sequence. Accordingly, the first line of the answer explanation gives the FAA question number and the citation of the authoritative source for the answer.

13.1 Takeoff Speeds and EPR

1.
8613. (Refer to figures 53, 54, and 55 on pages 605, 606, and 607.) What is the takeoff EPR for Operating Conditions R-1?

A—2.04.
B—2.01.
C—2.035.

Answer (C) is correct (8613). *(FTW Chap 8)*
Refer to operating conditions R-1 in Fig. 53. Find pressure altitude using Fig. 54 at field elevation 100 ft. and altimeter setting 29.50 in. Pressure altitude = 500 ft. (100 + 400).

Find the EPR by entering the takeoff EPR chart (Fig. 55). Move right horizontally in the OAT column to +50°F and then move down vertically to determine the temperature limit EPR of 2.04. Next, find the pressure altitude of 500 ft., which is between SL and 1,000 ft. Interpolate to determine that the pressure limit EPR at a pressure altitude of 500 ft. is 2.035. The takeoff EPR is the smaller of the two limits, which is 2.035. No EPR bleed corrections are necessary, and none of the other data in condition R-1 are relevant.

Answer (A) is incorrect because 2.04 is the temperature limit, not takeoff, EPR. Answer (B) is incorrect because 2.01 is the pressure limit EPR for sea level, not 500 ft.

2.
8614. (Refer to figures 53, 54, and 55 on pages 605, 606, and 607.) What is the takeoff EPR for Operating Conditions R-2?

A—2.19.
B—2.18.
C—2.16.

Answer (A) is correct (8614). *(FTW Chap 8)*
Refer to operating conditions R-2 in Fig. 53. Find pressure altitude using Fig. 54 at field elevation 4,000 ft. and altimeter setting 1,032 mb. Pressure altitude = 3,500 ft. (4,000 – 500).

Find the EPR by entering the takeoff EPR chart (Fig. 55). Move right horizontally in the OAT column to –15°C and then move down vertically to determine the temperature limit EPR of 2.19. Next, find the pressure altitude of 3,500 ft., which is between 3,000 ft. and 4,000 ft. Interpolate to determine that the pressure limit EPR at a pressure altitude of 3,500 ft. is 2.19. Since both temperature and pressure EPR are the same, the takeoff EPR is 2.19. No EPR bleed air corrections are necessary, and none of the other data in condition R-2 are relevant.

Answer (B) is incorrect because 2.18 is the temperature limit EPR at approximately –12°C, not –15°C. Answer (C) is incorrect because 2.16 is the pressure limit EPR at 3,000 ft., not 3,500 ft.

3.
8615. (Refer to figures 53, 54, and 55 on pages 605, 606, and 607.) What is the takeoff EPR for Operating Conditions R-3?

A—2.01.
B—2.083.
C—2.04.

Answer (C) is correct (8615). *(FTW Chap 8)*
Refer to operating conditions R-3 in Fig. 53. Find pressure altitude using Fig. 54 at field elevation 950 ft. and altimeter setting 29.40 in. Pressure altitude = 1,450 ft. (950 + 500).

Find the EPR by entering the takeoff EPR chart (Fig. 55). Move right horizontally in the OAT column to +59°F and then move down vertically to determine the temperature limit EPR of 2.01. Next, find the pressure altitude of 1,450 ft., which is between 1,000 ft. and 2,000 ft. Interpolate to determine that the pressure limit EPR at a pressure altitude of 1,450 ft. is 2.083. The takeoff EPR is the smaller of the two limits, which is 2.01. The EPR bleed correction for the air-conditioning OFF is +.03, so the corrected takeoff EPR is 2.04 (2.01 + .03).

Answer (A) is incorrect because 2.01 is the takeoff EPR with the air-conditioning ON, not OFF. Answer (B) is incorrect because 2.083 is the pressure limit, not takeoff, EPR.

4.
8616. (Refer to figures 53, 54, and 55 on pages 605, 606, and 607.) What is the takeoff EPR for Operating Conditions R-4?

A—2.06.
B—2.105.
C—2.11.

Answer (B) is correct (8616). *(FTW Chap 8)*

Refer to operating conditions R-4 in Fig. 53. Find pressure altitude using Fig. 54 at field elevation 2,000 ft. and altimeter setting 1,017 mb. Pressure altitude = 1,900 ft. (2,000 – 100).

Find the EPR by entering the takeoff EPR chart (Fig. 55). Move right horizontally in the OAT column to 0°C and then move down vertically to determine the temperature limit EPR of 2.11. Next, find the pressure altitude of 1,900 ft., which is between 1,000 ft. and 2,000 ft. Interpolate to determine that the pressure limit EPR at a pressure altitude of 1,900 ft. is 2.105. The takeoff EPR is the smaller of the two limits, which is 2.105. No EPR bleed corrections are necessary, and none of the other data in condition R-4 are relevant.

Answer (A) is incorrect because 2.06 is the pressure limit EPR for 1,000 ft., not 1,900 ft. Answer (C) is incorrect because 2.11 is the temperature limit, not takeoff, EPR.

5.
8617. (Refer to figures 53, 54, and 55 on pages 605, 606, and 607.) What is the takeoff EPR for Operating Conditions R-5?

A—1.98.
B—1.95.
C—1.96.

Answer (A) is correct (8617). *(FTW Chap 8)*

Refer to operating conditions R-5 in Fig. 53. Find pressure altitude using Fig. 54 at field elevation 50 ft. and altimeter setting 30.15 in. Pressure altitude = –150 ft. (50 – 200).

Find the EPR by entering the takeoff EPR chart (Fig. 55). Move right horizontally in the OAT column to +95°F and then move down vertically to determine the temperature limit EPR of 1.95. Next, find the pressure altitude of –150 ft., which is between SL and –1,000 ft. Interpolate to determine that the pressure limit EPR at a pressure altitude of –150 ft. is 2.003. Use the smaller of the two limits, which is 1.95. The EPR bleed air correction for the air-conditioning OFF is +.03. The takeoff EPR is 1.98 (1.95 + .03). None of the other data in condition R-5 are relevant.

Answer (B) is incorrect because 1.95 is the takeoff EPR with the air-conditioning ON, not OFF. Answer (C) is incorrect because 1.96 is the pressure limit EPR at –1,000 ft., not –150 ft.

6.
8618. (Refer to figures 53, 54, and 55 on pages 605, 606, and 607.) What is the takeoff safety speed for Operating Conditions R-1?

A—128 knots.
B—121 knots.
C—133 knots.

Answer (A) is correct (8618). *(FTW Chap 8)*

Takeoff safety speed is V_2. Refer to operating conditions R-1 in Fig. 53.

Find pressure altitude using Fig. 54 at field elevation 100 ft. and altimeter setting 29.50 in. Pressure altitude = 500 ft. (100 + 400).

On Fig. 55, enter V_1, V_R, V_2 chart under pressure altitude. Find –1 to 1 pressure altitude line; then proceed to the right to the +50°F OAT (+50°F is between –65°F and +91°F). Go down that column to flaps 15°, to 90,000 lb. (90) gross weight, then right to V_2 (takeoff safety speed). V_2 is 128 kt.

Answer (B) is incorrect because 121 kt. is the rotation (V_R) speed, not the safety speed. Answer (C) is incorrect because 133 kt. is the V_2 speed using 5°, not 15°, flaps.

7.
8619. (Refer to figures 53, 54, and 55 on pages 605, 606, and 607.) What is the rotation speed for Operating Conditions R-2?

A—147 knots.
B—152 knots.
C—146 knots.

Answer (C) is correct (8619). *(FTW Chap 8)*
Rotation speed is V_R. Refer to operating conditions R-2 in Fig. 53.
Find pressure altitude using Fig. 54 at field elevation 4,000 ft. and altimeter setting 1,032 mb. Pressure altitude = 3,500 ft. (4,000 – 500).
On Fig. 55, enter the V_1, V_R, V_2 chart under pressure altitude. Find the 3-to-5 pressure altitude line; then proceed to the right to the –15°C OAT (–15°C is between –54°C and –8°C). Go down that column to the flaps 5° and 110,000 lb. (110) gross weight, then right to V_R (rotation speed). V_R is 146 kt.
Answer (A) is incorrect because 147 kt. is the V_R speed using the pressure altitude line of 5 to 7, not 3 to 5. Answer (B) is incorrect because 152 kt. is the V_R speed using 1°, not 5°, flaps.

8.
8620. (Refer to figures 53, 54, and 55 on pages 605, 606, and 607.) What are V_1, V_R, and V_2 speeds for Operating Conditions R-3?

A—143, 143, and 147 knots.
B—138, 138, and 142 knots.
C—136, 138, and 143 knots.

Answer (B) is correct (8620). *(FTW Chap 8)*
The takeoff decision speed is V_1, the rotation speed is V_R, and the takeoff safety speed is V_2. Refer to the operating conditions R-3 in Fig. 53.
Find pressure altitude using Fig. 54 at field elevation 950 ft. and altimeter setting 29.40 in. Pressure altitude = 1,450 ft. (950 + 500).
On Fig. 55, enter the V_1, V_R, V_2 chart under pressure altitude. Find the 1-to-3 pressure altitude line; then proceed to the right to the +59°F OAT (+59°F is between +47°F and +89°F). Go down that column to 5° flaps and gross weight of 100,000 (100) lb. V_1 is 136 kt., V_R is 138 kt., and V_2 is 142 kt. V_1 adjustments must be made for wind and runway slope as indicated at the bottom of the chart. Add 1 kt. for the 20-kt. headwind and add 1 kt. for the 1% up-runway slope. The adjusted V_1 is 138 kt. (136 + 1 + 1).
Answer (A) is incorrect because V_1 and V_R of 143 kt. and V_2 of 147 kt. are the values using 1°, not 5°, flaps. Answer (C) is incorrect because V_1 of 136 kt. has not been adjusted for the wind component or the runway slope.

9.
8622. (Refer to figures 53, 54, and 55 on pages 605, 606, and 607.) What are rotation and V_2 bug speeds for Operating Conditions R-5?

A—138 and 143 knots.
B—136 and 138 knots.
C—134 and 141 knots.

Answer (A) is correct (8622). *(FTW Chap 8)*
Rotation speed is V_R, and takeoff safety speed is V_2. Refer to operating condition R-5 in Fig. 53.
Find pressure altitude using Fig. 54 at field elevation 50 ft. and altimeter setting 30.15 in. Pressure altitude = –150 ft. (50 – 200).
On Fig. 55, enter the V_1, V_R, V_2 chart under pressure altitude. Find the –1-to-1 pressure altitude line; then proceed to the right to +95°F OAT (+95°F is between 92°F and 105°F). Go down that column to flaps 1°. Since the gross weight is 95,000 (95) lb., you must interpolate between 90 and 100 gross weight. V_R at 90,000 lb. is 134 and at 100,000 lb. is 143. Interpolate to determine the actual V_R (rotation) speed is 138 kt. The same procedure provides the V_2 speed of 143 kt.
Answer (B) is incorrect because V_R of 136 kt. is for a gross weight below 95,000 lb., and V_2 of 138 kt. is for a gross weight of 90,000 lb. Answer (C) is incorrect because 134 kt. is V_R at 90,000 lb., and 141 kt. is V_2 below 95,000 lb.

10.
8621. (Refer to figure 53 below and figures 54 and 55 on pages 606 and 607.) What are critical engine failure and takeoff safety speeds for Operating Conditions R-4?

A—131 and 133 knots.
B—123 and 134 knots.
C—122 and 130 knots.

Answer (B) is correct (8621). *(FTW Chap 8)*

V_1 is the minimum speed in the takeoff, following a failure of the critical engine at V_{EF}, at which the pilot can continue the takeoff and achieve the required height above the takeoff surface within the takeoff distance. The takeoff safety speed is V_2. Refer to operating condition R-4 in Fig. 53.

Find pressure altitude using Fig. 54 at field elevation 2,000 ft. and altimeter setting 1,017 mb. Pressure altitude = 1,900 ft. (2,000 – 100).

On Fig. 55, enter the V_1, V_R, V_2 chart under pressure altitude. Find the 1-to-3 pressure altitude line; then proceed to the right to the 0°C OAT (0°C is between –54°C and +8°C). Go down that column to flaps 1° and gross weight of both 80 and 90. You will find V_1 at 80 of 122 kt. and at 90 of 131 kt. Because the actual gross weight is 85 (85,000 lb.), interpolate to determine the correct V_1 speed of 127 kt. Interpolate for V_2 to determine a speed of 134 kt. Next, adjust V_1 for wind and slope. Subtract 2 kt. for the 10-kt. tailwind and subtract 2 kt. for the 2% down-runway slope. Thus, V_1 is 123 kt. (127 – 2 – 2).

Answer (A) is incorrect because 131 kt. is V_1 at 90,000 lb. before any adjustments, and 133 kt. is V_R (not V_2) at 90,000, not 85,000, lb. Answer (C) is incorrect because 122 kt. is V_1 at 80,000 lb. before adjusting for the wind and runway slope, and 130 kt. is V_2 at 80,000, not 85,000, lb.

OPERATING CONDITIONS	R-1	R-2	R-3	R-4	R-5
FIELD ELEVATION	100	4,000	950	2,000	50
ALTIMETER SETTING	29.50"	1032 mb	29.40"	1017 mb	30.15"
TEMPERATURE (OAT)	+50 °F	–15 °C	+59 °F	0 °C	+95 °F
WEIGHT (X1000)	90	110	100	85	95
FLAP POSITION	15°	5°	5°	1°	1°
WIND COMPONENT (KTS)	5 HW	5 TW	20 HW	10 TW	7 HW
RUNWAY SLOPE %	1% UP	1% DN	1% UP	2% DN	1.5% UP
AIR CONDITIONING	ON	ON	OFF	ON	OFF
ENGINE ANTI-ICE	OFF	ON	OFF	ON	OFF
CG STATION	635.7	643.8	665.2	657.2	638.4
LEMAC STA 625.0, MAC 134.0					

FIGURE 53.—B-737 – Takeoff.

ALTIMETER SETTING TO STATION PRESSURE

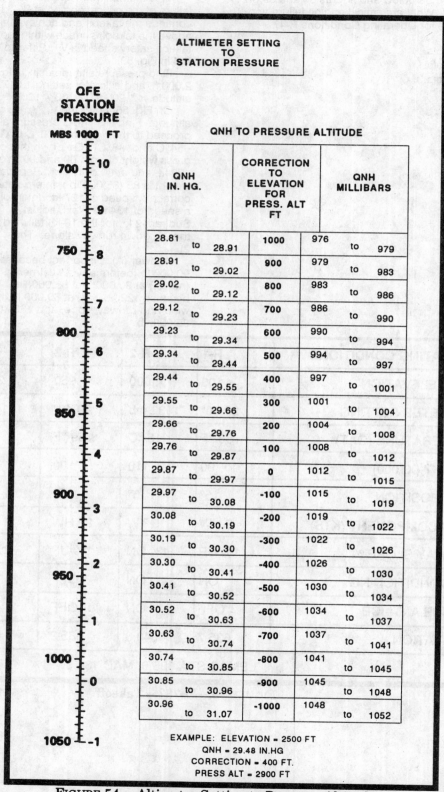

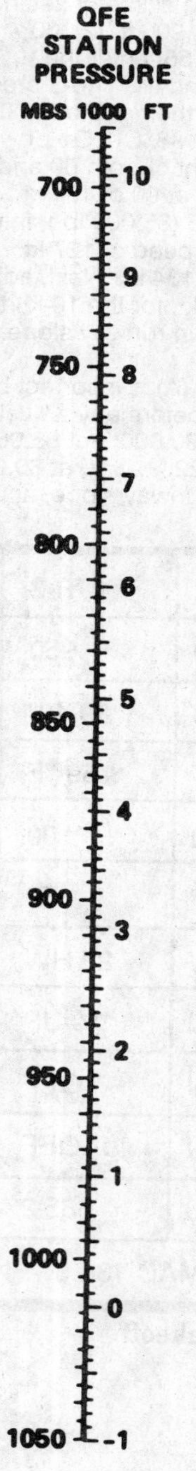

QNH TO PRESSURE ALTITUDE

QNH IN. HG.			CORRECTION TO ELEVATION FOR PRESS. ALT FT	QNH MILLIBARS		
28.81	to	28.91	1000	976	to	979
28.91	to	29.02	900	979	to	983
29.02	to	29.12	800	983	to	986
29.12	to	29.23	700	986	to	990
29.23	to	29.34	600	990	to	994
29.34	to	29.44	500	994	to	997
29.44	to	29.55	400	997	to	1001
29.55	to	29.66	300	1001	to	1004
29.66	to	29.76	200	1004	to	1008
29.76	to	29.87	100	1008	to	1012
29.87	to	29.97	0	1012	to	1015
29.97	to	30.08	-100	1015	to	1019
30.08	to	30.19	-200	1019	to	1022
30.19	to	30.30	-300	1022	to	1026
30.30	to	30.41	-400	1026	to	1030
30.41	to	30.52	-500	1030	to	1034
30.52	to	30.63	-600	1034	to	1037
30.63	to	30.74	-700	1037	to	1041
30.74	to	30.85	-800	1041	to	1045
30.85	to	30.96	-900	1045	to	1048
30.96	to	31.07	-1000	1048	to	1052

EXAMPLE: ELEVATION = 2500 FT
QNH = 29.48 IN.HG
CORRECTION = 400 FT.
PRESS ALT = 2900 FT

FIGURE 54.—Altimeter Setting to Pressure Altitude.

TAKEOFF EPR

0 TO 60 KTS

A/C ON

EPR BLEED CORRECTIONS	Δ EPR
AIR CONDITIONING OFF	+.03
ENGINE ANTI-ICE	ZERO

OAT																				
°F	-65	-49	-40	-31	-22	-13	-4	5	14	23	32	41	50	59	68	77	86	95	104	120
°C	-54	-45	-40	-35	-30	-25	-20	-15	-10	-5	0	5	10	15	20	25	30	35	40	49
TEMP LIMIT EPR	2.31	2.31	2.31	2.29	2.27	2.24	2.22	2.19	2.17	2.14	2.11	2.07	2.04	2.01	2.01	2.01	2.00	1.95	1.91	1.82

PRESS LIMIT EPR							
ALT	5660 AND ABOVE	4000	3000	2000	1000	S.L.	-1000
EPR	2.31	2.22	2.16	2.11	2.06	2.01	1.96

1. FIND TEMP LIMIT EPR
2. FIND PRESS LIMIT EPR
3. USE THE SMALLER OF THE TWO LIMITS

V_1, V_R, V_2

ANTI-SKID ON

PRESSURE ALTITUDE 1000 FT		OAT					
9 to 10	F° C°			-65 to -19 -54 to -28	-18 to 18 -27 to -8	19 to 45 -7 to 7	46 to 86 8 to 30
7 to 9	F° C°		-65 to -21 -54 to -29	-20 to 10 -28 to -23	11 to 39 -22 to 4	40 to 87 5 to 31	88 to 101 32 to 38
5 to 7	F° C°	-65 to -15 -54 to -26	-14 to 15 -27 to -9	16 to 40 -8 to 4	41 to 87 5 to 31	88 to 105 32 to 40	106 to 109 41 to 43
3 to 5	F° C°	-65 to 20 -54 to -8	21 to 42 -7 to 6	43 to 88 7 to 31	89 to 103 32 to 39	104 to 116 40 to 46	
1 to 3	F° C°	-65 to 46 -54 to 8	47 to 89 9 to 32	90 to 104 33 to 40	105 to 120 41 to 49		
-1 to 1	F° C°	-65 to 91 -54 to 33	92 to 105 34 to 40	106 to 120 41 to 49			

FLAPS	GROSS WT -1000 LB	V_1 V_R V_2	V_1 V_R V_2	V_1 V_R V_2	V_1 V_R V_2	V_1 V_R V_2	V_1 V_R V_2
1	120	159 161 164	160 162 164				
	110	150 152 155	151 153 155	152 154 155			
	100	141 143 147	142 143 147	142 144 147	143 145 147	144 146 147	
	90	131 133 138	132 134 138	133 135 138	133 136 138	134 136 138	135 137 138
	80	122 124 130	122 125 130	123 126 130	124 126 130	125 127 130	125 128 130
	70	112 116 123	113 117 123	113 117 122	114 118 122	115 119 122	116 119 122
5	120	153 155 158	154 156 158				
	110	144 146 150	145 147 150				
	100	135 137 142	136 138 142	137 139 142	138 140 142		
	90	126 128 133	127 129 133	128 130 133	129 131 133	130 132 133	
	80	116 118 125	117 119 125	118 121 125	119 122 125	120 123 125	121 124 125
	70	106 109 118	107 110 118	108 111 117	109 112 117	110 113 117	112 114 117
15	100	130 130 135	131 131 135	132 132 135			
	90	120 121 128	121 122 128	123 123 128	124 124 128	125 125 128	126 126 128
	80	111 112 119	112 113 119	113 114 119	114 115 119	115 116 119	117 117 119
	70	105 105 112	101 103 112	102 105 112	103 106 112	105 107 112	106 108 112
25	100	124 126 132	126 127 132				
	90	115 117 124	116 118 124	117 119 124	118 120 124		
	80	105 108 116	107 109 116	108 110 116	109 111 116	110 112 116	111 113 116
	70	105 105 108	104 104 108	101 101 108	99 102 108	100 103 108	101 104 108

SHADED AREA INDICATES PERFORMANCE AFFECTED BY MINIMUM CONTROL SPEED, MINIMUM FIELD LENGTH FOR LIGHTEST WEIGHT ABOVE SHADED AREA IS REQUIRED.

V_1 ADJUSTMENTS*	
WIND	SLOPE
ADD 1 KT PER 20 KTS HEADWIND	ADD 1 KT PER 1% UP SLOPE
SUBTRACT 1 KT PER 5 KTS TAILWIND	SUBTRACT 1 KT PER 1% DOWN SLOPE

*V_1 MUST NOT EXCEED V_R

SPEEDS NOT VALID WHEN WEIGHTS ARE PREDICTED ON USE OF CLEARWAY, STOPWAY, IMPROVED CLIMB OR ARE LIMITED BY BRAKE ENERGY

FLAP RETRACTION/ MANEUVERING SPEED

FLAP POS	KTS IAS
0	210
1	190
2	180
5	170
10	160
15	150
25	140

FOR MANEUVERS IMMEDIATELY AFTER TAKE-OFF EXCEEDING 15° BANK, MAINTAIN AT LEAST V2 + 15 AT TAKEOFF FLAPS

STAB, TRIM SETTING -UNITS AIRPLANE NOSE UP

CG	FLAPS ALL
6	8
8	7-3/4
10	7-1/2
12	7
14	6-3/4
16	6-1/4
18	5-3/4
20	5-1/2
22	5
24	4-1/2
26	4
28	3-1/2
30	3
32	2-1/2

FIGURE 55.—B-737 – Takeoff Performance.

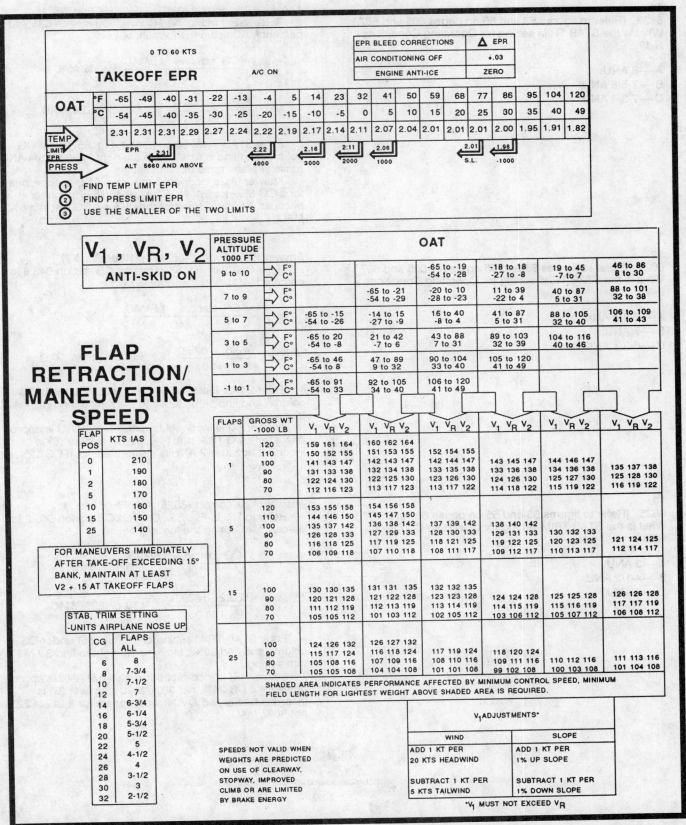

13.2 STAB TRIM Setting

11.
8623. (Refer to figures 53 and 55 on pages 605 and 607.) What is the STAB TRIM setting for Operating Conditions R-1?

A—8 ANU.
B—7-5/8 ANU.
C—7-3/4 ANU.

Answer (C) is correct (8623). *(PWBH Chap 7)*

Refer to R-1 in Fig. 53. Convert CG station 635.7 to percent MAC using the formula below:

$$\frac{\textit{CG station} - \textit{LEMAC}}{\textit{MAC}} = \textit{\% MAC}$$

$$\frac{635.7 - 625.0}{134.0} = .079 \textit{ or } 8.0\% \textit{ MAC}$$

Enter STAB TRIM setting chart (Fig. 55) under CG column and find 8%. Move to the right to find 7-3/4 ANU (units airplane nose-up) trim setting.

Answer (A) is incorrect because 8 ANU is appropriate for a CG 6%, not 8%, MAC. Answer (B) is incorrect because 7-5/8 ANU is appropriate for a CG 9%, not 8%, MAC.

12.
8624. (Refer to figures 53 and 55 on pages 605 and 607.) What is the STAB TRIM setting for Operating Conditions R-2?

A—5-3/4 ANU.
B—7 ANU.
C—6-3/4 ANU.

Answer (C) is correct (8624). *(PWBH Chap 7)*

Refer to R-2 in Fig. 53. Convert CG station 643.8 to percent MAC using the formula below:

$$\frac{\textit{CG station} - \textit{LEMAC}}{\textit{MAC}} = \textit{\% MAC}$$

$$\frac{643.8 - 625.0}{134.0} = .140 \textit{ or } 14.0\% \textit{ MAC}$$

Enter STAB TRIM setting chart (Fig. 55) under CG column and find 14%. Move to the right to find 6-3/4 ANU trim setting.

Answer (A) is incorrect because 5-3/4 ANU is appropriate for a CG 18%, not 14%, MAC. Answer (B) is incorrect because 7 ANU is appropriate for a CG 12%, not 14%, MAC.

13.
8625. (Refer to figures 53 and 55 on pages 605 and 607.) What is the STAB TRIM setting for Operating Conditions R-3?

A—3 ANU.
B—4-1/2 ANU.
C—5 ANU.

Answer (A) is correct (8625). *(PWBH Chap 7)*

Refer to R-3 in Fig. 53. Convert CG station 665.2 to percent MAC using the formula below:

$$\frac{\textit{CG station} - \textit{LEMAC}}{\textit{MAC}} = \textit{\% MAC}$$

$$\frac{665.2 - 625.0}{134.0} = .30 \textit{ or } 30\% \textit{ MAC}$$

Enter STAB TRIM setting chart (Fig. 55) under CG column and find 30%. Move to the right to find 3 ANU trim setting.

Answer (B) is incorrect because 4-1/2 ANU is appropriate for a CG 24%, not 30%, MAC. Answer (C) is incorrect because 5 ANU is appropriate for a CG of 22%, not 30%, MAC.

14.
8626. (Refer to figures 53 and 55 on pages 605 and 607.) What is the STAB TRIM setting for Operating Conditions R-4?

A—4-1/4 ANU.
B—4-1/2 ANU.
C—5 ANU.

Answer (B) is correct (8626). *(PWBH Chap 7)*
Refer to R-4 in Fig. 53. Convert CG station 657.2 to percent MAC using the formula below:

$$\frac{\textit{CG station} - \textit{LEMAC}}{\textit{MAC}} = \textit{\% MAC}$$

$$\frac{657.2 - 625.0}{134.0} = .240 \textit{ or } 24.0\% \textit{ MAC}$$

Enter STAB TRIM setting chart (Fig. 55) under CG column and find 24%. Move to the right to find 4-1/2 ANU trim setting.
Answer (A) is incorrect because 4-1/4 ANU is appropriate for a CG 25%, not 24%, MAC. Answer (C) is incorrect because 5 ANU is appropriate for a CG 22%, not 24%, MAC.

15.
8627. (Refer to figures 53 and 55 on pages 605 and 607.) What is the STAB TRIM setting for Operating Conditions R-5?

A—6-3/4 ANU.
B—8 ANU.
C—7-1/2 ANU.

Answer (C) is correct (8627). *(PWBH Chap 7)*
Refer to R-5 in Fig. 53. Convert CG station 638.4 to percent MAC using the formula below:

$$\frac{\textit{CG station} - \textit{LEMAC}}{\textit{MAC}} = \textit{\% MAC}$$

$$\frac{638.4 - 625.0}{134.0} = .10 \textit{ or } 10.0\% \textit{ MAC}$$

Enter STAB TRIM setting chart (Fig. 55) under CG column and find 10%. Move to the right to find 7-1/2 ANU trim setting.
Answer (A) is incorrect because 6-3/4 ANU is appropriate for a CG 14%, not 10%, MAC. Answer (B) is incorrect because 8 ANU is appropriate for a CG 6%, not 10%, MAC.

13.3 En Route Climb Distance, Fuel

16.
8628. (Refer to figures 56, 57, and 58 on pages 612 and 613.) What is the ground distance covered during en route climb for Operating Conditions V-1?

A—145 NM.
B—137 NM.
C—134 NM.

Answer (A) is correct (8628). *(FTW Chap 10)*
Refer to V-1 in Fig. 56. The chart in Fig. 58 is used for en route climb ISA +10°C.

Find pressure altitude of 33,000 ft. at the left edge of the chart; then move right horizontally to the brake release weight of 110,000 lb. The distance is 154 NM (lower left number), and the time is 26 min. (upper left number).

Adjust the distance for the 20-kt. average headwind component by multiplying the wind by the time (in hours) to determine a distance of 9 NM [20 x (26 ÷ 60)]. A headwind will reduce the distance; thus the ground distance covered is 145 NM (154 – 9).

Answer (B) is incorrect because 137 NM is the ground distance covered with an average headwind component of 40, not 20, kt. Answer (C) is incorrect because 134 NM is the ground distance covered for a cruise pressure altitude of 32,000, not 33,000, ft.

17.
8629. (Refer to figures 56, 57, and 58 on pages 612 and 613.) What is the ground distance covered during en route climb for Operating Conditions V-2?

A—84 NM.
B—65 NM.
C—69 NM.

Answer (C) is correct (8629). *(FTW Chap 10)*
Refer to V-2 in Fig. 56. The chart in Fig. 57 is used for en route climb ISA.

Find pressure altitude of 27,000 ft. at the left edge of the chart; then move right horizontally to the brake release weight of 95,000 lb. The distance is 65 NM (lower left number), and the time is 13 min. (upper right number).

Adjust the distance for the 20-kt. average tailwind component by multiplying the wind by the time (in hours) to determine a distance of 4 NM [20 x (13 ÷ 60)]. A tailwind will increase the distance; thus the ground distance covered is 69 NM (65 + 4).

Answer (A) is incorrect because 84 NM is the approximate ground distance covered at ISA +10°C, not ISA. Answer (B) is incorrect because 65 NM is the ground distance covered before adjusting for the 20-kt. tailwind component.

18.
8630. (Refer to figures 56, 57, and 58 on pages 612 and 613.) What is the ground distance covered during en route climb for Operating Conditions V-3?

A—95 NM.
B—79 NM.
C—57 NM.

Answer (B) is correct (8630). *(FTW Chap 10)*
Refer to V-3 in Fig. 56. The chart in Fig. 57 is used for en route climb ISA.

Find pressure altitude of 35,000 ft. at the left edge of the chart; then move right horizontally to the brake release weight of 85,000 lb. The distance is 87 NM (lower left number), and the time is 16 min. (upper left number).

Adjust the distance for the 30-kt. average headwind component by multiplying the wind by the time (in hours) to determine a distance of 8 NM [30 x (16 ÷ 60)]. A headwind will decrease the distance; thus the ground distance covered is 79 NM.

Answer (A) is incorrect because 95 NM is the ground distance covered for a 30-kt. tailwind, not headwind. Answer (C) is incorrect because 57 NM is the approximate ground distance covered at a pressure altitude of 30,000, not 35,000, ft.

19.
8631. (Refer to figures 56, 57, and 58 on pages 612 and 613.) What is the ground distance covered during en route climb for Operating Conditions V-4?

A—63 NM.
B—53 NM.
C—65 NM.

Answer (A) is correct (8631). *(FTW Chap 10)*
Refer to V-4 in Fig. 56. The chart in Fig. 58 is used for en route climb ISA +10°C.
Find pressure altitude of 22,000 ft. at the left edge of the chart; then move right horizontally to the brake release weight of 105,000 lb. The distance is 61 NM (lower left number), and the time is 13 min. (upper left number).
Adjust the distance for the 10-kt. average tailwind component by multiplying the wind by the time (in hours) to determine a distance of 2 NM [10 x (13 ÷ 60)]. A tailwind will increase the distance; thus the ground distance covered is 63 NM (61 + 2).
Answer (B) is incorrect because 53 NM is the ground distance covered at ISA, not ISA +10°C. Answer (C) is incorrect because 65 NM is the ground distance covered at a pressure altitude of 22,300, not 22,000, ft.

20.
8632. (Refer to figures 56, 57, and 58 on pages 612 and 613.) What is the ground distance covered during en route climb for Operating Conditions V-5?

A—70 NM.
B—47 NM.
C—61 NM.

Answer (C) is correct (8632). *(FTW Chap 10)*
Refer to V-5 in Fig. 56. The chart in Fig. 58 is used for en route climb ISA +10°C.
Find pressure altitude of 31,000 ft. at the left edge of the chart; then move right horizontally to the brake release weight of 75,000 lb. The distance is 70 NM (lower left number), and the time is 13 min. (upper left number).
Adjust the distance for the 40-kt. average headwind component by multiplying the wind by the time (in hours) to determine a distance of 9 NM [40 x (13 ÷ 60)]. A headwind will decrease the distance; thus the ground distance covered is 61 NM (70 – 9).
Answer (A) is incorrect because 70 NM is the ground distance covered before adjusting for the 40-kt. headwind. Answer (B) is incorrect because 47 NM is the ground distance covered at a pressure altitude of 27,000, not 31,000, ft.

21.
8633. (Refer to figures 56, 57, and 58 on pages 612 and 613.) How much fuel is burned during en route climb for Operating Conditions V-1?

A—4,100 pounds.
B—3,600 pounds.
C—4,000 pounds.

Answer (C) is correct (8633). *(FTW Chap 10)*
Refer to V-1 in Fig. 56. The chart in Fig. 58 is used for en route climb at ISA +10°C.
Find pressure altitude of 33,000 ft. at the left edge of the chart; then move right horizontally to the brake release weight of 110,000 lb. The fuel used is 4,100 lb. (upper right number).
Adjust the fuel burned for the 2,000-ft. airport elevation (at the bottom of the chart), which is –100 lb. Thus, the fuel burned during the en route climb is 4,000 lb. (4,100 – 100).
Answer (A) is incorrect because 4,100 lb. is the fuel burned before the adjustment is made for high-elevation airports. Answer (B) is incorrect because 3,600 lb. is the fuel burned during the en route climb at ISA, not ISA +10°C.

OPERATING CONDITIONS	V-1	V-2	V-3	V-4	V-5
BRK REL WEIGHT (X1000)	110	95	85	105	75
CRUISE PRESS ALT	33,000	27,000	35,000	22,000	31,000
AIRPORT ELEVATION	2,000	3,000	2,000	4,000	2,000
ISA TEMPERATURE	+10°	ISA	ISA	+10°	+10°
AVG WIND COMP (KTS)	20 HW	20 TW	30 HW	10 TW	40 HW

FIGURE 56.—B-737 – En Route Climb.

EN ROUTE CLIMB 280/.70 ISA

PRESSURE ALTITUDE -FT	UNITS MIN/LB NM/KNOTS	BRAKE RELEASE WEIGHT - LB										
		120000	115000	110000	105000	100000	95000	90000	85000	80000	75000	65000
37000	TIME/FUEL DIST./TAS		41/5700 251/387	32/4700 192/384	27/4100 162/382	24/3700 140/380	21/3400 124/379	19/3100 111/378	17/2800 100/377	16/2500 90/376	14/2300 82/375	12/1900 67/374
36000	TIME/FUEL DIST./TAS	41/ 5900 246/386	33/4900 194/383	28/4300 164/381	25/3900 143/379	22/3500 127/378	20/3200 114/377	18/2900 103/376	16/2700 93/375	15/2500 84/374	14/2300 77/374	11/1900 63/373
35000	TIME/FUEL DIST./TAS	33/5100 197/382	29/4500 168/380	25/4100 147/378	23/3700 131/377	21/3400 117/376	19/3100 106/375	17/2800 96/374	16/2600 87/373	14/2400 80/373	13/2200 73/372	11/1800 60/371
34000	TIME/FUEL DIST./TAS	29/4700 171/379	26/4300 150/377	23/3900 134/376	21/3500 120/375	19/3200 109/374	18/3000 99/373	16/2700 90/372	15/2500 82/372	14/2300 75/371	12/2100 69/371	10/1800 57/370
33000	TIME/FUEL DIST./TAS	27/4400 153/376	24/4000 137/375	22/3700 123/374	20/3400 112/373	18/3100 102/372	17/2900 93/371	15/2700 85/370	14/2500 78/370	13/2300 71/369	12/2100 65/369	10/1700 54/368
32000	TIME/FUEL DIST./TAS	25/4200 139/374	23/3900 126/372	21/3600 114/371	19/3300 104/370	17/3000 95/370	16/2800 87/369	15/2600 80/368	14/2400 74/368	12/2200 67/367	11/2000 62/367	10/1700 51/366
31000	TIME/FUEL DIST./TAS	23/4000 128/371	21/3700 117/370	19/3400 107/369	18/3200 98/368	16/2900 90/367	15/2700 82/367	14/2500 76/366	13/2300 70/366	12/2100 64/365	11/2000 59/365	9/1700 49/364
30000	TIME/FUEL DIST./TAS	22/3900 119/368	20/3600 109/367	18/3300 100/366	17/3100 92/365	16/2800 84/365	15/2600 78/364	13/2400 72/364	12/2300 66/363	11/2100 61/363	11/1900 56/363	9/1600 47/362
29000	TIME/FUEL DIST./TAS	21/3700 111/365	19/3400 102/364	18/3200 93/363	16/3000 86/363	15/2700 79/362	14/2500 73/362	13/2400 68/361	12/2200 62/361	11/2000 57/361	10/1900 53/360	9/1600 44/360
28000	TIME/FUEL DIST./TAS	19/3600 103/362	18/3300 95/361	17/3100 88/360	15/2900 81/360	14/2700 75/359	13/2500 69/359	12/2300 64/359	11/2100 59/358	11/2000 54/358	10/1800 50/358	8/1500 42/357
27000	TIME/FUEL DIST./TAS	19/3400 96/358	17/3200 89/358	16/3000 82/357	15/2800 76/357	14/2600 71/356	13/2400 65/356	12/2200 60/356	11/2100 56/356	10/1900 52/355	9/1800 47/355	8/1500 40/355
26000	TIME/FUEL DIST./TAS	17/3300 88/354	16/3000 82/354	15/2800 76/353	14/2600 70/353	13/2500 65/352	12/2300 60/352	11/2100 56/352	10/2000 52/352	10/1800 48/351	9/1700 44/351	7/1400 37/351
25000	TIME/FUEL DIST./TAS	16/3100 81/350	15/2900 75/350	14/2700 70/349	13/2500 65/349	12/2400 60/349	11/2200 56/348	11/2000 52/348	10/1900 48/348	9/1800 45/348	8/1600 41/348	7/1400 35/347
24000	TIME/FUEL DIST./TAS	15/3000 75/346	14/2800 69/346	13/2600 65/345	12/2400 60/345	12/2300 56/345	11/2100 52/345	10/2000 48/345	9/1800 45/344	9/1700 41/344	8/1600 38/344	7/1300 32/344
23000	TIME/FUEL DIST./TAS	14/2800 69/342	13/2700 64/342	13/2500 60/342	12/2300 56/342	11/2200 52/342	10/2000 48/341	9/1900 45/341	9/1800 41/341	8/1600 38/341	8/1500 35/341	6/1300 30/341
22000	TIME/FUEL DIST./TAS	14/2700 63/339	13/2500 59/339	12/2400 55/338	11/2200 51/338	10/2100 48/338	10/1900 45/338	9/1800 41/338	8/1700 38/338	8/1600 36/338	7/1400 33/338	6/1200 28/337
6000	TIME/FUEL DIST./TAS	4/1000 9/295	4/1000 9/295	4/900 8/295	4/800 8/295	3/800 7/295	3/700 7/295	3/700 6/295	3/700 6/295	3/600 5/295	2/600 5/295	2/500 4/295
1500	TIME/FUEL	2/600	2/600	2/500	2/500	2/500	2/400	2/400	2/400	1/400	1/300	1/300

FUEL ADJUSTMENT FOR HIGH ELEVATION AIRPORTS	AIRPORT ELEVATION	2000	4000	6000	8000	10000	12000
EFFECT ON TIME AND DISTANCE IS NEGLIGIBLE	FUEL ADJUSTMENT	-100	-200	-400	-500	-600	-700

FIGURE 57.—En Route Climb 280/.70 ISA.

EN ROUTE CLIMB 280/.70 ISA +10 °C

PRESSURE ALTITUDE -FT	UNITS MIM/LB NM/KNOTS	BRAKE RELEASE WEIGHT - LB 120000	115000	110000	105000	100000	95000	90000	85000	80000	75000	65000
37000	TIME/FUEL DIST./TAS			42/5700 263/395	34/4700 206/391	29/4100 174/389	25/3700 151/388	23/3300 133/386	20/3000 119/385	18/2700 107/384	16/2500 96/384	13/2100 78/382
36000	TIME/FUEL DIST./TAS		43/5900 266/394	35/5000 211/391	30/4400 179/389	26/3900 156/387	23/3500 138/385	21/3200 123/384	19/2900 111/383	17/2700 100/383	16/2400 90/382	13/2000 74/381
35000	TIME/FUEL DIST./TAS	45/6200 275/394	36/5300 219/390	31/4600 186/388	27/4100 162/386	24/3700 143/385	22/3400 128/384	20/3100 115/383	10/2800 104/382	16/2600 94/381	15/2400 85/380	12/2000 70/379
34000	TIME/FUEL DIST./TAS	38/5600 228/390	32/4900 193/387	28/4400 168/386	25/3900 149/384	23/3600 133/383	21/3300 120/382	19/3000 108/381	17/2700 98/380	16/2500 89/379	14/2300 81/379	12/1900 67/378
33000	TIME/FUEL DIST./TAS	34/5100 200/387	30/4600 174/385	26/4100 154/383	24/3800 138/382	22/3400 124/381	20/3100 113/380	18/2900 102/379	16/2600 93/378	15/2400 85/378	14/2200 77/377	11/1900 64/376
32000	TIME/FUEL DIST./TAS	31/4800 180/384	28/4400 160/382	25/4000 143/381	23/3600 129/379	21/3300 116/378	19/3000 106/378	17/2800 96/377	16/2600 88/376	14/2400 80/376	13/2200 73/375	11/1800 61/374
31000	TIME/FUEL DIST./TAS	29/4600 165/381	26/4200 147/379	23/3800 133/378	21/3500 120/377	20/3200 109/376	18/2900 100/375	16/2700 91/375	15/2500 83/374	14/2300 76/374	13/2100 70/373	11/1800 58/372
30000	TIME/FUEL DIST./TAS	27/4400 152/378	24/4000 137/376	22/3700 124/375	20/3400 113/374	19/3100 103/374	17/2900 94/373	16/2600 86/372	14/2400 79/372	13/2200 72/371	12/2100 66/371	10/1700 55/370
29000	TIME/FUEL DIST./TAS	25/4200 141/375	23/3800 128/374	21/3500 116/373	19/3200 106/372	18/3000 97/371	16/2800 89/370	15/2600 82/370	14/2400 75/369	13/2200 69/369	12/2000 63/369	10/1700 52/368
28000	TIME/FUEL DIST./TAS	24/4000 131/371	22/3700 119/370	20/3400 109/369	18/3100 100/369	17/2900 91/368	16/2700 84/368	14/2500 77/367	13/2300 71/367	12/2100 65/366	11/1900 60/366	9/1600 50/365
27000	TIME/FUEL DIST./TAS	22/3800 121/368	21/3500 111/367	19/3300 102/366	18/3000 93/366	16/2800 86/365	15/2600 79/364	14/2400 73/364	13/2200 67/364	12/2000 61/363	11/1900 56/363	9/1600 47/363
26000	TIME/FUEL DIST./TAS	21/3600 110/363	19/3400 101/362	18/3100 93/362	16/2900 86/361	15/2700 79/361	14/2500 73/360	13/2300 67/360	12/2100 62/360	11/2000 57/359	10/1800 52/359	9/1500 44/359
25000	TIME/FUEL DIST./TAS	19/3400 101/358	18/3200 93/358	17/3000 85/357	15/2800 79/357	14/2600 73/357	13/2400 67/356	12/2200 62/356	11/2000 57/356	10/1900 53/356	10/1700 48/355	8/1500 41/355
24000	TIME/FUEL DIST./TAS	18/3300 92/354	17/3000 85/354	16/2800 78/353	15/2600 72/353	13/2400 67/353	12/2300 62/352	12/2100 57/352	11/1900 53/352	10/1800 49/352	9/1700 45/352	8/1400 38/351
23000	TIME/FUEL DIST./TAS	17/3100 84/350	16/2900 78/350	15/2900 72/350	14/2500 67/349	13/2300 62/349	12/2200 57/349	11/2000 53/349	10/1900 49/348	9/1700 45/348	9/1600 42/348	7/1300 35/348
22000	TIME/FUEL DIST./TAS	16/3000 77/346	15/2800 71/346	14/2600 66/346	13/2400 61/346	12/2200 57/345	11/2100 53/345	10/1900 49/345	10/1800 45/345	9/1700 42/345	8/1500 38/345	7/1300 32/344
6000	TIME/FUEL DIST./TAS	5/1100 10/301	4/1000 10/301	4/900 9/301	4/900 9/301	4/800 8/301	3/800 8/301	3/700 7/301	3/700 7/301	3/600 6/301	3/600 6/301	2/500 5/301
1500	TIME/FUEL	3/600	2/600	2/500	2/500	2/500	2/500	2/400	2/400	2/400	1/300	1/300

FUEL ADJUSTMENT FOR HIGH ELEVATION AIRPORTS	AIRPORT ELEVATION	2000	4000	6000	8000	10000	12000
EFFECT ON TIME AND DISTANCE IS NEGLIGIBLE	FUEL ADJUSTMENT	-100	-300	-400	-500	-600	-800

FIGURE 58.—En Route Climb 280/.70 ISA +10 °C.

22.
8634. (Refer to figures 56 and 57 on page 612 and figure 58 above.) How much fuel is burned during en route climb for Operating Conditions V-2?

A—2,250 pounds.
B—2,600 pounds.
C—2,400 pounds.

Answer (A) is correct (8634). *(FTW Chap 10)*

Refer to V-2 in Fig. 56. The chart in Fig. 57 is used for en route climb at ISA.

Find pressure altitude of 27,000 ft. at the left edge of the chart; then move right horizontally to the brake release weight of 95,000 lb. The fuel burned is 2,400 lb. (upper right number).

Adjust the fuel burned for the 3,000-ft. airport elevation (at bottom of chart), which is interpolated between 2,000 ft. and 4,000 ft. to be –150 lb. Thus, the fuel burned during the en route climb is 2,250 lb.

Answer (B) is incorrect because 2,600 lb. is the fuel burned during an en route climb at ISA +10°C, not ISA, and with no adjustment made for the airport elevation. Answer (C) is incorrect because 2,400 lb. is the fuel burned during an en route climb before adjusting for the airport elevation.

23.
8635. (Refer to figures 56, 57, and 58 on pages 612 and 613.) What is the aircraft weight at the top of climb for Operating Conditions V-3?

A—82,100 pounds.
B—82,500 pounds.
C—82,200 pounds.

Answer (B) is correct (8635). *(FTW Chap 10)*

Refer to V-3 in Fig. 56. The chart in Fig. 57 is used for en route climb at ISA.

Find pressure altitude of 35,000 ft. at the left edge of the chart; then move right horizontally to the brake release weight of 85,000 lb. The fuel burned is 2,600 lb. (upper right number).

Adjust the fuel burned for the 2,000-ft. airport elevation (at bottom of chart), which is –100 lb. The total fuel burned during the climb is 2,500 lb.

The aircraft weight at the top of the climb is the brake release weight minus the fuel burned during climb, or 82,500 lb. (85,000 – 2,500).

Answer (A) is incorrect because 82,100 lb. is the aircraft weight at the top of the climb when 2,900, not 2,500, lb. of fuel is burned during the en route climb. Answer (C) is incorrect because 82,200 lb. is the aircraft weight at the top of the climb when 2,800 lb. of fuel is burned during a climb at a temperature of ISA +10°C, not ISA.

24.
8636. (Refer to figures 56, 57, and 58 on pages 612 and 613.) What is the aircraft weight at the top of climb for Operating Conditions V-4?

A—102,900 pounds.
B—102,600 pounds.
C—103,100 pounds.

Answer (A) is correct (8636). *(FTW Chap 10)*

Refer to V-4 in Fig. 56. The chart in Fig. 58 is used for en route climb at ISA +10°C.

Find pressure altitude of 22,000 ft. at the left edge of the chart; then move right horizontally to the brake release weight of 105,000 lb. The fuel burned is 2,400 lb. (upper right number).

Adjust the fuel burned for the 4,000-ft. airport elevation (at bottom of chart), which is –300 lb. The total fuel burned during the climb is 2,100 lb. (2,400 – 300).

Aircraft weight at the top of the climb is the brake release weight minus fuel burned, or 102,900 lb. (105,000 – 2,100).

Answer (B) is incorrect because 102,600 lb. is the aircraft weight at the top of the climb before the adjustment is made to the fuel burned for the airport elevation. Answer (C) is incorrect because 103,100 lb. is the aircraft weight at the top of the climb if the brake release weight was 100,000, not 105,000, lb.

25.
8637. (Refer to figures 56, 57, and 58 on pages 612 and 613.) What is the aircraft weight at the top of climb for Operating Conditions V-5?

A—73,000 pounds.
B—72,900 pounds.
C—72,800 pounds.

Answer (A) is correct (8637). *(FTW Chap 10)*

Refer to V-5 in Fig. 56. The chart in Fig. 58 is used for en route climb at ISA +10°C.

Find pressure altitude of 31,000 ft. at the left edge of the chart; then move right horizontally to the brake release weight of 75,000 lb. The fuel burned is 2,100 lb. (upper right number).

Adjust the fuel burned for the 2,000-ft. airport elevation (at bottom of chart), which is –100 lb. The total fuel burned during the climb is 2,000 lb. (2,100 – 100).

Aircraft weight at the top of the climb is the brake release weight minus the fuel burned, or 73,000 lb. (75,000 – 2,000).

Answer (B) is incorrect because 72,900 lb. is the aircraft weight at the top of the climb before the airport elevation adjustment is made. Answer (C) is incorrect because 72,800 lb. is the aircraft weight at the top of the climb for a cruise pressure altitude of 34,000, not 31,000, ft.

13.4 Climb and Cruise Power

26.
8638. (Refer to figures 59 and 60 on page 616.) What is the max climb EPR for Operating Conditions T-1?

A—1.82.
B—1.96.
C—2.04.

Answer (A) is correct (8638). *(FTW Chap 10)*

Refer to operating conditions T-1 in Fig. 59. Use the Max Climb and Max Continuous EPR chart in Fig. 60. Find the Max Climb column at the left edge of the chart. Move down vertically to 10,000 ft. (SL to 30,000) and move right horizontally to the total air temperature (TAT) column of +10°C. The temperature limit EPR is 1.90. At the bottom center of the chart, find the pressure limit EPR altitude of 10,000 ft. (5,660 ft. and above). The number above is the pressure limit EPR of 2.30. Use the smaller of the two limits, which is 1.90.

Next, apply the bleed air correction for engine anti-ice ON, which is –.08. Thus, the max climb EPR is 1.82.

Answer (B) is incorrect because 1.96 is the max continuous, not climb, EPR. Answer (C) is incorrect because 2.04 is the max continuous, not climb, EPR without the bleed air correction for the engine anti-ice ON.

27.
8639. (Refer to figures 59 and 60 on page 616.) What is the max continuous EPR for Operating Conditions T-2?

A—2.10.
B—1.99.
C—2.02.

Answer (C) is correct (8639). *(FTW Chap 10)*

Refer to operating conditions T-2 in Fig. 59. Use the Max Climb and Max Continuous chart in Fig. 60. Find the Max Cont. column at the left side of the chart and move down vertically to the altitude of 5,000 ft. (1,500 to 20,000). Move right horizontally to the TAT column of 0°C to determine the temperature limit EPR of 2.10. At the bottom center of the same chart, find the pressure limit altitude of 5,000 ft. (4,000) to determine the pressure limit EPR of 2.20. Use the smaller of the two limits, which is 2.10.

Make the necessary bleed air corrections for the engine anti-ice ON (–.08), wing anti-ice "2 engines ON" (–.04), and the air-conditioning OFF (+.04). Thus, the max continuous EPR is 2.02 (2.10 – .08 – .04 + .04).

Answer (A) is incorrect because 2.10 is the max continuous EPR before making the necessary bleed air corrections. Answer (B) is incorrect because 1.99 is the max continuous temperature limit EPR for an altitude from SL to 1,500 ft. and 20,000 ft. to 30,000 ft., not 5,000 ft.

28.
8640. (Refer to figures 59 and 60 below.) What is the max cruise EPR for Operating Conditions T-3?

A—2.11.
B—2.02.
C—1.90.

Answer (C) is correct (8640). *(FTW Chap 10)*

Refer to operating conditions T-3 in Fig. 59. Use the max cruise EPR chart in Fig. 60. Find the pressure altitude of 25,000 ft. (6 to 30) at the left edge of the chart, and move right horizontally to the TAT column of −15°C to determine an EPR of 2.02.

Make the necessary bleed air corrections for the engine anti-ice ON (−.08), and the wing anti-ice "2 engine ON" (−.04). Thus, the max cruise EPR is 1.90.

Answer (A) is incorrect because 2.11 is the max cruise EPR at an altitude of either 35,000 ft. or 37,000 ft., not 25,000 ft., and no bleed air corrections applied.
Answer (B) is incorrect because 2.02 is the max cruise EPR before making the necessary bleed air corrections.

OPERATING CONDITIONS	T-1	T-2	T-3	T-4	T-5
TOTAL AIR TEMP (TAT)	+10 °C	0 °C	−15 °C	−30 °C	+15 °C
ALTITUDE	10,000	5,000	25,000	35,000	18,000
ENGINE ANTI-ICE	ON	ON	ON	ON	OFF
WING ANTI-ICE	OFF	2 ON	2 ON	1 ON	OFF
AIR CONDITIONING	ON	OFF	ON	ON	OFF

FIGURE 59.—B-737 – Climb and Cruise Power.

EN ROUTE

MAX CLIMB & MAX CONTINUOUS EPR

A/C AIRBLEED ON

MAX. CLIMB	MAX. CONT.	TAT °C -40	-35	-30	-25	-20	-15	-10	-5	0	5	10	15	20	25	30	35	40	45	50
S.L. TO 30000	S.L. TO 1500 20000 TO 30000	2.25	2.23	2.21	2.18	2.15	2.12	2.09	2.04	1.99	1.94	1.90	1.86	1.82	1.79	1.76	1.73	1.70	1.67	1.64
	1500 TO 20000	2.30	2.28	2.26	2.24	2.21	2.19	2.16	2.13	2.10	2.07	2.04	2.00	1.95	1.91	1.86	1.81	1.75	1.71	1.66
	35000 & 37000	2.24	2.22	2.20	2.17	2.14	2.11	2.07	2.02	1.97	1.92									

2.30	2.20	2.14	2.09	2.04	1.98
5660 AND ABOVE	4000	3000	2000	1000	S.L.

TEMP / PRESS LIMIT EPR

1. FIND TEMP LIMIT EPR
2. FIND PRESS LIMIT EPR
3. USE THE SMALLER OF THE TWO LIMITS

MAX CRUISE EPR

TAT °C		-50	-45	-40	-35	-30	-25	-20	-15	-10	-5	0	5	10	15	20	25	30	35	40
PRESS ALT 1000 FT	6 TO 30	2.18	2.16	2.14	2.12	2.10	2.07	2.05	2.02	1.99	1.95	1.91	1.85	1.79	1.73	1.68	1.64	1.61	1.57	1.54
	35 & 37	2.28	2.26	2.24	2.22	2.20	2.17	2.14	2.11	2.07	2.02	1.97	1.92	1.87	1.84	1.80				

ANTI-ICE BLEED CORRECTIONS	Δ EPR
ENGINE ANTI-ICE	-.08
WING ANTI-ICE	2 ENG -.04
	1 ENG -.06

AIR COND-BLEED CORRECTIONS Δ EPR	A/C OFF
S. L. TO 37000	+ .04

BLEED CORRECTIONS APPLY TO MAX CLIMB, MAX CONTINUOUS, AND MAX CRUISE EPR SETTINGS

FIGURE 60.—B-737 – Climb and Cruise Power.

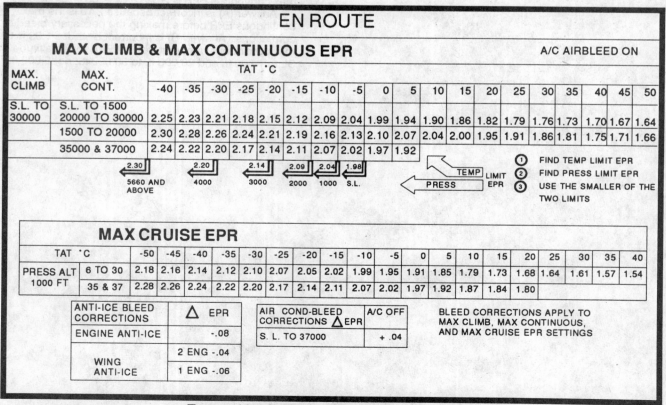

29.
8641. (Refer to figures 59 and 60 on page 616.) What is the max climb EPR for Operating Conditions T-4?

A—2.20.
B—2.07.
C—2.06.

Answer (C) is correct (8641). *(FTW Chap 10)*
Refer to operating conditions T-4 in Fig. 59. Use the max climb and max continuous chart in Fig. 60. Find the Max Climb column at the left edge of the chart, and move down vertically to the pressure altitude of 35,000 ft. (35,000 and 37,000). Move right horizontally to the TAT column of −30°C to determine the temperature limit EPR of 2.20. At the bottom center of the chart, find the pressure limit EPR altitude of 35,000 ft. (5,660 and above) to determine the pressure limit EPR of 2.30. Use the smaller of the two limits, which is 2.20.

Make the necessary bleed air corrections for the engine anti-ice ON (−.08) and the wing anti-ice "1 engine ON" (−.06). Thus, the max climb EPR is 2.06.

Answer (A) is incorrect because 2.20 is the max climb EPR before making the necessary bleed air corrections. Answer (B) is incorrect because 2.07 is the max climb EPR for a TAT of −32.5°C, not −30°C.

30.
8642. (Refer to figures 59 and 60 on page 616.) What is the max continuous EPR for Operating Conditions T-5?

A—2.00.
B—2.04.
C—1.96.

Answer (B) is correct (8642). *(FTW Chap 10)*
Refer to operating conditions T-5 in Fig. 59. Use the max climb and max continuous EPR chart in Fig. 60. Find the Max Cont. column at the left edge of the chart, and move down vertically to the pressure altitude of 18,000 ft. (1,500 to 20,000). Then move right horizontally to the TAT column of +15°C to determine a temperature limit EPR of 2.00. At the bottom center of the chart, find the pressure limit EPR altitude of 18,000 ft. (5,660 and above) to determine the pressure limit EPR of 2.30. Use the smaller of the two limits, which is 2.00.

Make the necessary bleed air correction for the air-conditioning OFF of +.04. Thus, the max continuous EPR is 2.04.

Answer (A) is incorrect because 2.00 is the max continuous EPR before making the necessary bleed air correction. Answer (C) is incorrect because an EPR of 1.96 is determined by subtracting, not adding, the .04 bleed air correction for the air-conditioning OFF.

OPERATING CONDITIONS	X-1	X-2	X-3	X-4	X-5
DISTANCE (NM)	2,000	2,400	1,800	2,800	1,200
WIND COMPONENT (KTS)	50 TW	50 HW	20 HW	50 TW	30 HW
CRUISE PRESS ALTITUDE	27,000	35,000	20,000	29,000	37,000
ISA TEMPERATURE	+10°	ISA	+20°	–10°	+10°
LANDING WEIGHT (X1000)	70	75	75	65	90

FIGURE 61.—Flight Planning at .78 Mach Cruise.

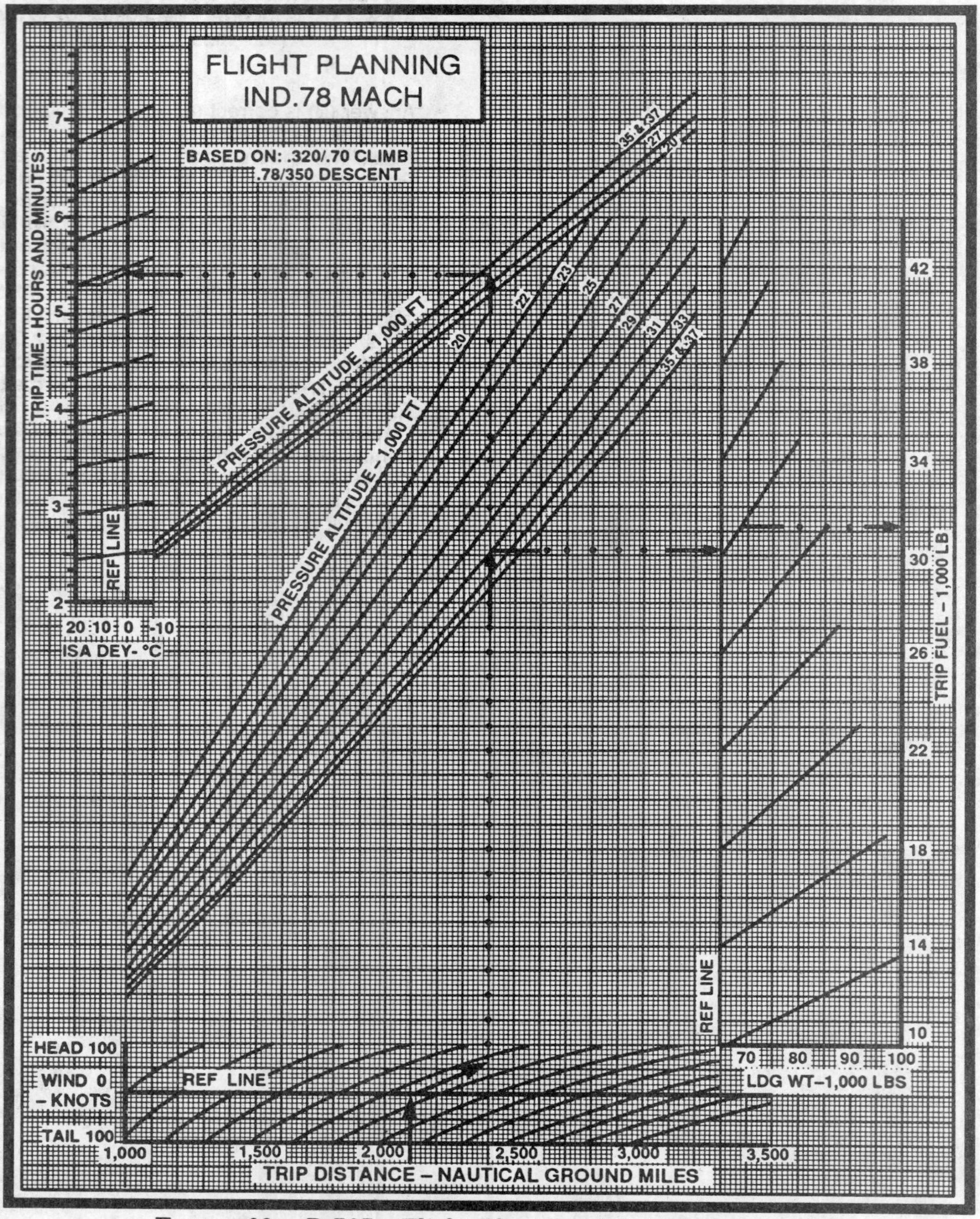

FIGURE 62.—B-737 – Flight Planning .78 Mach Indicated.

13.5 Flight Planning at .78 Mach Cruise

31.
8643. (Refer to figures 61 and 62 on page 618.) What is the trip time for Operating Conditions X-1?

A—4 hours 5 minutes.
B—4 hours 15 minutes.
C—4 hours.

Answer (C) is correct (8643). *(FTW Chap 10)*

Refer to operating conditions X-1 in Fig. 61. Fig. 62 provides a flight planning chart.

Find the trip distance of 2,000 NM at the bottom of the chart, and move up vertically to the reference line. Move down (tailwind) and to the left (parallel to the guide line) to 50 kt. Move up vertically to the second set of pressure altitude lines to 27,000 ft. (27). Move left horizontally to the reference line; then move down and to the left (parallel to the guide line) to +10°C. Then move horizontally to the left edge of the chart to determine a trip time of 4 hr.

Answer (A) is incorrect because a trip time of 4 hr. 5 min. is for a temperature of ISA, not ISA +10°C. Answer (B) is incorrect because 4 hr. 15 min. is the trip time in calm wind, not a 50-kt. tailwind.

32.
8648. (Refer to figures 61 and 62 on page 618.) What is the trip fuel for Operating Conditions X-1?

A—25,000 pounds.
B—26,000 pounds.
C—24,000 pounds.

Answer (B) is correct (8648). *(FTW Chap 10)*

Refer to operating conditions X-1 in Fig. 61. Fig. 62 provides a flight planning chart.

Find the trip distance of 2,000 NM at the bottom of the chart, and move up vertically to the reference line. Move down (tailwind) and to the left (parallel to the guide line) to 50 kt. Move up vertically to the first set of pressure altitude lines to 27,000 ft. (27). Move right horizontally to the reference line; then move up and to the right (parallel to the guide line) to 70,000 lb. Then move horizontally to the right edge of the chart to determine a trip fuel of 25,600 lb. or round up to 26,000 lb.

Answer (A) is incorrect because 25,000 lb. is the trip fuel with a landing weight of 75,000, not 70,000, lb. Answer (C) is incorrect because 24,000 lb. is the trip fuel with a tailwind component of 80, not 50, kt.

33.
8644. (Refer to figures 61 and 62 on page 618.) What is the trip time for Operating Conditions X-2?

A—5 hours 5 minutes.
B—6 hours 15 minutes.
C—5 hours 55 minutes.

Answer (B) is correct (8644). *(FTW Chap 10)*

Refer to operating conditions X-2 in Fig. 61. Fig. 62 provides a flight planning chart.

Find the trip distance of 2,400 NM at the bottom of the chart, and move up vertically to the reference line. Move up (headwind) and to the right (parallel to the guide line) to 50 kt. Move up vertically to the second set of pressure altitude lines to 35,000 ft. (35). Then move horizontally to the left edge of the chart to determine a trip time of 6 hr. 15 min.

Answer (A) is incorrect because 5 hr. 5 min. is the trip time with a 40-kt. tailwind, not a 50-kt. headwind. Answer (C) is incorrect because 5 hr. 55 min. is the trip time at a temperature of ISA +20°C, not ISA.

34.
8649. (Refer to figures 61 and 62 on page 618.) What is the trip fuel for Operating Conditions X-2?

A—33,000 pounds.
B—28,000 pounds.
C—35,000 pounds.

Answer (C) is correct (8649). *(FTW Chap 10)*
Refer to operating conditions X-2 in Fig. 61. Fig. 62 provides a flight planning chart.
Find the trip distance of 2,400 NM at the bottom of the chart, and move up vertically to the reference line. Move up (headwind) and to the left (parallel to the guide line) to 50 kt. Move up vertically to the first set of pressure altitude lines to 35,000 ft. (35). Move right horizontally to the reference line; then move up and to the right (parallel to the guide line) to 75,000 lb. Then move horizontally to the right edge of the chart to determine a trip fuel of 35,000 lb.
Answer (A) is incorrect because 33,000 lb. is the trip fuel at a landing weight of 65,000, not 75,000, lb. Answer (B) is incorrect because 28,000 lb. is the trip fuel with a tailwind, not headwind, component of 50 kt.

35.
8645. (Refer to figures 61 and 62 on page 618.) What is the trip time for Operating Conditions X-3?

A—4 hours 15 minutes.
B—3 hours 40 minutes.
C—4 hours.

Answer (C) is correct (8645). *(FTW Chap 10)*
Refer to operating conditions X-3 in Fig. 61. Fig. 62 provides a flight planning chart.
Find the trip distance of 1,800 NM at the bottom of the chart, and move up vertically to the reference line. Move up (headwind) and to the right (parallel to the guide line) to 20 kt. Move up vertically to the second set of pressure altitude lines to 20,000 ft. (20). Move left horizontally to the reference line; then move down and to the left (parallel to the guide line) to +20°C (the left edge of the chart) to determine a trip time of 4 hr.
Answer (A) is incorrect because 4 hr. 15 min. is the trip time with a 50-kt., not 20-kt., headwind. Answer (B) is incorrect because 3 hr. 40 min. is the trip time in a calm wind, not a 20-kt. headwind.

36.
8650. (Refer to figures 61 and 62 on page 618.) What is the trip fuel for Operating Conditions X-3?

A—36,000 pounds.
B—34,500 pounds.
C—33,000 pounds.

Answer (B) is correct (8650). *(FTW Chap 10)*
Refer to operating conditions X-3 in Fig. 61. Fig. 62 provides a flight planning chart.
Find the trip distance of 1,800 NM at the bottom of the chart, and move up vertically to the reference line. Move up (headwind) and to the left (parallel to the guide line) to 20 kt. Move up vertically to the first set of pressure altitude lines to 20,000 ft. (20). Move right horizontally to the reference line; then move up and to the right (parallel to the guide line) to 75,000 lb. Then move horizontally to the right edge of the chart to determine a trip fuel of 34,500 lb.
Answer (A) is incorrect because 36,000 lb. is the trip fuel at a landing weight of 80,000, not 75,000, lb. Answer (C) is incorrect because 33,000 lb. is the trip fuel at a landing weight of 70,000, not 75,000, lb.

37.
8646. (Refer to figures 61 and 62 on page 618.) What is the trip time for Operating Conditions X-4?

A—6 hours 50 minutes.
B—5 hours 45 minutes.
C—5 hours 30 minutes.

Answer (B) is correct (8646). *(FTW Chap 10)*

Refer to operating conditions X-4 in Fig. 61. Fig. 62 provides a flight planning chart.

Find the trip distance of 2,800 NM at the bottom of the chart, and move up vertically to the reference line. Move down (tailwind) and to the left (parallel to the guide line) to 50 kt. Move up vertically to the second set of pressure altitude lines to 29,000 ft. Move left horizontally to the reference line; then move up and to the right (parallel to the guide line) to −10°C. Then move horizontally to the left edge of the chart to determine a trip time of 5 hr. 45 min.

Answer (A) is incorrect because 6 hr. 50 min. is the trip time with a 40-kt. headwind, not a 50-kt. tailwind. Answer (C) is incorrect because 5 hr. 30 min. is the trip time with a temperature of ISA +10°C, not −10°C.

38.
8651. (Refer to figures 61 and 62 on page 618.) What is the trip fuel for Operating Conditions X-4?

A—33,000 pounds.
B—31,500 pounds.
C—34,000 pounds.

Answer (A) is correct (8651). *(FTW Chap 10)*

Refer to operating conditions X-4 in Fig. 61. Fig. 62 provides a flight planning chart.

Find the trip distance of 2,800 NM at the bottom of the chart, and move up vertically to the reference line. Move down (tailwind) and to the left (parallel to the guide line) to 50 kt. Move up vertically to the first set of pressure altitude lines to 29,000 ft. (29). Move right horizontally to the reference line, which is 65,000 lb.; then move horizontally to the right edge of the chart to determine a trip fuel of 33,000 lb.

Answer (B) is incorrect because 31,500 lb. is the trip fuel with a tailwind component of 70, not 50, kt. Answer (C) is incorrect because 34,000 lb. is the trip fuel with a landing weight of 70,000, not 65,000, lb.

39.
8647. (Refer to figures 61 and 62 on page 618.) What is the trip time for Operating Conditions X-5?

A—2 hours 55 minutes.
B—3 hours 10 minutes.
C—2 hours 50 minutes.

Answer (A) is correct (8647). *(FTW Chap 10)*

Refer to operating conditions X-5 in Fig. 61. Fig. 62 provides a flight planning chart.

Find the trip distance of 1,200 NM at the bottom of the chart, and move up vertically to the reference line. Move up (headwind) and to the right (parallel to the guide line) to 30 kt. Move up vertically to the second set of pressure altitude lines to 37,000 ft. (37). Move left horizontally to the reference line; then move down and to the left (parallel to the guide line) to +10°C. Then move horizontally to the left edge of the chart to determine a trip time of 2 hr. 55 min.

Answer (B) is incorrect because 3 hr. 10 min. is the trip time with a 60-kt., not 30-kt., headwind. Answer (C) is incorrect because 2 hr. 50 min. is the trip time with a 20-kt., not 30-kt., headwind.

40.
8652. (Refer to figures 61 and 62 on page 618.) What is the trip fuel for Operating Conditions X-5?

A—15,000 pounds.
B—20,000 pounds.
C—19,000 pounds.

Answer (C) is correct (8652). *(FTW Chap 10)*

Refer to operating conditions X-5 in Fig. 61. Fig. 62 provides a flight planning chart.

Find the trip distance of 1,200 NM at the bottom of the chart, and move up vertically to the reference line. Move up (headwind) and to the right (parallel to the guide line) to 30 kt. Move up vertically to the first set of pressure altitude lines to 37,000 ft. (37). Move right horizontally to the reference line; then move up and to the right (parallel to the guide line) to 90,000 lb. Then move horizontally to the right edge of the chart to determine a trip fuel of 19,000 lb.

Answer (A) is incorrect because 15,000 lb. is the trip fuel at a landing weight of 65,000, not 90,000, lb. Answer (B) is incorrect because 20,000 lb. is the trip fuel with a headwind component of 50, not 30, kt.

13.6 Turbulent Air Penetration RPM

41.
8653. (Refer to figures 63 and 64 below.) What is the turbulent air penetration N_1 power setting for Operating Conditions Q-1?

A—82.4 percent.
B—84.0 percent.
C—84.8 percent.

Answer (C) is correct (8653). *(FTW Chap 10)*
Refer to operating conditions Q-1 in Fig. 63. Fig. 64 provides a chart to determine the N_1 power setting for turbulent air penetration.

Find the pressure altitude column, and move down vertically to 30,000 ft. Move right horizontally to a gross weight of 110,000 (110) lb. to determine the approximate power setting of 82.4%. Move right horizontally to determine the ISA TAT is −23°C, and move right to find an adjustment of 1.6% per 10°C variation is required. The TAT variation is 15° (23 − 8), which is an adjustment of 2.4% [(15 ÷ 10) x 1.6]. Since actual TAT is warmer than ISA TAT, the adjustment is added. Thus, the N_1 power setting is 84.8%.

Answer (A) is incorrect because 82.4% is the approximate power setting before adjustment is made for TAT variation. Answer (B) is incorrect because 84.0% is the N_1 power setting with an actual TAT of −13°C, not −8°C.

OPERATING CONDITIONS	Q–1	Q–2	Q–3	Q–4	Q–5
WEIGHT (X1000)	110	70	90	80	100
PRESSURE ALTITUDE	30,000	25,000	35,000	20,000	10,000
TOTAL AIR TEMP (TAT)	–8 °C	–23 °C	–16 °C	+4 °C	–6 °C

FIGURE 63.—B-737– Turbulent Air RPM.

TURBULENT AIR PENETRATION

TARGET SPEED IAS/MACH	PRESS ALT -1000 FT	GROSS WEIGHT - 1000 LB: 70	80	90	100	110	ISA TAT -°C	% N_1 ADJUSTMENT PER 10 °C VARIATION FROM TABLE TAT COLDER - WARMER +
		APPROXIMATE POWER SETTING -%N_1 RPM						
280/.70	35	77.1	79.0	81.0	83.4		-36	1.6
	30	77.2	78.2	79.4	81.1	82.4	-23	1.6
	25	76.7	77.5	78.3	79.2	80.1	-13	1.5
	20	74.7	75.4	76.1	77.0	77.9	-6	1.4
	15	72.7	73.5	74.2	74.8	75.7	1	1.2
	10	70.5	71.3	72.1	72.9	73.9	9	1.3

FIGURE 64.—B-737 – Turbulent Air Penetration.

42.
8654. (Refer to figures 63 and 64 on page 622.) What is the turbulent air penetration N_1 power setting for Operating Conditions Q-2?

A—78.2 percent.
B—75.2 percent.
C—76.7 percent.

Answer (B) is correct (8654). *(FTW Chap 10)*
Refer to operating conditions Q-2 in Fig. 63. Fig. 64 provides a chart to determine the N_1 power setting for turbulent air penetration.

Find the pressure altitude column, and move down vertically to 25,000 ft. Move right horizontally to a gross weight of 70,000 (70) lb. to determine the approximate power setting of 76.7%. Move right horizontally to determine the ISA TAT is −13°C, and move right to find an adjustment of 1.5% per 10°C variation is required. The TAT variation is 10° (23 − 13), which is an adjustment of 1.5% [(10 ÷ 10) x 1.5]. Since actual TAT is colder than ISA TAT, the adjustment is subtracted. Thus, the N_1 power setting is 75.2%.

Answer (A) is incorrect because 78.2% is the N_1 power setting with an actual TAT of −3°C, not −23°C. Answer (C) is incorrect because 76.7% is the approximate N_1 power setting before adjustment is made for TAT variation.

43.
8655. (Refer to figures 63 and 64 on page 622.) What is the turbulent air penetration N_1 power setting for Operating Conditions Q-3?

A—77.8 percent.
B—82.6 percent.
C—84.2 percent.

Answer (C) is correct (8655). *(FTW Chap 10)*
Refer to operating conditions Q-3 in Fig. 63. Fig. 64 provides a chart to determine the N_1 power setting for turbulent air penetration.

Find the pressure altitude column, and move down vertically to 35,000 ft. Move right horizontally to a gross weight of 90,000 (90) lb. to determine the approximate power setting of 81.0%. Move right horizontally to determine the ISA TAT is −36°C, and move right to find an adjustment of 1.6% per 10°C variation is required. The TAT variation is 20° (36 − 16), which is an adjustment of 3.2% [(20 ÷ 10) x 1.6]. Since actual TAT is warmer than ISA TAT, the adjustment is added. Thus, the N_1 power setting is 84.2%.

Answer (A) is incorrect because 77.8% is the N_1 power setting with an actual TAT of −56°C, not −16°C. Answer (B) is incorrect because 82.6% is the N_1 power setting with an actual TAT of −26°C, not −16°C.

44.
8656. (Refer to figures 63 and 64 on page 622.) What is the turbulent air penetration N_1 power setting for Operating Conditions Q-4?

A—76.8 percent.
B—75.4 percent.
C—74.0 percent.

Answer (A) is correct (8656). *(FTW Chap 10)*
Refer to operating conditions Q-4 in Fig. 63. Fig. 64 provides a chart to determine the N_1 power setting for turbulent air penetration.

Find the pressure altitude column, and move down vertically to 20,000 ft. Move right horizontally to a gross weight of 80,000 (80) lb. to determine the approximate power setting of 75.4%. Move right horizontally to determine the ISA TAT is −6°C, and move right to find an adjustment of 1.4% per 10°C variation is required. The TAT variation is 10° [+4 − (−6)], which is an adjustment of 1.4% [(10 ÷ 10) x 1.4]. Since actual TAT is warmer than ISA TAT, the adjustment is added. Thus, the N_1 power setting is 76.8%.

Answer (B) is incorrect because 75.4% is the approximate N_1 power setting before adjustment is made for the TAT variation. Answer (C) is incorrect because 74.0% is the N_1 power setting with an actual TAT of −16°C, not +4°C.

45.
8657. (Refer to figures 63 and 64 on page 622.) What is the turbulent air penetration N_1 power setting for Operating Conditions Q-5?

A—70.9 percent.
B—72.9 percent.
C—71.6 percent.

Answer (A) is correct (8657). *(FTW Chap 10)*
Refer to operating conditions Q-5 in Fig. 63. Fig. 64 provides a chart to determine the N_1 power setting for turbulent air penetration.

Find the pressure altitude column, and move down vertically to 10,000 ft. Move right horizontally to a gross weight of 100,000 (100) lb. to determine the approximate power setting of 72.9%. Move right horizontally to determine the ISA TAT is +9°C, and move right to find an adjustment of 1.3% per 10°C variation is required. The TAT variation is 15° [+9 – (–6)], which is an adjustment of 2.0% [(15 ÷ 10) x 1.3]. Since actual TAT is colder than ISA TAT, the adjustment is subtracted. Thus, the N_1 power setting is 70.9%.

Answer (B) is incorrect because 72.9% is the N_1 power setting before adjustment is made for the TAT variation. Answer (C) is incorrect because 71.6% is the N_1 power setting for an actual TAT of –1°C, not –6°C.

13.7 Flight Planning at .74 Mach Cruise

46.
8658. (Refer to figures 66 and 67 on page 625.) What is the trip time corrected for wind under Operating Conditions Z-1?

A—58.1 minutes.
B—51.9 minutes.
C—54.7 minutes.

Answer (B) is correct (8658). *(FTW Chap 10)*
Refer to operating conditions Z-1 in Fig. 66. Fig. 67 provides a chart for flight planning at .74 Mach cruise.

Find 340 NM under the distance column on the left side of the chart, and move right to determine a TAS of 438 kt. and an air time of 55 min.

Correct the time for the 25-kt. tailwind with the formula at the bottom of the chart.

$$\Delta\ Time = \frac{Time \times Wind\ component}{TAS}$$

$$\Delta\ Time = \frac{55 \times 25}{438} = 3.1\ min.$$

Subtract ΔTime for the tailwind. Thus, the adjusted trip time is 51.9 min. (55 – 3.1).

Answer (A) is incorrect because 58.1 min. is the adjusted trip time for a 25-kt. headwind, not tailwind. Answer (C) is incorrect because 54.7 min. is the approximate air time before adjusting for the 25-kt. tailwind.

47.
8663. (Refer to figures 66 and 67 on page 625.) What is the estimated fuel consumption for Operating Conditions Z-1?

A—5,230 pounds.
B—5,970 pounds.
C—5,550 pounds.

Answer (A) is correct (8663). *(FTW Chap 10)*
Refer to operating conditions Z-1 in Fig. 66. Fig. 67 provides a chart for flight planning at .74 Mach cruise.

Find 340 NM under the distance column on the left side of the chart, and move right to determine a TAS of 438 kt., an air time of 55 min., and fuel consumption of 5,550 lb.

Correct the fuel for the 25-kt. tailwind with the formula at the bottom of the chart.

$$\Delta\ Fuel = \frac{Fuel \times Wind\ component}{TAS}$$

$$\Delta\ Fuel = \frac{5{,}550 \times 25}{438} = 317\ (320)\ lb.$$

Subtract ΔFuel for the tailwind. Thus, the estimated fuel consumption is 5,230 lb. (5,550 – 320).

Answer (B) is incorrect because 5,970 lb. is the estimated fuel consumption for a distance of 350, not 340, NM and a 25-kt. headwind, not tailwind. Answer (C) is incorrect because 5,550 lb. is the estimated fuel consumption before adjusting for the 25-kt. tailwind.

OPERATING CONDITIONS	Z-1	Z-2	Z-3	Z-4	Z-5
DISTANCE (NM)	340	650	900	290	400
AVG WIND COMP (KTS)	25 TW	45 HW	35 TW	25 HW	60 HW

FIGURE 66.—Flight Planning at .74 Mach Cruise.

ABBREVIATED FLIGHT PLANNING
.280/.70 CLIMB
.74/320/340 DESCENT
250 KTS CRUISE BELOW 10000 FT.
320 KTS CRUISE 10000 THRU 23000 FT.
.74 MACH CRUISE 24000 FT. AND ABOVE

DIST. N. MI.	REC. ALT.	TAS KTS	AIR TIME MINS.	FUEL LBS.
50	6000-7000	279	16	1800
60	6000-7000	279	18	1950
260	26000-27000	447	44	4600
270	26000-27000	447	45	4750
280	27000-28000	445	47	4850
290	28000-29000	443	48	4950
300	28000-29000	443	49	5100
310	28000-29000	443	51	5200
320	29000-31000	441	52	5300
330	29000-31000	441	53	5400
340	31000-33000	438	55	5550
350	31000-33000	438	56	5650
400	33000-35000	433	62	6250
450	33000-35000	433	69	6850
500	33000-35000	433	76	7500
550	33000-35000	433	82	8100
600	33000-35000	433	89	8700
650	33000-35000	433	96	9300
700	33000-35000	433	102	9900
750	33000-35000	433	109	10500
800	33000-35000	433	115	11100
850	33000-35000	433	122	11700
900	33000-35000	433	129	12300
950	33000-35000	433	135	12900
1000	33000-35000	433	142	13500

TIME AND FUEL CORRECTION FOR WIND

Δ TIME = TIME X WIND COMPONENT + TAS

Δ FUEL = FUEL X WIND COMPONENT + TAS

EXAMPLE: DIST. = 250
STILL AIR TIME = 43 MIN.
STILL AIR FUEL = 4500 LBS.
WIND COMPONENT = 20 KTS.

Δ TIME = 43 X 20 + 449 = MIN.

Δ FUEL = 4500 X 20 = 449 = 200 LBS.

ADD Δ TIME AND Δ FUEL FOR THE HEADWIND; SUBTRACT FOR TAILWIND

FIGURE 67.—Abbreviated Flight Planning.

48.
8659. (Refer to figures 66 and 67 on page 625.) What is the trip time corrected for wind under Operating Conditions Z-2?

A—1 hour 35 minutes.
B—1 hour 52 minutes.
C—1 hour 46 minutes.

Answer (C) is correct (8659). *(FTW Chap 10)*
Refer to operating conditions Z-2 in Fig. 66. Fig. 67 provides a chart for flight planning at .74 Mach cruise.
Find 650 NM under the distance column on the left side of the chart, and move right to determine a TAS of 433 kt. and an air time of 96 min.
Correct the time for the 45-kt. headwind with the formula at the bottom of the chart.

$$\Delta\ Time = \frac{Time \times Wind\ component}{TAS}$$

$$\Delta\ Time = \frac{96 \times 45}{433} = 10\ min.$$

Add ΔTime for the headwind. Thus, the adjusted trip time is 106 min. (96 + 10), or 1 hr. 46 min.
Answer (A) is incorrect because 1 hr. 35 min. is the approximate air time before adjustment is made for the 45-kt. headwind. Answer (B) is incorrect because 1 hr. 52 min. is the adjusted trip time for a distance of 700, not 650, NM.

49.
8664. (Refer to figures 66 and 67 on page 625.) What is the estimated fuel consumption for Operating Conditions Z-2?

A—10,270 pounds.
B—9,660 pounds.
C—10,165 pounds.

Answer (A) is correct (8664). *(FTW Chap 10)*
Refer to operating conditions Z-2 in Fig. 66. Fig. 67 provides a chart for flight planning at .74 Mach cruise.
Find 650 NM under the distance column on the left side of the chart, and move right to determine a TAS of 433 kt., an air time of 96 min., and fuel consumption of 9,300 lb.
Correct the fuel for the 45-kt. headwind with the formula at the bottom of the chart.

$$\Delta\ Fuel = \frac{Fuel \times Wind\ component}{TAS}$$

$$\Delta\ Fuel = \frac{9{,}300 \times 45}{433} = 967\ (970)\ lb.$$

Add ΔFuel for the headwind. Thus, the estimated fuel consumption is 10,270 lb. (9,300 + 970).
Answer (B) is incorrect because 9,660 lb. is the estimated fuel consumption with a headwind of 17, not 45, kt. Answer (C) is incorrect because 10,165 lb. is the estimated fuel consumption with a headwind of 40, not 45, kt.

50.
8660. (Refer to figures 66 and 67 on page 625.) What is the trip time corrected for wind under Operating Conditions Z-3?

A—2 hours 9 minutes.
B—1 hour 59 minutes.
C—1 hour 52 minutes.

Answer (B) is correct (8660). *(FTW Chap 10)*
Refer to operating conditions Z-3 in Fig. 66. Fig. 67 provides a chart for flight planning at .74 Mach cruise.
Find 900 NM under the distance column on the left side of the chart, and move right to determine a TAS of 433 kt. and an air time of 129 min.
Correct the time for the 35-kt. headwind with the formula at the bottom of the chart.

$$\Delta \text{ Time} = \frac{\text{Time} \times \text{Wind component}}{\text{TAS}}$$

$$\Delta \text{ Time} = \frac{129 \times 35}{433} = 10 \text{ min.}$$

Subtract ΔTime for the tailwind. Thus, the adjusted trip time is 119 min. (129 – 10), or 1 hr. 59 min.
Answer (A) is incorrect because 2 hr. 9 min. is the air time before adjustment is made for the 35-kt. tailwind. Answer (C) is incorrect because 1 hr. 52 min. is the adjusted trip time for a distance of 850, not 900, NM.

51.
8665. (Refer to figures 66 and 67 on page 625.) What is the estimated fuel consumption for Operating Conditions Z-3?

A—12,300 pounds.
B—11,300 pounds.
C—13,990 pounds.

Answer (B) is correct (8665). *(FTW Chap 10)*
Refer to operating conditions Z-3 in Fig. 66. Fig. 67 provides a chart for flight planning at .74 Mach cruise.
Find 900 NM under the distance column on the left side of the chart, and move right to determine a TAS of 433 kt., an air time of 129 min., and fuel consumption of 12,300 lb.
Correct the fuel for the 35-kt. tailwind with the formula at the bottom of the chart.

$$\Delta \text{ Fuel} = \frac{\text{Fuel} \times \text{Wind component}}{\text{TAS}}$$

$$\Delta \text{ Fuel} = \frac{12{,}300 \times 35}{433} = 994 \text{ (1,000) } lb.$$

Subtract ΔFuel for the tailwind. Thus, the estimated fuel consumption is 11,300 lb. (12,300 – 1,000).
Answer (A) is incorrect because 12,300 lb. is the estimated fuel consumption before adjustment is made for the 35-kt. tailwind. Answer (C) is incorrect because 13,990 lb. is the estimated fuel consumption at a distance of 950, not 900, NM.

52.
8661. (Refer to figures 66 and 67 on page 625.) What is the trip time corrected for wind under Operating Conditions Z-4?

A—48.3 minutes.
B—50.7 minutes.
C—51.3 minutes.

Answer (B) is correct (8661). *(FTW Chap 10)*
Refer to operating conditions Z-4 in Fig. 66. Fig. 67 provides a chart for flight planning at .74 Mach cruise.
Find 290 NM under the distance column on the left side of the chart, and move right to determine a TAS of 443 kt. and an air time of 48 min.
Correct the time for the 25-kt. headwind with the formula at the bottom of the chart.

$$\Delta\ Time = \frac{Time \times Wind\ component}{TAS}$$

$$\Delta\ Time = \frac{48 \times 25}{443} = 2.7\ min.$$

Add ΔTime for the headwind. Thus, the adjusted trip time is 50.7 min. (48 + 2.7).
Answer (A) is incorrect because 48.3 min. is the approximate air time before adjustment is made for the 25-kt. headwind. Answer (C) is incorrect because 51.3 min. is the adjusted trip time for a headwind of 30, not 25, kt.

53.
8666. (Refer to figures 66 and 67 on page 625.) What is the estimated fuel consumption for Operating Conditions Z-4?

A—4,950 pounds.
B—5,380 pounds.
C—5,230 pounds.

Answer (C) is correct (8666). *(FTW Chap 10)*
Refer to operating conditions Z-4 in Fig. 66. Fig. 67 provides a chart for flight planning at .74 Mach cruise.
Find 290 NM under the distance column on the left side of the chart, and move right to determine a TAS of 443 kt., an air time of 48 min., and fuel consumption of 4,950 lb.
Correct the fuel for the 25-kt. headwind with the formula at the bottom of the chart.

$$\Delta\ Fuel = \frac{Fuel \times Wind\ component}{TAS}$$

$$\Delta\ Fuel = \frac{4{,}950 \times 25}{443} = 279\ (280)\ lb.$$

Add ΔFuel for the headwind. Thus, the estimated fuel consumption is 5,230 lb. (4,950 + 280).
Answer (A) is incorrect because 4,950 lb. is the estimated fuel consumption before adjustment is made for the 25-kt. headwind. Answer (B) is incorrect because 5,380 lb. is the estimated fuel consumption for a distance of about 300, not 290, NM.

54.
8662. (Refer to figures 66 and 67 on page 625.) What is the trip time corrected for wind under Operating Conditions Z-5?

A—1 hour 11 minutes.
B—56 minutes.
C—62 minutes.

Answer (A) is correct (8662). *(FTW Chap 10)*
Refer to operating conditions Z-5 in Fig. 66. Fig. 67 provides a chart for flight planning at .74 Mach cruise.
Find 400 NM under the distance column on the left side of the chart, and move right to determine a TAS of 433 kt. and an air time of 62 min.
Correct the time for the 60-kt. headwind with the formula at the bottom of the chart.

$$\Delta\ Time = \frac{Time \times Wind\ component}{TAS}$$

$$\Delta\ Time = \frac{62 \times 60}{433} = 9\ min.$$

Add ΔTime for the headwind. Thus, the adjusted trip time is 71 min. (62 + 9), or 1 hr. 11 min.
Answer (B) is incorrect because 56 min. is the air time before any wind adjustment is made for a distance of 350, not 400, NM. Answer (C) is incorrect because 62 min. is the air time before adjustment is made for the 60-kt. headwind.

55.
8667. (Refer to figures 66 and 67 on page 625.) What is the estimated fuel consumption for Operating Conditions Z-5?

A—6,250 pounds.
B—5,380 pounds.
C—7,120 pounds.

Answer (C) is correct (8667). *(FTW Chap 10)*
Refer to operating conditions Z-5 in Fig. 66. Fig. 67 provides a chart for flight planning at .74 Mach cruise.
Find 400 NM under the distance column on the left side of the chart, and move right to determine a TAS of 433 kt., an air time of 62 min., and fuel consumption of 6,250 lb.
Correct the fuel for the 60-kt. headwind with the formula at the bottom of the chart.

$$\Delta\ Fuel = \frac{Fuel \times Wind\ component}{TAS}$$

$$\Delta\ Fuel = \frac{6{,}250 \times 60}{433} = 866\ (870)\ lb.$$

Add ΔFuel for the headwind. Thus, the estimated fuel consumption is 7,120 lb. (6,250 + 870).
Answer (A) is incorrect because 6,250 lb. is the estimated fuel consumption before adjustment is made for the 60-kt. headwind. Answer (B) is incorrect because 5,380 lb. is the estimated fuel consumption with a 60-kt. tailwind, not headwind.

OPERATING CONDITIONS	O-1	O-2	O-3	O-4	O-5
ALTITUDE	31,000	23,000	17,000	8,000	4,000
WEIGHT (X1000)	102	93	104	113	109
ENGINES OPERATING	2	2	2	2	2
HOLDING TIME (MIN)	20	40	35	15	25

FIGURE 68.—B-737 – Holding.

HOLDING

EPR
IAS KNOTS
FF PER ENGINE LB/HR

FLIGHT LEVEL	GROSS WEIGHT 1000 LB									
	115	110	105	100	95	90	85	80	75	70	65
350	2.13	2.07	2.01	1.95	1.90	1.85	1.80	1.76	1.71	1.67	1.64
	234	228	223	217	211	210	210	210	210	210	210
	2830	2810	2630	2460	2290	2180	2070	1960	1870	1780	1700
300	1.86	1.82	1.79	1.75	1.71	1.67	1.64	1.60	1.57	1.54	1.51
	231	226	220	215	210	210	210	210	210	210	210
	2740	2600	2470	2370	2250	2140	2050	1960	1880	1790	1720
250	1.69	1.66	1.63	1.60	1.57	1.54	1.51	1.48	1.45	1.43	1.41
	229	224	218	213	210	210	210	210	210	210	210
	2710	2610	2490	2370	2260	2180	2080	1980	1920	1840	1780
200	1.56	1.53	1.50	1.48	1.45	1.43	1.40	1.38	1.36	1.34	1.32
	227	222	217	211	210	210	210	210	210	210	210
	2716	2590	2490	2390	2310	2230	2130	2060	2000	1920	1860
150	1.45	1.43	1.40	1.38	1.36	1.34	1.32	1.31	1.29	1.27	1.26
	226	221	216	210	210	210	210	210	210	210	210
	2790	2680	2570	2470	2380	2290	2220	2140	2070	2000	1990
100	1.36	1.34	1.33	1.31	1.29	1.28	1.26	1.25	1.24	1.22	1.21
	225	220	215	210	210	210	210	210	210	210	210
	2860	2780	2670	2560	2470	2390	2310	2240	2170	2100	2030
050	1.29	1.28	1.27	1.25	1.24	1.23	1.21	1.20	1.19	1.18	1.17
	224	219	214	210	210	210	210	210	210	210	210
	2960	2870	2770	2670	2580	2500	2420	2350	2290	2230	2150
015	1.25	1.24	1.23	1.22	1.21	1.20	1.19	1.18	1.17	1.16	1.15
	224	219	214	210	210	210	210	210	210	210	210
	3050	2950	2850	2790	2670	2590	2510	2430	2370	2300	2240

FIGURE 69.—B-737 – Holding Performance Chart.

13.8 Holding Performance

56.
8668. (Refer to figures 68 and 69 on page 630.) What are the recommended IAS and EPR settings for holding under Operating Conditions O-1?

A—221 knots and 1.83 EPR.
B—223 knots and 2.01 EPR.
C—217 knots and 1.81 EPR.

Answer (C) is correct (8668). *(FTW Chap 10)*

Refer to operating conditions O-1 in Fig. 68. Fig. 69 provides a holding performance chart to determine IAS, EPR, and fuel flow per engine. Since neither 31,000 ft. (FL 310) nor 102,000 lb. is on the performance chart, you must interpolate.

At FL 350, the EPR value for 102,000 lb. is 1.97. At FL 300, the EPR value for 102,000 lb. is 1.77. Interpolating for FL 310 yields an EPR value of 1.81.

At FL 350, the IAS for 102,000 lb. is 219 kt. At FL 300, the IAS for 102,000 lb. is 217 kt. Interpolating for FL 310 yields an IAS value of 217 kt.

Answer (A) is incorrect because 221 kt. and 1.83 EPR are the recommended settings for holding at 105,000, not 102,000, lb. Answer (B) is incorrect because 223 kt. and 2.01 EPR are the recommended settings for holding at FL 350, not FL 310, and at a weight of 105,000, not 102,000, lb.

57.
8673. (Refer to figures 68 and 69 on page 630.) What is the approximate fuel consumed when holding under Operating Conditions O-1?

A—1,625 pounds.
B—1,950 pounds.
C—2,440 pounds.

Answer (A) is correct (8673). *(FTW Chap 10)*

Refer to operating conditions O-1 in Fig. 68. Fig. 69 provides a performance chart to determine fuel flow (lb./hr.) per engine. The total fuel flow is found by multiplying the number of engines (2) by the fuel flow. Since neither 31,000 ft. (FL 310) nor 102,000 lb. is found on the chart, you must interpolate.

At FL 350, the fuel flow for 102,000 lb. is 2,528 lb./hr./engine. At FL 300, the fuel flow for 102,000 lb. is 2,410 lb./hr./engine. Interpolating for FL 310 yields a fuel flow of 2,434 lb./hr./engine or for two engines a fuel flow of 4,868 lb./hr. (2 x 2,434).

The approximate fuel consumed while holding for 20 min. is 1,625 lb. [4,868 x (20 min. ÷ 60 min./hr.)].

Answer (B) is incorrect because 1,950 lb. is the approximate fuel consumed while holding for 24, not 20, min. Answer (C) is incorrect because 2,440 lb. is the approximate fuel consumed per hr. per engine while holding under operating conditions O-1.

58.
8669. (Refer to figures 68 and 69 on page 630.) What are the recommended IAS and EPR settings for holding under Operating Conditions O-2?

A—210 knots and 1.57 EPR.
B—210 knots and 1.51 EPR.
C—210 knots and 1.45 EPR.

Answer (B) is correct (8669). *(FTW Chap 10)*

Refer to operating conditions O-2 in Fig. 68. Fig. 69 provides a holding performance chart to determine IAS, EPR, and fuel flow per engine. Since neither 23,000 ft. (FL 230) nor 93,000 lb. is on the performance chart, you must interpolate.

At FL 250, the EPR value for 93,000 lb. is 1.56. At FL 200, the EPR value for 93,000 lb. is 1.44. Interpolating for FL 230 yields an EPR value of 1.51.

At FL 250, the IAS for 93,000 lb. is 210 kt. At FL 200, the IAS for 93,000 lb. is 210 kt. Interpolating for FL 230 yields an IAS value of 210 kt.

Answer (A) is incorrect because 210 kt. and 1.57 EPR are the recommended settings for holding at FL 250, not FL 230, and at a weight of 95,000, not 93,000, lb. Answer (C) is incorrect because 210 kt. and 1.45 EPR are the recommended settings for holding at FL 200, not FL 230, and at a weight of 95,000, not 93,000, lb.

59.
8674. (Refer to figures 68 and 69 on page 630.) What is the approximate fuel consumed when holding under Operating Conditions O-2?

A—2,250 pounds.
B—2,500 pounds.
C—3,000 pounds.

Answer (C) is correct (8674). *(FTW Chap 10)*

Refer to operating conditions O-2 in Fig. 68. Fig. 69 provides a performance chart to determine fuel flow (lb./hr.) per engine. The total fuel flow is found by multiplying the number of engines (2) by the fuel flow. Since neither 23,000 ft. (FL 230) nor 93,000 lb. is found on the chart, you must interpolate.

At FL 250, the fuel flow for 93,000 lb. is 2,228 lb./hr./engine. At FL 200, the fuel flow for 93,000 lb. is 2,278 lb./hr./engine. Interpolating for FL 230 yields a fuel flow of 2,258 lb./hr./engine or for two engines a fuel flow of 4,516 lb./hr. (2 x 2,258).

The approximate fuel consumed while holding for 40 min. is 3,000 lb. [4,516 x (40 min. ÷ 60 min./hr.)].

Answer (A) is incorrect because 2,250 lb. is the approximate fuel consumed per hr. per engine while holding and not the total amount consumed for 40 min. Answer (B) is incorrect because 2,500 lb. is the approximate fuel consumed while holding at FL 250, not FL 230, and at a weight of 95,000, not 93,000, lb.

60.
8670. (Refer to figures 68 and 69 on page 630.) What are the recommended IAS and EPR settings for holding under Operating Conditions O-3?

A—217 knots and 1.50 EPR.
B—215 knots and 1.44 EPR.
C—216 knots and 1.40 EPR.

Answer (B) is correct (8670). *(FTW Chap 10)*

Refer to operating conditions O-3 in Fig. 68. Fig. 69 provides a holding performance chart to determine IAS, EPR, and fuel flow per engine. Since neither 17,000 ft. (FL 170) nor 104,000 lb. is on the performance chart, you must interpolate.

At FL 200, the EPR value for 104,000 lb. is 1.50. At FL 150, the EPR value for 104,000 lb. is 1.40. Interpolating for FL 170 yields an EPR value of 1.44.

At FL 200, the IAS for 104,000 lb. is 216 kt. At FL 150, the IAS for 104,000 lb. is 215 kt. Interpolating for FL 170 yields an IAS value of 215 kt.

Answer (A) is incorrect because 217 kt. and 1.50 EPR are the recommended settings for holding at FL 200, not FL 170, and at a weight of 105,000, not 104,000, lb. Answer (C) is incorrect because 216 kt. and 1.40 EPR are the recommended settings for holding at FL 150, not FL 170, and at a weight of 105,000, not 104,000, lb.

61.
8675. (Refer to figures 68 and 69 on page 630.) What is the approximate fuel consumed when holding under Operating Conditions O-3?

A—2,940 pounds.
B—2,520 pounds.
C—3,250 pounds.

Answer (A) is correct (8675). *(FTW Chap 10)*

Refer to operating conditions O-3 in Fig. 68. Fig. 69 provides a performance chart to determine fuel flow (lb./hr.) per engine. The total fuel flow is found by multiplying the number of engines (2) by the fuel flow. Since neither 17,000 ft. (FL 170) nor 104,000 lb. is found on the chart, you must interpolate.

At FL 200, the fuel flow for 104,000 lb. is 2,470 lb./hr./engine. At FL 150, the fuel flow for 104,000 lb. is 2,550 lb./hr./engine. Interpolating for FL 170 yields a fuel flow of 2,502 lb./hr./engine or for two engines a fuel flow of 5,004 lb./hr. (2 x 2,502).

The approximate fuel consumed while holding for 35 min. is 2,940 lb. [5,004 x (35 min. ÷ 60 min./hr.)].

Answer (B) is incorrect because 2,520 lb. is the approximate fuel consumed per hr., not 35 min., per engine, not two engines, while holding. Answer (C) is incorrect because 3,250 lb. is the approximate fuel consumed while holding for about 40, not 35, min.

62.
8671. (Refer to figures 68 and 69 on page 630.) What are the recommended IAS and EPR settings for holding under Operating Conditions O-4?

A—223 knots and 1.33 EPR.
B—225 knots and 1.33 EPR.
C—220 knots and 1.28 EPR.

Answer (A) is correct (8671). *(FTW Chap 10)*
Refer to operating conditions O-4 in Fig. 68. Fig. 69 provides a holding performance chart to determine IAS, EPR, and fuel flow per engine. Since neither 8,000 ft. (FL 080) nor 113,000 lb. is on the performance chart, you must interpolate.
At FL 100, the EPR value for 113,000 lb. is 1.35. At FL 050, the EPR value for 113,000 lb. is 1.29. Interpolating for FL 080 yields an EPR value of 1.33.
At FL 100, the IAS for 113,000 lb. is 223 kt. At FL 050, the IAS for 113,000 lb. is 222 kt. Interpolating for FL 080 yields an IAS value of 223 kt.
Answer (B) is incorrect because 225 kt. and 1.33 EPR are the recommended settings for holding at a weight of 115,000, not 113,000, lb. Answer (C) is incorrect because 220 kt. and 1.28 EPR are the approximate recommended settings for holding at a weight of 111,000, not 113,000, lb. at FL 050, not FL 080.

63.
8676. (Refer to figures 68 and 69 on page 630.) What is the approximate fuel consumed when holding under Operating Conditions O-4?

A—2,870 pounds.
B—2,230 pounds.
C—1,440 pounds.

Answer (C) is correct (8676). *(FTW Chap 10)*
Refer to operating conditions O-4 in Fig. 68. Fig. 69 provides a performance chart to determine fuel flow (lb./hr.) per engine. The total fuel flow is found by multiplying the number of engines (2) by the fuel flow. Since neither 8,000 ft. (FL 080) nor 113,000 lb. is found on the chart, you must interpolate.
At FL 100, the fuel flow for 113,000 lb. is 2,828 lb./hr./engine. At FL 050, the fuel flow for 113,000 lb. is 2,924 lb./hr./engine. Interpolating for FL 080 yields a fuel flow of 2,886 lb./hr./engine or for two engines a fuel flow of 5,772 lb./hr. (2 x 2,886).
The approximate fuel consumed while holding for 15 min. is 1,440 lb. [5,772 x (15 min. ÷ 60 min./hr.)].
Answer (A) is incorrect because 2,870 lb. is the approximate fuel consumed while holding for 30, not 15, min., and the approximate fuel consumed by one engine, not two, per hr. Answer (B) is incorrect because 2,230 lb. is the approximate fuel consumed while holding for 23, not 15, min.

64.
8672. (Refer to figures 68 and 69 on page 630.) What are the recommended IAS and EPR settings for holding under Operating Conditions O-5?

A—219 knots and 1.28 EPR.
B—214 knots and 1.26 EPR.
C—218 knots and 1.27 EPR.

Answer (C) is correct (8672). *(FTW Chap 10)*
Refer to operating conditions O-5 in Fig. 68. Fig. 69 provides a holding performance chart to determine IAS, EPR, and fuel flow per engine. Since neither 4,000 ft. (FL 040) nor 109,000 lb. is on the performance chart, you must interpolate.
At FL 050, the EPR value for 109,000 lb. is 1.28. At FL 015, the EPR value for 109,000 lb. is 1.24. Interpolating for FL 040 yields an EPR value of 1.27.
At FL 050, the IAS for 109,000 lb. is 218 kt. At FL 015, the IAS for 109,000 lb. is 218 kt. Interpolating for FL 040 yields an IAS value of 218 kt.
Answer (A) is incorrect because 219 kt. and 1.28 EPR are the recommended settings for holding at FL 050, not FL 040, and at a weight of 110,000, not 109,000, lb. Answer (B) is incorrect because 214 kt. and 1.26 EPR are the recommended settings for holding at FL 050, not FL 040, and at a weight of 105,000, not 109,000, lb.

65.
8677. (Refer to figures 68 and 69 on page 630.) What is the approximate fuel consumed when holding under Operating Conditions O-5?

A—2,950 pounds.
B—2,870 pounds.
C—2,400 pounds.

Answer (C) is correct (8677). *(FTW Chap 10)*
Refer to operating conditions O-5 in Fig. 68. Fig. 69 provides a performance chart to determine fuel flow (lb./hr.) per engine. The total fuel flow is found by multiplying the number of engines (2) by the fuel flow. Since neither 4,000 ft. (FL 040) nor 109,000 lb. is found on the chart, you must interpolate.
At FL 050, the fuel flow for 109,000 lb. is 2,850 lb./hr./engine. At FL 015, the fuel flow for 109,000 lb. is 2,930 lb./hr./engine. Interpolating for FL 040 yields a fuel flow of 2,914 lb./hr./engine or for two engines a fuel flow of 5,828 lb./hr. (2 x 2,914).
The approximate fuel consumed while holding for 25 min. is 2,400 lb. [5,828 x (25 min. ÷ 60 min./hr.)].
Answer (A) is incorrect because 2,950 lb. is the amount of fuel consumed per hr. per engine at FL 015, not FL 040, and at a weight of 110,000, not 109,000, lb. Answer (B) is incorrect because 2,870 lb. is the amount of fuel consumed per hr. per engine at FL 050, not FL 040, at a weight of 110,000, not 109,000, lb.

13.9 Fuel Dump Time

66.
8678. (Refer to figure 70 on page 635.) How many minutes of dump time is required to reach a weight of 144,500 pounds?

Initial weight	180,500 lb
Zero fuel weight	125,500 lb

A—13 minutes.
B—15 minutes.
C—16 minutes.

Answer (B) is correct (8678). *(TCAS Chap 6)*
Fig. 70 provides a chart to calculate fuel dump time.

1. Subtract the zero fuel weight from the initial weight to determine the initial fuel weight of 55,000 lb. (180,500 – 125,500).
2. Subtract the zero fuel weight from the desired weight to determine the ending fuel weight of 19,000 lb. (144,500 – 125,500).
3. Since neither 55,000 lb. nor 19,000 lb. is on the chart, you must interpolate.
4. At an initial fuel weight of 58,000 lb. and an ending fuel weight of 19,000 lb., the fuel dump time is 17.5 min. At an initial fuel weight of 54,000 lb. and an ending fuel weight of 19,000 lb., the fuel dump time is 14.5 min.
5. Interpolate for the initial fuel weight of 55,000 lb. to determine a fuel dump time of 15 min.

Answer (A) is incorrect because 13 min. is the fuel dump time for an initial fuel weight of 54,000, not 55,000, lb. and an ending fuel weight of 22,000, not 19,000, lb. Answer (C) is incorrect because 16 min. is the fuel dump time for an initial fuel weight of 58,000, not 55,000, lb. and an ending fuel weight of 22,000, not 19,000, lb.

67.
8680. (Refer to figure 70 below.) How many minutes of dump time is required to reach a weight of 151,500 pounds?

Initial weight .... 181,500 lb
Zero fuel weight .... 126,000 lb

A—15 minutes.
B—14 minutes.
C—13 minutes.

Answer (C) is correct (8680). *(TCAS Chap 6)*
Fig. 70 provides a chart to calculate fuel dump time.

1. Subtract the zero fuel weight from the initial weight to determine the initial fuel weight of 55,500 lb. (181,500 – 126,000).
2. Subtract the zero fuel weight from the desired weight to determine the ending fuel weight of 25,500 lb. (151,500 – 126,000).
3. Since neither 55,500 lb. nor 25,500 lb. is on the chart, you must interpolate.
4. At an initial fuel weight of 58,000 lb. and an ending fuel weight of 25,500 lb., the fuel dump time is 15.1 min. At an initial fuel weight of 54,000 lb. and an ending fuel weight of 25,500 lb., the fuel dump time is 12.1 min.
5. Interpolate for the initial fuel weight of 55,500 lb. to determine a fuel dump time of 13 min.

Answer (A) is incorrect because 15 min. is the fuel dump time for an initial fuel weight of 58,000, not 55,000, lb. and an ending fuel weight of 26,000, not 25,500, lb. Answer (B) is incorrect because 14 min. is the fuel dump time for an initial weight of 55,500 lb. and an ending fuel weight of 22,000, not 25,500, lb.

INITIAL FUEL WEIGHT — **ENDING FUEL WEIGHT - 1000 LB**

1000 LB	10	14	18	22	26	30	34	38	42	46	50	54	58	62	64	70
70	28	27	25	23	22	20	18	17	15	13	12	10	8	5	3	0
66	26	25	23	21	20	18	16	15	13	12	10	8	5	3	0	
62	23	23	20	18	17	15	13	11	10	8	7	5	3	0		
58	21	20	18	16	15	13	11	10	8	6	5	3	0			
54	18	16	15	13	12	10	8	7	5	3	2	0				
50	16	15	13	12	10	8	7	5	3	2	0					
46	15	13	12	10	8	7	5	3	2	0						
42	13	12	10	8	7	5	3	2	0							
38	12	10	8	7	5	3	2	0								
34	10	8	7	5	3	2	0									
30	8	7	5	3	2	0										
26	7	5	3	2	0											
22	5	3	2	0												
18	3	2	0													
14	2	0														
10	0															

FUEL DUMP TIME

FUEL JETTISON TIME-MINUTES

FIGURE 70.—Fuel Dump Time.

68.
8679. (Refer to figure 70 on page 635.) How many minutes of dump time is required to reduce fuel load to 25,000 pounds?

Initial weight .... 179,500 lb
Zero fuel weight .... 136,500 lb

A—10 minutes.
B—9 minutes.
C—8 minutes.

Answer (C) is correct (8679). *(TCAS Chap 6)*
Fig. 70 provides a chart to calculate fuel dump time.

1. Subtract the zero fuel weight from the initial weight to determine the initial fuel weight of 43,000 lb. (179,500 – 136,500).
2. The ending fuel weight is 25,000 lb.
3. Since neither 43,000 lb. nor 25,000 lb. is on the chart, you must interpolate.
4. At an initial fuel weight of 46,000 lb. and an ending fuel weight of 25,000 lb., the fuel dump time is 8.5 min. At an initial fuel weight of 42,000 lb. and an ending fuel weight of 25,000 lb., the fuel dump time is 7.25 min.
5. Interpolate for the initial fuel weight of 43,000 lb. to determine a fuel dump time of 8 min.

Answer (A) is incorrect because 10 min. is the fuel dump time for an initial fuel weight of 46,000, not 43,000, lb. and an ending fuel weight of 22,000, not 25,000, lb. Answer (B) is incorrect because 9 min. is the fuel dump time for an initial weight of 44,000, not 43,000, lb. and an ending fuel weight of 22,000, not 25,000, lb.

69.
8681. (Refer to figure 70 on page 635.) How many minutes of dump time is required to reduce fuel load to 16,000 pounds?

Initial weight .... 175,500 lb
Zero fuel weight .... 138,000 lb

A—9 minutes.
B—10 minutes.
C—8 minutes.

Answer (A) is correct (8681). *(TCAS Chap 6)*
Fig. 70 provides a chart to calculate fuel dump time.

1. Subtract the zero fuel weight from the initial weight to determine the initial fuel weight of 37,500 lb. (175,500 – 138,000).
2. The ending fuel weight is 16,000 lb.
3. Since neither 37,500 lb. nor 16,000 lb. is on the chart, you must interpolate.
4. At an initial fuel weight of 38,000 lb. and an ending fuel weight of 16,000 lb., the fuel dump time is 9.0 min. At an initial fuel weight of 34,000 lb. and an ending fuel weight of 16,000 lb., the fuel dump time is 7.5 min.
5. Interpolate for the initial fuel weight of 37,500 lb. to determine a fuel dump time of 9 min.

Answer (B) is incorrect because 10 min. is the fuel dump time for an initial fuel weight of 38,000, not 37,500, lb. and an ending fuel weight of 14,000, not 16,000, lb. Answer (C) is incorrect because 8 min. is the fuel dump time for an initial fuel weight of 38,000, not 37,500, lb. and an ending fuel weight of 18,000, not 16,000, lb.

13.10 Drift-Down Performance

70.
8682. (Refer to figures 71 and 72 on pages 637 and 638.) What is the approximate level-off pressure altitude after drift-down under Operating Conditions D-1?

A—19,400 feet.
B—18,000 feet.
C—20,200 feet.

Answer (A) is correct (8682). *(FTP Chap 6)*
Refer to operating conditions D-1 in Fig. 71. Fig. 72 provides a chart to determine the approximate level-off pressure altitude after drift-down.

For engine anti-ice (A/I) ON, use the middle chart in Fig. 72. Find the gross weight at engine failure of 100,000 (100) lb. on the left side of the chart. Then move right horizontally to the ISA deviation of 0°C to determine the level-off pressure altitude of 19,400 ft.

Answer (B) is incorrect because 18,000 ft. is the level-off pressure altitude after drift-down with the engine A/I ON, and the wing A/I ON, not OFF. Answer (C) is incorrect because 20,200 ft. is the level-off pressure altitude after drift-down when the 800-ft. correction is incorrectly applied for the air-conditioning bleed air OFF. This correction is applied only when the level-off is below 17,000 ft.

71.
8683. (Refer to figure 71 below and figure 72 on page 638.) What is the approximate level-off pressure altitude after drift-down under Operating Conditions D-2?

A—14,700 feet.
B—17,500 feet.
C—18,300 feet.

Answer (B) is correct (8683). *(FTP Chap 6)*
Refer to operating conditions D-2 in Fig. 71. Fig. 72 provides a chart to determine the approximate level-off pressure altitude after drift-down.

For engine anti-ice (A/I) OFF, use the top chart in Fig. 72. Find the gross weight at engine failure of 110,000 (110) lb. on the left side of the chart. Then move right horizontally to the ISA deviation of +10°C to determine the level-off pressure altitude of 17,500 ft.

Answer (A) is incorrect because 14,700 ft. is the level-off pressure altitude with the engine A/I ON, not OFF, and before the correction is made for the air-conditioning bleed air OFF. Answer (C) is incorrect because 18,300 ft. is the level-off pressure altitude after drift-down when the 800-ft. correction is incorrectly applied for the air-conditioning bleed air OFF. The correction is made if level-off is below, not above, 17,000 ft.

72.
8684. (Refer to figure 71 below and figure 72 on page 638.) What is the approximate level-off pressure altitude after drift-down under Operating Conditions D-3?

A—22,200 feet.
B—19,800 feet.
C—21,600 feet.

Answer (C) is correct (8684). *(FTP Chap 6)*
Refer to operating conditions D-3 in Fig. 71. Fig. 72 provides a chart to determine the approximate level-off pressure altitude after drift-down.

For engine and wing anti-ice (A/I) ON, use the bottom chart in Fig. 72. Find the gross weight at engine failure of 90,000 (90) lb. on the left side of the chart. Then move right horizontally to the ISA deviation of −10°C to determine the level-off pressure altitude of 21,600 ft.

Answer (A) is incorrect because 22,200 ft. is the level-off pressure altitude after drift-down with the wing A/I OFF, not ON, at an ISA deviation of 0°C, not −10°C, and with the 800-ft. altitude correction incorrectly applied for the air-conditioning bleed air OFF. Answer (B) is incorrect because 19,800 ft. is the level-off pressure altitude after drift-down for an ISA deviation of +10°C, not −10°C.

73.
8685. (Refer to figure 71 below and figure 72 on page 638.) What is the approximate level-off pressure altitude after drift-down under Operating Conditions D-4?

A—27,900 feet.
B—22,200 feet.
C—24,400 feet.

Answer (C) is correct (8685). *(FTP Chap 6)*
Refer to operating conditions D-4 in Fig. 71. Fig. 72 provides a chart to determine the approximate level-off pressure altitude after drift-down.

For engine and wing anti-ice (A/I) ON, use the bottom chart in Fig. 72. Find the gross weight at engine failure of 80,000 (80) lb. on the left side of the chart. Then move right horizontally to the ISA deviation of −10°C to determine the level-off pressure altitude of 24,400 ft.

Answer (A) is incorrect because 27,900 ft. is the level-off pressure altitude after drift-down with the engine and wing A/I OFF, not ON. Answer (B) is incorrect because 22,200 ft. is the level-off pressure altitude after drift-down for an ISA deviation of +4°C, not −10°C.

OPERATING CONDITIONS	D-1	D–2	D–3	D–4	D–5
WT AT ENG FAIL (X1000)	100	110	90	80	120
ENGINE ANTI-ICE	ON	OFF	ON	ON	ON
WING ANTI-ICE	OFF	OFF	ON	ON	OFF
ISA TEMPERATURE	ISA	+10°	−10°	−10°	+20°
AIR CONDITIONING	OFF	OFF	OFF	OFF	OFF

FIGURE 71. —B-737– Drift-Down.

1 ENGINE INOP

ENGINE A/I OFF

GROSS WEIGHT 1000 LB		OPTIMUM DRIFTDOWN SPEED KIAS	ISA DEV °C			
AT ENGINE FAILURE	AT LEVEL OFF (APPROX)		-10	0	10	20
			APPROX GROSS LEVEL OFF PRESS ALT FT			
80	77	184	27900	26800	25400	22800
90	86	195	25000	23800	21700	20000
100	96	206	22000	20500	20000	18500
110	105	216	20000	19100	17500	15400
120	114	224	18200	16600	14700	12200

ENGINE A/I ON

GROSS WEIGHT 1000 LB		OPTIMUM DRIFTDOWN SPEED KIAS	ISA DEV °C			
AT ENGINE FAILURE	AT LEVEL OFF (APPROX)		-10	0	10	20
			APPROX GROSS LEVEL OFF PRESS ALT FT			
80	77	184	25500	24600	22800	20000
90	86	195	23000	21400	20000	19400
100	96	206	20000	19400	18700	15600
110	105	216	18100	16600	14700	12200
120	114	224	15500	13800	11800	8800

ENGINE AND WING A/I ON

GROSS WEIGHT 1000 LB		OPTIMUM DRIFTDOWN SPEED KIAS	ISA DEV °C			
AT ENGINE FAILURE	AT LEVEL OFF (APPROX)		-10	0	10	20
			APPROX GROSS LEVEL OFF PRESS ALT FT			
80	77	184	24400	23400	21400	20000
90	86	195	21600	20100	19800	18000
100	96	206	19600	18000	16400	14200
110	105	216	16800	15100	13300	10700
120	114	224	14000	12200	10300	7200

NOTE:

WHEN ENGINE BLEED FOR AIR CONDITIONING IS OFF BELOW 17,000 FT., INCREASE LEVEL-OFF ALTITUDE BY 800 FT.

FIGURE 72.—Drift-Down Performance Chart.

74.
8686. (Refer to figures 71 and 72 on pages 637 and 638.) What is the approximate level-off pressure altitude after drift-down under Operating Conditions D-5?

A—8,800 feet.
B—9,600 feet.
C—13,000 feet.

Answer (B) is correct (8686). *(FTP Chap 6)*
Refer to operating conditions D-5 in Fig. 71. Fig. 72 provides a chart to determine the approximate level-off pressure altitude after drift-down.
For engine anti-ice (A/I) ON, use the middle chart in Fig. 72. Find the gross weight at engine failure of 120,000 (120) lb. on the left side of the chart. Then move right horizontally to the ISA deviation of +20°C to determine the level-off pressure altitude of 8,800 ft. The note at the bottom of Fig. 72 states that, when engine bleed air for air-conditioning is OFF below 17,000 ft., increase level-off altitude by 800 ft. Thus, the level-off pressure altitude is 9,600 ft. (8,800 + 800).
Answer (A) is incorrect because 8,800 ft. is the level-off pressure altitude before adjustment is made for air-conditioning bleed air OFF below 17,000 ft. Answer (C) is incorrect because 13,000 ft. is the level-off pressure altitude for engine A/I OFF, not ON.

13.11 Landing Performance

75.
8687. (Refer to figures 73 and 75 on pages 642 and 643.) What is the go-around EPR for Operating Conditions L-1?

A—2.01 EPR.
B—2.03 EPR.
C—2.04 EPR.

Answer (B) is correct (8687). *(FTW Chap 15)*
Refer to operating conditions L-1 in Fig. 73. The top portion in Fig. 75 provides a chart to determine the go-around EPR.
Find the TAT column on the left side of the chart, and move right horizontally to the temperature of +15°C. Move down vertically to determine the temperature limit EPR of 2.00. At the bottom of the chart, find the pressure altitude of 500 ft., which is between SL and 1,000 ft. Interpolate to determine that the pressure limit EPR at a pressure altitude of 500 ft. is 2.01. Use the smaller of the two limits, which is 2.00.
Make the necessary EPR bleed corrections as indicated in the top right corner of the chart. The adjustment for the air-conditioning OFF is +.03; thus the go-around EPR is 2.03 (2.00 + .03).
Answer (A) is incorrect because 2.01 is the pressure limit, not the go-around, EPR. Answer (C) is incorrect because 2.04 is the pressure limit EPR (2.01), not the lower temperature limit EPR (2.00), with the appropriate EPR bleed correction.

76.
8692. (Refer to figures 73, 74, and 75 on pages 642 and 643.) What is V_{REF} for Operating Conditions L-1?

A—143 knots.
B—144 knots.
C—145 knots.

Answer (A) is correct (8692). *(FTW Chap 8)*
Refer to operating conditions L-1 in Fig. 73. Fig. 74 provides a wind component chart, and Fig. 75 provides a chart to determine the landing speed (V_{REF}).
Find the gross weight of 100,000 (100) lb. at the left side of the landing speed chart (Fig. 75, lower right), and move right horizontally to the 30° flap setting column to determine V_{REF} of 135 kt. At the bottom of the chart, the note states the wind factor (½ of the headwind component) is added to V_{REF}.
The headwind component is determined by using the chart in Fig. 74. Find the 50° angle between the wind direction and runway (350-300), and move up and to the right to the 20-kt. wind velocity arc. Then move left horizontally to the left edge of the chart to determine a headwind component of 13 kt. Thus, the wind factor is 6.5 kt. (13 ÷ 2).
The corrected V_{REF} is 142 kt. (135 + 7).
Answer (B) is incorrect because 144 kt. is V_{REF} with 25°, not 30°, flap position and 0, not 13, kt. headwind component. Answer (C) is incorrect because 145 kt. is V_{REF} with a 20-kt., not 13-kt., headwind component.

77.
8688. (Refer to figures 73 and 75 on pages 642 and 643.) What is the go-around EPR for Operating Conditions L-2?

A—2.115 EPR.
B—2.10 EPR.
C—2.06 EPR.

Answer (C) is correct (8688). *(FTW Chap 15)*
Refer to operating conditions L-2 in Fig. 73. The top portion in Fig. 75 provides a chart to determine the go-around EPR.

Find the reported OAT column on the left side of the chart, and move right horizontally to the temperature of +27°F. Move down vertically to determine the temperature limit EPR of 2.10. At the bottom of the chart, find the pressure altitude of 3,100 ft., which is between 3,000 and 4,000 ft. Interpolate to determine that the pressure limit EPR at a pressure altitude of 3,100 ft. is 2.115. Use the smaller of the two limits, which is 2.10.

Make the necessary EPR bleed corrections as indicated in the top right corner of the chart. The adjustment for the two-engine wing anti-ice ON is –.04; thus, the go-around EPR is 2.06 (2.10 – .04).

Answer (A) is incorrect because 2.115 is the pressure limit, not go-around, EPR. Answer (B) is incorrect because 2.10 is the temperature limit EPR without the EPR bleed correction for the two-engine wing anti-ice ON.

78.
8693. (Refer to figures 73, 74, and 75 on pages 642 and 643.) What is the reference speed for Operating Conditions L-2?

A—140 knots.
B—145 knots.
C—148 knots.

Answer (B) is correct (8693). *(FTW Chap 8)*
Refer to operating conditions L-2 in Fig. 73. Fig. 74 provides a wind component chart, and Fig. 75 provides a chart to determine the landing speed (V_{REF}).

Find the gross weight of 95,000 (95) lb. at the left side of the landing speed chart (Fig. 75, lower right), and move right horizontally to the 25° flap setting column to determine V_{REF} of 140 kt. At the bottom of the chart, the note states the wind factor (½ of the headwind component) is added to V_{REF}.

The headwind component is determined by using the chart in Fig. 74. Find the 50° angle between the wind direction and runway [(360-350) + 40], and move up and to the right to the 15-kt. wind velocity arc. Then move left horizontally to the left edge of the chart to determine a headwind component of 9.5 kt. Thus, the wind factor is 4.75 kt. (9.5 ÷ 2).

The corrected V_{REF} is 145 kt. (140 + 5).

Answer (A) is incorrect because 140 kt. is V_{REF} before the wind factor of 5 kt. is added. Answer (C) is incorrect because 148 kt. is V_{REF} using the wind velocity, not headwind component, of 15 kt.

79.
8689. (Refer to figures 73 and 75 on pages 642 and 643.) What is the go-around EPR for Operating Conditions L-3?

A—2.06 EPR.
B—2.07 EPR.
C—2.09 EPR.

Answer (A) is correct (8689). *(FTW Chap 15)*
Refer to operating conditions L-3 in Fig. 73. The top portion in Fig. 75 provides a chart to determine the go-around EPR.

Find the reported OAT column on the left side of the chart, and move right horizontally to the temperature of –8°C. Move down vertically to determine the temperature limit EPR of 2.13. At the bottom of the chart, find the pressure altitude of 2,500 ft., which is between 2,000 and 3,000 ft. Interpolate to determine that the pressure limit EPR at a pressure altitude of 2,500 ft. is 2.12. Use the smaller of the two limits, which is 2.12.

Make the necessary EPR bleed corrections as indicated in the top right corner of the chart. The adjustment for the one-engine wing anti-ice ON is –.06; thus, the go-around EPR is 2.06 (2.12 – .06).

Answer (B) is incorrect because 2.07 is the go-around EPR when the temperature limit EPR is used in error. The smaller of the two limits (in this question, the pressure limit) must be used. Answer (C) is incorrect because 2.09 is the go-around EPR for two-engine, not one, wing anti-ice ON and the air-conditioning OFF, not ON.

80.
8694. (Refer to figures 73, 74, and 75 on pages 642 and 643.) What is V_{REF} +20 for Operating Conditions L-3?

A—151 knots.
B—169 knots.
C—149 knots.

Answer (B) is correct (8694). *(FTW Chap 8)*

Refer to operating conditions L-3 in Fig. 73. Fig. 74 provides a wind component chart, and Fig. 75 provides a chart to determine the landing speed (V_{REF}).

Find the gross weight of 90,000 (90) lb. at the left side of the landing speed chart (Fig. 75, lower right), and move right horizontally to the 15° flap setting column to determine V_{REF} of 141 kt. At the bottom of the chart, the note states that the wind factor (½ of the headwind component) is added to V_{REF}.

The headwind component is determined by using the chart in Fig. 74. Find the 40° angle between the wind direction and runway (310-270), and move up and to the right to the 20-kt. wind velocity arc. Then move left horizontally to the left edge of the chart to determine a headwind component of 15.5 kt. Thus, the wind factor is 7.75 kt. (15.5 ÷ 2).

The corrected V_{REF} is 149 kt. (141 + 8). Thus, V_{REF} + 20 is 169 kt. (149 + 20).

Answer (A) is incorrect because 151 kt. is V_{REF} + 20 before the wind factor of 8 kt. (½ of headwind component) is added. Answer (C) is incorrect because 149 kt. is V_{REF}, not V_{REF} + 20.

81.
8690. (Refer to figures 73 and 75 on pages 642 and 643.) What is the go-around EPR for Operating Conditions L-4?

A—2.056 EPR.
B—2.12 EPR.
C—2.096 EPR.

Answer (A) is correct (8690). *(FTW Chap 15)*

Refer to operating conditions L-4 in Fig. 73. The top portion in Fig. 75 provides a chart to determine the go-around EPR.

Find the TAT column on the left side of the chart, and move right horizontally to the temperature of –10°C. Move down vertically to determine the temperature limit EPR of 2.16. At the bottom of the chart, find the pressure altitude of 2,100 ft., which is between 2,000 and 3,000 ft. Interpolate to determine that the pressure limit EPR at a pressure altitude of 2,100 ft. is 2.096. Use the smaller of the two limits, which is 2.096.

Make the necessary EPR bleed corrections as indicated in the top right corner of the chart. The adjustment for the two-engine wing anti-ice ON is –.04; thus, the go-around EPR is 2.056 (2.096 – .04).

Answer (B) is incorrect because 2.12 is the go-around EPR if the temperature, not pressure, limit is the lower of the two EPR limits. Answer (C) is incorrect because 2.096 is the EPR before the EPR bleed correction for the two-engine wing anti-ice ON.

OPERATING CONDITIONS	L-1	L-2	L-3	L-4	L-5
TEMPERATURE	+15 °C TAT	+27 °F OAT	−8 °C OAT	−10 °C TAT	+55 °F OAT
PRESSURE ALTITUDE	500	3,100	2,500	2,100	1,200
AIR CONDITIONING	OFF	ON	ON	ON	ON
WING ANTI-ICE	OFF	2 ON	1 ON	2 ON	OFF
WEIGHT (X1000)	100	95	90	105	85
FLAP SETTING	30°	25°	15°	40°	30°
RUNWAY ASSIGNED	35	04	27	34	09
SURFACE WIND	300/20	350/15	310/20	030/10	130/15

FIGURE 73.—B-737 – Landing.

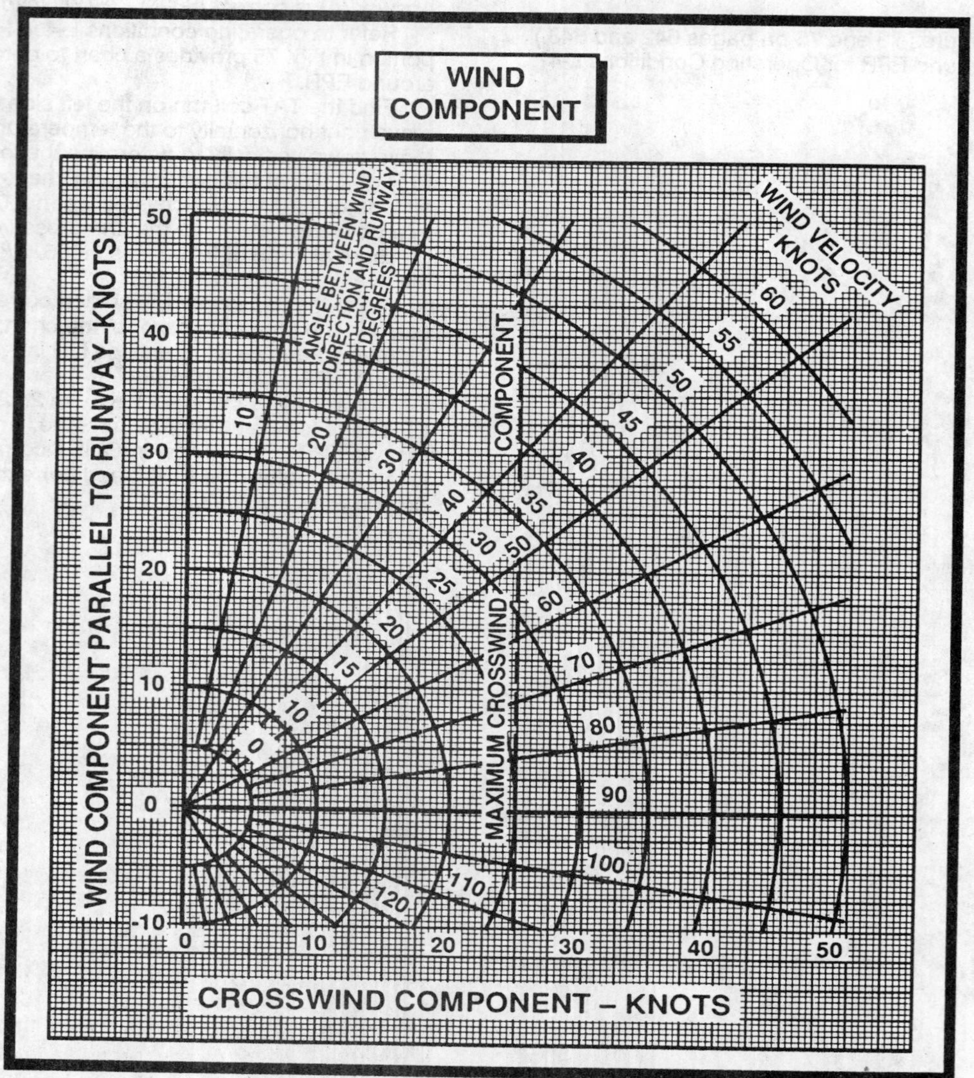

FIGURE 74.—Wind Component Chart.

LANDING

GO AROUND EPR

A/C BLEED ON

EPR BLEED CORRECTIONS	1 ENG	2 ENG
AIR CONDITIONING OFF	+.03	+.03
ENGINE ANTI-ICE ON	ZERO	ZERO
WING ANTI-ICE ON (FLT)	-.06	-.04

REPORTED OAT °F	-61	-52	-43	-35	-25	-17	-10	0	10	18	27	38	47	55	64	73	83	91	100	119
REPORTED OAT °C	-52	-47	-42	-37	-32	-27	-23	-18	-13	-8	-3	3	8	13	18	23	28	33	38	48
TAT °C	-50	-45	-40	-35	-30	-25	-20	-15	-10	-5	0	5	10	15	20	25	30	35	40	50
TEMP LIMIT EPR	2.30	2.30	2.30	2.29	2.26	2.24	2.21	2.19	2.16	2.13	2.10	2.07	2.04	2.00	1.98	1.98	1.98	1.94	1.90	1.80

PRESS	5660 AND ABOVE	4000	3000	2000	1000	S.L.	-1000
LIMIT EPR	2.30	2.20	2.15	2.09	2.04	1.98	1.93

1. FIND TEMP LIMIT EPR
2. FIND PRESS LIMIT EPR
3. USE THE SMALLER OF THE TWO LIMITS

FLAP EXTENSION/ MANEUVERING SPEED

NORMAL MANEUVER AND FLAP EXTENSION SPEEDS

FLAP POS	NORMAL MANEUVER	SELECT FLAP
0	210	1
1	190	5
5	170	10/15
10	160	15
15	150	25/30/40
25	140	30/40
30	VREF	40
40	VREF	—

LANDING SPEED

GROSS WT -1000 LB	REFERENCE SPEED AT FLAP POSITION 40	30	25	15
110	138	142	153	158
105	134	138	149	154
100	130	135	144	150
95	127	131	140	145
90	123	127	136	141
85	119	124	132	136
80	115	120	127	132
75	113	116	123	127
70	109	112	119	123

ADD WIND FACTOR OF: 1/2 HEADWIND COMPONENT + GUST (MAX: 20 KTS)

FIGURE 75.—B-737 – Landing Performance Chart.

82.
8695. (Refer to figures 73 and 74 on page 642, and 75 above.) What is V_{REF} +10 for Operating Conditions L-4?

A—152 knots.
B—138 knots.
C—148 knots.

Answer (C) is correct (8695). *(FTW Chap 8)*

Refer to operating conditions L-4 in Fig. 73. Fig. 74 provides a wind component chart, and Fig. 75 provides a chart to determine the landing speed (V_{REF}).

Find the gross weight of 105,000 (105) lb. at the left side of the landing speed chart (Fig. 75, lower right), and move right horizontally to the 40° flap setting column to determine V_{REF} of 134 kt. At the bottom of the chart, the note states that the wind factor (½ of the headwind component) is added to V_{REF}.

The headwind component is determined by using the chart in Fig. 74. Find the 50° angle between the wind direction and runway [(360 – 340) + 30], and move up and to the right to the 10-kt. wind velocity arc. Then move horizontally to the left edge of the chart to determine a headwind component of 6.5 kt. Thus, the wind factor is 3.25 kt. (6.5 ÷ 2).

The corrected V_{REF} is 138 kt. (134 + 4). Thus, V_{REF} + 10 is 148 kt. (138 + 10).

Answer (A) is incorrect because 152 kt. is V_{REF} + 10 at a flap setting of 30°, not 40°. Answer (B) is incorrect because 138 kt. is V_{REF}, not V_{REF} + 10.

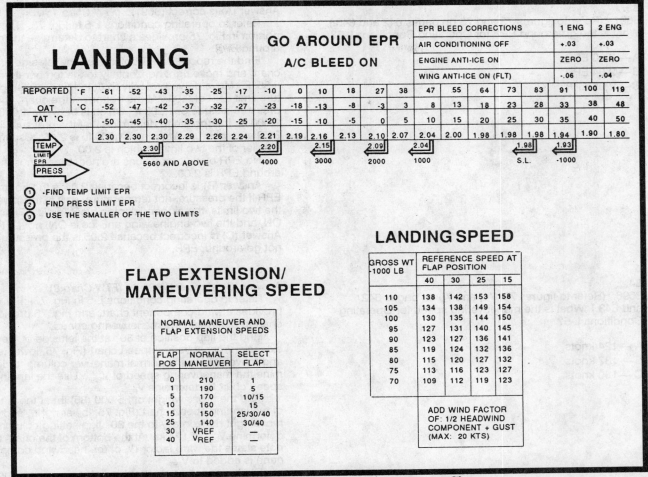

83.
8691. (Refer to figures 73 and 75 on pages 642 and 643.) What is the go-around EPR for Operating Conditions L-5?

A—2.00 EPR.
B—2.04 EPR.
C—2.05 EPR.

Answer (A) is correct (8691). *(FTW Chap 15)*

Refer to operating conditions L-5 in Fig. 73. The top portion in Fig. 75 provides a chart to determine the go-around EPR.

Find the reported OAT column on the left side of the chart, and move right horizontally to the temperature of +55°F. Move down vertically to determine the temperature limit EPR of 2.00. At the bottom of the chart, find the pressure altitude of 1,200 ft., which is between 1,000 and 2,000 ft. Interpolate to determine that the pressure limit EPR at a pressure altitude of 1,200 ft. is 2.05. Use the smaller of the two limits, which is 2.00.

No EPR bleed corrections are necessary; thus the go-around EPR is 2.00.

Answer (B) is incorrect because 2.04 is the go-around EPR if the pressure, not temperature, limit is the lower of the two limits, the air-conditioning bleed air is OFF, not ON, and the two-engine wing anti-ice is ON, not OFF. Answer (C) is incorrect because 2.05 is the pressure limit, not go-around, EPR.

84.
8696. (Refer to figures 73, 74, and 75 on pages 642 and 643.) What is the maneuvering speed for Operating Conditions L-5?

A—124 knots.
B—137 knots.
C—130 knots.

Answer (C) is correct (8696). *(FTW Chap 8)*

Refer to operating conditions L-5 in Fig. 73. Fig. 74 provides a wind component chart, and Fig. 75 provides a chart to determine the maneuvering speed.

Find the flap position of 30° at the left side of the flap extension/maneuvering speed chart (Fig. 75, lower left), and move right to the normal maneuver column to determine the maneuvering speed of V_{REF}. Use the landing speed chart to determine V_{REF}.

Find the gross weight of 85,000 (85) lb. at the left side of the landing speed chart (Fig. 75, lower right), and move right horizontally to the 30° flap setting column to determine V_{REF} of 124 kt. At the bottom of the chart, the note states the wind factor (½ of the headwind component) is added to V_{REF}.

The headwind component is determined by using the chart in Fig. 74. Find the 40° angle between the wind direction and runway (130 – 90), and move up and to the right to the 15-kt. wind velocity arc. Then move horizontally to the left edge of the chart to determine a headwind component of 11.5 kt. Thus, the wind factor is 5.75 kt. (11.5 ÷ 2).

The corrected V_{REF} is 130 kt. (124 + 6).

Answer (A) is incorrect because 124 kt. is V_{REF} before the wind factor of 6 kt. (½ of the headwind component) is added. Answer (B) is incorrect because 137 kt. is V_{REF} when the wind velocity, not the headwind component, is used to determine the wind factor.

END OF CHAPTER

CHAPTER FOURTEEN
BOEING 727 OPERATING/PERFORMANCE DATA

This chapter contains outlines of major concepts tested, all FAA test questions and answers regarding Boeing 727 operating/performance data, and an explanation of each answer. Each module, or subtopic, within this chapter is listed above with the number of questions from the FAA pilot knowledge test pertaining to that particular module. For each module, the first number following the parentheses is the page number on which the outline begins, and the next number is the page number on which the questions begin.

There are 70 questions in this chapter. We separate and organize the FAA questions into meaningful study units, i.e., chapters and modules. As an analogy, it is easier to deal with the "trees" if you understand the "forest." In this context, "trees" are individual FAA questions and the "forest" is the ATP knowledge test. The organizational units between the overall ATP knowledge test and individual ATP test questions are chapters and modules in this book.

CAUTION: The **sole purpose** of this book is to expedite your passing the FAA pilot knowledge test for the ATP certificate. Topics or regulations not directly tested on the FAA pilot knowledge test are omitted. Much more information and knowledge are necessary to fly safely. This additional material is presented in Gleim's other pilot training books (see the order form on page 818) and in many FAA books and circulars, as well as in airplane *POH*s and other commercial textbooks.

14.1 CG COMPUTATIONS (Questions 1-15)

1. There are 15 questions on CG computations requiring one of the following:
   a. CG as a percentage of MAC
   b. CG in inches
   c. Gross weight index (simply the total moments)
2. Fifteen different loading assumptions are presented on Figs. 76, 77, and 78. Based on each of these loading computations, you need to do a CG computation wherein you compute total weight and total moments, and then divide total weight into total moments to determine the CG, which is the answer for the CG in inches questions.
   a. For CG as a percentage of MAC, put the distance of CG aft of LEMAC over MAC to determine % MAC.
   b. For the gross weight index questions, stop as soon as you add up the total moments; i.e., you do not have to compute CG.
3. Weights and moments are given on Fig. 80 on page 661 for
   a. Passenger
      1) Forward
      2) Aft
   b. Cargo
      1) Forward
      2) Aft
   c. Fuel
      1) Tanks 1 and 3
      2) Tank 2
4. EXAMPLE: Fig. 76 on page 659 provides loading conditions (passengers, cargo, and fuel). The information from the first column, WT-1, is used to determine weight and arm in the schedule below. Fig. 79 on page 660 provides B-727 weights and limits, including LEMAC of 860.5 in. Fig. 80 on page 661 provides B-727 loading tables. Compute the CG and then the percent of MAC as illustrated below.

Item	Weight	Arm	Mom./1,000
B.O.W.	105,500		92,837.0
Psgr. Fwd. (18 x 170)	3,060	582.0	1,780.9
Psgr. Aft (95 x 170)	16,150	1,028.0	16,602.2
CGO, Fwd.	1,500	680.0	1,020.0
CGO, Aft	2,500	1,166.0	2,915.0
Fuel (1 + 3)	21,000		20,902.0
Fuel 2	28,000	913.9	25,589.0
Totals	177,710		161,646.1

$$CG = \frac{Total\ mom./1{,}000}{Total\ wt.} \times 1{,}000 = \frac{161{,}646.1}{177{,}710} \times 1{,}000 = 909.6\ in.$$

$$\%\ MAC = \frac{CG - LEMAC}{MAC} = \frac{909.6 - 860.5}{180.9} = .271\ or\ 27.1\%\ MAC$$

14.2 MAX TAKEOFF EPR (Questions 16-20)

1. **EPR** is engine-pressure ratio. It indicates thrust being developed by the engine: the pressure differential between the engine inlet and the turbine exhaust.
2. Determine max takeoff EPR settings, using Fig. 83 on page 668, after you have computed pressure altitude using Fig. 82 on page 667.

a. Pressure altitude, Fig. 82, page 667

1) On the left side, find the appropriate altimeter setting. Immediately to the right is the correction factor (which corrects airport elevation to pressure altitude).

b. Max takeoff EPR, top of Fig. 83, page 668

1) Note the pressure altitude along the vertical axis.

2) On the horizontal axis at the top of the chart are temperatures which determine the EPR setting. You may have to interpolate.

3) Note that there are adjustments to be made for

a) Air-conditioning, engines 1 and 3
b) Anti-ice, engine 2
c) Six-stage bleed, engine 2

c. EXAMPLE: Find pressure altitude using Fig. 82 on page 667 at field elevation 1,050 ft. and altimeter 29.36 in. Pressure altitude = 1,550 ft.

Find the EPR setting for 1 and 3 by entering the max takeoff EPR chart (Fig. 83 on page 668). Under the pressure altitude column, go down to both 1,000 ft. and 2,000 ft. Go right, stopping under the temperature column at +23°F. You will find an EPR setting at 1,000 ft. of 2.15 and at 2,000 ft. of 2.21. Because the actual pressure altitude is 1,550 ft., interpolate to find the correct EPR of 2.18.

The same procedure provides the EPR for engine 2 of 2.19.

Make the necessary bleed correction adjustments to the above EPR settings: Engines 1 and 3 air-conditioning OFF is +.04 EPR per engine added to the previous value of 2.18, so EPR = 2.22. Engine 2 anti-ice ON is –.03, so EPR = 2.16 (2.19 – .03). None of the other data in condition G-1 are relevant.

14.3 TAKEOFF SPEEDS (Questions 21-25)

1. On Fig. 83, page 668, use the chart on the right side, based on your determined pressure altitude on Fig. 82, page 667.

2. On Fig. 83, lower right, enter the V_1, V_R, V_2 chart under the appropriate pressure altitude (upper left of this chart).

a. Proceed to the right to the appropriate temperature, which is on the horizontal axis.

b. Proceed down that column to the appropriate flap setting sections (5°, 15°, 20°, 25°).

c. Within the flap setting sections, find the appropriate gross weight to determine your V_1, V_R, and/or V_2. You may have to interpolate.

1) **V_1** is the maximum speed in the takeoff at which the pilot must take the first action (e.g., apply brakes, reduce thrust, deploy speed brakes) to stop the airplane within the accelerate-stop distance.

a) V_1 is also the minimum speed in the takeoff, following a failure of the critical engine at V_{EF}, at which the pilot can continue the takeoff and achieve the required height above the takeoff surface within the takeoff distance.

2) **V_R** is rotation speed.

3) **V_2** is takeoff safety speed.

3. EXAMPLE: Find pressure altitude using Fig. 82 on page 667 at field elevation 1,050 ft. and altimeter 29.36 in. Pressure altitude = 1,550 ft.

On Fig. 83 on page 668, enter V_1, V_R, V_2 chart under pressure altitude. Find the 1-to-3 pressure altitude line; then proceed to the right to the 23°F OAT (23°F is between –65°F and 83°F). Go down that column to flaps 15°, to 140,000 lb. gross weight (140), then right to V_2 (takeoff safety speed). V_2 is 137 kt.

14.4 STAB TRIM SETTINGS (Questions 26-30)

1. The STAB TRIM is a stabilizer trim setting for takeoff, and it is determined by the CG as a percent of MAC.
2. On Fig. 83, page 668, use the STAB TRIM chart in the middle left.
   a. Find the appropriate CG in the left column and then move to the right under the appropriate flap setting and determine the trim setting (ANU means Airplane Nose Up).
3. EXAMPLE: Convert CG station 911.2 in. to percent MAC using the following formula:

$$\frac{CG - LEMAC}{MAC} = \%\ MAC$$

$$\frac{911.2 - 860.5}{180.9} = .280 \text{ or } 28.0\%\ MAC$$

Enter STAB TRIM setting chart under CG% column and find 28%. Move to the right under flaps 15° to find 4½ ANU trim setting.

14.5 HOLDING IAS AND EPR (Questions 31-35)

1. Holding speeds and EPR settings are indicated on Fig. 85, page 671.
   a. Altitude is on the vertical axis of the holding performance chart.
   b. Gross weight is on the horizontal axis of the chart.
   c. For each intersection, the EPR, IAS in knots, and fuel burn per engine per hour are presented.
2. Questions 31 through 35 require only IAS and EPR settings. Interpolation is required, both as to altitude and as to weight.
3. EXAMPLE: Given 24,000 ft., 195,000 lb., three engines operating, and 15 min. of holding (H-1 on Fig. 84 on page 670), what are recommended holding IAS and EPR settings? Since neither 24,000 ft. nor 195,000 lb. is on Fig. 85 on page 671, interpolate.

At 25,000 ft., the EPR value for 195,000 lb. is 1.83. At 20,000 ft., the EPR value for 195,000 lb. is 1.68. Interpolating for 24,000 ft. yields an EPR value of 1.80.

At 25,000 ft., the IAS for 195,000 lb. is 264.5 kt. At 20,000 ft., the IAS for 195,000 lb. is 261.5 kt. Interpolating for 24,000 ft. yields 264 kt.

14.6 HOLDING FUEL CONSUMPTION (Questions 36-40)

1. Fuel consumption during holding is determined by Fig. 85 on page 671. See Module 14.5, Holding IAS and EPR.
2. EXAMPLE: H-1 on Fig. 84 on page 670 specifies 24,000 ft., 195,000 lb., three engines operating, and 15 min. holding. Compute the fuel burn during holding by using Fig. 85 on page 671.

At 25,000 ft. and 195,000 lb., fuel flow is 3,500 lb./hr. per engine. At 20,000 ft. and 195,000 lb., fuel flow is 3,540 lb./hr. per engine. Interpolating for 24,000 ft., fuel flow is 3,508 lb./hr. per engine. Multiply by 3 (three engines) and multiply by .25 (15 min.):

$$3{,}508\ lb. \times 3 \times .25 = 2{,}631\ lb.$$

14.7 DESCENT TIME, FUEL, AND DISTANCE (Questions 41-45)

1. Fig. 87 on page 674 contains a descent performance chart.
   a. Four descent profiles are given based on descent rate and airspeed.
      1) .80M/250 KIAS
      2) .80M/280/250 KIAS
      3) .80M/320/250 KIAS
      4) .80M/350/250 KIAS
2. Given one of the descent profiles, the distance is determined by altitude, which is on the vertical axis, and weight, which is on the horizontal axis and stated at only three levels, 120,000 lb., 140,000 lb., and 160,000 lb.
3. Choose whichever of the four charts is appropriate.
4. Enter the chart at the correct flight level and interpolate for the amount of landing weight to determine the time, fuel, and distance.
5. EXAMPLE: S-1 of Fig. 86 on page 674 indicates FL 370, 130,000 lb. landing weight, and .80M/250 descent. On Fig. 87 on page 674, use .80M/250 KIAS, enter FL 370 row, and find 26 min. Interpolating the distance for 130,000 lb., which is between 123 NAM (120,000 lb.) and 128 NAM (140,000 lb.), gives 125 NAM.

14.8 LANDING DISTANCES (Questions 46-60)

1. There are four charts:
   a. Fig. 88 on page 676 -- Normal Landing, Dry Runway
   b. Fig. 89 on page 678 -- Normal Landing, Wet Runway
   c. Fig. 90 on page 680 -- Normal Landing, Icy Runway
   d. Fig. 91 on page 682 -- Normal Landing Distance Comparison
2. Landing charts have gross weight on the horizontal axis and landing distance on the vertical axis.
3. Landing distance is determined by distance lines for use of
   a. Three reversers only
   b. Brakes
   c. Brakes and reversers
   d. Brakes and spoilers
   e. Brakes and spoilers plus reversers
4. To determine landing distance, find the gross weight at the bottom of the chart and proceed up vertically to the appropriate distance line. From the intersection, move horizontally to the left of the chart to determine landing distance.
5. EXAMPLE: Fig. 88 on page 676 provides a chart to compare landing distances on a dry runway. At the bottom of the chart, find 114 (gross weight/1,000 lb.) and move up vertically to the brakes line. Move left horizontally to the edge of the chart to find a landing distance of 2,900 ft. Repeat the process, except use the brakes and reversers line to determine a landing distance of 2,600 ft. The difference is 300 ft. (2,900 – 2,600).

14.9 THRUST REQUIRED (Questions 61-70)

1. There are two charts:
   a. Fig. 92 on page 684 -- Landing Thrust -- 140,000 lb.
   b. Fig. 93 on page 688 -- Landing Thrust -- 110,000 lb.
2. Landing thrust charts have indicated airspeed on the horizontal axis and thrust required on the vertical axis.
3. Thrust is determined by configuration curves for
   a. 40° flaps, gear down (level flight)
   b. 30° flaps, gear down (level flight)
   c. 25° flaps, gear down (level flight)
   d. 25° flaps, gear up (level flight)
   e. 15° flaps, gear up (level flight)
   f. 5° flaps, gear up (level flight)
   g. 2° flaps, gear up (level flight)
   h. 0° flaps, gear up (level flight)
   i. 40° flaps, gear down (3° glide slope)
   j. 30° flaps, gear down (3° glide slope)
4. For any IAS, go up vertically to the appropriate configuration curve. From the intersection, move horizontally to the left side of the chart to determine required thrust.
5. EXAMPLE: Figure 92 on page 684 provides a chart to determine the landing thrust required at a gross weight of 140,000 lb. The 3° glide slope curve is shown as a dashed line. There are two 3° glide slope curves, and the curve for 30° flaps and gear down is the lower curve. Find V_{REF} on the curve, which is depicted as a circle with a line through it, and then move down vertically to determine an airspeed of 127 kt. At the bottom of the chart, find 157 kt. (127 + 30) and move up vertically to the 30° glide slope curve with flaps 30° and gear down. Note that this is greater than the maximum speed to maintain the glide slope. Using the maximum of 156 kt., move left horizontally to the edge of the chart to determine a required thrust of 16,200 lb.

QUESTIONS AND ANSWER EXPLANATIONS

All the FAA questions from the pilot knowledge test for the ATP certificate relating to the Boeing 727 operating/performance data and the material outlined previously are reproduced on the following pages in the same modules as the outlines. To the immediate right of, or below, each question are the correct answer and answer explanation. You should cover these answers and answer explanations while responding to the questions. Refer to the general discussion in Chapter 1 on how to take the FAA pilot knowledge test.

Remember that the questions from the FAA pilot knowledge test bank have been reordered by topic, and the topics are organized into a meaningful sequence. Accordingly, the first line of the answer explanation gives the FAA question number and the citation of the authoritative source for the answer.

14.1 CG Computations

1.
8697. (Refer to figures 76, 79, and 80 on pages 659, 660, and 661.) What is the CG in percent of MAC for Loading Conditions WT-1?

A—26.0 percent MAC.
B—27.1 percent MAC.
C—27.9 percent MAC.

Answer (B) is correct (8697). *(PWBH Chap 7)*
CG as a percent of MAC is required. Fig. 76 provides loading conditions (passengers, cargo, and fuel). The information from the first column, WT-1, is used to determine weight and arm in the schedule below. Fig. 79 provides B-727 weights and limits, including LEMAC of 860.5 in. Fig. 80 provides B-727 loading tables. Compute the CG and then the percent of MAC as illustrated below.

Item	Weight	Arm	Mom./1,000
B.O.W.	105,500		92,837.0
Psgr. Fwd. (18 x 170)	3,060	582.0	1,780.9
Psgr. Aft (95 x 170)	16,150	1,028.0	16,602.2
CGO, Fwd.	1,500	680.0	1,020.0
CGO, Aft	2,500	1,166.0	2,915.0
Fuel (1 + 3)	21,000		20,902.0
Fuel 2	28,000	913.9	25,589.0
Totals	177,710		161,646.1

$$CG = \frac{\textit{Total mom./1,000}}{\textit{Total wt.}} \times 1{,}000$$

$$CG = \frac{161{,}646.1}{177{,}710} \times 1{,}000 = 909.6 \textit{ in.}$$

$$\frac{CG - LEMAC}{MAC} = \% \ MAC$$

$$\frac{909.6 - 860.5}{180.9} = .271 \textit{ or } 27.1\% \ MAC$$

Answer (A) is incorrect because 26.0% MAC requires a CG of 907.5 in. Answer (C) is incorrect because 27.9% MAC requires a CG of 911.0 in.

2.
8698. (Refer to figures 76, 79, and 80 on pages 659, 660, and 661.) What is the CG in inches aft of datum for Loading Conditions WT-2?

A—908.8 inches.
B—909.6 inches.
C—910.7 inches.

Answer (C) is correct (8698). *(PWBH Chap 7)*
CG in inches aft of datum is required. Fig. 76 provides loading conditions (passengers, cargo, and fuel). The information from the second column, WT-2, is used to determine weight and arm in the schedule below. Fig. 79 provides B-727 weights and limits. Fig. 80 provides B-727 loading tables. Compute the CG as illustrated below.

Item	Weight	Arm	Mom./1,000
B.O.W.	105,500		92,837.0
Psgr. Fwd. (23 x 170)	3,910	582.0	2,275.6
Psgr. Aft (112 x 170)	19,040	1,028.0	19,573.1
CGO, Fwd.	2,500	680.0	1,700.0
CGO, Aft	3,500	1,166.0	4,081.0
Fuel (1 + 3)	22,000		21,914.0
Fuel 2	27,000	914.0	24,678.0
Totals	183,450		167,058.7

$$CG = \frac{\textit{Total mom./1,000}}{\textit{Total wt.}} \times 1{,}000$$

$$CG = \frac{167{,}058.1}{183{,}450} \times 1{,}000 = 910.7 \textit{ in.}$$

Answer (A) is incorrect because 908.8 in. requires a total mom./1,000 of 166,719 with a total weight of 183,450 lb. Answer (B) is incorrect because 909.6 in. requires a total mom./1,000 of 166,866 with a total weight of 183,450 lb.

3.
8699. (Refer to figures 76, 79, and 80 on pages 659, 660, and 661.) What is the CG in percent of MAC for Loading Conditions WT-3?

A—27.8 percent MAC.
B—28.9 percent MAC.
C—29.1 percent MAC.

Answer (A) is correct (8699). *(PWBH Chap 7)*
CG as a percent of MAC is required. Fig. 76 provides loading conditions (passengers, cargo, and fuel). The information from the third column, WT-3, is used to determine weight and arm in the schedule below. Fig. 79 provides B-727 weights and limits, including LEMAC of 860.5 in. Fig. 80 provides B-727 loading tables. Compute the CG and then the percent of MAC as illustrated below.

Item	Weight	Arm	Mom./1,000
B.O.W.	105,500		92,837.0
Psgr. Fwd. (12 x 170)	2,040	582.0	1,187.3
Psgr. Aft (75 x 170)	12,750	1,028.0	13,107.0
CGO, Fwd.	3,500	680.0	2,380.0
CGO, Aft	4,200	1,166.0	4,897.2
Fuel (1 + 3)	24,000		23,940.0
Fuel 2	24,250	914.3	22,171.8
Totals	176,240		160,520.3

$$CG = \frac{\textit{Total mom./1,000}}{\textit{Total wt.}} \times 1{,}000$$

$$CG = \frac{160{,}520.3}{176{,}240} \times 1{,}000 = 910.8\ in.$$

$$\frac{CG - LEMAC}{MAC} = \%\ MAC$$

$$\frac{910.8 - 860.5}{180.9} = .278 \text{ or } 27.8\%\ MAC$$

Answer (B) is incorrect because 28.9% MAC requires a CG of 912.8 in. Answer (C) is incorrect because 29.1% MAC requires a CG of 913.1 in.

4.
8700. (Refer to figures 76, 79, and 80 on pages 659, 660, and 661.) What is the CG in inches aft of datum for Loading Conditions WT-4?

A—908.4 inches.
B—909.0 inches.
C—909.5 inches.

Answer (A) is correct (8700). *(PWBH Chap 7)*
CG in inches aft of datum is required. Fig. 76 provides loading conditions (passengers, cargo, and fuel). The information from the fourth column, WT-4, is used to determine weight and arm in the schedule below. Fig. 79 provides B-727 weights and limits. Fig. 80 provides B-727 loading tables. Compute the CG as illustrated below.

Item	Weight	Arm	Mom./1,000
B.O.W.	105,500		92,837.0
Psgr. Fwd. (28 x 170)	4,760	582.0	2,770.3
Psgr. Aft (122 x 170)	20,740	1,028.0	21,320.7
CGO, Fwd.	850	680.0	578.0
CGO, Aft	1,500	1,166.0	1,749.0
Fuel (1 + 3)	20,000		19,894.0
Fuel 2	26,200	914.1	23,949.4
Totals	179,550		163,098.4

$$CG = \frac{\textit{Total mom./1,000}}{\textit{Total wt.}} \times 1{,}000$$

$$CG = \frac{163{,}098.4}{179{,}550} \times 1{,}000 = 908.4\ in.$$

Answer (B) is incorrect because 909.0 in. requires a total mom./1,000 of 163,211 with a total weight of 179,550 lb. Answer (C) is incorrect because 909.5 in. requires a total mom./1,000 of 163,301 with a total weight of 179,550 lb.

5.
8701. (Refer to figures 76, 79, and 80 on pages 659, 660, and 661.) What is the CG in percent of MAC for Loading Conditions WT-5?

A—25.6 percent MAC.
B—26.7 percent MAC.
C—27.2 percent MAC.

Answer (B) is correct (8701). *(PWBH Chap 7)*
CG as a percent of MAC is required. Fig. 76 provides loading conditions (passengers, cargo, and fuel). The information from the fifth column, WT-5, is used to determine weight and arm in the schedule below. Fig. 79 provides B-727 weights and limits, including LEMAC of 860.5 in. Fig. 80 provides B-727 loading tables. Compute the CG and then the percent of MAC as illustrated below.

Item	Weight	Arm	Mom./1,000
B.O.W.	105,500		92,837.0
Psgr. Fwd. (26 x 170)	4,420	582.0	2,572.4
Psgr. Aft (103 x 170)	17,510	1,028.0	18,000.3
CGO, Fwd.	1,400	680.0	952.0
CGO, Aft	2,200	1,166.0	2,565.2
Fuel (1 + 3)	23,000		22,926.0
Fuel 2	25,200	914.2	23,037.8
Totals	179,230		162,890.7

$$CG = \frac{Total\ mom./1,000}{Total\ wt.} \times 1,000$$

$$CG = \frac{162,890.7}{179,230} \times 1,000 = 908.8\ in.$$

$$\frac{CG - LEMAC}{MAC} = \%\ MAC$$

$$\frac{908.8 - 860.5}{180.9} = .267\ or\ 26.7\%\ MAC$$

Answer (A) is incorrect because 25.6% MAC requires a CG of 906.8 in. Answer (C) is incorrect because 27.2% MAC requires a CG of 909.7 in.

6.
8702. (Refer to figures 77, 79, and 80 on pages 659, 660, and 661.) What is the gross weight index for Loading Conditions WT-6?

A—181,340.5 index.
B—156,545.0 index.
C—165,991.5 index.

Answer (C) is correct (8702). *(PWBH Chap 7)*
Gross weight index (total moment) is required. Fig. 77 provides loading conditions (passengers, cargo, and fuel). The information from the first column, WT-6, is used to determine weight and arm in the schedule below. Fig. 79 provides B-727 weights and limits. Fig. 80 provides B-727 loading tables. Compute the gross weight index as illustrated below.

Item	Weight	Arm	Mom./1,000
B.O.W.	105,500		92,837.0
Psgr. Fwd. (10 x 170)	1,700	582.0	989.4
Psgr. Aft (132 x 170)	22,440	1,028.0	23,068.3
CGO, Fwd.	5,000	680.0	3,400.0
CGO, Aft	6,000	1,166.0	6,966.0
Fuel (1 + 3)	19,000		18,884.0
Fuel 2	21,700	914.6	19,846.8
Totals	181,340		165,991.5

Note: The mom./1,000 given for 6,000 lb. in the aft cargo compartment is 6,966, but, if it is calculated using wt. x arm (6,000 x 1,166), the mom./1,000 is 6,996. Use the mom./1,000 given in the chart to get the correct answer.

Gross weight index (total mom./1,000) is 165,991.5.

Answer (A) is incorrect because 181,340.5 is approximately the gross weight, not the gross weight index or total moments/1,000. Answer (B) is incorrect because a gross weight index of 156,545.0 would require a gross weight less than 181,340 lb.

7.
8703. (Refer to figures 77, 79, and 80 on pages 659, 660, and 661.) What is the CG in percent of MAC for Loading Conditions WT-7?

A—21.6 percent MAC.
B—22.9 percent MAC.
C—24.0 percent MAC.

Answer (C) is correct (8703). *(PWBH Chap 7)*
CG as a percent of MAC is required. Fig. 77 provides loading conditions (passengers, cargo, and fuel). The information from the second column, WT-7, is used to determine weight and arm in the schedule below. Fig. 79 provides B-727 weights and limits, including LEMAC of 860.5 in. Fig. 80 provides B-727 loading tables. Compute the CG and then the percent of MAC as illustrated below.

Item	Weight	Arm	Mom./1,000
B.O.W.	105,500		92,837.0
Psgr. Fwd. (27 x 170)	4,590	582.0	2,671.4
Psgr. Aft (83 x 170)	14,110	1,028.0	14,505.1
CGO, Fwd.	4,500	680.0	3,060.0
CGO, Aft	5,500	1,166.0	6,413.0
Fuel (1 + 3)	18,000		17,874.0
Fuel 2	19,800	914.9	18,115.0
Totals	172,000		155,475.5

$$CG = \frac{\textit{Total mom./1,000}}{\textit{Total wt.}} \times 1{,}000$$

$$CG = \frac{155{,}475.5}{172{,}000} \times 1{,}000 = 903.9 \textit{ in.}$$

$$\frac{CG - LEMAC}{MAC} = \%\ MAC$$

$$\frac{903.9 - 860.5}{180.9} = .24 \textit{ or } 24.0\%\ MAC$$

Answer (A) is incorrect because 21.6% MAC requires a CG of 899.6 in. Answer (B) is incorrect because 22.9% MAC requires a CG of 901.9 in.

8.
8704. (Refer to figures 77, 79, and 80 on pages 659, 660, and 661.) What is the CG in percent of MAC for Loading Conditions WT-8?

A—29.4 percent MAC.
B—30.0 percent MAC.
C—31.3 percent MAC.

Answer (C) is correct (8704). *(PWBH Chap 7)*
CG as a percent of MAC is required. Fig. 77 provides loading conditions (passengers, cargo, and fuel). The information from the third column, WT-8, is used to determine weight and arm in the schedule below. Fig. 79 provides B-727 weights and limits, including LEMAC of 860.5 in. Fig. 80 provides B-727 loading tables. Compute the CG and then the percent of MAC as illustrated below.

Item	Weight	Arm	Mom./1,000
B.O.W.	105,500		92,837.0
Psgr. Fwd. (6 x 170)	1,020	582.0	593.6
Psgr. Aft (98 x 170)	16,660	1,028.0	17,126.5
CGO, Fwd.	1,300	680.0	884.0
CGO, Aft	3,300	1,166.0	3,847.8
Fuel (1 + 3)	24,000		23,940.0
Fuel 2	12,000	916.1	10,993.0
Totals	163,780		150,221.9

$$CG = \frac{\textit{Total mom./1,000}}{\textit{Total wt.}} \times 1{,}000$$

$$CG = \frac{150{,}221.9}{163{,}780} \times 1{,}000 = 917.2 \textit{ in.}$$

$$\frac{CG - LEMAC}{MAC} = \%\ MAC$$

$$\frac{917.2 - 860.5}{180.9} = .313 \textit{ or } 31.3\%\ MAC$$

Answer (A) is incorrect because 29.4% MAC requires a CG of 913.7 in. Answer (B) is incorrect because 30.0% MAC requires a CG of 914.8 in.

9.
8705. (Refer to figures 77, 79, and 80 on pages 659, 660, and 661.) What is the gross weight index for Loading Conditions WT-9?

A—169,755.2 index.
B—158,797.9 index.
C—186,565.5 index.

Answer (A) is correct (8705). *(PWBH Chap 7)*
Gross weight index (total moment) is required. Fig. 77 provides loading conditions (passengers, cargo, and fuel). The information from the fourth column, WT-9, is used to determine weight and arm in the schedule below. Fig. 79 provides B-727 weights and limits. Fig. 80 provides B-727 loading tables. Compute the gross weight index as illustrated below.

Item	Weight	Arm	Mom./1,000
B.O.W.	105,500		92,837.0
Psgr. Fwd. (29 x 170)	4,930	582.0	2,869.3
Psgr. Aft (133 x 170)	22,610	1,028.0	23,243.0
CGO, Fwd.	975	680.0	663.0
CGO, Aft	1,250	1,166.0	1,457.5
Fuel (1 + 3)	22,000		21,914.0
Fuel 2	29,300	913.7	26,771.4
Totals	186,565		169,755.2

Gross weight index (total mom./1,000) is 169,755.2.

Answer (B) is incorrect because a gross weight index of 158,797.2 would require a gross weight less than 186,565 lb. Answer (C) is incorrect because 186,565.5 is approximately the gross weight, not the gross weight index or total moments/1,000.

10.
8706. (Refer to figures 77, 79, and 80 on pages 659, 660, and 661.) What is the CG in percent of MAC for Loading Conditions WT-10?

A—27.0 percent MAC.
B—27.8 percent MAC.
C—28.0 percent MAC.

Answer (C) is correct (8706). *(PWBH Chap 7)*
CG as a percent of MAC is required. Fig. 77 provides loading conditions (passengers, cargo, and fuel). The information from the fifth column, WT-10, is used to determine weight and arm in the schedule below. Fig. 79 provides B-727 weights and limits, including LEMAC of 860.5 in. Fig. 80 provides B-727 loading tables. Compute the CG and then the percent of MAC as illustrated below.

Item	Weight	Arm	Mom./1,000
B.O.W.	105,500		92,837.0
Psgr. Fwd. (21 x 170)	3,570	582.0	2,077.7
Psgr. Aft (127 x 170)	21,590	1,028.0	22,194.5
CGO, Fwd.	2,300	680.0	1,564.0
CGO, Aft	2,400	1,166.0	2,798.4
Fuel (1 + 3)	21,000		20,902.0
Fuel 2	22,700	914.5	20,759.2
Totals	179,060		163,132.8

$$CG = \frac{Total\ mom./1{,}000}{Total\ wt.} \times 1{,}000$$

$$CG = \frac{163{,}132.8}{179{,}060} \times 1{,}000 = 911.1\ in.$$

$$\frac{CG - LEMAC}{MAC} = \%\ MAC$$

$$\frac{911.1 - 860.5}{180.9} = .28\ or\ 28.0\%\ MAC$$

Answer (A) is incorrect because 27.0% MAC requires a CG of 909.3 in. Answer (B) is incorrect because 27.8% MAC requires a CG of 910.8 in.

11.
8707. (Refer to figures 78, 79, and 80 on pages 659, 660, and 661.) What is the CG in percent of MAC for Loading Conditions WT-11?

A—26.8 percent MAC.
B—27.5 percent MAC.
C—28.6 percent MAC.

Answer (C) is correct (8707). *(PWBH Chap 7)*
CG as a percent of MAC is required. Fig. 78 provides loading conditions (passengers, cargo, and fuel). The information from the first column, WT-11, is used to determine weight and arm in the schedule below. Fig. 79 provides B-727 weights and limits, including LEMAC of 860.5 in. Fig. 80 provides B-727 loading tables. Compute the CG and then the percent of MAC as illustrated below.

Item	Weight	Arm	Mom./1,000
B.O.W.	105,500		92,837.0
Psgr. Fwd. (11 x 170)	1,870	582.0	1,088.3
Psgr. Aft (99 x 170)	16,830	1,028.0	17,301.2
CGO, Fwd.	3,100	680.0	2,108.0
CGO, Aft	5,500	1,166.0	6,413.0
Fuel (1 + 3)	17,000		16,866.0
Fuel 2	19,600	914.9	17,932.0
Totals	169,400		154,545.5

$$CG = \frac{\textit{Total mom./1,000}}{\textit{Total wt.}} \times 1{,}000$$

$$CG = \frac{154{,}545.5}{169{,}400} \times 1{,}000 = 912.3 \textit{ in.}$$

$$\frac{CG - LEMAC}{MAC} = \%\ MAC$$

$$\frac{912.3 - 860.5}{180.9} = .286 \textit{ or } 28.6\%\ MAC$$

Answer (A) is incorrect because 26.8% MAC requires a CG of 909.0 in. Answer (B) is incorrect because 27.5% MAC requires a CG of 910.2 in.

12.
8708. (Refer to figures 78, 79, and 80 on pages 659, 660, and 661.) What is the CG in percent of MAC for Loading Conditions WT-12?

A—25.8 percent MAC.
B—26.3 percent MAC.
C—27.5 percent MAC.

Answer (B) is correct (8708). *(PWBH Chap 7)*
CG as a percent of MAC is required. Fig. 78 provides loading conditions (passengers, cargo, and fuel). The information from the second column, WT-12, is used to determine weight and arm in the schedule below. Fig. 79 provides B-727 weights and limits, including LEMAC of 860.5 in. Fig. 80 provides B-727 loading tables. Compute the CG and then the percent of MAC as illustrated below.

Item	Weight	Arm	Mom./1,000
B.O.W.	105,500		92,837.0
Psgr. Fwd. (28 x 170)	4,760	582.0	2,770.3
Psgr. Aft (105 x 170)	17,850	1,028.0	18,349.8
CGO, Fwd.	4,200	680.0	2,856.0
CGO, Aft	4,400	1,166.0	5,130.4
Fuel (1 + 3)	23,000		22,926.0
Fuel 2	27,800	913.9	25,406.4
Totals	187,510		170,275.9

$$CG = \frac{\textit{Total mom./1,000}}{\textit{Total wt.}} \times 1{,}000$$

$$CG = \frac{170{,}275.9}{187{,}510} \times 1{,}000 = 908.1 \textit{ in.}$$

$$\frac{CG - LEMAC}{MAC} = \%\ MAC$$

$$\frac{908.1 - 860.5}{180.9} = .263 \textit{ or } 26.3\%\ MAC$$

Answer (A) is incorrect because 25.8% MAC requires a CG of 907.2 in. Answer (C) is incorrect because 27.5% MAC requires a CG of 910.2 in.

13.
8709. (Refer to figures 78, 79, and 80 on pages 659, 660, and 661.) What is the CG in percent of MAC for Loading Conditions WT-13?

A—28.6 percent MAC.
B—29.4 percent MAC.
C—30.1 percent MAC.

Answer (A) is correct (8709). *(PWBH Chap 7)*
CG as a percent of MAC is required. Fig. 78 provides loading conditions (passengers, cargo, and fuel). The information from the third column, WT-13, is used to determine weight and arm in the schedule below. Fig. 79 provides B-727 weights and limits, including LEMAC of 860.5 in. Fig. 80 provides B-727 loading tables. Compute the CG and then the percent of MAC as illustrated below.

Item	Weight	Arm	Mom./1,000
B.O.W.	105,500		92,837.0
Psgr. Fwd. (22 x 170)	3,740	582.0	2,176.7
Psgr. Aft (76 x 170)	12,920	1,028.0	13,281.8
CGO, Fwd.	1,600	680.0	1,088.0
CGO, Aft	5,700	1,166.0	6,646.2
Fuel (1 + 3)	24,000		23,940.0
Fuel 2	29,100	913.7	26,588.7
Totals	182,560		166,558.4

$$CG = \frac{Total\ mom./1,000}{Total\ wt.} \times 1,000$$

$$CG = \frac{166,558.4}{182,560} \times 1,000 = 912.4\ in.$$

$$\frac{CG - LEMAC}{MAC} = \%\ MAC$$

$$\frac{912.4 - 860.5}{180.9} = .286\ or\ 28.6\%\ MAC$$

Answer (B) is incorrect because 29.4% MAC requires a CG of 913.7 in. Answer (C) is incorrect because 30.1% MAC requires a CG of 915.0 in.

14.
8710. (Refer to figures 78, 79, and 80 on pages 659, 660, and 661.) What is the CG in percent of MAC for Loading Conditions WT-14?

A—30.1 percent MAC.
B—29.5 percent MAC.
C—31.5 percent MAC.

Answer (B) is correct (8710). *(PWBH Chap 7)*
CG as a percent of MAC is required. Fig. 78 provides loading conditions (passengers, cargo, and fuel). The information from the fourth column, WT-14, is used to determine weight and arm in the schedule below. Fig. 79 provides B-727 weights and limits, including LEMAC of 860.5 in. Fig. 80 provides B-727 loading tables. Compute the CG and then the percent of MAC as illustrated below.

Item	Weight	Arm	Mom./1,000
B.O.W.	105,500		92,837.0
Psgr. Fwd. (17 x 170)	2,890	582.0	1,682.0
Psgr. Aft (124 x 170)	21,080	1,028.0	21,670.2
CGO, Fwd.	3,800	680.0	2,584.0
CGO, Aft	4,800	1,166.0	5,596.8
Fuel (1 + 3)	22,000		21,914.0
Fuel 2	25,400	914.2	23,220.7
Totals	185,470		169,504.7

$$CG = \frac{Total\ mom./1,000}{Total\ wt.} \times 1,000$$

$$CG = \frac{169,504.7}{185,470} \times 1,000 = 913.9\ in.$$

$$\frac{CG - LEMAC}{MAC} = \%\ MAC$$

$$\frac{913.9 - 860.5}{180.9} = .295\ or\ 29.5\%\ MAC$$

Answer (A) is incorrect because 30.1% MAC requires a CG of 915.0 in. Answer (C) is incorrect because 31.5% MAC requires a CG of 917.5 in.

15.
8711. (Refer to figures 78, 79, and 80 on pages 659, 660, and 661.) What is the CG in Percent of MAC for Loading Conditions WT-15?

A—32.8 percent MAC.
B—31.5 percent MAC.
C—29.5 percent MAC.

Answer (A) is correct (8711). *(PWBH Chap 7)*
CG as a percent of MAC is required. Fig. 78 provides loading conditions (passengers, cargo, and fuel). The information from the fifth column, WT-15, is used to determine weight and arm in the schedule below. Fig. 79 provides B-727 weights and limits, including LEMAC of 860.5 in. Fig. 80 provides B-727 loading tables. Compute the CG and then the percent of MAC as illustrated below.

Item	Weight	Arm	Mom./1,000
B.O.W.	105,500		92,837.0
Psgr. Fwd. (3 x 170)	510	582.0	296.8
Psgr. Aft (130 x 170)	22,100	1,028.0	22,718.8
CGO, Fwd.	1,800	680.0	1,224.0
CGO, Aft	3,800	1,166.0	4,430.8
Fuel (1 + 3)	21,000		20,902.0
Fuel 2	21,900	914.6	20,029.7
Totals	176,610		162,439.1

$$CG = \frac{\textit{Total mom./1,000}}{\textit{Total wt.}} \times 1{,}000$$

$$CG = \frac{162{,}439.1}{176{,}610} \times 1{,}000 = 919.8 \textit{ in.}$$

$$\frac{CG - LEMAC}{MAC} = \%\ MAC$$

$$\frac{919.8 - 860.5}{180.9} = .328 \text{ or } 32.8\%\ MAC$$

Answer (B) is incorrect because 31.5% MAC requires a CG of 917.5 in. Answer (C) is incorrect because 29.5% MAC requires a CG of 913.9 in.

LOADING CONDITIONS	WT-1	WT-2	WT-3	WT-4	WT-5
PASSENGERS					
FORWARD COMPT	18	23	12	28	26
AFT COMPT	95	112	75	122	103
CARGO					
FORWARD HOLD	1,500	2,500	3,500	850	1,400
AFT HOLD	2,500	3,500	4,200	1,500	2,200
FUEL					
TANKS 1 AND 3 (EACH)	10,500	11,000	FULL	10,000	11,500
TANK 2	28,000	27,000	24,250	26,200	25,200

FIGURE 76.—B-727 – Loading.

LOADING CONDITIONS	WT-6	WT-7	WT-8	WT-9	WT-10
PASSENGERS					
FORWARD COMPT	10	27	6	29	21
AFT COMPT	132	83	98	133	127
CARGO					
FORWARD HOLD	5,000	4,500	1,300	975	2,300
AFT HOLD	6,000	5,500	3,300	1,250	2,400
FUEL					
TANKS 1 AND 3 (EACH)	9,500	9,000	FULL	11,000	10,500
TANK 2	21,700	19,800	12,000	29,300	22,700

FIGURE 77.—B-727 – Loading.

LOADING CONDITIONS	WT-11	WT-12	WT-13	WT-14	WT-15
PASSENGERS					
FORWARD COMPT	11	28	22	17	3
AFT COMPT	99	105	76	124	130
CARGO					
FORWARD HOLD	3,100	4,200	1,600	3,800	1,800
AFT HOLD	5,500	4,400	5,700	4,800	3,800
FUEL					
TANKS 1 AND 3 (EACH)	8,500	11,500	12,000	11,000	10,500
TANK 2	19,600	27,800	29,100	25,400	21,900

FIGURE 78.—B-727 – Loading.

AIRPLANE DATUM CONSTANTS

MAC	180.9 inches
L.E. of MAC	860.5 inches
Basic Operating Index	92,837.0 / 1,000

OPERATING LIMITATIONS

Maximum Takeoff Slope	±2%
Maximum Takeoff / Landing Crosswind Component	32 knots
Maximum Takeoff / Landing Tailwind Component	12 knots

WEIGHT LIMITATIONS

Basic Operating Weight	105,500 pounds
Maximum Zero Fuel Weight	138,500 pounds
Maximum Taxi Weight	185,700 pounds
Maximum Takeoff Weight (Brake Release)	184,700 pounds
Maximum In-flight Weight (Flaps 30)	155,500 pounds
(Flaps 40)	144,000 pounds
Maximum Landing Weight (Flaps 30)	155,000 pounds
(Flaps 40)	143,000 pounds

FIGURE 79.—B-727 – Table of Weights and Limits.

PASSENGER LOADING TABLE

Number of Pass.	Weight Lbs.	Moment 1000
Forward Compartment Centroid-582.0		
5	850	495
10	1,700	989
15	2,550	1,484
20	3,400	1,979
25	4,250	2,473
29	4,930	2,869
AFT Compartment Centroid-1028.0		
10	1,700	1,748
20	3,400	3,495
30	5,100	5,243
40	6,800	6,990
50	8,500	8,738
60	10,200	10,486
70	11,900	12,233
80	13,600	13,980
90	15,300	15,728
100	17,000	17,476
110	18,700	19,223
120	20,400	20,971
133	22,610	23,243

CARGO LOADING TABLE

Weight Lbs.	Moment 1000 — Forward Hold Arm 680.0	Moment 1000 — Aft Hold Arm 1166.0
6,000		6,966
5,000	3,400	5,830
4,000	2,720	4,664
3,000	2,040	3,498
2,000	1,360	2,332
1,000	680	1,166
900	612	1,049
800	544	933
700	476	816
600	408	700
500	340	583
400	272	466
300	204	350
200	136	233
100	68	117

NOTE: These computations are to be used for testing purposes only.

FUEL LOADING TABLE

TANKS 1 & 3 (EACH)

Weight Lbs.	Arm	Moment 1000
8,500	992.1	8,433
9,000	993.0	8,937
9,500	993.9	9,442
10,000	994.7	9,947
10,500	995.4	10,451
11,000	996.1	10,957
11,500	996.8	11,463
12,000	997.5	11,970
FULL CAPACITY		

****Note: Computations for Tank 2 weights for 12,500 lbs. to 18,000 lbs. have been purposely omitted.**

TANKS 2 (3 CELL)

Weight Lbs.	Arm	Moment 1000	Weight Lbs.	Arm	Moment 1000
8,500	917.5	7,799	22,500	914.5	20,576
9,000	917.2	8,255	23,000	914.5	21,034
9,500	917.0	8,711	23,500	914.4	21,488
10,000	916.8	9,168	24,000	914.3	21,943
10,500	916.6	9,624	24,500	914.3	22,400
11,000	916.5	10,082	25,000	914.2	22,855
11,500	916.3	10,537	25,500	914.2	23,312
12,000	916.1	10,993	26,000	914.1	23,767
**(See note at lower left)			26,500	914.1	24,244
			27,000	914.0	24,678
18,500	915.1	16,929	27,500	913.9	25,132
19,000	915.0	17,385	28,000	913.9	25,589
19,500	914.9	17,841	28,500	913.8	26,043
20,000	914.9	18,298	29,000	913.7	26,497
20,500	914.8	18,753	29,500	913.7	26,954
21,000	914.7	19,209	30,000	913.6	27,408
21,500	914.6	19,664	**FULL CAPACITY**		
22,000	914.6	20,121			

FIGURE 80.—Loading Tables.

14.2 Max Takeoff EPR

16.
8712. (Refer to figures 81, 82, and 83 on pages 666, 667, and 668.) What is the max takeoff EPR for Operating Conditions G-1?

A—Engines 1 and 3, 2.22; engine 2, 2.16.
B—Engines 1 and 3, 2.22; engine 2, 2.21.
C—Engines 1 and 3, 2.15; engine 2, 2.09.

Answer (A) is correct (8712). *(FTW Chap 8)*

Refer to the first column, G-1, in Fig. 81. Find pressure altitude using Fig. 82 at field elevation 1,050 ft. and altimeter 29.36 in. Pressure altitude = 1,550 ft.

Find the EPR setting for 1 and 3 by entering the max takeoff EPR chart (Fig. 83). Under the pressure altitude column, go down to both 1,000 ft. and 2,000 ft. Go right, stopping under the temperature column at +23°F. You will find an EPR setting at 1,000 ft. of 2.15 and at 2,000 ft. of 2.21. Because the actual pressure altitude is 1,550 ft., interpolate to find the correct EPR of 2.18.

The same procedure provides the EPR for engine 2 of 2.19.

Make the necessary bleed correction adjustments to the above EPR settings: Engines 1 and 3 air-conditioning OFF is +.04 EPR per engine added to the previous value of 2.18, so EPR = 2.22. Engine 2 anti-ice ON is –.03, so EPR = 2.16 (2.19 – .03). None of the other data in condition G-1 are relevant.

Answer (B) is incorrect because engine 2 anti-ice is ON, which requires a reduction, not an addition, to the engine EPR. Answer (C) is incorrect because an EPR for engines 1 and 3 of 2.15 is for a temperature of approximately 23°C, not 23°F, at 1,550 ft. with the correct bleed correction. The same is true for engine number 2 EPR of 2.09.

17.
8713. (Refer to figures 81, 82, and 83 on pages 666, 667, and 668.) What is the max takeoff EPR for Operating Conditions G-2?

A—Engines 1 and 3, 2.15; engine 2, 2.16.
B—Engines 1 and 3, 2.18; engine 2, 2.13.
C—Engines 1 and 3, 2.14; engine 2, 2.11.

Answer (C) is correct (8713). *(FTW Chap 8)*

Refer to the first column, G-2, in Fig. 81. Find pressure altitude using Fig. 82 at field elevation 2,000 ft. and altimeter 1016 mb. Pressure altitude = 1,900 ft.

Find the EPR setting for 1 and 3 by entering the max takeoff EPR chart (Fig. 83). Under the pressure altitude column, go down to both 1,000 ft. and 2,000 ft. Go right, stopping under the temperature column at +10°C. You will find an EPR setting at 1,000 ft. of 2.13 and at 2,000 ft. of 2.14. Because the actual pressure altitude is 1,900 ft., interpolate to find the correct EPR of 2.14.

The same procedure provides the EPR for engine 2 of 2.16.

Make the necessary bleed correction adjustments to the above EPR settings: For engines 1 and 3, no adjustments are necessary because the air-conditioning is ON. Engine 2 EPR is reduced by .05 for +10°C OAT and warmer with 6th stage bleed ON, so EPR = 2.11 (2.16 – .05). None of the other data in condition G-2 are relevant.

Answer (A) is incorrect because engines 1 and 3 EPR of 2.15 and engine 2 EPR of 2.16 are the values at 1,000-ft. pressure altitude at –10°C. Answer (B) is incorrect because engines 1 and 3 EPR of 2.18 is the EPR with the air-conditioning ON, not OFF. Engine 2 EPR of 2.13 is corrected for anti-ice ON, not OFF, and no correction was made for the OAT +10°C or warmer.

18.
8714. (Refer to figures 81, 82, and 83 on pages 666, 667, and 668.) What is the max takeoff EPR for Operating Conditions G-3?

A—Engines 1 and 3, 2.08; engine 2, 2.05.
B—Engines 1 and 3, 2.14; engine 2, 2.10.
C—Engines 1 and 3, 2.18; engine 2, 2.07.

Answer (B) is correct (8714). *(FTW Chap 8)*
Refer to the first column, G-3, in Fig. 81. Find pressure altitude using Fig. 82 at field elevation 4,350 ft. and altimeter 30.10 in. Pressure altitude = 4,150 ft.

Find the EPR setting for 1 and 3 by entering the max takeoff EPR chart (Fig. 83). Under the pressure altitude column, go down to 3,856 ft. and above. Go right, stopping under the temperature column at +68°F. You will find an EPR setting of 2.14.

The same procedure provides the EPR for engine 2 of 2.15.

Make the necessary bleed correction adjustments to the above EPR settings: For engines 1 and 3, no adjustments are necessary because the air-conditioning is ON. Engine 2 anti-ice is OFF, but the 6th stage bleed is on so EPR must be reduced by .05 for 50°F OAT or warmer as indicated in the instructions for reducing engine 2 EPR below the EPR bleed corrections table. Thus, engine 2 EPR = 2.10 (2.15 – .05). None of the other data in condition G-3 are relevant.

Answer (A) is incorrect because engines 1 and 3 EPR of 2.08 and engine 2 EPR of 2.05 are corrected for a temperature of 86°F, not 68°F, at 4,350-ft. pressure altitude. Answer (C) is incorrect because engines 1 and 3 EPR of 2.18 is corrected for the air conditioner OFF, not ON. Engine 2 EPR of 2.07 has also been corrected for anti-ice ON, not OFF.

19.
8715. (Refer to figures 81, 82, and 83 on pages 666, 667, and 668.) What is the max takeoff EPR for Operating Conditions G-4?

A—Engines 1 and 3, 2.23; engine 2, 2.21.
B—Engines 1 and 3, 2.26; engine 2, 2.25.
C—Engines 1 and 3, 2.24; engine 2, 2.24.

Answer (A) is correct (8715). *(FTW Chap 8)*
Refer to the first column, G-4, in Fig. 81. Find pressure altitude using Fig. 82 at field elevation 3,050 ft. and altimeter 1010 mb. Pressure altitude = 3,150 ft.

Find the EPR setting for 1 and 3 by entering the max takeoff EPR chart (Fig. 83). Under the pressure altitude column, go down to both 3,000 ft. and 3,856 ft. and above. Go right, stopping under the temperature column at –5°C. You will find an EPR setting at both 3,000 ft. and 3,856 ft. of 2.23.

The same procedure provides the EPR for engine 2 of 2.24.

Make the necessary bleed correction adjustments to the above EPR settings: For engines 1 and 3, no adjustments are necessary because the air-conditioning is ON. Engine 2 anti-ice ON is –.03, so EPR = 2.21 (2.24 – 0.03). None of the other data in condition G-4 are relevant.

Answer (B) is incorrect because engines 1 and 3 EPR of 2.26 and engine 2 EPR of 2.25 are adjusted for an OAT of +5°F, not –5°C. Answer (C) is incorrect because engines 1 and 3 EPR of 2.24 is for an OAT between –10°C and –5°C. Engine 2 EPR of 2.24 has not been adjusted by –.03 for anti-ice ON.

20.
8716. (Refer to figures 81, 82, and 83 on pages 666, 667, and 668.) What is the max takeoff EPR for Operating Conditions G-5?

A—Engines 1 and 3, 2.27; engine 2, 2.18.
B—Engines 1 and 3, 2.16; engine 2, 2.14.
C—Engines 1 and 3, 2.23; engine 2, 2.22.

Answer (C) is correct (8716). *(FTW Chap 8)*
Refer to the first column, G-5, in Fig. 81. Find pressure altitude using Fig. 82 at field elevation 2,150 ft. and altimeter 29.54 in. Pressure altitude = 2,550 ft.
Find the EPR setting for 1 and 3 by entering the max takeoff EPR chart (Fig. 83). Under the pressure altitude column, go down to both 2,000 ft. and 3,000 ft. Go right, stopping under the temperature column at +5°F. You will find an EPR setting at 2,000 ft. of 2.21 and at 3,000 ft. of 2.26. Because the actual pressure altitude is 2,550 ft., interpolate to find the correct EPR of 2.23.
The same procedure provides the EPR for engine 2 of 2.25.
Make the necessary bleed correction adjustments to the above EPR settings: For engines 1 and 3, no adjustments are necessary because the air-conditioning is ON. Engine 2 anti-ice ON is –.03, so EPR = 2.22 (2.25 – .03). None of the other data in condition G-5 are relevant.
Answer (A) is incorrect because engines 1 and 3 EPR of 2.27 has been adjusted for the air-conditioning OFF, not ON. Engine 2 EPR of 2.18 appears to have been adjusted for both anti-ice ON and 6th stage bleed on with an OAT above 50°F. Answer (B) is incorrect because engines 1 and 3 EPR of 2.16 and engine 2 EPR of 2.14 are corrected for +5°C, not +5°F, and a pressure altitude of 1,750 ft., not 2,150 ft.

14.3 Takeoff Speeds

21.
8717. (Refer to figures 81, 82, and 83 on pages 666, 667, and 668.) What is the takeoff safety speed for Operating Conditions G-1?

A—122 knots.
B—137 knots.
C—133 knots.

Answer (B) is correct (8717). *(FTW Chap 8)*
Takeoff safety speed is V_2. Refer to the first column, G-1, in Fig. 81.
Find pressure altitude using Fig. 82 at field elevation 1,050 ft. and altimeter 29.36 in. Pressure altitude = 1,550 ft.
On Fig. 83, enter V_1, V_R, V_2 chart under pressure altitude. Find the 1-to-3 pressure altitude line; then proceed to the right to the 23°F OAT (23°F is between –65°F and 83°F). Go down that column to flaps 15°, to 140,000 lb. gross weight (140), then right to V_2 (takeoff safety speed). V_2 is 137 kt.
Answer (A) is incorrect because 122 kt. is V_1, V_R speed. Answer (C) is incorrect because 133 kt. is the V_2 speed for 130,000 lb.

22.
8718. (Refer to figures 81, 82, and 83 on pages 666, 667, and 668.) What is the rotation speed for Operating Conditions G-2?

A—150 knots.
B—154 knots.
C—155 knots.

Answer (C) is correct (8718). *(FTW Chap 8)*
Rotation speed is V_R. Refer to the second column, G-2, in Fig. 81.
Find pressure altitude using Fig. 82 at field elevation 2,000 ft. and altimeter 1016 mb. Pressure altitude = 1,900 ft.
On Fig. 83, enter V_1, V_R, V_2 chart under pressure altitude. Find the 1-to-3 pressure altitude line; then proceed to the right to the 10°C OAT (10°C is between –54°C to 28°C). Go down that column to flaps 5°, to 190,000 lb. gross weight (190), then right to V_R (rotation speed). V_R is 155 kt.
Answer (A) is incorrect because 150 kt. is the V_R speed for 180,000 lb. Answer (B) is incorrect because 154 kt. is the V_2 speed for 160,000 lb.

23.
8719. (Refer to figures 81, 82, and 83 on pages 666, 667, and 668.) What are V_1, V_R, and V_2 speeds for Operating Conditions G-3?

A—134, 134, and 145 knots.
B—134, 139, and 145 knots.
C—132, 132, and 145 knots.

Answer (A) is correct (8719). *(FTW Chap 8)*
Takeoff decision speed is V_1, rotation speed is V_R, and takeoff safety speed is V_2. Refer to the third column, G-3, in Fig. 81.
Find pressure altitude using Fig. 82 at field elevation 4,350 ft. and altimeter 30.10 in. Pressure altitude = 4,150 ft.
On Fig. 83, enter V_1, V_R, V_2 chart under pressure altitude. Find the 3-to-5 pressure altitude line; then proceed to the right to the 68°F OAT (68°F is between 33°F and 90°F). Go down that column to flaps 25°, to 180,000 lb. gross weight (180), then right to $V_1 = V_R$ and V_2. V_1 is 134 kt., V_R is 134 kt., and V_2 is 145 kt.
Answer (B) is incorrect because throughout the chart $V_1 = V_R$; thus V_1 is 134 kt. and V_R is also 134 kt., not 139 kt. Answer (C) is incorrect because 132, 132, and 145 kt. are V_1, V_R, and V_2 speeds using the 1-to-3, not 3-to-5, pressure altitude line.

24.
8720. (Refer to figures 81, 82, and 83 on pages 666, 667, and 668.) What are V_1 and V_2 speeds for Operating Conditions G-4?

A—133 and 145 knots.
B—127 and 141 knots.
C—132 and 146 knots.

Answer (C) is correct (8720). *(FTW Chap 8)*
Takeoff decision speed is V_1, and takeoff safety speed is V_2. Refer to the fourth column, G-4, in Fig. 81.
Find pressure altitude using Fig. 82 at field elevation 3,050 ft. and altimeter 1010 mb. Pressure altitude = 3,150 ft.
On Fig. 83, enter V_1, V_R, V_2 chart under pressure altitude. Find the 3-to-5 pressure altitude line; then proceed to the right to the –5°C OAT (–5°C is between –54°C to 0°C). Go down that column to flaps 15°, to 160,000 lb. gross weight (160), then right to V_1 and V_2. V_1 is 132 kt. and V_2 is 146 kt.
Answer (A) is incorrect because V_1 of 133 kt. and V_2 of 145 kt. is using an OAT of +5°C, not –5°C. Answer (B) is incorrect because V_1 of 127 kt. and V_2 of 141 kt. are for 150,000 lb., not 160,000 lb.

25.
8721. (Refer to figures 81, 82, and 83 on pages 666, 667, and 668.) What are rotation and V_2 bug speeds for Operating Conditions G-5?

A—120 and 134 knots.
B—119 and 135 knots.
C—135 and 135 knots.

Answer (B) is correct (8721). *(FTW Chap 8)*
Rotation speed is V_R, and takeoff safety speed is V_2. Refer to the fifth column, G-5, in Fig. 81.
Find pressure altitude using Fig. 82 at field elevation 2,150 ft. and altimeter 29.54 in. Pressure altitude = 2,550 ft.
On Fig. 83, enter V_1, V_R, V_2 chart under pressure altitude. Find the 1-to-3 pressure altitude line; then proceed to the right to the 5°F OAT (5°F is between –65°F and 83°F). Go down that column to flaps 5°, to 120,000 lb. gross weight (120), then right to V_R and V_2. V_R is 119 kt. and V_2 is 135 kt.
Answer (A) is incorrect because V_R of 120 kt. and V_2 of 134 kt. are found by using the 3-to-5 pressure altitude line with an OAT of 5°C. Answer (C) is incorrect because rotation speed is equal to V_1 (takeoff decision speed), not V_2.

14.4 STAB TRIM Settings

26.
8722. (Refer to figures 81 below and 83 on page 668.) What is the STAB TRIM setting for Operating Conditions G-1?

A—4 ANU.
B—4-1/2 ANU.
C—4-3/4 ANU.

Answer (B) is correct (8722). *(FTW Chap 8)*
Refer to column G-1 in Fig. 81.
Convert CG station 911.2 in. to percent MAC using the following formula:

$$\frac{CG - LEMAC}{MAC} = \% \ MAC$$

$$\frac{911.2 - 860.5}{180.9} = .280 \ \text{or} \ 28.0\% \ MAC$$

Enter STAB TRIM setting chart under CG% column and find 28%. Move to the right under flaps 15° to find 4½ ANU trim setting.

Answer (A) is incorrect because 4 ANU is appropriate for 5° flaps. Answer (C) is incorrect because 4¾ ANU is appropriate for 25° flaps.

27.
8723. (Refer to figures 81 below and 83 on page 668.) What is the STAB TRIM setting for Operating Conditions G-2?

A—6-1/2 ANU.
B—7-1/4 ANU.
C—5-3/4 ANU.

Answer (A) is correct (8723). *(FTW Chap 8)*
Refer to column G-2 in Fig. 81.
Convert CG station 882.2 in. to percent MAC using the following formula:

$$\frac{CG - LEMAC}{MAC} = \% \ MAC$$

$$\frac{882.2 - 860.5}{180.9} = .12 \ \text{or} \ 12.0\% \ MAC$$

Enter STAB TRIM setting chart under CG% column and find 12%. Move to the right under flaps 5° to find 6½ ANU trim setting.

Answer (B) is incorrect because 7¼ ANU is appropriate for 15°/20° flaps. Answer (C) is incorrect because 5¾ ANU is appropriate for CG station of 18% MAC.

OPERATING CONDITIONS	G-1	G-2	G-3	G-4	G-5
FIELD ELEVATION FT	1,050	2,000	4,350	3,050	2,150
ALTIMETER SETTING	29.36"	1016 mb	30.10"	1010 mb	29.54"
TEMPERATURE	+23 °F	+10 °C	+68 °F	–5 °C	+5 °F
AIR COND ENGS 1 AND 3	OFF	ON	ON	ON	ON
ANTI-ICE ENG 2	ON	OFF	OFF	ON	ON
GROSS WEIGHT (X1000)	140	190	180	160	120
6TH STAGE BLEED	OFF	ON	ON	OFF	OFF
FLAP POSITION	15°	5°	25°	15°	5°
CG STATION	911.2	882.2	914.8	932.9	925.6
LEMAC – STA 860.5, MAC 180.9"					

FIGURE 81.—B-727 – Takeoff.

ALTIMETER SETTING TO STATION PRESSURE

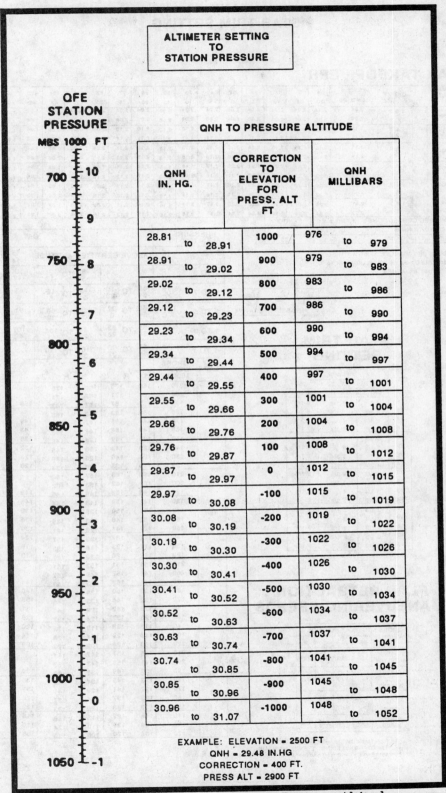

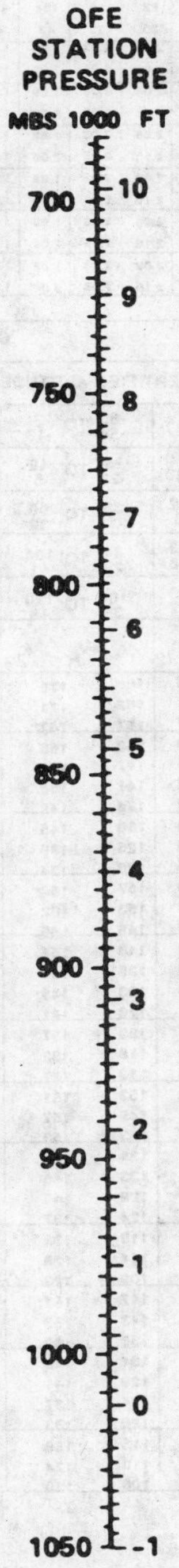

QNH TO PRESSURE ALTITUDE

QNH IN. HG.	CORRECTION TO ELEVATION FOR PRESS. ALT FT	QNH MILLIBARS
28.81 to 28.91	1000	976 to 979
28.91 to 29.02	900	979 to 983
29.02 to 29.12	800	983 to 986
29.12 to 29.23	700	986 to 990
29.23 to 29.34	600	990 to 994
29.34 to 29.44	500	994 to 997
29.44 to 29.55	400	997 to 1001
29.55 to 29.66	300	1001 to 1004
29.66 to 29.76	200	1004 to 1008
29.76 to 29.87	100	1008 to 1012
29.87 to 29.97	0	1012 to 1015
29.97 to 30.08	-100	1015 to 1019
30.08 to 30.19	-200	1019 to 1022
30.19 to 30.30	-300	1022 to 1026
30.30 to 30.41	-400	1026 to 1030
30.41 to 30.52	-500	1030 to 1034
30.52 to 30.63	-600	1034 to 1037
30.63 to 30.74	-700	1037 to 1041
30.74 to 30.85	-800	1041 to 1045
30.85 to 30.96	-900	1045 to 1048
30.96 to 31.07	-1000	1048 to 1052

EXAMPLE: ELEVATION = 2500 FT
QNH = 29.48 IN.HG
CORRECTION = 400 FT.
PRESS ALT = 2900 FT

FIGURE 82.—Altimeter Setting to Pressure Altitude.

TAKEOFF EPR, SPEEDS AND STAB TRIM SETTING

MAX TAKEOFF EPR

PRESS ALT FT	OAT °F / °C	-67 TO -9 / -55 TO -23	-4 / -20	5 / -15	14 / -10	23 / -5	32 / 0	41 / 5	50 / 10	59 / 15	68 / 20	77 / 25	86 / 30	95 / 35	104 / 40	113 / 45	120 / 49
-1000	1 & 3	2.04	2.04	2.04	2.04	2.04	2.04	2.04	2.04	2.04	2.04	2.04	2.04	2.03	1.99	1.94	1.91
	2	2.06	2.06	2.06	2.06	2.06	2.06	2.06	2.06	2.06	2.06	2.06	2.06	2.05	2.00	1.96	1.92
S.L.	1 & 3	2.10	2.10	2.10	2.10	2.10	2.10	2.10	2.10	2.10	2.10	2.10	2.08	2.03	1.99	1.94	1.91
	2	2.11	2.11	2.11	2.11	2.11	2.11	2.11	2.11	2.11	2.11	2.11	2.10	2.05	2.00	1.96	1.92
1000	1 & 3	2.15	2.15	2.15	2.15	2.15	2.15	2.15	2.13	2.12	2.12	2.11	2.08	2.03	1.99	1.94	1.91
	2	2.16	2.16	2.16	2.16	2.16	2.16	2.16	2.15	2.13	2.13	2.12	2.10	2.05	2.00	1.96	1.92
2000	1 & 3	2.21	2.21	2.21	2.21	2.21	2.20	2.17	2.14	2.14	2.14	2.11	2.08	2.03	1.99	1.94	1.91
	2	2.22	2.22	2.22	2.22	2.22	2.21	2.18	2.16	2.16	2.15	2.12	2.10	2.05	2.00	1.96	1.92
3000	1 & 3	2.26	2.26	2.26	2.25	2.23	2.20	2.17	2.14	2.14	2.14	2.11	2.08	2.03	1.99	1.94	1.91
	2	2.28	2.28	2.28	2.27	2.24	2.21	2.18	2.16	2.16	2.15	2.12	2.10	2.05	2.00	1.96	1.92
3856 & ABOVE	1 & 3	2.31	2.29	2.27	2.25	2.23	2.20	2.17	2.14	2.14	2.14	2.11	2.08	2.03	1.99	1.94	1.91
	2	2.32	2.31	2.29	2.27	2.24	2.21	2.18	2.16	2.16	2.15	2.12	2.10	2.05	2.00	1.96	1.92

EPR BLEED CORRECTIONS	ENG 1 & 3	ENG 2
AIR CONDITIONING	OFF +.04	-
ENGINE ANTI-ICE ON	-	-.03

REDUCE ENG 2 EPR BY .05 WITH 6TH STAGE BLEED ON (IF INSTALLED) FOR 10 °C (50 °F) OAT & WARMER

V_1, V_R, V_2

ANTI-SKID OPERATIVE

PRESSURE ALT - 1000 FT		OAT			
9 TO 11	°F / °C	(ABOVE CERTIFIED ALTITUDE)		-65 TO 25 / -54 TO -4	26 TO 87 / -3 TO 31
7 TO 9	°F / °C		-65 TO 9 / -54 TO -13	10 TO 75 / -12 TO 24	76 TO 104 / 25 TO 40
5 TO 7	°F / °C	-65 TO -10 / -54 TO -23	-8 TO 42 / -22 TO 5	43 TO 97 / 6 TO 36	98 TO 111 / 37 TO 44
3 TO 5	°F / °C	-65 TO 32 / -54 TO 0	33 TO 90 / 1 TO 32	91 TO 113 / 33 TO 45	114 TO 120 / 46 TO 49
1 TO 3	°F / °C	-65 TO 83 / -54 TO 28	84 TO 106 / 29 TO 41	107 TO 120 / 42 TO 49	
-1 TO 1	°F / °C	-65 TO 99 / -54 TO 37	100 TO 120 / 38 TO 49		

FLAPS	GROSS WEIGHT 1000 LB	$V_1 = V_R$	V_2	$V_1 = V_R$	V_2	$V_1 = V_R$	V_2	$V_1 = V_R$	V_2
5	210	165	175	166	175				
	200	160	171	162	171				
	190	155	167	157	167	158	167		
	180	150	163	152	163	154	163		
	170	144	159	147	159	149	159	150	158
	160	140	154	141	153	143	153	145	153
	150	135	149	136	149	138	149	140	148
	140	129	145	130	145	132	144	134	144
	130	124	140	125	139	126	138	128	138
	120	119	135	120	134	120	134	121	133
15	210	156	166	157	166				
	200	151	162	153	162				
	190	146	158	148	158	149	158		
	180	141	154	143	154	145	154		
	170	136	150	138	150	140	150	141	149
	160	132	146	133	145	135	145	137	145
	150	127	141	128	141	130	141	132	140
	140	122	137	123	137	124	136	126	136
	130	117	133	118	132	118	131	120	131
	120	112	128	113	127	113	127	115	126
20	210	151	161	152	161				
	200	146	157	148	157				
	190	141	153	143	153	144	153		
	180	136	150	138	150	140	149		
	170	132	146	133	146	135	145	136	145
	160	128	142	129	141	131	141	133	141
	150	123	137	124	137	126	136	128	136
	140	118	133	119	133	120	132	122	132
	130	113	129	114	128	114	127	116	127
	120	109	124	109	123	109	123	111	122
25	210	146	157	147	157				
	200	141	153	143	153				
	190	137	149	138	149	139	149		
	180	132	145	134	145	136	145		
	170	127	141	129	141	131	141	132	140
	160	123	137	124	137	126	137	128	136
	150	119	133	120	133	122	133	124	132
	140	114	129	115	129	116	128	118	128
	130	109	125	110	124	110	124	112	123
	120	105	120	106	120	106	119	108	118

STAB TRIM SETTING

CG	FLAPS 5	FLAPS 15 / 20	FLAPS 25
	UNITS AIRPLANE NOSE UP		
10	6 3/4	7 1/2	8 1/4
12	6 1/2	7 1/4	8
14	6 1/4	7	7 3/4
16	6	6 3/4	7 1/2
18	5 3/4	6 1/2	7
20	5 1/2	6	6 1/2
22	5	5 3/4	6 1/4
24	4 3/4	5 1/4	5 3/4
26	4 1/2	4 3/4	5 1/4
28	4	4 1/2	4 3/4
30	3 3/4	4	4 1/4
32	3 1/2	3 3/4	4
34	3 1/4	3 1/4	3 1/2
36	2 3/4	3	3
38	2 1/2	2 1/2	2 1/2
40	2 1/2	2 1/2	2 1/2
42	2 1/2	2 1/2	2 1/2

FLAP RETRACTION/ MANEUVERING SPEEDS

GROSS WEIGHT LB	FLAP POSITION 15	5	2	0
154500 & BELOW	150	160	190	200
154501 TO 176000	160	170	200	210
176001 TO 191000	170	180	210	220
ABOVE 191000	180	190	225	235

FOR MANEUVERS IMMEDIATELY AFTER TAKEOFF EXCEEDING 15° BANK MAINTAIN AT LEAST V_2 +10 AT TAKEOFF FLAPS

FIGURE 83.—Takeoff Performance.

28.
8724. (Refer to figures 81 and 83 on pages 666 and 668.) What is the STAB TRIM setting for Operating Conditions G-3?

A—3-3/4 ANU.
B—4 ANU.
C—4-1/4 ANU.

Answer (C) is correct (8724). *(FTW Chap 8)*
Refer to column G-3 in Fig. 81.
Convert CG station 914.8 in. to percent MAC using the following formula:

$$\frac{CG - LEMAC}{MAC} = \% \ MAC$$

$$\frac{914.8 - 860.5}{180.9} = .30 \ \text{or} \ 30.0\% \ MAC$$

Enter STAB TRIM setting chart under CG% column and find 30%. Move to the right under flaps 25° to find 4¼ ANU trim setting.
Answer (A) is incorrect because 3¾ ANU is appropriate for 5° flaps. Answer (B) is incorrect because 4 ANU is appropriate for 15°/20° flaps.

29.
8725. (Refer to figures 81 and 83 on pages 666 and 668.) What is the STAB TRIM setting for Operating Conditions G-4?

A—2-3/4 ANU.
B—4 ANU.
C—2-1/2 ANU.

Answer (C) is correct (8725). *(FTW Chap 8)*
Refer to column G-4 in Fig. 81.
Convert CG station 932.9 in. to percent MAC using the following formula:

$$\frac{CG - LEMAC}{MAC} = \% \ MAC$$

$$\frac{932.9 - 860.5}{180.9} = .40 \ \text{or} \ 40.0\% \ MAC$$

Enter STAB TRIM setting chart under CG% column and find 40%. Move to the right under flaps 15° to find 2½ ANU trim setting.
Answer (A) is incorrect because 2¾ ANU is appropriate for 5° flaps with a CG of 36% MAC. Answer (B) is incorrect because 4 ANU is appropriate for a CG at 30% MAC.

30.
8726. (Refer to figures 81 and 83 on pages 666 and 668.) What is the STAB TRIM setting for Operating Conditions G-5?

A—3-1/4 ANU.
B—2-3/4 ANU.
C—2-1/2 ANU.

Answer (B) is correct (8726). *(FTW Chap 8)*
Refer to column G-5 in Fig. 81.
Convert CG station 925.6 in. to percent MAC using the following formula:

$$\frac{CG - LEMAC}{MAC} = \% \ MAC$$

$$\frac{925.6 - 860.5}{180.9} = .359 \ \text{or} \ 36.0\% \ MAC$$

Enter STAB TRIM setting chart under CG% column and find 36%. Move to the right under flaps 5° to find 2¾ ANU trim setting.
Answer (A) is incorrect because 3¼ ANU is appropriate for a CG at 34% MAC. Answer (C) is incorrect because 2½ ANU is appropriate for a CG at 38% MAC.

14.5 Holding IAS and EPR

31.
8727. (Refer to figure 84 below, and 85 on page 671.) What are the recommended IAS and EPR settings for holding under Operating Conditions H-1?

A—264 knots and 1.80 EPR.
B—259 knots and 1.73 EPR.
C—261 knots and 1.81 EPR.

Answer (A) is correct (8727). *(FTW Chap 10)*
Given 24,000 ft., 195,000 lb., three engines operating, and 15 min. of holding (H-1 on Fig. 84), what are recommended holding IAS and EPR settings? Since neither 24,000 ft. nor 195,000 lb. is on Fig. 85, interpolate.
At 25,000 ft., the EPR value for 195,000 lb. is 1.83. At 20,000 ft, the EPR value for 195,000 lb. is 1.68. Interpolating for 24,000 ft. yields an EPR value of 1.80.
At 25,000 ft., the IAS for 195,000 lb. is 264.5 kt. At 20,000 ft., the IAS for 195,000 lb. is 261.5 kt. Interpolating for 24,000 ft. yields 264 kt.
Answer (B) is incorrect because 259 kt. is appropriate for lower altitudes. Answer (C) is incorrect because 261 kt. and 1.81 EPR are specified for 190,000 lb. at 25,000 ft.

32.
8728. (Refer to figure 84 below, and 85 on page 671.) What are the recommended IAS and EPR settings for holding under Operating Conditions H-2?

A—257 knots and 1.60 EPR.
B—258 knots and 1.66 EPR.
C—253 knots and 1.57 EPR.

Answer (C) is correct (8728). *(FTW Chap 10)*
Given 17,000 ft., 185,000 lb., three engines operating, and 30 min. of holding (H-2 on Fig. 84), what are recommended holding IAS and EPR settings? Since neither 17,000 ft. nor 185,000 lb. is on Fig. 85, interpolate.
At 20,000 ft., the EPR value for 185,000 lb. is 1.64. At 15,000 ft., the EPR value for 185,000 lb. is 1.52. Interpolating for 17,000 ft. yields an EPR value of 1.57.
At 20,000 ft., the IAS for 185,000 lb. is 254.5 kt. At 15,000 ft., the IAS for 185,000 lb. is 252.5 kt. Interpolating for 17,000 ft. yields 253 kt.
Answer (A) is incorrect because 257 kt. is appropriate for higher altitudes. Answer (B) is incorrect because 258 kt. and 1.66 EPR are specified for 190,000 lb. at 20,000 ft.

33.
8729. (Refer to figure 84 below, and 85 on page 671.) What are the recommended IAS and EPR settings for holding under Operating Conditions H-3?

A—226 knots and 1.30 EPR.
B—230 knots and 1.31 EPR.
C—234 knots and 1.32 EPR.

Answer (B) is correct (8729). *(FTW Chap 10)*
Given 8,000 ft., 155,000 lb., three engines operating, and 45 min. of holding (H-3 on Fig. 84), what are recommended holding IAS and EPR settings? Since neither 8,000 ft. nor 155,000 lb. is on Fig. 85, interpolate.
At 10,000 ft., the EPR value for 155,000 lb. is 1.34. At 5,000 ft., the EPR value for 155,000 lb. is 1.27. Interpolating for 8,000 ft. yields an EPR value of 1.31.
At 10,000 ft., the IAS for 155,000 lb. is 230 kt. At 5,000 ft., the IAS for 155,000 lb. is 229 kt. Interpolating for 8,000 ft. yields 230 kt.
Answer (A) is incorrect because 226 kt. is appropriate for lower altitudes. Answer (C) is incorrect because 234 kt. is appropriate for higher altitudes.

OPERATING CONDITIONS	H-1	H-2	H-3	H-4	H-5
ALTITUDE	24,000	17,000	8,000	18,000	22,000
WEIGHT (X1000)	195	185	155	135	175
ENGINES OPERATING	3	3	3	3	3
HOLDING TIME (MIN)	15	30	45	25	35

FIGURE 84.—B-727 – Holding.

34.
8730. (Refer to figure 84 on page 670, and 85 below.) What are the recommended IAS and EPR settings for holding under Operating Conditions H-4?

A—219 knots and 1.44 EPR.
B—216 knots and 1.42 EPR.
C—220 knots and 1.63 EPR.

Answer (B) is correct (8730). *(FTW Chap 10)*
Given 18,000 ft., 135,000 lb., three engines operating, and 25 min. of holding (H-4 on Fig. 84), what are recommended holding IAS and EPR settings? Since neither 18,000 ft. nor 135,000 lb. is on Fig. 85, interpolate.
At 20,000 ft., the EPR value for 135,000 lb. is 1.46. At 15,000 ft., the EPR value for 135,000 lb. is 1.36. Interpolating for 18,000 ft. yields an EPR value of 1.42.
At 20,000 ft., the IAS for 135,000 lb. is 216 kt. At 15,000 ft., the IAS for 135,000 lb. is 215 kt. Interpolating for 18,000 ft. yields 216 kt.
Answer (A) is incorrect because 219 kt. is appropriate for higher altitudes. Answer (C) is incorrect because 1.63 EPR is appropriate for a higher altitude and gross weight.

35.
8731. (Refer to figure 84 on page 670, and 85 below.) What are the recommended IAS and EPR settings for holding under Operating Conditions H-5?

A—245 knots and 1.65 EPR.
B—237 knots and 1.61 EPR.
C—249 knots and 1.67 EPR.

Answer (C) is correct (8731). *(FTW Chap 10)*
Given 22,000 ft., 175,000 lb., three engines operating, and 35 min. of holding (H-5 on Fig. 84), what are recommended holding IAS and EPR settings? Since neither 22,000 ft. nor 175,000 lb. is on Fig. 85, interpolate.
At 25,000 ft., the EPR value for 175,000 lb. is 1.75. At 20,000 ft., the EPR value for 175,000 lb. is 1.61. Interpolating for 22,000 ft. yields an EPR value of 1.67.
At 25,000 ft., the IAS for 175,000 lb. is 249.5 kt. At 20,000 ft., the IAS for 175,000 lb. is 247.5 kt. Interpolating for 22,000 ft. yields 249 kt.
Answer (A) is incorrect because 245 kt. is appropriate for lower altitudes. Answer (B) is incorrect because 237 kt. is appropriate for a lower altitude and gross weight.

EPR IAS - KTS FF PER ENG - LB/HR	HOLDING						B-727	
PRESSURE ALTITUDE FT	**GROSS WEIGHT - 1000 LB**								

PRESSURE ALTITUDE FT	200	190	180	170	160	150	140	130	120
25000	1.85 268 3600	1.81 261 3400	1.77 253 3210	1.73 246 3030	1.69 238 2860	1.64 230 2680	1.60 222 2510	1.55 213 2340	1.51 205 2180
20000	1.69 265 3630	1.66 258 3450	1.62 251 3280	1.59 244 3110	1.55 236 2940	1.51 228 2770	1.48 220 2600	1.44 212 2440	1.40 204 2270
15000	1.56 263 3670	1.53 256 3500	1.50 249 3340	1.47 242 3170	1.44 235 3000	1.41 227 2850	1.38 219 2680	1.35 211 2520	1.32 203 2350
10000	1.45 262 3800	1.43 255 3640	1.40 248 3460	1.38 241 3310	1.35 234 3140	1.33 226 2970	1.30 218 2810	1.28 210 2640	1.25 202 2480
5000	1.36 260 3890	1.34 254 3720	1.32 247 3550	1.30 240 3380	1.28 233 3220	1.26 225 3060	1.24 218 2890	1.22 210 2730	1.20 201 2560

FIGURE 85.—B-727 – Holding Performance Chart.

14.6 Holding Fuel Consumption

36.
8732. (Refer to figures 84 and 85 on pages 670 and 671.) What is the approximate fuel consumed when holding under Operating Conditions H-1?

A—3,500 pounds.
B—4,680 pounds.
C—2,630 pounds.

Answer (C) is correct (8732). *(FTW Chap 10)*
H-1 on Fig. 84 specifies 24,000 ft., 195,000 lb., three engines operating, and 15 min. holding. Compute the fuel burn during holding by using Fig. 85.
At 25,000 ft. and 195,000 lb., fuel flow is 3,500 lb./hr. per engine. At 20,000 ft. and 195,000 lb., fuel flow is 3,540 lb./hr. per engine. Interpolating for 24,000 ft., fuel flow is 3,508 lb./hr. per engine. Multiply by 3 (three engines) and multiply by .25 (15 min.):

$$3{,}508\ lb. \times 3 \times .25 = 2{,}631\ lb.$$

Answer (A) is incorrect because 3,500 lb. means a per-engine fuel flow of 4,667 lb./hr. Answer (B) is incorrect because 4,680 lb. means a per-engine fuel flow of 6,240 lb./hr.

37.
8733. (Refer to figures 84 and 85 on pages 670 and 671.) What is the approximate fuel consumed when holding under Operating Conditions H-2?

A—5,100 pounds.
B—3,400 pounds.
C—5,250 pounds.

Answer (A) is correct (8733). *(FTW Chap 10)*
H-2 on Fig. 84 specifies 17,000 ft., 185,000 lb., three engines operating, and 30 min. holding. Compute the fuel burn during holding by using Fig. 85.
At 20,000 ft. and 185,000 lb., fuel flow is 3,365 lb./hr. per engine. At 15,000 ft. and 185,000 lb., fuel flow is 3,420 lb./hr. per engine. Interpolating for 17,000 ft., fuel flow is 3,398 lb./hr. per engine. Multiply by 3 (three engines) and multiply by .5 (30 min.):

$$3{,}398\ lb. \times 3 \times .5 = 5{,}097\ lb.$$

Answer (B) is incorrect because 3,400 lb. means a per-engine fuel flow of 2,267 lb./hr. Answer (C) is incorrect because 5,250 lb. means a per-engine fuel flow of 3,500 lb./hr.

38.
8734. (Refer to figures 84 and 85 on pages 670 and 671.) What is the approximate fuel consumed when holding under Operating Conditions H-3?

A—3,090 pounds.
B—6,950 pounds.
C—6,680 pounds.

Answer (B) is correct (8734). *(FTW Chap 10)*
H-3 on Fig. 84 specifies 8,000 ft., 155,000 lb., three engines operating, and 45 min. holding. Compute the fuel burn during holding by using Fig. 85.
At 10,000 ft. and 155,000 lb., fuel flow is 3,055 lb./hr. per engine. At 5,000 ft. and 155,000 lb., fuel flow is 3,140 lb./hr. per engine. Interpolating for 8,000 ft., fuel flow is 3,089 lb./hr. per engine. Multiply by 3 (three engines) and multiply by .75 (45 min.):

$$3{,}089\ lb. \times 3 \times .75 = 6{,}950\ lb.$$

Answer (A) is incorrect because 3,090 lb. means a per-engine fuel flow of 1,374 lb./hr. Answer (C) is incorrect because 6,680 lb. means a per-engine fuel flow of 2,969 lb./hr.

39.
8735. (Refer to figures 84 and 85 on pages 670 and 671.) What is the approximate fuel consumed when holding under Operating Conditions H-4?

A—3,190 pounds.
B—3,050 pounds.
C—2,550 pounds.

Answer (A) is correct (8735). *(FTW Chap 10)*
H-4 on Fig. 84 specifies 18,000 ft., 135,000 lb., three engines operating, and 25 min. holding. Compute the fuel burn during holding by using Fig. 85.

At 20,000 ft. and 135,000 lb., fuel flow is 2,520 lb./hr. per engine. At 15,000 ft. and 135,000 lb., fuel flow is 2,600 lb./hr. per engine. Interpolating for 18,000 ft., fuel flow is 2,552 lb./hr. per engine. Multiply by 3 (three engines) and multiply by .417 (25 min.):

$$2{,}552\ \textit{lb.} \times 3 \times .417 = 3{,}190\ \textit{lb.}$$

Answer (B) is incorrect because 3,050 lb. means a per-engine fuel flow of 2,445 lb./hr. Answer (C) is incorrect because 2,550 lb. means a per-engine fuel flow of 2,043 lb./hr.

40.
8736. (Refer to figures 84 and 85 on pages 670 and 671.) What is the approximate fuel consumed when holding under Operating Conditions H-5?

A—3,170 pounds.
B—7,380 pounds.
C—5,540 pounds.

Answer (C) is correct (8736). *(FTW Chap 10)*
H-5 on Fig. 84 specifies 22,000 ft., 175,000 lb., three engines operating, and 35 min. holding. Compute the fuel burn during holding by using Fig. 85.

At 25,000 ft. and 175,000 lb., fuel flow is 3,120 lb./hr. per engine. At 20,000 ft. and 175,000 lb., fuel flow is 3,195 lb./hr. per engine. Interpolating for 22,000 ft., fuel flow is 3,165 lb./hr. per engine. Multiply by 3 (three engines) and multiply by .583 (35 min.):

$$3{,}165\ \textit{lb.} \times 3 \times .583 = 5{,}539\ \textit{lb.}$$

Answer (A) is incorrect because 3,170 lb. means a per-engine fuel flow of 1,813 lb./hr. Answer (B) is incorrect because 7,380 lb. means a per-engine fuel flow of 4,220 lb./hr.

OPERATING CONDITIONS	S–1	S–2	S–3	S–4	S–5
FLIGHT LEVEL	370	350	410	390	330
LANDING WEIGHT (X1000)	130	150	135	155	125
DESCENT TYPE	.80M/ 250	.80M/ 280/250	.80M/ 320/250	.80M/ 350/250	.80M/ 320/250

FIGURE 86.—Descent Performance.

.80M/250 KIAS

FLIGHT LEVEL	TIME MIN	FUEL LB	DISTANCE NAM AT LANDING WEIGHTS		
			120,000 LB	140,000 LB	160,000 LB
410	27	1610	133	137	138
390	27	1600	130	134	136
370	26	1570	123	128	129
350	25	1540	116	120	122
330	24	1510	110	113	115
310	23	1480	103	107	108
290	22	1450	97	100	101
270	21	1420	90	93	95
250	20	1390	84	87	88
230	19	1360	78	80	81
210	18	1320	72	74	75
190	17	1280	66	68	68
170	16	1240	60	62	62
150	14	1190	54	56	56
100	11	1050	39	40	40
050	8	870	24	24	24
015	5	700	12	12	12

.80M/280/250 KIAS

FLIGHT LEVEL	TIME MIN	FUEL LB	DISTANCE NAM AT LANDING WEIGHTS		
			120,000 LB	140,000 LB	160,000 LB
410	25	1550	123	129	132
390	24	1540	121	127	130
370	24	1520	115	121	125
350	23	1500	111	117	120
330	23	1480	106	111	115
310	22	1450	100	105	108
290	21	1430	94	99	102
270	20	1400	88	93	95
250	19	1370	83	87	89
230	18	1350	77	81	83
210	17	1310	72	75	76
190	16	1280	66	69	70
170	15	1240	61	63	64
150	14	1200	55	57	58
100	12	1080	42	42	42
050	8	870	24	24	24
015	5	700	12	12	12

.80M/320/250 KIAS

FLIGHT LEVEL	TIME MIN	FUEL LB	DISTANCE NAM AT LANDING WEIGHTS		
			120,000 LB	140,000 LB	160,000 LB
410	22	1490	113	120	123
390	22	1480	111	117	121
370	21	1460	105	112	116
350	21	1440	101	107	111
330	20	1420	96	103	107
310	20	1400	92	98	102
290	19	1390	89	94	98
270	19	1370	85	90	94
250	18	1350	80	85	88
230	17	1330	75	79	82
210	17	1300	71	74	77
190	16	1270	66	69	71
170	15	1240	61	64	65
150	14	1210	56	59	60
100	12	1110	45	46	46
050	8	870	24	24	24
015	5	700	12	12	12

.80M/350/250 KIAS

FLIGHT LEVEL	TIME MIN	FUEL LB	DISTANCE NAM AT LANDING WEIGHTS		
			120,000 LB	140,000 LB	160,000 LB
410	21	1440	106	112	116
390	21	1430	103	110	114
370	20	1420	99	106	110
350	20	1400	95	101	106
330	19	1390	91	98	102
310	19	1380	88	94	98
290	18	1360	85	90	95
270	18	1350	82	87	91
250	17	1330	78	83	87
230	17	1310	74	78	81
210	16	1290	70	74	76
190	16	1270	65	69	71
170	15	1240	61	64	66
150	14	1210	57	60	61
100	13	1130	47	48	49
050	8	870	24	24	24
015	5	700	12	12	12

NOTE: FUEL FOR A STRAIGHT-IN APPROACH IS INCLUDED

FIGURE 87.—Descent Performance Chart.

14.7 Descent Time, Fuel, and Distance

41.
8737. (Refer to figures 86 and 87 on page 674.) What are descent time and distance under Operating Conditions S-1?

A—24 minutes, 118 NAM.
B—26 minutes, 125 NAM.
C—25 minutes, 118 NAM.

Answer (B) is correct (8737). *(FTW Chap 10)*
S-1 of Fig. 86 indicates FL 370, 130,000 lb. landing weight, and .80M/250 descent. On Fig. 87, use .80M/250 KIAS, enter FL 370 row, and find 26 min. Interpolating the distance for 130,000 lb., which is between 123 NAM (120,000 lb.) and 128 NAM (140,000 lb.), gives 125 NAM.
Answer (A) is incorrect because 24 min. is the time to descend from FL 330, not FL 370. Answer (C) is incorrect because 25 min. is the time to descend from FL 350, not FL 370.

42.
8738. (Refer to figures 86 and 87 on page 674.) What are descent fuel and distance under Operating Conditions S-2?

A—1,440 pounds, 104 NAM.
B—1,500 pounds, 118 NAM.
C—1,400 pounds, 98 NAM.

Answer (B) is correct (8738). *(FTW Chap 10)*
S-2 of Fig. 86 indicates FL 350, 150,000 lb. landing weight, and .80M/280/250 descent. On Fig. 87, use .80M/280/250 KIAS, enter FL 350 row, and find descent fuel is 1,500 lb. Interpolating the distance for 150,000 lb., which is between 117 NAM (140,000 lb.) and 120 NAM (160,000 lb.), gives 118 NAM.
Answer (A) is incorrect because 1,440 lb. is the descent fuel from FL 350 using a .80M/320/250 KIAS-type descent. Answer (C) is incorrect because 1,400 lb. is the descent fuel from FL 350 using a .80M/350/250 KIAS-type descent.

43.
8739. (Refer to figures 86 and 87 on page 674.) What are descent fuel and distance under Operating Conditions S-3?

A—1,490 pounds, 118 NAM.
B—1,440 pounds, 110 NAM.
C—1,550 pounds, 127 NAM.

Answer (A) is correct (8739). *(FTW Chap 10)*
S-3 of Fig. 86 indicates FL 410, 135,000 lb. landing weight, and .80M/320/250 descent. On Fig. 87, use .80M/320/250 KIAS, enter FL 410 row, and find descent fuel is 1,490 lb. Interpolating the distance for 135,000 lb., which is between 113 NAM (120,000 lb.) and 120 NAM (140,000 lb.), gives 118 NAM.
Answer (B) is incorrect because 1,440 lb. is the descent fuel from FL 410 using a .80M/350/250 KIAS-type descent. Answer (C) is incorrect because 1,550 lb. is the descent fuel from FL 410 using a .80M/280/250 KIAS-type descent.

44.
8740. (Refer to figures 86 and 87 on page 674.) What are descent time and distance under Operating Conditions S-4?

A—22 minutes, 110 NAM.
B—21 minutes, 113 NAM.
C—24 minutes, 129 NAM.

Answer (B) is correct (8740). *(FTW Chap 10)*
S-4 of Fig. 86 indicates FL 390, 155,000 lb. landing weight, and .80M/350/250 descent. On Fig. 87, use .80M/350/250 KIAS. Enter FL 390 row, and find 21 min. Interpolating the distance for 155,000 lb., which is between 110 NAM (140,000 lb.) and 114 NAM (160,000 lb.), gives 113 NAM.
Answer (A) is incorrect because 22 min. is the time to descend from FL 390 using a .80M/320/250 KIAS-type descent. Answer (C) is incorrect because 24 min. is the time to descend from FL 390 using a .80M/280/250 KIAS-type descent.

45.
8741. (Refer to figures 86 and 87 on page 674.) What are descent fuel and distance under Operating Conditions S-5?

A—1,420 pounds, 97 NAM.
B—1,440 pounds, 102 NAM.
C—1,390 pounds, 92 NAM.

Answer (A) is correct (8741). *(FTW Chap 10)*
S-5 of Fig. 86 indicates FL 330, 125,000 lb. landing weight, and .80M/320/250 descent. On Fig. 87, use .80M/320/250 KIAS, enter FL 370 row, and find descent fuel is 1,420 lb. Interpolating the distance for 125,000 lb., which is between 96 NAM (120,000 lb.) and 103 NAM (140,000 lb.), gives 97 NAM.
Answer (B) is incorrect because 1,440 lb. is the descent fuel from FL 350 using a .80M/320/250 KIAS-type descent. Answer (C) is incorrect because 1,390 lb. is the descent fuel from FL 330 using a .80M/350/250 KIAS-type descent.

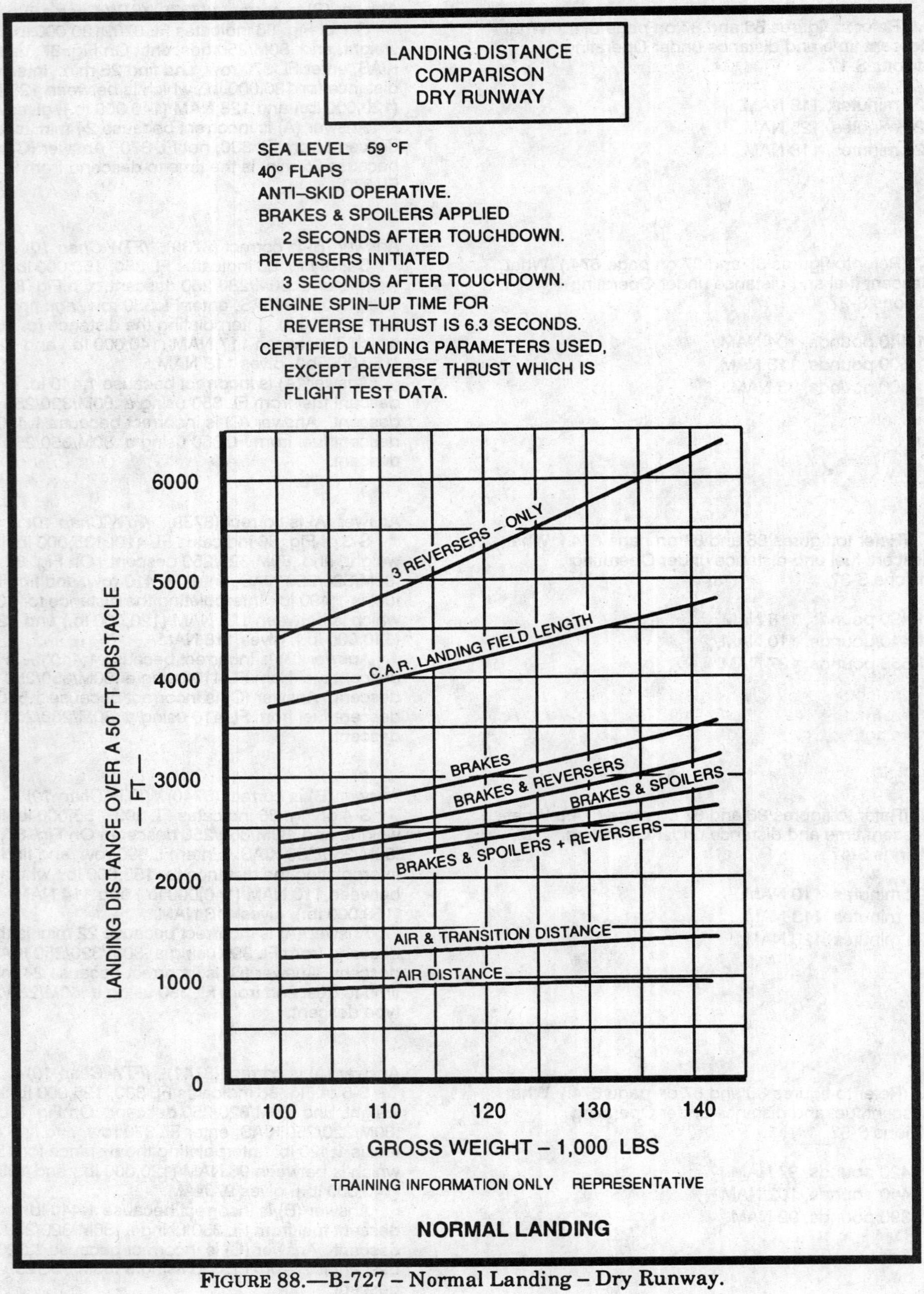

FIGURE 88.—B-727 – Normal Landing – Dry Runway.

14.8 Landing Distances

46.
8743. (Refer to figure 88 on page 676.) How much longer is the dry runway landing distance using brakes only compared to using brakes and reversers at 114,000 pounds gross weight?

A—1,150 feet.
B—500 feet.
C—300 feet.

Answer (C) is correct (8743). *(FTW Chap 15)*
Fig. 88 provides a chart to compare landing distances on a dry runway. At the bottom of the chart, find 114 (gross weight/1,000 lb.) and move up vertically to the brakes line. Move horizontally to the left edge of the chart to find a landing distance of 2,900 ft. Repeat the process, except use the brakes and reversers line to determine a landing distance of 2,600 ft. The difference is 300 ft. (2,900 – 2,600).
Answer (A) is incorrect because 1,150 ft. is the difference between using brakes only and the CAR landing field length. Note: CAR (Civil Air Regulations) is an outdated term for FAR (Federal Aviation Regulations). Answer (B) is incorrect because 500 ft. is the difference between using brakes only and using brakes and spoilers.

47.
8744. (Refer to figure 88 on page 676.) How many feet will remain after landing on a 7,200-foot dry runway with spoilers inoperative at 118,000 pounds gross weight?

A—4,200 feet.
B—4,500 feet.
C—4,750 feet.

Answer (B) is correct (8744). *(FTW Chap 15)*
Fig. 88 provides a chart to compare landing distances on a dry runway. At the bottom of the chart, find 118 (gross weight/1,000 lb.) and move up vertically to the brakes and reversers (spoilers inoperative) line. Move horizontally to the left edge of the chart to find a landing distance of 2,700 ft. Landing on a 7,200-ft. runway, a total of 4,500 ft. will remain (7,200 – 2,700). This is the shortest landing distance with spoilers inoperative.
Answer (A) is incorrect because 4,200 ft. of runway would remain if brakes only were used. Answer (C) is incorrect because 4,750 ft. of runway would remain if brakes and spoilers were operative and used.

48.
8745. (Refer to figure 88 on page 676.) What is the maximum landing weight which will permit stopping 2,000 feet short of the end of a 5,400-foot dry runway with reversers and spoilers inoperative?

A—117,500 pounds.
B—136,500 pounds.
C—139,500 pounds.

Answer (B) is correct (8745). *(FTW Chap 15)*
Fig. 88 provides a chart to compare landing distances on a dry runway. The required landing distance is 3,400 ft. (5,400 – 2,000). On the left margin of the chart, find the landing distance of 3,400 ft. and move right horizontally to intersect the brakes only line. Move down vertically to the bottom of the chart to determine the maximum landing (gross weight) of 136.5/1,000 lb. or 136,500 lb.
Answer (A) is incorrect because a landing weight of 117,500 lb. would require a landing distance less than 3,400 ft. Answer (C) is incorrect because a landing weight of 139,500 lb. would require a landing distance greater than 3,400 ft.

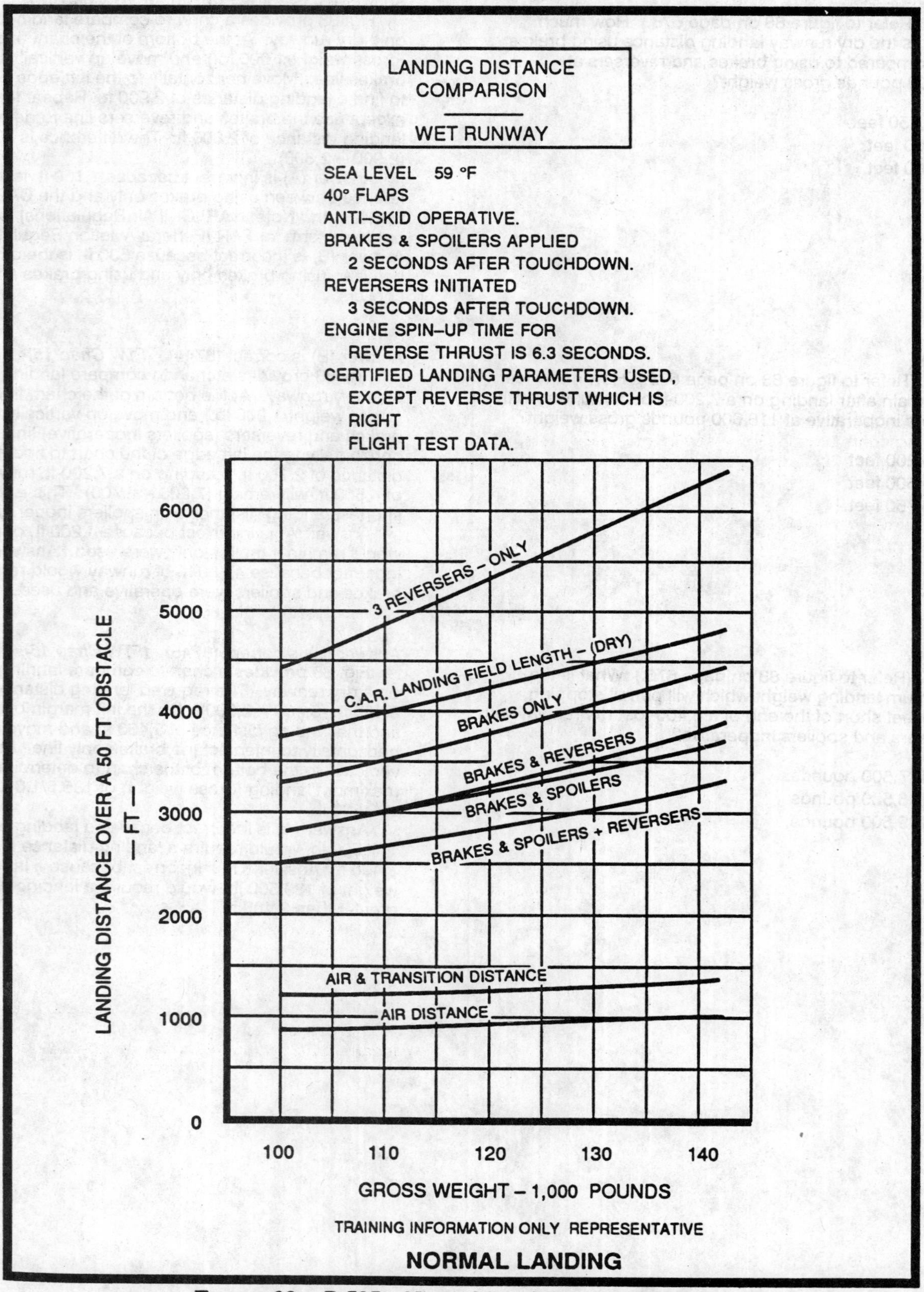

FIGURE 89.—B-727 – Normal Landing – Wet Runway.

49.
8742. (Refer to figures 88 and 89 on pages 676 and 678.) Which conditions will result in the shortest landing distance at a weight of 132,500 pounds?

A—Dry runway using brakes and reversers.
B—Dry runway using brakes and spoilers.
C—Wet runway using brakes, spoilers and reversers.

Answer (B) is correct (8742). *(FTW Chap 15)*
Fig. 88 provides a chart to compare landing distances on a dry runway. At the bottom of the chart, find 132.5 (gross weight/1,000 lb.) and move up vertically to the brakes and reversers line. Move horizontally to the left edge of the chart and find a landing distance of approximately 2,900 ft. Repeat the process except use the brakes and spoilers line to find a landing distance of approximately 2,750 ft. Fig 89 provides a chart to compare landing distances on a wet runway. Repeat the same procedures using the brakes, spoilers, and reversers line to find a landing distance of approximately 3,150 ft. Thus, the shortest landing distance will be on a dry runway using brakes and spoilers.
Answer (A) is incorrect because a longer landing distance is required when using brakes and reversers than when using brakes and spoilers on a dry runway. Answer (C) is incorrect because a longer landing distance is required when using brakes on a wet runway compared to a dry runway.

50.
8746. (Refer to figure 89 on page 678.) Which of the following configurations will result in the shortest landing distance over a 50-foot obstacle to a wet runway?

A—Brakes and spoilers at 122,500 pounds gross weight.
B—Brakes and reversers at 124,000 pounds gross weight.
C—Brakes, spoilers, and reversers at 131,000 pounds gross weight.

Answer (C) is correct (8746). *(FTW Chap 15)*
Fig. 89 provides a chart to compare landing distances over a 50-ft. obstacle to a wet runway. First, at the bottom of the chart, find 122.5 (gross weight/1,000 lb.) and move up vertically to the brakes and spoilers line. Move horizontally to the left edge of the chart and find a landing distance of 3,250 ft. Next, repeat the process using a gross weight of 124 and the brakes and reversers line to determine a landing distance of 3,400 ft. Finally, repeat the same process, this time using a gross weight of 131 and the brakes, spoilers, and reversers line to determine a landing distance of 3,100 ft. Now compare the distances to determine that the shortest landing distance will result in a configuration of brakes, spoilers, and reversers at 131,000 lb. gross weight (3,100 ft.).
Answer (A) is incorrect because using brakes and spoilers at 122,500 lb. gross weight does not produce the shortest landing distance. Answer (B) is incorrect because using brakes and reversers at 124,000 lb. gross weight results in the longest, not shortest, landing distance.

51.
8747. (Refer to figure 89 on page 678.) How many feet will remain after landing on a 6,000-foot wet runway with reversers inoperative at 122,000 pounds gross weight?

A—2,200 feet.
B—2,750 feet.
C—3,150 feet.

Answer (B) is correct (8747). *(FTW Chap 15)*
Fig. 89 provides a chart to compare landing distances on a wet runway. At the bottom of the chart, find 122 (gross weight/1,000 lb.) and move up vertically to the brakes and spoilers line (reverse inoperative). Move horizontally to the left edge of the chart to determine the landing distance of 3,250 ft. On a 6,000-ft. runway, 2,750 ft. will remain (6,000 – 3,250) after landing.
Answer (A) is incorrect because 2,200 ft. of runway would remain if brakes only were used. Answer (C) is incorrect because 3,150 ft. would remain if brakes, spoilers, and reversers were used.

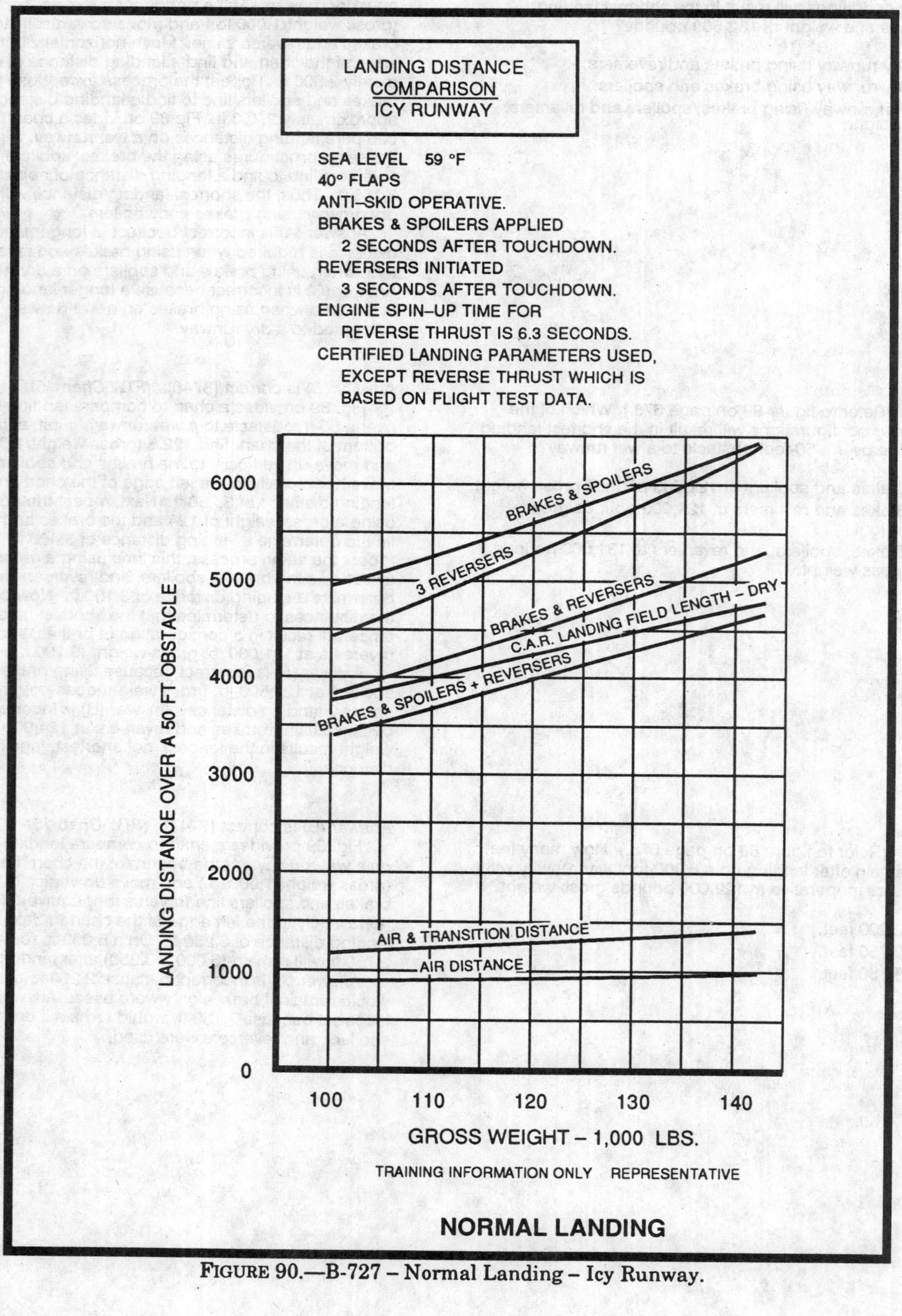

FIGURE 90.—B-727 – Normal Landing – Icy Runway.

52.
8748. (Refer to figure 90 on page 680.) Which configuration will result in a landing distance of 5,900 feet over a 50-foot obstacle to an icy runway?

A—Use of three reversers at 131,000 pounds gross weight.
B—Use of brakes and spoilers at 125,000 pounds gross weight.
C—Use of three reversers at 133,000 pounds gross weight.

Answer (C) is correct (8748). *(FTW Chap 15)*

Fig. 90 provides a chart to compare landing distances over a 50-ft. obstacle to an icy runway. First, at the bottom of the chart, find 131 (gross weight/1,000 lb.) and move up vertically to the three reversers line. Move horizontally to the left edge of the chart to determine a landing distance of 5,800 ft. Next, repeat the process using a gross weight of 125 and the brakes and spoilers line to determine a landing distance of 5,800 ft. Finally, repeat the process using a gross weight of 133 and the three reversers line to determine a landing distance of 5,900 ft. You are required to select the configuration that would require a landing distance of 5,900 ft., which is using three reversers at 133,000 lb. gross weight.

Answer (A) is incorrect because use of three reversers at 131,000 lb. would require less than 5,900 ft. of landing distance. Answer (B) is incorrect because use of brakes and spoilers at 125,000 lb. would require a landing distance of less than 5,900 ft.

53.
8749. (Refer to figure 90 on page 680.) What is the transition distance when landing on an icy runway at a gross weight of 134,000 pounds?

A—400 feet.
B—950 feet.
C—1,350 feet.

Answer (A) is correct (8749). *(FTW Chap 15)*

Fig. 90 provides a chart to compare landing distances on an icy runway. The transition distance is the difference between the air and transition distance and the air distance. At the bottom of the chart, find 134 (gross weight/1,000 lb.) and move up vertically to the air and transition line to determine a distance of 1,350 ft. Repeat the same process, only this time use the air line to determine a distance of 950 ft. The transition distance is 400 ft. (1,350 – 950).

Answer (B) is incorrect because 950 ft. is the air distance at a gross weight of 134,000 lb. Answer (C) is incorrect because 1,350 ft. is the air and transition distance at a gross weight of 134,000 lb.

54.
8750. (Refer to figure 90 on page 680.) What is the maximum landing weight which will permit stopping 700 feet short of the end of a 5,200-foot icy runway?

A—124,000 pounds.
B—137,000 pounds.
C—108,000 pounds.

Answer (B) is correct (8750). *(FTW Chap 15)*

Fig. 90 provides a chart to compare landing distances on an icy runway. Determine the maximum landing (gross) weight which will permit a landing distance of 4,500 ft. (700 ft. short of the end of a 5,200-ft. runway). At the left margin of the chart, find the landing distance of 4,500 ft. and move right horizontally to the brakes, spoilers, and reversers line. Move down vertically to determine the gross weight is 137,000 lb.

Answer (A) is incorrect because 124,000 lb. gross weight would permit stopping 1,100 ft. short of the end of a 5,200-ft. icy runway using brakes, spoilers, and reversers. Answer (C) is incorrect because 108,000 lb. gross weight would permit stopping 1,550 ft. short of the end of a 5,200 ft. icy runway using brakes, spoilers, and reversers.

55.
8751. (Refer to figure 90 on page 680.) What is the landing distance on an icy runway with reversers inoperative at a landing weight of 125,000 pounds?

A—4,500 feet.
B—4,750 feet.
C—5,800 feet.

Answer (C) is correct (8751). *(FTW Chap 15)*

Fig. 90 provides a chart to compare landing distances on an icy runway. Since reversers are inoperative, brakes and spoilers will provide the braking. At the bottom of the chart, find 125 (gross weight/1,000 lb.) and move up vertically to the brakes and spoilers line. Move horizontally to the left edge of the chart to determine a landing distance of 5,800 ft.

Answer (A) is incorrect because a landing distance of 4,500 ft. is achieved at a gross weight of 120,000 lb. using brakes and reversers, which are inoperative. Answer (B) is incorrect because a landing distance of 4,750 ft. is achieved by using brakes and reversers, which are inoperative.

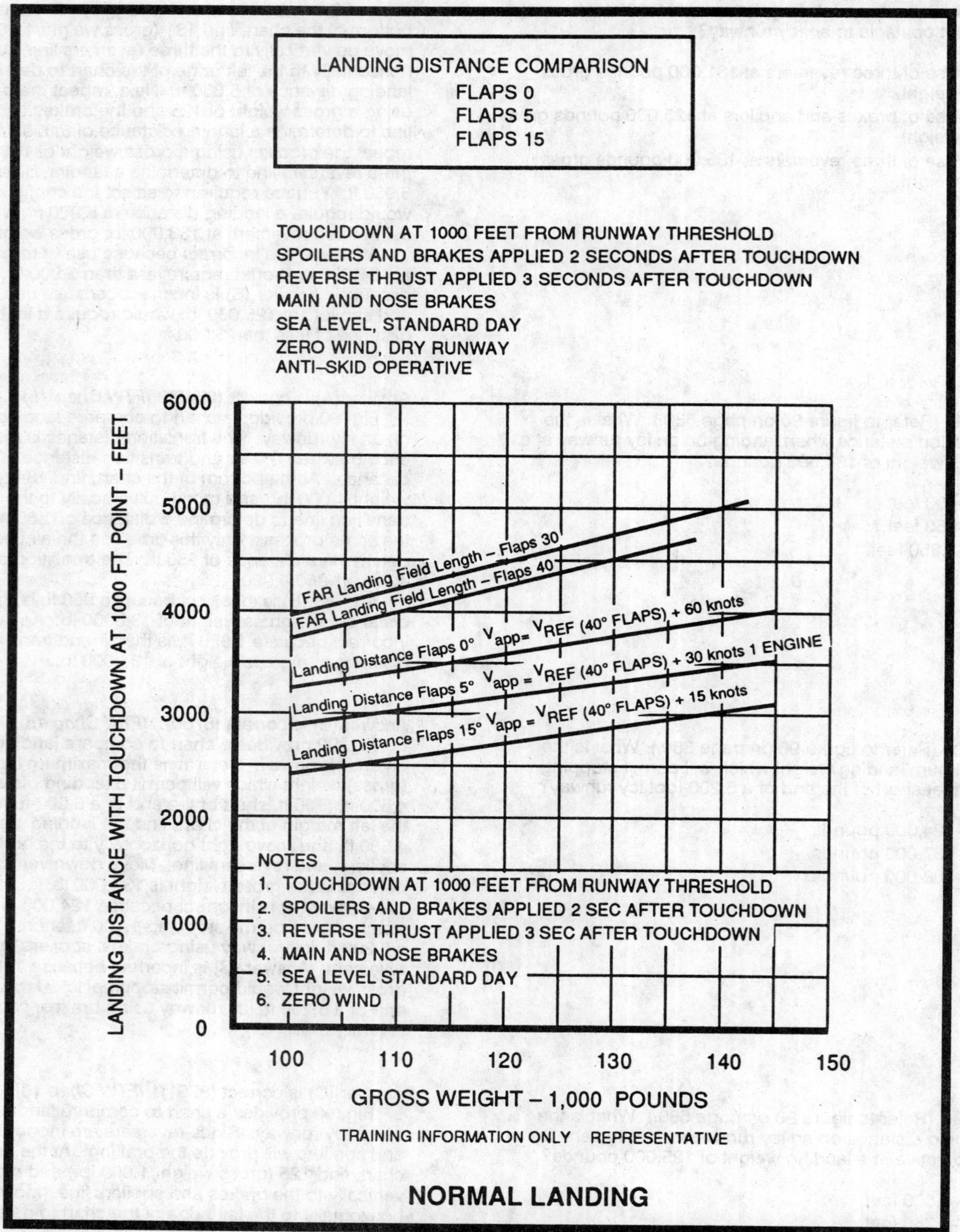

FIGURE 91.—B-727 – Normal Landing Distance Comparison.

56.
8752. (Refer to figure 91 on page 682.) How much will landing distance be reduced by using 15° of flaps rather than 0° flaps at a landing weight of 119,000 pounds?

A—500 feet.
B—800 feet.
C—2,700 feet.

Answer (B) is correct (8752). *(FTW Chap 15)*
Fig. 91 provides a chart to compare landing distances using various flap settings on a dry runway. Determine the landing distance reduction by using 15° flaps rather than 0° flaps. First, at the bottom of the chart, find 119 (gross weight/1,000 lb.) and move up vertically to landing distance flaps 0° line. Move horizontally to the left edge of the chart to determine a landing distance of 3,550 ft. Next, repeat the process using the landing distance flaps 15° line to determine a landing distance of 2,750 ft. The landing distance is reduced 800 ft. (3,550 – 2,750) by using 15° flaps rather than 0° flaps.
Answer (A) is incorrect because 500 ft. is the approximate reduction of the landing distance using 5°, not 15°, flaps and 0° flaps. Answer (C) is incorrect because 2,700 ft. is the approximate landing distance using 15° flaps.

57.
8753. (Refer to figure 91 on page 682.) What is the ground roll when landing with 15° of flaps at a landing weight of 122,000 pounds?

A—1,750 feet.
B—2,200 feet.
C—2,750 feet.

Answer (A) is correct (8753). *(FTW Chap 15)*
Fig. 91 provides a chart to compare landing distances using various flap settings. The ground roll is 1,000 ft. less than the landing distance since the touchdown point is 1,000 ft. from the runway threshold (see note 1). At the bottom of the chart, find 122 (gross weight/1,000 lb.) and move up vertically to the landing distance flaps 15° line. Then move horizontally to the left edge of the chart to determine a landing distance of 2,750 ft. The ground roll is 1,750 ft. (2,750 – 1,000).
Answer (B) is incorrect because 2,200 ft. is the ground roll when landing with 5°, not 15°, flaps. Answer (C) is incorrect because 2,750 ft. is the total landing distance, not the ground roll, using 15° flaps.

58.
8755. (Refer to figure 91 on page 682.) How much more runway will be used to land with 0° flaps rather than 15° of flaps at a landing weight of 126,000 pounds?

A—900 feet.
B—1,800 feet.
C—2,700 feet.

Answer (A) is correct (8755). *(FTW Chap 15)*
Fig. 91 provides a chart to compare landing distances using various flap settings. Determine the increase in landing distance with 0° flaps rather than 15° flaps. First, at the bottom of the chart, find 126 (gross weight/1,000 lb.) and move up vertically to the landing distance flaps 0° line. Move horizontally to the left edge of the chart to determine a landing distance of 3,700 ft. Next, repeat the process using the landing distance 15° line to determine a landing distance of 2,800 ft. The landing distance is increased 900 ft. (3,700 – 2,800) by using 0° flaps rather than 15° flaps.
Answer (B) is incorrect because 1,800 ft. is the ground roll distance using 15° flaps at a landing weight of 126,000 lb. Answer (C) is incorrect because 2,700 ft. is the ground roll distance using 0° flaps at a landing weight of 126,000 lb.

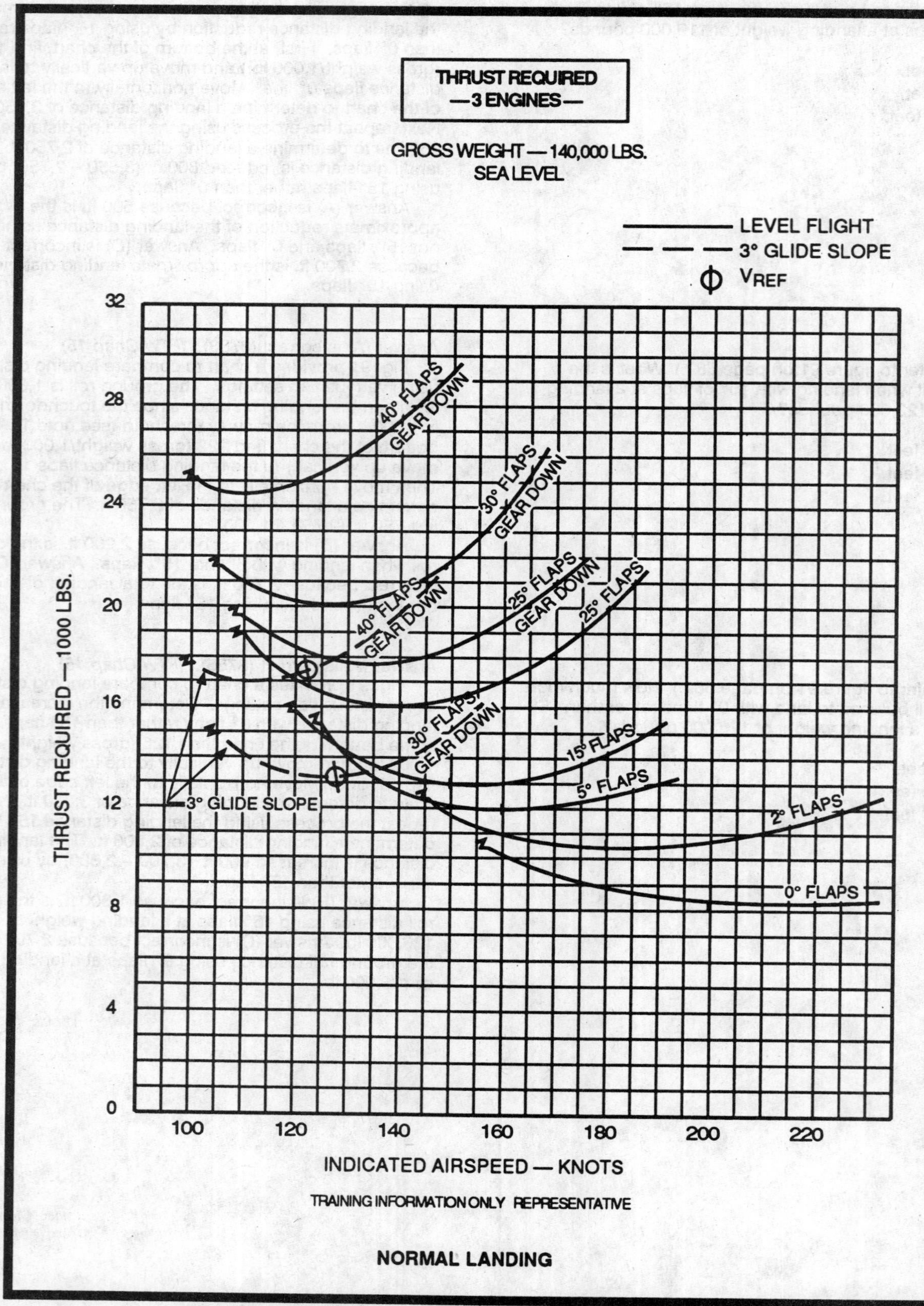

FIGURE 92.—B-727 – Landing Thrust – 140,000 Pounds.

59.
8754. (Refer to figures 91 and 92 on pages 682 and 684.) What approach speed and ground roll will be needed when landing at a weight of 140,000 pounds if flaps are not used?

A—138 knots and 3,900 feet.
B—153 knots and 2,900 feet.
C—183 knots and 2,900 feet.

Answer (C) is correct (8754). *(FTW Chap 15)*

Fig. 91 provides a chart to determine landing distances at various flap settings. Determine the ground roll when using 0° flaps. The ground roll distance is found by subtracting the threshold-to-touchdown distance of 1,000 ft. (see note 1) from the total landing distance. At the bottom of the chart, find 140 (gross weight/1,000 lb.) and move up vertically to the landing distance flaps 0° line. Then move horizontally to the left edge of the chart to determine a landing distance of 3,900 ft. Thus, the ground roll distance is 2,900 ft. (3,900 – 1,000). Next, compute the required approach speed. Information provided on the landing distance flaps 0° states $V_{APP} = V_{REF}$ (40° flaps) + 60 kt. Fig. 92 provides V_{REF} speed at various flap settings. Use the 3° glide slope (dashed line) at 40° flaps and find V_{REF}, which is depicted by a circle with a line through it. Move down vertically to the bottom of the chart to determine V_{REF} of 123 kt. The approach speed (V_{APP}) is 183 kt. (123 + 60).

Answer (A) is incorrect because 138 kt. is V_{APP} for 15° flaps and 3,900 ft. is the total landing distance, not ground roll, using 0° flaps at a weight of 140,000 lb. Answer (B) is incorrect because 153 kt. is V_{APP} for 5°, not 0°, flaps.

60.
8756. (Refer to figures 91 and 92 on pages 682 and 684.) What approach speed and landing distance will be needed when landing at a weight of 140,000 pounds with 15° of flaps?

A—123 knots and 3,050 feet.
B—138 knots and 3,050 feet.
C—153 knots and 2,050 feet.

Answer (B) is correct (8756). *(FTW Chap 15)*

Fig. 91 provides a chart to determine landing distances at various flap settings. At the bottom of the chart, find 140 (gross weight/1,000 lb.) and move up vertically to the landing distance flaps 15° line. Then move horizontally to the left edge of the chart to determine a landing distance of 3,050 ft. Next, compute the required approach speed (V_{APP}). Information from the landing distance flaps 15° states $V_{APP} = V_{REF}$ (40° flaps) + 15 kt. Fig. 92 provides V_{REF} speed at various flap settings. Use the 3° glide slope (dashed line) at 40° flaps and find V_{REF}, which is depicted by a circle with a line through it. Move down vertically to the bottom of the chart to determine V_{REF} of 123 kt. V_{APP} is 138 kt. (123 + 15).

Answer (A) is incorrect because 123 kt. is the V_{REF} speed for a 3° glide slope using 40° flaps. Answer (C) is incorrect because 153 kt. is used as V_{APP} when landing with 5°, not 15°, flaps, and 2,050 ft. is the ground roll, not landing, distance.

14.9 Thrust Required

61.
8757. (Refer to figure 92 on page 684.) What is the maximum charted indicated airspeed while maintaining a 3° glide slope at a weight of 140,000 pounds?

A—127 knots.
B—149 knots.
C—156 knots.

Answer (C) is correct (8757). *(FTW Chap 15)*

Fig. 92 provides a chart to determine landing thrust required and indicated airspeed at a weight of 140,000 lb. The chart has two 3° glide slope (dashed) curves, one at 40° flaps and the other at 30° flaps. Find the 40° flaps curve and follow it up and right to the end. Then move down vertically to the bottom of the chart to determine an airspeed of 149 kt. Follow the same procedures using the 30° flap curve (3° glide slope) to find a maximum airspeed of 156 kt. Thus, the maximum charted indicated airspeed while maintaining a 3° glide slope is 156 kt.

Answer (A) is incorrect because 127 kt. is the V_{REF} speed on the 3° glide slope curve using 30° flaps. Answer (B) is incorrect because 149 kt. is the maximum indicated airspeed using 40° flaps, but a higher airspeed is available using only 30° flaps.

62.
8758. (Refer to figure 92 on page 684.) What is the thrust required to maintain a 3° glide slope at 140,000 pounds, with gear down, flaps 30°, and an airspeed of V_{REF} +30 knots?

A—13,300 pounds.
B—16,200 pounds.
C—17,700 pounds.

Answer (B) is the best answer (8758). *(FTW Chap 15)*
Fig. 92 provides a chart to determine the landing thrust required at a gross weight of 140,000 lb. The 3° glide slope curve is shown as a dashed line. There are two 3° glide slope curves, and the curve for 30° flaps and gear down is the lower curve. Find V_{REF} on the curve, which is depicted as a circle with a line through it, and then move down vertically to determine an airspeed of 127 kt. At the bottom of the chart, find 157 kt. (127 + 30) and move up vertically to the 30° glide slope curve with flaps 30° and gear down. Note that this is greater than the maximum speed to maintain the glide slope. Using the maximum of 156 kt., move horizontally to the left edge of the chart to determine a required thrust of 16,200 lb.
Answer (A) is incorrect because 13,300 lb. is the thrust required to maintain a 3° glide slope with gear down, flaps 30°, and an airspeed of V_{REF}, not V_{REF} + 30 kt. Answer (C) is incorrect because 17,700 lb. is the thrust required to maintain a 3° glideslope with gear down, flaps 40°, not 30°, and an airspeed of V_{REF}.

63.
8759. (Refer to figure 92 on page 684.) What thrust is required to maintain level flight at 140,000 pounds, with gear up, flaps 25°, and an airspeed of 172 knots?

A—13,700 pounds.
B—18,600 pounds.
C—22,000 pounds.

Answer (B) is correct (8759). *(FTW Chap 15)*
Fig. 92 provides a chart to determine the thrust required at a gross weight of 140,000 lb. Level flight is depicted by solid lines, and the 25° flaps and gear up line is in the middle of the chart above the 15° flaps (level flight) line and below the 25° flaps and gear down line. At the bottom of the chart, find 172 kt. and move up vertically to the 25° flaps solid line. Then move horizontally to the left edge of the chart to determine a required thrust of 18,600 lb.
Answer (A) is incorrect because 13,700 lb. is the required thrust for level flight at 172 kt. with gear up and 15°, not 25°, flaps. Answer (C) is incorrect because 22,000 lb. is the required thrust for level flight at 177 kt., not 172 kt., with gear down, not up, and 25° flaps.

64.
8760. (Refer to figure 92 on page 684.) What thrust is required to maintain level flight at 140,000 pounds, with gear down, flaps 25°, and an airspeed of 162 knots?

A—17,400 pounds.
B—19,500 pounds.
C—22,200 pounds.

Answer (B) is correct (8760). *(FTW Chap 15)*
Fig. 92 provides a chart to determine the thrust required at a gross weight of 140,000 lb. Level flight is depicted by a solid line, and the gear down with flaps 25° line is above the gear up with 25° flaps line and below the gear down with 30° flaps line. At the bottom of chart, find 162 kt. and move up vertically to the 25° flaps and gear down solid line. Then move horizontally to the left edge of the chart to determine a required thrust of 19,500 lb.
Answer (A) is incorrect because 17,400 lb. is the required thrust for level flight at 162 kt. with gear up, not down, and 25° flaps. Answer (C) is incorrect because 22,200 lb. is the required thrust for level flight at 150 kt., not 162 kt., with gear down and 30°, not 25°, flaps.

65.
8761. (Refer to figure 92 on page 684.) What thrust is required to maintain level flight at 140,000 pounds, with gear down, flaps 25°, and an airspeed of 145 knots?

A—16,500 pounds.
B—18,100 pounds.
C—18,500 pounds.

Answer (B) is correct (8761). *(FTW Chap 15)*
Fig. 92 provides a chart to determine the thrust required at a gross weight of 140,000 lb. Level flight is depicted by a solid line, and the gear down with flaps 25° line is above gear up with flaps 25° line and below the gear down with flaps 30° line. At the bottom of the chart, find 145 kt. and move up vertically to the gear down with flaps 25° line; then move horizontally to the left edge of the chart to determine a required thrust of 18,100 lb.
Answer (A) is incorrect because 16,500 lb. is the required thrust for level flight at 125 kt. and 150 kt. with gear up, not down, and 25° flaps. Answer (C) is incorrect because 18,500 lb. is the required thrust for level flight at 117 kt. and 151 kt. with gear down and 25° flaps.

66.
8762. (Refer to figure 92 on page 684.) What is the change of total drag for a 140,000-pound airplane when configuration is changed from flaps 30°, gear down, to flaps 0°, gear up, at a constant airspeed of 160 knots?

A—13,500 pounds.
B—13,300 pounds.
C—15,300 pounds.

Answer (A) is correct (8762). *(FTW Chap 15)*
Fig. 92 provides a chart to determine the thrust required at a gross weight of 140,000 lb. Determine the thrust required first for gear down with flaps 30° at 160 kt., then for gear up, flaps 0°. Find 160 kt. at the bottom of the chart, and move up vertically to the gear down with flaps 30° line. Then move horizontally to the left edge of the chart to determine a required thrust of 23,800 lb. Repeat this process using the gear up with 0° flaps line to determine a required thrust of 10,300 lb. In level flight at a constant airspeed, thrust is equal to drag. Thus, the change in total drag is 13,500 lb. (23,800 – 10,300).
Answer (B) is incorrect because 13,300 lb. would be the change in total drag at a constant airspeed less than 160 kt. Answer (C) is incorrect because 15,300 lb. would be the change in total drag at a constant airspeed greater than 160 kt.

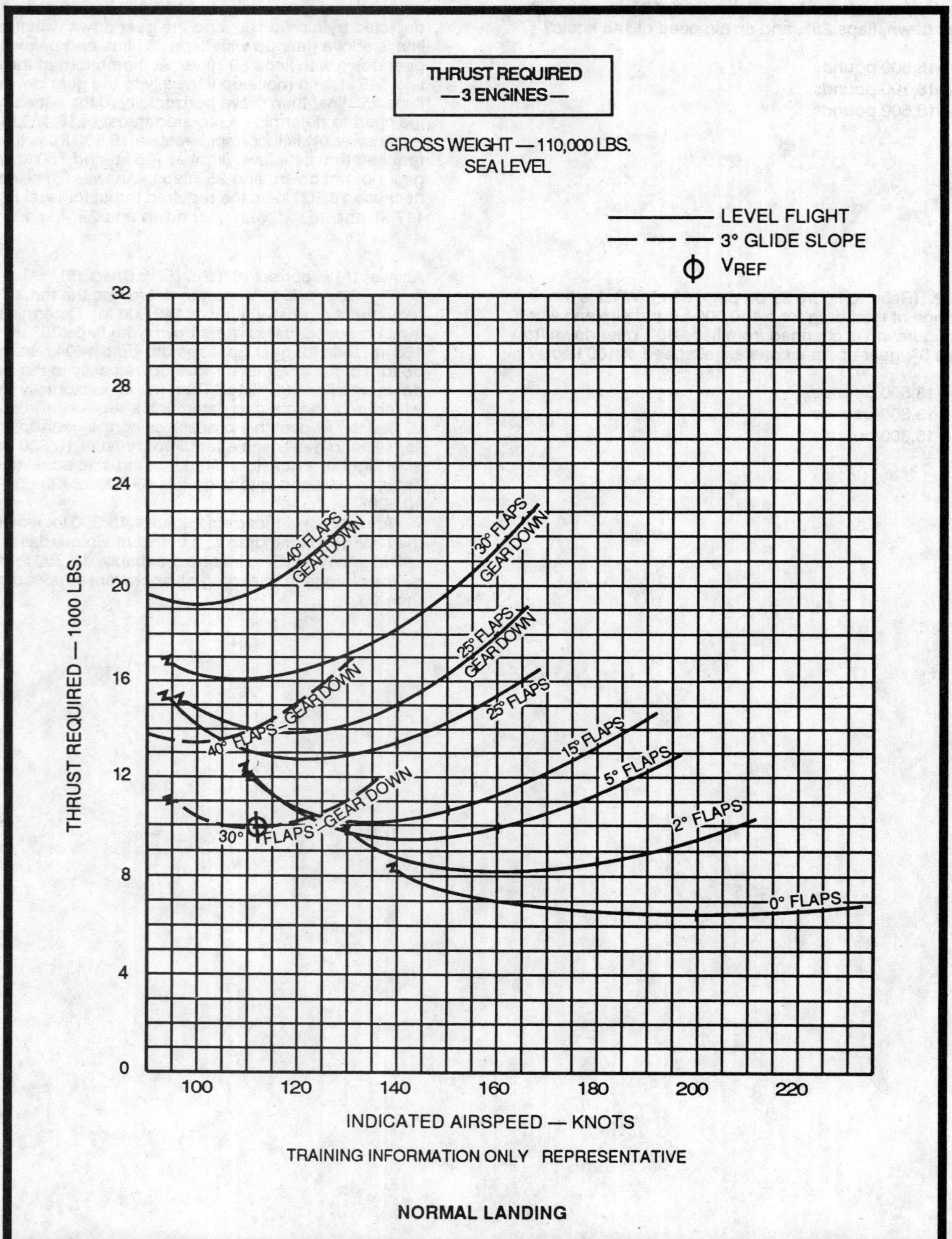

FIGURE 93.—B-727 – Landing Thrust – 110,000 Pounds.

67.
8763. (Refer to figure 93 on page 688.) What is the maximum charted indicated airspeed while maintaining a 3° glide slope at a weight of 110,000 pounds?

A—136 knots.
B—132 knots.
C—139 knots.

Answer (A) is correct (8763). *(FTW Chap 15)*
Fig. 93 provides a chart to determine the landing thrust required at a gross weight of 110,000 lb. The chart has two 3° glide slope (dashed) curves, one at 40° flaps and the other at 30° flaps. Find the 40° flaps curve and move along the curve up and right to the end. Then move down vertically to the bottom edge of the chart to determine the maximum indicated airspeed using 40° flaps of 132 kt. Repeat the procedure using the 30° flaps line to determine the maximum indicated airspeed using 30° flaps of 136 kt. Thus, the maximum charted indicated airspeed while maintaining a 3° glide slope is 136 kt.
Answer (B) is incorrect because 132 kt. is the maximum indicated airspeed using 40° flaps. A higher airspeed is available when using 30° flaps. Answer (C) is incorrect because 139 kt. is above the maximum airspeed available to maintain a 3° glide slope.

68.
8764. (Refer to figure 93 on page 688.) What is the thrust required to maintain a 3° glide slope at 110,000 pounds, with gear down, flaps 30°, and an airspeed of V_{REF} +20 knots?

A—9,800 pounds.
B—11,200 pounds.
C—17,000 pounds.

Answer (B) is correct (8764). *(FTW Chap 15)*
Fig. 93 provides a chart to determine the landing thrust required at a gross weight of 110,000 lb. The 3° glide slope curve is depicted as a dashed line, and the 30° flaps curve is the lowest of the two curves. Find V_{REF} on the 30° flaps curve, which is depicted as a circle with a line through it. Move down vertically to determine V_{REF} speed of 111 kt. Next, find 131 kt. (V_{REF} +20 kt.) at the bottom of the chart and move up vertically to the 3° glide slope using the 30° flaps and gear down line. Then move horizontally to the left edge of the chart to determine a required thrust of 11,200 lb.
Answer (A) is incorrect because 9,800 lb. is the required thrust to maintain a 3° glide slope, gear down with flaps 30° at V_{REF}, not V_{REF} +20 kt. Answer (C) is incorrect because 17,000 lb. is the required thrust to maintain a 3° glide slope at 131 kt., gear down, and 40°, not 30°, flaps.

69.
8765. (Refer to figure 93 on page 688.) What thrust is required to maintain level flight at 110,000 pounds, with gear down, flaps 40°, and an airspeed of 118 knots?

A—17,000 pounds.
B—20,800 pounds.
C—22,300 pounds.

Answer (B) is correct (8765). *(FTW Chap 15)*
Fig. 93 provides a chart to determine the landing thrust required at a gross weight of 110,000 lb. Level flight is depicted by a solid line, and the gear down with flaps 40° line is above the gear down with flaps 30° line on the upper left side of the chart. At the bottom of the chart, find 118 kt. and move up vertically to the gear down with flaps 40° line. Then move horizontally to the left edge of the chart to determine a required thrust of 20,800 lb.
Answer (A) is incorrect because 17,000 lb. is the required thrust for level flight at 118 kt., gear down, and 30°, not 40°, flaps. Answer (C) is incorrect because 22,300 lb. is the required thrust for level flight at 128 kt., not 118 kt., gear down, and 40° flaps.

70.
8766. (Refer to figure 93 on page 688.) What thrust is required to maintain level flight at 110,000 pounds, with gear up, flaps 25°, and an airspeed of 152 knots?

A—14,500 pounds.
B—15,900 pounds.
C—16,700 pounds.

Answer (A) is correct (8766). *(FTW Chap 15)*
Fig. 93 provides a chart to determine the landing thrust required at a gross weight of 110,000 lb. Level flight is depicted by a solid line. The gear up with flaps 25° line is above the gear up with 15° flaps line and below the gear down with flaps 25° line. At the bottom of the chart, find 152 kt. and move up vertically to the gear up with flaps 25° line. Then move horizontally to the left side of the chart to determine a required thrust of 14,500 lb.

Answer (B) is incorrect because 15,900 lb. is the required thrust for level flight at 146 kt., not 152 kt., gear down, not up, and 25° flaps. Answer (C) is incorrect because 16,700 lb. is the required thrust for level flight at 152 kt., gear down, not up, and 25° flaps.

END OF CHAPTER

CHAPTER FIFTEEN
AVIATION WEATHER

This chapter contains outlines of major concepts tested, all FAA test questions and answers regarding aviation weather, and an explanation of each answer. Each module, or subtopic, within this chapter is listed above with the number of questions from the FAA pilot knowledge test pertaining to that particular module. For each module, the first number following the parentheses is the page number on which the outline begins, and the next number is the page number on which the questions begin.

There are 80 questions in this chapter. We separate and organize the FAA questions into meaningful study units, i.e., chapters and modules. As an analogy, it is easier to deal with the "trees" if you understand the "forest." In this context, "trees" are individual FAA questions and the "forest" is the ATP knowledge test. The organizational units between the overall ATP knowledge test and individual ATP test questions are chapters and modules in this book.

CAUTION: The **sole purpose** of this book is to expedite your passing the FAA pilot knowledge test for the ATP certificate. Topics or regulations not directly tested on the FAA pilot knowledge test are omitted. Much more information and knowledge are necessary to fly safely. This additional material is presented in Gleim's other pilot training books (see the order form on page 818) and in many FAA books and circulars, as well as in airplane *POH*s and other commercial textbooks.

15.1 PRESSURE SYSTEMS (Questions 1-5)

1. Unequal solar heating of the Earth's surface causes all changes in the Earth's weather.
2. A **trough** is defined as an elongated area of low pressure.
3. An **anticyclone** is a high-pressure area.
4. High-pressure areas are areas where air descends toward the surface, then outward.
5. Thermal lows are relatively shallow with weak pressure gradients and are usually found over the surface of a dry, sunny region.

15.2 WEATHER FRONTS (Questions 6-12)

1. Surface winds tend to flow parallel to the frontal zone at a stationary front.
2. After an aircraft passes through a front into colder air, atmospheric pressure usually increases.
3. Upper winds blowing across the front usually cause rapid movement of surface fronts.
4. Frontal waves and low-pressure areas usually form along small slow-moving cold fronts or stationary fronts.
5. **Frontolysis** is the process in which the adjacent air masses modify, i.e., equalize, and the front dissipates.
6. A squall line is an example of a nonfrontal instability band.
7. There is a dew point difference on each side of a "dry line."

15.3 CORIOLIS FORCE (Questions 13-15)

1. At lower levels of the atmosphere, i.e., near the surface, friction causes the wind to blow across isobars into a low because the friction decreases the wind speed and Coriolis force.
2. Coriolis force has the least effect on wind direction at the equator.
3. The Coriolis force results in clockwise rotation around a low in the Southern Hemisphere.

15.4 CLOUDS AND FOG (Questions 16-22)

1. If precipitation is reported as light or greater intensity, the minimum thickness of the cloud layer is 4,000 ft.
2. Warm air flowing over a colder lake may produce fog on the lee side of a large lake.
3. A **rotor cloud** is the lowest cloud in the stationary group associated with a mountain wave.
4. **Standing lenticular clouds** are indicative of very strong turbulence.
5. Winds stronger than 15 kt. may tend to dissipate advection fog into low stratus clouds.
6. **Upslope fog** is the result of moist, stable air being moved over gradually rising ground by wind.
7. Haze layers are cleared or dispersed by wind or the movement of air.

15.5 TEMPERATURE CHANGES AND STABILITY (Questions 23-32)

1. The minimum temperature usually occurs after sunrise.
2. **Adiabatic heating or cooling** means the temperature of the air changes by compression or expansion with no heat added or removed.
   a. Expansion of air as it rises causes adiabatic cooling.
   b. Unsaturated air will cool flowing upslope at about 3°C per 1,000 ft.
3. Cloud bases form at the altitude where the dew point lapse rate and the dry adiabatic lapse rate converge.
4. **Katabatic wind** flows downslope becoming warmer and drier.

5. When saturated air moves downhill, its temperature increases at a slower rate than dry air because vaporization uses heat.
6. An air mass is stable if the temperature remains unchanged or decreases slightly as altitude is increased.
   a. Stable air resists convection.
7. The ambient temperature lapse rate is used to determine the stability of the atmosphere.

15.6 TEMPERATURE INVERSION (Questions 33-37)

1. In the stratosphere, one commonly finds a temperature inversion.
2. A stable layer of air is associated with a temperature inversion.
3. Poor visibility characterizes a ground-based inversion.
4. Terrestrial radiation on a clear, relatively calm night produces the most frequent type of ground- or surface-based temperature inversion.
5. A calm or light wind near the surface and a relatively strong wind just above the inversion are necessary conditions for the occurrence of low-level temperature inversion wind shear.

15.7 DENSITY, PRESSURE, AND CORRECTED ALTITUDE (Questions 38-42)

1. Atmospheric pressure decreases about 1 in. Hg for every 1,000 ft. of altitude gained.
   a. Changing the altimeter setting changes the indicated altitude in the same direction and by 1,000 ft. for every inch of change.
   b. For example, changing from 29.92 in. to 30.92 in. increases indicated altitude by 1,000 ft., or from 30.15 in. to 30.25 in. increases indicated altitude by 100 ft.
2. Since altimeter readings are adjusted for changes in barometric pressure but not for temperature changes, an airplane will be at lower-than-indicated altitude when flying in colder-than-standard air.
   a. On warm days, an airplane will be at a higher altitude than the altimeter indicates.
   b. And density altitude will be higher than pressure altitude.
3. Corrected altitude is the indicated altitude of an airplane's altimeter corrected for temperature variation from standard atmospheric temperature.
   a. Corrected altitude is an approximation of true altitude.
4. **Station pressure** is the actual atmospheric pressure at field elevation.

15.8 THUNDERSTORMS (Questions 43-57)

1. Thunderstorm updrafts result in water vapor changing to liquid, or condensation, which releases latent heat into the atmosphere.
2. A stratus layer may form in a mildly stable layer while convective clouds penetrate the layer and form thunderstorms, which may be entirely embedded in a massive stratus layer and pose an unseen threat to instrument flight.
3. **Embedded thunderstorms** means that the thunderstorms are embedded in clouds or thick haze layers and cannot be seen.

4. Thunderstorms have three stages: cumulus, mature, and dissipating.
   a. During the **cumulus stage** of a thunderstorm, a cumulus cloud is building and there are continuous updrafts.
   b. The **mature stage** of a thunderstorm begins when rain begins falling at the surface.
      1) During the mature stage, the cold rain slows the compressional heating of the downdraft, and the downdraft remains cooler than the surrounding air, causing acceleration of the downdraft.
   c. In the **dissipating stage**, the storm is characterized predominantly by downdrafts as the storm rains itself out.
5. In an **air mass thunderstorm**, the rain falls through or immediately beside the updraft. This retards the updraft and reverses it to a downdraft.
   a. In a **steady-state thunderstorm**, the rain falls outside the updraft, allowing the updraft to continue unabated.
6. Funnel clouds or tornadoes normally form with steady-state thunderstorms associated with cold fronts or squall lines.
7. **Cumulonimbus mamma** is a cumulonimbus cloud having hanging protuberances like pouches, testes, or udders, on the underside of the cloud, usually indicative of severe turbulence.
   a. This type of cloud can produce a tornado.
8. A **squall line** is a nonfrontal, narrow band of active thunderstorms.
   a. Most often, squall lines develop ahead of a cold front in moist, unstable air.
9. The maximum hazard zone caused by wind shear associated with a thunderstorm is found on all sides and directly under the thunderstorm cell.
10. Pressure usually falls rapidly with the approach of a thunderstorm, then rises sharply with the onset of the first gust and arrival of the cold downdraft and heavy rain showers, falling back to normal as the storm moves on.
11. Weather radar detects droplets of precipitation.
    a. If a radarscope displays a clear area, it indicates an area where no precipitation drops are detected.
12. The top of a known or suspected severe thunderstorm should be cleared by at least 1,000 ft. of altitude for each 10 kt. of wind speed at the cloud top.

15.9 ICING (Questions 58-66)

1. **Freezing rain** is rain that falls through colder air and becomes supercooled, freezing on impact.
2. **Ice pellets** always indicate freezing rain at higher altitudes.
3. When wet snow is encountered, it indicates the temperature is above freezing at flight altitude.
4. Frost forms when the temperature of the collecting surface is below the dew point and the dew point is below freezing.
   a. Frost is the direct sublimation of water vapor to ice crystals.
5. Frost will most likely form on aircraft surfaces on clear nights with stable air and light winds.

6. Water droplets that are colder than 0°C are considered supercooled, and when they strike an exposed object, they freeze on impact, i.e., freezing rain.
7. Two conditions are necessary for structural icing in flight:
   a. The aircraft must be flying through visible water such as rain or cloud droplets.
   b. The temperature at the point where the moisture strikes the aircraft must be 0°C or colder.
8. Rime ice forms when drops are small, such as those found in low-level stratus clouds.

15.10 HIGH-ALTITUDE WEATHER (Questions 67-75)

1. The **troposphere** is the layer from the surface to an average altitude of 7 mi., and it is characterized by an overall decrease of temperature with an increase in altitude.
2. The **tropopause** is characterized by an abrupt change in temperature lapse rate.
3. Temperature and wind vary greatly in the vicinity of the tropopause, and maximum winds and narrow wind shear zones generally occur near the tropopause.
4. Maximum winds associated with the jet stream occur in the vicinity of breaks in the tropopause on the polar side of the jet core.
5. The jet stream typically occurs at the tropopause in an area of intensified temperature gradients.
6. The jet stream is usually to the north of surface lows and fronts.
7. The development of a surface low usually is south of the jet stream and moves nearer as the low deepens.
   a. The occluding low moves north of the jet stream, and the jet stream crosses the frontal system near the point of occlusion.
8. When high-level moisture is available, cirrus clouds form on the equatorial side of the jet stream.
9. A strong wind shear can be expected on the low-pressure side of a 100-kt. jet stream core.

15.11 ARCTIC WEATHER (Questions 76-78)

1. In the Northern Hemisphere, weather systems generally move east to west in the arctic and subtropical regions.
2. Summer thunderstorms in the Arctic generally move from northeast to southwest in the polar easterlies, which is opposite the general movement in midlatitudes.
3. **Whiteout** is a visibility-restricting phenomenon that occurs in the Arctic when a cloud layer of uniform thickness overlies a snow- or ice-covered surface.

15.12 TROPICAL WEATHER (Questions 79-80)

1. To be upgraded to a hurricane, a tropical storm must have sustained winds of 65 kt. or more.
2. Hurricanes located in the Caribbean or Gulf of Mexico move in a direction between west and northwest while in low latitudes.
   a. As the hurricane moves toward the midlatitudes, the prevailing westerlies will gain control, and the hurricane will curve to the northeast.

QUESTIONS AND ANSWER EXPLANATIONS

All the FAA questions from the pilot knowledge test for the ATP certificate relating to aviation weather and the material outlined previously are reproduced on the following pages in the same modules as the outlines. To the immediate right of each question are the correct answer and answer explanation. You should cover these answers and answer explanations while responding to the questions. Refer to the general discussion in Chapter 1 on how to take the FAA pilot knowledge test.

Remember that the questions from the FAA pilot knowledge test bank have been reordered by topic, and the topics are organized into a meaningful sequence. Accordingly, the first line of the answer explanation gives the FAA question number and the citation of the authoritative source for the answer.

15.1 Pressure Systems

1.
9152. What is the primary cause of all changes in the Earth's weather?

A—Variations of solar energy at the Earth's surface.
B—Changes in air pressure over the Earth's surface.
C—Movement of air masses from moist areas to dry areas.

Answer (A) is correct (9152). *(AvW Chap 2)*
Every physical process of weather is accompanied by or is the result of a heat exchange. Unequal solar heating of the Earth's surface causes differences in air pressure which result in all changes in the Earth's weather.
Answer (B) is incorrect because changes in air pressure are a result of the unequal solar heating of the Earth's surface. Answer (C) is incorrect because movement of air masses is a result of unequal solar heating of the Earth's surface.

2.
9165. What term describes an elongated area of low pressure?

A—Trough.
B—Ridge.
C—Hurricane or typhoon.

Answer (A) is correct (9165). *(AvW Chap 3)*
A trough is defined as an elongated area of low pressure with the lowest pressure along a line marking maximum cyclonic curvature.
Answer (B) is incorrect because a ridge is an elongated area of high, not low, pressure. Answer (C) is incorrect because a hurricane or typhoon is a tropical cyclone (low) with highest sustained winds of 65 kt. or greater.

3.
9178. Which weather condition is defined as an anticyclone?

A—Calm.
B—High pressure area.
C—COL.

Answer (B) is correct (9178). *(AvW Chap 3)*
An anticyclone is an area of high atmospheric pressure. The circulation is clockwise in the Northern Hemisphere, counterclockwise in the Southern Hemisphere, and undefined at the Equator.
Answer (A) is incorrect because calm is defined as the absence of wind or of apparent motion of the air. Answer (C) is incorrect because COL is the neutral area between two highs or two lows. It is also the intersection of a trough and a ridge.

4.
9159. What is a feature of air movement in a high pressure area?

A—Ascending from the surface high to lower pressure at higher altitudes.
B—Descending to the surface and then outward.
C—Moving outward from the high at high altitudes and into the high at the surface.

Answer (B) is correct (9159). *(AvW Chap 4)*
The air movement out of a high-pressure area depletes the quantity of air because the air is heavier than the low-pressure air surrounding it. Therefore high-pressure areas are areas of descending air toward the surface, then outward from the high.
Answer (A) is incorrect because air descends, not ascends, from a high-pressure area, at all altitudes. Answer (C) is incorrect because the air always moves outward, not inward, from a high, regardless of altitude.

5.
9160. Where is the usual location of a thermal low?

A—Over the arctic region.
B—Over the eye of a hurricane.
C—Over the surface of a dry, sunny region.

Answer (C) is correct (9160). *(AvW Chap 4)*
A dry, sunny region becomes quite warm from intense surface heating, thus generating a surface low-pressure area known as a thermal low. Thermal lows are relatively shallow with weak pressure gradients and without well-defined cyclonic circulation.
Answer (A) is incorrect because thermal lows develop over dry, sunny regions, not in the Arctic. Answer (B) is incorrect because an eye of a hurricane marks the center of a well-developed tropical cyclone, not a thermal low.

15.2 Weather Fronts

6.
9191. What is a feature of a stationary front?

A—The warm front surface moves about half the speed of the cold front surface.
B—Weather conditions are a combination of strong cold front and strong warm front weather.
C—Surface winds tend to flow parallel to the frontal zone.

Answer (C) is correct (9191). *(AvW Chap 8)*
The opposing forces exerted by adjacent air masses of different densities are such that the frontal surface between them shows little or no movement and a stationary front results. The surface winds tend to flow parallel to this frontal zone.
Answer (A) is incorrect because the movement of a warm front surface at about half the speed of the cold front surface is a feature of the movement of a warm, not stationary, front when the general wind flow is the same in each case. Answer (B) is incorrect because weather conditions that are a combination of strong cold front and strong warm front weather are a feature of an occluded, not stationary, front.

7.
9192. Which event usually occurs after an aircraft passes through a front into the colder air?

A—Temperature/dewpoint spread decreases.
B—Wind direction shifts to the left.
C—Atmospheric pressure increases.

Answer (C) is correct (9192). *(AvW Chap 8)*
A front lies in a pressure trough, and pressure generally is higher in cold air. Thus, when you cross a front directly into colder air, barometric pressure usually increases.
Answer (A) is incorrect because the temperature/dew point spread usually differs across a front. But it may not decrease if you fly into a cold, dry air mass. Answer (B) is incorrect because, in the Northern Hemisphere, the wind always shifts to the right, not left, due to the Coriolis force.

8.
9215. Which atmospheric factor causes rapid movement of surface fronts?

A—Upper winds blowing across the front.
B—Upper low located directly over the surface low.
C—The cold front overtaking and lifting the warm front.

Answer (A) is correct (9215). *(AvW Chap 8)*
The upper wind flow dictates to a great extent the movement of the front. Systems tend to move with the upper winds. When winds aloft blow across a front, it tends to move with the wind.
Answer (B) is incorrect because an upper low located directly over a surface low is a factor in how extensive the weather will be, not in how fast it will move. Answer (C) is incorrect because a cold front overtaking and lifting the warm front is a characteristic of an advancing cold front.

9.
9216. In which meteorological conditions can frontal waves and low pressure areas form?

A—Warm fronts or occluded fronts.
B—Slow-moving cold fronts or stationary fronts.
C—Cold front occlusions.

Answer (B) is correct (9216). *(AvW Chap 8)*
Frontal waves and areas of low pressure usually form on slow-moving cold fronts or on stationary fronts.
Answer (A) is incorrect because occluded fronts are formed by frontal waves and areas of low pressure which cause a cold front to close together with a warm front. Frontal waves and low-pressure areas normally form on slow-moving cold, not warm, fronts. Answer (C) is incorrect because a cold front occlusion occurs when the air behind the cold front is colder than the air in advance of the warm front, lifting the warm front aloft.

10.
9213. What type weather change is to be expected in an area where frontolysis is reported?

A—The frontal weather is becoming stronger.
B—The front is dissipating.
C—The front is moving at a faster speed.

Answer (B) is correct (9213). *(AvW Chap 8)*
Frontolysis is the process in which the adjacent air masses modify, and as temperature and pressure equalize across a front, the front dissipates.
Answer (A) is incorrect because frontal weather becoming stronger is a weather change that is to be expected in an area where frontogenesis, not frontolysis, is reported. Answer (C) is incorrect because a front moving at a fast speed is a weather change that is expected in an area of frontogenesis, not frontolysis.

11.
9214. Which weather condition is an example of a nonfrontal instability band?

A—Squall line.
B—Advective fog.
C—Frontogenesis.

Answer (A) is correct (9214). *(AvW Chap 8)*
An instability line is a narrow, nonfrontal line or band of convective activity. If this activity is fully developed thunderstorms, it is called a squall line.
Answer (B) is incorrect because advective fog occurs when warm moist air moves over a cool surface. It forms in stable, not unstable, air. Answer (C) is incorrect because frontogenesis is the generation of a frontal, not nonfrontal, zone.

12.
9217. What weather difference is found on each side of a "dry line"?

A—Extreme temperature difference.
B—Dewpoint difference.
C—Stratus versus cumulus clouds.

Answer (B) is correct (9217). *(AvW Chap 8)*
A "dry line" is common in Western Texas and New Mexico northward over the Plains. Moist air flowing north from the Gulf of Mexico meets the drier and slightly denser air flowing from the southwest. Except for moisture (dew point) differences, there is seldom any significant weather difference found on each side.
Answer (A) is incorrect because, except for a moisture difference, not an extreme temperature difference, there is seldom any significant air mass contrast across the "dry line." Answer (C) is incorrect because the side with moisture may have clouds, while generally clear skies mark the dry side.

15.3 Coriolis Force

13.
9157. At lower levels of the atmosphere, friction causes the wind to flow across isobars into a low because the friction

A—decreases windspeed and Coriolis force.
B—decreases pressure gradient force.
C—creates air turbulence and raises atmospheric pressure.

Answer (A) is correct (9157). *(AvW Chap 4)*
Surface friction decreases the wind speed and Coriolis force but does not affect pressure gradient force. The stronger pressure gradient turns the wind across the isobars toward lower pressure.
Answer (B) is incorrect because friction does not affect the pressure gradient force. Answer (C) is incorrect because surface obstructions, not surface friction, cause air turbulence.

14.
9176. At which location does Coriolis force have the least effect on wind direction?

A—At the poles.
B—Middle latitudes (30° to 60°).
C—At the Equator.

Answer (C) is correct (9176). *(AvW Chap 4)*
The Coriolis force affects the wind direction everywhere except immediately at the Equator.
Answer (A) is incorrect because the Coriolis force has the most (not least) effect on wind direction at the poles. Answer (B) is incorrect because the effects of the Coriolis force are quite pronounced in middle latitudes.

15.
9177. How does Coriolis force affect wind direction in the Southern Hemisphere?

A—Causes clockwise rotation around a low.
B—Causes wind to flow out of a low toward a high.
C—Has exactly the same effect as in the Northern Hemisphere.

Answer (A) is correct (9177). *(AvW Chap 4)*
Coriolis force deflects air to the left in the Southern Hemisphere, which is the opposite from the Northern Hemisphere. In the Southern Hemisphere, the wind blows clockwise around a low.
Answer (B) is incorrect because the wind flows from a high to a low, not a low to a high, in both the Northern and Southern Hemispheres. Answer (C) is incorrect because the Coriolis force deflects air to the left in the Southern Hemisphere, which is the opposite, not the same, effect as in the Northern Hemisphere.

15.4 Clouds and Fog

16.
9193. What minimum thickness of cloud layer is indicated if precipitation is reported as light or greater intensity?

A—4,000 feet thick.
B—2,000 feet thick.
C—A thickness which allows the cloud tops to be higher than the freezing level.

Answer (A) is correct (9193). *(AvW Chap 5)*
When arriving at or departing an airport reporting precipitation of light or greater intensity, expect clouds to be at least 4,000 ft. thick.
Answer (B) is incorrect because, to produce significant precipitation (light or greater intensity), clouds are normally at least 4,000 ft., not 2,000 ft., thick. Answer (C) is incorrect because a cloud thickness resulting in cloud tops above the freezing level means ice droplets and supercooled water will develop.

17.
9194. Which condition produces weather on the lee side of a large lake?

A—Warm air flowing over a colder lake may produce fog.
B—Cold air flowing over a warmer lake may produce advection fog.
C—Warm air flowing over a cool lake may produce rain showers.

Answer (A) is correct (9194). *(AvW Chap 5)*
Warm air flowing over a colder lake may become saturated by evaporation from the water while also becoming cooler in the low levels by contact with the cooler water. Fog often becomes extensive and dense to the lee side of the lake. The lee side is the side to which the wind is going.
Answer (B) is incorrect because cold air flowing over a warmer lake may produce rain showers, not advection fog, on the lee side of the lake. Answer (C) is incorrect because warm air flowing over a cool lake may produce fog, not rain showers, on the lee side of the lake.

18.
9226. What is the lowest cloud in the stationary group associated with a mountain wave?

A—Rotor cloud.
B—Standing lenticular.
C—Low stratus.

Answer (A) is correct (9226). *(AvW Chap 9)*
When moisture is sufficient to produce clouds on the lee side of a mountain, the lowest clouds associated with mountain wave are rotor clouds. These are found under each crest of the standing wave.
Answer (B) is incorrect because the standing lenticular clouds mark the crest, i.e., the top, of each standing wave. Answer (C) is incorrect because low stratus clouds are not associated with a mountain wave.

19.
9190. Which type clouds are indicative of very strong turbulence?

A—Nimbostratus.
B—Standing lenticular.
C—Cirrocumulus.

Answer (B) is correct (9190). *(AvW Chap 7)*
Standing lenticular clouds are formed on the crests of mountain waves. Wind can be quite strong blowing through these clouds, and their presence is a good indication of very strong turbulence.
Answer (A) is incorrect because nimbostratus is a gray or dark massive cloud layer, diffused by continuous rain, snow, or ice pellets. The stratus feature indicates very little turbulence. Answer (C) is incorrect because cirrocumulus describes thin clouds appearing as small white flakes or patches of cotton. Their presence indicates some turbulence and possible icing.

20.
9206. When advection fog has developed, what may tend to dissipate or lift the fog into low stratus clouds?

A—Temperature inversion.
B—Wind stronger than 15 knots.
C—Surface radiation.

Answer (B) is correct (9206). *(AvW Chap 12)*
Advection fog forms when moist air moves over colder ground or water. It deepens as wind speed increases up to about 15 kt. Wind stronger than 15 kt. lifts the fog into a layer of low stratus or stratocumulus.
Answer (A) is incorrect because winds stronger than 15 kt., not a temperature inversion, tend to dissipate or lift advection fog. Answer (C) is incorrect because surface temperature radiation is a factor in radiation fog, not advection fog.

21.
9207. Which conditions are necessary for the formation of upslope fog?

A—Moist, stable air being moved over gradually rising ground by a wind.
B—A clear sky, little or no wind, and 100 percent relative humidity.
C—Rain falling through stratus clouds and a 10- to 25-knot wind moving the precipitation up the slope.

Answer (A) is correct (9207). *(AvW Chap 12)*
Upslope fog is formed by moist, stable air being cooled as it is gradually moved up sloping terrain by a wind. Once the upslope wind ceases, the fog dissipates.
Answer (B) is incorrect because clear skies, calm wind, and high humidity are conditions necessary for the formation of radiation fog, not upslope fog. Answer (C) is incorrect because upslope fog is formed by moist air being moved gradually over rising ground, not by rain falling through stratus clouds and not by a wind blowing the precipitation up the slope.

22.
9208. How are haze layers cleared or dispersed?

A—By convective mixing in cool night air.
B—By wind or the movement of air.
C—By evaporation similar to the clearing of fog.

Answer (B) is correct (9208). *(AvW Chap 12)*
Haze layers may be cleared or dispersed by the wind, or heating during the day may cause convective movement of the air, spreading the haze to a higher altitude.
Answer (A) is incorrect because convective mixing is caused by heating during the day, not by the cool night air. Answer (C) is incorrect because haze must be dispersed by movement of air. It cannot evaporate in a manner similar to the clearing of fog.

15.5 Temperature Changes and Stability

23.
9155. When does minimum temperature normally occur during a 24-hour period?

A—After sunrise.
B—About 1 hour before sunrise.
C—At midnight.

Answer (A) is correct (9155). *(AvW Chap 2)*
Diurnal variation is the change in temperature within a 24-hr. period. The minimum temperature normally occurs after sunrise, sometimes as much as 1 hr. after.
Answer (B) is incorrect because the minimum temperature normally occurs after, not before, sunrise. Answer (C) is incorrect because the minimum temperature normally occurs after sunrise, not at midnight.

24.
9170. Which term applies when the temperature of the air changes by compression or expansion with no heat added or removed?

A—Katabatic.
B—Advection.
C—Adiabatic.

Answer (C) is correct (9170). *(AvW Chap 6)*
When air expands, it cools; when compressed, it warms. These changes are adiabatic, meaning that no heat is removed from or added to the air.
Answer (A) is incorrect because katabatic is a wind blowing down an incline caused by cold, heavier air spilling down the incline displacing warmer, less dense air. Answer (B) is incorrect because advection is the horizontal flow in a convective current, i.e., wind.

25.
9171. What is the approximate rate unsaturated air will cool flowing upslope?

A—3 °C per 1,000 feet.
B—2 °C per 1,000 feet.
C—4 °C per 1,000 feet.

Answer (A) is correct (9171). *(AvW Chap 6)*
Unsaturated air moving upward and downward cools and warms at about 3°C (5.4°F) per 1,000 ft. This is the dry adiabatic rate of temperature change.
Answer (B) is incorrect because unsaturated air will cool flowing upslope at 3°C, not 2°C, per 1,000 ft. Answer (C) is incorrect because unsaturated air will cool flowing upslope at 3°C, not 4°C, per 1,000 ft.

26.
9186. Which process causes adiabatic cooling?

A—Expansion of air as it rises.
B—Movement of air over a colder surface.
C—Release of latent heat during the vaporization process.

Answer (A) is correct (9186). *(AvW Chap 6)*
Adiabatic cooling is caused by the expansion of air as it rises. Anytime air is moved upward, it expands because of decreasing atmospheric pressure. When air expands, it cools.
Answer (B) is incorrect because adiabatic cooling means that no heat is removed from the air, as would be the case if the air were moved over a colder surface. Answer (C) is incorrect because adiabatic is the process in which no heat is removed from or added to the air.

27.
9185. What weather condition occurs at the altitude where the dewpoint lapse rate and the dry adiabatic lapse rate converge?

A—Cloud bases form.
B—Precipitation starts.
C—Stable air changes to unstable air.

Answer (A) is correct (9185). *(AvW Chap 6)*
The altitude where the dew point lapse rate and the dry adiabatic lapse rate converge is where convective cloud bases form. Unsaturated air in a convective current cools at about 3.0°C (5.4°F) per 1,000 ft.; dew point decreases at about 5/9°C (1°F) per 1,000 ft. When they converge, cloud bases form.
Answer (B) is incorrect because precipitation starts when precipitation particles have grown to a size and weight that the atmosphere can no longer suspend and the particles fall as precipitation. Answer (C) is incorrect because air stability depends on the ambient or existing temperature lapse rate, not the convergence of the dew point lapse rate and the dry adiabatic lapse rate.

28.
9158. Which type wind flows downslope becoming warmer and dryer?

A—Land breeze.
B—Valley wind.
C—Katabatic wind.

Answer (C) is correct (9158). *(AvW Chap 4)*
Katabatic wind forms because cold, heavy air spills down sloping terrain displacing warmer, less dense air ahead of it. The cold, heavy air is adiabatically heated and dried as it flows downslope because of heating due to the downward air being compressed by increasing pressure.
Answer (A) is incorrect because a land breeze is a wind that flows from the cooler land toward warmer water. Answer (B) is incorrect because a valley wind is wind flowing up out of a valley because colder, denser air settles downward and forces the warmer air near the ground up a mountain slope.

29.
9187. When saturated air moves downhill, its temperature increases

A—at a faster rate than dry air because of the release of latent heat.
B—at a slower rate than dry air because vaporization uses heat.
C—at a slower rate than dry air because condensation releases heat.

Answer (B) is correct (9187). *(AvW Chap 6)*
When saturated air moves downhill, its temperature increases at a slower rate than dry air because vaporization uses heat known as the "latent heat of vaporization." The water removal cools the air from which the water is removed.
Answer (A) is incorrect because, when saturated air moves downhill, its temperature increases at a slower, not faster, rate than dry air because of the absorption, not release, of latent heat. Answer (C) is incorrect because, as air moves downhill, its temperature increases at a slower rate than dry air because vaporization uses heat, not because of the release of heat through condensation.

30.
9184. What is indicated about an air mass if the temperature remains unchanged or decreases slightly as altitude is increased?

A—The air is unstable.
B—A temperature inversion exists.
C—The air is stable.

Answer (C) is correct (9184). *(AvW Chap 6)*
If the air temperature remains unchanged or decreases only slightly as altitude is increased, the air mass tends to be stable.
Answer (A) is incorrect because unstable air would have a uniform decrease (approaching 3°C/1,000 ft.) in temperature with an increase in altitude. Answer (B) is incorrect because in a temperature inversion the temperature increases with increases in altitude.

31.
9188. Which condition is present when a local parcel of air is stable?

A—The parcel of air resists convection.
B—The parcel of air cannot be forced uphill.
C—As the parcel of air moves upward, its temperature becomes warmer than the surrounding air.

Answer (A) is correct (9188). *(AvW Chap 6)*
Stable air resists convection. If a parcel of air is lifted, it is cooler than the surrounding air and will return to its original position when the lifting force is removed. Spontaneous convection is impossible in stable air.
Answer (B) is incorrect because stable air can be forced uphill to form a mountain wave. Answer (C) is incorrect because rising air warmer than the surrounding air describes unstable, not stable, air.

32.
9195. How can the stability of the atmosphere be determined?

A—Ambient temperature lapse rate.
B—Atmospheric pressure at various levels.
C—Surface temperature/dewpoint spread.

Answer (A) is correct (9195). *(AvW Chap 6)*
The difference between the ambient temperature lapse rate of a given mass of air and the adiabatic rates of cooling in upward-moving air determines the stability of the air. For example, surface heating or cooling aloft tends to make the air unstable, while surface cooling or warming aloft tends to make the air more stable.
Answer (B) is incorrect because the difference between ambient temperature and adiabatic lapse rate, not atmospheric pressure at various levels, determines stability. Answer (C) is incorrect because the surface temperature/dew point spread is used to indicate probability of fog, not atmospheric stability.

15.6 Temperature Inversion

33.
9168. Where is a common location for an inversion?

A—At the tropopause.
B—In the stratosphere.
C—At the base of cumulus clouds.

Answer (B) is correct (9168). *(AvW Chap 2)*
Inversions may occur at any altitude and are common in the stratosphere. An inversion is an increase in temperature with an increase in altitude.
Answer (A) is incorrect because a common location for an inversion is in the stratosphere, not at the tropopause. Answer (C) is incorrect because the base of cumulus clouds is where the dew point lapse rate and the dry adiabatic lapse rate converge. It is not a common location for an inversion.

34.
9154. What feature is associated with a temperature inversion?

A—A stable layer of air.
B—An unstable layer of air.
C—Air mass thunderstorms.

Answer (A) is correct (9154). *(AvW Chaps 2, 6)*
A temperature inversion is defined as an increase in temperature with height; i.e., the normal lapse rate is inverted. Thus, any warm air rises to its own temperature and forms a stable layer of air.
Answer (B) is incorrect because instability occurs when the temperature decreases, not increases as in a temperature inversion, with an increase in altitude and the rising air continues to rise. Answer (C) is incorrect because air mass thunderstorms result from instability. They do not occur when there is a temperature inversion.

35.
9153. What characterizes a ground-based inversion?

A—Convection currents at the surface.
B—Cold temperatures.
C—Poor visibility.

Answer (C) is correct (9153). *(AvW Chap 12)*
A ground-based inversion is characterized by poor visibility as a result of trapping fog, smoke, and other restrictions into low levels of the atmosphere.
Answer (A) is incorrect because convective currents at the surface do not occur when there is a ground-based inversion. Answer (B) is incorrect because, when the temperature is cold, it is difficult for the earth to radiate enough heat to become colder than the overlying air.

36.
9169. What condition produces the most frequent type of ground- or surface-based temperature inversion?

A—The movement of colder air under warm air or the movement of warm air over cold air.
B—Widespread sinking of air within a thick layer aloft resulting in heating by compression.
C—Terrestrial radiation on a clear, relatively calm night.

Answer (C) is correct (9169). *(AvW Chap 2)*
An inversion often develops near the ground on clear, cool nights when the wind is relatively calm. The ground radiates heat and cools much faster than the overlying air. Air in contact with the ground becomes cold, while the temperature a few hundred feet above changes very little.
Answer (A) is incorrect because the movement of colder air under warm air is what happens when a cold front is advancing, and the movement of warm air over cold air is the process of an advancing warm front. Answer (B) is incorrect because widespread sinking of air describes compressional or adiabatic heating.

37.
9225. Which is a necessary condition for the occurrence of a low-level temperature inversion wind shear?

A—The temperature differential between the cold and warm layers must be at least 10°C.
B—A calm or light wind near the surface and a relatively strong wind just above the inversion.
C—A wind direction difference of at least 30° between the wind near the surface and the wind just above the inversion.

Answer (B) is correct (9225). *(AvW Chap 9)*
A temperature inversion forms near the surface on a clear night with calm or light surface wind, and a relatively strong wind just above the inversion is necessary to form a low-level temperature inversion wind shear.
Answer (A) is incorrect because magnitude of temperature differential in the inversion is not important; the wind shear is caused by the variation in wind speed. Answer (C) is incorrect because surface wind and a relatively strong wind just above the inversion, not a wind direction difference of at least 30°, are needed to form a low-level temperature inversion wind shear. The wind shear is caused by wind speed variation, not variation in wind direction.

15.7 Density, Pressure, and Corrected Altitude

38.
9163. En route at FL 270, the altimeter is set correctly. On descent, a pilot fails to set the local altimeter setting of 30.57. If the field elevation is 650 feet, and the altimeter is functioning properly, what will it indicate upon landing?

A—585 feet.
B—1,300 feet.
C—Sea level.

Answer (C) is correct (9163). *(AvW Chap 3)*
If an altimeter is set to 29.92 for flight at FL 270 and is not adjusted to the correct altimeter setting of 30.57 during descent, the altimeter will indicate an altitude lower than actual by 650 ft. (1,000 ft. x the difference between the two altimeter settings, which is .65). Thus, if the airplane lands at an airport with a field elevation of 650 ft., the altimeter will indicate sea level (650 ft. airport elevation – 650 ft. altimeter setting error).
Answer (A) is incorrect because 585 ft. is obtained by subtracting 65 ft. rather than subtracting 650 ft. Answer (B) is incorrect because 1,300 ft. is obtained by adding 650 ft. rather than subtracting 650 ft.

39.
9173. If the ambient temperature is colder than standard at FL 310, what is the relationship between true altitude and pressure altitude?

A—They are both the same, 31,000 feet.
B—True altitude is lower than 31,000 feet.
C—Pressure altitude is lower than true altitude.

Answer (B) is correct (9173). *(AvW Chap 3)*
At FL 310, the altimeter is set to pressure altitude (29.92). If the outside air temperature (ambient) is colder than standard, the air is compressed and heavier in weight per unit volume than on a warm day. Thus, in colder-than-standard air, the true altitude is lower than the pressure altitude.
Answer (A) is incorrect because both true and pressure altitudes are the same at FL 310 if the ambient air temperature is standard, not colder than standard. Answer (C) is incorrect because pressure altitude is lower than true altitude in warmer-, not colder-, than-standard air temperature.

40.
9172. If the ambient temperature is warmer than standard at FL 350, what is the density altitude compared to pressure altitude?

A—Lower than pressure altitude.
B—Higher than pressure altitude.
C—Impossible to determine without information on possible inversion layers at lower altitudes.

Answer (B) is correct (9172). *(AvW Chap 3)*
Density altitude, by definition, is pressure altitude adjusted for nonstandard temperature. When the ambient air temperature is warmer than standard, the expanded air is lighter in weight per unit volume than on a cold day, and the pressure levels are raised. Thus, the pressure level where the altimeter indicates FL 350 is higher on a warm day than under standard conditions.
Answer (A) is incorrect because density altitude is higher, not lower, when air temperature is warmer than standard. Answer (C) is incorrect because density altitude is pressure altitude corrected for nonstandard temperatures. Pressure altitude is based on a standard pressure atmosphere at a particular altitude, and inversion layers at lower levels have no effect on pressure altitude.

41.
9164. What is corrected altitude (approximate true altitude)?

A—Pressure altitude corrected for instrument error.
B—Indicated altitude corrected for temperature variation from standard.
C—Density altitude corrected for temperature variation from standard.

Answer (B) is correct (9164). *(AvW Chap 3)*
Corrected altitude is the indicated altitude of an airplane's altimeter corrected for temperature variation from standard atmospheric temperature. This is an approximation of true altitude.
Answer (A) is incorrect because pressure altitude corrected for instrument error is a nonsense concept. Answer (C) is incorrect because density altitude is pressure altitude corrected for temperature variation from standard. Density altitude is a final figure and not subject to additional adjustments.

42.
9174. Which pressure is defined as station pressure?

A—Altimeter setting.
B—Actual pressure at field elevation.
C—Station barometric pressure reduced to sea level.

Answer (B) is correct (9174). *(AvW Chap 3)*
Pressure can be measured only at the point of measurement. The pressure measured at a station or airport is "station pressure," or the actual pressure at field elevation.
Answer (A) is incorrect because altimeter setting is the value to which the scale of a pressure altimeter is adjusted to read field elevation. Answer (C) is incorrect because station barometric pressure reduced to sea level is a method to readily compare station pressures between stations at different altitudes.

15.8 Thunderstorms

43.
9182. What is the result when water vapor changes to the liquid state while being lifted in a thunderstorm?

A—Latent heat is released to the atmosphere.
B—Latent heat is transformed into pure energy.
C—Latent heat is absorbed from the surrounding air by the water droplet.

Answer (A) is correct (9182). *(AvW Chap 11)*
In a thunderstorm, the updrafts (lifting action) result in water vapor changing to liquid or condensation. Condensation releases latent heat to the atmosphere, which partially offsets cooling in the saturated updraft and increases buoyancy within the cloud.
Answer (B) is incorrect because latent heat cannot create pure energy. Latent heat is returned to the surrounding atmosphere. Answer (C) is incorrect because this is the process of latent heat of vaporization, which is changing liquid water to vapor.

44.
9189. Convective clouds which penetrate a stratus layer can produce which threat to instrument flight?

A—Freezing rain.
B—Clear air turbulence.
C—Embedded thunderstorms.

Answer (C) is correct (9189). *(AvW Chap 6)*
A stratus layer may sometimes form in a mildly stable layer while convective clouds penetrate the layer and possibly form thunderstorms. These thunderstorms may be almost or entirely embedded in a massive stratus layer and pose an unseen threat to instrument flight.
Answer (A) is incorrect because the formation of freezing rain is dependent on rain falling through colder air. Convective clouds that penetrate a stratus layer may or may not produce precipitation. Answer (B) is incorrect because clear air turbulence is turbulence encountered in air where no clouds are present.

45.
9199. What is indicated by the term "embedded thunderstorms"?

A—Severe thunderstorms are embedded in a squall line.
B—Thunderstorms are predicted to develop in a stable air mass.
C—Thunderstorms are obscured by other types of clouds.

Answer (C) is correct (9199). *(AvW Chap 11)*
The term "embedded thunderstorms" means that the thunderstorms are embedded in clouds or thick haze layers and cannot be seen.
Answer (A) is incorrect because a squall line consists of severe thunderstorms which can always be seen. Answer (B) is incorrect because thunderstorms do not occur in stable air masses.

46.
9198. What feature is normally associated with the cumulus stage of a thunderstorm?

A—Beginning of rain at the surface.
B—Frequent lightning.
C—Continuous updraft.

Answer (C) is correct (9198). *(AvW Chap 11)*
During the cumulus stage of a thunderstorm, the cumulus cloud is building, and there are continuous updrafts.
Answer (A) is incorrect because the beginning of rain at a surface marks the beginning of the mature stage. Answer (B) is incorrect because frequent lightning occurs after the downdrafts have developed, producing the static electricity which causes lightning.

47.
9196. Which weather phenomenon signals the beginning of the mature stage of a thunderstorm?

A—The appearance of an anvil top.
B—The start of rain at the surface.
C—Growth rate of the cloud is at its maximum.

Answer (B) is correct (9196). *(AvW Chap 11)*
The mature stage of a thunderstorm begins when rain begins falling at the surface. This means that downdrafts have developed sufficiently to carry water all the way through the thunderstorm.
Answer (A) is incorrect because the appearance of an anvil top occurs during the dissipating stage. Answer (C) is incorrect because the growth rate of a thunderstorm is at its greatest during the cumulus stage.

48.
9203. Why are downdrafts in a mature thunderstorm hazardous?

A—Downdrafts are kept cool by cold rain which tends to accelerate the downward velocity.
B—Downdrafts converge toward a central location under the storm after striking the surface.
C—Downdrafts become warmer than the surrounding air and reverse into an updraft before reaching the surface.

Answer (A) is correct (9203). *(AvW Chap 11)*
During the mature stage, cold rain in the downdraft slows compressional heating, and the downdraft remains colder than the surrounding air. Thus, its downward speed is accelerated and may exceed 2,500 fpm.
Answer (B) is incorrect because, after striking the ground, the downdrafts will move away from the storm's center (not converge). Answer (C) is incorrect because downdrafts remain colder, not warmer, than the surrounding air and accelerate downward, not reverse into an updraft.

49.
9197. During the life cycle of a thunderstorm, which stage is characterized predominately by downdrafts?

A—Cumulus.
B—Dissipating.
C—Mature.

Answer (B) is correct (9197). *(AvW Chap 11)*
Thunderstorms have three life cycles: cumulus, mature, and dissipating. In the dissipating stage, the storm is characterized by downdrafts as the storm rains itself out.
Answer (A) is incorrect because the cumulus stage is the building stage characterized by updrafts. Answer (C) is incorrect because the mature stage has both updrafts and downdrafts, which create strong wind shears.

50.
9204. What is a difference between an air mass thunderstorm and a steady-state thunderstorm?

A—Air mass thunderstorms produce precipitation which falls outside of the updraft.
B—Air mass thunderstorm downdrafts and precipitation retard and reverse the updrafts.
C—Steady-state thunderstorms are associated with local surface heating.

Answer (B) is correct (9204). *(AvW Chap 11)*
The rain associated with an air mass thunderstorm falls through or immediately beside the updraft. Falling precipitation induces frictional drag, retards the updraft, and reverses it to a downdraft. During a steady-state thunderstorm, precipitation falls outside the updraft, allowing the updraft to continue unabated.
Answer (A) is incorrect because steady-state, not air mass, thunderstorms produce precipitation which falls outside the updraft. Answer (C) is incorrect because air mass, not steady-state, thunderstorms are associated with local surface heating.

51.
9205. Which type storms are most likely to produce funnel clouds or tornadoes?

A—Air mass thunderstorms.
B—Cold front or squall line thunderstorms.
C—Storms associated with icing and supercooled water.

Answer (B) is correct (9205). *(AvW Chap 11)*
Funnel clouds or tornadoes normally form with steady-state thunderstorms associated with cold fronts or squall lines. The mature stage updrafts in a steady-state thunderstorm are stronger and last longer than those in air mass storms and may persist for several hours.
Answer (A) is incorrect because, even though air mass thunderstorms may produce funnel clouds or tornadoes, they are most likely to occur with steady-state thunderstorms. Answer (C) is incorrect because all thunderstorms that have updrafts and carry water above the freezing level can produce icing and supercooled water. But thunderstorms associated with cold fronts and squall lines are most likely to produce funnel clouds or tornadoes.

52.
9210. Which type cloud is associated with violent turbulence and a tendency toward the production of funnel clouds?

A—Cumulonimbus mamma.
B—Standing lenticular.
C—Stratocumulus.

Answer (A) is correct (9210). *(AvW Chap 11)*
Cumulonimbus mamma is a cumulonimbus cloud having hanging protuberances, like pouches, testes, or udders, on the underside of the cloud, usually indicative of severe turbulence. This type of cloud can produce a tornado.
Answer (B) is incorrect because standing lenticular clouds mark mountain waves that are the product of stable air flowing over an obstruction. Answer (C) is incorrect because stratocumulus clouds sometimes form from the breaking up of stratus or the spreading out of cumulus, and they are associated with some turbulence and possible icing at subfreezing levels.

53.
9200. Where do squall lines most often develop?

A—In an occluded front.
B—Ahead of a cold front.
C—Behind a stationary front.

Answer (B) is correct (9200). *(AvW Chap 11)*
A squall line is a nonfrontal, narrow band of active thunderstorms. Most often squall lines develop ahead of a cold front in moist, unstable air.
Answer (A) is incorrect because squall lines most often develop ahead of a cold front, not in an occluded front. Answer (C) is incorrect because squall lines most often develop ahead of a cold front, not behind a stationary front.

54.
9201. Where can the maximum hazard zone caused by wind shear associated with a thunderstorm be found?

A—In front of the thunderstorm cell (anvil side) and on the southwest side of the cell.
B—Ahead of the roll cloud or gust front and directly under the anvil cloud.
C—On all sides and directly under the thunderstorm cell.

Answer (C) is correct (9201). *(AvW Chap 11)*
Hazardous turbulence is present in all thunderstorms. The maximum hazard zone caused by wind shear associated with a thunderstorm is found on all sides and directly under the thunderstorm cell.
Answer (A) is incorrect because the wind shear associated with a thunderstorm is on all sides and directly under the cell, not just in the front and on the southwest side. Answer (B) is incorrect because the wind shear associated with a thunderstorm is on all sides and directly under the cell. A roll cloud is not present in all thunderstorms, and when present it marks the eddies of the shear zone between the plow wind and surrounding air.

55.
9202. Atmospheric pressure changes due to a thunderstorm will be at the lowest value

A—during the downdraft and heavy rain showers.
B—when the thunderstorm is approaching.
C—immediately after the rain showers have stopped.

Answer (B) is correct (9202). *(AvW Chap 11)*
Pressure usually falls rapidly with the approach of a thunderstorm, then rises sharply with the onset of the first gust and arrival of the cold downdraft and heavy rain showers, falling back to normal as the storm moves on.
Answer (A) is incorrect because, during the downdraft and heavy rain showers, the pressure rises sharply. Answer (C) is incorrect because, immediately after the rain showers have stopped, the pressure will return to normal.

56.
9211. A clear area in a line of thunderstorm echoes on a radar scope indicates

A—the absence of clouds in the area.
B—an area of no convective turbulence.
C—an area where precipitation drops are not detected.

Answer (C) is correct (9211). *(AvW Chap 11)*
Weather radar detects droplets of precipitation. If a radarscope displays a clear area, it indicates an area where no precipitation drops are detected.
Answer (A) is incorrect because weather radar detects only precipitation drops, not clouds. Answer (B) is incorrect because convective turbulence, which would not be detected by radar, could be found under cumulus clouds. Radar does not detect turbulence.

57.
9212. When flying over the top of a severe thunderstorm, the cloud should be overflown by at least

A—1,000 feet for each 10 knots windspeed.
B—2,500 feet.
C—500 feet above any moderate to severe turbulence layer.

Answer (A) is correct (9212). *(AvW Chap 11)*
The top of a known or suspected severe thunderstorm should be cleared by at least 1,000 ft. of altitude for each 10 kt. of wind speed at the cloud top. In some severe thunderstorms, this clearance may exceed the altitude capability of most aircraft.
Answer (B) is incorrect because the cloud should be overflown by at least 1,000 ft. for each 10 kt. wind speed, which would normally be greater than 2,500 ft. with a severe thunderstorm. Answer (C) is incorrect because the exact location of a turbulence layer will not usually be known.

15.9 Icing

58.
9161. Freezing rain encountered during climb is normally evidence that

A—a climb can be made to a higher altitude without encountering more than light icing.
B—a layer of warmer air exists above.
C—ice pellets at higher altitudes have changed to rain in the warmer air below.

Answer (B) is correct (9161). *(AvW Chap 5)*
Freezing rain is rain that falls through colder air and becomes supercooled, freezing on impact. If encountered, it means that there is a layer of warmer air above.
Answer (A) is incorrect because freezing rain means only that a layer of warmer air exists above. It does not indicate the amount of icing that may be encountered during a climb. Answer (C) is incorrect because freezing rain is formed by rain falling through colder air, not from ice pellets melting through warmer air.

59.
9180. What condition is indicated when ice pellets are encountered during flight?

A—Thunderstorms at higher levels.
B—Freezing rain at higher levels.
C—Snow at higher levels.

Answer (B) is correct (9180). *(AvW Chap 5)*
Ice pellets always indicate freezing rain at higher altitudes. Ice pellets are formed when rain freezes during descent.
Answer (A) is incorrect because ice pellets always indicate freezing rain, not thunderstorms, at higher altitudes. Answer (C) is incorrect because freezing rain, not snow, is indicated at higher altitudes when ice pellets are encountered.

60.
9162. What temperature condition is indicated if precipitation in the form of wet snow occurs during flight?

A—The temperature is above freezing at flight altitude.
B—The temperature is above freezing at higher altitudes.
C—There is an inversion with colder air below.

Answer (A) is correct (9162). *(AvW Chap 5)*
Falling snow may melt in warmer layers of air. When wet snow is encountered, it indicates that the temperature is above freezing at flight altitude.
Answer (B) is incorrect because wet snow indicates above-freezing temperature at flight level, not at higher altitudes. The temperature was below freezing at the altitudes where the snow formed. Answer (C) is incorrect because wet snow indicates falling snow that has begun to melt due to above-freezing temperature at flight level. An inversion may or may not be the cause of the warmer air.

61.
9179. Which conditions result in the formation of frost?

A—The temperature of the collecting surface is at or below freezing and small droplets of moisture are falling.
B—Dew collects on the surface and then freezes because the surface temperature is lower than the air temperature.
C—Temperature of the collecting surface is below the dewpoint and the dewpoint is also below freezing.

Answer (C) is correct (9179). *(AvW Chap 5)*
Frost forms when both the temperature of the collecting surface is below the dew point and the dew point is also below freezing. Frost is the direct sublimation of water vapor to ice crystals.
Answer (A) is incorrect because moisture that falls on a collecting surface that is at or below freezing will form ice. Answer (B) is incorrect because frozen dew is hard and transparent, while frost is the sublimation from vapor to ice and is white and opaque.

62.
9181. When will frost most likely form on aircraft surfaces?

A—On clear nights with stable air and light winds.
B—On overcast nights with freezing drizzle precipitation.
C—On clear nights with convective action and a small temperature/dewpoint spread.

Answer (A) is correct (9181). *(AvW Chap 10)*
Frost will most likely form on aircraft surfaces on clear nights with stable air and light winds. These are conditions which in all other respects make weather ideal for flying.
Answer (B) is incorrect because freezing drizzle would produce ice on the aircraft surfaces, not frost. Answer (C) is incorrect because stable air is required. Convective action requires unstable conditions.

63.
9183. What is a feature of supercooled water?

A—The water drop sublimates to an ice particle upon impact.
B—The unstable water drop freezes upon striking an exposed object.
C—The temperature of the water drop remains at 0 °C until it impacts a part of the airframe, then clear ice accumulates.

Answer (B) is correct (9183). *(AvW Chap 5)*
Water droplets that are colder than 0°C are considered supercooled. When they strike an exposed object, they freeze on impact. Aircraft icing results if supercooled water strikes an airplane.
Answer (A) is incorrect because sublimation is the process of changing water vapor to ice crystals, not liquid water to ice (the latter is freezing). Answer (C) is incorrect because supercooled water temperature is below, not at, 0°C.

64.
9223. Which type precipitation is an indication that supercooled water is present?

A—Wet snow.
B—Freezing rain.
C—Ice pellets.

Answer (B) is correct (9223). *(AvW Chap 5)*
Rain falling through colder air may become supercooled, freezing on impact as freezing rain. Supercooled water is liquid water that is colder than 0°C, and its impact on an object induces freezing.
Answer (A) is incorrect because wet snow is an indication that temperature is above freezing at present level. Answer (C) is incorrect because ice pellets indicate that water has frozen, not become/remained supercooled.

65.
9221. What condition is necessary for the formation of structural icing in flight?

A—Supercooled water drops.
B—Water vapor.
C—Visible water.

Answer (C) is correct (9221). *(AvW Chap 10)*
Two conditions are necessary for structural icing in flight: (1) The aircraft must be flying through visible water such as rain or cloud droplets, and (2) the temperature at the point where the moisture strikes the aircraft must be 0°C or colder.
Answer (A) is incorrect because supercooled water drops increase the rate of icing but are not a condition necessary for the formation of structural icing. Answer (B) is incorrect because water must be visible, not in a gaseous (vapor) state.

66.
9224. Which type of icing is associated with the smallest size of water droplet similar to that found in low-level stratus clouds?

A—Clear ice.
B—Frost ice.
C—Rime ice.

Answer (C) is correct (9224). *(AvW Chap 10)*
Rime ice forms when drops are small, such as those found in low-level stratus clouds. Its irregular shape makes it very effective in decreasing aerodynamic efficiency of airfoils.
Answer (A) is incorrect because clear ice forms when drops are large, not small, as found in rain or cumuliform clouds. Answer (B) is incorrect because frost is not a structural icing condition found in flight; it occurs to airplanes parked on the ground.

15.10 High-Altitude Weather

67.
9151. What is a characteristic of the troposphere?

A—It contains all the moisture of the atmosphere.
B—There is an overall decrease of temperature with an increase of altitude.
C—The average altitude of the top of the troposphere is about 6 miles.

Answer (B) is correct (9151). *(AvW Chap 1)*
The troposphere is the layer from the surface to an average altitude of 7 mi. It is characterized by an overall decrease of temperature with an increase in altitude.
Answer (A) is incorrect because moisture can be found in the stratosphere, as evidenced by some of the largest thunderstorms. Answer (C) is incorrect because the average altitude of the top of the troposphere is about 7 mi., not 6 mi.

68.
9209. Which feature is associated with the tropopause?

A—Absence of wind and turbulence.
B—Absolute upper limit of cloud formation.
C—Abrupt change of temperature lapse rate.

Answer (C) is correct (9209). *(AvW Chap 13)*
The tropopause is characterized by an abrupt change in temperature lapse rate. The temperature above the tropical tropopause increases with height, and the temperature above the polar tropopause remains about constant with height.
Answer (A) is incorrect because the jet stream (wind) and clear air turbulence are found extensively in the tropopause. Answer (B) is incorrect because clouds can be present into the stratosphere, as in very large thunderstorms and cirrus clouds made up of ice crystals.

69.
9240. What weather feature occurs at altitude levels near the tropopause?

A—Maximum winds and narrow wind shear zones.
B—Abrupt temperature increase above the tropopause.
C—Thin layers of cirrus (ice crystal) clouds at the tropopause level.

Answer (A) is correct (9240). *(AvW Chap 13)*
Temperature and wind vary greatly in the vicinity of the tropopause. Maximum winds generally occur near the tropopause. These winds create narrow zones of wind shear which often generate hazardous turbulence.
Answer (B) is incorrect because abrupt temperature increase does not occur above the tropopause. Answer (C) is incorrect because thin layers of cirrus (ice crystal) clouds can develop at altitudes below the tropopause level and extend into the lower stratosphere.

70.
9238. Where do the maximum winds associated with the jetstream usually occur?

A—In the vicinity of breaks in the tropopause on the polar side of the jet core.
B—Below the jet core where a long straight stretch of the jetstream is located.
C—On the equatorial side of the jetstream where moisture has formed cirriform clouds.

Answer (A) is correct (9238). *(AvW Chap 13)*
Maximum winds associated with the jet stream occur in the vicinity of breaks between the tropical and polar tropopause. Maximum wind speed in the jet stream is found in the core on the polar side due to very strong temperature gradients.
Answer (B) is incorrect because, in the jet stream, the maximum winds are found in, not below, the core. Answer (C) is incorrect because, when moisture is available, cirriform clouds will form on the upward motion of air of the jet stream on the equatorial side. This will occur in the slower winds of the jet stream.

71.
9241. Where are jetstreams normally located?

A—In areas of strong low pressure systems in the stratosphere.
B—At the tropopause where intensified temperature gradients are located.
C—In a single continuous band, encircling the Earth, where there is a break between the equatorial and polar tropopause.

Answer (B) is correct (9241). *(AvW Chap 13)*
The jet stream is a narrow, shallow, meandering river of maximum winds extending around the Earth in a wave-like pattern. The jet stream typically occurs in a break in the tropopause in an area of intensified temperature gradients characteristic of the break.
Answer (A) is incorrect because a jet stream is located in a break in the tropopause, not in the stratosphere. Answer (C) is incorrect because there may be more than one jet stream at any time; up to three at one time are not uncommon.

72.
9227. Where is the normal location of the jetstream relative to surface lows and fronts?

A—The jetstream is located north of the surface systems.
B—The jetstream is located south of the low and warm front.
C—The jetstream is located over the low and crosses both the warm front and the cold front.

Answer (A) is correct (9227). *(AvW Chap 13)*
Strong, long-trajectory jet streams usually are associated with well-developed surface lows and frontal systems beneath upper troughs or lows. The jet stream is to the north as a surface low develops, and the low moves nearer the jet stream as the low deepens. The occluding low moves north of the jet stream, and the jet stream crosses the frontal system near the point of occlusion.
Answer (B) is incorrect because the jet stream is located to the north, not south, of the low and warm front. Answer (C) is incorrect because the jet stream crosses the occlusion of the warm and the cold fronts at the point of occlusion.

73.
9228. Which type frontal system is normally crossed by the jetstream?

A—Cold front and warm front.
B—Warm front.
C—Occluded front.

Answer (C) is correct (9228). *(AvW Chap 13)*
The development of a surface low usually is south of the jet stream and moves nearer as the low deepens. The occluding low moves north of the jet stream, and the jet stream crosses the frontal system near the point of occlusion.
Answer (A) is incorrect because the jet stream crosses an occluded front, not both warm and cold fronts. Answer (B) is incorrect because the jet normally crosses an occluded, not a warm, front.

74.
9229. Which type clouds may be associated with the jetstream?

A—Cumulonimbus cloud line where the jetstream crosses the cold front.
B—Cirrus clouds on the equatorial side of the jetstream.
C—Cirrostratus cloud band on the polar side and under the jetstream.

Answer (B) is correct (9229). *(AvW Chap 13)*
Air travels in a "corkscrew" path around the jet stream with upward motion on the equatorial side. Thus, when high-level moisture is available, cirrus clouds form on the equatorial side of the jet stream.
Answer (A) is incorrect because cirriform, not cumulonimbus, clouds are associated with the jet stream. Answer (C) is incorrect because cirrostratus clouds form on the equatorial, not polar, side of the jet stream.

75.
9236. A strong wind shear can be expected

A—on the low pressure side of a 100-knot jetstream core.
B—where the horizontal wind shear is 15 knots, in a distance equal to 2.5° longitude.
C—if the 5°C isotherms are spaced 100 NM or closer together.

Answer (A) is correct (9236). *(AvW Chap 13)*
Wind speed decreases outward from the jet stream core, and the rate of decrease is greater on the polar (low-pressure) side than on the equatorial (high-pressure) side. Thus, a strong wind shear can be expected on the low-pressure side of a 100-kt. jet stream core.
Answer (B) is incorrect because, on a tropopause data chart, a strong wind shear can be expected where the horizontal wind shear is greater than 18 kt., not 15 kt., in a distance equal to 2.5° longitude (or about 150 NM). Answer (C) is incorrect because, on a tropopause data chart, a strong wind shear can be expected if the 20-kt. isotachs, not 5°C isotherms, are spaced 100 NM or closer.

15.11 Arctic Weather

76.
9156. Which area or areas of the Northern Hemisphere experience a generally east to west movement of weather systems?

A—Arctic only.
B—Arctic and subtropical.
C—Subtropical only.

Answer (B) is correct (9156). *(AvW Chap 4)*
The high-pressure belt at about 30° north latitude forces air outward at the surface to the north and to the south. The southward moving air is deflected by the Coriolis force, becoming the well-known subtropical northeast (moving northeast to southwest) trade winds.
In the arctic region (60° north latitude and above), the heavier, denser air moves south at a low level toward the Equator but is turned to the right by the Coriolis force, causing the low-level polar easterlies (moving east to west).
Answer (A) is incorrect because, in the Northern Hemisphere, both the arctic and subtropical areas experience a general east-to-west movement of weather systems. Answer (C) is incorrect because, in the Northern Hemisphere, both the arctic and subtropical areas experience a general east-to-west movement of weather systems.

77.
9233. Summer thunderstorms in the arctic region will generally move

A—northeast to southwest in polar easterlies.
B—southwest to northeast with the jetstream flow.
C—directly north to south with the low-level polar airflow.

Answer (A) is correct (9233). *(AvW Chap 14)*
During summer afternoons, scattered cumulus clouds forming over the interior of the arctic region occasionally grow into thunderstorms. These thunderstorms generally move from northeast to southwest in the polar easterlies, which is opposite the general movement in midlatitudes.
Answer (B) is incorrect because thunderstorms in the Arctic generally move northeast to southwest in the polar easterlies, not southwest to northeast with the jet stream flow. Answer (C) is incorrect because thunderstorms in the Arctic generally move northeast to southwest in polar easterlies, not directly north to south.

78.
9234. Which arctic flying hazard is caused when a cloud layer of uniform thickness overlies a snow or ice covered surface?

A—Ice fog.
B—Whiteout.
C—Blowing snow.

Answer (B) is correct (9234). *(AvW Chap 14)*

Whiteout is a visibility-restricting phenomenon that occurs in the Arctic when a cloud layer of uniform thickness overlies a snow- or ice-covered surface. Parallel rays of the sun are broken up and diffused when passing through the cloud layer so that they strike the snow surface from many angles, resulting in a loss of depth perception.

Answer (A) is incorrect because ice fog forms in moist air during extremely cold conditions. It is not formed by a cloud layer overlying a snow-covered surface. Answer (C) is incorrect because blowing snow is snow that is blown by light or greater winds, causing decreased visibility. It is not formed by a cloud layer overlying a snow-covered surface.

15.12 Tropical Weather

79.
9259. Which weather condition is present when the tropical storm is upgraded to a hurricane?

A—Highest windspeed, 100 knots or more.
B—A clear area or hurricane eye has formed.
C—Sustained winds of 65 knots or more.

Answer (C) is correct (9259). *(AvW Chap 15)*

Tropical cyclones are classified by their intensity based on average 1-min. wind speeds. To be classified as a hurricane, the cyclone must have sustained winds of 65 kt. or more.

Answer (A) is incorrect because tropical cyclones are classified based on the sustained winds, not the highest wind speed. Answer (B) is incorrect because a clear area, or eye, usually forms in the tropical storm stage and continues through the hurricane stage.

80.
9260. What is the general direction of movement of a hurricane located in the Caribbean or Gulf of Mexico region?

A—Northwesterly curving to northeasterly.
B—Westerly, until encountering land, then easterly.
C—Counterclockwise over open water, then dissipating outward over land.

Answer (A) is correct (9260). *(AvW Chap 15)*

Hurricanes located in the Caribbean or Gulf of Mexico move in a direction between west and northwest while in low latitudes. As the hurricane moves toward the mid-latitudes, the prevailing westerlies will gain control, and the hurricane will curve to the northeast.

Answer (B) is incorrect because a hurricane will curve easterly because of prevailing winds, not because of land. Answer (C) is incorrect because the windflow in the hurricane is counterclockwise, not the general movement of the hurricane itself.

END OF CHAPTER

CHAPTER SIXTEEN
WEATHER REPORTS AND FORECASTS

This chapter contains outlines of major concepts tested, all FAA test questions and answers regarding weather reports and forecasts, and an explanation of each answer. Each module, or subtopic, within this chapter is listed above with the number of questions from the FAA pilot knowledge test pertaining to that particular module. For each module, the first number following the parentheses is the page number on which the outline begins, and the next number is the page number on which the questions begin.

There are 90 questions in this chapter. We separate and organize the FAA questions into meaningful study units, i.e., chapters and modules. As an analogy, it is easier to deal with the "trees" if you understand the "forest." In this context, "trees" are individual FAA questions and the "forest" is the ATP knowledge test. The organizational units between the overall ATP knowledge test and individual ATP test questions are chapters and modules in this book.

CAUTION: The **sole purpose** of this book is to expedite your passing the FAA pilot knowledge test for the ATP certificate. Topics or regulations not directly tested on the FAA pilot knowledge test are omitted. Much more information and knowledge are necessary to fly safely. This additional material is presented in Gleim's other pilot training books (see the order form on page 818) and in many FAA books and circulars, as well as in airplane *POH*s and other commercial textbooks.

16.1 PILOT WEATHER REPORT (PIREP) (Questions 1-5)

1. Structural icing is one type of observed weather that can be directly observed only during flight and then reported in a PIREP.
2. **Intermittent light turbulence** causes momentary slight, erratic changes in altitude and/or attitude, one-third to two-thirds of the time.
3. **Occasional light chop** causes slight, rapid, and somewhat rhythmic bumpiness without appreciable changes in attitude or altitude less than one-third of the time.
4. **Continuous moderate turbulence** causes changes in altitude and/or attitude more than two-thirds of the time, with the aircraft remaining in positive control at all times.
5. The **/SK** section of a PIREP describes cloud layers as follows:
   a. Height of cloud base in hundreds of feet. If unknown, use UNKN.
   b. Cloud cover symbol
   c. Height of cloud tops in hundreds of feet, if known
   d. A slash (/) to separate layers
   e. EXAMPLE: **/SK 036 OVC 060/075 OVC** means there are two overcast layers. The first has a base of 3,600 ft. with tops at 6,000 ft. The second has a base at 7,500 ft. and no report of cloud tops.

16.2 EN ROUTE WEATHER ADVISORIES (Questions 6-9)

1. En Route Flight Advisory Service (EFAS) provides weather advisories pertinent to the type of flight, intended route of flight, and altitude.
   a. Below FL 180, en route weather advisories should be obtained from an FSS on 122.0 MHz.
2. Hazardous Inflight Weather Advisory Service (HIWAS) is a continuous broadcast over selected VORs of convective SIGMETs, SIGMETs, AIRMETs, severe weather forecast alerts (AWW), and center weather advisories (CWA).

16.3 TWEB ROUTE FORECASTS (Questions 10-11)

1. TWEB Route Forecast information is obtained from the TEL TWEB and Telephone Voice Response Systems (VRS).
2. The TWEB Route Forecasts and Synopses are issued by Weather Forecast Offices (WFOs) (formerly known as Weather Service Forecast Offices) three times per day according to time zone.
   a. The TWEB forecast is valid for a 15-hr. period.

16.4 RADAR SUMMARY CHART (Questions 12-15)

1. A radar summary chart graphically displays a collection of radar weather reports (SDs). See Fig. 152 on page 728.
2. A radar summary chart displays the type of precipitation echoes, their intensity, intensity trend, configuration, coverage, echo tops and bases, and movement.
   a. Severe weather watches are plotted if they are in effect when the chart is valid.
3. The **type of precipitation** can be determined by the radar operator from the scope presentation in combination from other sources.
   a. EXAMPLE: **TRW** means thunderstorms and rain showers.

4. The **echo intensity** is obtained from the video integrator processor (VIP) and is indicated on the chart by contours.
   a. The six VIP levels are combined into three contours as indicated below.

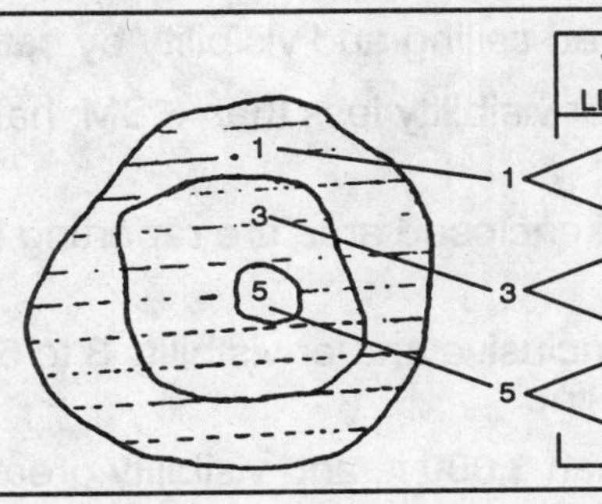

VIP LEVEL	ECHO INTENSITY	PRECIPITATION INTENSITY
1	Weak	Light
2	Moderate	Moderate
3	Strong	Heavy
4	Very strong	Very heavy
5	Intense	Intense
6	Extreme	Extreme

NOTE: The numbers representing the intensity level do not appear on the chart.

   b. The first contour line represents intensity level 1 to 2, or weak to moderate echoes.
   c. The second contour is intensity level 3 to 4, or strong to very strong.
   d. The third contour is intensity level 5 to 6, or intense to extreme.

5. The **intensity trend** of echoes is indicated by a symbol plotted beside the precipitation type.
   a. A plus (+) means the intensity is increasing; a minus (–) means the intensity is decreasing; and no sign means no change.
   b. EXAMPLE: **RW+** means rain showers increasing in intensity.

6. The heights of the **tops and bases** of echoes are shown on the chart in hundreds of feet above mean sea level.
   a. A horizontal line is used with the heights shown above and below the line denoting the top and base heights, respectively.
   b. No number below the line means the echo base is at or near the surface.
   c. EXAMPLES:

$\underline{450}$ Bases at surface; maximum top 45,000 ft.

$\frac{220}{080}$ Bases 8,000 ft.; maximum top 22,000 ft.

$\overline{020}$ Bases 2,000 ft.; maximum top either missing or reported in another place

7. **Echo Movement**
   a. Individual cell movement is indicated by an arrow with the speed in knots entered as a number at the top of the arrowhead.
   b. Line or area movement is indicated by a shaft and barb combination with the shaft indicating the direction and the barbs the speed.
      1) A half barb is 5 kt., a whole barb is 10 kt., and a pennant is 50 kt.
   c. EXAMPLES:

Individual echo movement to the northeast at 35 kt.

Line or area movement to the east at 15 kt.

16.5 WEATHER DEPICTION CHART (Questions 16-19)

1. A weather depiction chart is a map of the United States depicting actual sky conditions, visibility restrictions, and type of precipitation at reporting stations at the time stated on the chart. See Fig. 150 on page 730.
2. The weather depiction chart shows observed ceiling and visibility by categories as follows:
   a. **IFR** -- ceiling less than 1,000 ft. and/or visibility less than 3 SM; hatched area outlined by a smooth area
      1) All reporting stations within the enclosed area are reporting IFR conditions at the time of the report.
   b. **MVFR** -- ceiling 1,000 ft. to 3,000 ft. inclusive and/or visibility 3 to 5 SM inclusive; non-hatched area outlined by a smooth line
   c. **VFR** -- no ceiling or ceiling greater than 3,000 ft. and visibility greater than 5 SM; not outlined
3. The amount of sky cover is shown by shading in the station circle.
   a. If the sky cover is clear, the circle is open; if overcast, the circle is solid; if scattered, the circle is 1/4 shaded; and if broken, the circle is 3/4 shaded.
   b. If the sky is obscured, there is an "X" in the circle rather than shading.
4. Cloud height of the sky cover is entered under the station circle in hundreds of feet.
5. Weather and obstructions to vision symbols are entered to the left of the station circle.
   a. EXAMPLES: = means fog.
      •• means continuous rain.
6. When visibility is 6 SM or less, it is entered to the left of the weather or obstructions to vision symbol.
7. **Example Sky Symbols and Related Weather Data**

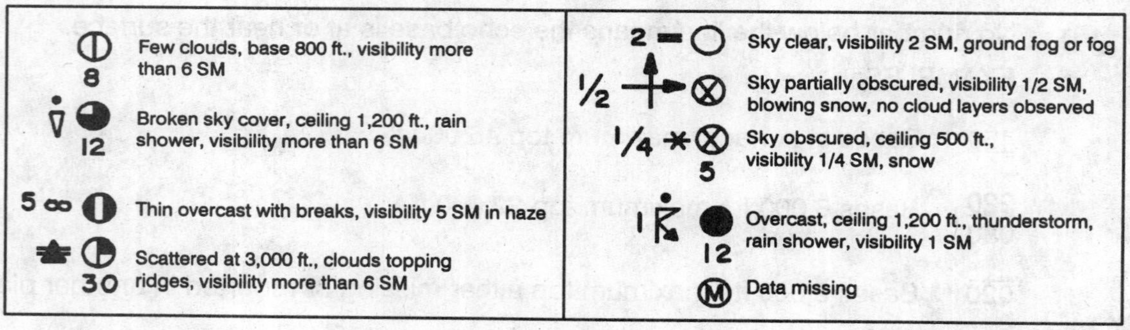

16.6 LOW-LEVEL SIGNIFICANT WEATHER PROGNOSTIC CHART (Questions 20-24)

1. The low-level prognostic chart is a four-panel chart. The panels show weather conditions that are forecast to exist at a specific time shown on the chart.
   a. The two upper panels forecast significant weather from the surface up to 24,000 ft. MSL: one for 12 hr. and the other for 24 hr. from the time of issuance.

b. The two lower panels forecast surface conditions: one for 12 hr. and the other for 24 hr. from time of issuance.

c. See Fig. 151 on page 733.

2. The significant weather, or upper, panels depict IFR, MVFR, turbulence, and freezing levels.

   a. **IFR** -- areas enclosed by a smooth line

      1) IFR means forecast conditions of ceilings less than 1,000 ft. and/or visibility less than 3 SM.

   b. **MVFR** -- areas enclosed by a scalloped line

   c. Non-convective turbulence of moderate or greater intensity -- areas enclosed by long, dashed lines

      1) Numbers below and/or above a short line show expected base and/or top of the turbulence in hundreds of feet MSL.

         a) EXAMPLE: <u>**120**</u> means expected top is 12,000 ft. MSL.

   d. Freezing level height contours for the highest freezing level -- contours drawn at 4,000-ft. intervals as short, dashed lines

      1) Interpolate for freezing levels between the given contours.

3. The surface, or lower, panels depict highs, lows, fronts, and areas of precipitation.

   a. Solid lines enclose areas of expected continuous or intermittent (stable) precipitation.

      1) Additionally, areas of continuous or intermittent precipitation with embedded showers and thunderstorms are also enclosed by solid lines.

   b. Dash-dot lines enclose areas of showers and thunderstorms, i.e., unstable precipitation.

   c. If precipitation affects half or more of an area, that area is shaded.

4. The following are some standard weather symbols:

Symbol	*Meaning*	*Symbol*	*Meaning*
	**Moderate Turbulence**		**Rain Shower**
	**Severe Turbulence**		**Snow Shower**
	**Moderate Icing**		**Thunderstorm**
	**Severe Icing**		**Freezing Rain**
	**Rain**		**Tropical Storm**
	**Snow**		**Hurricane (typhoon)**
	**Drizzle**		

16.7 WINDS AND TEMPERATURES ALOFT FORECASTS (FD) (Questions 25-35)

1. Forecast winds and temperatures at specified altitudes for specific locations in the United States are presented in table form. See Fig. 149 on page 736.
2. A four-digit group (used when temperatures are not forecast) shows wind direction with reference to true north and the wind speed in knots.
   a. The first two digits indicate wind direction after a zero is added.
   b. The next two digits indicate the wind speed.
3. A six-digit group includes the forecast temperature aloft.
   a. The last two digits indicate the temperature in degrees Celsius.
   b. Plus or minus is indicated before the temperature, except at higher altitudes (above 24,000 ft. MSL) where it is always below freezing.
4. When the wind speed is less than 5 kt., the forecast is coded **9900**, which means that the wind is light and variable.
5. Note that, at some of the lower levels, the wind and temperature information is omitted.
   a. Winds aloft are not forecast for levels within 1,500 ft. of the station elevation.
   b. No temperatures are forecast for the 3,000-ft. level or for a level within 2,500 ft. of the station elevation.
6. If the wind speed is forecast to be from 100 to 199 kt., the forecaster adds 50 to the direction and subtracts 100 from the speed. To decode, you must do the reverse: subtract 50 from the direction and add 100 to the speed.
   a. EXAMPLE: If the forecast for 39,000 ft. appears as **731960**, subtract 50 from 73 and add 100 to 19. The wind would be 230° at 119 kt. with a temperature of –60°C.
   b. It is easy to know when the coded direction has been increased by 50. Coded direction (in tens of degrees) normally ranges from 01 (010°) to 36 (360°). Any coded direction with a numerical value greater than 36 indicates a wind of 100 kt. or greater. The coded direction for winds of 100 to 199 kt. thus ranges from 51 through 86.
7. If the wind speed is forecast to be 199 kt. or more, the wind group is coded as 199 kt.
   a. EXAMPLE: The forecast for FL 390 is to be 280° at 205 kt., temperature at –51°C. This would be encoded in the FD as **789951**.
8. EXAMPLES:

Coded	Decoded
9900+00	Winds light and variable, temperature 0°C
2707	270° at 7 kt.
850552	85 – 50 = 35; 05 + 100 = 105 350° at 105 kt., temperature –52°C

9. International Standard Atmosphere (ISA) temperature at sea level is 15°C and decreases at a lapse rate of 2°C/1,000 ft.
   a. Compute the ISA temperature by multiplying the given altitude (per 1,000 ft.) by the lapse rate of 2°C/1,000 ft., and subtract that amount from the sea level ISA temperature of 15°C.
      1) EXAMPLE: What is ISA temperature at FL 270?

$$\begin{aligned} \text{ISA} &= 15 - [(27{,}000 \div 1{,}000)(2)] \\ &= 15 - (27 \times 2) \\ &= 15 - 54 \\ &= -39°\text{C} \end{aligned}$$

b. In the tropopause (36,000 ft. and above), the ISA temperature is approximately −56°C.

10. You will be asked to determine wind and temperature at altitudes not given on the chart, which means you must interpolate.

a. Additionally, you will be asked for the wind and temperature trend over a given route, which may also require interpolation.

16.8 AVIATION ROUTINE WEATHER REPORT (METAR) (Questions 36-55)

1. Aviation routine weather reports (METARs) are actual weather observations at the time indicated on the report. There are two types of reports.
   a. **METAR** is a routine weather report.
   b. **SPECI** is a special METAR (nonroutine) weather observation concerning significant weather changes.
2. Following the type of report are the elements listed below:
   a. The four-letter ICAO station identifier
      1) In the contiguous 48 states, the three-letter domestic identifier is prefixed with a "K."
   b. Date/time group that the observation was taken. It is appended with a "Z" to denote Coordinated Universal Time (UTC).
      1) EXAMPLE: **131753Z** means the observation was taken on the 13th day at 1753 UTC.
      2) Subtract 6 hr. from UTC for Central Standard Time.
   c. Report modifier
      1) **AUTO** indicates a fully automated weather reporting station, with no human intervention.
         a) The type of sensor equipment used at the station is indicated in the remarks (RMK) section; i.e., **AO2** means the automated weather station has a precipitation (rain/snow) discriminator.
   d. Wind
   e. Visibility
      1) Prevailing visibility is reported in statute miles with a space and then fractions of statute miles, as needed, with **SM** appended to it.
      2) Automated reporting stations will show visibility less than 1/4 SM as **M1/4SM**.
   f. Weather and obstructions to visibility
      1) **−SHRA** means light rain showers.
      2) **+TSRA** means thunderstorm with heavy rain.
   g. Sky condition
      1) A ceiling layer is not designated in the METAR code.
         a) The ceiling is the lowest broken or overcast layer, or vertical visibility into an obscuration.
      2) Cloud bases are reported with three digits in hundreds of feet AGL.
         a) EXAMPLE: **OVC010** means overcast clouds at 1,000 ft. AGL.

3) Total obscurations are reported in the format "VVhhh" with VV meaning vertical visibility and "hhh" being the vertical visibility in hundreds of feet.

a) EXAMPLES:

i) **VV010** means vertical visibility of 1,000 ft.
ii) **VV001** means vertical visibility (spoken as an indefinite ceiling) of 100 ft.

h. Temperature and dew point

i. Altimeter

1) Altimeter settings are reported in a four-digit format and prefixed with an "A" to denote the unit of measure as inches of mercury.

2) EXAMPLE: **A3007** means altimeter setting of 30.07 in. of Hg.

j. Remarks

1) **RAB57** means rain began at 57 min. past the hour.

2) **RAE44** means rain ended at 44 min. past the hour.

3) **PK WND 32039/43** means peak wind, 320° true at 39 kt., occurred at 43 min. past the hour.

a) PK WND remark is included whenever the peak wind exceeds 25 kt.

4) A maintenance indicator (dollar) sign, **$**, is included when an automated weather reporting station detects that maintenance is needed on the system.

3. EXAMPLE: METAR KDAL 131755Z 16005KT 7SM SCT023 OVC100 30/22 A3007

a. METAR is routine weather report.

b. KDAL is Dallas, TX.

c. 131755Z means the report was taken on the 13th day at 1755 UTC (or Zulu).

d. 16005KT means the wind is from 160° true at 5 kt.

e. 7SM means visibility is 7 SM.

f. SCT023 OVC100 means a scattered cloud layer at 2,300 ft. and the ceiling is an overcast layer at 10,000 ft.

g. 30/22 means the temperature is 30°C and the dew point is 22°C.

h. A3007 means the altimeter setting is 30.07 in. of Hg.

4. **Transparent sky cover** is clouds or obscuring phenomena aloft through which blue sky or a high sky cover is visible.

5. A **squall** is a sudden increase of at least 15 kt. in average wind speed to a sustained speed of 20 kt. or more for at least 1 minute.

6. **Runway visibility** is the distance down the runway that a pilot can see unlighted objects.

7. As a general rule, the data that may be manually added to the Automated Weather Observing Station (AWOS) report by an observer are limited to

a. Thunderstorms (intensity and direction)
b. Precipitation (type and intensity)
c. Obstructions to vision when the visibility is 3 SM or less

16.9 TERMINAL AERODROME FORECAST (TAF) (Questions 56-64)

1. Terminal aerodrome forecasts (TAF) are weather forecasts for selected airports throughout the country. They are a source of weather to expect at your destination airport at your ETA.
2. Forecasts are issued three times a day for the next 24-hr. period.
3. **The Format of a TAF**
   a. Type of report
      1) **TAF** is a routine forecast.
      2) **TAF AMD** is an amended forecast.
   b. ICAO station identifier
   c. Issuance date/time
      1) The first two digits are the date and the last four digits are the time in UTC when the forecast is issued.
   d. Valid period
      1) The first two digits are the date followed by the two-digit beginning hour and the two-digit ending hour.
   e. The first forecast group follows the valid period and always includes the wind, visibility, and sky condition elements.
4. The forecast portion of the TAF includes the following:
   a. Wind
      1) A calm wind (3 kt. or less) is forecast as **00000KT.**
   b. Visibility (expressed in statute miles)
   c. Weather
      1) The term **VC** applies to weather conditions expected to occur in the vicinity of the airport (within a 5-to-10 SM radius of the airport) but not at the airport itself.
      2) EXAMPLE: **VCTS** means thunderstorms are expected within a 5-to-10 SM radius of the airport but not at the airport itself.
   d. Sky condition
      1) If cumulonimbus clouds are expected at the airport, the contraction **CB** is appended to the cloud layer, which represents the base of the cumulonimbus cloud(s).
         a) Cumulonimbus clouds are the only cloud type forecast in TAFs.
5. A PROB40 (PROBability) HHhh group in a TAF indicates the probability of thunderstorms or other precipitation.
6. EXAMPLE: TAF

   KSJT 031745Z 031818 12012KT 6SM HZ BKN016
   FM2000 17018KT BKN025
   FM2200 BKN030 OVC250 PROB40 2303 1SM +TSRA OVC008CB
   FM0900 27020G34KT 2SM OVC010CB RA BR=

   a. TAF is a routine forecast issuance.
   b. KSJT is San Angelo, TX.
   c. 031745Z 031818 means the TAF was issued on the third day at 1745 UTC and is valid from the third day at 1800 UTC until the following day at 1800 UTC.

d. 12012KT 6SM HZ BKN016 means the forecast from 1800 UTC to 2000 UTC, wind 120° true at 12 kt., visibility 6 SM in haze, broken cloud layer base at 1,600 ft.

e. FM2000 17018KT BKN025 means the forecast from 2000 UTC to 2200 UTC, wind 170° true at 18 kt., broken cloud layer base at 2,500 ft.

f. FM2200 BKN030 OVC250 PROB40 2303 1SM +TSRA OVC008CB means the forecast from 2200 UTC to 0900 UTC, broken cloud layer base at 3,000 ft., overcast cloud layer base at 25,000 ft. Between the hours of 2300 UTC and 0300 UTC, there is a 40% probability of visibility reduced to 1 SM, thunderstorm, heavy rain, and overcast cumulonimbus cloud layer base at 800 ft.

g. FM0900 27020G34KT 2SM OVC010CB RA BR= means the forecast from 0900 UTC until 1800 UTC, wind 270° true at 20 kt., gusts to 34 kt., visibility 2 SM in rain and mist, overcast cumulonimbus clouds at 1,000 ft. The equal sign (=) indicates the end of the TAF.

16.10 MISCELLANEOUS CHARTS AND FORECASTS (Questions 65-75)

1. **In-flight aviation weather advisories** contain information regarding volcanic eruption, turbulence, and icing conditions for a specific region.
2. Isobars on a surface weather chart represent lines of equal pressure reduced to sea level.
3. A prognostic chart depicts the conditions forecast to exist at a specific time in the future.
4. For international flights, a High-Level Significant Weather Prognostic Chart is prepared for use between 25,000 ft. and 60,000 ft. pressure altitude (FL 250 to FL 600).
5. Forecast winds and temperatures aloft for an international flight may be obtained by consulting Winds and Temperatures Aloft Charts prepared by the U.S. National Meteorological Center (NMC).
6. Thunderstorm activity that may grow to severe intensity is indicated on the Severe Weather Outlook Chart as **APCHG**.
7. A convective outlook (AC) provides perspectives of both general and severe thunderstorm activity during the following 24 hr.
8. PIREPs, AIRMETs, and SIGMETs reflect the most accurate information on current and forecast icing conditions.
9. The tropopause data chart is issued once daily with a valid time of 1800 UTC and may be used from 1800 UTC, plus or minus 6 hr. (i.e., 1200 to 2400 UTC).
   a. Vertical wind shear can be determined directly from the dashed lines on the tropopause data chart.
      1) The vertical wind shear critical for probable turbulence is 6 kt. or more per 1,000 ft.
   b. Horizontal wind shear can be determined from the spacing of the isotachs.
      1) The horizontal wind shear critical for turbulence (moderate or greater) is greater than 18 kt. per 150 NM.

16.11 CONSTANT PRESSURE ANALYSIS CHARTS (Questions 76-85)

1. Constant pressure analysis charts provide information about the observed upper-air temperature, wind, and temperature/dew point spread along the proposed route.
2. Height contours (solid lines) depict highs, lows, troughs, and ridges aloft in the same manner as isobars on a surface chart.

a. Height of a pressure system center is denoted with a bold three-digit code below the pressure system symbol.

1) On 300-mb and 500-mb charts, add a zero to the code; e.g., **912** means 9,120 meters MSL.

2) Height is expressed in meters MSL.

3) On a 200-mb chart, add a prefix of 1 and a 0 at the end; e.g., **210** means 12,100 meters MSL.

b. A three-dimensional picture can be developed by interpreting the solid height contour lines.

3. Isotachs appear only on the 300- and 200-mb charts.

a. They are marked by dashed lines.
b. They are lines of equal wind speed.
c. Areas of strong winds are denoted by hatching (70-110 kt.).
d. A clear area within a hatched area denotes 110-150 kt.
e. To interpret the jet stream path, find the winds of 50 kt. and greater.

4. Determine vertical development of a low-pressure area by comparing the 500-, 300-, and 200-mb charts.

a. A low that tilts little with height, with upper winds encircling the low, identifies a slow-moving storm which may cause extensive and persistent cloudiness, precipitation, and adverse flying conditions.

5. The temperature, temperature/dew point spread (moisture content), and winds aloft are shown on constant pressure charts for various flight levels. Note that these are given in pressure altitude, not true altitude.

a. 500 mb (18,000 ft.)
b. 300 mb (30,000 ft.)
c. 200 mb (39,000 ft.)

6. Weather stations which send up radiosondes (i.e., small weather balloons) are indicated on the chart and provide

a. Temperature
b. Temperature/dew point spread
c. Wind
d. Height of pressure surface
e. Height of pressure surface change over previous 12 hr.
f. EXAMPLE:

Wind	210° at 10 kt.
Temperature	–03°C
Temperature/dew point spread	+8°C
Height of constant pressure surface	5,900 meters
Previous 12-hr. height change	+20 meters

7. On the constant pressure analysis chart, satellite and aircraft observations are used in the analysis over areas of sparse data.

a. A satellite observation is plotted using a star at the cloud top location.
b. An aircraft observation is plotted using a square at the aircraft location.

16.12 AIRMETS AND SIGMETS (Questions 86-90)

1. SIGMETs and AIRMETs are issued to notify en route pilots of the possibility of encountering hazardous flying conditions.
   a. If a SIGMET alert is announced by an ARTCC or terminal facilities, you should contact the nearest FSS to obtain the information contained in the SIGMET.
2. AIRMETs apply to light aircraft to notify of
   a. Moderate icing
   b. Moderate turbulence
   c. Visibility less than 3 SM or ceilings less than 1,000 ft. affecting over 50% of the area at one time
   d. Sustained surface winds of 30 kt. or more
   e. Extensive mountain obscurement
3. SIGMET advisories include weather phenomena potentially hazardous to all aircraft.
   a. Convective SIGMETs
      1) Severe thunderstorm due to
         a) Surface winds greater than or equal to 50 kt.
         b) Hail at the surface greater than or equal to ¾ in. in diameter
         c) Tornadoes
      2) A line of thunderstorms
      3) Embedded thunderstorms
      4) Thunderstorm areas greater than or equal to thunderstorm intensity level 4 with coverage of 40% or more of an area at least 3,000 square miles
   b. SIGMETs
      1) Severe icing not associated with thunderstorms
      2) Severe or extreme turbulence or clear air turbulence (CAT) not related to thunderstorms
      3) Duststorms, sandstorms, or volcanic ash lowering surface or in-flight visibilities to below 3 SM
      4) Volcanic eruption
4. Convective SIGMETs indicating a LVL 5 (level 5) means an intense thunderstorm. The outlook section of a convective SIGMET is for 2 to 6 hr. after the valid time.

QUESTIONS AND ANSWER EXPLANATIONS

All the FAA questions from the pilot knowledge test for the ATP certificate relating to aviation weather reports and forecasts and the material outlined previously are reproduced on the following pages in the same modules as the outlines. To the immediate right of each question are the correct answer and answer explanation. You should cover these answers and answer explanations while responding to the questions. Refer to the general discussion in Chapter 1 on how to take the FAA pilot knowledge test.

Remember that the questions from the FAA pilot knowledge test bank have been reordered by topic, and the topics are organized into a meaningful sequence. Accordingly, the first line of the answer explanation gives the FAA question number and the citation of the authoritative source for the answer.

16.1 Pilot Weather Report (PIREP)

1.
9250. Which type of weather can only be directly observed during flight and then reported in a PIREP?

A—Structural icing.
B—Jetstream-type winds.
C—Level of the tropopause.

Answer (A) is correct (9250). *(AWS Sect 3)*
Pilots are urged to volunteer directly observed reports of thunderstorms, icing, turbulence, wind shear, cloud bases (tops and layers), visibility, precipitation, wind, and temperature at altitude. The question requires the condition observable only by a pilot, which is structural icing. Weather observers cannot observe structural icing, but they can observe the jet stream and tropopause level.
Answer (B) is incorrect because a pilot would not be able to determine from observation if jet stream-type winds or other CAT were encountered. Answer (C) is incorrect because the level of the tropopause is determined by radiosondes released by ground weather observing stations. It is not a type of weather that can be directly observed by a pilot during flight.

2.
9264. What type turbulence should be reported when it momentarily causes slight, erratic changes in altitude and/or attitude, one-third to two-thirds of the time?

A—Occasional light chop.
B—Moderate chop.
C—Intermittent light turbulence.

Answer (C) is correct (9264). *(AIM Para 7-1-21)*
Light turbulence is defined as turbulence that momentarily causes slight, erratic changes in altitude and/or attitude. Intermittent is defined as occurring from one-third to two-thirds of the time.
Answer (A) is incorrect because light chop does not cause any appreciable changes in altitude and/or attitude, and occasional is less than one-third of the time.
Answer (B) is incorrect because moderate chop does not cause any appreciable changes in altitude and/or attitude.

3.
9262. What type turbulence should be reported when it causes slight, rapid, and somewhat rhythmic bumpiness without appreciable changes in attitude or altitude, less than one-third of the time?

A—Occasional light chop.
B—Moderate turbulence.
C—Moderate chop.

Answer (A) is correct (9262). *(AIM Para 7-1-21)*
Light chop is turbulence that causes slight, rapid, and somewhat rhythmic bumpiness without appreciable changes in attitude or altitude. Occasional is defined as occurring less than one-third of the time.
Answer (B) is incorrect because moderate turbulence causes a change in the aircraft's attitude and/or altitude. Answer (C) is incorrect because moderate chop causes rapid, not rhythmic, bumps or jolts, which are not "slight."

4.
9263. What type turbulence should be reported when it causes changes in altitude and/or attitude more than two-thirds of the time, with the aircraft remaining in positive control at all times?

A—Continuous severe chop.
B—Continuous moderate turbulence.
C—Intermittent moderate turbulence.

Answer (B) is correct (9263). *(AIM Para 7-1-21)*
Moderate turbulence is defined as turbulence that causes changes in altitude and/or attitude, but the aircraft remains in positive control at all times. Continuous is defined as occurring more than two-thirds of the time.
Answer (A) is incorrect because severe chop is not a turbulence reporting term. Answer (C) is incorrect because intermittent means that turbulence is occurring from one-third to two-thirds of the time.

5.
9713.
KFTW UA/OV DFW/TM 1753/FL095/TP PA30
/SK 036 OVC 060/075 OVC/RM TOPS UNKN.

This pilot report to Fort Worth (KFTW) indicates

A—several overcast layers including one above 9,500 feet.
B—a clear layer between 3,600 feet and 6,000 feet.
C—the base of an overcast layer at 7,500 feet.

Answer (C) is correct (9713). *(AWS Sect 3)*
In the PIREP, the sky cover is coded as /SK 036 OVC 060/075 OVC, which means two overcast layers are reported. The first has a base of 3,600 ft. with tops at 6,000 ft., and the second overcast layer has a base of 7,500 ft. A remark states the tops are unknown.
Answer (A) is incorrect because, while several overcast layers are reported, only the top of the second overcast layer is above the airplane's altitude of 9,500 ft. The pilot cannot observe that there is an overcast layer above 9,500 ft. Answer (B) is incorrect because an overcast layer, not a clear layer, is between 3,600 ft. and 6,000 ft.

16.2 En Route Weather Advisories

6.
9258. What type service should normally be expected from an En Route Flight Advisory Service?

A—Weather advisories pertinent to the type of flight, intended route of flight, and altitude.
B—Severe weather information, changes in flight plans, and receipt of position reports.
C—Radar vectors for traffic separation, route weather advisories, and altimeter settings.

Answer (A) is correct (9258). ***(AIM Para 7-1-4)***
En Route Flight Advisory Service (EFAS) is specifically designed to provide en route aircraft with timely and meaningful weather advisories pertinent to the type of flight, intended route of flight, and altitude. EFAS is also a central collection and distribution point for pilot-reported weather information (PIREP).
Answer (B) is incorrect because flight plan changes are services provided through Flight Service Stations, not by EFAS. Answer (C) is incorrect because radar vectors and altimeter settings are services that can be provided by ATC, not EFAS.

7.
9261. Below FL 180, en route weather advisories should be obtained from an FSS on

A—122.1 MHz.
B—122.0 MHz.
C—123.6 MHz.

Answer (B) is correct (9261). ***(AIM Para 7-1-4)***
En Route Flight Advisory Service (EFAS) provides communications capabilities for aircraft flying 5,000 ft. AGL to 17,500 ft. MSL on a common frequency of 122.0 MHz. EFAS is normally available from 6 a.m. to 10 p.m.
Answer (A) is incorrect because 122.1 MHz is normally a remote frequency used by FSS at a NAVAID site. A pilot transmits on 122.1 MHz, and the FSS receives on this frequency. The FSS transmits back to the pilot on the NAVAID frequency. Answer (C) is incorrect because 123.6 MHz is the CTAF frequency used by an FSS located on an airport without an operating control tower.

8.
9705. The Hazardous Inflight Weather Advisory Service (HIWAS) is a continuous broadcast over selected VORs of

A—SIGMETs, CONVECTIVE SIGMETs, AIRMETs, Severe Weather Forecast Alerts (AWW), and Center Weather Advisories (CWA).
B—SIGMETs, CONVECTIVE SIGMETs, AIRMETs, Wind Shear Advisories, and Severe Weather Forecast Alerts (AWW).
C—Wind Shear Advisories, Radar Weather Reports, SIGMETs, CONVECTIVE SIGMETs, AIRMETs, and Center Weather Advisories (CWA).

Answer (A) is correct (9705). ***(AIM Para 7-1-9)***
The Hazardous Inflight Weather Advisory Service (HIWAS) is a continuous broadcast service over selected VORs of in-flight weather advisories, i.e., SIGMETs, convective SIGMETs, AIRMETs, severe weather forecast alerts (AWW), and center weather advisories (CWA).
Answer (B) is incorrect because a runway wind shear advisory is given by a tower controller, not HIWAS, to arriving and departing aircraft. Answer (C) is incorrect because radar weather reports are available from En Route Flight Advisory Service (EFAS), not HIWAS.

9.
9256. At what time are current AIRMETs broadcast in their entirety by the Hazardous Inflight Weather Advisory Service (HIWAS)?

A—15 and 45 minutes after the hour during the first hour after issuance, and upon receipt.
B—Every 15 minutes until the AIRMET is canceled.
C—There is a continuous broadcast over selected VORs of Inflight Weather Advisories.

Answer (C) is correct (9256). ***(AIM Para 7-1-9)***
HIWAS is a continuous broadcast over selected VORs of in-flight weather advisories including AIRMETs, SIGMETs, convective SIGMETs, center weather advisories, urgent PIREPs, and summarized severe weather forecast alerts.
Answer (A) is incorrect because, in those areas without HIWAS, an FSS will broadcast a current AIRMET in its entirety upon receipt and at 15 and 45 min. past the hour during the first hour of issuance. Answer (B) is incorrect because a HIWAS is a continuous broadcast, not every 15 min., of in-flight weather advisories.

16.3 TWEB Route Forecasts

10.
9282. How can the pilot obtain TWEB Route Forecast information?

A—From the TEL TWEB and Telephone Voice Response Systems (VRS).
B—From the ATIS and Pilots Automatic Telephone Weather.
C—From ARTCC and Automated Flight Service Station briefings.

Answer (A) is correct (9282). *(AIM Para 7-1-8)*
A pilot can obtain TWEB Route Forecast information by telephone access to the TWEB (TEL TWEB) and Telephone Voice Response Systems (VRS). These numbers are found in the FSS and National Weather Service telephone numbers section of the *Airport/Facility Directory*.
Answer (B) is incorrect because ATIS provides only weather information and non-control information in selected high-activity terminal areas. Pilots Automatic Telephone Weather Answering Service (PATWAS) contains a weather summary for a 50-NM area of the parent station. Answer (C) is incorrect because ARTCC (air route traffic control center) provides air traffic control, not weather, information to pilots.

11.
9703. The TWEB Route Forecasts and Synopses are issued by the Weather Service Forecast Offices (WSFOs) three times per day according to time zone. The TWEB forecast is valid for an

A—8-hour period.
B—12-hour period.
C—15-hour period.

Answer (C) is correct (9703). *(AWS Sect 4)*
The TWEB Route Forecasts and Synopses are issued by Weather Forecast Offices (WFO, formerly known as a WSFO) three times per day according to time zone. The TWEB forecast is valid for a 15-hr. period. This schedule provides 24-hr. coverage with most frequent updating during the hours of greatest general aviation activity.
Answer (A) is incorrect because the TWEB forecast is valid for a 15-hr., not an 8-hr., period. Answer (B) is incorrect because an area forecast (FA), not a TWEB forecast, contains a 12-hr. specific forecast (followed by a 6-hr. categorical outlook) in the VFR clouds and weather section.

16.4 Radar Summary Chart

12.
9306. (Refer to figure 152 on page 728.) What weather conditions are depicted in the area indicated by arrow A on the Radar Summary Chart?

A—Moderate to strong echoes; echo tops 30,000 feet MSL; line movement toward the northwest.
B—Weak to moderate echoes; average echo bases 30,000 feet MSL; cell movement toward the southeast; rain showers with thunder.
C—Strong to very strong echoes; echo tops 30,000 feet MSL; thunderstorms and rain showers.

Answer (C) is correct (9306). *(AWS Chap 7)*
On Fig. 152, find point A (SE S. Dakota). Note that it points to a dot indicating the highest top in hundreds of feet, which is 30,000 (00 has been dropped). It lies within the second ring in a circuit, making it level 3 to 4, which is strong to very strong. The entire area is TRW, which is thunderstorms and rainshowers.
Answer (A) is incorrect because an area within the first contour is level 1 to 2, or weak to moderate echo intensity. Strong echo intensity is a level 3, which is indicated within the second contour. The line movement is to the northeast, not northwest, as indicated by the shaft and barb combination located in southern Nebraska. Answer (B) is incorrect because weak to moderate echoes are located in the first contour. The "300" over the line indicates the tops, not bases, at 30,000 ft. MSL.

13.
9309. (Refer to figure 152 on page 728.) What weather conditions are depicted in the area indicated by arrow B on the Radar Summary Chart?

A—Weak echoes; heavy rain showers; area movement toward the southeast.
B—Weak to moderate echoes; rain showers increasing in intensity.
C—Strong echoes; moderate rain showers; no cell movement.

Answer (B) is correct (9309). *(AWS Chap 7)*
The arrow from B (eastern S. Dakota) on Fig. 152 points to the first level of contours, which is weak to moderate intensity with rainshowers increasing in intensity as indicated by RW+.
Answer (A) is incorrect because only intensity of precipitation (increasing or decreasing), not heavy or light, is depicted on a radar summary chart. The area of movement is to the northeast, not southeast, as indicated by the shaft and barb combination located in southern Nebraska. Answer (C) is incorrect because strong echoes are level 3, which is indicated by the second contour line on the radar summary chart. Precipitation is indicated by increasing or decreasing, not moderate.

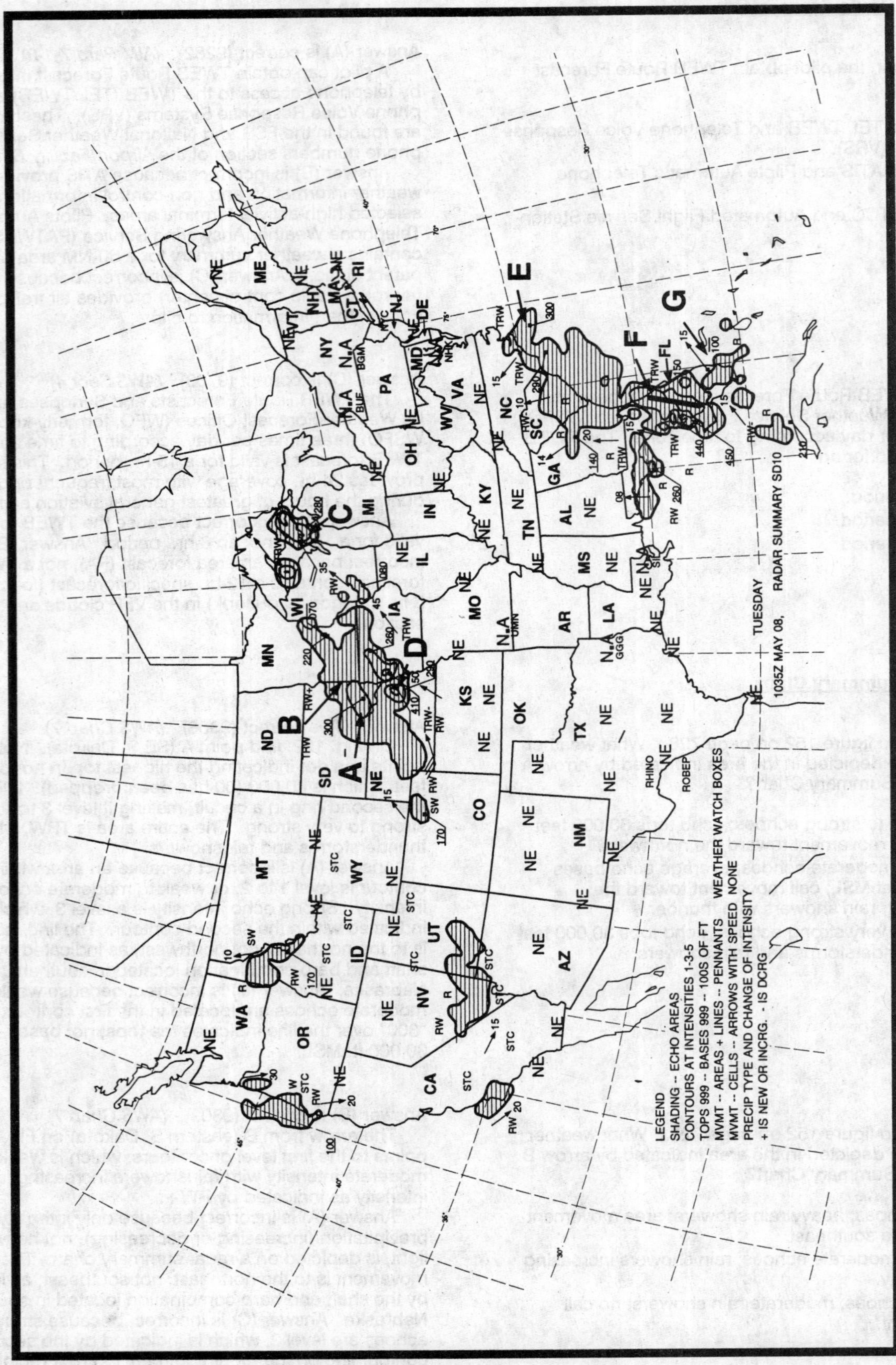

FIGURE 152.—Radar Summary Chart.

14.
9308. (Refer to figure 152 on page 728.) What weather conditions are depicted in the area indicated by arrow C on the Radar Summary Chart?

A—Average echo bases 2,800 feet MSL; thundershowers; intense to extreme echo intensity.
B—Cell movement toward the northwest at 20 knots; intense echoes; echo bases 28,000 feet MSL.
C—Area movement toward the northeast at 20 knots; strong to very strong echoes; echo tops 28,000 feet MSL.

Answer (C) is correct (9308). *(AWS Chap 7)*
The point of the arrow from C (N. Michigan) on Fig. 152 is in the second level of contours, which indicates strong to very strong echo intensity. The 280 indicates 28,000 ft. MSL tops. The arrow with two feathers indicates 20-kt. northeast movement.
Answer (A) is incorrect because 280 indicates tops of 28,000 ft. MSL, not bases of 2,800 ft. MSL. Answer (B) is incorrect because point C would be in the third, not second, level of contour if the echoes were intense.

15.
9307. (Refer to figure 152 on page 728.) What weather conditions are depicted in the area indicated by arrow D on the Radar Summary Chart?

A—Echo tops 4,100 feet MSL; strong to very strong echoes within the smallest contour; area movement toward the northeast at 50 knots.
B—Intense to extreme echoes within the smallest contour; echo tops 29,000 feet MSL; cell movement toward the northeast at 50 knots.
C—Strong to very strong echoes within the smallest contour; echo bases 29,000 feet MSL; cell in northeast Nebraska moving northeast at 50 knots.

Answer (B) is correct (9307). *(AWS Chap 7)*
The arrow extending from D (NE Nebraska) in Fig. 152 is in the third contour, which means that the echo intensity is intense to extreme. The 290 indicates tops of 29,000 ft. MSL. The arrow with the 50 on top of it indicates movement to the northeast at 50 kt.
Answer (A) is incorrect because the 410 is for another area of echoes to the northeast of the D arrow, with tops of 41,000 ft. MSL, not 4,100 ft. MSL. Answer (C) is incorrect because the tops, not bases, are 29,000 ft. MSL, and the echoes are intense to extreme, not strong to very strong.

16.5 Weather Depiction Chart

16.
9265. What conditions are indicated on a Weather Depiction Chart?

A—Actual sky cover, visibility restrictions, and type of precipitation at reporting stations.
B—Forecast ceilings and visibilities over a large geographic area.
C—Actual en route weather conditions between reporting stations.

Answer (A) is correct (9265). *(AWS Sect 6)*
The weather depiction chart is computer prepared from the observations reported by both manual and automated observation locations to provide a broad overview of observed conditions as of the time the chart was prepared. The chart indicates actual sky cover, visibility restrictions, and type of precipitation at reporting stations.
Answer (B) is incorrect because the weather depiction chart is not a forecast but an overview of observed conditions at a specified time. Answer (C) is incorrect because the weather depiction chart indicates actual weather conditions at a reporting station only as of a specified time.

17.
9299. What is indicated on the Weather Depiction Chart by a continuous smooth line enclosing a hatched geographic area?

A—The entire area has ceilings less than 1,000 feet and/or visibility less than 3 miles.
B—More than 50 percent of the area enclosed by the smooth line is predicted to have IFR conditions.
C—Reporting stations within the enclosed area are all showing IFR conditions at the time of the report.

Answer (C) is correct (9299). *(AWS Sect 6)*
A continuous smooth line enclosing a hatched area indicates that all reporting stations within the enclosed area are reporting IFR weather conditions at the time of the report.
Answer (A) is incorrect because the weather depiction chart indicates observed weather at reporting stations at the time of the chart. There may be some areas without a reporting station within the enclosed area that are not IMC. Answer (B) is incorrect because the weather depiction chart reflects only observed weather, not forecast weather, at reporting stations.

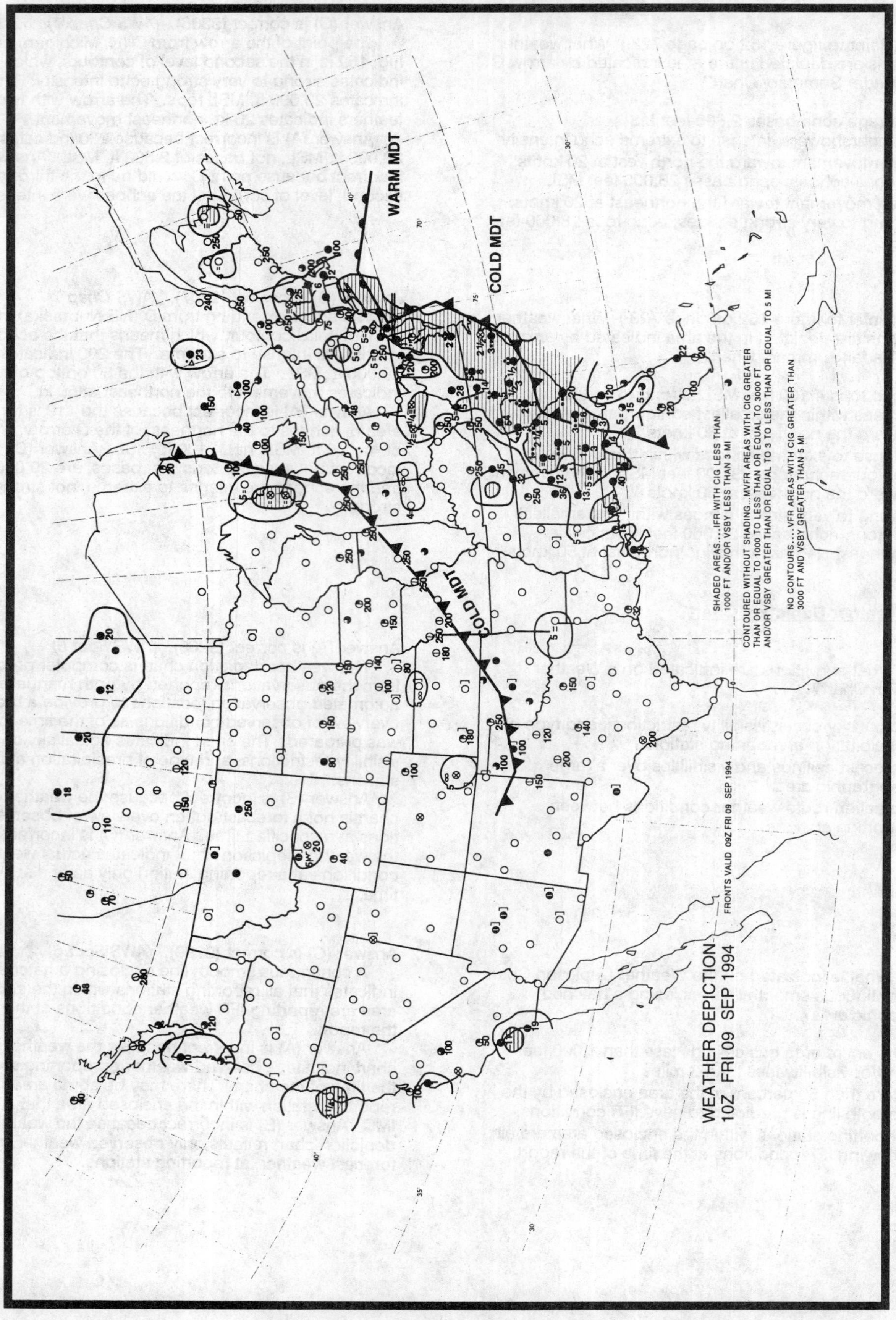

FIGURE 150.—Weather Depiction Chart.

18.
9298. (Refer to figure 150 on page 730.) The Weather Depiction Chart indicates that the coastal sections of Texas and Louisiana are reporting

A—all ceilings at or above 20,000 feet with visibilities of 20 miles or more.
B—marginal VFR conditions due to broken ceilings of 3,200 feet.
C—VFR conditions with scattered clouds at 3,200 feet.

Answer (C) is the best answer (9298). *(AWS Sect 6)*
The station in southwest Louisiana is reporting a sky cover that is scattered with the base of the lowest layer at 3,200 ft. Since the area is not contoured, the conditions are VFR.
Answer (A) is incorrect because a station with the visibility data missing means only that visibility is greater than 6 SM, not 20 SM, and most of the coast is reporting clear skies, not ceilings at or above 20,000 ft. Answer (B) is incorrect because the station in southeast Louisiana is reporting overcast, not broken, skies with a ceiling of 1,600, not 3,200, ft.

19.
9297. (Refer to figure 150 on page 730.) The IFR conditions in the vicinity of Lakes Superior, Huron, and Michigan were caused by

A—overcast sky and haze.
B—convective action during the front's passage.
C—obscured skies and fog.

Answer (C) is correct (9297). *(AWS Sect 6)*
The area off the northern tip of Michigan shows obscured skies, by the "X" in the station circle, and fog, by the "=" symbol to the left of the station circle. Since the area is shaded, the conditions are IFR.
Answer (A) is incorrect because an "X" in the station model indicates an obscured, not overcast, sky, and "=" indicates fog, not haze. Answer (B) is incorrect because the weather depiction chart does not indicate convective action, only sky conditions and visibility.

16.6 Low-Level Significant Weather Prognostic Chart

20.
9254. The U.S. Low-Level Significant Weather Prognostic Chart depicts weather conditions

A—that are forecast to exist at a specific time shown on the chart.
B—as they existed at the time the chart was prepared.
C—that are forecast to exist 6 hours after the chart was prepared.

Answer (A) is correct (9254). *(AWS Sect 8)*
A low-level prognostic chart contains four panels: the two on the left are for 12 hr. after the time of issuance, and the two on the right are for 24 hr. after issuance. The two on the top are significant weather progs, and the two on the bottom are surface progs.
Answer (B) is incorrect because prognostic charts forecast conditions, not report observed conditions (as does a weather depiction chart). Answer (C) is incorrect because the low-level prognostic chart forecasts conditions 12 and 24 hr., not 6 hr., after the time of issuance.

21.
9301. (Refer to figure 151 on page 733.) The 12-Hour Significant Weather Prognostic Chart indicates that eastern Kentucky and eastern Tennessee can expect probable ceilings

A—less than 1,000 feet and/or visibility less than 3 miles.
B—less than 1,000 feet and/or visibility less than 3 miles, and moderate turbulence below 10,000 feet MSL.
C—less than 1,000 feet and/or visibility less than 3 miles, and moderate turbulence above 10,000 feet MSL.

Answer (A) is correct (9301). *(AWS Chap 8)*
The 12-hour significant weather prognostic is on panel A of Fig. 151. Eastern Kentucky and eastern Tennessee are enclosed in a solid line, which indicates IFR, i.e., ceiling less than 1,000 ft. and/or visibility less than 3 SM.
Answer (B) is incorrect because no turbulence is forecast for eastern Kentucky and eastern Tennessee on the 12-hr. significant weather prog. Turbulence is indicated by a dashed line, such as the one which includes parts of western Kentucky and Tennessee. Answer (C) is incorrect because no turbulence is forecast for eastern Kentucky and eastern Tennessee. Turbulence is indicated by a dashed line such as the one which includes parts of western Kentucky and Tennessee.

22.
9302. (Refer to figure 151 on page 733.) The chart symbols over southern California on the 12-Hour Significant Weather Prognostic Chart indicate

A—expected top of moderate turbulent layer to be 12,000 feet MSL.
B—expected base of moderate turbulent layer to be 12,000 feet MSL.
C—light turbulence expected above 12,000 feet MSL.

Answer (A) is correct (9302). *(AWS Chap 8)*

On the 12-hour significant weather prognostic chart (panel A of Fig. 151), the symbol "_/_" indicates moderate turbulence. The expected top and base of the turbulent layer appear above and below a short line in hundreds of ft. MSL. Absence of a figure below the line (as here) indicates turbulence from the surface up. No figure above the line indicates turbulence extending above the upper limit of the chart. Thus, in southern California, moderate turbulence is expected from the surface up to 12,000 ft. MSL.

Answer (B) is incorrect because 12,000 ft. MSL is the top of the turbulence, not the base. Answer (C) is incorrect because the symbol shows moderate, not light, turbulence that is below, not above, 12,000 ft. MSL.

23.
9300. (Refer to figure 151 on page 733.) The 12-Hour Significant Weather Prognostic Chart indicates that West Virginia will likely experience

A—continuous or showery precipitation covering half or more of the area.
B—thunderstorms and rain showers covering half or more of the area.
C—continuous rain covering less than half of the area.

Answer (A) is correct (9300). *(AWS Chap 8)*

The shaded area covering West Virginia on the 12-hour surface prognostic chart (panel B of Fig. 151) indicates 50% or more coverage (because of the shading). The two solid dots indicate continuous rain. The small dot over the triangle indicates rain showers.

Answer (B) is incorrect because thunderstorms are indicated by an R with an arrow on its front leg. Answer (C) is incorrect because coverage of less than half of the area is indicated by the absence of shading. An area of continuous rain is outlined in a solid, not dash-dot, line.

24.
9303. (Refer to figure 151 on page 733.) A planned low-altitude flight from central Oklahoma to western Tennessee at 1200Z is likely to encounter

A—continuous or intermittent rain or rain showers, moderate turbulence, and freezing temperatures below 8,000 feet.
B—continuous or showery rain over half or more of the area, moderate turbulence, and freezing temperatures above 10,000 feet.
C—showery precipitation covering less than half the area, no turbulence below 18,000 feet, and freezing temperatures above 12,000 feet.

Answer (B) is correct (9303). *(AWS Chap 8)*

1200Z is on the right panels of Fig. 151. The lower panel (panel D) shows continuous rain as indicated by two dots in the shaded area. Additionally, rain showers are shown by the triangle with the dot above it. Now look on panel C. The route of flight appears to be halfway between the 8,000-ft. freezing level and the 12,000-ft. freezing level. Thus, freezing temperatures should be above 10,000 ft. Also, there is a symbol indicating moderate turbulence.

Answer (A) is incorrect because the route of flight is south of the 8,000-ft. freezing level. Answer (C) is incorrect because the shading indicates more, not less, than 50% rain coverage, the turbulence is up to, not above, 18,000 ft., and temperatures are probably freezing above 10,000 ft., not 12,000 ft.

16.7 Winds and Temperatures Aloft Forecasts (FD)

25.
9296. What wind direction and speed aloft are forecast by this WINDS AND TEMPERATURE ALOFT FORECAST (FD) report for FL 390 – "731960"?

A—230° at 119 knots.
B—131° at 96 knots.
C—073° at 196 knots.

Answer (A) is correct (9296). *(AWS Sect 4)*

The first two digits are the direction group, and since it is greater than 36, the wind speed must be 100 kt. or greater. Subtract 50 from the direction group to determine wind direction of 230° (73 – 50 = 23). The second two digits are the wind speed; since it was determined that the wind was 100 kt. or greater, add 100 to this group. Thus, the wind speed is 119 kt. (100 + 19 = 119).

Answer (B) is incorrect because coded directions with wind speed over 100 kt. range from 51 through 86. The direction is 230°, not 131°, at 119 kt., not 96 kt. Answer (C) is incorrect because 50 must be subtracted from the first two digits and 100 added to the second two digits. The last two digits are the temperature.

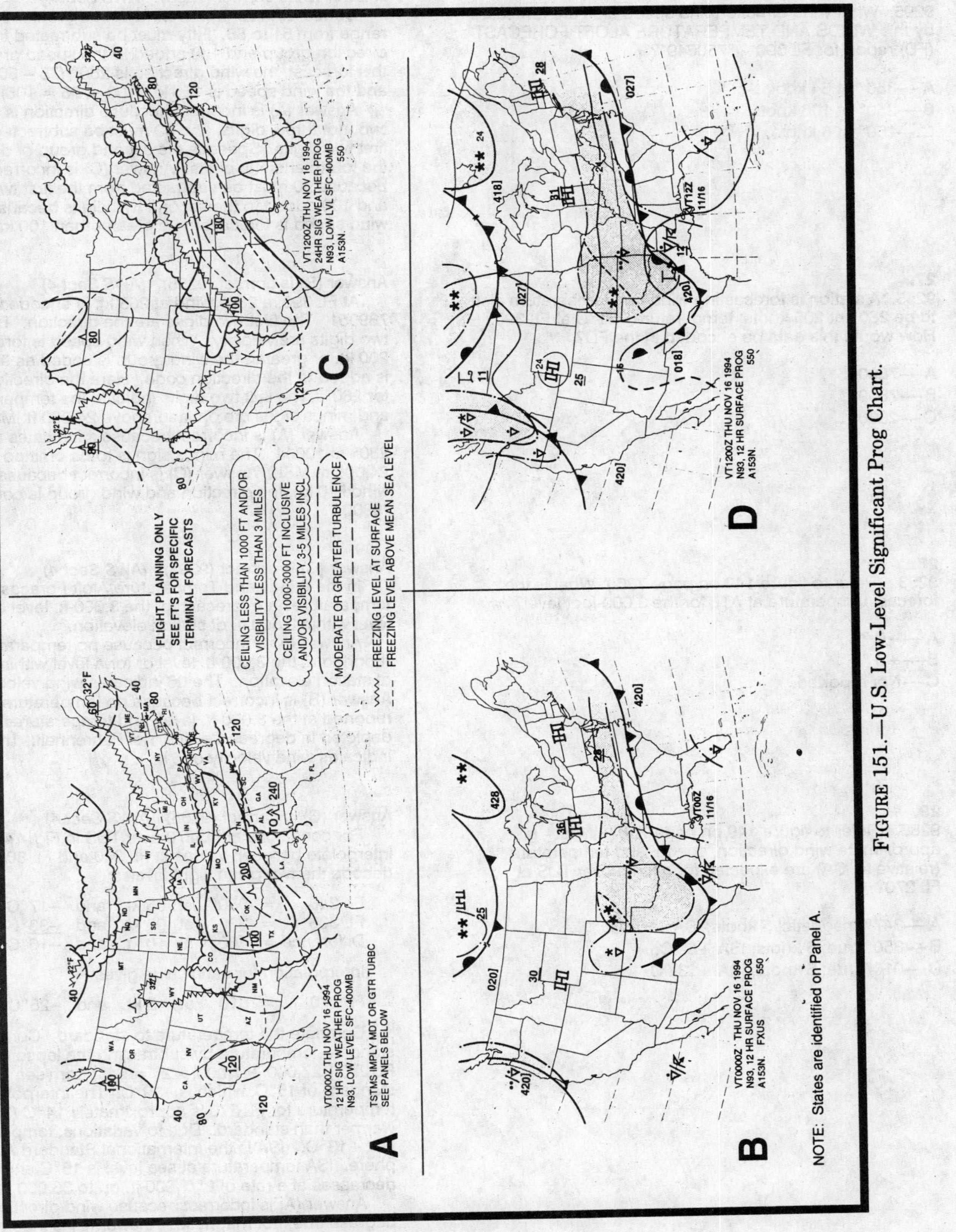

FIGURE 151.—U.S. Low-Level Significant Prog Chart.

26.
9295. What wind direction and speed aloft are forecast by this WINDS AND TEMPERATURE ALOFT FORECAST (FD) report for FL 390 – "750649"?

A—350° at 64 knots.
B—250° at 106 knots.
C—150° at 6 knots.

Answer (B) is correct (9295). *(AWS Sect 4)*

Coded directions with wind speed greater than 100 kt. range from 51 to 86. Fifty must be subtracted from the direction group and 100 added to the speed group. In this forecast, the wind direction is 250° (75 – 50 = 25), and the wind speed is 106 kt. (100 + 06 = 106).

Answer (A) is incorrect because direction is the first two, not three, digits, and 50 must be subtracted from the first two digits. Speed is the second group of digits, not the fourth and fifth digits. Answer (C) is incorrect because 50 must be subtracted from the first two digits and 100 added to the second two digits because the wind speed is forecast to be greater than 100 kt.

27.
9255. A station is forecasting wind and temperature aloft to be 280° at 205 knots; temperature –51°C at FL 390. How would this data be encoded in the FD?

A—7800–51.
B—789951.
C—280051.

Answer (B) is correct (9255). *(AWS Sect 4)*

At FL 390, a 280° wind at 205 kt. is encoded as 789951. The first two digits are the direction. The second two digits are velocity. When wind speed is forecast at 200 kt. or greater, the wind group is coded as 99, and 50 is added to the direction code. Here the direction is 78 for 280°. The last two digits indicate the temperature, and minus signs are omitted above 24,000 ft. MSL.

Answer (A) is incorrect because it indicates a wind at 280° at 100 kt. The minus sign is to be omitted above 24,000 ft. MSL. Answer (C) is incorrect because, if the wind is 0 kt., the direction and wind group is coded "9900."

28.
9293. (Refer to figure 149 on page 736.) What is the forecast temperature at ATL for the 3,000-foot level?

A—+6 °C.
B—+6 °F.
C—Not reported.

Answer (C) is correct (9293). *(AWS Sect 4)*

In the Winds and Temperature Aloft Forecasts, no temperatures are forecast for the 3,000-ft. level or for a level within 2,500 ft. of station elevation.

Answer (A) is incorrect because no temperature is reported at the 3,000-ft. level or for a level within 2,500 ft. of station elevation. The 06 indicates wind velocity of 6 kt. Answer (B) is incorrect because no temperature is reported at the 3,000-ft. level, and temperatures are depicted in degrees Celsius, not Fahrenheit. The 06 indicates wind velocity of 6 kt.

29.
9288. (Refer to figure 149 on page 736.) What approximate wind direction, speed, and temperature (relative to ISA) are expected for a flight over TUS at FL 270?

A—347° magnetic; 5 knots; ISA –10 °C.
B—350° true; 5 knots; ISA +5 °C.
C—010° true; 5 knots; ISA +13 °C.

Answer (C) is correct (9288). *(AWS Sect 4)*

For conditions at FL 270 over TUS in Fig. 149, interpolate between values at FL 240 and FL 300. First decode the two given flight levels:

FL 240	=	050°	at	05 kt.	and	–17°C
FL 300	=	330°	at	05 kt.	and	–33°C
Difference	=	80°	at	0 kt.	and	–16°C

Interpolation for each value gives:

FL 270	=	010°	at	5 kt.	and	–25°C

Compare the temperature to standard. Compute the standard temperature by subtracting the lapse rate at FL 270 [(27,000 ÷ 1,000) x 2° = 54°] from sea level standard of 15°C, which is –39°C. The interpolated temperature for FL 270 is approximately 14°C (39 – 25) warmer than standard. Due to variations, temperature is ISA +13°C. (ISA is the International Standard Atmosphere. ISA temperature at sea level is 15°C and decreases at a rate of 2°/1,000 ft. up to 36,000 ft. MSL.)

Answer (A) is incorrect because wind direction is degrees true, not magnetic. Answer (B) is incorrect because wind direction is 010° true, not 350° true.

30.
9294. (Refer to figure 149 on page 736.) What approximate wind direction, speed, and temperature (relative to ISA) are expected for a flight over MKC at FL 260?

A—260° true; 43 knots; ISA +10 °C.
B—260° true; 45 knots; ISA –10 °C.
C—260° magnetic; 42 knots; ISA +9 °C.

Answer (A) is correct (9294). *(AWS Sect 4)*
For conditions at FL 260 over MKC in Fig. 149, interpolate between values at FL 240 and FL 300. First decode the two given flight levels:

FL 240	=	260°	at	38 kt.	and	–21°C
FL 300	=	260°	at	50 kt.	and	–36°C
Difference	=	0°	at	12 kt.	and	–15°C

Interpolation for each value gives:

FL 260	=	260°	at	42 kt.	and	–26°C

To compare the temperature to standard, subtract the lapse rate at FL 260 [(26,000 ÷ 1,000) x 2° = 52°] from sea level standard of 15°C to get FL 260 standard of –37°C. The interpolated temperature for FL 270 of about –26°C is 11°C warmer than standard. The best answer is 260° true; 43 kt.; ISA +10. (ISA is the International Standard Atmosphere. ISA temperature at sea level is 15°C and decreases at a rate of 2°/1,000 ft. up to 36,000 ft. MSL.)
Answer (B) is incorrect because forecast temperature is warmer, not colder, than ISA. Answer (C) is incorrect because wind direction is degrees true, not magnetic.

31.
9291. (Refer to figure 149 on page 736.) What will be the wind and temperature trend for a DEN-ICT-OKC flight at 11,000 feet?

A—Temperature decrease.
B—Windspeed increase slightly.
C—Wind shift from calm to a westerly direction.

Answer (B) is correct (9291). *(AWS Sect 4)*
To determine the wind and temperature trend, the winds and temperatures aloft must be interpolated for 11,000 ft. The table below shows data for 9,000 and 12,000 ft. and the interpolated data for 11,000 ft.

	9,000	12,000	11,000
DEN	9900+09	9900+04	9900+06
ICT	0607+08	9900+04	0602+05
OKC	1106+10	9900+05	1102+07

The best answer is that wind speed increases slightly from light and variable in DEN to 2 kt. at ICT and OKC.
Answer (A) is incorrect because the temperature increases at OKC to a temperature higher than DEN. Answer (C) is incorrect because the wind shifts from calm to an easterly, not westerly, direction.

32.
9292. (Refer to figure 149 on page 736.) What will be the wind and temperature trend for a DSM-LIT-SHV flight at 12,000 feet?

A—Windspeed decrease.
B—Temperature decrease.
C—Wind direction shift from northwest to southeast.

Answer (A) is correct (9292). *(AWS Sect 4)*
In determining the wind and temperature trend, it is easier to view in a table format. Note that, in this question, no interpolation is needed since 12,000 ft. is an altitude at which data are supplied from the Winds and Temperatures Aloft Forecast. Below is a table of the data:

	DSM	LIT	SHV
12,000 ft.	3022+00	2808+06	2106+06

During this flight, the wind speed decreases from 22 kt. to 8 kt. to 6 kt.
Answer (B) is incorrect because the temperature increases, not decreases, en route. Answer (C) is incorrect because the wind direction shifts from northwest to southwest, not southeast.

33.
9287. (Refer to figure 149 below.) What approximate wind direction, speed, and temperature (relative to ISA) are expected for a flight over OKC at FL 370?

A—265° true; 27 knots; ISA +1 °C.
B—260° true; 27 knots; ISA +6 °C.
C—260° magnetic; 27 knots; ISA +10 °C.

Answer (B) is correct (9287). *(AWS Sect 4)*
For conditions at FL 370 over OKC in Fig. 149, interpolate between values at FL 340 and FL 390. First decode the two given flight levels:

FL 340	=	250°	at	27 kt.	and	–43°C
FL 390	=	270°	at	27 kt.	and	–54°C
Difference	=	20°	at	0 kt.	and	–11°C

Interpolation for each value gives:

FL 370	=	262°	at	27 kt.	and	–50°C

Since the FD is rounded to the nearest 10°, the wind direction is 260°. To compare the temperature to standard temperature, remember that the temperature in the tropopause (36,000 ft. MSL and above) is approximately –56°C. Thus, –50°C is ISA +6°C. (ISA is the International Standard Atmosphere. ISA temperature at sea level is 15°C and decreases at a rate of 2°/1,000 ft. up to 36,000 ft. MSL.)

Answer (A) is incorrect because the direction is rounded to the nearest 10°, not 5°, and temperature is ISA +6°C, not +1°C. Answer (C) is incorrect because winds are in degrees true, not magnetic, and temperature is ISA +6°C, not +10°C.

WINDS AND TEMPERATURES ALOFT FORECASTS

DATA BASED ON Ø312ØØZ
VALID Ø4ØØØØZ FOR USE 18ØØ–Ø3ØØZ. TEMPS NEG ABV 24ØØØ

FT	3ØØØ	6ØØØ	9ØØØ	12ØØØ	18ØØØ	24ØØØ	3ØØØØ	34ØØØ	39ØØØ
ABI		13Ø6+16	16Ø7+11	18Ø7+Ø6	21Ø8-Ø7	22Ø8-18	24Ø833	25Ø942	3ØØ753
ABO			Ø81Ø+14	Ø511+Ø8	3415-Ø6	322Ø-18	312333	312543	3Ø2554
AMA		Ø614	Ø814+1Ø	Ø7Ø9+Ø5	321Ø-Ø7	2914-19	281934	282243	292554
ATL	Ø9Ø6	99ØØ+17	99ØØ+12	Ø2Ø5+Ø7	35Ø7-Ø7	33Ø5-19	29Ø534	28Ø543	99ØØ54
BNA	99ØØ	99ØØ+17	32Ø5+12	31Ø9+Ø7	3Ø18-Ø7	2918-19	272134	262444	262855
BRO	151Ø	1614+2Ø	1611+14	17Ø8+Ø8	99ØØ-Ø7	99ØØ-19	99ØØ34	99ØØ43	99ØØ55
DAL	Ø91Ø	17Ø6+17	2ØØ9+11	2Ø11+Ø6	2Ø15-Ø8	2214-19	231333	241342	271153
DEN			99ØØ+Ø9	99ØØ+Ø4	3Ø2Ø-1Ø	3Ø29-21	3Ø3636	3Ø4145	294756
DSM	3615	3315+Ø7	3118+Ø4	3Ø22+ØØ	2835-12	2748-24	276438	277348	277957
ELP		Ø61Ø	Ø614+13	Ø615+Ø8	Ø113-Ø5	3614-17	361433	361442	251354
GCK		Ø611+11	Ø8Ø9+Ø8	99ØØ+Ø3	2817-Ø9	2823-2Ø	273135	273644	284155
HLC		Ø4Ø9+Ø9	Ø4Ø5+Ø7	31Ø6+Ø2	2822-1Ø	273Ø-21	273936	274545	275256
HOU	Ø9Ø9	16Ø7+19	16Ø6+13	16Ø6+Ø7	16Ø5-Ø8	99ØØ-2Ø	99ØØ34	99ØØ43	99ØØ54
ICT	Ø516	Ø613+12	Ø6Ø7+Ø8	99ØØ+Ø4	2718-Ø9	2626-2Ø	263635	264144	274655
IND	3611	32Ø7+12	2912+Ø8	2818+Ø3	2733-Ø9	2643-21	265635	265944	256255
INK		Ø6Ø9+16	Ø7Ø9+12	Ø6Ø8+Ø7	Ø1Ø7-Ø6	36Ø7-18	35Ø833	34Ø842	35Ø855
JAN	3612	3613+18	3611+13	36Ø9+Ø7	Ø1Ø5-Ø8	99ØØ-19	99ØØ34	99ØØ43	23Ø854
LIT	Ø31Ø	36Ø8+16	32Ø6+11	28Ø8+Ø6	2517-Ø8	2518-19	252Ø34	252243	262454
LOU	Ø1Ø5	99ØØ+15	29Ø8+1Ø	2913+Ø5	2825-Ø8	2731-2Ø	263834	264143	254454
MEM	Ø1Ø9	Ø1Ø8+17	34Ø8+12	311Ø+Ø6	2916-Ø7	2717-19	261934	262144	262555
MKC	Ø316	Ø211+11	34Ø9+Ø7	3Ø13+Ø3	2728-1Ø	2638-21	265Ø36	265645	276356
MSY	Ø315	Ø216+19	Ø315+13	Ø414+Ø7	Ø51Ø-Ø8	Ø6Ø5-2Ø	99ØØ34	99ØØ43	21Ø854
OKC	Ø715	Ø81Ø+14	11Ø6+1Ø	99ØØ+Ø5	2414-Ø8	2419-19	252534	252743	272754
SAT	11Ø7	1713+18	1813+13	1911+Ø7	2ØØ6-Ø7	19Ø6-19	18Ø734	17Ø743	99ØØ54
SGF	Ø414	Ø41Ø+14	36Ø5+Ø9	29Ø8+Ø4	2624-Ø9	2632-2Ø	254135	264444	264655
SHV	Ø5Ø9	99ØØ+18	99ØØ+12	21Ø6+Ø6	2Ø12-Ø8	21Ø9-19	22Ø734	24Ø743	26Ø754
STL	Ø314	Ø11Ø+12	321Ø+Ø8	2915+Ø3	273Ø-Ø9	2741-21	265435	265744	266Ø55
TUS		Ø8Ø7+23	Ø814+16	Ø814+1Ø	Ø81Ø-Ø5	Ø5Ø5-17	33Ø533	31Ø842	29Ø954

FIGURE 149.—Winds and Temperatures Aloft Forecast.

34.
9289. (Refer to figure 149 on page 736.) What will be the wind and temperature trend for an SAT-ELP-TUS flight at 16,000 feet?

A—Temperature decrease slightly.
B—Windspeed decrease.
C—Wind direction shift from southwest to east.

Answer (C) is correct (9289). *(AWS Sect 4)*
To determine the wind and temperature trend, the winds and temperatures aloft must be interpolated for 16,000 ft. The table below shows data for 12,000 and 18,000 ft. and the interpolated data for 16,000 ft.

	12,000	18,000	16,000
SAT	1911+07	2006–07	2008–02
ELP	0615+08	0113–05	0314–01
TUS	0814+10	0810–05	0811+00

On this route, the wind direction shifts from southwest (200°) to east (080°).
Answer (A) is incorrect because temperatures increase, not decrease, slightly. Answer (B) is incorrect because wind speed increases between SAT and ELP but decreases from ELP to TUS.

35.
9290. (Refer to figure 149 on page 736.) What will be the wind and temperature trend for an STL-MEM-MSY flight at FL 330?

A—Windspeed decrease.
B—Wind shift from west to north.
C—Temperature increase 5 °C.

Answer (A) is correct (9290). *(AWS Sect 4)*
To determine the wind and temperature trend, the winds and temperatures aloft must be interpolated for FL 330. The table below shows data for FL 300 and FL 340 and the interpolated data for FL 330.

	FL 300	FL 340	FL 330
STL	265435	265744	265642
MEM	261934	262144	262142
MSY	990034	990043	990041

During this flight, the wind speed decreases from 56 kt. to light and variable.
Answer (B) is incorrect because the wind remains westerly in direction and becomes light and variable; it does not shift to the north. Answer (C) is incorrect because temperature increases 1°C, not 5°C.

16.8 Aviation Routine Weather Report (METAR)

36.
9267. (Refer to figure 145 on page 738.) What type of report is listed for Lubbock (KLBB) at 1818Z?

A—A report made by an automatic weather reporting system.
B—A special report concerning very low station pressure.
C—A special METAR weather observation, concerning significant weather changes.

Answer (C) is correct (9267). *(AWS Sect 2)*
At 1818Z (or 1818 UTC), KLBB issued a SPECI report, which is a special METAR weather observation. It was issued because of significant weather changes since the routine report at 1750Z (i.e., lower visibility, change in type of precipitation, and a drop in temperature).
Answer (A) is incorrect because a report made by an automatic weather reporting system is identified by the contraction AUTO following the date/time group. Answer (B) is incorrect because the special METAR was issued because of significant weather changes, not because of a very low station pressure. The altimeter setting at 1818Z is 29.46 in. of Hg.

AVIATION ROUTINE WEATHER REPORTS (METAR)

TX

METAR KAMA 131755Z 33025G35KT 3/4SM IC OVC003 M02/M01 A2952 RMK PK WND 32039/43 WSHFT 1735 PRESFR P0003.

METAR KAUS 131753Z 19011G17KT 8SM SCT040 BKN250 31/21 A3006 RMK SLPNO.

METAR KBPT 131755Z 17004KT 7SM FEW001 SCT030 BKN250 34/23 A2979 RMK VIS E 2.

METAR KBRO 131755Z 14015KT 6SM HZ SCT034 OVC250 34/30 A2985 RMK PRESRR.

METAR KCDS 131758Z 11013KT 7SM-SHRA OVC180 23/21 A3012 RMK RAB42 VIRGA SW.

METAR KCLL 131749Z 21011KT 7SM SCT003 BKN025 OVC100 34/21 A3008 RMK BKN025 V OVC.

METAR KCOT 131749Z 13010KT 10SM SCT040 SCT200 31/21 A3002 RMK RAE24.

METAR KCRP 131753Z 16016KT 10SM SCT028 BKN250 32/24 A3003.

METAR KDAL 131755Z 16005KT 7SM SCT023 OVC100 30/22 A3007.

METAR KDFW 131800Z 17007KT 10SM SCT035 OVC120 29/20 A3008.

METAR KDHT 131756Z 0401KT 15SM BKN025 22/15 A3026.

METAR KDRT 131756Z 12012KT 10SM FEW006 SCT020 BKN100 OVC250 29/22 A3000 RMK CONS LTG DSTN ESE TS SE MOVG NW VIRGA W.

METAR KELP 131755Z 09007KT 60SM VCBLDU FEW070 SCT170 BKN210 29/13 A3015.

METAR KFTW 131750Z 18007KT 7SM SCT025 OVC100 29/20 A3008.

FTW 131815Z UA/OV DFW/TM 1803/FL095/TP PA30/SK 036 OVC 060/075 OVC/RM TOPS UNKN.

METAR KGGG 131745Z 15008KT 15SM SKC 32/21 A3011.

METAR KGLS 131750Z VRB04KT 6SM VCSH SCT041 BKN093 26/22 A2995.

SPECI KGLS 131802Z 10012G21KT 060V140 2SM+SHRA SCT005 BKN035 OVC050CB 24/23 A2980 RMK RAB57 WSHFT 58FROPA.

METAR KHOU 131752Z 15008KT 7SM SCT030 OVC250 31/27 A3008.

METAR KHRL 131753Z 14015KT 8SM SKC 30/25 A3010.

METAR KIAH 131755Z VRB03KT 1/4SM R33L/1200FT BCFG VV007 27/26 A3005.

METAR KINK 131755Z 04027G36KT 2SM BLSA PO OVC015TCU 24/13 A2985.

METAR KLBB 131750Z 06029G43KT 1SM BLSNDU SQ VV010 03/M01 A2949.

LBB 131808Z UUA/OV LBB /TM 1800/FL UNKN /TP B737 /TB MDT /RM LLWS -17KT SFC-010 DURC RWY 36 LBB.

SPECI KLBB 131818Z 35031G40KT 1/2SM FZDZ VV030 M01/M01 A2946 RMK WSHFT 12 FROPA.

LBB 131821Z UUA/OV LBB/TM1817/FL011/TP B727/SK UNKN OVC/TA -06 /TB MOD/IC MDT CLR.

METAR KLFK 131756Z 24007KT 7SM BKN100 33/19 A3008.

METAR KMAF 131756Z 02020KT 12SM BKN025 OVC250 27/18 A3009 RMK RAE44.

METAR KMFE 131756Z 13015KT 7SM BKN125 33/19 A2998.

METAR KMRF 131752Z 09012G20KT 60SM SKC 28/14 A3000.

MRF 131801Z UUA/OV MRF/TM1758/FL450/TP B767/TB MDT CAT.

Figure 145.—Aviation Routine Weather Reports (METAR).

37.
9266. (Refer to figure 145 on page 738.) What was the local Central Standard Time of the Aviation Routine Weather Report at Austin (KAUS)?

A—11:53 a.m.
B—5:53 p.m.
C—10:53 p.m.

Answer (A) is correct (9266). *(AWS Sect 2)*
The date/time after Austin (KAUS) on Fig. 145 is 131753Z. The first two digits are the date and the last four digits are the time, followed by Z to denote coordinated universal time (UTC). Thus, the report was issued at 1753 UTC. To determine Central Standard Time, you must subtract 6 hr. from UTC; thus the time is 11:53 a.m. (1753 – 6 = 1153) CST.
Answer (B) is incorrect because this is UTC adjusted to 24-hr. clock time (1753 = 5:53 p.m.). Answer (C) is incorrect because Central Standard Time is 6 hr. behind, not 5 hr. ahead of, UTC.

38.
9273. (Refer to figure 145 on page 738.) What weather improvement was reported at Lubbock (KLBB) between 1750 and 1818 UTC?

A—The wind shift and frontal passage at 1812Z.
B—The vertical visibility improved by 2,000 feet.
C—The temperature and dew point spread improved.

Answer (B) is correct (9273). *(AWS Sect 2)*
The vertical visibility at KLBB at 1750 UTC was reported to be 1,000 ft. (VV010). At 1818 UTC, the vertical visibility was reported to be 3,000 ft. (VV030), an improvement of 2,000 ft. from the 1750 UTC report.
Answer (A) is incorrect because, while the wind did shift at 1812Z due to a frontal passage, wind is not a weather element. Answer (C) is incorrect because, at 1750 UTC, the temperature was +3°C and the dew point was –01°C (03/M01), or a spread of 4°C. At 1818 UTC, both the temperature and dew point were –1°C (M01/M01), or a spread of 0°C. Thus, the temperature/dew point spread decreased, not increased or improved.

39.
9270. (Refer to figure 145 on page 738.) What condition is reported at Dallas (KDAL)?

A—The tops of the overcast is 10,000 feet.
B—Temperature/dewpoint spread is 8°F.
C—Altimeter setting is 30.07.

Answer (C) is correct (9270). *(AWS Sect 2)*
Altimeter settings are reported in a four-digit format in inches of mercury prefixed with an "A" to denote the units of pressure. KDAL altimeter setting is coded as A3007, which means 30.07 inches of mercury.
Answer (A) is incorrect because the base, not the top, of the overcast layer is 10,000 ft. Answer (B) is incorrect because the temperature/dew point spread is 8°C, not 8°F.

40.
9269. (Refer to figure 145 on page 738.) What condition is reported at Childress (KCDS)?

A—Light rain showers.
B—Heavy rain showers began 42 minutes after the hour.
C—The ceiling is solid overcast at an estimated 1,800 feet above sea level.

Answer (A) is correct (9269). *(AWS Sect 2)*
In the METAR for KCDS is the code –SHRA, which means there are light (–) showers (SH) and the precipitation type is rain (RA).
Answer (B) is incorrect because light, not heavy, rain showers began at 42 min. past the hour. Answer (C) is incorrect because cloud height is expressed in AGL, not MSL. KCDS reports the bases of an overcast layer at 18,000 ft., not 1,800 ft., and METARs do not state whether the bases are estimated or measured.

41.
9271. (Refer to figure 145 on page 738.) The peak wind at KAMA was reported to be from 320° true at 39 knots,

A—which occurred at 1743Z.
B—with gusts to 43 knots.
C—with .43 of an inch liquid precipitation since the last report.

Answer (A) is correct (9271). *(AWS Sect 2)*
Whenever the peak wind exceeds 25 kt., **PK WND** will be included in the remarks with three digits for direction and two or three digits for speed followed by the time (in hours and minutes or just minutes past the hour) of occurrence. The time of the METAR report for KAMA is 1755Z, and the remark **PK WND 32039/43** means the peak wind 320° true at 39 kt. occurred at 43 min. past the hour, or at 1743Z.
Answer (B) is incorrect because the peak wind occurred at 43 min. past the hour, or 1743Z. Gusts are not reported in a peak wind remark. Answer (C) is incorrect because the remark means that the peak wind occurred at 43 min. past the hour, not that .43 of an inch of precipitation has accumulated since the last report.

42.
9268. (Refer to figure 146 on page 741.) What method was used to obtain the METAR at Tyler (KTYR) at 1753Z?

A—Automated Surface Observing System (ASOS), having a precipitation discriminator.
B—Automatic Meteorological Observing Station (AMOS), with a precipitation discriminator.
C—Automated Weather Observing System (AWOS), without a precipitation discriminator.

Answer (A) is correct (9268). *(AIM Para 7-1-10)*
After the date/time group on the METAR for KTYR is the contraction AUTO, which means that the METAR is a fully automated report. Currently, an ASOS is the only automated station that performs the basic observing functions necessary to generate a METAR report. Additionally, the remark A02 means the automated station has a precipitation discriminator.

Answer (B) is incorrect because an AMOS is used at some sites, but it is not able to generate a METAR report. Currently, ASOS stations generate METAR reports. Answer (C) is incorrect because, currently, only the ASOS, not the AWOS, can perform the functions necessary to generate a METAR report. In the future, selected AWOS sites may be incorporated into the nationwide data collection network, and these stations will generate METAR reports. Additionally, a remark of A01, not A02, means that the automated station is without a precipitation discriminator.

43.
9276. (Refer to figure 146 on page 741.) What was the ceiling at Walnut Ridge (KARG)?

A—1,000 feet AGL.
B—2,400 feet AGL.
C—1,000 feet MSL.

Answer (A) is correct (9276). *(AWS Sect 2)*
The ceiling is the lowest broken or overcast layer (measured in hundreds of feet above ground level) or vertical visibility (measured in hundreds of feet) into an obscuration. The ceiling at KARG is reported to be overcast clouds at 1,000 ft. AGL (OVC010).

Answer (B) is incorrect because the runway visual range for RWY 28 at KARG is 2,400 ft. (R28/2400 FT), not the ceiling. Answer (C) is incorrect because the ceiling is measured in hundreds of feet above ground level (AGL), not above mean sea level (MSL).

44.
9272.
SPECI KGLS 131802Z 10012G21KT 060V140 2SM +SHRA SCT005 BKN035 OVC050CB 24/23 A2980 RMK RAB57 WS TKO RW09L WSHFT 58 FROPA.

This SPECI report at Galveston (KGLS) indicates which condition?

A—Wind steady at 100° magnetic at 12 knots, gusts to 21.
B—Precipitation started at 57 after the hour.
C—5,000 feet overcast with towering cumulus.

Answer (B) is correct (9272). *(AWS Sect 2)*
The remarks (RMK) section of the SPECI report at KGLS indicates rain began at 57 min. past the hour (RAB57); wind shear occurred during takeoff on RWY 09L (WS TKO RW09L); and the wind shifted in direction at 58 min. past the hour due to a frontal passage (WSHFT 58 FROPA).

Answer (A) is incorrect because the wind is variable, not steady, from 060° to 140° with the prevailing wind at 100°. Wind direction is referenced to true, not magnetic, north. Answer (C) is incorrect because the 5,000 ft. overcast layer is the base of cumulonimbus clouds (CB), not tower cumulus clouds (TCU).

45.
9274.
METAR KMAF 131756Z 02020KT 12SM BKN025 OVC250 27/18 A3009 RMK RAE44.

Which weather condition is indicated by this METAR report at Midland (KMAF)?

A—Rain of unknown intensity ended 16 minutes before the hour.
B—The ceiling was at 25,000 feet MSL.
C—Wind was 020° magnetic at 20 knots.

Answer (A) is correct (9274). *(AWS Sect 2)*
The report at KMAF indicates RMK RAE44, which means remarks follow: rain ended 44 min. past the hour (or 16 min. before the hour).

Answer (B) is incorrect because the ceiling is a broken layer at 2,500 ft. AGL (BKN025), not 25,000 ft. MSL. Answer (C) is incorrect because wind direction is referenced to true, not magnetic, north.

AVIATION ROUTINE WEATHER REPORTS (METAR)

TX

METAR KABI 131755Z AUTO 21016G24KT 180V240 1SM R11/P6000FT -RA BR BKN015 OVC025 19/15 A2990 RMK AO2 PK WND 20035/25 WSHFT 1715 VIS 3/4V1 1/2 VIS 3/4 RWY11 RAB07 CIG 013V 017 CIG 014 RWY11 PRESFR SLP125 P0003 60009 T01940154 10196 20172 58033 TSNO $.

METAR KMWL 131756Z 13011KT 10SM BKN011 OVC050 25/23 A3006.

METAR KPSX 131755Z 20010KT 7SM SCT018 OVC200 31/24 A3007.

METAR KPVW 131750Z 05006KT 10SM SCT012 OVC030 30/20 A3011 RMK RAE47.

METAR KSAT 131756Z 15016KT 7SM SCT028 OVC250 30/20 A3005.

SAT 131756Z UA/OV SAT/TM 1739Z/FL UNKN/TP UNKN/SK OVC 040.

METAR KSJT 131755Z 22012KT 7SM BKN018 OVC070 25/23 A3002.

METAR KSPS 131757Z 09014KT 6SM -RA SCT025 OVC090 24/22 A3005.

SPECI KSPS 131820Z 01025KT 2SM+RA OVC015TCU 22/21 A3000 RMK DSNT TORNADO B15 N MOV E.

SPS 131820Z UA/OV SPS/TM 1818/FL090/TP C402/SK OVC 075.

METAR KTPL 131751Z 17015KT 15SM SCT015 SCT100 OVC250 31/20 A3007.

METAR KTYR 131753Z AUTO 26029G41KT 2SM +TSRA BKN008 OVC020 31/24 A3001 RMK A02 TSB44 RAB46.

METAR KVCT 131755Z 17013KT 7SM SCT030 OVC250 30/24 A3005.

AR

METAR KARG 131753Z AUTO 22015G25KT 3/4SM R28/2400FT +RA OVC010 29/28 A2985 RMK AO2.

METAR KELD 131755Z 06005G10KT 3SM FU BKN050 OVC100 30/21 A3010.

METAR KFSM 131756Z 00000KT 5SM SKC 30/20 A2982.

FSM 131830Z UA/OV HRO-FSM/TM 1825/FL290/TP B737/SK SCT 290.

METAR KFYV 131755Z 170018G32KT 2SM +TSRA SQ SCT030 BKN060OVC100CB 28/21 A2978 RMK RAB47.

FYV 131801Z UA/OV 1 E DAK/TM 1755Z/FL 001/TP CV440/RM WS LND RWY16 FYV.

METAR KHOT 131751Z 34006KT 18SM SCT040 OVC150 32/18 A3010.

METAR KHRO 131753Z 09007KT 7SM FEW020 BKN040CB 30/27 A3001.

SPECI KHRO 131815Z 13017G26KT 2SM +TSRA SCT020 BKN045TCU 29/24A2983 RMK RAB12 FRQ LTGICCG VC PRESFR.

HRO 131830Z UUA/OV 6 S HRO/TM 1825Z/FL 001/TP DC6/RM WS TKO RWY 18.

METAR KLIT 131754Z 07004KT 10SM SCT030 BKN250 34/29 A3007.

METAR KPBF 131753Z 29007KT 5SM SCT040 BKN100 35/19 A3008.

METAR KTXK 131753Z 25003KT 7SM SCT100 BKN200 33/19 A3010.

Figure 146.—Aviation Routine Weather Reports (METAR).

46.
9275.
METAR KSPS 131757Z 09014KT 6SM –RA SCT025 OVC090 24/22 A3005.

SPECI KSPS 131820Z 01025KT 3SM +RA FC OVC015 22/21 A3000.

What change took place at Wichita Falls (KSPS) between 1757 and 1820 UTC?

A—The rain became lighter.
B—Atmospheric pressure increased.
C—A funnel cloud was observed.

Answer (C) is correct (9275). *(AWS Sect 2)*
The special report (SPECI) for KSPS at 1820 UTC reports that a funnel cloud (FC) was observed.

Answer (A) is incorrect because the rain intensity increased, not decreased, between 1757 and 1820 UTC. At 1757 UTC the rain was light (–RA), and at 1820 UTC the rain was heavy (+RA). Answer (B) is incorrect because the atmospheric pressure decreased, not increased. At 1757 UTC the altimeter setting was 30.05 in. of Hg (A3005), and at 1820 UTC the altimeter setting was 30.00 in. of Hg (A3000).

47.
9277.
METAR KHRO 131753Z 09007KT 7SM FEW020 BKN040 30/27 A3001.

SPECI KHRO 131815Z 13017G26KT 3SM +TSRA SCT020 BKN045TCU 29/24 A2983 RMK RAB12 WS TKO LDG RW14R FRQ LTGICCG VC.

What change has taken place between 1753 and 1815 UTC at Harrison (KHRO)?

A—The ceiling lowered and cumulonimbus clouds developed.
B—Thundershowers began at 12 minutes past the hour.
C—Visibility reduced to IFR conditions.

Answer (B) is correct (9277). *(AWS Sect 2)*
The special report (SPECI) taken at 1815 UTC at KHRO reports thunderstorm with heavy rain (+TSRA), and the remarks state that the rain began at 12 min. past the hour (RAB12).

Answer (A) is incorrect because, while the ceiling decreased from 4,000 ft. to 3,500 ft., towering cumulus clouds (TCU), not cumulonimbus clouds (CB), were reported at 1815 UTC. Answer (C) is incorrect because visibility reduced to 3 SM, which is VFR, not IFR.

48.
9716. The prevailing visibility in the following METAR is

METAR KFSM 131756Z AUTO 00000KT M1/4SM R25/0600V1000FT -RA FG VV004 06/05 A2989 RMK A02 $.

A—less than 1/4 statute mile.
B—measured 1/4 statute mile.
C—a mean (average) of 1/4 statute mile.

Answer (A) is correct (9716). *(AIM Para 7-1-28)*
Prevailing visibility is reported in statute miles with a space and then fractions of statute miles, as needed, with SM appended to it. This METAR was produced at an automated station, as indicated by the modifier AUTO. At an automated station, visibility of less than 1/4 SM is reported as M1/4SM.

Answer (B) is incorrect because the letter M means that the visibility is less than 1/4 SM, not measured 1/4 SM. Answer (C) is incorrect because the letter M means that the visibility is less than 1/4 SM, not that the visibility is a mean (average) of 1/4 SM.

49.
9717. The symbol ($) at the end of the following METAR indicates that

METAR KFSM 131756Z AUTO 00000KT M1/4SM R25/0600V1000FT -RA FG VV004 06/05 A2989 RMK A02 $.

A—the latest information is transmitted over a discrete VHF frequency at KFSM.
B—the latest information is broadcast on the voice portion of a local NAVAID at KFSM.
C—maintenance is needed on the system.

Answer (C) is correct (9717). *(AIM Para 7-1-10)*
A maintenance indicator (dollar) sign, $, is included when an automated weather reporting station detects that maintenance is needed on the system.

Answer (A) is incorrect because the $ symbol indicates that maintenance is needed on the system, not that the latest information is transmitted over a discrete VHF frequency at KFSM. Answer (B) is incorrect because the $ symbol indicates that maintenance is needed on the system, not that the latest information is broadcast on the voice portion of a local NAVAID at KFSM.

50.
9718. The VV001 in the following METAR indicates

METAR KFSM 131756Z AUTO 00000KT M1/4SM
R25/0600V1000FT -RA FG VV001 A2989 RMK AO2
VIS 3/4 RWY19 CHINO RWY19 $

A—an observer reported the vertical visibility as 100 feet.
B—a 100-foot indefinite ceiling.
C—the variability value is 100 feet.

Answer (B) is correct (9718). *(AIM Para 7-1-10)*
The sky condition in the METAR is shown as VV001, which means a vertical visibility (spoken as an indefinite ceiling) of 100 ft.
Answer (A) is incorrect because the METAR was produced by a fully automated station without any human intervention, as indicated by the AUTO modifier. Thus, there is no observer. Answer (C) is incorrect because the vertical visibility, not variability value, is 100 ft.

51.
9712. Clouds or obscuring phenomena aloft, through which blue sky or higher sky cover is visible, is known as a

A—thin overcast.
B—partial obscuration.
C—"transparent" sky cover.

Answer (C) is correct (9712). *(AWS Sect 2)*
Clouds or obscuring phenomena aloft, through which blue sky or higher sky cover is visible, are known as transparent sky cover.
Answer (A) is incorrect because clouds or obscuring phenomena aloft, through which blue sky or higher sky cover is visible, are known as transparent sky cover, not thin overcast. There is no provision for reporting thin layers in the METAR code. Answer (B) is incorrect because clouds or obscuring phenomena aloft, through which blue sky or higher sky cover is visible, are known as transparent sky cover, not partial obscuration. There is no provision in the METAR code to report partial obscurations.

52.
9708. A squall is a sudden increase of at least 15 knots in average wind speed to a sustained speed of

A—25 knots or more for at least 1 minute.
B—20 knots or more for at least 2 minutes.
C—20 knots or more for at least 1 minute.

Answer (C) is correct (9708). *(AWS Sect 2)*
A squall is a sudden increase of at least 15 kt. in average wind speed to a sustained speed of 20 kt. or more for at least 1 minute. Squalls are reported in the METAR as weather phenomena by the code SQ.
Answer (A) is incorrect because a squall is a sudden increase of at least 15 kt. in average wind speed to a sustained speed of 20 kt., not 25 kt., or more for at least 1 minute. Answer (B) is incorrect because a squall is a sudden increase of at least 15 kt. in average wind speed to a sustained speed of 20 kt. or more for at least 1, not 2, minutes.

53.
9249. If squalls are reported at the destination airport, what wind conditions existed at the time?

A—Sudden increases in wind speed of at least 15 knots, to a sustained wind speed of 20 knots, lasting for at least 1 minute.
B—Peak gusts of at least 35 knots for a sustained period of 1 minute or longer.
C—Rapid variation in wind direction of at least 20° and changes in speed of at least 10 knots between peaks and lulls.

Answer (A) is correct (9249). *(AWS Sect 2)*
A squall is a sudden increase in wind speed of at least 15 kt. to a sustained wind speed of 20 kt. or more, lasting for at least 1 min.
Answer (B) is incorrect because a sudden increase in wind speed of at least 15 kt., not a peak gust, is needed for classification as a squall. Answer (C) is incorrect because a gust, not a squall, has a variation in wind speed of at least 10 kt. between peaks and lulls.

54.
9242. Which measurement is reported as runway visibility?

A—Visibility reported by a ground observer from the airport control tower.
B—Slant range visibility in the landing area of the active runway.
C—Distance down the runway a pilot can see unlighted objects.

Answer (C) is correct (9242). *(AWS Sect 2)*
Runway visibility is the distance down the runway from which the pilot can see unlighted objects or unfocused lights of moderate intensity.
Answer (A) is incorrect because runway visibility is measured from a location along an identified runway, not from the airport control tower. Answer (B) is incorrect because slant range is the pilot's visibility when looking outside the cockpit while in the air.

55.
9704. Data that may be added (manual weather augmentation) to the Automated Weather Observing System (AWOS) report is limited to

A—the precipitation accumulation report, an automated variable visibility, and wind direction remark.
B—thunderstorms (intensity and direction), precipitation (type and intensity), and obstructions to visibility (dependent on the visibility being 3 miles or less).
C—density altitude, NOTAMs, and reported slant range visibility.

Answer (B) is correct (9704). *(AWS Sect 2)*
Manual weather augmentation remarks added to an AWOS-generated METAR are located in the remarks section. As a general rule, the manual remarks are limited to thunderstorms (intensity and direction), precipitation (type and intensity), and obstructions to vision when the visibility is 3 SM or less.
Answer (A) is incorrect because wind direction is an automated feature, not manually added data, of the AWOS. Answer (C) is incorrect because density altitude is an automated, not a manually inputted, remark.

16.9 Terminal Aerodrome Forecast (TAF)

56.
9244. Which primary source contains information regarding the expected weather at the destination airport at the ETA?

A—Low-Level Prog Chart.
B—Radar Summary and Weather Depiction Charts.
C—Terminal Aerodrome Forecast.

Answer (C) is correct (9244). *(AWS Sect 4)*
A Terminal Aerodrome Forecast (TAF) is a concise statement of the expected meteorological conditions at an airport during a specified period (usually 24 hr.). Thus, a TAF contains information regarding the expected weather at the destination airport at the ETA.
Answer (A) is incorrect because a low-level prog chart is a forecast of significant weather for the United States. It is not a forecast for a specific destination. Answer (B) is incorrect because weather depiction charts and radar summary charts are national weather maps of observed weather at a specific time. They are useful for flight planning but do not provide specific information about a particular destination.

57.
9245. Weather conditions expected to occur in the vicinity of the airport, but not at the airport, are denoted by the letters "VC." When VC appears in a Terminal Aerodrome Forecast, it covers a geographical area of

A—a 5 to 10 statute mile radius from the airport.
B—a 5-mile radius of the center of a runway complex.
C—10 miles of the station originating the forecast.

Answer (A) is correct (9245). *(AWS Sect 4)*
When VC appears in a TAF, it applies to weather conditions expected to occur in an area within a 5-to-10 SM radius of the airport, but not at the airport itself.
Answer (B) is incorrect because VC applies to weather conditions expected to occur in an area within a 5-to-10 SM radius from the airport, not within a 5-mile radius of the runway complex. Answer (C) is incorrect because VC applies to weather conditions expected to occur in the vicinity of the airport (within a 5-to-10 SM radius of the airport), not within 10 miles of the station originating the forecast.

58.
9248. What weather is predicted by the term VCTS in a Terminal Aerodrome Forecast?

A—Thunderstorms are expected between a 5 to 10 statute mile radius of the airport, but not at the airport itself.
B—Rain showers may occur over the station and within 50 miles of the station.
C—Thunderstorms are expected between 5 and 25 miles of the runway complex.

Answer (A) is correct (9248). *(AWS Sect 4)*
The term VC (vicinity) applies to weather conditions expected within a 5-to-10 SM radius of the airport, but not at the airport itself. Thus, VCTS in a TAF means thunderstorms are expected within a 5-to-10 SM radius of the airport, but not at the airport itself.
Answer (B) is incorrect because VC means within 5-to-10 SM from the airport, not 50 miles, and TS means thunderstorms, not rain showers. Answer (C) is incorrect because a geographic area between 5 and 25 miles of the runway complex was the definition of the term vicinity in the U.S. terminal forecast (FT), not the TAF.

59.
9246. Which are the only cloud types forecast in the Terminal Aerodrome Forecast?

A—Altocumulus
B—Cumulonimbus
C—Stratocumulus

Answer (B) is correct (9246). *(AWS Sect 4)*
If cumulonimbus clouds are expected at the airport, the contraction CB is appended to the cloud layer which represents the base of the cumulonimbus cloud(s). Cumulonimbus clouds are the only cloud type forecast in the TAF.
Answer (A) is incorrect because the only cloud type forecast in the TAF is cumulonimbus, not altocumulus. Answer (C) is incorrect because the only cloud type forecast in the TAF is cumulonimbus, not stratocumulus.

60.
9709. A calm wind is forecast, in the International Terminal Aerodrome Forecast (TAF), if a wind speed of

A—6 knots or less is expected.
B—3 knots or less is expected.
C—5 knots or less is expected.

Answer (B) is correct (9709). *(AWS Sect 4)*
A wind forecast of **00000KT** is included in the TAF if a calm wind (3 kt. or less) is expected.
Answer (A) is incorrect because a calm wind is forecast if a wind speed of 3 kt., not 6 kt., or less is expected. Answer (C) is incorrect because a calm wind is forecast if a wind speed of 3 kt., not 5 kt., or less is expected.

61.
9710. In the International Terminal Aerodrome Forecast (TAF), a variable wind direction is noted by "VRB" where the three digit direction usually appears. A calm wind (3 knots or less) appears in the TAF as

A—"00003KT."
B—"CALM."
C—"00000KT."

Answer (C) is correct (9710). *(AWS Sect 4)*
In the International Terminal Aerodrome Forecast (TAF), a calm wind (3 kt. or less) appears in the TAF as "00000KT."
Answer (A) is incorrect because, in the TAF, a calm wind (3 kt. or less) appears in the TAF as "00000KT," not "00003KT." Answer (B) is incorrect because, in the TAF, a calm wind (3 kt. or less) appears in the TAF as "00000KT," not "CALM."

62.
9278. A PROB40 (PROBability) HHhh group in an International Terminal Aerodrome Forecast (TAF) indicates the probability of

A—thunderstorms or other precipitation.
B—precipitation or low visibility.
C—thunderstorms or high wind.

Answer (A) is correct (9278). *(AWS Sect 4)*
A PROB40 (PROBability) HHhh group in a TAF indicates the probability of thunderstorms or other precipitation events. The PROB group is used when the occurrence of thunderstorms or precipitation is in the 30% to less than 50% range; thus the probability value of 40 is appended to the PROB contraction. PROB40 is followed by a four-digit group giving the beginning time (HH) and ending time (hh) of the period during which thunderstorms or precipitation is expected.
Answer (B) is incorrect because a PROB40 group in a TAF indicates the probability of thunderstorms or other precipitation events, not low visibility. Answer (C) is incorrect because a PROB40 group in a TAF indicates the probability of thunderstorms or other precipitation events, not high winds.

INTERNATIONAL TERMINAL AERODROME FORECAST (TAF)

TX

TAF
KALI 031745Z 031818 14015KT 6SM HZ BKN012
FM2000 15015G25KT P6SM BKN030 WS009/02045KT
FM2200 16011G21KT 4SM SCT040 BKN250 TEMPO 2301 3SM TSGS BKN020
FM0100 13015KT 5SM SCT015
FM0700 12008KT 5SM BKN008 BECMG 0912 3SM BKN015

TAF
KAMA 031745Z 031818 05012KT 5SM RA BR BKN010 BKN080 TEMPO1803 03015KT 2SM +TSRA OVC010
FM0400 03015KT 3SM BKN020 OVC080 TEMPO 0410 2SM +TSRA OVC010
FM1100 03012KT 5SM RA BR OVC010 BECMG 1618 1/2SM RA FG OVC008

TAF
KAUS 031745Z COR 031818 17010KT P6SM BKN025 OVC100
FM2100 15008KT 4 SM BKN030 OVC100 TEMPO 2223 1SM TSPE OVC010
FM0100 16005KT 5SM BKN014 TEMPO 0809 1SM +TSRA BKN014 BECMG 1214 3SM TSRA BKN020
FM1500 17008KT 5SM SCT050

TAF
KCRP 031745Z 031818 15015G20KT P6SM SCT020 BKN250
FM2300 16015G25KT 4SM SCT030 BKN250 TEMPO 0001 TSRA
FM0100 16015KT 2SM BKN015 BECMG 0911 5SM SCT030

TAF
KDAL 031745Z 031818 00000KT P6SM SCT030 BKN100
FM2200 17007KT 5SM BR BKN030 OVC100 PROB40 0002 2SM TSRA OVC010
FM0200 09005KT 4SM -RA BKN020 PROB30 0407 3SM TSRA
FM0700 07004KT 1/2SM FG OVC002 BECMG 0912 3SM TSRA SCT040

TAF AMD
KDRT 031745Z 031818 14010KT P6SM OVC014
FM1900 VRB05KT 5SM BKN020 OVC100 TEMPO 2021 2SM +TSRA
FM2300 14012KT 5SM HZ BKN030 BKN100 PROB40 0205 3SM TSRA BKN020
FM0500 27006KT 6SM BR SCT035 BKN080 TEMPO 0709 2SM FU BR BKN020
FM1000 00000KT 4SM OVC030 BECMG 1416 3SM TSRA OVC020

TAF
KELP 031745Z 031818 08012KT P6SM SCT070 SCT100
FM2000 13010KT 6SM SCT070 BKN120 TEMPO 2223 15026G35KT 3SM BLSA BKN050
FM0600 07012KT 5SM BKN070 PROB40 0709 2SM -TSRA BKN025
FM1200 07020G34KT 1SM +TSRA BKN020CB WS008/25040KT

TAF
KHOU 031745Z 031818 18010KT 6SM HZ SCT020
FM2100 18015KT 4SM HZ SCT035 SCT250
FM0100 19010KT 3SM HZ SCT250
FM0700 20005KT 1SM BR FU BKN005 OVC025
FM1300 13007KT 4SM HZ BKN040

TAF
KIAH 031745Z 031818 18010KT 5SM HZ SCT020
FM2000 16008KT 4SM HZ SCT015 SCT250
FM0500 17012KT 1SM BR FU BKN008 OVC020
FM1000 00000KT 1/4SM -RA FG BKN010 OVC031
FM1400 14005KT 5SM BKN004 OVC080 BECMG 1618 NSW

TAF
KINK 031745Z 031818 10010KT P6SM SCT020 SCT100
FM2100 08013KT 3SM DZ BKN025 BKN080 PROB40 0002 06026G35KT 1SM +TSRAGR
FM0400 05019KT 2SM DU BKN020 OVC050 PROB40 0709 1SM +TSRA FEW002 OVC010
FM0900 02004KT 1/2SM RA FG SCT025 BKN045 OVC100CB
FM1400 34035G45KT 2SM SS SKC

TAF
KLBB 031745Z 031818 06012KT 3SM -TSRA SCT010 OVC020
FM2100 04015KT 5SM BR BKN020 OVC060 PROB40 0103 06025G35KT 1/8SM +SHRASNPE OVC003
FM0400 05018KT 3SM -RA BR OVC010 PROB30 0608 07020KT 1SM +TSRA
FM0900 00000KT 1/4SM -RA FG VV002
FM1300 01005G12KT 1SM FZRA
FM1600 VRB04KT 1/8SM FG VV001

TAF
KSAT 031745Z 031818 17010KT 6SM HZ BKN016 OVC030
FM2000 17015KT P6SM BKN025
FM2200 19012KT 4SM FU BKN030 OVC250 PROB40 0104 07020G30KT 3SM TSRA BKN020
FM0500 12015KT 3SM SG BKN010 BKN035 PROB40 0709 05015G23KT 1SM +TSRA OVC010
FM1000 35008G16KT 4SM BLSN OVC020

TAF
KSJT 031745Z 031818 12012KT 6SM HZ BKN016
FM2000 17018KT 4SM BR BKN025
FM2200 14020G28KT 3SM GS BKN030 OVC250 PROB40 0103 16025G32KT 1SM +TSRA OVC008CB
FM0900 17020G34KT 2SM RA BR OVC010CB

TAF
KSPS 031745Z 031818 07012KT 4S -RA FG SCT030 BKN080 TEMPO 0203 09022G30KT 1SM FZDZ OVC020
FM0900 05015KT 2SM BR SCT001 BKN005 OVC010 SNRA WS090/09035KT

FIGURE 147 -- International Terminal Aerodrome Forecast (TAF)

63.
9280. (Refer to figure 147 on page 746.) What type conditions can be expected for a flight scheduled to land at San Angelo (KSJT) at 1500Z?

A—Chance of 1 statute mile visibility and cumulonimbus clouds.
B—IFR conditions due to low visibility, rain, and mist.
C—IFR conditions due to low ceilings, rain, and fog.

Answer (B) is correct (9280). *(AWS Sect 4)*
At KSJT from 0900 to 1800Z (UTC), the forecast is wind 270° at 20 kt. with gusts to 34 kt., visibility 2 SM, overcast cumulonimbus clouds at 1,000 ft. with rain and mist. Thus, the expected conditions are IFR conditions due to low visibility, rain, and mist.
Answer (A) is incorrect because visibility is forecast to be 2 SM, not 1 SM. Answer (C) is incorrect because IFR conditions are due to low visibility in rain and mist, not low ceilings and fog.

64.
9279. (Refer to figure 147 on page 746.) At which time is IFR weather first predicted at Lubbock (KLBB)?

A—2100Z.
B—0100Z.
C—0400Z.

Answer (B) is correct (9279). *(AWS Sect 4)*
The forecast for KLBB between the hours of 0100Z to 0300Z is a 40% probability of visibility 1/8 SM (IFR) in thunderstorms and heavy rain showers, with snow and ice pellets, and an overcast layer at 300 ft. Thus, the first IFR weather predicted at KLBB is at 0100Z.
Answer (A) is incorrect because at 2100Z the forecast is wind from 040° at 15 kt., 5 SM visibility, broken clouds at 2,000 ft., and an overcast layer at 6,000 ft., which is VFR weather, not IFR weather. Answer (C) is incorrect because at 0400Z the forecast is 3 SM visibility and an overcast layer at 1,000 ft., which is MVFR, not IFR.

16.10 Miscellaneous Charts and Forecasts

65.
9243. What is the single source reference that contains information regarding volcanic eruption, turbulence, and icing conditions for a specific region?

A—Weather Depiction Chart.
B—In-Flight Weather Advisories.
C—Area Forecast.

Answer (B) is correct (9243). *(AWS Sect 4)*
In-flight aviation weather advisories provide information on volcanic eruption, turbulence, and icing conditions for a specific region.
Answer (A) is incorrect because a weather depiction chart is prepared from METAR reports and gives only a broad overview of the observed condition at the valid time of the chart. It does not provide any information on volcanic eruption, turbulence, and icing conditions for a specific region. Answer (C) is incorrect because in-flight weather advisories, not an area forecast, provides information on volcanic eruption, turbulence, and icing conditions for a specific region.

66.
9175. Isobars on a surface weather chart represent lines of equal pressure

A—at the surface.
B—reduced to sea level.
C—at a given atmospheric pressure altitude.

Answer (B) is correct (9175). *(AWS Sect 5)*
Isobars on a surface analysis (weather) chart represent the sea level pressure pattern, usually spaced at 4-mb, or 4-hPa, intervals. This allows a comparison to be made of pressure reports by stations at various altitudes.
Answer (A) is incorrect because the isobars are depicted at the sea level pressure pattern at 4-mb (4-hPa) intervals, not just at the surface. Answer (C) is incorrect because the isobars are reduced to sea level pressure, not any given atmospheric pressure altitude.

67.
9304. A prognostic chart depicts the conditions

A—existing at the surface during the past 6 hours.
B—which presently exist from the 1,000-millibar through the 700-millibar level.
C—forecast to exist at a specific time in the future.

Answer (C) is correct (9304). *(AWS Sect 8)*
Prognostic charts show conditions as they are forecast to be at the valid time (UTC or Zulu) for the chart. The charts are issued four times daily.
Answer (A) is incorrect because prognostic charts relate to the future, not the past. Answer (B) is incorrect because low-level prognostic charts are issued for the surface and 24,000 ft., which is 400 mb. 1,000 mb is very close to the surface; i.e., sea level is 1,013 mb. 700 mb is approximately 10,000 ft. MSL.

68.
9253. For international flights, a U.S. High-Level Significant Weather Prognostic Chart is prepared for use

A—at any altitude above 29,000.
B—between 25,000 feet and 60,000 feet pressure altitude.
C—between FL 180 and FL 600.

Answer (B) is correct (9253). *(AWS Sect 8)*
High-Level Significant Weather Prognostic Charts are manually produced by the U.S. National Meteorological Center for international flights. They are prepared for flights between 25,000 ft. and 60,000 ft. pressure altitude (or FL 250 to FL 600).
Answer (A) is incorrect because high-level prognostics for international flight are prepared for FL 250 to FL 600, not any altitude above 29,000. Answer (C) is incorrect because the base of the International High-Level Prognostic is FL 250, not FL 180.

69.
9251. Forecast winds and temperatures aloft for an international flight may be obtained by consulting

A—Area Forecasts published by the departure location host country.
B—the current International Weather Depiction Chart appropriate to the route.
C—Wind and Temperature Aloft Charts prepared by the U.S. National Meteorological Center (NMC).

Answer (C) is correct (9251). *(AWS Sect 9)*
Information on forecast winds and temperatures aloft is found in a Wind and Temperature Aloft Chart. For international flights, this chart is prepared by the U.S. National Meteorological Center (NMC), which is a component of the World Area Forecast System.
Answer (A) is incorrect because area forecasts are forecasts of general weather conditions over an area of several states and do not contain forecasts of the winds and temperatures aloft. Answer (B) is incorrect because the International Weather Depiction Chart indicates current weather and does not forecast winds and temperatures aloft.

70.
9252. How will an area of thunderstorm activity, that may grow to severe intensity, be indicated on the Severe Weather Outlook Chart?

A—SLGT within cross-hatched areas.
B—APCHG within any area.
C—SVR within any area.

Answer (B) is correct (9252). *(AWS Sect 11)*
On a Severe Weather Outlook Chart, an area will be labeled APCHG to indicate probable general thunderstorm activity that may approach severe intensity. Approaching means winds greater than or equal to 35 kt., but less than 50 kt., and/or hail greater than or equal to ½ in. in diameter, but less than ¾ in. (surface conditions).
Answer (A) is incorrect because a cross-hatched area identifies a tornado watch area. Answer (C) is incorrect because the term SVR is not used on the Severe Weather Outlook Chart.

71.
9305. What information is provided by a Convective Outlook (AC)?

A—It describes areas of probable severe icing and severe or extreme turbulence during the next 24 hours.
B—It provides prospects of both general and severe thunderstorm activity during the following 24 hours.
C—It indicates areas of probable convective turbulence and the extent of instability in the upper atmosphere (above 500 mb).

Answer (B) is correct (9305). *(AWS Sect 4)*
The convective outlook describes the prospects for general thunderstorm activity during the following 24 hr. Areas with a high, moderate, or slight risk of severe thunderstorms are included, as well as areas where thunderstorms may approach severe limits.
Answer (A) is incorrect because severe icing and severe or extreme turbulence are the subjects of SIGMETs. Answer (C) is incorrect because it describes a 500-mb Constant Pressure Analysis Chart.

72.
9247. What sources reflect the most accurate information on current and forecast icing conditions?

A—Low-Level Sig Weather Prog Chart, RADAT's, and the Area Forecast.
B—PIREP's, Area Forecast, and the Freezing Level Chart.
C—PIREP's, AIRMET's, and SIGMET's.

Answer (C) is correct (9247). *(AWS Sect 4)*
Pilot reports (PIREPs) can reflect the most current icing conditions for a specific area, including type and intensity. AIRMET Zulu is for icing and freezing levels for a specified time and normally an outlook. A SIGMET is issued for areas of severe icing.
Answer (A) is incorrect because low-level sig weather prog charts do not forecast icing conditions but do forecast freezing levels, and an area forecast does not provide any information on icing conditions. Answer (B) is incorrect because a freezing level chart cannot be used to determine current or forecast icing conditions, and an area forecast does not provide any information on icing conditions.

73.
9702. The tropopause data chart is a two-panel chart containing a maximum wind prog and a vertical wind shear prog. The progs are issued once daily with a valid time of 1800 UTC and may be used from

A—1800 to 0600 UTC.
B—1800 UTC plus 24 hours.
C—1800 UTC +/– 6 hours.

Answer (C) is correct (9702). *(AWS Sect 13)*
The tropopause data chart is prepared for the contiguous 48 states and is available once a day with a valid time of 1800 UTC (or Z). The progs may be used for a period from 1800 UTC, plus or minus 6 hr.
Answer (A) is incorrect because the progs may be used for a period of up to plus or minus 6 hrs. from the valid time (i.e., 1200 to 2400 UTC), not 1800 to 0600 UTC. Answer (B) is incorrect because the progs may be used for a period of up to plus or minus 6 hr., not plus 24 hr., from the valid time (1800 UTC).

74.
9283. Vertical wind shear can be determined directly from the dashed lines on the tropopause data chart. The vertical wind shear that is critical for probable turbulence is

A—4 knots or greater per 1,000 feet.
B—6 knots or more per 1,000 feet.
C—greater than 8 knots per 1,000 feet.

Answer (B) is correct (9283). *(AWS Sect 13)*
Vertical wind shear can be determined directly from the dashed lines on the tropopause data chart. The vertical wind shear critical for probable turbulence is 6 kt. or more per 1,000 ft.
Answer (A) is incorrect because the vertical wind shear critical for probable turbulence is 6 kt. or more per 1,000 ft., not 4 kt. or more per 1,000 ft. Answer (C) is incorrect because the vertical wind shear critical for probable turbulence is 6 kt. or more per 1,000 ft., not greater than 8 kt. per 1,000 ft.

75.
9701. The horizontal wind shear, critical for turbulence (moderate or greater) per 150 miles is

A—18 knots or less.
B—greater than 18 knots.
C—not a factor, only vertical shear is a factor.

Answer (B) is correct (9701). *(AWS Sect 13)*
The horizontal wind shear critical for turbulence (moderate or greater) is greater than 18 kt. per 150 NM.
Answer (A) is incorrect because the horizontal wind shear critical for turbulence is greater than 18 kt., not 18 kt. or less. Answer (C) is incorrect because both horizontal and vertical wind shears are critical for turbulence.

16.11 Constant Pressure Analysis Charts

76.
9281. Constant Pressure Analysis Charts contain contours, isotherms and some contain isotachs. The contours depict

A—ridges, lows, troughs, and highs aloft.
B—highs, lows, troughs, and ridges on the surface.
C—highs, lows, troughs, and ridges corrected to MSL.

Answer (A) is correct (9281). *(AWS Sect 12)*
Constant pressure analysis charts contain contours and isotherms, and some contain isotachs. Contours are lines of equal height and depict highs, lows, troughs, and ridges aloft in the same manner as isobars on the surface chart.
Answer (B) is incorrect because contours depict highs, lows, troughs, and ridges aloft, not on the surface. Answer (C) is incorrect because contour heights are expressed as pressure altitudes in a standard atmosphere, not corrected to MSL.

77.
9707. On the constant pressure analysis chart, satellite and aircraft observations are used in the analysis, over areas of sparse data. A satellite observation is plotted using

A—a station circle at the cloud top location.
B—a square at the cloud top location.
C—a star at the cloud top location.

Answer (C) is correct (9707). *(AWS Sect 12)*
On the constant pressure analysis chart, satellite and aircraft observations are used in analysis over areas of sparse data. A satellite observation is plotted using a star at the cloud top location, with the cloud height, wind estimate, and time of report.
Answer (A) is incorrect because a station circle represents the location of a reporting station, not a satellite observation. Answer (B) is incorrect because a square is used to indicate an aircraft observation, not a satellite observation.

78.
9711. On the constant pressure analysis chart, aircraft and satellite observations are used in the analysis, over areas of sparse data. An aircraft observation is plotted using

A—a station circle at the aircraft location.
B—a square at the aircraft location.
C—a star at the aircraft location.

Answer (B) is correct (9711). *(AWS Sect 12)*
On the constant pressure analysis chart, aircraft and satellite observations are used in analysis over areas of sparse data. An aircraft observation is plotted using a square at the aircraft location, with the flight level of aircraft, temperature, and wind data.
Answer (A) is incorrect because a station circle represents the location of a reporting station, not an aircraft location. Answer (C) is incorrect because a star represents a satellite observation, not an aircraft observation.

79.
9312. (Refer to figure 153 on page 752.) What type weather system is approaching the California Coast from the west?

A—LOW.
B—HIGH.
C—Cold front.

Answer (A) is correct (9312). *(AWS Sect 12)*
A three-dimensional picture can be developed by following the change in height of the height contours. These are the solid lines on Fig. 153, and the height is indicated in the black box. The contour that is approaching the California coast is lower than the contours over the southwestern and northwestern U.S. Thus, a low-pressure area must be approaching.
Answer (B) is incorrect because the height contours would increase, not decrease, for a high. Answer (C) is incorrect because pressure systems, not fronts, are depicted on a constant pressure chart.

80.
9310. (Refer to figure 154 on page 753.) What is the height of the 300-millibar level at the low pressure center in Canada?

A—9,120 meters MSL.
B—18,000 meters MSL.
C—11,850 meters MSL.

Answer (A) is correct (9310). *(AWS Sect 12)*
On Fig. 154, the low-pressure center in Canada is marked by the bold "L" in the upper center of the chart. The height of the low-pressure center is indicated by the three bold numbers under the "L," which are 912. For a 300-mb level, add a zero to the end of the number. Heights are expressed in meters MSL. Thus, 912 indicates 9,120 meters MSL.
Answer (B) is incorrect because the height of the 300-mb level of the low-pressure center is 9,120 meters MSL, not 18,000 meters MSL. Answer (C) is incorrect because Fig. 155 is the 200-mb, not 300-mb, pressure chart. The "185" below the "L" indicates the height of the 200-mb low-pressure center to be 18,500 meters MSL.

81.
9313. (Refer to figures 153 through 155 on pages 752 through 754.) What type weather is inferred by the almost vertical extent of the LOW in Canada?

A—A rapid-moving system with little chance of developing cloudiness, precipitation, and adverse flying conditions.
B—A slow-moving storm which may cause extensive and persistent cloudiness, precipitation, and generally adverse flying weather.
C—A rapid-moving storm, leaning to west with altitude, which encourages line squalls ahead of the system with a potential of severe weather.

Answer (B) is correct (9313). *(AWS Sect 12)*
By comparing the 500-, 300-, and 200-MB pressure chart, it is determined that the low pressure is tilting little with height. The upper winds are not blowing across but are almost encircling the low. Because of these conditions, the storm moves very slowly and usually causes extensive and persistent cloudiness, precipitation, and generally adverse flying weather.
Answer (A) is incorrect because the wind aloft is encircling the low, which means it is a slow-, not rapid-, moving system. Answer (C) is incorrect because the low is leaning very little, and the winds are encircling the low, which means it is a slow-, not rapid-, moving system.

82.
9311. (Refer to figures 153 through 155 on pages 752 through 754.) Interpret the path of the jetstream.

A—Southern California, Nevada, Utah, Nebraska/Kansas, and then southeastward.
B—Oregon, Idaho, Wyoming, Nebraska, Iowa, and across the Great Lakes.
C—The Alaska area, across Canada to Montana, North Dakota, then across the Great Lakes area.

Answer (C) is correct (9311). *(AWS Sect 12)*
To interpret the path of the jet stream, compare the isotachs on the 300- and 200-mb charts. The jet stream has winds of 50 kt. or greater. These greater wind speeds are found in a band from the Alaska area across Canada to Montana and North Dakota, then across the Great Lakes region.
Answer (A) is incorrect because the isotachs in the southern California area are between 30 and 50 kt. Answer (B) is incorrect because Oregon has isotachs between 10 and 30 kt.

83.
9314. (Refer to figures 153 through 155 on pages 752 through 754.) What is the approximate temperature for a flight from southern California to central Kansas at FL 350?

A— –16°C.
B— –39°C.
C— –41°C.

Answer (C) is correct (9314). *(AWS Sect 12)*
You will need to use the 300-mb (FL 300) chart and the 200-mb (FL 390) chart. You will then need to interpolate for FL 350.
The temperature is located in the upper left corner of the station on a constant pressure chart. On the 300-mb chart, the station in southern California is reporting a temperature of –30°C, and along the line to central Kansas, the temperature at the stations remains at –30°C. On the 200-mb chart, the southern California station reports a temperature of –53°C, and the station in central Kansas reports a temperature of –47°C. The average is –50°C.
Interpolate for FL 350 for an approximate temperature of –41°C.
Answer (A) is incorrect because –16°C is the approximate temperature at FL 230, not FL 350, from southern California to central Kansas. Answer (B) is incorrect because –39°C is the approximate temperature at FL 340, not FL 350.

84.
9315. (Refer to figures 153 through 155 on pages 752 through 754.) Determine the approximate wind direction and velocity at FL 240 over the station in central Oklahoma.

A—280° at 10 knots.
B—320° at 10 knots.
C—330° at 13 knots.

Answer (B) is correct (9315). *(AWS Sect 12)*
To determine the approximate wind direction, you must interpolate between values for FL 180 (500-mb chart) and FL 300 (300-mb chart). The wind direction and speed are determined by the flag at the reporting station. First decode the two given pressure levels:

FL 180 (500 mb)	=	280°	at	10 kt.
FL 300 (300 mb)	=	360°	at	10 kt.
Difference	=	80°	at	0 kt.

Interpolation for each value gives:

FL 240	=	320°	at	10 kt.

Answer (A) is incorrect because 280° at 10 kt. is the wind direction and speed at the 500-mb pressure level (FL 180). Answer (C) is incorrect because 330° at 13 kt. is the interpolation between the 200- and 300-mb charts, not the 300- and 500-mb charts.

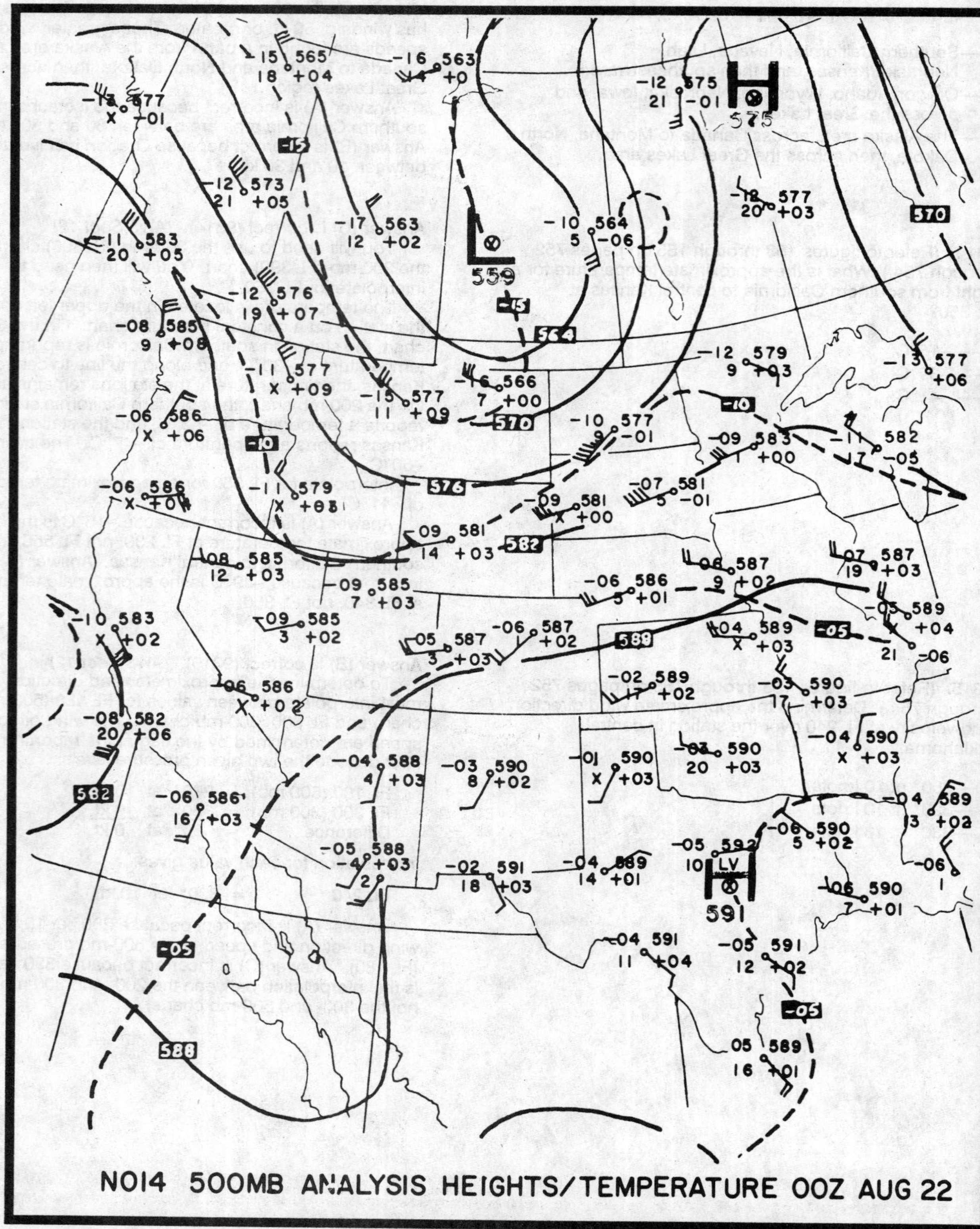

FIGURE 153.—500 MB Analysis Heights / Temperature Chart.

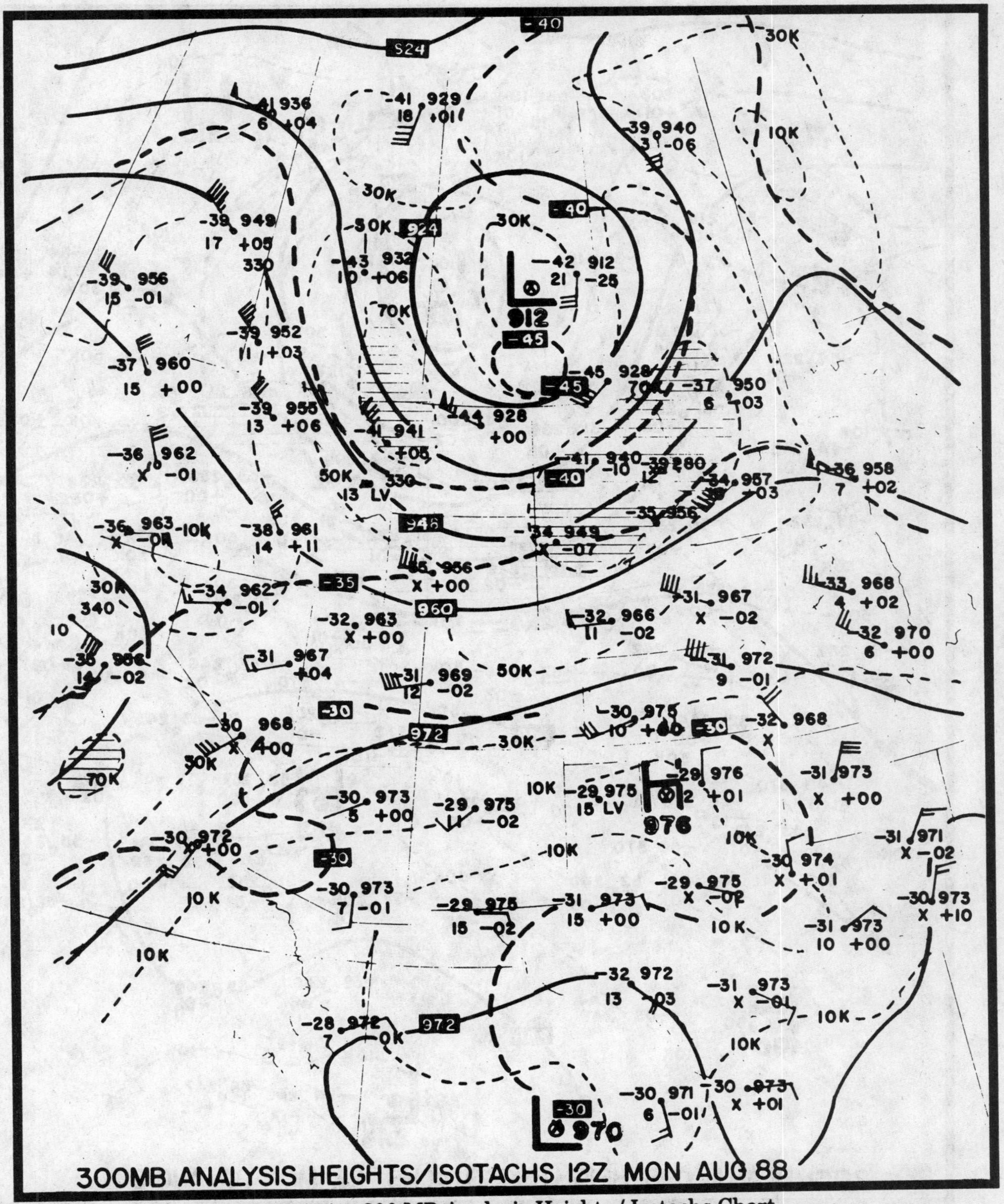

FIGURE 154.—300 MB Analysis Heights / Isotachs Chart.

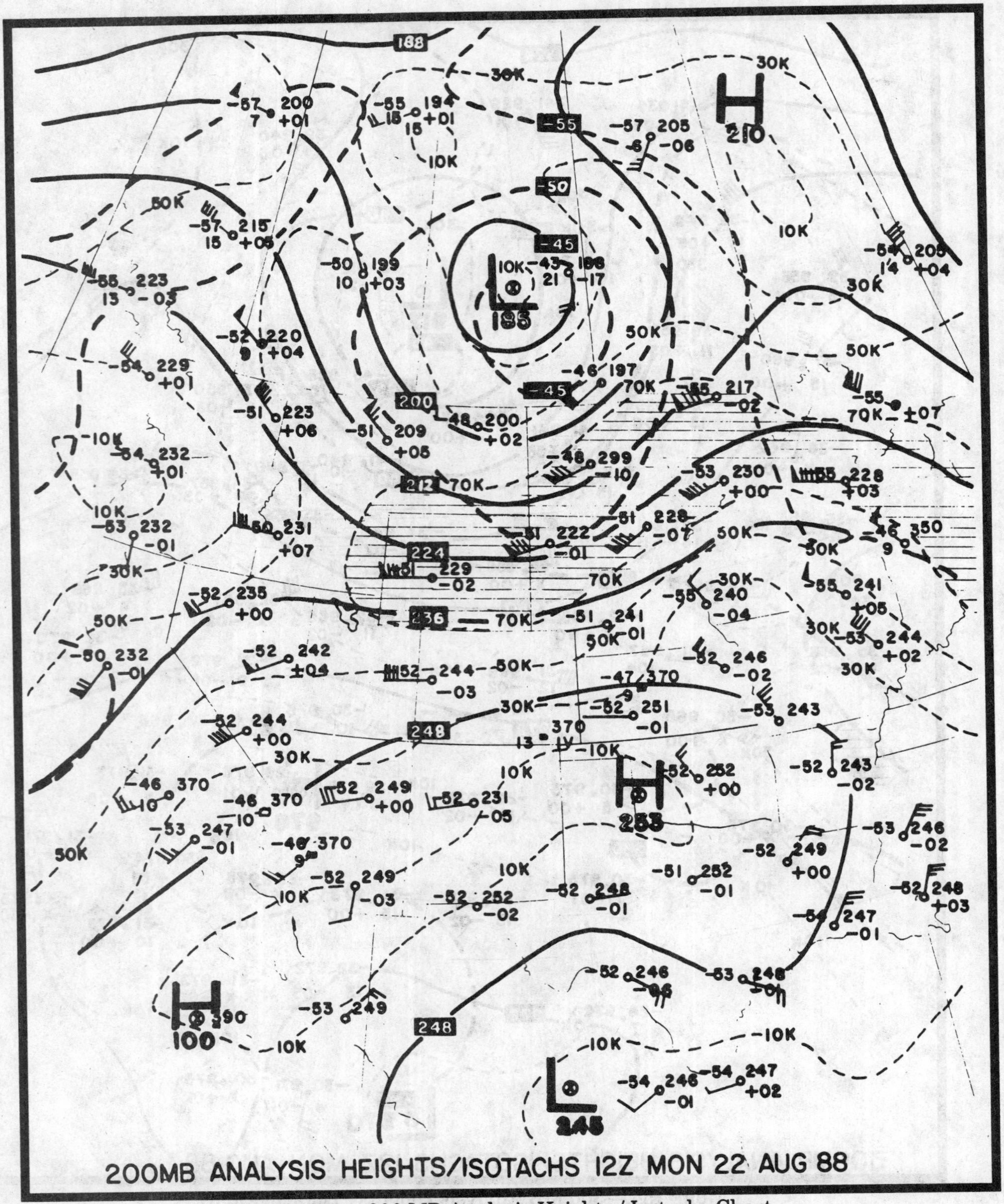

FIGURE 155.—200 MB Analysis Heights / Isotachs Chart.

85.
9316. (Refer to figures 153 through 155 on pages 752 through 754.) What is the relative moisture content of the air mass approaching the California coast?

A—Dry.
B—Moist enough for condensation.
C—Very wet with high potential for clouds and precipitation.

Answer (A) is correct (9316). *(AWS Sect 12)*
Determine the moisture content by comparing the temperature/dew point spread of the stations along the California coast at the 200-, 300-, and 500-mb pressure levels. The spread, if given, is located at the lower left of the station symbol. Both the 500-and 200-mb charts indicate relatively wide spread, thus dry conditions. The 300-mb chart shows that moisture is high in northern California. Overall the system is relatively dry.
Answer (B) is incorrect because there is very little moisture, as depicted by the wide temperature/dew point spread. Answer (C) is incorrect because the air mass is dry, not wet (note wide temperature/dew point spreads).

16.12 AIRMETs and SIGMETs

86.
9257. If a SIGMET alert is announced, how can information contained in the SIGMET be obtained?

A—ATC will announce the hazard and advise when information will be provided in the FSS broadcast.
B—By contacting a weather watch station.
C—By contacting the nearest AFSS.

Answer (C) is correct (9257). *(AIM Para 7-1-9)*
Pilots, upon hearing the alert notice, if they have not received the advisory or are in doubt, should contact the nearest FSS and ascertain whether the advisory is pertinent to their flights.
Answer (A) is incorrect because ATC does not advise when to listen to an FSS broadcast; rather they tell you to contact FSS. Answer (B) is incorrect because the pilot may monitor an FSS broadcast or contact any FSS. A weather watch station is a nonsense term.

87.
9286. Which type weather conditions are covered in the Convective SIGMET?

A—Embedded thunderstorms, lines of thunderstorms, and thunderstorms with 3/4-inch hail or tornadoes.
B—Cumulonimbus clouds with tops above the tropopause and thunderstorms with 1/2-inch hail or funnel clouds.
C—Any thunderstorm with a severity level of VIP 2 or more.

Answer (A) is correct (9286). *(AWS Sect 4)*
Convective SIGMETs are issued for (1) severe thunderstorm due to surface winds greater than 50 kt., hail at the surface equal to or greater than 3/4 in. in diameter, or tornadoes; (2) embedded thunderstorms; (3) line of thunderstorms; or (4) thunderstorms greater than or equal to VIP level 4 affecting 40% or more of an area at least 3,000 square mi.
Answer (B) is incorrect because cumulonimbus clouds with tops above the tropopause is not a weather condition covered in a convective SIGMET. Answer (C) is incorrect because thunderstorms must be at least VIP level 4, not level 2.

88.
9706. A severe thunderstorm is one in which the surface wind is

A—50 knots or greater and/or surface hail is 3/4 inch or more in diameter.
B—55 knots or greater and/or surface hail is 1/2 inch or more in diameter.
C—45 knots or greater and/or surface hail is 1 inch or more in diameter.

Answer (A) is correct (9706). *(AWS Sect 4)*
A severe thunderstorm is one in which the surface winds are greater than or equal to 50 kt., hail at the surface is greater than or equal to 3/4 in. in diameter, or tornadoes are present.
Answer (B) is incorrect because a severe thunderstorm is one in which the surface winds are 50 kt., not 55 kt., or greater or hail at the surface is 3/4 in., not 1/2 in., or more in diameter. Answer (C) is incorrect because a severe thunderstorm is one in which the surface winds are 50 kt., not 45 kt., or greater or hail at the surface is 3/4 in., not 1 in., or more in diameter.

89.
9284. (Refer to figure 148 below.) Which system in the Convective SIGMET listing has the potential of producing the most severe storm?

A — The storms in Texas and Oklahoma.
B — The storms in Colorado, Kansas, and Oklahoma.
C — The isolated storm 50 miles northeast of Memphis (MEM).

Answer (C) is correct (9284). *(AWS Sect 4)*
The isolated thunderstorm 50 mi. northeast of MEM is a VIP level 5 (intense) storm. With a top above 45,000 ft., extensive vertical development is taking place.
Answer (A) is incorrect because the storms in Texas and Oklahoma do not have such extensive development (tops 30,000 ft.) as the storm over Tennessee.
Answer (B) is incorrect because the storms in Colorado, Kansas, and Oklahoma do not have such extensive vertical development (tops of 38,000 ft.) as the storm over Tennessee.

90.
9285. (Refer to figure 148 below.) What time period is covered by the outlook section of the Convective SIGMET?

A — 24 hours after the valid time.
B — 2 to 6 hours after the valid time.
C — No more than 2 hours after the valid time.

Answer (B) is correct (9285). *(AIM Para 7-1-5)*
The outlook for a particular region is appended to the convective SIGMET. The outlook is a forecast and meteorological discussion for thunderstorm systems that are expected to require convective SIGMET issuances during a period 2 to 6 hr. after the valid time. Note that on Fig. 148 the outlook is good until 2355Z, which is 4 hr. after the valid time of 1955Z.
Answer (A) is incorrect because the outlook is for a period of 2 to 6 hr., not 24 hr., after the valid time.
Answer (C) is incorrect because the outlook can cover up to 6 hr. after the valid time.

CONVECTIVE SIGMET

MKCC WST Ø31755
CONVECTIVE SIGMET 42C
VALID UNTIL 1955Z
TX OK
FROM 5W MLC–PEQ–SJT–5W MLC
AREA SCT EMBDD TSTMS MOVG LTL. TOPS 3ØØ.

CONVECTIVE SIGMET 43C
VALID UNTIL 1955Z
CO KS OK
FROM AKO–OSW–3ØWNW OKC–AKO
AREA SCT TSTMS OCNLY EMBDD MOVG FROM 322Ø. TOPS 38Ø.

CONVECTIVE SIGMET 44C
VALID UNTIL 1955Z
5ØNE MEM
ISOLD INSTD LVL5 TSTM DIAM 1Ø MOVG FROM 2625. TOP ABV 45Ø.

OUTLOOK VALID UNTIL 2355Z
TSTMS OVR TX AND SE OK WL MOV SEWD 15 KTS.
TSTMS OVER CO, KS, AND N OK WL CONT MOVG SEWD 2Ø KTS.
TSTM OVR TN WL CONT MOVG EWD 25 KTS.

FIGURE 148.—Convective Sigmet.

END OF CHAPTER

CHAPTER SEVENTEEN
WIND SHEAR

This chapter contains outlines of major concepts tested, all FAA test questions and answers regarding wind shear, and an explanation of each answer. Each module, or subtopic, within this chapter is listed above with the number of questions from the FAA pilot knowledge test pertaining to that particular module. For each module, the first number following the parentheses is the page number on which the outline begins, and the next number is the page number on which the questions begin.

There are 45 questions in this chapter. We separate and organize the FAA questions into meaningful study units, e.g., wind shear, microbursts, etc. As an analogy, it is easier to deal with the "trees" if you understand the "forest." In this context, "trees" are individual FAA questions and the "forest" is the ATP knowledge test. The organizational units between the overall ATP knowledge test and individual ATP test questions are chapters and modules in this book.

CAUTION: The **sole purpose** of this book is to expedite your passing the FAA pilot knowledge test for the ATP certificate. Topics or regulations not directly tested on the FAA pilot knowledge test are omitted. Much more information and knowledge are necessary to fly safely. This additional material is presented in Gleim's other pilot training books (see the order form on page 818) and in many FAA books and circulars, as well as in airplane *POH*s and other commercial textbooks.

17.1 WIND SHEAR (Questions 1-13)

1. **Wind shear** is the rate of change of wind velocity.
   a. It may be associated with either a wind shift or a wind speed gradient (horizontally or vertically) at any level in the atmosphere.
2. A **severe wind shear** is defined as a rapid change in wind direction or velocity causing airspeed changes greater than 15 kt. or vertical speed changes greater than 500 fpm.
3. When surface wind directions vary at different places on the airport, there is a possibility of wind shear over or near the airport.
4. As the wind shears from a headwind to a calm wind, there is a quick reduction in the headwind component. The indications will be as follows:
   a. Decrease in indicated airspeed
   b. Pitch down of the airplane's nose
   c. Decrease in altitude
5. Increase in headwind component, e.g., shear from a tailwind to a headwind or a tailwind to a calm wind, results in the following:
   a. Increase in airspeed
   b. Increase in pitch
   c. Increase in altitude

6. During an approach in which thrust is being managed to maintain desired indicated airspeed and the glide slope is being flown, a tailwind shear to a constant headwind results in the following:
   a. Increase in pitch
   b. Decrease in vertical speed
   c. Initially an increase, then a decrease in airspeed
7. If airspeed and lift are lost due to wind shear, you should maintain or increase pitch attitude and accept the lower-than-normal airspeed indications.

17.2 CLEAR AIR TURBULENCE (CAT) (Questions 14-23)

1. **Clear air turbulence (CAT)** is best defined as turbulence encountered outside of convective clouds.
   a. The term CAT is used to describe the turbulence within and in the vicinity of cirrus and standing lenticular clouds.
   b. The term CAT is commonly applied to high-level turbulence associated with wind shear.
   c. CAT is often encountered in the vicinity of the jet stream.
2. Turbulence encountered above 15,000 ft. AGL, not associated with cloud formations, should be reported as CAT.
3. A preferred location of CAT is in an upper trough on the polar side of a jet stream.
4. A curving jet stream associated with a deep low-pressure trough can cause the greater turbulence.
5. CAT associated with a mountain wave may extend from the mountain crests to as high as 5,000 ft. above the tropopause and can range 100 NM or more downstream from the mountains.
6. When constant pressure charts show 20-kt. isotachs less than 60 NM apart, there is sufficient horizontal wind shear for CAT.
7. As the first ripple of CAT is encountered, you should adjust airspeed to that recommended for rough air.
8. In severe turbulence, you should attempt to maintain a constant attitude.
9. When encountering turbulence due to a wind shift associated with a sharp pressure trough, you should establish a course across the trough.
10. If jet stream turbulence is encountered with a direct headwind or tailwind, change altitude or course to avoid a possible elongated turbulent area.
11. When making an altitude change to get out of jet stream turbulence, you should
    a. Descend if the ambient temperature is falling.
    b. Climb if the ambient temperature is rising.

17.3 MICROBURSTS (Questions 24-35)

1. **Microbursts** are small-scale intense downdrafts from thunderstorms which, on reaching the surface, spread outward in all directions from the downdraft center.
   a. Hazard. Microbursts cause the presence of both vertical and horizontal wind shears that can be extremely hazardous to all types and categories of aircraft, especially at low altitudes.
   b. Intensity. The downdrafts can be as strong as 6,000 fpm.
   c. Duration. An individual microburst will seldom last longer than 15 min. from the time it strikes the ground until dissipation.
2. Horizontal winds near the surface can be as strong as 45 kt., resulting in a 90-kt. shear (headwind to tailwind change for a traversing aircraft) across the microburst.
3. The aircraft may encounter a headwind (performance increasing) followed by a downdraft and tailwind (both performance decreasing), possibly resulting in terrain impact.
   a. See Fig. 144 on page 767.

17.4 WINGTIP VORTICES/WAKE TURBULENCE (Questions 36-45)

1. Wingtip vortices (wake turbulence) are created when airplanes develop lift.
   a. The vortex characteristics may be altered by extending the flaps or changing the speed.
2. The greatest wingtip vortex strength occurs behind heavy, clean (flaps and gear up), and slow aircraft.
   a. For example, the takeoff of a jet transport airplane, when it has a high gross weight and a high angle of attack
3. Vortices circulate outward, upward, and around the wingtip (from the higher pressure below to the lower pressure above).
4. Wingtip vortices created by larger (transport category) aircraft tend to sink into the flight path of airplanes operating below the generating airplane.
5. A light crosswind can result in an upwind vortex remaining in the touchdown zone for a longer period of time.
6. Light quartering tailwinds hold the vortices of preceding aircraft on the runway for the longest period of time.
7. When taking off behind a departing jet, climb above and stay upwind of the jet aircraft's flight path until you are able to turn clear of the wake.
8. When taking off behind a jet that has just landed, plan to lift off beyond the point where the jet touched down.
9. To allow pilots of in-trail lighter aircraft to make flight path adjustments to avoid wake turbulence, pilots of heavy and large jet aircraft should fly
   a. On the established glide path
   b. On the approach course centerline or to the extended centerline of the runway of intended landing, as appropriate to conditions

QUESTIONS AND ANSWER EXPLANATIONS

All the FAA questions from the pilot knowledge test for the ATP certificate relating to wind shear, clear air turbulence, microbursts, and wake turbulence and the material outlined previously are reproduced on the following pages in the same modules as the outlines. To the immediate right of each question are the correct answer and answer explanation. You should cover these answers and answer explanations while responding to the questions. Refer to the general discussion in Chapter 1 on how to take the FAA pilot knowledge test.

Remember that the questions from the FAA pilot knowledge test bank have been reordered by topic, and the topics are organized into a meaningful sequence. Accordingly, the first line of the answer explanation gives the FAA question number and the citation of the authoritative source for the answer.

17.1 Wind Shear

1.
9166. What is an important characteristic of wind shear?

A—It is primarily associated with the lateral vortices generated by thunderstorms.
B—It usually exists only in the vicinity of thunderstorms, but may be found near a strong temperature inversion.
C—It may be associated with either a wind shift or a windspeed gradient at any level in the atmosphere.

Answer (C) is correct (9166). *(AvW Chap 9)*

Wind shear is the rate of change of wind velocity. The differences may be in wind speed, wind direction, or both. An important characteristic is that wind shear may be associated with either a wind shift or a wind speed gradient at any level in the atmosphere.

Answer (A) is incorrect because wind shear can be vertical (as well as lateral) in thunderstorm clouds between the updrafts and downdrafts, as well as in other areas such as frontal zones and low-level temperature inversions. Answer (B) is incorrect because wind shear can be encountered in areas other than thunderstorms, e.g., within a frontal zone, in and near the jet stream, in low-level inversions.

2.
9139. Which is a definition of “severe wind shear”?

A—Any rapid change of horizontal wind shear in excess of 25 knots; vertical shear excepted.
B—Any rapid change in wind direction or velocity which causes airspeed changes greater than 15 knots or vertical speed changes greater than 500 ft/min.
C—Any change of airspeed greater than 20 knots which is sustained for more than 20 seconds or vertical speed changes in excess of 100 ft/min.

Answer (B) is correct (9139). *(AC 00-54)*

A severe wind shear is defined as a rapid change in wind direction or velocity causing airspeed changes greater than 15 kt. or vertical speed changes greater than 500 fpm.

Answer (A) is incorrect because a severe wind shear can occur with both horizontal and vertical shears. Answer (C) is incorrect because a severe wind shear causes airspeed changes greater than 15 kt., not 20 kt., or vertical speed changes greater than 500 fpm, not 100 fpm.

3.
9167. What information from the control tower is indicated by the following transmission?

“SOUTH BOUNDARY WIND ONE SIX ZERO AT TWO FIVE, WEST BOUNDARY WIND TWO FOUR ZERO AT THREE FIVE.”

A—A downburst is located at the center of the airport.
B—Wake turbulence exists on the west side of the active runway.
C—There is a possibility of wind shear over or near the airport.

Answer (C) is correct (9167). *(AIM Para 4-3-7)*

The information for the transmission was provided by the Low-Level Wind Shear Alert System (LLWAS). This system detects the possibility of low-level wind shear over or near the airport. The system compares the wind measured around the airport with the wind measured at the center field location. When conditions exist, the tower controller will provide the site's location and wind. Note that the transmission in the question indicates wind from different directions at the airport.

Answer (A) is incorrect because a downburst is a vertical movement of air which is not measured by the LLWAS until it has horizontal movement. Also the wind direction is toward the center of the airport, not away from it. Answer (B) is incorrect because wake turbulence does not produce wind. It is generated by an aircraft that is producing lift, which could be on either side of the active runway.

4.
9054. What airport condition is reported by the tower when more than one wind condition at different positions on the airport is reported?

A—Light and variable.
B—Wind shear.
C—Frontal passage.

Answer (B) is correct (9054). ***(AIM Para 4-3-7)***
When the tower reports more than one wind condition at different positions on the airport, it means that wind shear is probable. Various sensors of the Low-Level Wind Shear Alert System measure the wind, and when differences become excessive, the tower will provide more than one wind condition at different positions.
Answer (A) is incorrect because light and variable is used to report the wind conditions when wind speed is less than 5 kt. Answer (C) is incorrect because a frontal passage is normally indicated by a change in wind direction, but it is usually not reported by the tower.

5.
9133. Which INITIAL cockpit indications should a pilot be aware of when a headwind shears to a calm wind?

A—Indicated airspeed decreases, aircraft pitches up, and altitude decreases.
B—Indicated airspeed increases, aircraft pitches down, and altitude increases.
C—Indicated airspeed decreases, aircraft pitches down, and altitude decreases.

Answer (C) is correct (9133). ***(AC 00-54)***
As the wind shears from a headwind to a calm wind, there is a quick reduction in the headwind component and a decrease in aircraft performance. The indications will be a decrease in indicated airspeed, a pitch down of the airplane's nose, and a decrease in altitude.
Answer (A) is incorrect because the aircraft will pitch down, not up, due to the relatively small angle of attack used during the headwind and the sudden decrease in the airflow over the wing when the wind shears to calm. Answer (B) is incorrect because less power is required to maintain an indicated airspeed in a headwind than in calm air because of ram air; thus a shear from a headwind to calm is indicated by a decrease in airspeed and a decrease, not an increase, in altitude.

6.
9134. Which condition would INITIALLY cause the indicated airspeed and pitch to increase and the sink rate to decrease?

A—Sudden decrease in a headwind component.
B—Tailwind which suddenly increases in velocity.
C—Sudden increase in a headwind component.

Answer (C) is correct (9134). ***(AC 00-54)***
A sudden increase in a headwind component, i.e., a tailwind shearing to a headwind, is initially indicated by an increase in airspeed, pitch, and altitude. A sudden increase in a headwind component will increase aircraft performance.
Answer (A) is incorrect because a sudden decrease in a headwind component decreases aircraft performance and is indicated by a decrease in airspeed, pitch, and altitude. Answer (B) is incorrect because an increase in tailwind velocity decreases performance and is indicated by a decrease in airspeed, pitch, and altitude.

7.
9135. Which INITIAL cockpit indications should a pilot be aware of when a constant tailwind shears to a calm wind?

A—Altitude increases; pitch and indicated airspeed decrease.
B—Altitude, pitch, and indicated airspeed decrease.
C—Altitude, pitch, and indicated airspeed increase.

Answer (C) is correct (9135). ***(AC 00-54)***
When a constant tailwind shears to a calm wind, the shear increases indicated airspeed and thus increases performance. The airplane tends to pitch up and gain altitude.
Answer (A) is incorrect because pitch and indicated airspeed also increase. Answer (B) is incorrect because altitude, pitch, and indicated airspeed decrease when a headwind, not tailwind, shears to a calm wind.

8.
9138. Which wind-shear condition results in an increase in airspeed?

A—Increasing tailwind and decreasing headwind.
B—Increasing tailwind and headwind.
C—Decreasing tailwind and increasing headwind.

Answer (C) is correct (9138). *(AC 00-54)*
When a tailwind shears to a headwind, the airspeed initially increases, the aircraft pitches up, and the altitude increases.
Answer (A) is incorrect because, when a headwind shears to a tailwind, increasing tailwind component and decreasing headwind component, the reduction of the ram air pressure on the pitot tube causes an initial reduction of indicated airspeed. The reduced headwind component will also cause a pitch down moment and a decrease in altitude. Answer (B) is incorrect because, when a headwind shears to a tailwind, increasing tailwind component and decreasing headwind component, the reduction of the ram air pressure on the pitot tube causes an initial reduction of indicated airspeed. The reduced headwind component will also cause a pitch down moment and a decrease in altitude.

9.
9137. Which wind-shear condition results in a loss of airspeed?

A—Decreasing headwind or tailwind.
B—Decreasing headwind and increasing tailwind.
C—Increasing headwind and decreasing tailwind.

Answer (B) is correct (9137). *(AC 00-54)*
When the headwind component decreases or the tailwind component increases, initially the airspeed decreases, the aircraft pitches down, and the altitude decreases.
Answer (A) is incorrect because, in a decreasing tailwind condition, airspeed initially increases, not decreases. Answer (C) is incorrect because both an increasing headwind and a decreasing tailwind increase, not decrease, airspeed initially.

10.
9141. Which airplane performance characteristics should be recognized during takeoff when encountering a tailwind shear that increases in intensity?

A—Loss of, or diminished, airspeed performance.
B—Decreased takeoff distance.
C—Increased climb performance immediately after takeoff.

Answer (A) is correct (9141). *(AC 00-54)*
As a tailwind shear increases in intensity, the aircraft performance decreases. More power will be required to counter the decrease in airspeed. As the tailwind intensity increases, there will be a loss of, or diminished, airspeed performance.
Answer (B) is incorrect because, as a tailwind shear increases, takeoff distance is increased, not decreased, because more power or distance is required to attain lift-off speed. Answer (C) is incorrect because, as a tailwind shear increases during climbout, the climb performance will decrease, not increase.

11.
9142. Thrust is being managed to maintain desired indicated airspeed and the glide slope is being flown. Which characteristics should be observed when a tailwind shears to a constant headwind?

A—PITCH ATTITUDE: Increases. VERTICAL SPEED: Increases. INDICATED AIRSPEED: Decreases, then increases to approach speed.
B—PITCH ATTITUDE: Increases. VERTICAL SPEED: Decreases. INDICATED AIRSPEED: Increases, then decreases.
C—PITCH ATTITUDE: Decreases. VERTICAL SPEED: Decreases. INDICATED AIRSPEED: Decreases, then increases to approach speed.

Answer (B) is correct (9142). *(AC 00-54)*
When a tailwind shears to a constant headwind, the indicated airspeed will initially increase, then decrease. The vertical speed will decrease, and pitch attitude will increase. Initially, thrust will be reduced to slow the airspeed, then increase as more power and a slower rate of descent are needed to maintain the glide slope in a constant headwind.
Answer (A) is incorrect because indicated airspeed will initially increase, not decrease, and vertical speed will decrease, not increase. Answer (C) is incorrect because both pitch and indicated airspeed will initially increase, not decrease.

12.
9220. In comparison to an approach in a moderate headwind, which is an indication of a possible wind shear due to a decreasing headwind when descending on the glide slope?

A—Less power is required.
B—Higher pitch attitude is required.
C—Lower descent rate is required.

Answer (B) is correct (9220). *(AC 00-54)*
A decreasing headwind shear will decrease indicated airspeed and performance capability. Due to a loss of airspeed, the airplane will tend to pitch down. Thus, a higher pitch attitude is required.
Answer (A) is incorrect because, as airspeed decreases, more, not less, power is required. Answer (C) is incorrect because, as the headwind decreases, groundspeed will increase, requiring a higher, not a lower, descent rate.

13.
9136. What is the recommended technique to counter the loss of airspeed and resultant lift from wind shear?

A—Lower the pitch attitude and regain lost airspeed.
B—Avoid overstressing the aircraft, "pitch to airspeed," and apply maximum power.
C—Maintain, or increase, pitch attitude and accept the lower-than-normal airspeed indications.

Answer (C) is correct (9136). *(AC 00-54)*
A loss of airspeed and resultant lift indicates an increasing tailwind (or decreasing headwind) shear. Successful recovery from a wind-shear encounter requires maintaining or increasing pitch attitude and accepting lower-than-normal airspeed indications.
Answer (A) is incorrect because lowering the pitch attitude to regain lost airspeed is a result of past training emphasis on airspeed control; it is not the recommended technique for recovering from a wind shear. Answer (B) is incorrect because the recommended technique to recover from a wind shear is to maintain or increase pitch attitude and not "pitch to airspeed," which may decrease pitch to regain lost airspeed.

17.2 Clear Air Turbulence (CAT)

14.
9235. Turbulence encountered above 15,000 feet AGL, not associated with cloud formations, should be reported as

A—convective turbulence.
B—high altitude turbulence.
C—clear air turbulence.

Answer (C) is correct (9235). *(AWS Sec 14)*
High-level turbulence encountered above 15,000 ft. AGL, not associated with cumuliform cloudiness, should be reported as clear air turbulence.
Answer (A) is incorrect because convective turbulence is normally associated with cumuliform clouds and is reported as turbulence. Answer (B) is incorrect because turbulence above 15,000 ft. AGL, not associated with clouds, is termed clear air turbulence, not high-altitude turbulence.

15.
9237. What is a likely location of clear air turbulences?

A—In an upper trough on the polar side of a jetstream.
B—Near a ridge aloft on the equatorial side of a high pressure flow.
C—Downstream of the equatorial side of a jetstream.

Answer (A) is correct (9237). *(AvW Chap 13)*
A preferred location of clear air turbulence is in an upper trough on the polar side of the jet stream. Cold and warm advection along with strong wind shears develop near the jet stream, especially where the curvature of the jet stream sharply increases in deepening upper troughs.
Answer (B) is incorrect because CAT is likely to occur on the polar side of a jet stream in an upper trough, not near a ridge aloft on the equatorial side of a high-pressure flow. Answer (C) is incorrect because CAT is likely on the polar, not equatorial, side of a jet stream.

16.
9239. Which type jetstream can be expected to cause the greater turbulence?

A—A straight jetstream associated with a high pressure ridge.
B—A jetstream associated with a wide isotherm spacing.
C—A curving jetstream associated with a deep low pressure trough.

Answer (C) is correct (9239). *(AvW Chap 13)*
Cold outbreaks colliding with warm air from the south intensify weather systems in the vicinity of the jet stream along the boundary between cold and warm air. Cold and warm advection along with strong wind shears (turbulence) develop near the jet stream, especially where curvature of the jet stream sharply increases in deepening upper troughs.
Answer (A) is incorrect because greater turbulence is expected in a curved, not straight, jet stream. Answer (B) is incorrect because greater turbulence is more pronounced when isotherm spacing is narrow, not wide.

17.
9232. Clear air turbulence (CAT) associated with a mountain wave may extend as far as

A—1,000 miles or more downstream of the mountain.
B—5,000 feet above the tropopause.
C—100 miles or more upwind of the mountain.

Answer (B) is correct (9232). *(AvW Chap 13)*
Mountain waves can create clear air turbulence (CAT). Mountain wave CAT may extend from the mountain crests to as high as 5,000 ft. above the tropopause and can range 100 mi. or more downstream from the mountains.
Answer (A) is incorrect because mountain wave CAT can range 100, not 1,000, mi. or more downstream of the mountain. Answer (C) is incorrect because mountain wave CAT is downwind, not upwind, of the mountain.

18.
9218. Under what conditions would clear air turbulence (CAT) most likely be encountered?

A—When constant pressure charts show 20-knot isotachs less than 60 NM apart.
B—When constant pressure charts show 60-knot isotachs less than 20 NM apart.
C—When a sharp trough is moving at a speed less than 20 knots.

Answer (A) is correct (9218). *(AC 00-30)*
When constant pressure charts show 20-kt. isotachs less than 60 NM apart, there is sufficient horizontal shear for CAT. These conditions normally occur on the polar side of the jet stream.
Answer (B) is incorrect because, when constant pressure charts show 20-kt., not 60-kt., isotachs less than 60 NM, not 20 NM, apart, CAT is most likely to be encountered. Answer (C) is incorrect because CAT can be expected upwind of the base of a deep upper trough, not because a sharp trough is moving.

19.
9128. What action is appropriate when encountering the first ripple of reported clear air turbulence (CAT)?

A—Extend flaps to decrease wind loading.
B—Extend gear to provide more drag and increase stability.
C—Adjust airspeed to that recommended for rough air.

Answer (C) is correct (9128). *(AvW Chap 13)*
When encountering the first ripple of clear air turbulence (CAT), it is appropriate to reduce airspeed to that recommended for rough air. This action decreases the amount of stress that is put on the airplane while in turbulence.
Answer (A) is incorrect because use of flaps increases the camber of the wing and angle of attack but does not decrease the amount of wing loading. Cruise airspeed usually exceeds the flap operating airspeed. This slow airspeed with a higher angle of attack greatly increases the possibility of a stall due to a vertical gust of wind exceeding the airplane's critical angle of attack.
Answer (B) is incorrect because extending the gear increases the drag but does not change the stability of the airplane. The reduced airspeed to extend the gear requires a higher angle of attack, which may cause the critical angle of attack to be exceeded during a wind shear.

20.
9129. If severe turbulence is encountered, which procedure is recommended?

A—Maintain a constant altitude.
B—Maintain a constant attitude.
C—Maintain constant airspeed and altitude.

Answer (B) is correct (9129). *(AvW Chap 11)*
When severe turbulence is encountered, as in a thunderstorm, it is almost impossible to hold a constant altitude. Maneuvering in an attempt to do so greatly increases stress on the aircraft. Stresses will be least if the aircraft is held in a constant attitude and allowed to ride the waves of updrafts and downdrafts.
Answer (A) is incorrect because severe turbulence causes large abrupt changes in altitude, and attempting to hold a constant altitude may overstress the airplane. Answer (C) is incorrect because severe turbulence causes large variations in both indicated airspeed and altitude. Any attempt to maintain constant airspeed and altitude may overstress the aircraft.

21.
9219. What action is recommended when encountering turbulence due to a wind shift associated with a sharp pressure trough?

A—Establish a course across the trough.
B—Climb or descend to a smoother level.
C—Increase speed to get out of the trough as soon as possible.

Answer (A) is correct (9219). *(AC 00-30A)*
If turbulence is encountered in an abrupt wind shift associated with a sharp pressure trough line, you should establish a course across the trough. This action is recommended because the turbulence normally is parallel to the trough and by crossing it you will minimize the turbulence.
Answer (B) is incorrect because climbing or descending to a smoother level is recommended when encountering jet stream turbulence with direct tailwinds or headwinds, not because of a wind shift associated with a sharp pressure trough. Answer (C) is incorrect because speed should be decreased, not increased, to the recommended airspeed for rough air to avoid over-stressing the airplane.

22.
9230. Which action is recommended if jetstream turbulence is encountered with a direct headwind or tailwind?

A—Increase airspeed to get out of the area quickly.
B—Change course to fly on the polar side of the jetstream.
C—Change altitude or course to avoid a possible elongated turbulent area.

Answer (C) is correct (9230). *(AC 00-30)*
If jet stream turbulence is encountered with direct tailwinds or headwinds, a change of altitude or course should be initiated since these turbulent areas are elongated with the wind and are shallow and narrow.
Answer (A) is incorrect because an increase in airspeed may overstress the airplane in turbulent conditions. Normally, a reduction in airspeed is required for turbulent air penetration. Answer (B) is incorrect because CAT is normally on the polar side of the jet stream, so you would be flying into more turbulent weather.

23.
9231. Which action is recommended regarding an altitude change to get out of jetstream turbulence?

A—Descend if ambient temperature is falling.
B—Descend if ambient temperature is rising.
C—Maintain altitude if ambient temperature is not changing.

Answer (A) is correct (9231). *(AC 00-30)*
If turbulence is due to a sloping tropopause, watch the temperature gauge. The point of coldest temperature will be the tropopause penetration. Turbulence will be more pronounced in the temperature-change zone on the stratospheric (upper) side of the sloping tropopause. To get out of this turbulence, descend if the ambient temperature is falling, and climb with a rising temperature.
Answer (B) is incorrect because, to get out of jet stream turbulence with a rising ambient temperature, you would climb, not descend. Answer (C) is incorrect because you would need to make an altitude change due to jet stream turbulence, and there should be a temperature change due to a sloping tropopause.

17.3 Microbursts

24.
9143. Maximum downdrafts in a microburst encounter may be as strong as

A—8,000 ft/min.
B—7,000 ft/min.
C—6,000 ft/min.

Answer (C) is correct (9143). *(AC 00-54)*
Downdrafts in a microburst can be as strong as 6,000 fpm. Horizontal winds near the surface can be as strong as 45 kt., resulting in a 90-kt. wind shear. The strong horizontal winds occur within a few hundred feet of the ground.
Answer (A) is incorrect because maximum downdrafts in a microburst may be as strong as 6,000, not 8,000, fpm. Answer (B) is incorrect because maximum downdrafts in a microburst may be as strong as 6,000, not 7,000, fpm.

25.
9131. Maximum downdrafts in a microburst encounter may be as strong as

A—1,500 ft/min.
B—4,500 ft/min.
C—6,000 ft/min.

Answer (C) is correct (9131). *(AIM Para 7-1-23)*
Downdrafts in a microburst can be as strong as 6,000 fpm. Horizontal winds near the surface can be as strong as 45 kt., resulting in a 90-kt. wind shear. The strong horizontal winds occur within a few hundred feet of the ground.
Answer (A) is incorrect because maximum downdrafts in a microburst may be as strong as 6,000, not 1,500, fpm. Answer (B) is incorrect because maximum downdrafts in a microburst may be as strong as 6,000, not 4,500, fpm.

26.
9130. What is the expected duration of an individual microburst?

A—Five minutes with maximum winds lasting approximately 2 to 4 minutes.
B—One microburst may continue for as long as an hour.
C—Seldom longer than 15 minutes from the time the burst strikes the ground until dissipation.

Answer (C) is correct (9130). *(AIM Para 7-1-23)*
An individual microburst will seldom last longer than 15 min. from the time it strikes ground until dissipation. The horizontal winds continue to increase during the first 5 min., with maximum-intensity winds lasting approximately 2 to 4 min.
Answer (A) is incorrect because individual microbursts seldom last longer than 15 min., not 5 min. Answer (B) is incorrect because, when microbursts are concentrated into a line structure (not an individual microburst), activity may continue for as long as 1 hr.

27.
9150. What is the expected duration of an individual microburst?

A—Two minutes with maximum winds lasting approximately 1 minute.
B—One microburst may continue for as long as 2 to 4 hours.
C—Seldom longer than 15 minutes from the time the burst strikes the ground until dissipation.

Answer (C) is correct (9150). *(AC 00-54)*
An individual microburst will seldom last longer than 15 min. from the time it strikes ground until dissipation. The horizontal winds continue to increase during the first 5 min., with maximum-intensity winds lasting approximately 2 to 4 min.
Answer (A) is incorrect because microbursts last 15, not 2 min., and maximum winds last 2 to 4 min., not 1 min. Answer (B) is incorrect because the maximum winds last 2 to 4 min., not 2 to 4 hr., and the microburst is usually limited to about 15 min.

28.
9140. Doppler wind measurements indicate that the windspeed change a pilot may expect when flying through the peak intensity of a microburst is approximately

A—15 knots.
B—25 knots.
C—45 knots.

Answer (C) is correct (9140). *(AC 00-54)*
Doppler radar wind measurements indicate that the wind speed change a pilot might expect when flying through the average microburst at its point of peak intensity is about 45 kt. However, microburst wind speed differences of almost 100 kt. have been measured.
Answer (A) is incorrect because a pilot may expect a 45-kt., not a 15-kt., wind speed change when flying through the peak intensity of a microburst. Answer (B) is incorrect because a pilot may expect a 45-kt., not a 25-kt., wind speed change when flying through the peak intensity of a microburst.

29.
9144. An aircraft that encounters a headwind of 45 knots, within a microburst, may expect a total shear across the microburst of

A—40 knots.
B—80 knots.
C—90 knots.

Answer (C) is correct (9144). *(AC 00-54)*
If a headwind in a microburst is 45 kt., the wind will be going in the opposite direction on the other side of the microburst at presumably the same 45 kt., resulting in a wind shear between the headwind and tailwind of 90 kt.
Answer (A) is incorrect because the total shear is the total headwind to tailwind change of a traversing aircraft; thus a 45-kt. headwind would shear 90 kt., not 40 kt., to a 45-kt. tailwind. Answer (B) is incorrect because the total shear is the total headwind to tailwind change of a traversing aircraft; thus a 45-kt. headwind would shear 90 kt., not 80 kt., to a 45-kt. tailwind.

30.
9132. An aircraft that encounters a headwind of 40 knots, within a microburst, may expect a total shear across the microburst of

A—40 knots.
B—80 knots.
C—90 knots.

Answer (B) is correct (9132). *(AIM Para 7-1-23)*
If a headwind in a microburst is 40 kt., the wind will be going in the opposite direction on the other side of a microburst at presumably the same 40 kt., resulting in an 80-kt. shear (headwind to tailwind change for a traversing aircraft) across the microburst.
Answer (A) is incorrect because the total shear is the total headwind to tailwind change of a traversing airplane; thus a 40-kt. headwind would shear 80 kt., not 40 kt., to a 40-kt. tailwind. Answer (C) is incorrect because the total shear is the total headwind to tailwind change of a traversing airplane; thus a 40-kt. headwind would shear 80 kt., not 90 kt., to a 40-kt. tailwind.

31.
9145. (Refer to figure 144 on page 767.) If involved in a microburst encounter, in which aircraft positions will the most severe downdraft occur?

A—4 and 5.
B—2 and 3.
C—3 and 4.

Answer (C) is correct (9145). *(AC 00-54)*
In Fig. 144, the most severe downdrafts occur at the center of the microburst, indicated by points 3 and 4.
Answer (A) is incorrect because point 5 has significantly less downdraft even though it has considerably more tailwind. Answer (B) is incorrect because point 2 has not as significant a downdraft as 3 and 4, but it contains a significant headwind even though it is decreasing.

32.
9146. (Refer to figure 144 below.) When penetrating a microburst, which aircraft will experience an increase in performance without a change in pitch or power?

A—3.
B—2.
C—1.

Answer (C) is correct (9146). *(AC 00-54)*
Point 1 on Fig. 144 indicates the position where the airplane first encounters a headwind and experiences increasing performance. This point is where the headwind component is the greatest, providing an increase in performance without a change in pitch or power.
Answer (A) is incorrect because point 3 indicates the point where the most severe downdraft occurs, which results in a decrease in performance. Answer (B) is incorrect because point 2 does not have as significant a headwind component as point 1, and thus performance is less than at point 1.

33.
9147. (Refer to figure 144 below.) What effect will a microburst encounter have upon the aircraft in position 3?

A—Decreasing headwind.
B—Increasing tailwind.
C—Strong downdraft.

Answer (C) is correct (9147). *(AC 00-54)*
At point 3 in Fig. 144, the airplane is experiencing a strong downdraft as it is approaching the center of the microburst.
Answer (A) is incorrect because at point 2, not 3, the airplane encounters decreasing headwind. Answer (B) is incorrect because at point 5 the airplane encounters an increasing tailwind, and it may result in an extreme situation as pictured, i.e., just before impact.

34.
9148. (Refer to figure 144 below.) What effect will a microburst encounter have upon the aircraft in position 4?

A—Strong tailwind.
B—Strong updraft.
C—Significant performance increase.

Answer (A) is correct (9148). *(AC 00-54)*
At point 4 in Fig. 144, the airplane is encountering a strong tailwind in addition to a strong downdraft and a decrease in airplane performance.
Answer (B) is incorrect because updrafts will occur in thunderstorms, not in microbursts from thunderstorms. Answer (C) is incorrect because the significant increase in performance occurs at point 1 where the headwind component is the greatest.

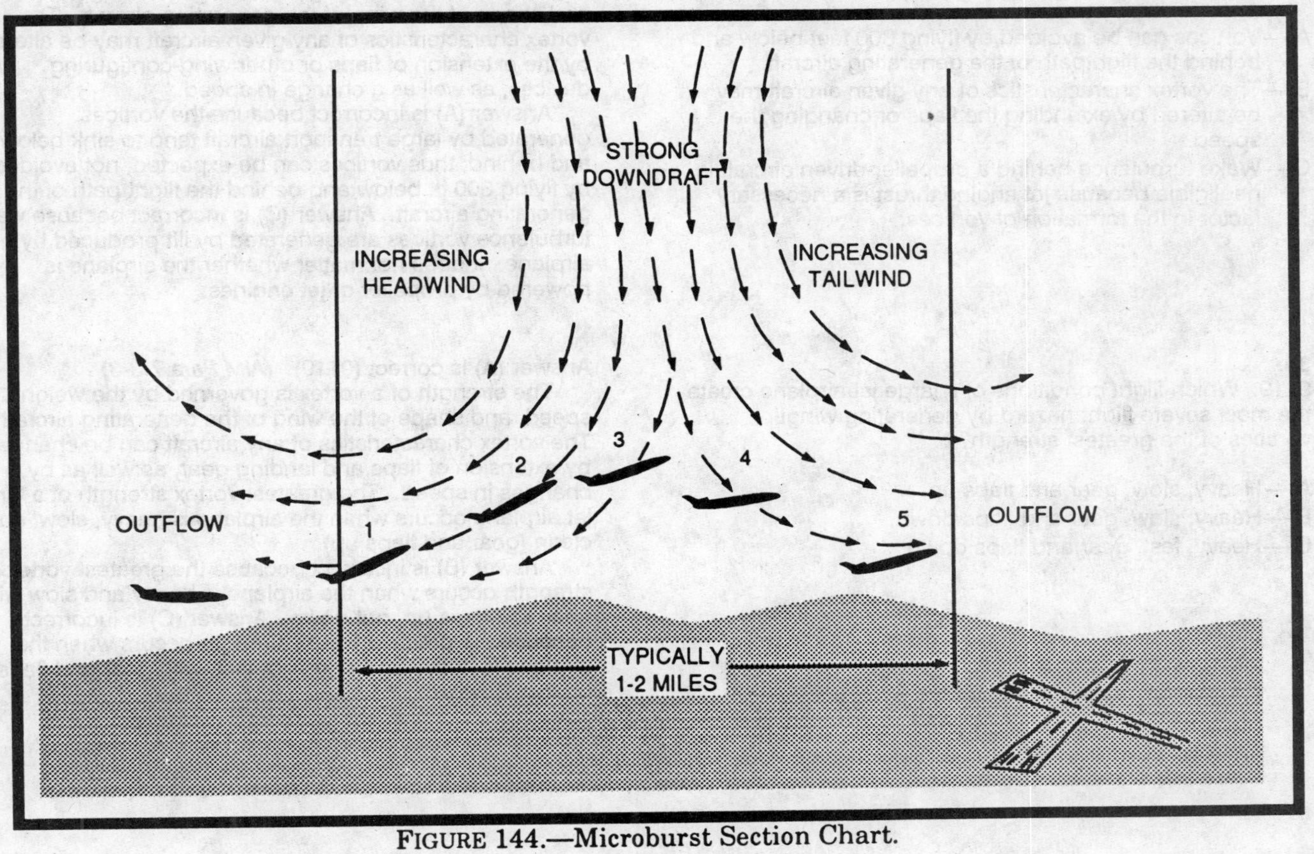

FIGURE 144.—Microburst Section Chart.

35.
9149. (Refer to figure 144 on page 767.) How will the aircraft in position 4 be affected by a microburst encounter?

A—Performance increasing with a tailwind and updraft.
B—Performance decreasing with a tailwind and downdraft.
C—Performance decreasing with a headwind and downdraft.

Answer (B) is correct (9149). *(AC 00-54)*
The aircraft at point 4 on Fig. 144 is affected by the microburst's causing a decrease in airplane performance due to a tailwind and downdraft.
Answer (A) is incorrect because performance will decrease, not increase, with a tailwind, and thunderstorms, not microbursts, have updrafts. Answer (C) is incorrect because the airplane at point 2 on Fig. 144 indicates the position where performance will decrease due to a headwind and downdraft.

17.4 Wingtip Vortices/Wake Turbulence

36.
9120. Hazardous vortex turbulence that might be encountered behind large aircraft is created only when that aircraft is

A—developing lift.
B—operating at high airspeeds.
C—using high power settings.

Answer (A) is correct (9120). *(AIM Para 7-3-2)*
Lift is generated by the creation of a pressure differential over the wing's, or other airfoil's, surface. The lowest pressure occurs over the upper wing surface and the highest pressure under the wing. This pressure differential triggers the roll up of the airflow aft of the wing resulting in swirling air masses trailing downstream from the wingtips. An airplane's wake consists of two counter-rotating vortices.
Answer (B) is incorrect because hazardous vortex turbulence is created only when that aircraft is developing lift, which can be while operating at low or high airspeeds. A slow, heavy, and clean airplane will generate the most hazardous vortex turbulence. Answer (C) is incorrect because most takeoff rolls are at high power settings, but the generation of vortices does not occur until lift is produced. Also landing approaches are conducted at lower power settings; vortex turbulence is produced whenever an airplane is producing lift.

37.
9123. Which statement is true concerning the wake turbulence produced by a large transport aircraft?

A—Vortices can be avoided by flying 300 feet below and behind the flightpath of the generating aircraft.
B—The vortex characteristics of any given aircraft may be altered by extending the flaps or changing the speed.
C—Wake turbulence behind a propeller-driven aircraft is negligible because jet engine thrust is a necessary factor in the formation of vortices.

Answer (B) is correct (9123). *(AIM Para 7-3-3)*
The strength of the wake turbulence produced by a large transport aircraft is governed by the weight, speed, and shape of the wing of the generating aircraft. The vortex characteristics of any given aircraft may be altered by the extension of flaps or other wing-configuring devices, as well as a change in speed.
Answer (A) is incorrect because the vortices generated by large transport aircraft tend to sink below and behind; thus vortices can be expected, not avoided, by flying 300 ft. below and behind the flight path of the generating aircraft. Answer (C) is incorrect because wake turbulence vortices are generated by lift produced by any airplane. It does not matter whether the airplane is powered by propeller or jet engines.

38.
9119. Which flight conditions of a large jet airplane create the most severe flight hazard by generating wingtip vortices of the greatest strength?

A—Heavy, slow, gear and flaps up.
B—Heavy, slow, gear and flaps down.
C—Heavy, fast, gear and flaps down.

Answer (A) is correct (9119). *(AIM Para 7-3-3)*
The strength of a vortex is governed by the weight, speed, and shape of the wing of the generating aircraft. The vortex characteristics of any aircraft can be changed by extension of flaps and landing gear, as well as by changes in speed. The greatest vortex strength of a large jet airplane occurs when the airplane is heavy, slow, and clean (gear and flaps up).
Answer (B) is incorrect because the greatest vortex strength occurs when the airplane is heavy and slow with gear and flaps up, not down. Answer (C) is incorrect because the greatest vortex strength occurs when the airplane is heavy and slow, not fast, with gear and flaps up, not down.

39.
9122. How does the wake turbulence vortex circulate around each wingtip?

A—Inward, upward, and around the wingtip.
B—Counterclockwise when viewed from behind the aircraft.
C—Outward, upward, and around the wingtip.

Answer (C) is correct (9122). ***(AIM Para 7-3-4)***

Since the pressure differential is caused by a lower pressure above the wing and a higher pressure below the wing, the air from the bottom moves out, up, and around each wingtip.

Answer (A) is incorrect because the air moves out around the edge of the wing, not in underneath the wing. Answer (B) is incorrect because the air moves out around the edge of the wing. From behind, the left wingtip vortex is clockwise, and the right wingtip vortex is counterclockwise.

40.
9121. Wingtip vortices created by large aircraft tend to

A—sink below the aircraft generating the turbulence.
B—rise from the surface to traffic pattern altitude.
C—accumulate and remain for a period of time at the point where the takeoff roll began.

Answer (A) is correct (9121). ***(AIM Para 7-3-4)***

The vortices created by large aircraft sink at a rate of several hundred feet per minute, slowing their descent and diminishing in strength with time and distance behind the generating aircraft. Pilots should fly at or above the preceding aircraft's flight path, avoiding the area behind and below the vortex-generating aircraft.

Answer (B) is incorrect because vortices created by large aircraft tend to sink, not rise, into the traffic pattern altitude. Answer (C) is incorrect because wingtip vortices are not generated until the aircraft's wings develop lift, so no wingtip vortices are generated at the point where the takeoff roll begins.

41.
9124. What effect would a light crosswind have on the wingtip vortices generated by a large airplane that has just taken off?

A—The upwind vortex will tend to remain on the runway longer than the downwind vortex.
B—A crosswind will rapidly dissipate the strength of both vortices.
C—The downwind vortex will tend to remain on the runway longer than the upwind vortex.

Answer (A) is correct (9124). ***(AIM Para 7-3-4)***

When vortices of large aircraft sink close to the ground (within about 200 ft.), they tend to move laterally over the ground at a speed of about 2 or 3 kt. in the direction of each generating wing. Thus, the downwind vortex on a crosswind is blown away quickly, but the upwind vortex remains on the runway longer.

Answer (B) is incorrect because a crosswind will hold the upwind vortex in the vicinity of the runway. Answer (C) is incorrect because the downwind vortex moves away at a faster rate than the upwind vortex.

42.
9126. What wind condition prolongs the hazards of wake turbulence on a landing runway for the longest period of time?

A—Direct tailwind.
B—Light quartering tailwind.
C—Light quartering headwind.

Answer (B) is correct (9126). ***(AIM Para 7-3-4)***

Light quartering tailwinds require the maximum caution because they can move the vortices of preceding aircraft forward into the touchdown zone and hold the upwind vortex on the runway.

Answer (A) is incorrect because, even though a direct tailwind can move the vortices of a preceding aircraft forward into the touchdown zone, it is not as hazardous because both vortices would move to the sides and not remain on the runway. Answer (C) is incorrect because a light quartering headwind would move the vortices away, i.e., toward the runway threshold, from, not into, the touchdown zone on a landing runway.

43.
9125. To avoid the wingtip vortices of a departing jet airplane during takeoff, the pilot should

A—lift off at a point well past the jet airplane's flightpath.
B—climb above and stay upwind of the jet airplane's flightpath.
C—remain below the flightpath of the jet airplane.

Answer (B) is correct (9125). *(AIM Para 7-3-6)*

A departing jet airplane's rotation point is where full vortices are first generated. On your takeoff, rotate prior to that point. Climb above and remain upwind of the jet airplane's flight path to avoid the descending wingtip vortices. Avoid subsequent headings which will cross below and behind the jet airplane (i.e., the jet will climb faster than a propeller airplane).

Answer (A) is incorrect because, if you rotate beyond the jet's rotation point, you will have to fly up into the jet's vortices. Answer (C) is incorrect because the jet airplane's vortices will sink. If you stay below the jet's flight path, you will fly in the area of the vortices.

44.
9127. If you take off behind a heavy jet that has just landed, you should plan to lift off

A—prior to the point where the jet touched down.
B—beyond the point where the jet touched down.
C—at the point where the jet touched down and on the upwind edge of the runway.

Answer (B) is correct (9127). *(AIM Para 7-3-6)*

You should ensure that an interval of at least 2 min. has elapsed before your takeoff behind a heavy jet that has just landed. Note the point where the heavy jet touched down and plan to lift off beyond that point. The vortices developed by the heavy jet will no longer be generated when lift is no longer produced (which is at the point of touchdown of the jet's nose gear).

Answer (A) is incorrect because a liftoff prior to the point where the jet touched down would force you to climb through the jet's vortices. Answer (C) is incorrect because liftoff should be planned beyond, not at, the point of touchdown to ensure you avoid the vortices, and you should remain on the center, not upwind edge, of the runway during takeoff.

45.
9715. To allow pilots of in-trail lighter aircraft to make flight path adjustments to avoid wake turbulence, pilots of heavy and large jet aircraft should fly

A—below the established glidepath and slightly to either side of the on-course centerline.
B—on the established glidepath and on the approach course centerline or runway centerline extended.
C—above the established glidepath and slightly downwind of the on-course centerline.

Answer (B) is correct (9715). *(AIM Para 7-3-8)*

To allow pilots of in-trail lighter aircraft to make flight path adjustments to avoid wake turbulence, pilots of aircraft that produce strong wake vortices, which include heavy and large jet aircraft, should fly on the established glide path and on the approach course centerline or the extended centerline of the runway.

Answer (A) is incorrect because pilots of heavy and large jet aircraft should fly on, not below, the established glide path and on the approach course centerline, not to either side of the centerline. Answer (C) is incorrect because pilots of heavy and large jet aircraft should fly on, not above, the established glide path and on the approach course centerline, not slightly downwind of the centerline.

END OF CHAPTER

CHAPTER EIGHTEEN
AEROMEDICAL FACTORS

This chapter contains outlines of major concepts tested, all FAA test questions and answers regarding aeromedical factors, and an explanation of each answer. Each module, or subtopic, within this chapter is listed above with the number of questions from the FAA pilot knowledge test pertaining to that particular module. For each module, the first number following the parentheses is the page number on which the outline begins, and the next number is the page number on which the questions begin.

There are 21 questions in this chapter. We separate and organize the FAA questions into meaningful study units, i.e., chapters and modules. As an analogy, it is easier to deal with the "trees" if you understand the "forest." In this context, "trees" are individual FAA questions and the "forest" is the ATP knowledge test. The organizational units between the overall ATP knowledge test and individual ATP test questions are chapters and modules in this book.

CAUTION: The **sole purpose** of this book is to expedite your passing the FAA pilot knowledge test for the ATP certificate. Topics or regulations not directly tested on the FAA pilot knowledge test are omitted. Much more information and knowledge are necessary to fly safely. This additional material is presented in Gleim's other pilot training books (see the order form on page 818) and in many FAA books and circulars, as well as in airplane *POH*s and other commercial textbooks.

18.1 HYPOXIA (Questions 1-3)

1. **Hypoxia** is a state of oxygen deficiency in the body sufficient to impair functions of the brain and other organs.
2. Hypoxia is caused by reduced barometric pressure at increased altitudes. With decreased atmospheric pressures, less oxygen is available to be absorbed by the lungs.
   a. For example, loss of cabin pressure in a pressurized aircraft results in an increase in cabin pressure altitude (or decrease in cabin pressure) and a decrease in the oxygen availability (or oxygen partial pressure).

18.2 CARBON MONOXIDE AND ALCOHOL (Questions 4-5)

1. The symptoms of carbon monoxide poisoning include headache, drowsiness, and dizziness.
2. Alcohol has an adverse effect on pilots, especially as altitude increases. Alcohol decreases mental capability and renders pilots more susceptible to disorientation and hypoxia.

18.3 HYPERVENTILATION (Questions 6-7)

1. **Hyperventilation** results from an abnormal increase in the volume of breathing. The result is an excessive amount of carbon dioxide being removed from the body.
   a. A stressful situation causing anxiety will most likely result in hyperventilation.
2. The symptoms of hyperventilation are lightheadedness, suffocation, drowsiness, tingling of the extremities, and coolness.

18.4 COLLISION AVOIDANCE (Questions 8-11)

1. Scanning procedures for effective collision avoidance should constitute looking outside for 15 seconds, then inside for 5 seconds, on a repeating basis.
2. At night, one should scan for traffic slowly to permit off-center viewing.
3. A threat of collision exists if an aircraft ahead appears to have no lateral or vertical movement and is increasing in size.
4. Another collision threat is an aircraft that is on the horizon and is increasing in size.

18.5 SPATIAL DISORIENTATION (Questions 12-13)

1. Pilots who use body sensations to interpret flight attitudes are more subject to spatial disorientation.
2. A recommended procedure to prevent or overcome spatial disorientation is to rely entirely on the indications of the flight instruments.

18.6 VISUAL ILLUSIONS (Questions 14-21)

1. The **Coriolis illusion** describes the effect of a prolonged constant-rate turn under IFR conditions followed by an abrupt head movement which creates the illusion of rotation on an entirely different axis.
2. The **somatogravic illusion** may occur during a rapid acceleration takeoff and creates the illusion that the airplane is in a nose-up attitude.
3. **Autokinesis** can occur in the dark when a pilot stares at a stationary light for a period of time with the result that the light appears to move about.
4. **Illusions Leading to Landing Errors**
   a. A narrower-than-usual runway can create the illusion that the airplane is at a higher-than-actual altitude.
   b. When landing over darkened or featureless terrain, such as water or snow, a pilot may be susceptible to the illusion that the airplane appears to be at an altitude higher than it actually is, which would result in a hard landing.
   c. Haze can give the illusion that the airplane is farther from the runway than it actually is.
   d. Sudden penetration of fog can create the illusion of pitching up.
   e. Rain on the windscreen can create the illusion of being at a higher-than-actual altitude.

QUESTIONS AND ANSWER EXPLANATIONS

All the FAA questions from the pilot knowledge test for the ATP certificate relating to aeromedical factors and the material outlined previously are reproduced on the following pages in the same modules as the outlines. To the immediate right of, or below, each question are the correct answer and answer explanation. You should cover these answers and answer explanations while responding to the questions. Refer to the general discussion in Chapter 1 on how to take the FAA pilot knowledge test.

Remember that the questions from the FAA pilot knowledge test bank have been reordered by topic, and the topics are organized into a meaningful sequence. Accordingly, the first line of the answer explanation gives the FAA question number and the citation of the authoritative source for the answer.

18.1 Hypoxia

1.
9106. Hypoxia is the result of which of these conditions?

A—Insufficient oxygen reaching the brain.
B—Excessive carbon dioxide in the bloodstream.
C—Limited oxygen reaching the heart muscles.

Answer (A) is correct (9106). *(MHP Chap 4)*
Hypoxia is a state of oxygen deficiency in the body sufficient to impair functions of the brain and other organs.
Answer (B) is incorrect because insufficient, not excessive, carbon dioxide in the blood stream describes hyperventilation. Answer (C) is incorrect because it is insufficient, not limited, oxygen to the brain, not heart muscles.

2.
9103. What causes hypoxia?

A—Excessive carbon dioxide in the atmosphere.
B—An increase in nitrogen content of the air at high altitudes.
C—A decrease of oxygen partial pressure.

Answer (C) is correct (9103). *(MHP Chap 4)*
Hypoxia from exposure to altitude is due only to the reduced barometric pressures encountered at altitude. With the decrease in barometric pressure, less oxygen is absorbable by the lungs.
Answer (A) is incorrect because the percentage of carbon dioxide and oxygen in the atmosphere remains constant with changes in altitude. There is just less pressure as you increase in altitude. Answer (B) is incorrect because relative nitrogen content also remains constant at high altitudes. There is just less pressure.

3.
9105. Loss of cabin pressure may result in hypoxia because as cabin altitude increases

A—the percentage of nitrogen in the air is increased.
B—the percentage of oxygen in the air is decreased.
C—oxygen partial pressure is decreased.

Answer (C) is correct (9105). *(MHP Chap 4)*
Hypoxia from exposure to altitude is due only to the reduced barometric pressures encountered at altitude. With the decrease in barometric pressure, less oxygen is absorbable by the lungs.
Answer (A) is incorrect because the percentage of nitrogen, carbon dioxide, and oxygen in the atmosphere remains constant with changes in altitude. There is just less pressure as you increase in altitude. Answer (B) is incorrect because oxygen remains at about 21% in the atmosphere, i.e., from the ground out to space. The amount of oxygen decreases, however, due to lower barometric pressure.

18.2 Carbon Monoxide and Alcohol

4.
9101. What is a symptom of carbon monoxide poisoning?

A—Rapid, shallow breathing.
B—Pain and cramping of the hands and feet.
C—Dizziness.

Answer (C) is correct (9101). *(AIM Para 8-1-4)*
Symptoms of carbon monoxide poisoning include headache, drowsiness, and dizziness. Pilots should be alert to the possibility that they may be experiencing carbon monoxide poisoning. Carbon monoxide poisoning generally occurs as a result of a defective cabin heater.

Answer (A) is incorrect because rapid breathing can result in hyperventilation, but it is not a symptom of carbon monoxide poisoning. Answer (B) is incorrect because tingling in the extremities, not pain and cramping, is one symptom of hyperventilation, not carbon monoxide poisoning.

5.
9111. What is the effect of alcohol consumption on functions of the body?

A—Alcohol has an adverse effect, especially as altitude increases.
B—Small amounts of alcohol in the human system increase judgment and decision-making abilities.
C—Alcohol has little effect if followed by equal quantities of black coffee.

Answer (A) is correct (9111). *(MHP Chap 8)*
Alcohol impairs flying skills. Even small amounts of alcohol render pilots more susceptible to disorientation and hypoxia.

Answer (B) is incorrect because even small amounts of alcohol impair, not increase, judgment and decision-making abilities. Answer (C) is incorrect because there is no way, including drinking black coffee, of increasing the body's metabolism of alcohol or of alleviating a hangover.

18.3 Hyperventilation

6.
9104. Which is a common symptom of hyperventilation?

A—Tingling of the hands, legs, and feet.
B—Increased vision keenness.
C—Decreased breathing rate.

Answer (A) is correct (9104). *(MHP Chap 5)*
Hyperventilation results from an abnormal increase in the volume of air breathed in and out of the lungs. It can occur subconsciously when a stressful situation is encountered. The result is an excessive amount of carbon dioxide removed from the body. The symptoms are lightheadedness, suffocation, drowsiness, tingling of the extremities, and coolness.

Answer (B) is incorrect because hyperventilation distorts one's abilities, not increases them. Answer (C) is incorrect because decreasing the breathing rate overcomes hyperventilation and is not a symptom of it.

7.
9102. Which would most likely result in hyperventilation?

A—A stressful situation causing anxiety.
B—The excessive consumption of alcohol.
C—An extremely slow rate of breathing and insufficient oxygen.

Answer (A) is correct (9102). *(MHP Chap 5)*
Hyperventilation results from an abnormal increase in the volume of air breathed in and out of the lungs. It can occur subconsciously when a stressful situation is encountered. The result is an excessive amount of carbon dioxide removed from the body. The symptoms are lightheadedness, suffocation, drowsiness, tingling of the extremities, and coolness.

Answer (B) is incorrect because excessive consumption of alcohol would most likely result in hypoxia, not hyperventilation. Answer (C) is incorrect because a slow rate of breathing is the cure for hyperventilation, and insufficient oxygen is the cause of hypoxia, not hyperventilation.

18.4 Collision Avoidance

8.
9117. Scanning procedures for effective collision avoidance should constitute

A—looking outside for 15 seconds, then inside for 5 seconds, then repeat.
B—1 minute inside scanning, then 1 minute outside scanning, then repeat.
C—looking outside every 30 seconds except in radar contact when outside scanning is unnecessary.

Answer (A) is correct (9117). *(AIM Para 8-1-6)*
Studies show that the amount of time the pilot spends on visual tasks inside the cabin should be no more than one-fourth to one-third of scan time outside, or no more than 4 to 5 seconds on the instrument panel for every 16 seconds of outside scanning when in VFR conditions.
Answer (B) is incorrect because pilots should spend the majority of scan time outside the airplane when in VFR conditions. Answer (C) is incorrect because pilots should spend the majority of scan time outside the airplane, and outside scanning is necessary when in radar contact in VFR conditions.

9.
9114. What is the most effective way to use the eyes during night flight?

A—Look only at far away, dim lights.
B—Scan slowly to permit offcenter viewing.
C—Concentrate directly on each object for a few seconds.

Answer (B) is correct (9114). *(FTH Chap 14)*
Physiologically, the eyes are most effective at seeing objects off center at night. Accordingly, a pilot should scan slowly to permit off-center viewing.
Answer (A) is incorrect because pilots must look at their gauges and instruments, which are about 2 ft. in front of them. Answer (C) is incorrect because peripheral (off-center) vision is more effective at night.

10.
9116. Which observed target aircraft would be of most concern with respect to collision avoidance?

A—One which appears to be ahead and moving from left to right at high speed.
B—One which appears to be ahead and moving from right to left at slow speed.
C—One which appears to be ahead with no lateral or vertical movement and is increasing in size.

Answer (C) is correct (9116). *(AIM Para 8-1-8)*
Any aircraft that appears to have no relative motion and stays in one scan quadrant is likely to be on a collision course. If the target shows no lateral or vertical motion but increases in size, take evasive action.
Answer (A) is incorrect because an airplane which is ahead of you and is moving from left to right should pass in front of you. Answer (B) is incorrect because an airplane which is ahead of you and is moving from right to left should pass in front of you.

11.
9118. When using the Earth's horizon as a reference point to determine the relative position of other aircraft, most concern would be for aircraft

A—above the horizon and increasing in size.
B—on the horizon with little relative movement.
C—on the horizon and increasing in size.

Answer (C) is correct (9118). *(AIM Para 8-1-8)*
Many pilots use the horizon as a reference point to determine the relative altitude of other aircraft. If the aircraft is above the horizon, it is probably on a higher flight path than you. An aircraft which appears to be below the horizon is probably flying at lower altitude. Accordingly, an airplane which appears to be on the horizon and does not show much relative movement may be at your altitude. Any aircraft which appears to increase in size is coming toward you.
Answer (A) is incorrect because an airplane above the horizon is probably at a higher altitude. Answer (B) is incorrect because an airplane on the horizon without movement may be traveling in the same direction as you.

18.5 Spatial Disorientation

12.
9112. A pilot is more subject to spatial disorientation when

A—ignoring or overcoming the sensations of muscles and inner ear.
B—eyes are moved often in the process of cross-checking the flight instruments.
C—body sensations are used to interpret flight attitudes.

Answer (C) is correct (9112). *(MHP Chap 14)*
Spatial disorientation is a state of temporary confusion resulting from misleading information being sent to the brain by various sensory organs. Using body sensations to interpret flight attitudes makes pilots more susceptible to spatial disorientation.
Answer (A) is incorrect because ignoring or overcoming the sensations of muscles and inner ear is a means of avoiding (not becoming subject to) spatial disorientation. Answer (B) is incorrect because rapid eye movements have little or no impact on spatial disorientation, and visual reference to reliable flight instruments helps avoid spatial disorientation.

13.
9113. Which procedure is recommended to prevent or overcome spatial disorientation?

A—Reduce head and eye movement to the greatest possible extent.
B—Rely on the kinesthetic sense.
C—Rely entirely on the indications of the flight instruments.

Answer (C) is correct (9113). *(AIM Para 8-1-5)*
The best way to overcome the effects of spatial disorientation is to rely entirely on the airplane's flight instruments and/or ground references (if available) and not on body sensations.
Answer (A) is incorrect because head and eye movement has little effect on spatial disorientation. Answer (B) is incorrect because relying on the kinesthetic sense encourages, rather than prevents, spatial disorientation.

18.6 Visual Illusions

14.
9107. When making an approach to a narrower-than-usual runway, without VASI assistance, the pilot should be aware that the approach

A—altitude may be higher than it appears.
B—altitude may be lower than it appears.
C—may result in leveling off too high and landing hard.

Answer (B) is correct (9107). *(AIM Para 8-1-5)*
A narrower-than-usual runway can create the illusion that the aircraft is at a higher altitude than it actually is. A pilot who does not recognize this illusion will fly a lower approach, with the risk of striking objects along the approach path.
Answer (A) is incorrect because wider-than-usual runways, not narrower-than-usual runways, may result in higher-than-desired approaches. Answer (C) is incorrect because leveling off too high is a result of not recognizing the illusion created by a wider-, not a narrower-, than-usual runway.

15.
9115. While making prolonged constant rate turns under IFR conditions, an abrupt head movement can create the illusion of rotation on an entirely different axis. This is known as

A—autokinesis.
B—Coriolis illusion.
C—the leans.

Answer (B) is correct (9115). *(AIM Para 8-1-5)*
Abrupt head movement in a prolonged constant-rate turn that has ceased stimulating the motion-sensing system can create the illusion of rotation or movement on an entirely different axis. This is known as the Coriolis illusion. The disoriented pilot could maneuver the aircraft in a dangerous attitude in an attempt to stop rotation. This effect may be prevented by not making sudden, extreme head movements, particularly while making prolonged constant-rate turns under IFR conditions.
Answer (A) is incorrect because autokinesis refers to a static light appearing to move about when stared at for many seconds in the dark. Answer (C) is incorrect because the term "leans" refers to an abrupt correction of a banked attitude which has been entered too slowly to stimulate the motion-sensing system in the inner ear and can create the illusion of bank in the opposite direction.

16.
9108. The illusion of being in a noseup attitude which may occur during a rapid acceleration takeoff is known as

A—inversion illusion.
B—autokinesis.
C—somatogravic illusion.

Answer (C) is correct (9108). *(AIM Para 8-1-5)*
A rapid acceleration during takeoff can create the illusion of being in a nose-up attitude. The disoriented pilot could push the airplane into a nose-low or dive attitude.
Answer (A) is incorrect because the inversion illusion results from an abrupt change from climb to straight-and-level flight, which can create an illusion of tumbling backwards. Answer (B) is incorrect because autokinesis refers to a static light appearing to move about when stared at for many seconds in the dark.

17.
9109. In the dark, a stationary light will appear to move when stared at for a period of time. This illusion is known as

A—somatogravic illusion.
B—ground lighting illusion.
C—autokinesis.

Answer (C) is correct (9109). *(AIM Para 8-1-5)*
In the dark, a static light will appear to move about when stared at for many seconds. The disoriented pilot may lose control of the aircraft in attempting to align it with the light.
Answer (A) is incorrect because somatogravic illusion occurs with a rapid acceleration during takeoff, creating the illusion of being in a nose-up attitude. Answer (B) is incorrect because a ground lighting illusion refers to lights on a straight path, such as a road, being mistaken by a pilot for runway or approach lights.

18.
9110. When making a landing over darkened or featureless terrain such as water or snow, a pilot should be aware of the possibility of illusion. The approach may appear to be too

A—high.
B—low.
C—shallow.

Answer (A) is correct (9110). *(AIM Para 8-1-5)*
The absence of ground features as when landing over water, darkened areas, and terrain made featureless by snow can create the illusion that the airplane is at a higher altitude than it actually is. The pilot who does not recognize this illusion will fly a lower-than-appropriate approach.
Answer (B) is incorrect because the illusion is that the aircraft is at a higher altitude than it is, not too low. Answer (C) is incorrect because the illusion is that the aircraft is at a higher altitude than it is, not too shallow.

19.
9433. Haze can give the illusion that the aircraft is

A—closer to the runway than it actually is.
B—farther from the runway than it actually is.
C—the same distance from the runway as when there is no restriction to visibility.

Answer (B) is correct (9433). *(AIM Para 8-1-5)*
Atmospheric haze can create the illusion of being at a greater distance from the runway. The pilot who does not recognize this illusion will fly a lower approach.
Answer (A) is incorrect because bright runway and approach lights or a wider-than-usual runway, not haze, can give the illusion of being closer to the runway. Answer (C) is incorrect because haze can give the illusion of being farther, not the same distance, from the runway.

20.
9434. Sudden penetration of fog can create the illusion of

A—pitching up.
B—pitching down.
C—leveling off.

Answer (A) is correct (9434). *(AIM Para 8-1-5)*
Penetration of fog can create the illusion of pitching up. The pilot who does not recognize this illusion will steepen the approach, often quite abruptly.
Answer (B) is incorrect because sudden penetration of fog can create the illusion of pitching up, not down. Answer (C) is incorrect because sudden penetration of fog can create the illusion of pitching up, not leveling off.

21.
9435. What illusion, if any, can rain on the windscreen create?

A—Does not cause illusions.
B—Lower than actual.
C—Higher than actual.

Answer (C) is correct (9435). *(AIM Para 8-1-5)*
Rain on the windscreen can create the illusion of greater height above the runway. The pilot who does not recognize this illusion will fly a lower approach.
Answer (A) is incorrect because rain on the windscreen can create the illusion of being higher than actual. Answer (B) is incorrect because rain on the windscreen can create the illusion of being higher, not lower, than actual.

END OF CHAPTER

APPENDIX A
AIRLINE TRANSPORT PILOT (PART 121) PRACTICE TEST

The following 80 questions have been randomly selected from the airplane questions in the FAA's ATP test bank. You will be referred to figures (charts, tables, etc.) throughout this book. Be careful not to consult the answers or answer explanations when you look for and at the figures. Topical coverage in this practice test is similar to that of the ATP (Part 121) knowledge test. Use the correct answer listing on page 786 to grade your practice test. The ATP (Part 135) practice knowledge test is on pages 787 through 794.

1.
8134. For which of these aircraft is the "clearway" for a particular runway considered in computing takeoff weight limitations?

A—Those passenger-carrying transport aircraft certificated between August 26, 1957 and August 30, 1959.
B—Turbine-engined-powered transport airplanes certificated after September 30, 1958.
C—U.S. certified air carrier airplanes certificated after August 29, 1959.

2.
8144. The emergency lights on a passenger-carrying airplane must be armed or turned on during

A—taxiing, takeoff, cruise, and landing.
B—taxiing, takeoff, and landing.
C—takeoff, cruise, and landing.

3.
8154. Which airplanes are required to be equipped with a ground proximity warning glide slope deviation alerting system?

A—All turbine-powered airplanes.
B—Passenger-carrying turbine-powered airplanes only.
C—Large turbine-powered airplanes only.

4.
8181. A passenger briefing by a crewmember shall be given, instructing passengers on the necessity of using oxygen in the event of cabin depressurization, prior to flights conducted above

A—FL 200.
B—FL 240.
C—FL 250.

5.
8185. For a 2-hour flight in a reciprocating-engine-powered airplane at a cabin pressure altitude of 12,000 feet, how much supplemental oxygen for sustenance must be provided? Enough oxygen for

A—30 minutes for 10 percent of the passengers.
B—10 percent of the passengers for 1.5 hours.
C—each passenger for 30 minutes.

6.
8190. When the need for a flight engineer is determined by aircraft weight, what is the takeoff weight that requires a flight engineer?

A—80,000 pounds.
B—more than 80,000 pounds.
C—300,000 pounds.

7.
8195. An air carrier operates a flight in VFR over-the-top conditions. What radio navigation equipment is required to be a dual installation?

A—VOR.
B—VOR and ILS.
C—VOR and DME.

8.
8200. The required crewmember functions that are to be performed in the event of an emergency shall be assigned by the

A—pilot in command.
B—air carrier's chief pilot.
C—certificate holder.

9.
8203. An air carrier that elects to use an Inertial Navigational System (INS) must meet which equipment requirement prior to takeoff on a proposed flight?

A—The INS system must consist of two operative INS units.
B—Only one INS is required to be operative, if a Doppler Radar is substituted for the other INS.
C—A dual VORTAC/ILS system may be substituted for an inoperative INS.

10.
8207. A pilot flight crewmember, other than pilot in command, must have received a proficiency check or line-oriented simulator training within the preceding

A—6 calendar months.
B—12 calendar months.
C—24 calendar months.

11.
8225. Which passenger announcement(s) must be made after each takeoff?

A—Keep safety belts fastened while seated and no smoking in the aircraft lavatories.
B—Passengers should keep seat belts fastened while seated.
C—How to use the passenger oxygen system and that there is a $1,000 fine for tampering with a smoke detector.

12.
8227. How does deadhead transportation, going to or from a duty assignment, affect the computation of flight time limits for air carrier flight crewmembers? It is

A—considered part of the rest period if the flightcrew includes more than two pilots.
B—considered part of the rest period for flight engineers and navigators.
C—not considered part of a rest period.

13.
8270. What is the fuel reserve requirement for a commercially operated reciprocating-engine-powered airplane flying within the 48 contiguous United States upon arrival at the most distant alternate airport specified in the flight release? Enough fuel to fly

A—30 minutes plus 15 percent of total time required to fly at normal cruising consumption to the alternate.
B—to fly for 90 minutes at normal cruising fuel consumption.
C—45 minutes at normal cruising fuel consumption.

14.
8282. During a supplemental air carrier flight, who is responsible for obtaining information on meteorological conditions?

A—Aircraft dispatcher.
B—Pilot in command.
C—Director of operations or flight follower.

15.
8286. Which documents are required to be carried aboard each domestic air carrier flight?

A—Load manifest (or information from it) and flight release.
B—Dispatch release and weight and balance release.
C—Dispatch release, load manifest (or information from it), and flight plan.

16.
8289. When a pilot's flight time consists of 80 hours' pilot in command in a particular type airplane, how does this affect the minimums for the destination airport?

A—Has no effect on destination but alternate minimums are no less than 300 and 1.
B—Minimums are decreased by 100 feet and 1/2 mile.
C—Minimums are increased by 100 feet and 1/2 mile.

17.
8311. What is the maximum, if any, number of packages of ORM material that may be transported in a passenger-carrying aircraft?

A—No limit applies.
B—A number whose combined transportation indices total 50.
C—A number whose combined transportation indices total 100.

18.
8319. Which of the following constitutes "substantial damage" according to NTSB Part 830?

A—Ground damage to landing gear, wheels, or tires.
B—Damage to wingtips (or rotor blades, in the case of a helicopter).
C—Failure of a component which would adversely affect the performance, and which would require replacement.

19.
8325. When are outboard ailerons normally used?

A—Low-speed flight only.
B—High-speed flight only.
C—Low-speed and high-speed flight.

20.
8574. (Refer to figure 44 on page 571.) What is the new CG if the weight is shifted from the aft to the forward compartment under Loading Conditions WS-2?

A—26.1 percent MAC.
B—20.5 percent MAC.
C—22.8 percent MAC.

21.
8590. (Refer to figures 45, 46, and 47 on pages 579, 580, and 581.) What is the STAB TRIM setting for Operating Conditions A-3?

A—18 percent MAC.
B—20 percent MAC.
C—22 percent MAC.

22.
8606. (Refer to figures 51 and 52 on page 591.) What is the total time from starting to the alternate through completing the approach for Operating Conditions L-4?

A—35 minutes.
B—19 minutes.
C—20 minutes.

23.
8653. (Refer to figures 63 and 64 on page 622.) What is the turbulent air penetration N_1 power setting for Operating Conditions Q-1?

A—82.4 percent.
B—84.0 percent.
C—84.8 percent.

24.
8680. (Refer to figure 70 on page 635.) How many minutes of dump time is required to reach a weight of 151,500 pounds?

Initial weight .... 181,500 lb
Zero fuel weight .... 126,000 lb

A—15 minutes.
B—14 minutes.
C—13 minutes.

25.
8700. (Refer to figures 76, 79, and 80 on pages 659, 660, and 661.) What is the CG in inches aft of datum for Loading Conditions WT-4?

A—908.4 inches.
B—909.0 inches.
C—909.5 inches.

26.
8710. (Refer to figures 78, 79, and 80 on pages 659, 660, and 661.) What is the CG in percent of MAC for Loading Conditions WT-14?

A—30.1 percent MAC.
B—29.5 percent MAC.
C—31.5 percent MAC.

27.
8734. (Refer to figures 84 and 85 on pages 670 and 671.) What is the approximate fuel consumed when holding under Operating Conditions H-3?

A—3,090 pounds.
B—6,950 pounds.
C—6,680 pounds.

28.
8756. (Refer to figures 91 and 92 on pages 682 and 684.) What approach speed and landing distance will be needed when landing at a weight of 140,000 pounds with 15° of flaps?

A—123 knots and 3,050 feet.
B—138 knots and 3,050 feet.
C—153 knots and 2,050 feet.

29.
8846. What is the minimum floor load limit that an aircraft must have to carry the following pallet of cargo?

Pallet dimensions are 48.5 x 33.5 inches.
Pallet weight – 44 lb
Tie-down devices – 27 lb
Cargo weight – 786.5 lb

A—79 lb/sq ft.
B—76 lb/sq ft.
C—73 lb/sq ft.

30.
8851. (Refer to figure 122 on page 454.) At what altitude and indicated airspeed would you expect to cross PIVOT INT on the approach to ORD?

A—FL 200 and 300 KIAS.
B—10,000 feet and 250 KIAS.
C—12,000 feet and 200 KIAS.

31.
8857. Maximum holding speed for a civil turbojet aircraft at a joint use airport (civil/Navy) between 7,000 and 14,000 ft is

A—200 knots.
B—265 knots.
C—230 knots.

32.
8869. (Refer to figure 125 on page 288.) What is the magnetic bearing TO the station as indicated by illustration 4?

A—285°.
B—055°.
C—235°.

33.
8889. What restriction applies to a large, turbine-powered airplane operating to or from a primary airport in Class B airspace?

A—Must not exceed 200 knots within Class B airspace.
B—Must operate above the floor when within lateral limits of Class B airspace.
C—Must operate in accordance with IFR procedures regardless of weather conditions.

34.
8910. What are the indications of the pulsating VASI?

A—High - pulsing white, on glidepath - green; low - pulsing red.
B—High - pulsing white, on glidepath - steady white, slightly below glide slope - steady red; low - pulsing red.
C—High - pulsing white, on course and on glidepath - steady white, off course but on glidepath - pulsing white and red; low - pulsing red.

35.
8932. (Refer to figure 131 on page 236.) What is the runway distance remaining at "C" for a nighttime takeoff on runway 9?

A—1,000 feet.
B—1,500 feet.
C—1,800 feet.

36.
8940. (Refer to figure 132 on page 331 and legend 22 on page 333.) Which navigation frequency must be used for the LORAN RNAV RWY 10R to Portland Intl Airport?

A—MWX 9940.
B—104.3 MHz.
C—133.0 MHz.

37.
8973. (Refer to figures 137 and 138 on page 322.) Which displacement from the localizer and glide slope at the outer marker is indicated?

A—1,550 feet to the left of the localizer centerline and 210 feet below the glide slope.
B—1,550 feet to the right of the localizer centerline and 210 feet above the glide slope.
C—775 feet to the left of the localizer centerline and 420 feet below the glide slope.

38.
8985. (Refer to figure 139 on page 290.) On which radial is the aircraft as indicated by the No. 1 NAV?

A—R-175.
B—R-165.
C—R-345.

39.
8987. (Refer to figure 139 on page 290.) What is the lateral displacement in degrees from the desired radial on the No. 2 NAV?

A—1°.
B—2°.
C—4°.

40.
8992. (Refer to figures 140 and 141 on pages 294 and 295.) To which aircraft position does HSI presentation "C" correspond?

A—9.
B—4.
C—12.

41.
9000. (Refer to figures 142 and 143 on page 292.) To which aircraft position does HSI presentation "E" correspond?

A—5.
B—6.
C—15.

42.
9014. Where are position reports required on an IFR flight on airways or routes?

A—Over all designated compulsory reporting points.
B—Only where specifically requested by ARTCC.
C—When requested to change altitude or advise of weather conditions.

43.
9024. Where does the DME indicator have the greatest error between the ground distance and displayed distance to the VORTAC?

A—High altitudes close to the VORTAC.
B—Low altitudes close to the VORTAC.
C—Low altitudes far from the VORTAC.

44.
9026. How are RNAV routes below FL 390 defined on the IFR flight plan?

A—Define each waypoint using degree-distance fixes based on appropriate navigational aids or by latitude/longitude.
B—List the initial and final fix with at least one waypoint each 200 NM.
C—Begin and end over appropriate arrival and departure transition fixes or navigation aids for the altitude being flown, define the random route waypoints by using degree-distance fixes based on navigation aids appropriate for the altitude being flown.

45.
9036. What action(s) should a pilot take if vectored across the final approach course during an IFR approach?

A—Continue on the last heading issued until otherwise instructed.
B—Contact approach control, and advise that the flight is crossing the final approach course.
C—Turn onto final, and broadcast in the blind that the flight has proceeded on final.

46.
9059. What effect would a change in ambient temperature or air density have on gas-turbine-engine performance?

A—As air density decreases, thrust increases.
B—As temperature increases, thrust increases.
C—As temperature increases, thrust decreases.

47.
9102. Which would most likely result in hyperventilation?

A—A stressful situation causing anxiety.
B—The excessive consumption of alcohol.
C—An extremely slow rate of breathing and insufficient oxygen.

48.
9132. An aircraft that encounters a headwind of 40 knots, within a microburst, may expect a total shear across the microburst of

A—40 knots.
B—80 knots.
C—90 knots.

49.
9139. Which is a definition of "severe wind shear"?

A—Any rapid change of horizontal wind shear in excess of 25 knots; vertical shear excepted.
B—Any rapid change in wind direction or velocity which causes airspeed changes greater than 15 knots or vertical speed changes greater than 500 ft/min.
C—Any change of airspeed greater than 20 knots which is sustained for more than 20 seconds or vertical speed changes in excess of 100 ft/min.

50.
9165. What term describes an elongated area of low pressure?

A—Trough.
B—Ridge.
C—Hurricane or typhoon.

51.
9171. What is the approximate rate unsaturated air will cool flowing upslope?

A—3 °C per 1,000 feet.
B—2 °C per 1,000 feet.
C—4 °C per 1,000 feet.

52.
9202. Atmospheric pressure changes due to a thunderstorm will be at the lowest value

A—during the downdraft and heavy rain showers.
B—when the thunderstorm is approaching.
C—immediately after the rain showers have stopped.

53.
9228. Which type frontal system is normally crossed by the jetstream?

A—Cold front and warm front.
B—Warm front.
C—Occluded front.

54.
9235. Turbulence encountered above 15,000 feet AGL, not associated with cloud formations, should be reported as

A—convective turbulence.
B—high altitude turbulence.
C—clear air turbulence.

55.
9253. For international flights, a U.S. High-Level Significant Weather Prognostic Chart is prepared for use

A—at any altitude above 29,000.
B—between 25,000 feet and 60,000 feet pressure altitude.
C—between FL 180 and FL 600.

56.
9271. (Refer to figure 145 on page 738.) The peak wind at KAMA was reported to be from 320° true at 39 knots,

A—which occurred at 1743Z.
B—with gusts to 43 knots.
C—with .43 of an inch liquid precipitation since the last report.

57.
9279. (Refer to figure 147 on page 746.) At which time is IFR weather first predicted at Lubbock (KLBB)?

A—2100Z.
B—0100Z.
C—0400Z.

58.
9292. (Refer to figure 149 on page 736.) What will be the wind and temperature trend for a DSM-LIT-SHV flight at 12,000 feet?

A—Windspeed decrease.
B—Temperature decrease.
C—Wind direction shift from northwest to southeast.

59.
9308. (Refer to figure 152 on page 728.) What weather conditions are depicted in the area indicated by arrow C on the Radar Summary Chart?

A—Average echo bases 2,800 feet MSL; thundershowers; intense to extreme echo intensity.
B—Cell movement toward the northwest at 20 knots; intense echoes; echo bases 28,000 feet MSL.
C—Area movement toward the northeast at 20 knots; strong to very strong echoes; echo tops 28,000 feet MSL.

60.
9325. Which is a definition of the term "crewmember"?

A—Only a pilot, flight engineer, or flight navigator assigned to duty in an aircraft during flight time.
B—A person assigned to perform duty in an aircraft during flight time.
C—Any person assigned to duty in an aircraft during flight except a pilot or flight engineer.

61.
9332. How soon after the conviction for driving while intoxicated by alcohol or drugs shall it be reported to the FAA, Civil Aviation Security Division?

A—No later than 30 working days after the motor vehicle action.
B—No later than 60 days after the motor vehicle action.
C—Required to be reported upon renewal of medical certificate.

62.
9335. An applicant who is taking a practical test for a type rating to be added to a commercial pilot certificate, in an approved simulator, is

A—required to have a first-class medical certificate.
B—required to have a second-class medical certificate.
C—not required to have a medical certificate.

63.
9345. To be eligible for the practical test for the renewal of a Category II authorization, what recent instrument approach experience is required?

A—Within the previous 6 months, six ILS approaches, three of which may be flown to the Category I DH by use of an approach coupler.
B—Within the previous 6 months, six ILS approaches flown by use of an approach coupler to the Category I DH.
C—Within the previous 12 calendar months, three ILS approaches flown by use of an approach coupler to the Category II DH.

64.
9355. Which operational requirement must be observed by a commercial operator when ferrying a large, three-engine, turbojet-powered airplane from one facility to another to repair an inoperative engine?

A—The computed takeoff distance to reach V_1 must not exceed 70 percent of the effective runway length.
B—The existing and forecast weather for departure, en route, and approach must be VFR.
C—No passengers may be carried.

65.
9364. A pilot is flying in IFR weather conditions and has two-way radio communications failure. What altitude should be used?

A—Last assigned altitude, altitude ATC has advised to expect, or the MEA, whichever is highest.
B—An altitude that is at least 1,000 feet above the highest obstacle along the route.
C—A VFR altitude that is above the MEA for each leg.

66.
9384. Under which condition, if any, may a pilot descend below DH or MDA when using the ALSF-1 approach light system as the primary visual reference for the intended runway?

A—Under no condition can the approach light system serve as a necessary visual reference for descent below DH or MDA.
B—Descent to the intended runway is authorized as long as any portion of the approach light system can be seen.
C—The approach light system can be used as a visual reference, except that descent below 100 feet above TDZE requires that the red light bars be visible and identifiable.

67.
9399. What is the maximum indicated airspeed a turbine-powered aircraft may be operated below 10,000 feet MSL?

A—288 knots.
B—250 knots.
C—230 knots.

68.
9402. What action should a pilot take when a clearance is received from ATC that appears to be contrary to a regulation?

A—Read the clearance back in its entirety.
B—Request a clarification from ATC.
C—Do not accept the clearance.

69.
9435. What illusion, if any, can rain on the windscreen create?

A—Does not cause illusions.
B—Lower than actual.
C—Higher than actual.

70.
9441. Which is a disadvantage of the one-step over the two-step process when deicing/anti-icing an airplane?

A—It is more complicated.
B—The holding time is increased.
C—More fluid is used with the one-step method when large deposits of ice and snow must be flushed off airplane surfaces.

71.
9570. (Refer to figure 112 on page 304.) While arcing left on the IAH 10 DME Arc, the pilot experiences a left crosswind component. Where should the bearing pointer be referenced relative to the 90° (wingtip) position to maintain the 10 DME range?

A—On the left wingtip reference.
B—Behind the left wingtip reference.
C—Ahead of the left wingtip reference.

72.
9584. (Refer to figures 107, 115, 116, 117, 118, and 118C on pages 372, 442, 443, 416, 444, and 447.) What is the ETE at .82 Mach?

A—1 hour 05 minutes.
B—1 hour 07 minutes.
C—1 hour 03 minutes.

73.
9585. (Refer to figures 115, 116, 117,118, and 118C on pages 372, 442, 443, 416, 444, and 447.) What is the total fuel required at .82 Mach?

A—22,420 pounds.
B—22,284 pounds.
C—22,700 pounds.

74.
9646. (Refer to figures 190, 195, 195A, 196 and 196A on pages 459, 465, 466, 467, and 468.) The PIC of PIL 10 has 87.5 hours and 26 landings as PIC in the B-767, while operating under Part 121. The PIC has 1,876 hours and 298 landings, as PIC in the L-1011 while operating under Part 121. What are the minimums for the ILS/DME RWY 35R approach at DEN for the PIC?

A—5567/18.
B—5667/42.
C—5631/20.

75.
9669. (Refer to legend 15 and figure 205 on pages 483 and 477.) San Francisco Intl (SFO) is an FAR Part 139 airport. What is the minimum number of aircraft rescue and fire fighting vehicles, and the type and amount of fire fighting agents that the airport should have?

A—Three vehicles and 500 pounds of dry chemical (DC) or Halon 1211 or 450 pounds DC and 4,000 gallons of water.
B—Three vehicles and 500 pounds of dry chemical (DC) or Halon 1211 or 500 pounds of DC plus 5,000 gallons of water.
C—Three vehicles and 500 pounds of dry chemical (DC) or Halon 1211 or 450 pounds DC plus 6,000 gallons of water.

76.
9670. (Refer to figure 210 on page 431.) The route between FIS (near Key West) and MTH, which is labeled B646, is an example of a

A—LF/MF Airway.
B—LF/MF Oceanic Route.
C—Military Training Route.

77.
9685. (Refer to figures 214, 183, and 183A on pages 490, 496, and 497.) The weather at PHL goes below the PIC's minimums and TNA 90 (a CAT C aircraft operating under FAR Part 121) diverts to the alternate ACY. Upon arrival at ACY, TNA 90 is cleared for an ILS RWY 13 approach. The PIC has less than 100 hours of PIC time in the MD-90. What are the landing minimums?

A—376/18.
B—376/50.
C—376/42.

78.
9694. The weather forecast requires an alternate for LUKACHUKAI (GPS RWY 25) ARIZONA. The alternate airport must have an approved instrument approach procedure, which is anticipated to be operational and available at the estimated time of arrival, other than

A—GPS or VOR.
B—ILS or GPS.
C—GPS or Loran C.

79.
9706. A severe thunderstorm is one in which the surface wind is

A—50 knots or greater and/or surface hail is 3/4 inch or more in diameter.
B—55 knots or greater and/or surface hail is 1/2 inch or more in diameter.
C—45 knots or greater and/or surface hail is 1 inch or more in diameter.

80.
9715. To allow pilots of in-trail lighter aircraft to make flight path adjustments to avoid wake turbulence, pilots of heavy and large jet aircraft should fly

A—below the established glidepath and slightly to either side of the on-course centerline.
B—on the established glidepath and on the approach course centerline or runway centerline extended.
C—above the established glidepath and slightly downwind of the on-course centerline.

For additional practice tests, use Gleim's *FAA Test Prep* software. Call (800) 87-GLEIM or use the order form at the back of this book to obtain your copy of this software. This software does not let you cheat (yourself). You can make up as many tests as you desire, and you can also have the software rearrange the question sequence and answer order. The questions on each test are randomly selected from the FAA's actual test questions so that the coverage of topics is the same as on the actual FAA test.

PART 121 PRACTICE TEST LIST OF ANSWERS

Q. #	Answer	Page	Q. #	Answer	Page	Q. #	Answer	Page	Q. #	Answer	Page
1.	B	80	21.	C	582	41.	B	293	61.	B	28
2.	B	83	22.	A	590	42.	A	257	62.	C	29
3.	A	93	23.	C	622	43.	A	287	63.	A	31
4.	C	87	24.	C	635	44.	C	251	64.	C	56
5.	A	84	25.	A	652	45.	B	264	65.	A	52
6.	B	94	26.	B	657	46.	C	209	66.	C	48
7.	A	89	27.	B	672	47.	A	774	67.	B	40
8.	C	97	28.	B	685	48.	B	766	68.	B	256
9.	B	122	29.	B	199	49.	B	760	69.	C	777
10.	C	100	30.	B	451	50.	A	696	70.	C	219
11.	B	107	31.	C	300	51.	A	700	71.	C	305
12.	C	102	32.	B	289	52.	B	707	72.	B	438
13.	C	116	33.	B	227	53.	C	710	73.	B	438
14.	B	110	34.	B	242	54.	C	763	74.	A	458
15.	C	121	35.	A	237	55.	B	748	75.	C	472
16.	C	119	36.	A	330	56.	A	739	76.	B	319
17.	A	63	37.	A	323	57.	B	747	77.	B	489
18.	C	25	38.	C	290	58.	A	735	78.	C	336
19.	A	187	39.	C	291	59.	C	729	79.	A	755
20.	C	572	40.	C	295	60.	B	26	80.	B	770

The listing above gives the correct answers for your ATP (Part 121) practice knowledge test and the page number in this book on which you will find each question with the complete Gleim answer explanation.

APPENDIX B
AIRLINE TRANSPORT PILOT (PART 135) PRACTICE TEST

The following 80 questions have been randomly selected from the airplane questions in the FAA's ATP test bank. You will be referred to figures (charts, tables, etc.) throughout this book. Be careful not to consult the answers or answer explanations when you look for and at the figures. Topical coverage in this practice test is similar to that of the ATP (Part 135) knowledge test. Use the correct answer listing on page 794 to grade your practice test. The ATP (Part 121) practice knowledge test is on pages 779 through 785.

1.
8007. Where must a certificate holder keep copies of completed load manifests and for what period of time?

A—1 month at its principal operations base, or at a location approved by the Administrator.
B—30 days at its principal operations base, or another location used by it and approved by the Administrator.
C—30 days, at the flight's destination.

2.
8011. Who is responsible for keeping copies of the certificate holder's manual up to date with approved changes or additions?

A—Each of the certificate holder's employees who are furnished a manual.
B—An employee designated by the certificate holder.
C—A representative of the certificate holder approved by the Administrator.

3.
8017. The maximum altitude loss for a malfunctioning autopilot without an approach coupler is 45 feet. If the MDA is 1,620 feet MSL and the TDZE is 1,294 feet, to which minimum altitude may you use the autopilot?

A—1,510 feet MSL.
B—1,339 feet MSL.
C—1,570 feet MSL.

4.
8026. A flight attendant crewmember is required on aircraft having a passenger seating configuration, excluding any pilot seat, of

A—15 or more.
B—19 or more.
C—20 or more.

5.
8054. In airplanes where a third gyroscopic bank-and-pitch indicator is required, that instrument must

A—continue reliable operation for at least 30 minutes after the output of the airplane's electrical generating system falls below an optimum level.
B—be operable by a selector switch which may be actuated from either pilot station.
C—continue reliable operation for a minimum of 30 minutes after total failure of the electrical generating system.

6.
8055. The two pilot stations of a pressurized aircraft are equipped with approved quick-donning oxygen masks. What is the maximum altitude authorized if one pilot is not wearing an oxygen mask and breathing oxygen?

A—41,000 feet MSL.
B—35,000 feet MSL.
C—25,000 feet MSL.

7.
8072. A pressurized airplane being operated at FL 330 can descend safely to 15,000 feet MSL in 3.5 minutes. What oxygen supply must be carried for all occupants other than the pilots?

A—60 minutes.
B—45 minutes.
C—30 minutes.

8.
8075. Which airplanes must have a shoulder harness installed at each flight crewmember station?

A—All airplanes used in commuter air service, having a passenger seating configuration of 9, excluding any pilot seat.
B—All airplanes operating under FAR Part 135, having a seating configuration for 10 persons.
C—All turbojet-powered airplanes.

9.
8089. If the weather forecasts require the listing of an alternate airport on an IFR flight, the airplane must carry enough fuel to fly to the first airport of intended landing, then to the alternate, and fly thereafter for a minimum of

A—45 minutes at normal holding speed.
B—45 minutes at normal cruise speed and then complete an approach and landing.
C—45 minutes at normal cruise speed.

10.
8093. If a certificate holder makes arrangements for another person to perform aircraft maintenance, that maintenance shall be performed in accordance with the

A—certificate holder's manual and FAR Parts 43, 91, and 135.
B—provisions of a contract prepared by a certificate holder and approved by the supervising FAA district office.
C—provisions and standards outlined in the certificate holder's manual.

11.
8108. A person is acting as pilot in command of a multiengine, reciprocating engine-powered airplane operated in passenger-carrying service by a commuter air carrier. If five takeoffs and landings have been accomplished in that make and basic model, which additional pilot-in-command experience meets the requirement for designation as the pilot in command?

A—Two takeoffs and landings, and 8 hours.
B—Five takeoffs and landings, and 5 hours.
C—Three takeoffs and landings, and 7 hours.

12.
8121. (Refer to figure 1 on page 172.) What is the maximum landing distance that may be used by a turbine-engine-powered, small transport category airplane to land on Rwy 24 (dry) at the destination airport?

A—5,460 feet.
B—5,490 feet.
C—6,210 feet.

13.
8132. When a person in the custody of law enforcement personnel is scheduled on a flight, what procedures are required regarding boarding of this person and the escort?

A—They shall be boarded before all other passengers board, and deplaned after all the other passengers have left the aircraft.
B—They shall be boarded after all other passengers board, and deplaned before all the other passengers leave the aircraft.
C—They shall board and depart before the other passengers.

14.
8300. (Refer to legend 34 on page 59, excerpt from CFR 49, Part 172.) What is the maximum, if any, net quantity of acetyl bromide in one package that may be carried in a cargo-only aircraft?

A—1 quart.
B—1 gallon.
C—No limit is specified.

15.
8316. What is the maximum quantity of flammable liquid fuel that may be carried in the cabin of a small, nonscheduled, passenger-carrying aircraft being operated in a remote area of the United States?

A—10 gallons.
B—15 gallons.
C—20 gallons.

16.
8317. What period of time must a person be hospitalized before an injury may be defined by the NTSB as a "serious injury"?

A—72 hours; commencing within 10 days after date of injury.
B—48 hours; commencing within 7 days after date of the injury.
C—10 days, with no other extenuating circumstances.

17.
8331. Which is a purpose of leading-edge flaps?

A—Increase the camber of the wing.
B—Reduce lift without increasing airspeed.
C—Direct airflow over the top of the wing at high angles of attack.

18.
8357. In a light, twin-engine airplane with one engine inoperative, when is it acceptable to allow the ball of a slip-skid indicator to be deflected outside the reference lines?

A—While maneuvering at minimum controllable airspeed to avoid overbanking.
B—When operating at any airspeed greater than V_{MC}.
C—When practicing imminent stalls in a banked attitude.

19.
8380. What are some characteristics of an airplane loaded with the CG at the aft limit?

A—Lowest stall speed, highest cruise speed, and least stability.
B—Highest stall speed, highest cruise speed, and least stability.
C—Lowest stall speed, lowest cruise speed, and highest stability.

20.
8433. What is the maximum allowable weight that may be carried on a pallet which has the dimensions of 81 X 83 inches?

Floor load limit – 180 lb/sq ft
Pallet weight – 82 lb
Tie-down devices – 31 lb

A—8,403.7 pounds.
B—8,321.8 pounds.
C—8,290.8 pounds.

21.
8435. (Refer to figures 3, 6, 8, 9, 10, and 11 on pages 515, 516, 518, 519, 520, and 521.) What is the CG in inches from datum under Loading Conditions BE-2?

A—Station 295.2.
B—Station 292.9.
C—Station 293.0.

22.
8442. (Refer to figures 3, 6, 8, 9, 10, and 11 on pages 515, 516, 518, 519, 520, and 521.) What is the CG shift if all passengers in rows 2 and 4 are deplaned under Loading Conditions BE-4?

A—2.5 inches aft.
B—2.5 inches forward.
C—2.0 inches aft.

23.
8445. (Refer to figures 4, 7, 9, 10, and 11 on pages 515, 517, 519, 520, and 521.) What is the CG in inches from datum under Loading Conditions BE-7?

A—Station 296.0.
B—Station 297.8.
C—Station 299.9.

24.
8453. (Refer to figures 4, 7, 9, 10, and 11 on pages 515, 517, 519, 520, and 521.) What is the CG shift if the cargo in section G is moved to section J under Loading Conditions BE-10?

A—2.7 inches aft.
B—2.4 inches aft.
C—3.2 inches aft.

25.
8467. (Refer to figure 13 on page 532.) Given the following conditions, what is the takeoff ground roll and V_1 speed?

Pressure altitude	3,000 ft
Temperature (OAT)	–10 °C
Weight	15,000 lb
Wind component	8 kts TW
Ice vanes	Extended

A—2,200 feet, 105 knots.
B—2,000 feet, 113 knots.
C—1,900 feet, 103 knots.

26.
8476. (Refer to figures 15, 16, and 17 on pages 539 and 540.) What is the two-engine rate of climb after takeoff in climb configuration for Operating Conditions BE-23?

A—1,500 ft/min.
B—2,600 ft/min.
C—2,490 ft/min.

27.
8484. (Refer to figures 19 and 20 on page 547.) At what altitude is the service ceiling with one engine inoperative for Operating Conditions BE-26?

A—13,000 feet.
B—14,200 feet.
C—13,600 feet.

28.
8507. (Refer to figures 27 and 28 on pages 563 and 564.) What are the approach speed and ground roll when landing under Operating Conditions B-37?

A—108 knots and 1,400 feet.
B—109 knots and 900 feet.
C—107 knots and 1,350 feet.

29.
8807. Which document would constitute an approved change to the type design without requiring a recertification?

A—An approved Minimum Equipment List.
B—The Operations Specifications as approved by the Administrator.
C—A special flight permit.

30.
8815. What is the maximum number of hours that a commuter air carrier may schedule a flight crewmember to fly in scheduled operations and other commercial flying in any calendar month?

A—100.
B—110.
C—120.

31.
8816. (Refer to figure 112 on page 304.) What effect on approach minimums, if any, does an inoperative MALSR have for an aircraft with an approach speed of 120 knots at IAH?

A—None.
B—Increases RVR to 5,000 feet.
C—Increases RVR to 6,000 feet.

32.
8832. What requirement must be met regarding cargo that is carried anywhere in the passenger compartment of a commuter air carrier airplane?

A—Cargo may not be carried anywhere in the rear of the passenger compartment.
B—The bin in which the cargo is carried may not be installed in a position that restricts access to, or use of the aisle between the crew and the passenger compartment.
C—The container or bin in which the cargo is carried must be made of material which is at least flash resistant.

33.
8838. What emergency equipment is required for extended overwater operations?

A—A portable survival emergency locator transmitter for each liferaft.
B—A pyrotechnic signaling device for each life preserver.
C—A life preserver equipped with a survivor locator light, for each person on the airplane.

34.
8853. What action should a pilot take if within 3 minutes of a clearance limit and further clearance has not been received?

A—Assume lost communications and continue as planned.
B—Plan to hold at cruising speed until further clearance is received.
C—Start a speed reduction to holding speed in preparation for holding.

35.
8865. (Refer to figure 124 on page 298.) A pilot receives this ATC clearance:

"...CLEARED TO THE ABC VORTAC. HOLD WEST ON THE TWO SEVEN ZERO RADIAL..."

What is the recommended procedure to enter the holding pattern?

A—Parallel or teardrop.
B—Parallel only.
C—Direct only.

36.
8871. (Refer to figure 125 on page 288.) Which RMI illustration indicates the aircraft is located on the 055° radial of the station and heading away from the station?

A—1.
B—2.
C—3.

37.
8893. What is the required flight visibility and distance from clouds if you are operating in Class E airspace at 9,500 feet with a VFR-on-Top clearance during daylight hours?

A—3 statute miles, 1,000 feet above, 500 feet below, and 2,000 feet horizontal.
B—5 statute miles, 500 feet above, 1,000 feet below, and 2,000 feet horizontal.
C—3 statute miles, 500 feet above, 1,000 feet below, and 2,000 feet horizontal.

38.
8915. Identify REIL.

A—Amber lights for the first 2,000 feet of runway.
B—Green lights at the threshold and red lights at far end of runway.
C—Synchronized flashing lights laterally at each side of the runway threshold.

39.
8922. (Refer to figure 129 on page 234.) What is the runway distance remaining at "A" for a daytime takeoff on runway 9?

A—1,000 feet.
B—1,500 feet.
C—2,000 feet.

40.
8958. What aural and visual indications should be observed over an ILS inner marker?

A—Continuous dots at the rate of six per second.
B—Continuous dashes at the rate of two per second.
C—Alternate dots and dashes at the rate of two per second.

41.
8966. What functions are provided by ILS?

A—Azimuth, distance, and vertical angle.
B—Azimuth, range, and vertical angle.
C—Guidance, range, and visual information.

42.
8970. What facilities may be substituted for an inoperative middle marker during a Category I ILS approach?

A—ASR and PAR.
B—The middle marker has no effect on straight-in minimums.
C—Compass locator, PAR, and ASR.

43.
8984. (Refer to figure 139 on page 290.) What is the lateral displacement of the aircraft in nautical miles from the radial selected on the No. 1 NAV?

A—5.0 NM.
B—7.5 NM.
C—10.0 NM.

44.
8998. (Refer to figures 140 and 141 on pages 294 and 295.) To which aircraft position does HSI presentation "I" correspond?

A—4.
B—12.
C—11.

45.
9003. (Refer to figures 142 and 143 on page 292.) To which aircraft position does HSI presentation "B" correspond?

A—9.
B—13.
C—19.

46.
9005. Under what condition may a pilot cancel an IFR flight plan prior to completing the flight?

A—Anytime it appears the clearance will cause a deviation from FAR's.
B—Anytime within controlled airspace by contacting ARTCC.
C—Only if in VFR conditions in other than Class A airspace.

47.
9019. What would be the identification when a VORTAC is undergoing routine maintenance and is considered unreliable?

A—A test signal, "TESTING", is sent every 30 seconds.
B—Identifier is preceded by "M" and an intermittent "OFF" flag would appear.
C—The identifier would be removed.

48.
9031. What is the suggested time interval for filing and requesting an IFR flight plan?

A—File at least 30 minutes prior to departure and request the clearance not more than 10 minutes prior to taxi.
B—File at least 30 minutes prior to departure and request the clearance at least 10 minutes prior to taxi.
C—File at least 1 hour prior to departure and request the clearance at least 10 minutes prior to taxi.

49.
9039. When cleared for an IFR approach to an uncontrolled airport with no FSS, what precaution should the pilot take after being advised to change to advisory frequency?

A—Monitor ATC for traffic advisories as well as UNICOM.
B—Broadcast intentions and continually update position reports on UNICOM.
C—Wait until visual contact is made with the airport and broadcast intentions to land.

50.
9086. What are FDC NOTAMs?

A—Conditions of facilities en route that may cause delays.
B—Time critical aeronautical information of a temporary nature from distant centers.
C—Regulatory amendments to published IAP's and charts not yet available in normally published charts.

51.
9107. When making an approach to a narrower-than-usual runway, without VASI assistance, the pilot should be aware that the approach

A—altitude may be higher than it appears.
B—altitude may be lower than it appears.
C—may result in leveling off too high and landing hard.

52.
9111. What is the effect of alcohol consumption on functions of the body?

A—Alcohol has an adverse effect, especially as altitude increases.
B—Small amounts of alcohol in the human system increase judgment and decision-making abilities.
C—Alcohol has little effect if followed by equal quantities of black coffee.

53.
9122. How does the wake turbulence vortex circulate around each wingtip?

A—Inward, upward, and around the wingtip.
B—Counterclockwise when viewed from behind the aircraft.
C—Outward, upward, and around the wingtip.

54.
9133. Which INITIAL cockpit indications should a pilot be aware of when a headwind shears to a calm wind?

A—Indicated airspeed decreases, aircraft pitches up, and altitude decreases.
B—Indicated airspeed increases, aircraft pitches down, and altitude increases.
C—Indicated airspeed decreases, aircraft pitches down, and altitude decreases.

55.
9150. What is the expected duration of an individual microburst?

A—Two minutes with maximum winds lasting approximately 1 minute.
B—One microburst may continue for as long as 2 to 4 hours.
C—Seldom longer than 15 minutes from the time the burst strikes the ground until dissipation.

56.
9156. Which area or areas of the Northern Hemisphere experience a generally east to west movement of weather systems?

A—Arctic only.
B—Arctic and subtropical.
C—Subtropical only.

57.
9170. Which term applies when the temperature of the air changes by compression or expansion with no heat added or removed?

A—Katabatic.
B—Advection.
C—Adiabatic.

58.
9173. If the ambient temperature is colder than standard at FL 310, what is the relationship between true altitude and pressure altitude?

A—They are both the same, 31,000 feet.
B—True altitude is lower than 31,000 feet.
C—Pressure altitude is lower than true altitude.

59.
9192. Which event usually occurs after an aircraft passes through a front into the colder air?

A—Temperature/dewpoint spread decreases.
B—Wind direction shifts to the left.
C—Atmospheric pressure increases.

60.
9232. Clear air turbulence (CAT) associated with a mountain wave may extend as far as

A—1,000 miles or more downstream of the mountain.
B—5,000 feet above the tropopause.
C—100 miles or more upwind of the mountain.

61.
9273. (Refer to figure 145 on page 738.) What weather improvement was reported at Lubbock (KLBB) between 1750 and 1818 UTC?

A—The wind shift and frontal passage at 1812Z.
B—The vertical visibility improved by 2,000 feet.
C—The temperature and dew point spread improved.

62.
9280. (Refer to figure 147 on page 746.) What type conditions can be expected for a flight scheduled to land at San Angelo (KSJT) at 1500Z?

A—Chance of 1 statute mile visibility and cumulonimbus clouds.
B—IFR conditions due to low visibility, rain, and mist.
C—IFR conditions due to low ceilings, rain, and fog.

63.
9286. Which type weather conditions are covered in the Convective SIGMET?

A—Embedded thunderstorms, lines of thunderstorms, and thunderstorms with 3/4-inch hail or tornadoes.
B—Cumulonimbus clouds with tops above the tropopause and thunderstorms with 1/2-inch hail or funnel clouds.
C—Any thunderstorm with a severity level of VIP 2 or more.

64.
9288. (Refer to figure 149 on page 736.) What approximate wind direction, speed, and temperature (relative to ISA) are expected for a flight over TUS at FL 270?

A—347° magnetic; 5 knots; ISA –10 °C.
B—350° true; 5 knots; ISA +5 °C.
C—010° true; 5 knots; ISA +13 °C.

65.
9297. (Refer to figure 150 on page 730.) The IFR conditions in the vicinity of Lakes Superior, Huron, and Michigan were caused by

A—overcast sky and haze.
B—convective action during the front's passage.
C—obscured skies and fog.

66.
9324. What is the name of a plane beyond the end of a runway which does not contain obstructions and can be considered when calculating takeoff performance of turbine-powered aircraft?

A—Clearway.
B—Stopway.
C—Obstruction clearance plane.

67.
9331. The flight instruction of other pilots in air transportation service by an airplane transport pilot is restricted to

A—36 hours in any 7-consecutive-day period.
B—7 hours in any 24-consecutive-hour period.
C—30 hours in any 7-consecutive-day period.

68.
9347. A Category II ILS pilot authorization, when originally issued, is normally limited to

A—Category II operations not less than 1600 RVR and a 150-foot DH.
B—pilots who have completed an FAA-approved Category II training program.
C—Category II operations not less than 1200 RVR and a 100-foot DH.

69.
9349. When a type rating is to be added to an airline transport pilot certificate, and the practical test is scheduled in an approved flight simulator and an aircraft, the applicant is

A—required to have at least a current third-class medical certificate.
B—required to have a current first-class medical certificate.
C—not required to hold a medical certificate.

70.
9382. Assuming that all ILS components are operating and the required visual references are not acquired, the missed approach should be initiated upon

A—arrival at the DH on the glide slope.
B—arrival at the visual descent point.
C—expiration of the time listed on the approach chart for missed approach.

71.
9423. Hold line markings at the intersection of taxiways and runways consist of four lines (two solid and two dashed) that extend across the width of the taxiway. These lines are

A—white in color and the dashed lines are nearest the runway.
B—yellow in color and the dashed lines are nearest the runway.
C—yellow in color and the solid lines are nearest the runway.

72.
9546. (Refer to figures 94, 95, and 96 on pages 343, 344, and 414.) What is the ETE from Chicago Midway Airport to Greater Buffalo Intl?

A—2 hours 12 minutes.
B—2 hours 15 minutes.
C—2 hours 18 minutes.

73.
9547. (Refer to figures 94, 95, and 96 on pages 343, 344, and 414.) What are the fuel requirements from Chicago Midway Airport to Greater Buffalo Intl?

A—2,224 pounds.
B—1,987 pounds.
C—1,454 pounds.

74.
9563. (Refer to figure 104 on page 366.) If communications are lost soon after takeoff on RWY 11R at Tucson Intl, what altitude restrictions apply, in IMC conditions?

A—Fly assigned heading for vectors to intercept appropriate transition, maintain 17,000 feet to GBN, then climb to assigned altitude.
B—Fly assigned heading for vectors to intercept the Gila Bend transition; climb to 17,000 feet or lower assigned altitude; climb to FL 220, 10 minutes after departure.
C—Fly assigned heading for vectors to intercept the Gila Bend transition; climb to 17,000 feet; 10 minutes after departure, climb to FL 220.

75.
9602. (Refer to figure 161A on page 410.) For landing on RWY 31L at JFK, how much RWY is available?

A—11,248 feet.
B—11,966 feet.
C—14,572 feet.

76.
9612. (Refer to figures 168, 171, 172, and 173 on pages 380, 421, 385, and 387.) What TAS should PTZ 70 maintain to arrive at FNT 30 minutes after passing PMM?

A—255 knots.
B—265 knots.
C—260 knots.

77.
9623. (Refer to figure 175 on page 422.) Four airways (V298, V25, V448, and V204) near YKM have a series of dots that overlay the airway. What do these dots indicate?

A—That the airways penetrate a Prohibited and Restricted Airspace.
B—That 2 miles either side of the airway, where shaded, is a Controlled Firing Area.
C—That the airways penetrate a Military Operations Area (MOA) and a special clearance must be received from ATC.

78.
9634. (Refer to figures 183 and 183A on pages 400 and 401.) When the weather at PHL goes below the PIC's minimums, the flight diverts to ACY. Upon arrival at ACY, EAB 90 is cleared for the ILS RWY 13 approach. The PIC has 89 hours of PIC time in the BE 1900. What are the PIC's minimums?

A—700-2.
B—276/18.
C—376/42.

79.
9693. The Instrument Approach Procedure Chart top margin identification is VOR or GPS RWY 25, AL-5672 (FAA), LUKACHUKAI, ARIZONA. In what phase of the approach overlay program is this GPS approach?

A—Phase I.
B—Phase III.
C—Phase II.

80.
9711. On the constant pressure analysis chart, aircraft and satellite observations are used in the analysis, over areas of sparse data. An aircraft observation is plotted using

A—a station circle, at the aircraft location.
B—a square, at the aircraft location.
C—a star, at the aircraft location.

PART 135 PRACTICE TEST
LIST OF ANSWERS

Q. #	Answer	Page	Q. #	Answer	Page	Q. #	Answer	Page	Q. #	Answer	Page
1.	B	139	21.	B	510	41.	C	320	61.	B	739
2.	A	137	22.	C	523	42.	B	325	62.	B	747
3.	C	145	23.	C	513	43.	A	290	63.	A	755
4.	C	147	24.	B	526	44.	C	296	64.	C	734
5.	C	149	25.	A	534	45.	C	293	65.	C	731
6.	B	143	26.	B	537	46.	C	252	66.	A	26
7.	C	152	27.	A	545	47.	C	287	67.	A	32
8.	C	154	28.	A	561	48.	A	250	68.	A	28
9.	C	160	29.	A	157	49.	B	264	69.	A	29
10.	A	176	30.	C	167	50.	C	244	70.	A	48
11.	A	164	31.	B	305	51.	B	776	71.	B	232
12.	B	173	32.	B	141	52.	A	774	72.	A	339
13.	A	58	33.	C	153	53.	C	769	73.	A	340
14.	B	58	34.	C	256	54.	C	761	74.	B	360
15.	C	64	35.	C	298	55.	C	766	75.	A	405
16.	B	24	36.	B	289	56.	B	711	76.	C	377
17.	A	189	37.	A	43	57.	C	700	77.	A	307
18.	B	208	38.	C	240	58.	B	703	78.	C	393
19.	A	202	39.	A	234	59.	C	697	79.	B	336
20.	C	195	40.	A	321	60.	B	763	80.	B	750

The listing above gives the correct answers for your ATP (Part 135) practice knowledge test and the page number in this book on which you will find each question with the complete Gleim answer explanation.

FAA LISTING OF SUBJECT MATTER KNOWLEDGE CODES

These five pages reprint the FAA's subject matter codes relating to the ATP knowledge test. These are the codes that will appear on your Airman Computer Test Report. See the illustration on page 11. Your test report will list the subject matter codes of the questions answered incorrectly. The total number of questions answered incorrectly may differ from the subject matter codes shown on the test report, since you may have missed more than one question in a certain subject matter code.

When you receive your Airman Computer Test Report, you can trace the subject matter codes listed on it to these five pages to find out which topics you had difficulty with. You should discuss your knowledge test results with your instructor.

Additionally, you should cross-reference the subject knowledge codes on your Airman Computer Test Report to our listing of FAA ATP test question numbers beginning on page 800. Determine which Gleim study modules you need to review.

The publications listed in the following pages contain study material you need to be familiar with when preparing for the ATP knowledge test. All of these publications can be purchased through U.S. Government bookstores, commercial aviation supply houses, or industry organizations.

Title 14, Code of Federal Regulations (14 CFR PART 1) —Definitions and Abbreviations

A01 General Definitions
A02 Abbreviations and Symbols

14 CFR PART 61—Certification: Pilots, Flight Instructors, and Ground Instructors

A20 General
A21 Aircraft Ratings and Pilot Authorizations
A22 Student Pilots
A23 Private Pilots
A24 Commercial Pilots
A25 Airline Transport Pilots
A26 Flight Instructors
A27 Ground Instructors
A29 Recreational Pilot

14 CFR PART 91—General Operating and Flight Rules

B07 General
B08 Flight Rules - General
B09 Visual Flight Rules
B10 Instrument Flight Rules
B11 Equipment, Instrument, and Certificate Requirements
B12 Special Flight Operations
B13 Maintenance, Preventive Maintenance, and Alterations
B14 Large and Turbine-powered Multiengine Airplanes
B15 Additional Equipment and Operating Requirements for Large and Transport Category Aircraft
B16 Appendix A - Category II Operations: Manual, Instruments, Equipment, and Maintenance
B17 Foreign Aircraft Operations and Operations of U.S.-Registered Civil Aircraft Outside of the U.S.

14 CFR PART 108—Airplane Operator Security

C10 General

14 CFR PART 119—Certification: Air Carriers and Commercial Operators

C20 General
C21 Applicability of Operating Requirements to Different Kinds of Operations Under Parts 121, 125, and 135
C22 Certification, Operations Specifications, and Certain Other Requirements for Operations Conducted Under Parts 121 or 135.

14 CFR PART 121—Certification and Operations: Domestic, Flag, and Supplemental Air Carriers and Commercial Operators of Large Aircraft

D01 General
D02 Certification Rules for Domestic and Flag Air Carriers
D03 Certification Rules for Supplemental Air Carriers and Commercial Operators
D04 Rules Governing All Certificate Holders Under This Part
D05 Approval of Routes: Domestic and Flag Air Carriers
D06 Approval of Areas and Routes for Supplemental Air Carriers and Commercial Operators
D07 Manual Requirements
D08 Aircraft Requirements
D09 Airplane Performance Operating Limitations
D10 Special Airworthiness Requirements
D11 Instrument and Equipment Requirements
D12 Maintenance, Preventive Maintenance, and Alterations
D13 Airman and Crewmember Requirements
D14 Training Program
D15 Crewmember Qualifications

D16 Aircraft Dispatcher Qualifications and Duty Time Limitations: Domestic and Flag Air Carriers
D17 Flight Time Limitations and Rest Requirements: Domestic Air Carriers
D18 Flight Time Limitations: Flag Air Carriers
D19 Flight Time Limitations: Supplemental Air Carriers and Commercial Operators
D20 Flight Operations
D21 Dispatching and Flight Release Rules
D22 Records and Reports
D23 Crewmember Certificate: International
D24 Special Federal Aviation Regulation SFAR No. 14

14 CFR PART 135—Operating Requirements: Commuter and On-Demand Operations

E01 General
E02 Flight Operations
E03 Aircraft and Equipment
E04 VFR/IFR Operating Limitations and Weather Requirements
E05 Flight Crewmember Requirements
E06 Flight Crewmember Flight Time Limitations and Rest Requirements
E07 Crewmember Testing Requirements
E08 Training
E09 Airplane Performance Operating Limitations
E10 Maintenance, Preventive Maintenance, and Alterations
E11 Appendix A: Additional Airworthiness Standards for 10 or More Passenger Airplanes
E12 Special Federal Aviation Regulations SFAR No. 36
E13 Special Federal Aviation Regulations SFAR No. 38

US HMR 172—Hazardous Materials Table

F02 General

US HMR 175—Materials Transportation Bureau Hazardous Materials Regulations (HMR)

G01 General Information and Regulations
G02 Loading, Unloading, and Handling
G03 Specific Regulation Applicable According to Classification of Material

NTSB 830—Rules Pertaining to the Notification and Reporting of Aircraft Accidents or Incidents and Overdue Aircraft, and Preservation of Aircraft Wreckage, Mail, Cargo, and Records

G10 General
G11 Initial Notification of Aircraft Accidents, Incidents, and Overdue Aircraft
G12 Preservation of Aircraft Wreckage, Mail, Cargo, and Records
G13 Reporting of Aircraft Accidents, Incidents, and Overdue Aircraft

AC 91-23—Pilot's Weight and Balance Handbook

H10 Weight and Balance Control
H11 Terms and Definitions
H12 Empty Weight Center of Gravity
H13 Index and Graphic Limits
H14 Change of Weight
H15 Control of Loading — General Aviation
H16 Control of Loading — Large Aircraft

AC 61-23—Pilot's Handbook of Aeronautical Knowledge

H300 Forces Acting on the Airplane in Flight
H301 Turning Tendency (Torque Effect)
H302 Airplane Stability
H303 Loads and Load Factors
H304 Airplane Structure
H305 Flight Control Systems
H306 Electrical System
H307 Engine Operation
H308 Propeller
H309 Starting the Engine
H310 Exhaust Gas Temperature Gauge
H311 Aircraft Documents, Maintenance, and Inspections
H312 The Pitot-Static System and Associated Instruments
H313 Gyroscopic Flight Instruments
H314 Magnetic Compass
H315 Weight Control
H316 Balance, Stability, and Center of Gravity
H317 Airplane Performance
H318 Observations
H319 Service Outlets
H320 Weather Briefings
H321 Nature of the Atmosphere
H322 The Cause of Atmospheric Circulation
H323 Moisture and Temperature
H324 Air Masses and Fronts
H325 Aviation Weather Reports, Forecasts, and Weather Charts
H326 Types of Airports
H327 Sources for Airport Data
H328 Airport Markings and Signs
H329 Airport Lighting
H330 Wind Direction Indicators
H331 Radio Communications
H332 Air Traffic Services
H333 Wake Turbulence
H334 Collision Avoidance
H335 Controlled Airspace
H336 Uncontrolled Airspace
H337 Special Use Airspace
H338 Other Airspace Areas
H339 Aeronautical Charts
H340 Latitude and Longitude
H341 Effect of Wind
H342 Basic Calculations
H343 Pilotage
H344 Dead Reckoning
H345 Flight Planning
H346 Charting the Course
H347 Filing a VFR Flight Plan
H348 Radio Navigation
H349 Obtaining a Medical Certificate
H350 Health Factors Affecting Pilot Performance
H351 Environmental Factors Which Affect Pilot Performance

AC 61-21—Flight Training Handbook

H50 Introduction to Flight Training
H51 Introduction to Airplanes and Engines
H52 Introduction to the Basics of Flight
H53 The Effect and Use of Controls
H54 Ground Operations

H55 Basic Flight Maneuvers
H56 Airport Traffic Patterns and Operations
H57 Takeoffs and Departure Climbs
H58 Landing Approaches and Landings
H59 Faulty Approaches and Landings
H60 Proficiency Flight Maneuvers
H61 Cross-Country Flying
H62 Emergency Flight by Reference to Instruments
H63 Night Flying
H64 Seaplane Operations
H65 Transition to Other Airplanes
H66 Principles of Flight and Performance Characteristics

AC 61-27—Instrument Flying Handbook

I01 Training Considerations
I02 Instrument Flying: Coping with Illusions in Flight
I03 Aerodynamic Factors Related to Instrument Flying
I04 Basic Flight Instruments
I05 Attitude Instrument Flying — Airplanes
I06 Attitude Instrument Flying — Helicopters
I07 Electronic Aids to Instrument Flying
I08 Using the Navigation Instruments
I09 Radio Communications Facilities and Equipment
I10 The Federal Airways System and Controlled Airspace
I11 Air Traffic Control
I12 ATC Operations and Procedures
I13 Flight Planning
I14 Appendix: Instrument Instructor Lesson Guide — Airplanes
I15 Segment of En Route Low Altitude Chart

AC 00-6—Aviation Weather

I20 The Earth's Atmosphere
I21 Temperature
I22 Atmospheric Pressure and Altimetry
I23 Wind
I24 Moisture, Cloud Formation, and Precipitation
I25 Stable and Unstable Air
I26 Clouds
I27 Air Masses and Fronts
I28 Turbulence
I29 Icing
I30 Thunderstorms
I31 Common IFR Producers
I32 High Altitude Weather
I33 Arctic Weather
I34 Tropical Weather
I35 Soaring Weather
I36 Glossary of Weather Terms

AC 00-45—Aviation Weather Services

I40 The Aviation Weather Service Program
I41 Surface Aviation Weather Reports
I42 Pilot and Radar Reports and Satellite Pictures
I43 Aviation Weather Forecasts
I44 Surface Analysis Chart
I45 Weather Depiction Chart
I46 Radar Summary Chart
I47 Significant Weather Prognostics
I48 Winds and Temperatures Aloft
I49 Composite Moisture Stability Chart
I50 Severe Weather Outlook Chart
I51 Constant Pressure Charts
I52 Tropopause Data Chart
I53 Tables and Conversion Graphs

AIM—Aeronautical Information Manual

J01 Air Navigation Radio Aids
J02 Radar Services and Procedures
J03 Airport Lighting Aids
J04 Air Navigation and Obstruction Lighting
J05 Airport Marking Aids and Signs
J06 Airspace — General
J07 Class G Airspace
J08 Controlled Airspace
J09 Special Use Airspace
J10 Other Airspace Areas
J11 Service Available to Pilots
J12 Radio Communications Phraseology and Techniques
J13 Airport Operations
J14 ATC Clearance/Separations
J15 Preflight
J16 Departure Procedures
J17 En Route Procedures
J18 Arrival Procedures
J19 Pilot/Controller Roles and Responsibilities
J20 National Security and Interception Procedures
J21 Emergency Procedures — General
J22 Emergency Services Available to Pilots
J23 Distress and Urgency Procedures
J24 Two-Way Radio Communications Failure
J25 Meteorology
J26 Altimeter Setting Procedures
J27 Wake Turbulence
J28 Bird Hazards, and Flight Over National Refuges, Parks, and Forests
J29 Potential Flight Hazards
J30 Safety, Accident, and Hazard Reports
J31 Fitness for Flight
J32 Type of Charts Available
J33 Pilot Controller Glossary

Other Documents

J34 Airport/Facility Directory
J35 En Route Low Altitude Chart
J36 En Route High Altitude Chart
J37 Sectional Chart
J39 Terminal Area Chart
J40 Standard Instrument Departure (SID) Chart
J41 Standard Terminal Arrival (STAR) Chart
J42 Instrument Approach Procedures
J43 Helicopter Route Chart

AC 67-2—Medical Handbook for Pilots

J52 Hypoxia
J53 Hyperventilation
J55 The Ears
J56 Alcohol
J57 Drugs and Flying
J58 Carbon Monoxide
J59 Vision
J60 Night Flight
J61 Cockpit Lighting
J62 Disorientation (Vertigo)

J63 Motion Sickness
J64 Fatigue
J65 Noise
J66 Age
J67 Some Psychological Aspects of Flying
J68 The Flying Passenger

ADDITIONAL ADVISORY CIRCULARS

K01 AC 00-24, Thunderstorms
K02 AC 00-30, Rules of Thumb for Avoiding or Minimizing Encounters with Clear Air Turbulence
K03 AC 00-34, Aircraft Ground Handling and Servicing
K04 AC 00-54, Pilot Wind Shear Guide
K05 AC 00-55, Announcement of Availability: FAA Order 8130.21A
K11 AC 20-34, Prevention of Retractable Landing Gear Failure
K12 AC 20-32, Carbon Monoxide (CO) Contamination in Aircraft — Detection and Prevention
K13 AC 20-43, Aircraft Fuel Control
K20 AC 20-103, Aircraft Engine Crankshaft Failure
K23 AC 20-121, Airworthiness Approval of Airborne Loran C Systems for Use in the U.S. National Airspace System
K26 AC 20-138, Airworthiness Approval of Global Positioning System (GPS) Navigation Equipment for Use as a VFR and IFR Supplemental Navigation System
K40 AC 25-4, Inertial Navigation System (INS)
K45 AC 39-7, Airworthiness Directives
K46 AC 43-9, Maintenance Records
K47 AC 43.9-1, Instructions for Completion of FAA Form 337
K48 AC 43-11, Reciprocating Engine Overhaul Terminology and Standards
K49 AC 43.13-1, Acceptable Methods, Techniques, and Practices - Aircraft Inspection and Repair
K50 AC 43.13-2, Acceptable Methods, Techniques, and Practices - Aircraft Alterations
K80 AC 60-4, Pilot's Spatial Disorientation
L05 AC 60-22, Aeronautical Decision Making
L10 AC 61-67, Stall and Spin Awareness Training
L11 AC 61-101, Presolo Written Test
L15 AC 61-107, Operations of Aircraft at Altitudes Above 25,000 Feet MSL and/or MACH numbers (Mmo) Greater Than .75
L25 AC 65-19, Inspection Authorization Study Guide
L34 AC 90-48, Pilots' Role in Collision Avoidance
L42 AC 90-87, Helicopter Dynamic Rollover
L44 AC 90-94, Guidelines for Using Global Positioning System Equipment for IFR En Route and Terminal Operations and for Nonprecision Instrument Approaches in the U.S. National Airspace System
L45 AC 90-95, Unanticipated Right Yaw in Helicopters
L50 AC 91-6, Water, Slush, and Snow on the Runway
L52 AC 91-13, Cold Weather Operation of Aircraft
L53 AC 91-14, Altimeter Setting Sources
L57 AC 91-43, Unreliable Airspeed Indications
L59 AC 91-46, Gyroscopic Instruments — Good Operating Practices
L61 AC 91-50, Importance of Transponder Operation and Altitude Reporting
L62 AC 91-51, Airplane Deice and Anti-Ice Systems
L70 AC 91-67, Minimum Equipment Requirements for General Aviation Operations Under FAR Part 91
L80 AC 103-4, Hazard Associated with Sublimation of Solid Carbon Dioxide (Dry Ice) Aboard Aircraft
L90 AC 105-2, Sport Parachute Jumping
M01 AC 120-12, Private Carriage Versus Common Carriage of Persons or Property
M02 AC 120-27, Aircraft Weight and Balance Control
M08 AC 120-58, Pilot Guide — Large Aircraft Ground Deicing
M13 AC 121-195-1, Operational Landing Distances for Wet Runways; Transport Category Airplanes
M35 AC 135-17, Pilot Guide — Small Aircraft Ground Deicing
M51 AC 20-117, Hazards Following Ground Deicing and Ground Operations in Conditions Conducive to Aircraft Icing
M52 AC 00-2, Advisory Circular Checklist

The Aircraft Gas Turbine Engine and Its Operation — United Technologies Corporation, Pratt Whitney, 1988

T01 Gas Turbine Engine Fundamentals
T02 Gas Turbine Engine Terms
T03 Gas Turbine Engine Components
T04 Gas Turbine Engine Operation
T05 Operational Characteristics of Jet Engines
T06 Gas Turbine Engine Performance

Aircraft Powerplants — Glencoe/McGraw-Hill, Seventh Edition

T07 Aircraft Powerplant Classification and Progress
T08 Reciprocating-Engine Construction and Nomenclature
T09 Internal-Combustion Engine Theory and Performance
T10 Lubricants and Lubricating Systems
T11 Induction Systems, Superchargers, Turbochargers, and Cooling and Exhaust Systems
T12 Basic Fuel Systems and Carburetors
T13 Fuel Injection Systems
T14 Reciprocating-Engine Ignition and Starting Systems
T15 Operation, Inspection, Maintenance, and Troubleshooting of Reciprocating Engines
T16 Reciprocating-Engine Overhaul Practices
T17 Gas Turbine Engine: Theory, Construction, and Nomenclature
T18 Gas Turbine Engine: Fuels and Fuel Systems
T19 Turbine-Engine Lubricants and Lubricating Systems
T20 Ignition and Starting Systems of Gas-Turbine Engines
T21 Turbofan Engines
T22 Turboprop Engines
T23 Turboshaft Engines
T24 Gas-Turbine Operation, Inspection, Troubleshooting, Maintenance, and Overhaul
T25 Propeller Theory, Nomenclature, and Operation
T26 Turbopropellers and Control Systems
T27 Propeller Installation, Inspection, and Maintenance
T29 Engine Indicating, Warning, and Control Systems

Aircraft Basic Science — Glencoe/McGraw-Hill, Seventh Edition

T31 Fundamentals of Mathematics
T32 Science Fundamentals
T33 Basic Aerodynamics
T34 Airfoils and Their Applications
T35 Aircraft in Flight
T36 Aircraft Drawings
T37 Weight and Balance
T38 Aircraft Materials
T39 Fabrication Techniques and Processes
T40 Standard Aircraft Hardware
T41 Aircraft Fluid Lines and Their Fittings
T42 Federal Aviation Regulations and Publications
T43 Ground Handling and Safety
T44 Aircraft Inspection and Servicing

Aircraft Maintenance and Repair — Glencoe/McGraw-Hill, Sixth Edition

T45 Aircraft Structures
T46 Aircraft Fluid Power Systems
T47 Aircraft Landing-Gear Systems
T48 Aircraft Fuel Systems
T49 Environmental Systems
T50 Aircraft Instruments and Instrument Systems
T51 Auxiliary Systems
T52 Assembly and Rigging

TCAS—Transport Category Aircraft Systems—Jeppesen Sanderson, Inc.

T53 Types, Design Features and Configurations of Transport Aircraft
T54 Auxiliary Power Units, Pneumatic, and Environmental Control Systems
T55 Anti-Icing Systems and Rain Protection
T56 Electrical Power Systems
T57 Flight Control Systems
T58 Fuel Systems
T59 Hydraulic Systems
T60 Oxygen Systems
T61 Warning and Fire Protection Systems
T62 Communications, Instruments, and Navigational Systems
T63 Miscellaneous Aircraft Systems and Maintenance Information

FAA Accident Prevention Program Bulletins

V01 FAA-P-8740-2, Density Altitude
V02 FAA-P-8740-5, Weight and Balance
V03 FAA-P-8740-12, Thunderstorms
V04 FAA-P-8740-19, Flying Light Twins Safely
V05 FAA-P-8740-23, Planning Your Takeoff
V06 FAA-P-8740-24, Tips on Winter Flying
V07 FAA-P-8740-25, Always Leave Yourself an Out
V08 FAA-P-8740-30, How to Obtain a Good Weather Briefing
V09 FAA-P-8740-40, Wind Shear
V10 FAA-P-8740-41, Medical Facts for Pilots
V11 FAA-P-8740-44, Impossible Turns
V12 FAA-P-8740-48, On Landings, Part I
V13 FAA-P-8740-49, On Landings, Part II
V14 FAA-P-8740-50, On Landings, Part III
V15 FAA-P-8740-51, How to Avoid a Midair Collision
V16 FAA-P-8740-52, The Silent Emergency

FTP—Flight Theory for Pilots—Jeppesen Sanderson, Inc.

W01 Introduction
W02 Air Flow and Airspeed Measurement
W03 Aerodynamic Forces on Airfoils
W04 Lift and Stall
W05 Drag
W06 Jet Aircraft Basic Performance
W07 Jet Aircraft Applied Performance
W08 Prop Aircraft Basic Performance
W09 Prop Aircraft Applied Performance
W10 Helicopter Aerodynamics
W11 Hazards of Low Speed Flight
W12 Takeoff Performance
W13 Landing Performance
W14 Maneuvering Performance
W15 Longitudinal Stability and Control
W16 Directional and Lateral Stability and Control
W17 High Speed Flight

Fly the Wing — Iowa State University Press/Ames, Second Edition

X01 Basic Aerodynamics
X02 High-Speed Aerodynamics
X03 High-Altitude Machs
X04 Approach Speed Control and Target Landings
X05 Preparation for Flight Training
X06 Basic Instrument Scan
X07 Takeoffs
X08 Rejected Takeoffs
X09 Climb, Cruise, and Descent
X10 Steep Turns
X11 Stalls
X12 Unusual Attitudes
X14 Maneuvers at Minimum Speed
X15 Landings: Approach Technique and Performance
X16 ILS Approaches
X17 Missed Approaches and Rejected Landings
X18 Category II and III Approaches
X19 Nonprecision and Circling Approaches
X20 Weight and Balance
X21 Flight Planning
X22 Icing
X23 Use of Anti-ice and Deice
X24 Winter Operation
X25 Thunderstorm Flight
X26 Low-Level Wind Shear

NOTE: AC 00-2, *Advisory Circular Checklist*, transmits the status of all FAA advisory circulars (AC's), as well as FAA internal publications and miscellaneous flight information such as *Aeronautical Information Manual*, *Airport/Facility Directory*, knowledge test guides, practical test standards, and other material directly related to a certificate or rating. To obtain a free copy of AC 00-2, send your request to:

U.S. Department of Transportation
Subsequent Distribution Office, SVC-121.23
Ardmore East Business Center
3341 Q 75th Ave.
Landover, MD 20785

CROSS-REFERENCES TO THE FAA PILOT KNOWLEDGE TEST QUESTION NUMBERS

Pages 800 through 813 contain the FAA question numbers from the ATP knowledge test bank. The questions are numbered 8001 to 9720. To the right of each FAA question number, we have added the FAA's subject matter knowledge code. To the right of the subject matter knowledge code, we have listed our answer and our chapter and question numbers. For example, the FAA's question 8001 is cross-referenced to the FAA's subject matter knowledge code E01, FAR Part 135–General. The correct answer is B, and the question appears with answer explanations in our book under 5-6, which means it is reproduced in Chapter 5 as question 6. Helicopter questions (omitted from this book) are denoted with an H. Flight navigator questions (omitted from this book) are denoted with an N.

The first line of each of our answer explanations in Chapters 2 through 18 contains

1. The correct answer
2. The FAA question number
3. A reference for the answer explanation, e.g., *FTH Chap 1*

Thus, our question numbers are cross-referenced throughout this book to the FAA question numbers, and these 14 pages cross-reference the FAA question numbers back to this book.

FAA		GLEIM		FAA		GLEIM		FAA		GLEIM	
Q. No.	Subject Code	Answer	Chap/ Q. No.	Q. No.	Subject Code	Answer	Chap/ Q. No.	Q. No.	Subject Code	Answer	Chap/ Q. No.
8001	E01	B	5-6	8021	E02	B	5-26	8041	E02	A	5-19
8002	E06	H		8022	E02	A	5-24	8042	E02	C	5-20
8003	C22	A	2-45	8023	E02	C	5-23	8043	E02	B	5-11
8004	E01	B	5-4	8024	E02	C	5-28	8044	E02	C	5-38
8005	E01	C	5-14	8025	E02	B	5-29	8045	E02	C	5-56
8006	E02	C	5-12	8026	E02	C	5-44	8046	E03	B	5-54
8007	E02	B	5-9	8027	E02	B	5-47	8047	E03	C	5-57
8008	E02	A	5-10	8028	E02	A	5-46	8048	E03	B	5-52
8009	E02	C	5-8	8029	E02	C	5-48	8049	E03	A	5-86
8010	E01	B	5-1	8030	E02	A	5-30	8050	E03	B	5-85
8011	E01	A	5-3	8031	E02	B	5-31	8051	E03	C	5-84
8012	E01	C	5-5	8032	E02	A	5-16	8052	E03	B	5-82
8013	E02	B	5-32	8033	E02	B	5-49	8053	E03	A	5-50
8014	E02	A	5-33	8034	E02	C	5-43	8054	E03	C	5-51
8015	E02	C	5-34	8035	E02	B	5-42	8055	E02	B	5-25
8016	E02	B	5-36	8036	E02	B	5-39	8056	E02	B	5-22
8017	E02	C	5-35	8037	E02	C	5-37	8057	E03	B	5-90
8018	E02	B	5-45	8038	E02	A	5-15	8058	E03	B	5-80
8019	E02	A	5-13	8039	E02	B	5-21	8059	E03	B	5-78
8020	E02	B	5-27	8040	E02	B	5-17	8060	E03	C	5-79

H - Helicopter question
N - Flight navigator question

FAA		GLEIM		FAA		GLEIM		FAA		GLEIM	
Q. No.	Subject Code	Answer	Chap/ Q. No.	Q. No.	Subject Code	Answer	Chap/ Q. No.	Q. No.	Subject Code	Answer	Chap/ Q. No.
8061	E03	A	5-77	8105	E05	B	5-114	8149	D11	A	4-41
8062	E03	C	5-76	8106	E02	C	5-40	8150	D11	C	4-48
8063	E04	B	5-98	8107	E05	A	5-108	8151	D11	A	4-49
8064	E04	C	5-94	8108	E05	A	5-112	8152	D11	C	4-42
8065	E04	A	5-92	8109	E05	B	5-109	8153	D11	B	4-16
8066	E04	B	5-93	8110	E05	C	5-111	8154	D11	A	4-54
8067	E03	C	5-87	8111	E05	B	5-113	8155	D11	B	4-25
8068	E03	C	5-89	8112	E11	A	5-155	8156	D11	C	4-26
8069	E03	B	5-58	8113	E02	B	5-41	8157	D11	A	4-13
8070	E03	A	5-59	8114	E04	C	5-88	8158	D11	C	4-14
8071	E03	B	5-60	8115	E09	C	5-136	8159	D11	B	4-15
8072	E03	C	5-61	8116	E09	A	5-137	8160	D11	C	4-7
8073	E03	C	5-65	8117	E09	C	5-151	8161	D11	A	4-8
8074	E03	B	5-63	8118	E09	A	5-139	8162	D11	C	4-9
8075	E03	C	5-73	8119	E09	C	5-152	8163	D11	B	4-17
8076	E03	B	5-75	8120	E09	A	5-140	8164	D11	B	4-32
8077	E03	A	5-74	8121	E09	B	5-143	8165	D11	C	4-33
8078	E03	B	5-72	8122	E09	A	5-144	8166	D11	A	4-34
8079	E03	B	5-67	8123	E09	C	5-145	8167	D11	B	4-43
8080	E03	C	5-62	8124	E09	A	5-138	8168	D11	C	4-44
8081	E03	C	5-64	8125	E09	A	5-146	8169	D11	C	4-35
8082	E05	C	5-106	8126	E09	A	5-147	8170	D11	B	4-46
8083	E05	B	5-107	8127	E09	A	5-148	8171	D11	C	4-47
8084	E04	C	5-104	8128	E09	B	5-149	8172	D11	A	4-45
8085	E04	C	5-103	8129	E09	B	5-153	8173	D11	A	4-23
8086	E04	A	5-100	8130	E09	A	5-150	8174	D11	A	4-21
8087	E04	A	5-97	8131	C10	B	3-64	8175	D10	B	4-6
8088	E04	B	5-95	8132	C10	A	3-66	8176	D11	C	4-10
8089	E04	C	5-96	8133	D09	B	4-3	8177	D11	C	4-11
8090	E04	A	5-102	8134	D09	B	4-2	8178	D11	C	4-19
8091	E04	C	5-101	8135	D05	C	4-1	8179	D11	B	4-18
8092	E04	B	5-99	8136	C10	B	3-65	8180	D11	A	4-29
8093	E10	A	5-154	8137	C10	B	3-63	8181	D11	C	4-30
8094	E09	B	5-142	8138	D10	C	4-4	8182	D11	B	4-31
8095	E07	C	5-127	8139	D10	B	4-5	8183	D11	C	4-27
8096	E07	B	5-128	8140	D11	A	4-51	8184	D11	A	4-28
8097	E07	A	5-126	8141	D11	B	4-52	8185	D11	A	4-20
8098	E07	B	5-121	8142	D11	B	4-36	8186	D11	B	4-22
8099	E07	C	5-124	8143	D11	A	4-53	8187	D11	B	4-24
8100	E07	B	5-123	8144	D11	B	4-12	8188	D13	B	4-56
8101	E07	C	5-122	8145	D11	A	4-37	8189	D13	C	4-59
8102	E07	A	5-125	8146	D11	B	4-39	8190	D13	B	4-60
8103	E05	B	5-110	8147	D11	C	4-40	8191	D13	A	4-55
8104	E05	A	5-118	8148	D11	B	4-50	8192	D13	B	4-64

H - Helicopter question
N - Flight navigator question

FAA		GLEIM		FAA		GLEIM		FAA		GLEIM	
Q. No.	Subject Code	Answer	Chap/ Q. No.	Q. No.	Subject Code	Answer	Chap/ Q. No.	Q. No.	Subject Code	Answer	Chap/ Q. No.
8193	D13	B	4-65	8237	D20	C	4-108	8281	D21	C	4-120
8194	D11	C	4-164	8238	D20	B	4-84	8282	D21	B	4-121
8195	D11	A	4-38	8239	D20	B	4-104	8283	D21	A	4-117
8196	D13	C	4-61	8240	D20	C	4-103	8284	D21	B	4-119
8197	D13	A	4-62	8241	D20	B	4-107	8285	D21	C	4-150
8198	D13	B	4-68	8242	D20	C	4-101	8286	D21	C	4-159
8199	D13	C	4-63	8243	D20	B	4-96	8287	D21	B	4-163
8200	D13	C	4-69	8244	D20	B	4-99	8288	D21	A	4-161
8201	D13	B	4-66	8245	D20	A	4-105	8289	D21	C	4-151
8202	D13	A	4-67	8246	D20	C	4-102	8290	D22	A	4-154
8203	D11	B	4-165	8247	D21	C	4-126	8291	D21	A	4-157
8204	D14	C	4-74	8248	D21	A	4-122	8292	D22	A	4-153
8205	D15	A	4-80	8249	D21	B	4-123	8293	D22	B	4-155
8206	D15	B	4-76	8250	D21	B	4-125	8294	D22	A	4-156
8207	D15	C	4-81	8251	D21	B	4-129	8295	D22	B	4-158
8208	D15	B	4-78	8252	D21	A	4-124	8296	D22	C	4-160
8209	D15	B	4-77	8253	D21	B	4-152	8297	D20	A	4-98
8210	D15	A	4-79	8254	D21	C	4-130	8298	D20	C	4-97
8211	D16	C	4-83	8255	D21	B	4-131	8299	F02	C	3-67
8212	D13	A	4-57	8256	D21	C	4-127	8300	F02	B	3-68
8213	D13	C	4-58	8257	D21	A	4-136	8301	F02	A	3-69
8214	D14	B	4-73	8258	D21	B	4-133	8302	F02	B	3-70
8215	D14	C	4-70	8259	D21	C	4-114	8303	F02	C	3-71
8216	D14	A	4-71	8260	D21	B	4-113	8304	G01	C	3-72
8217	D14	B	4-72	8261	D21	A	4-135	8305	G01	C	3-73
8218	D14	C	4-75	8262	D21	B	4-128	8306	G01	A	3-74
8219	D18	C	4-90	8263	D21	C	4-137	8307	G01	C	3-75
8220	D18	A	4-88	8264	D21	C	4-138	8308	G01	C	3-76
8221	D18	B	4-89	8265	D21	B	4-134	8309	G02	B	3-77
8222	D19	A	4-92	8266	D21	C	4-115	8310	G02	A	3-78
8223	D19	B	4-93	8267	D21	C	4-116	8311	G02	A	3-79
8224	D19	C	4-94	8268	D21	B	4-139	8312	G03	B	3-80
8225	D20	B	4-109	8269	D21	A	4-144	8313	L80	C	3-81
8226	D22	B	4-162	8270	D21	C	4-141	8314	G03	B	3-82
8227	D18	C	4-91	8271	D21	A	4-145	8315	G03	B	3-83
8228	D17	A	4-87	8272	D21	B	4-146	8316	G03	C	3-84
8229	D16	C	4-85	8273	D21	A	4-147	8317	G11	B	2-2
8230	D16	B	4-82	8274	D21	C	4-140	8318	G11	A	2-5
8231	D16	B	4-86	8275	D21	B	4-143	8319	G10	C	2-3
8232	D21	A	4-112	8276	D21	B	4-148	8320	G10	B	2-1
8233	D20	B	4-110	8277	D21	A	4-142	8321	G10	B	2-4
8234	D20	B	4-111	8278	D21	C	4-132	8322	G13	C	2-6
8235	D20	C	4-100	8279	D21	C	4-149	8323	G13	C	2-7
8236	D20	A	4-106	8280	D21	A	4-118	8324	T45	C	6-4

H - Helicopter question
N - Flight navigator question

FAA		GLEIM		FAA		GLEIM		FAA		GLEIM	
Q. No.	Subject Code	Answer	Chap/ Q. No.	Q. No.	Subject Code	Answer	Chap/ Q. No.	Q. No.	Subject Code	Answer	Chap/ Q. No.
8325	T45	A	6-5	8369	H65	B	6-102	8413	H78	H	
8326	T45	B	6-1	8370	H65	B	6-97	8414	H78	H	
8327	T45	C	6-3	8371	H65	B	6-96	8415	H78	H	
8328	T45	A	6-7	8372	H66	A	6-73	8416	H78	H	
8329	T45	C	6-12	8373	H66	B	6-74	8417	H77	H	
8330	T45	B	6-10	8374	H66	A	6-80	8418	H77	H	
8331	T45	A	6-15	8375	H66	A	6-29	8419	H76	H	
8332	T45	B	6-20	8376	H66	C	6-76	8420	H71	H	
8333	T45	A	6-21	8377	H66	C	6-23	8421	H71	H	
8334	T45	A	6-18	8378	H66	B	6-24	8422	H72	C	6-39
8335	T45	C	6-19	8379	H66	B	6-25	8423	H72	H	
8336	T45	A	6-22	8380	H66	A	6-75	8424	H73	H	
8337	T45	A	6-13	8381	H66	C	6-83	8425	H73	H	
8338	T45	B	6-11	8382	H66	B	6-26	8426	H74	H	
8339	T45	C	6-9	8383	H66	A	6-28	8427	H74	H	
8340	T45	C	6-8	8384	W04	B	6-14	8428	H74	H	
8341	T34	A	6-31	8385	W04	A	6-16	8429	C20	B	2-42
8342	T57	B	6-6	8386	W04	B	6-17	8430	C20	C	2-43
8343	T45	C	6-2	8387	W17	B	6-117	8431	H16	A	6-40
8344	H303	A	6-33	8388	W17	B	6-119	8432	H16	A	6-41
8345	H303	C	6-65	8389	W17	C	6-118	8433	H16	C	6-42
8346	H300	A	6-27	8390	W17	A	6-116	8434	H16	B	11-1
8347	H303	C	6-35	8391	W17	A	6-122	8435	H15	B	11-2
8348	H60	A	6-32	8392	W17	B	6-120	8436	H15	A	11-3
8349	H55	C	6-66	8393	W17	B	6-123	8437	H15	C	11-4
8350	H55	A	6-69	8394	W16	C	6-124	8438	H15	C	11-5
8351	H55	B	6-68	8395	W03	B	6-121	8439	H14	B	11-11
8352	H55	A	6-67	8396	W14	C	6-37	8440	H14	C	11-12
8353	H303	B	6-38	8397	W07	B	6-30	8441	H14	A	11-13
8354	H303	B	6-36	8398	W05	C	6-82	8442	H14	C	11-14
8355	H71	H		8399	W06	B	6-63	8443	H14	B	11-15
8356	W04	C	6-34	8400	W06	A	6-64	8444	H15	A	11-6
8357	H65	B	6-99	8401	W06	C	6-85	8445	H15	C	11-7
8358	H65	C	6-101	8402	H81	H		8446	H15	C	11-8
8359	H65	A	6-103	8403	H80	H		8447	H15	C	11-9
8360	H65	A	6-94	8404	H78	H		8448	H15	A	11-10
8361	H65	A	6-98	8405	H78	H		8449	H14	A	11-16
8362	H65	C	6-95	8406	H78	H		8450	H14	C	11-17
8363	H65	A	6-92	8407	H78	H		8451	H14	B	11-18
8364	H65	A	6-93	8408	H78	H		8452	H14	A	11-19
8365	H66	C	6-72	8409	H78	H		8453	H14	B	11-20
8366	H66	A	6-71	8410	H74	H		8454	H13	C	11-21
8367	H66	B	6-70	8411	H71	H		8455	H13	A	11-22
8368	H66	A	6-87	8412	H78	H		8456	H13	B	11-23

H - Helicopter question
N - Flight navigator question

FAA		GLEIM		FAA		GLEIM		FAA		GLEIM	
Q. No.	Subject Code	Answer	Chap/ Q. No.	Q. No.	Subject Code	Answer	Chap/ Q. No.	Q. No.	Subject Code	Answer	Chap/ Q. No.
8457	H13	B	11-24	8501	H317	C	11-67	8545	H66	H	
8458	H13	A	11-25	8502	H317	B	11-70	8546	H66	H	
8459	H317	A	11-26	8503	H317	C	11-68	8547	H66	H	
8460	H317	A	11-27	8504	H317	A	11-71	8548	H66	H	
8461	H317	B	11-28	8505	H317	A	11-72	8549	H66	H	
8462	H317	B	11-29	8506	H317	B	11-73	8550	H66	H	
8463	H317	C	11-30	8507	H317	A	11-74	8551	H66	H	
8464	H317	C	11-31	8508	H317	B	11-75	8552	H66	H	
8465	H317	A	11-35	8509	H317	C	11-76	8553	H66	H	
8466	H317	B	11-32	8510	H317	C	11-77	8554	H66	H	
8467	H317	A	11-34	8511	H317	B	11-78	8555	H66	H	
8468	H317	A	11-33	8512	H317	C	11-79	8556	H66	H	
8469	H317	C	11-36	8513	H15	H		8557	H66	H	
8470	H317	C	11-37	8514	H15	H		8558	H66	H	
8471	H317	A	11-38	8515	H15	H		8559	H66	H	
8472	H317	B	11-39	8516	H15	H		8560	H66	H	
8473	H317	C	11-40	8517	H15	H		8561	H66	H	
8474	H317	C	11-41	8518	H14	H		8562	H66	H	
8475	H317	C	11-45	8519	H14	H		8563	H66	H	
8476	H317	B	11-42	8520	H14	H		8564	H66	H	
8477	H317	A	11-43	8521	H14	H		8565	H66	H	
8478	H317	C	11-44	8522	H14	H		8566	H66	H	
8479	H317	B	11-46	8523	H13	H		8567	H66	H	
8480	H317	B	11-47	8524	H13	H		8568	H66	H	
8481	H317	B	11-48	8525	H13	H		8569	H66	H	
8482	H317	C	11-49	8526	H13	H		8570	H66	H	
8483	H317	C	11-50	8527	H13	H		8571	H66	H	
8484	H317	A	11-51	8528	H14	H		8572	H66	H	
8485	H317	B	11-54	8529	H14	H		8573	H14	B	12-1
8486	H317	C	11-52	8530	H14	H		8574	H14	C	12-2
8487	H317	A	11-55	8531	H14	H		8575	H14	A	12-3
8488	H317	C	11-53	8532	H14	H		8576	H14	B	12-4
8489	H317	B	11-56	8533	H66	H		8577	H14	A	12-5
8490	H317	A	11-58	8534	H66	H		8578	H14	A	12-6
8491	H317	C	11-60	8535	H66	H		8579	H14	C	12-7
8492	H314	A	11-62	8536	H66	H		8580	H14	B	12-8
8493	H314	C	11-64	8537	H66	H		8581	H14	B	12-9
8494	H314	A	11-57	8538	H66	H		8582	H14	A	12-10
8495	H317	C	11-59	8539	H66	H		8583	X07	A	12-11
8496	H317	B	11-61	8540	H66	H		8584	X07	C	12-12
8497	H317	B	11-63	8541	H66	H		8585	X07	A	12-13
8498	H317	C	11-65	8542	H66	H		8586	X07	B	12-14
8499	H317	A	11-66	8543	H66	H		8587	X07	B	12-15
8500	H317	B	11-69	8544	H66	H		8588	X07	A	12-16

H - Helicopter question
N - Flight navigator question

FAA		GLEIM		FAA		GLEIM		FAA		GLEIM	
Q. No.	Subject Code	Answer	Chap/ Q. No.	Q. No.	Subject Code	Answer	Chap/ Q. No.	Q. No.	Subject Code	Answer	Chap/ Q. No.
8589	X07	B	12-17	8633	X09	C	13-21	8677	X09	C	13-65
8590	X07	C	12-18	8634	X09	A	13-22	8678	T58	B	13-66
8591	X07	A	12-19	8635	X09	B	13-23	8679	T58	C	13-68
8592	X07	C	12-20	8636	X09	A	13-24	8680	T58	C	13-67
8593	X09	A	12-21	8637	X09	A	13-25	8681	T58	A	13-69
8594	X09	C	12-22	8638	X09	A	13-26	8682	W06	A	13-70
8595	X09	A	12-23	8639	X09	C	13-27	8683	W06	B	13-71
8596	X09	B	12-24	8640	X09	C	13-28	8684	W06	C	13-72
8597	X09	C	12-25	8641	X09	C	13-29	8685	W06	C	13-73
8598	X09	B	12-26	8642	X09	B	13-30	8686	W06	B	13-74
8599	X09	C	12-27	8643	X09	C	13-31	8687	X15	B	13-75
8600	X09	B	12-28	8644	X09	B	13-33	8688	X15	C	13-77
8601	X09	B	12-29	8645	X09	C	13-35	8689	X15	A	13-79
8602	X09	A	12-30	8646	X09	B	13-37	8690	X15	A	13-81
8603	X09	B	12-31	8647	X09	A	13-39	8691	X15	A	13-83
8604	X09	B	12-32	8648	X09	B	13-32	8692	X07	A	13-76
8605	X09	B	12-33	8649	X09	C	13-34	8693	X07	B	13-78
8606	X09	A	12-34	8650	X09	B	13-36	8694	X07	B	13-80
8607	X09	A	12-35	8651	X09	A	13-38	8695	X07	C	13-82
8608	X15	C	12-36	8652	X09	C	13-40	8696	X07	C	13-84
8609	X15	B	12-37	8653	X09	C	13-41	8697	H16	B	14-1
8610	X15	A	12-38	8654	X09	B	13-42	8698	H16	C	14-2
8611	X15	A	12-39	8655	X09	C	13-43	8699	H16	A	14-3
8612	X15	B	12-40	8656	X09	A	13-44	8700	H16	A	14-4
8613	X07	C	13-1	8657	X09	A	13-45	8701	H16	B	14-5
8614	X07	A	13-2	8658	X09	B	13-46	8702	H16	C	14-6
8615	X07	C	13-3	8659	X09	C	13-48	8703	H16	C	14-7
8616	X07	B	13-4	8660	X09	B	13-50	8704	H16	C	14-8
8617	X07	A	13-5	8661	X09	B	13-52	8705	H16	A	14-9
8618	X07	A	13-6	8662	X09	A	13-54	8706	H16	C	14-10
8619	X07	C	13-7	8663	X09	A	13-47	8707	H16	C	14-11
8620	X07	B	13-8	8664	X09	A	13-49	8708	H16	B	14-12
8621	X07	B	13-10	8665	X09	B	13-51	8709	H16	A	14-13
8622	X07	A	13-9	8666	X09	C	13-53	8710	H16	B	14-14
8623	X07	C	13-11	8667	X09	C	13-55	8711	H16	A	14-15
8624	X07	C	13-12	8668	X09	C	13-56	8712	X07	A	14-16
8625	X07	A	13-13	8669	X09	B	13-58	8713	X07	C	14-17
8626	X07	B	13-14	8670	X09	B	13-60	8714	X07	B	14-18
8627	X07	C	13-15	8671	X09	A	13-62	8715	X07	A	14-19
8628	X09	A	13-16	8672	X09	C	13-64	8716	X07	C	14-20
8629	X09	C	13-17	8673	X09	A	13-57	8717	X07	B	14-21
8630	X09	B	13-18	8674	X09	C	13-59	8718	X07	C	14-22
8631	X09	A	13-19	8675	X09	A	13-61	8719	X07	A	14-23
8632	X09	C	13-20	8676	X09	C	13-63	8720	X07	C	14-24

H - Helicopter question
N - Flight navigator question

FAA		GLEIM		FAA		GLEIM		FAA		GLEIM	
Q. No.	Subject Code	Answer	Chap/ Q. No.	Q. No.	Subject Code	Answer	Chap/ Q. No.	Q. No.	Subject Code	Answer	Chap/ Q. No.
8721	X07	B	14-25	8765	X15	B	14-69	8809	E05	A	5-116
8722	X07	B	14-26	8766	X15	A	14-70	8810	J41	A	9-50
8723	X07	A	14-27	8767	C20	C	2-44	8811	J41	C	9-52
8724	X07	C	14-28	8768	C22	A	2-46	8812	J41	A	9-51
8725	X07	C	14-29	8769	H16	C	6-43	8813	E05	B	5-117
8726	X07	B	14-30	8770	H16	B	6-44	8814	E06	B	5-119
8727	X09	A	14-31	8771	H16	B	6-45	8815	E06	C	5-120
8728	X09	C	14-32	8772	H16	A	6-46	8816	J42	B	9-56
8729	X09	B	14-33	8773	H16	A	6-47	8817	J18	B	9-57
8730	X09	B	14-34	8774	A02	C	2-19	8818	J42	C	9-58
8731	X09	C	14-35	8775	A02	B	2-20	8819	E01	B	5-2
8732	X09	C	14-36	8776	H16	B	6-48	8820	E08	C	5-129
8733	X09	A	14-37	8777	H16	C	6-49	8821	E08	A	5-130
8734	X09	B	14-38	8778	H16	A	6-50	8822	I13	H	
8735	X09	A	14-39	8779	H16	B	6-51	8823	I13	H	
8736	X09	C	14-40	8780	A02	C	2-18	8824	J35	C	9-60
8737	X09	B	14-41	8781	H16	C	6-52	8825	J35	B	9-61
8738	X09	B	14-42	8782	J35	C	10-15	8826	J35	C	9-62
8739	X09	A	14-43	8783	J35	C	10-16	8827	E08	B	5-132
8740	X09	B	14-44	8784	J35	B	10-17	8828	E08	C	5-133
8741	X09	A	14-45	8785	J34	A	10-18	8829	E08	A	5-134
8742	X15	B	14-49	8786	J41	A	10-19	8830	E05	B	5-115
8743	X15	C	14-46	8787	H16	B	6-53	8831	E09	B	5-141
8744	X15	B	14-47	8788	H16	A	6-54	8832	E02	B	5-18
8745	X15	B	14-48	8789	H16	A	6-55	8833	E03	A	5-55
8746	X15	C	14-50	8790	H16	C	6-56	8834	E03	B	5-81
8747	X15	B	14-51	8791	H16	C	6-57	8835	I13	B	10-78
8748	X15	C	14-52	8792	E03	C	5-53	8836	J42	C	10-81
8749	X15	A	14-53	8793	J40	A	10-24	8837	J42	A	10-79
8750	X15	B	14-54	8794	J40	C	10-25	8838	E03	C	5-68
8751	X15	C	14-55	8795	I13	B	10-26	8839	J42	B	10-80
8752	X15	B	14-56	8796	J34	B	10-27	8840	E03	A	5-69
8753	X15	A	14-57	8797	J34	B	10-28	8841	E03	C	5-70
8754	X15	C	14-59	8798	J34	C	10-29	8842	E03	A	5-71
8755	X15	A	14-58	8799	J41	C	10-30	8843	E04	B	5-91
8756	X15	B	14-60	8800	J42	C	10-31	8844	H16	A	6-58
8757	X15	C	14-61	8801	A20	B	10-32	8845	H16	C	6-59
8758	X15	B	14-62	8802	J42	B	10-33	8846	H16	B	6-60
8759	X15	B	14-63	8803	J42	C	10-34	8847	H16	B	6-61
8760	X15	B	14-64	8804	J42	A	10-35	8848	H16	C	6-62
8761	X15	B	14-65	8805	J41	A	10-36	8849	J42	A	10-94
8762	X15	A	14-66	8806	J15	C	10-37	8850	J42	C	10-95
8763	X15	A	14-67	8807	E03	A	5-83	8851	J42	B	10-93
8764	X15	B	14-68	8808	E03	B	5-66	8852	J42	A	10-96

H - Helicopter question
N - Flight navigator question

FAA Q. No.	FAA Subject Code	GLEIM Answer	GLEIM Chap/ Q. No.	FAA Q. No.	FAA Subject Code	GLEIM Answer	GLEIM Chap/ Q. No.	FAA Q. No.	FAA Subject Code	GLEIM Answer	GLEIM Chap/ Q. No.
8853	J17	C	8-25	8897	B09	A	3-15	8941	J42	C	9-110
8854	J17	A	8-26	8898	B09	B	3-14	8942	J18	C	9-107
8855	J17	A	9-42	8899	B09	C	3-19	8943	J42	B	9-111
8856	J17	C	9-43	8900	B09	B	3-13	8944	J42	C	9-112
8857	J17	C	9-44	8901	J03	B	7-45	8945	J01	A	9-106
8858	J17	A	9-47	8902	J03	A	7-43	8946	J01	B	9-105
8859	J17	C	9-49	8903	J03	B	7-42	8947	J01	C	9-103
8860	J17	B	9-48	8904	J03	B	7-44	8948	J01	C	9-104
8861	J17	A	9-35	8905	J03	C	7-48	8949	J01	B	9-108
8862	J17	B	9-36	8906	J03	A	7-49	8950	J42	A	9-89
8863	J17	C	9-37	8907	J05	A	7-30	8951	J42	C	9-90
8864	J17	B	9-38	8908	J03	A	7-61	8952	J42	B	9-91
8865	J17	C	9-39	8909	J03	C	7-58	8953	J18	A	9-93
8866	J17	C	9-40	8910	J03	B	7-59	8954	J18	C	9-95
8867	J17	A	9-41	8911	J03	B	7-50	8955	J18	A	9-94
8868	I08	B	9-10	8912	J03	B	7-52	8956	J01	B	9-79
8869	I08	B	9-11	8913	J03	C	7-51	8957	J01	C	9-78
8870	I08	A	9-12	8914	J03	A	7-46	8958	J01	A	9-81
8871	I08	B	9-13	8915	J03	C	7-47	8959	J01	C	9-82
8872	J06	B	7-15	8916	J03	B	7-53	8960	J01	B	9-83
8873	J06	A	7-16	8917	J03	B	7-54	8961	J01	B	9-77
8874	J06	B	7-14	8918	J03	C	7-55	8962	J01	A	9-80
8875	J06	C	7-18	8919	J03	A	7-56	8963	J01	B	9-97
8876	J06	C	7-17	8920	J03	A	7-57	8964	J01	C	9-98
8877	J06	B	7-20	8921	J03	B	7-60	8965	J01	A	9-99
8878	J08	A	7-22	8922	J03	A	7-31	8966	J01	C	9-76
8879	J08	A	7-21	8923	J03	B	7-41	8967	J01	B	9-102
8880	J08	A	7-19	8924	J03	C	7-32	8968	I07	B	9-88
8881	J06	B	7-10	8925	J03	B	7-33	8969	V12	A	9-87
8882	J06	B	7-12	8926	J03	B	7-34	8970	B11	B	9-92
8883	J06	B	7-11	8927	J03	B	7-36	8971	I07	B	9-84
8884	J06	C	7-7	8928	J03	B	7-38	8972	I07	C	9-85
8885	J06	B	7-8	8929	J03	A	7-35	8973	I07	A	9-86
8886	J06	A	7-9	8930	J03	B	7-40	8974	J01	B	9-118
8887	B07	C	7-13	8931	J03	C	7-37	8975	J01	A	9-120
8888	J08	C	7-6	8932	J03	A	7-39	8976	J01	C	9-121
8889	J08	B	7-5	8933	V14	B	6-127	8977	J01	C	9-122
8890	J09	C	7-4	8934	V14	A	6-131	8978	J01	A	9-113
8891	J09	B	7-2	8935	V14	B	6-129	8979	J01	B	9-117
8892	J09	C	7-3	8936	V14	C	6-130	8980	J01	B	9-119
8893	B09	A	3-12	8937	V14	C	6-132	8981	J01	B	9-116
8894	B09	C	3-16	8938	V14	B	6-128	8982	J01	C	9-114
8895	B09	B	3-18	8939	V14	C	6-133	8983	J01	A	9-115
8896	B09	C	3-17	8940	J42	A	9-109	8984	I08	A	9-14

H - Helicopter question
N - Flight navigator question

FAA		GLEIM		FAA		GLEIM		FAA		GLEIM	
Q. No.	Subject Code	Answer	Chap/ Q. No.	Q. No.	Subject Code	Answer	Chap/ Q. No.	Q. No.	Subject Code	Answer	Chap/ Q. No.
8985	I08	C	9-15	9029	J15	C	8-3	9073	T11	B	6-91
8986	I08	B	9-16	9030	J15	C	8-1	9074	T03	A	6-125
8987	I08	C	9-17	9031	J15	A	8-4	9075	H317	C	6-78
8988	I08	A	9-18	9032	J15	A	8-5	9076	W12	A	6-79
8989	I08	C	9-19	9033	J15	B	8-6	9077	X09	B	6-86
8990	I08	A	9-26	9034	J18	B	8-13	9078	W06	A	6-84
8991	I08	B	9-27	9035	J18	A	8-14	9079	W13	B	6-126
8992	I08	C	9-28	9036	J18	B	8-52	9080	L57	B	6-154
8993	I08	C	9-29	9037	J18	C	8-55	9081	L57	A	6-155
8994	I08	B	9-30	9038	J18	A	8-53	9082	L57	A	6-156
8995	I08	A	9-31	9039	J18	B	8-54	9083	W12	A	6-77
8996	I08	B	9-32	9040	J18	B	8-9	9084	X15	A	6-81
8997	I08	B	9-33	9041	J18	A	8-56	9085	L50	A	6-100
8998	I08	C	9-34	9042	J13	H		9086	J15	C	7-62
8999	I08	C	9-23	9043	J13	H		9087	J15	A	7-65
9000	I08	B	9-24	9044	J13	B	8-60	9088	J15	B	7-64
9001	I08	C	9-25	9045	J14	A	8-23	9089	J15	C	7-63
9002	I08	A	9-20	9046	J14	B	8-35	9090	J18	A	8-57
9003	I08	C	9-21	9047	J14	A	8-36	9091	J18	B	8-58
9004	I08	C	9-22	9048	J14	C	8-37	9092	J18	C	8-59
9005	J15	C	8-10	9049	J10	A	7-1	9093	J14	C	8-38
9006	J16	C	8-16	9050	J11	B	8-46	9094	J14	B	8-32
9007	J16	A	8-17	9051	J11	B	8-43	9095	J14	C	8-33
9008	J16	C	8-15	9052	J11	C	8-42	9096	J14	C	8-34
9009	J16	A	8-18	9053	J12	C	8-11	9097	J21	A	8-44
9010	J19	C	8-39	9054	J13	B	17-4	9098	J30	B	8-45
9011	J19	C	8-40	9055	J13	C	8-61	9099	J26	A	8-31
9012	J16	A	8-12	9056	J13	A	8-19	9100	J31	C	8-30
9013	J17	C	8-27	9057	J13	B	8-20	9101	J31	C	18-4
9014	J17	A	8-28	9058	T24	C	6-104	9102	J31	A	18-7
9015	J17	C	8-29	9059	T01	C	6-105	9103	J31	C	18-2
9016	J17	A	8-51	9060	T05	B	6-108	9104	J31	A	18-6
9017	J01	B	9-3	9061	T01	C	6-107	9105	J31	C	18-3
9018	J18	B	9-4	9062	T01	A	6-210	9106	J31	A	18-1
9019	J01	C	9-8	9063	T01	A	6-106	9107	J31	B	18-14
9020	J01	A	9-9	9064	T03	C	6-112	9108	J31	C	18-16
9021	J18	C	9-1	9065	T03	A	6-113	9109	J31	C	18-17
9022	J11	C	9-2	9066	T03	C	6-114	9110	J31	A	18-18
9023	I07	B	9-7	9067	T03	A	6-115	9111	J31	A	18-5
9024	I07	A	9-6	9068	H317	A	6-88	9112	J31	C	18-12
9025	J01	C	9-5	9069	H317	B	6-89	9113	J31	C	18-13
9026	J15	C	8-7	9070	T05	B	6-109	9114	H63	B	18-9
9027	J15	B	8-8	9071	W06	B	6-111	9115	J31	B	18-15
9028	J15	B	8-2	9072	T11	A	6-90	9116	J31	C	18-10

H - Helicopter question
N - Flight navigator question

FAA		GLEIM		FAA		GLEIM		FAA		GLEIM	
Q. No.	Subject Code	Answer	Chap/ Q. No.	Q. No.	Subject Code	Answer	Chap/ Q. No.	Q. No.	Subject Code	Answer	Chap/ Q. No.
9117	J31	A	18-8	9161	I24	B	15-58	9205	I30	B	15-51
9118	J31	C	18-11	9162	I24	A	15-60	9206	I31	B	15-20
9119	J27	A	17-38	9163	I22	C	15-38	9207	I31	A	15-21
9120	J27	A	17-36	9164	I22	B	15-41	9208	I31	B	15-22
9121	J27	A	17-40	9165	I22	A	15-2	9209	I32	C	15-68
9122	J27	C	17-39	9166	I23	C	17-1	9210	I30	A	15-52
9123	J27	B	17-37	9167	J13	C	17-3	9211	I30	C	15-56
9124	J27	A	17-41	9168	I20	B	15-33	9212	I30	A	15-57
9125	J27	B	17-43	9169	I21	C	15-36	9213	I27	B	15-10
9126	J27	B	17-42	9170	I25	C	15-24	9214	I27	A	15-11
9127	J27	B	17-44	9171	I25	A	15-25	9215	I27	A	15-8
9128	I28	C	17-19	9172	I22	B	15-40	9216	I27	B	15-9
9129	I30	B	17-20	9173	I22	B	15-39	9217	I27	B	15-12
9130	J25	C	17-26	9174	I22	B	15-42	9218	I28	A	17-18
9131	J25	C	17-25	9175	I44	B	16-66	9219	K01	A	17-21
9132	J25	B	17-30	9176	I23	C	15-14	9220	K04	B	17-12
9133	K04	C	17-5	9177	I23	A	15-15	9221	I29	C	15-65
9134	K04	C	17-6	9178	I23	B	15-3	9222	L57	A	6-157
9135	K04	C	17-7	9179	I24	C	15-61	9223	I29	B	15-64
9136	K04	C	17-13	9180	I24	B	15-59	9224	I29	C	15-66
9137	K04	B	17-9	9181	I24	A	15-62	9225	I28	B	15-37
9138	K04	C	17-8	9182	I24	A	15-43	9226	I28	A	15-18
9139	K04	B	17-2	9183	I24	B	15-63	9227	I32	A	15-72
9140	K04	C	17-28	9184	I25	C	15-30	9228	I32	C	15-73
9141	K04	A	17-10	9185	I25	A	15-27	9229	I32	B	15-74
9142	K04	B	17-11	9186	I25	A	15-26	9230	K02	C	17-22
9143	K04	C	17-24	9187	I25	B	15-29	9231	K02	A	17-23
9144	K04	C	17-29	9188	I25	A	15-31	9232	I32	B	17-17
9145	K04	C	17-31	9189	I25	C	15-44	9233	I33	A	15-77
9146	K04	C	17-32	9190	I26	B	15-19	9234	I33	B	15-78
9147	K04	C	17-33	9191	I27	C	15-6	9235	I32	C	17-14
9148	K04	A	17-34	9192	I27	C	15-7	9236	I32	A	15-75
9149	K04	B	17-35	9193	I24	A	15-16	9237	I32	A	17-15
9150	K04	C	17-27	9194	I24	A	15-17	9238	I32	A	15-70
9151	I20	B	15-67	9195	I25	A	15-32	9239	I32	C	17-16
9152	I21	A	15-1	9196	I30	B	15-47	9240	I32	A	15-69
9153	I21	C	15-35	9197	I30	B	15-49	9241	I32	B	15-71
9154	I21	A	15-34	9198	I30	C	15-46	9242	I41	C	16-54
9155	I21	A	15-23	9199	I30	C	15-45	9243	I43	B	16-65
9156	I23	B	15-76	9200	I30	B	15-53	9244	I43	C	16-56
9157	I23	A	15-13	9201	I30	C	15-54	9245	I43	A	16-57
9158	I23	C	15-28	9202	I30	B	15-55	9246	I43	B	16-59
9159	I23	B	15-4	9203	I30	A	15-48	9247	I43	C	16-72
9160	I23	C	15-5	9204	I30	B	15-50	9248	I43	A	16-58

H - Helicopter question
N - Flight navigator question

FAA Q. No.	FAA Subject Code	GLEIM Answer	GLEIM Chap/ Q. No.
9249	I41	A	16-53
9250	I42	A	16-1
9251	I48	C	16-69
9252	I50	B	16-70
9253	I47	B	16-68
9254	I47	A	16-20
9255	I43	B	16-27
9256	I40	C	16-9
9257	J25	C	16-86
9258	J25	A	16-6
9259	I34	C	15-79
9260	I34	A	15-80
9261	J25	B	16-7
9262	J25	A	16-3
9263	J25	B	16-4
9264	J25	C	16-2
9265	I45	A	16-16
9266	I41	A	16-37
9267	I41	C	16-36
9268	I41	A	16-42
9269	I41	A	16-40
9270	I41	C	16-39
9271	I41	A	16-41
9272	I41	B	16-44
9273	I41	B	16-38
9274	I41	A	16-45
9275	I41	C	16-46
9276	I41	A	16-43
9277	I41	B	16-47
9278	I43	A	16-62
9279	I43	B	16-64
9280	I43	B	16-63
9281	I51	A	16-76
9282	J25	A	16-10
9283	I52	B	16-74
9284	I43	C	16-89
9285	I43	B	16-90
9286	I43	A	16-87
9287	I43	B	16-33
9288	I43	C	16-29
9289	I43	C	16-34
9290	I43	A	16-35
9291	I43	B	16-31
9292	I43	A	16-32
9293	I43	C	16-28
9294	I43	A	16-30
9295	I43	B	16-26
9296	I43	A	16-25
9297	I45	C	16-19
9298	I45	C	16-18
9299	I45	C	16-17
9300	I47	A	16-23
9301	I47	A	16-21
9302	I47	A	16-22
9303	I47	B	16-24
9304	I47	C	16-67
9305	I43	B	16-71
9306	I46	C	16-12
9307	I46	B	16-15
9308	I46	C	16-14
9309	I46	B	16-13
9310	I51	A	16-80
9311	I51	C	16-82
9312	I51	A	16-79
9313	I51	B	16-81
9314	I51	C	16-83
9315	I51	B	16-84
9316	I51	A	16-85
9317	A02	B	2-13
9318	A02	H	
9319	A02	A	2-15
9320	A02	B	2-14
9321	A02	A	2-12
9322	A02	C	2-17
9323	A02	B	2-16
9324	A01	A	2-8
9325	A01	B	2-9
9326	A01	B	2-10
9327	A01	B	2-11
9328	A25	C	2-38
9329	A25	B	2-39
9330	A25	A	2-40
9331	A25	A	2-41
9332	A21	B	2-24
9333	A20	B	2-25
9334	A21	C	2-36
9335	A20	C	2-26
9336	A20	H	
9337	A20	H	
9338	A20	A	2-35
9339	A20	C	2-34
9340	A20	B	2-30
9341	A20	H	
9342	A20	A	2-32
9343	A20	B	2-27
9344	A20	A	2-33
9345	A21	A	2-37
9346	A20	A	2-23
9347	A20	A	2-22
9348	A20	B	2-21
9349	A20	A	2-31
9350	A20	B	2-29
9351	A20	B	2-28
9352	B17	C	3-61
9353	B17	B	3-62
9354	B07	A	3-1
9355	B15	C	3-59
9356	B15	B	3-54
9357	B15	A	3-55
9358	B15	B	3-60
9359	B15	A	3-56
9360	B15	A	3-57
9361	B15	A	3-58
9362	B10	A	3-43
9363	B10	C	3-39
9364	B10	A	3-42
9365	B10	C	3-44
9366	B10	H	
9367	B10	H	
9368	B10	C	3-33
9369	B10	B	3-31
9370	B10	B	3-27
9371	B10	H	
9372	B10	H	
9373	B10	H	
9374	B10	B	3-26
9375	B10	A	3-22
9376	B10	C	3-21
9377	B10	A	3-20
9378	B08	C	3-9
9379	B08	C	3-8
9380	B10	C	3-47

H - Helicopter question
N - Flight navigator question

FAA		GLEIM		FAA		GLEIM		FAA		GLEIM	
Q. No.	Subject Code	Answer	Chap/ Q. No.	Q. No.	Subject Code	Answer	Chap/ Q. No.	Q. No.	Subject Code	Answer	Chap/ Q. No.
9381	B10	A	3-48	9425	J14	B	8-47	9469	H345	N	
9382	B10	A	3-28	9426	J14	A	8-48	9470	H345	N	
9383	B10	B	3-29	9427	J14	C	8-49	9471	H345	N	
9384	B10	C	3-30	9428	J14	C	8-50	9472	H345	N	
9385	B10	B	3-32	9429	J01	C	9-134	9473	H345	N	
9386	B10	B	3-46	9430	J01	A	9-127	9474	H345	N	
9387	B10	C	3-45	9431	J01	A	9-128	9475	H345	N	
9388	B08	A	3-7	9432	J01	A	9-129	9476	H345	N	
9389	B10	A	3-41	9433	J31	B	18-19	9477	H345	N	
9390	B10	C	3-40	9434	J31	A	18-20	9478	H345	N	
9391	B10	A	3-37	9435	J31	C	18-21	9479	H345	N	
9392	B10	B	3-36	9436	J05	B	7-28	9480	H345	N	
9393	B10	B	3-35	9437	J05	C	7-29	9481	H345	N	
9394	B10	C	3-34	9438	J18	B	9-96	9482	H345	N	
9395	B08	A	3-10	9439	J33	B	8-22	9483	H345	N	
9396	B08	C	3-6	9440	M51	C	6-134	9484	H345	N	
9397	B08	B	3-5	9441	T55	C	6-149	9485	H345	N	
9398	B08	C	3-2	9442	M51	B	6-146	9486	H345	N	
9399	B08	B	3-3	9443	T55	A	6-150	9487	H345	N	
9400	B08	B	3-4	9444	T55	A	6-151	9488	H345	N	
9401	B08	B	3-11	9445	T55	C	6-152	9489	H345	N	
9402	B08	B	8-24	9446	T55	C	6-147	9490	H345	N	
9403	B10	C	3-38	9447	T55	B	6-148	9491	H345	N	
9404	B10	B	3-23	9448	M51	C	6-144	9492	H345	N	
9405	B10	B	3-24	9449	M51	A	6-135	9493	I08	N	
9406	B10	A	3-25	9450	M08	B	6-139	9494	I08	N	
9407	B11	C	3-51	9451	M08	C	6-138	9495	I08	N	
9408	B11	A	3-50	9452	M08	B	6-145	9496	I08	N	
9409	B11	B	3-52	9453	M08	C	6-140	9497	I08	N	
9410	B15	C	3-53	9454	M08	C	6-141	9498	I08	N	
9411	B10	C	9-101	9455	D13	N		9499	H345	N	
9412	B10	C	3-49	9456	B17	N		9500	H345	N	
9413	B10	C	9-100	9457	D13	N		9501	H339	N	
9414	B11	H		9458	D13	N		9502	I04	N	
9415	B11	H		9459	D13	N		9503	I04	N	
9416	J05	B	7-24	9460	D17	N		9504	I08	N	
9417	J05	C	7-25	9461	D20	N		9505	H339	N	
9418	J17	A	9-45	9462	H339	N		9506	H339	N	
9419	J17	C	9-46	9463	H339	N		9507	K40	N	
9420	J19	C	8-41	9464	H345	N		9508	K40	N	
9421	J05	A	7-26	9465	H345	N		9509	H339	N	
9422	J05	C	7-27	9466	H345	N		9510	H339	N	
9423	J05	B	7-23	9467	H345	N		9511	H339	N	
9424	J13	A	8-21	9468	H345	N		9512	I08	N	

H - Helicopter question
N - Flight navigator question

FAA		GLEIM		FAA		GLEIM		FAA		GLEIM	
Q. No.	Subject Code	Answer	Chap/ Q. No.	Q. No.	Subject Code	Answer	Chap/ Q. No.	Q. No.	Subject Code	Answer	Chap/ Q. No.
9513	I08	N		9557	I13	B	10-12	9601	J42	C	10-66
9514	I13	N		9558	I13	B	10-13	9602	J34	A	10-69
9515	I13	N		9559	I13	A	10-14	9603	J42	C	10-68
9516	I13	N		9560	I13	B	10-21	9604	J42	A	10-67
9517	I13	N		9561	I13	B	10-20	9605	E02	H	
9518	I13	N		9562	J34	B	10-38	9606	E02	H	
9519	I13	N		9563	J40	B	10-22	9607	I13	H	
9520	I13	N		9564	J40	A	10-23	9608	I13	H	
9521	I13	N		9565	J34	C	10-39	9609	J34	C	9-63
9522	I13	N		9566	I13	H		9610	I13	B	10-40
9523	I13	N		9567	I13	H		9611	I13	A	10-41
9524	I13	N		9568	I13	H		9612	I13	C	10-42
9525	I13	N		9569	J41	C	9-53	9613	B10	A	10-43
9526	I43	N		9570	I08	C	9-54	9614	J40	B	10-44
9527	I43	N		9571	J42	A	9-55	9615	J40	C	10-45
9528	I51	N		9572	J34	H		9616	B10	B	10-46
9529	I51	N		9573	J42	C	9-59	9617	J42	C	10-47
9530	I51	N		9574	I13	H		9618	E04	B	10-48
9531	I51	N		9575	I13	H		9619	I07	B	10-49
9532	I51	N		9576	E02	H		9620	J36	C	10-50
9533	I51	N		9577	E03	H		9621	I13	H	
9534	I51	N		9578	I13	A	10-70	9622	I13	H	
9535	A32	N		9579	I13	B	10-71	9623	J35	A	9-64
9536	A32	N		9580	W06	B	10-72	9624	J35	C	9-65
9537	H339	N		9581	I13	C	10-73	9625	J34	B	9-66
9538	H340	N		9582	I13	B	10-74	9626	I13	C	10-51
9539	H339	N		9583	I13	C	10-77	9627	I13	A	10-52
9540	H339	N		9584	I13	B	10-75	9628	I13	B	10-53
9541	I08	N		9585	I13	B	10-76	9629	J42	B	10-55
9542	I08	N		9586	I13	B	10-86	9630	J42	A	10-56
9543	K40	N		9587	J42	A	10-84	9631	J42	C	10-57
9544	H345	N		9588	J42	B	10-85	9632	E04	A	10-58
9545	A32	N		9589	D21	B	10-83	9633	E04	C	10-59
9546	I13	A	10-1	9590	J42	A	10-82	9634	E04	C	10-60
9547	I13	A	10-2	9591	I13	C	10-87	9635	I13	A	10-54
9548	I13	C	10-3	9592	I13	B	10-88	9636	J34	B	10-61
9549	J40	C	10-4	9593	W06	A	10-89	9637	E02	H	
9550	J42	C	10-6	9594	I13	B	10-90	9638	E03	H	
9551	J42	B	10-10	9595	I13	C	10-91	9639	I13	H	
9552	J42	B	10-5	9596	J36	C	10-92	9640	I13	H	
9553	J42	A	10-7	9597	I13	C	10-62	9641	J35	A	9-70
9554	J42	A	10-8	9598	I13	B	10-63	9642	I13	A	10-97
9555	J42	A	10-9	9599	I07	C	10-64	9643	I13	A	10-98
9556	I13	B	10-11	9600	J42	B	10-65	9644	J36	B	10-99

H - Helicopter question
N - Flight navigator question

FAA		GLEIM		FAA		GLEIM		FAA		GLEIM	
Q. No.	Subject Code	Answer	Chap/ Q. No.	Q. No.	Subject Code	Answer	Chap/ Q. No.	Q. No.	Subject Code	Answer	Chap/ Q. No.
9645	J42	C	10-101	9674	J35	A	9-74	9703	I43	C	16-11
9646	D21	A	10-102	9675	J35	B	9-75	9704	I41	B	16-55
9647	J41	B	10-100	9676	J15	A	10-116	9705	I40	A	16-8
9648	J42	C	10-103	9677	I13	B	10-117	9706	I41	A	16-88
9649	J34	B	10-104	9678	I13	B	10-118	9707	I51	C	16-77
9650	E02	H		9679	I13	C	10-119	9708	I41	C	16-52
9651	E03	H		9680	D21	B	10-125	9709	I43	B	16-60
9652	I13	H		9681	J42	C	10-122	9710	I43	C	16-61
9653	I13	H		9682	J42	B	10-123	9711	I51	B	16-78
9654	J42	C	9-71	9683	J42	A	10-124	9712	I41	C	16-51
9655	J34	A	9-72	9684	D21	C	10-126	9713	I41	C	16-5
9656	I13	B	10-108	9685	D21	B	10-130	9714	D19	B	4-95
9657	I13	C	10-107	9686	J42	A	10-120	9715	J27	B	17-45
9658	J34	A	9-69	9687	J42	B	10-129	9716	J25	A	16-48
9659	J34	B	9-68	9688	J34	C	10-127	9717	J25	C	16-49
9660	J40	C	10-109	9689	J34	B	10-128	9718	J25	B	16-50
9661	J34	A	10-114	9690	J34	C	10-121	9719	E08	A	5-131
9662	J42	C	10-110	9691	J01	C	9-124	9720	E08	B	5-135
9663	D21	B	10-111	9692	J01	A	9-123	9721	J01	H	
9664	J15	B	10-105	9693	J01	B	9-125	9722	J01	B	9-132
9665	J15	A	10-106	9694	J01	C	9-126	9723	J01	C	9-130
9666	J34	C	10-113	9695	M35	C	6-136	9724	J01	B	9-131
9667	J42	B	10-115	9696	M35	B	5-105	9725	J01	A	9-133
9668	J34	A	9-67	9697	M35	C	6-153	9726	J01	H	
9669	J34	C	10-112	9698	M35	B	6-143	9727	J01	B	9-135
9670	J35	B	9-73	9699	M35	B	6-137	9728	J01	C	9-136
9671	I13	H		9700	M35	C	6-142	9729	J01	C	9-138
9672	I13	H		9701	I52	B	16-75	9730	J01	C	9-137
9673	I13	H		9702	I52	C	16-73				

H - Helicopter question
N - Flight navigator question

AUTHOR'S RECOMMENDATION

The Experimental Aircraft Association, Inc. is a very successful and effective nonprofit organization that represents and serves those of us interested in flying, in general, and in sport aviation, in particular. I personally invite you to enjoy becoming a member:

$35 for a 1-year membership
$20 per year for individuals under 19 years old
Family membership available for $45 per year

Membership includes the monthly magazine *Sport Aviation*.

Write to: Experimental Aircraft Association, Inc.
P.O. Box 3086
Oshkosh, Wisconsin 54903-3086

Or call: (414) 426-4800
(800) 564-6322

The annual EAA Oshkosh AirVenture is an unbelievable aviation spectacular with over 12,000 airplanes at one airport! Virtually everything aviation-oriented you can imagine! Plan to spend at least 1 day (not everything can be seen in a day) in Oshkosh (100 miles northwest of Milwaukee).

Convention dates: 1999 -- July 22 through August 2
2000 -- July 26 through August 1

The annual Sun 'n Fun EAA Fly-In is also highly recommended. It is held at the Lakeland, FL (KLAL) airport (between Orlando and Tampa). Visit the Sun 'n Fun web site at http://www.sun-n-fun.com.

Convention dates: 1999 -- April 11 through 17
2000 -- April 9 through 15
2001 -- April 8 through 14

BE-A-PILOT: INTRODUCTORY FLIGHT

Be-A-Pilot is an industry-sponsored marketing program designed to inspire people to "Stop dreaming, start flying." Be-A-Pilot has sought flight schools to participate in the program and offers a $35 introductory flight certificate that can be redeemed at a participating flight school.

The goal of this program is to encourage people to experience their dreams of flying through an introductory flight and to begin taking flying lessons.

For more information, you can visit the Be-A-Pilot home page at http://www.beapilot.com or call 1-888-BE-A-PILOT.

CIVIL AIR PATROL: CADET ORIENTATION FLIGHT PROGRAM

The Civil Air Patrol (CAP) Cadet Orientation Flight Program is designed to introduce CAP cadets to general aviation operations. The program is voluntary and primarily motivational, and it is designed to stimulate the cadet's interest in and knowledge of aviation.

Each orientation flight includes at least 30 min. of actual flight time, usually in the local area of the airport. Except for takeoff, landing, and a few other portions of the flight, cadets are encouraged to handle the controls. The Cadet Orientation Flight Program is designed to allow five front-seat and four back-seat flights. But you may be able to fly more.

For more information about the CAP cadet program nearest you, visit the CAP home page at http://www.cap.af.mil or call 1-800-FLY-2338.

PILOT KNOWLEDGE (WRITTEN EXAM) BOOKS AND SOFTWARE

Before pilots take their FAA pilot knowledge tests, they want to understand the answer to every FAA test question. Gleim's pilot knowledge test books are widely used because they help pilots learn and understand exactly what they need to know to pass. Each chapter opens with an outline of exactly what you need to know to pass the test. Additional information can be found in our reference books and flight maneuver/practical test prep books.

Use ***FAA Test Prep*** software with the appropriate Gleim book to prepare for success on your FAA pilot knowledge test.

PRIVATE PILOT AND RECREATIONAL PILOT FAA WRITTEN EXAM ($13.95)

The test for the private pilot certificate consists of 60 questions out of the 711 questions in our book. Also, the FAA's pilot knowledge test for the recreational pilot certificate consists of 50 questions from this book.

INSTRUMENT PILOT FAA WRITTEN EXAM ($16.95)

The test consists of 60 questions out of the 900 questions in our book. Also, become an instrument-rated flight instructor (CFII) or an instrument ground instructor (IGI) by taking the FAA's pilot knowledge test of 50 questions from this book.

COMMERCIAL PILOT FAA WRITTEN EXAM ($14.95)

The test consists of 100 questions out of the 595 questions in our book.

FUNDAMENTALS OF INSTRUCTING FAA WRITTEN EXAM ($9.95)

The test consists of 50 questions out of the 160 questions in our book. This test is required for any person to become a flight instructor or ground instructor. The test needs to be taken only once. For example, if someone is already a flight instructor and wants to become a ground instructor, taking the FOI test a second time is not required.

FLIGHT/GROUND INSTRUCTOR FAA WRITTEN EXAM ($14.95)

The test consists of 100 questions out of the 833 questions in our book. This book is to be used for the Flight Instructor--Airplane (FIA), Basic Ground Instructor (BGI), and the Advanced Ground Instructor (AGI) knowledge tests.

AIRLINE TRANSPORT PILOT FAA WRITTEN EXAM ($26.95)

The test consists of 80 questions each for the ATP Part 121, ATP Part 135, and the flight dispatcher certificate. Studying for the ATP will now be a learning and understanding experience rather than a memorization marathon -- at a lower cost and with higher test scores and less frustration!!

FLIGHT ENGINEER FAA WRITTEN EXAM ($26.95)

The FAA's flight engineer turbojet and basic knowledge test consists of 80 questions out of the 688 questions in our book. This book is to be used for the turbojet and basic (FEX) and the turbojet-added rating (FEJ) knowledge tests.

REFERENCE AND FLIGHT MANEUVERS/PRACTICAL TEST PREP BOOKS

Our Flight Maneuvers and Practical Test Prep books are designed to simplify and facilitate your flight training and will help prepare pilots for FAA practical tests as much as the Gleim written exam books help prepare pilots for FAA pilot knowledge tests. Each task, objective, concept, requirement, etc., in the FAA's practical test standards is explained, analyzed, illustrated, and interpreted so pilots will gain practical test proficiency as quickly as possible.

Private Pilot Flight Maneuvers and Practical Test Prep	352 pages	($16.95)
Instrument Pilot Flight Maneuvers and Practical Test Prep	288 pages	($17.95)
Commercial Pilot Flight Maneuvers and Practical Test Prep	336 pages	($14.95)
Flight Instructor Flight Maneuvers and Practical Test Prep	544 pages	($17.95)

PILOT HANDBOOK ($13.95)

A complete pilot ground school text in outline format with many diagrams for ease in understanding. This book is used in preparation for private, commercial, and flight instructor certificates and the instrument rating. A complete, detailed index makes it more useful and saves time. It contains a special section on biennial flight reviews.

AVIATION WEATHER AND WEATHER SERVICES ($18.95)

A complete rewrite of the FAA's *Aviation Weather 00-6A* and *Aviation Weather Services 00-45E* into a single easy-to-understand book complete with maps, diagrams, charts, and pictures. Learn and understand the subject matter much more easily and effectively with this book.

FAR/AIM REPRINT ($14.95)

The purpose of this book is to consolidate the common Federal Aviation Regulations (FAR) parts and the *Aeronautical Information Manual* into one easy-to-use reference book. The Gleim book is better because of bigger type, better presentation, improved indexes, and full-color figures. FAR Parts 1, 43, 61, 67, 71, 73, 91, 97, 103, 105, 119, 121 (Appendices I and J only), 135, 137, 141, and 142 are included.

GLEIM'S PRIVATE PILOT KIT

Gleim's *Private Pilot FAA Written Exam* book and software, *Private Pilot Flight Maneuvers and Practical Test Prep*, *Pilot Handbook*, *FAR/AIM Reprint*, a combined syllabus/logbook, a flight computer, a navigational plotter, and a durable, all-purpose flight bag. Our introductory price (30% savings over purchasing items separately) is far lower than similarly equipped kits found elsewhere. The Gleim Kit retails for **$99.95**. Gleim's *FAR/AIM Reprint*, *Private Pilot Syllabus/Logbook*, flight computer, navigational plotter, and flight bag are also available for individual sale. See our order form for details.

A/FD	*Airport/Facility Directory*
A/I	anti-ice
AC	convective outlook
ADF	automatic direction finder
ADIZ	Air Defense Identification Zone
AFSS	Automated Flight Service Station
AIRMET	Airman's Meteorological Information
ANU	airplane nose-up
ARTCC	Air Route Traffic Control Center
ASR	airport surveillance radar
ATC	Air Traffic Control
ATIS	Automatic Terminal Information Service
ATP	airline transport pilot
BC	back course
BCM	back course marker
BMEP	brake mean effective pressure
CAS	calibrated airspeed
CAT	clear air turbulence
CDI	course deviation indicator
CFR	Code of Federal Regulations
CG	center of gravity
COP	changeover point
DH	decision height
DME	distance measuring equipment
DME/P	precision distance measuring equipment
EFAS	En Route Flight Advisory Service
EFC	expect further clearance
ELT	emergency locator transmitter
EPR	engine pressure ratio
ESHP	equivalent shaft horsepower
ETA	estimated time of arrival
ETE	estimated time en route
FAF	final approach fix
FAR	Federal Aviation Regulation
FD	Winds and Temperatures Aloft Forecast
FDC NOTAM	Flight Data Center Notice to Airmen
FL	flight level
FPD	freezing point depressant
FSDO	Flight Standards District Office
FSS	Flight Service Station
GPS	global positioning system
GPWS	ground proximity warning system
GS	glide slope
HAT	height above touchdown
Hg	mercury
HIRL	high-intensity runway lights
HIWAS	Hazardous Inflight Weather Advisory Service
HS	high speed
HSI	horizontal situation indicator
IAP	instrument approach procedure
IAS	indicated airspeed
ICAO	International Civil Aviation Organization
IFR	instrument flight rules
ILS	instrument landing system
IMC	instrument meteorological conditions
INS	inertial navigation system
INT	intersection
IR	instrument route
ISA	International Standard Atmosphere
ISMLS	interim standard microwave landing system
L/D	lift-to-drag ratio
L/D_{MAX}	maximum lift-to-drag ratio
LDA	localizer-type directional aid
LEMAC	leading edge of MAC
LLWAS	low-level wind shear alert system
LOC	localizer
LORAN	long range navigation
LR	long range
LRC	long-range cruise
MAC	mean aerodynamic chord
MALSR	medium-intensity approach lighting system
MAP	missed approach point
MAP	manifold absolute pressure
mb	millibar
MC	magnetic course
MCA	minimum crossing altitude
MDA	minimum descent altitude
MEA	minimum en route altitude
MEL	minimum equipment list
METAR	aviation routine weather report
MHA	minimum holding altitude
MIRL	medium-intensity runway lights
MLS	microwave landing system
MM	middle marker
MNPS	minimum navigation performance specifications
MOA	military operations area
MOCA	minimum obstruction clearance altitude
MSL	mean sea level
MTR	military training routes
N_1	RPM of low-pressure compressor (turbine)
NAM	nautical air miles
NAT	North Atlantic
NAVAID	navigational aid
NDB	nondirectional radiobeacon
NGM	nautical ground miles
NM	nautical mile
NMC	National Meteorological Center
NOAA	National Oceanographic and Atmospheric Administration
NOTAM	Notice to Airmen
NTSB	National Transportation Safety Board
OAT	outside air temperature
OBS	omnibearing selector
OM	outer marker
ORM	other regulated material
PAPI	precision approach path indicator
PAR	precision approach radar
PIC	pilot in command
PIREP	pilot weather report
PPH	pounds per hour
PT	procedure turn
RAIL	runway alignment indicator lights
RCLS	runway centerline light system
REIL	runway end identifier lights
RMI	radio magnetic indicator
RNAV	area navigation
RVR	runway visual range
SDF	simplified directional facility
SIC	second in command
SID	standard instrument departure
SIGMET	Significant Meteorological Information
SL	sea level
SM	statute mile
STAB	stabilizer
STAR	standard terminal arrival route
TACAN	Tactical Air Navigation
TAF	terminal aerodrome forecast
TAS	true airspeed
TAT	total air temperature
TCAS	traffic alert and collision avoidance system
TD	time distance
TDZ	touchdown zone
TDZE	touchdown zone elevation
TDZL	touchdown zone lighting
TWEB	Transcribed Weather Broadcast
UTC	Coordinated Universal Time
V_1	maximum speed in the takeoff at which the pilot must take the first action to stop the airplane within the accelerate-stop distance
V_2	takeoff safety speed
V_{APP}	approach speed
VASI	visual approach slope indicator
V_C	design cruising speed
VDP	visual descent point
VHF	very high frequency
VLF	very low frequency
V_{MC}	minimum control speed with the critical engine inoperative
V_{MU}	minimum unstick speed
V_{MO}/M_{MO}	maximum operating limit speed
VOR	VHF omnidirectional range
VORTAC	collocated VOR and TACAN
VOT	VOR test facility
VR	visual route
V_R	rotation speed
V_{REF}	reference speed
VRS	Telephone Voice Response Systems
V_S	stalling speed or the minimum steady flight speed at which the airplane is controllable
V_{S0}	stalling speed or the minimum steady flight speed in the landing configuration
V_Y	best rate-of-climb speed
V_{YSE}	single-engine best rate-of-climb speed
Z	Zulu or UTC

Thank you FOR CHOOSING GLEIM

We dedicate ourselves to providing pilots with knowledge transfer systems, enabling them to pass the FAA pilot knowledge (written) tests and FAA practical (flight) tests. We solicit your feedback. Use the last page in this book to make notes as you use *Airline Transport Pilot FAA Written Exam* and other Gleim products. Tear out the page and mail it to us when convenient. Alternatively, e-mail (irvin@gleim.com) or FAX (352-375-6940) your feedback to us.

GLEIM'S E-MAIL UPDATE SERVICE

update@gleim.com

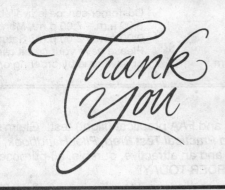

Your message to Gleim must include (in the subject or body) the acronym for your book or software, followed by the edition-printing for books and version for software. The edition-printing is indicated on the book's spine and at the bottom right corner of the cover. The software version is indicated on the diskette label.

	Written Exam Book	Written Exam Software	Flight Maneuvers Book
Private Pilot	PPWE	FAATP PP	PPPT
Instrument Pilot	IPWE	FAATP IP	IPFM
Commercial Pilot	CPWE	FAATP CP	CPPT
Flight/Ground Instructor	FIGI	FAATP FIGI	FIPT
Fundamentals of Instructing	FOI	FAATP FOI	
Airline Transport Pilot	ATP	FAATP ATP	

	Reference Book
Pilot Handbook	PH
Aviation Weather and Weather Services	AWWS
Private Pilot Syllabus and Logbook	SYLLOG
FAR/AIM Reprint	FARAIM

EXAMPLES

For ***Airline Transport Pilot FAA Written Exam***, third edition-seventh printing:

To: update@gleim.com
From: your e-mail address
Subject: ATP 3-7

For ***FAA Test Prep*** software, Airline Transport Pilot, version 3.1:

To: update@gleim.com
From: your e-mail address
Subject: FAATP ATP 3-1

IT ONLY TAKES A MINUTE

If you do not have e-mail, have a friend send e-mail to us and print our response for you.

Gleim Publications, Inc.
P.O. Box 12848
Gainesville, FL 32604

TOLL FREE: (800) 87-GLEIM
LOCAL: (352) 375-0772
FAX: (352) 375-6940
INTERNET: www.gleim.com
E-MAIL: sales@gleim.com

Customer service is available:
8:00 a.m. - 7:00 p.m., Mon. - Fri.
9:00 a.m. - 2:00 p.m., Saturday
Please have your credit card ready or save time by ordering online.

GLEIM'S PRIVATE PILOT KIT

Includes everything you need to pass the FAA pilot knowledge (written) test and FAA practical (flight) test: Gleim's *Private Pilot FAA Written Exam* book and software, *Private Pilot Flight Maneuvers and Practical Test Prep*, *Pilot Handbook*, *FAR/AIM Reprint*, a combined syllabus/logbook, flight computer, navigational plotter, and an attractive, durable, all-purpose flight bag. Our price is far lower than similarly equipped kits found elsewhere. ORDER TODAY!

30% savings ➡
Diskette version (For DOS-based operating systems or Windows 3.1) .... $ 99.95 ______
CD-ROM version (For Windows 95, Windows 98, or NT 4.0) .... $119.95 ______

WRITTEN TEST BOOKS AND SOFTWARE

		Books	*FAA Test Prep* Software: Diskette*	*FAA Test Prep* Software: CD-ROM‡ ☐ free demo	Audio ☐ free demo	
Private/Recreational Pilot	Eighth Edition	☐ @ $13.95	☐ @ $30.00	☐ @ $49.95	☐ @ $60.00	______
Instrument Pilot	Sixth Edition	☐ @ 16.95	☐ @ 30.00	☐ @ 59.95		______
Commercial Pilot	Seventh Edition	☐ @ 14.95	☐ @ 30.00	☐ @ 59.95		______
Fundamentals of Instructing	Sixth Edition	☐ @ 9.95	☐ @ 30.00	☐ @] $59.95 for both		______
Flight/Ground Instructor	Sixth Edition	☐ @ 14.95	☐ @ 30.00			______
Airline Transport Pilot	Third Edition	☐ @ 26.95	☐ @ 30.00	☐ @ 59.95		______
Flight Engineer	First Edition	☐ @ 26.95	☐ @ 30.00	☐ @ 59.95		______

*Requires appropriate Gleim book for access to charts, figures, etc.
‡Our new CD-ROM version will only install under Windows 95, Windows 98, or NT 4.0. This new Windows version includes all questions, figures, charts, and outlines for each of the pilot knowledge tests.

FLIGHT MANEUVERS/PRACTICAL TEST PREP BOOKS

Private Pilot Flight Maneuvers and Practical Test Prep .... (Third Edition) .... $16.95 ______
Instrument Pilot Flight Maneuvers and Practical Test Prep .... (Second Edition) .... 17.95 ______
Commercial Pilot Flight Maneuvers and Practical Test Prep .... (Third Edition) .... 14.95 ______
Flight Instructor Flight Maneuvers and Practical Test Prep .... (Second Edition) .... 17.95 ______

REFERENCE BOOKS AND SYLLABUS

FAR/AIM Reprint .... (Most Recent Edition) .... $14.95 ______
Aviation Weather and Weather Services .... (Second Edition) .... 18.95 ______
Pilot Handbook .... (Sixth Edition) .... 13.95 ______
Private Pilot Syllabus and Logbook .... 9.95 ______

OTHER

Flight Computer .... $ 9.95 ______
Navigational Plotter .... 5.95 ______
Flight Bag .... 29.95 ______

Shipping and Handling (nonrefundable): 1 item = $5; each additional item = $1 ______

Add applicable sales tax for shipments within the State of Florida. Sales Tax ______

Please FAX or write for additional charges for outside the 48 contiguous United States.

Printed 12/98. Prices subject to change without notice.

TOTAL $______

1. *We process and ship orders (via UPS in the 48 contiguous states) within 1 business day over 98.8% of the time. Call by noon for same-day service!*
2. *Please copy this order form for friends and others. Orders from individuals must be prepaid. No CODs.*
3. *Gleim Publications, Inc. guarantees the immediate refund of all resalable texts and unopened software and audiotapes returned in 30 days. Applies only to items purchased direct from Gleim. No refunds on shipping and handling.*
4. *If your local FBO or aviation bookstore does not stock the books you are ordering from us directly, please provide us with a name and address, so we can invite them to stock Gleim.*

Name ______________________
(please print)

Shipping Address ______________________
(street address required for UPS) Apt. #

____

City ____________ State ______ Zip ______

☐ VISA/MC/DISC/AMEX ☐ Check/M.O. Daytime Phone (______) ______________

Credit Card No. ________ - ________ - ________ - ________

Expiration Date (month/year) ____/____

Signature ______________________

020

INDEX

łaze																			7	72
- 11	lusion												• •		• •	• • •		٠.	6	92
L	ayers														٠.				2	69
lead	ing set knob, HS wind affecting pe														•	•		•	1	82
lead	wind affecting pent above touchdo	enormar	ice												•	•	•	•	4	40
leigr	ort identification	own												•					2	25
1:																				
ligh,	Altitude weather																69	5,	7	09
	lovation airports	•																	. 1	02
1.	ntongity runway	lighte																	~	20
1	aval cignificant	weather	progr	nost	IC C	cha	rt												1	22
1	ift devices																			10
	חבספנונים מדממה																		O	91
	Palative humidity	nower	outpu	ıt .															- 1	02
Highe	act anot alevation	n NOS I	AP ch	art															~	10
JIDI																			~	25
Histo	ny cuhmenu FA	A Test P	ren so	offw	are															10
HIWA	AS					• •	٠.			• •							2	3,	1	14
Hold																			9	17
308	For release						٠.												0	24
ales	Line markings						٠.	٠.									2	37	2	71
Hold	ing						٠.									•	-	٠, ,	6	48
148	Fuel consumption AS and EPR, B-	n, B-/2/																	6	348
100 W 500	Darfarmanaa P	727										201								000
1	Position signs																2	24,	, 4	112
I Invi	contal aituation in	adicator																	. 6	03
LICI	nterpretation																		. 6	209
LICIA	coolizor									13									. 6	2/1.
Liveri	canes																		٠, ر	990
Lhide	onlaning																			184
Hype	erventilation																1	12	, 1	14
Нуро	oxia																7	71	, 1	773
MR.A.																			M.	
IAS.	holding, B-727																		. 6	548
ICAC	nonprecision a	nnroach	runw	avs	:														. 6	223
Ice p	ollote								. 3.3										. (094
Icino																	0	94	,	101
	Condition opera	tions, FA	AR 12	1						٠.					• •	• • •		• •	. :	122
	Conditions, FAR	135											• •	• •						132
IFR																				267
	Approaches ATC clearance,	FAD O1	• • • • •									•		٠.	in			•	i	36
	Cancellation	FAR 91												•	9	ile y		:		246
	Charts																			272
	Clearances, pick	king up																	. :	246
	Clicht																			
	Plan closing	a																		363
	Plane							100												240
	Flighte																			337
	In controlled air	space F	AR 91																	. 01
	Navigation equi	pment .												٠.			٠.	• •		26/
	Operating limita	tions. FA	AR 13	5																131
	Operations, rad	io failure	, FAH	91				• • •					٠.		٠.			٠.		363
	Preferred routes Weather depicti							• • •		• • •										716
ILS																				
ILS	Approach minin	nume														100			è	488
	Approaches	iuiiis			• • •		•									100		Ų.		274
	Critical area box	undary s	ians .																	224
	DMF minimums						2													458
	Minimums												3	379), 3	393	, 4	187	7,	489
Imm	nediate notification	on. NTSE	3 830																	. 22
Inbo	pard ailerons																			178
Indi	cated stall speed	i														٠.				179
Indu	ced drag						٠.													1/9
Iner	tial navigation sy	stem					٠.			• •	• •		• • •	٠.	• •					70
480	FAR 121							• •	٠.	• •	• •			• •	• •					722
		itner adv	risorie	5 .			• •	• •		٠.										122
initia	al training FAR 121																H			. 72
	FAR 135																	00		134
Inne	er marker IIS																			2/4
Inor	perable instrume	ents and	equip	me	nt.	FA	R	13	5											130
Ino	perative instrume	ents and	equip	ome	ent.	FA	R	91												. 37
INS		1000000																7	9,	268
Inst	ruction, FAR 61																			. 23
Inst	ructions for FAA	Test Pre	p sof	twa	re															. 13
	rument																			
	A																			0770
	Chart lege	nds																		2/8
	Light syste	m locali	zer b	ack	CO	urs	e													441
	Equipment, and	certific	ate re	quir	en	en	ts,	F	AH	9.	١.			• •			٠	• • •		134
	Proficiency che	CK requi	reme	its,	FA	H 1	35					• •	• •				•	• • •		68

ntensity trend, echoes	/13	0
ntensity trend, echoes		٦
ntermittent light turbulence	/1	4
nternational Flights	12	5
Standard atmosphere	/ 1	d
nterphone system, crewmember	. 202	
FAD 101	6	9
FAR 135	12	8
Intersection identification Inversion temperature	36	9
Inversion temperature	. 693, 70	4
loohoro	12	4
Isotachs		4
J et stream	. 695, 75	8
Katabatic wind		
Katabatic wind	69	32
Knowledge codes, subject matter	79	35
Nilowiedge codes, subject matter		
Landing Approach, and takeoff minimums, FAR 135	13	3:
Distance B-727	6/	16
B-727		1
BE-1900		-
Limitations	40	3
FAR 135 FAR 131		2
Turbine engine transport alforatt. FAR 121		
Minimums, localizer back course	42	P
Performance		2
P.737	00	и
Under IFR, FAR 91		3
Weather minimums, FAR 121		5
Weight, DC-9	5	_
1 AC to CEO	4	OI
1 accrCrodo		
Leteral etability	10	ᆲ
law enforcement escort of prisoners		u
LAWRE	2	
I AV to PHY	4	u
I DA	6	Γ
LID		а
Loading adge flane and slots	1	1
LEMAC DC-9	5	a
Level off oltitude P 727	0	C
1 F/MF accord routes	6	. /
LIEECLIADD flights		34
1:4		- 61
Lighted heliport identification		и
Limitations and privileges FAR 61	20,	4
Limited aviation weather reporting station		ш
Line checks pilot FAR 121		1
Line checks pilot in command FAR 135	1	V
Load factor	1	1
Legalizar approach minimums	4	ы
Legalizar type directional aid	2	и
Longitudinal stability	1	а
I ORAN RNAV instrument approach procedure		4
LOBANIC		4
Loss of signal	2	
Loct		
Communications	3	3-
Medical certificate		4
Pilot certificate FAR 61 (tel no to call)		2
Low-level significant weather prog chart	716, 7	:
Lowest		
Allowable altitude	4	н
Altitude for alide slope interception	4	н
Lubber line, HSI	2	20
MAC, DC-9	5	51
Mach speed flight	1	14
Magnetic compass and variation	186. 3	3!
Magnetized materials		
49 CFR		
EAD 101		- 1
Maintenance, FAR 135		1
Malfunction reports FAR 91		
		2
MALSR Manipulation of controls, FAR 135		1
Manual contents and requirements, FAR 135		1
		2
MAP Mature stage, thunderstorm		6
Max takeoff EPR, B-727		6
Wax landon EFR, D-121	- SY (12-11)

Please forward your suggestions, corrections, and comments concerning typographical errors, etc., to **Irvin N. Gleim • c/o Gleim Publications, Inc. • P.O. Box 12848 • University Station • Gainesville, Florida • 32604**. Please include your name and address below so we can properly thank you for your interest. Also, please refer to both the page number and the FAA question number for each item.

1. ______________________________

2. ______________________________

3. ______________________________

4. ______________________________

5. ______________________________

6. ______________________________

7. ______________________________

8. ______________________________

9. ______________________________

10. ______________________________

Remember for superior service: Mail, e-mail, or fax questions about our books or software. Telephone questions about orders, prices, shipments, or payments.

Name: ______________________________

Address: ______________________________

City/State/Zip: ______________________________

Telephone: Home: __________ Work: __________ FAX: __________

E-mail ______________________________